Con[illegible]aries

Engli[illegible] – Français
French – Anglais

Rosalind Williams BA

Pan Books London and Sydney

Trademarks
The symbol ® designates entered words that we have reason to believe constitute trademarks. However, neither the presence or absence of such designation should be regarded as affecting the legal status of any trademark.

Marques déposées
Le symbole ® désigne les mots enregistrés qui, nous avons lieu de croire, constituent des marques déposées. Néanmoins, ni la présence ni l'absence de ce symbole n'indique le statut
légal d'aucune marque déposée.

First published 1982 by Pan Books Ltd,
Cavaye Place, London SW10 9PG,
9 8 7 6 5 4 3 2

ISBN 0 330 26648 9
Printed and bound in Great Britain by Hunt Barndard Printing Ltd., Aylesbury, Bucks.

Abbreviations/Abréviations

adj adjective, adjectif
admin administration
adv adverb, adverbe
aero aeronautics
aéro aéronautique
anat anatomy, anatomie
arch architecture
art article
astrol astrology, astrologie
astron astronomy, astronomie
auto automobile
aux auxiliary, auxiliaire
bot botany, botanique
chem chemistry
chim chimie
coll colloquial
comm commerce
conj conjunction, conjonction
derog derogatory
econ economics
écon économie
elec electricity
élec électricité
f feminine, féminin
fam familiar, familier
geog geography
géog géographie
geol geology
géol géologie
gramm grammar, grammaire
impol impolite, impoli
interj interjection
invar invariable
m masculine, masculin
math mathematics, mathématiques
med medicine
méd médicine
mil military, militaire
n noun, nom
naut nautical, nautique
péj péjoratif
phone telephone
phot photography, photographie
pl plural, pluriel
pol politics, politique
prep preposition, préposition
pron pronoun, pronom
psych psychology, psychologie
rail railways
rel religion
sing singular, singulier
tech technical, technique
v verb, verbe
V vide (see, voir)
zool zoology, zoologie

French pronunciation

ɑ pate [pɑt]
a rame [ram]
ɛ baie [bɛ]
e pré [pre]
i fiche [fiʃ]
ɔ col [kɔl]
o pot [po]
u route [rut]
y vue [vy]
ə me [mə]
ø deux [dø]
œ jeune [ʒœn]
ɑ̃ vent [vɑ̃]
ɛ̃ fin [fɛ̃]
ɔ̃ ton [tɔ̃]
œ̃ brun [brœ̃]
' hibou ['ibu] (no liaison)
b bière [bjɛr]
d dame [dam]
f faîte [fɛt]
g gant [gɑ̃]
h hola [hɔla]
j pierre [pjɛr]
k conte [kɔ̃t]
l lieu [ljø]
m mon [mɔ̃]
n nid [ni]
p poli [pɔli]
r rage [raʒ]
s sein [sɛ̃]
t tube [tyb]
v vite [vit]
w oui [wi]
z zone [zon]
ɥ lui [lɥi]
ʃ chou [ʃu]
ʒ neige [nɛʒ]
ɲ ligne [liɲ]
ŋ parking [parkiŋ]

In French, the stress always falls on the final syllable of a word or group of words.

Prononciation de l'anglais

a hat [hat]	g gaze [geiz]
e bell [bel]	h hop [hop]
i big [big]	j yell [jel]
o dot [dot]	k cat [kat]
ʌ bun [bʌn]	l life [laif]
u book [buk]	m mouse [maus]
ə alone [ə'loun]	n night [nait]
a: card [ka:d]	p pick [pik]
ə: word [wə:d]	r rose [rouz]
i: team [ti:m]	s sit [sit]
o: torn [to:n]	t toe [tou]
u: spoon [spu:n]	v vest [vest]
ai die [dai]	w week [wi:k]
ei ray [rei]	z zoo [zu:]
oi toy [toi]	θ think [θiŋk]
au how [hau]	ð those [ðouz]
ou road [roud]	ʃ shoe [ʃu:]
eə lair [leə]	ʒ treasure ['treʒə]
iə fear [fiə]	tʃ chalk [tʃo:k]
uə poor [puə]	dʒ jump [dʒʌmp]
b back [bak]	ŋ sing [siŋ]
d dull [dʌl]	
f find [faind]	

Le signe ' est placé devant la syllabe qui porte l'accent tonique.
Le signe ˌ est placé devant la syllabe qui porte l'accent secondaire.

Guide to the dictionary

Irregular plural forms are shown at the headword and in the text. The following categories of French plural forms are considered regular:

main	mains
prix	prix
chev**al**	chev**aux**
feu	**feux**
seau	**seaux**

Irregular feminine forms of adjectives are shown at the headword and in the text. The following categories are considered regular:

brun	brun**e**
digne	digne
préci**eux**	préci**euse**
vi**f**	vi**ve**
artifici**el**	artifici**elle**
anci**en**	anci**enne**
premi**er**	premi**ère**

Irregular verbs marked with an asterisk in the headword list are listed in the verb tables, with the following exceptions:

For verbs ending in **-aindre**, **-eindre**, or **-oindre** see **atteindre**.
For verbs ending in **-aître** (except **naître**) see **connaître**.
For verbs ending in **-cevoir** see **apercevoir**.
For verbs ending in **-clure** see **conclure**.
For verbs ending in **-crire** see **écrire**.
For verbs ending in **-entir** (also **dormir**, **partir**, **servir**, **sortir**) see **mentir**.
For verbs ending in **-quérir** see **acquérir**.
For verbs ending in **-uire** (except **luire**, **nuire**) see **conduire**.

Adverbs are shown only if their formation is irregular. English adverbs are considered regular if they are formed by adding *-ly* to the adjective. French adverbs are considered regular if they are formed by adding *-ment* to the feminine form of the adjective.

Guide au dictionnaire

Les formes irrégulières au pluriel sont indiquées après le mot cherché et dans le texte. Les catégories suivantes des formes plurielles sont considérées régulières en anglais:

cat	cats
glass	glasses
fly	flies
half	halves
wife	wives

Les formes irrégulières des adjectifs au féminin sont indiquées après le mot cherché et dans le texte. Les catégories suivantes des formes féminines sont considérées régulières:

brun	brune
digne	digne
precieux	précieuse
vif	vive
artificiel	artificielle
ancien	ancienne
premier	première

Les verbes irréguliers se trouvant dans la liste des verbes sont marqués d'un astérisque dans la liste des mots du dictionnaire.

Les adverbes se construisant régulièrement ne sont pas indiqués. Les adverbes anglais sont considérés réguliers s'ils sont construits en ajoutant *-ly* à l'adjectif. Les adverbes français sont considérés réguliers s'ils sont construits en ajoutant *-ment* à la forme féminine de l'adjectif.

French irregular verbs

Infinitive	Present	Imperfect	Past Participle	Future
absoudre	absous	absolvais	absous	absoudrai
acquérir	acquiers	acquérais	acquis	acquerrai
aller	vais	allais	allé	irai
apercevoir	aperçois	apercevais	aperçu	apercevrai
assaillir	assaille	assaillais	assailli	assaillirai
asseoir	assieds	asseyais	assis	assiérai
atteindre	atteins	atteignais	atteint	atteindrai
avoir	ai	avais	eu	aurai
battre	bats	battais	battu	battrai
boire	bois	buvais	bu	boirai
bouillir	bous	bouillais	bouilli	bouillirai
braire	brais	brayais	brait	brairai
circoncire	circoncis	circoncisais	circoncis	circoncirai
clore	clos		clos	clorai
conclure	conclus	concluais	conclu	conclurai
conduire	conduis	conduisais	conduit	conduirai
confire	confis	confisais	confit	confirai
connaître	connais	connaissais	connu	connaîtrai
coudre	couds	cousais	cousu	coudrai
courir	cours	courais	couru	courrai
couvrir	couvre	couvrais	couvert	couvrirai
croire	crois	croyais	cru	croirai
croître	croîs	croissais	crû	croîtrai
cueillir	cueille	cueillais	cueilli	cueillerai
devoir	dois	devais	dû	devrai
dire	dis	disais	dit	dirai
dissoudre	dissous	dissolvais	dissous	dissoudrai
échoir	il échoit		échu	il échoira
écrire	écris	écrivais	écrit	écrirai
envoyer	envoie	envoyais	envoyé	enverrai
être	suis	étais	été	serai
faillir			failli	faillirai
faire	fais	faisais	fait	ferai
falloir	il faut	il fallait	fallu	il faudra
foutre	fous	foutais	foutu	foutrai
frire	fris		frit	frirai
fuir	fuis	fuyais	fui	fuirai

Infinitive	Present	Imperfect	Past Participle	Future
gésir	gis	gisais		
haïr	hais	haïssais	haï	haïrai
importer	il importe			
lire	lis	lisais	lu	lirai
luire	luis	luisais	lui	luirai
maudire	maudis	maudissais	maudit	maudirai
mentir	mens	mentais	menti	mentirai
mettre	mets	mettais	mis	mettrai
moudre	mouds	moulais	moulu	moudrai
mourir	meurs	mourais	mort	mourrai
mouvoir	meus	mouvais	mû	mouvrai
naître	nais	naissais	né	naîtrai
nuire	nuis	nuisais	nui	nuirai
offrir	offre	offrais	offert	offrirai
ouïr	ois	oyais	ouï	oirrai
ouvrir	ouvre	ouvrais	ouvert	ouvrirai
plaire	plais	plaisais	plu	plairai
pleuvoir	il pleut	il pleuvait	plu	il pleuvra
pouvoir	peux *or* puis	pouvais	pu	pourrai
prendre	prends	prenais	pris	prendrai
résoudre	résous	résolvais	résolu	résoudrai
rire	ris	riais	ri	rirai
savoir	sais	savais	su	saurai
seoir	il sied	il seyait		
souffrir	souffre	souffrais	souffert	souffrirai
suffire	suffis	suffisais	suffi	suffirai
suivre	suis	suivais	suivi	suivrai
surseoir	sursois	sursoyais	sursis	surseoirai
taire	tais	taisais	tu	tairai
tenir	tiens	tenais	tenu	tiendrai
traire	trais	trayais	trait	trairai
tressaillir	tressaille	tressaillais	tressailli	tressaillirai
vaincre	vaincs	vainquais	vaincu	vaincrai
valoir	vaux	valais	valu	vaudrai
venir	viens	venais	venu	viendrai
vêtir	vêts	vêtais	vêtu	vêtirai
vivre	vis	vivais	vécu	vivrai
voir	vois	voyais	vu	verrai
vouloir	veux	voulais	voulu	voudrai

Verbes irréguliers anglais

Infinitif	Prétérit	Participe Passé	Infinitif	Prétérit	Participe Passé
abide	abode	abode	**deal**	dealt	dealt
arise	arose	arisen	**dig**	dug	dug
awake	awoke	awoken	**do**	did	done
be	was	been	**draw**	drew	drawn
bear	bore	borne *or* born	**dream**	dreamed *or* dreamt	dreamed *or* dreamt
beat	beat	beaten	**drink**	drank	drunk
become	became	become	**drive**	drove	driven
begin	began	begun	**dwell**	dwelt	dwelt
behold	beheld	beheld	**eat**	ate	eaten
bend	bent	bent	**fall**	fell	fallen
bet	bet	bet	**feed**	fed	fed
beware			**feel**	felt	felt
bid	bid	bidden *or* bid	**fight**	fought	fought
			find	found	found
bind	bound	bound	**flee**	fled	fled
bite	bit	bitten	**fling**	flung	flung
bleed	bled	bled	**fly**	flew	flown
blow	blew	blown	**forbid**	forbade	forbidden
break	broke	broken	**forget**	forgot	forgotten
breed	bred	bred	**forgive**	forgave	forgiven
bring	brought	brought	**forsake**	forsook	forsaken
build	built	built	**freeze**	froze	frozen
burn	burnt *or* burned	burnt *or* burned	**get**	got	got
			give	gave	given
burst	burst	burst	**go**	went	gone
buy	bought	bought	**grind**	ground	ground
can	could		**grow**	grew	grown
cast	cast	cast	**hang**	hung *or* hanged	hung *or* hanged
catch	caught	caught			
choose	chose	chosen	**have**	had	had
cling	clung	clung	**hear**	heard	heard
come	came	come	**hide**	hid	hidden
cost	cost	cost	**hit**	hit	hit
creep	crept	crept	**hold**	held	held
cut	cut	cut	**hurt**	hurt	hurt

Infinitif	Prétérit	Participe Passé	Infinitif	Prétérit	Participe Passé
keep	kept	kept	**say**	said	said
kneel	knelt	knelt	**see**	saw	seen
knit	knitted	knitted	**seek**	sought	sought
	or knit	*or* knit	**sell**	sold	sold
know	knew	known	**send**	sent	sent
lay	laid	laid	**set**	set	set
lead	led	led	**sew**	sewed	sewn
lean	leant	leant			*or* sewed
	or leaned	*or* leaned	**shake**	shook	shaken
leap	leapt	leapt	**shear**	sheared	sheared
	or leaped	*or* leaped			*or* shorn
learn	learnt	learnt	**shed**	shed	shed
	or learned	*or* learned	**shine**	shone	shone
leave	left	left	**shoe**	shod	shod
lend	lent	lent	**shoot**	shot	shot
let	let	let	**show**	showed	shown
lie	lay	lain	**shrink**	shrank	shrunk
light	lit	lit	**shut**	shut	shut
	or lighted	*or* lighted	**sing**	sang	sung
lose	lost	lost	**sink**	sank	sunk
make	made	made	**sit**	sat	sat
may	might		**sleep**	slept	slept
mean	meant	meant	**slide**	slid	slid
meet	met	met	**sling**	slung	slung
mow	mowed	mown	**slink**	slunk	slunk
must			**slit**	slit	slit
ought			**smell**	smelt	smelt
pay	paid	paid		*or* smelled	*or* smelled
put	put	put	**sow**	sowed	sown
quit	quitted	quitted			*or* sowed
	or quit	*or* quit	**speak**	spoke	spoken
read	read	read	**speed**	sped	sped
rid	rid	rid		*or* speeded	*or* speeded
ride	rode	ridden	**spell**	spelt	spelt
ring	rang	rung		*or* spelled	*or* spelled
rise	rose	risen	**spend**	spent	spent
run	ran	run	**spill**	spilt	spilt
saw	sawed	sawn		*or* spilled	*or* spilled
		or sawed	**spin**	spun	spun

Infinitif	Prétérit	Participe Passé	Infinitif	Prétérit	Participe Passé
spit	spat	spat	**swim**	swam	swum
spilt	split	split	**swing**	swung	swung
spread	spread	spread	**take**	took	taken
spring	sprang	sprung	**teach**	taught	taught
stand	stood	stood	**tear**	tore	torn
steal	stole	stolen	**tell**	told	told
stick	stuck	stuck	**think**	thought	thought
sting	stung	stung	**throw**	threw	thrown
stink	stank *or* stunk	stunk	**thrust**	thrust	thrust
			tread	trod	trodden
stride	strode	stridden	**wake**	woke	woken
strike	struck	struck	**wear**	wore	worn
string	strung	strung	**weave**	wove	woven
strive	strove	striven	**weep**	wept	wept
swear	swore	sworn	**win**	won	won
sweep	swept	swept	**wind**	wound	wound
swell	swelled	swollen *or* swelled	**wring**	wrung	wrung
			write	wrote	written

English–Français

A

a [ə], **an** *art* un, une.
aback [ə'bak] *adv* **be taken aback** être déconcerté.
abandon [ə'bandən] *v* abandonner; (*hope, etc.*) renoncer à.
abashed [ə'baʃt] *adj* décontenancé, confus.
abate [ə'beit] *v* (*storm*) s'apaiser; (*fever*) baisser; (*courage*) diminuer. **abatement** *n* suppression *f*; réduction *f*.
abattoir ['abətwaː] *n* abattoir *m*.
abbey ['abi] *n* abbaye *f*. **abbess** *n* abbesse *f*. **abbot** *n* abbé *m*.
abbreviate [ə'briːvieit] *v* abréger. **abbreviation** *n* abréviation *f*.
abdicate ['abdikeit] *v* (*king, etc.*) abdiquer; (*give up*) renoncer à. **abdication** *n* abdication *f*; renonciation *f*.
abdomen ['abdəmən] *n* abdomen *m*. **abdominal** *adj* abdominal.
abduct [əb'dʌkt] *v* enlever. **abduction** *n* enlèvement *m*.
aberration [abə'reiʃən] *n* aberration *f*. **aberrant** *adj* aberrant.
abet [ə'bet] *v* encourager. **abettor** *n* complice *m, f*.
abeyance [ə'beiəns] *n* **be in abeyance** rester en suspens. **fall into abeyance** tomber en désuétude.
abhor [əb'hoː] *v* abhorrer. **abhorrence** *n* horreur *f*. **abhorrent** *adj* odieux.
***abide** [ə'baid] *v* (*tolerate*) supporter. **abide by** (*rule*) se conformer à; (*promise*) rester fidèle à.
ability [ə'biləti] *n* capacité *f*; talent *m*. **to the best of one's ability** de son mieux.
abject ['abdʒekt] *adj* abject; misérable; (*apology*) servile. **in abject poverty** dans la misère noire.
ablaze [ə'bleiz] *adv, adj* en feu.
able ['eibl] *adj* capable. **be able** pouvoir; (*know how to*) savoir. **able-bodied** *adj* robuste.
abnormal [ab'noːml] *adj* anormal. **abnormality** *n* anomalie *f*; malformation *f*.
aboard [ə'boːd] *adv* à bord. *prep* à bord de. **go aboard** s'embarquer.
abode [ə'boud] *V* **abide**. *n* demeure *f*; (*law*) domicile *m*.
abolish [ə'boliʃ] *v* abolir; supprimer. **abolition** *n* abolition *f*; suppression *f*.
abominable [ə'bominəbl] *adj* abominable. **abomination** *n* abomination *f*.
Aborigine [abə'ridʒini] *n* aborigène *m, f*.
abort [ə'boːt] *v* avorter. **abortion** *n* avortement *m*. **have an abortion** se faire avorter. **abortive** *adj* manqué.
abound [ə'baund] *v* abonder.
about [ə'baut] *adv* (*approximately*) vers, environ; (*here and there*) ça et là; (*around*) autour. *prep* (*concerning*) au sujet de; (*around*) autour de. **about to** sur le point de. **what is it about?** de quoi s'agit-il?
above [ə'bʌv] *adv, prep* au-dessus (de). **above all** surtout. **above-mentioned** *adj* ci-dessus.
abrasion [ə'breiʒən] *n* frottement *m*; (*med*) écorchure *f*. **abrasive** *nm, adj* abrasif.
abreast [ə'brest] *adv* de front. **keep abreast of** se tenir au courant de.
abridge [ə'bridʒ] *v* abréger. **abridgment** *n* résumé *m*.
abroad [ə'broːd] *adv* à l'étranger.
abrupt [ə'brʌpt] *adj* soudain; brusque; (*slope*) abrupt.
abscess ['abses] *n* abscès *m*.
abscond [əb'skond] *v* s'enfuir.
absent ['absənt] *adj* absent. **absent-minded** *adj* distrait. **absent-mindedness** *n* distraction *f*. **absence** *n* absence *f*. **in the**

absence of faute de. **absentee** *n* absent, -e *m, f.*
absolute ['absəluːt] *adj* absolu; complet, -ète. **absolutely** *adv* absolument, tout à fait.
absolve [əb'zolv] *v* absoudre; (*law*) acquitter. **absolution** *n* absolution *f.*
absorb [əb'zoːb] *v* absorber. **absorbent** *adj* absorbant. **absorbing** *adj* (*book, etc.*) passionnant. **absorption** *n* absorption *f.*
abstain [əb'stein] *v* s'abstenir. **abstention** *n* abstention *f.* **abstinence** *n* abstinence *f.*
abstract ['abstrakt; *v* ab'strakt] *adj* abstrait. *n* abstrait *m*; résumé *m. v* isoler. **abstraction** *n* (*removal*) extraction *f*; (*absent-mindedness*) distraction *f*; (*concept*) abstraction *f.*
absurd [əb'səːd] *adj* absurde.
abundance [ə'bʌndəns] *n* abondance *f.* **abundant** *adj* abondant. **abundantly** *adv* abondamment; (*grow*) à foison; (*completely*) tout à fait.
abuse [ə'bjuːz; *n* ə'bjuːs] *v* (*misuse*) abuser de; (*insult*) injurier, insulter. *n* abus *m*; insultes *f pl.* **abusive** *adj* abusif; injurieux.
abyss [ə'bis] *n* abîme *m.*
academy [ə'kadəmi] *n* académie *f.* **academic** *adj* académique; théorique; (*studies*) scolaire, universitaire.
accede [ak'siːd] *v* **accede to** agréer.
accelerate [ək'seləreit] *v* accélérer. **acceleration** *n* accélération *f.* **accelerator** *n* accélérateur *m.*
accent ['aksənt] *n* accent *m. v also* **accentuate** accentuer.
accept [ək'sept] *v* accepter. **acceptable** *adj* acceptable. **acceptance** *n* acceptation *f*; approbation *f.*
access ['akses] *n* accès *m.* **accessible** *adj* accessible. **accession** *n* accession *f*; (*to throne*) avènement *m.*
accessory [ək'sesəri] *nm, adj* accessoire.
accident ['aksidənt] *n* accident *m.* **by accident** par hasard. **accidental** *adj* accidentel.
acclaim [ə'kleim] *v* acclamer. *n also* **acclamation** acclamation *f.*
acclimatize [ə'klaimətaiz] *v* acclimater; habituer.
accolade ['akəleid] *n* accolade *f.*
accommodate [ə'komədeit] *v* loger; (*adapt*) accommoder. **accommodating** *adj* obligeant. **accommodation** *n* logement *m*, chambres *f pl.*
accompany [ə'kʌmpəni] *v* accompagner. **accompaniment** *n* accompagnement *m.* **accompanist** *n* accompagnateur, -trice *m, f.*
accomplice [ə'kʌmplis] *n* complice *m, f.*
accomplish [ə'kʌmpliʃ] *v* accomplir; réaliser. **accomplished** *adj* (*skilled*) doué; accompli. **accomplishment** *n* accomplissement *m*; talent *m.*
accord [ə'koːd] *v* (s')accorder. *n* accord *m.* **of one's own accord** de son plein gré. **accordance** *n* conformité *f.* **in accordance with** conformément à. **according to** selon.
accordion [ə'koːdiən] *n* accordéon *m.*
accost [ə'kost] *v* accoster.
account [ə'kaunt] *n* compte *m*; (*report*) exposé *m.* **on account of** à cause de. **on no account** en aucun cas. **take into account** tenir compte de. *v* **account for** justifier; expliquer. **accountant** *n* comptable *m, f.*
accrue [ə'kruː] *v* revenir; s'accumuler. **accrued interest** intérêt couru *m.*
accumulate [ə'kjuːmjuleit] *v* (s')accumuler. **accumulation** *n* accumulation *f.*
accurate ['akjurət] *adj* exact, précis. **accuracy** *n* exactitude *f*, précision *f.*
accuse [ə'kjuːz] *v* accuser. **accusation** *n* accusation *f.* **accusing** *adj* accusateur, -trice.
accustom [ə'kʌstəm] *v* habituer.
ace [eis] *n* as *m.*
ache [eik] *v* faire mal. *n* douleur *f.*
achieve [ə'tʃiːv] *v* (*task*) accomplir; (*aim*) atteindre. **achievement** *n* (*feat*) exploit *m*; (*completion*) exécution *f.*
acid ['asid] *nm, adj* acide.
acknowledge [ək'nolidʒ] *v* reconnaître; (*letter, etc.*) accuser réception de, répondre à. **acknowledgment** *n* reconnaissance *f*; (*of error*) aveu *m*; (*receipt*) reçu *m.*
acne ['akni] *n* acné *f.*
acorn ['eikoːn] *n* gland *m.*
acoustic [ə'kuːstik] *adj* acoustique. **acoustics** *pl n* acoustique *f sing.*
acquaint [ə'kweint] *v* (*inform*) aviser. **acquaint with** mettre au courant de. **be acquainted with** (*a fact*) savoir; (*a place or person*) connaître. **become acquainted with** faire la connaissance de. **acquaintance** *n* connaissance *f*, relation *f.*
acquiesce [akwi'es] *v* acquiescer. **acquiescence** *n* consentement *m.*

acquire [ə'kwaiə] *v* acquérir; prendre. **acquired taste** goût qui s'acquiert *m*. **acquisition** *n* acquisition *f*. **acquisitive** *adj* âpre au gain

acquit [ə'kwit] *v* acquitter. **acquittal** *n* acquittement *m*.

acrid ['akrid] *adj* âcre; (*biting*) acerbe.

acrimony ['akriməni] *n* acrimonie *f*. **acrimonious** *adj* acrimonieux.

acrobat ['akrəbat] *n* acrobate *m*, *f*. **acrobatic** *adj* acrobatique. **acrobatics** *pl n* acrobatie *f sing*.

across [ə'kros] *prep* en travers de, à travers; de l'autre côté. *adv* (*width*) de large. **go across** traverser.

acrylic [ə'krilik] *adj* acrylique.

act [akt] *n* acte *m*, action *f*; (*law*) loi *f*; (*theatre*) acte *m*. **in the act of** en train de. *v* agir; (*theatre*) jouer. **act the fool** faire l'idiot. **acting** *adj* (*temporary*) suppléant, par intérim. **actor** *n* acteur *m*. **actress** *n* actrice *f*.

action ['akʃən] *n* action *f*; (*law*) procès *m*; (*mil*) combat *m*. **out of action** hors d'usage.

active ['aktiv] *adj* actif. **activate** *v* activer. **activity** *n* activité *f*.

actual ['aktʃuəl] *adj* réel; (*factual*) positif. **actually** *adv* effectivement; à vrai dire.

actuary ['aktjuəri] *n* actuaire *m*.

acumen [ə'kjuːmen] *n* perspicacité *f*.

acupuncture ['akjupʌŋktʃə] *n* acupuncture *f*.

acute [ə'kjuːt] *adj* aigu, -guë; (*mind*) pénétrant; (*pain, etc.*) vif.

adamant ['adəmənt] *adj* inflexible.

Adam's apple [adəm'zapl] *n* pomme d'Adam *f*.

adapt [ə'dapt] *v* (s')adapter. **adaptable** *adj* adaptable. **adaptation** *n* adaptation *f*. **adaptor** *n* (*elec*) prise multiple *f*.

add [ad] *v* ajouter; (*numbers*) additionner. **addition** *n* addition *f*. **in addition** de plus. **in addition to** en plus de. **additional** *adj* additionnel; supplémentaire.

addendum [ə'dendəm] *n* addendum *m invar*.

adder ['adə] *n* vipère *f*.

addict ['adikt; *v* ə'dikt] *n* (*drugs*) toxicomane *m*, *f*; fanatique *m*, *f*. *v* **become addicted to** s'adonner à. **addiction** *n* (*med*) dépendance *f*.

additive ['aditiv] *nm*, *adj* additif.

address [ə'dres] *n* adresse *f*; (*talk*) discours *m*. *v* (s')adresser (à).

adenoids ['adənoidz] *pl n* végétations adénoïdes *f pl*.

adept [ə'dept] *adj* expert, versé.

adequate ['adikwət] *adj* suffisant.

adhere [əd'hiə] *v* adhérer. **adherent** *n* adhérent, -e *m*, *f*. **adhesion** *n* adherence *f*. **adhesive** *nm*, *adj* adhésif.

adjacent [ə'dʒeisənt] *adj* adjacent, contigu, -guë.

adjective ['adʒiktiv] *n* adjectif *m*.

adjoin [ə'dʒoin] *v* être contigu à. **adjoining** *adj* voisin.

adjourn [ə'dʒəːn] *v* ajourner; (*meeting*) suspendre la séance; (*move*) se retirer.

adjudicate [ə'dʒuːdikeit] *v* juger. **adjudication** *n* jugement *m*. **adjudicator** *n* juge *m*.

adjust [ə'dʒʌst] *v* ajuster; (s')adapter; (*correct*) régler. **adjustment** *n* réglage *m*.

ad-lib ['ad'lib] *adv* à volonté. *v* improviser.

administer [əd'ministə] *v* administrer; (*business, etc.*) gérer. **administration** *n* administration *f*; gestion *f*. **administrative** *adj* administratif. **administrator** *n* administrateur, -trice *m*, *f*.

admiral ['admərəl] *n* amiral *m*. **Admiralty** *n* ministère de la Marine *m*.

admire [əd'maiə] *v* admirer. **admirable** *adj* admirable. **admiration** *n* admiration *f*. **admiring** *adj* admiratif.

admit [əd'mit] *v* (*let in*) laisser entrer; (*acknowledge*) admettre. **admission** *n* admission *f*.

adolescence [adə'lesns] *n* adolescence *f*. **adolescent** *n*, *adj* adolescent, -e.

adopt [ə'dopt] *v* adopter. **adopted** *adj* (*child*) adoptif. **adoption** *n* adoption *f*.

adore [ə'doː] *v* adorer. **adorable** *adj* adorable. **adoration** *n* adoration *f*.

adorn [ə'doːn] *v* orner, parer.

adrenalin [ə'drenəlin] *n* adrénaline *f*.

adrift [ə'drift] *adv* à la dérive. **come adrift** (*wire, etc.*) se détacher.

adroit [ə'droit] *adj* adroit.

adulation [adju'leiʃən] *n* adulation *f*.

adult ['adʌlt] *n* (*m*+*f*), *adj* adulte.

adulterate [ə'dʌltəreit] *v* adultérer, falsifier.

adultery [ə'dʌltəri] *n* adultère *m*. **adulterer** *n* adultère *m*, *f*.

advance [əd'vaːns] *v* (s')avancer. *n* avance *f*. **advance booking office** location *f*. **book in advance** retenir à l'avance. **luggage in advance** bagages enregistrés *m pl*.

advantage [əd'vaːntidʒ] *n* avantage *m*. **take advantage of** profiter de. **advantageous** *adj* avantageux.
advent ['advənt] *n* venue *f*. **Advent** *n* (*rel*) Avent *m*.
adventure [əd'ventʃə] *n* aventure *f*. **adventurer** *n* aventurier, -ère *m, f*. **adventurous** *adj* aventureux.
adverb ['advəːb] *n* adverbe *m*.
adversary ['advəsəri] *n* adversaire *m, f*.
adverse ['advəːs] *adj* défavorable, hostile. **adversity** *n* adversité *f*.
advertise ['advətaiz] *v* (*comm*) faire de la publicité (pour); (*newspaper, etc.*) insérer une annonce. **advertisement** *n* (*comm*) réclame *f*, publicité *f*; (*newspaper*) annonce *f*. **advertising** *n* publicité *f*.
advise [əd'vaiz] *v* conseiller; recommander; (*inform*) aviser. **advice** *n* conseils *m pl*; avis *m*. **advisable** *adj* recommandable. **adviser** *n* conseiller, -ère *m, f*. **advisory** *adj* consultatif.
advocate ['advəkeit] *v* recommander.
aerial ['eəriəl] *adj* aérien. *n* antenne *f*.
aerodynamics [eərədai'namiks] *n* aérodynamique *f*.
aeronautics [eərə'noːtiks] *n* aéronautique *f*.
aeroplane ['eərəplein] *n* avion *m*.
aerosol ['eərəsol] *n* bombe *f*; (*perfume*) atomiseur *m*.
aesthetic [iːs'θetik] *adj* esthétique.
affair [ə'feə] *n* affaire *f*. **have an affair with** avoir une liaison avec.
affect[1] [ə'fekt] *v* (*influence*) affecter, toucher.
affect[2] [ə'fekt] *v* (*feign*) affecter, feindre. **affected** *adj* affecté, maniéré.
affection [ə'fekʃən] *n* affection *f*. **affectionate** *adj* affectueux.
affiliate [ə'filieit] *v* affilier. **affiliated company** filiale *f*. **affiliation** *n* affiliation *f*.
affinity [ə'finəti] *n* affinité *f*.
affirm [ə'fəːm] *v* affirmer. **affirmative** *nm, adj* affirmatif.
affix [ə'fiks; *n* 'afiks] *v* apposer; (*stick*) coller. *n* (*gramm*) affixe *m*.
afflict [ə'flikt] *v* affliger. **affliction** *n* affliction *f*; infirmité *f*.
affluent ['afluənt] *adj* abondant; riche. **affluence** *n* abondance *f*; richesse *f*.
afford [ə'foːd] *v* avoir les moyens d'acheter; (*provide*) fournir.
affront [ə'frʌnt] *v* insulter. *n* affront *m*.
afield [ə'fiːld] *adv* **far afield** très loin. **farther afield** plus loin.
afloat [ə'flout] *adv* à flot.
afoot [ə'fut] *adv* **there's something afoot** il se prépare quelque chose.
aforesaid [ə'foːsed] *adj* susdit.
afraid [ə'freid] *adj* effrayé. **be afraid** avoir peur; (*polite regret*) regretter.
afresh [ə'freʃ] *adv* de nouveau. **start afresh** recommencer.
Africa ['afrikə] *n* Afrique *f*. **African** *adj* africain; *n* Africain, -e *m, f*.
aft [aːft] *adv* sur *or* à l'arrière.
after ['aːftə] *prep, conj* après. *adv* après; ensuite. **after all** après tout.
after-effect *n* suite *f*.
aftermath ['aːftəmaθ] *n* conséquences *f pl*.
afternoon [ˌaːftə'nuːn] *n* après-midi *m*.
afterthought ['aːftəθoːt] *n* pensée après coup *f*.
afterwards ['aːftəwədz] *adv* ensuite.
again [ə'gen] *adv* de nouveau, encore. **again and again** à plusieurs reprises.
against [ə'genst] *prep* contre. **against the law** contraire à la loi.
age [eidʒ] *n* âge *m*; (*historical*) époque *f*. **for ages** pendant une éternité. **of age** majeur, -e. **under age** mineur, -e. *v* vieillir. **aged** *adj* âgé.
agency ['eidʒənsi] *n* agence *f*, bureau *m*.
agenda [ə'dʒendə] *n* ordre du jour *m*.
agent ['eidʒənt] *n* agent, -e *m, f*; représentant, -e *m, f*.
aggravate ['agrəveit] *v* aggraver; (*increase*) augmenter; (*annoy*) agacer. **aggravation** *n* aggravation *f*; agacement *m*.
aggregate ['agrigət] *n* ensemble *m*. *adj* collectif.
aggression [ə'greʃən] *n* agression *f*. **aggressive** *adj* agressif.
aghast [ə'gaːst] *adj* atterré.
agile ['adʒail] *adj* agile. **agility** *n* agilité *f*.
agitate ['adʒiteit] *v* (*shake*) agiter; (*worry*) troubler. **agitated** *adj* inquiet, -ète. **agitation** *n* agitation *f*; émotion *f*. **agitator** *n* agitateur, -trice *m, f*.
agnostic [ag'nostik] *n*(*m*+*f*), *adj* agnostique.
ago [ə'gou] *adv* il y a: *il y a deux mois*.
agog [ə'gog] *adj, adv* en émoi. **be all agog** être impatient.
agony ['agəni] *n* (*mental*) angoisse *f*; (*med*) agonie *f*. **be in agony** souffrir le martyre. **agonizing** *adj* angoissant.

agree ['ə'griː] *v* être d'accord; consentir; (*concur*) convenir, s'accorder. **agreeable** *adj* agréable. **agreement** *n* accord *m*.
agriculture ['agrikʌltʃə] *n* agriculture *f*. **agricultural** *adj* agricole.
aground [ə'graund] *adv* échoué. **run aground** s'échouer.
ahead [ə'hed] *adv* en avant; (*time*) en avance.
aid [eid] *v* aider. **aid and abet** être complice de. *n* aide *f*. **in aid of** au profit de.
aim [eim] *v* viser; aspirer. *n* (*purpose*) but *m*. **take aim (at)** viser. **aimless** *adj* (*person*) sans but; (*action*) futile.
air [eə] *n* air *m*. **by air** par avion. *v* aérer; (*opinion*) faire connaître. **airy** *adj* bien aéré.
airbed ['eəbed] *n* matelas pneumatique *m*.
airborne ['eəbɔːn] *adj* aéroporté. **become airborne** (*aircraft*) décoller.
air-conditioned *adj* climatisé. **air-conditioning** *n* climatisation *f*.
aircraft ['eəkraːft] *n* avion *m*. **aircraft-carrier** *n* porte-avions *m invar*.
airfield ['eəfiːld] *n* terrain d'aviation *m*.
air force *n* armée de l'air *f*.
air-hostess *n* hôtesse de l'air *f*.
airing cupboard *n* placard-séchoir *m*.
air lift *n* pont aérien *m*.
airline ['eəlain] *n* ligne aérienne *f*.
airmail ['eəmeil] *n* poste aérienne *f*. **airmail letter** lettre par avion *f*. **by airmail** par avion.
airport ['eəpoːt] *n* aéroport *m*.
air-raid *n* attaque aérienne *f*. **air-raid shelter** abri antiaérien *m*.
airtight ['eətait] *adj* hermétique.
aisle [ail] *n* (*church*) allée centrale *f*, bas-côté *m*; (*theatre*) passage *m*; (*train, etc.*) couloir central *m*.
ajar [ə'dʒaː] *adj*, *adv* entrouvert.
akin [ə'kin] *adj* **be akin to** (*resemble*) tenir de, ressembler à; (*family*) être parent de.
alabaster ['aləbaːstə] *n* albâtre *m*.
alarm [ə'laːm] *n* alarme *f*. **alarm clock** *n* réveil *m*. *v* alarmer. **alarmist** *n* alarmiste *m*, *f*.
alas [ə'las] *interj* hélas!
Albania [al'beinjə] *n* Albanie *f*. **Albanian** *nm*, *adj* albanais; *n* (*people*) Albanais, -e *m*, *f*.
albatross ['albətros] *n* albatros *m*.
albino [al'biːnou] *n* albinos *m*, *f*.
album ['albəm] *n* album *m*.
alchemy ['alkəmi] *n* alchimie *f*. **alchemist** *n* alchimiste *m*.
alcohol ['alkəhol] *n* alcool *m*. **alcoholic** *n*(*m*+*f*), *adj* alcoolique. **alcoholism** *n* alcoolisme *m*.
alcove ['alkouv] *n* (*room*) alcôve *f*; (*wall*) niche *f*.
alderman ['oːldəmən] *n* conseiller municipal *m*.
ale [eil] *n* bière *f*.
alert [ə'ləːt] *adj* alerte; vigilant. *n* alerte *f*. **on the alert** sur le qui-vive. *v* alerter, éveiller l'attention de.
algebra ['aldʒibrə] *n* algèbre *f*. **algebraic** *adj* algébrique.
Algeria [al'dʒiəriə] *n* Algérie *f*. **Algerian** *n* Algérien, -enne *m*, *f*; *adj* algérien.
Algiers [al'dʒiəz] *n* Alger.
alias ['eiliəs] *adv* alias. *n* faux nom *m*.
alibi ['alibai] *n* alibi *m*.
alien ['eiliən] *n*, *adj* étranger, -ère. **alien to** contraire à. **alienate** *v* aliéner. **alienation** *n* aliénation *f*, éloignement *m*.
alight[1] [ə'lait] *v* descendre; (*bird*) se poser.
alight[2] [ə'lait] *adj* allumé; en feu. **set alight** mettre le feu à.
align [ə'lain] *v* (s')aligner. **alignment** *n* alignement *m*.
alike [ə'laik] *adj* semblable. *adv* pareillement, de la même façon. **be alike** se ressembler.
alimentary canal [ali'mentəri] *n* tube digestif *m*.
alimony ['aliməni] *n* pension alimentaire *f*.
alive [ə'laiv] *adj* vivant.
alkali ['alkəlai] *n* alcali *m*. **alkaline** *adj* alcaline.
all [oːl] *pron*, *adj* tout, toute (*pl* tous, toutes). *adv* tout, complètement. **all right** ça va. **All Saints' Day** le Toussaint. **all the same** tout de même. **not at all** pas du tout.
allay [ə'lei] *v* apaiser; (*suspicion*) dissiper.
allege [ə'ledʒ] *v* alléguer. **allegation** *n* allégation *f*. **alleged** *adj* prétendu, allégué; présumé.
allegiance [ə'liːdʒəns] *n* fidélité *f*.
allegory ['aligəri] *n* allégorie *f*. **allegorical** *adj* allégorique.
allergy ['alədʒi] *n* allergie *f*. **allergic** *adj* allergique.
alleviate [ə'liːvieit] *v* soulager.
alley ['ali] *n* ruelle *f*.

alliance [ə'laiəns] *n* alliance *f.*
alligator ['aligeitə] *n* alligator *m.*
alliteration [əlitə'reiʃən] *n* allitération *f.*
allocate ['aləkeit] *v* (*allot*) allouer; (*share*) répartir. **allocation** *n* allocation *f*; (*share*) part *f.*
allot [ə'lot] *v* assigner. **allotment** *n* (*land*) parcelle de terre *f.*
allow [ə'lau] *v* permettre; (*give*) accorder. **allow for** tenir compte de. **allowance** *n* allocation *f*; (*subsistence*) indemnité *f*, pension *f*; (*comm*) rabais *m.*
alloy ['aloi; *v* ə'loi] *n* alliage *m.* *v* allier; faire un alliage de.
allude [ə'luːd] *v* faire allusion. **allusion** *n* allusion *f.*
allure [ə'ljuə] *v* attirer. *n* charme *m.* **alluring** *adj* séduisant.
ally ['alai; *v* ə'lai] *n* allié, -ée *m, f.* *v* allier. **allied** *adj* allié; (*connected*) apparenté.
almanac ['oːlmənak] *n* almanach *m.*
almighty [oːl'maiti] *adj* tout-puissant; (*coll*) fameux.
almond ['aːmənd] *n* (*nut*) amande *f*; (*tree*) amandier *m.*
almost ['oːlmoust] *adv* presque, à peu près.
alms [aːmz] *n* aumône *f.* **almshouse** *n* hospice *m.*
aloft [ə'loft] *adv* en haut.
alone [ə'loun] *adj, adv* seul. **leave alone** laisser tranquille. **let alone** sans parler de.
along [ə'loŋ] *prep* le long de. **alongside** *prep* à côté de.
aloof [ə'luːf] *adj* distant. *adv* à l'écart.
aloud [ə'laud] *adv* (*reading*) à voix haute; (*think*) tout haut.
alphabet ['alfəbit] *n* alphabet *m.* **alphabetical** *adj* alphabétique. **in alphabetical order** par ordre alphabétique.
already [oːl'redi] *adv* déjà.
Alsatian [al'seiʃən] *n* (*dog*) chien-loup *m.*
also ['oːlsou] *adv* aussi.
altar ['oːltə] *n* autel *m.*
alter ['oːltə] *v* changer; (*dress, etc.*) retoucher. **alteration** *n* changement *m*; retouchage *m.*
alternate [oːl'təːnət; *v* 'oːltəneit] *adj* alternatif, alterné; (*every other*) tous les deux. *v* alterner. **alternating current** courant alternatif *m.* **alternator** *n* alternateur *m.*
alternative [oːl'təːnətiv] *n* (*of two*) alternative *f*; (*of several*) choix *m*; autre solution *f.* *adj* autre, alternatif.
although [oːl'ðou] *conj* bien que, quoique.
altitude ['altitjuːd] *n* altitude *f.*
alto ['altou] *n* (*male*) haute-contre *f*; (*female*) contralto *m*; (*instrument*) alto *m.*
altogether [oːltə'geðə] *adv* (*completely*) entièrement; (*including everything*) en tout.
altruistic [altru'istik] *adj* altruiste.
aluminium [alju'miniəm] *n* aluminium *m.*
always ['oːlweiz] *adv* toujours.
am [am] *V* **be.**
amalgamate [ə'malgəmeit] *v* (*companies*) fusionner; (*metals*) amalgamer. **amalgamation** *n* fusionnement *m*; amalgamation *f.*
amass [ə'mas] *v* amasser.
amateur ['amətə] *n* amateur *m.*
amaze [ə'meiz] *v* stupéfier. **amazed** *adj* stupéfait. **amazement** *n* stupéfaction *f.* **amazing** *adj* stupéfiant, ahurissant.
ambassador [am'basədə] *n* ambassadeur *m.*
amber ['ambə] *n* ambre; (*traffic lights*) feu orange *m.*
ambidextrous [ambi'dekstrəs] *adj* ambidextre.
ambiguous [am'bigjuəs] *adj* ambigu, -guë. **ambiguity** *n* ambiguïté *f.*
ambition [am'biʃən] *n* ambition *f.* **ambitious** *adj* ambitieux.
ambivalent [am'bivələnt] *adj* ambivalent. **ambivalence** *n* ambivalence *f.*
amble ['ambl] *v* marcher d'un pas tranquille; (*horse*) ambler. *n* pas tranquille *m*; (*horse*) amble *m.*
ambulance ['ambjuləns] *n* ambulance *f.*
ambush ['ambuʃ] *n* embuscade *f.* **in ambush** en embuscade. *v* attirer dans une embuscade.
ameliorate [ə'miːliəreit] *v* (s')améliorer. **amelioration** *n* amélioration *f.*
amenable [ə'miːnəbl] *adj* (*cooperative*) maniable; (*answerable*) responsable.
amend [ə'mend] *v* (s')amender; (*revise*) modifier; (*correct*) corriger. **amendment** *n* amendement *m*; modification *f.*
amenity [ə'miːnəti] *n* agrément *m.* **amenities** *pl n* commodités *f pl.*
America [ə'merikə] *n* Amérique *f*; (*United States*) Etats-Unis *m pl.* **American** *n* Américain, -e *m, f*; *adj* américain.

amethyst ['aməθist] *n* améthyste *f.*
amiable ['eimiəbl] *adj* aimable.
amicable ['amikəbl] *adj* amical; (*law*) à l'amiable.
amid [ə'mid] *prep* au milieu de.
amiss [ə'mis] *adv* de travers. *adj* mal à propos. **something is amiss** quelque chose ne va pas.
ammonia [ə'mouniə] *n* (*gas*) ammoniac *m*; (*liquid*) ammoniaque *f.*
ammunition [amju'niʃən] *n* munitions *f pl.*
amnesia [am'niːziə] *n* amnésie *f.*
amnesty ['amnəsti] *n* amnistie *f.*
amoeba [ə'miːbə] *n* amibe *f.*
among [ə'mʌŋ] *prep* entre, parmi.
amoral [ei'morəl] *adj* amorale.
amorous ['amərəs] *adj* amoureux.
amorphous [ə'moːfəs] *adj* amorphe; (*ideas, etc.*) sans forme.
amount [ə'maunt] *n* quantité *f*; (*total*) montant *m.* *v* **amount to** s'élever à; (*be equivalent to*) revenir à, équivaloir à.
ampere ['ampeə] *n* ampère *m.*
amphetamine [am'fetəmiːn] *n* amphétamine *f.*
amphibian [am'fibiən] *nm, adj* amphibie. **amphibious** *adj* amphibie.
amphitheatre ['amfiθiətə] *n* amphithéâtre *m.*
ample ['ampl] *adj* (*plenty*) bien assez de; (*large*) ample.
amplify ['amplifai] *v* amplifier; développer. **amplifier** *n* amplificateur *m.*
amputate ['ampjuteit] *v* amputer. **amputation** *n* amputation *f.*
Amsterdam ['amstə'dam] *n* Amsterdam.
amuse [ə'mjuːz] *v* (*cause laughter*) faire rire; (*entertain*) distraire. **amuse oneself** s'amuser. **amused** *adj* amusé. **amusement** *n* amusement *m*; distraction *f.*
an [ən] *V* a.
anachronism [ə'nakrənizəm] *n* anachronisme *m.* **anachronistic** *adj* anachronique.
anaemia [ə'niːmiə] *n* anémie *f.* **anaemic** *adj* anémique.
anaesthetic [anəs'θetik] *nm, adj* anesthésique. **under anaesthetic** sous anesthésie. **anaesthetist** *n* anesthésiste *m, f.* **anaesthetize** *v* anesthésier.
anagram ['anəgram] *n* anagramme *f.*
anal ['einl] *adj* anal.
analogy [ə'nalədʒi] *n* analogie *f.*
analysis [ən'aləsis] *n* analyse *f.* **analyse** *v* analyser, faire l'analyse de. **analytical** *adj* analytique.
anarchy ['anəki] *n* anarchie *f.* **anarchist** *n* anarchiste *m, f.*
anathema [ə'naθəmə] *n* anathème *m.* **it is anathema to me** je l'ai en abomination.
anatomy [ə'natəmi] *n* (*med*) anatomie *f*; structure *f.*
ancestor ['ansestə] *n* ancêtre *m*, aïeul, -e *m, f.* **ancestral** *adj* ancestral. **ancestry** *n* ascendance *f*; ancêtres *m pl*, aïeux *m pl.*
anchor ['aŋkə] *n* ancre *f.* *v* (*naut*) (se) mettre à l'ancre; (*fasten*) ancrer.
anchovy ['antʃəvi] *n* anchois *m.*
ancient ['einʃənt] *adj* antique; ancien.
ancillary [an'siləri] *adj* auxiliaire.
and [and] *conj* et.
Andorra [an'doːrə] *n* Andorre *f.*
anecdote ['anikdout] *n* anecdote *f.*
anemone [ə'neməni] *n* anémone *f.*
anew [ə'njuː] *adv* de nouveau.
angel ['eindʒəl] *n* ange *m.* **angelic** *adj* angélique.
angelica [an'dʒelikə] *n* angélique *f.*
anger ['aŋgə] *n* colère *f.* *v* mettre en colère.
angina [an'dʒainə] *n* angine de poitrine *f.*
angle ['aŋgl] *n* angle *m*; aspect *m.*
angling ['aŋgliŋ] *n* pêche à la ligne *f.* **angler** *n* pêcheur, -euse *m, f.*
angry ['aŋgri] *adj* en colère; furieux. **become angry** se fâcher.
anguish ['aŋgwiʃ] *n* angoisse *f.*
angular ['aŋgjulə] *adj* anguleux.
animal ['animəl] *nm, adj* animal.
animate ['animət; *v* 'animeit] *adj* animé. *v* animer. **animation** *n* animation *f.*
animosity [ani'mosəti] *n* animosité *f.*
aniseed ['anisiːd] *n* graine d'anis *f*; (*as modifier*) à l'anis.
ankle ['aŋkl] *n* cheville *f.*
annals ['anlz] *pl n* annales *f pl.*
annex [ə'neks; *n* 'aneks] *v* annexer. **annexe** *n* annexe *f.*
annihilate [ə'naiəleit] *v* (*mil*) anéantir; annihiler. **annihilation** *n* anéantissement *m.*
anniversary [ani'vəːsəri] *n* anniversaire *m.*
annotate ['anəteit] *v* annoter. **annotation** *n* annotation *f.*
announce [ə'nauns] *v* annoncer. **announcement** *n* annonce *f*; (*official*) avis *m*; (*of birth, etc.*) faire-part *m.* **announcer** *n* (*radio, TV*) speaker, -erine *m, f.*

annoy [ə'noi] *v* ennuyer, agacer. **annoyance** *n* mécontentement *m*; (*nuisance*) tracas *m*. **annoyed** *adj* mécontent. **annoying** *adj* agaçant, ennuyeux.
annual ['anjuəl] *adj* annuel. *n* (*bot*) plante annuelle *f*; (*children's book*) album *m*.
annul [ə'nʌl] *v* (*marriage*) annuler; (*law*) abroger. **annulment** *n* annulation *f*; abrogation *f*.
anode ['anoud] *n* anode *f*.
anomaly [ə'noməli] *n* anomalie *f*. **anomalous** *adj* anormal.
anonymous [ə'noniməs] *adj* anonyme. **anonymity** *n* anonymat *m*.
anorak ['anərak] *n* anorak *m*.
another [ə'nʌðə] *pron*, *adj* (*different*) un autre; (*extra*) encore un. **one another** l'un l'autre, les uns les autres.
answer ['aːnsə] *n* réponse *f*; solution *f*. *v* répondre (à). **answerable** *adj* responsable.
ant [ant] *n* fourmi *f*. **anthill** *n* fourmilière *f*.
antagonize [an'tagənaiz] *v* contrarier. **antagonism** *n* antagonisme *m*. **antagonist** *n* antagoniste *m*, *f*. **antagonistic** *adj* opposé.
antecedent [anti'siːdənt] *adj* antérieur, -e. *n* antécédent *m*.
antelope ['antəloup] *n* antilope *f*.
antenna [an'tenə] *n* antenne *f*.
anthem ['anθəm] *n* (*national*) hymne *m*; motet *m*.
anthology [an'θolədʒi] *n* anthologie *f*.
anthropology [anθrə'polədʒi] *n* anthropologie *f*. **anthropological** *adj* anthropologique. **anthropologist** *n* anthropologiste *m*, *f*.
anti-aircraft [anti'eəkraːft] *adj* antiaérien.
antibiotic [antibai'otik] *nm*, *adj* antibiotique.
antibody ['anti,bodi] *n* anticorps *m*.
anticipate [an'tisipeit] *v* (*foresee*) prévoir; (*act in advance*) prévenir, anticiper. **anticipation** *n* attente *f*; appréhension *f*. **in anticipation** par anticipation, d'avance.
anticlimax [anti'klaimaks] *n* chute *f*.
anticlockwise [anti'klokwaiz] *adj* dans le sens inverse des aiguilles d'une montre.
antics ['antiks] *pl n* singeries *f pl*, cirque *m sing*.
anticyclone [anti'saikloun] *n* anticyclone *m*.
antidote ['antidout] *n* antidote *m*.
antifreeze ['antifriːz] *n* antigel *m*.
antihistamine [anti'histəmin] *n* antihistaminique *m*.
antipathy [an'tipəθi] *n* antipathie *f*. **antipathetic** *adj* antipathique.
antique [an'tiːk] *adj* ancien; antique. *n* (*ornament*) objet d'art ancien *m*; (*furniture*) meuble ancien *m*. **antique dealer** *n* antiquaire *m*, *f*. **antique shop** *n* magasin d'antiquités *m*. **antiquated** *adj* vieilli. **antiquity** *n* antiquité *f*.
anti-Semitic [antisə'mitik] *adj* antisémite. **anti-Semite** *n* antisémite *m*, *f*. **anti-Semitism** *n* antisémitisme *m*.
antiseptic [anti'septik] *nm*, *adj* antiseptique.
antisocial [anti'souʃəl] *adj* antisocial.
antithesis [an'tiθəsis] *n* antithèse *f*.
antlers ['antləz] *pl n* bois *m pl*, ramure *f sing*.
antonym ['antənim] *n* antonyme *m*.
anus ['einəs] *n* anus *m*.
anvil ['anvil] *n* enclume *f*.
anxious ['aŋkʃəs] *adj* (*worry*) anxieux; (*desire*) impatient. **anxiety** *n* anxiété *f*; grand désir *m*. **anxiously** *adv* avec inquiétude; avec impatience.
any ['eni] *adj* (*interrogative*) du, de la, des; (*negative*) de; (*whichever*) n'importe quel. *pron* en: *je n'en ai pas*; aucun; n'importe lequel. **anybody** *or* **anyone** *pron* n'importe qui; (*somebody*) quelqu'un; (*negative*) personne. **anyhow** *or* **anyway** *adv* en tout cas; quand même. **any more** encore (de); (*negative*) plus. **anything** *pron* n'importe quoi; (*something*) quelque chose; (*negative*) rien. **anywhere** *adv* n'importe où; (*somewhere*) quelque part; (*negative*) nulle part. **at any rate** en tout cas. **in any case** de toute façon.
apart [ə'paːt] *adv* à part; à distance; séparément; en pièces. **apart from** en dehors de. **come apart** se défaire. **take apart** démonter. **tell apart** distinguer l'un de l'autre.
apartment [ə'paːtmənt] *n* (*room*) pièce *f*; (*flat*) appartement *m*.
apathy ['apəθi] *n* apathie *f*, indifférence *f*. **apathetic** *adj* apathique.
ape [eip] *n* singe *m*, *f*. *v* singer, imiter.
aperture ['apətjuə] *n* (*phot*) ouverture *f*; orifice *m*.

apex ['eipeks] *n* sommet *m*.
aphid ['eifid] *n* aphidé *m*.
aphrodisiac [afrə'diziak] *nm, adj* aphrodisiaque.
apiece [ə'piːs] *adv* chacun; par personne; la pièce.
apology [ə'polədʒi] *n* excuses *f pl*; (*defence*) apologie *f*. **apologize** *v* s'excuser. **be apologetic** se répandre en excuses.
apoplexy ['apəpleksi] *n* apoplexie *f*. **fit of apoplexy** coup de sang *m*.
apostle [ə'posl] *n* apôtre *m*.
apostrophe [ə'postrəfi] *n* apostrophe *f*.
appal [ə'poːl] *v* (*shock*) consterner; (*frighten*) épouvanter. **appalling** *adj* consternant; épouvantable.
apparatus [apə'reitəs] *n* appareil *m*, dispositif *m*.
apparent [ə'parənt] *adj* (*not real*) apparent; (*obvious*) évident, manifeste. **apparently** *adv* apparemment; paraît-il.
apparition [apə'riʃən] *n* apparition *f*.
appeal [ə'piːl] *v* faire (un) appel. **appeal to** (*please*) plaire à; (*request*) s'adresser à. **appealing** *adj* (*moving*) attendrissant; (*attractive*) attirant.
appear [ə'piə] *v* (*be seen*) apparaître, se montrer; (*seem*) paraître. **appearance** *n* apparition *f*; (*aspect*) apparence *f*.
appease [ə'piːz] *v* apaiser. **appeasement** *n* apaisement *m*.
appendix [ə'pendiks] *n* appendice *m*. **appendicitis** *n* appendicite *f*.
appetite ['apitait] *n* appétit *m*. **appetizer** *n* apéritif *m*. **appetizing** *adj* appétissant.
applaud [ə'ploːd] *v* applaudir. **applause** *n* applaudissements *m pl*.
apple ['apl] *n* (*fruit*) pomme *f*; (*tree*) pommier *m*.
apply [ə'plai] *v* appliquer; (*paint, etc.*) mettre; (*ask*) s'adresser; (*refer*) s'appliquer. **appliance** *n* appareil *m*. **applicable** *adj* applicable. **applicant** *n* candidat, -e *m, f*. **application** *n* application *f*; (*job*) demande *f*.
appoint [ə'point] *v* désigner, nommer. **at the appointed time** à l'heure convenue. **appointment** *n* (*meeting*) rendez-vous *m*; (*job*) poste.
apportion [ə'poːʃən] *v* partager, répartir; assigner.
appraise [ə'preiz] *v* estimer, évaluer. **appraisal** *n* évaluation *f*; appréciation *f*.
appreciate [ə'priːʃieit] *v* (*value*) apprécier; (*be aware of*) se rendre compte de; (*be grateful for*) être reconnaissant de; (*rise in value*) prendre de la valeur. **appreciation** *n* appréciation *f*; reconnaissance *f*.
apprehend [apri'hend] *v* (*arrest*) arrêter, appréhender; (*understand*) comprendre. **apprehension** *n* (*fear*) appréhension *f*; arrestation *f*. **apprehensive** *adj* inquiet, -ète; appréhensif.
apprentice [ə'prentis] *v* placer *or* mettre en apprentissage (chez). *n* apprenti, -e *m, f*. **apprenticeship** *n* apprentissage *m*.
approach [ə'proutʃ] *v* (s')approcher (de). *n* approche *f*, accès *m*.
appropriate [ə'prouprieit; *adj* ə'proupriət] *v* s'approprier. *adj* (*name, etc.*) juste, bien choisi; (*correct*) approprié.
approve [ə'pruːv] *v* approuver. **approval** *n* approbation *f*. **on approval** à l'essai.
approximate [ə'proksimeit; *adj* ə'proksimət] *v* se rapprocher (de). *adj* approximatif.
apricot ['eiprikot] *n* (*fruit*) abricot *m*; (*tree*) abricotier *m*.
April ['eiprəl] *n* avril *m*. **April fool** *n* poisson d'avril *m*.
apron ['eiprən] *n* tablier *m*; (*aero*) aire de manœuvre *f*.
apt [apt] *adj* (*fitting*) juste, convenable; (*inclined*) enclin, porté. **aptly** *adv* à propos.
aptitude ['aptitjuːd] *n* aptitude *f*.
aqualung ['akwəlʌŋ] *n* scaphandre autonome *m*.
aquarium [ə'kweəriəm] *n* aquarium *m*.
Aquarius [ə'kweəriəs] *n* Verseau *m*.
aquatic [ə'kwatik] *adj* aquatique
aqueduct ['akwidʌkt] *n* aqueduc *m*.
Arab ['arəb] *n* Arabe *m, f*. *adj* arabe. **Arabia** *n* Arabie *f*. **Arabian** *or* **Arabic** *adj* arabe.
arable ['arəbl] *adj* arable.
arbitrary ['aːbitrəri] *adj* arbitraire.
arbitrate ['aːbitreit] *v* arbitrer, juger. **arbitration** *n* arbitrage *m*. **arbiter** *n* arbitre *m*.
arc [aːk] *n* arc *m*. **arc lamp** lampe à arc *f*. **arc light** arc voltaïque *m*.
arcade [aː'keid] *n* arcade *m*; (*shopping*) passage.
arch [aːtʃ] *v* (s')arquer. *n* (*church, etc.*) voûte *f*, cintre *m*; (*bridge*) arche *f*.
archaeology [aːki'olədʒi] *n* archéologie *f*. **archaeological** *adj* archéologique. **archaeologist** *n* archéologue *m, f*.

archaic [aːˈkeiik] *adj* archaïque. **archaism** *n* archaïsme *m*.
archbishop [aːtʃˈbiʃəp] *n* archevêque *m*.
archduke [aːtʃˈdjuːk] *n* archiduc *m*. **archduchess** *n* archiduchesse *f*.
archery [ˈaːtʃəri] *n* tir à l'arc *m*. **archer** *n* archer *m*.
archetype [ˈaːkitaip] *n* archétype *m*.
archipelago [aːkiˈpeləgou] *n* archipel *m*.
architect [ˈaːkitekt] *n* architecte *m*. **architecture** *n* architecture *f*.
archives [ˈaːkaivz] *pl n* archives *f pl*. **archivist** *n* archiviste *m*, *f*.
ardent [ˈaːdənt] *adj* ardent.
ardour [ˈaːdə] *n* ardeur *f*.
arduous [ˈaːdjuəs] *adj* ardu.
are [aː] *V* **be**.
area [ˈeəriə] *n* aire *f*; (*region*) étendue *f*, région *f*.
arena [əˈriːnə] *n* arène *f*.
argue [ˈaːgjuː] *v* se disputer, discuter. **argument** *n* dispute *f*; (*debate*) discussion *f*; (*reasons*) argument *m*.
arid [ˈarid] *adj* aride. **aridity** *n* aridité *f*.
Aries [ˈeəriːz] *n* Bélier *m*.
***arise** [əˈraiz] *v* s'élever; (*question*) se présenter; resulter.
arisen [əˈrizn] *V* **arise**.
aristocracy [ariˈstokrəsi] *n* aristocratie *f*. **aristocrat** *n* aristocrate *m*, *f*. **aristocratic** *adj* aristocratique.
arithmetic [əˈriθmətik] *n* arithmétique *f*, calcul *m*.
arm[1] [aːm] *n* bras *m*. **armchair** *n* fauteuil *m*. **arm in arm** bras dessus bras dessous. **armpit** *n* aisselle *f*.
arm[2] [aːm] *n* arme *f*. **be up in arms against** s'élever contre. *v* armer.
armistice [ˈaːmistis] *n* armistice *m*.
armour [ˈaːmə] *n* armure *f*. **suit of armour** armure complète *f*. **armoured** *adj* cuirassé, blindé. **armoury** *n* arsenal *m*.
army [ˈaːmi] *n* armée *f*.
aroma [əˈroumə] *n* arome *m*; (*wine*) bouquet.
arose [əˈrouz] *V* **arise**.
around [əˈraund] *prep* autour de; (*approximately*) à peu près. *adv* autour, à l'entour.
arrange [əˈreindʒ] *v* arranger; (*meeting, etc.*) fixer; (*make plans*) s'arranger. **arrangement** *n* arrangement *m*. **make arrangements** faire des préparatifs, prendre des mesures.
array [əˈrei] *v* (*adorn*) orner; (*mil*) ranger. *n* (*display*) étalage *m*; (*mil*) ordre *m*.
arrears [əˈriəz] *pl n* arriéré *m sing*. **in arrears** arriéré; en retard.
arrest [əˈrest] *v* arrêter. *n* arrestation *f*. **under arrest** en état d'arrestation.
arrive [əˈraiv] *v* arriver. **arrival** *n* arrivée *f*; (*person*) arrivant, -e *m*, *f*.
arrogant [ˈarəgənt] *adj* arrogant. **arrogance** *n* arrogance *f*.
arrow [ˈarou] *n* flèche *f*.
arse [aːs] *n* (*vulgar*) cul *m*.
arsenal [ˈaːsənl] *n* arsenal *m*.
arsenic [ˈaːsnik] *n* arsenic *m*.
arson [ˈaːsn] *n* incendie criminel *m*.
art [aːt] *n* art *m*; (*painting, etc.*) beaux-arts *m pl*; (*cunning*) artifice *m*. **art gallery** musée d'art *m*. **arts and crafts** artisanat *m sing*. **art school** école des beaux-arts *f*. **Arts degree** licence ès lettres *f*. **artful** *adj* rusé.
artefact [ˈaːtifakt] *n* objet fabriqué *m*.
artery [ˈaːtəri] *n* artère *f*.
arthritis [aːˈθraitis] *n* arthrite *f*.
artichoke [ˈaːtitʃouk] *n* artichaut *m*.
article [ˈaːtikl] *n* article *m*; objet *m*.
articulate [aːˈtikjuleit; *adj* aːˈtikjulət] *v* articuler. **articulated lorry** semi-remorque *m*. *adj* bien articulé; net, nette. **be articulate** s'exprimer bien. **articulation** *n* articulation *f*.
artifice [ˈaːtifis] *n* artifice *f*, stratagème *m*.
artificial [aːtiˈfiʃəl] *adj* artificiel; synthétique; (*affected*) factice, forcé. **artificial respiration** respiration artificielle *f*.
artillery [aːˈtiləri] *n* artillerie *f*.
artisan [aːtiˈzan] *n* artisan *m*.
artist [ˈaːtist] *n* artiste *m*, *f*. **artistic** *adj* artistique.
as [az] *conj* (*while*) comme, tandis que, à mesure que; (*because*) puisque; (*like*) comme, en. *adv* aussi. **as . . . as . . .** aussi . . . que . . . . **as for** quant à. **as if** comme si. **as it were** pour ainsi dire. **as usual** comme d'habitude. **as well** aussi.
asbestos [azˈbestos] *n* amiante *f*.
ascend [əˈsend] *v* monter. **ascension** *n* ascension *f*. **Ascension Day** jour de l'Ascension *m*. **ascent** *n* ascension *f*; montée *f*.
ascertain [asəˈtein] *v* établir; vérifier.
ascetic [əˈsetik] *adj* ascétique. *n* ascète *m*, *f*.
ash[1] [aʃ] *n* cendre *f*. **ashtray** *n* cendrier *m*. **Ash Wednesday** mercredi des cendres *m*.

ash[2] [aʃ] *n* (*tree*) frêne *m*.
ashamed [əˈʃeimd] *adj* honteux. **be ashamed** avoir honte.
ashore [əˈʃɔː] *adv* à terre. **go ashore** débarquer.
Asia [ˈeiʃə] *n* Asie *f*. **Asian** *n* Asiatique *m, f*; *adj* asiatique.
aside [əˈsaid] *adv* de côté. à part. *n* aparté *m*.
ask [aːsk] *v* demander; inviter. **ask about** s'informer de. **ask after** demander des nouvelles de. **ask a question** poser une question. **ask for** demander.
askew [əˈskjuː] *adv* de travers.
asleep [əˈsliːp] *adj* endormi. **be asleep** dormir. **fall asleep** s'endormir.
asparagus [əsparəgəs] *n* asperge *f*.
aspect [ˈaspekt] *n* aspect *m*; (*of house*) orientation *f*.
asphalt [ˈasfalt] *n* asphalte *m*. *v* asphalter.
asphyxiate [əsˈfiksieit] *v* (s')asphyxier. **asphyxia** *or* **asphyxiation** *n* asphyxie *f*.
aspire [əˈspaiə] *v* aspirer, ambitionner. **aspirate** *adj* aspiré. **aspiration** *n* aspiration *f*. **aspiring** *adj* ambitieux.
aspirin [ˈasperin] *n* aspirine *f*.
ass [as] *n* âne, -esse *m, f*; (*coll*) imbécile *m*.
assail [əˈseil] *v* assaillir. **assailant** *n* agresseur *m*.
assassinate [əˈsasineit] *v* assassiner. **assassin** *n* assassin *m*. **assassination** *n* assassinat *m*.
assault [əˈsoːlt] *n* attaque *f*; (*mil*) assaut *m*; (*law*) voies de fait *f pl*. *v* attaquer.
assemble [əˈsembl] *v* (*things*) (s')assembler; (*people*) (se) rassembler; (*put together*) monter. **assembly** *n* assemblée *f*; rassemblement *m*; montage *m*. **assembly line** chaîne de montage *f*.
assent [əˈsent] *n* assentiment *m*. *v* consentir.
assert [əˈsəːt] *v* (*declare*) affirmer; (*rights, etc.*) revendiquer. **assertion** *n* affirmation *f*; revendication *f*.
assess [əˈses] *v* évaluer; (*payment, etc.*) fixer le montant de; (*property*) calculer la valeur imposable de. **assessment** *n* évaluation *f*; calcul *m*.
asset [ˈaset] *n* avantage *m*. **assets** *pl n* biens *m pl*; (*comm*) actif *m sing*.
assiduous [əˈsidjuəs] *adj* assidu. **assiduity** *n* assiduité *f*.
assign [əˈsain] *v* (*job, etc.*) assigner; (*meaning*) attribuer; (*person*) nommer. **assignation** *n* (*meeting*) rendez-vous *m*. **assignment** mission *f*; (*school*) devoir *m*.
assimilate [əˈsimileit] *v* (s')assimiler. **assimilation** *n* assimilation *f*.
assist [əˈsist] *v* aider. **assistance** *n* aide *f*, secours *m*. **assistant** *n* auxiliaire *m, f*; (*school*) assistant, -e *m, f*; (*shop*) vendeur, -euse *m, f*; (*as modifier*) adjoint, sous-.
associate [əˈsousiət; *v* əˈsousieit] *n* associé, -e *m, f*, collègue *m, f*. *v* associer. **be associated with** (*things*) être associé à; (*people*) s'associer avec. **association** *n* association *f*.
assorted [əˈsoːtid] *adj* assorti. **assortment** *n* assortiment *m*; mélange *m*.
assume [əˈsjuːm] *v* supposer, présumer; (*take on*) assumer, adopter. **assumption** *n* supposition *f*.
assure [əˈʃuə] *v* assurer. **assurance** *n* assurance *f*.
asterisk [ˈastərisk] *n* astérisque *m*. *v* marquer d'un astérisque.
asthma [ˈasmə] *n* asthme *m*. **asthmatic** *n*(*m+f*), *adj* asthmatique.
astonish [əˈstoniʃ] *v* étonner. **astonishment** *n* étonnement *m*.
astound [əˈstaund] *v* stupéfier, abasourdir.
astray [əˈstrei] *adv* **go astray** s'égarer.
astride [əˈstraid] *adv* à califourchon. *prep* à califourchon sur.
astringent [əˈstrindʒənt] *nm, adj* astringent.
astrology [əˈstrolədʒi] *n* astrologie *f*. **astrologer** *n* astrologue *m*. **astrological** *adj* astrologique.
astronaut [ˈastrənoːt] *n* astronaute *m, f*.
astronomy [əˈstronəmi] *n* astronomie *f*. **astronomer** *n* astronome *m*. **astronomical** *adj* astronomique.
astute [əˈstjuːt] *adj* fin, astucieux. **astuteness** *n* finesse *f*, astuce *f*.
asunder [əˈsʌndə] *adv* (*in two*) en deux; (*in pieces*) en morceaux.
asylum [əˈsailəm] *n* asile *m*.
at [at] *prep* à; chez: *chez le docteur*; (*towards*) vers. **at first** d'abord. **at last** enfin. **at least** au moins. **at once** tout de suite.
ate [et] *V* **eat**.
atheism [ˈeiθiizəm] *n* athéisme *m*. **atheist** *n* athée *m, f*. **atheistic** *adj* athée.
Athens [ˈaθinz] *n* Athènes. **Athenian** *adj* athénien; *n* Athénien, -enne *m, f*.

athlete ['aθliːt] *n* athlète *m, f.* **athlete's foot** *n* mycose *f.* **athletic** *adj* sportif, athlétique. **athletics** *n* athlétisme *m.*
Atlantic [ət'lantik] *adj* atlantique. **the Atlantic (Ocean)** l'(océan) Atlantique *m.*
atlas ['atləs] *n* atlas *m.*
atmosphere ['atməsfiə] *n* atmosphère *f*; ambiance *f.* **atmospheric** *adj* atmosphérique.
atom ['atəm] *n* atome *m*; (*tiny part*) grain *m.* **atom bomb** bombe atomique *f.* **atomic** *adj* atomique. **atomizer** *n* atomiseur *m.*
atone [ə'toun] *v* **atone for** expier; réparer. **atonement** *n* expiation *f*; réparation *f.*
atrocious [ə'trouʃəs] *adj* atroce. **atrocity** *n* atrocité *f.*
attach [ə'tatʃ] *v* attacher, joindre. **attached** *adj* (*letter, etc.*) ci-joint; (*fond*) attaché. **attachment** *n* accessoire *m*; affection *f.*
attaché [ə'taʃei] *n* attaché, -e *m, f.* **attaché case** mallette *f.*
attack [ə'tak] *n* attaque *f*; (*med*) accès *m*, crise *f.* *v* attaquer, combattre. **attacker** *n* attaquant *m.*
attain [ə'tein] *v* atteindre (à). **attainments** *pl n* résultats *m pl.*
attempt [ə'tempt] *v* tenter (de), essayer (de). *n* tentative *f*, essai *m.*
attend [ə'tend] *v* (*meeting*) assister à; (*school*) aller à; servir; faire attention. **attend to** s'occuper de. **attendance** *n* présence *f*; (*number present*) assistance *f*; service *m.* **attendant** *n* gardien, -enne *m, f.* **attendants** *pl n* suite *f sing.*
attention [ə'tenʃən] *n* attention *f*; (*mil*) garde-à-vous *m.* **pay attention** faire attention. **attentive** *adj* (*caring*) prévenant; (*listening*) attentif.
attic ['atik] *n* grenier *m.* **attic room** mansarde *f.*
attire [ə'taiə] *v* parer (de). *n* habits *m pl*; (*ceremonial*) tenue *f.*
attitude ['atitjuːd] *n* attitude *f.*
attorney [ə'təːni] *n* mandataire *m*; (*US*) avoué *m.* **Attorney General** Procureur Général *m.*
attract [ə'trakt] *v* attirer. **attract attention** éveiller l'intérêt. **attraction** *n* attraction *f*; (*charm*) attrait *m.* **attractive** *adj* attrayant; (*price, etc.*) intéressant.
attribute [ə'tribjuːt; *n* 'atribjuːt] *v* attribuer; (*crime, etc.*) imputer. *n* attribut *m.* **attribution** *n* attribution *f*; imputation *f.*
attrition [ə'triʃən] *n* usure *f.*
atypical [ei'tipikl] *adj* atypique.
aubergine ['oubəʒiːn] *n* aubergine *f.*
auburn ['oːbən] *adj* auburn *invar*; roux, rousse.
auction ['oːkʃən] *n* vente aux enchères *f.* *v* vendre aux enchères. **auctioneer** *n* commissaire-priseur *m.*
audacious [oː'deiʃəs] *adj* (*brave*) audacieux; (*impudent*) effronté. **audacity** *n* audace *f*; effronterie *f.*
audible ['oːdəbl] *adj* audible, distinct.
audience ['oːdjəns] *n* spectateurs *m pl*, auditeurs *m pl*; (*interview*) audience *f.*
audiovisual [oːdiou'viʒuəl] *adj* audiovisuel. **audiovisual aids** support audiovisuel *m sing.*
audit ['oːdit] *v* vérifier. *n* vérification *f.* **auditor** *n* expert-comptable *m.*
audition [oː'diʃən] *n* audition *f.* *v* auditionner.
auditorium [oːdi'toːriəm] *n* salle *f.*
augment [oːg'ment] *v* (s')augmenter.
August ['oːgəst] *n* août *m.*
aunt [aːnt] *n* tante *f.*
au pair [ou 'peə] *adv* au pair. *n* jeune fille au pair *f.*
aura ['oːrə] *n* aura *f*; ambiance *f.*
auspicious [oː'spiʃəs] *adj* favorable, de bon augure.
austere [oː'stiə] *adj* austère. **austerity** *n* austérité *f.*
Australia [o'streiljə] *n* Australie *f.* **Australian** *n* Australien, -enne *m, f*; *adj* australien.
Austria ['ostriə] *n* Autriche *f.* **Austrian** *n* Autrichien, -enne *m, f*; *adj* autrichien.
authentic [oː'θentik] *adj* authentique. **authenticity** *n* authenticité *f.*
author ['oːθə] *n* auteur *m.*
authority [oː'θorəti] *n* (*power*) autorité *f*; (*permission*) autorisation *f.* **authoritative** *adj* (*source, etc.*) autorisé; (*person*) autoritaire.
authorize ['oːθəraiz] *v* autoriser. **authorization** *n* autorisation *f*; (*legal*) mandat *m.*
autobiography [oːtoubai'ogrəfi] *n* autobiographie *f.* **autobiographical** *adj* autobiographique.
autocratic [oːtou'kratik] *adj* autocratique. **autocracy** *n* autocratie *f.* **autocrat** *n* autocrate *m.*
autograph ['oːtəgraːf] *v* dédicacer, signer. *n* autographe *m.*
automatic [oːtə'matik] *adj* automatique. *n* (*car*) voiture automatique *f.* **automation** *n* automatisation *f.*

automobile ['ɔːtəməbiːl] *n* automobile *f*.
autonomous [ɔː'tɔnəməs] *adj* autonome. **autonomy** *n* autonomie *f*.
autopsy ['ɔːtɔpsi] *n* autopsie *f*.
autumn ['ɔːtəm] *n* automne *m*.
auxiliary [ɔːg'ziljəri] *n*(*m*+*f*), *adj* auxiliaire.
avail [ə'veil] *v* **avail oneself of** utiliser; profiter de. *n* **to no avail** sans résultat.
available [ə'veiləbl] *adj* disponible. **availability** *n* disponibilité *f*.
avalanche ['ævəlaːnʃ] *n* avalanche *f*.
avarice ['avəris] *n* avarice *f*. **avaricious** *adj* avare.
avenge [ə'vendʒ] *v* venger. **avenge oneself** prendre sa revanche.
avenue ['avinjuː] *n* avenue *f*.
average ['avəridʒ] *n* moyenne *f*. *adj* moyen.
aversion [ə'vəːʃən] *n* aversion *f*. **averse** *adj* adversaire (de). **be averse to** avoir horreur de.
avert [ə'vəːt] *v* (*avoid*) prévenir; (*turn away*) écarter; (*eyes, etc.*) détourner.
aviary ['eiviəri] *n* volière *f*.
aviation [eivi'eiʃən] *n* aviation *f*.
avid ['avid] *adv* avide. **avidity** *n* avidité *f*.
avocado [avə'kaːdou] *n* (*pear*) avocat *m*; (*tree*) avocatier *m*.
avoid [ə'void] *v* éviter. **avoidable** *adj* évitable.
await [ə'weit] *v* attendre.
***awake** [ə'weik] *v* (s')éveiller. *adj* éveillé. **awake to** conscient de.
award [ə'wɔːd] *v* décerner; (*damages*) accorder. *n* récompense *f*, prix *m*.
aware [ə'weə] *adj* conscient; au courant. **be aware of** savoir. **awareness** *n* conscience *f*.
away [ə'wei] *adv* au loin, à une distance de; absent. *adj* (*sport*) à l'extérieur.
awe [ɔː] *n* crainte révérentielle *f*. **awe-inspiring** *adj* impressionnant. **awe-struck** *adj* stupéfait. **be in awe of** être intimidé par.
awful ['ɔːful] *adj* affreux, épouvantable. **awfully** *adv* (*very*) vraiment.
awkward ['ɔːkwəd] *adj* (*difficult*) peu commode; (*situation*) délicat; (*inconvenient*) inopportun; (*clumsy*) maladroit. **awkwardness** *n* maladresse *f*; embarras *m*.
awning ['ɔːniŋ] *n* (*shop*) banne *f*; (*tent*) auvent *m*; (*naut*) taud *m*.
awoke [ə'wouk] *V* **awake**.
awoken [ə'woukn] *V* **awake**.
axe [aks] *n* hache *f*.
axiom ['aksiəm] *n* axiome *m*.
axis ['aksis] *n* axe *m*.
axle ['aksl] *n* axe *m*; (*mot*) essieu *m*.

B

babble ['babl] *v* bredouiller; (*baby*) babiller; (*stream*) gazouiller. *n* babil *m*; (*noise*) rumeur *f*.
baboon [bə'buːn] *n* babouin *m*.
baby ['beibi] *n* bébé *m*. **babyish** *adj* enfantin.
bachelor ['batʃələ] *n* célibataire *m*. **Bachelor of Arts/Science** licencié, -e ès lettres/sciences *m*, *f*.
back [bak] *n* dos, derrière *m*; (*reverse side*) revers *m*, verso *m*; (*furthest part*) fond *m*. *adj* arrière. *adv* en arrière. *v* renforcer; financer; (*bet on*) parier sur. **back away** se reculer. **back out** (*car, etc.*) sortir en marche arrière; (*duty, etc.*) se dérober (à).
backache ['bakeik] *n* mal aux reins *m*.
backdate [ˌbak'deit] *v* (*cheque*) antidater. **backdated to** avec rappel à.
backfire [ˌbak'faiə] *v* (*mot*) pétarader; (*plan, etc.*) échouer.
backgammon ['bakˌgamən] *n* trictrac *m*.
background ['bakgraund] *n* fond *m*, arrière-plan *m*; (*social*) milieu *m*. **background music** musique de fond *f*.
backhand ['bakhand] *adj*, *adv* (*sport*) en revers. *n* revers *m*.
backlog ['baklog] *n* arriéré *m*.
backside ['baksaid] *n* arrière *m*; (*coll*) derrière *m*.
backstage ['baksteidʒ] *adv* derrière la scène. **go backstage** aller dans la coulisse.
backstroke ['bakstrouk] *n* dos crawlé *m*.
backward ['bakwəd] *adj* en arrière; (*retarded*) arriéré. **backwardness** *n* arriération mentale *f*.
backwards ['bakwədz] *adv* en arrière; (*back first*) à rebours, à reculons; (*in reverse order*) à l'envers.
backwater ['bakwoːtə] *n* (*place*) trou perdu *m*; (*pool*) eau stagnante *f*.

bacon ['beikən] *n* bacon *m*. **bacon and eggs** œufs au jambon *m pl*.
bacteria [bak'tiəriə] *pl n* bactéries *f pl*.
bad [bad] *adj* mauvais; (*naughty*) méchant; (*serious*) grave; (*decayed*) gâté, carié. **bad-mannered** *adj* mal élevé. **bad-tempered** *adj* acariâtre. **badly** *adv* mal; (*seriously*) grièvement; (*very much*) absolument.
badge [badʒ] *n* insigne *m*; (*scouting*) badge *m*; (*police, etc*.) plaque *f*.
badger ['badʒə] *n* blaireau *m*. *v* harceler.
badminton ['badmintən] *n* badminton *m*.
baffle ['bafl] *v* déconcerter.
bag [bag] *n* sac *m*. **baggage** *n* bagages *m pl*. **baggy** *adj* bouffant; trop ample.
bagpipes ['bagpaips] *pl n* cornemuse *f sing*.
bail[1] [beil] *n* (*law*) caution *f*. **on bail** sous caution. **stand bail for** se rendre garant de. *v* **bail out** faire mettre en liberté provisoire sous caution.
bail[2] *or* **bale** [beil] *v* **bail out** (*flooded boat*) écoper; (*from aircraft*) sauter en parachute.
bailiff ['beilif] *n* (*law*) huissier *m*; (*of estate*) régisseur *m*.
bait [beit] *n* (*fishing*) amorce *f*; (*lure*) appât *m*. *v* amorcer; (*annoy*) tourmenter.
bake [beik] *v* (faire) cuire au four. **baked beans** haricots blancs à la sauce tomate *m pl*. **baker** *n* boulanger, -ère *m, f*. **bakery** *n* boulangerie *f*.
balance ['baləns] *n* equilibre *m*; (*scales*) balance *f*; (*comm*) solde *m*. **balance of payments** balance des paiements *f*. *v* (se) tenir en équilibre; (*equal*) équilibrer; (*comm*) balancer, solder. **balance the books** dresser le bilan.
balcony ['balkəni] *n* balcon *m*; (*theatre*) fauteils de deuxième balcon *m pl*.
bald [boːld] *adj* chauve; (*tyre*) lisse; (*style*) plat.
bale[1] [beil] *n* ballot *m*; (*hay*) balle *f*. *v* emballotter.
bale[2] *V* **bail**[2].
ball[1] [boːl] *n* balle *f*, boule *f*; (*football*) ballon *m*; (*wool, etc*.) pelote *f*; (*of foot*) plante *f*. **ball bearings** roulement à billes *m sing*. **ball-point pen** stylo bille *m*.
ball[2] [boːl] *n* (*dance*) bal *m*. **ballroom** *n* salle de danse *f*.
ballad ['baləd] *n* ballade *f*; (*music*) romance *f*.
ballast ['baləst] *n* (*naut*) lest *m*; (*rail*) ballast *m*. *v* lester; ballaster.
ballet ['balei] *n* ballet *m*. **ballerina** *n* ballerine *f*.
ballistic [bə'listik] *adj* balistique. **ballistic missile** engin balistique *m*.
balloon [bə'luːn] *n* ballon *m*. **balloonist** *n* aéronaute *m, f*.
ballot ['balət] *n* scrutin *m*; (*paper*) bulletin de vote *m*. **ballot box** urne électorale *f*. *v* voter au scrutin secret.
bamboo [bam'buː] *n* bambou *m*.
ban [ban] *v* interdire. *n* interdit *m*. **put a ban on** interdire.
banal [bə'naːl] *adj* banal. **banality** *n* banalité *f*.
banana [bə'naːnə] *n* (*fruit*) banane *f*; (*tree*) bananier *m*.
band[1] [band] (*group*) bande *f*; (*music*) orchestre *m*; (*mil*) fanfare *f*. **bandstand** *n* kiosque à musique *m*. **jump on the bandwagon** prendre le train en marche.
band[2] [band] *n* (*strip*) bande *f*.
bandage ['bandidʒ] *n* pansement *m*, bandage *m*. *v* mettre un pansement sur.
bandit ['bandit] *n* bandit *m*.
bandy ['bandi] *adj also* **bandy-legged** bancal, arqué. *v* échanger. **bandy about** faire circuler. **bandy words** discuter.
bang [baŋ] *n* (*noise*) claquement *m*, détonation *f*; (*blow*) coup *m*. *interj* pan! *v* (*hit*) frapper, cogner; (*door*) claquer; (*gun, etc*.) détoner.
bangle ['baŋgl] *n* bracelet *m*, jonc *m*.
banish ['baniʃ] *v* bannir; exiler. **banishment** *n* bannissement *m*, exil *m*.
banister ['banistə] *n* rampe *f*.
banjo ['bandʒou] *n* banjo *m*.
bank[1] [baŋk] *n* (*edge*) bord *m*; (*river*) rive *f*; (*sand*) banc *m*; (*earth, etc*.) talus *m*.
bank[2] [baŋk] *n* banque *f*. **bank account** compte en banque *m*. **bank holiday** jour férié *m*. **bank statement** relevé de compte *m*. *v* mettre en banque. **bank on** compter sur. **bank with** avoir un compte à. **banker** *n* banquier *m*. **banker's order** ordre de virement bancaire *m*.
bankrupt ['baŋkrʌpt] *adj* failli, en faillite. **go bankrupt** faire faillite. *n* failli, -e *m, f*. *v* mettre en faillite. **bankruptcy** *n* faillite *f*.
banner ['banə] *n* bannière *f*.
banquet ['baŋkwit] *n* banquet *m*.
banter ['bantə] *v* plaisanter. *n* badinage *m*.

baptize [bap'taiz] *v* baptiser. **baptism** *n* baptême *m* **Baptist** *n*(*m*+*f*), *adj* baptiste.

bar [baː] *n* (*rod*) barreau *f*, barre *f*; obstacle *m*; (*law*) barreau *m*; (*chocolate*) tablette *f*; (*for drinks*) bar *m*, comptoir *m*; (*music*) mesure *f*. *v* barrer; défendre. *prep* sauf.

barbarian [baː'beəriən] *n*(*m*+*f*), *adj* barbare. **barbaric** *or* **barbarous** *adj* barbare. **barbarism** *or* **barbarity** *n* barbarie *f*.

barbecue ['baːbikjuː] *n* barbecue *m*. *v* griller au charbon de bois.

barbed wire [baːbd] *n* fil de fer barbelé *m*.

barber ['baːbə] *n* coiffeur pour hommes *m*.

barbiturate [baː'bitjurət] *n* barbiturique *m*.

bare [beə] *v* mettre à nu. **bare one's teeth** montrer les dents. *adj* nu; dénudé. **barefaced** *adj* éhonté. **barefoot** *adv* nu-pieds. **the bare necessities** le strict nécessaire *m*. **barely** *adv* à peine.

bargain ['baːgin] *n* (*transaction*) marché; (*offer*) occasion. **into the bargain** par-dessus le marché. *v* négocier. **bargain for** (*expect*) s'attendre à. **bargain with** marchander avec.

barge [baːdʒ] *n* chaland *m*, péniche *f*. *v* **barge in** faire irruption, entrer sans façons. **barge through** traverser comme un ouragan.

baritone ['baritoun] *n* baryton *m*.

bark[1] [baːk] *v* (*dog*) aboyer. *n* aboiement *m*.

bark[2] [baːk] *n* (*tree*) écorce *f*.

barley ['baːli] *n* orge *f*. **barley sugar** sucre d'orge *m*. **barley water** orgeat *m*.

barn [baːn] *n* grange *f*.

barometer [bə'romitə] *n* baromètre *m*.

baron ['barən] *n* baron *m*. **baroness** *n* baronne *f*. **baronet** *n* baronnet *m*.

barracks ['barəks] *n* (*mil*) caserne *f*, quartier *m*.

barrage ['baraːʒ] *n* barrage *m*; (*of questions*) pluie *f*; (*of words*) flot *m*.

barrel ['barəl] *n* (*cask*) tonneau *m*; (*gun, etc.*) canon *m*.

barren ['barən] *adj* stérile; aride. **barrenness** *n* stérilité *f*; aridité *f*.

barricade [bari'keid] *n* barricade *f*. *v* barricader.

barrier ['bariə] *n* barrière *f*; (*rail*) portillon *m*.

barrister ['baristə] *n* avocat *m*.

barrow ['barou] *n* voiture de quatre saisons *f*.

barter ['baːtə] *v* troquer, faire un troc. *n* troc *m*.

base[1] [beis] *n* base *f*. *v* baser. **baseless** *adj* sans fondement.

base[2] [beis] *adj* bas, basse; ignoble. **baseness** *n* bassesse *f*.

baseball ['beisboːl] *n* base-ball *m*.

basement ['beismənt] *n* sous-sol *m*.

bash [baʃ] *v* cogner. *n* coup *m*. **have a bash** (*try*) essayer un coup.

bashful ['baʃful] *adj* timide.

basic ['beisik] *adj* fondamental; (*salary, etc.*) de base; (*chem*) basique.

basil ['bazl] *n* basilic *m*.

basin ['beisin] *n* cuvette *f*; (*bowl*) bol *m*; (*bathroom*) lavabo; (*geog*) bassin *m*.

basis ['beisis] *n* base *f*.

bask [baːsk] *v* (*in the sun*) se dorer; (*in glory, etc.*) jouir (de).

basket ['baːskit] *n* (*shopping*) panier *m*; (*linen, etc.*) corbeille *f*. **basketball** *n* basket *m*.

bass[1] [beis] *n* (*voice*) basse *f*.

bass[2] [bas] *n* (*freshwater*) perche *f*; (*sea*) bar *m*.

bassoon [bə'suːn] *n* basson *m*.

bastard ['baːstəd] *n* bâtard, -e *m, f*; (*derog*) salaud *m*; (*coll*) type *m*.

baste [beist] *v* (*cookery*) arroser.

bastion ['bastjən] *n* bastion *m*.

bat[1] [bat] *n* (*sport*) batte *f*. **off one's own bat** de sa propre initiative. *v* frapper; manier la batte. **bat an eyelid** sourciller.

bat[2] [bat] *n* chauve-souris *f*.

batch [batʃ] *n* (*loaves*) fournée *f*; (*letters*) paquet *m*; (*goods*) lot *m*.

bath [baːθ] *n* bain *m*; (*tub*) baignoire *f*. **bathchair** *n* fauteuil roulant *m*. **bathroom** *n* salle de bains *f*. **baths** *pl n* (*swimming*) piscine *f sing*. *v* baigner; prendre un bain.

bathe [beið] *v* (se) baigner; (*wound*) laver. **bather** *n* baigneur, -euse *m, f*. **bathing** *n* baignade *f*. **bathing costume** maillot *m*. **bathing trunks** slip de bain *m*.

baton ['batn] *n* bâton *m*; (*police*) matraque *f*; (*race*) témoin *m*.

battalion [bə'taljən] *n* bataillon *m*.

batter[1] ['batə] *v* battre. **battered** *adj* délabré.

batter[2] ['batə] *n* pâte à frire *f*; (*pancakes*) pâte à crêpes *f*.
battery ['batəri] *n* (*elec*) pile *f*; (*mot*) batterie *f*; (*mil*) batterie *f*.
battle ['batl] *n* bataille *f*. **battlefield** *n* champ de bataille *m*. **battlements** *pl n* remparts *m pl*. **battleship** *n* cuirassé *m*. *v* se battre, lutter.
bawl [boːl] *v* brailler.
bay[1] [bei] *n* (*geog*) baie *f*.
bay[2] [bei] *v* aboyer. *n* aboi *m*. **at bay** à distance.
bay[3] [bei] *n* laurier *m*. **bay leaf** feuille de laurier *f*.
bayonet ['beiənit] *n* baïonnette *f*.
bay window *n* fenêtre en saillie *f*.
bazaar [bə'zaː] *n* (*charity sale*) vente de charité *f*; (*eastern*) bazar *m*.
***be** [biː] *v* être.
beach [biːtʃ] *n* plage *f*. *v* échouer.
beacon ['biːkən] *n* phare *m*; (*naut*) balise *f*.
bead [biːd] *n* perle *f*; (*rosary*) grain *m*.
beak [biːk] *n* bec *m*.
beaker ['biːkə] *n* gobelet *m*.
beam [biːm] *n* (*arch*) poutre *f*; (*light*) rayon *m*, faisceau *m*; (*smile*) sourire épanoui *m*. *v* rayonner.
bean [biːn] *n* haricot *m*; (*coffee*) grain *m*. **full of beans** en pleine forme.
***bear**[1] [beə] *v* (*carry*) porter; (*support*) soutenir; (*tolerate*) supporter; (*give birth*) donner naissance à. **bear right/left** prendre à droit/gauche. **bearable** *adj* supportable. **bearing** *n* (*behaviour*) maintien *m*; (*relation*) rapport *m*; (*direction*) relèvement *m*. **lose one's bearings** être désorienté.
bear[2] [beə] *n* ours *m*.
beard [biəd] *n* barbe *f*. **bearded** *adj* barbu.
beast [biːst] *n* bête *f*; (*person*) brute *f*. **beastly** *adj* abominable; (*unkind*) sale.
***beat** [biːt] *v* battre. *n* battement *m*; rythme *m*; (*police*) ronde *f*. **beating** *n* (*as punishment*) rossée *f*; (*defeat*) défaite *f*.
beaten ['biːtn] *V* **beat**.
beauty ['bjuːti] *n* beauté *f*. **beautician** *n* esthéticien, -enne *m*, *f*. **beautiful** *adj* beau, belle; magnifique. **beautify** *v* embellir.
beaver ['biːvə] *n* castor *m*.
became [bi'keim] *V* **become**.
because [bi'koz] *conj* parce que. **because of** à cause de.
beckon ['bekən] *v* faire signe (à).
***become** [bi'kʌm] *v* devenir; (*suit*) aller à. **becoming** *adj* convenable; (*clothes*) seyant.
bed [bed] *n* lit *m*; (*coal, etc.*) couche *f*; (*flowers*) parterre *m*. **bedclothes** *pl n* literie *f sing*. **bedridden** *adj* alité. **bedroom** *n* chambre *f*. **bedside** *n* chevet *m*. **bed-sitter** *n* studio *m*. **bedspread** *n* couvre-lit *m*. **go to bed** se coucher.
bedraggled [bi'dragld] *adj* débraillé.
bee [biː] *n* abeille *f*. **beehive** *n* ruche *f*. **have a bee in one's bonnet** avoir une marotte. **make a beeline for** filer droit sur.
beech [biːtʃ] *n* hêtre *m*.
beef [biːf] *n* bœuf *m*.
been [biːn] *V* **be**.
beer [biə] *n* bière *f*.
beetle ['biːtl] *n* coléoptère *m*.
beetroot ['biːtruːt] *n* betterave *f*.
before [bi'foː] *prep* avant; (*in front of*) devant. *adv* auparavant, avant. *conj* avant de, avant que. **beforehand** *adv* à l'avance.
befriend [bi'frend] *v* traiter en ami; (*help*) venir en aide à.
beg [beg] *v* mendier; (*entreat*) supplier, demander. **beggar** *n* mendiant, -e *m*, *f*.
began [bi'gan] *V* **begin**.
***begin** [bi'gin] *v* commencer. **to begin with** pour commencer. **beginner** *n* novice *m*, *f*. **beginning** *n* commencement *m*, début *m*; origine *f*.
begrudge [bi'grʌdʒ] *v* envier. **begrudge doing** faire à contre-cœur.
begun [bi'gʌn] *V* **begin**.
behalf [bi'haːf] *n* part *f*. **on behalf of** de la part de; en faveur de.
behave [bi'heiv] *v* se conduire. **behave yourself!** sois sage! **behaviour** *n* conduite *f*.
behead [bi'hed] *v* décapiter.
behind [bi'haind] *adv*, *prep* derrière, en arrière (de); (*late*) en retard. *n* (*coll*) postérieur *m*. **behindhand** *adv*, *adj* en retard.
***behold** [bi'hould] *v* voir.
beige [beiʒ] *nm*, *adj* beige.
being ['biːiŋ] *n* existence *f*; être *m*. **for the time being** pour le moment.
belated [bi'leitid] *adj* tardif.
belch [beltʃ] *v* roter; (*smoke, etc.*) vomir. *n* renvoi *m*.

belfry ['belfri] *n* beffroi *m*; (*church*) clocher *m*.
Belgium ['beldʒəm] *n* Belgique *f*. **Belgian** *n* Belge *m*, *f*. *adj* belge.
Belgrade ['belgreid] *n* Belgrade.
believe [bi'liːv] *v* croire. **believe in** (*God*) croire en; (*ghosts, etc.*) croire à; (*approve of*) être partisan de. **belief** *n* croyance *f*; (*rel*) credo *m*, foi *f*; opinion *f*. **believable** *adj* croyable. **believer** *n* partisan, -e *m*, *f*; (*rel*) croyant, -e *m*, *f*.
bell [bel] *n* cloche *f*, clochette *f*; (*door*) sonnette *f*; (*telephone*) sonnerie *f*; (*bicycle*) timbre *m*.
belligerent [bi'lidʒərənt] *n*, *adj* belligérant, -e. **belligerence** *n* belligérance *f*.
bellow ['belou] *v* mugir; (*cow*) beugler; (*person*) brailler. *n* mugissement *m*; beuglement *m*; (*person*) hurlement *m*.
bellows ['belouz] *pl n* (*organ*) soufflerie *f sing*; (*fire*) soufflet *m sing*.
belly ['beli] *n* ventre *m*.
belong [bi'loŋ] *v* appartenir; (*club*) être membre (de). **belongings** *pl n* affaires *f pl*.
beloved [bi'lʌvid] *adj* bien aimé. *n* bien-aimé, -e *m*, *f*.
below [bi'lou] *prep* sous, au-dessous de. *adv* en bas, en dessous; (*letters, etc.*) ci-dessous. **hit below the belt** porter un coup bas (à).
belt [belt] *n* ceinture *f*; (*land*) zone *f*, région *f*; (*tech*) courroie *f*. *v* (*slang*: *hit*) flanquer un gnon à; (*slang*: *rush*) se carapater.
bench [bentʃ] *n* banc *m*; (*workshop*) établi *m*; (*law*) tribunal *m*.
***bend** [bend] *n* coude *m*; (*road*) virage *m*; (*arm, knee*) pli *m*. *v* (se) courber; plier. **bend over** se pencher. **bend over backwards** se mettre en quatre.
beneath [bi'niːθ] *prep* sous, au-dessous de; (*unworthy*) indigne de. *adv* au-dessous, en bas.
benefactor ['benəfaktə] *n* bienfaiteur *m*. **benefactress** *n* bienfaitrice *f*.
benefit ['benəfit] *n* avantage *m*; (*money*) allocation *f*. **for the benefit of** dans l'intérêt de. **the benefit of the doubt** le bénéfice du doute. *v* faire du bien à; gagner (à). **beneficial** *adj* salutaire.
benevolent [bi'nevələnt] *adj* (*kindly*) bienveillant; (*charitable*) bienfaisant. **benevolence** *n* bienveillance *f*; bienfaisance *f*.
benign [bi'nain] *adj* (*med*) bénin, -igne; (*kindly*) bienveillant.
bent [bent] *V* **bend**. *adj* courbé; (*slang*: *dishonest*) véreux; (*slang*: *homosexual*) homosexuel. **be bent on** vouloir absolument. *n* aptitude *f*, disposition *f*.
bequeath [bi'kwiːð] *v* léguer. **bequest** *n* legs *m*.
bereaved [bi'riːvd] *adj* endeuillé. **bereavement** *n* deuil *m*.
beret ['berei] *n* béret *m*.
Berlin [bəː'lin] *n* Berlin.
Bern [bəːn] *n* Berne.
berry ['beri] *n* baie *f*.
berserk [bə'səːk] *adj* fou furieux, folle furieuse. **go berserk** devenir fou furieux; (*with anger*) se mettre en rage.
berth [bəːθ] *n* couchette *f*; (*naut*) mouillage *m*. **give a wide berth to** éviter. *v* (*naut*) mouiller, amarrer.
beside [bi'said] *prep* à côté de. **beside oneself** (*with anger*) hors de soi. **besides** *adv* (*as well*) de plus; (*moreover*) d'ailleurs.
besiege [bi'siːdʒ] *v* (*town*) assiéger; (*pester*) assaillir.
best [best] *adj* le meilleur, la meilleure. **best man** garçon d'honneur *m*. *adv* le mieux. *n* mieux *m*. **at best** au mieux. **do one's best** faire de son mieux. **make the best of** s'accommoder de; profiter de.
bestow [bi'stou] *v* accorder; (*title*) conférer.
bet [bet] *v* parier. *n* pari *m*. **betting shop** bureau de paris *m*.
betray [bi'trei] *v* trahir. **betrayal** *n* trahison *f*.
better ['betə] *adj* meilleur. *nm*, *adv* mieux. **be better** (*after illness*) aller mieux. **get the better of** triompher de. *v* améliorer, dépasser.
between [bi'twiːn] *prep* entre.
beverage ['bevəridʒ] *n* boisson *f*.
***beware** [bi'weə] *v* prendre garde. *interj* attention (à)!
bewilder [bi'wildə] *v* dérouter, abasourdir. **bewilderment** *n* confusion *f*; abasourdissement *m*.
beyond [bi'jond] *prep* au delà de; (*exceeding*) au-dessus de. *adv* au delà. **be beyond** dépasser.
bias ['baiəs] *n* tendance *f*; préjugé *m*; (*sewing*) biais *m*. *v* influencer; (*prejudice*) prévenir. **biased** *adj* partial. **be biased** avoir un préjugé.

bib [bib] *n* bavoir *m*; (*of apron*) bavette *f*.
Bible ['baibl] *n* Bible *f*. **biblical** *adj* biblique.
bibliography [bibli'ogrəfi] *n* bibliographie *f*. **bibliographer** *n* bibliographe *m*, *f*. **bibliographical** *adj* bibliographique.
biceps ['baiseps] *n* biceps *m*.
bicker ['bikə] *v* se chamailler. **bickering** *n* chamailleries *f pl*.
bicycle ['baisikl] *n* bicyclette *f*, vélo *m*.
***bid** [bid] *n* offre *f*; (*auction*) enchère *f*; (*cards*) demande *f*; (*attempt*) tentative *f*. *v* faire une offre *or* enchère (de); (*cards*) demander; (*command*) ordonner; (*greeting*) dire, souhaiter. **bidder** *n* offrant *m*. **bidding** *n* enchères *f pl*; ordre *m*.
bidet ['biːdei] *n* bidet *m*.
biennial [bai'eniəl] *adj* biennal.
bifocals [bai'foukəlz] *pl n* lunettes bifocales *f pl*.
big [big] *adj* grand; gros, grosse.
bigamy ['bigəmi] *n* bigamie. **bigamist** *n* bigame *m*, *f*. **bigamous** *adj* bigame.
bigot ['bigət] *n* fanatique *m*, *f*. **bigoted** *adj* fanatique.
bikini [bi'kiːni] *n* bikini *m*.
bilingual [bai'liŋgwəl] *adj* bilingue.
bilious ['biljəs] *adj* bilieux. **bilious attack** crise de foie *f*. **biliousness** *n* affection hépatique *f*.
bill[1] [bil] (*hotel, shop*) note *f*; (*restaurant*) addition *f*; (*fuel, etc.*) facture *f*; (*pol*) projet de loi *m*; (*poster*) affiche *f*.
bill[2] [bil] *n* bec *m*.
billiards ['biljədz] *n* billard *m*.
billion ['biljən] *n* (10^{12}) billion *m*; (10^9) milliard *m*.
billow ['bilou] *n* flot *m*; (*sail*) gonflement *m*. *v* (*sail*) se gonfler; (*smoke*) tournoyer.
bin [bin] *n* (*rubbish*) poubelle *f*; (*coal*) coffre *m*; (*wine*) casier *m*.
binary ['bainəri] *adj* binaire.
***bind** [baind] *v* lier; (*book*) relier; (*neaten edge*) border; (*force*) obliger. *n* (*coll*) barbe *f*.
binding ['baindiŋ] *n* (*book*) reliure *f*; (*tape*) extra-fort *m*; (*skis*) fixation *f*. *adj* obligatoire.
binoculars [bi'nokjuləz] *pl n* jumelles *f pl*.
biography [bai'ogrəfi] *n* biographie *f*. **biographer** *n* biographe *m*, *f*. **biographical** *adj* biographique.
biology [bai'olədʒi] *n* biologie *f*. **biological** *adj* biologique. **biologist** *n* biologiste *m*, *f*.
birch [bəːtʃ] *n* bouleau *m*; (*punishment*) verge *f*.
bird [bəːd] *n* oiseau *m*.
birth [bəːθ] *n* naissance *f*; (*confinement*) accouchement *m*. **birth certificate** acte de naissance *m*. **birth control** contrôle des naissances *m*. **birthday** *n* anniversaire *m*. **birthmark** *n* tache de vin *f*. **birthplace** *n* lieu de naissance *m*. **birth rate** natalité *f*. **give birth to** donner naissance à.
biscuit ['biskit] *n* petit gâteau sec *m*; biscuit *m*.
bishop ['biʃəp] *n* évêque *m*.
bison ['baisən] *n* bison *m*.
bit[1] [bit] *V* **bite**. *n* (*horse*) mors *m*; (*drill*) mèche *f*.
bit[2] [bit] *n* morceau *m*, bout *m*, brin *m*. **a bit** *adv* un peu. **bit by bit** petit à petit. **do one's bit** fournir sa part d'effort.
bitch [bitʃ] *n* (*dog*) chienne *f*; (*slang*) garce *f*.
***bite** [bait] *v* mordre; (*insect*) piquer. *n* morsure *f*; piqûre *f*; (*mouthful*) bouchée *f*. **biting** *adj* (*remark, etc.*) mordant; (*wind*) cinglant; (*cold*) âpre.
bitten ['bitn] *V* **bite**.
bitter ['bitə] *adj* amer; (*cold*) glacial. **to the bitter end** jusqu'au bout. **bitterness** *n* amertume *f*.
bizarre [bi'zaː] *adj* bizarre.
black ['blak] *adj* noir. *n* noir *m*; (*person*) Noir, -e *m*, *f*. *v* (*comm*) boycotter. **blacken** *v* noircir. **blackness** *n* noirceur *f*; (*darkness*) obscurité *f*.
blackberry ['blakbəri] *n* (*fruit*) mûre *f*; (*bush*) mûrier *m*.
blackbird ['blakbəːd] *n* merle *m*.
blackboard ['blakboːd] *n* tableau (noir) *m*.
blackcurrant [ˌblak'kʌrənt] *n* cassis *m*.
black eye *n* œil poché *m*.
blackhead ['blakhed] *n* point noir *m*.
black ice *n* verglas *m*.
blackleg ['blakleg] *n* jaune *m*.
blackmail ['blakmeil] *n* chantage *m*. *v* faire chanter. **blackmailer** *n* maître-chanteur *m*.
black market *n* marché noir *m*.
blackout ['blakaut] *n* (*med*) étourdissement *m*; (*war*) black-out *m*; (*power cut*) panne d'électricité *f*.
blacksmith ['blaksmiθ] *n* (*iron*) forgeron *m*; (*horses*) maréchal-ferrant *m*.
bladder ['bladə] *n* vessie *f*.

blade [bleid] *n* lame *f*; (*oar*) plat *m*; (*grass*) brin *m*; (*propeller*) pale *f*.
blame [bleim] *v* attribuer (à), rejeter la responsabilité (sur); (*censure*) blâmer. *n* responsabilité *f*; blâme *m*.
blank [blaŋk] *adj* blanc, blanche; (*cheque*) en blanc; (*empty*) vide; (*puzzled*) déconcerté. *n* blanc *m*, vide *m*; (*gun*) cartouche à blanc *f*.
blanket ['blaŋkit] *n* couverture *f*. *v* recouvrir; (*muffle*) étouffer.
blare [bleə] *n* vacarme *m*; (*trumpet*) sonnerie *f*. *v* retentir; (*radio, etc.*) beugler.
blaspheme [blas'fiːm] *v* blasphémer. **blasphemous** *adj* blasphématoire. **blasphemy** *n* blasphème *m*.
blast [blaːst] *n* explosion *f*; (*noise, wind*) coup *m*; (*trumpet*) fanfare *f*; (*steam*) jet *m*. *v* (*rocks*) faire sauter; (*hopes, etc.*) détruire. *interj* la barbe!
blatant ['bleitənt] *adj* (*obvious*) flagrant; (*shameless*) éhonté.
blaze [bleiz] *n* (*flare*) flambée *f*; (*large fire*) incendie *m*; (*sun*) flamboiement *m*; (*anger*) explosion *f*. *v* flamber; flamboyer; (*light*) resplendir. **blazing** *adj* en flammes; (*sun*) éclatant; (*coll*) furibond.
bleach [bliːtʃ] *n* blanchir; (*hair*) décolorer. *n* décolorant *m*; (*household*) eau de Javel *f*.
bleak [bliːk] *adj* (*landscape*) morne, désolé; (*bare*) austère; (*prospect*) triste; (*weather*) froid.
bleat [bliːt] *v* bêler. *n* bêlement *m*.
bled [bled] *V* **bleed**.
***bleed** [bliːd] *v* saigner. **bleeding** *n* saignement *m*, hémorragie *f*.
blemish ['blemiʃ] *n* défaut *m*; (*reputation*) souillure *f*; (*fruit*) tache *f*. *v* gâter; (*reputation*) ternir.
blend [blend] *v* (se) mélanger; (*ideas*) fusionner; (*colours*) (se) fondre, aller bien ensemble. *n* mélange *m*.
bless [bles] *v* bénir. **bless you!** à vos souhaits! **blessed** (*rel*) béni, bienheureux; (*coll*) sacré. **blessing** *n* bénédiction *f*; (*at meal*) bénédicité; (*benefit*) bien *m*. **what a blessing!** quelle chance!
blew [bluː] *V* **blow**².
blind [blaind] *adj* aveugle. **blind spot** (*mot*) angle mort *m*. *v* aveugler. *n* (*window*) store *m*; (*mask*) feinte *f*. **the blind** les aveugles *m pl*. **blindness** cécité *f*.
blindfold ['blaindfould] *v* bander les yeux à. *n* bandeau *m*. *adv* les yeux bandés.
blink [bliŋk] *v* cligner des yeux. *n* clignotement *m*. **blinkers** *pl n* œillères *f pl*.
bliss [blis] *n* bonheur suprême *m*. **blissful** *adj* merveilleux, divin.
blister ['blistə] *n* ampoule *f*; (*paint*) boursouflure *f*. *v* se couvrir d'ampoules; se boursoufler.
blizzard ['blizəd] *n* tempête de neige *f*.
blob [blob] *n* goutte *f*.
bloc [blok] *n* (*pol*) bloc *m*.
block [blok] *n* bloc *m*; (*wood*) billot *m*; (*flats*) immeuble *m*; (*houses*) pâté *m*; obstruction *f*. **block letters** majuscules *f pl*. *v* (*obstruct*) bloquer, boucher; (*hinder*) gêner. **blockage** *n* obstruction *f*.
bloke [blouk] *n* (*coll*) type *m*.
blond [blond] *adj* blond. **blonde** *nf, adj* blonde.
blood [blʌd] *n* sang *m*. **bloody** *adj* sanglant, ensanglanté; (*slang*) foutu.
bloodcurdling ['blʌdkəːdliŋ] *adj* à figer le sang.
blood donor *n* donneur, -euse de sang *m, f*.
blood group *n* groupe sanguin *m*.
bloodhound ['blʌdhaund] *n* limier *m*.
blood poisoning *n* empoisonnement du sang *m*.
blood pressure *n* tension *f*. **have high/low blood pressure** faire de l'hypertension/hypotension.
bloodshed ['blʌdʃəd] *n* effusion de sang *f*.
bloodshot ['blʌdʃot] *adj* injecté de sang.
bloodstream ['blʌdstriːm] *n* système sanguin *m*.
bloodthirsty ['blʌdθəːsti] *adj* sanguinaire.
bloom [bluːm] *v* fleurir. *n* floraison *f*; (*single flower*) fleur *f*. **in full bloom** en pleine floraison.
blot [blot] *n* tache *f*; (*ink*) pâté *m*. *v* tacher; (*dry*) sécher. **blot out** effacer. **blotting paper** papier buvard *m*.
blouse [blauz] *n* chemisier *m*.
blow¹ [blou] *n* (*hit*) coup. **come to blows** en venir aux mains.
***blow**² [blou] *v* souffler; (*trumpet*) sonner; (*whistle*) siffler. **blow away** chasser. **blow off** (faire) s'envoler. **blow one's nose** se moucher. **blow out** (s')éteindre. **blow up** (*explode*) (faire) sauter; (*inflate*) gonfler.
blown [bloun] *V* **blow**².

blubber ['blʌbə] *n* blanc de baleine *m*. *v* pleurer comme un veau.
blue [bluː] *adj* bleu; (*coarse*) grivois. *n* bleu *m*. **bluebell** *n* jacinthe des bois *f*. **blueprint** *n* bleu *m*; plan *m*.
bluff [blʌf] *n* bluff *m*. *v* bluffer.
blunder [blʌndə] *n* bévue *f*; (*coll*) gaffe *f*; (*social*) impair *m*. *v* faire une bévue.
blunt [blʌnt] *adj* (*blade*) émoussé; (*point*) épointé; (*frank*) carré, brusque. *v* émousser; épointer.
blur [bləː] *n* tache floue *f*. *v* estomper. **blurred** *adj* flou.
blush [blʌʃ] *v* rougir. *n* rougeur *f*.
boar [boː] *n* sanglier *m*.
board [boːd] *v* (*ship, plane*) monter à bord de; (*train, bus*) monter dans; (*lodge*) prendre en pension. *n* (*wood*) planche *f*; (*meals*) pension *f*; (*officials*) conseil *m*; (*naut*) bord *m*. **above board** régulier. **across the board** de portée générale. **boardroom** *n* salle du conseil *f*. **go on board** (s')embarquer. **on board** à bord. **boarder** *n* pensionnaire *m, f*. **boarding card** carte d'embarquement *f*. **boarding house** pension *f*. **boarding school** pensionnat *m*.
boast [boust] *v* se vanter. *n* fanfaronnade *f*. **boastful** *adj* vantard.
boat [bout] *n* bateau *m*. **all in the same boat** tous logés à la même enseigne. **boater** *n* (*hat*) canotier *m*. **boating** *n* canotage *m*.
bob[1] [bob] *v* (*up and down*) sautiller; (*curtsy*) faire une révérence. *n* révérence *f*.
bob[2] [bob] *v* (*hair*) couper court; (*tail*) écourter. *n* (*hairstyle*) coiffure à la Jeanne d'Arc *f*.
bobbin ['bobin] *n* bobine *f*.
bodice ['bodis] *n* corsage *m*.
body ['bodi] *n* corps *m*; (*corpse*) cadavre *m*. **bodyguard** *n* garde du corps *m*. **bodywork** *n* (*mot*) carrosserie *f*.
bog [bog] *n* marais *m*. **get bogged down** s'embourber. **boggy** *adj* marécageux.
bogus ['bougəs] *adj* faux, fausse.
bohemian [bə'hiːmiən] *n*(*m*+*f*), *adj* (*artist*) bohème; (*gipsy*) bohémien, -enne.
boil[1] [boil] *v* (faire) bouillir; (*vegetables, etc.*) cuire à l'eau. **boil down to** revenir à. **boil over** déborder. **boiled egg** œuf à la coque *m*. **boiler** *n* chaudière *f*. **boiler suit** bleus *m pl*. **boiling point** point d'ébullition *m*.
boil[2] [boil] *n* furoncle *m*.
boisterous ['boistərəs] *adj* (*person*) turbulent; (*sea*) tumultueux.
bold [bould] *adj* hardi. **boldness** *n* hardiesse *f*.
bolster ['boulstə] *n* (*pillow*) traversin *m*. *v* **bolster up** soutenir.
bolt [boult] *n* (*door*) verrou *m*; (*for nut*) boulon *m*; (*dash*) bond *m*. *v* verrouiller; (*food*) engouffrer; (*run away*) se sauver.
bomb [bom] *v* bombarder. *n* bombe *f*. **bomber** *n* (*aircraft*) bombardier *m*.
bombard [bəm'baːd] *v* bombarder. **bombardier** *n* (*mil*) caporal d'artillerie *m*. **bombardment** *n* bombardement *m*.
bond [bond] *n* (*agreement*) engagement *m*; (*tie*) lien *m*; (*comm*) bon *m*; (*glue*) adhérence *f*. **bondage** *n* esclavage *m*.
bone [boun] *n* os *m*; (*fish*) arête *f*. **bone china** porcelaine tendre *f*. **bone-dry** *adj* absolument sec, absolument sèche. **have a bone to pick with** avoir un compte à régler avec. **boned** *or* **boneless** *adj* désossé. **bony** *adj* osseux; (*person*) anguleux.
bonfire ['bonfaiə] *n* feu de joie *m*.
Bonn [bon] *n* Bonn.
bonnet ['bonit] *n* (*hat*) capote *f*; (*mot*) capot *m*.
bonus ['bounəs] *n* prime *f*.
booby trap ['buːbi] *n* traquenard *m*; (*mil*) object piégé *m*.
book [buk] *n* livre *m*; (*writing*) cahier *m*; (*tickets*) carnet *m*. *v* retenir, réserver. **booked up** complet, -ète.
bookcase ['bukkeis] *n* bibliothèque *f*.
booking ['bukiŋ] *n* réservation *f*. **booking office** location *f*.
book-keeper ['buk,kiːpə] *n* comptable *m, f*. **book-keeping** *n* comptabilité *f*.
booklet ['buklit] *n* brochure *f*.
bookmaker ['bukmeikə] *n* bookmaker *m*.
bookmark ['bukmaːk] *n* marque *f*.
bookseller ['bukselə] *n* libraire *m, f*.
bookshop ['bukʃop] *n* librairie *f*.
bookstall ['bukstoːl] *n* kiosque à livres *m*.
boom [buːm] *v* (*noise*) gronder; (*comm*) prospérer. *n* grondement *m*; (*comm*) forte hausse *f*; (*econ*) boom *m*.
boost [buːst] *v* (*confidence*) renforcer; (*comm*) faire monter; (*publicize*) faire de la réclame pour.
boot [buːt] *n* (*shoe*) botte *f*; (*mot*) coffre *m*.

bye-law ['bailoː] *n* arrêté municipal *m*.
by-election ['baiiˌlekʃən] *n* election partielle *f*.
bypass ['baiˌpaːs] *n* route de contournement *f*. *v* contourner.
bystander ['baiˌstandə] *n* spectateur, -trice *m*, *f*.

C

cab [kab] *n* taxi *m*; (*lorry*) cabine *f*.
cabaret ['kabərei] *n* cabaret *m*; (*show*) spectacle *m*.
cabbage ['kabidʒ] *n* chou (*pl* choux) *m*.
cabin ['kabin] *n* cabine *f*; (*hut*) cabane *f*.
cabinet ['kabinit] *n* cabinet *m*; (*filing*) classeur *m*; (*pol*) cabinet *m*. **cabinet-maker** *n* ébéniste *m*. **cabinet minister** membre du cabinet *m*.
cable ['keibl] *n* câble *m*. **cablecar** *n* téléphérique *m*. *v* câbler.
cackle ['kakl] *v* caqueter; (*laugh*) glousser. *n* caquet *m*; gloussement *m*.
cactus ['kaktəs] *n* cactus *m*.
caddie ['kadi] *n* caddie *m*.
cadence ['keidəns] *n* cadence *f*; (*voice*) modulation *f*.
cadet [kə'det] *n* élève officier *m*.
café ['kafei] *n* café *m*.
cafeteria [kafə'tiəriə] *n* cafétéria *f*.
caffeine ['kafiːn] *n* caféine *f*.
cage [keidʒ] *n* cage *f*.
cake [keik] *n* gâteau *m*; (*soap*, *etc*) pain *m*. **cake shop** pâtisserie *f*. **it's a piece of cake** c'est du gâteau. **like hot cakes** comme des petits pains. **caked** *adj* coagulé. **caked with** raidi par.
calamine ['kaləmain] *n* calamine *f*. **calamine lotion** lotion calmante à la calamine *f*.
calamity [kə'laməti] *n* calamité *f*.
calcium ['kalsiəm] *n* calcium *m*.
calculate ['kalkjuleit] *v* calculer; (*reckon*) évaluer. **calculable** *adj* calculable. **calculated** *adj* délibéré. **calculating** *adj* (*scheming*) calculateur, -trice. **calculation** *n* calcul *m*. **calculator** *n* machine à calculer *f*, calculatrice *f*.
calendar ['kaləndə] *n* calendrier *m*. **calendar month** mois de calendrier *m*.
calf[1] [kaːf] *n* (*animal*) veau *m*.
calf[2] [kaːf] *n* (*anat*) mollet *m*.
calibre ['kalibə] *n* calibre *m*.
call [koːl] *n* appel *m*; cri *m*; visite *f*. **call-box** *n* cabine téléphonique *f*. *v* appeler; (*waken*) réveiller; (*visit*) passer. **be called** s'appeler. **call for** (*need*) demander; (*person*) passer prendre. **call off** (*cancel*) annuler. **call on** (*visit*) passer voir. **call up** (*mil*) mobiliser. **caller** *n* visiteur, -euse *m*, *f*; (*phone*) demandeur, -euse *m*, *f*. **calling** *n* vocation *f*; (*job*) métier *m*.
callous ['kaləs] *adj* dur, sans pitié.
calm [kaːm] *adj* calme. *n* calme *m*; période de tranquillité *f*. *v* calmer. **calm down** (se) calmer. **calmness** *n* calme *m*; sang-froid *m*.
calorie ['kaləri] *n* calorie *f*.
came [keim] *V* **come**.
camel ['kaməl] *n* chameau, -elle *m*, *f*. **camel-hair** *n* poil de chameau *m*.
camera ['kamərə] *n* appareil-photo *m*; (*cine*) caméra *f*.
Cameroon [kamə'ruːn] *n* Cameroun *m*.
camouflage ['kaməflaːʒ] *n* camouflage *m*. *v* camoufler.
camp[1] [kamp] *v* camper. **go camping** faire du camping. *n* camp *m*. **camp-bed** *n* lit de camp *m*. **campsite** *n* camping *m*.
camp[2] [kamp] *adj* affecté; efféminé; (*slang*: *homosexual*) pédé.
campaign [kam'pein] *n* campagne *f*. *v* faire campagne.
campus ['kampəs] *n* campus *m*.
camshaft ['kamʃaːft] *n* (*mot*) arbre à cames *m*.
***can**[1] [kan] *v* (*be able*) pouvoir; (*know how to*) savoir.
can[2] [kan] *n* (*oil*) bidon *m*; (*beer*, *fruit*) boîte *f*. **can-opener** *n* ouvre-boîtes *m* *invar*. *v* mettre en boîte.
Canada ['kanədə] *n* Canada *m*. **Canadian** *n* Canadien, -enne *m*, *f*; *adj* canadien.
canal [kə'nal] *n* canal *m*.
canary [kə'neəri] *n* serin *m*.
Canberra ['kanbərə] *n* Canberra.
cancel ['kansəl] *v* annuler; (*order*) décommander; (*contract*) résilier; (*train*) supprimer; (*cheque*) faire opposition à. **cancellation** *n* annulation *f*; suppression *f*.
cancer ['kansə] *n* cancer *m*. **Cancer** *n* Cancer *m*.
candid ['kandid] *adj* franc, franche.
candidate ['kandidət] *n* candidat *m*.

candle ['kandl] *n* (*wax*) bougie *f*; (*tallow*) chandelle *f*. **candle-light** *n* lumière de bougie *f*. **candlestick** *n* bougeoir *m*; chandelier *m*. **candlewick** *n* chenille de coton *f*.
candour ['kandə] *n* franchise *f*.
candy ['kandi] *n* (*US*) bonbons *m pl*. **candied** *adj* glacé, confit.
cane [kein] *n* canne *f*; (*school*) verge *f*. *v* fouetter.
canine ['keinain] *adj* canin. *n* (*tooth*) canine *f*.
canister ['kanistə] *n* boîte *f*.
cannabis ['kanəbis] *n* (*drug*) cannabis *m*; (*plant*) chanvre indien *m*.
cannibal ['kanibəl] *n*(*m*+*f*), *adj* cannibale. **cannibalism** *n* cannibalisme *m*.
cannon ['kanən] *n* canon *m*. **cannonball** *n* boulet de canon *m*.
canoe [kə'nuː] *n* canoë *m*; (*sport*) kayac *m*. *v* faire du canoë; faire du kayac.
canon ['kanən] *n* canon *m*. **canonical** *adj* canonique. **canonize** *v* canoniser.
canopy ['kanəpi] *n* baldaquin *m*, dais *m*.
canteen [kan'tiːn] *n* (*dining place*) cantine *f*; (*flask*) bidon *m*; (*cutlery*) ménagère *f*.
canter ['kantə] *n* petit galop *m*. *v* aller au petit galop.
canton ['kantən] *n* canton *m*.
canvas ['kanvəs] *n* toile *f*.
canvass ['kanvəs] *v* (*pol*) faire du démarchage électoral; (*for orders, votes*) solliciter. **canvasser** *n* (*pol*) agent électoral *m*; (*comm*) démarcheur *m*. **canvassing** *n* démarchage *m*.
canyon ['kanjən] *n* cañon *m*.
cap [kap] *n* (*hat*) casquette *f*; (*bottle*) capsule *f*; (*pen*) capuchon *m*. *v* capsuler; surpasser.
capable ['keipəbl] *adj* capable; (*situation*) susceptible. **capability** *n* capacité *f*; aptitude *f*.
capacity [kə'pasəti] *n* capacité *f*; (*status*) qualité *f*.
cape[1] [keip] *n* (*cloak*) pèlerine *f*.
cape[2] [keip] *n* (*geog*) cap *m*.
caper ['keipə] *n* (*cookery*) câpre *f*.
capital ['kapitl] *n* (*city*) capitale *f*; (*letter*) majuscule *f*; (*money*) capital *m*. *adj* capital. **capitalism** *n* capitalisme *m*. **capitalist** *n* capitaliste *m, f*. **capitalize** *v* capitaliser; (*word*) mettre une majuscule à. **capitalize on** tirer parti de.
capitulate [kə'pitjuleit] *v* capituler. **capitulation** *n* capitulation *f*.
capricious [kə'priʃəs] *adj* capricieux.
Capricorn ['kaprikoːn] *n* Capricorne *m*.
capsicum ['kapsikəm] *n* piment *m*.
capsize [kap'saiz] *v* (*naut*) (faire) chavirer.
capsule ['kapsjuːl] *n* capsule *f*.
captain ['kaptin] *n* capitaine *m*.
caption ['kapʃən] *n* légende *f*; (*title*) sous-titre *m*.
captive ['kaptiv] *n* captif, -ive *m, f*. *adj* captif. **captivate** *v* captiver. **captivity** *n* captivité *f*.
capture ['kaptʃə] *v* prendre, capturer; (*attention*) capter. *n* capture *f*. **captor** *n* ravisseur *m*.
car [kaː] *n* voiture *f*; (*rail*) wagon *m*. **car park** parking *m*. **car wash** lave-auto *m*.
caramel ['karəmel] *n* caramel *m*.
carat ['karət] *n* carat *m*.
caravan ['karəvan] *n* caravane *f*; (*gipsy*) roulotte *f*.
caraway ['karəwei] *n* cumin *m*, carvi *m*.
carbohydrates [kaːbə'haidreits] *pl n* farineux *m pl*, féculents *m pl*.
carbon ['kaːbən] *n* carbone *m*. **carbon copy** (*typing*) carbone *m*; (*identical thing*) réplique *f*. **carbon dioxide** gaz carbonique *m*. **carbon paper** papier carbone *m*.
carburettor ['kaːbjuretə] *n* carburateur *m*.
carcass ['kaːkəs] *n* carcasse *f*.
card [kaːd] *n* carte *f*; (*index*) fiche *f*. **cardboard** *n* carton *m*. **card trick** tour de cartes. **it's on the cards** il y a de grandes chances. **play one's cards right** bien mener son jeu.
cardiac ['kaːdiak] *adj* cardiaque. **cardiac arrest** arrêt du cœur *m*.
cardigan ['kaːdigən] *n* cardigan *m*.
cardinal ['kaːdənl] *nm, adj* cardinal.
care [keə] *v* se soucier (de). **care for** (*like*) aimer; (*tend*) soigner; (*look after*) s'occuper de. *n* soin *m*, attention *f*; (*worry*) souci *m*. **care of** chez. **take care** faire attention. **take care of** s'occuper de. **carefree** *adj* sans souci, insouciant. **careful** *adj* prudent; conscientieux. **be careful!** faites attention! **careless** *adj* négligent; (*work*) peu soigné.
career [kə'riə] *n* carrière *f*.
caress [kə'res] *v* caresser. *n* caresse *f*.
caretaker ['keəteikə] *n* gardien, -enne *m, f*; concierge *m, f*.
cargo ['kaːgou] *n* cargaison *m*.

caricature ['karikətjuə] *n* caricature *f.* *v* caricaturer. **caricaturist** *n* caricaturiste *m, f.*
carnage ['kaːnidʒ] *n* carnage *m.*
carnal ['kaːnl] *adj* charnel. **carnal knowledge** (*law*) relations sexuelles *f pl.*
carnation [kaː'neiʃən] *n* œillet *m.*
carnival ['kaːnivəl] *n* carnaval *m.*
carnivorous [kaː'nivərəs] *adj* carnivore. **carnivore** *n* carnivore *m.*
carol ['karəl] *n* chant joyeux *m.* **Christmas carol** chant de Noël *m.*
carpenter ['kaːpəntə] *n* charpentier *m.* **carpentry** *n* charpenterie *f.*
carpet ['kaːpit] *n* tapis *m.* **carpet-sweeper** *n* balai mécanique *m.* *v* moquetter.
carriage ['karidʒ] *n* (*horse-drawn*) voiture *f*; (*rail*) wagon *m*; (*comm*) transport *m*; (*person*) maintien *m.* **carriageway** *n* chaussée *f.* **dual carriageway** route à chaussées séparées *f.*
carrier ['kariə] *n* (*comm*) entreprise de transports *f*; (*med*) porteur, -euse *m, f.* **carrier-bag** *n* sac en plastique *m.*
carrot ['karət] *n* carotte *f.*
carry ['kari] *v* porter; transporter. **carry away** emporter. **carrycot** *n* porte-bébé *m.* **carry on** continuer. **carry out** exécuter. **get carried away** (*coll*) s'emballer.
cart [kaːt] *n* (*horse-drawn*) charrette *f.* **cart-horse** *n* cheval de trait *m.* **turn a cart-wheel** faire la roue. *v* transporter; (*coll*) trimballer.
cartilage ['kaːtəlidʒ] *n* cartilage *m.*
cartography [kaː'togrəfi] *n* cartographie *f.* **cartographer** *n* cartographe *m, f.*
carton ['kaːtən] *n* (*cream, etc.*) pot *m*; (*milk*) carton *m.*
cartoon [kaː'tuːn] *n* dessin *m*; (*film*) dessin animé *m.* **cartoonist** *n* dessinateur, -trice *m, f*; animateur, -trice *m, f.*
cartridge ['kaːtridʒ] *n* cartouche *f*; (*camera*) chargeur *m.* **cartridge paper** papier à cartouche *m.*
carve [kaːv] *v* (*meat*) découper; (*wood, etc.*) tailler; sculpter; (*initials*) graver. **carving** *n* sculpture *f.* **carving knife** couteau à découper *m.*
cascade [kas'keid] *n* cascade *f.* *v* tomber en cascade.
case[1] [keis] *n* cas *m*; (*law*) affaire *f*; arguments *m pl.* **in any case** en tout cas. **in case** à tout hasard. **in case of** en cas de. **in that case** dans ce cas-là.
case[2] [keis] *n* (*luggage*) valise *f*; (*crate*) caisse *f*; (*violin, camera, etc.*) étui *m.*
cash [kaʃ] *n* (*money*) argent *m*; (*not cheque*) espèces *f pl*; (*immediate payment*) argent comptant *m.* **cash desk** caisse *f.* **cash register** caisse enregistreuse *f.* *v* encaisser.
cashier[1] [ka'ʃiə] *n* caissier *m.*
cashier[2] [ka'ʃiə] *v* renvoyer; (*mil*) casser.
cashmere [kaʃ'miə] *n* cachemire *m.*
casino [kə'siːnou] *n* casino *m.*
cask [kaːsk] *n* fût *m.*
casket ['kaːskit] *n* coffret *m.*
casserole ['kasəroul] *n* (*dish*) cocotte *f*; (*food*) ragoût en cocotte *m.* *v* cuire en cocotte.
cassette [kə'set] *n* cassette *f.*
cassock ['kasək] *n* soutane *f.*
***cast** [kaːst] *n* (*mould*) moulage *m*; (*theatre*) distribution *f*; (*throw*) coup *m.* *v* (*throw*) jeter, lancer; (*plaster, etc.*) couler; (*theatre*) distribuer les rôles (de). **cast away** rejeter. **castaway** *n* naufragé, -e *m, f.* **casting vote** voix prépondérante *f.* **cast-iron** *adj* en fonte; (*excuse, etc.*) inattaquable.
caste [kaːst] *n* caste *f.*
castle ['kaːsl] *n* château fort *m.*
castor oil ['kaːstə] *n* huile de ricin *f.*
castrate [kə'streit] *v* châtrer; émasculer. **castration** *n* castration *f.*
casual ['kaʒuəl] *adj* (*chance*) fortuit, fait par hasard; (*informal*) sans-gêne, désinvolte. **casually** *adv* par hasard; avec désinvolture.
casualty ['kaʒuəlti] *n* (*injured*) blessé, -e *m, f*; (*dead*) mort, -e *m, f*; (*of accident*) victime *f*; (*hospital ward*) salle des accidentés *f.*
cat [kat] *n* chat, chatte *m, f.* **cat's eyes** (*road*) cataphotes *m pl.* **catsuit** *n* combinaison-pantalon *f.* **let the cat out of the bag** vendre la mèche.
catalogue ['katəlog] *n* catalogue *m.* *v* cataloguer.
catalyst ['katəlist] *n* catalyse *f.*
catamaran [katəmə'ran] *n* catamaran *m.*
catapult ['katəpʌlt] *n* lance-pierres *m invar*; (*aero, mil*) catapulte *f.* *v* catapulter.
cataract ['katərakt] *n* cataracte *f.*
catarrh [kə'taː] *n* catarrhe *m.*
catastrophe [kə'tastrəfi] *n* catastrophe *f.* **catastrophic** *adj* catastrophique.

***catch** [katʃ] *v* attraper; (*by surprise*) prendre; (*train, etc.*) ne pas manquer; (*on nail*) (s')accrocher; (*hear*) saisir. **catch fire** prendre feu. **catch on** devenir populaire; (*understand*) comprendre. **catch up** (se) rattraper. *n* prise *f*; (*drawback*) attrape *f*; (*window*) loqueteau *m*. **catching** *adj* contagieux.
category ['katəgəri] *n* catégorie *f*. **categorical** *adj* catégorique. **categorize** *v* classer par catégories.
cater ['keitə] *v* **cater for** (*needs*) pourvoir à. **caterer** *n* fournisseur *m*, traiteur *m*. **catering** *n* restauration *f*.
caterpillar ['katəpilə] *n* chenille *f*.
cathedral [kə'θiːdrəl] *n* cathédrale *f*.
cathode ['kaθoud] *n* cathode *f*. **cathode ray tube** tube cathodique *m*.
catholic ['kaθəlik] *adj* (*rel*) catholique; (*tastes, etc.*) éclectique. *n* catholique *m, f*. **catholicism** *n* catholicisme *m*.
catkin ['katkin] *n* chaton *m*.
cattle ['katl] *pl n* bétail *m sing*.
catty ['kati] *adj* (*slang*) vache.
caught [koːt] *V* **catch**.
cauliflower ['koliflauə] *n* chou-fleur (*pl* choux-fleurs) *m*.
cause [koːz] *v* causer. *n* cause *f*.
causeway ['koːzwei] *n* chaussée *f*.
caustic ['koːstik] *adj* caustique.
caution ['koːʃən] *n* prudence *f*; (*warning*) avertissement *m*; réprimande *f*. *v* avertir. **cautious** *adj* prudent.
cavalry ['kavəlri] *n* cavalerie *f*.
cave [keiv] *n* caverne *f*, grotte *f*. *v* **cave in** s'effondrer; (*wall*) céder.
caviar ['kaviaː] *n* caviar *m*.
cavity ['kavəti] *n* cavité *f*. **cavity wall** mur creux *m*.
cayenne [kei'en] *n* cayenne *m*.
cease [siːs] *v* cesser. **cease-fire** *n* cessez-le-feu *m invar*. **ceaseless** *adj* incessant. **ceaselessly** *adv* sans cesse.
cedar ['siːdə] *n* cèdre *m*.
cedilla [si'dilə] *n* cédille *f*.
ceiling ['siːliŋ] *n* plafond *m*.
celebrate ['seləbreit] *v* célébrer. **celebrated** *adj* célèbre. **celebration** *n* célébration *f*; (*occasion*) festivités *f pl*. **celebrity** *n* célébrité *f*.
celery ['seləri] *n* céleri *m*. **stick of celery** côte de céleri *f*.
celestial [sə'lestiəl] *adj* céleste.
celibate ['selibət] *n*(*m*+*f*), *adj* célibataire. **celibacy** *n* célibat *m*.
cell [sel] *n* cellule *f*; (*elec*) élément *m*.
cellar ['selə] *n* cave *f*.
cello ['tʃelou] *n* violoncelle *m*. **cellist** *n* violoncelliste *m, f*.
cellular ['seljulə] *adj* cellulaire; (*blanket*) en cellular.
cement [sə'ment] *n* ciment *m*. **cement-mixer** *n* bétonnière *f*. *v* cimenter.
cemetery ['semətri] *n* cimetière *m*.
cenotaph ['senətaːf] *n* cénotaphe *m*.
censor ['sensə] *n* censeur *m*. *v* censurer. **censorship** *n* censure *f*.
censure ['senʃə] *v* blâmer. *n* critique *f*.
census ['sensəs] *n* recensement *m*.
cent [sent] *n* cent *m*. **per cent** pour cent.
centenary [sen'tiːnəri] *nm, adj* centenaire.
centigrade ['sentigreid] *adj* centigrade.
centimetre ['sentimiːtə] *n* centimètre *m*.
centipede ['sentipiːd] *n* mille-pattes *m invar*.
central ['sentrəl] *adj* central. **central heating** chauffage central *m*. **centralization** *n* centralisation *f*. **centralize** *v* (se) centraliser.
centre ['sentə] *n* centre *m*. *v* centrer. **centre on** (*thoughts*) se concentrer sur; (*problem*) tourner autour de.
centrifugal [sen'trifjugəl] *adj* centrifuge.
century ['sentʃuri] *n* siècle *m*.
ceramic [sə'ramik] *adj* (en) céramique. **ceramics** *n* céramique *f*.
cereal ['siəriəl] *n* céréale *f*.
ceremonial [ˌserə'mouniəl] *n* cérémonial *m*. *adj* cérémoniel; de cérémonie.
ceremony ['serəməni] *n* (*event*) cérémonie *f*; (*formality*) cérémonies *f pl*. **stand on ceremony** faire des façons. **ceremonious** *adj* solennel; (*over-polite*) cérémonieux.
certain ['səːtn] *adj* certain. **certainly** *adv* certainement; (*willingly*) volontiers. **certainty** *n* certitude *f*.
certificate [sə'tifikət] *n* certificat *m*; diplôme *m*. **certify** *v* certifier.
cervix ['səːviks] *n* col de l'utérus *m*.
cesspool ['sespuːl] *n* fosse d'aisances *f*.
chafe [tʃeif] *v* (*rub*) frotter; (*make sore*) gratter.
chaffinch ['tʃafintʃ] *n* pinson *m*.
chain [tʃein] *n* chaîne *f*. **chain smoke** fumer cigarette sur cigarette. **chain store** magasin à succursales multiples *m*.
chair [tʃeə] *n* chaise *f*; (*university*) chaire *f*; (*meeting*) présidence. **chairlift** *n* télésiège *m*. **chairman** *n* président. *v* présider.

chalet ['ʃalei] *n* chalet *m*; (*motel*) bungalow *m*.
chalk [tʃoːk] *n* craie *f*. **chalky** *adj* crayeux.
challenge ['tʃalindʒ] *n* défi *m*. *n* défier; (*sport*) inviter; (*question*) contester.
chamber ['tʃeimbə] *n* chambre *f*. **chambermaid** *n* femme de chambre *f*. **chamber music** musique de chambre *f*. **chamberpot** *n* pot de chambre *m*.
chameleon [kəmiːliən] *n* caméléon *m*.
chamois ['ʃamwaː] *n* chamois *m*. **chamois leather** peau de chamois *m*.
champagne [ʃam'pein] *n* champagne *m*.
champion ['tʃampiən] *n* champion, -onne *m*, *f*. *v* défendre. **championship** *n* championnat *m*.
chance [tʃaːns] *n* (*luck*) hasard *m*; (*possibility*) chance *f*; (*opportunity*) occasion *f*. **by chance** par hasard. *adj* fortuit. *v* prendre le risque de.
chancellor [tʃaːnsələ] *n* chancelier *m*.
chandelier [ʃandə'liə] *n* lustre *m*.
change [tʃeindʒ] *n* changement *m*; (*money*) monnaie *f*. *v* changer; échanger; (*clothes*) se changer. **changeable** *adj* changeant; (*weather*) variable. **changing-room** *n* vestiaire *m*.
channel ['tʃanl] *n* chenal *m*; (*duct*) conduit *m*; (*TV*) chaîne *f*. **the Channel Islands** les îles anglo-normandes *f pl*. **the English Channel** la Manche. *v* (*efforts, etc.*) canaliser.
chant [tʃaːnt] *v* (*rel*) psalmodier; (*crowd*) scander. *n* psalmodie *f*; chant scandé *m*.
chaos ['keios] *n* chaos *m*. *adj* chaotique.
chap[1] [tʃap] *v* (*skin*) (se) gercer. *n* gerçure *f*.
chap[2] [tʃap] *n* (*coll*) type *m*.
chapel ['tʃapəl] *n* chapelle *f*.
chaperon ['ʃapəroun] *n* chaperon *m*. *v* chaperonner.
chaplain ['tʃaplin] *n* aumônier *m*.
chapter ['tʃaptə] *n* chapitre *m*.
char[1] [tʃaː] *v* (*burn*) carboniser.
char[2] [tʃaː] *v* faire des ménages. **charwoman** *n* femme de ménage *f*.
character ['karəktə] *n* caractère *m*; (*theatre, etc.*) personnage *m*. **characteristic** *nf*, *adj* caractéristique. **caracterize** *v* caractériser.
charcoal ['tʃaːkoul] *n* charbon de bois *m*.
charge [tʃaːdʒ] *n* (*law*) accusation *f*; (*mil*) charge *f*; (*cost*) prix *m*; responsabilité *f*; (*battery*) charge *f*. **in charge** responsable. **take charge of** se charger de. *v* (*law*) accuser (de); (*mil*) charger; (*person*) faire payer; (*amount*) demander; (*battery*) (se) charger. **charge in/out** entrer/sortir en coup de vent.
chariot ['tʃariət] *n* char *m*.
charity ['tʃarəti] *n* charité *f*; (*society*) œuvre charitable *f*. **charitable** *adj* charitable.
charm [tʃaːm] *n* charme *m*; (*on bracelet*) breloque *f*. *v* charmer. **charming** *adj* charmant.
chart [tʃaːt] *n* (*map*) carte *f*; (*graph, etc.*) graphique *m*, diagramme *m*. *v* (*journey*) porter sur la carte; (*sales, etc.*) faire le graphique de.
charter ['tʃaːtə] *v* (*boat, etc.*) affréter. **chartered accountant** expert-comptable *m*. *n* affrètement; (*document*) charte *f*. **charter flight** charter *m*.
chase [tʃeis] *v* chasser, poursuivre. *n* chasse *f*, poursuite *f*.
chasm ['kazəm] *n* gouffre *m*.
chassis ['ʃasi] *n* (*mot*) châssis *m*.
chaste [tʃeist] *adj* chaste, pur. **chastity** *n* chasteté *f*.
chastise [tʃas'taiz] *v* châtier. **chastisement** *n* châtiment *m*.
chat [tʃat] *n* causette *f*. *v* bavarder.
chatter ['tʃatə] *v* jacasser; (*teeth*) claquer. *n* jacassement *m*; bavardage *m*. **chatterbox** *n* bavard, -e *m*, *f*.
chauffeur ['ʃoufə] *n* chauffeur *m*.
chauvinism ['ʃouvinizəm] *n* chauvinisme *m*. **chauvinist** *n*, *adj* chauvin, -e **male chauvinist** (*slang*) phallocrate *m*.
cheap [tʃiːp] *adj* bon marché *invar*; (*reduced*) réduit. **cheapen** *v* baisser le prix de; (*degrade*) déprécier. **cheaply** *adv* à bon marché.
cheat [tʃiːt] *v* (*deceive*) tromper; (*at games*) tricher; frauder. *n* tricheur, -euse *m*, *f*; fraude *f*.
check [tʃek] *n* contrôle *m*, vérification *f*; (*restraint*) arrêt *m*; (*chess*) échec *m*; (*US: cheque*) chèque *m*; (*US: bill*) addition *f*. **checkmate** *n* échec et mat. **checkpoint** *n* contrôle *m*. **checks** *pl n* (*pattern*) carreaux *m pl*. *v* vérifier; contrôler; (*restrain*) maîtriser. **check-in** *n* (*aero*) enregistrement *m*. **check-out** *n* (*supermarket*) caisse *f*. **check out** (*hotel*) régler sa note. **check-up** *n* (*med*) bilan de santé *m*. **check up on** (*thing*) vérifier; (*person*) se renseigner sur. **checked** *adj* (*pattern*) à carreaux.

cheek [tʃiːk] *n* (*anat*) joue *f*; (*coll*: *impudence*) toupet *m*. **cheekbone** *n* pommette *f*. **cheeky** *adj* effronté.
cheer [tʃiə] *v* (*shout*) acclamer, pousser des hourras. **cheer up** (s')égayer; prendre courage; (*comfort*) consoler. *n* gaieté *f*; (*shout*) acclamation *f*. **cheerio!** *interj* salut! **cheers!** *interj* à la vôtre! **cheerful** *adj* gai; (*news*) réconfortant. **cheerless** *adj* morne. **cheery** *adj* joyeux.
cheese [tʃiːz] *n* fromage *m*. **cheesecake** *n* tarte au fromage blanc *f*. **cheesecloth** *n* (*for clothes*) toile à beurre *f*.
cheetah ['tʃiːtə] *n* guépard *m*.
chef [ʃef] *n* chef (de cuisine) *m*.
chemistry ['kemistri] *n* chimie *f*. **chemist** *n* chimiste *m*, *f*; pharmacien, -enne *m*, *f*. **chemist's shop** pharmacie *f*.
cheque *or US* **check** [tʃek] *n* chèque *m*. **chequebook** *n* chéquier *m*. **cheque card** carte d'identité bancaire *f*.
cherish ['tʃeriʃ] *v* chérir; (*hope, etc.*) nourrir.
cherry ['tʃeri] *n* (*fruit*) cerise *f*; (*tree*) cerisier *m*.
chess [tʃes] *n* échecs *m pl*. **chessboard** *n* échiquier *m*. **chessman** *n* pièce *f*.
chest [tʃest] *n* (*anat*) poitrine *f*; (*box*) caisse *f*. **chest of drawers** commode *f*. **chesty** *adj* (*cough*) de poitrine.
chestnut ['tʃesnʌt] *n* (*fruit*) châtaigne *f*, marron *m*; (*tree*) châtaigner *m*, marronnier *m*. *adj* (*hair*) châtain.
chew [tʃuː] *v* mâcher. **chewing gum** chewing-gum *m*. **chew over** ruminer. **chew the cud** ruminer. **chew up** mâchonner.
chicken ['tʃikin] *n* poulet *m*, (*very young*) poussin *m*. **chicken pox** *n* varicelle *f*. *v* **chicken out** (*slang*) se dégonfler.
chicory ['tʃikəri] *n* chicorée *f*.
chief [tʃiːf] *n* chef *m*. *adj* principal; en chef. **chiefly** *adv* principalement; surtout.
chilblain ['tʃilblein] *n* engelure *f*.
child [tʃaild] *n pl* **children** enfant. **childbirth** *n* accouchement *m*. **childhood** *n* enfance *f*. **childish** *adj* puéril. **childless** *adj* sans enfants.
chill [tʃil] *n* fraîcheur *f*, froid *m*; (*fear*) frisson *m*; (*med*) refroidissement *m*. *v* (*wine*) rafraîchir; (*champagne*) frapper. **chilled to the bone** transi jusqu'aux os. **chilly** *adj* froid.
chilli ['tʃili] *n* piment *m*.
chime [tʃaim] *v* carillonner; (*hours*) sonner. *n* carillon *m*.
chimney ['tʃimni] *n* cheminée *f*. **chimney pot** tuyau de cheminée *m*. **chimney sweep** ramoneur *m*.
chimpanzee [tʃimpən'ziː] *n* chimpanzé *m*.
chin [tʃin] *n* menton *m*.
china ['tʃainə] *n* porcelaine *f*.
China ['tʃainə] *n* Chine *f*. **Chinese** *nm*, *adj* chinois. **the Chinese** les Chinois *m pl*.
chink[1] [tʃiŋk] *n* (*slit*) fente *f*; (*door*) entrebâillement *m*.
chink[2] [tʃiŋk] *n* (*sound*) tintement *m*. *v* (faire) tinter.
chip [tʃip] *n* (*fragment*) éclat *m*; (*in cup, etc.*) ébréchure *f*; (*poker, etc.*) jeton *m*. **chipboard** *n* bois aggloméré *m*. **chips** *pl n* (*cookery*) frites *f pl*. *v* (s')ébrécher. **chip in** (*interrupt*) dire son mot; (*money*) contribuer.
chiropody [ki'ropədi] *n* soins du pied *m pl*. **chiropodist** *n* pédicure *m*, *f*.
chirp [tʃəːp] *v* pépier. *n* pépiement *m*. **chirpy** *adj* gai.
chisel ['tʃizl] *n* ciseau *m*. *v* ciseler.
chivalry ['ʃivəlri] *n* chevalerie *f*. **chivalrous** *adj* chevaleresque.
chive [tʃaiv] *n* ciboulette *f*.
chlorine ['kloːriːn] *n* chlore *m*. **chlorinate** *v* javelliser.
chloroform ['klorəfoːm] *n* chloroforme *m*. *v* chloroformer.
chlorophyll ['klorəfil] *n* chlorophylle *f*.
chocolate ['tʃokələt] *n* chocolat *m*.
choice [tʃois] *n* choix *m*. *adj* (*fruit*) de choix *invar*; (*word*) bien choisi.
choir ['kwaiə] *n* chœur *m*; chorale *f*. **choirboy** *n* jeune choriste *m*. **choir-stall** *n* stalle *f*.
choke [tʃouk] *v* (s')étrangler, étouffer; (*block*) boucher. *n* (*mot*) starter *m*.
cholera ['kolərə] *n* choléra *m*.
***choose** [tʃuːz] *v* choisir.
chop[1] [tʃop] *n* (*meat*) côtelette *f*; (*blow*) coup *m*. *v* trancher; (*wood*) couper à la hache; (*vegetables, etc.*) hacher. **chop down** (*tree*) abattre. **chopper** *n* hachoir *m*.
chop[2] [tʃop] *v* **chop and change** changer constamment. **chop logic** ergoter. **choppy** *adj* (*sea*) un peu agité.
chops [tʃops] *pl n* (*jaws*) mâchoires *f pl*. **lick one's chops** se lécher les babines.
chopstick ['tʃopstik] *n* baguette *f*.
chord [koːd] *n* (*anat*) corde *f*; (*music*) accord *m*.

chore [tʃoː] *n* (*unpleasant*) corvée *f*. **chores** *pl n* (*household*) travaux du ménage *m pl*.
choreography [koriˈogrəfi] *n* chorégraphie *f*. **choreographer** *n* chorégraphe *m, f*.
chorus [ˈkoːrəs] *n* refrain *m*; (*singers*) chœur *m*; (*dancers*) troupe *f*. **choral** *adj* choral.
chose [tʃouz] *V* **choose**.
chosen [ˈtʃouzn] *V* **choose**.
christen [ˈkrisn] *v* baptiser; (*nickname*) surnommer. **christening** *n* baptême *m*.
Christian [ˈkristʃən] *n, adj* chrétien, -enne. **Christian name** prénom *m*. **Christianity** *n* christianisme *m*.
Christmas [ˈkrisməs] *n* Noël *m*. **Christmas Day** le jour de Noël *m*. **Christmas Eve** la veille de Noël *f*.
chromatic [krəˈmatik] *adj* chromatique.
chrome [kroum] *n* chrome *m*.
chromium [ˈkroumiəm] *n* chrome *m*. **chromium-plated** *adj* chromé. **chromium-plating** *n* chromage *m*.
chromosome [ˈkrouməsoum] *n* chromosome *m*.
chronic [ˈkronik] *adj* chronique; (*coll*) atroce.
chronicle [ˈkronikl] *n* chronique *f*.
chronological [kronəˈlodʒikəl] *adj* chronologique. **in chronological order** par ordre chronologique.
chrysalis [ˈkrisəlis] *n* chrysalide *f*.
chrysanthemum [kriˈsanθəməm] *n* chrysanthème *m*.
chubby [ˈtʃʌbi] *adj* potelé.
chuck [tʃʌk] (*coll*) *v* (*throw*) lancer; (*give up*) laisser tomber. **chuck out** (*thing*) balancer; (*person*) vider.
chuckle [ˈtʃʌkl] *v* glousser. *n* petit rire *m*.
chunk [tʃʌŋk] *n* gros morceau *m*; (*bread*) quignon *m*.
church [tʃəːtʃ] *n* église *f*. **churchgoer** *n* pratiquant, -e *m, f*. **church hall** salle paroissiale *f*. **churchyard** *n* cimetière *m*.
churn [tʃəːn] *n* baratte *f*. *v* baratter; (*water*) (faire) bouillonner. **churn out** (*coll: books, etc.*) pondre en série.
chute [ʃuːt] *n* glissière *f*.
cider [ˈsaidə] *n* cidre *m*.
cigar [siˈgaː] *n* cigare *m*.
cigarette [sigəˈret] *n* cigarette *f*. **cigarette lighter** briquet *m*.
cinder [ˈsində] *n* cendre *f*. **burnt to a cinder** réduit en cendres.
cine camera [ˈsini] *n* caméra *f*.
cinema [ˈsinəmə] *n* cinéma *m*.
cinnamon [ˈsinəmən] *n* cannelle *f*.
circle [ˈsəːkl] *n* cercle *m*; (*theatre*) balcon *m*. *v* (*surround*) encercler; (*move round*) tourner autour de; (*aircraft*) tourner. **circular** *nf, adj* circulaire.
circuit [ˈsəːkit] *n* tour *m*; (*law*) tournée *f*; (*elec, sport*) circuit *m*. **circuitous** *adj* indirect.
circulate [ˈsəːkjuleit] *v* (faire) circuler. **circulation** *n* circulation *f*; (*newspaper*) tirage *m*.
circumcise [ˈsəːkəmsaiz] *v* circoncire. **circumcision** *n* circoncision *f*.
circumference [səˈkʌmfərəns] *n* circonférence *f*.
circumflex [ˈsəːkəmfleks] *adj* circonflexe. *n* accent circonflexe *m*.
circumscribe [ˈsəːkəmskraib] *v* circonscrire.
circumspect [ˈsəːkəmspekt] *adj* circonspect.
circumstance [ˈsəːkəmstans] *n* circonstance *f*. **circumstances** *pl n* (*financial*) moyens *m pl*. **under no circumstances** en aucun cas. **under the circumstances** vu l'état des choses.
circus [ˈsəːkəs] *n* cirque *m*.
cistern [ˈsistən] *n* citerne *f*; (*toilet*) chasse d'eau *f*.
cite [sait] *v* citer. **citation** *n* citation *f*.
citizen [ˈsitizn] *n* (*town*) habitant, -e *m, f*; (*state*) citoyen, -enne *m, f*. **citizenship** *n* citoyenneté *f*.
citrus [ˈsitrəs] *n* citrus *m pl*. **citrus fruits** agrumes *m pl*. **citric acid** acide citrique *m*.
city [ˈsiti] *n* ville *f*, cité *f*. **city centre** centre ville *m*.
civic [ˈsivik] *adj* (*authorities*) municipal; (*rights*) civique. **civic centre** centre administratif *m*.
civil [ˈsivl] *adj* civil; poli. **civil engineering** travaux publics *m pl*. **civil rights** droits civiques *m pl*. **civil servant** fonctionnaire *m, f*. **civil service** administration *f*. **civil war** guerre civile *f*.
civilian [səˈviljən] *n, adj* civil, -e.
civilization [ˌsivilaiˈzeiʃən] *n* civilisation *f*.
civilize *v* civiliser.
clad [klad] *adj* habillé.
claim [kleim] *v* (*right, prize, etc.*) revendiquer; (*damages*) réclamer; (*profess*) déclarer. *n* revendication *f*; réclamation

f; (*insurance*) déclaration de sinistre *f*; (*right*) droit *m*.
clairvoyant [kleə'voiənt] *n* voyant, -e *m, f*.
clam [klam] *n* praire *f*.
clamber ['klambə] *v* grimper en rampant.
clammy ['klami] *adj* moite.
clamour ['klamə] *n* clameur *f*. *v* vociférer.
clamp [klamp] *n* pince *f*, crampon *m*. *v* serrer, cramponner. **clamp down on** supprimer; restreindre.
clan [klan] *n* clan *m*.
clandestine [klan'destin] *adj* clandestin.
clang [klaŋ] *n* bruit métallique *m*. *v* résonner. **clanger** *n* (*coll*) gaffe *f*.
clap [klap] *v* applaudir. **clap one's hands** battre des mains. *n* (*noise*) claquement *m*; (*thunder*) coup *m*; (*applause*) applaudissements *m pl*.
claret ['klarət] *n* bordeaux *m*.
clarify ['klarəfai] *v* (se) clarifier; (*situation*) (s')éclaircir.
clarinet [klarə'net] *n* clarinette *f*.
clarity ['klarəti] *n* clarté *f*.
clash [klaʃ] *n* (*bang*) s'entrechoquer; (*conflict*) se heurter; (*colours*) jurer. *n* (*dispute*) accrochage *m*; (*personalities*) incompatibilité *f*; (*noise*) choc *m*.
clasp [klaːsp] *v* serrer. *n* (*fastening*) fermoir *m*; (*grip*) étreinte *f*.
class [klaːs] *n* classe *f*; catégorie *f*; (*school*) cours *m*. **class-room** *n* salle de classe *f*. *v* classer.
classic ['klasik] *nm, adj* classique. **classical** *adj* classique. **classics** *n* humanités *f pl*.
classify ['klasifai] *v* classifier. **classification** *n* classification *f*. **classified** *adj* classifié; secret, -ète. **classified advertisement** petite annonce *f*.
clatter ['klatə] *n* cliquetis *m*. *v* cliqueter.
clause [kloːz] *n* (*law*) clause *f*; (*gramm*) proposition *f*.
claustrophobia [kloːstrə'foubiə] *n* claustrophobie *f*. **claustrophobe** *n* claustrophobe *m, f*. **claustrophobic** *adj* claustrophobique.
claw [kloː] *n* griffe *f*; (*lobster*) pince *f*. *v* griffer.
clay [klei] *n* argile *f*.
clean [kliːn] *adj* propre; net, nette. *adv* entièrement. **clean-shaven** *adj* glabre. *v* nettoyer. **cleaner** *n* (*charwoman*) femme de ménage *f*. **cleaner's** *n* teinturerie *f*. **cleaning** *n* nettoyage *m*; (*housework*) ménage. **cleanliness** *or* **cleanness** *n* propreté *f*.
cleanse [klenz] *v* nettoyer; purifier. **cleanser** *n* (*cosmetic*) démaquillant *m*.
clear [kliə] *adj* clair; transparent; distinct; (*without obstacles*) libre. *v* (s')éclaircir; clarifier; (*remove obstacles*) débarrasser; (*law*) disculper; (*jump*) franchir. **clearance** *n* (*space*) espace (*m*) libre; (*customs*) dédouanement *m*; (*aero*) autorisation *f*. **clearing** *n* clairière *f*. **clearness** *n* clarté *f*.
clef [klef] *n* clef *f*.
clench [klentʃ] *v* empoigner. **clench one's fists/teeth** serrer les poings/dents.
clergy ['kləːdʒi] *n* clergé *m*. **clergyman** *n* (*Protestant*) pasteur *m*; (*Catholic*) prêtre *m*.
clerical ['klerikəl] *adj* (*office*) d'employé, de bureau; (*rel*) clérical.
clerk [klaːk] *n* employé, -e *m, f*.
clever ['klevə] *adj* intelligent; (*skilful*) habile; (*smart*) astucieux. **cleverness** *n* intelligence *f*; habileté *f*; astuce *f*.
cliché ['kliːʃei] *n* cliché *m*.
click [klik] *n* déclic *m*. *v* claquer, faire un déclic.
client ['klaiənt] *n* client, -e *m, f*. **clientele** *n* clientèle *f*.
cliff [klif] *n* falaise *f*.
climate ['klaimət] *n* climat *m*. **climatic** *adj* climatique.
climax ['klaimaks] *n* apogée *m*, point culminant *m*.
climb [klaim] *v* grimper, monter; (*mountain*) gravir. *n* montée *f*. **climbing** *n* (*sport*) alpinisme *m*.
***cling** [kliŋ] *v* se cramponner; (*stick*) (se) coller.
clinic ['klinik] *n* clinique *f*. **clinical** *adj* (*med*) clinique; (*attitude*) objectif.
clink [kliŋk] *v* (faire) tinter. *n* tintement *m*.
clip[1] [klip] *v* (*hedge*) tailler; (*hair*) couper; (*dog*) tondre. *n* (*coll*: *blow*) taloche *f*; (*cinema*) extrait *m*. **clipping** *n* (*newspaper*) coupure de presse *f*.
clip[2] [klip] *n* attache *f*. *v* attacher.
clitoris ['klitəris] *n* clitoris *m*.
cloak [klouk] *n* (*clothing*) cape *f*; (*mask*) manteau *m*. **cloakroom** *n* vestiaire *m*. *v* masquer.
clock [klok] *n* (*large*) horloge *f*; (*small*) pendule *f*. **against the clock** contre la montre. **clock-tower** *n* clocher *m*. **clock-**

wise *adj*, *adv* dans le sens des aiguilles d'une montre. **clockwork** *adj* mécanique. **like clockwork** comme sur des roulettes.
clog [klog] *n* sabot *m*. *v* boucher.
cloister ['kloistə] *n* cloître *m*. *v* cloîtrer.
close[1] [klous] *adj* (*near*) proche; (*friend*) intime; (*contest, etc.*) serré; (*atmosphere*) étouffant. *adv* de près. **close by** tout près. **close-fitting** *adj* ajusté. **close-up** *n* gros plan *m*. *n* cul-de-sac *m*. **closely** *adv* de près; attentivement.
close[2] [klouz] *n* (*end*) fin *f*. *v* (se) fermer; (*block*) boucher; (*finish*) (se) terminer. **close in** approcher; (*enclose*) clôturer. **close up** se rapprocher. **closing** *or* **closure** *n* fermeture *f*.
closet ['klozit] *n* placard *m*; (*room*) cabinet *m*. *v* enfermer.
clot [klot] *n* caillot *m*. *v* (se) coaguler.
cloth [kloθ] *n* (*fabric*) tissu *m*; (*linen*) toile *f*; (*cleaning*) chiffon *m*.
clothe [klouð] *v* vêtir, habiller. **clothes** *pl n* vêtements *m pl*. **clothes brush** brosse à habits *f*. **clothes horse** séchoir *m*. **clothes line** corde à linge *f*. **clothes peg** pince à linge *f*. **clothing** *n* vêtements *m pl*.
cloud [klaud] *n* nuage *m*. **cloudburst** *n* déluge de pluie *m*. *v* (*mind*) (s')obscurcir; (*face*) (s')assombrir. **cloud over** se couvrir de nuages. **cloudless** *adj* sans nuages. **cloudy** *adj* nuageux, couvert; (*liquid*) trouble.
clove[1] [klouv] *n* (*spice*) clou de girofle *m*. **oil of cloves** essence de girofle *f*.
clove[2] [klouv] *n* (*of garlic*) gousse *f*.
clover ['klouvə] *n* trèfle *m*.
clown [klaun] *n* clown *m*.
club [klʌb] *n* (*weapon*) massue *f*; (*cards*) trèfle; (*society*) club *m*. **club-foot** *n* pied-bot *m*. **clubhouse** *n* pavillon *m*. *v* matraquer. **club together** se cotiser.
clue [kluː] *n* indice *m*; (*crosswords*) définition *f*.
clump [klʌmp] *n* massif *m*; (*trees*) bouquet *m*; (*grass, flowers*) touffe *f*.
clumsy ['klʌmzi] *adj* maladroit, gauche. **clumsiness** *n* maladresse *f*, gaucherie *f*.
clung [klʌŋ] *V* **cling**.
cluster ['klʌstə] *n* (*flowers, fruit*) grappe *f*; groupe *m*. *v* se grouper.
clutch [klʌtʃ] *n* (*grip*) étreinte *f*; (*mot*) embrayage *m*. *v* empoigner, se cramponner à.
clutter ['klʌtə] *n* désordre *m*. *v* encombrer.
coach [koutʃ] *n* (*bus*) car *m*; (*rail*) voiture *f*; (*sport*) entraîneur *m*; (*school*) répétiteur, -trice *m, f*. *v* entraîner; (*for exam*) préparer. **coaching** *n* répétitions *f pl*; entraînement *m*.
coagulate [kou'agjuleit] *v* (se) coaguler. **coagulation** *n* coagulation *f*.
coal [koul] *n* charbon *m*, houille *f*. **coalman** *n* charbonnier *m*. **coalmine** *n* houillère *f*. **coalminer** *n* mineur *m*. **coalmining** *n* charbonnage *m*.
coalition [kouə'liʃən] *n* coalition *f*.
coarse [koːs] *adj* grossier; (*salt, etc.*) gros, grosse. **coarseness** *n* rudesse *f*.
coast [koust] *n* côte *f*. **coastguard** *n* garde maritime *m*. **coastline** *n* littoral *m*. **the coast is clear** la voie est libre. *v* (*mot*) descendre en roue libre. **coastal** *adj* côtier. **coaster** *n* (*mat*) dessous de verre *m*.
coat [kout] *n* manteau *m*; (*animal*) pelage *m*, poil *m*; (*horse*) robe *f*; (*paint, etc.*) couche *f*. **coat hanger** cintre *m*. *v* couvrir; (*cookery*) enrober. **coating** *n* couche *f*.
coax [kouks] *v* cajoler.
cobbler ['koblə] *n* cordonnier *m*.
cobra ['koubrə] *n* cobra *m*.
cobweb ['kobweb] *n* toile d'araignée *f*.
cocaine [kə'kein] *n* cocaïne *f*.
cock [kok] *n* coq *m*; mâle *m*; (*vulgar: penis*) bitte *f*. *v* (*gun*) armer; (*ears*) dresser.
cockle ['kokl] *n* coque *f*.
cockpit ['kokpit] *n* poste de pilotage *m*.
cockroach ['kokroutʃ] *n* blatte *f*.
cocktail ['kokteil] *n* cocktail *m*.
cocky ['koki] *adj* suffisant.
cocoa ['koukou] *n* cacao *m*.
coconut ['koukənʌt] *n* noix de coco *f*. **coconut palm** cocotier *m*.
cocoon [kə'kuːn] *n* cocon *m*.
cod [kod] *n* morue *f*. **cod-liver oil** huile de foie de morue *f*.
code [koud] *n* code *m*. *v* chiffrer.
codeine ['koudiːn] *n* codéine *f*.
coeducation [kouedju'keiʃən] *n* éducation mixte *f*. **coeducational** *adj* mixte.
coerce [kou'əːs] *v* contraindre. **coercion** *n* contrainte *f*. **coercive** *adj* coercitif.
coexist [kouig'zist] *v* coexister.
coffee ['kofi] *n* café *m*. **black/white coffee** café noir/au lait *m*. **coffee bar** café *m*. **coffee bean** grain de café *m*. **coffee pot** cafetière *f*. **coffee table** table basse *f*.

coffin ['kofin] *n* cercueil *m*.
cog [kog] *n* dent *f*.
cognac ['konjak] *n* cognac *m*.
cohabit [kou'habit] *v* cohabiter. **cohabitation** *n* cohabitation *f*.
coherent [kou'hiərənt] *adj* cohérent; (*account, etc*.) facile à suivre. **coherence** *n* cohérence *f*. **coherently** *adj* avec cohérence.
coil [koil] *n* rouleau *m*; (*elec*) bobine *f*; (*med*) stérilet *m*. *v* (s')enrouler; (*snake*) se lover.
coin [koin] *n* pièce (de monnaie) *f*. *v* (*money*) frapper; (*word, etc*.) inventer.
coincide [kouin'said] *v* coïncider. **coincidence** *n* coïncidence *f*. **coincidental** *adj* de coïncidence.
colander ['koləndə] *n* passoire *f*.
cold [kould] *adj* froid. **be cold** (*person*) avoir froid; (*weather*) faire froid. **cold-blooded** *adj* (*animal*) à sang froid; (*person*) insensible. **cold-hearted** *adj* impitoyable. **cold sore** *n* herpès *m*. *n* froid *m*; (*med*) rhume *m*. **have a cold** être enrhumé.
colic ['kolik] *n* colique *f*.
collaborate [kə'labəreit] *v* collaborer. **collaboration** *n* collaboration *f*. **collaborator** *n* collaborateur, -trice *m, f*.
collapse [ke'laps] *v* s'écrouler, s'éffondrer. *n* éffondrement *m*, écroulement *m*. **collapsible** *adj* pliant.
collar ['kolə] *n* (*on garment*) col *m*; (*dog, etc*.) collier *m*. **collarbone** *n* clavicule *f*.
collate [ko'leit] *v* collationner. **collation** *n* collation *f*.
colleague ['koliːg] *n* collègue *m, f*.
collect [kə'lekt] *v* (s')amasser; (se) rassembler; (*as hobby*) collectionner; (*pick up*) ramasser; (*gather*) recueillir; (*call for*) passer prendre. *adj, adv* (*US: phone*) en P.C.V. **collection** *n* rassemblement *m*; (*money*) quête *f*; (*stamps, etc*.) collection *f*; (*mail*) levée *f*. **collective** *adj* collectif. **collector** *n* (*stamps, etc*.) collectionneur, -euse *m, f*.
college ['kolidʒ] *n* collège *m*; (*professional*) école *f*.
collide [kə'laid] *v* se heurter. **collision** *n* collision *f*.
colloquial [kə'loukwiəl] *adj* familier. **colloquialism** *n* expression familière *f*.
colon ['koulon] *n* (*punctuation*) deux points *m invar*.
colonel ['kəːnl] *n* colonel *m*.
colony ['koləni] *n* colonie *f*. **colonial** *adj* colonial. **colonization** *n* colonisation *f*. **colonize** *v* coloniser.
colossal [kə'losəl] *adj* colossal.
colour ['kʌlə] *n* couleur *f*. **colour bar** discrimination raciale *f*. **colour-blind** *adj* daltonien. **colour scheme** combinaison de couleurs *f*. **colour television** (*set*) téléviseur couleur *m*. *v* colorer; (*picture*) colorier. **coloured** *adj* coloré; (*picture*) en couleur; (*person*) de couleur. **colourful** *adj* coloré. **colouring** *n* (*complexion*) teint *m*; coloration *f*. **colourless** *adj* incolore.
colt [koult] *n* poulain *m*.
column ['koləm] *n* colonne *f*. **columnist** *n* journaliste *m, f*.
coma ['koumə] *n* coma *m*. **in a coma** dans le coma.
comb [koum] *n* peigne *m*; (*bird*) crête *f*. *v* (*hair*) peigner; (*search*) fouiller.
combat ['kombat] *n* combat *m*. *v* combattre. **combatant** *n* combattant, -e *m, f*.
combine [kəm'bain; *n* 'kombain] *v* combiner; s'unir. *n* association *f*. **combination** *n* combinaison *f*. **combination lock** serrure à combinaison *f*.
combustion [kəm'bʌstʃən] *n* combustion *f*. **combustible** *adj* combustible.
***come** [kʌm] *n* venir; arriver. **come across** (*find*) tomber sur. **come back** revenir. **come-back** *n* rentrée *f*. **come down** descendre. **come-down** *n* déchéance *f*. **come in** entrer. **come off** se détacher; (*succeed*) réussir. **come out** sortir. **come to** (*from faint*) revenir à soi; (*total*) se monter à.
comedy ['komədi] *n* comédie *f*. **comedian** *n* comique *m*.
comet ['komit] *n* comète *f*.
comfort ['kʌmfət] *n* confort *m*; consolation *f*. *v* consoler; (*soothe*) soulager. **comfortable** *adj* confortable; (*person*) à l'aise.
comic ['komik] *adj* comique. *n* (*person*) comique *m*; (*magazine*) comic *m*. **comical** *adj* drôle.
comma ['komə] *n* virgule *f*.
command [kə'maːnd] *v* commander; ordonner; (*respect*) exiger. *n* commandement *m*; ordre *m*; (*mastery*) maîtrise *f*. **commander** *n* chef *m*; (*mil*) commandant *m*. **commandment** *n* commandement *m*.
commandeer [komən'diə] *v* réquisitionner.

commando [kə'maːndou] *n* commando *m*.
commemorate [kə'memәreit] *v* commémorer. **commemoration** *n* commémoration *f*. **commemorative** *adj* commémoratif.
commence [kə'mens] *v* commencer. **commencement** *n* commencement *m*.
commend [kə'mend] *v* (*praise*) louer; recommander; (*entrust*) confier. **commendable** *adj* louable; recommandable. **commendation** *n* louange *f*; recommandation *f*.
comment ['koment] *n* observation *f*, commentaire *m*. *v* remarquer. **comment on** commenter, faire des remarques sur. **commentary** *n* commentaire *m*; (*sport*) reportage *m*. **commentator** *n* reporter *m*.
commerce ['komәːs] *n* commerce *m*. **commercial** *adj* commercial; de commerce. **commercialize** *v* commercialiser.
commiserate [kə'mizәreit] *v* (*illness*) témoigner de la sympathie (à); (*bad luck*) s'apitoyer sur le sort (de). **commiseration** *n* commisération *f*.
commission [kə'miʃən] *n* commission *f*; ordres *m pl*; (*mil*) brevet *m*. *v* (*order*) commander; déléguer; (*mil*) nommer à un commandement. **commissioner** *n* commissaire *m*; (*police*) préfet *m*.
commit [kə'mit] *v* commettre; (*entrust*) confier. **commit oneself** s'engager. **commit suicide** se suicider. **commitment** *n* responsabilité *f*; (*comm*) engagement *m*.
committee [kə'miti] *n* commission *f*, comité *m*.
commodity [kə'modəti] *n* produit *m*, marchandise *f*.
common ['komən] *adj* commun; ordinaire; vulgaire. **Common Market** Marché Commun *m*. **commonplace** *adj* banal. **common-room** *n* salle commune *f*. **common sense** bon sens. **commonwealth** *n* république *f*; confédération *f*; (*British*) Commonwealth *m*.
commotion [kə'mouʃən] *n* commotion *f*; (*noise*) agitation *f*.
communal ['komjunəl] *adj* (*shared*) commun; (*of community*) communautaire.
commune[1] [kə'mjuːn] *v* communier; converser intimement.
commune[2] ['komjuːn] *n* communauté *f*; (*admin*) commune *f*.
communicate [kə'mjuːnikeit] *v* communiquer. **communication** *n* communication *f*.
communication cord sonnette d'alarme *f*. **communicative** *adj* communicatif, bavard.
communion [kə'mjuːnjən] *n* communion *f*.
communism ['komjunizəm] *n* communisme *m*. **communist** *n*(*m*+*f*), *adj* communiste.
community [kə'mjuːnəti] *n* communauté *f*; colonie *f*. **community centre** foyer socio-éducatif *m*.
commute [kə'mjuːt] *n* (*travel*) faire la navette; échanger; (*law*) commuer. **commuter** *n* banlieusard, -e *m*, *f*.
compact[1] [kəm'pakt; *n* 'kompakt] *adj* compact; concis. *v* condenser. *n* (*powder*) poudrier *m*.
compact[2] ['kompakt] *n* (*agreement*) contrat *m*.
companion [kəm'panjən] *n* compagnon *m*, compagne *f*. **companionship** *n* camaraderie *f*.
company ['kʌmpəni] *n* compagnie *f*; (*theatre*) troupe *f*.
compare [kəm'peə] *v* (se) comparer. **comparable** *adj* comparable. **comparative** *adj* comparatif; relatif. **comparison** *n* comparaison *f*.
compartment [kəm'paːtmənt] *n* compartiment *m*.
compass ['kʌmpəs] *n* boussole *f*; (*naut*) compas *m*; (*extent*) étendue *f*. **compasses** *pl n* (*math*) compas *m sing*.
compassion [kəm'paʃən] *n* compassion *f*. **compassionate** *adj* compatissant; (*leave, etc.*) pour raisons de famille.
compatible [kəm'patəbl] *adj* compatible. **compatibility** *n* compatibilité *f*.
compel [kəm'pel] *v* contraindre, forcer. **compelling** *adj* irrésistible.
compensate ['kompənseit] *v* compenser; (*money*) dédommager. **compensation** *n* compensation *f*.
compete [kəm'piːt] *v* concourir; (*comm*) faire concurrence. **competition** *n* compétition *f*; (*contest*) concours *m*; (*rivalry*) concurrence *f*. **competitive** *adj* (*price*) compétitif; (*selection*) par concours. **competitor** *n* concurrent, -e *m*, *f*.
competent ['kompətənt] *adj* compétent; suffisant. **competence** *n* compétence *f*.
compile [kəm'pail] *v* compiler; (*dictionary*) composer; (*list*) dresser. **compilation** *n* compilation *f*.

complacent [kəm'pleisnt] *adj* content de soi. **complacency** *n* contentement de soi *m*.
complain [kəm'plein] *v* se plaindre. **complaint** *n* plainte *f*; (*comm*) réclamation *f*; (*med*) maladie *f*.
complement ['kompləmənt] *n* complément *m*. *v* compléter. **complementary** *adj* complémentaire.
complete [kəm'pliːt] *adj* complet, -ète; (*finished*) achevé. *v* compléter; achever. **completion** *n* achèvement *m*.
complex ['kompleks] *nm*, *adj* complexe. **complexity** *n* complexité *f*.
complexion [kəm'plekʃən] *n* teint *m*; aspect *m*.
complicate ['komplikeit] *v* compliquer. **complication** *n* complication *f*.
complicity [kəm'plisəti] *n* complicité *f*.
compliment ['kompləmənt] *n* compliment *m*. *v* complimenter (de). **complimentary** *adj* flatteur, -euse; (*free*) gracieux. **complimentary copy** exemplaire offert en hommage *m*. **complimentary ticket** billet de faveur *m*.
comply [kəm'plai] *n* se soumettre (à); (*wishes*) se conformer (à); (*request*) accéder (à). **compliant** *adj* accommodant. **in compliance with** conformément à.
component [kəm'pounənt] *n* (*tech*) pièce *f*; (*chem*) composant *m*. *adj* constituent.
compose [kəm'pouz] *v* composer. **composed** *adj* calme. **composer** *n* compositeur, -trice *m*, *f*. **composition** *n* composition *f*; (*essay*) rédaction *f*.
compost ['kompost] *n* compost *m*. **compost heap** tas de compost *m*.
composure [kəm'pouʒə] *n* sang-froid *m*.
compound[1] ['kompaund; *v* kəm'paund] *n* composé *m*. *adj* composé; (*number*) complexe; (*fracture*) compliqué. *v* composer; (*make worse*) aggraver.
compound[2] ['kompaund] *n* enclos *m*.
comprehend [kompri'hend] *v* comprendre. **comprehensible** *adj* compréhensible. **comprehension** *n* compréhension *f*. **comprehensive** *adj* compréhensif; détaillé; (*insurance*) tous-risques. **comprehensive school** centre d'études secondaires *m*.
compress [kəm'pres; *n* 'kompres] *v* (se) comprimer; (se) condenser. *n* compresse *f*. **compression** *n* compression *f*; concentration *f*.
comprise [kəm'praiz] *v* comprendre.
compromise ['komprəmaiz] *v* transiger; (*risk*) compromettre. *n* compromis *m*.
compulsion [kəm'pʌlʃən] *n* contrainte *f*. **compulsive** *adj* (*gambler*, *etc*.) invétéré; (*psych*) compulsif; (*demand*) coercitif. **compulsory** *adj* obligatoire.
compunction [kəm'pʌŋkʃən] *n* remords *m*.
computer [kəm'pjuːtə] *n* ordinateur *m*. **computer science** informatique *f*. **computerization** *n* automatisation électronique *f*. **computerize** *v* informatiser.
comrade ['komrid] *n* camarade *m*, *f*. **comradeship** *n* camaraderie *f*.
concave [kon'keiv] *adj* concave.
conceal [kən'siːl] *v* dissimuler, cacher. **concealment** *n* dissimulation *f*.
concede [kən'siːd] *v* concéder.
conceit [kən'siːt] *n* vanité *f*. **conceited** *adj* vaniteux.
conceive [kən'siːv] *v* concevoir; (*understand*) comprendre. **conceivable** *adj* concevable.
concentrate ['konsəntreit] *v* (se) concentrer. *n* (*chem*) concentré *m*. **concentration** *n* concentration *f*. **concentration camp** camp de concentration *m*.
concentric [kən'sentrik] *adj* concentrique.
concept ['konsept] *n* concept *m*.
conception [kən'sepʃən] *n* conception *f*.
concern [kən'səːn] *v* concerner; regarder. *n* (*business*) affaire *f*; (*comm*) entreprise *f*; (*anxiety*) inquiétude *f*. **concerned** *adj* inquiet, -ète; affecté; en question. **concerning** *prep* en ce qui concerne.
concert ['konsət; *v* kən'səːt] *n* concert *m*. *v* concerter.
concertina [konsə'tiːnə] *n* concertina *m*.
concerto [kən'tʃəːtou] *n* concerto *m*.
concession [kən'seʃən] *n* concession *f*; (*comm*) réduction *f*. **concessionary** *adj* concessionnaire; (*cheap*) à prix réduit.
conciliate [kən'silieit] *v* (se) concilier; apaiser. **conciliation** *n* conciliation *f*; apaisement *m*. **conciliatory** *adj* conciliant.
concise [kən'sais] *adj* concis.
conclude [kən'kluːd] *v* conclure. **concluding** *adj* final. **conclusion** *n* conclusion *f*. **conclusive** *adj* définitif.
concoct [kən'kokt] *v* (*cookery*) confectionner; (*excuse*) fabriquer. **concoction** *n* confection *f*; (*excuse*) combinaison *f*.
concrete ['koŋkriːt] *adj* (*real*) concret,

-ète. *n* béton *m*. **concrete mixer** bétonnière *f*. *v* bétonner.
concur [kən'kəː] *v* (*agree*) être d'accord; coïncider. **concurrent** *adj* simultané.
concussion [kən'kʌʃən] *n* (*med*) commotion cérébrale *f*. *v* **be concussed** être commotionné.
condemn [kən'dem] *v* condamner. **condemnation** *n* condamnation *f*.
condense [kən'dens] *v* (se) condenser. **condensation** *n* condensation *f*. **condenser** *n* (*elec*) condensateur *m*.
condescend [kondi'send] *v* condescendre, daigner. **condescension** *n* condescendance *f*.
condition [kən'diʃən] *n* condition *f*; (*state*) état *m*. *v* conditionner. **conditional** *nm*, *adj* conditionnel. **be conditional on** dépendre de.
condolences [kən'dounlənsiz] *pl n* condoléances *f pl*.
condom ['kondom] *n* préservatif *m*.
condone [kən'doun] *v* pardonner; fermer les yeux sur.
conducive [kən'djuːsiv] *adj* contribuant. **be conducive to** conduire à.
conduct ['kondʌkt; *v* kən'dʌkt] *n* conduite *f*. *v* diriger; (*phys*) conduire. **conduct oneself** se conduire. **conducted tour** excursion accompagnée *f*; visite guidée *f*. **conduction** *n* conduction *f*.
conductor [kən'dʌktə] *n* (*music*) chef d'orchestre *m*; (*bus*) receveur *m*; (*phys*) conducteur *m*. **conductress** *n* (*bus*) receveuse *f*.
cone [koun] *n* cône *m*; (*ice cream*) cornet *m*.
confectioner [kən'fekʃənə] *n* (*cakes*) pâtissier, -ère *m*, *f*; (*sweets*) confiseur, -euse *m*, *f*. **confectionery** *n* confiserie *f*; pâtisserie *f*.
confederate [kən'fedərət] *n*, *adj* confédéré, -e. *v* (se) confédérer. **confederation** *n* confédération *f*.
confer [kən'fəː] *v* conférer. **conference** *n* conférence *f*.
confess [kən'fes] *v* confesser, avouer. **confession** *n* confession *f*; aveu *m*.
confetti [kən'feti] *n* confettis *m pl*.
confide [kən'faid] *v* confier; avouer en confidence. **confide in** (*tell*) se confier à; (*trust*) se fier à. **confidence** *n* (*trust*) confiance *f*; (*self-assurance*) assurance *f*; (*secret*) confidence *f*. **confident** *adj* assuré. **confidential** *adj* confidentiel. **confidently** *adv* avec confiance.
confine [kən'fain] *v* (*imprison*) enfermer; limiter. **be confined** (*childbirth*) accoucher. **confinement** *n* (*childbirth*) couches *f pl*; emprisonnement *m*.
confirm [kən'fəːm] *v* confirmer. **confirmation** *n* confirmation *f*. **confirmed** *adj* (*liar*, *etc*.) invétéré; (*bachelor*) endurci.
confiscate ['konfiskeit] *v* confisquer. **confiscation** *n* confiscation *f*.
conflict ['konflikt; *v* kən'flikt] *n* conflit *m*. *v* être en conflit; s'opposer. **conflicting** *adj* incompatible; contradictoire.
conform [kən'foːm] *v* (se) conformer. **conformity** *n* conformité *f*.
confound [kən'faund] *v* confondre.
confront [kən'frʌnt] *v* (*present*) confronter; (*face*) affronter. **confrontation** *n* confrontation *f*.
confuse [kən'fjuːz] *v* confondre; (*mix up*) embrouiller. **confused** *adj* confus; embrouillé. **confusing** *adj* déroutant. **confusion** *n* confusion *f*; désordre *m*.
congeal [kən'dʒiːl] *v* (se) figer; (*blood*) (se) coaguler; (*freeze*) (se) congeler.
congenial [kən'dʒiːmiəl] *adj* sympathique.
congenital [kən'dʒenitl] *adj* congénital.
congested [kən'dʒestid] *adj* encombré; (*med*) congestionné. **congestion** *n* encombrement *m*; (*med*) congestion *f*.
conglomeration [kən,glomə'reiʃən] *n* agglomération *f*.
congratulate [kən'gratjuleit] *v* féliciter. **congratulations** *pl n* félicitations *f pl*.
congregate ['koŋgrigeit] *v* (se) rassembler. **congregation** *n* assemblée *f*.
congress ['koŋgres] *n* congrès *m*.
conical ['konikəl] *adj* conique.
conifer ['konifə] *n* conifère *m*. **coniferous** *adj* conifère.
conjecture [kən'dʒektʃə] *v* conjecturer. *n* conjecture *f*. **conjectural** *adj* conjectural.
conjugal ['kondʒugəl] *adj* conjugal.
conjugate ['kondʒugeit] *v* (se) conjuguer. **conjugation** *n* conjugaison *f*.
conjunction [kən'dʒʌŋkʃən] *n* conjonction *f*.
conjunctivitis [kən,dʒʌŋkti'vaitis] *n* conjonctivite *f*.
conjure ['kʌndʒə; (*appeal to*) kən'dʒuə] *v* (*magic*) faire apparaître; (*appeal to*) conjurer. **conjurer** *n* prestidigitateur, -trice *m*, *f*. **conjuring** *n* prestidigitation *f*. **conjuring trick** tour de passe-passe *m*.

connect [kə'nekt] *v* (se) relier. **be connected with** avoir des rapports avec. **connection** *n* jonction *f*; (*elec*) connexion *f*; relation *f*; (*rail*) correspondance *f*.
connoisseur [konə'səː] *n* connaisseur, -euse *m, f*.
connotation [konə'teiʃən] *n* connotation *f*.
conquer ['koŋkə] *v* conquérir; vaincre. **conqueror** *n* conquérant *m*. **conquest** *n* conquête *f*.
conscience ['konʃəns] *n* conscience *f*.
conscientious [konʃi'enʃəs] *adj* consciencieux. **conscientious objector** objecteur de conscience *m*.
conscious ['konʃəs] *adj* conscient. **consciousness** *n* (*med*) connaissance *f*; (*awareness*) conscience *f*.
conscript ['konskript] *nm* conscrit. **conscription** *n* conscription *f*.
consecrate ['konsikreit] *v* consacrer. **consecration** *n* consécration *f*.
consecutive [kən'sekjutiv] *adj* consécutif.
consensus [kən'sensəs] *n* consensus *m*.
consent [kən'sent] *v* consentir. *n* consentement *m*.
consequence ['konsikwəns] *n* conséquence *f*; importance *f*. **consequent** *adj* résultant. **consequently** *adv* par conséquent.
conservative [kən'səːvətiv] *adj* (*pol*) conservateur, -trice; modeste; traditionnel. *n* (*pol*) conservateur, -trice *m, f*.
conserve [kən'səːv] *v* conserver. **conservation** *n* préservation *f*; défense de l'environnement *f*. **conservatoire** *n* (*music*) conservatoire *m*. **conservatory** *n* (*greenhouse*) serre *f*.
consider [kən'sidə] *v* considérer. **considerable** *adj* considérable. **considerate** *adj* prévenant. **consideration** *n* considération *f*. **considering** *prep* étant donné.
consign [kən'sain] *v* (*goods*) expédier; (*entrust*) confier. **consignment** *n* envoi *m*.
consist [kən'sist] *v* consister (en). **consistency** *n* (*of substance*) consistance *f*; (*of behaviour, etc.*) cohérence *f*. **consistent** *adj* logique; compatible.
console [kən'soul] *v* consoler. **consolation** *n* consolation *f*.
consolidate [kən'solideit] *v* (se) consolider. **consolidation** *n* consolidation *f*.
consommé [kən'somei] *n* consommé *m*.
consonant ['konsənənt] *n* consonne *f*. *adj* en accord.
conspicuous [kən'spikjuəs] *adj* remarquable; en vue. **be conspicuous** attirer les regards; se faire remarquer.
conspire [kən'spaiə] *v* conspirer. **conspiracy** *n* conspiration *f*. **conspirator** *n* conspirateur, -trice *m, f*.
constable ['kʌnstəbl] *n* agent de police *m*. **constabulary** *n* police *f*.
constant ['konstənt] *adj* (*unchanging*) constant; incessant. *n* constante *f*. **constancy** *n* constance *f*.
constellation [konstə'leiʃən] *n* constellation *f*.
consternation [konstə'neiʃən] *n* consternation *f*.
constipation [konsti'peiʃən] *n* constipation *f*. **constipated** *adj* constipé.
constituent [kən'stitjuənt] *adj* constituant. *n* élément constitutif *m*; (*pol*) electeur, -trice *m, f*. **constituency** *n* (*pol*) circonscription électorale *f*.
constitute ['konstitjuːt] *v* constituer. **constitution** *n* constitution *f*. **constitutional** *adj* constitutionnel.
constraint [kən'streint] *n* contrainte *f*.
constrict [kən'strikt] *v* resserrer. **constriction** *n* resserrement *m*.
construct [kən'strʌkt] *v* construire. **construction** *n* construction *f*; interprétation *f*. **constructive** *adj* constructif.
consul ['konsəl] *n* consul *m*. **consular** *adj* consulaire. **consulate** *n* consulat *m*.
consult [kən'sʌlt] *v* consulter. **consultant** *n* consultant *m*; (*med*) spécialiste *m*. **consultation** *n* consultation *f*.
consume [kən'sjuːm] *v* consommer; (*fire*) consumer. **consumer** *n* consommateur, -trice *m, f*. **consumer goods** biens de consommation *m pl*. **consumption** *n* consommation *f*.
contact ['kontakt] *n* contact *m*; (*acquaintance*) connaissance *f*. **contact lenses** verres de contact *m pl*. *v* se mettre en contact avec.
contagious [kən'teidʒəs] *adj* contagieux.
contain [kən'tein] *v* contenir. **container** *n* (*box, etc.*) récipient *m*; (*transport*) conteneur *m*.
contaminate [kən'taməneit] *v* contaminer. **contamination** *n* contamination *f*.
contemplate ['kontəmpleit] *v* (*consider*) envisager; (*look at*) contempler. **contemplation** *n* contemplation *f*. **contemplative** *adj* contemplatif.

contemporary [kən'tempərəri] *n, adj* contemporain, -e.
contempt [kən'tempt] *n* mépris *m*. **contempt of court** outrage à la Cour *m*. **contemptible** *adj* méprisable. **contemptuous** *adj* dédaigneux.
contend [kən'tend] *v* (*fight*) combattre (contre), faire face à; (*claim*) soutenir. **contention** *n* dispute *f*.
content[1] ['kontent] *n* contenu *m*. **contents** *pl n* contenu *m sing*; (*book*) table des matières *f*.
content[2] [kən'tent] *adj also* **contented** content, satisfait. **be content with** se contenter de. **contentment** *n* contentement *m*, satisfaction *f*.
contest [kən'test; *n* 'kontest] *v* contester; (se) disputer. *n* (*fight*) combat *m*; (*sport*) lutte *f*; (*competition*) concours *m*. **contestant** *n* concurrent, -e *m, f*.
context ['kontekst] *n* contexte *m*.
continent ['kontinənt] *n* continent *m*. **continental** *adj* continental. **continental breakfast** petit déjeuner à la française *m*. **continental quilt** couette *f*.
contingency [kən'tindʒənsi] *n* éventualité *f*. **contingent** *adj* contingent.
continue [kən'tinjuː] *v* continuer; (*after pause*) reprendre. **continual** *adj* continuel. **continuation** *n* continuation *f*; reprise *f*; (*serial*) suite *f*. **continuity** *n* continuité *f*. **continuous** *adj* continu.
contort [kən'toːt] *v* tordre. **contortion** *n* (*acrobat*) contorsion *f*; (*twisting*) torsion *f*.
contour ['kontuə] *n* contour *m*. **contour line** courbe de niveau *f*.
contraband ['kontrəband] *n* contrebande *f*.
contraception [kontrə'sepʃən] *n* contraception *f*. **contraceptive** *nm, adj* contraceptif.
contract ['kontrakt; *v* kən'trakt] *n* contrat *m*. *v* (se) contracter. **contraction** *n* contraction *f*. **contractor** *n* entrepreneur *m*.
contradict [kontrə'dikt] *v* contredire. **contradiction** *n* contradiction *f*. **contradictory** *adj* contradictoire.
contralto [kən'traltou] *n* contralto *m*.
contraption [kən'trapʃən] *n* (*coll*) machin *m*.
contrary ['kontrəri; (*perverse*) kən'treəri] *adj* contraire; (*perverse*) contrariant. *adv* contrairement. *n* contraire *m*. **on the contrary** au contraire.
contrast [kən'traːst; *n* 'kontraːst] *v* contraster. *n* contraste *m*. **contrasting** *adj* contrasté.
contravene [kontrə'viːn] *v* enfreindre. **contravention** *n* violation *f*.
contribute [kən'tribjut] *v* contribuer. **contribution** *n* contribution *f*. **contributor** *n* (*magazine, etc.*) collaborateur, -trice *m, f*; (*money*) donateur, -trice *m, f*.
contrive [kən'traiv] *v* (*invent*) combiner; (*manage*) s'arranger (pour). **contrived** *adj* artificiel.
control [kən'troul] *n* contrôle *m*; autorité *f*. **controls** *n* commandes *f pl*. *v* (*restrain*) maîtriser; (*prices, etc.*) contrôler; (*business*) diriger. **controller** *n* contrôleur *m*.
controversy [kən'trovəsi] *n* controverse *f*. **controversial** *adj* discuté; discutable.
convalesce [konvə'les] *v* se remettre. **convalescence** *n* convalescence *f*. **convalescent** *n, adj* convalescent, -e.
convector [kən'vektə] *n* radiateur à convection *m*.
convenience [kən'viːnjəns] *n* commodité *f*, convenance *f*. **convenient** *adj* commode, convenable. **be convenient** convenir (à).
convent ['konvənt] *n* couvent *m*.
convention [kən'venʃən] *n* (*meeting*) convention *f*; (*tradition*) usage *m*. **conventional** *adj* conventionnel, classique.
converge [kən'vəːdʒ] *v* converger. **convergence** *n* convergence *f*. **convergent** *adj* convergent.
converse[1] [kən'vəːs] *v* causer. **conversation** *n* conversation *f*.
converse[2] ['konvəːs] *nm, adj* contraire, inverse.
convert [kən'vəːt; *n* 'konvəːt] *v* convertir; (*house*) aménager. *n* converti, -e *m, f*. **conversion** *n* conversion *f*; aménagement *m*.
convertible [kən'vəːtəbl] *n* (*car*) voiture décapotable *f*.
convex ['konveks] *adj* convexe.
convey [kən'vei] *v* transmettre; transporter; communiquer. **conveyance** *n* transport *m*. **conveyor belt** tapis roulant *m*.
convict ['konvikt; *v* kən'vikt] *n* forçat *m*. *v* déclarer coupable.
conviction [kən'vikʃən] *n* (*law*) condamnation *f*; (*belief*) conviction *f*.
convince [kən'vins] *v* convaincre.

convoy ['konvoi] *n* convoi *m*.
convulsion [kən'vʌlʃən] *n* (*med*) convulsion *f*. **convulsive** *adj* convulsif.
cook [kuk] *n* cuisinier, -ère *m, f*. *v* (faire) cuire; faire la cuisine. **cooker** *n* cuisinière *f*. **cookery** *or* **cooking** *n* cuisine *f*. **cookie** *n* (*US*) petit gâteau sec *m*.
cool [kuːl] *adj* (*temperature*) frais, fraîche; calme; (*unfriendly*) froid. *v* (se) rafraîchir, (se) refroidir. **cooler** *n* glacière *f*. **coolness** *n* fraîcheur *f*; froideur *f*; (*calmness*) sang-froid *m*.
coop [kuːp] *n* poulailler *m*. *v* **coop up** cloîtrer.
cooperate [kou'opəreit] *v* coopérer. **cooperation** *n* coopération *f*. **cooperative** *adj* coopératif.
coordinate [kou'oːdineit] *v* coordonner. *adj* coordonné. *n* coordonnée *f*.
cope[1] [koup] *v* se débrouiller. **cope with** s'occuper de; (*solve*) venir à bout de.
cope[2] [koup] *n* chape *f*.
Copenhagen [koupən'heigən] *n* Copenhague.
copious ['koupiəs] *adj* copieux; abondant.
copper[1] ['kopə] *n* (*metal*) cuivre *m*. **coppers** *pl n* (*money*) petite monnaie *f sing*.
copper[2] ['kopə] *n also* **cop** (*slang*) flic *m*.
copulate ['kopjuːleit] *v* copuler. **copulation** *n* copulation *f*.
copy ['kopi] *n* copie *f*; (*phot*) épreuve *f*; (*of book, etc.*) exemplaire *m*. *v* copier. **copyright** *n* copyright *m*.
coral ['korəl] *n* corail (*pl* -aux) *m*. **coral reef** récif de corail *m*.
cord [koːd] *n* cordon *m*; (*windows*) corde *f*.
cordial ['koːdiəl] *nm, adj* cordial. **cordiality** *n* cordialité *f*.
cordon ['koːdn] *n* cordon *m*. *v* **cordon off** interdire l'accès à.
corduroy ['koːdəroi] *n* velours côtelé *m*.
core [koː] *n* (*fruit*) trognon *m*; (*earth*) noyau *m*; (*problem, etc*) essential *m*. *v* enlever le trognon de.
cork [koːk] *n* liège *m*; (*of bottle*) bouchon *m*. **corkscrew** *n* tire-bouchon *m*. *v* boucher.
corn[1] [koːn] *n* blé *m*; (*US*) maïs *m*. **cornflour** *n* farine de maïs *f*. **cornflower** *n* bleuet *m*. **corn on the cob** épi de maïs *m*.
corn[2] [koːn] *n* (*med*) cor *m*.
corner ['koːnə] *n* coin *m*; (*mot*) tournant *m*. *v* (*coll*) coincer; (*comm*) accaparer.
cornet ['koːnit] *n* cornet *m*.
Cornwall ['koːnwoːl] *n* Cornouailles *f*.
coronary ['korənəri] *adj* coronaire. **coronary thrombosis** infarctus (du myocarde) *m*.
coronation [korə'neiʃən] *n* couronnement *m*.
corporal[1] ['koːpərəl] *adj* corporel.
corporal[2] ['koːpərəl] *n* caporal-chef *m*.
corporation [ˌkoːpə'reiʃən] *n* (*town*) conseil municipal *m*; (*comm*) société commerciale *f*.
corps [koː] *n* corps *m*.
corpse [koːps] *n* cadavre *m*.
correct [kə'rekt] *adj* correct. *v* corriger. **correction** *n* correction *f*.
correlate ['korəleit] *v* correspondre; mettre en corrélation. **correlation** *n* corrélation *f*.
correspond [korə'spond] *v* correspondre. **correspondence** *n* correspondance *f*. **correspondent** *n* correspondant, -e *m, f*.
corridor ['koridoː] *n* couloir *m*.
corroborate [kə'robəreit] *v* corroborer. **corroboration** *n* confirmation *f*.
corrode [kə'roud] *v* (se) corroder. **corrosion** *n* corrosion *f*. **corrosive** *adj* corrosif.
corrugated ['korəgeitid] *adj* ondulé. **corrugated iron** tôle ondulée *f*.
corrupt [kə'rʌpt] *v* corrompre. *adj* corrompu. **corruption** *n* corruption *f*.
corset ['koːset] *n* corset *m*.
Corsica ['koːsikə] *n* Corse *f*. **Corsican** *n* Corse *m, f*; *adj* corse.
cosmetic [koz'metik] *adj* cosmétique; (*surgery*) plastique. **cosmetics** *pl n* produits de beauté *m pl*.
cosmic ['kozmik] *adj* cosmique.
cosmopolitan [kozmə'politən] *n*(*m*+*f*), *adj* cosmopolite.
***cost** [kost] *v* coûter. *n* coût *m*; frais *m pl*. **cost of living** coût de la vie *m*. **costly** *adj* coûteux.
costume ['kostjuːm] *n* costume *m*.
cosy ['kouzi] *adj* douillet, -ette.
cot [kot] *n* lit d'enfant *m*.
cottage ['kotidʒ] *n* cottage *m*; petite maison *f*; (*thatched*) chaumière *f*. **cottage cheese** fromage maigre *m*.
cotton ['kotn] *n* coton *m*; (*thread*) fil *m*. **cotton-wool** *n* ouate *f*.
couch [kautʃ] *n* canapé *m*. *v* exprimer.
cough [kof] *n* toux *f*. *v* tousser.
could [kud] *V* **can**[1].

council ['kaunsəl] *n* conseil *m*; (*of town*) conseil municipal *m*. **councillor** *n* conseiller, -ère *m, f*.
counsel ['kaunsəl] *n* conseil *m*; (*law*) avocat, -e *m, f*. *v* conseiller. **counsellor** *n* conseiller, -ère *m, f*; (*social*) orienteur *m*.
count[1] [kaunt] *v* compter; (*consider*) estimer. *n* compte *m*. **countdown** *n* compte à rebours *m* **countless** *adj* innombrable.
count[2] [kaunt] *n* comte *m*. **countess** *n* comtesse *f*.
counter[1] ['kauntə] *n* (*shop, etc.*) comptoir *m*; (*bank*) guichet *m*; (*disc*) jeton *m*.
counter[2] ['kauntə] *adj* contraire. *v* (*blow*) parer; (*boxing, etc.*) riposter. **counter to** à l'encontre de.
counteract [kauntə'rakt] *v* neutraliser.
counterattack ['kauntərə,tak] *v* contre-attaquer. *n* contre-attaque *f*.
counterfeit ['kauntəfit] *adj* faux, fausse. *v* contrefaire. *n* faux *m*.
counterfoil ['kauntə,foil] *n* talon *m*.
counterpart ['kauntə,paɪt] *n* contrepartie *f*; équivalent *m*; (*person*) homologue *m, f*.
country ['kʌntri] *n* pays *m*; (*not town*) campagne *f*; (*native land*) patrie *f*. **the countryside** la campagne *f*.
county ['kaunti] *n* comté *m*. **county town** chef-lieu *m*.
coup [kuː] *n* (*pol*) coup d'Etat *m*.
couple ['kʌpl] *n* couple *m*. *v* accoupler; (*animals*) s'accoupler.
coupon ['kuːpon] *n* (*comm*) bon *m*; (*advertisements, etc.*) coupon *m*.
courage ['kʌridʒ] *n* courage *m*. **courageous** *adj* courageux.
courgette [kuə'ʒet] *n* courgette *f*.
courier ['kuriə] *n* guide *m*; (*messenger*) courrier *m*.
course [koːs] *n* cours *m*; (*naut*) route *f*; (*meal*) plat *m*. **of course** bien entendu.
court [koːt] *v* (*woman*) courtiser; (*favour*) solliciter; (*danger*) s'exposer à. *n* cour *m*; (*tennis*) court *m*; (*other sports*) terrain *m*. **court-martial** *n* conseil de guerre *m*. **court-room** *n* salle de tribunal *f*. **courtyard** *n* cour *f*.
courteous ['kəːtiəs] *adj* courtois. **courtesy** *n* courtoisie *f*, politesse *f*.
cousin ['kʌzn] *n* cousin, -e *m, f*.
cove [kouv] *n* anse *f*.
cover ['kʌvə] *n* couverture *f*; (*lid*) couvercle *m*; (*protective*) housse *f*; (*shelter*) abri *m*. *v* couvrir. **coverage** *n* reportage *m*. **covering** *n* (*wrapping*) couverture *f*; (*layer*) couche *f*.
cow [kau] *n* vache *f*. **cowboy** *n* cow-boy *m*. **cowslip** *n* primevère *f*.
coward ['kauəd] *n* lâche *m, f*. **cowardice** *n* lâcheté *f*. **cowardly** *adj* lâche.
cower ['kauə] *v* trembler; se blottir.
coy [koi] *adj* timide.
crab [krab] *n* crabe *m*. **crab-apple** pomme sauvage *f*. **crabby** *adj* revêche.
crack [krak] *n* (*split*) fente *f*; (*glass, china, etc.*) fêlure *f*; (*noise*) craquement *m*. *v* (se) fêler; (*ground*) (se) crevasser; (*ice*) (se) craqueler; (*nut*) casser; (*noise*) (faire) craquer.
cracker ['krakə] *n* (*biscuit*) craquelin *m*; (*firework*) pétard *m*; (*Christmas*) diablotin *m*.
crackle ['krakl] *v* crépiter. *n* crépitement *m*.
cradle ['kreidl] *n* berceau *m*. *v* bercer.
craft [kraːft] *n* (*skill*) art *m*; (*job*) métier *m*; (*boat*) barque *f*; (*cunning*) astuce *f*. **craftsman** *n* artisan *m*. **crafty** astucieux.
cram [kram] *v* fourrer, bourrer; (*people*) (s')entasser; (*for exam*) (faire) bachoter.
cramp [kramp] *n* (*med*) crampe *f*. **cramped** *adj* à l'étroit.
cranberry ['kranbəri] *n* canneberge *f*.
crane [krein] *n* grue *f*. **cranefly** *n* tipule *f*. *v* **crane one's neck** tendre le cou.
crank [kraŋk] *n* (*tech*) manivelle *f*. **crankshaft** *n* vilebrequin *m*.
crap [krap] (*vulgar*) *n* merde *f*; (*nonsense*) conneries *f pl*. **crappy** *adj* merdique.
crash [kraʃ] *n* fracas *m*; (*car, etc.*) accident *m*, collision *f*. *v* (*car, etc.*) s'écraser; (*collide*) se percuter; (*smash*) (se) fracasser. **crash course** cours intensif *m*. **crash helmet** casque *m*. **crash landing** atterrissage forcé *m*.
crate [kreit] *n* cageot *m*.
crater ['kreitə] *n* cratère *m*; (*bomb*) entonnoir *m*.
cravat [krə'vat] *n* foulard *m*.
crave [kreiv] *v* avoir grand besoin de; (*beg*) solliciter. **craving** *n* besoin maladif *m*; désir insatiable *m*.
crawl [kroːl] *v* ramper; (*cars*) avancer au pas; (*babies*) aller à quatre pattes; (*with lice, etc.*) grouiller. *n* (*swimming*) crawl *m*.

crayfish ['kreifiʃ] *n* écrevisse *f*.
crayon ['kreiən] *n* crayon de couleur *m*. *v* colorier au crayon.
craze [kreiz] *n* engouement *m*.
crazy ['kreizi] *adj* fou, folle. **crazy paving** dallage irrégulier *m*.
creak [kriːk] *v* grincer. *n* grincement *m*.
cream [kriːm] *nf*, *adj* crème. **cream cheese** fromage blanc *m*. *v also* **cream off** écrémer. **creamy** *adj* crémeux.
crease [kriːs] *n* pli *m*. **crease-resistant** *adj* infroissable. *v* (se) froisser.
create [kri'eit] *v* créer. **creation** *n* création *f*. **creative** *adj* créatif.
creature ['kriːtʃə] *n* créature *f*; bête *f*.
credentials [kri'denʃəlz] *pl n* références *f pl*; pièce d'identité *f sing*.
credible ['kredəbl] *adj* croyable; plausible. **credibility** *n* crédibilité *f*.
credit ['kredit] *n* crédit *m*; honneur *m*. **credit card** carte de crédit *f*. **credits** *pl n* (*cinema*) générique *m sing*. *v* croire; attribuer; (*banking*) créditer. **creditable** *adj* honorable. **creditor** *n* créancier, -ère *m*, *f*.
credulous ['kredjuləs] *adj* crédule. **credulity** *n* crédulité *f*.
creed [kriːd] *n* credo *m*.
***creep** [kriːp] *v* se glisser. **creeper** *n* plante grimpante *f*. **creepy** *adj* qui fait frissonner.
cremate [kri'meit] *v* incinérer. **cremation** *n* crémation *f*. **crematorium** *n* crématorium *m*.
crêpe [kreip] *n* crêpe *m*. **crêpe paper** papier crêpon *m*.
crept [krept] *V* **creep**.
crescent ['kresnt] *n* croissant *m*.
cress [kres] *n* cresson *m*.
crest [krest] *n* crête *f*; (*mark*) timbre *m*. **crestfallen** *adj* découragé.
crevice ['krevis] *n* fissure *f*.
crew [kruː] *n* (*naut*) équipage *m*; (*group*) équipe *f*. *v* (*sailing*) être équipier. **crew-cut** *n* cheveux en brosse *m pl*. **crew-neck** *n* col ras *m*.
crib [krib] *n* (*baby's*) berceau *m*; (*manger*) mangeoire *f*; (*rel*) crèche *f*. *v* copier.
cricket[1] ['krikit] *n* (*insect*) grillon *m*.
cricket[2] ['krikit] *n* (*sport*) cricket *m*.
crime [kraim] *n* crime *m*. **criminal** *n*, *adj* criminel, -elle.
crimson ['krimzn] *nm*, *adj* cramoisi.
cringe [krindʒ] *v* reculer; s'humilier.
crinkle ['kriŋkl] *v* (se) froisser. *n* fronce *f*.
cripple ['kripl] *v* estropier; (*industry*, *etc*.) paralyser. *n* estropié, -e *m*, *f*.
crisis ['kraisis] *n* crise *f*.
crisp [krisp] *adj* (*biscuit*) croquant; (*snow*) craquant; (*weather*, *style*) vif. **crisps** *pl n* chips *f pl*.
criterion [krai'tiəriən] *n*, *pl* **-ria** critère *m*.
criticize ['kriti,saiz] *v* critiquer. **critic** *n* critique *m*. **critical** *adj* critique. **criticism** *n* critique *f*.
croak [krouk] *v* (*frog*) coasser; (*crow*) croasser. *n* coassement *m*; croassement *m*.
crochet ['krouʃei] *n* travail au crochet *m*. *v* (*activity*) faire du crochet; (*make*) faire au crochet. **crochet hook** crochet *m*.
crockery ['krokəri] *n* vaisselle *f*.
crocodile ['krokə,dail] *n* crocodile *m*.
crocus ['kroukəs] *n* crocus *m*.
crook [kruk] *n* (*shepherd's*) houlette *f*; (*bend*) angle *m*; (*coll*) escroc *m*.
crooked ['krukid] *adj* (*bent*) courbé; (*path*) tortueux; (*askew*) de travers; (*dishonest*) malhonnête.
crop [krop] *n* culture *f*; (*harvest*) récolte *f*; (*cereals*) moisson *f*; (*riding*) cravache *f*. *v* écourter, tondre; (*graze*) brouter; (*hair*) couper ras. **crop up** survenir.
croquet ['kroukei] *n* croquet *m*.
cross [kros] *n* croix *f*; hybride *m*; biais *m*. *adj* (*angry*) fâché; diagonal. *v* (se) croiser; (*go across*) traverser; (*cheque*) barrer.
cross-examine [,krosig'zamin] *v* interroger. **cross-examination** *n* contre-interrogatoire *m*.
cross-eyed [,kros'aid] *adj* louche.
crossfire ['kros,faiə] *n* feux croisés *m pl*.
crossing ['krosiŋ] *n* (*junction*) croisement *m*; (*for pedestrians*) passage clouté *m*; (*journey*) traversée *f*.
cross-legged [,kros'legid] *adj* les jambes croisées.
cross-reference [,kros'refərəns] *n* renvoi *m*. **cross-refer** *v* renvoyer.
crossroads ['kros,roudz] *n* carrefour *m*.
cross section *n* coupe transversale *f*; (*sample*) échantillon *m*.
crosswind ['kros,wind] *n* vent de travers *m*.
crossword ['kros,wəːd] *n* mots croisés *m pl*.
crotchet ['krotʃit] *n* noire *f*. **crotchety** *adj* grognon, -onne.

crouch [krautʃ] *v* s'accroupir. *n* accroupissement *m*.
crow[1] [krou] *n* corneille *f*. **as the crow flies** à vol d'oiseau. **crowbar** *n* levier *m*.
crow[2] [krou] *v* (*cock*) chanter; (*baby*) gazouiller. *n* chant du coq *m*.
crowd [kraud] *n* foule *f*. *v* (*gather round*) s'attrouper; (*fill up*) (s')entasser. **crowded** *adj* plein (de monde).
crown [kraun] *n* couronne *f*; (*road*) milieu *m*; (*hat*) fond *m*. *v* couronner. **crown jewels** joyaux de la couronne *m pl*. **crown prince** prince héritier *m*
crucial ['kruːʃəl] *adj* crucial.
crucify ['kruːsi,fai] *v* crucifier. **crucifix** *n* crucifix *m*. **crucifixion** *n* crucifixion *f*, crucifiement *m*.
crude [kruːd] *adj* (*materials*) brut; rudimentaire; (*behaviour*) grossier. **crudely** *adv* crûment; imparfaitement.
cruel ['kruːəl] *adv* cruel. **cruelty** *n* cruauté *f*.
cruise [kruːz] *n* croisière *f*. *v* (*ship*) croiser; (*mot*) rouler. **cruising speed** vitesse de croisière *f*. **cruiser** *n* (*ship*) croiseur *m*.
crumb [krʌm] *n* miette *f*.
crumble ['krʌmbl] *v* (*to crumbs*) (s')émietter; (*to dust*) (s')effriter; (*collapse*) s'écrouler.
crumple ['krʌmpl] *v* (se) chiffonner.
crunch [krʌntʃ] *v* (*food*) croquer; (*snow, etc.*) faire craquer. *n* craquement *m*. **the crunch** (*coll*) l'instant critique. **crunchy** *adj* croquant.
crusade [kruː'seid] *n* croisade *f*. *v* faire une croisade.
crush [krʌʃ] *v* (s')écraser. (*clothes*) (se) froiser. *n* cohue *f*. **crushing** *adj* (*defeat*) écrasant; (*remark*) percutant.
crust [krʌst] *n* croûte *f*. **crusty** *adj* (*bread*) croustillant; (*coll*) hargneux.
crutch [krʌtʃ] *n* béquille *f*; (*support*) soutien *m*.
cry [krai] *n* cri *m*. *v* (*shout*) crier; (*weep*) pleurer. **cry out** s'écrier, pousser un cri.
crypt [kript] *n* crypte *f*.
crystal ['kristl] *n* cristal *m*. **crystal-clear** *adj* clair comme le jour. **crystallize** *v* (se) cristalliser.
cub [kʌb] *n* petit, -e *m*, *f*; (*bear*) ourson *m*; (*fox*) renardeau *m*; (*lion*) lionceau *m*. **cub scout** louveteau *m*.
cube [kjuːb] *n* cube *m*. *v* (*maths*) cuber; (*cookery*) couper en cubes. **cubic** *adj* cubique; (*in units*) cube.
cubicle ['kjuːbikl] *n* (*for changing*) cabine *f*; (*for sleeping*) alcôve *f*.
cuckoo ['kukuː] *n* coucou *m*.
cucumber [kju'kʌmbə] *n* concombre *m*.
cuddle ['kʌdl] *n* étreinte *f*. *v* serrer dans les bras; (*child*) câliner. **cuddle up** se pelotonner.
cue[1] [kjuː] *n* signal *m*; (*theatre*) replique *f*.
cue[2] [kjuː] *n* (*billiards*) queue de billard *f*.
cuff[1] [kʌf] *n* (*shirt*) manchette *f*. **cuff-link** *n* bouton de manchette *m*. **off the cuff** à l'improviste.
cuff[2] [kʌf] *v* gifler. *n* gifle *f*.
culinary ['kʌlinəri] *adj* culinaire.
culminate ['kʌlmi,neit] *v* culminer. **culminate in** se terminer par. **culmination** *n* point culminant *m*; (*success*) apogée *m*.
culprit ['kʌlprit] *n* coupable *m*, *f*; (*law*) accusé, -e *m*, *f*.
cult [kʌlt] *n* culte *m*.
cultivate ['kʌlti,veit] *n* cultiver. **cultivation** *n* culture *f*.
culture ['kʌltʃə] *n* culture *f*. **cultural** *adj* culturel. **cultured** *adj* cultivé.
cumbersome ['kʌmbəsəm] *adj* encombrant.
cunning ['kʌniŋ] *adj* astucieux; rusé. *n* astuce *f*; ruse *f*.
cup [kʌp] *n* tasse *f*; (*prize*) coupe *f*.
cupboard ['kʌbəd] *n* placard *m*.
curate ['kjuərət] *n* vicaire *m*.
curator [kjuə'reitə] *n* conservateur *m*.
curb [kəːb] *v* refréner; restreindre. *n* frein *m*.
curdle ['kəːdl] *v* (*milk*) (se) cailler; (*blood*) (se) figer.
cure [kjuə] *v* guérir; (*salt*) saler; (*smoke*) fumer. *n* remède *m*; (*recovery*) guérison *f*. **curable** *adj* guérissable.
curfew ['kəːfjuː] *n* couvre-feu *m*.
curious ['kjuəriəs] *adj* curieux. **curiosity** *n* curiosité *f*.
curl [kəːl] *v* (*hair*) friser, boucler. **curl up** (s')enrouler; (*person, animal*) se pelotonner. *n* boucle *f*; spirale *f*. **curler** *n* (*hair*) rouleau *m*. **curly** *adj* bouclé, frisé.
currant ['kʌrənt] *n* (*dried fruit*) raisin de Corinthe *m*; (*berry*) groseille *f*; (*bush*) groseillier *m*.
currency ['kʌrənsi] *n* monnaie *f*; (*foreign*) devise *f*; circulation *f*.
current ['kʌrənt] *adj* courant; (*fashion, etc.*) actuel. **current affairs** questions

d'actualité *f pl.* *n* courant *m*; tendance *f*. **currently** *adv* en ce moment.
curry ['kʌri] *n* curry *m*. **curry powder** poudre de curry *f*. **curried** *adj* au curry.
curse [kəːs] *v* maudire; (*swear*) jurer. *n* malédiction *f*; juron *m*; (*bane*) fléau *m*.
curt [kəːt] *adj* brusque.
curtail [kəː'teil] *v* écourter; (*expenses*) réduire. **curtailment** *n* raccourcissement *m*; réduction *f*.
curtain ['kəːtn] *n* rideau *m*. **curtain call** rappel *m*. *v* garnir de rideaux.
curtsy ['kəːtsi] *n* révérence *f*. *v* faire une révérence.
curve [kəːv] *n* courbe *f*. *v* (se) courber.
cushion ['kuʃən] *n* coussin *m*. *v* amortir.
custard ['kʌstəd] *n* (*pouring*) crème anglaise *f*; (*with eggs*) flan *m*.
custody ['kʌstədi] *n* garde *f*; emprisonnement *m*.
custom ['kʌstəm] *n* coutume *f*; (*comm*) clientèle *f*. **customs** *n* douane *f*. **customs officer** douanier *m*. **customary** *adj* habituel. **customer** *n* client, -e *m, f*.
***cut** [kʌt] *n* (*slit*) coupure *f*; (*stroke*) coup *m*; réduction *f*; (*of clothes*) coupe *f*; (*of meat*) morceau *m*. *v* couper; (*slice*) découper; (*shape*, trim) tailler; réduire. **cutback** *n* réduction *f*. **cut down** (*tree*, *etc.*) abattre; réduire. **cut glass** cristal taillé *m*. **cut off** couper; isoler. **cut out** (*engine*) caler; (*picture*) découper; (*give up*) supprimer. **cut-price** *adv* à prix réduit.
cute [kjuːt] *adj* (*sweet*) mignon, -onne; (*clever*) rusé.
cutlery ['kʌtləri] *n* couverts *m pl*.
cutlet ['kʌtlit] *n* côtelette *f*.
cutting ['kʌtiŋ] *n* (*rail*) tranchée *f*; (*newspaper*) coupure *f*; (*plant*) bouture *f*. *adj* (*edge*) tranchant; (*wind*) cinglant; (*remark*) mordant.
cycle ['saikl] *n* cycle *m*; bicyclette *f*, vélo *m*. *v* faire de la bicyclette; aller à bicyclette. **cycling** *n* cyclisme *m*. **cyclist** *n* cycliste *m, f*.
cyclone ['saikloun] *n* cyclone *m*.
cylinder ['silində] *n* cylindre *m*. **cylinder head** (*mot*) culasse *f*. **cylindrical** *adj* cylindrique.
cymbal ['simbəl] *n* cymbale *f*.
cynic ['sinik] *n* cynique *m, f*. **cynical** *adj* cynique. **cynicism** *n* cynisme *m*.
cypress ['saiprəs] *n* cyprès *m*.
Cyprus ['saiprəs] *n* Chypre *f*. **Cypriot** *n* Cypriote *m, f*; *adj* cypriote.
cyst [sist] *n* (*med*) kyste *m*.
Czechoslovakia [ˌtʃekəslə'vakiə] *n* Tchécoslovaquie *f*. **Czech** *n* (*people*) Tchèque *m, f*; *nm, adj* tchèque. **Czechoslovak** *n* (*people*) Tchécoslovaque *m, f*; *nm, adj* tchécoslovaque.

D

dab [dab] *n* goutte *f*, petite touche *f*. *v* tamponner; appliquer à petits coups.
dabble ['dabl] *v* (*in water*) barboter; (*politics*, *etc.*) se mêler un peu (de).
dad [dad] *n* (*coll*) papa *m*.
daffodil ['dafədil] *n* jonquille *f*.
daft [daːft] *adj* idiot.
dagger ['dagə] *n* poignard *m*.
daily ['deili] *adj* quotidien. *n* (*newspaper*) quotidien *m*; (*cleaner*) femme de ménage *f*. *adv* tous les jours.
dainty ['deinti] *adj* délicat; (*small*) menu.
dairy ['deəri] *n* laiterie *f*; crémerie *f*. **dairy farming** industrie laitière *f*. **dairy produce** produits laitiers *m pl*.
daisy ['deizi] *n* marguerite *f*; (*wild*) pâquerette *f*.
dam [dam] *n* barrage *m*. *v* endiguer; construire un barrage (sur).
damage ['damidʒ] *n* dommage *m*. **damages** *pl n* (*law*) dommages-intérêts *m pl*. *v* endommager; (*health*, *etc.*) abîmer; (*reputation*) nuire à. **damaging** *adj* préjudiciable.
damn [dam] *v* (*rel*) damner; condamner. *interj* (*coll*) zut! *adj also* **damned** (*slang*) fichu. *adv* (*slang*) sacrément. **damn all** (*slang*) zéro. **I don't give a damn** (*slang*) je m'en fiche pas mal. **damnable** *adj* odieux. **damnation** *n* (*rel*) damnation *f*.
damp [damp] *adj* humide; (*skin*) moite. *n also* **dampness** humidité *f*. *v also* **dampen** (*moisten*) humecter; (*noise*) étouffer; (*courage*) refroidir. **damp-course** *n* couche isolante *f*. **put a damper on** jeter un froid sur.
damson ['damzən] *n* (*fruit*) prune de Damas *f*; (*tree*) prunier de Damas *m*.
dance [daːns] *v* danser. *n* danse *f*; bal *m*.

dance floor piste de danse *f.* **dancer** *n* danseur, -euse *m, f.* **dancing** *n* danse *f.*
dandelion ['dandi,laiən] *n* pissenlit *m.*
dandruff ['dandrəf] *n* pellicules *f pl.*
danger ['deindʒə] *n* danger *m.* **be in danger of** risquer de. **danger money** prime de risque *f.* **on the danger list** dans un état critique. **dangerous** *adj* dangereux.
dangle ['daŋgl] *v* (*be hanging*) pendre; (*let hang*) balancer.
Danish ['deiniʃ] *nm, adj* danois. **Dane** *n* Danois, -e *m, f.*
dare [deə] *v* oser; (*challenge*) défier. **I dare say** sans doute. *n* défi *m.*
daring ['deəriŋ] *n* audace *f. adj* audacieux.
dark [daːk] *adj* obscur; (*colour*) foncé; (*hair*) brun. **be dark** (*night*) faire nuit. **dark horse** quantité inconnue *f.* **darkroom** *n* (*phot*) chambre noire *f.* *n* obscurité *f*; nuit *f.* **in the dark** (*ignorant*) dans le noir. **darken** *v* (s')obscurcir; (*sky*) (s')assombrir; foncer. **darkness** *n* obscurité *f*, ténèbres *f pl.*
darling ['daːliŋ] *n, adj* chéri, -e.
darn [daːn] *v* (*socks*) repriser; (*clothes*) raccommoder. *n* reprise *f.* **darning** *n* raccommodage *m.*
dart [daːt] *n* (*game*) fléchette *f*; (*sewing*) pince *f.* **dartboard** *n* cible *f.* *v* s'élancer; (*rays*) darder.
dash [daʃ] *n* (*drop*) goutte *f*; (*writing*) tiret *m*; (*rush*) élan *m.* *v* (*rush*) se précipiter; (*throw*) (se) jeter; (*hopes*) anéantir. **dashboard** *n* (*mot*) tableau de bord *m.* **dashing** *adj* plein de panache.
data ['deitə] *n* données *f pl.* **data processing** informatique *f.*
date[1] [deit] *n* date *f*; (*meeting*) rendez-vous *m.* **out of date** (*invalid*) périmé; (*old-fashioned*) démodé. **up to date** moderne; (*books, etc.*) à jour. *v* dater; fixer la date de; (*boyfriend, etc.*) sortir avec. **dated** *adj* démodé.
date[2] [deit] *n* (*fruit*) datte *f*; (*tree*) dattier *m.*
daub [doːb] *v* barbouiller.
daughter ['doːtə] *n* fille *f.* **daughter-in-law** *n* belle-fille *f.*
daunt [doːnt] *v* décourager. **dauntless** *adj* intrépide.
dawdle ['doːdl] *v* traîner.
dawn [doːn] *n* aube *f*; point du jour *m.* *v* (*day*) poindre; (*hope*) naître. **dawn on** venir à.
day [dei] *n* jour *m*, journée *f.* **day after** lendemain *m.* **day before** veille *f.* **daylight** *n* jour *m.* **day-to-day** *adj* journalier.
daydream ['deidriːm] *v* rêvasser. *n* rêvasserie *f.*
daze [deiz] *v* hébéter; (*from blow*) étourdir; (*shock*) abasourdir. *n* hébétement *m*; étourdissement *m*; stupéfaction *f.*
dazzle ['dazl] *v* éblouir. *n* lumière aveuglante *f.*
dead [ded] *adj* mort. *adv* absolument. **dead-beat** *adj* (*coll*) claqué. **dead end** impasse *f.* **deadline** *n* date limite *f*; heure limite *f.* **deadlock** *n* impasse *f.* **deadpan** *adj, adv* sans expression. **deaden** *v* amortir; (*pain*) calmer. **deadly** *adj* mortel.
deaf [def] *adj* sourd. **deaf-mute** *n* sourd-muet, sourde-muette *m, f.* **deafen** *v* rendre sourd; (*noise*) assourdir. **deafness** *n* surdité *f.*
***deal** [diːl] *n* quantité *f*; (*bargain*) marché *m*; (*cards*) donne *f.* **a good deal** beaucoup. *v* (*cards*) distribuer. **deal in** être dans le commerce de. **deal with** (*comm*) négocier avec; (*handle*) se charger de; (*book, report, etc.*) traiter de. **dealer** *n* négociant *m*; (*cards*) donneur *m.* **dealings** *pl n* (*comm*) opérations *f pl*; (*people*) relations *f pl.*
dealt [delt] *V* deal.
dean [diːn] *n* doyen *m.*
dear [diə] *n, adj* cher, chère. **oh dear!** oh là là! **dearly** *adv* cher, chèrement.
death [deθ] *n* mort *f.* **death certificate** acte de décès *m.* **death duties** droits de succession *m pl.* **death penalty** peine de mort *f.* **death toll** chiffre des morts *m.* **deathly** *adj* cadavérique; mortel.
debase [di'beis] *v* avilir; (*lower quality*) rabaisser. **debasement** *n* avilissement *m*; baisse *f.*
debate [di'beit] *v* discuter. *n* débat *m*; discussion *f.* **debatable** *adj* contestable.
debit ['debit] *n* débit *m.* *v* débiter; porter au débit.
debris ['deibriː] *n* débris *m pl.*
debt [det] *n* dette *f.* **get into debt** s'endetter. **debtor** *n* débiteur, -trice *m, f.*
decade ['dekeid] *n* décade *f.*
decadent ['dekədənt] *adj* décadent. **decadence** *n* décadence *f.*
decant [di'kant] *v* décanter. **decanter** *n* carafe *f.*

decapitate [di'kapi,teit] *v* décapiter. **decapitation** *n* décapitation *f*.
decay [di'kei] *v* (*rot*) pourrir; décliner; tomber en ruines; (*tooth*) se carier. *n* pourrissement *m*; décadence *f*, carie *f*. **decaying** *adj* en pourriture; en décadence.
decease [di'siːs] *n* décès *m*. *v* décéder. **deceased** *n*, *adj* défunt, -e.
deceit [di'siːt] *n* tromperie *f*. **deceitful** *adj* trompeur, -euse. **deceitfully** *adv* faussement. **deceitfulness** *n* fausseté *f*.
deceive [di'siːv] *v* tromper.
December [di'sembə] *n* décembre *m*.
decent ['diːsənt] *adj* (*dress*) décent; (*respectable*) convenable; (*coll: nice*) chic. **decency** *n* décence *f*; convenances *f pl*; (*kindness*) gentillesse *f*.
deceptive [di'septiv] *adj* trompeur. **deception** *n* tromperie *f*; illusion *f*.
decibel ['desi,bel] *n* décibel *m*.
decide [di'said] *v* (se) décider. **decided** *adj* résolu; incontestable; marqué. **deciding** *adj* décisif.
deciduous [di'sidjuəs] *adj* à feuilles caduques.
decimal ['desiməl] *adj* décimal. *n* décimale *f*. **decimal point** virgule *f*. **decimalization** *n* décimalisation *f*. **decimalize** *v* décimaliser.
decipher [di'saifə] *v* déchiffrer.
decision [di'siʒən] *n* décision *f*. **decisive** *adj* décisif; (*manner*) décidé.
deck [dek] *n* (*naut*) pont *m*; (*records*) table de lecture *f*. **deck-chair** *n* transat *m*. *v* orner.
declare [di'kleə] *v* déclarer. **declaration** *n* déclaration *f*.
decline [di'klain] *n* déclin *m*; (*prices*) baisse *f*. *v* décliner; baisser. **declension** *n* déclinaison *f*.
decompose [,diːkəm'pouz] *v* (se) décomposer. **decomposition** *n* décomposition *f*.
decorate ['dekə,reit] *v* décorer; orner; (*room, house*) peindre et tapisser. **decorating** *n* décoration intérieure *f*. **decoration** *n* décoration *f*; ornement *m*; (*room*) décor *m*. **decorative** *adj* décoratif. **decorator** *n* décorateur *m*.
decoy ['diːkoi; *v* di'koi] *n* leurre *m*; (*person*) compère *m*. *v* leurrer.
decrease [di'kriːs] *v* diminuer, décroître. *n* diminution *f*, décroissance *f*.
decree [di'kriː] *n* décret *m*. *v* décréter.
decrepit [di'krepit] *adj* décrépit; (*building*) délabré. **decrepitude** *n* décrépitude *f*; délabrement *m*.
dedicate ['dedi,keit] *v* dédier; consacrer. **dedication** dédicace *f*; consécration *f*; dévouement *m*.
deduce [di'djuːs] *v* déduire. **deduction** *n* déduction *f*.
deduct [di'dʌkt] *v* déduire; (*numbers*) soustraire; (*from wage*) prélever (sur). **deductible** *adj* déductible. **deduction** *n* déduction *f*; prélèvement *m*.
deed [diːd] *n* action *f*; (*law*) contrat *m*. **deed poll** acte unilatéral *m*.
deep [diːp] *adj* profond; (*broad*) large; (*sound*) grave. *adv* profondément. **deep-freeze** *n* congélateur *m*. **deep-seated** *adj* profondément enraciné. **deepen** *v* (s')approfondir.
deer [diə] *n* cerf *m*, biche *f*.
deface [di'feis] *v* mutiler; (*poster, etc.*) barbouiller.
default [di'foːlt] *n* défaut *m*. **in default of** faute de. *v* faire défaut; être en défaut.
defeat [di'fiːt] *v* vaincre, battre. *n* défaite *f*. **defeatist** *n*(*m*+*f*), *adj* défaitiste.
defect ['diːfekt; *v* di'fekt] *n* défaut *m*. *v* faire défection. **defection** *n* défection *f*. **defective** *adj* défectueux. **defector** *n* transfuge *m*, *f*.
defend [di'fend] *v* défendre. **defence** *n* défense *f*. **defenceless** *adj* sans défense. **defendant** *n* défendeur, -eresse *m*, *f*. **defending** *adj* (*champion*) en titre; (*law*) de la défense.
defensive [di'fensiv] *n* défensive *f*. *adj* défensif.
defer [di'fəː] *v* (*put off*) différer. **deferment** *n* ajournement *m*; suspension *f*.
defiant [di'faiənt] *adj* rebelle; provocant. **defiance** *n* défi *m*. **in defiance of** au mépris de. **defiantly** *adv* d'un air *or* ton de défi.
deficient [di'fiʃənt] *adj* insuffisant. **be deficient in** manquer de. **deficiency** *n* manque *f*; (*med*) carence *f*.
deficit ['defisit] *n* déficit *m*.
define [di'fain] *v* définir. **definition** *n* définition *f*; délimitation *f*; (*clearness*) netteté *f*. **definitive** *adj* définitif.
definite ['definit] *adj* certain; déterminé; manifeste; (*gramm*) défini. **definitely** *adv* sans aucun doute; catégoriquement.
deflate [di'fleit] *v* (*tyre, etc.*) dégonfler; (*person*) démonter. **deflation** *n* (*econ*) déflation *f*; dégonflement *m*.

deform [di'fɔːm] *v* déformer. **deformation** *n* déformation *f*. **deformed** *adj* difforme. **deformity** *n* difformité *f*.
defraud [di'frɔːd] *v* (*state*) frauder; (*person*) escroquer.
defrost [diː'frost] *v* (*refrigerator, etc.*) dégivrer; (*frozen food*) décongeler.
deft [deft] *adj* habile. **deftness** *n* habileté *f*.
defunct [di'fʌŋkt] *adj* défunt.
defy [di'fai] *v* défier.
degenerate [di'dʒenəˌreit; *n, adj* di'dʒenərit] *v* dégénérer. *n, adj* dégénéré, -e. **degeneracy** *or* **degeneration** *n* dégénérescence *f*.
degrade [di'greid] *v* dégrader. **degradation** *n* (*person*) avilissement *m*; dégradation *f*.
degree [di'griː] *n* degré *m*; (*university*) licence *f*. **by degrees** petit à petit.
dehydrate [diː'haidreit] *v* déshydrater. **dehydration** *n* déshydratation *f*.
de-icer [diː'aisə] *n* dégivreur *m*. **de-ice** *v* dégivrer.
deity ['diːəti] *n* divinité *f*, déité *f*.
dejected [di'dʒektid] *adj* abattu. **dejection** *n* abattement *m*.
delay [di'lei] *v* (*make late*) retarder; (*put off*) différer. *n* délai *m*; retardement *m*; (*rail*) retard *m*. **delaying** *adj* dilatoire.
delegate ['deləgeit; *n, adj* 'deləgit] *v* déléguer. *n, adj* délégué, -e. **delegation** *n* délégation *f*; nomination *f*.
delete [di'liːt] *v* rayer. **deletion** *n* (*act*) suppression *f*; (*word, phrase, etc.*) rature *f*.
deliberate [di'libərət; *v* di'libəreit] *adj* (*intentional*) délibéré; réfléchi; mesuré. *v* délibérer (sur). **deliberately** *adv* exprès; avec mesure. **deliberation** *n* délibération *f*.
delicate ['delikət] *adj* délicat; (*health*) fragile. **delicacy** *n* délicatesse *f*; (*food*) friandise *f*.
delicious [di'liʃəs] *adj* délicieux.
delight [di'lait] *n* grand plaisir *m*, joie *f*. *v* enchanter; se délecter (à). **delighted** *adj* ravi. **delightful** *adj* charmant, ravissant.
delinquency [di'liŋkwənsi] *n* délinquance *f*. **delinquent** *n, adj* délinquant, -e.
delirious [di'liriəs] *adj* délirant. **be delirious** (*med*) avoir le délire; (*crowd, etc.*) être en délire. **delirium** *n* délire *m*.
deliver [di'livə] *v* (*message*) remettre; (*goods*) livrer; (*letters*) distribuer; (*save*) délivrer; (*speech*) prononcer; (*woman*) accoucher. **deliverance** *n* délivrance *f*. **delivery** *n* livraison *f*; distribution *f*; (*speech*) débit *m*; accouchement *m*.
delta ['deltə] *n* delta *m*.
delude [di'luːd] *v* tromper. **delude oneself** se faire des illusions. **deluded** *adj* induit en erreur. **delusion** *n* illusion *f*; (*psych*) fantasme *m*.
deluge ['deljuːdʒ] *n* déluge *n*. *v* inonder.
delve [delv] *v* creuser, fouiller.
demand [di'maːnd] *v* exiger, réclamer. *n* exigence *f*; (*claim*) réclamation *f*; (*comm*) demande *f*. **be in demand** être demandé.
democracy [di'mokrəsi] *n* démocratie *f*.
democrat *n* démocrate *m, f*. **democratic** *adj* démocratique.
demolish [di'moliʃ] *v* démolir. **demolition** *n* démolition *f*.
demon ['diːmən] *n* démon *m*. **demoniacal** *adj* démoniaque.
demonstrate ['demənˌstreit] *v* démontrer; (*machine, etc.*) faire une démonstration de; (*pol*) manifester. **demonstration** *n* démonstration *f*; manifestation *f*. **demonstrative** *adj* démonstratif.
demoralize [di'morəˌlaiz] *v* démoraliser. **become demoralized** perdre courage. **demoralization** *n* démoralisation *f*.
demure [di'mjuə] *adj* modeste, sage.
den [den] *n* tanière *f*, repaire *m*.
denim ['denim] *n* toile de jean *f*. **denims** *pl n* (*jeans*) blue-jean *m sing*.
Denmark ['denmaːk] *n* Danemark *m*.
denomination [diˌnomi'neiʃən] *n* dénomination *f*; (*money*) valeur *f*; (*rel*) secte *f*. **denominator** *n* dénominateur *m*.
denote [di'nout] *v* dénoter.
denounce [di'nauns] *v* dénoncer.
dense [dens] *adj* dense; (*coll*: *stupid*) bouché. **density** *n* densité *f*.
dent [dent] *n* bosselure *f*. *v* bosseler, cabosser.
dental ['dentl] *adj* dentaire. **dental surgeon** chirurgien dentiste *m*.
dentist ['dentist] *n* dentiste *m, f*. **dentistry** *n* art dentaire *m*.
denture ['dentʃə] *n* dentier *m*.
denude [di'njuːd] *v* dénuder.
denunciation [dinʌnsi'eiʃən] *n* dénonciation *f*.
deny [di'nai] *v* nier; refuser. **denial** *n* dénégation *f*; (*accusation, etc.*) démenti *m*.
deodorant [diː'oudərənt] *nm, adj* déodorant, désodorisant.

depart [di'paːt] *v* partir. **depart from** (*leave*) quitter; (*deviate*) s'écarter de. **departure** *n* départ *m*. **departure lounge** salle de départ *f*.

department [di'paːtmənt] *n* département *m*; (*shop*) rayon *m*; (*school, university*) section *f*; domaine *m*; (*comm*) service *m*. **department store** grand magasin *m*.

depend [di'pend] *v* dépendre. **depend on** dépendre de; (*rely*) compter sur. **dependant** *n* personne à charge *f*. **dependence** *n* dépendance *f*. **dependent** *adj* dépendant.

depict [di'pikt] *v* (*words*) peindre; (*picture*) représenter. **depiction** *n* peinture *f*; représentation *f*.

deplete [di'pliːt] *v* réduire. **depletion** *n* réduction *f*.

deplore [di'ploː] *v* déplorer. **deplorable** *adj* déplorable.

deport [di'poːt] *v* déporter; expulser. **deportation** *n* déportation *f*; expulsion *f*. **deportment** *n* maintien *m*.

depose [di'pouz] *v* déposer. **deposition** *n* déposition *f*.

deposit [di'pozit] *v* déposer. *n* dépôt *m*; (*against damage*) caution *f*; (*token payment*) acompte *m*. **deposit account** compte de dépôt *m*. **depositor** *n* déposant, -e *m, f*.

depot ['depou] *n* dépôt *m*.

deprave [di'preiv] *v* dépraver. **depravity** *n* dépravation *f*.

depreciate [di'priːʃi,eit] *v* (se) déprécier. **depreciation** *n* dépréciation *f*.

depress [di'pres] *v* déprimer; (*press down*) appuyer sur. **depression** *n* dépression *f*; découragement *m*; (*econ*) crise *f*.

deprive [di'praiv] *v* priver. **deprivation** *n* privation *f*.

depth [depθ] *n* profondeur *f*; (*breadth*) largeur *f*; intensité *f*.

deputy ['depjuti] *n* adjoint, -e *m, f*. **deputation** *n* délégation *f*. **deputize for** assurer l'intérim de.

derail [di'reil] *v* (faire) dérailler. **derailment** *n* déraillement *m*.

derelict ['derilikt] *adj* abandonné, délaissé.

deride [di'raid] *v* railler. **derision** *n* dérision *f*. **derisive** *adj* moqueur. **derisory** *adj* (*offer, etc.*) dérisoire.

derive [di'raiv] *v* (*gain*) trouver, tirer. **be derived from** dériver de, provenir de. **derivation** *n* dérivation *f*.

derogatory [di'rogətəri] *adj* dénigrant, désobligeant.

descend [di'send] *v* descendre. **descend to** (*crime, etc.*) s'abaisser à. **descendant** *n* descendant, -e *m, f*. **descent** *n* descente *f*; origine *f*.

describe [di'skraib] *v* décrire. **description** *n* description *f*. **descriptive** *adj* descriptif.

desert[1] ['dezət] *n* désert *m*.

desert[2] [di'zəːt] *v* déserter, abandonner. **deserted** *adj* désert. **deserter** *n* déserteur *m*. **desertion** *n* désertion *f*; abandon *m*.

desert[3] [di'zəːt] *n* dû *m*. **get one's just deserts** avoir ce que l'on mérite.

deserve [di'zəːv] *v* mériter.

design [di'zain] *n* modèle *m*, plan *m*; (*pattern*) dessin *m*; (*comm*) design *m*; (*machine, etc.*) conception *f*; (*intention*) dessein *m*. *v* dessiner; projeter; concevoir. **designer** *n* (*comm*) concepteur-projeteur *m*; (*art*) dessinateur, -trice *m, f*.

designate ['dezig,neit] *v* désigner. **designation** *n* désignation *f*.

desire [di'zaiə] *n* désir *m*. *v* désirer. **desirable** *adj* désirable.

desk [desk] *n* bureau *m*; (*school*) pupitre *m*.

desolate ['desələt] *adj* désert; sombre; (*person*) affligé. **desolation** *n* désolation *f*.

despair [di'speə] *n* désespoir *m*. *v* désespérer.

desperate ['despərət] *adj* désespéré. **desperation** *n* désespoir *m*.

despise [di'spaiz] *v* mépriser.

despite [di'spait] *prep* malgré.

despondent [di'spondənt] *adj* découragé. **despondency** *n* découragement *m*.

despot ['despot] *n* despote *m*. **despotic** *adj* despotique.

dessert [di'zəːt] *n* dessert *m*. **dessertspoon** *n* cuiller à dessert *f*.

destination [desti'neiʃən] *n* destination *f*.

destine ['destin] *v* destiner. **destiny** *n* destin *m*.

destitute ['destitjuːt] *adj* indigent. **destitution** *n* dénuement *m*.

destroy [di'stroi] *v* détruire. **destroyer** *n* (*ship*) contre-torpilleur *m*. **destruction** *n* destruction *f*. **destructive** *adj* destructeur, -trice; destructif.

detach [di'tatʃ] *v* détacher. **detachable** *adj* détachable. **detached** *adj* détaché; (*unbiased*) objectif; indifférent. **detached house** maison individuelle *f*. **detachment** *n* détachement *m*; séparation *f*.

detail ['diːtei] *n* détail *m*. *v* détailler; (*mil*) affecter.
detain [di'tein] *v* retenir; (*law*) détenir.
detect [di'tekt] *v* découvrir; distinguer. **detective** *n* agent de la sûreté *m*. **detective story** roman policier *m*. **detector** *n* detecteur *m*.
detention [di'tenʃən] *n* détention *f*; (*school*) retenue *f*.
deter [di'təː] *v* décourager; dissuader; (*prevent*) détourner. **deterrent** *n* force de dissuasion *f*.
detergent [di'təːdʒənt] *nm, adj* détersif.
deteriorate [di'tiəriəˌreit] *v* (se) détériorer. **deterioration** *n* détérioration *f*.
determine [di'təːmin] *v* déterminer; fixer; décider. **determination** *n* détermination *f*. **determined** *adj* déterminé; résolu.
detest [di'test] *v* détester.
detonate ['detəˌneit] *v* (faire) détoner. **detonation** *n* détonation *f*. **detonator** *n* détonateur *m*
detour ['diːtuə] *n* détour *m*. *v* faire un détour.
detract [di'trakt] *v* **detract from** diminuer.
detriment ['detrimənt] *n* détriment *m*. **detrimental** *adj* nuisible.
devalue [diː'valjuː] *v* dévaluer. **devaluation** *n* dévaluation *f*.
devastate ['devəˌsteit] *v* (*town, etc.*) dévaster; (*person*) terrasser. **devastating** *adj* (*power*) dévastateur, -trice; (*effect*) accablant. **devastation** *n* dévastation *f*.
develop [di'veləp] *v* (se) développer; contracter. **development** *n* développement *m*; exploitation *f*.
deviate ['diːviˌeit] *v* dévier. **deviation** *n* déviation *f*.
device [di'vais] *n* appareil *m*; (*scheme*) formule *f*.
devil ['devl] *n* diable *m*. **talk of the devil!** quand on parle du loup! **devilish** *adj* diabolique.
devise [di'vaiz] *v* inventer; (*plan*) combiner.
devious ['diːviəs] *adj* détourné, tortueux.
devoid [di'void] *adj* dénué.
devolution [ˌdiːvə'luːʃən] *n* (*pol*) décentralisation *f*.
devote [di'vout] *v* consacrer. **devoted** *adj* dévoué. **devotion** *n* dévouement *m*.
devour [di'vauə] *v* dévorer.
devout [di'vaut] *adj* (*person*) pieux; (*earnest*) fervent.
dew [djuː] *n* rosée *f*.
dexterous ['dekstrəs] *adj* adroit. **dexterity** *n* adresse *f*.
diabetes [ˌdaiə'biːtiːz] *n* diabète *m*. **diabetic** *n(m+f)*, *adj* diabétique.
diagnose [ˌdaiəg'nouz] *v* diagnostiquer. **diagnosis** *n* diagnostic *m*. **diagnostic** *adj* diagnostique.
diagonal [dai'agənəl] *adj* diagonal. *n* diagonale *f*.
diagram ['daiəˌgram] *n* diagramme *m*; (*math*) figure *f*. **diagrammatic** *adj* schématique.
dial ['daiəl] *n* cadran *m*. *v* (*number*) faire. **dial direct** appeler par l'automatique. **dial 999** appeler Police Secours. **dialling code** indicatif *m*. **dialling tone** tonalité *f*.
dialect ['daiəlekt] *n* dialecte *m*; (*rural*) patois *m*.
dialogue ['daiəlog] *n* dialogue *m*.
diameter [dai'amitə] *n* diamètre *m*. **diametrically opposed** diamétralement opposé.
diamond ['daiəmənd] *n* (*gem*) diamant *m*; (*cards*) carreau *m*; (*shape*) losange *m*.
diaper ['daiəpə] *n* (*US*) couche *f*.
diaphragm ['daiəˌfram] *n* diaphragme *m*.
diarrhoea [ˌdaiə'riə] *n* diarrhée *f*.
diary ['daiəri] *n* (*record*) journal *m*; (*appointments*) agenda *m*.
dice [dais] *n* dé *m*. *v* couper en dés. **dice with death** jouer avec la mort.
dictate [dik'teit] *v* dicter. **dictation** *n* dictée *f*. **dictator** *n* dictateur *m*. **dictatorship** *n* dictature *f*.
dictionary ['dikʃənəri] *n* dictionnaire *m*.
did [did] *V* **do**.
die [dai] *v* mourir. **be dying** se mourir. **be dying to** mourir d'envie de. **be dying for** avoir une envie folle de. **die down** s'apaiser. **die out** disparaître.
diesel ['diːzəl] *n* diesel *m*. **diesel oil** gas-oil *m*. **diesel train** autorail *m*.
diet ['daiət] *n* (*restricted*) régime *m*; (*normal food*) nourriture *f*. *v* suivre un régime.
differ ['difə] *v* différer; ne pas être d'accord. **difference** *n* différence *f*. **different** *adj* différent; (*another*) autre. **differential** *adj* différentiel. **differentials** *pl n* (*salary*) écarts salariaux *m pl*. **differentiate** *v* distinguer.
difficult ['difikəlt] *adj* difficile. **difficulty** *n* difficulté *f*.

***dig** [dig] *v* creuser; (*dog*) fouiller. **dig up** déterrer. *n* (*archaeol*) fouille *f*; (*coll: remark*) coup de patte *m*; (*with elbow*) coup de coude *m*.
digest [dai'dʒest] *v* digérer. **digestion** *n* digestion *f*.
digit ['didʒit] *n* (*math*) chiffre *m*; (*finger*) doigt *m*. **digital** *adj* (*clock, etc.*) à affichage numérique.
dignified ['digni,faid] *adj* digne.
dignity ['dignəti] *n* dignité *f*.
digress [dai'gres] *v* s'éloigner. **digression** *n* digression *f*.
digs [digz] *pl n* chambre *f sing*, logement *m sing*.
dilapidated [di'lapi,deitid] *adj* délabré.
dilate [dai'leit] *v* (se) dilater. **dilation** *n* dilatation *f*.
dilemma [di'lemə] *n* dilemme *m*.
diligent ['dilidʒent] *adj* assidu; laborieux. **diligence** *n* assiduité *f*, zèle *m*.
dilute [dai'luɪt] *v* diluer. *adj* dilué.
dim [dim] *adj* (*light*) faible; (*sound*) vague; (*coll: stupid*) bouché. **take a dim view of** voir d'un mauvais œil. *v* (*light*) baisser; (*sound*) affaiblir. **dimness** *n* faiblesse *f*; obscurité *f*.
dimension [di'menʃən] *n* dimension *f*. **two-/three-dimensional** à deux/trois dimensions.
diminish [di'miniʃ] *v* diminuer.
diminutive [di'minjutiv] *adj* (*small*) tout petit; (*gramm*) diminutif. *n* diminutif *m*.
dimple ['dimpl] *n* fossette *f*.
din [din] *n* vacarme *m*.
dine [dain] *v* dîner. **diner** *n* (*person*) dîneur, -euse *m, f*. **dining car** wagon-restaurant *m*. **dining room** salle à manger *f*.
dinghy ['diŋgi] *n* youyou *m*; (*with sail*) dériveur *m*.
dingy ['dindʒi] *adj* miteux.
dinner ['dinə] *n* dîner *m*; (*midday meal*) déjeuner *m*. **dinner jacket** smoking *m*.
dinosaur ['dainə,soɪ] *n* dinosaure *m*.
diocese ['daiəsis] *n* diocèse *m*.
dip [dip] *v* (*into water, etc.*) plonger; (*go down*) baisser. *n* (*coll: bathe*) baignade *f*; (*in ground*) déclivité *f*. **dip-stick** *n* jauge *f*.
diphthong ['difθoŋ] *n* diphtongue *f*.
diploma [di'ploumə] *n* diplôme *m*.
diplomacy [di'plouməsi] *n* diplomatie *f*. **diplomat** *n* diplomate *m*. **diplomatic** *adj* diplomatique; (*person*) diplomate.
dire [daiə] *adj* terrible; extrême. **in dire straits** dans une situation désespérée.
direct [di'rekt] *adj* direct. **direct object** complément direct *m*. *v* diriger; adresser; (*instruct*) charger. *adv* directement. **direction** *n* direction *f*; instruction *f*. **directly** *adv* directement; (*immediately*) tout de suite. **director** *n* directeur, -trice *m, f*; (*theatre*) metteur en scène *m*; (*film, TV, etc.*) réalisateur, -trice *m, f*. **directory** *n* (*phone*) annuaire *m*; (*addresses*) répertoire *m*. **directory enquiries** renseignements *m pl*.
dirt [dəɪt] *n* saleté *f*, crasse *f*.
dirty ['dəɪti] *adj* sale; (*vulgar*) grossier. *v* salir.
disability [disə'biləti] *n* incapacité *f*; infirmité *f*. **disabled** *adj* infirme, handicapé.
disadvantage [,disəd'vaɪntidʒ] *n* désavantage *m*. **at a disadvantage** dans une position désavantageuse.
disagree [,disə'griː] *v* ne pas être d'accord; (*be different*) ne pas concorder; (*food, etc.*) ne pas convenir (à). **disagreeable** *adj* désagréable. **disagreement** *n* désaccord *m*.
disappear [,disə'piə] *v* disparaître. **disappearance** *n* disparition *f*.
disappoint [,disə'point] *v* decevoir. **disappointment** *n* déception *f*.
disapprove [,disə'pruɪv] *v* désapprouver. **disapproval** *n* désapprobation *f*. **disapproving** *adj* désapprobateur, -trice *m, f*.
disarm [dis'aɪm] *v* désarmer. **disarmament** *n* désarmement *m*. **disarming** *adj* (*smile*) désarmant.
disaster [di'zaɪstə] *n* désastre *m*, catastrophe *f*. **disastrous** *adj* désastreux.
disband [dis'band] *v* (se) disperser.
disbelief [disbi'liɪf] *n* incrédulité *f*.
disc *or US* **disk** [disk] *n* disque *m*.
discard [dis'kaɪd; *n* 'diskaɪd] *v* se débarrasser de; abandonner; (*cards*) se défausser de. *n* défausse *f*.
discern [di'səɪn] *v* discerner. **discernible** *adj* perceptible. **discerning** *adj* judicieux. **discernment** *n* discernement *m*.
discharge [dis'tʃaɪdʒ] *v* (*patient, employee*) renvoyer; (*gun*) tirer; (*cargo*) décharger; (*duty*) remplir; (*law, mil*) libérer. *n* renvoi *m*; (*elec*) décharge *f*; (*med*) pertes *f pl*.
disciple [di'saipl] *n* disciple *m*.
discipline ['disiplin] *n* discipline *f*. *v* discipliner; punir. **disciplinary** *adj* disciplinaire.

disclaim [dis'kleim] *v* désavouer.
disclose [dis'klouz] *v* divulguer, révéler. **disclosure** *n* divulgation *f*, révélation *f*.
discolour [dis'kʌlə] *v* (se) décolorer; (*from white*) jaunir. **discolouration** *n* décoloration *f*; jaunissement *m*.
discomfort [dis'kʌmfət] *n* malaise *m*, gêne *f*.
disconcert [diskən'səːt] *v* déconcerter.
disconnect [diskə'nekt] *v* disjoindre; (*gas, phone, etc.*) couper; (*television, etc.*) débrancher. **disconnected** *adj* (*thoughts, etc.*) décousu.
disconsolate [dis'konsələt] *adj adj* inconsolable.
discontented [diskən'tentid] *adj* mécontent. **discontent** *or* **discontentment** *n* mécontentement *m*.
discontinue [diskən'tinjuː] *v* cesser; interrompre.
discord ['diskoːd] *n* discorde *f*; (*music*) dissonance *f*. **discordant** *adj* discordant; dissonant.
discotheque ['diskətek] *n* discothèque *f*.
discount ['diskaunt] *n* remise *f*, escompte *m*. **at a discount** au rabais. **discount store** magasin de demi-gros *m*. *v* ne pas tenir compte de.
discourage [dis'kʌridʒ] *v* décourager. **become discouraged** se laisser décourager. **discouragement** *n* désapprobation *f*.
discover [dis'kʌvə] *v* découvrir. **discovery** *n* découverte *f*.
discredit [dis'kredit] *v* discréditer. *n* discrédit *m*.
discreet [di'skriːt] *adj* discret, -ète. **discretion** *n* discrétion *f*. **use your own discretion** c'est à vous de juger. **discretionary** *adj* discrétionnaire.
discrepancy [di'skrepənsi] *n* divergence *f*, désaccord *m*.
discrete [di'skriːt] *adj* discret, -ète.
discriminate [di'skrimi,neit] *v* distinguer; (*unfairly*) établir une discrimination. **discrimination** *n* distinction *f*; discrimination *f*; discernement *m*.
discus ['diskəs] *n* disque *m*.
discuss [di'skʌs] *v* discuter. **discussion** *n* discussion *f*.
disdain [dis'dein] *n* dédain *m*. **disdainful** *adj* dédaigneux. **disdainfully** *adv* avec dédain.
disease [di'ziːz] *n* maladie *f*. **diseased** *adj* malade.
disembark [disim'baːk] *v* débarquer. **disembarkation** *n* débarquement *m*.
disengage [disin'geidʒ] *v* dégager; (*tech*) débrayer. **disengaged** *adj* libre; débrayé.
disentangle [disin'taŋgl] *v* débrouiller.
disfigure [dis'figə] *v* défigurer. **disfigurement** *n* défigurement *m*.
disgrace [dis'greis] *n* honte *f*; (*disfavour*) disgrâce *f*. **in disgrace** (*child, etc.*) en pénitence. *v* faire honte à; déshonorer. **disgraceful** *adj* honteux, scandaleux.
disgruntled [dis'grʌntld] *adj* mécontent.
disguise [dis'gaiz] *v* déguiser. *n* déguisement *m*; masque *m*. **in disguise** déguisé.
disgust [dis'gʌust] *n* dégoûter. **disgusting** *adj* dégoûtant, écœurant.
dish [diʃ] *n* plat *m*. **do the dishes** faire la vaisselle. **dishcloth** *n* lavette *f*. **dishwasher** *n* lave-vaisselle *m invar*. *v* **dish up** servir.
dishearten [dis'haːtn] *v* décourager.
dishevelled [di'ʃevəld] *adj* échevelé.
dishonest [dis'onist] *adj* malhonnête. **dishonesty** malhonnêteté *f*.
dishonour [dis'onə] *n* déshonneur *m*. *v* déshonorer. **dishonourable** *adj* déshonorant.
disillusion [disi'luːʒən] *v* désillusionner. *n* désillusion *f*.
disinfect [disin'fekt] *v* désinfecter. **disinfectant** *nm, adj* désinfectant. **disinfection** *n* désinfection *f*.
disinherit [disin'herit] *v* déshériter.
disintegrate [dis'inti,greit] *v* (se) désintégrer. **disintegration** *n* désintégration *f*.
disinterested [dis'intristid] *adj* désintéressé.
disjointed [dis'dʒointid] *adj* décousu.
disk *V* **disc**.
dislike [dis'laik] *v* ne pas aimer. *n* aversion *f*. **take a dislike to** prendre en grippe.
dislocate ['dislə,keit] *v* disloquer. **dislocation** *n* dislocation *f*.
dislodge [dis'lodʒ] *v* faire bouger.
disloyal [dis'loiəl] *adj* déloyal. **disloyalty** *n* déloyauté *f*.
dismal ['dizməl] *adj* morne, lugubre.
dismantle [dis'mantl] *v* démonter.
dismay [dis'mei] *n* consternation *f*. *v* consterner.
dismiss [dis'mis] *v* (*send away*) renvoyer, congédier; (*meeting*) dissoudre; (*reject*) écarter. **dismissal** *n* renvoi *m*, congédiement *m*.

dismount [dis'maunt] *v* descendre.
disobey [disə'bei] *v* désobeir à. **disobedience** *n* désobéissance *f*. **disobedient** *adj* désobéissant.
disorder [dis'oːdə] *n* désordre *m*; (*med*) trouble *m*. **disorderly** *adj* désordonné.
disorganized [dis'oːgənaizd] *adj* désorganisé.
disown [dis'oun] *v* renier.
disparage [di'sparidʒ] *v* dénigrer. **disparagement** *n* dénigrement *m*. **disparaging** *adj* désobligeant.
disparity [dis'pariti] *n* disparité *f*.
dispassionate [dis'paʃənit] *adj* calme; impartial. **dispassionately** *adv* sans émotion; impartialement.
dispatch [di'spatʃ] *v* expédier. *n* expédition *f*; (*report*) dépêche *f*.
dispel [di'spel] *v* dissiper.
dispense [di'spens] *v* distribuer, administrer; (*medicine*) préparer. **dispense with** se passer de. **dispensary** *n* pharmacie *f*. **dispensation** *n* (*decree*) décret *m*; (*rel*) dispense *f*.
disperse [di'spəːs] *v* (se) disperser; (se) dissiper. **dispersal** *n* dispersion *f*.
displace [dis'pleis] *v* déplacer. **displacement** *n* déplacement *m*.
display [di'splei] *v* étaler; (*courage, etc.*) faire preuve de. *n* exposition *f*; (*comm*) étalage; (*courage, etc.*) manifestation *f*.
displease [dis'pliːz] *v* déplaire à. **displeasure** *n* mécontentement *m*.
dispose [di'spouz] *v* disposer. **dispose of** se débarrasser de. **disposable** *adj* à jeter. **disposal** *n* disposition *f*; (*rubbish*) enlèvement *m*; (*bomb*) désamorçage *m*. **disposition** *n* tempérament *m*; inclination *f*.
disproportion [disprə'poːʃən] *n* disproportion *f*. **disproportionate** *adj* disproportionné.
disprove [dis'pruːv] *v* réfuter.
dispute [di'spjuːt] *n* dispute *f*, (*argument*) discussion *f*; (*industrial*) conflit *m*. **beyond dispute** incontestable. *v* contester; discuter. **disputable** *adj* discutable.
disqualify [dis'kwoliˌfai] *v* disqualifier. **disqualification** *n* disqualification *f*.
disregard [disrə'gaːd] *v* (*ignore*) mépriser; négliger. *n* indifférence *f*; mépris.
disreputable [dis'repjutəbl] *adj* louche; (*clothes*) miteux.
disrespect [disrə'spekt] *n* manque de respect *m*. **disrespectful** *adj* irrespectueux. **be disrespectful to** manquer de respect envers.
disrupt [dis'rʌpt] *v* perturber, interrompre. **disruption** *n* perturbation *f*; interruption *f*. **disruptive** *adj* perturbateur, -trice.
dissatisfied [di'satisˌfaid] *adj* mécontent. **dissatisfaction** *n* mécontentement *m*.
dissect [di'sekt] *v* disséquer. **dissection** *n* dissection *f*.
dissent [di'sent] *v* différer. *n* dissentiment *m*. **dissension** *n* dissension *f*.
dissident ['disidənt] *n, adj* dissident, -e. **dissidence** *n* dissidence *f*.
dissimilar [di'similə] *adj* dissemblable. **dissimilarity** *n* dissemblance *f*.
dissociate [di'sousieit] *v* dissocier. **dissociation** *n* dissociation *f*.
dissolve [di'zolv] *v* (se) dissoudre.
dissuade [di'sweid] *v* dissuader. **dissuasion** *n* dissuasion *f*.
distance ['distəns] *n* distance *f*. **in the distance** au loin. **distant** *adj* lointain, éloigné; (*reserved*) distant.
distaste [dis'teist] *n* dégoût *m*. **distasteful** *adj* déplaisant.
distemper [di'stempə] *n* (*paint*) détrempe *f*. *v* peindre en détrempe.
distended [di'stendid] *adj* (*med*) dilaté; distendu. **distension** *n* dilatation *f*; distension *f*.
distil [di'stil] *v* (se) distiller. **distillery** *n* distillerie *f*.
distinct [di'stiŋkt] *adj* distinct; net, nette. **distinction** *n* distinction *f*. **distinctive** *adj* distinctif.
distinguish [di'stiŋgwiʃ] *v* distinguer; caractériser.
distort [di'stoːt] *v* déformer. **distortion** *n* distorsion *f*; déformation *f*.
distract [di'strakt] *v* distraire. **distracting** *adj* gênant. **distraction** *n* distraction *f*; interruption *f*.
distraught [di'stroːt] *adj* éperdu.
distress [di'stres] *n* douleur *f*, affliction *f*; (*poverty, danger*) détresse *f*. *v* affliger. **distressing** *adj* pénible.
distribute [di'stribjut] *v* distribuer; (*share*) répartir. **distribution** *n* distribution *f*; répartition *f*. **distributor** *n* (*mot*) distributeur *m*.
district ['distrikt] *n* (*of town*) quartier *m*; (*admin*) arrondissement *m*; (*of country*) région *f*. **district nurse** infirmière visiteuse *f*.

distrust [dis'trʌst] *v* se méfier de. *n* méfiance *f*. **distrustful** *adj* méfiant.
disturb [di'stəːb] *v* déranger; troubler. **disturbance** *n* dérangement *m*; (*noise*) tapage *m*. **disturbing** *adj* inquiétant.
disuse [dis'juːs] *n* désuétude *f*. **fall into disuse** tomber en désuétude. **disused** *adj* désaffecté.
ditch [ditʃ] *n* fossé *m*.
ditto ['ditou] *adv* idem.
divan [di'van] *n* divan *m*.
dive [daiv] *v* plonger. *n* plongeon *m*; (*submarine*) plongée *f*. **diver** *n* plongeur *m*. **diving board** plongeoir *m*.
diverge [dai'vəːdʒ] *v* diverger. **divergence** *n* divergence *f*. **divergent** *adj* divergent.
diverse [dai'vəːs] *adj* divers. **diversity** *n* diversité *f*.
divert [dai'vəːt] *v* détourner; (*traffic*) dévier; (*amuse*) divertir. **diversion** *n* déviation *f*; divertissement *m*. **create a diversion** faire une diversion.
divide [di'vaid] *v* (se) diviser; (se) séparer. **divided** *adj* (*country*) désuni. **dividers** *pl n* compas à pointes sèches *m sing*. **dividing** *adj* (*wall, etc.*) mitoyen. **divisible** *adj* divisible. **division** *n* division *f*; séparation *f*.
dividend ['dividend] *n* dividende *m*.
divine [di'vain] *adj* divin. **divinity** *n* divinité *f*; théologie *f*.
divorce [di'voːs] *n* divorce *m*. *v* divorcer (avec). **divorcee** *n* divorcé, -e *m, f*.
divulge [dai'vʌldʒ] *v* divulguer.
dizzy ['dizi] *adj* pris de vertige; (*height*) vertigineux. **dizziness** *n* vertige *m*.
***do** [duː] *v* faire; (*suffice*) suffire (à); (*coll: cheat*) refaire. **do away with** supprimer. **do up** (*clothes*) (se) fermer; (*parcel*) emballer; (*house*) remettre à neuf. **do without** se passer de. **how do you do?** (*on introduction*) enchanté. **that will do!** ça suffit!
docile ['dousail] *adj* docile.
dock[1] [dok] *n* (*ships*) dock *m*, bassin *m*. **dockyard** *n* chantier naval *m*. *v* mettre à quai; (*space*) s'arrimer. **docker** *n* docker *m*.
dock[2] [dok] *n* (*law*) banc des accusés *m*.
dock[3] [dok] *v* écourter; (*wages*) rogner.
doctor ['doktə] *n* docteur *m*, médecin *m*; (*university*) docteur *m*. **doctorate** *n* doctorat *m*.
doctrine ['doktrin] *n* doctrine *f*.
document ['dokjumənt] *n* document *m*. *v* documenter. **documentary** *nm, adj* documentaire. **documentation** *n* documentation *f*.
dodge [dodʒ] *v* (s')esquiver; (*tax*) éviter de payer. *n* détour *m*; (*sport*) esquive *f*; (*coll: trick*) truc *m*. **dodgy** *adj* délicat; douteux.
dog [dog] *n* chien *m*. **dog-eared** *adj* écorné. **dogfish** *n* chien de mer *m*. **dog rose** églantine *f*. *v* (*follow*) suivre de près; (*plague*) harceler.
dogged ['dogid] *adj* tenace. **doggedly** *adv* avec ténacité.
dogma ['dogmə] *n* dogme *m*. **dogmatic** *adj* dogmatique.
do-it-yourself [ˌduːitjoː'self] *n* bricolage *m*.
dole [doul] *n* allocation de chômage *f*. **on the dole** au chômage. *v* **dole out** distribuer.
doll [dol] *n* poupée *f*. *v* **doll up** bichonner.
dollar ['dolə] *n* dollar *m*.
dolphin ['dolfin] *n* dauphin *m*.
domain [də'mein] *n* domaine *m*.
dome [doum] *n* dôme *m*.
domestic [də'mestik] *adj* domestique; (*not foreign*) intérieur. **domestic science** arts ménagers *m pl*. *n* domestique.
dominate ['domiˌneit] *v* dominer. **dominance** *n* dominance *f*. **dominant** *adj* dominant. **domination** *n* domination *f*.
domineering [domi'niəriŋ] *adj* dominateur, -trice.
dominion [də'minjən] *n* dominion *m*, territoire *m*.
domino ['dominou] *n* domino *m*.
don [don] *v* revêtir.
donate [də'neit] *v* faire don de; (*blood*) donner. **donation** *n* don *m*.
done [dʌn] *V* **do**.
donkey ['doŋki] *n* âne, -esse *m, f*.
donor ['dounə] *n* (*med*) donneur, -euse *m, f*; (*charity*) donateur, -euse *m, f*.
doom [duːm] *v* condamner. *n* destin *m*. **doomed** *adj* voué à l'échec.
door [doː] *n* porte *f*; (*car, train*) portière *f*. **doorbell** *n* sonnette *f*. **doorknob** *n* poignée de porte *f*. **door-knocker** *n* heurtoir *m*. **doormat** *n* essuie-pieds *m invar*. **doorstep** *n* pas de porte *m*. **door-to-door** *adj, adv* à domicile. **doorway** *n* embrasure de porte *f*.
dope [doup] *v* doper. *n* dopant *m*; (*slang: drugs*) drogue *f*; (*slang: person*) andouille *f*.

dormant ['doːmənt] *adj* en sommeil.
dormitory ['doːmitəri] *n* dortoir *m*. **dormitory town** ville dortoir *f*.
dormouse ['doːˌmaus] *n*, *pl* **-mice** loir *m*.
dose [dous] *n* dose *f*. *v* administrer un médicament à. **dosage** *n* dosage *m*; (*on bottle*) posologie *f*.
dot [dot] *n* point *m*. *v* pointiller. **dotted line** pointillé *m*.
dote [dout] *v* **dote on** raffoler de. **dotage** *n* (*senility*) gâtisme *m*.
double ['dʌbl] *adj*, *adv* double; deux fois. *n* double *m*. *v* doubler; plier en deux.
double-barrelled [ˌdʌbl'barəld] *adj* (*coll*: *name*) à rallonges; (*gun*) à deux coups.
double bass [beis] *n* contrebasse *f*.
double bed *n* grand lit *m*.
double cream *n* crème à fouetter *f*.
double-cross [ˌdʌbl'kros] *v* (*coll*) doubler.
double-decker [ˌdʌbl'dekə] *n* autobus à impériale *m*.
double dutch *n* baragouin *m*. **talk double dutch** baragouiner.
double-glazing [ˌdʌbl'gleiziŋ] *n* doubles fenêtres *f pl*.
double-jointed [ˌdʌbl'dʒointid] *adj* désarticulé.
double room *n* chambre à deux personnes *f*.
doubt [daut] *n* doute *m*. **no doubt** sans doute. *v* douter (de). **doubtful** *adj* douteux; incertain. **doubtless** *adv* sans aucun doute.
dough [dou] *n* pâte *f*; (*slang*: *money*) fric *m*. **doughnut** *n* beignet *m*.
dove [dʌv] *n* colombe *f*. **dovecote** *n* colombier *m*.
Dover ['douvə] *n* Douvres.
dowdy ['daudi] *adj* sans élégance; démodé.
down[1] [daun] *adv* en bas; (*to ground*) par terre. *prep* en bas de; (*along*) le long de. *v* (*coll*: *drink*) s'envoyer. **down tools** cesser le travail.
down[2] [daun] *n* duvet *m*. **downy** *adj* duveté.
downcast ['daunˌkaːst] *adj* abattu.
downfall ['daunˌfoːl] *n* chute *f*.
downhearted [ˌdaun'haːtid] *adj* abattu.
downhill [ˌdaun'hil] *adj* en pente. **go downhill** descendre la pente; (*deteriorate*) être sur le déclin; (*business*) péricliter.
down payment *n* acompte *m*.
downpour ['daunˌpoː] *n* averse *f*.
downright ['daunˌrait] *adj* catégorique. *adv* carrément; purement et simplement.
downstairs ['daunˌsteəz; *adv* ˌdaun'steəz] *adj* (*ground floor*) du rez-de-chaussée; (*below*) d'en bas. *adv* au rez-de-chaussée; en bas. **go downstairs** descendre.
downstream [ˌdaun'striːm] *adv* en aval. **go downstream** descendre le courant.
down-to-earth [ˌdauntə'əːθ] *adj* terre à terre.
downtrodden ['daunˌtrodn] *adj* opprimé.
downward ['daunwəd] *adj* vers le bas; (*glance*) baissé.
downwards ['daunwədz] *adv* vers le bas, en bas.
dowry ['dauəri] *n* dot *f*.
doze [douz] *v* sommeiller. *n* somme *m*.
dozen ['dʌzn] *n* douzaine *f*.
drab [drab] *adj* terne.
draft[1] [draːft] *n* (*letter*) brouillon *m*; (*sketch*) ébauche *f*; (*money*) retrait *m*; (*mil*) détachement *m*. *v* faire le brouillon de; (*plan*) esquisser; (*comm*) rédiger; (*mil*) détacher.
draft[2] *V* **draught**.
drag [drag] *v* traîner; (*river*) draguer. *n* résistance; (*coll*: *bore*) corvée *f*; (*coll*: *smoke*) bouffée *f*. **in drag** en travesti.
dragon ['dragən] *n* dragon *m*. **dragonfly** *n* libellule *f*.
drain [drein] *n* (*pipe*) égout *m*; (*grid*) bouche d'égout *f*. *v* drainer, vider. **draining board** égouttoir *m*. **drainpipe** *n* tuyau d'écoulement *m*. **drainage** *n* drainage *m*; (*in town*) système d'égouts *m*.
drama ['draːmə] *n* drame *m*; art dramatique *m*. **dramatic** *adj* dramatique; (*effect*) théâtral. **dramatist** *n* dramaturge *m*. **dramatize** *v* adapter pour la scène; (*exaggerate*) dramatiser.
drank [draŋk] *V* **drink**.
drape [dreip] *v* draper. **drapes** *pl n* (*US*) rideaux *m pl*.
draper ['dreipə] *n* marchand de nouveautés *m*. **draper's shop** magasin de nouveautés *m*. **drapery** *n* draperie *f*.
drastic ['drastik] *adj* energique, radical.
draught *or US* **draft** [draːft] *n* courant d'air *m*; (*drink*) coup *m*. **draughts** *pl n* dames *f pl*. **draught beer** bière à la pression *f*. **draughtboard** *n* damier *m*. **draught excluder** bourrelet *m*. **draughtsman** *n* dessinateur *m*.
***draw** [droː] *v* (*art*) dessiner; (*pull*) tirer; (*attract*) attirer; (*be equal*) être ex aequo.

draw back reculer. **draw near** s'approcher (de). **draw out** prolonger. **draw up** (*plan*) dresser. *n* (*sport*) match nul *m*; (*lottery*) tirage au sort *m*.
drawback ['drɔːbak] *n* inconvénient *m*.
drawbridge ['drɔːbridʒ] *n* pont-levis *m*.
drawer ['drɔːə] *n* tiroir *m*.
drawing ['drɔːiŋ] *n* dessin *m*. **drawing board** planche à dessin *f*. **drawing pin** punaise *f*. **drawing room** salon *m*.
drawl [drɔːl] *n* voix traînante *f*. *v* parler d'une voix traînante.
drawn [drɔːn] *V* **draw**.
dread [dred] *v* redouter. *n* terreur *f*. **dreadful** *adj* épouvantable, atroce. **dreadfully** *adv* terriblement.
***dream** [driːm] *n* rêve *m*. *v* rêver; (*imagine*) songer. **dreamy** *adj* rêveur, -euse.
dreamt [dremt] *V* **dream**.
dreary ['driəri] *adj* morne; monotone.
dredge [dredʒ] *v* draguer. *n* drague *f*.
dregs [dregz] *pl n* lie *f sing*.
drench [drentʃ] *v* tremper.
dress [dres] *n* robe; (*clothing*) tenue *f*. **dress circle** premier balcon *m*. **dressmaker** *n* couturière *f*. **dressmaking** *n* couture *f*. **dress rehearsal** répétition générale *f*. *v* (s')habiller; (*salad*) assaisonner; (*wound*) panser. **dress up as** se déguiser en. **dressy** *adj* élégant.
dresser[1] ['dresə] *n* (*furniture*) buffet *m*.
dresser[2] ['dresə] *n* (*theatre*) habilleur, -euse *m*, *f*.
dressing ['dresiŋ] *n* (*wound*) pansement *m*; (*cookery*) assaisonnement *m*. **dressing gown** robe de chambre *f*. **dressing room** (*theatre*) loge *f*; (*in house*) dressing-room *m*. **dressing table** coiffeuse *f*.
drew [druː] *V* **draw**.
dribble ['dribl] *v* (*child*) baver; (*liquid*) couler lentement; (*sport*) dribbler. *n* bave *f*; petite goutte *f*; dribble *m*.
dried [draid] *adj* séché; déshydraté; (*milk*) en poudre. **dried fruit** fruits secs *m pl*.
drier ['draiə] *n* séchoir *m*.
drift [drift] *v* dériver, aller à la dérive. *n* (*heap*) amoncellement *m*; (*deviation*) dérive *f*; (*gist*) but *m*. **driftwood** *n* bois flotté *m*.
drill [dril] *v* (*hole*) forer; (*tooth*) fraiser. *n* foret *m*; fraise *f*; (*mil*) exercice *m*.
***drink** [driŋk] *v* boire. *n* boisson *f*. **drinkable** *adj* potable. **drinking water** eau potable *f*.
drip [drip] *v* dégoutter. *n* (*drop*) goutte *f*; (*coll*: *person*) nouille *f*; (*med*) goutte-à-goutte *m invar*. **drip-dry** *adj* (*on label*) ne pas repasser. **dripping** *n* (*fat*) graisse *f*.
***drive** [draiv] *v* conduire; (*push*) chasser; (*nail*) enfoncer. *n* (*trip*) promenade en voiture *f*; (*to house*) allée *f*; (*energy*) dynamisme *m*. **driver** *n* conducteur, -trice *m*, *f*. **driving** *n* conduite *f*. **driving licence** permis de conduire *m*. **driving school** auto-école *f*. **driving test** examen du permis de conduire *m*.
drivel ['drivl] *v* radoter. *n* radotage *m*.
driven ['drivn] *V* **drive**.
drizzle ['drizl] *v* bruiner. *n* bruine *f*.
drone [droun] *v* ronronner, vrombir; (*bee*) bourdonner. *n* ronronnement *m*, vrombissement *m*; bourdonnement *m*.
droop [druːp] *v* s'affaisser, retomber.
drop [drop] *n* (*liquid*) goutte *f*; (*fall*) baisse *f*. *v* (*fall*) tomber; (*let fall*) laisser tomber; (*price*) baisser. **drop off** (*sleep*) s'endormir. **dropper** *n* compte-gouttes *m invar*. **droppings** *pl n* crottes *f pl*; (*bird*) fiente *f sing*.
drought [draut] *n* sécheresse *f*.
drove [drouv] *V* **drive**.
drown [draun] *v* (se) noyer.
drowsy ['drauzi] *adj* somnolent. **grow drowsy** s'assoupir. **drowsiness** *n* somnolence *f*.
drudgery ['drʌdʒəri] *n* corvée *f*.
drug [drʌg] *n* drogue *f*. **be on drugs** se droguer. **drug addict** drogué, -e *m*, *f*. *v* droguer.
drum [drʌm] *n* tambour *m*; (*oil*) tonnelet *m*. **drumstick** *n* baguette de tambour *f*; (*chicken*) pilon *m*. *v* tambouriner. **drummer** *n* tambour *m*.
drunk [drʌŋk] *V* **drink**. *adj* ivre. **get drunk** s'enivrer. *n also* **drunkard** ivrogne, -esse *m*, *f*. **drunkenness** *n* ivresse *f*.
dry [drai] *adj* sec, sèche; (*wit*) caustique; (*dull*) aride. **dry-clean** *v* nettoyer à sec. **dry cleaner's** teinturerie *f*. **dry rot** pourriture sèche *f*. **dry ski slope** piste artificielle *f*. *v* sécher. **dry up** se dessécher, se tarir; (*dishes*) essuyer la vaisselle.
dual ['djuəl] *adj* double.
dubbed ['dʌbd] *adj* (*film*) doublé. **dubbing** *n* doublage *m*.
dubious ['djuːbiəs] *adj* douteux.
Dublin ['dʌblin] *n* Dublin.

duchess ['dʌtʃis] *n* duchesse *f.*
duck[1] [dʌk] *n* canard *m.* **duckling** *n* caneton, canette *m, f.* **duckpond** *n* mare aux canards *f.*
duck[2] [dʌk] *v* (*dodge*) se baisser subitement; (*submerge*) plonger.
duct [dʌkt] *n* conduite *f*; (*anat*) conduit *m.*
dud [dʌd] *adj* raté; faux, fausse.
due [djuː] *adj* dû, due; (*suitable*) qui convient. **be due** devoir arriver. *adv* droit. **dues** *pl n* droits *m pl.*
duel ['djuəl] *n* duel *m.* *v* se battre en duel. **duellist** *n* duelliste *m.*
duet [dju'et] *n* duo *m.*
dug [dʌg] *V* **dig.**
duke [djuːk] *n* duc *m.*
dull [dʌl] *adj* terne; (*sound*) sourd; (*weather*) gris. (se) ternir; (s')assourdir; (*blunt*) (s')émousser.
dumb [dʌm] *adj* muet, muette; (*slang: stupid*) bêta, -asse. **dumbbell** *n* haltère *m.* **dumbfound** *v* confondre. **dumbness** *n* mutisme *m.*
dummy ['dʌmi] *n* (*comm*) factice *m*; (*dressmaker's*) mannequin *m*; (*ventriloquist's*) pantin *m*; (*baby's*) sucette *f.* **dummy run** coup d'essai *m.*
dump [dʌmp] *n* (*tip*) décharge *f*; (*coll: place*) trou. **be down in the dumps** avoir le cafard. *v* déposer.
dumpling ['dʌmpliŋ] *n* (*savoury*) boulette de pâte *f*; (*fruit*) chausson *m.*
dunce [dʌns] *n* âne *m.* **dunce's cap** bonnet d'âne *m.*
dune [djuːn] *n* dune *f.*
dung [dʌŋ] *n* crotte *f*; (*manure*) fumier *m.*
dungarees [ˌdʌŋgə'riːz] *pl n* salopette *f sing.*
dungeon ['dʌndʒən] *n* cachot *m.*
Dunkirk ['dʌnkəːk] *n* Dunkerque.
duplicate ['djuːplikeit; *n, adj* 'djuːplikət] *v* faire un double de; (*photocopy*) polycopier. *n* double *m.* *adj* en double; (*comm*) en duplicata.
durable ['djuərəbl] *adj* solide; durable.
duration [dju'reiʃən] *n* durée *f.*
during ['djuriŋ] *prep* pendant.
dusk [dʌsk] *n* crépuscule *m.* **dusky** *adj* sombre.
dust [dʌst] *n* poussière *f.* **dustbin** *n* poubelle *f.* **dustman** *n* éboueur *m.* **dustpan** *n* pelle à poussière *f.* **dust sheet** housse *f.* *v* épousseter. **duster** *n* chiffon *m.* **dusty** *adj* poussiéreux.
Dutch [dʌtʃ] *nm, adj* hollandais, néerlandais. **the Dutch** les Hollandais *m pl,* les Néerlandais *m pl.*
duty ['djuːti] *n* devoir *m*; (*job*) fonction *f*; (*tax*) droit *m.* **duty-free** exempté de douane. **duty-free shop** magasin hors-taxe *m.* **off duty** libre. **on duty** de service. **dutiful** *adj* respectueux; consciencieux.
duvet ['duːvei] *n* couette *f.*
dwarf [dwoːf] *n, adj* nain, -e *m, f.* *v* écraser.
***dwell** [dwel] *v* habiter. **dwell on** s'arrêter sur. **dwelling** *n* habitation *f.*
dwelt [dwelt] *V* **dwell.**
dwindle ['dwindl] *v* diminuer.
dye [dai] *n* teinture *f.* *v* teindre.
dyke [daik] *n* (*ditch*) fossé *m*; (*barrier*) digue *f.*
dynamic [dai'namik] *adj* dynamique. **dynamism** *n* dynamisme *m.*
dynamite ['dainəˌmait] *n* dynamite *f.*
dynamo ['dainəˌmou] *n* dynamo *f.*
dynasty ['dinəsti] *n* dynastie *f.*
dysentery ['disəntri] *n* dysenterie *f.*
dyslexia [dis'leksiə] *n* dyslexie *f.* **dyslexic** *n*(*m*+*f*), *adj* dyslexique.
dyspepsia [dis'pepsiə] *n* dyspepsie *f.*

E

each [iːtʃ] *adj* chaque. *pron* chacun, -e. **each other** l'un l'autre, les uns les autres.
eager ['iːgə] *adj* avide; ardent; impatient. **eagerness** *n* désir ardent *m*; impatience *f.*
eagle ['iːgl] *n* aigle *m.*
ear[1] [iə] *n* oreille *f.* **earache** *n* mal d'oreille *m.* **eardrum** *n* tympan *m.* **earmark** *v* réserver; (*money*) assigner. **earphones** *pl n* casque *m sing.* **earring** *n* boucle d'oreille *f.* **earshot** *n* portée de voix *f.*
ear[2] [iə] *n* (*grain*) épi *m.*
earl [əːl] *n* comte *m.*
early ['əːli] *adv* de bonne heure, tôt. *adj* tôt; prématuré; précoce.
earn [əːn] *v* gagner; mériter. **earnings** *pl n* salaire *m sing*; profits *m pl.*
earnest ['əːnist] *adj* sérieux; ardent; sincère. **in earnest** sérieusement.

earth [əːθ] *n* terre *f*; (*of fox*) terrier *m*. **earthenware** *n* faïence *f*. **earthquake** *n* tremblement de terre *m*. *v* (*elec*) mettre à la terre.
earwig ['iəwig] *n* perce-oreille *m*.
ease [iːz] *n* aise *f*; (*easiness*) aisance *f*. **at ease** à l'aise; (*mil*) repos. **with ease** facilement. *v* (*pain*) soulager; calmer; diminuer; (*relax*) se détendre.
easel ['iːzl] *n* chevalet *m*.
east [iːst] *n* est *m*. *adj also* **easterly**, **eastern** oriental; d'est; à l'est. *adv* à *or* vers l'est. **eastbound** *adj* est *invar*.
Easter ['iːstə] *n* Pâques *f pl*. **Easter egg** œuf de Pâques *m*.
easy ['iːzi] *adj* facile. **easy chair** fauteuil *m*. **easy-going** *adj* accommodant. **take it easy** ne pas se fatiguer. **easily** *adv* sans difficulté; sans aucun doute. **easiness** *n* facilité *f*.
***eat** [iːt] *v* manger. **eat out** aller au restaurant. **eat up** finir. **eatable** *adj* mangeable.
eaten ['iːtn] *V* **eat**.
eavesdrop ['iːvzdrop] *v* écouter de façon indiscrète. **eavesdropper** *n* oreille indiscrète *f*.
ebb [eb] *n* reflux *m*. *v* refluer; (*courage, etc.*) décliner.
ebony ['ebəni] *n* ébène *f*.
eccentric [ik'sentrik] *n*(*m*+*f*), *adj* excentrique. **eccentricity** *n* excentricité *f*.
ecclesiastical [ikliːzi'astikl] *adj* ecclésiastique.
echo ['ekou] *n* écho *m*. *v* répercuter; répéter; résonner.
eclair [ei'kleə] *n* éclair *m*.
eclipse [i'klips] *n* éclipse *f*. *v* éclipser.
ecology [i'kolədʒi] *n* écologie *f*. **ecological** *adj* écologique. **ecologist** *n* écologiste *m*, *f*.
economy [i'konəmi] *n* économie *f*. **economic** *adj* économique; (*profitable*) rentable. **economical** *adj* économe, économique. **economics** *n* économique *f*. **economist** *n* économiste *m*, *f*. **economize** *v* économiser.
ecstasy ['ekstəsi] *n* extase *f*. **ecstatic** *adj* extasié. **be ecstatic about** s'extasier sur.
eczema ['eksimə] *n* eczéma *m*.
edge [edʒ] *n* bord *m*; (*of blade*) tranchant *m*. **on edge** énervé. *v* border; (*move*) se glisser. **edging** *n* bordure *f*. **edgy** *adj* énervé.
edible ['edəbl] *adj* comestible.
Edinburgh ['edinbərə] *n* Edimbourg.
edit ['edit] *v* (*text*) éditer; (*film*) monter; (*magazine*) diriger. **editor** *n* rédacteur, -trice *m*, *f*, éditeur, -trice *m*, *f*; (*newspaper*) rédacteur, -trice en chef *m f*. **editorial** *n* éditorial *m*. **editorial staff** rédaction *f*.
edition [i'diʃən] *n* édition *f*.
educate ['edjukeit] *v* instruire. **educated** *adj* instruit; cultivé. **education** *n* éducation *f*; (*teaching*) enseignement *m*; (*studies*) études *f pl*. **educational** *adj* (*methods*) pédagogique; (*game, etc.*) éducatif.
eel [iːl] *n* anguille *f*.
eerie ['iəri] *adj* étrange; sinistre.
effect [i'fekt] *n* effet *m*. **take effect** (*drug*) faire son effet; (*rule, etc.*) entrer en vigueur. *v* effectuer. **effective** *adj* efficace. **effectiveness** *n* efficacité *f*.
effeminate [i'feminət] *adj* efféminé.
effervescent [,efə'vesənt] *adj* effervescent; (*drink*) gazeux. **effervescence** *n* effervescence *f*; (*drink*) pétillement *m*.
efficient [i'fiʃənt] *adj* efficace; compétent. **efficiency** *n* efficacité *f*; compétence *f*.
effigy ['efidʒi] *n* effigie *f*.
effort ['efət] *n* effort *m*. **effortless** *adj* facile.
egg [eg] *n* œuf *m*. **egg-cup** *n* coquetier *m*. **egg-shaped** *adj* ovoïde. **eggshell** *n* coquille d'œuf *f*.
egotism ['egətizm] *n* égotisme *m*. **egotist** *n* égotiste *m*, *f*.
Egypt ['iːdʒipt] *n* Egypte *f*. **Egyptian** *n* Egyptien, -enne *m*, *f*; *adj* égyptien.
eiderdown ['aidədaun] *n* édredon *m*.
eight [eit] *nm*, *adj* huit. **eighth** *n*(*m*+*f*), *adj* huitième.
eighteen [ei'tiːn] *nm*, *adj* dix-huit. **eighteenth** *n*(*m*+*f*), *adj* dix-huitième.
eighty ['eiti] *nm*, *adj* quatre-vingts. **eightieth** *n*(*m*+*f*), *adj* quatre-vingtième.
either ['aiðə] *adj* l'un ou l'autre; (*each*) chaque. *pron* l'un ou l'autre. *adv* non plus. *conj* ou. **either ... or ...** ou ... ou ....
ejaculate [i'dʒakjuleit] *v* éjaculer; (*shout*) s'exclamer. **ejaculation** *n* éjaculation *f*; exclamation *f*.
eject [i'dʒekt] *v* éjecter; expulser. **ejection** *n* éjection *f*; expulsion *f*. **ejector seat** siège éjectable *m*.
eke [iːk] *v* **eke out** (*add to*) augmenter; (*make last*) faire durer.

elaborate [i'labərət; *v* i'labəreit] *adj* compliqué, minutieux. *v* élaborer; donner des détails. **elaborately** *adv* en détail.
elapse [i'laps] *v* s'écouler.
elastic [i'lastik] *nm, adj* élastique. **elastic band** *n* élastique *m*. **elasticity** *n* élasticité *f*.
elated [i'leitid] *adj* transporté. **elation** *n* exultation *f*.
elbow ['elbou] *n* coude *m*. **elbow grease** (*coll*) huile de coude *f*.
elder[1] ['eldə] *n, adj* aîné, -e.
elder[2] ['eldə] *n* sureau *m*. **elderberry** *n* baie de sureau *f*.
elderly ['eldəli] *adj* âgé.
eldest ['eldist] *adj* aîné.
elect [i'lekt] *v* élire; choisir. *adj* futur. **election** *n* élection *f*. **electoral** *adj* électoral. **electorate** *n* électorat *m*.
electric [ə'lektrik] *adj* électrique. **electric blanket** couverture chauffante *f*. **electric fire** radiateur électrique *m*. **electric shock** décharge électrique *f*. **electrical** *adj* électrique. **electrician** *n* électricien *m*. **electricity** *n* électricité *f*. **electrify** *v* électriser; (*rail*) électrifier.
electrocute [i'lektrəkjuːt] *v* électrocuter. **electrocution** *n* électrocution *f*.
electrode [i'lektroud] *n* électrode *f*.
electronic [elək'tronik] *adj* électronique. **electronics** *n* électronique *f*.
elegant ['eligənt] *adj* élégant. **elegance** *n* élégance *f*.
elegy ['elidʒi] *n* élégie *f*.
element ['eləmənt] *n* élément *m*; (*elec*) résistance *f*. **elementary** *adj* élémentaire.
elephant ['elifənt] *n* éléphant *m*.
elevate ['eliveit] *v* élever. **elevation** *n* élévation *f*; altitude *f*. **elevator** *n* (*US*) ascenseur *m*.
eleven [i'levn] *nm, adj* onze. **eleventh** *n*(*m*+*f*), *adj* onzième.
elf [elf] *n* elfe *m*. **elfin** *adj* d'elfe.
eligible ['elidʒəbl] *adj* éligible.
eliminate [i'limineit] *v* éliminer. **elimination** *n* élimination *f*.
elite [ei'liːt] *n* élite *f*.
ellipse [i'lips] *n* ellipse *f*. **elliptical** *adj* elliptique.
elm [elm] *n* orme *m*.
elocution [elə'kjuːʃən] *n* élocution *f*.
elope [i'loup] *v* s'enfuir.
eloquent ['eləkwənt] *adj* éloquent. **eloquence** *n* éloquence *f*.
else [els] *adv* autre, d'autre. **or else** autrement, ou bien. **elsewhere** *adv* ailleurs.
elude [i'luːd] *v* éluder, échapper à. **elusive** *adj* insaisissable.
emaciated [i'meisieitid] *adj* émacié. **emaciation** *n* émaciation *f*.
emanate ['eməneit] *v* émaner. **emanation** *n* émanation *f*.
emancipate [i'mansipeit] *v* émanciper. **emancipation** *n* émancipation *f*.
embalm [im'baːm] *v* embaumer.
embankment [im'baŋkmənt] *n* (*rail*) talus *m*; (*river*) quai *m*; (*canal*) digue *f*.
embargo [im'baːgou] *n* embargo *m*.
embark [im'baːk] *v* (s')embarquer. **embark on** commencer; s'engager dans. **embarkation** *n* embarquement *m*.
embarrass [im'barəs] *v* embarrasser, gêner. **embarrassment** *n* embarras *m*, gêne *f*.
embassy ['embəsi] *n* ambassade *f*.
embellish [im'beliʃ] *v* embellir. **embellishment** *n* embellissement *m*.
ember ['embə] *n* charbon ardent *m*. **embers** *pl n* braise *f sing*.
embezzle [im'bezl] *v* détourner. **embezzlement** *n* détournement de fonds *m*. **embezzler** *n* escroc *m*.
embitter [im'bitə] *v* (*person*) aigrir; (*relationship*) envenimer.
emblem ['embləm] *n* emblème *m*.
embody [im'bodi] *v* exprimer; réunir. **embodiment** *n* incarnation *f*, personnification *f*.
emboss [im'bos] *v* (*metal*) repousser; (*paper, etc.*) gaufrer. **embossed** *adj* (*letterhead, etc.*) en relief.
embrace [im'breis] *v* (s')embrasser. *n* enlacement *m*.
embroider [im'broidə] *v* broder; (*truth*) broder sur. **embroidery** *n* broderie *f*. **embroidery silk** soie à broder *f*.
embryo ['embriou] *n* embryon *m*. **in embryo** (*project, etc.*) en germe.
emerald ['emərəld] *n* émeraude *f*.
emerge [i'məːdʒ] *v* émerger, surgir.
emergency [i'məːdʒənsi] *n* cas urgent *m*; (*med*) urgence *f*. **emergency exit** sortie de secours *f*. **emergency landing** atterrissage forcé *m*. **in case of emergency** en cas d'urgence.
emigrate ['emigreit] *v* émigrer. **emigration** *n* émigration *f*.
eminent ['eminənt] *adj* éminent. **eminence** *n* distinction *f*.

emit [i'mit] *v* émettre.
emotion [i'mouʃən] *n* émotion *f.* **emotional** *adj* (*state*) émotionnel; (*shock*) émotif. **emotionally** *adv* avec émotion.
empathy ['empəθi] *n* communion d'idées *f.*
emperor ['empərə] *n* empereur *m.* **empress** *n* impératrice *f.*
emphasis ['emfəsis] *n* accent *m*; importance *f.* **emphasize** *v* appuyer sur; accentuer. **emphatic** *adj* énergique.
empire ['empaiə] *n* empire *m.*
empirical [impirikəl] *adj* empirique.
employ [im'ploi] *v* employer. **employee** *n* employé, -e *m, f.* **employer** *n* patron, -onne *m, f.* **employment** *n* emploi *m.* **employment agency** agence de placement *f.*
empower [im'pauə] *v* autoriser.
empty ['empti] *adj* vide; vacant. **empty-handed** *adj* bredouille. *v* vider. **emptiness** *n* vide *m.*
emu ['iːmjuː] *n* émeu *m.*
emulate ['emjuleit] *v* imiter. **emulation** *n* émulation *f.*
emulsion [i'mʌʃən] *n* émulsion *f.*
enable [i'neibl] *v* permettre à.
enact [i'nakt] *v* (*play*) jouer; (*decree*) décréter.
enamel [i'naməl] *n* émail (*pl* -aux) *m.* *v* émailler.
enamour [i'namə] *v* enchanter. **be enamoured of** être épris de.
encase [in'keis] *v* recouvrir (de).
enchant [in'tʃaːnt] *v* enchanter. **enchanting** *adj* ravissant. **enchantment** *n* enchantement *m.*
encircle [in'səːkl] *v* entourer.
enclose [in'klouz] *v* enclore; (*surround*) entourer; (*in letter*) joindre. **enclosed** *adj* ci-joint. **enclosure** *n* enceinte *f*; (*document*) pièce jointe *f.*
encore ['oŋkoː] *nm, interj* bis. *v* bisser.
encounter [in'kauntə] *v* affronter, rencontrer. *n* rencontre *f.*
encourage [in'kʌridʒ] *v* encourager. **encouragement** *n* encouragement *m.*
encroach [in'kroutʃ] *v* empiéter. **encroachment** *n* empiètement *m.*
encumber [in'kʌmbə] *v* encombrer. **encumbrance** *n* embarras *m.*
encyclopedia [insaiklə'piːdiə] *n* encyclopédie *f.*
end [end] *n* (*tip*) bout *m*; (*finish*) fin *f.* **end product** (*comm*) produit fini *m*; (*result*) résultat *m.* **make ends meet** joindre les deux bouts. *v* finir; (se) terminer. **ending** *n* fin *f*; (*of word*) terminaison *f.* **endless** *adj* interminable; incessant.
endanger [in'deindʒə] *v* mettre en danger; compromettre.
endeavour [in'devə] *n* effort *m.* *v* s'efforcer (de).
endemic [en'demik] *adj* endémique. *n* endémie *f.*
endive ['endiv] *n* endive *f*; (*curly*) chicorée *f.*
endorse [in'doːs] *v* (*cheque, etc.*) endosser; approuver. **endorsement** *n* endossement *m*; sanction *f*; (*mot*) contravention *f.*
endow [in'dau] *v* doter (de); (*prize, etc*) fonder. **endowment** *n* dotation *f*; fondation *f.*
endure [in'djuə] *v* supporter; (*last*) durer. **endurance** *n* endurance *f,* résistance *f.*
enemy ['enəmi] *n* ennemi, -e *m, f.*
energy ['enədʒi] *n* énergie *f.* **energetic** *adj* énergique.
enfold [in'fould] *v* envelopper.
enforce [in'foːs] *v* (*law*) faire obéir; (*discipline*) imposer.
engage [in'geidʒ] *v* (s')engager; (*employee*) embaucher; (*clutch*) s'embrayer. **engaged** *adj* fiancé; occupé. **get engaged** se fiancer. **engagement** *n* rendez-vous *m invar*; fiançailles *f pl*; (*actor*) engagement *m.*
engine ['endʒin] *n* machine *f*; moteur *m.* **engine driver** mécanicien *m.* **engine room** (*on ship*) salle des machines *f.*
engineer [endʒi'niə] *n* ingénieur *m*; (*mechanic*) technicien *m.* *v* machiner. **engineering** *n* ingénierie *f.*
England ['iŋglənd] *n* Angleterre *f.* **English** *nm, adj* anglais. **the English** les Anglais.
engrave [in'greiv] *v* graver. **engraver** *n* graveur *m.* **engraving** *n* gravure *f.*
engrossed [in'groust] *adj* absorbé.
engulf [in'gʌlf] *v* engouffrer.
enhance [in'haːns] *v* mettre en valeur, rehausser.
enigma [i'nigmə] *n* énigme *f.* **enigmatic** *adj* énigmatique.
enjoy [in'dʒoi] *v* aimer; (*good health, etc.*) jouir de. **enjoy oneself** s'amuser. **enjoyable** *adj* agréable. **enjoyment** *n* plaisir *m.*
enlarge [in'laːdʒ] *v* (s')agrandir. **enlargement** *n* agrandissement *m.*

enlighten [in'laitn] *v* éclairer. **enlightenment** *n* éclaircissement *m.*
enlist [in'list] *v* (s')engager; recruter. **enlistment** *n* engagement *m.*
enmity ['enməti] *n* inimitié *f.*
enormous [i'noːməs] *adj* énorme. **enormously** *adv* énormément.
enough [i'nʌf] *adj, adv, n* assez. **be enough** suffire.
enquire [in'kwaiə] *V* **inquire.**
enrage [in'reidʒ] *v* mettre en rage.
enrich [in'ritʃ] *v* enrichir; (*soil*) fertiliser.
enrol [in'roul] *v* (s')inscrire; (*mil*) (s')enrôler. **enrolment** *n* inscription *f*; enrôlement *m.*
ensign ['ensain] *n* (*emblem*) insigne *m*; (*flag*) drapeau *m*; (*naut*) pavillon *m.*
enslave [in'sleiv] *v* asservir. **enslavement** *n* asservissement *m.*
ensue [in'sjuː] *v* s'ensuivre.
ensure [in'ʃuə] *v* assurer.
entail [in'teil] *v* occasionner, comporter.
entangle [in'taŋgl] *v* empêtrer, emmêler.
enter ['entə] *v* entrer (dans); (*register*) inscrire. **enter for** (*exam*) (se) présenter à.
enterprise ['entəˌpraiz] *n* entreprise *f*; initiative *f.* **enterprising** *adj* entreprenant.
entertain [ˌentə'tein] *v* (*amuse*) divertir; (*guests*) recevoir; (*idea*) considérer. **entertainer** *n* artiste *m, f.* **entertainment** *n* divertissement *m.*
enthral [in'θroːl] *v* captiver.
enthusiasm [in'θuːziˌazəm] *n* enthousiasme *m.* **enthusiast** *n* enthousiaste *m, f.* **enthusiastic** *adj* enthousiaste, passionné.
entice [in'tais] *v* attirer, entraîner. **enticing** *adj* attrayant; (*food*) alléchant.
entire [in'taiə] *adj* entier. **in its entirety** en entier.
entitle [in'taitl] *v* autoriser, donner droit à; (*book*) intituler.
entity ['entəti] *n* entité *f.*
entrails ['entreilz] *pl n* entrailles *f pl.*
entrance[1] ['entrəns] *n* entrée *f.*
entrance[2] [in'traːns] *v* ravir.
entrant ['entrənt] *n* (*competition, exam*) candidat, -e *m, f*; (*race*) concurrent, -e *m, f*; (*profession*) débutant, -e *m, f.*
entreat [in'triːt] *v* supplier. **entreaty** *n* supplication *f.*
entrench [in'trentʃ] *v* (*mil*) retrencher. **entrenched** *adj* (*custom*) implanté; indélogeable.
entrepreneur [ˌontrəprə'nəː] *n* entrepreneur *m.*
entrust [in'trʌst] *v* confier; (*with task*) charger.
entry ['entri] *n* entrée *f*; (*on list*) inscription *f.* **entry form** feuille d'inscription *f.* **no entry** (*road*) sens interdit; (*gate, etc.*) défense d'entrer.
entwine [in'twain] *v* (s')entrelacer.
enunciate [i'nʌnsiˌeit] *v* articuler; (*theory*) énoncer. **enunciation** *n* articulation *f*; énonciation *f.*
envelop [in'veləp] *v* envelopper.
envelope ['envəˌloup] *n* enveloppe *f.*
environment [in'vaiərənmənt] *n* milieu *m*, environnement *m.*
envisage [in'vizidʒ] *v* (*foresee*) prévoir; (*imagine*) envisager.
envoy ['envoi] *n* envoyé, -e *m, f.*
envy ['envi] *n* envie *f.* *v* envier. **enviable** *adj* enviable. **envious** *adj* envieux. **enviously** *adv* avec envie.
enzyme ['enzaim] *n* enzyme *f.*
ephemeral [i'femərəl] *adj* éphémère.
epic ['epik] *adj* épique. *n* épopée *f.*
epidemic [epi'demik] *n* épidémie *f.* *adj* épidémique.
epilepsy ['epilepsi] *n* épilepsie *f.* **epileptic** *n(m+f)*, *adj* épileptique. **epileptic fit** crise d'epilepsie *f.*
epilogue ['epilog] *n* épilogue *m.*
Epiphany [i'pifəni] *n* Epiphanie *f*, fête des Rois *f.*
episcopal [i'piskəpəl] *adj* épiscopal.
episode ['episoud] *n* épisode *m.* **episodic** *adj* épisodique.
epitaph ['epiˌtaːf] *n* épitaphe *f.*
epitome [i'pitəmi] *n* modèle *m*; quintessence *f.* **epitomize** *v* incarner.
epoch ['iːpok] *n* époque *f.*
equable ['ekwəbl] *adj* égal.
equal ['iːkwəl] *adj* égal, -e. *v* égaler. **equality** *n* égalité *f.* **equalize** *v* égaliser.
equanimity [ekwə'niməti] *n* sérénité *f.*
equate [i'kweit] *v* assimiler; (*make equal*) égaler. **equation** *n* équation *f.*
equator [i'kweitə] *n* équateur *m.* **equatorial** *adj* équatorial.
equestrian [i'kwestriən] *adj* équestre. *n* cavalier, -ère *m, f.*
equilateral [ˌiːkwi'latərəl] *adj* équilatéral.
equilibrium [ˌiːkwi'libriəm] *n* équilibre *m.*
equinox ['ekwinoks] *n* équinoxe *m.* **equinoctial** *adj* équinoxial.

equip [i'kwip] *v* équiper. **equipment** *n* équipement *m*; matériel *m*.
equity ['ekwəti] *n* équité *f*.
equivalent [i'kwivələnt] *nm, adj* équivalent.
era ['iərə] *n* ère *f*; époque *f*.
eradicate [i'radi,keit] *v* extirper, supprimer.
erase [i'reiz] *v* effacer; (*with rubber*) gommer. **eraser** *n* gomme *f*.
erect [i'rekt] *adj* droit. *v* (*statue, etc.*) ériger; (*build*) bâtir; (*tent, etc.*) dresser. **erection** *n* érection *f*; construction *f*.
ermine ['əːmin] *n* hermine *f*.
erode [i'roud] *v* éroder, ronger. **erosion** *n* érosion *f*. **erosive** *adj* érosif.
erotic [i'rotik] *adj* érotique.
err [əː] *v* se tromper; (*sin*) pécher.
errand ['erənd] *n* course *f*. **errand boy** garçon de courses *m*.
erratic [i'ratik] *adj* irrégulier.
error ['erə] *n* erreur *f*.
erudite ['erudait] *adj* savant. **erudition** *n* érudition *f*.
erupt [i'rupt] *v* (*volcano*) entrer en éruption; (*quarrel*) éclater. **eruption** *n* éruption *f*.
escalate ['eskə,leit] *v* (s')intensifier. **escalation** *n* escalade *f*. **escalator** *n* escalier roulant *m*.
escalope ['eskə,lop] *n* escalope *f*.
escape [is'keip] *v* (s')échapper (à). *n* fuite *f*, évasion *f*.
escort ['eskoːt; *v* i'skoːt] *n* escorte *f*. *v* escorter.
esoteric [esə'terik] *adj* ésotérique.
especial [i'speʃəl] *adj* particulier. **especially** *adv* particulièrement, surtout.
espionage ['espiə,naːʒ] *n* espionnage *m*.
esplanade [,esplə'neid] *n* esplanade *f*.
essay ['esei] *n* essai *m*; (*school*) rédaction *f*, dissertation *f*. **essayist** *n* essayiste *m, f*.
essence ['esns] *n* essence *f*.
essential [i'senʃəl] *adj* essentiel. **essentials** *pl n* essentiel *m sing*.
establish [i'stabliʃ] *v* établir; fonder. **establishment** *n* établissement *m*; fondation *f*.
estate [i'steit] *n* propriété *f*; (*houses*) lotissement *m*; (*law*) biens *m pl*. **estate agent** agent immobilier *m*. **estate car** break *m*.
esteem [i'stiːm] *v* estimer. *n* estime *f*.
estimate ['estimət; *v* 'esti,meit] *n* évaluation *f*; (*comm*) devis *m*. *v* estimer. **estimation** *n* jugement *m*; (*esteem*) estime *f*.
estuary ['estjuəri] *n* estuaire *m*.
eternal [i'təːnl] *adj* éternel. **eternity** *n* éternité *f*.
ether ['iːθə] *n* éther *m*.
ethereal [i'θiəriəl] *adj* éthéré.
ethical ['eθikl] *adj* moral. **ethics** *pl n* morale *f sing*.
ethnic ['eθnik] *adj* ethnique.
etiquette ['eti,ket] *n* étiquette *f*.
etymology [,eti'molədʒi] *n* étymologie *f*. **etymological** *adj* étymologique.
Eucharist ['juːkərist] *n* Eucharistie *f*.
eunuch ['juːnək] *n* eunuque *m*.
euphemism ['juːfə,mizəm] *n* euphémisme *m*. **euphemistic** *adj* euphémique.
euphoria [ju'foːriə] *n* euphorie *f*. **euphoric** *adj* euphorique.
Europe ['juərəp] *n* Europe *f*. **European** *n* Européen, -enne *m, f*; *adj* européen. **European Economic Community (EEC)** Communauté Économique Européenne (CEE) *f*.
euthanasia [juːθə'neiziə] *n* euthanasie *f*.
evacuate [i'vakju,eit] *v* évacuer. **evacuation** *n* évacuation *f*. **evacuee** *n* évacué, -e *m, f*.
evade [i'veid] *v* éviter. **evasion** *n* fuite *f*. **evasive** *adj* évasif.
evaluate [i'valju,eit] *v* évaluer. **evaluation** *n* évaluation *f*.
evangelical [,iːvan'dʒelikəl] *adj* évangélique. **evangelist** *n* évangéliste *m*
evaporate [i'vapə,reit] *v* s'évaporer; (*fade away*) se volatiliser. **evaporated milk** lait concentré *m*. **evaporation** *n* évaporation *f*.
eve [iːv] *n* veille *f*.
even ['iːvən] *adj* (*surface*) uni; régulier; égal; (*number*) pair. *adv* même; (*more, etc.*) encore. **even so** quand même. **even-tempered** *adj* placide. *v* égaliser.
evening ['iːvniŋ] *n* soir *m*, soirée *f*. **evening class** cours du soir *m*. **evening dress** (*man*) tenue de soirée *f*; (*woman*) robe du soir *f*.
evensong ['iːvən,soŋ] *n* office du soir *m*.
event [i'vent] *n* événement *m*; cas *m*; (*race*) course *f*. **in the event of** en cas de; au cas où. **eventful** *adj* mouvementé.
eventual [i'ventʃuəl] *adj* qui s'ensuit. **eventuality** *n* éventualité *f*. **eventually** *adv* finalement.
ever ['evə] *adv* jamais; (*always*) toujours.

evergreen ['evəgriːn] *adj* vert, à feuilles persistantes. *n* arbre vert *m*.
everlasting [ˌevə'laːstiŋ] *adj* éternel.
every ['evri] *adj* (*all*) tous les, toutes les; (*each*) chaque, tout. **everybody** *or* **everyone** *pron* tout le monde. **everyday** *adj* banal; de tous les jours. **every other day** tous les deux jours, un jour sur deux. **everything** *pron* tout. **everywhere** *adv* partout.
evict [i'vikt] *v* expulser. **eviction** *n* expulsion *f*.
evidence ['evidəns] *n* évidence *f*; (*testimony*) témoignage *m*; signe *m*. **give evidence** témoigner. **evident** *adj* évident. **evidently** *adv* évidemment; à ce qu'il paraît.
evil ['iːvl] *adj* mauvais. *n* mal *m*.
evoke [i'vouk] *v* évoquer. **evocation** *n* évocation *f*. **evocative** *adj* évocateur, -trice.
evolve [i'volv] *v* (se) développer. **evolution** *n* évolution *f*. **evolutionary** *adj* évolutionniste.
ewe [juː] *n* brebis *f*.
exacerbate [ig'zasəˌbeit] *v* exacerber.
exact [ig'zakt] *adj* exact. *v* exiger. **exacting** *adj* exigeant; (*task*) astreignant. **exactly** *adv* précisément, exactement.
exaggerate [ig'zadʒəˌreit] *v* exagérer; accentuer. **exaggeration** *n* exagération *f*.
exalt [ig'zolt] *v* élever; (*praise*) exalter.
examine [ig'zamin] *v* examiner; (*law*) interroger. **examination** *n* examen *m*. **examiner** *n* examinateur, -trice *m*, *f*.
example [ig'zaːmpl] *n* exemple *m*. **for example** par exemple. **set a good example** donner l'exemple.
exasperate [ig'zaːspəˌreit] *v* exaspérer. **exasperation** *n* exaspération *f*.
excavate ['ekskəˌveit] *v* excaver; (*dig*) creuser; (*archaeol*) fouiller, faire des fouilles. **excavation** *n* creusage *m*; fouille *f*.
exceed [ik'siːd] *v* dépasser. **exceedingly** *adv* extrêmement.
excel [ik'sel] *v* briller; surpasser. **excellence** *n* excellence *f*. **excellent** *adj* excellent.
Excellency ['eksələnsi] *n* Excellence *f*.
except [ik'sept] *prep* sauf, excepté; (*but*) sinon. *v* excepter. **exception** *n* exception *f*. **take exception to** s'offenser de. **exceptional** *adj* exceptionnel.
excerpt ['eksəːpt] *n* extrait *m*.
excess [ik'ses] *n* excès *m*. **excess fare** supplément *m*. **excess luggage** excédent de bagages *m*. **excessive** *adj* excessif.
exchange [iks'tʃeindʒ] *v* échanger; faire un échange (de). *n* échange *m*; (*phone*) central *m*; (*finance*) change *m*. **exchange rate** taux de change *m*.
exchequer [iks'tʃekə] *n* ministère des finances *m*.
excise ['eksaiz] *n* taxe *f*; (*department*) régie *f*. **excise duties** contributions indirectes *f pl*.
excite [ik'sait] *v* exciter. **excited** *adj* excité, agité. **get excited** s'exciter, s'agiter. **excitement** *n* excitation *f*. **exciting** *adj* passionnant.
exclaim [ik'skleim] *v* s'exclamer, s'écrier.
exclamation [ˌeksklə'meiʃən] *n* exclamation *f*. **exclamation mark** point d'exclamation *m*.
exclude [ik'skluːd] *v* exclure. **exclusion** *n* exclusion *f*. **exclusive** *adj* exclusif; select; (*dates, numbers, etc.*) exclusivement; (*price, charge*) non compris.
excommunicate [ekskə'mjuːniˌkeit] *v* excommunier. **excommunication** *n* excommunication *f*.
excrete [ik'skriːt] *v* excréter. **excrement** *n* excrément *m*. **excretion** *n* excrétion *f*.
excruciating [ik'skruːʃieitiŋ] *adj* (*pain*) atroce; (*noise*) infernal.
excursion [ik'skəːʃən] *n* excursion *f*.
excuse [ik'skjuːz] *v* excuser. **excuse me!** excusez-moi! *n* excuse *f*. **excusable** *adj* excusable.
execute ['eksiˌkjuːt] *n* exécuter; accomplir. **execution** *n* exécution *f*; (*of duties*) exercice *m*. **executioner** *n* bourreau *m*.
executive [ig'zekjutiv] *adj* (*power*) exécutif; (*job*) administratif. *n* (*person*) cadre *m*; (*group*) bureau *m*.
exemplify [ig'zempliˌfai] *v* exemplifier.
exempt [ig'zempt] *adj* exempt. *v* exempter. **exemption** *n* exemption *f*.
exercise ['eksəˌsaiz] *n* exercice *m*. **exercises** *pl n* (*physical*) gymnastique *f sing*. **exercise book** cahier *m*. *v* exercer.
exert [ig'zəːt] *v* exercer; (*force*) employer. **exert onself** se dépenser; s'appliquer. **exertion** *n* effort *m*; exercice *m*; emploi *m*.
exhale [eks'heil] *v* (*give off*) exhaler; (*breathe out*) expirer.
exhaust [ig'zoːst] *v* épuiser. *n* (*system*) échappement *m*; (*pipe*) tuyau d'échappement *m*. **exhaustion** *n* épuise-

ment *m*. **exhaustive** *adj* complet, -ète. **exhaustively** *adv* à fond.
exhibit [ig'zibit] *v* exposer; (*skill, etc.*) faire preuve de. *n* objet exposé *m*. **exhibition** *n* exposition *f*. **make an exhibition of oneself** se donner en spectacle. **exhibitionist** *n*(*m*+*f*), *adj* exhibitionniste. **exhibitor** *n* exposant, -e *m, f*.
exhilarate [ig'zilə,reit] *v* vivifier, stimuler. **exhilaration** *n* ivresse *f*.
exile ['eksail] *v* exiler. *n* exil *m*; (*person*) exilé, -e *m, f*. **go into exile** s'exiler.
exist [ig'zist] *v* exister; (*live*) vivre. **existence** *n* existence *f*. **existentialism** *n* existentialisme *m*. **existing** *adj* (*current*) actuel.
exit ['egzit] *n* sortie *f*.
exonerate [ig'zonə,reit] *v* (*from blame*) disculper; (*from obligation*) exempter. **exoneration** *n* disculpation *f*; exemption *f*.
exorbitant [ig'zoːbitənt] *adj* exorbitant.
exorcise ['eksoː,saiz] *v* exorciser. **exorcism** *n* exorcisme *m*. **exorcist** *n* exorciste *m*.
exotic [ig'zotik] *adj* exotique.
expand [ik'spand] *v* (se) dilater; (se) développer; (s')étendre. **expansion** *n* expansion *f*; développement *m*. **expansive** *adj* expansif.
expanse [ik'spans] *n* étendue *f*.
expatriate [eks'peitrieit; *n, adj* eks'peitriət] *v* expatrier. *n, adj* expatrié, -e.
expect [ik'spekt] *v* attendre; supposer; (*demand*) exiger. **expectancy** *or* **expectation** *n* attente *f*.
expedient [ik'spiːdiənt] *adj* (*convenient*) opportun; politique. *n* expédient *m*.
expedition [,ekspi'diʃən] *n* expédition *f*.
expel [ik'spel] *v* expulser; (*school*) renvoyer.
expenditure [ik'spenditʃə] *n* dépense *f*.
expense [ik'spens] *n* frais *m pl*. **at the expense of** aux dépens de. **expense account** frais de représentation *m pl*. **expensive** *adj* cher. **be expensive** coûter cher.
experience [ik'spiəriəns] *n* expérience *f*. *v* (*encounter*) rencontrer; (*feel*) éprouver. **experienced** *adj* expérimenté.
experiment [ik'sperimənt] *n* expérience *f*. *v* faire une expérience; expérimenter. **experimental** *adj* expérimental.
expert ['ekspəːt] *nm, adj* expert.
expertise [,ekspəː'tiːz] *n* adresse *f*.
expire [ik'spaiə] *v* expirer. **expiry** *n* expiration *f*.
explain [ik'splein] *v* expliquer. **explanation** *n* explication *f*. **explanatory** *adj* explicatif.
expletive [ek'spliːtiv] *n* (*oath*) juron *m*; exclamation *f*.
explicit [ik'splisit] *adj* explicite.
explode [ik'sploud] *v* (faire) exploser. **explosion** *n* explosion *f*. **explosive** *nm, adj* explosif.
exploit ['exploit; *v* ik'sploit] *n* exploit *m*. *v* exploiter. **exploitation** *n* exploitation *f*.
explore [ik'sploː] *v* explorer. **exploration** *n* exploration *f*. **explorer** *n* explorateur, -trice *m, f*.
exponent [ik'spounənt] *n* interprète *m*.
export [ik'spoːt; *n* 'ekspoːt] *v* exporter. *n* exportation *f*. **exporter** *n* (*person*) exportateur, -trice *m, f*; (*country*) pays exportateur *m*.
expose [ik'spouz] *v* exposer; révéler; (*uncover*) découvrir. **exposure** *n* exposition *f*; (*phot*) pose *f*. **die of exposure** mourir de froid.
express [ik'spres] *v* exprimer. *n* (*train*) rapide *m*. *adj, adv* exprès. **expression** *n* expression *f*. **expressive** *adj* expressif.
expulsion [ik'spʌlʃən] *n* expulsion *f*; (*school*) renvoi *m*.
exquisite ['ekswizit] *adj* exquis.
extend [ik'stend] *v* (s')étendre; (se) prolonger. **extension** *n* prolongation *f*; (*flex, etc.*) rallonge *f*; (*to house*) agrandissements *m pl*; (*phone*) poste *m*. **extensive** *adj* étendu; considérable.
extent [ik'stent] *n* étendue *f*, longueur *f*; (*range*) importance *f*; (*degree*) mesure *f*.
exterior [ik'stiəriə] *nm, adj* extérieur, -e.
exterminate [ik'stəːmi,neit] *v* exterminer. **extermination** *n* extermination *f*.
external [ik'stəːnl] *adj* externe, extérieur, -e. **for external use only** pour l'usage externe.
extinct [ik'stiŋkt] *adj* (*species*) disparu; (*volcano*) éteint. **extinction** *n* extinction *f*.
extinguish [ik'stiŋgwiʃ] *v* éteindre; (*hopes*) anéantir. **extinguisher** *n* extincteur *m*.
extort [ik'stoːt] *v* extorquer. **extortion** *n* extorsion *f*. **extortionate** *adj* exorbitant.
extra ['ekstrə] *adj* de plus; supplémentaire; de réserve. *n* supplément *m*; (*theatre, cinema*) figurant, -e *m, f*.

extract [ik'strakt; *n* 'ekstrakt] *v* extraire; (*tooth*) arracher. *n* extrait *m*. **extraction** *n* extraction *f*.
extradite ['ekstrə,dait] *v* extrader. **extradition** *n* extradition *f*.
extramural [,ekstrə'mjuərəl] *adj* (*course*) hors faculté; (*district*) extra-muros.
extraordinary [ik'stroːdənəri] *adj* extraordinaire.
extravagant [ik'stravəgənt] *adj* (*person*) dépensier; (*taste*) dispendieux; (*ideas, dress*) extravagant. **extravagance** *n* prodigalité *f*; (*expensive thing*) folie *f*; extravagance *f*.
extreme [ik'striːm] *nm, adj* extrême. **extremist** *n*(*m*+*f*), *adj* extrémiste. **extremity** *n* extrémité *f*.
extricate ['ekstri,keit] *v* dégager; tirer.
extrovert ['ekstrəvəːt] *n, adj* extraverti, -e.
exuberant [ig'zjuːbərənt] *adj* exubérant. **exuberance** *n* exubérance *f*.
exude [ig'zjuːd] *v* exsuder, suinter.
exult [ig'zʌlt] *v* se réjouir. **exultant** *adj* triomphant. **exultation** *n* exultation *f*.
eye [ai] *n* œil (*pl* yeux) *m*. **as far as the eye can see** à perte de vue. **keep an eye on** surveiller. *v* regarder.
eyeball ['aiboːl] *n* globe oculaire *m*.
eyebrow ['aibrau] *n* sourcil *m*.
eye-catching ['aikatʃiŋ] *adj* accrocheur, -euse.
eyelash ['ailaʃ] *n* cil *m*.
eyelid ['ailid] *n* paupière *f*.
eye shadow *n* fard à paupières *m*.
eyesight ['aisait] *n* vue *f*.
eyesore ['aisoː] *n* horreur *f*.
eyewitness ['ai,witnis] *n* témoin oculaire *m*.

F

fable ['feibl] *n* fable *f*.
fabric ['fabrik] *n* tissu *m*. **fabricate** *v* fabriquer. **fabrication** *n* fabrication *f*.
fabulous ['fabjuləs] *adj* fabuleux; (*coll: wonderful*) formidable.
façade [fə'saːd] *n* façade *f*.
face [feis] *n* visage *m*, figure *f*. **facecloth** *n* gant de toilette *m*. **facelift** *n* lifting *m*. **face pack** masque de beauté *m*. **face-to-face** *nm, adv* face à face. **face value** (*coin*) valeur nominale *f*. **at face value** au pied de la lettre. **in the face of** face à, devant. *v* faire face à; (*building*) donner sur. **face the facts** regarder les choses en face.
facet ['fasit] *n* facette *f*.
facetious [fə'siːʃəs] *adj* facétieux.
facial ['feiʃəl] *adj* facial. *n* soin de visage *m*.
facilitate [fə'sili,teit] *v* faciliter.
facility [fə'siləti] *n* facilité *f*. **facilities** *pl n* installations *f pl*, équipements *m pl*.
facing ['feisiŋ] *n* (*sewing*) revers *m*; (*building*) revêtement *m*.
facsimile [fak'siməli] *n* fac-similé *m*.
fact [fakt] *n* fait *m*; réalité *f*. **as a matter of fact** à vrai dire. **in fact** en fait. **factual** *adj* basé sur les faits.
faction ['fakʃən] *n* faction *f*.
factor ['faktə] *n* facteur *m*.
factory ['faktəri] *n* usine *f*; (*smaller*) fabrique *f*.
faculty ['fakəlti] *n* faculté *f*; aptitude *f*.
fad [fad] *n* marotte *f*. **faddy** *adj* capricieux.
fade [feid] *v* (*light*) baisser; (*colour*) passer; (*flower*) se faner; (*sound*) s'affaiblir.
fag [fag] (*coll*) *n* (*cigarette*) sèche *f*; (*boring task*) barbe *f*. **fag end** (*of cigarette*) mégot *m*. **fagged out** claqué.
fail [feil] *v* (not succeed) échouer; (*grow weak*) faiblir, baisser; (*neglect*) manquer (de). *n* échec *m*. **without fail** à coup sûr; inévitablement. **failing** *n* défaut *m*. **failure** *n* échec *m*; (*person*) raté, -e *m, f*; (*breakdown*) panne *f*.
faint [feint] *adj* faible; (*colour*) pâle; (*idea*) vague. **I haven't the faintest idea** je n'en ai pas la moindre idée. *v* s'évanouir. *n* évanouissement *m*.
fair[1] [feə] *adj* juste, équitable; (*average*) passable; (*hair*) blond; (*skin*) clair; (*fine*) beau, belle. **by fair means or foul** par tous les moyens. **fair copy** copie au propre *f*. **fair-sized** *adj* assez grand. **play fair** jouer franc jeu. **fairly** *adv* avec justice; (*reasonably*) assez. **fairness** *n* justice *f*; blondeur *f*.
fair[2] [feə] *n* foire *f*. **fairground** *n* champ de foire *m*.
fairy ['feəri] *n* fée *f*. *adj* féerique. **fairy lights** guirlande électrique *f*. **fairy tale** conte de fées *m*.
faith [feiθ] *n* foi *f*. **have faith in** avoir confiance en. **faithful** *adj* fidèle. **faithfulness** *n* fidelité *f*.

fake [feik] *n* (*picture*) faux *m*; article truqué *m*; (*person*) imposteur *m*. *adj* faux, fausse; (*photo, interview, etc.*) truqué; falsifié. *v* faire un faux de; truquer; falsifier; (*illness*) faire semblant (de).
falcon ['fo:lkən] *n* faucon *m*.
***fall** [fo:l] *v* tomber. **fall apart** tomber en morceaux; (*plans, life, etc.*) se désagréger. **fall back on** avoir recours à. **fall through** échouer. *n* chute *f*; (*US*) automne *m*; (*price, etc.*) baisse *f*.
fallacy ['faləsi] *n* erreur *f*.
fallen ['fo:lən] *V* **fall**.
fallible ['faləbl] *adj* faillible. **fallibility** *n* faillibilité *f*.
fallow ['falou] *adj* (*land*) en jachère; (*idea, etc.*) en friche.
false [fo:ls] *adj* faux, fausse; artificiel. **false alarm** fausse alerte *f*. **false teeth** fausses dents *f pl*. **under false pretences** par des moyens frauduleux. **falsehood** *n* mensonge *m*. **falseness** *n* fausseté *f*. **falsify** *v* falsifier. **falsification** *n* falsification *f*.
falsetto [fo:l'setou] *n* fausset *m*.
falter ['fo:ltə] *v* chanceler; (*voice*) hésiter.
fame [feim] *n* renommée *f*.
familiar [fə'miljə] *adj* familier. **be familiar with** bien connaître. **familiarity** *n* familiarité *f*. **familiarize** *v* familiariser.
family ['faməli] *n* famille *f*. **family allowance** allocations familiales *f pl*. **family planning** planning familial *m*. **family tree** arbre généalogique *m*.
famine ['famin] *n* famine *f*.
famished ['famiʃt] *adj* affamé. **be famished** (*coll*) avoir une faim de loup.
famous ['feiməs] *adj* célèbre; (*coll: excellent*) fameux.
fan[1] [fan] *n* ventilateur *m*; (*hand-held*) éventail *m*. **fan belt** courroie de ventilateur *f*. **fan heater** radiateur soufflant *m*. *v* éventer.
fan[2] [fan] *n* fan *m, f*, passionné, -e *m, f*, admirateur, -trice *m, f*. **fan club** club de fans *m*.
fanatic [fə'natik] *n* fanatique *m, f*. **fanatical** *adj* fanatique.
fancy ['fansi] *n* caprice *m*; (*desire*) envie *f*; imagination *f*. *v* (*imagine*) se figurer, croire; avoir envie de. **fancy oneself** se gober. *adj* de fantaisie. **fancy dress** travesti *m*. **fanciful** *adj* imaginaire; fantasque, bizarre.
fanfare ['fanfeə] *n* fanfare *f*.
fang [faŋ] *n* (*dog*) croc *m*; (*snake*) crochet *m*.
fantastic [fan'tastik] *adj* fantastique.
fantasy ['fantəsi] *n* fantaisie *f*.
far [fa:] *adv* loin; (*much*) beaucoup. *adj* lointain; (*opposite*) autre. **as far as** jusqu'à, autant que. **far and wide** partout. **far away** *adv* au loin. **faraway** *adj* lointain. **Far East** Extrême Orient *m*. **far-fetched** *adj* tiré par les cheveux. **far-off** *adj* eloigné. **far-reaching** *adj* d'une grande portée. **so far so good** jusqu'ici ça va.
farce [fa:s] *n* farce *f*. **farcical** *adj* risible, grotesque.
fare [feə] *n* prix du billet *m*. **fare stage** section *f*.
farewell [feə'wel] *nm, interj* adieu.
farm [fa:m] *n* ferme *f*. **farmhouse** *n* ferme *f*. **farmland** *n* terres cultivées *f pl*. **farmyard** *n* cour de ferme *f*. *v* cultiver; être fermier. **farmer** *n* fermier *m*. **farmer's wife** fermière *f*. **farming** *n* agriculture *f*.
fart [fa:t] (*vulgar*) *n* pet *m*. *v* péter.
farther ['fa:ðə] *adv* plus loin. *adj* plus lointain.
farthest ['fa:ðist] *adv* le plus loin. *adj* le plus lointain.
farthing ['fa:ðiŋ] *n* sou *m*.
fascinate ['fasineit] *v* fasciner. **fascination** *n* fascination *f*.
fascism ['faʃizəm] *n* fascisme *m*. **fascist** *n*(*m*+*f*), *adj* fasciste.
fashion ['faʃən] *n* mode *f*; (*manner*) façon *f*. **after a fashion** tant bien que mal. **fashion show** présentation de collections *f*. **in fashion** à la mode. *v* façonner. **fashionable** *adj* à la mode.
fast[1] [fa:st] *adj* rapide; (*colour*) bon teint *invar*. **be fast** (*clock, etc.*) avancer. *adv* vite; (*securely*) ferme. **fast asleep** profondément endormi.
fast[2] [fa:st] *v* jeûner. *n* jeûne *m*.
fasten ['fa:sn] *v* (s')attacher; (*close*) (se) fermer. **fastener** *or* **fastening** *n* attache *f*; fermeture *f*.
fastidious [fa'stidiəs] *adj* méticuleux, exigeant.
fat [fat] *n* graisse *f*; (*on meat*) gras *m*. *adj* gros, grosse; gras, grasse. **get fat** grossir. **fatten** *v* engraisser. **fattening** *adj* (*food*) qui fait grossir.
fatal ['feitl] *adj* fatal, mortel. **fatality** *n* mort *m*; accident mortel *m*.

fate [feit] *n* sort *m*. **fated** *adj* destiné; (*condemned*) voué au malheur. **fateful** *adj* fatal.
father ['faːðə] *n* père *m*. **Father Christmas** le père Noël. **father-in-law** *n* beau-père *m*. **fatherland** *n* patrie *f*. *v* engendrer. **fatherhood** *n* paternité *f*. **fatherly** *adj* paternel.
fathom ['faðəm] *n* brasse *f*. *v* **fathom out** sonder.
fatigue [fə'tiːg] *n* fatigue *f*. *v* fatiguer.
fatuous ['fatjuəs] *adj* imbécile, stupide.
fault [foːlt] *n* (*failing*) défaut *m*; (*blame*) faute *f*. **at fault** fautif. **faultless** *adj* impeccable; irréprochable. **faulty** *adj* défectueux.
fauna ['foːnə] *n* faune *f*.
favour ['feivə] *n* faveur *f*; service *m*; avantage *m*. **be in favour of** être partisan de. *v* favoriser; préférer. **favourable** *adj* favorable; (*wind, etc.*) propice. **favourite** *n, adj* favori, -ite.
fawn [foːn] *n* faon *m*. *adj* fauve.
fear [fiə] *n* peur *f*, crainte *f*. *v* craindre. **fearful** *adj* (*terrible*) affreux; (*frightened*) peureux. **fearless** *adj* intrépide.
feasible ['fiːzəbl] *adj* faisable; plausible. **feasibility** *n* possibilité *f*; plausibilité *f*.
feast [fiːst] *n* festin *m*; (*rel*) fête *f*.
feat [fiːt] *n* exploit *m*.
feather ['feðə] *n* plume *f*. **feather bed** lit de plume *m*. **feathery** *adj* plumeux.
feature ['fiːtʃə] *n* trait *m*, caractéristique *f*; specialité *f*. **feature film** grand film *m*. *v* (faire) figurer; (*make prominent*) mettre en vedette.
February ['februəri] *n* février *m*.
fed [fed] *V* **feed**.
federal ['fedərəl] *nm, adj* fédéral.
federate ['fedəˌreit] *v* (se) fédérer. *adj* fédéré. **federation** *n* fédération *f*.
fee [fiː] *n* droits *m pl*, frais *m pl*; (*doctor, etc.*) honoraires *m pl*.
feeble ['fiːbl] *adj* faible; (*excuse*) pauvre. **feebleness** *n* faiblesse *f*.
***feed** [fiːd] *v* (se) nourrir; (*machine, fire*) alimenter. **be fed up** (*coll*) en avoir marre. *n* nourriture *f*; (*baby's*) tétée *f*, biberon *m*. **feedback** *n* feed-back *m*.
***feel** [fiːl] *v* (se) sentir; (*touch*) palper; (*think*) avoir l'impression. *n* toucher *m*; sensation *f*. **feeler** *n* antenne *f*. **feeling** *n* sentiment *m*; sensation *f*.
feet [fiːt] *V* **foot**.
feign [fein] *v* feindre, simuler.
feline ['fiːlain] *n, adj* félin, -e.
fell[1] [fel] *V* **fall**.
fell[2] [fel] *v* abattre.
fellow ['felou] *n* compagnon *m*; (*coll*) type *m*; (*of society*) membre *m*. **fellowship** *n* amitié *f*; association *f*.
felony ['feləni] *n* crime *m*. **felon** *n* criminel, -elle *m, f*.
felt[1] [felt] *V* **feel**.
felt[2] [felt] *n* feutre *m*. **felt-tip pen** feutre *m*.
female ['fiːmeil] *adj* femelle, féminin. *n* femelle *f*; (*person*) femme *f*.
feminine ['feminin] *nm, adj* féminin. **femininity** *n* féminité *f*. **feminism** *n* féminisme *m*. **feminist** *n* féministe *m, f*.
fence [fens] *n* clôture *f*; (*horse-racing*) obstacle *m*. *v* clôturer; (*sport*) faire de l'escrime. **fencing** *n* (*sport*) escrime *f*.
fend [fend] *v* **fend for oneself** se débrouiller. **fend off** parer; (*attacker*) repousser.
fender ['fendə] *n* garde-feu *m invar*; (*US*) garde-boue *m invar*.
fennel ['fenl] *n* fenouil *m*.
ferment [fə'ment; *n* 'fəːment] *v* (faire) fermenter. *n* ferment *m*; agitation *f*. **fermentation** *n* fermentation *f*.
fern [fəːn] *n* fougère *f*.
ferocious [fə'rouʃəs] *adj* féroce. **ferocity** *n* férocité *f*.
ferret ['ferit] *n* furet *m*. *v* fureter. **ferret out** dénicher.
ferry ['feri] *n* ferry *m*; (*smaller*) bac *m*. *v* transporter.
fertile ['fəːtail] *adj* (*land*) fertile; (*person*) fécond. **fertility** *n* fertilité *f*; fécondité *f*. **fertilization** *n* fertilisation *f*. **fertilize** *v* fertiliser; féconder. **fertilizer** *n* engrais *m*.
fervent ['fəːvənt] *adj* fervent. **fervour** *n* ferveur *f*.
fester ['festə] *v* suppurer; (*anger, etc.*) couver.
festival ['festəvəl] *n* festival *m*; (*rel*) fête *f*.
festoon [fə'stuːn] *v* festonner. *n* feston *m*.
fetch [fetʃ] *v* aller chercher; (*person*) amener; (*thing*) apporter; (*sell for*) rapporter. **fetching** *adj* ravissant.
fête [feit] *n* fête *f*.
fetid ['fiːtid] *adj* fétide.
fetish ['fetiʃ] *n* fétiche *m*.
fetter ['fetə] *v* entraver. **fetters** *pl n* entraves *f pl*; (*irons*) fers *m pl*.
feud [fjuːd] *n* querelle *f*. *v* se quereller.

feudal ['fjuːdl] *adj* féodal.
fever ['fiːvə] *n* fièvre *f*. **feverish** *adj* fiévreux.
few [fjuː] *nm, adj* peu (de). **a few** quelques; quelques-uns, quelques-unes. **quite a few** pas mal (de). **fewer** *nm, adj* moins (de). **fewest** le moins (de).
fiancé [fi'onsei] *n* fiancé *m*. **fiancée** *n* fiancée *f*.
fiasco [fi'askou] *n* fiasco *m*.
fib [fib] *n* blague *f*. *v* raconter des blagues.
fibre ['faibə] *n* fibre *f*. **fibreglass** *n* fibre de verre *f*.
fickle ['fikl] *adj* inconstant.
fiction ['fikʃən] *n* (*stories*) romans *m pl*; (*invention*) fiction *f*. **fictional** *or* **fictitious** *adj* fictif.
fiddle ['fidl] *n* violon *m*; (*coll: fraud*) combine *f*. *v* jouer du violon; (*coll: cheat*) traficoter; (*coll: falsify*) truquer. **fiddle with** tripoter. **fiddly** *adj* minutieux.
fidelity [fi'deləti] *n* fidélité *f*.
fidget ['fidʒit] *v* se trémousser. **fidgety** *adj* remuant.
field [fiːld] *n* champ *m*; (*sport*) terrain *m*; (*of knowledge, etc.*) domaine *f*. **field glasses** jumelles *f pl*. **field marshal** maréchal *m*. **fieldwork** *n* recherches sur le terrain *f pl*.
fiend [fiːnd] *n* démon *m*; (*coll: enthusiast*) enragé, -e *m, f*. **fiendish** *adj* diabolique.
fierce [fiəs] *adj* féroce; violent; (*struggle*) acharné. **fierceness** *n* férocité *f*; violence *f*; acharnement *m*.
fiery ['faiəri] *adj* ardent, brûlant; (*temper*) violent.
fifteen [fif'tiːn] *nm, adj* quinze. **fifteenth** *n(m+f), adj* quinzième.
fifth [fifθ] *n(m+f), adj* cinquième.
fifty ['fifti] *nm, adj* cinquante. **fifty-fifty** *adj, adv* moitié-moitié, cinquante pour cent. **fiftieth** *n(m+f), adj* cinquantième.
fig [fig] *n* (*fruit*) figue *f*; (*tree*) figuier *m*.
***fight** [fait] *v* se battre, combattre; (*argue*) se disputer. *n* combat *m*; (*struggle*) lutte *f*.
figment ['figmənt] *n* création *f*. **figment of the imagination** invention *f*.
figure ['figə] *n* figure *f*; (*number*) chiffre *m*; (*slimness*) ligne *f*; (*human*) forme *f*. **figurehead** *n* figure de proue *f*; (*derog*) prête-nom *m*. **figure skating** patinage artistique *m*. *v* (*appear*) figurer; (*think*) penser. **figure out** arriver à comprendre. **figurative** *adj* figuré.
filament ['filəmənt] *n* filament *m*.
file[1] [fail] *n* (*folder*) dossier *m*; (*card index*) fichier *m*; (*in office*) classeur *m*. **in single file** à la file. *v* classer; (*claim, etc.*) déposer, intenter. **file past** défiler; passer un à un. **filing** *n* classement *m*. **filing cabinet** classeur *m*. **filing clerk** documentaliste *m, f*.
file[2] [fail] *n* lime *f*. *v* limer. **filings** *pl n* limaille *f sing*.
filial ['filiəl] *adj* filial.
fill [fil] *v* (se) remplir; (*tooth*) plomber. **fill in** (*form*) remplir; (*hole*) boucher. **fill up** (*petrol tank*) faire le plein; (*cup, etc.*) remplir.
fillet ['filit] *n* filet *m*. **fillet steak** tournedos *m*. *v* désosser.
filling ['filiŋ] *n* plombage *m*; (*of pie, etc.*) garniture *f*. *adj* (*food*) substantiel. **filling station** poste d'essence *m*.
film [film] *n* film *m*; (*phot*) pellicule *f*; (*layer*) couche *f*. **film star** vedette *f*. **filmstrip** *n* film fixe *m*. *v* filmer.
filter ['filtə] *n* filtre *m*. **filter paper** papier filtre *m*. **filter-tipped** *adj* à bout filtre. *v* filtrer; purifier.
filth [filθ] *n* saleté *f*. **filthy** *adj* crasseux; (*language*) ordurier.
fin [fin] *n* nageoire *f*.
final ['fainl] *adj* (*last*) dernier; définitif. *n* finale *f*. **finalist** *n* finaliste *m, f*. **finalize** *v* mettre la dernière main à. **finally** *adv* enfin, finalement.
finance [fai'nans] *n* finance *f*. *v* financer. **financial** *adj* financier. **financial year** année budgétaire *f*. **financier** *n* financier *m*.
finch [fintʃ] *n* fringillidé *m*.
***find** [faind] *v* trouver. **find out** se renseigner (sur); découvrir. *n* trouvaille *f*. **findings** *pl n* conclusions *f pl*.
fine[1] [fain] *adj* fin, délicat; (*sunny, excellent*) beau, belle. *adv* bien. **fine arts** beaux arts *m pl*. **finely** *adv* magnifiquement; (*small*) menu. **finery** *n* parure *f*.
fine[2] [fain] *n* amende *f*. *v* **be fined** avoir une amende.
finesse [fi'nes] *n* finesse *f*; (*cards*) impasse *f*.
finger ['fiŋgə] *n* doigt *m*. **finger bowl** rince-doigts *m invar*. **fingermark** *n* trace de doigt *f*. **fingernail** *n* ongle *m*. **finger-**

print *n* empreinte digitale *f.* **fingertip** *n* bout du doigt *m.* *v* toucher.
finish ['finiʃ] *v* finir, (se) terminer. **finishing line** ligne d'arrivée *f.* **finishing touch** touche finale *f.* *n* fin *f*; (*sport*) arrivée *f*; surface *f.*
finite ['fainait] *adj* fini.
Finland ['finlənd] *n* Finlande *f.* **Finn** *n* Finlandais, -e *m, f*; (*Finnish speaker*) Finnois, -e *m, f.* **Finnish** *adj* finlandais; *nm, adj* (*language*) finnois.
fir [fəː] *n* sapin *m.* **fir cone** pomme de pin *f.*
fire ['faiə] *n* feu *m*; (*uncontrolled*) incendie *m.* **set fire to** mettre le feu à. *v* (*enthusiasm, etc.*) enflammer; (*pottery*) cuire; (*gun*) tirer; (*coll*: *dismiss*) vider.
fire alarm *n* avertisseur d'incendie *m.*
firearm ['faiərˌaːm] *n* arme à feu *f.*
fire brigade *n* pompiers *m pl.*
fire door *n* porte anti-incendie *f.*
fire drill *n* exercice anti-incendie *m.*
fire engine *n* pompe à incendie *f.*
fire escape *n* (*stairs*) escalier de secours *m*; (*ladder*) échelle d'incendie *f.*
fire exit *n* sortie de secours *f.*
fire extinguisher *n* extincteur *m.*
fire-guard ['faiəˌgaːd] *n* garde-feu *m invar.*
firelight ['faiəˌlait] *n* lueur du feu *f.*
fireman ['faiəmən] *n* pompier *m.*
fireplace ['faiəˌpleis] *n* cheminée *f.*
fireproof ['faiəˌpruːf] *v* ignifuger. *adj* ignifuge.
fireside ['faiəˌsaid] *n* foyer *m.*
fire station *n* caserne de pompiers *f.*
firewood ['faiəˌwud] *n* bois à brûler *m.*
firework ['faiəˌwəːk] *n* feu d'artifice *m.*
firing squad *n* peloton d'exécution *m.*
firm[1] [fəːm] *adj* ferme; solide. **firmness** *n* fermeté *f*; solidité *f.*
firm[2] [fəːm] *n* (*comm*) compagnie *f,* firme *f.*
first [fəːst] *n, adj* premier. *adv* d'abord; pour la première fois. **at first** d'abord. **first aid** premiers secours *m pl.* **first-class** *adj* (*ticket*) de première classe; (*mail*) tarif normal. **first floor** premier étage *m.* **first-hand** *adj* de première main. **first name** prénom *m.* **first-rate** *adj* excellent, de premier ordre. **in the first place** en premier lieu.
fiscal ['fiskəl] *adj* fiscal.
fish [fiʃ] *n* poisson *m.* *v* pêcher. **fish out** extirper. **fishy** *adj* (*coll*) louche.
fishbone ['fiʃˌboun] *n* arête *f.*
fish cake *n* croquette de poisson *f.*
fisherman ['fiʃəmən] *n* pêcheur *m.*
fish fingers *pl n* bâtonnets de poisson *m pl.*
fishing ['fiʃiŋ] *n* pêche *f.* **fishing boat** barque de pêche *f.* **fishing line** ligne de pêche *f.* **fishing rod** canne à pêche *f.* **fishing tackle** attirail de pêche *m.* **go fishing** aller à la pêche.
fishmonger ['fiʃˌmʌŋgə] *n* marchand de poisson *m.*
fishpond ['fiʃˌpond] *n* étang à poissons *m.*
fish shop *n* poissonnerie *f.*
fish slice *n* pelle à poisson *f.*
fish tank *n* aquarium *m.*
fission ['fiʃən] *n* fission *f.*
fissure ['fiʃə] *n* fissure *f.*
fist [fist] *n* poing *m.* **fistful** *n* poignée *f.*
fit[1] [fit] *adj* (*suitable*) convenable; (*competent*) capable; (*worthy*) digne; (*healthy*) en bonne santé. *v* (*clothes, etc.*) aller à; ajuster; (*match*) correspondre à; équiper; (faire) entrer. **fitness** *n* santé *f,* forme *f*; aptitudes *f pl.* **fitter** *n* (*tech*) monteur *m*; (*clothes*) essayeur, -euse *m, f.* **fitting** *adj* approprié. **fitting room** salon d'essayage *m.* **fittings** *pl n* installations *f pl.*
fit[2] [fit] *n* accès *m,* crise *f.* **fitful** *adj* intermittent; (*sleep*) troublé.
five [faiv] *nm, adj* cinq.
fix [fiks] *v* fixer; arranger; réparer. *n* (*coll*) embêtement *m*; (*slang*: *drugs*) piqûre *f.*
fixation *n* fixation *f.* **fixed** *adj* fixe. **fixture** *n* installation *f*; (*sport*) épreuve *f.*
fizz [fiz] *v* pétiller. *n* pétillement *m.* **fizzy** *adj* pétillant.
flabbergasted ['flabeˌgaːstid] *adj* (*coll*) sidéré.
flabby ['flabi] *adj* mou, molle; (*person*) flasque.
flag[1] [flag] *n* drapeau *m*; (*naut*) pavillon *m.* **flagpole** *n* mât *m.* **flagship** *n* vaisseau amiral *m.* *v* **flag down** héler.
flag[2] [flag] *v* languir; (*tire*) s'alanguir; (*interest*) faiblir.
flagon ['flagən] *n* grande bouteille *f*; (*jug*) cruche *f.*
flagrant ['fleigrənt] *adj* flagrant.
flair [fleə] *n* flair *m.*
flake [fleik] *n* (*snow, etc.*) flocon *m*; (*paint, plaster, etc.*) écaille *f.* *v* s'écailler; (*skin*) peler. **flake out** (*coll*) tomber dans les pommes. **flaky** *adj* floconneux; (*pastry*) feuilleté.

flamboyant [flam'boiənt] *adj* flamboyant.
flame [fleim] *n* flamme *f*. **burst into flames** s'enflammer. *v* flamber. **flaming** *adj* ardent; (*slang*) foutu. **flammable** *adj* inflammable.
flamingo [flə'miŋgou] *n* flamant *m*.
flan [flan] *n* tarte *f*.
flank [flaŋk] *n* flanc *m*. *v* flanquer.
flannel ['flanl] *n* (*fabric*) flanelle *f*; (*facecloth*) gant de toilette *m*. **flannels** *pl n* pantalon de flanelle *m sing*. *v* (*slang*) baratiner.
flap [flap] *v* battre; (*sails*) claquer; (*coll*) paniquer. *n* (*envelope, etc.*) rabat *m*; battement *m*; claquement *m*; (*table*) abattant *m*; (*coll*) panique *f*.
flare [fleə] *n* signal lumineux *m*; (*clothes*) évasement *m*. *v* s'enflammer; (*clothes*) (s')évaser. **flare up** (*anger, etc.*) éclater; (*person*) s'emporter; (*fire*) s'embraser.
flash [flaʃ] *n* éclat *m*, éclair *m*; (*phot*) flash *m*. **flashback** *n* flashback *m invar*. **flash bulb** ampoule de flash *f*. **flash cube** cube-flash *m*. **flashlight** *n* (*torch*) lampe électrique *f* *v* (*light*) projeter, (*intermittently*) clignoter; (*sparkle*) étinceler; (*show off*) étaler; (*mot*) faire un appel de phares. **flashy** *adj* tapageur, -euse; tape-à-l'œil *invar*.
flask [flaːsk] *n* flacon *m*; thermos ® *m*.
flat[1] [flat] *adj* plat; (*tyre, battery*) à plat; (*music*) faux, fausse; (*beer*) éventé. *n* (*music*) bémol *m*. **flat-fish** *n* poisson plat *m*. **flat-footed** *adj* aux pieds plats. **flat rate** taux fixe *m*. **go flat out** (*car*) être à sa vitesse de pointe. **work flat out** travailler d'arrache-pied. **flatly** *adv* carrément, catégoriquement. **flatten** *v* (s')aplatir; (*smooth*) (s')aplanir.
flat[2] [flat] *n* appartement *m*. **flatlet** *n* studio *m*.
flatter ['flatə] *v* flatter. **flatterer** *n* flatteur, -euse *m, f*. **flattering** *adj* flatteur, -euse. **flattery** *n* flatterie *f*.
flatulence ['flatjuləns] *n* flatulence *f*.
flaunt [floːnt] *v* étaler, faire étalage de. **flaunt oneself** poser.
flautist ['floːtist] *n* flûtiste *m, f*.
flavour ['fleivə] *n* goût *m*; (*ice-cream, etc.*) parfum *m*. *v* parfumer; assaisonner. **flavouring** *n* parfum *m*; assaisonnement *m*.
flaw [floː] *n* défaut *m*. **flawed** *adj* imparfait. **flawless** *adj* parfait.
flax [flaks] *n* lin *m*. **flaxen** *adj* de lin.
flea [fliː] *n* puce *f*.
fleck [flek] *n* (*colour*) moucheture *f*; particule *f*. *v* moucheter.
fled [fled] *V* **flee**.
***flee** [fliː] *v* fuir; s'enfuir (de).
fleece [fliːs] *n* toison *f*. *v* (*coll*) tondre. **fleecy** *adj* (*cloud*) floconneux; (*woolly*) laineux.
fleet [fliːt] *n* flotte *f*.
fleeting ['fliːtiŋ] *adj* fugace, passager.
Flemish ['flemiʃ] *nm, adj* flamand. **the Flemish** les Flamands *m pl*.
flesh [fleʃ] *n* chair *f*. **flesh-coloured** *adj* couleur chair *invar*. **in the flesh** en chair et en os. **fleshy** *adj* charnu.
flew [fluː] *V* **fly**[1].
flex [fleks] *n* fil souple *m*; (*telephone*) cordon *m*. *v* fléchir; (*muscles*) tendre. **flexibility** *n* flexibilité *f*. **flexible** *adj* flexible, souple.
flick [flik] *v* donner un petit coup à. **flick through** (*book*) feuilleter. *n* petit coup *m*; (*with finger*) chiquenaude *f*. **the flicks** (*coll*) le ciné *m*.
flicker ['flikə] *v* danser, trembloter. *n* vacillement *m*; (*of hope, etc.*) lueur *f*.
flight[1] [flait] *n* (*of bird, etc.*) vol *m*; (*of stairs*) escalier *m*. **flight path** trajectoire *f*.
flight[2] [flait] *n* (*fleeing*) fuite *f*.
flimsy ['flimzi] *adj* peu solide; (*cloth, paper*) léger, mince; (*excuse*) piètre.
flinch [flintʃ] *v* broncher.
***fling** [fliŋ] *v* lancer, jeter. **have one's fling** se payer du bon temps.
flint [flint] *n* silex *m*.
flip [flip] *v* donner un petit coup à. **flip through** (*book*) feuilleter. *n* petit coup *m*; (*with finger*) chiquenaude *f*. **flipping** *adv* (*coll*) fichu.
flippant ['flipənt] *adj* désinvolte. **flippancy** *n* désinvolture *f*.
flipper ['flipə] *n* (*seal, etc.*) nageoire *f*; (*swimmer's*) palme *f*.
flirt [fləːt] *v* flirter. *n* flirteur, -euse *m, f*. **flirtation** *n* flirt *m*.
flit [flit] *v* voleter. **do a moonlight flit** déménager à la cloche de bois
float [flout] *v* (faire) flotter; (*swimmer*) faire la planche. *n* (*fishing*) flotteur *m*; (*in procession*) char *m*.
flock[1] [flok] *n* (*animals*) troupeau *m*; (*birds*) volée *f*; (*people*) foule *f*. *v* s'attrouper.

flock² [flok] *n* (*wool*) bourre de laine *f*; (*cotton*) bourre de coton *f*.
flog [flog] *v* flageller. **flogging** *n* flagellation *f*; (*law*) fouet *m*.
flood [flʌd] *n* inondation *f*; (*sudden rush*) déluge *m*. **open the floodgates** ouvrir les vannes. *v* inonder; (*river*) (faire) déborder. **flooding** *n* inondation *f*.
***floodlight** ['flʌdˌlait] *v* illuminer; (*sport*) éclairer. *n* projecteur *m*. **floodlighting** *n* illumination *f*; éclairage *m*.
floor [floː] *n* plancher *m*; (*ground*) sol *m*; (*storey*) étage *m*. **floorboard** *n* planche *f*. *v* terrasser; stupéfier.
flop [flop] *n* (*coll*) fiasco *m*. *v* s'effondrer; (*coll*) faire fiasco. **floppy** *adj* flottant; (*hat*) à bords flottants.
flora ['floːrə] *n* flore *f*.
floral [floːrəl] *adj* floral.
florist ['florist] *n* fleuriste *m, f*.
flounce¹ [flauns] *v* **flounce in/out** entrer/sortir dans un mouvement d'humeur. *n* geste impatient *m*.
flounce² [flauns] *n* (*of dress*) volant *m*.
flounder¹ ['flaundə] *v* patauger.
flounder² ['flaundə] *n* flet *m*.
flour ['flauə] *n* farine *f*. **floury** *adj* enfariné; (*potatoes*) farineux.
flourish ['flʌriʃ] *v* prospérer; (*wave*) brandir. *n* fioriture *f*; (*gesture*) moulinet *m*. **flourishing** *adj* florissant.
flout [flaut] *v* se moquer de.
flow [flou] *v* couler; circuler. *n* écoulement *m*; circulation *f*. **flow chart** organigramme *m*. **flowing** *adj* gracieux; (*hair, etc.*) flottant.
flower ['flauə] *n* fleur *f*. **flower arrangement** composition florale *f*. **flower bed** plate-bande *f*. **flowerpot** *n* pot à fleurs *m*. **flower show** floralies *f pl*. *v* fleurir. **flowery** *adj* fleuri.
flown [floun] *V* **fly¹**.
flu [fluː] *n* grippe *f*.
fluctuate ['flʌktjuˌeit] *v* fluctuer, varier. **fluctuating** *n* fluctuation *f*, variation *f*.
flue [fluː] *n* tuyau *m*, conduit *m*.
fluent ['fluənt] *adj* coulant. **fluency** *n* aisance *f*. **fluently** *adv* couramment.
fluff [flʌf] *n* (*on animal, bird*) duvet *m*; (*from fabric*) peluche *f*. *v* (*coll*: *fail*) louper. **fluffy** *adj* duveteux; pelucheux.
fluid ['fluid] *nm, adj* fluide.
fluke [fluːk] *n* coup de chance *m*, hasard extraordinaire *m*.
flung [flʌŋ] *V* **fling**.
fluorescent [fluə'resnt] *adj* fluorescent. **fluorescence** *n* fluorescence *f*.
fluoride ['fluəraid] *n* fluor *m*.
flush¹ [flʌʃ] *n* (*blush*) rougeur *f*; (*burst*) éclat *m*. *v* rougir; (*wash out*) nettoyer à grande eau; (*toilet*) tirer la chasse. **flushed** *adj* rouge.
flush² [flʌʃ] *adj* à ras (de); (*slang*: *rich*) plein de fric.
fluster ['flʌstə] *v* énerver. **get flustered** s'énerver. *n* agitation *f*.
flute [fluːt] *n* flûte *f*.
flutter ['flʌtə] *v* voleter; (*wings*) battre; (*heart*) palpiter. *n* battement *m*; palpitation *f*; agitation *f*.
flux [flʌks] *n* flux *m*. **be in a state of flux** changer sans arrêt.
***fly¹** [flai] *v* voler; (*aeroplane*) piloter; (*kite*) faire voler; (*time*) passer vite; (*flee*) fuir. **fly across** *or* **over** survoler. **fly away** s'envoler. **flyaway** *adj* (*hair*) difficile. **flyleaf** *n* page de garde *f*. **flyover** *n* (*mot*) autopont *m*. **flysheet** *n* feuille volante *f*. **flywheel** *n* (*tech*) volant *m*. *n also* **flies** (*on trousers*) braguette *f*.
fly² [flai] *n* mouche *f*.
foal [foul] *n* poulain *m*.
foam [foum] *n* mousse *f*; (*sea, animal*) écume *f*. **foam rubber** caoutchouc mousse *m*. *v* mousser; écumer. **foamy** *adj* mousseux; écumeux.
focal ['foukəl] *adj* focal. **focal point** foyer *m*; (*of attention*) point central *m*.
focus ['foukəs] *n* foyer *m*; (*of interest*) centre *m*. **in focus** au point. *v* (*phot, etc.*) mettre au point; (*rays*) (faire) converger; concentrer.
fodder ['fodə] *n* fourrage *m*.
foe [fou] *n* ennemi, -e *m, f*.
foetus ['fiːtəs] *n* fœtus *m*. **foetal** *adj* fœtal.
fog [fog] *n* brouillard *m*. **fogbound** *adj* bloqué par le brouillard. **foghorn** *n* corne de brume *f*. **foglamp** *n* (*mot*) phare antibrouillard *m*. **foggy** *adj* brumeux. **it's foggy** il fait du brouillard.
foible ['foibl] *n* marotte *f*.
foil¹ [foil] *v* déjouer.
foil² [foil] *n* feuille de métal *f*; (*cooking*) papier d'aluminium *m*.
foil³ [foil] *n* (*fencing*) fleuret *m*.
foist [foist] *v* refiler.
fold¹ [fould] *n* pli *m*. *v* (se) plier. **fold one's arms** se croiser les bras. **fold up** plier; (*coll*: *collapse*) s'écrouler. **folder** *n*

dossier *m*, chemise *f*. **folding** *adj* pliant. **folding door** porte en accordéon *f*.
fold² [fould] *n* (*sheep*) parc à moutons *m*.
foliage ['fouliidʒ] *n* feuillage *m*.
folk [fouk] *pl n* gens *f pl*. **folk dance** danse folklorique *f*. **folklore** *n* folklore *m*. **folk music** musique folk *f*. **folks** *pl n* (*coll*) famille *f sing*. **folk singer** chanteur, -euse de folk *m*, *f*.
follicle ['folikl] *n* follicule *m*.
follow ['folou] *v* suivre; (*result*) s'ensuivre. **follow up** exploiter; (*faire*) suivre. **follower** *n* disciple *m*.
folly ['foli] *n* folie *f*.
fond [fond] *adj* tendre, affectueux. **be fond of** aimer. **fondness** *n* (*for person*) affection *f*; (*for thing*) prédilection *f*.
fondant ['fondənt] *n* fondant *m*.
fondle ['fondl] *v* caresser.
font [font] *n* fonts baptismaux *m pl*.
food [fuːd] *n* nourriture *f*, aliments *m pl*. **food poisoning** intoxication alimentaire *f*. **foodstuffs** *pl n* aliments *m pl*.
fool [fuːl] *n* imbécile *m*, *f*. **foolproof** *adj* infaillible. *v* (*deceive*) duper. **fool around** faire l'imbécile. **foolhardy** *adj* téméraire. **foolish** *adj* idiot. **foolishly** *adv* bêtement. **foolishness** *n* bêtise *f*.
foolscap ['fuːlskap] *n* papier pot *m*.
foot [fut] *n*, *pl* **feet** pied *m*; (*bird*, *animal*) patte *f*; (*of page*) bas *m*. **get off on the right/wrong foot** être bien/mal parti. **on foot** à pied. **put one's foot in it** mettre les pieds dans le plat.
foot-and-mouth disease *n* fièvre aphteuse *f*.
football ['fut,boːl] *n* (*game*) football *m*; (*ball*) ballon *m*. **footballer** *n* footballeur *m*.
footbridge ['fut,bridʒ] *n* passerelle *f*.
foothold ['fut,hould] *n* prise de pied *f*.
footing ['futiŋ] *n* position *f*; relations *f pl*. **equal footing** pied d'égalité *m*.
footlights ['fut,laits] *pl n* rampe *f sing*.
footnote ['fut,nout] *n* note en bas de la page *f*.
footpath ['fut,paːθ] *n* sentier *m*.
footprint ['fut,print] *n* empreinte du pied *f*.
footstep ['fut,step] *n* pas *m*.
footwear ['fut,weə] *n* chaussures *f pl*.
for [foː] *prep* pour; (*exchange*) contre; (*distance*) pendant. *conj* car.
forage ['foridʒ] *v* fourrager. *n* fourrage *m*.
forbade [fo'bad] *V* **forbid**.
***forbear** [foː'beə] *v* s'abstenir. **forbearance** *n* patience *f*.
***forbid** [fo'bid] *v* défendre, interdire. **forbidding** *adj* menaçant; (*look*) rébarbatif.
forbidden [fo'bidn] *V* **forbid**.
force [foːs] *n* force *f*. **in force** en vigueur. *v* forcer; imposer; (*thrust*) pousser. **force-feed** *v* nourrir de force. **forceful** *adj* énergique, puissant. **forcibly** *adv* de force.
forceps ['foːseps] *pl n* forceps *m sing*.
ford [foːd] *n* gué *m*. *v* passer à gué.
fore [foː] *adj* antérieur, de devant. *n* (*naut*) avant *m*. **come to the fore** se faire remarquer. *adv* à l'avant.
forearm ['foːraːm] *n* avant-bras *m invar*.
forebears ['foːbeəz] *pl n* ancêtres *m pl*.
foreboding [foː'boudiŋ] *n* pressentiment *m*.
***forecast** ['foːkaːst] *n* prévision *f*. **weather forecast** bulletin météorologique *m*. *v* prévoir.
forecourt ['foːkoːt] *n* avant-cour *m*; (*of garage*) devant *m*.
forefathers ['foːfaːðəz] *pl n* ancêtres *m pl*.
forefinger ['foːfiŋgə] *n* index *m*.
forefront ['foːfrʌnt] *n* premier rang *m*.
foregone ['foːgon] *adj* **be a foregone conclusion** être à prévoir.
foreground ['foːgraund] *n* premier plan *m*.
forehand ['foːhand] *n* (*tennis*) coup droit *m*.
forehead ['forid] *n* front *m*.
foreign ['forən] *adj* étranger. **foreigner** *n* étranger, -ère *m*, *f*.
foreleg ['foːleg] *n* jambe antérieure *f*; patte de devant *f*.
foreman ['foːmən] *n* contremaître *m*.
foremost ['foːmoust] *adj* principal. **first and foremost** tout d'abord.
forename ['foːneim] *n* prénom *m*.
forensic [fə'rensik] *adj* (*medicine*) légal; (*evidence*) médico-légal.
forerunner ['foːrʌnə] *n* précurseur *m*.
***foresee** [foː'siː] *v* prévoir. **forseeable** *adj* prévisible.
foreshadow [foː'ʃadou] *v* présager.
foresight ['foːsait] *n* prévoyance *f*.
foreskin ['foːskin] *n* prépuce *m*.
forest ['forist] *n* forêt *f*. **forester** *n* forestier *m*. **forestry** *n* sylviculture *f*. **Forestry Commission** Eaux et Forêts *f pl*.

forestall [fo:'sto:l] *v* devancer, anticiper.
foretaste ['fo:teist] *n* avant-goût *m*.
***foretell** [fo:'tel] *v* prédire.
forethought ['fo:θo:t] *n* prévoyance.
forever [fo:'evə] *adv* toujours.
foreword ['fo:wə:d] *n* avant-propos *m*.
forfeit ['fo:fit] *v* perdre. *n* peine *f*; (*game*) gage *m*.
forgave [fə'geiv] *V* **forgive**.
forge[1] [fo:dʒ] *v* (*counterfeit*) contrefaire; (*metal*) forger. *n* forge *f*. **forger** *n* faussaire *m, f*; (*law*) contrefacteur *m*. **forgery** *n* (*act*) contrefaçon *f*; (*thing forged*) faux *m*.
forge[2] [fo:dʒ] *v* **forge ahead** pousser de l'avant.
***forget** [fə'get] *v* oublier. **forget-me-not** *n* myosotis *m*. **forgetful** *adj* distrait.
***forgive** [fə'giv] *v* pardonner. **forgiveness** *n* pardon *m*; clémence *f*.
forgiven [fə'givn] *V* **forgive**.
***forgo** [fo:'gou] *v* renoncer à.
forgot [fə'got] *V* **forget**.
forgotten [fə'gotn] *V* **forget**.
fork [fo:k] *n* (*cutlery*) fourchette *f*; (*branch*) fourche *f*; (*roads*) embranchement *m*. *v* (*road*) bifurquer. **fork out** (*slang: pay*) allonger. **forked** *adj* fourchu.
forlorn [fə'lo:n] *adj* malheureux; abandonné.
form [fo:m] *n* forme *f*; (*document*) formulaire *m*; (*bench*) banc *m*; (*school*) classe *f*. *v* (se) former. **formation** *n* formation *f*. **formative** *adj* formateur, -trice.
formal ['fo:məl] *adj* (*dress*) de cérémonie; officiel; (*person, manner*) compassé; (*in form only*) formel. **formality** *n* formalité *f*.
format ['fo:mat] *n* format *m*.
former ['fo:mə] *adj* (*previous*) ancien; (*first*) premier. *pron* celui-là, celle-là. **formerly** *adv* autrefois.
formidable ['fo:midəbl] *adj* redoutable.
formula ['fo:mjulə] *n* formule *f*.
formulate ['fo:mju,leit] *v* formuler. **formulation** *n* formulation *f*.
***forsake** [fə'seik] *v* abandonner.
forsaken [fə'seikn] *V* **forsake**.
forsook [fə'suk] *V* **forsake**.
fort [fo:t] *n* fort *m*.
forte ['fo:tei] *n* fort *m*.
forth [fo:θ] *adv* en avant. **and so forth** et ainsi de suite. **forthcoming** *adj* à venir, prochain; (*person*) ouvert. **forthright** *adj* franc, franche. **forthwith** *adv* sur-le-champ.
fortify ['fo:ti,fai] *v* fortifier. **fortification** *n* fortification *f*.
fortitude ['fo:ti,tju:d] *n* courage *m*.
fortnight ['fo:tnait] *n* quinzaine *f*. **fortnightly** *adv* tous les quinze jours.
fortress ['fo:tris] *n* forteresse *f*.
fortuitous [fo:'tju:itəs] *adj* fortuit.
fortunate ['fo:tjunət] *adj* heureux. **be fortunate** avoir de la chance. **fortunately** *adv* heureusement.
fortune ['fo:tʃən] *n* fortune *f*; (*luck*) chance *f*. **fortune-teller** *n* diseur, -euse de bonne aventure *m, f*.
forty ['fo:ti] *nm, adj* quarante. **forty winks** un petit somme. **fortieth** *n(m+f), adj* quarantième.
forum ['fo:rəm] *n* forum *m*; (*meeting*) tribune *f*.
forward ['fo:wəd] *adj* en avant; (*impudent*) effronté. **come forward** se présenter. *v* expédier; (*send on*) faire suivre. **please forward** prière de faire suivre.
forwards ['fo:wədz] *adv* en avant.
fossil ['fosl] *n* fossile *m*. **fossilized** *adj* fossilisé.
foster ['fostə] *v* (*child*) élever; encourager; (*idea*) entretenir.
fought [fo:t] *V* **fight**.
foul [faul] *adj* infect; (*language*) ordurier; (*weather*) sale. **foul play** acte criminel *m*; (*sport*) jeu déloyal *m*. *n* (*sport*) coup défendu. *v* infecter; (*entangle*) (s')emmêler.
found[1] [faund] *V* **find**.
found[2] [faund] *v* fonder. **foundation** *n* fondation *f*; base *f*, fondement *m*. **founder** *n* fondateur, -trice *m, f*.
founder ['faundə] *v* (*ship*) sombrer; (*collapse*) s'effondrer.
foundry ['faundri] *n* fonderie *f*.
fountain ['fauntin] *n* fontaine *f*. **fountain pen** stylo à encre *m*.
four [fo:] *nm, adj* quatre. **foursome** *n* (*game*) partie à quatre *f*; deux couples *m pl*. **on all fours** à quatre pattes. **fourth** *n(m+f), adj* quatrième.
fourteen [fo:'ti:n] *nm, adj* quatorze. **fourteenth** *n(m+f), adj* quatorzième.
fowl [faul] *n* volaille *f*.
fox [foks] *n* renard *m*. **foxglove** *n* digitale *f*. **foxhunting** *n* chasse au renard *f*. **foxtrot** *n* slow *m*. *v* (*coll*) mystifier.
foyer ['foiei] *n* foyer *m*.

fraction ['frakʃən] *n* fraction *f*. **fractionally** *adv* un tout petit peu.
fracture ['fraktʃə] *n* fracture *f*. *v* (se) fracturer.
fragile ['fradʒail] *adj* fragile. **fragility** *n* fragilité *f*.
fragment ['fragmənt] *n* fragment *m*. **fragmented** *adj* morcelé.
fragrant ['freigrənt] *adj* parfumé. **fragrance** *n* parfum *m*.
frail [freil] *adj* frêle, fragile. **frailty** *n* fragilité *f*; (*moral*) faiblesse *f*.
frame [freim] *n* cadre *m*; (*house*) charpente *f*; (*car*) châssis *m*; (*spectacles*) monture *f*; (*film*) image *f*. **frame of mind** humeur *f*. **framework** *n* charpente *f*; structure *f*. *v* encadrer.
franc [fraŋk] *n* franc *m*.
France [frains] *n* France *f*.
franchise ['frantʃaiz] *n* droit de suffrage *m*.
frank [fraŋk] *adj* franc, franche. **frankness** *n* franchise *f*.
frantic ['frantik] *adj* frénétique; (*person*) hors de soi.
fraternal [frə'təːnl] *adj* fraternel. **fraternity** *n* fraternité *f*; (*community*) confrérie *f*. **fraternize** *v* fraterniser.
fraud [froːd] *n* (*law*) fraude *f*; (*deception*) supercherie *f*; (*financial*) escroquerie *f*; (*person*) imposteur *m*. **fraudulent** *adj* frauduleux.
fraught [froːt] *adj* (*tense*) tendu. **fraught with** chargé de.
fray[1] [frei] *v* (s')effilocher; (*cuff*, *etc.*) (s')effranger.
fray[2] [frei] *n* rixe *f*.
freak [friːk] *n* phénomène *m*; anomalie *f*. **freak of nature** accident de la nature *m*. *adj* insolite, inattendu.
freckle ['frekl] *n* tache de son *f*. **freckled** *adj* taché de son.
free [friː] *adj* libre; gratuit. **free-for-all** *n* mêlée générale *f*. **freehand** *adj*, *adv* à main levée. **freehold** *n* propriété foncière libre *f*. **freelance** *n*, *adj* indépendant, -e. **freemason** *n* francmaçon *m*. **freestyle** *n* nage libre *f*. **of one's own free will** de son propre gré. *v* libérer. **freedom** *n* liberté *f*.
freesia ['friːziə] *n* freesia *m*.
***freeze** [friːz] *v* geler; (*food*) congeler; (*prices*, *etc.*) bloquer. *n* gel *m*; blocage *m*. **freezer** *n* congélateur *m*. **freezing** *adj* glacial. **freezing point** point de congélation *m*.
freight [freit] *n* fret *m*; transport *m*; (*goods*) marchandises *f pl*. **freight train** train de marchandises *m*. *v* affréter; transporter. **freighter** *n* (*ship*) cargo *m*; (*aircraft*) avion-cargo *m*.
French [frentʃ] *nm*, adj français. **the French** les Français *m pl*. **French bean** haricot vert *m*. **French dressing** vinaigrette *f*. **French horn** cor d'harmonie *m*. **French-polish** *v* vernir à l'alcool. **French window** *or* *US* **door** porte-fenêtre *f*.
frenzy ['frenzi] *n* frénésie *f*. **frenzied** *adj* frénétique.
frequent ['friːkwənt; *v* fri'kwent] *adj* fréquent. *v* fréquenter. **frequency** *n* fréquence *f*. **frequently** *adv* fréquemment.
fresco ['freskou] *n* fresque *f*.
fresh [freʃ] *adj* frais, fraîche; (*new*) nouveau, -elle. **freshwater** *adj* (*fish*) d'eau douce. **freshen up** faire un brin de toilette. **freshness** *n* fraîcheur *f*.
fret[1] [fret] *v* se tracasser. **fretful** *adj* agité; (*child*) pleurnicheur, -euse.
fret[2] [fret] *v* découper, chantourner. **fretsaw** *n* scie à découper *f*. **fretwork** *n* découpage *m*.
friar ['fraiə] *n* frère *m*, moine *m*.
friction ['frikʃən] *n* friction *f*; désaccord *m*.
Friday ['fraidei] *n* vendredi *m*.
fridge [fridʒ] *n* (*coll*) frigo *m*.
friend [frend] *n* ami, -e *m*, *f*. **make friends with** devenir ami avec. **friendliness** *n* bienveillance *f*. **friendly** *adj* amical; (*kind*) gentil, -ille. **friendship** *n* amitié *f*.
frieze [friːz] *n* frise *f*.
frigate ['frigit] *n* frégate *f*.
fright [frait] *n* effroi *m*, peur *f*. **frighten** *v* effrayer. **be frightened** avoir peur. **frightening** *adj* effrayant. **frightful** *adj* affreux.
frigid ['fridʒid] *adj* glacial; (*manner*) froid; (*woman*) frigide. **frigidity** *n* froideur *f*; frigidité *f*.
frill [fril] *n* (*dress*) ruche *f*; (*shirt*) jabot *m*. **frilly** *adj* à fanfreluches.
fringe [frindʒ] *n* frange *f*; (*edge*) bord *m*. **fringe benefits** avantages supplémentaires *m pl*. *v* franger; border.
frisk [frisk] *v* gambader; (*search*) fouiller. **frisky** *adj* vif.
fritter[1] ['fritə] *v* **fritter away** gaspiller.
fritter[2] ['fritə] *n* (*cookery*) beignet *m*.
frivolity [fri'voliti] *n* frivolité *f*. **frivolous** *adj* frivole.

frizz [friz] *v* (*hair*) friser. **frizzy** *adj* crépu.
fro [frou] *adv* **to and fro** de long en large. **go to and fro between** aller et venir entre.
frock [frok] *n* robe *f*.
frog [frog] *n* grenouille *f*. **frogman** *n* homme-grenouille *m*. **frogs' legs** cuisses de grenouille *f pl*.
frolic ['frolik] *v* folâtrer. *n* ébats *m pl*.
from [from] *prep* de; (*starting from*) à partir de; (*extract*) dans, à.
front [frʌnt] *n* devant *m*, avant *m*; (*mil, weather*) front *m*; (*promenade*) front de mer *m*. **in front of** devant. *adj* de devant, en avant; (*first*) premier. **front view** vue de face *f*. **frontage** *n* façade *f*; (*shop*) devanture *f*.
frontier ['frʌntiə] *n* frontière *f*.
frost [frost] *n* gelée *f*. **frostbite** *n* gelure *f*. *v* geler. **frosted glass** verre dépoli *m*. **frosty** *adj* glacial.
froth [froθ] *n* écume *f*, mousse *f*. *v* écumer, mousser. **frothy** *adj* écumeux, mousseux.
frown [fraun] *n* froncement de sourcils *m*. *v* froncer les sourcils, se renfrogner. **frown on** désapprouver.
froze [frouz] *V* **freeze**.
frozen ['frouzn] *V* **freeze**. *adj* gelé. **frozen food** aliments congelés *m pl*.
frugal ['fruːgəl] *adj* (*meal, etc.*) frugal; (*person*) économe. **frugality** *n* frugalité *f*.
fruit [fruːt] *n* fruit *m*. **fruit cake** cake *m*. **fruit machine** machine à sous *f*. **fruit salad** salade de fruits *f*. **fruitful** *adj* fructueux. **fruition** *n* réalisation *f*. **fruitless** *adj* stérile.
frustrate [frʌ'streit] *v* frustrer; (*plans, etc.*) faire échouer. **frustration** *n* frustration *f*.
fry [frai] *v* (faire) frire. **fried** *adj* frit. **fried egg** œuf sur le plat *m*. **frying** *n* friture *f*. **frying pan** poêle *f*.
fuchsia ['fjuːʃə] *n* fuchsia *m*.
fuck [fʌk] (*vulgar*) *v* baiser. **fuck off!** va te faire foutre!
fudge [fʌdʒ] *n* fondant *m*.
fuel ['fjuəl] *n* combustible *m*; (*mot*) carburant *m*. **fuel gauge** indicateur de niveau de carburant *m*. **fuel pump** pompe à essence *f*. *v* (*stove, etc.*) alimenter; (*aircraft*) (se) ravitailler en combustible.
fugitive ['fjuːdʒitiv] *n, adj* fugitif, -ive.
fulcrum ['fulkrəm] *n* pivot *m*.
fulfil [ful'fil] *v* accomplir; exécuter; satisfaire. **fulfilment** *n* accomplissement *m*; exécution *f*; contentement *m*.
full [ful] *adj* plein; complet, -ète. **full blast** *adv* (*radio, etc.*) à pleines tubes. **full-length** *adj* (*picture*) en pied; (*film*) long métrage. **full moon** pleine lune *f*. **full name** nom et prénoms. **full-scale** *adj* de grande envergure. **full stop** point *m*. **full-time** *adj, adv* à plein temps. **fully** *adv* entièrement.
fumble ['fʌmbl] *v* (*feel*) tâtonner; (*search*) fouiller.
fume [fjuːm] *v* fumer; (*coll: rage*) être furibond. **fumes** *pl n* vapeurs *f pl*.
fun [fʌn] *n* amusement *m*. **for fun** pour rire. **funfair** *n* fête foraine *f*. **have fun** bien s'amuser. **make fun of** se moquer de.
function ['fʌŋkʃən] *n* fonction *f*; réception *f*. *v* fonctionner. **functional** *adj* fonctionnel.
fund [fʌnd] *n* fond *m*, caisse *f*. **funds** *pl n* fonds *m pl*.
fundamental [fʌndə'mentl] *adj* fondamental.
funeral ['fjuːnərəl] *n* enterrement *m*; (*state*) funérailles *f pl*. **funeral parlour** dépôt mortuaire *m*. **funeral service** service funèbre *m*.
fungus ['fʌŋgəs] *n*, *pl* **fungi** champignon *m*.
funnel ['fʌnl] *n* (*pouring*) entonnoir *m*; (*ship*) cheminée *f*.
funny ['fʌni] *adj* drôle; bizarre.
fur [fəː] *n* fourrure *f*; (*kettle*) incrustation *f*. *v* s'incruster. **furrier** *n* fourreur *m*. **furry** *adj* à poil.
furious ['fjuəriəs] *adj* furieux.
furnace ['fəːnis] *n* fourneau *m*.
furnish ['fəːniʃ] *v* (*house, etc.*) meubler; (*supply*) fournir. **furnishings** *pl n* mobilier *m sing*.
furniture ['fəːnitʃə] *n* meubles *m pl*, mobilier *m*.
furrow ['fʌrou] *n* sillon *m*; (*brow*) ride *f*. *v* sillonner; rider.
further ['fəːðə] *adv* (*farther*) plus loin; (*more*) davantage. *adj* (*farther*) plus lointain; additionnel. **further education** enseignement post-scolaire *m*. **furthermore** en outre. **until further notice** jusqu'à nouvel ordre. *v* avancer.
furthest ['fəːðist] *adv* le plus loin. *adj* le plus lointain.
furtive ['fəːtiv] *adj* furtif.

fury ['fjuəri] *n* fureur *f*.
fuse[1] [fjuːz] *v* (*blend*) fusionner; (*melt*) fondre; (*elec*) faire sauter. **fused** *adj* (*plug*) avec fusible incorporé. *n* (*elec*) plomb *m*. **fuse box** boîte à fusibles *f*. **fuse wire** fusible *m*.
fuse[2] [fjuːz] *v* (*bomb*) amorcer. *n* amorce *f*.
fuselage ['fjuːzəˌlaːʒ] *n* fuselage *m*.
fusion ['fjuːʒən] *n* fusion *f*.
fuss [fʌs] *n* façons *f pl*; agitation *f*. **make a fuss** faire des histoires. *v* s'affairer; (*worry*) se tracasser. **fussy** *adj* tatillon, -onne; (*overelaborate*) tarabiscoté.
futile ['fjuːtail] *adj* futile, vain. **futility** *n* futilité *f*.
future ['fjuːtʃə] *n* avenir *m*; (*gramm*) futur *m*. **in future** à l'avenir. *adj* futur, à venir. **futuristic** *adj* futuriste.
fuzz [fʌz] *n* (*hair*) cheveux crépus *m pl*; (*on body*) duvet *m*; (*slang: police*) flicaille *f*. **fuzzy** *adj* crépu; (*photo*) flou.

G

gabble ['gabl] *v* bredouiller. *n* baragouin *m*.
gable ['geibl] *n* pignon *m*.
gadget ['gadʒit] *n* gadget *m*.
gag[1] [gag] *v* bâillonner. *n* bâillon *m*.
gag[2] [gag] (*coll*) *n* (*joke*) plaisanterie *f*. *v* plaisanter.
gaiety ['geiəti] *n* gaieté *f*.
gain [gein] *n* gain *m*, profit *m*. *v* gagner; (*speed, weight*) prendre; (*clock, watch*) avancer.
gait [geit] *n* démarche *f*.
gala ['gaːlə] *n* gala *m*.
galaxy ['galəksi] *n* galaxie *f*.
gale [geil] *n* coup de vent *m*.
gallant ['galənt] *adj* courageux; noble; (*to women*) galant. **gallantry** *n* courage *m*; galanterie *f*.
gall-bladder ['goːlˌbladə] *n* vésicule biliaire *f*.
galleon ['galiən] *n* galion *m*.
gallery ['galəri] *n* galerie *f*; (*spectators*) tribune *f*; (*theatre*) dernier balcon *m*.
galley ['gali] *n* (*ship*) galère *f*; (*kitchen*) cuisine *f*.
gallon ['galən] *n* gallon *m*.
gallop ['galəp] *n* galop *m*. *v* galoper.
gallows ['galouz] *n* gibet *m*.
gallstone ['goːlstoun] *n* calcul biliaire *m*.
galore [gə'loː] *adv* (*coll*) à gogo.
galvanize ['galvənaiz] *v* galvaniser. **galvanize into action** donner le coup de fouet à.
gamble ['gambl] *v* jouer. **gamble on** compter sur. *n* jeu (de hasard) *m*; entreprise risquée *f*. **gambler** *n* joueur, -euse *m, f*. **gambling** *n* jeu *m*.
game [geim] *n* jeu *m*; (*of cards, tennis, etc.*) partie *f*; (*hunting*) gibier *m*. **gamekeeper** *n* garde-chasse *m*. **games** *n* (*school*) sport *m*. *adj* courageux. **be game for** être prêt à.
gammon ['gamən] *n* jambon salé *m*; (*smoked*) jambon fumé *m*.
gang [gaŋ] *n* bande *f*. *v* **gang up on** se liguer contre. **gangster** *n* gangster *m*.
gangrene ['gaŋgriːn] *n* gangrène *f*.
gangway ['gaŋwei] *n* passage *m*; (*naut*) passerelle *f*.
gaol *V* **jail**.
gap [gap] *n* trou *m*, vide *m*.
gape [geip] *v* (*stare*) rester bouche bée; (*open wide*) bâiller. **gaping** *adj* béant.
garage ['garaːdʒ] *n* garage *m*.
garbage ['gaːbidʒ] (*US*) *n* ordures *f pl*. **garbage can** poubelle *f*.
garble ['gaːbl] *v* déformer, embrouiller. **garbled** *adj* confus; incompréhensible.
garden ['gaːdn] *n* jardin *m*. **garden party** garden-party *f*. **gardens** *pl n* parc *m sing*, jardin public *m sing*. **gardener** *n* jardinier, -ère *m, f*. **gardening** *n* jardinage *m*.
gargle ['gaːgl] *v* se gargariser. *n* gargarisme *m*.
gargoyle ['gaːgoil] *n* gargouille *f*.
garland ['gaːlənd] *n* guirlande *f*. *v* enguirlander.
garlic ['gaːlik] *n* ail (*pl* aulx) *m*.
garment ['gaːmənt] *n* vêtement *m*.
garnish ['gaːniʃ] *v* garnir. *n* garniture *f*.
garrison ['garisn] *n* garnison *f*. *v* mettre en garnison.
garter ['gaːtə] *n* jarretière *f*; (*for socks*) fixe-chaussette *m*; (*US*) jarretelle *f*. **garter belt** (*US*) porte-jarretelles *m invar*.
gas [gas] *n* gaz *m*; (*US: petrol*) essence *f*. **gasmask** *n* masque à gaz *m*. **gas ring** (*cooker*) brûleur *m*. **gasworks** *n* usine à gaz *f*. *v* asphyxier. **gaseous** *adj* gazeux. **gassy** *adj* gazeux.

gash [gaʃ] *n* entaille *f.* *v* entailler.
gasket ['gaskit] *n* joint (d'étanchéité) *m.*
gasoline ['gasəˌliːn] *n* (*US*) essence *f.*
gasp [gaːsp] *v* haleter; (*from surprise*) avoir le souffle coupé. *n* halètement *m*; souffle *m.*
gastric ['gastrik] *adj* gastrique. **gastric ulcer** ulcère de l'estomac *m.* **gastroenteritis** *n* gastro-entérite *f.*
gastronomic [gastrə'nomik] *adj* gastronomique. **gastronomy** *n* gastronomie *f.*
gate [geit] *n* (*garden*) porte *f*; (*field*) barrière *f*; (*iron*) grille *f*; (*airport*) sortie *f.* **gatecrash** *v* s'introduire sans invitation. **gateway** *n* porte *f.*
gateau ['gatou] *n* gâteau *m.*
gather ['gaðə] *v* ramasser; (*people*) (se) rassembler; (*sewing*) froncer; (*infer*) déduire. **gathering** *n* rassemblement *m*, réunion *f.*
gaudy ['goːdi] *adj* criard.
gauge [geidʒ] *n* (*instrument*) jauge *f*; (*rail*) écartement *m*; (*measurement*) calibre *m.* *v* jauger, mesurer.
gaunt [goːnt] *adj* décharné; (*face*) creux; (*grim*) lugubre.
gauze [goːz] *n* gaze *f.*
gave [geiv] *V* **give.**
gay [gei] *adj* gai; (*slang*) homo. *n* (*slang*) homosexuel, -elle *m, f.*
gaze [geiz] *n* regard fixe *m.* *v* regarder.
gazelle [gə'zel] *n* gazelle *f.*
gazetteer [gazə'tiə] *n* index géographique *m.*
gear [giə] *n* (*equipment*) matériel *m*; (*belongings*) affaires *f pl*; (*mot*) vitesse *f.* **gearbox** *n* boîte de vitesses *f.* **gear lever** levier de vitesse *m.* **in gear** en prise. *v* adapter; préparer.
geese [giːs] *V* **goose.**
gelatine ['dʒeləˌtiːn] *n* gélatine *f.*
gelignite ['dʒeligˌnait] *n* gélignite *f.*
gem [dʒem] *n* gemme *f*; (*delightful thing*) bijou (*pl* -oux) *m*, perle *f.*
Gemini ['dʒemini] *n* Gémeaux *m pl.*
gender ['dʒendə] *n* genre *m.*
gene [dʒiːn] *n* gène *m.*
genealogy [dʒiːniˌalədʒi] *n* généalogie *f.* **genealogical** *adj* généalogique.
general ['dʒenərəl] *nm, adj* général. **general election** elections législatives *f pl.* **general hospital** centre hospitalier *m.* **general knowledge** connaissances générales *f pl.* **general practitioner** généraliste *m.* **in general** en général. **generalization** *n* généralisation *f.* **generalize** *v* généraliser.
generate ['dʒenəreit] *v* engendrer; produire. **generation** *n* génération *f*; production *f.* **generator** *n* (*elec*) génératrice *f*; (*steam*) générateur *m.*
generic [dʒi'nerik] *adj* générique.
generous ['dʒenərəs] *adj* généreux. **generosity** *n* générosité *f.*
genetic [dʒi'netik] *adj* génétique. **genetics** *n* génétique *f.*
Geneva [dʒi'niːvə] *n* Genève. **Lake Geneva** le lac Léman.
genial ['dʒiːniəl] *adj* cordial.
genital ['dʒenitl] *adj* génital. **genitals** *pl n* organes génitaux *m pl.*
genius ['dʒiːnjəs] *n* génie *m.*
genteel [dʒen'tiːl] *adj* distingué.
gentle ['dʒentl] *adj* doux, douce; (*light*) léger. **gentleman** *n* monsieur (*pl* messieurs) *m*; (*courteous man*) gentleman *m.* **gentleness** *n* douceur *f.*
gentry ['dʒentri] *n* petite noblesse *f.*
gents [dʒents] *n* (*sign*) messieurs *m.*
genuine ['dʒenjuin] *adj* véritable, authentique; sincère.
genus ['dʒiːnəs] *n* genre *m.*
geography [dʒi'ogrəfi] *n* géographie *f.* **geographer** *n* géographe *m, f.* **geographical** *adj* géographique.
geology [dʒi'olədʒi] *n* géologie *f.* **geological** *adj* géologique. **geologist** *n* géologue *m, f.*
geometry [dʒi'omətri] *n* géométrie *f.* **geometrical** *adj* géométrique.
geranium [dʒə'reiniəm] *n* géranium *m.*
geriatric [dʒeri'atrik] *adj* gériatrique. **geriatrics** *n* gériatrie *f.*
germ [dʒəːm] *n* (*med*) microbe *m*; germe *m.*
Germany ['dʒəːməni] *n* Allemagne *f.* **German** *nm, adj* allemand; *n* (*people*) Allemand, -e *m, f.* **German measles** rubéole *f.* **Germanic** *adj* germanique.
germinate ['dʒəːmineit] *v* (faire) germer. **germination** *n* germination *f.*
gerund ['dʒerənd] *n* gérondif *m.*
gesticulate [dʒe'stikjuˌleit] *v* gesticuler. **gesticulation** *n* gesticulation *f.*
gesture ['dʒestʃə] *n* geste *m.* *v* faire signe.
***get** [get] *v* avoir; obtenir; recevoir; (*fetch*) aller chercher; (*go*) aller; (*become*) devenir. **get across** (*cross*) traverser; communiquer. **get at** (*reach*) atteindre; (*tease*) s'en prendre à. **getaway** *n* fuite *f.*

get back (*return*) revenir; (*recover*) retrouver. **get down** descendre. **get down to** se mettre à. **get off** descendre. **get on** continuer; (*horse, etc.*) monter (*sur*); (*agree*) s'accorder. **get out** sortir. **get up** se lever.

geyser ['gi:zə] *n* geyser *m*; (*water-heater*) chauffe-bain *m invar.*

ghastly ['ga:stli] *adj* horrible; (*pale*) blême.

gherkin ['gə:kin] *n* cornichon *m.*

ghetto ['getou] *n* ghetto *m.*

ghost [goust] *n* fantôme *m.* **ghostly** *adj* spectral.

giant ['dʒaiənt] *nm, adj* géant.

gibberish ['dʒibəriʃ] *n* baragouin *m.*

gibe [dʒaib] *n* raillerie *f.* *v* **gibe at** railler.

giblets ['dʒiblits] *pl n* abattis *m pl.*

giddy ['gidi] *adj* (*dizzy*) pris de vertige; (*height*) vertigineux; (*scatterbrained*) étourdi. **giddiness** *n* vertiges *m pl.*

gift [gift] *n* cadeau *m*; (*talent*) don *m.* **gift token** chèque-cadeau *m.* **gifted** *adj* doué.

gigantic [dʒai'gantik] *adj* gigantesque.

giggle ['gigl] *v* rire nerveusement, glousser. *n* gloussement *m.* **get the giggles** avoir le fou rire.

gill [gil] *n* (*fish*) branchie *f*; (*mushroom*) lamelle *f.*

gilt [gilt] *n* dorure *f.* *adj* doré.

gimmick ['gimik] *n* (*coll*) truc *m.*

gin [dʒin] *n* gin *m.*

ginger ['dʒindʒə] *n* gingembre *m.* **gingerbread** *n* pain d'épice *m.* *adj* (*hair*) roux, rousse.

gingerly ['dʒindʒəli] *adv* avec précaution.

gipsy ['dʒipsi] *n* bohémien, -enne *m, f.*

giraffe [dʒi'ra:f] *n* girafe *f.*

girder ['gə:də] *n* poutre *f.*

girdle ['gə:dl] *n* ceinture *f*; (*corset*) gaine *f.* *v* ceindre.

girl [gə:l] *n* fille *f*; (*pupil*) élève *f.* **girlfriend** *n* petite amie *f.* **girlhood** *n* enfance *f.*

girth [gə:θ] *n* (*tree*) circonférence *f*; (*waist, etc.*) tour *m*; (*saddle*) sangle *m.*

gist [dʒist] *n* essentiel *m.*

***give** [giv] *v* donner; offrir; céder. **give-and-take** *n* concessions mutuelles *f pl.* **give away** faire cadeau de; révéler. **give back** rendre. **give in** se rendre. **give off** émettre. **give out** distribuer. **give up** abandonner. **give way** céder; (*collapse*) s'affaisser.

given ['givn] *V* **give.**

glacier ['glasiə] *n* glacier *m.* **glaciation** *n* glaciation *f.*

glad [glad] *adj* heureux. **gladden** *v* réjouir. **gladly** *adv* avec plaisir.

glamour ['glamə] *n* prestige *m*, éclat *m*; (*person*) fascination *f.* **glamorous** *adj* (*life*) brillant; (*person*) séduisant; (*job*) prestigieux; (*dress*) splendide.

glance [gla:ns] *n* coup d'œil *m.* *v* jeter un coup d'œil.

gland [gland] *n* glande *f.* **glandular** *adj* glandulaire. **glandular fever** mononucléose infectieuse *f.*

glare [gleə] *v* lancer un regard furieux; (*light*) éblouir. *n* regard furieux *m*; éblouissement *m.*

glass [gla:s] *n* verre *m.* **glasses** *pl n* lunettes *f pl.* **glassworks** *n* verrerie *f.* **glassy** *adj* vitreux.

glaze [gleiz] *v* (*window*) vitrer; (*pottery, etc.*) vernisser; (*cookery*) glacer. *n* vernis *m*; glaçage *m.* **glazier** *n* vitrier *m.*

gleam [gli:m] *v* luire. *n* lueur *f.* **gleaming** *adj* brillant.

glean [gli:n] *v* glaner.

glee [gli:] *n* joie *f.* **gleeful** *adj* joyeux.

glib [glib] *adj* désinvolte. **glibly** *adv* avec aisance, avec désinvolture.

glide [glaid] *v* (*aero*) planer (*slide*) glisser. *n* vol plané *m*; glissement *m.* **glider** *n* planeur *m.*

glimmer ['glimə] *v* luire faiblement; miroiter. *n* faible lueur *f*; miroitement *m.*

glimpse [glimps] *v* entrevoir. *n* vision rapide *f.*

glint [glint] *v* étinceler. *n* reflet *m.*

glisten ['glisn] *v* briller.

glitter ['glitə] *v* scintiller. *n* scintillement *m.*

gloat [glout] *v* jubiler.

globe [gloub] *n* globe *m.* **globe artichoke** artichaut *m.* **globe-trotter** *n* globe-trotter *m.* **global** *adj* global; universel.

gloom [glu:m] *n* obscurité *f*; mélancolie *f.* **gloomy** *adj* sombre, lugubre.

glory ['glo:ri] *n* gloire *f*; splendeur *f.* **glorify** *v* glorifier. **glorious** *adj* magnifique, glorieux.

gloss [glos] *n* lustre *m*; (*paint*) brillant *m.* **glossy** *adj* brillant, lustré.

glossary ['glosəri] *n* glossaire *m.*

glove [glʌv] *n* gant *m.* **glove compartment** vide-poches *m invar.*

glow [glou] *v* rougeoyer. *n* rougeoiement *m*. **glowing** *adj* rougeoyant; (*words*) chaleureux.
glucose ['gluːkous] *n* glucose *m*.
glue [gluː] *n* colle *f*. *v* coller.
glum [glʌm] *adj* triste.
glut [glʌt] *n* surplus *m*.
glutton ['glʌtən] *n* glouton, -onne *m*, *f*. **gluttonous** *adj* glouton. **gluttony** gloutonnerie *f*.
gnarled [naːld] *adj* noueux.
gnash [naʃ] *v* **gnash one's teeth** grincer les dents.
gnat [nat] *n* moucheron *m*.
gnaw [noː] *v* ronger. **gnawing** *adj* tenaillant.
gnome [noum] *n* gnome *m*.
***go** [gou] *v* aller; (*leave*) partir; (*work*) marcher; (*become*) devenir; (*make sound*) faire. **go away** s'en aller. **go back** retourner. **go-between** *n* intermédiaire *m*, *f*. **go by** passer; (*judge by*) se fonder sur. **go down** descendre; (*temperature, etc.*) baisser. **go in** entrer. **go off** (*food*) se gâter; (*cease to like*) perdre le goût de. **go on** continuer. **go out** sortir. **go up** monter. **go with** (*match*) s'assortir avec. **go without** se passer de. *n* énergie *f*; (*try*) coup *m*. **it's your go** c'est à toi de jouer. **on the go** sur la brèche.
goad [goud] *v* aiguillonner. *n* aiguillon *m*.
goal [goul] *n* but *m*. **goalkeeper** *n* gardien de but *m*. **goal post** montant de but *m*.
goat [gout] *n* chèvre *f*. **act the goat** (*coll*) faire l'imbécile.
gobble ['gobl] *v* engloutir.
goblin ['goblin] *n* lutin *m*.
god [god] *n* dieu *m*. **goddaughter** *n* filleule *f*. **godfather** *n* parrain *m*. **godmother** *n* marraine *f*. **godsend** *n* aubaine *f*. **godson** *n* filleul *m*. **goddess** *n* déesse *f*.
goggles ['goglz] *pl n* lunettes protectrices *f pl*.
gold [gould] *n* or *m*. **goldfinch** *n* chardonneret *m*. **goldfish** *n* poisson rouge *m*. **goldfish bowl** bocal *m*. **gold mine** mine d'or *f*. **goldsmith** *n* orfèvre *m*. **golden** *adj* d'or, doré. **golden opportunity** occasion magnifique *f*. **golden rule** règle d'or *f*. **golden syrup** mélasse raffinée *f*.
golf [golf] *n* golf *m*. **golf course** terrain de golf *m*. **golfer** *n* golfeur, -euse *m*, *f*.
gondola ['gondələ] *n* gondole *f*. **gondolier** *n* gondolier *m*.
gone [gon] *V* **go**.
gong [goŋ] *n* gong *m*.
gonorrhoea [ˌgonə'riə] *n* blennorragie *f*.
good [gud] *adj* bon, bonne; (*person*) brave; (*well-behaved*) sage. **good afternoon** bonjour; (*later*) bonsoir. **goodbye** *interj* au revoir. **good evening** bonsoir. **good-for-nothing** *nm*, *adj* propre à rien. **Good Friday** vendredi saint *m*. **good-looking** *adj* beau, belle. **good morning** bonjour. **goodnight** *interj* bonsoir; (*bedtime*) bonne nuit. **goodwill** *n* bonne volonté *f*; (*comm*) incorporels *m pl*. *n* bien *m*. **be no good** ne servir à rien. **for good** pour de bon. **goodness** *n* bonté *f*.
goods [gudz] *pl n* (*comm*) marchandises *f pl*, articles *m pl*; (*law*) biens *m pl*. **goods train** train de marchandises *m*.
goose [guːs] *n*, *pl* **geese** oie *f*.
gooseberry ['guzbəri] *n* (*fruit*) groseille à maquereau *f*; (*bush*) groseiller *m*. **play gooseberry** tenir la chandelle.
gore [goː] *v* encorner.
gorge [goːdʒ] *n* gorge *f*. *v* se gorger.
gorgeous ['goːdʒəs] *adj* magnifique.
gorilla [gə'rilə] *n* gorille *m*.
gorse [goːs] *n* ajonc *m*.
gory [goːri] *adj* sanglant.
gospel ['gospəl] *n* évangile *m*.
gossip ['gosip] *n* (*chat*) bavardage *m*; (*unkind*) commérage *m*; (*person*) commère *f*. *v* bavarder; (*unkindly*) potiner.
got [got] *V* **get**.
Gothic ['goθik] *adj* gothique.
goulash ['guːlaʃ] *n* goulache *f*.
gourd [guəd] *n* gourde *f*.
gourmet ['guəmei] *n* gourmet *m*.
gout [gaut] *n* goutte *f*.
govern ['gʌvən] *v* gouverner; administrer; déterminer. **governess** *n* gouvernante *f*. **government** *n* gouvernement *m*. **governor** *n* gouverneur *m*; (*school*) administrateur, -trice *m*, *f*; (*coll: boss*) patron *m*.
gown [gaun] *n* robe *f*; (*law, university*) toge *f*.
grab [grab] *v* saisir. *n* mouvement vif pour saisir *m*.
grace [greis] *n* grâce *f*; (*before meal*) bénédicité *m*. **graceful** *adj* gracieux, élégant. **gracious** *adj* gracieux; courtois.
grade [greid] *n* catégorie *f*; échelon *m*; qualité *f*; (*mark*) note *f*. *v* classer.
gradient ['greidiənt] *n* (*measurement*) inclinaison *f*; (*slope*) pente *f*.

gradual ['gradjuəl] *adj* graduel.
graduate ['gradju,eit; *n, adj* 'gradjuət] *v* graduer; (*university*) obtenir sa licence. *n, adj* licencié, -e.
graffiti [grə'fi:ti:] *pl n* graffiti *m pl.*
graft [gra:ft] *n* greffe *f.* *v* greffer.
grain [grein] *n* grain *m*; (*wood*) fibre *f.*
gram [gram] *n* gramme *m.*
grammar ['gramə] *n* grammaire *f.* **grammar school** lycée *m.* **grammatical** *adj* grammatical.
gramophone ['graməfoun] *n* phonographe *f.*
granary ['granəri] *n* grenier *m.*
grand [grand] *adj* magnifique; grandiose. **grandeur** *n* splendeur *f.*
grandchild ['grantʃaild] *n* petit-enfant, petite-enfant *m, f.*
grand-dad ['grandad] *n also* **grandpa** (*coll*) pépé.
granddaughter ['grando:tə] *n* petite-fille *f.*
grandfather ['gran,fa:ðə] *n* grand-père *m.*
grandma ['granma:] *n also* **granny** (*coll*) mémé *f.*
grandmother ['gran,mʌðə] *n* grande-mère *f.*
grandparent ['gran,peərənt] *n* grand-parent *m.*
grand piano *n* piano à queue *m.*
grandson ['gransʌn] *n* petit-fils *m.*
grandstand ['granstand] *n* tribune *f.*
grand total *n* somme globale *f.*
granite ['granit] *n* granit *m.*
grant [gra:nt] *v* accorder; admettre. *n* subvention *f*; (*student*) bourse *f.*
granule ['granju:l] *n* granule *m.* **granulated sugar** sucre semoule *m.*
grape [greip] *n* raisin *m.* **grapevine** *n* vigne *f*; (*coll*) téléphone arabe *f.*
grapefruit ['greipfru:t] *n* pamplemousse *m.*
graph [graf] *n* graphique *f.* **graph paper** papier quadrillé *m*; papier millimétré *m.* **graphic** *adj* graphique; (*description*) vivant.
grapple ['grapl] *v* **grapple with** affronter résolument.
grasp [gra:sp] *v* saisir. *n* prise *f*; compréhension *f.* **grasping** *adj* avare.
grass [gra:s] *n* herbe *f*; (*lawn*) gazon *m.* **grasshopper** *n* sauterelle *f.* **grass snake** couleuvre *f.* **grassy** *adj* herbeux.
grate[1] [greit] *n* grille de foyer *f.* **grating** *n* grille *f.*
grate[2] [greit] *v* (*food*) râper; (*metal*) (faire) grincer. **grater** *n* râpe *f.*
grateful ['greitful] *adj* reconnaissant.
gratify ['grati,fai] *v* satisfaire; faire plaisir à. **gratifying** *adj* agréable.
gratitude ['gratitju:d] *n* reconnaissance *f.*
gratuity [grə'tjuəti] *n* pourboire *m.*
grave[1] [greiv] *n* tombe *f.* **gravedigger** *n* fossoyeur *m.* **gravestone** *n* pierre tombale *f.* **graveyard** *n* cimetière *m.*
grave[2] [greiv] *adj* grave.
gravel ['gravəl] *n* gravier *m.* *v* couvrir de gravier.
gravity ['gravəti] *n* (*physics*) pesanteur *f*; (*seriousness*) gravité *f.*
gravy ['greivi] *n* jus de viande *m*; sauce *f.*
graze[1] [greiz] *v* (*scrape*) écorcher; (*touch*) frôler. *n* écorchure *f.*
graze[2] [greiz] *v* (*animal*) brouter, paître.
grease [gri:s] *n* graisse *f.* **grease-paint** *n* fard gras *m.* **greaseproof paper** papier parcheminé *m.* *v* graisser. **greasy** *adj* graisseux; (*hair, road*) gras, grasse.
great [greit] *adj* grand; magnifique. **Great Britain** Grande-Bretagne *f.* **greatly** *adv* fort, très. **greatness** *n* grandeur *f.*
Greece [gri:s] *n* Grèce *f.* **Greek** *nm, adj* grec, grecque; *n* (*people*) Grec, Grecque *m, f.*
greed [gri:d] *n* avidité *f*; (*for food*) gourmandise *f.* **greedy** *adj* avide; (*for food*) vorace.
green [gri:n] *adj* vert; naïf, naïve; (*bacon*) non fumé. *n* vert *m*; (*grass*) gazon *m.* **greenfly** *n* puceron *m.* **greengage** *n* reine-claude *f.* **greengrocer's** *n* fruiterie *f.* **greenhouse** *n* serre *f*; **green light** feu vert *m.* **greens** *pl n* légumes verts *m pl.* **have green fingers** avoir le pouce vert. **greenery** *n* verdure *f.*
Greenland ['gri:nlənd] *n* Groenland *m.* **Greenlander** *n* Groenlandais, -e *m, f.*
greet [gri:t] *v* saluer, accueillir. **greeting** *n* salutation *f.* **greetings card** carte de vœux *f.*
gregarious [gri'geəriəs] *adj* grégaire.
grenade [grə'neid] *n* grenade *f.*
grew [gru:] *V* **grow.**
grey [grei] *nm, adj* gris. **greyhound** *n* lévrier, levrette *m, f.* **go grey** (*hair*) grisonner.
grid [grid] *n* grille *f*; (*elec*) réseau *m.*
grief [gri:f] *n* chagrin *m.*
grieve [gri:v] *v* (*upset*) peiner; (*sorrow*) s'affliger. **grieve for** pleurer. **grievance** *n*

grief *m*; injustice *f*. **grievous** *adj* affreux; grave. **grievous bodily harm** coups et blessures *m pl*.
grill [gril] *v* (faire) griller. *n* gril *m*; (*meal*) grillade *f*. **grillroom** *n* rôtisserie *f*.
grille [gril] *n* grille *f*.
grim [grim] *adj* sinistre; (*coll*) désagréable. **grimly** *adv* d'un air mécontent.
grimace [gri'meis] *n* grimace *f*. *v* grimacer.
grime [graim] *n* crasse *f*. **grimy** *adj* crasseux.
grin [grin] *n* sourire *m*. *v* sourire.
***grind** [graind] *v* (*coffee, etc.*) moudre; (*crush*) écraser; (*knife*) aiguiser; (*teeth*) grincer. *n* grincement *m*; (*coll*) boulot *m*. **grinder** *n* broyeur *m*, moulin *m*.
grip [grip] *n* (*of hand*) poigne *f*; (*hold*) prise *f*; (*bag*) trousse *f*. *v* saisir; (*hold*) serrer; (*tyres*) adhérer. **gripping** *adj* passionnant.
gripe [graip] *n* colique *f*. *v* (*coll*) rouspéter.
grisly ['grizli] *adj* macabre; horrible.
gristle ['grisl] *n* cartilage *m*. **gristly** *adj* cartilagineux.
grit [grit] *n* sable *m*; gravillon *m*; (*coll*: *courage*) cran *m*. *v* (*teeth*) serrer; (*road*) répandre du gravillon sur.
groan [groun] *n* (*pain*) gémissement *m*; (*dismay*) grognement *m*. *v* gémir; grogner.
grocer ['grousə] *n* épicier, -ère *m*, *f*. **grocer's** *n* (*shop*) épicerie *f*. **groceries** *pl n* provisions *f pl*.
groin [groin] *n* aine *f*.
groom [gruːm] *n* (*for horse*) palefrenier *m*; (*of bride*) marié *m*. *v* (*horse*) panser; préparer.
groove [gruːv] *n* cannelure *f*, rainure *f*; (*record*) sillon *m*. *v* canneler.
grope [group] *v* tâtonner. **grope for** chercher à tâtons.
gross [grous] *adj* (*not net*) brut; flagrant; obèse; (*coarse*) grossier. *n* grosse *f*.
grotesque [grə'tesk] *nm*, *adj* grotesque.
grotto ['grotou] *n* grotte *f*.
ground[1] [graund] *V* **grind**.
ground[2] [graund] *n* terre *f*; (*area*) terrain *m*. **ground floor** rez-de-chaussée *m*. **ground frost** gelée blanche *f*. **grounds** *pl n* parc *m sing*; motifs *m pl*; (*coffee*) marc *m sing*. **groundsheet** *n* tapis de sol *m*. **groundwork** *n* base *f*. *v* (*aircraft*) retenir au sol; fonder; (*ship*) s'échouer. **groundless** *adj* sans fond.
group [gruːp] *n* groupe *m*. *v* (se) grouper.
grouse[1] [graus] *n* grouse *f*.
grouse[2] [graus] (*coll*) *v* rouspéter. *n* grief *m*.
grove [grouv] *n* bocage *m*.
grovel ['grovl] *v* ramper.
***grow** [grou] *v* pousser; grandir; (*become*) devenir; cultiver. **grown-up** *n*(*m*+*f*), *adj* adulte. **growth** *n* croissance *f*; (*thing grown*) pousse *f*; (*med*) grosseur *f*.
growl [graul] *v* grogner. *n* grognement *m*.
grown [groun] *V* **grow**.
grub [grʌb] *n* larve *f*; (*slang*: *food*) bouffe *f*. **grubby** *adj* sale.
grudge [grʌdʒ] *v* donner à contre-cœur. *n* rancune *f*. **bear a grudge against** en vouloir à. **grudgingly** *adv* de mauvaise grâce.
gruelling ['gruəliŋ] *adj* exténuant.
gruesome ['gruːsəm] *adj* horrible.
gruff [grʌf] *adj* bourru.
grumble ['grʌmbl] *v* grommeler. *n* grognement *m*.
grumpy ['grʌmpi] *adj* maussade.
grunt [grʌnt] *v* grogner. *n* grognement *m*.
guarantee [garən'tiː] *n* garantie *f*. *n* garantir. **guarantor** *n* garant, -e *m*, *f*.
guard [gaːd] *n* garde *f*; (*rail*) chef de train *m*. **guard dog** chien de garde *m*. **guard's van** fourgon *m*. *v* garder; défendre. **guarded** *adj* (*remark, etc.*) prudent. **guardian** *n* gardien, -enne *m*, *f*; (*of child*) tuteur, -trice *m*, *f*. **guardian angel** ange gardien *m*.
Guernsey ['gəːnzi] *n* Guernesey *m*.
guerrilla [gə'rilə] *n* guérillero *m*. **guerrilla warfare** guérilla *f*.
guess [ges] *n* conjecture *f*. **at a guess** au jugé. **guesswork** *n* conjecture *f*. *v* deviner; estimer; supposer; (*believe*) croire.
guest [gest] *n* invité, -e *m*, *f*; (*hotel*) client, -e *m*, *f*. **guesthouse** *n* pension de famille *f*. **guest room** chambre d'ami *f*.
guide [gaid] *n* guide *m*; manuel *m*; (*girl*) éclaireuse *f*. **guidebook** *n* guide *m*. **guide dog** chien d'aveugle *m*. *v* guider. **guidance** *n* conseils *m pl*. **guided** *adj* (*missile*) téléguidé. **guided tour** visite guidée *f*.
guild [gild] *n* confrérie *f*; (*craftsmen, etc.*) guilde *f*.
guillotine ['gilətiːn] *n* (*beheading*) guillotine *f*; (*paper*) massicot *m*. *v* guillotiner; massicoter.

guilt [gilt] *n* culpabilité *f*. **guilty** *adj* coupable.
Guinea ['gini] *n* Guinée *f*.
guinea pig *n* cochon d'Inde *m*; (*for experiment*) cobaye *m*.
guitar [gi'taː] *n* guitare *f*. **guitarist** *n* guitariste *m, f*.
gulf [gʌlf] *n* golfe *m*; (*abyss*) gouffre *m*.
gull [gʌl] *n* mouette *f*.
gullet ['gʌlit] *n* œsophage *m*; (*throat*) gosier *m*.
gullible ['gʌləbl] *adj* crédule. **gullibility** *n* crédulité *f*.
gully ['gʌli] *n* ravine *f*.
gulp [gʌlp] *v* avaler; (*food*) engloutir; (*drink*) lamper. *n* (*food*) bouchée *f*; (*drink*) gorgée *f*; (*action*) coup (de gosier) *m*.
gum[1] [gʌm] *n* (*glue*) gomme *f*. **gumboots** *pl n* bottes de caoutchouc *f pl*. *v* gommer.
gum[2] [gʌm] *n* (*mouth*) gencive *f*.
gun [gʌn] *n* pistolet *m*; (*rifle*) fusil *m*. **gunfire** *n* fusillade *f*. **gunman** *n* bandit armé *m*. **gunpowder** *n* poudre à canon *f*. **gunrunning** *n* contrebande d'armes *f*. **gunshot wound** blessure de balle *f*.
gurgle ['gəːgl] *n* gargouillis *m*. *v* gargouiller.
gush [gʌʃ] *v* jaillir. *n* jaillissement *m*. **gushing** *adj* (*person*) trop exubérant.
gust [gʌst] *n* (*wind*) rafale *f*; (*smoke*) bouffée *f*; (*laughter*) éclat *m*. *v* souffler en bourrasque.
gut [gʌt] *n* (*anat*) boyau *m*. **guts** *pl n* (*coll*) cran *m sing*. *v* vider.
gutter ['gʌtə] *n* (*roof*) gouttière *f*; (*street*) caniveau *m*.
guy[1] [gai] *n* (*coll*) type *m*.
guy[2] [gai] *n* (*rope*) corde de tente *f*.
gymnasium [dʒim'neiziəm] *n* gymnase *m*. **gymnast** *n* gymnaste *m, f*. **gymnastic** *adj* gymnastique. **gymnastics** *n* gymnastique *f*.
gynaecology [gainə'kolədʒi] *n* gynécologie *f*. **gynaecological** *adj* gynécologique. **gynaecologist** *n* gynécologue *m, f*.
gypsum ['dʒipsəm] *n* gypse *m*.
gyrate [ˌdʒai'reit] *v* tournoyer. **gyration** *n* giration *f*.
gyroscope ['dʒairəˌskoup] *n* gyroscope *m*.

H

haberdasher ['habədaʃə] *n* mercier, -ère *m, f*. **haberdashery** *n* mercerie *f*.
habit ['habit] *n* habitude *f*; (*clothes*) habit *m*. **habitual** *adj* habituel.
habitable ['habitəbl] *adj* habitable.
habitat ['habitat] *n* habitat *m*.
hack[1] [hak] *v* hacher, tailler. *n* entaille *f*. **hacksaw** *n* scie à métaux *f*.
hack[2] [hak] *n* (*horse*) cheval de selle *m*; (*writer*) nègre *m*.
hackneyed ['haknid] *adj* usé, rebattu.
had [had] *V* **have**.
haddock ['hadək] *n* églefin *m*.
haemorrhage ['heməridʒ] *n* hémorragie *f*.
haemorrhoids ['hemərroidz] *pl n* hémorroïdes *f pl*.
hag [hag] *n* (*coll*) chameau *m*.
haggard ['hagəd] *adj* hagard.
haggle ['hagl] *v* marchander, chicaner. **haggling** *n* marchandage *m*.
Hague [heig] *n* **The Hague** La Haye.
hail[1] [heil] *n* grêle *f*. **hailstone** *n* grêlon *m*. *v* grêler.
hail[2] [heil] *v* saluer; (*taxi*) héler. **hail from** être originaire de.
hair [heə] *n* cheveux *m pl*; (*single strand*) cheveu *m*; (*of body, animal*) poil *m*; (*animal coat*) pelage *m*. **hairy** *adj* velu; (*person*) hirsute.
hairbrush ['heəbrʌʃ] *n* brosse à cheveux *f*.
haircut ['heəkʌt] *n* coupe *f*. **have a haircut** se faire couper les cheveux.
hairdresser ['heəˌdresə] *n* coiffeur, -euse *m, f*. **hairdresser's** *n* salon de coiffure *m*. **hairdressing** *n* coiffure *f*.
hair-dryer ['heəˌdraiə] *n* sèche-cheveux *m*.
hairnet ['heənet] *n* filet à cheveux *m*.
hair-piece ['heəˌpiːs] *n* postiche *m*.
hairpin ['heəpin] *n* épingle à cheveux *f*. **hairpin bend** virage en épingle à cheveux *m*.
hair-raising ['heəˌreiziŋ] *adj* horrifique.
hair spray *n* laque *f*.
hairstyle ['heəstail] *n* coiffure *f*.
Haiti ['heiti] *n* Haïti *f*.
hake [heik] *n* colin *m*.
half [haːf] *n* moitié *f*; demi, -e *m f*. **go halves** se mettre de moitié. **in half** en deux. *adj* demi. *adv* à moitié, à demi.
half-and-half *adv* moitié-moitié.

half-baked [ˌhaːfˈbeikt] (*coll*) *adj* (*idea*) à la noix; (*person*) mal dégrossi.
half-breed [ˈhaːfbriːd] *n* (*person*) métis, -isse *m, f*; (*horse*) demi-sang *m invar*.
half-hearted [ˌhaːfˈhaːtid] *adj* (*person*) sans enthousiasme; (*attempt*) sans conviction.
half-hour [ˌhaːfˈauə] *n* demi-heure *f*.
half-mast [ˌhaːfˈmaːst] *n* **at half-mast** en berne.
half-open [ˌhaːfˈoupən] *adj* entrouvert.
half-price [ˌhaːfˈprais] *adj, adv* demi-tarif; à moitié prix.
half-term [ˌhaːfˈtəːm] *n* congé de demi-trimestre *m*.
half-time [ˌhaːfˈtaim] *adv, adj* à mi-temps.
halfway [ˌhaːfˈwei] *adj* à mi-chemin. **meet halfway** (*compromise*) couper la poire en deux.
half-wit [ˈhaːfwit] *n* idiot, -e *m, f*.
halibut [ˈhalibət] *n* flétan *m*.
hall [hoːl] *n* vestibule *m*; (*room*) salle *f*; (*corridor*) couloir *m*.
hallmark [ˈhoːlmaːk] *n* poinçon *m*; (*of genius, etc.*) sceau *m*. *v* poinçonner.
hallowed [ˈhaloud] *adj* saint, sanctifié.
Halloween [halouˈiːn] *n* veille de la Toussaint *f*.
hallucination [həˌluːsiˈneiʃən] *n* hallucination *f*.
halo [ˈheilou] *n* auréole *f*; (*astron*) halo *m*.
halt [hoːlt] *n* halte *f*. *v* faire halte; (*car, etc.*) faire arrêter; interrompre.
halter [ˈhoːltə] *n* licou *m*.
halve [haːv] *v* diviser en deux; réduire de moitié.
ham [ham] *n* jambon *m*.
hamburger [ˈhambəːgə] *n* hamburger *m*.
hammer [ˈhamə] *n* marteau *m*. *v* marteler. **hammer in** enfoncer. **hammer out** (*disputes, etc.*) démêler.
hammock [ˈhamək] *n* hamac *m*.
hamper[1] [ˈhampə] *v* gêner.
hamper[2] [ˈhampə] *n* panier *m*.
hamster [ˈhamstə] *n* hamster *m*.
hand [hand] *n* main *f*; (*worker*) travailleur, -euse *m, f*; (*clock*) aiguille *f*; (*measure*) paume *f*; (*coll: assistance*) coup de main *m*. **by hand** à la main. **keep one's hand in** garder la main. **on the other hand** par contre. **to hand** sous la main. *v* passer. **hand down** transmettre. **hand in** remettre. **hand over** céder. **handful** *n* poignée *f*.
handbag [ˈhandbag] *n* sac à main *m*.
handbook [ˈhandbuk] *n* manuel *m*; guide *m*.
handbrake [ˈhandbreik] *n* frein à main *m*.
handcuff [ˈhandkʌf] *v* mettre les menottes à. **handcuffs** *pl n* menottes *f pl*.
handicap [ˈhandikap] *n* handicap *m*. *v* handicaper.
handicraft [ˈhandikraːft] *n* artisanat *m*.
handiwork [ˈhandiwəːk] *n* œuvre *f*, ouvrage *m*.
handkerchief [ˈhaŋkətʃif] *n* mouchoir *m*.
handle [ˈhandl] *n* (*broom, etc.*) manche *m*; (*door, drawer*) poignée *f*; (*basket*) anse *f*. *v* manier; (*control*) manœuvrer. **handlebars** *pl n* guidon *m sing*.
handmade [ˌhandˈmeid] *adj* fait main.
hand-out [ˈhandaut] *n* (*leaflet*) prospectus *m*; charité *f*. *v* **hand out** distribuer.
hand-pick [handˈpik] *v* trier sur le volet.
handrail [ˈhandreil] *n* rampe *f*.
handshake [ˈhandʃeik] *n* poignée de main *f*.
handsome [ˈhansəm] *adj* beau, belle.
handstand [ˈhandˌstand] *n* **do a handstand** faire l'arbre droit.
handwriting [ˈhandˌraitiŋ] *n* écriture *f*. **handwritten** *adj* manuscrit.
handy [ˈhandi] *adj* (*useful*) commode; accessible; (*to hand*) sous la main; adroit.
***hang** [haŋ] *v* pendre; (*picture, etc.*) accrocher. **hang around** rôder. **hang fire** traîner en longueur. **hang-gliding** *n* vol libre *m*. **hangman** *n* bourreau *m*. **hang on** (*coll: wait*) attendre; (*hold out*) tenir bon; dépendre de. **hangover** *n* (*slang*) gueule de bois *f*. **hang up** accrocher; (*phone*) raccrocher. **hang-up** *n* (*coll*) complexe *m*. **hanger** *n* cintre *m*.
hangar [ˈhaŋə] *n* hangar *m*.
hanker [ˈhaŋkə] *v* **hanker for** *or* **after** aspirer à. **hankering** *n* envie *f*.
haphazard [ˌhapˈhazəd] *adj* (fait) au petit bonheur.
happen [ˈhapən] *v* arriver, se passer. **happening** *n* événement *m*.
happy [ˈhapi] *adj* heureux. **happy birthday/Christmas!** joyeux anniversaire/Noël! **happy-go-lucky** *adj* insouciant. **happily** *adv* tranquillement; joyeusement. **happiness** *n* bonheur *m*.
harass [ˈharəs] *v* harceler.
harbour [ˈhaːbə] *n* port *m*. *v* héberger; (*hope, suspicions, etc.*) entretenir.

hard [haːd] *adj* dur; difficile. *adv* fort, ferme. **hard-and-fast** *adj* (*rule*) absolu; inflexible. **hardback** *n* livre relié *m*. **hard-boiled** *adj* (*egg*) dur. **hard-hearted** *adj* impitoyable. **hard up** (*coll*) fauché. **hardware** *n* (*ironmongery*) quincaillerie *f*; (*computers*) hardware *m*. **try hard** faire un gros effort. **work hard** travailler dur. **harden** *v* durcir. **hardness** *n* dureté *f*; difficulté *f*. **hardship** *n* épreuves *f pl*; privation *f*.
hardly ['haːdli] *adv* à peine.
hardy ['haːdi] *adj* robuste; (*plant*) résistant au gel; (*bold*) hardi.
hare [heə] *n* lièvre *m*. **hare-brained** *adj* (*person*) écervelé; (*scheme*) insensé. **harelip** *n* bec-de-lièvre *m*.
haricot ['harikou] *n* haricot blanc *m*.
harm [haːm] *n* mal *m*. *v* faire du mal à. **harmful** *adj* nuisible. **harmless** *adj* innocent; pas méchant.
harmonic [haː'monik] *nm*, *adj* harmonique.
harmonica [haː'monikə] *n* harmonica *m*.
harmonize ['haːmənaiz] *v* (s')harmoniser.
harmony ['haːməni] *n* harmonie *f*. **harmonious** *adj* harmonieux.
harness ['haːnis] *n* harnais *m*. *v* harnacher; (*power, etc.*) exploiter.
harp [haːp] *n* harpe *f*. **harpist** *n* harpiste *m*, *f*.
harpoon [haː'puːn] *n* harpon *m*. *v* harponner.
harpsichord ['haːpsiˌkoːd] *n* clavecin *m*.
harrowing ['harouiŋ] *adj* poignant; (*cry*) déchirant.
harsh [haːʃ] *adj* dur; (*texture*) rêche, rugueux; (*sound*) discordant, criard. **harshness** *n* dureté *f*; rugosité *f*; discordance *f*.
harvest ['haːvist] *n* moisson *f*; (*fruit*) récolte *f*; (*grapes*) vendange *f*. *v* moissonner; récolter; vendanger.
has [haz] *V* **have**.
hash [haʃ] *n* (*food*) hachis *m*; (*coll: mess*) gâchis *m*.
hashish ['haʃiːʃ] *n* haschisch *m*.
haste [heist] *n* hâte *f*. **hasten** *v* (se) hâter. **hastily** *adv* en hâte; sans réfléchir. **hasty** *adj* hâtif; rapide.
hat [hat] *n* chapeau *m*.
hatch[1] [hatʃ] *v* (faire) éclore; (*plot*) ourdir.
hatch[2] [hatʃ] *n* (*canteen*) passe-plats *m invar*; (*naut*) écoutille *f*. **hatchback** *adj* (*car*) avec hayon arrière *m*.
hatchet ['hatʃit] *n* hachette *f*.
hate [heit] *v* haïr, détester. *n also* **hatred** haine *f*. **pet hate** (*coll*) bête noire *f*. **hateful** *adj* haïssable, odieux.
haughty ['hoːti] *adj* hautain. **haughtiness** *n* hauteur *f*.
haul [hoːl] *v* traîner; (*naut*) haler. *n* (*fish*) prise *f*; (*stolen goods*) butin *m*. **haulage** *n* (*transport*) roulage *m*; (*naut*) halage *m*.
haunch [hoːntʃ] *n* hanche *f*. **haunches** *pl n* derrière *m sing*.
haunt [hoːnt] *v* hanter. *n* repaire *m*. **haunting** *adj* obsédant.
***have** [hav] *v* avoir; (*meal*) prendre; (*cause to be*) faire. **have on** (*wear*) porter; (*coll: tease*) faire marcher. **have to** devoir, être obligé de.
haven ['heivn] *n* havre *m*.
haversack ['havəsak] *n* havresac *m*, sac à dos *m*.
havoc ['havək] *n* ravages *m pl*. **play havoc with** désorganiser complètement.
hawk [hoːk] *n* faucon *m*.
hawthorn ['hoːθoːn] *n* aubépine *f*.
hay [hei] *n* foin *m*. **go haywire** (*plans*) mal tourner; (*machine*) se détraquer. **hay fever** rhume des foins *m*. **haystack** *n* meule de foin *f*.
hazard ['hazəd] *n* risque *m*; (*chance*) hasard *m*. *v* hasarder, risquer. **hazardous** *adj* hasardeux, risqué.
haze [heiz] *n* brume *f*. **hazy** *adj* brumeux; vague.
hazel ['heizl] *n* noisetier *m*. **hazel-nut** *n* noisette *f*. *adj* (*colour*) noisette *invar*.
he [hiː] *pron* il; (*emphatic*) lui. **he who** celui qui. *n* (*coll*) mâle *m*.
head [hed] *n* tête *f*; (*leader*) chef *m*; (*coin*) face *f*. *adj* principal. *v* se diriger; venir en tête de; intituler. **headed** *adj* (*paper*) à en-tête. **heading** *n* titre *m*. **heady** *adj* capiteux.
headache ['hedeik] *n* mal de tête *m*. **have a headache** avoir mal à la tête.
headfirst [ˌhed'fəːst] *adv* la tête la première.
headlamp ['hedlamp] *n also* **headlight** (*mot*) phare *m*.
headland ['hedlənd] *n* promontoire *m*.
headline ['hedlain] *n* (*newspaper*) manchette *f*; (*news*) grand titre *m*.
headlong ['hedloŋ] *adv* la tête la première; (*rush*) à toute allure.

headmaster [ˌhed'maːstə] *n* directeur *m*. **headmistress** *n* directrice *f*.
head-on *adj*, *adv* de plein fouet.
headphones ['hedfounz] *n* casque *m sing*.
headquarters [ˌhed'kwoːtəz] *n* bureau principal *m*.
headrest ['hedrest] *n* appui-tête *m*.
headscarf ['hedskaːf] *n* foulard *m*.
headstrong ['hedstroŋ] *adj* têtu.
headway ['hedwei] *n* progrès *m*.
heal [hiːl] *v* guérir; (*wound*) (se) cicatriser.
health [helθ] *n* santé *f*. **health foods** aliments naturels *m pl*. **healthy** *adj* sain, en bonne santé; (*appetite*) robuste.
heap [hiːp] *n* tas *m*. *v* entasser, empiler.
***hear** [hiə] *v* entendre. **hear from** avoir des nouvelles de. **hear of** entendre parler de. **hearing** *n* (*sense*) ouïe *f*; audition *f*. **hearing aid** appareil acoustique *m*. **hearsay** *n* ouï-dire *m invar*.
heard [həːd] *V* **hear**.
hearse [həːs] *n* corbillard *m*.
heart [haːt] *n* cœur *m*. **by heart** par cœur. **set one's heart on** vouloir à tout prix. **to one's heart's content** tout son content. **hearten** *v* encourager. **heartless** *adj* cruel. **hearty** *adj* (*welcome, etc.*) chaleureux; (*meal*) copieux.
heart attack *n* crise cardiaque *f*.
heartbeat ['haːtbiːt] *n* battement de cœur *m*.
heart-breaking ['haːtbreikiŋ] *adj* navrant. **heart-broken** *adj* navré.
heartburn ['haːtbəːn] *n* brûlures d'estomac *f pl*.
heart failure *n* arrêt du cœur *m*.
heartfelt ['haːtfelt] *adj* sincère.
hearth [haːθ] *n* foyer *m*. **hearthrug** *n* devant de foyer *m*.
heart-throb ['haːtθrob] *n* (*coll*) idole *f*.
heart-to-heart *adj*, *adv* à cœur ouvert. *n* **have a heart-to-heart** parler à cœur ouvert.
heartwarming ['haːtwoːmiŋ] *adj* réconfortant.
heat [hiːt] *n* chaleur *f*; (*sport*) épreuve éliminatoire *f*. **heatwave** *n* vague de chaleur *f*. *v* chauffer. **heated** *adj* chauffé; (*argument*) passionné. **heater** *n* appareil de chauffage *m*. **heating** *n* chauffage *m*.
heath [hiːθ] *n* lande *f*.
heathen ['hiːðn] *n*, *adj* païen, -enne.
heather ['heðə] *n* bruyère *f*.
heave [hiːv] *v* (*lift*) lever avec effort; (*pull*) tirer avec effort; (*sea*) se soulever; (*sigh*) pousser; (*retch*) avoir des haut-le-cœur. *n* (*sea*) houle *f*; haut-le-cœur *m invar*; effort *m*.
heaven ['hevn] *n* ciel *m*. **heavenly** *adj* céleste; (*excellent*) divin.
heavy ['hevi] *adj* lourd; (*rain*) fort; (*cold*) gros, grosse. **heavyweight** *nm*, *adj* poids lourd. **heaviness** *n* lourdeur *f*.
Hebrew ['hiːbruː] *n* (*people*) Hébreu *m*, (*language*) hébreu *m*. *adj* hébreu, hébraïque.
heckle ['hekl] *v* chahuter; interrompre. **heckler** *n* interrupteur, -trice *m, f*. **heckling** *n* interpellations *f pl*.
hectare ['hektaː] *n* hectare *m*.
hectic ['hektik] *adj* mouvementé, très bousculé.
hedge [hedʒ] *n* haie *f*. *v* entourer d'une haie; (*be evasive*) répondre à côté; (*bet*) couvrir.
hedgehog ['hedʒhog] *n* hérisson *m*.
heed [hiːd] *v* faire attention à. *n* attention *f*. **heedless** *adj* étourdi, insouciant.
heel [hiːl] *n* talon *m*. *v* (*shoe*) remettre un talon à.
hefty ['hefti] *adj* (*person*) costaud; (*heavy*) lourd; (*large*) gros, grosse.
heifer ['hefə] *n* génisse *f*.
height [hait] *n* hauteur *f*; (*person*) taille *f*; (*aircraft*) altitude *f*; (*of success, etc.*) sommet *m*, point culminant *m*. **heighten** *v* augmenter; (*make higher*) relever.
heir [eə] *n* héritier *m*. **heiress** *n* héritière *f*. **heirloom** *n* héritage *m*.
held [held] *V* **hold**¹.
helicopter ['helikoptə] *n* hélicoptère *m*.
hell [hel] *n* enfer *m*. **go to hell!** (*impol*) va te faire voir! **hell for leather** au triple galop. **hellish** *adj* infernal.
hello [hə'lou] *interj* bonjour! (*coll*) salut! (*phone*) allô!
helm [helm] *n* barre *f*. **be at the helm** tenir la barre.
helmet ['helmit] *n* casque *m*.
help [help] *n* aide *f*, secours *m*. *interj* au secours! *v* aider; (*at meal, etc.*) servir; (*prevent oneself from*) s'empêcher de. **can I help you?** (*in shop*) vous désirez? **help yourself!** servez-vous! **it can't be helped!** tant pis! **helper** *n* aide *m, f*. **helpful** *adj* utile, efficace. **helping** *n* portion *f*. **helpless** *adj* impuissant.
Helsinki [hel'siŋki] *n* Helsinki.

hem [hem] *n* ourlet *m.* *v* ourler.
hemisphere ['hemi,sfiə] *n* hémisphère *m.*
hemp [hemp] *n* (*plant*) chanvre *m*; (*drug*) haschish *m.*
hen [hen] *n* poule *f*; femelle *f.* **henhouse** *n* poulailler *m.* **hen party** réunion de femmes *f.* **henpecked** *adj* mené par le bout du nez.
hence [hens] *adv* (*therefore*) d'où; (*from now*) d'ici. **henceforth** *adv* désormais.
henna ['henə] *n* henné *m.*
her [həː] *pron* elle; (*direct object*) la; (*indirect object*) lui. *adj* son, sa; (*pl*) ses.
herald ['herəld] *n* héraut *m.* *v* annoncer. **heraldic** *adj* héraldique. **heraldry** *n* héraldique *f.*
herb [həːb] *n* herbe *f.* **herbal** *adj* d'herbes.
herd [həːd] *n* troupeau *m.* *v* mener. **herd together** s'attrouper.
here [hiə] *adv* ici. **hereafter** *adv* ci-après. **here and now** en ce moment même. **here and there** çà et là. **here goes!** allons-y! **here is/are** voici. **here, there, and everywhere** un peu partout.
hereditary [hi'redətəri] *adj* héréditaire.
heredity [hi'redəti] *n* hérédité *f.*
heresy ['herəsi] *n* hérésie *f.* **heretic** *n* hérétique *m, f.* **heretical** *adj* hérétique.
heritage ['heritidʒ] *n* héritage *m.*
hermit ['həːmit] *n* ermite *m.*
hernia ['həːniə] *n* hernie *f.*
hero ['hiərou] *n* héros *m.* **heroine** *n* héroïne *f.* **hero-worship** *n* culte du héros *m.* **heroic** *adj* héroïque. **heroism** *n* héroïsme *m.*
heroin ['herouin] *n* héroïne *f.*
heron ['herən] *n* héron *m.*
herring ['heriŋ] *n* hareng *m.*
hers [həːz] *pron* le sien, la sienne.
herself [həː'self] *pron* se; (*emphatic*) elle-même. **by herself** toute seule.
hesitate ['heziteit] *v* hésiter. **hesitant** *adj* hésitant. **hesitation** *n* hésitation *f.*
heterosexual [hetərə'sekʃuəl] *n, adj* hétérosexuel, -elle.
hexagon ['heksəgən] *n* hexagone *m.* **hexagonal** *adj* hexagonal.
heyday ['heidei] *n* (*of person*) apogée *m*; (*of thing*) âge d'or *m.*
hiatus [hai'eitəs] *n* lacune *f.*
hibernate ['haibəneit] *v* hiberner. **hibernation** *n* hibernation *f.*
hiccup ['hikʌp] *n* hoquet *m.* **have hiccups** avoir le hoquet. *v* hoqueter.
hid [hid] *V* **hide**[1].
***hide**[1] [haid] *v* (se) cacher. **hide-and-seek** *n* cache-cache *m.* **hide-out** *n* cachette *f.*
hide[2] [haid] *n* peau *f*; (*leather*) cuir *m.*
hidden ['hidn] *V* **hide**[1].
hideous ['hidiəs] *adj* hideux.
hiding[1] ['haidiŋ] *n* **be in hiding** se tenir caché. **go into hiding** se cacher. **hiding place** cachette *f.*
hiding[2] ['haidiŋ] *n* (*beating*) correction *f.*
hierarchy ['haiərɑːki] *n* hiérarchie *f.* **hierarchical** *adj* hiérarchique.
hi-fi ['hai,fai] *n* hi-fi *f invar*; (*system*) chaîne hi-fi *f.*
high [hai] *adj* haut; (*speed*) grand; (*price, etc.*) élevé. *adv* (en) haut. **highly** *adv* (*very*) fort; (*recommend*) chaudement.
highbrow ['haibrau] *n, adj* intellectuel, -elle.
high chair *n* chaise haute *f.*
high-frequency [,hai'friːkwənsi] *adj* de haute fréquence.
high-heeled [,hai'hiːld] *adj* à hauts talons.
high jump *n* saut en hauteur *m.*
highland ['hailənd] *n* région montagneuse *f.* **the Highlands** (*Scotland*) les Highlands *m pl.*
highlight ['hailait] *v* mettre en lumière. *n* (*art*) rehaut *m*; (*hair*) reflet *m*; (*of evening, etc.*) clou *m.*
Highness ['hainis] *n* Altesse *f.*
high-pitched [,hai'pitʃd] *adj* aigu, -uë.
high-rise block *n* tour *f.*
high-speed [,hai'spiːd] *adj* ultra-rapide.
high-spirited [,hai'spiritid] *adj* plein d'entrain. **high spirits** entrain *m.*
high street *n* rue principale *f.*
highway ['haiwei] *n* grande route *f*; voie publique *f.* **highway code** code de la route *m.* **highwayman** *n* voleur de grand chemin *m.*
hijack ['haidʒæk] *v* détourner. *n* détournement *m.*
hike [haik] *n* excursion à pied *f.* *v* excursionner à pied. **hiker** *n* excursionniste à pied *m, f.* **hiking** *n* randonnées à pied *f pl.*
hilarious [hi'leəriəs] *adj* (*merry*) hilare; (*funny*) désopilant. **hilarity** *n* hilarité *f.*
hill [hil] *n* colline *f*; (*slope*) côte *f.* **hillside** *n* flanc de coteau *m.* **hilly** *adj* accidenté.
him [him] *pron* lui; (*direct object*) le.
himself [him'self] *pron* se; (*emphatic*) lui-même. **by himself** tout seul.

hind [haind] *adj* postérieur, -e; de derrière. **hindsight** *n* sagesse rétrospective *f*.
hinder ['hində] *v* gêner, entraver. **hindrance** *n* gêne *f*, entrave *f*.
Hindu [hin'duː] *n* Hindou, -e *m*, *f*. *adj* hindou. **Hinduism** *n* hindouisme *m*.
hinge [hindʒ] *n* charnière *f*; (*door*) gond *m*. *v* **hinge on** dépendre de.
hint [hint] *n* allusion *f*; (*tip*) conseil *m*; (*trace*) nuance *f*. *v* laisser entendre, insinuer.
hip [hip] *n* hanche *f*.
hippopotamus [hipə'potəməs] *n* hippopotame *m*.
hire [haiə] *v* louer; (*person*) engager. **hire out** louer. *n* location *f*; (*boat*) louage *m*. **for hire** à louer. **hire purchase** achat à crédit *m*.
his [hiz] *adj* son, sa; (*pl*) ses. *pron* le sien, la sienne.
hiss [his] *v* siffler. *n* sifflement *m*.
history ['histəri] *n* histoire *f*. **historian** *n* historien, -enne *m*, *f*. **historic** *adj* historique.
***hit** [hit] *n* coup *m*; succès *m*, coup réussi *m*; (*slang: song*) tube *m*. *v* frapper; (*bump*) (se) heurter; (*reach*) atteindre. **hit-or-miss** *adv* au petit bonheur.
hitch [hitʃ] *n* (*obstacle*) anicroche *f*. *v* (*lift*) remonter; (*fasten*) accrocher. **hitch-hike** *v* faire du stop. **hitch-hiker** *n* auto-stoppeur, -euse *m*, *f*. **hitch-hiking** *n* auto-stop *m*.
hitherto [ˌhiðə'tuː] *adv* jusqu'ici.
hive [haiv] *n* ruche *f*.
hoard [hoːd] *n* réserve *f*; trésor *m*. *v* amasser.
hoarding ['hoːdiŋ] *n* (*advertising*) panneau d'affichage *m*; (*fence*) palissade *f*.
hoarse [hoːs] *adj* enroué, rauque. **hoarsely** *adv* d'une voix rauque. **hoarseness** *n* enrouement *m*.
hoax [houks] *n* canular *m*.
hobble ['hobl] *v* clopiner; (*horse*) entraver.
hobby ['hobi] *n* passe-temps *m*.
hock[1] [hok] *n* jarret *m*.
hock[2] [hok] *n* vin du Rhin *m*.
hockey ['hoki] *n* hockey *m*. **hockey stick** crosse de hockey *f*.
hoe [hou] *n* houe *f*. *v* biner.
hog [hog] *n* porc *m*. *v* (*coll*) accaparer, monopoliser.
hoist [hoist] *v* hisser. *n* treuil *m*; (*for goods*) monte-charge *m invar*.
***hold**[1] [hould] *n* prise *f*; influence *f*. **get hold of** saisir. *v* tenir; contenir; (*have*) avoir. **holdall** *n* fourre-tout *m invar*. **hold back** (se) retenir. **hold forth** pérorer. **hold on** (*wait*) attendre; maintenir en place; (*grip*) tenir bon. **hold out** tendre; (*resist*) tenir bon. **hold up** (*raise*) lever; (*support*) soutenir; (*delay*) retarder. **hold-up** *n* retard *m*; (*traffic*) bouchon *m*; (*robbery*) hold-up *m invar*. **holder** *n* (*person*) détenteur, -trice *m*, *f*; (*for object*) support *m*.
hold[2] [hould] *n* (*naut*) cale *f*.
hole [houl] *n* trou *m*; (*rabbit*) terrier *m*. *v* (se) trouer.
holiday ['holədi] *n* vacances *f pl*; (*day off*) jour de congé *m*. **holiday-maker** *n* vacancier, -ère *m*, *f*. **holiday resort** villégiature *f*.
Holland ['holənd] *n* Hollande *f*.
hollow ['holou] *adj*, *adv* creux. *n* creux *m*; (*in ground*) dépression *f*. *v* creuser.
holly ['holi] *n* houx *m*. **hollyhock** *n* rose trémière *f*.
holster ['houlstə] *n* étui de revolver *m*.
holy ['houli] *adj* saint. **holiness** *n* sainteté *f*.
homage ['homidʒ] *n* hommage *m*. **pay homage to** rendre hommage à.
home [houm] *n* maison *f*, foyer *m*. **at home** chez soi. **make oneself at home** faire comme chez soi. *adv* à la maison; (*right in*) à fond. **go home** rentrer. *adj* familial; domestique; (*not foreign*) intérieur, -e, national. **homeless** *adj* sans abri. **homely** *adj* simple, confortable; (*US: ugly*) laid.
home address *n* domicile permanent *m*; adresse personnelle *f*.
homecoming ['houmˌkʌmiŋ] *n* retour *m*.
home-grown [houm'groun] *adj* du jardin.
home help *n* aide ménagère *f*.
homeland ['houmland] *n* patrie *f*.
home-made [houm'meid] *adj* fait à la maison.
Home Office *n* ministère de l'Intérieur *m*.
home rule *n* autonomie *f*.
homesick ['houmsik] *adj* nostalgique. **homesickness** *n* mal du pays *m*; nostalgie *f*.
homework ['houmwəːk] *n* devoirs *m pl*.
homicide ['homisaid] *n* homicide *m*. **homicidal** *adj* homicide.

homogeneous [homə'dʒiːniəs] *adj* homogène.
homosexual [homə'sekʃuəl] *n, adj* homosexuel, -elle. **homosexuality** *n* homosexualité *f.*
honest ['onist] *adj* honnête; sincère; franc, franche. **honesty** *n* honnêteté *f;* sincérité *f.*
honey ['hʌni] *n* miel *m.* **honeycomb** *n* rayon de miel *m.* **honeymoon** *n* lune de miel *f.* **honeysuckle** *n* chèvrefeuille *m.*
honour ['onə] *n* honneur *m.* *v* honorer. **honorary** *adj* honoraire. **honourable** *adj* honorable.
hood [hud] *n* capuchon *m;* (*car roof*) capote *f;* (*US: car bonnet*) capot *m.*
hoof [huːf] *n* sabot *m.*
hook [huk] *n* crochet *m;* (*on dress*) agrafe *f;* (*fishing*) hameçon *m.* *v* accrocher; agrafer; (*fishing*) prendre. **hooked** *adj* crochu.
hooligan ['huːligən] *n* voyou *m.* **hooliganism** *n* vandalisme *m.*
hoop [huːp] *n* cerceau *m;* (*for barrel*) cercle *m.*
hoot [huːt] *v* (*owl*) hululer; (*car*) klaxonner; (*boo*) huer. *n* hululement *m;* coup de klaxon *m;* huée *f.* **hooter** *n* klaxon *m;* (*factory*) sirène *f.*
hop[1] [hop] *v* sauter à cloche-pied; (*jump*) sauter, sautiller. *n* saut *m,* sautillement *m;* (*coll: dance*) sauterie *f.*
hop[2] [hop] *n* (*bot*) houblon *m.*
hope [houp] *n* espoir *m.* *v* espérer. **hopeful** *adj* plein d'espoir; encourageant. **hopeless** *adj* désespéré; (*coll: bad*) nul.
horde [hoːd] *n* horde *f.*
horizon [hə'raizn] *n* horizon *m.*
horizontal [hori'zontl] *adj* horizontal. *n* horizontale *f.*
hormone ['hoːmoun] *n* hormone *f.*
horn [hoːn] *n* corne *f;* (*music*) cor *m;* (*car, etc.*) klaxon *m.*
hornet ['hoːnit] *n* frelon *m.*
horoscope ['horəskoup] *n* horoscope *m.*
horrible ['horibl] *adj* horrible, affreux.
horrid ['horid] *adj* méchant, vilain.
horrify ['horifai] *v* horrifier. **horrific** *adj* horrifique.
horror ['horə] *n* horreur *f.* *adj* (*story, film, etc.*) d'épouvante.
horse [hoːs] *n* cheval *m.*
horseback ['hoːsbak] *n* **on horseback** à cheval.
horse-box ['hoːsboks] *n* fourgon à chevaux *m.*
horse chestnut *n* (*nut*) marron d'Inde *m;* (*tree*) marronnier d'Inde *m.*
horse-drawn ['hoːsdroːn] *adj* à chevaux.
horsefly ['hoːsflai] *n* taon *m.*
horsehair ['hoːsheə] *n* crin *m.*
horseman ['hoːsmən] *n* cavalier *m.*
horsepower ['hoːs,pauə] *n* cheval-vapeur *m.*
horseradish ['hoːs,radiʃ] *n* raifort *m.*
horseshoe ['hoːʃʃuː] *n* fer à cheval *m.*
horsewoman ['hoːs,wumən] *n* cavalière *f.*
horticulture ['hoːtikʌltʃə] *n* horticulture *f.* **horticultural** *adj* horticole.
hose [houz] *n* tuyau *m;* (*mot*) durite *f;* (*stockings*) bas *m pl.* *v* arroser au jet.
hosiery ['houziəri] *n* bas *m pl;* (*business*) bonneterie *f.*
hospitable [hospitəbl] *adj* hospitalier.
hospital ['hospitl] *n* hôpital *m.* **hospitalize** *v* hospitaliser.
hospitality [,hospi'taliti] *n* hospitalité *f.*
host[1] [houst] *n* hôte *m.* **hostess** *n* hôtesse *f.*
host[2] [houst] *n* (*crowd*) foule *f.*
hostage ['hostidʒ] *n* otage *m.*
hostel ['hostəl] *n* foyer *m.* **youth hostel** auberge de jeunesse *f.*
hostile ['hostail] *adj* hostile. **hostility** *n* hostilité *f.*
hot [hot] *adj* chaud; (*curry, etc.*) fort; (*temper*) violent. **be hot** (*person*) avoir chaud; (*weather*) faire chaud. **hot dog** hot-dog *m.* **hot-house** *n* serre *f.* **hotplate** *n* chauffe-plats *m invar.* **hot-tempered** *adj* emporté. **hot-water bottle** bouillotte *f.*
hotel [hou'tel] *n* hôtel *m.*
hound [haund] *n* chien de meute *m.* *v* chasser, s'acharner sur.
hour ['auə] *n* heure *f.* **hourglass** *n* sablier *m.* **hourly** *adj, adv* toutes les heures.
house [haus; *v* hauz] *n* maison *f;* (*theatre*) salle *f.* *v* loger.
houseboat ['hausbout] *n* péniche aménagée *f.*
housebound ['hausbaund] *adj* confiné chez soi.
housecoat ['hauskout] *n* peignoir *m.*
household ['haushould] *n* maison *f,* ménage *m.*
housekeeper ['haus,kiːpə] *n* gouvernante *f.* **housekeeping** *n* (*work*) ménage *m;* (*money*) argent du ménage *m.*

housemaid ['hausmeid] *n* bonne *f*.
house-to-house *adj*, *adv* porte à porte.
house-trained ['haustreind] *adj* propre.
house-warming ['haus͵wo:miŋ] *n* **have a house-warming** (**party**) pendre la crémaillère.
housewife ['hauswaif] *n* ménagère *f*.
housework ['hauswə:k] *n* ménage *m*.
housing ['hauziŋ] *n* logement *m*. **housing estate** cité *f*.
hovel ['hovəl] *n* taudis *m*.
hover ['hovə] *v* planer; (*person*) rôder. **hovercraft** *n* aéroglisseur *m*.
how [hau] *adv* comment, comme. **how are you?** comment allez-vous? **how do you do?** bonjour; (*on introduction*) enchanté. **how much?** combien?
however [hau'evə] *conj* cependant. *adv* de quelque manière que.
howl [haul] *v* hurler. *n* hurlement *m*.
hub [hʌb] *n* moyeu *m*; pivot *m*. **hubcap** *n* (*mot*) enjoliveur *m*.
huddle ['hʌdl] *v* se blottir. *n* petit groupe *m*.
hue [hju:] *n* teinte *f*.
huff [hʌf] *n* **in a huff** froissé.
hug [hʌg] *v* étreindre. *n* étreinte *f*.
huge [hju:dʒ] *adj* énorme.
hulk [hʌlk] *n* épave *f*, carcasse *f*; (*derog: person*) mastodonte *m*. **hulking** *adj* balourd.
hull [hʌl] *n* (*naut*) coque *f*.
hum [hʌm] *v* bourdonner; (*tune*) fredonner; (*engine*) vrombir. *n* bourdonnement *m*; vrombissement *m*. **humming-bird** *n* oiseau-mouche *m*.
human ['hju:mən] *nm*, *adj* humain. **human being** être humain *m*.
humane [hju:'mein] *adj* humain.
humanity [hju:'manəti] *n* humanité *f*. **humanitarian** *n*(*m*+*f*), *adj* humanitaire.
humble ['hʌmbl] *adj* humble. *v* humilier.
humdrum ['hʌmdrʌm] *adj* monotone.
humid ['hju:mid] *adj* humide. **humidity** *n* humidité *f*.
humiliate [hju:'milieit] *v* humilier. **humiliation** *n* humiliation *f*.
humility [hju:'miləti] *n* humilité *f*.
humour ['hju:mə] *n* humour *m*; (*mood*) humeur *f*. *v* ménager. **humorist** *n* humoriste *m*, *f*. **humorous** *adj* humoristique.
hump [hʌmp] *n* bosse *f*. **humpbacked** *adj* (*bridge*) en dos d'âne. *v* arrondir, voûter.
hunch [hʌntʃ] *v* arrondir, voûter. *n* pressentiment *m*. **hunchback** *n* bossu, -e *m*, *f*. **hunchbacked** *adj* bossu.
hundred ['hʌndrəd] *nm*, *adj* cent. **hundreds** *pl n* (*coll*) centaines *f pl*. **hundredth** *n*(*m*+*f*), *adj* centième.
hung [hʌŋ] *V* **hang**.
Hungary ['hʌŋgəri] *n* Hongrie *f*. **Hungarian** *nm*, *adj* hongrois; *n* (*people*) Hongrois, -e *m*, *f*.
hunger ['hʌŋgə] *n* faim *f*. *v* avoir faim. **be hungry** avoir faim. **hungrily** *adv* avidement.
hunt [hʌnt] *n* chasse *f*; (*search*) recherche *f*. *v* chasser; chercher. **hunting** *n* chasse *f*. **huntsman** *n* chasseur *m*.
hurdle ['hə:dl] *n* obstacle *m*; (*sport*) haie *f*.
hurl [hə:l] *v* jeter, précipiter. **hurl abuse** lancer des injures.
hurricane ['hʌrikən] *n* ouragan *m*.
hurry ['hʌri] *n* hâte *f*. **be in a hurry** être pressé. *v* (faire) se dépêcher, (se) presser. **hurried** *adj* précipité, pressé. **hurriedly** *adv* précipitamment.
***hurt** [hə:t] *v* faire mal (à), blesser. *n* mal *m*. *adj* blessé.
husband ['hʌzbənd] *n* mari *m*.
hush [hʌʃ] *n* silence *m*. *interj* chut! *v* faire taire. **hush up** (*news*) étouffer. **hushed** *adj* étouffé.
husk [hʌsk] *n* (*wheat*) balle *f*; (*rice, maize*) enveloppe *f*; (*nut*) écale *f*. *v* (*grain*) vanner; (*rice, maize*) décortiquer; écaler.
husky ['hʌski] *adj* enroué. **huskily** *adv* d'une voix rauque. **huskiness** *n* enrouement *m*.
hussar [hə'za:] *n* hussard *m*.
hustle ['hʌsl] *v* (se) bousculer. *n* bousculade *f*. **hustle and bustle** tourbillon *m*.
hut [hʌt] *n* hutte *f*.
hutch [hʌtʃ] *n* clapier *m*.
hyacinth ['haiəsinθ] *n* jacinthe *f*.
hybrid ['haibrid] *nm*, *adj* hybride.
hydraulic [hai'dro:lik] *adj* hydraulique.
hydrocarbon [͵haidrou'ka:bən] *n* hydrocarbure *m*.
hydro-electric [͵haidroui'lektrik] *adj* hydro-électrique.
hydrofoil ['haidroufoil] *n* hydrofoil *m*.
hydrogen ['haidrədʒən] *n* hydrogène *m*.
hyena [hai'i:nə] *n* hyène *f*.
hygiene ['haidʒi:n] *n* hygiène *f*. **hygienic** *adj* hygiénique.

hymn [him] *n* hymne *f*. **hymn-book** *n* livre de cantiques *m*.
hyphen ['haifən] *n* trait d'union *m*.
hypnosis [hip'nousis] *n* hypnose *f*. **under hypnosis** en état d'hypnose. **hypnotic** *adj* hypnotique. **hypnotism** *n* hypnotisme *m*. **hypnotist** *n* hypnotiseur, -euse *m, f*. **hypnotize** *v* hypnotiser.
hypochondria [haipə'kondriə] *n* hypochondrie *f*. **hypochondriac** *n(m+f)*, *adj* hypochondriaque.
hypocrisy [hi'pokrəsi] *n* hypocrisie *f*. **hypocrite** *n* hypocrite *m, f*. **hypocritical** *adj* hypocrite.
hypodermic [haipə'dəːmik] *adj* hypodermique. *n* seringue hypodermique *f*.
hypothesis [hai'poθəsis] *n*, *pl* **-ses** hypothèse *f*. **hypothetical** *adj* hypothétique.
hysterectomy [histə'rektəmi] *n* hystérectomie *f*.
hysteria [his'tiəriə] *n* hystérie *f*. **hysterical** *adj* hystérique; (*laughter, crying*) convulsif. **hysterics** *pl n* (*crying*) crise de nerfs *f sing*; (*laughter*) crise de rire *f sing*.

I

I [ai] *pron* je; (*emphatic*) moi.
ice [ais] *n* glace *f*; (*on road*) verglas *m*. **iceberg** *n* iceberg *m*. **ice-cold** *adj* glacé. **ice cream** glace *f*. **ice cube** glaçon *m*. **ice rink** patinoire *f*. **ice-skate** *n* patin à glace *m*. **ice-skating** *n* patinage sur glace *m*. *v* (*chill*) rafraîchir; (*cake*) glacer. **ice over** *or* **up** (*lake*) geler; (*windscreen, etc.*) givrer. **iced** *adj* glacé; (*champagne*) frappé; (*melon*) rafraîchi. **icing** *n* glaçage *m*. **icing sugar** sucre glace *m*. **icy** *adj* glacial; (*road*) verglacé.
Iceland ['aislənd] *n* Islande *f*. **Icelander** *n* Islandais, -e *m, f*. **Icelandic** *nm, adj* islandais.
icicle ['aisikl] *n* glaçon *m*.
icon ['aikon] *n* icône *f*.
idea [ai'diə] *n* idée *f*.
ideal [ai'diəl] *nm, adj* idéal. **idealist** *n* idéaliste *m, f*. **idealistic** *adj* idéaliste.
identical [ai'dentikəl] *adj* identique. **identical twins** vrais jumeaux *m pl*, vraies jumelles *f pl*.
identify [ai'dentifai] *v* identifier. **identify with** s'identifier à *or* avec. **identification** *n* identification *f*; (*papers*) pièce d'identité *f*.
identity [ai'dentiti] *n* identité *f*. **identity card** carte d'identité *f*. **identity parade** séance d'identification *f*.
ideology [aidi'olədʒi] *n* idéologie *f*.
idiom ['idiəm] *n* (*expression*) idiotisme *m*; (*language*) idiome *m*. **idiomatic** *adj* idiomatique.
idiosyncrasy [ˌidiə'siŋkrəsi] *n* particularité *f*.
idiot ['idiət] *n* idiot, -e *m, f*. **idiotic** *adj* idiot.
idle ['aidl] *adj* (*doing nothing*) désœuvré; (*lazy*) oisif; (*machine*) en repos; (*talk, etc.*) oiseux. *v* fainéanter; (*engine*) tourner au ralenti. **idleness** *n* désœuvrement *m*; (*laziness*) paresse *f*.
idol ['aidl] *n* idole *f*. **idolatry** *n* idolâtrie *f*. **idolize** *v* idolâtrer.
idyllic [i'dilik] *adj* idyllique.
if [if] *conj* si. **as if** comme si. **if not** sinon. **if so** s'il en est ainsi.
ignite [ig'nait] *v* (*light*) mettre le feu à; (*catch fire*) prendre feu.
ignition [ig'niʃən] *n* ignition *f*; (*mot*) allumage *m*. **ignition key** clef de contact *f*. **ignition switch** contact *m*. **turn on the ignition** mettre le contact.
ignorant ['ignərənt] *adj* ignorant. **ignorance** *n* ignorance *f*.
ignore [ig'noː] *v* (*remark, etc.*) ne pas relever; (*person*) faire semblant de ne pas reconnaître; (*rule*) ne pas respecter.
ill [il] *adj* (*sick*) malade; (*bad*) mauvais. *nm, adv* mal. **ill-at-ease** *adj* mal à l'aise. **ill-bred** *or* **ill-mannered** *adj* mal élevé. **ill-gotten gains** biens mal acquis *m pl*. **ill-treat** *v* maltraiter. **illness** *n* maladie *f*.
illegal [i'liːgəl] *adj* illégal.
illegible [i'ledʒəbl] *adj* illisible.
illegitimate [ˌili'dʒitimit] *adj* illégitime. **illegitimacy** *n* illégitimité *f*.
illicit [i'lisit] *adj* illicite.
illiterate [i'litərit] *n, adj* illettré, -e. **illiteracy** *n* analphabétisme *m*.
illogical [i'lodʒikəl] *adj* illogique.
illuminate [i'luːmiˌneit] *v* éclairer; (*building*) illuminer. **illumination** *n* éclairage *m*; illumination *f*.

illusion [i'luːʒən] *n* illusion *f.*
illustrate ['ilə,streit] *v* illustrer. **illustration** *n* illustration *f.* **illustrator** *n* illustrateur, -trice *m, f.*
illustrious [i'lʌstriəs] *adj* illustre.
image ['imidʒ] *n* image *f*; (*public personality*) image de marque *f*; (*double*) portrait vivant *m.* **imagery** *n* images *f pl.*
imagine [i'madʒin] *v* (s')imaginer. **imaginary** *adj* imaginaire. **imagination** *n* imagination *f.* **imaginative** *adj* plein d'imagination.
imbalance [im'baləns] *n* déséquilibre *m.*
imbecile ['imbə,siːl] *n* imbécile *m, f.*
imitate ['imi,teit] *v* imiter. **imitation** *n* imitation *f.*
immaculate [i'makjulit] *adj* impeccable; (*rel*) immaculé.
immaterial [,imə'tiəriəl] *adj* insignifiant, indifférent.
immature [,imə'tjuə] *adj* pas mûr. **be immature** (*person*) manquer de maturité. **immaturity** *n* manque de maturité *m.*
immediate [i'miːdiət] *adj* immédiat. **immediately** *adv* tout de suite; directement.
immense [i'mens] *adj* immense.
immerse [i'məːs] *v* immerger, plonger. **immersion** *n* immersion *f.* **immersion heater** chauffe-eau électrique *m invar.*
immigrate ['imi,greit] *v* immigrer. **immigrant** *n* immigrant, -e *m, f.* **immigration** *n* immigration *f.*
imminent ['iminənt] *adj* imminent.
immobile [i'moubail] *adj* immobile. **immobilize** *v* immobiliser.
immoral [i'morəl] *adj* immoral. **immorality** *n* immoralité *f.*
immortal [i'moːtl] *adj* immortel. **immortality** *n* immortalité *f.* **immortalize** *v* immortaliser.
immovable [i'muːvəbl] *adj* fixe; inflexible.
immune [i'mjuːn] *adj* immunisé. **immunity** *n* immunité *f.* **immunization** *n* immunisation *f.* **immunize** *v* immuniser.
imp [imp] *n* diablotin *m.*
impact ['impakt] *n* impact *m.*
impair [im'peə] *v* détériorer, abîmer.
impale [im'peil] *v* empaler.
impart [im'paːt] *v* communiquer; (*give*) donner.
impartial [im'paːʃəl] *adj* impartiel. **impartiality** *n* impartialité *f.*
impasse [am'paːs] *n* impasse *f.*
impassive [im'pasiv] *adj* impassible.
impatient [im'peiʃənt] *adj* impatient. **get impatient** s'impatienter. **impatience** *n* impatience *f.*
impeach [im'piːtʃ] *v* accuser; (*question*) mettre en doute. **impeachment** *n* accusation *f*; (*US*) procédure d'impeachment *f.*
impeccable [im'pekəbl] *adj* impeccable.
impede [im'piːd] *v* empêcher, gêner.
impediment [im'pedimənt] *n* obstacle *m.* **speech impediment** défaut d'élocution *m.*
impel [im'pel] *v* pousser, obliger.
impending [im'pendiŋ] *adj* imminent; menaçant.
imperative [im'perətiv] *adj* urgent, impérieux. *n* impératif *m.*
imperfect [im'pəːfikt] *adj* imparfait; défectueux. *n* imparfait *m.*
imperial [im'piəriəl] *adj* impérial; majestueux. **imperialism** *n* impérialisme *m.*
impersonal [im'pəːsənl] *adj* impersonnel.
impersonate [im'pəːsə,neit] *v* se faire passer pour; (*theatre*) imiter. **impersonation** *n* imitation *f.*
impertinent [im'pəːtinənt] *adj* impertinent. **impertinence** *n* impertinence *f.*
impervious [im'pəːviəs] *adj* imperméable; (*to criticism, etc.*) fermé.
impetuous [im'petjuəs] *adj* impétueux.
impetus ['impətəs] *n* impulsion *f,* élan *m.*
impinge [im'pindʒ] *v* **impinge on** empiéter sur; affecter.
implement ['implimənt; *v* 'impliment] *n* instrument *m.* **implements** *pl n* matériel *m sing. v* exécuter.
implication [impli'keiʃən] *n* insinuation *f,* implication *f.*
implicit [im'plisit] *adj* implicite; absolu.
implore [im'ploː] *v* implorer. **imploring** *adj* suppliant.
imply [im'plai] *v* (laisser) supposer; suggérer; insinuer. **implied** *adj* implicite, tacite.
impolite [impə'lait] *adj* impoli.
import [im'poːt] *n* (*comm*) importation *f*; sens *m*; importance *f. v* (*comm*) importer; signifier.
importance [im'poːtəns] *n* importance *f.* **important** *adj* important.
impose [im'pouz] *v* imposer; (*fine, etc.*) infliger. **impose on** abuser de. **imposition** *n* imposition *f.*
impossible [im'posəbl] *nm, adj* impossible.

impostor [im'postə] *n* imposteur *m*.
impotent ['impətənt] *adj* impuissant. **impotence** *n* impuissance *f*.
impound [im'paund] *v* confisquer.
impoverish [im'povəriʃ] *v* appauvrir.
impregnate ['impreg,neit] *v* imprégner. **impregnation** *n* imprégnation *f*.
impress [im'pres] *v* impressionner; (*print*) imprimer. **impression** *n* impression *f*. **impressive** *adj* impressionnant.
imprint [im'print; *n* 'imprint] *v* imprimer. *n* empreinte *f*.
imprison [im'prizn] *v* emprisonner. **imprisonment** *n* emprisonnement *m*.
improbable [im'probəbl] *adj* improbable; (*story, etc.*) invraisemblable.
impromptu [im'promptjuː] *adv, adj* impromptu.
improper [im'propə] *adj* indécent; malhonnête; incorrect.
improve [im'pruːv] *v* (s')améliorer; perfectionner. **improvement** *n* amélioration *f*; progrès *m*.
improvise ['imprə,vaiz] *v* improviser. **improvisation** *n* improvisation *f*.
impudent ['impjudənt] *adj* impudent. **impudence** *n* impudence *f*.
impulse ['impʌls] *n* impulsion *f*. **impulsive** *adj* impulsif; irréfléchi.
impure [im'pjuə] *adj* impur. **impurity** *n* impureté *f*.
in [in] *prep* dans, en; (*town*) à. *adv* (*inside*) dedans; (*at home*) chez soi.
inability [,inə'biləti] *n* incapacité *f*.
inaccessible [,inak'sesəbl] *adj* inaccessible.
inaccurate [in'akjurit] *adj* inexact. **inaccuracy** *n* inexactitude *f*.
inactive [in'aktiv] *adj* inactif, peu actif. **inaction** *n* inaction *f*. **inactivity** *n* inactivité *f*.
inadequate [in'adikwit] *adj* insuffisant. **inadequacy** *n* insuffisance *f*.
inadvertent [,inəd'vəːtənt] *adj* inattentif. **inadvertently** *adv* par inadvertance.
inane [in'ein] *adj* inepte. **inanity** *n* ineptie *f*.
inanimate [in'animit] *adj* inanimé.
inarticulate [,inaː'tikjulit] *adj* (*sound*) inarticulé; (*person*) incapable de s'exprimer.
inasmuch [,inəz'mʌtʃ] *adv* **inasmuch as** attendu que.
inaudible [in'oːdəbl] *adj* inaudible.
inaugurate [i'noːgju,reit] *v* inaugurer.
inaugural *adj* inaugural. **inauguration** *n* inauguration *f*.
inborn [,in'boːn] *adj* inné; congénital.
incapable [in'keipəbl] *adj* incapable.
incendiary [in'sendiəri] *adj* incendiaire. **incendiary device** dispositif incendiaire *m*.
incense[1] ['insens] *n* encens *m*.
incense[2] [in'sens] *v* courroucer, exaspérer. **incensed by** outré de.
incentive [in'sentiv] *n* objectif *m*, stimulant *m*.
incessant [in'sesənt] *adj* incessant.
incest ['insest] *n* inceste *m*. **incestuous** *adj* incestueux.
inch [intʃ] *n* pouce *m*. **inch by inch** petit à petit. *v* **inch forward** avancer petit à petit.
incident ['insidənt] *n* incident *m*; épisode *m*. **incidental** *adj* accessoire; accidental. **incidental music** musique de fond *f*. **incidentally** *adv* (*by the way*) à propos.
incinerator [in'sinə,reitə] *n* incinérateur *m*. **incinerate** *v* incinérer. **incineration** *n* incinération *f*.
incite [in'sait] *v* pousser, inciter.
incline [in'klain] *v* (s')incliner. **be inclined to** incliner à. *n* pente *f*. **inclination** *n* inclination *f*; (*hill*) inclinaison *f*.
include [in'kluːd] *v* inclure, comprendre. **including** *prep* y compris. **inclusion** *n* inclusion *f*. **inclusive** *adj* inclus.
incognito [,inkog'niːtou] *adv* incognito.
incoherent [,inkə'hiərənt] *adj* incohérent. **incoherently** *adv* sans cohérence.
income ['inkʌm] *n* revenu *m*. **income tax** impôt sur le revenu *m*. **private income** rente *f*.
incompatible [inkəm'patəbl] *adj* incompatible. **incompatibility** *n* incompatibilité *f*.
incompetent [in'kompitənt] *adj* incompétent. **incompetence** *n* incompétence *f*.
incomplete [,inkəm'pliːt] *adj* incomplet, -ète.
incomprehensible [in,kompri'hensəbl] *adj* incompréhensible.
inconceivable [inkən'siːvəbl] *adj* inconcevable.
incongruous [in'koŋgruəs] *adj* incongru; peu approprié.
inconsiderate [,inkən'sidərit] *adj* inconsidéré; (*person*) sans égards.
inconsistent [,inkən'sistənt] *adj* inconsistant. **inconsistency** *n* inconsistance *f*.

incontinence [in'kontinəns] *n* incontinence *f*. **incontinent** *adj* incontinent.
inconvenience [inkən'viːnjəns] *n* inconvénient *m*; (*trouble*) dérangement *m*. *v* déranger. **inconvenient** *adj* inopportun, incommode.
incorporate [in'koːpəˌreit] *v* incorporer, contenir; (*comm*) fusionner.
incorrect [inkə'rekt] *adj* incorrect.
increase [in'kriːs] *v* augmenter; (s')intensifier. *n* augmentation *f*. **increasing** *adj* croissant. **increasingly** *adv* de plus en plus.
incredible [in'kredəbl] *adj* incroyable.
incredulous [in'kredjuləs] *adj* incrédule. **incredulity** *n* incrédulité *f*.
increment ['iŋkrəmənt] *n* augmentation *f*.
incriminate [in'krimineit] *v* incriminer. **incriminating** *adj* compromettant; (*evidence, etc.*) à conviction.
incubate ['iŋkjuˌbeit] *v* incuber, couver. **incubation** *n* incubation *f*. **incubator** *n* couveuse *f*.
incur [in'kəː] *v* encourir; contracter; (*risk*) courir.
incurable [in'kjuərəbl] *adj* incurable.
indecent [in'diːsnt] *adj* indécent. **indecency** *n* indécence *f*.
indeed [in'diːd] *adv* en effet, vraiment.
indefinite [in'definit] *adj* indéfini, indéterminé.
indelible [in'deləbl] *adj* indélébile; (*memory, etc.*) ineffaçable.
indemnity [in'demnəti] *n* indemnité *f*.
indent [in'dent] *v* denteler; (*printing*) renfoncer. **indentation** *n* dentelure *f*; renfoncement *m*.
independent [ˌindi'pendənt] *adj* indépendant. **independence** *n* indépendance *f*.
index ['indeks] *n* index *m*, catalogue *m*; (*ratio*) indice *m*. **index finger** index *m*. **index-linked** *adj* indexé. *v* classer; (*book*) mettre un index à.
India ['indjə] *n* Inde *f*. **Indian** *n* Indien, -enne *m, f*; *adj* indien. **Indian ink** encre de Chine *f*.
indicate ['indikeit] *v* indiquer. **indication** *n* indication *f*, signe *m*. **indicative** *nm, adj* indicatif. **indicator** *n* indicateur *m*; (*mot*) clignotant *m*.
indict [in'dait] *v* accuser. **indictment** *n* mise en accusation *f*.
indifferent [in'difrənt] *adj* indifférent; (*derog*) médiocre. **indifference** *n* indifférence *f*.
indigenous [in'didʒinəs] *adj* indigène.
indigestion [ˌindi'dʒestʃən] *n* dyspepsie *f*, indigestion *f*.
indignant [in'dignənt] *adj* indigné. **get indignant** s'indigner. **indignantly** *adv* avec indignation. **indignation** *n* indignation *f*.
indignity [in'dignəti] *n* indignité *f*.
indirect [ˌindi'rekt] *adj* indirect.
indiscreet [ˌindi'skriːt] *adj* indiscret, -ète. **indiscretion** *n* indiscrétion *f*.
indiscriminate [ˌindi'skriminit] *adj* fait au hasard; (*blind*) aveugle.
indispensable [ˌindi'spensəbl] *adj* indispensable.
indisposed [ˌindi'spouzd] *adj* (*ill*) indisposé; (*unwilling*) peu disposé. **indisposition** *n* indisposition *f*.
individual [ˌindi'vidjuəl] *adj* individuel; original. *n* individu *m*. **individuality** *n* individualité *f*.
indoctrinate [in'doktriˌneit] *v* endoctriner. **indoctrination** *n* endoctrination *f*.
indolent ['indələnt] *adj* indolent. **indolence** *n* indolence *f*.
indoor ['indoː] *adj* d'intérieur; (*swimming pool, etc.*) couvert. **indoors** *adv* à l'intérieur, à la maison.
induce [in'djuːs] *v* persuader; provoquer; (*med: labour*) déclencher. **inducement** *n* encouragement *m*; (*incentive*) motif *m*.
indulge [in'dʌldʒ] *v* satisfaire; (*give way to*) céder à. **indulge in** se livrer à. **indulgence** *n* indulgence *f*; satisfaction *f*. **indulgent** *adj* indulgent.
industry ['indəstri] *n* industrie *f*; zèle *m*. **industrial** *adj* industriel. **industrial action** action revendicative *f*. **industrialize** *v* industrialiser. **industrious** *adj* industrieux.
inebriated [i'niːbrieitid] *adj* ivre.
inedible [in'edibl] *adj* non comestible.
inefficient [ˌini'fiʃnt] *adj* inefficace; incompétent. **inefficiency** *n* inefficacité *f*; incompétence *f*.
inept [i'nept] *adj* inepte.
inequality [ˌini'kwoləti] *n* inégalité *f*.
inert [i'nəːt] *adj* inerte. **inertia** *n* inertie *f*.
inevitable [in'evitəbl] *adj* inévitable.
inexpensive [ˌinik'spensiv] *adj* pas cher.
inexperienced [ˌinik'spiəriənst] *adj* inexpérimenté.
infallible [in'faləbl] *adj* infaillible.

infamous ['infəməs] *adj* infâme. **infamy** *n* infamie *f*.
infancy ['infənsi] *n* petite enfance *f*; (*of idea, etc.*) enfance *f*.
infant ['infənt] *n* bébé *m*; enfant en bas âge *m, f*. **infantile** *adj* enfantin, infantile.
infantry ['infəntri] *n* infanterie *f*.
infatuate [in'fatjueit] *v* **be infatuated with** (*person*) être entiché de; (*idea*) être engoué de. **infatuation** *n* engouement *m*.
infect [in'fekt] *v* infecter. **infection** *n* infection *f*. **infectious** *adj* infectieux, contagieux.
infer [in'fəː] *v* déduire. **inference** *n* déduction *f*.
inferior [in'fiəriə] *n*(*m*+*f*), *adj* inférieur, -e. **inferiority** *n* infériorité *f*.
infernal [in'fəːnl] *adj* infernal.
infest [in'fest] *v* infester. **infestation** *n* infestation *f*.
infidelity [ˌinfi'deliti] *n* infidelité *f*.
infiltrate [in'filˌtreit] *v* (s')infiltrer. **infiltration** *n* infiltration *f*; (*pol*) noyautage *m*.
infinite ['infinit] *nm, adj* infini. **infinity** *n* infinité *f*; (*maths*) infini *m*.
infinitive [in'finitiv] *nm, adj* infinitif.
infirm [in'fəːm] *adj* infirme. **infirmity** *n* infirmité *f*.
inflame [in'fleim] *v* (s')enflammer. **inflammable** *adj* inflammable. **inflammation** *n* inflammation *f*.
inflate [in'fleit] *v* gonfler; (*prices*) faire monter. **inflation** *n* (*econ*) inflation *f*; (*of tyre, etc.*) gonflement *m*.
inflection [in'flekʃən] *n* inflexion *f*; (*word ending*) désinence *f*.
inflict [in'flikt] *v* infliger. **infliction** *n* infliction *f*.
influence ['influəns] *n* influence *f*. *v* influencer. **influential** *adj* influent.
influenza [ˌinflu'enzə] *n* grippe *f*.
influx ['inflʌks] *n* flot *m*, afflux *m*.
inform [in'foːm] *v* informer. **informative** *adj* instructif. **informer** *n* dénonciateur, -trice *m, f*.
informal [in'foːml] *adj* familier; dénué de formalité; (*unofficial*) officieux.
information [ˌinfə'meiʃən] *n* renseignements *m pl*.
infra-red [ˌinfrə'red] *adj* infrarouge.
infringe [in'frindʒ] *v* enfreindre. **infringe on** empiéter sur. **infringement** *n* infraction *f*.
infuriate [in'fjuəriˌeit] *v* rendre furieux. **infuriating** *adj* exaspérant.
ingenious [in'dʒiːnjəs] *adj* ingénieux. **ingenuity** *n* ingéniosité *f*.
ingot ['iŋgət] *n* lingot *m*.
ingredient [in'griːdjənt] *n* ingrédient *m*.
inhabit [in'habit] *v* habiter. **inhabitant** *n* habitant, -e *m, f*.
inhale [in'heil] *v* inhaler; (*smoke*) avaler; (*perfume*) aspirer.
inherent [in'hiərənt] *adj* inhérent.
inherit [in'herit] *v* hériter (de). **inheritance** *n* héritage *m*; succession *f*.
inhibit [in'hibit] *v* inhiber, gêner. **inhibition** *n* inhibition *f*.
inhuman [in'hjuːmən] *adj* inhumain. **inhumanity** *n* inhumanité *f*.
iniquity [i'nikwəti] *n* iniquité *f*.
initial [i'niʃl] *adj* initial, premier *n* initiale *f*. *v* parafer.
initiate [i'niʃiˌeit] *v* initier; inaugurer; commencer. **initiation** *n* initiation *f*; commencement *m*; inauguration *f*.
initiative [i'niʃiətiv] *n* initiative *f*.
inject [in'dʒekt] *v* injecter. **injection** *n* injection *f*, piqûre *f*.
injure ['indʒə] *v* blesser. **injury** *n* blessure *f*.
injustice [in'dʒʌstis] *n* injustice *f*.
ink [iŋk] *n* encre *f*. **ink-well** *n* encrier *m*. *v* encrer.
inkling ['iŋkliŋ] *n* soupçon *m*.
inland ['inlənd; *adv* in'land] *adj* intérieur, -e. **Inland Revenue** fisc *m*. *adv* à l'intérieur.
in-laws ['inˌloːs] *pl n* (*coll*) beaux-parents *m pl*, belle-famille *f sing*.
inlay [ˌin'lei] *v* incruster; marqueter. *n* incrustation *f*; marqueterie *f*.
inlet ['inlet] *n* crique *f*.
inmate ['inmeit] *n* occupant, -e *m, f*; (*prison*) détenu, -e *m, f*; hospitalisé, -e *m, f*.
inn [in] *n* auberge *f*. **innkeeper** *n* aubergiste *m, f*.
innate [ˌi'neit] *adj* inné.
inner ['inə] *adj* intérieur, -e; (*thoughts, etc.*) intime. **inner tube** chambre à air *f*.
innocent ['inəsnt] *adj* innocent. **innocence** *n* innocence *f*.
innocuous [i'nokjuəs] *adj* inoffensif.
innovation [inə'veiʃən] *n* innovation *f*.
innuendo [ˌinju'endou] *n* insinuation *f*.
innumerable [i'njuːmərəbl] *adj* innombrable.

inoculate [i'nokju,leit] *v* inoculer. **inoculation** *n* inoculation *f*.
inorganic [,ino:'ganik] *adj* inorganique.
input ['input] *n* (*elec*) énergie *f*; (*tech*) consommation *f*; (*computer*) input *m*.
inquest ['inkwest] *n* enquête *f*.
inquire [in'kwaiə] *v* s'informer (de), demander. **inquiring** *adj* (*mind*) curieux; (*look*) interrogateur, -trice. **inquiry** *n* (*official*) enquête *f*; (*individual*) demande de renseignements *f*. **inquiry desk** renseignements *m pl*.
inquisition [,inkwi'ziʃən] *n* investigation *f*. **the Inquisition** l'Inquisition *f*.
inquisitive [in'kwizətiv] *adj* curieux.
insane [in'sein] *adj* (*med*) aliéné; (*crazy*) fou, folle. **insanity** *n* aliénation *f*; folie *f*.
insatiable [in'seiʃəbl] *adj* insatiable.
inscribe [in'skraib] *v* inscrire, graver. **inscription** *n* inscription *f*.
insect ['insekt] *n* insecte *m*. **insecticide** *n* insecticide *m*.
insecure [,insi'kjuə] *adj* (*future, etc.*) incertain; (*person*) anxieux; (*structure*) peu solide. **insecurity** *n* insécurité *f*.
inseminate [in'semineit] *v* inséminer. **insemination** *n* insémination *f*.
insensitive [in'sensətiv] *adj* insensible. **insensitivity** *n* insensibilité *f*.
inseparable [in'sepərəbl] *adj* inséparable.
insert [in'sə:t; *n* 'insə:t] *v* insérer. *n* insertion *f*; (*page*) encart *m*. **insertion** *n* insertion *f*.
inshore [,in'ʃo:] *adj* côtier.
inside [,in'said] *adv* dedans. *prep* à l'intérieur de. *adj* intérieur, -e. *n* dedans *m*, intérieur *m*. **inside out** à l'envers.
insidious [in'sidiəs] *adj* insidieux.
insight ['insait] *n* perspicacité *f*.
insignificant [,insig'nifikənt] *adj* insignifiant. **insignificance** *n* insignifiance *f*.
insincere [,insin'siə] *adj* hypocrite; faux, fausse.
insinuate [in'sinjueit] *v* insinuer. **insinuation** *n* insinuation *f*.
insipid [in'sipid] *adj* insipide.
insist [in'sist] *v* insister; affirmer. **insistence** *n* insistance *f*. **insistent** *adj* insistant. **insistently** *adv* avec insistance.
insolent ['insələnt] *adj* insolent. **insolence** *n* insolence *f*.
insoluble [in'soljubl] *adj* insoluble.
insomnia [in'somniə] *n* insomnie *f*. **insomniac** *n*(*m*+*f*), *adj* insomniaque.
inspect [in'spekt] *v* inspecter, examiner. **inspection** *n* inspection *f*; examen *m*. **inspector** *n* inspecteur, -trice *m, f*.
inspire [in'spaiə] *v* inspirer. **inspiration** *n* inspiration *f*.
instability [,instə'biləti] *n* instabilité *f*.
install [in'sto:l] *v* installer. **installation** *n* installation *f*.
instalment [in'sto:lmənt] *n* (*comm*) acompte *m*; (*of serial*) épisode *m*.
instance ['instəns] *n* exemple *m*, cas *m*. **for instance** par exemple.
instant ['instənt] *adj* immédiat; (*comm*) courant; (*coffee*) soluble. *n* instant *m*. **instantaneous** *adj* instantané. **instantly** *adv* sur-le-champ.
instead [in'sted] *adv* à la place, plutôt. **instead of** au lieu de.
instep ['instep] *n* (*anat*) cou-de-pied *m*; (*shoe*) cambrure *f*.
instigate ['instigeit] *v* inciter; provoquer. **instigation** *n* instigation *f*. **instigator** *n* instigateur, -trice *m, f*.
instil [in'stil] *v* insuffler, inculquer.
instinct ['instiŋkt] *n* instinct *m*. **instinctive** *adj* instinctif.
institute ['institju:t] *v* instituer, fonder. *n* institut *m*. **institution** *n* institution *f*; (*school, home*) établissement *m*.
instruct [in'strʌkt] *v* instruire; (*order*) charger. **instruction** *n* instruction *f*. **instructions** *pl n* directives *f pl*; (*comm*) indications *f pl*; (*for use*) mode d'emploi *m sing*. **instructive** *adj* instructif. **instructor** *n* professeur *m*; (*skiing*) moniteur, -trice *m, f*.
instrument ['instrəmənt] *n* instrument *m*. **instrumental** *adj* (*music*) instrumental. **be instrumental in** contribuer à.
insubordinate [,insə'bo:dənət] *adj* insubordonné. **insubordination** *n* insubordination *f*.
insufficient [,insə'fiʃənt] *adj* insuffisant.
insular ['insjulə] *adj* insulaire; (*outlook*) borné.
insulate ['insjuleit] *v* isoler. **insulation** *n* isolation *f*; (*against cold*) calorifugeage *m*; (*material*) isolant *m*.
insulin ['insjulin] *n* insuline *f*.
insult [in'sʌlt; *n* 'insʌlt] *v* insulter. *n* insulte *f*.
insure [in'ʃuə] *v* (faire) assurer. **insurance** *n* assurance *f*. **insurance certificate** (*mot*) carte d'assurance *f*.

intact [in'takt] *adj* intact.
intake ['inteik] *n* (*tech*) adduction *f*; (*school*) admission *f*; (*food*) consommation *f*.
intangible [in'tandʒəbl] *adj* intangible.
integral ['intigrəl] *adj* intégral; (*part*) intégrant. *n* intégrale *f*.
integrate ['intigreit] *v* intégrer. **integration** *n* intégration *f*.
integrity [in'tegrəti] *n* intégrité *f*.
intellect ['intilekt] *n* intellect *m*, intelligence *f*. **intellectual** *n*, *adj* intellectuel, -elle.
intelligent [in'telidʒənt] *adj* intelligent. **intelligence** *n* intelligence *f*; (*information*) renseignements *m pl*. **intelligence test** test d'aptitude intellectuelle *m*.
intelligible [in'telidʒəbl] *adj* intelligible.
intend [in'tend] *v* avoir l'intention (de). **intended** *adj* intentionnel; projeté.
intense [in'tens] *adj* intense; (*person*) véhément. **intensify** *v* (s')intensifier. **intensity** *n* intensité *f*; véhémence *f*. **intensive** *adj* intensif. **intensive care** service de réanimation *m*.
intent[1] [in'tent] *n* intention *f*.
intent[2] [in'tent] *adj* attentif; résolu; absorbé.
intention [in'tenʃən] *n* intention *f*. **intentional** *adj* intentionnel, voulu.
inter [in'təː] *v* enterrer. **interment** *n* enterrement *m*.
interact [ˌintər'akt] *v* agir réciproquement. **interaction** *n* interaction *f*.
intercede [ˌintə'siːd] *v* intercéder.
intercept [ˌintə'sept] *v* intercepter. **interception** *n* interception *f*.
interchange [ˌintə'tʃeindʒ] *n* échange *m*; (*motorway*) échangeur *m*. *v* échanger. **interchangeable** *adj* interchangeable.
intercom ['intəˌkom] *n* interphone *m*.
intercourse ['intəkoːs] *n* relations *f pl*; (*sexual*) rapports *m pl*.
interest ['intrist] *n* intérêt *m*; (*comm*) intérêts *m pl*. *v* intéresser. **be interested in** s'intéresser à.
interfere [ˌintə'fiə] *v* s'immiscer. **interfere with** (*plans*) contrecarrer; (*work*) empiéter sur; (*meddle*) tripoter. **interference** *n* intrusion *f*; (*radio*) parasites *m pl*. **interfering** *adj* importun.
interim ['intərim] *n* intérim *m*. *adj* provisoire, intérimaire.
interior [in'tiəriə] *adj* intérieur, -e. *n* intérieur *m*.
interjection [ˌintə'dʒekʃən] *n* interjection *f*.
interlude ['intəluːd] *n* intervalle *m*; (*theatre*) intermède *m*; (*musical*) interlude *m*.
intermediate [ˌintə'miːdiət] *adj* intermédiaire.
interminable [in'təːminəbl] *adj* interminable.
intermission [ˌintə'miʃən] *n* interruption *f*; (*cinema*) entracte *m*.
intermittent [ˌintə'mitənt] *adj* intermittent. **intermittently** *adv* par intermittence.
intern [in'təːn] *v* interner. **internment** *n* internement *m*.
internal [in'təːnl] *adj* interne, intérieur, -e. **internal combustion engine** moteur à explosion *m*.
international [ˌintə'naʃənl] *adj* international.
interpose [ˌintə'pouz] *v* intervenir; (*remark, etc.*) intercaler.
interpret [in'təːprit] *v* interpréter. **interpretation** *n* interprétation *f*. **interpreter** *n* interprète *m*, *f*.
interrogate [in'terəgeit] *v* interroger. **interrogation** *n* interrogation *f*; (*police*) interrogatoire *m*. **interrogator** *n* interrogateur, -trice *m*, *f*.
interrogative [ˌintə'rogətiv] *adj* interrogateur, -trice; (*gramm*) interrogatif. *n* interrogatif *m*.
interrupt [ˌintə'rʌpt] *v* interrompre. **interruption** *n* interruption *f*.
intersect [ˌintə'sekt] *v* (se) couper; (*math*) (s')intersecter. **intersection** *n* croisement *m*; intersection *f*.
intersperse [ˌintə'spəːs] *v* parsemer.
interval ['intəvəl] *n* intervalle *m*; (*theatre*) entracte *m*.
intervene [ˌintə'viːn] *v* intervenir, survenir. **intervention** *n* intervention *f*.
interview ['intəvjuː] *n* entrevue; (*press, radio, etc.*) interview *f*. *v* interviewer.
intestine [in'testin] *n* intestin *m*. **intestinal** *adj* intestinal.
intimate[1] ['intimət] *adj* intime; (*detailed*) approfondi. **intimacy** *n* intimité *f*.
intimate[2] ['intimeit] *v* faire connaître; suggérer. **intimation** *n* annonce *f*; suggestion *f*.
intimidate [in'timideit] *v* intimider. **intimidation** *n* intimidation *f*.
into ['intu] *prep* dans, en.

intolerable [in'tolərəbl] *adj* intolérable.
intolerant [in'tolərənt] *adj* intolérant. **intolerance** *n* intolérance *f*.
intonation [ˌintə'neiʃən] *n* intonation *f*.
intoxicate [in'toksikeit] *v* enivrer. **intoxicated** *adj* ivre. **intoxication** *n* ivresse *f*.
intransitive [in'transitiv] *nm*, *adj* intransitif.
intravenous [ˌintrə'viːnəs] *adj* intraveineux.
intrepid [in'trepid] *adj* intrépide.
intricate ['intriket] *adj* complexe, compliqué. **intricacy** *n* complexité *f*, complication *f*.
intrigue ['intriːg; *v* in'triːg] *n* intrigue *f*. *v* intriguer.
intrinsic [in'trinsik] *adj* intrinsèque.
introduce [ˌintrə'djuːs] *v* presenter, introduire. **introduction** *n* introduction *f*, présentation *f*. **introductory** *adj* préliminaire.
introspective [ˌintrə'spektiv] *adj* introspectif. **introspection** *n* introspection *f*.
introvert ['intrəˌvəːt] *n* introverti, -e *m*, *f*.
intrude [in'truːd] *v* s'imposer, s'immiscer. **intruder** *n* intrus, -e *m*, *f*. **intrusion** *n* intrusion *f*.
intuition [ˌintju'iʃən] *n* intuition *f*. **intuitive** *adj* intuitif.
inundate ['inʌndeit] *v* inonder. **inundation** *n* inondation *f*.
invade [in'veid] *v* envahir. **invader** *n* envahisseur, -euse *m*, *f*. **invasion** *n* invasion *f*.
invalid[1] ['invəlid] *n(m+f)*, *adj* malade; (*disabled*) infirme, invalide.
invalid[2] [in'valid] *adj* non valide.
invaluable [in'valjuəbl] *adj* inestimable.
invariable [in'veəriəbl] *adj* invariable.
invective [in'vektiv] *n* invective *f*.
invent [in'vent] *v* inventer. **invention** *n* invention *f*. **inventor** *n* inventeur, -trice *m*, *f*.
inventory ['invəntri] *n* inventaire *m*.
invert [in'vəːt] *v* intervertir, renverser. **inverted commas** guillemets *m pl*. **inversion** *n* inversion *f*, renversement *m*.
invertebrate [in'vəːtibrət] *nm*, *adj* invertébré.
invest [in'vest] *v* investir, placer. **investment** *n* investissement *m*, placement *m*. **investor** *n* actionnaire *m*, *f*.
investigate [in'vestigeit] *v* examiner; (*crime*) enquêter sur. **investigation** *n* investigation *f*.
invigorating [in'vigəreitiŋ] *adj* vivifiant, tonifiant.
invincible [in'vinsəbl] *adj* invincible.
invisible [in'vizəbl] *adj* invisible.
invite [in'vait] *v* inviter. **invitation** *n* invitation *f*. **inviting** *adj* engageant, tentant.
invoice ['invois] *n* facture *f*. *v* facturer.
invoke [in'vouk] *v* invoquer. **invocation** *n* invocation *f*.
involuntary [in'voləntəri] *adj* involontaire.
involve [in'volv] *v* impliquer, mêler; (*entail*) entraîner. **involved** *adj* compliqué. **involvement** *n* rôle *m*; problème *m*.
inward ['inwəd] *adj* vers l'intérieur; (*thoughts*) intime. **inwardly** *adv* secrètement. **inwards** *adv* vers l'intérieur.
iodine ['aiədiːn] *n* iode *m*.
ion ['aiən] *n* ion *m*.
irate [ai'reit] *adj* furieux.
Ireland ['aiələnd] *n* Irlande *f*. **Irish** *nm*, *adj* irlandais. **Irish Sea** mer d'Irlande *f*. **the Irish** les Irlandais *m pl*.
iris ['aiəris] *n* iris *m*.
irk [əːk] *v* contrarier. **irksome** *adj* ennuyeux.
iron ['aiən] *n* fer *m*. **Iron Curtain** rideau de fer *m*. **ironmonger's** *n* quincaillerie *f*. *v* repasser. **iron out** faire disparaître. **ironing** *n* repassage *m*. **ironing board** planche à repasser *f*.
irony ['aiərəni] *n* ironie *f*. **ironic** *adj* ironique.
irrational [i'raʃənl] *adj* pas rationnel, déraisonnable; (*math*) irrationnel.
irregular [i'regjulə] *adj* irrégulier. **irregularity** *n* irrégularité *f*.
irrelevant [i'reləvənt] *adj* sans rapport, hors de propos.
irreparable [i'repərəbl] *adj* irréparable.
irresistible [ˌiri'zistəbl] *adj* irrésistible.
irrespective [ˌiri'spektiv] *adj* **irrespective of** sans tenir compte de.
irresponsible [ˌiri'sponsəbl] *adj* irréfléchi.
irrevocable [i'revəkəbl] *adj* irrévocable.
irrigate ['irigeit] *v* irriguer. **irrigation** *n* irrigation *f*.
irritate ['iriteit] *v* irriter. **irritable** *adj* irritable. **irritation** *n* irritation *f*.
is [iz] *V* **be**.
Islam ['izlaːm] *n* Islam *m*. **Islamic** *adj* islamique.

island ['ailənd] *n* île *f*; (*in road*) refuge *m*.
isolate ['aisəleit] *v* isoler. **isolation** *n* isolement *m*.
issue ['iʃuː] *n* question *f*; résultat *m*; (*copy*) numéro *m*; (*stamps, etc.*) émission *f*. *v* distribuer; émettre; (*writ, etc.*) lancer.
isthmus ['isməs] *n* isthme *m*.
it [it] *pron* (*subject*) il, elle; (*direct object*) le, la; (*indirect object*) lui. **it is** c'est, il est.
italic [i'talik] *adj* italique. **italics** *pl n* italique *m sing*.
Italy ['itəli] *n* Italie *f*. **Italian** *nm, adj* italien; (*people*) Italien, -enne *m, f*.
itch [itʃ] *n* démangeaison *f*. *v* démanger.
item ['aitəm] *n* article *m*; question *f*.
itinerary [ai'tinərəri] *n* itinéraire *m*.
its [its] *adj* son, sa; (*pl*) ses. *pron* le sien, la sienne.
itself [it'self] *pron* se; (*emphatic*) lui-même, elle-même. **by itself** en soi; (*alone*) tout seul.
ivory ['aivəri] *n* ivoire *m*. **Ivory Coast** Côte d'Ivoire *f*.
ivy ['aivi] *n* lierre *m*.

J

jab [dʒab] *v* enfoncer. *n* coup de pointe *m*; (*coll*: *injection*) piqûre *f*.
jack [dʒak] *n* (*mot*) cric *m*; (*cards*) valet *m*. *v* **jack up** soulever avec un cric.
jackal ['dʒakoːl] *n* chacal *m*.
jackdaw ['dʒakdoː] *n* choucas *m*.
jacket ['dʒakit] *n* (*man's*) veston *m*; (*woman's*) jaquette *f*; (*of book*) couverture *f*. **jacket potato** pomme de terre au four *f*.
jackpot ['dʒakpot] *n* gros lot *m*.
jade [dʒeid] *nm* jade.
jaded ['dʒeidid] *adj* épuisé.
jagged ['dʒagid] *adj* déchiqueté.
jaguar ['dʒagjuə] *n* jaguar *m*.
jail *or* **gaol** [dʒeil] *n* prison *f*. *v* emprisonner. **jailer** *n* geôlier, -ère *m, f*.
jam[1] [dʒam] *v* (se) coincer; (*cram*) entasser; (*block*) encombrer. *n* embouteillage *m*.
jam[2] [dʒam] *n* confiture *f*.
janitor ['dʒanitə] *n* portier *m*.
January ['dʒanjuəri] *n* janvier *m*
Japan [dʒə'pan] *n* Japon *m*. **Japanese** *nm, adj* japonais. **the Japanese** les Japonais *m pl*.
jar[1] [dʒaː] *n* pot *m*, bocal *m*.
jar[2] [dʒaː] *v* (*sound*) grincer; (*knock*) cogner; (*shake*) ébranler; (*irritate*) agacer.
jargon ['dʒaːgən] *n* jargon *m*.
jasmine ['dʒazmin] *n* jasmin *m*.
jaundice ['dʒoːndis] *n* jaunisse *f*.
jaunt [dʒoːnt] *n* (*coll*) balade *f*.
jaunty ['dʒoːnti] *adj* enjoué, vif.
javelin ['dʒavəlin] *n* javelot *m*.
jaw [dʒoː] *n* mâchoire *f*. **jawbone** *n* maxillaire *m*.
jay [dʒei] *n* geai *m*.
jazz [dʒaz] *n* jazz *m*.
jealous ['dʒeləs] *adj* jaloux, -ouse. **jealousy** *n* jalousie *f*.
jeans [dʒiːns] *pl n* blue-jean *m sing*.
jeep [dʒiːp] *n* jeep *f*.
jeer [dʒiə] *v* railler, huer. *n* raillerie *f*, huée *f*.
jelly ['dʒeli] *n* gelée *f*. **jellyfish** *n* méduse *f*.
jeopardize ['dʒepədaiz] *v* mettre en danger. **jeopardy** *n* danger *m*, péril *m*.
jerk [dʒəːk] *n* saccade *f*, secousse *f*. *v* tirer brusquement; donner une secousse à. **jerky** *adj* saccadé. **jerkily** *adv* par saccades.
jersey ['dʒəːzi] *n* tricot *m*. **Jersey** *n* Jersey *f*.
jest [dʒest] *n* plaisanterie *f*. *v* plaisanter. **jester** *n* bouffon *m*.
jet[1] [dʒet] *n* jet *m*. **jet lag** décalage horaire *m*. **jet-propelled** *adj* à réaction.
jet[2] [dʒet] *n* jais *m*.
jetty ['dʒeti] *n* jetée *f*.
Jew [dʒuː] *n* Juif, Juive *m, f*. **Jewish** *adj* juif.
jewel ['dʒuːəl] *n* bijou (*pl* -oux) *m*. **jeweller** *n* bijoutier *m*. **jeweller's** *n* bijouterie *f*. **jewellery** *n* bijoux *m pl*.
jig [dʒig] *n* gigue *f*. *v* danser la gigue; sautiller.
jigsaw ['dʒigsoː] *n* (*puzzle*) puzzle *m*; (*saw*) scie à chantourner *f*.
jilt [dʒilt] *v* laisser tomber.
jingle ['dʒiŋgl] *n* tintement *m*; (*verse*) petit couplet *m*. *v* (faire) tinter.
jinx [dʒiŋks] *n* (*coll*) porte-guigne *m*. **jinxed** *adj* ensorcelé.

job [dʒob] *n* travail (*pl* -aux) *m*; poste *m*. **jobcentre** *n* agence pour l'emploi *f*. **job lot** lot d'articles divers *m*.
jockey ['dʒoki] *n* jockey *m*.
jocular ['dʒokjulə] *adj* jovial; facétieux.
jodhpurs ['dʒodpəz] *pl n* culotte de cheval *f sing*.
jog [dʒog] *n* (*jerk*) secousse *f*; (*with elbow*) coup de coude *m*. **jogtrot** *n* petit trot *m*. *v* secouer; (*elbow*) pousser; (*memory*) rafraîcher. **jogging** *n* footing *m*. **go jogging** faire du footing.
join [dʒoin] *v* (se) joindre, (s')unir; devenir membre (de), s'inscrire (à); (*roads, rivers, etc.*) (se) rejoindre. **join in** participer (à). **join up** assembler; (*mil*) s'engager. **joiner** *n* menuisier *m*.
joint [dʒoint] *n* jointure *f*; (*anat*) articulation *f*; (*of meat*) rôti *m*; (*slang*: *place*) boîte *f*. *adj* commun. **jointly** *adv* en commun.
joist [dʒoist] *n* solive *f*.
joke [dʒouk] *n* plaisanterie *f*; (*trick*) farce *f*. *v* plaisanter. **joker** *n* blagueur, -euse *m, f*; (*cards*) joker *m*.
jolly ['dʒoli] *adj* enjoué. *adv* (*coll*) drôlement. **jollity** *n* gaieté *f*.
jolt [dʒoult] *v* cahoter. *n* secousse *f*, cahot *m*; choc *m*.
jostle ['dʒosl] *v* (se) bousculer. *n* bousculade *f*.
jot [dʒot] *v* **jot down** noter. *n* iota *m*. **jotter** *n* bloc-notes *m*.
journal ['dʒəːnl] *n* revue *f*; (*comm*) livre de comptes *m*; (*diary*) journal *m*. **journalism** *n* journalisme *m*. **journalist** *n* journaliste *m, f*.
journey ['dʒəːni] *n* voyage *m*; (*distance*) trajet *m*. *v* voyager.
jovial ['dʒouviəl] *adj* jovial. **joviality** *n* jovialité *f*.
joy [dʒoi] *n* joie *f*; plaisir *m*. **joyful** *or* **joyous** *adj* joyeux.
jubilant ['dʒuːbilənt] *adj* débordant de joie. **be jubilant** jubiler. **jubilation** *n* jubilation *f*.
jubilee ['dʒuːbiliː] *n* jubilé *m*.
Judaism ['dʒuːdei,izəm] *n* judaïsme *m*.
judge [dʒʌdʒ] *n* juge *m*. *v* juger. **judging by** à en juger par. **judgment** *n* jugement *m*; discernement *m*.
judicial [dʒuː'diʃəl] *adj* judiciaire.
judicious [dʒuː'diʃəs] *adj* judicieux.
judo ['dʒuːdou] *n* judo *m*.
jug [dʒʌg] *n* cruche *f*; (*for milk*) pot *m*; (*slang*: *prison*) taule *f*.
juggernaut ['dʒʌgənoːt] *n* (*lorry*) mastodonte *m*.
juggle ['dʒʌgl] *v* jongler. **juggler** *n* jongleur, -euse *m, f*. **jugglery** *n* jonglerie *f*.
jugular ['dʒʌgjulə] *nf, adj* jugulaire.
juice [dʒuːs] *n* jus *m*. **juicy** *adj* juteux.
jukebox ['dʒuːkboks] *n* juke-box *m*.
July [dʒu'lai] *n* juillet *m*.
jumble ['dʒʌmbl] *v* brouiller. *n* mélange *m*, fouillis *m*. **jumble sale** vente de charité *f*.
jump [dʒʌmp] *n* saut *m*; (*start*) sursaut *m*. *v* sauter; sursauter. **jump at** (*offer, etc.*) sauter sur. **jumped-up** *adj* (*derog*) parvenu. **jumpy** *adj* (*coll*) nerveux.
jumper ['dʒʌmpə] *n* pull *m*.
junction ['dʒʌŋktʃən] *n* jonction *f*; (*roads*) bifurcation *f*; (*rail*) embranchement *m*.
juncture ['dʒʌŋkʃə] *n* conjoncture *f*. **at this juncture** à ce moment-là.
June [dʒuːn] *n* juin *m*.
jungle ['dʒʌŋgl] *n* jungle *f*.
junior ['dʒuːnjə] *adj* (*younger*) cadet, -ette; (*lower rank*) subalterne. *n* cadet, -ette *m, f*; (*clerk*) petit commis *m*; (*in names*) fils *m*.
juniper ['dʒuːnipə] *n* genévrier *m*. **juniper berry** baie de genièvre *f*.
junk[1] [dʒʌŋk] *n* bric-à-brac *m invar*; (*coll*: *rubbish*) camelote *f*. **junk-shop** *n* brocanteur *m*.
junk[2] [dʒʌŋk] *n* (*boat*) jonque *f*.
junta ['dʒʌntə] *n* junte *f*.
jurisdiction [dʒuəris'dikʃən] *n* juridiction *f*.
jury ['dʒuəri] *n* jury *m*. **juror** *n* juré, femme juré *m, f*.
just [dʒʌst] *adv* juste; simplement. **have just** venir de: *il vient de partir*. *adj* juste.
justice ['dʒʌstis] *n* justice *f*. **Justice of the Peace** juge de paix *m*.
justify ['dʒʌstifai] *v* justifier. **justifiable** *adj* justifiable. **justification** *n* justification *f*.
jut [dʒʌt] *v* **jut out** saillir, dépasser.
jute [dʒuːt] *n* jute *m*.
juvenile ['dʒuːvənail] *n* adolescent, -e *m, f*. *adj* juvénile. **juvenile delinquent** mineur délinquant, mineure délinquante *m, f*.
juxtapose [,dʒʌkstə'pouz] *v* juxtaposer. **justaposition** *n* juxtaposition *f*.

K

kaftan ['kaftan] *n* kaftan *m*.
kaleidoscope [kə'laidəskoup] *n* kaléidoscope *m*.
kangaroo [kaŋgə'ruː] *n* kangourou *m*.
karate [kə'raːti] *n* karaté *m*.
kayak ['kaiak] *n* kayak *m*.
kebab [ki'bab] *n* kébab *m*.
keel [kiːl] *n* quille *f*. *v* **keel over** (*naut*) chavirer; (*coll*: *faint*) tomber dans les pommes.
keen [kiːn] *adj* vif; enthousiaste; (*sharp*) aiguisé; (*sight*, *judgment*) pénétrant. **keenly** *adv* vivement, profondément; avec enthousiasme. **keenness** *n* finesse *f*; intensité *f*; enthousiasme *m*.
***keep** [kiːp] *v* garder; (*observe*, *maintain*) tenir; (*support*) entretenir; (*remain*) rester; (*food*, *etc.*) se garder. **keep-fit** *n* culture physique *f*. **keep on** continuer. **keep out!** (*on notice*) défense d'entrer! **keepsake** *n* souvenir *m*. **keep up with** suivre; aller aussi vite que. **keeper** *n* gardien, -enne *m*, *f*.
keg [keg] *n* tonnelet *m*.
kennel ['kenl] *n* niche *f*. **kennels** *pl n* chenil *m sing*.
kept [kept] *V* **keep**.
kerb [kəːb] *n* bordure du trottoir *f*.
kernel ['kəːnl] *n* (*nut*) amande *f*; (*seed*) graine *m*.
kerosene ['kerəsiːn] *n* kérosène *m*.
ketchup ['ketʃəp] *n* ketchup *m*.
kettle ['ketl] *n* bouilloire *f*. **kettledrum** *n* timbale *f*.
key [kiː] *n* clef *f*; (*piano*) touche *f*; (*music*) ton *m*. **keyboard** *n* clavier *m*. **keyhole** *n* trou de serrure *m*. **key-ring** *n* porte-clefs *m invar*. *adj* clef. *v* **key up** surexciter.
khaki ['kaːki] *nm*, *adj* kaki.
kick [kik] *n* coup de pied *m*; (*gun*) recul *m*. *v* donner un coup de pied (à). **kick off** (*football*) donner le coup d'envoi; (*coll*: *party*, *etc.*) démarrer. **kick-off** *n* coup d'envoi *m*; (*coll*) démarrage *m*. **kick out** (*coll*) flanquer dehors.
kid[1] [kid] *n* (*goat*, *leather*) chevreau *m*; (*coll*: *child*) gosse *m*, *f*.
kid[2] [kid] *v* (*coll*) faire marcher.
kidnap ['kidnap] *v* kidnapper. **kidnapper** *n* kidnappeur, -euse *m*, *f*. **kidnapping** *n* enlèvement *m*.
kidney ['kidni] *n* (*anat*) rein *m*; (*as food*) rognon *m*. **kidney bean** haricot rouge *m*. **kidney machine** rein artificiel *m*.
kill [kil] *v* tuer. **killjoy** *n* rabat-joie *m invar*. **killer** *n* tueur, -euse *m*, *f*; assassin *m*. **killing** *n* meutre *m*; massacre *m*.
kiln [kiln] *n* four *m*.
kilo ['kiːlou] *n* kilo *m*.
kilogram ['kiləgram] *n* kilogramme *m*.
kilometre ['kiləmiːtə] *n* kilomètre *m*.
kilt [kilt] *n* kilt *m*.
kin [kin] *n* parents *m pl*. **kinship** *n* parenté *f*.
kind[1] [kaind] *adj* aimable, gentil, -ille. **kind-hearted** *adj* bon, bonne. **kindness** *n* bonté *f*, gentillesse *f*.
kind[2] [kaind] *n* genre *m*; (*brand*) marque *f*. **in kind** en nature.
kindergarten ['kindəgaːtn] *n* jardin d'enfants *m*.
kindle ['kindl] *v* (s')allumer, (s')enflammer.
kindred ['kindrid] *n* parents *m pl*. *adj* (*related*) apparenté; similaire. **kindred spirit** âme sœur *f*.
kinetic [kin'etik] *adj* cinétique.
king [kiŋ] *n* roi *m*; (*draughts*) dame *f*. **kingfisher** *n* martin-pêcheur *m*. **kingdom** *n* royaume *m*; (*plant*, *animal*) règne *m*.
kink [kiŋk] *n* (*rope*) entortillement *m*; (*hair*) crêpelure *f*. *v* s'entortiller. **kinky** *adj* crêpelé; bizarre.
kiosk ['kiːosk] *n* kiosque *m*.
kipper ['kipə] *n* hareng fumé *m*.
kiss [kis] *v* (s')embrasser. *n* baiser *m*. **kiss of life** bouche à bouche *m*.
kit [kit] *n* (*equipment*) matériel *m*; (*sport*) affaires *f pl*; (*tools*, *first-aid*, *etc.*) trousse *f*; (*do-it-yourself*) kit *m*. *v* **kit out** équiper.
kitchen ['kitʃin] *n* cuisine *f*. **kitchen sink** évier *m*.
kite [kait] *n* cerf-volant *m*; (*bird*) milan *m*.
kitten ['kitn] *n* chaton *m*.
kitty ['kiti] *n* cagnotte *f*.
kleptomania [kleptə'meiniə] *n* kleptomanie *f*. **kleptomaniac** *n*(*m*+*f*), *adj* kleptomane.
knack [nak] *n* tour de main *m*, truc *m*. **get the knack of** attraper le tour de main pour.
knapsack [napsak] *n* sac à dos *m*.
knead [niːd] *v* pétrir.

knee [niː] *n* genou (*pl* -oux) *m*. **kneecap** *n* rotule *f*.
***kneel** [niːl] *v* s'agenouiller.
knelt [nelt] *V* **kneel**.
knew [njuː] *V* **know**.
knickers ['nikəz] *pl n* culotte *f sing*; (*briefs*) slip *m sing*.
knife [naif] *n* couteau *m*. *v* donner un coup de couteau à.
knight [nait] *n* chevalier *m*. *v* faire chevalier. **knighthood** *n* titre de chevalier *m*. **get a knighthood** être fait chevalier.
knit [nit] *v* tricoter. **knit together** lier; (*bone*) se souder. **knitting** *n* tricot *m*. **knitting machine** tricoteuse *f*. **knitting needle** aiguille à tricoter *f*.
knob [nob] *n* bouton *m*; (*of butter*) noix *f*.
knobbly ['nobli] *adj* noueux.
knock [nok] *n* coup *m*. *v* frapper; (*bump*) heurter. **knock down** abattre; (*mot*) renverser. **knock knees** genoux cagneux *m pl*. **knock out** (*stun*) assommer; (*from contest*) éliminer. **knockout** *n* (*boxing*) knock-out *m*. **knock over** renverser. **knocker** *n* marteau de porte *m*.
knot [not] *n* nœud *m*. *v* nouer.
***know** [nou] *v* (*facts*) savoir; (*places, people*) connaître; (*recognize*) reconnaître. **know-all** *n* (*coll*) je-sais-tout *m, f*. **know-how** *n* (*coll*) technique *f*. **know how to** savoir. **knowing** *adj* fin; (*look*) entendu.
knowledge ['nolidʒ] *n* connaissance *f*, savoir *m*. **knowledgeable** *adj* bien informé.
known [noun] *V* **know**.
knuckle ['nʌkl] *n* articulation du doigt *f*.

L

label ['leibl] *n* étiquette *f*. *v* étiqueter.
laboratory [lə'borətəri] *n* laboratoire *m*.
labour ['leibə] *n* travail (*pl* -aux) *m*; (*workers*) main-d'œuvre *f*. **Labour** *nm, adj* (*pol*) travailliste. **labour pains** douleurs de l'accouchement *f pl*. **labour-saving device** appareil ménager *m*. *v* peiner. **laborious** *adj* laborieux. **labourer** *n* ouvrier *m*.
laburnum [lə'bəːnəm] *n* cytise *m*.
labyrinth ['labərinθ] *n* labyrinthe *m*.
lace [leis] *n* dentelle *f*; (*for shoe*) lacet *m*. *v* lacer; (*drink*) arroser.
lacerate ['lasəreit] *v* lacérer. **laceration** *n* (*act*) lacération *f*; (*tear*) déchirure *f*.
lack [lak] *n* manque *m*. **for lack of** faute de. *v* manquer (de).
lackadaisical [ˌlakə'deizikəl] *adj* apathique; indolent.
lacquer ['lakə] *n* laque *f*. *v* laquer.
lad [lad] *n* (*coll*) gars *m*.
ladder ['ladə] *n* échelle *f*. *v* (*stocking*) filer. **ladderproof** *adj* indémaillable.
laden ['leidn] *adj* chargé.
ladle ['leidl] *n* louche *f*.
lady ['leidi] *n* dame *f*. **ladies** *n* (*sign*) dames *f*. **ladies and gentlemen!** mesdames, messieurs! **ladybird** *n* coccinelle *f*. **lady-in-waiting** *n* dame d'honneur *f*.
lag[1] [lag] *v* traîner. *n* retard *m*; (*time difference*) décalage *m*.
lag[2] [lag] *v* calorifuger. **lagging** *n* calorifuge *m*.
lager ['laːgə] *n* bière blonde *f*.
lagoon [lə'guːn] *n* lagune *f*.
laid [leid] *V* **lay**[1].
lain [lein] *V* **lie**[1].
lair [leə] *n* tanière *f*.
laity ['leiəti] *n* laïcs *m pl*.
lake [leik] *n* lac *m*.
lamb [lam] *n* agneau *m*.
lame [leim] *adj* boîteux; (*excuse, etc.*) faible. **be lame** boîter. *v* estropier. **lamely** *adv* maladroitement. **lameness** *n* boîterie *f*; faiblesse *f*.
lament [lə'ment] *n* lamentation *f*. *v* se lamenter, pleurer. **lamentable** *adj* lamentable; regrettable.
laminate ['lamineit] *v* laminer. **laminated** *adj* laminé; (*glass*) feuilleté; (*windscreen*) en verre feuilleté.
lamp [lamp] *n* lampe *f*. **lamppost** *n* réverbère *m*. **lampshade** *n* abat-jour *m invar*.
lance [laːns] *n* lance *f*. *v* (*blister, etc.*) ouvrir.
land [land] *n* terre *f*; (*country*) pays *m*. **landlady** *n* propriétaire *f*; (*boarding house*) patronne *f*. **landlord** *n* propriétaire *m*; (*pub*) patron *m*. **landmark** *n* point de repère *m*. **landscape** *n* paysage *m*. *v* (*boat*) débarquer; (*aircraft*) atterrir; (*fall*) tomber. **landing** *n* débarquement *m*; atterrissage *m*; (*between floors*) palier *m*. **landing stage** débarcadère *m*.

lane [lein] *n* chemin *m*; (*on motorway, etc.*) voie *f*; (*line of traffic*) file *f*.
language ['laŋgwidʒ] *n* (*means of expression*) langage *m*; (*of a nation*) langue *f*.
languish ['laŋgwiʃ] *v* languir.
lanky ['laŋki] *adj* dégingandé.
lantern ['lantən] *n* lanterne *f*.
Laos ['laɪos] *n* Laos *m*.
lap[1] [lap] *n* (*sport*) tour de piste *m*. *v* (*wrap*) enrouler. **lap over** se chevaucher.
lap[2] [lap] *v* (*drink*) laper; (*waves*) clapoter.
lap[3] [lap] *n* genoux *m pl*.
lapel [lə'pel] *n* revers *m*.
Lapland ['lapland] *n* Laponie *f*. **Lapp** *nm, adj* lapon; *n* (*people*) Lapon, -e *m, f*.
lapse [laps] *n* (*fault*) défaillance *f*; (*time*) intervalle *m*; (*of custom*) disparition *f*. *v* (*expire*) se périmer; (*fall*) tomber; (*commit fault*) faire un écart.
larceny ['laːsəni] *n* vol simple *m*.
larch [laːtʃ] *n* mélèze *m*.
lard [laːd] *n* saindoux *m*.
larder ['laːdə] *n* garde-manger *m invar*.
large [laːdʒ] *adj* grand, gros, grosse. **at large** en liberté; en général. **large-scale** *adj* à grande échelle; fait sur une grande échelle.
lark[1] [laːk] *n* (*bird*) alouette *f*.
lark[2] [laːk] (*coll*) *n* blague *f*. *v* **lark around** faire le petit fou, faire la petite folle.
larva ['laːvə] *n, pl* **larvae** larve *f*.
larynx ['lariŋks] *n* larynx *m*. **laryngitis** *n* laryngite *f*.
laser ['leizə] *n* laser *m*.
lash [laʃ] *n* coup de fouet *m*; (*thong*) mèche *f*; (*of eye*) cil *m*. *v* (*whip*) fouetter; (*rain, etc.*) cingler; attacher. **lash out** envoyer un coup; (*coll: money*) lâcher. **lashing** *n* flagellation *f*. **lashings of** (*coll*) des tas de.
lass [las] *n* jeune fille *f*.
lassitude ['lasitjuːd] *n* lassitude *f*.
lasso [la'suː] *n* lasso *m*. *v* prendre au lasso.
last[1] [laːst] *adj* dernier. **last-minute** *adj* de dernière minute. **last night** (*evening*) hier soir. *adv* en dernier; finalement; la dernière fois. *n* dernier, -ière *m, f*. **at last** enfin. **lastly** *adv* pour terminer.
last[2] [laːst] *v* durer. **last out** *v* (*person*) tenir, (*money, food, etc.*) faire. **lasting** *adj* durable.
latch [latʃ] *n* loquet *m*. *v* fermer au loquet.
late [leit] *adj* en retard; récent; (*former*) ancien; (*dead*) feu. *adv* (*not on time*) en retard; (*not early*) tard. **lately** *adv* récemment. **lateness** *n* retard *m*. **later** *adj* plus tard. **see you later!** à tout à l'heure! **latest** *adj* (*most recent*) dernier. **at the latest** au plus tard.
latent ['leitənt] *adj* latent.
lateral ['latərəl] *adj* latéral.
lathe [leið] *n* tour *m*.
lather ['laːðə] *n* mousse *f*. *v* (*apply soap*) savonner; (*foam*) mousser.
Latin ['latin] *nm, adj* latin.
latitude ['latitjuːd] *n* latitude *f*.
latrine [lə'triːn] *n* latrine *f*.
latter ['latə] *adj* dernier, deuxième. **the latter** celui-ci, celle-ci *m, f*.
lattice ['latis] *n* treillis *m*; (*frame*) treillage *m*.
laugh [laːf] *v* rire. **laugh at** rire de; se moquer de. *n* rire *m*; éclat de rire *m*. **laughable** *adj* ridicule. **it's no laughing matter** il n'y a pas de quoi rire. **laughing-stock** *n* risée *f*. **laughter** *n* rires *m pl*.
launch[1] [loːntʃ] *v* lancer. **launching** *n* lancement *m*.
launch[2] [loːntʃ] *n* vedette *f*; (*of warship*) chaloupe *f*.
launder ['loːndə] *v* blanchir. **launderette** *n* laverie automatique *f*. **laundry** *n* (*clothes, etc.*) linge *m*; (*place*) blanchisserie *f*.
laurel ['lorəl] *n* laurier *m*.
lava ['laːvə] *n* lave *f*.
lavatory ['lavətəri] *n* toilettes *f pl*, cabinets *m pl*.
lavender ['lavində] *n* lavende *f*.
lavish ['laviʃ] *adj* prodigue; somptueux. *v* prodiguer.
law [loː] *n* loi *f*; (*profession*) droit *m*; justice *f*. **law-abiding** *adj* respectueux des lois. **lawsuit** *n* procès *m*. **lawful** *adj* légal, légitime. **lawyer** *n* avocat *m*.
lawn [loːn] *n* pelouse *f*. **lawn-mower** *n* tondeuse *f*.
lax [laks] *adj* relâché. **laxity** *n* relâchement *m*.
laxative ['laksətiv] *nm, adj* laxatif.
***lay**[1] [lei] *v* poser; (*eggs*) pondre. **layabout** *n* fainéant, -e *m, f*. **lay-by** *n* petite aire de stationnement *f*. **lay off** (*workers*) licencier. **lay on** (*provide*) fournir. **layout** *n* (*of house, etc.*) disposition *f*; (*of page*) mise en page *f*. **lay the table** mettre la table.

lay² [lei] *adj* laïque. **layman** *n* profane *m*.
lay³ [lei] *V* **lie¹**.
layer ['leiə] *n* couche *f*. *v* (*hair*) couper en dégradé.
lazy ['leizi] *adj* paresseux. **laze around** paresser. **laziness** *n* paresse *f*.
***lead¹** [liːd] *v* mener, conduire; être à la tête de; (*sport*) être en tête. **lead on** (*tease*) faire marcher; (*encourage*) amener. **lead up to** conduire à; précéder. *n* (*sport*) tête *f*; exemple *m*; (*clue*) piste *f*; (*for dog*) laisse *f*; rôle principal *m*; (*elec*) fil *m*. **leader** *n* chef *m*; guide *m*; (*newspaper*) éditorial *m*. **leadership** *n* direction *f*. **leading** *adj* principal; majeur, -e.
lead² [led] *n* plomb *m*; (*pencil*) mine *f*.
leaf [liːf] *n* feuille *f*; page *f*; (*of table*) rallonge *f*, rabat *m*. *v* **leaf through** feuilleter. **leaflet** *n* prospectus *m*.
league [liːg] *n* ligue *f*; (*sport*) championnat *m*.
leak [liːk] *n* fuite *f*. *v* fuir; (*information*) divulguer. **leakage** *n* fuite *f*.
***lean¹** [liːn] *v* (se) pencher; (*support*) (s')appuyer. *n* inclinaison *f*. **leaning** *n* penchant *m*.
lean² [liːn] *nm*, *adj* maigre. **leanness** *n* maigreur *f*.
leant [lent] *V* **lean¹**.
***leap** [liːp] *n* saut *m*, bond *m*. **by leaps and bounds** à pas de géant. *v* sauter, bondir. **leap-frog** *n* saute-mouton *m*. **leap year** année bissextile *f*.
leapt [lept] *V* **leap**.
***learn** [ləːn] *v* apprendre. **learned** *adj* savant. **learner** *n* débutant, -e *m*, *f*. **learning** *n* érudition *f*.
learnt [ləːnt] *V* **learn**.
lease [liːs] *n* bail *m*. *v* louer à bail. **leasehold** *adj* loué à bail.
leash [liːʃ] *n* laisse *f*.
least [liːst] *adj* (*amount*) le moins de; (*smallest*) le moindre, la moindre. *pron*, *adv* le moins. **at least** au moins.
leather ['leðə] *n* cuir *m*. **leathery** *adj* coriace; (*skin*) parcheminé.
***leave¹** [liːv] *v* laisser; (*go away from*) quitter; (*depart*) partir. **be left** rester. **leave out** omettre, exclure. **left-luggage office** consigne *f*. **left-overs** *pl n* restes *m pl*.
leave² [liːv] *n* permission *f*; (*holiday*) congé *m*.
lecherous ['letʃərəs] *adj* lubrique. **lecher** *n* débauché *m*. **lechery** *n* luxure *f*.
lectern ['lektən] *n* lutrin *m*.
lecture ['lektʃə] *n* conférence *f*; réprimande *f*. **lecture theatre** amphithéâtre *m*. *v* faire un cours; réprimander. **lecturer** *n* conférencier, -ère *m*, *f*; (*university*) maître assistant *m*.
led [led] *V* **lead¹**.
ledge [ledʒ] *n* rebord *m*, saillie *f*.
ledger ['ledʒə] *n* grand livre *m*.
lee [liː] *n* abri *m*; (*naut*) côté sous le vent *m*. **leeward** *adj*, *adv* sous le vent.
leech [liːtʃ] *n* sangsue *f*.
leek [liːk] *n* poireau *m*.
leer [liə] *v* lorgner. *n* regard mauvais *m*.
leeway ['liːwei] *n* (*naut*) dérive *f*; liberté d'action *f*.
left¹ [left] *V* **leave¹**.
left² [left] *nf*, *adj* gauche. *adv* à gauche. **left-hand** *adj* à gauche. **left-handed** *adj* gaucher. **left-wing** *adj* de gauche.
leg [leg] *n* (*person*) jambe *f*; (*animal*) patte *f*; (*pork*, *chicken*) cuisse *f*; (*lamb*) gigot *m*; (*furniture*) pied *m*.
legacy ['legəsi] *n* legs *m*.
legal ['liːgəl] *adj* légal; judiciaire. **legality** *n* légalité *f*. **legalize** *v* légaliser.
legend ['ledʒənd] *n* légende *f*. **legendary** *adj* légendaire.
legible ['ledʒəbl] *adj* lisible. **legibility** *n* lisibilité *f*.
legion ['liːdʒən] *n* légion *f*.
legislate ['ledʒisleit] *v* faire des lois, légiférer. **legislation** *n* législation *f*.
legitimate [lə'dʒitimət] *adj* légitime. **legitimacy** *n* légitimité *f*.
leisure ['leʒə] *n* loisir *m*.
lemon ['lemən] *n* (*fruit*) citron *m*; (*tree*) citronnier *m*. *adj* (*colour*) citron *invar*. **lemonade** *n* limonade *f*. **lemon sole** limande-sole *f*. **lemon tea** thé au citron *m*.
***lend** [lend] *v* prêter.
length [leŋθ] *n* longueur *f*; (*time*) durée *f*; (*piece*) morceau *m*. **lengthen** *v* (s')allonger, rallonger. **lengthy** *adj* long, longue.
lenient ['liːniənt] *adj* indulgent. **leniency** *n* indulgence *f*.
lens [lenz] *n* lentille *f*; (*camera*) objectif *m*; (*spectacles*) verre *m*; (*eye*) cristallin *m*. **lens hood** parasoleil *m*.
lent [lent] *V* **lend**.
Lent [lent] *n* Carême *m*.

lentil ['lentil] *n* lentille *f.*
Leo ['li:ou] *n* Lion *m.*
leopard ['lepəd] *n* léopard *m.*
leotard ['li:ətaːd] *n* collant *m.*
leper ['lepə] *n* lépreux, -euse *m, f.* **leprosy** *n* lèpre *f.* **leprous** *adj* lépreux.
lesbian ['lezbiən] *n* lesbienne *f. adj* lesbien. **lesbianism** *n* lesbianisme *m.*
less [les] *nm, adv, prep* moins. *adj* moins de. **less and less** de moins en moins. **lessen** *v* diminuer. **lesser** *adj* moindre.
lesson ['lesn] *n* leçon *f,* cours *m.*
lest [lest] *conj* de peur que.
***let** [let] *v* laisser; (*rent out*) louer. **let down** (*lower*) descendre; (*disappoint*) décevoir; (*dress*) rallonger. **let-down** *n* déception *f.* **let in** faire entrer. **let out** faire sortir; (*shout, cry*) laisser échapper; (*clothes*) élargir.
lethal ['li:θəl] *adj* mortel.
lethargy ['leθədʒi] *n* léthargie *f.* **lethargic** *adj* léthargique.
letter ['letə] *n* lettre *f.* **letter-box** *n* boîte aux lettres *f.*
lettuce ['letis] *n* laitue *f.*
leukaemia [luː'kiːmiə] *n* leucémie *f.*
level ['levl] *n* niveau *m;* (*road, rail*) palier *m. adj* (*flat*) plat; horizontal; (*spoonful*) ras; (*equal*) à égalité. **be level with** être au niveau de; être à la hauteur de. **level crossing** passage à niveau *m.* **level-headed** *adj* équilibré. *v* niveler.
lever ['liːvə] *n* levier *m.*
levy ['levi] *n* taxation *f,* taxe *f. v* prélever, imposer.
lewd [luːd] *adj* obscène.
liable ['laiəbl] *adj* sujet, -ette; (*law*) responsable. **be liable to** risquer de. **liability** *n* responsabilité *f;* handicap *m.*
liaison [li'eizon] *n* liaison *f.*
liar ['laiə] *n* menteur, -euse *m, f.*
libel ['laibəl] *n* (*act*) diffamation *f;* (*writing*) libelle *m. v* diffamer; (*insult*) calomnier. **libellous** *adj* diffamatoire.
liberal ['libərəl] *adj* libéral; généreux. **Liberal** *n, adj* (*pol*) libéral, -e.
liberate ['libəreit] *v* libérer. **liberation** *n* libération *f.*
liberty ['libəti] *n* liberté *f.* **at liberty** en liberté, libre.
Libra ['liːbrə] *n* Balance *f.*
library ['laibrəri] *n* bibliothèque *f.* **librarian** *n* bibliothécaire *m, f.*
libretto [li'bretou] *n* livret *m.*
lice [lais] *V* **louse.**
licence ['laisəns] *n* permis *m;* (*comm*) licence *f.* **license** *v* donner une licence à; autoriser. **be licensed** (*shop, etc.*) détenir une licence. **licensee** *n* (*pub*) patron, -onne *m, f.*
lichen ['laikən] *n* lichen *m.*
lick [lik] *n* coup de langue *m. v* lécher.
lid [lid] *n* couvercle *m.*
lido ['liːdou] *n* complexe balnéaire *m.*
***lie**[1] [lai] *v* s'allonger, se coucher; (*be lying*) être allongé, être couché; (*be*) être. **lie around** traîner. **lie down** s'allonger, se coucher. **lie in** faire la grasse matinée.
lie[2] [lai] *n* mensonge *m. v* mentir.
Liechtenstein ['liktən,stain] *n* Liechtenstein *m.*
lieutenant [ləf'tenənt] *n* lieutenant *m.*
life [laif] *n* vie *f.* **lifeless** *adj* sans vie, inanimé.
lifebelt ['laifbelt] *n* bouée de sauvetage *f.*
lifeboat ['laifbout] *n* canot de sauvetage *m;* (*on ship*) chaloupe de sauvetage *f.*
lifeguard ['laifgaːd] *n* surveillant de baignade *m.*
life insurance *n* assurance-vie *f.*
life-jacket *n* gilet de sauvetage *m.*
lifeline ['laiflain] *n* main courante *f;* (*diver's*) corde de sécurité *f.*
lifelong ['laifloŋ] *adj* de toujours.
life-saving *n* sauvetage *m.*
life story *n* biographie *f.*
lifetime ['laiftaim] *n* vie *f;* éternité *f.*
lift [lift] *n* ascenseur *m.* **give someone a lift** prendre quelqu'un en voiture. *v* (se) lever, soulever.
ligament ['ligəmənt] *n* ligament *m.*
***light**[1] [lait] *n* lumière *f;* (*mot*) feu *m. adj* clair. **light bulb** ampoule *f.* **lighthouse** *n* phare m **light meter** photomètre *m.* **light-year** *n* année-lumineuse *f. v* (*set fire to*) allumer; (*room, etc.*) éclairer. **lighten** *v* (s')éclaircir. **lighter** *n* (*for cigarette*) briquet *m.* **lighting** *n* éclairage *m.*
light[2] [lait] *adj* léger. **light-headed** *adj* étourdi. **light-hearted** *adj* gai, joyeux. **lightweight** *adj* léger; (*boxing*) poids léger. **lighten** *v* alléger. **lightness** *n* légèreté *f.*
***light**[3] [lait] *v* **light upon** tomber sur.
lightning ['laitniŋ] *n* éclair *m,* foudre *f.* **lightning conductor** paratonnerre *m.*
like[1] [laik] *adj* semblable. *prep* comme. **be** *or* **look like** ressembler à **liken** *v* comparer. **likeness** *n* ressemblance *f;* forme *f;* portrait *m.* **likewise** *adv* également.

like² [laik] *v* aimer; (*want*) vouloir. **likeable** *adj* sympathique. **liking** *n* goût *m*.
likely ['laikli] *adj* probable; plausible. **be likely to** risquer de. *adv* probablement. **likelihood** *n* probabilité *f*.
lilac ['lailək] *nm, adj* lilas.
lily ['lili] *n* lis *m*. **lily-of-the-valley** *n* muguet *m*.
limb [lim] *n* membre *m*.
limbo ['limbou] *n* (*rel*) limbes *m pl*; oubli *m*.
lime¹ [laim] *n* chaux *f*. **limestone** *n* pierre à chaux *f*.
lime² [laim] *n* (*fruit*) lime *f*; (*tree*) limettier *m*; (*linden*) tilleul *m*. **lime green** *nm, adj* vert jaune. **lime juice** jus de citron vert *m*.
limelight ['laim,lait] *n* **in the limelight** en vedette.
limerick ['limərik] *n* poème humoristique *m*.
limit ['limit] *n* limite *f*. *v* limiter. **limitation** *n* limitation *f*. **limitless** *adj* illimité.
limousine ['limə,ziːn] *n* limousine *f*.
limp¹ [limp] *v* boîter.
limp² [limp] *adj* mou, molle. **limpness** *n* mollesse *f*.
limpet ['limpit] *n* patelle *f*.
line¹ [lain] *n* ligne *f*; corde *f*; (*of poem*) vers *m*; (*row*) rangée *f*, file *f*. *v* régler; (*wrinkle*) rider. **line up** (s')aligner. **linear** *adj* linéaire.
line² [lain] *v* (*clothes*) doubler; (*brakes*) garnir.
linen ['linin] *n* lin *m*; (*sheets, etc.*) linge *m*. **linen basket** panier à linge *m*.
liner ['lainə] *n* liner *m*.
linger ['liŋgə] *v* (*person*) s'attarder; (*pain, memory, etc.*) persister; (*dawdle*) traîner.
lingerie ['lãʒəriː] *n* lingerie *f*.
linguist ['liŋgwist] *n* linguiste *m, f*. **linguistic** *adj* linguistique. **linguistics** *n* linguistique *f*.
lining ['lainiŋ] *n* (*clothes*) doublure *f*; (*brakes*) garniture *f*.
link [liŋk] *n* lien *m*, liaison *f*; (*of chain*) maillon *m*. *v* lier.
linoleum [li'nouliəm] *n* linoléum *m*. **lino** *n* (*coll*) lino *m*.
linseed ['lin,siːd] *n* graines de lin *f pl*. **linseed oil** huile de lin *f*.
lint [lint] *n* tissu ouaté *m*.
lion ['laiən] *n* lion *m*. **lioness** *n* lionne *f*.
lip [lip] *n* lèvre *f*; (*edge*) bord *m*. **lip-read** *v* lire sur les lèvres. **lipstick** *n* rouge à lèvres *m*.
liqueur [li'kjuə] *n* liqueur *f*.
liquid ['likwid] *nm, adj* liquide. **liquidate** *v* liquider. **liquidation** *n* liquidation *f*. **liquidizer** *n* centrifugeuse *f*.
liquor ['likə] *n* spiritueux *m*.
liquorice ['likəris] *n* réglisse *f*.
lira ['liərə] *n* lire *f*.
Lisbon ['lizbən] *n* Lisbonne.
lisp [lisp] *v* zézayer.
list¹ [list] *n* liste *f*. *v* cataloguer, énumérer.
list² [list] *v* (*naut*) gîter. *n* inclinaison *f*.
listen ['lisn] *v* écouter. **listener** *n* auditeur, -trice *m, f*.
listless ['listlis] *adj* sans énergie; indolent, apathique.
lit [lit] *V* **light¹**, **light³**.
litany ['litəni] *n* litanie *f*.
literacy ['litərəsi] *n* degré d'alphabétisation *m*. **be literate** savoir lire et écrire.
literal ['litərəl] *adj* littéral.
literary ['litərəri] *adj* littéraire.
literature ['litrətʃə] *n* littérature *f*; (*brochures*) documentation *f*.
litigation [liti'geiʃən] *n* litige *m*.
litre ['liːtə] *n* litre *m*.
litter ['litə] *n* détritus *m pl*; (*zool*) portée *f*; (*bedding*) litière *f*. **litter-bin** *n* boîte à ordures *f*. *v* joncher; (*make untidy*) mettre en désordre.
little ['litl] *adj* (*small*) petit; (*not much*) peu de. *nm, adv* peu. **little by little** peu à peu.
liturgy ['litədʒi] *n* liturgie *f*. **liturgical** *adj* liturgique.
live¹ [liv] *v* vivre; habiter. **live down** faire oublier. **live on** vivre de.
live² [laiv] *adj* vivant; (*broadcast*) en direct; (*coal*) ardent; (*wire*) sous tension. *adv* en direct.
livelihood ['laivlihud] *n* gagne-pain *m invar*.
lively ['laivli] *adj* vif, plein d'entrain. **liveliness** *n* vivacité *f*, entrain *m*.
liven ['laivn] *v* **liven up** égayer, (s')animer.
liver ['livə] *n* foie *m*.
livestock ['laivstok] *n* bétail *m*.
livid ['livid] *adj* livide; furieux.
living ['liviŋ] *adj* vivant, en vie. *n* vie *f*. **living room** salle de séjour *f*.
lizard ['lizəd] *n* lézard *m*.
load [loud] *n* charge *f*; (*weight*) poids *m*; (*coll*) tas *m*. *v* charger. **loaded** *adj* chargé;

(*dice*) pipé; (*question*) insidieux; (*slang*: *rich*) bourré de fric.
loaf[1] [louf] *n* pain *m*.
loaf[2] [louf] *v* **loaf around** fainéanter. **loafer** *n* (*coll*) flemmard, -e *m*, *f*.
loan [loun] *n* prêt *m*. *v* prêter.
loathe [louð] *v* détester. **loathing** *n* dégoût *m*. **loathsome** *adj* détestable.
lob [lob] *v* lancer; (*tennis*) lober. *n* lob *m*.
lobby ['lobi] *n* vestibule *m*, foyer *m*; groupe de pression *m*. *v* faire pression (sur).
lobe [loub] *n* lobe *m*.
lobster ['lobstə] *n* homard *m*.
local ['loukəl] *adj* local; du pays. *n* (*coll*: *pub*) café du coin *m*. **the locals** (*coll*: *people*) les gens du coin. **locality** *n* (*region*) environs *m pl*; (*place*) lieu *m*. **localize** *v* localiser. **locally** *adv* localement; (*nearby*) dans les environs.
locate [lə'keit] *v* (*find*) repérer, localiser; situer. **location** *n* emplacement *m*; (*cinema*) extérieur *m*. **on location** en extérieur.
lock[1] [lok] *n* serrure *f*; (*canal*) écluse *f*. **locksmith** *n* serrurier *m*. **lock, stock, and barrel** en bloc. **under lock and key** sous clef. *v* fermer à clef; (*tech*) (se) bloquer. **lock away** mettre sous clef. **lock in** enfermer. **lock out** enfermer dehors. **lock up** tout fermer; (*jewels, etc.*) enfermer.
lock[2] [lok] *n* (*of hair*) mèche *f*; (*curl*) boucle *f*.
locker ['lokə] *n* casier *m*.
locket ['lokit] *n* médaillon *m*.
locomotive [ˌloukə'moutiv] *n* locomotive *f*. *adj* locomotif. **locomotion** *n* locomotion *f*.
locust ['loukəst] *n* locuste *f*.
lodge [lodʒ] *n* loge *f*; (*small house*) maison de gardien *f*. *v* (se) loger; (*report*) présenter. **lodge a complaint** porter plainte. **lodger** *n* locataire *m*, *f*; (*boarder*) pensionnaire *m*, *f*. **lodgings** *pl n* (*room*) chambre *f sing*; (*flatlet*) logement *m sing*.
loft [loft] *n* grenier *m*. **lofty** *adj* haut, élevé; (*haughty*) hautain.
log [log] *n* bûche *f*. **logbook** *n* registre *m*; (*naut*) livre de bord *m*; (*aero*) carnet de vol *m*; (*mot*) carnet de route *m*. **log cabin** cabane en rondins *f*. *v* noter.
logarithm ['logəriðəm] *n* logarithme *m*.
loggerheads ['logəhedz] *pl n* **at loggerheads** en désaccord.
logic ['lodʒik] *n* logique *f*. **logical** *adj* logique.
loins [loins] *pl n* reins *m pl*. **loin chop** côte première *f*. **loincloth** *n* pagne *m*.
loiter ['loitə] *v* traîner.
lollipop ['loli,pop] *n* sucette *f*.
London ['lʌndən] *n* Londres *m*.
lonely ['lounli] *adj* seul, solitaire. **loneliness** *n* solitude *f*.
long[1] [loŋ] *adj* long, longue. *adv* longtemps. **as long as** pourvu que. **long-distance** *adj* (*race*) de fond; (*phone*) interurbain. **long-playing record** 33 tours *m invar*. **long-range** *adj* à longue portée; (*weather forecast*) à long terme. **long-sighted** *adj* hypermétrope; (*having foresight*) prévoyant. **long-sleeved** *adj* à manches longues. **long-standing** *adj* de longue date. **long-term** *adj* à long terme. **long-winded** *adj* (*person*) intarissable; (*speech*) interminable.
long[2] [loŋ] *v* avoir très envie. **long for** désirer ardemment. **longing** *n* désir *m*, envie *f*.
longevity [lon'dʒevəti] *n* longévité *f*.
longitude ['londʒitjuːd] *n* longitude *f*. **longitudinal** *adj* longitudinal.
loo [luː] *n* (*coll*) cabinets *m pl*.
look [luk] *n* regard *m*; (*glance*) coup d'œil *m*; air *m*, allure *f*. *v* regarder; sembler, avoir l'air. **look after** s'occuper de; (*possessions*) prendre soin de. **look at** regarder. **look down on** mépriser. **look for** chercher. **look forward to** attendre avec impatience. **look out** faire attention. **look out of** regarder par. **look up** lever les yeux; (*word, etc.*) chercher; s'améliorer.
loom[1] [luːm] *v* apparaître indistinctement; menacer.
loom[2] [luːm] *n* métier à tisser *m*.
loop [luːp] *n* boucle *f*. *v* boucler; former une boucle. **loop the loop** (*aero*) faire un looping.
loophole ['luːphoul] *n* (*in law, etc.*) lacune *f*, échappatoire *f*.
loose [luːs] *adj* lâche; (*knot*) desserré; (*tooth*) branlant. **come loose** se desserrer; branler. **get loose** s'échapper. **let loose** lâcher. **loose change** petite monnaie *f*. **loose chippings** gravillons *m pl*. **loose covers** housses *f pl*. **loose-leaf** *adj* à feuilles volantes. *v* (*free*) lâcher; (*undo*) défaire. **loosely** *adv* lâchement; approximativement. **loosen** *v* relâcher; (se) desserrer; (se) défaire.

loot [luːt] *n* butin *m*. *v* piller. **looter** *n* pillard *m*. **looting** *n* pillage *m*.
lop [lop] *v* couper.
lopsided [ˌlop'saidid] *adj* de travers.
lord [loːd] *n* seigneur *m*; (*as title*) lord *m*.
lorry ['lori] *n* camion *m*. **lorry-driver** *n* camionneur *m*, routier *m*.
***lose** [luːz] *v* perdre; (*watch, clock*) retarder. **loser** *n* perdant, -e *m, f*. **lost property** objets trouvés *m pl*.
loss [los] *n* perte *f*. **be at a loss** être embarrassé.
lost [lost] *V* **lose**.
lot [lot] *n* (*destiny*) sort *m*; (*auction*) lot *m*. **a lot** beaucoup. **lots of** beaucoup de. **quite a lot of** pas mal de. **the lot** tout *m*.
lotion ['louʃən] *n* lotion *f*.
lottery ['lotəri] *n* loterie *f*.
lotus ['loutəs] *n* lotus *m*.
loud [laud] *adj* fort, sonore; (*gaudy*) voyant. *adv* fort. **loud hailer** porte-voix *m invar*. **loud-mouthed** *adj* braillard. **loudspeaker** *n* haut-parleur *m*. **loudly** *adv* fort. **loudness** *n* force *f*.
lounge [laundʒ] *n* salon *m*. **lounge suit** complet-veston *m*. *v* (*on bed*) se prélasser; (*idle*) paresser, flâner. **lounger** *n* (*bed*) lit de plage *m*.
louse [laus] *n, pl* **lice** pou (*pl* poux) *m*. **lousy** *adj* pouilleux; (*slang: bad*) moche, dégueulasse.
lout [laut] *n* rustre *m*.
love [lʌv] *n* amour *m*; (*tennis*) zéro *m*. **fall in love** tomber amoureux. **love affair** liaison *f*. **make love** faire l'amour. **with love from** (*in letter*) affectueusement. *v* aimer. **lovable** *adj* adorable. **lover** *n* amant *m*; (*enthusiast*) amateur *m*. **loving** *adj* affectueux.
lovely ['lʌvli] *adj* charmant, agréable.
low [lou] *adj* bas, basse; faible. *adv* bas. **low-cut** *adj* décolleté. **lowland** *n* plaine *f*. **low-lying** *adj* à basse altitude. **low-paid** *adj* mal payé. **lowly** *adj* humble, modeste.
lower ['louə] *adj* inférieur, -e. *v* baisser; (*on rope*) descendre.
loyal ['loiəl] *adj* loyal, fidèle. **loyalty** *n* loyauté *f*; fidélité *f*.
lozenge ['lozindʒ] *n* pastille *f*.
lubricate ['luːbrikeit] *v* lubrifier; (*mot*) graisser. **lubricant** *nm, adj* lubrifiant. **lubrication** *n* lubrification *f*; graissage *m*.
lucid ['luːsid] *adj* lucide. **lucidity** *n* lucidité *f*.
luck [lʌk] *n* chance *f*, hasard *m*. **bad luck** malchance *f*, malheur *m*. **good luck** bonne chance *f*, bonheur *m*. **lucky** *adj* heureux; (*charm*) porte-bonheur *m invar*. **be lucky** avoir de la chance.
lucrative ['luːkrətiv] *adj* lucratif.
ludicrous ['luːdikrəs] *adj* ridicule.
lug [lʌg] *v* traîner.
luggage ['lʌgidʒ] *n* bagages *m pl*. **luggage label** étiquette à bagages *f*. **luggage rack** porte-bagages *m invar*.
lukewarm ['luːkwoːm] *adj* tiède.
lull [lʌl] *n* arrêt *m*; (*storm*) accalmie *f*. *v* apaiser.
lullaby ['lʌləˌbai] *n* berceuse *f*.
lumbago [lʌm'beigou] *n* lumbago *m*.
lumber[1] ['lʌmbə] *n* (*wood*) bois de charpente *m*; (*junk*) bric-à-brac *m invar*. **lumberjack** *n* bûcheron *m*. **lumber yard** chantier de scierie *m*. *v* **lumber with** (*coll*) coller à.
lumber[2] ['lʌmbə] *v* marcher pesamment.
luminous ['luːminəs] *adj* lumineux.
lump [lʌmp] *n* morceau *m*, masse *f*; (*med*) grosseur *f*. **lump sum** somme globale *f*. **lumpy** *adj* grumeleux.
lunacy ['luːnəsi] *n* folie *f*, démence *f*.
lunar ['luːnə] *adj* lunaire.
lunatic ['lunətik] *n, adj* fou, folle; dément, -e. **lunatic asylum** asile d'aliénés *m*.
lunch [lʌntʃ] *n* déjeuner *m*. *v* déjeuner.
lung [lʌŋ] *n* poumon *m*.
lunge [lʌndʒ] *v* faire un mouvement brusque en avant. *n* coup en avant *m*.
lurch[1] [ləːtʃ] *v* (*person*) vaciller, tituber; (*car, ship*) faire une embardée. *n* vacillement *m*; embardée *f*.
lurch[2] [ləːtʃ] *n* **leave in the lurch** faire faux bond à.
lure [luə] *v* attirer par la ruse. *n* attrait *m*; (*decoy*) leurre *m*.
lurid ['luərid] *adj* affreux, horrible; à sensation.
lurk [ləːk] *v* (*person*) se tapir; (*danger*) menacer; (*doubt*) persister. **lurking** *adj* vague.
luscious ['lʌʃəs] *adj* succulent.
lush [lʌʃ] *adj* luxuriant, riche.
lust [lʌst] *n* (*sexual*) luxure *f*; (*for power, etc.*) soif *f*. *v* **lust after** convoiter; avoir soif de. **lusty** *adj* vigoureux.
lustre ['lʌstə] *n* lustre *m*.
lute [luːt] *n* luth *m*.

Luxembourg ['lʌksəm,bəːg] *n* Luxembourg *m*.
luxury ['lʌkʃəri] *n* luxe *m*. **luxuriant** *adj* luxuriant. **luxurious** *adj* luxueux.
lynch [lintʃ] *v* lyncher.
lynx [links] *n* lynx *m invar*.
lyre [laiə] *n* lyre *f*.
lyrical ['lirikəl] *adj* lyrique.
lyrics ['liriks] *pl n* paroles *f pl*. **lyricist** *n* parolier, -ère *m, f*.

M

mac [mak] *n* (*coll*) imper *m*.
macabre [mə'kaːbr] *adj* macabre.
macaroni [makə'rouni] *n* macaroni *m*.
mace[1] [meis] *n* (*staff*) masse *f*; (*club*) massue *f*.
mace[2] [meis] *n* (*spice*) macis *m*.
machine [mə'ʃiːn] *n* machine *f*. **machine-gun** *n* mitrailleuse *f*. **machinery** *n* machinerie *f*; mécanisme *m*.
mackerel ['makrəl] *n* maquereau *m*.
mackintosh ['makin,toʃ] *n* imperméable *m*.
mad [mad] *adj* fou, folle; (*angry*) furieux. **madden** *v* rendre fou; exaspérer. **madly** *adv* follement, éperdument. **madness** *n* folie *f*.
madam ['madəm] *n* madame *f*.
Madrid [mə'drid] *n* Madrid.
made [meid] *V* **make**.
Madeira [mə'diərə] *n* (*place*) Madère *f*; (*wine*) madère *m*.
magazine [,magə'ziːn] *n* revue *f*, magazine *m*; (*mil*) magasin *m*.
maggot ['magət] *n* ver *m*.
magic ['madʒik] *n* magie *f*. *adj also* **magical** magique. **magician** *n* magicien, -enne *m, f*.
magistrate ['madʒistreit] *n* magistrat *m*.
magnanimous [mag'naniməs] *adj* magnanime. **magnanimity** *n* magnanimité *f*.
magnate ['magneit] *n* magnat *m*.
magnet ['magnət] *n* aimant *m*. **magnetic** *adj* magnétique. **magnetism** *n* magnétisme *m*. **magnetize** *v* magnétiser.
magnificent [mag'nifisnt] *adj* magnifique. **magnificence** *n* magnificence *f*.
magnify ['magnifai] *v* grossir. **magnifying glass** loupe *f*. **magnification** *n* grossissement *m*.
magnitude ['magnitjuːd] *n* ampleur *f*.
magnolia [mag'nouliə] *n* magnolia *m*.
magpie ['magpai] *n* pie *f*.
mahogany [mə'hogəni] *n* acajou *m*.
maid [meid] *n* bonne *f*. **old maid** vieille fille *f*.
maiden ['meidən] *n* jeune fille *f*. *adj* (*first*) premier. **maiden aunt** tante célibataire *f*. **maiden name** nom de jeune fille *m*.
mail [meil] *n* (*letters*) courrier *m*; (*service*) poste *f*. **mail-bag** *n* sac postal *m*. **mailbox** *n* (*US*) boîte aux lettres *f*. **mailman** *n* (*US*) facteur *m*. **mail order** vente par correspondence *f*. *v* envoyer par la poste. **mailing list** liste d'adresses *f*.
maim [meim] *v* estropier.
main [mein] *adj* principal. **main course** plat principal *m*. **mainland** *n* continent *m*. **main-line station** gare de grande ligne *f*. **main road** grande route *f*. **mainstay** *n* soutien *m*. *n* (*gas, water*) conduite *f*. **in the main** en général. **mains** *n* (*elec*) secteur *m*.
maintain [mein'tein] *v* maintenir; (*car, family*) entretenir; continuer. **maintenance** *n* maintien *m*; entretien *m*; (*alimony*) pension alimentaire *f*.
maisonette [meizə'net] *n* duplex *m*.
maize [meiz] *n* maïs *m*.
majesty ['madʒəsti] *n* majesté *f*. **majestic** *adj* majestueux.
major ['meidʒə] *adj* majeur, -e. *n* (*mil*) commandant *m*.
majority [mə'dʒoriti] *n* majorité *f*. **be in the majority** être majoritaire.
***make** [meik] *n* marque *f*. *v* faire; rendre; obliger; arriver à. **make believe** faire semblant. **make out** (*draw up*) dresser; discerner; prétendre. **makeshift** *adj* de fortune. **make up** inventer (*face*) (se) maquiller; composer; assembler. **make-up** *n* maquillage *m*. **make up for** compenser. **maker** *n* fabricant *m*. **making** *n* fabrication *f*.
maladjusted [malə'dʒʌstid] *adj* inadapté.
malaria [mə'leəriə] *n* malaria *m*.
male [meil] *nm, adj* mâle.
malevolent [mə'levələnt] *adj* malveillant. **malevolence** *n* malveillance *f*. **malevolently** *adv* avec malveillance.
malfunction [mal'fʌŋkʃən] *n* mauvaise fonction *f*. *v* mal fonctionner.

Mali ['maːli] *n* Mali *m*.
malice ['malis] *n* malice *f*. **malicious** *adj* méchant, malveillant.
malignant [mə'lignənt] *adj* malfaisant; (*med*) malin, -igne. **malignancy** *n* malfaisance *f*; malignité *f*.
malinger [mə'liŋgə] *v* faire le malade. **malingerer** *n* faux malade, fausse malade *m, f*.
mallet ['malit] *n* maillet *m*.
malnutrition [malnju'triʃən] *n* sous-alimentation *f*.
malt [moːlt] *n* malt *m*.
Malta ['moːltə] *n* Malte *f*. **Maltese** *nm, adj* maltais. **the Maltese** les Maltais.
maltreat [mal'triːt] *v* maltraiter. **maltreatment** *n* mauvais traitement *m*.
mammal ['maməl] *n* mammifère *m*.
mammoth ['maməθ] *n* mammouth *m*. *adj* géant.
man [man] *n, pl* **men** homme *m*. *v* armer. **manhood** *n* âge d'homme *m*. **manly** *adj* viril.
manage ['manidʒ] *v* (*business, etc.*) gérer, administrer; (*cope*) se débrouiller. **manage to** réussir à. **manageable** *adj* maniable. **management** *n* gestion *f*, administration *f*, direction *f*; (*not workers*) cadres *m pl*. **manager** *n* directeur *m*, gérant *m*. **manageress** *n* directrice *f*, gérante *f*. **managerial** *adj* directorial. **managing director** directeur général *m*.
mandarin ['mandərin] *n* mandarin *m*. **mandarin orange** (*fruit*) mandarine *f*; (*tree*) mandarinier *m*.
mandate ['mandeit] *n* mandat *m*. **mandatory** *adj* obligatoire; (*power, etc.*) mandataire.
mandolin ['mandəlin] *n* mandoline *f*.
mane [mein] *n* crinière *f*.
mange [meindʒ] *n* gale *f*. **mangy** *adj* galeux; (*coll*) minable, miteux.
manger ['meindʒə] *n* mangeoire *f*; (*rel*) crèche *f*.
mangle[1] ['maŋgl] *n* (*wringer*) essoreuse *f*. *v* essorer.
mangle[2] ['maŋgl] *v* mutiler, estropier.
mango ['maŋgou] *n* (*fruit*) mangue *f*; (*tree*) manguier *m*.
manhandle [man'handl] *v* maltraiter; (*goods*) manutentionner.
manhole ['manhoul] *n* trou d'homme *m*.
mania ['meiniə] *n* manie *f*. **maniac** *n* (*psych*) maniaque *m, f*; (*coll*: *madman*) fou, folle *m, f*; (*coll*: *enthusiast*) mordu *m*.
manicure ['manikjuə] *n* soin des mains *m*. *v* (*nails*) faire. **manicurist** *n* manucure *m, f*.
manifest ['manifest] *adj* manifeste. *v* manifester. **manifestation** *n* manifestation *f*.
manifesto [mani'festou] *n* manifeste *m*.
manifold ['manifould] *adj* divers; multiple. *n* **exhaust manifold** (*mot*) collecteur d'échappement *m*.
manipulate [mə'nipjuleit] *v* manipuler; manœuvrer. **manipulation** *n* manipulation *f*; manœuvre *f*.
mankind [ˌman'kaind] *n* le genre humain *m*.
man-made [ˌman'meid] *adj* synthétique; artificiel.
manner ['manə] *n* manière *f*; attitude *f*; sorte *f*. **manners** *pl n* manières *f pl*.
mannerism ['manəˌrizəm] *n* trait particulier *m*.
manoeuvre *or US* **maneuver** [mə'nuːvə] *n* manœuvre *f*. *v* manœuvrer.
manor ['manə] *n* manoir *m*.
manpower ['manˌpauə] *n* main-d'œuvre *m*; force physique *f*.
mansion ['manʃən] *n* (*country*) château *m*; (*town*) hôtel particulier *m*.
manslaughter ['manˌsloːtə] *n* homicide involontaire *m*.
mantelpiece ['mantlpiːs] *n* cheminée *f*.
mantle ['mantl] *n* (*of snow*) manteau *m*; (*cloak*) cape *f*; (*of gas lamp*) manchon *m*.
manual ['manjuəl] *nm, adj* manuel. **manually** *adv* à la main.
manufacture [manju'faktʃə] *n* fabrication *f*; (*clothes*) confection *f*. *v* fabriquer; confectionner. **manufacturer** *n* fabricant *m*.
manure [mə'njuə] *n* fumier *m*; (*artificial*) engrais *m*. *v* fumer.
manuscript ['manjuskript] *nm, adj* manuscrit.
many ['meni] *adj* beaucoup de, un grand nombre de. *pron* beaucoup, un grand nombre. **as many** autant (de). **how many** combien (de). **so many** tant (de). **too many** trop (de).
map [map] *n* carte *f*; (*of town*) plan *m*. *v* faire la carte de. **map out** tracer.
maple ['meipl] *n* érable *m*.
mar [maː] *v* gâter.
marathon ['marəθən] *nm, adj* marathon.

marble ['maːbl] *n* marbre *m*; (*toy*) bille *f*. *v* marbrer.
march [maːtʃ] *n* marche *f*. *v* marcher au pas. **march-past** défilé *m*.
March [maːtʃ] *n* mars *m*.
marchioness [ˌmaːʃə'nes] *n* marquise *f*.
mare [meə] *n* jument *f*.
margarine [ˌmaːdʒə'riːn] *n* margarine *f*.
margin ['maːdʒin] *n* marge *f*. **marginal** *adj* marginal. **marginally** *adv* de très peu.
marguerite [ˌmaːgə'riːt] *n* marguerite *f*.
marigold ['marigould] *n* souci *m*.
marijuana [mari'waːnə] *n* marihuana *f*.
marina [mə'riːnə] *n* marina *f*.
marinade [ˌmari'neid] *n* marinade *f*. *v* mariner.
marine [mə'riːn] *adj* (*animal*, *plant*) marin; (*products*) de mer; maritime. *n* (*naut*) marine marchande *f*; (*mil*) fusilier marin *m*.
marital ['maritl] *adj* conjugal, matrimonial.
maritime ['maritaim] *adj* maritime.
marjoram ['maːdʒərəm] *n* marjolaine *f*.
mark[1] [maːk] *n* marque *f*; (*school*) note *f*, point *m*; (*model*) série *f*. **marksman** *n* bon tireur *m*. *v* marquer; (*school*) corriger, noter. **marked** *adj* marqué, sensible. **marking** *n* correction *f*; (*of animal*) marque *f*.
mark[2] [maːk] *n* (*currency*) mark *m*.
market ['maːkit] *n* marché *m*. **market day** jour de marché *m*. **market gardening** culture maraîchère *f*. **market place** place du marché *f*. **market research** étude de marché *f*. **market value** valeur marchande *f*. *v* vendre. **marketing** *n* commercialisation *f*.
marmalade ['maːməleid] *n* confiture d'orange *f*.
maroon[1] [mə'ruːn] *adj* bordeaux *invar*.
maroon[2] [mə'ruːn] *v* abandonner.
marquee [maː'kiː] *n* grande tente *f*; (*circus*) chapiteau *m*.
marquess *or* **marquis** ['maːkwis] *n* marquis *m*.
marquetry ['maːkətri] *n* marqueterie *f*.
marriage ['maridʒ] *n* mariage *m*. **by marriage** par alliance. **marriage certificate** extrait d'acte de mariage *m*. **marriage guidance counsellor** conseiller conjugal, conseillère conjugale *m*, *f*. **marriage licence** dispense de bans *f*.
marrow ['marou] *n* (*of bone*) moelle *f*; (*vegetable*) courge *f*.
marry ['mari] *v* se marier; (*husband*, *wife*) épouser; (*priest*, *vicar*) marier. **married** *adj* marié; conjugal. **get married** se marier. **married name** nom de femme mariée *m*.
Mars [maːz] *n* Mars *f*. **Martian** *n* Martien, -enne; *adj* martien.
marsh [maːʃ] *n* marais *m*. **marshland** *n* marécage *m*. **marshmallow** *n* guimauve *f*. **marshy** *adj* marécageux.
marshal ['maːʃəl] *n* (*mil*) maréchal *m*; (*sports*, *etc.*) membre du service d'ordre *m*. *v* rassembler.
martial ['maːʃəl] *adj* martial.
martin ['maːtin] *n* martinet *m*.
martyr ['maːtə] *n* martyr, -e *m*, *f*. *v* martyriser. **martyrdom** *n* martyre *m*.
marvel ['maːvəl] *n* merveille *f*. *v* s'étonner (de).
marvellous ['maːvələs] *adj* merveilleux.
marzipan [maːzi'pan] *n* pâte d'amandes *f*.
mascara [ma'skaːrə] *n* mascara *m*.
mascot ['maskət] *n* mascotte *f*.
masculine ['maskjulin] *nm*, *adj* masculin. **masculinity** *n* masculinité *f*.
mash [maʃ] *v* écraser; (*potatoes*) faire en purée. **mashed potatoes** puree *f sing*. *n* (*animal feed*) pâtée *f*; purée *f*.
mask [maːsk] *n* masque *m*. *v* masquer. **masking tape** papier-cache adhésif *m*.
masochist ['masəkist] *n* masochiste *m*, *f*. **masochism** *n* masochisme *m*. **masochistic** *adj* masochiste.
mason ['meisn] *n* maçon *m*. **masonry** *n* maçonnerie *f*.
masquerade [maskə'reid] *n* (*pretence*) mascarade *f*. *v* **masquerade as** se faire passer pour.
mass[1] [mas] *n* masse *f*. **mass hysteria** hystérie collective *f*. **mass media** media *m pl*. **mass-produce** *v* fabriquer en série. **mass production** fabrication en série *f*. *v* (se) masser.
mass[2] [mas] *n* (*rel*) messe *f*.
massacre ['masəkə] *n* massacre *m*. *v* massacrer.
massage ['masaːʒ] *n* massage *m*. *v* masser. **masseur** *n* masseur *m*. **masseuse** *n* masseuse *f*.
massive ['masiv] *adj* massif, énorme.
mast [maːst] *n* (*naut*) mât *m*; (*radio*, *etc.*) pylône *m*.
master ['maːstə] *n* maître *m*; (*teacher*) professeur *m*. **master copy** original *m*. **master key** passe-partout *m invar*. **mas-**

terpiece *n* chef-d'œuvre *m*. **master plan** stratégie d'ensemble *f*. *v* maîtriser; surmonter; (*learn, understand*) posséder à fond. **masterly** *adj* magistral. **mastery** *n* maîtrise *f*, domination *f*; (*skill*) virtuosité *f*.
mastermind ['maːstə,maind] *n* cerveau *m*. *v* diriger.
masturbate ['mastəbeit] *v* se masturber. **masturbation** *n* masturbation *f*.
mat [mat] *n* (*floor*) tapis *m*; (*door*) paillasson *m*; (*table*) dessous-de-plat *m invar*; (*cloth*) napperon *m*. **matted** *adj* (*hair*) emmêlé; (*cloth*) feutré.
match¹ [matʃ] *n* allumette *f*. **matchbox** *n* boîte à allumettes *f*.
match² [matʃ] *n* (*sport*) match *m*, partie *f*; (*equal*) égal, -e *m, f*. *v* égaler; (*clothes*) s'assortir à, aller bien ensemble; (*pair*) s'apparier. **matchless** *adj* sans égal.
mate [meit] *n* mâle, femelle *m, f*; camarade *m, f*; aide *f*; (*coll: friend*) copain, -ine *m, f*. *v* (s')accoupler.
material [mə'tiəriəl] *n* (*fabric*) tissu *m*; (*substance*) matière *f*; (*for book, etc.*) matériaux *m pl*. **materials** *n pl* fournitures *f pl*. *adj* matériel. **materialist** *n* matérialiste *m, f*. **materialistic** *adj* matérialiste. **materialize** *v* se matérialiser.
maternal [mə'təːnl] *adj* maternel.
maternity [mə'təːnəti] *n* maternité *f*. **maternity clothes** vêtements de grossesse *m pl*. **maternity hospital** maternité *f*.
mathematics [maθə'matiks] *n* mathématiques *f pl*. **mathematical** *adj* mathématique. **mathematician** *n* mathématicien, -enne *m, f*. **maths** *n* (*coll*) maths *f pl*.
matinee ['matinei] *n* matinée *f*. **matinée coat** veste de bébé *f*.
matins ['matinz] *n* matines *f pl*.
matriarch ['meitriaːk] *n* matrone *f*. **matriarchal** *adj* matriarcal.
matrimony ['matriməni] *n* mariage *m*. **matrimonial** *adj* matrimonial.
matrix ['meitriks] *n* matrice *f*.
matron ['meitrən] *n* matrone *f*; (*hospital*) infirmière en chef *f*; (*school*) infirmière *f*; (*home*) directrice *f*.
matt [mat] *adj* mat.
matter ['matə] *n* (*substance*) matière *f*; affaire *f*; contenu *m*. **as a matter of fact** à vrai dire. **matter-of-fact** *adj* (*tone*) neutre; (*person*) terre à terre. **what's the matter?** qu'est-ce qu'il y a? *v* importer. **it doesn't matter** ça ne fait rien.
mattress ['matris] *n* matelas *m*.
mature [mə'tjuə] *adj* mûr. *v* mûrir. **maturity** *n* maturité *f*.
maudlin ['moːdlin] *adj* larmoyant.
maul [moːl] *v* mutiler, malmener.
mausoleum [moːsə'liəm] *n* mausolée *m*.
mauve [mouv] *nm, adj* mauve.
maxim ['maksim] *n* maxime *f*.
maximum ['maksiməm] *nm, adj* maximum.
***may** [mei] *v* pouvoir.
May [mei] *n* mai *m*. **May Day** le Premier mai.
maybe ['meibiː] *adv* peut-être.
mayday ['meidei] *n* mayday *m*.
mayonnaise [,meiə'neiz] *n* mayonnaise *f*.
mayor [meə] *n* maire *m*.
maze [meiz] *n* labyrinthe *m*.
me [miː] *pron* moi; (*direct object*) me.
mead [miːd] *n* (*drink*) hydromel *m*.
meadow ['medou] *n* pré *m*.
meagre ['miːgə] *adj* maigre.
meal¹ [miːl] *n* (*food*) repas *m*. **make a meal of** (*labour*) faire tout un plat de.
meal² [miːl] *n* (*flour*) farine *f*.
***mean¹** [miːn] *v* (*signify*) vouloir dire; avoir l'intention (de); destiner.
mean² [miːn] *n* (*not generous*) avare; (*unkind*) mesquin; (*poor*) minable. **meanness** *n* avarice *f*; mesquinerie *f*.
mean³ [miːn] *n* milieu *m*; (*math*) moyenne *f*. *adj* moyen.
meander [mi'andə] *v* (*river*) serpenter; (*person*) errer. *n* méandre *m*.
meaning ['miːniŋ] *n* sens *m*, signification *f*. **meaningful** *adj* significatif. **meaningless** *adj* dénué de sens; (*senseless*) insensé.
means [miːnz] *n* (*way*) moyen *m*; (*wealth*) moyens *m pl*. **by all means** certainement. **by means of** au moyen de. **by no means** pas du tout. **means test** enquête sur les ressources *f*.
meant [ment] *V* **mean¹**.
meanwhile ['miːnwail] *adv* en attendant.
measles ['miːzlz] *n* rougeole *f*.
measure ['meʒə] *n* mesure *f*. **made to measure** fait sur mesure. *v* mesurer. **measurement** *n* mesure *f*.
meat [miːt] *n* viande *f*. **meatball** *n* boulette de viande *f*. **meat pie** pâté en croûte *m*.
mechanic [mi'kanik] *n* mécanicien *m*. **mechanical** *adj* mécanique. **mechanics** *pl n* mécanisme *m sing*; (*sing: science*)

mécanique *f.* **mechanism** *n* mécanisme *m.* **mechanize** *v* mécaniser.
medal ['medl] *n* médaille *f.* **medallist** *n* médaillé, -e *m, f.*
meddle ['medl] *v* (*interfere*) se mêler (de); toucher (à). **meddlesome** *adj* indiscret, -ète.
media ['miːdiə] *pl n* media *m pl.*
mediate ['miːdieit] *v* s'entremettre; servir de médiateur. **mediation** *n* médiation *f.* **mediator** *n* médiateur, -trice *m, f.*
medical ['medikəl] *adj* médical. **medical officer** médecin du travail *m.* **medical school** école de médecine *f.* *n* visite médicale *f.* examen médical *m.* **medicate** *v* médicamenter. **medicated** *adj* (*shampoo, etc.*) médical.
medicine ['medsən] *n* (*science*) médecine *f*; (*drug*) médicament *m.* **medicine chest** pharmacie *f.* **medicinal** *adj* médicinal.
medieval [medi'iːvəl] *adj* médiéval.
mediocre [miːdi'oukə] *adj* médiocre. **mediocrity** *n* médiocrité *f.*
meditate ['mediteit] *v* méditer. **meditation** *n* méditation *f.* **meditative** *adj* méditatif.
Mediterranean [ˌmeditə'reiniən] *adj* méditerranéen. *n* Méditerranée *f.*
medium ['miːdiəm] *n* milieu *m*; (*means*) moyen *m*; (*spirits*) médium *m.* **happy medium** juste milieu *m.* *adj* moyen. **medium-dry** *adj* (*wine*) demi-sec. **medium wave** (*radio*) onde moyenne *f.*
medley ['medli] *n* mélange *m*; (*music*) pot-pourri *m.*
meek [miːk] *adj* doux, douce. **meekness** *n* douceur *f.*
***meet** [miːt] *v* (se) rencontrer; (*by arrangement*) (se) retrouver; (*gather*) se réunir; (*expenses, etc.*) faire face à. **meeting** *n* réunion *f*, assemblée *f*; (*appointment*) rendez-vous *m.*
megaphone ['megəfoun] *n* porte-voix *m invar.*
melancholy ['melənkəli] *n* mélancolie *f.* *adj also* **melancholic** mélancolique.
mellow ['melou] *adj* moelleux, velouté; (*matured*) mûr. *v* mûrir; se velouter; (*person*) s'adoucir.
melodrama ['melədraːmə] *n* mélodrame *m.* **melodramatic** *adj* mélodramatique. **melodramatically** *adv* d'un air mélodramatique.
melody ['melədi] *n* mélodie *f.* **melodious** *adj* mélodieux.
melon ['melən] *n* melon *m.*
melt [melt] *v* (se) fondre. **melting** *n* fusion *f.*
member ['membə] *n* membre *m.* **membership** *n* adhésion *f.* **membership card** carte d'adhérent *f.* **membership fee** cotisation *f.*
membrane ['membrein] *n* membrane *f.* **membranous** *adj* membraneux.
memento [mə'mentou] *n* souvenir *m.*
memo ['memou] *n* (*coll*) note *f.*
memoirs ['memwaːz] *pl n* mémoires *m pl.*
memorable ['memərəbl] *adj* mémorable.
memorandum [memə'randəm] *n* mémorandum *m,* note *f.*
memorial [mi'moːriəl] *n* monument *m,* mémorial *m.* *adj* commémoratif.
memory ['meməri] *n* (*faculty*) mémoire *f*; (*thing remembered*) souvenir *m.* **memorize** *v* apprendre par cœur.
men [men] *V* **man.**
menace ['menis] *n* menace *f.* *v* menacer.
menagerie [mi'nadʒəri] *n* ménagerie *f.*
mend [mend] *v* raccommoder, réparer. *n* raccommodage *m.* **be on the mend** s'améliorer. **mending** *n* raccommodage *m.*
menial ['miːniəl] *adj* (*task*) de domestique; (*person*) servile.
meningitis [ˌmenin'dʒaitis] *n* méningite *f.*
menopause ['menəpoːz] *n* ménopause *f.*
menstrual ['menstruəl] *adj* menstruel. **menstruate** *v* avoir ses règles. **menstruation** *n* menstruation *f.*
mental ['mentl] *adj* mental; (*coll: mad*) timbré. **mental arithmetic** calcul mental *m.* **mental home** *or* **hospital** clinique psychiatrique *f.* **mentality** *n* mentalité *f.* **mentally** *adv* mentalement.
menthol ['menθəl] *n* menthol *m.*
mention ['menʃən] *v* mentionner. **don't mention it!** il n'y a pas de quoi! **not to mention** sans compter. *n* mention *f.*
menu ['menjuː] *n* menu *m.*
mercantile ['məːkənˌtail] *adj* marchand; commercial.
mercenary ['məːsinəri] *nm, adj* mercenaire.
merchandise ['məːtʃəndaiz] *n* marchandises *f pl.* **merchandizing** *n* techniques marchandes *f pl.*
merchant ['məːtʃənt] *n* négociant *m,* commerçant *m.* **merchant navy** marine marchande *f.*

mercury ['mɑːkjuri] *n* mercure *m*.
mercy ['mɑːsi] *n* pitié *f*, merci *f*; (*rel*) miséricorde *f*. **at the mercy of** à la merci de. **merciful** *adj* miséricordieux. **merciless** *adj* impitoyable.
mere [miə] *adj* simple. **it's a mere formality** ce n'est qu'une formalité.
merge [məːdʒ] *v* se mêler; (*comm*) fusionner; unifier. **merger** *n* fusion *f*.
meridian [mə'ridiən] *nm*, *adj* méridien.
meringue [mə'raŋ] *n* meringue *f*.
merit ['merit] *n* mérite *m*. *v* mériter.
mermaid ['məːmeid] *n* sirène *f*.
merry ['meri] *adj* gai, joyeux; (*coll*: *drunk*) éméché. **merry-go-round** *n* manège *m*. **merriment** *n* gaieté *f*; hilarité *f*.
mesh [meʃ] *n* maille *f*; (*network*) réseau *m*; (*gears*) engrenage *m*.
mesmerize ['mezməraiz] *v* hypnotiser.
mess [mes] *n* désordre *m*, gâchis *m*; (*dirt*) saleté *f*; (*mil*) mess *m*. **make a mess of** gâcher. *v* **mess up** salir; gâcher, mettre en désordre. **messy** *adj* en désordre; sale.
message ['mesidʒ] *n* message *m*; (*errand*) course *f*. **messenger** *n* messager, -ère *m*, *f*.
met [met] *V* **meet**.
metabolism [mi'tabəlizm] *n* métabolisme *m*.
metal ['metl] *n* métal *m*. **metallic** *adj* métallique. **metallurgist** *n* métallurgiste *m*. **metallurgy** *n* métallurgie *f*.
metamorphosis [metə'moːfəsis] *n* métamorphose *f*.
metaphor ['metəfə] *n* métaphore *f*. **metaphorical** *adj* métaphorique.
metaphysics [ˌmetə'fiziks] *n* métaphysique *f*. **metaphysical** *adj* métaphysique.
meteor ['miːtiə] *n* météore *m*. **meteoric** *adj* météorique; (*rapid*) fulgurant. **meteorite** *n* météorite *m*.
meteorology [ˌmiːtiə'rolədʒi] *n* météorologie *f*. **meteorological** *adj* météorologique. **meteorologist** *n* météorologue *m*, *f*.
meter ['miːtə] *n* compteur *m*.
methane ['miːθein] *n* méthane *m*.
method ['meθəd] *n* méthode *f*. **methodical** *adj* méthodique.
Methodist ['meθədist] *n* méthodiste *m*, *f*. **Methodism** *n* méthodisme *m*.
methylated spirits ['meθileitid] *n* alcool à brûler *m*.
meticulous [mi'tikjuləs] *adj* méticuleux.
metre ['miːtə] *n* mètre *m*. **metric** *adj* métrique.
metronome ['metrənoum] *n* métronome *m*.
metropolis [mə'tropəlis] *n* métropole *m*. **metropolitan** *adj* métropolitain.
mew [mjuː] *v* miauler. *n* miaulement *m*.
mice [mais] *V* **mouse**.
microbe ['maikroub] *n* microbe *m*.
microfilm ['maikrəˌfilm] *n* microfilm *m*.
microphone ['maikrəfoun] *n* microphone *m*.
microscope ['maikrəskoup] *n* microscope *m*. **microscopic** *adj* microscopique.
microwave ['maikrəweiv] *n* micro-onde *f*.
mid [mid] *adj* du milieu. **mid-June, July, etc.** mi-juin, juillet, etc.
mid-air [ˌmid'eə] *n* **in mid-air** en plein ciel.
midday [ˌmid'dei] *n* midi *m*.
middle ['midl] *n* milieu *m*. **in the middle** au milieu. *adj* du milieu. **middle-aged** *adj* d'un certain âge. **the Middle Ages** le moyen âge *m sing*. **middle-class** *adj* bourgeois. **Middle East** Moyen-Orient *m*. **middleman** *n* intermédiaire *m*. **middle-of-the-road** *adj* modéré. **middle-sized** *adj* de grandeur moyenne. **middling** *adj* comme ci comme ça.
midge [midʒ] *n* moucheron *m*.
midget ['midʒit] *n* nain, -e *m*, *f*.
midnight ['midnait] *n* minuit *m*.
midriff ['midrif] *n* diaphragme *m*; (*waist*) taille *f*.
midst [midst] *n* milieu *m*. **in our midst** parmi nous. **in the midst of** au milieu de.
midstream [ˌmid'striːm] *n* **in midstream** au milieu du courant.
midsummer ['midˌsʌmə] *n* cœur de l'été *m*. **Midsummer Day** la Saint-Jean *f*.
midway [ˌmid'wei] *adv*, *adj* à mi-chemin.
midweek [ˌmid'wiːk] *n* milieu de la semaine *m*.
midwife ['midwaif] *n* sage-femme *f*. **midwifery** *n* obstétrique *f*.
midwinter [ˌmid'wintə] *n* milieu de l'hiver *m*.
might[1] [mait] *V* **may**.
might[2] [mait] *n* puissance *f*.
mighty ['maiti] *adj* puissant; vaste. *adv* (*coll*) rudement.
migraine ['miːgrein] *n* migraine *f*.

migrate [mai'greit] *v* émigrer. **migration** *n* migration *f*.
mike [maik] *n* (*coll*: *microphone*) micro *m*.
mild [maild] *adj* doux, douce. **mildness** *n* douceur *f*.
mildew ['mildjuː] *n* (*vine*) mildiou *m*; (*plants*) rouille *f*; (*cloth*) moisissure *f*.
mile [mail] *n* mille *m*. **mileage** *n* distance en milles *f*; (*petrol*) consommation aux cent *f*. **mileometer** *n* compteur de milles *m*. **milestone** *n* borne *f*; (*of life, etc.*) jalon *m*.
militant ['militənt] *n*, *adj* militant, -e.
military ['militəri] *adj* militaire.
milk [milk] *n* lait *m*. **milk chocolate** chocolat au lait *m*. **milkman** *n* laitier *m*. **milk shake** lait parfumé fouetté *m*. *v* traire. **milking** *n* traite *f*. **milky** *adj* laiteux.
mill [mil] *n* moulin *m*; (*larger*) minoterie *f*; (*factory*) usine *f*. **like a millpond** comme un lac. **millstone** *n* meule *f*; (*burden*) boulet *m*. *v* moudre. **mill round** grouiller autour de. **miller** *n* meunier *m*.
millennium [mi'leniəm] *n* millénaire *m*. **the millennium** le millénium *m*.
millet ['milit] *n* millet *m*.
milligram ['mili,gram] *n* milligramme *m*.
millilitre ['mili,liːtə] *n* millilitre *m*.
millimetre ['mili,miːtə] *n* millimètre *m*.
milliner ['milinə] *n* modiste *f*. **millinery** *n* modes *f pl*.
million ['miljən] *n* million *m*. **millionaire** *n* millionnaire *m*. **millions of** des milliers de. **millionth** *n*(*m*+*f*), *adj* millionième.
mime [maim] *n* mime *m*. *v* mimer.
mimic ['mimik] *n* imitateur, -trice *m*, *f*. *v* imiter. **mimicry** *n* imitation *f*; (*zool*) mimétisme *m*.
minaret [minə'ret] *n* minaret *m*.
mince [mins] *n* (*meat*) hachis *m*. **mincemeat** *n* hachis de fruit secs, de pommes et de graisse *m*. **mince pie** tarte anglaise au mincemeat *f*. *v* hacher; (*walk*) marcher à petits pas maniérés. **mince words** mâcher ses mots. **mincer** *n* hachoir *m*. **mincing** *adj* affecté.
mind [maind] *n* esprit *m*. **bear in mind** tenir compte de. **go out of one's mind** perdre la tête. **have a good mind to** avoir bien envie de. **in mind** dans l'idée. **make up one's mind** décider. **read someone's mind** lire la pensée de quelqu'un. **to my mind** à mon avis. *v* (*look out*) faire attention (à), prendre garde (à); (*look after*) garder. **do you mind?** cela ne vous fait rien? **I don't mind** ça m'est égal. **never mind** ça ne fait rien.
mine[1] [main] *pron* le mien, la mienne.
mine[2] [main] *n* mine *f*. **minefield** *n* champ de mines *m*. **mineshaft** *n* puits de mine *m*. **minesweeper** dragueur de mines. *m*. *v* extraire; (*mil*) miner. **miner** *n* mineur *m*. **mining** *n* exploitation minière *f*. **mining town** ville miniere *f*.
mineral ['minərəl] *nm*, *adj* minéral. **minerals** *pl n* (*drinks*) boissons gazeuses *f pl*.
mingle ['miŋgl] *v* (se) mêler (à).
miniature ['minitʃə] *n* miniature *f*; (*bottle*) mini-bouteille *f*. *adj* miniature; minuscule.
minim ['minim] *n* blanche *f*.
minimum ['minimәm] *nm*, *adj* minimum. **minimal** *adj* minime. **minimize** *v* minimiser.
minister ['ministə] *n* ministre *m*. **ministerial** *adj* ministériel. **ministry** *n* ministère *m*.
mink [miŋk] *n* vison *m*.
minor ['mainə] *adj* mineur, -e; (*unimportant*) petit, secondaire. *n* mineur, -e *m*, *f*.
minority [mai'noriti] *n* minorité *f*. **in the minority** en minorité. *adj* minoritaire.
minstrel ['minstrəl] *n* ménestrel *m*.
mint[1] [mint] *n* (*bot*) menthe *f*.
mint[2] [mint] *n* Monnaie *f*. **in mint condition** à l'état neuf. *v* battre.
minuet [minju'et] *n* menuet *m*.
minus ['mainəs] *prep* moins. **minus quantity** quantité négative *f*. **minus sign** moins *m*.
minute[1] ['minit] *n* minute *f*. **minutes** *pl n* compte rendu *m sing*. *v* (*meeting*) rédiger le compte rendu de.
minute[2] [mai'njuːt] *adj* (*tiny*) minuscule; (*detailed*) minutieux.
miracle ['mirəkl] *n* miracle *m* **miraculous** *adj* miraculeux.
mirage ['miraːʒ] *n* mirage *m*.
mirror ['mirə] *n* miroir *m*, glace *f*; (*mot*) rétroviseur *m*. **mirror image** image invertie *f*. *v* refléter.
mirth [məːθ] *n* hilarité *f*.
misadventure [misəd'ventʃə] *n* mésaventure *f*. **death by misadventure** mort accidentelle *f*.
misanthropist [miz'anθrəpist] *n* misanthrope *m*, *f*. **misanthropic** *adj* misanthrope. **misanthropy** *n* misanthropie *f*.

misapprehension [misapri'henʃən] *n* malentendu *m.*
misbehave [misbi'heiv] *v* se conduire mal.
miscalculate [mis'kalkjuleit] *v* mal calculer; se tromper.
miscarriage [mis'karidʒ] *n* (*med*) fausse couche *f*; (*plans, etc.*) insuccès *m.* **miscarriage of justice** erreur judiciaire *f.*
miscellaneous [misə'leiniəs] *adj* divers.
mischief ['mistʃif] *n* malice *f*; (*of child*) sottises *f pl*; (*damage*) mal *m.* **get into mischief** faire des sottises. **make mischief** semer la discorde. **mischievous** *adj* espiègle, malicieux.
misconception [miskən'sepʃən] *n* idée fausse *f.*
misconduct [mis'kondʌkt] *n* inconduite *f.*
misconstrue [miskən'struː] *v* mal interpréter.
misdeed [mis'diːd] *n* méfait *m.*
misdemeanour [misdi'miːnə] *n* incartade *f*; (*law*) infraction *f.*
miser ['maizə] *n* avare *m, f.* **miserly** *adj* avare.
miserable ['mizərəbl] *adj* (*sad*) malheureux; pitoyable; (*wretched*) misérable; dérisoire.
misery ['mizəri] *n* (*sadness*) tristesse *f*; (*wretchedness*) misère *f*; (*coll: person*) grincheux, -euse *m, f.*
misfire [mis'faiə] *v* rater; (*mot*) avoir des ratés.
misfit ['misfit] *n* inadapté, -e *m, f.*
misfortune [mis'foːtʃən] *n* malheur *m.*
misgiving [mis'giviŋ] *n* doute *m*, appréhension *f.*
misguided [mis'gaidid] *adj* malencontreux.
mishap ['mishap] *n* mésaventure *f.*
misinterpret [misin'təːprit] *v* mal interpréter. **misinterpretation** *n* interprétation erronée *f.*
misjudge [mis'dʒʌdʒ] *v* mal évaluer; (*person*) méjuger.
***mislay** [mis'lei] *v* égarer.
***mislead** [mis'liːd] *v* tromper. **misleading** *adj* trompeur, -euse.
misnomer [mis'noumə] *n* nom mal approprié *m.*
misogynist [mi'sodʒənist] *n* misogyne *m, f.* **misogyny** *n* misogynie *f.*
misplace [mis'pleis] *v* mal placer; (*lose*) égarer.
misprint ['misprint] *n* coquille *f.*
miss[1] [mis] *v* manquer; (*long for*) regretter. **miss out** sauter; omettre. *n* coup manqué *m.* **missing** *adj* absent, manquant.
miss[2] [mis] *n* mademoiselle *f*; (*abbrev*) Mlle.
misshapen [miʃ'ʃeipən] *adj* difforme.
missile ['misail] *n* projectile *m*; (*mil*) missile *m.*
mission ['miʃən] *n* mission *f.* **missionary** *n* missionnaire *m, f.*
mist [mist] *n* (*weather*) brume *f*; (*on glass*) buée *f.* *v* **mist over** *or* **up** (s')embuer. **misty** *adj* brumeux; embué.
***mistake** [mi'steik] *n* erreur *f*, faute *f.* **by mistake** par erreur. **make a mistake** faire une faute, se tromper. *v* mal interpréter; ne pas reconnaître; confondre. **mistaken** *adj* erroné. **be mistaken** se tromper, faire erreur.
mistletoe ['misltou] *n* gui *m.*
mistress ['mistris] *n* maîtresse *f*; (*teacher*) professeur *m.*
mistrust [mis'trʌst] *n* méfiance *f.* *v* se méfier de.
***misunderstand** [misʌndə'stand] *v* mal comprendre. **misunderstanding** *n* méprise *f.*
misuse [mis'juːs; *v* mis'juːz] *n* abus *m*; usage impropre *m.* *v* abuser de; employer improprement.
mitigate ['mitigeit] *v* atténuer.
mitre ['maitə] *n* (*rel*) mitre *f*; (*carpentry*) onglet *m.* *v* tailler à onglet.
mitten ['mitn] *n* moufle *f.*
mix [miks] *v* (se) mélanger; (*cookery*) préparer; (*salad*) remuer. **mix up** mélanger; confondre; (*person*) embrouiller. **mix-up** *n* confusion *f.* **mixed** *adj* mixte; assorti. **mixed feelings** sentiments contraires *m pl.* **mixed grill** assortiment de grillades *m.* **mixer** *n* (*cookery*) mixer *m*; (*cement*) malaxeur *m.* **mixture** *n* mélange *m.*
moan [moun] *v* gémir; (*coll: complain*) rouspéter. *n* gémissement *m*; (*complaint*) plainte *f.*
moat [mout] *n* douves *f pl.*
mob [mob] *n* cohue *f.*
mobile ['moubail] *nm, adj* mobile. **mobility** *n* mobilité *f.* **mobilize** *v* mobiliser.
moccasin ['mokəsin] *n* mocassin *m.*
mock [mok] *v* se moquer (de); ridiculiser. *adj* faux, fausse; simulé. **mockery** *n* moquerie *f*; travestissement *m.* **mocking** *adj* moqueur, -euse.

mode [moud] *n* mode *m*.
model ['modl] *n* modèle *m*; (*fashion*) mannequin *m*. *adj* modèle; en miniature. *v* modeler; être mannequin; poser.
moderate ['modərət; *v* 'modəreit] *n*, *adj* modéré, -e. *v* (se) modérer. **moderately** *adv* modérément; (*fairly*) plus ou moins. **moderation** *n* modération *f*. **in moderation** modérément.
modern ['modən] *adj* moderne. **modern languages** langues vivantes *f pl*. **modernization** *n* modernisation *f*. **modernize** *v* moderniser.
modest ['modist] *adj* modeste. **modesty** *n* modestie *f*.
modify ['modifai] *v* modifier; modérer. **modification** *n* modification *f*.
modulate ['modjuleit] *v* moduler. **modulation** *n* modulation *f*.
module ['modjuːl] *n* module *m*.
mohair ['mouheə] *n* mohair *m*.
moist [moist] *adj* moite, humide. **moisten** *v* humecter. **moisture** *n* humidité *f*. **moisturize** *v* humidifier; (*skin*) hydrater.
molasses [mə'lasiz] *n* mélasse *f*.
mold (*US*) *V* **mould**.
mole[1] [moul] *n* (*on skin*) grain de beauté *m*.
mole[2] [moul] *n* (zool) taupe *f*. **molehill** *n* taupinière *f*.
molecule ['molikjuːl] *n* molécule *f*. **molecular** *adj* moléculaire.
molest [mə'lest] *v* molester; (*law*) attenter à la pudeur de.
mollusc ['moləsk] *n* mollusque *m*.
molt (*US*) *V* **moult**.
molten ['moultən] *adj* en fusion.
moment ['moumənt] *n* moment *m*, instant *m*. **at the moment** en ce moment. **momentary** *adj* momentané. **momentous** *adj* considérable.
Monaco ['monəˌkou] *n* Monaco *f*.
monarch ['monək] *n* monarque *m*. **monarchist** *n* monarchiste *m*, *f*. **monarchy** *n* monarchie *f*.
monastery ['monəstəri] *n* monastère *m*. **monastic** *adj* monastique.
Monday ['mʌndi] *n* lundi *m*.
money ['mʌni] *n* argent *m*, monnaie *f*. **get one's money back** être remboursé. **get one's money's worth** en avoir pour son argent. **money-box** *n* tirelire *f*. **money-lender** *n* prêteur sur gages *m*. **money-making** *adj* lucratif.
mongol ['moŋgəl] *n*, *adj* (*med*) mongolien, -enne. **mongolism** *n* mongolisme *m*.
mongrel ['mʌŋgrəl] *n* (*dog*) chien bâtard *m*.
monitor ['monitə] *n* (*device*) moniteur *m*. *v* contrôler.
monk [mʌŋk] *n* moine *m*.
monkey ['mʌŋki] *n* singe *m*. *v* **monkey around** perdre son temps; faire l'idiot.
monogamy [mə'nogəmi] *n* monogamie *f*. **monogamous** *adj* monogame.
monogram ['monəgram] *n* monogramme *m*.
monologue ['monəlog] *n* monologue *m*.
monopolize [mə'nopəlaiz] *v* monopoliser. **monopoly** *n* monopole *m*.
monosyllable ['monəsiləbl] *n* monosyllabe *m*. **monosyllabic** *adj* (*word*) monosyllabe; (*reply*) monosyllabique.
monotone ['monətoun] *n* ton monocorde *m*. **monotonous** *adj* monotone. **monotony** *n* monotonie *f*.
monsoon [mon'suːn] *n* mousson *f*.
monster ['monstə] *n* monstre *m*. **monstrosity** *n* monstruosité *f*. **monstrous** *adj* monstrueux; colossal.
month [mʌnθ] *n* mois *m*.
monthly ['mʌnθli] *adj* mensuel. *adv* mensuellement, tous les mois.
monument ['monjumənt] *n* monument *m*. **monumental** *adj* monumental.
mood[1] [muːd] *n* humeur *f*. **be in the mood for** avoir envie de, être d'humeur à. **moody** *adj* maussade.
mood[2] [muːd] *n* (*gramm*) mode *m*.
moon [muːn] *n* lune *f*. **moonbeam** *n* rayon de lune *m*. **moonlight** *n* clair de lune *m*. **moonlighting** *n* (*coll*) travail noir *m*.
moor[1] [muə] *n* lande *f*. **moorhen** *n* poule d'eau *f*.
moor[2] [muə] *v* amarrer, mouiller.
mop [mop] *n* (*floor*) balai laveur *m*; (*dishes*) lavette *f*. **mop of hair** tignasse *f*. *v* essuyer. **mop up** éponger.
mope [moup] *v* se morfondre.
moped ['mouped] *n* cyclomoteur *m*.
moral ['morəl] *adj* moral. **moral support** soutien moral *m*. *n* (*fable*) morale *f*. **morals** *pl n* moralité *f sing*. **moralist** *n* moraliste *m*, *f*. **morality** *n* moralité *f*. **moralize** *v* moraliser.
morale [mə'raːl] *n* moral *m*.
morbid ['moːbid] *adj* morbide.
more [moː] *adj* (*larger number*) plus de; (*in addition*) encore de. *pron*, *adv* plus,

davantage; encore. **all the more** d'autant plus. **and what's more** et qui plus est. **even more** encore plus. **more and more** de plus en plus. **once more** une fois de plus.
moreover [moːˈrouvə] *adv* de plus; (*besides*) d'ailleurs.
morgue [moːg] *n* morgue *f*.
Mormon [ˈmoːmən] *n, adj* mormon, -e.
morning [ˈmoːniŋ] *n* matin *m*, matinée *f*. **morning dress** habit *m*. **morning sickness** nausées matinales *f pl*.
Morocco [məˈrokou] *n* Maroc *m*. **Moroccan** *n* Marocain, -e *m, f*; *adj* marocain.
moron [ˈmoːron] *n* crétin, -e *m, f*. **moronic** *adj* crétin.
morose [məˈrous] *adj* morose.
morphine [ˈmoːfiːn] *n* morphine *f*.
Morse code [moːs] *n* morse *m*.
morsel [ˈmoːsəl] *n* petit morceau *m*.
mortal [ˈmoːtl] *nm, adj* mortel. **mortality** *n* mortalité *f*.
mortar [ˈmoːtə] *n* mortier *m*.
mortgage [ˈmoːgidʒ] *n* (*loan*) emprunt-logement *m*; (*law*) hypothèque *f*. *v* hypothéquer.
mortify [ˈmoːtifai] *v* mortifier. **mortification** *n* mortification *f*.
mortuary [ˈmoːtʃuəri] *n* morgue *f*.
mosaic [məˈzeiik] *n* mosaïque *f*.
Moscow [ˈmoskou] *n* Moscou.
mosque [mosk] *n* mosquée *f*.
mosquito [məˈskiːtou] *n* moustique *m*. **mosquito net** moustiquaire *f*.
moss [mos] *n* mousse *f*. **mossy** *adj* moussu.
most [moust] *adj* le plus de; (*majority*) la plupart de. *pron* le plus; la plupart. *adv* le plus; (*very*) bien, fort. **at most** au maximum. **make the most of** profiter de; utiliser au mieux. **mostly** *adv* surtout, pour la plupart; en général.
motel [mouˈtel] *n* motel *m*.
moth [moθ] *n* papillon de nuit *m*. **clothes moth** mite *f*. **mothball** *n* boule de naphtaline *f*. **moth-eaten** *adj* mité.
mother [ˈmʌðə] *n* mère *f*. **mother-in-law** *n* belle-mère *f*. **mother-of-pearl** *n* nacre *f*. **Mother's Day** la fête des Mères *f*. **mother-to-be** *n* future maman *f*. *v* dorloter. **motherhood** *n* maternité *f*. **motherly** *adj* maternel.
motion [ˈmouʃən] *n* mouvement *m*; (*proposal*) motion *f*. **set in motion** mettre en marche. *v* faire signe. **motionless** *adj* immobile.
motivate [ˈmoutiveit] *v* motiver; (*person*) pousser. **motivation** *n* motivation *f*.
motive [ˈmoutiv] *n* motif *m*; (*law*) mobile *m*. *adj* moteur, -trice.
motor [ˈmoutə] *n* moteur *m*. **motorbike** *n* (*coll*) moto *f*. **motorboat** *n* canot automobile *m*. **motorcyclist** *n* motocycliste *m, f*. **motor racing** course automobile *f*. **motorway** *n* autoroute *f*. **motorist** *n* automobiliste *m, f*. **motorize** *v* motoriser.
mottled [ˈmotld] *adj* tacheté.
motto [ˈmotou] *n* devise *f*.
mould[1] *or US* **mold** [mould] *n* (*shape*) moule *m*. *v* mouler; modeler.
mould[2] *or US* **mold** [mould] *n* (*fungus*) moisissure *f*. **mouldy** *adj* moisi; (*coll: nasty*) moche. **go mouldy** moisir.
moult *or US* **molt** [moult] *v* muer. *n* mue *f*.
mound [maund] *n* (*natural*) tertre *m*; (*artificial*) remblai *m*; (*heap*) tas *m*; (*burial*) tumulus *m*.
mount[1] [maunt] *v* monter (sur). **mount up** s'accumuler. *n* monture *f*; (*for painting*) carton de montage *m*; (*for machine*) support *m*.
mount[2] [maunt] *n* mont *m*.
mountain [ˈmauntən] *n* montagne *f*. **mountaineer** *n* alpiniste *m, f*. **mountaineering** *n* alpinisme *m*. **mountainous** *adj* montagneux; énorme.
mourn [moːn] *v* pleurer. **mournful** *adj* (*person*) mélancolique; (*sound*) lugubre. **mourning** *n* deuil *m*.
mouse [maus] *n, pl* **mice** souris *f*. **mousetrap** *n* souricière *f*. **mousy** *adj* timide; (*hair*) châtain clair *invar*.
mousse [muːs] *n* mousse *f*.
moustache [məˈstaːʃ] *n* moustache *f*.
mouth [mauθ] *n* bouche *f*; (*dog, cat, etc.*) gueule *f*; (*river*) embouchure *f*. **mouth organ** harmonica *m*. **mouthpiece** *n* bec *m*; (*spokesman*) porte-parole *m invar*. **mouthwash** *n* eau dentifrice *f*. **mouthwatering** *adj* appétissant. *v* dire du bout des lèvres. **mouthful** *n* bouchée *f*.
move [muːv] *n* mouvement *m*; (*house*) déménagement *m*; (*game*) coup *m*; (*step*) pas *m*. *v* bouger, (se) déplacer, (se) mouvoir; (*emotionally*) émouvoir; proposer; déménager; (*act*) agir. **move back** reculer; (faire) retourner. **move forward** (faire) avancer. **move in** emménager.

move out déménager. **move over** (s')écarter; (*to make room*) se pousser. **move up** (faire) monter. **movable** *adj* mobile. **movement** *n* mouvement *m*. **moving** *adj* émouvant; mobile; (*pavement, etc.*) roulant.
movie ['muːvi] (*US*) *n* film *m*. **go to the movies** (*coll*) aller au ciné.
***mow** [mou] *v* (*lawn*) tondre. **mow down** faucher.
mown [moun] *V* **mow**.
Mr ['mistə] *n* Monsieur *m*; (*abbrev*) M.
Mrs ['misiz] *n* Madame *f*; (*abbrev*) Mme.
much [mʌtʃ] *adj* beaucoup de. *pron, adv* beaucoup. **as much** autant (que). **how much** combien (de). **much as** bien que. **so much** tant (de). **too much** trop (de).
muck [mʌk] *n* (*manure*) fumier *m*; (*dirt*) saleté *f*. *v* **muck about** (*coll*) perdre son temps. **muck in** (*slang*) mettre la main à la pâte. **muck out** nettoyer. **mucky** *adj* sale.
mucus ['mjuːkəs] *n* mucus *m*. **mucous** *adj* muqueux.
mud [mʌd] *n* boue *f*. **mudguard** *n* garde-boue *m invar*. **muddy** *adj* boueux.
muddle ['mʌdl] *n* désordre *m*; confusion *f*. *v* brouiller; confondre.
muff [mʌf] *n* manchon *m*.
muffle ['mʌfl] *v* assourdir. **muffle up** emmitoufler. **muffler** *n* cache-nez *m invar*; (*US*: *mot*) silencieux *m*.
mug [mʌg] *n* chope *f*; (*slang*: *fool*) poire *f*. *v* agresser. **mugging** *n* agression *f*.
muggy ['mʌgi] *adj* mou, molle.
mulberry ['mʌlbəri] *n* (*fruit*) mûre *f*; (*bush*) mûrier *m*.
mule[1] [mjuːl] *n* (*animal*) mulet, mule *m, f*. **mulish** *adj* têtu.
mule[2] [mjuːl] *n* (*slipper*) mule *f*.
multicoloured [ˌmʌlti'kʌləd] *adj* multicolore.
multilingual [ˌmʌlti'liŋgwəl] *adj* polyglotte.
multiple ['mʌltipl] *nm, adj* multiple. **multiple sclerosis** sclérose en plaques *f*.
multiply ['mʌltiplai] *v* (se) multiplier. **multiplication** *n* multiplication *f*.
multiracial [ˌmʌlti'reiʃəl] *adj* multiracial.
multi-storey [ˌmʌlti'stoːri] *adj* à étages.
multitude ['mʌltitjuːd] *n* multitude *f*.
mumble ['mʌmbl] *v* marmotter. *n* marmottement *m*.
mummy[1] ['mʌmi] *n* (*corpse*) momie *f*.
mummification *n* momification *f*. **mummify** *v* momifier.
mummy[2] ['mʌmi] *n* (*coll*: *mother*) maman *f*.
mumps [mʌmps] *n* oreillons *m pl*.
munch [mʌntʃ] *v* mastiquer.
mundane [mʌn'dein] *adj* mondain, banal.
municipal [mju'nisipəl] *adj* municipal. **municipality** *n* municipalité *f*.
mural ['mjuərəl] *adj* mural. *n* peinture murale *f*.
murder ['məːdə] *n* meurtre *m*. *v* assassiner. **murderer** *n* meurtrier, -ère *m, f*. **murderous** *adj* meutrier.
murky ['məːki] *adj* sombre; (*water*) trouble.
murmur ['məːmə] *n* murmure *m*. *v* murmurer.
muscle ['mʌsl] *n* muscle *m*. **muscular** *adj* musculaire; (*person*) musclé.
muse [mjuːz] *v* méditer, songer. *n* muse *f*.
museum [mju'ziəm] *n* musée *m*.
mushroom ['mʌʃrum] *n* champignon *m*.
music ['mjuːzik] *n* musique *f*. **music centre** chaîne compacte stéréo *f*. **music hall** music-hall *m*. **music stand** pupitre à musique *m*. **musical** *adj* musical; (*gifted*) musicien. **musical box** boîte à musique *f*. **musical (comedy)** comédie musicale *f*. **musical instrumental** instrument de musique *m*. **musician** *n* musicien, -enne *m, f*.
musk [mʌsk] *n* musc *m*.
musket ['mʌskit] *n* mousquet *m*. **musketeer** *n* mousquetaire *m*.
Muslim ['mʌzlim] *n, adj* musulman, -e.
muslin ['mʌzlin] *n* mousseline *f*.
mussel ['mʌsl] *n* moule *f*.
***must** [mʌst] *v* devoir. *n* (*coll*) chose indispensable *f*.
mustard ['mʌstəd] *n* moutarde *f* **mustard pot** moutardier *m*.
muster ['mʌstə] *v* (se) rassembler, (se) réunir. *n* assemblée *f*. **pass muster** être acceptable.
musty ['mʌsti] *adj* de moisi. **smell musty** sentir le moisi.
mute [mjuːt] *adj* muet, -ette. *n* muet, -ette *m, f*; (*music*) sourdine *f*. *v* assourdir.
mutilate ['mjuːtileit] *v* mutiler. **mutilation** *n* mutilation *f*.
mutiny ['mjuːtini] *n* mutinerie *f*; révolte *f*. *v* se mutiner; se révolter. **mutinous** *adj* mutiné; rebelle.

mutter ['mʌtə] *n* marmonner. *n* marmonnement *m*.
mutton ['mʌtn] *n* mouton *m*.
mutual ['mjuːtʃuəl] *adj* mutuel; commun.
muzzle ['mʌzl] *n* (*nose*) museau *m*; (*device*) muselière *f*; (*gun*) bouche *f*. *v* museler.
my [mai] *adj* mon, ma; (*pl*) mes.
myself [mai'self] *pron* me; (*emphatic*) moi-même. **by myself** tout seul.
mystery ['mistəri] *n* mystère *m*. **mysterious** *adj* mystérieux.
mystic ['mistik] *n* mystique *m, f*. *adj also* **mystical** mystique; occulte; surnaturel. **mysticism** *n* mysticisme *m*.
mystify ['mistifai] *v* rendre perplexe, mystifier.
mystique [mi'stiːk] *n* mystique *f*.
myth [miθ] *n* mythe *m*. **mythical** *adj* mythique. **mythological** *adj* mythologique. **mythology** *n* mythologie *f*.

N

nag [nag] *v* harceler.
nail [neil] *n* clou *m*; (*anat*) ongle *m*. **bite one's nails** se ronger les ongles. **nailbrush** *n* brosse à ongles *f*. **nail-file** *n* lime à ongles *f*. **nail polish** vernis à ongles *m*. **nail-scissors** *pl n* ciseaux à ongles *m pl*. *v* clouer.
naive [nai'iːv] *adj* naïf. **naivety** *n* naïveté *f*.
naked ['neikid] *adj* nu; dénudé. **nakedness** *n* nudité *f*.
name [neim] *n* nom *m*. **my name is . . .** je m'appelle . . . . **namesake** *n* homonyme *m*. **what's your name?** comment vous appelez-vous? *v* nommer, appeler; donner un nom à. **nameless** *adj* sans nom; anonyme; inexprimable. **namely** *adv* à savoir.
nanny ['nani] *n* bonne d'enfants *f*.
nap[1] [nap] *n* petit somme *m*. *v* sommeiller. **catch napping** prendre à l'improviste.
nap[2] [nap] *n* (*of cloth*) poil *m*.
nape [neip] *n* nuque *f*.
napkin ['napkin] *n* serviette *f*.
nappy ['napi] *n* couche *f*.
narcotic [naː'kotic] *nm, adj* narcotique.
narrate [nə'reit] *v* raconter. **narration** *n* narration *f*. **narrator** *n* narrateur, -trice *m, f*.
narrative ['narətiv] *n* narration *f*. *adj* narratif.
narrow ['narou] *adj* étroit. **narrow-minded** *adj* borné. *v* (se) rétrécir. **narrow down** se ramener. **narrowly** *adv* (*only just*) de justesse; strictement.
nasal ['neizəl] *adj* nasal; (*voice*) nasillard. **nasalize** *v* nasaliser.
nasturtium [nə'stəːʃəm] *n* capucine *f*.
nasty ['naːsti] *adj* (*unpleasant*) mauvais, vilain; (*unkind*) méchant.
nation ['neiʃən] *n* nation *f*. **national** *n, adj* national. **national anthem** hymne national *m*. **nationalism** *n* nationalisme *m*. **nationalist** *n* nationaliste *m, f*. **nationality** *n* nationalité *f*. **nationalization** *n* nationalisation *f*. **nationalize** *v* nationaliser.
native ['neitiv] *adj* (*town*) natal; (*language*) maternel; indigène; inné. *n* autochtone *m, f*; indigène *m, f*.
nativity [nə'tivəti] *n* nativité *f*. **nativity play** miracle de la Nativité *m*.
natural ['natʃərəl] *adj* naturel. **naturalism** *n* naturalisme *m*. **naturalist** *n* naturaliste *m, f*. **naturally** *adv* naturellement; de nature.
nature ['neitʃə] *n* nature *f*. **nature study** histoire naturelle *f*. **nature trail** circuit forestier éducatif *m*.
naughty ['noːti] *adj* méchant. **naughtiness** *n* désobéissance *f*.
nausea ['noːziə] *n* nausée *f*. **nauseate** *v* écœurer.
nautical ['noːtikəl] *adj* nautique.
naval ['neivəl] *adj* naval; maritime. **naval officer** officier de marine *m*.
nave [neiv] *n* nef *f*.
navel ['neivəl] *n* nombril *m*. **navel orange** navel *f*.
navigate ['navigeit] *v* naviguer; (*steer*) diriger. **navigable** *adj* navigable. **navigation** *n* navigation *f*. **navigator** *n* navigateur *m*.
navy ['neivi] *n* marine *f*. **navy blue** bleu marine.
near [niə] *adv* près, proche. *prep* près de. *adj* proche. *v* approcher (de). **draw near** s'approcher (de). **in the near future** dans un proche avenir. **nearly** *adv* presque. **not nearly** loin de.
nearby [niə'bai] *adj* proche. *adv* près.
neat [niːt] *adj* net, nette; soigné; (*drink*) sec, sèche. **neaten** *v* ajuster; (*tidy*) ranger.

neatly *adv* avec soin; (*with skill*) habilement. **neatness** *n* netteté *f*.
necessary ['nesisəri] *adj* nécessaire. **if necessary** s'il le faut. **it is necessary** il faut. **necessitate** *v* nécessiter. **necessity** *n* nécessité *f*, chose nécessaire *f*.
neck [nek] *n* cou *m*; (*of shirt, etc.*) encolure *f*; (*of bottle, vase*) col *m*. **neck and neck** à égalité. **necklace** *n* collier *m*. **neckline** *n* encolure *f*. *v* (*slang*) se peloter.
nectar ['nektə] *n* nectar *m*.
née [nei] *adj* née.
need [niːd] *n* besoin *m*. *v* avoir besoin de; demander. **needless** *adj* inutile. **needy** *nm, adj* nécessiteux.
needle ['niːdl] *n* aiguille *f*. **needlework** *n* travaux d'aiguille *m pl*. *v* (*coll*) asticoter.
negative ['negətiv] *adj* négatif. *n* (*gramm*) négation *f*; (*photo*) négatif *m*; (*reply*) réponse négative *f*.
neglect [ni'glekt] *v* négliger. *n* manque de soins *m*. **in a state of neglect** à l'abandon. **neglected** *adj* abandonné. **negligible** *adj* négligeable.
négligée ['negliʒei] *n* négligé *m*.
negligence ['neglidʒəns] *n* négligence *f*. **negligent** *adj* négligent.
negotiate [ni'gouʃieit] *v* négocier; (*obstacle*) franchir. **negotiable** *adj* négociable; franchissable. **negotiation** *n* négociation *f*.
Negro ['niːgrou] *nm, adj* nègre. **Negress** *n* négresse *f*.
neigh [nei] *v* hennir. *n* hennissement *m*.
neighbour ['neibə] *n* voisin, -e *m, f*. **neighbourhood** *n* voisinage *m*. **neighbouring** *adj* avoisinant. **neighbourly** *adj* (de) bon voisin.
neither ['naiðə] *adv* ni. **neither . . . nor . . .** ni . . . ni . . . . *conj* ni, non plus. *adj, pron* ni l'un ni l'autre.
neon ['niːon] *n* néon *m*.
nephew ['nefjuː] *n* neveu *m*.
nepotism ['nepətizəm] *n* népotisme *m*.
nerve [nəːv] *n* nerf *m*; courage *m*; (*coll: cheek*) toupet *m*. **get on someone's nerves** taper sur les nerfs à quelqu'un. **lose one's nerve** (*coll*) se dégonfler. **nerve-racking** *adj* éprouvant. **nerves** *pl n* (*coll: before performance*) trac *m sing*. **nervous** *adj* nerveux; (*apprehensive*) inquiet, -ète. **nervous breakdown** dépression nerveuse *f*.
nest [nest] *n* nid *m*. **nest egg** pécule *m*. **nest of tables** table gigogne *f*. *v* nicher.
nestle ['nesl] *v* se nicher, se blottir.
net[1] [net] *n* filet *m*. **netball** *n* netball *m*. **net curtains** voilage *m sing*. **network** *n* réseau *m*. *v* prendre au filet.
net[2] [net] *adj* net.
Netherlands ['neðələndz] *pl n* **the Netherlands** les Pays-Bas *m pl*.
nettle ['netl] *n* ortie *f*. **nettle-rash** *n* urticaire *f*. *v* agacer.
neuralgia [nju'raldʒə] *n* névralgie *f*.
neurosis [nju'rousis] *n* névrose *f*. **neurotic** *adj* névrosé.
neuter ['njuːtə] *nm, adj* neutre. *v* châtrer.
neutral ['njuːtrəl] *adj* neutre. *n* (*mot*) point mort *m*. **in neutral** au point mort. **neutrality** *n* neutralité *f*. **neutralize** *v* neutraliser.
never ['nevə] *adj* (ne . . .) jamais. **never-ending** *adj* sans fin.
nevertheless [nevəðə'les] *adv* néanmoins, malgré tout.
new [njuː] *adj* nouveau, -elle; (*brand-new*) neuf; (*fresh*) frais, fraîche.
new-born ['njuːbom] *adj* nouveau-né.
newcomer ['njuːkʌmə] *n* nouveau venu, nouvelle venue *m, f*.
New Delhi *n* New Delhi.
new-fangled ['njuːˌfaŋgəld] *adj* nouveau genre.
new-laid [njuː'leid] *adj* (*egg*) du jour.
newly-weds ['njuːliwedz] *pl n* nouveaux mariés *m pl*.
news [njuːz] *n* nouvelles *f pl*; (*press, TV, etc.*) informations *f pl*, actualités *f pl*. **newsagent** *n* marchand, -e de journaux *m, f*. **newsletter** *n* bulletin *m*. **newspaper** *n* journal *m*. **newsreader** *n* speaker, -erine *m, f*.
newt [njuːt] *n* triton *m*.
New Testament *n* Nouveau Testament *m*.
New Year *n* nouvel an *m*. **Happy New Year!** bonne année! **New Year's Day** le jour de l'an *m*. **New Year's Eve** la Saint-Sylvestre *f*.
New Zealand [njuː'ziːlənd] *n* Nouvelle-Zélande *f*. **New Zealander** *n* Néo-Zélandais, -e *m, f*.
next [nekst] *adj* prochain, suivant; (*adjoining*) voisin. *adv* ensuite. *n* prochain, -e *m, f*. **the next day** le lendemain. **next-door** *adj* voisin, d'à

côté. **next-of-kin** *n* plus proche parent *m*. **next to** à côté de.
nib [nib] *n* plume *f*.
nibble ['nibl] *v* grignoter, mordiller.
nice [nais] *adj* beau, belle; agréable; (*kind*) gentil, -ille; (*food*) bon, bonne. **nicely** *adv* bien.
niche [nitʃ] *n* niche *f*.
nick [nik] *n* (*notch*) encoche *f*; (*cut*) entaille *f*; (*slang*: *prison*) taule *f*. **in the nick of time** juste à temps. *v* entailler; (*slang*: *steal*) piquer; (*slang*: *arrest*) pincer.
nickel ['nikl] *n* nickel *m*; (*US*: *coin*) pièce de cinq cents *f*.
nickname ['nikneim] *n* surnom *m*. *v* surnommer.
Nicosia [nikə'siə] *n* Nicosie.
nicotine ['nikətiːn] *n* nicotine *f*.
niece [niːs] *n* nièce *f*.
niggle ['nigl] *v* tatillonner. **niggling** *adj* (*detail*) insignifiant; (*doubt*) insinuant; (*pain*) persistant.
night [nait] *n* nuit *f*; (*evening*) soir *m*. **night after night** des nuits durant. **work nights** être de nuit.
night-club ['naitklʌb] *n* boîte de nuit *f*.
nightdress ['naitdres] *n* chemise de nuit *f*.
nightfall ['naitfoːl] *n* tombée du jour *f*.
nightie ['naiti] *n* (*coll*) nuisette *f*.
nightingale ['naitiŋ,geil] *n* rossignol *m*.
night-life ['naitlaif] *n* vie nocturne *f*.
night-light ['naitlait] *n* veilleuse *f*.
nightly ['naitli] *adj* de tous les soirs. *adv* tous les soirs.
nightmare ['naitmeə] *n* cauchemar *m*.
night-school ['nait,skuːl] *n* cours du soir *m pl*.
night-time ['nait,taim] *n* nuit *f*.
night-watchman [nait'wotʃmən] *n* veilleur de nuit *m*.
nil [nil] *n* rien *m*; (*sport*) zéro *m*.
nimble ['nimbl] *adj* agile; (*mind*) vif. **nimbleness** *n* agilité *f*.
nine [nain] *nm*, *adj* neuf. **dressed up to the nines** sur son trente et un. **ninth** *n*(*m*+*f*), *adj* neuvième.
nineteen [nain'tiːn] *nm*, *adj* dix-neuf. **nineteenth** *n*(*m*+*f*), *adj* dix-neuvième.
ninety ['nainti] *nm*, *adj* quatre-vingt-dix. **ninetieth** *n*(*m*+*f*), *adj* quatre-vingt-dixième.
nip[1] [nip] *v* pincer; (*bite*) donner un coup de dent à; (*coll*: *go quickly*) faire un saut. **nip in the bud** tuer dans l'œuf. *n* pinçon *m*; (*bite*) morsure *f*. **nippy** *adj* (*cold*) piquant; (*quick*) preste.
nip[2] [nip] *n* (*drop*) goutte *f*.
nipple ['nipl] *n* mamelon *m*; (*mot*) graisseur *m*.
nit [nit] *n* lente *f*; (*coll*) crétin, -e *m*, *f*.
nitrogen ['naitrədʒən] *n* azote *m*.
no [nou] *adv* non; (*with comparative*) ne ... pas. *adj* aucun, point de, pas de; (*on sign*) défense de, interdit. **no-claims bonus** bonification pour non-sinistre *f*. **no more** *or* **longer** ne ... plus.
noble ['noubl] *nm*, *adj* noble. **nobleness** *or* **nobility** *n* noblesse *f*.
nobody ['noubodi] *pron* (ne ...) personne. *n* (*insignificant person*) rien du tout *m*.
nocturnal [nok'təːnəl] *adj* nocturne.
nod [nod] *v* faire un signe de tête; (*affirmative*) faire signe que oui. **nod off** s'endormir. *n* signe de tête *m*.
noise [noiz] *n* bruit *m*; (*loud*) tapage *m*. **noiseless** *adj* silencieux. **noisy** *adj* bruyant.
nomad ['noumad] *n* nomade *m*, *f*. **nomadic** *adj* nomade.
nominal ['nominl] *adj* nominal; (*in name only*) de nom.
nominate ['nomineit] *v* proposer; (*appoint*) nommer. **nomination** *n* proposition de candidat *f*; nomination *f*.
nonchalant ['nonʃələnt] *adj* nonchalant. **nonchalance** *n* nonchalance *f*.
nonconformist [nonkən'foːmist] *n*(*m*+*f*), *adj* non-conformiste.
nondescript ['nondiskript] *adj* quelconque.
none [nʌn] *pron* aucun.
nonentity [non'entəti] *n* nullité *f*.
nonetheless [,nʌnðə'les] *adv* néanmoins.
non-existent [nonig'zistənt] *adj* non-existant.
non-fiction [non'fikʃən] *n* littérature non-romanesque *f*.
non-resident [non'rezidənt] *n* (*hotel*) client, -e de passage *m*, *f*.
nonsense ['nonsəns] *n* absurdités *f pl*, sottises *f pl*. **nonsensical** *adj* absurde.
non-smoker [non'smoukə] *n* (*person*) non-fumeur *m*; (*rail*) compartiment "non-fumeurs" *m*.
non-stop [non'stop] *adj* sans arrêt; (*train, flight*) direct. *adv* sans arrêt.

noodles ['nuːdlz] *pl n* nouilles *f pl.*
noon [nuːn] *n* midi *m.*
no-one ['nouwʌn] *pron* (ne...) personne.
noose [nuːs] *n* nœud coulant *m*; (*hangman's*) corde *f.*
nor [noː] *conj* ni.
norm [noːm] *n* norme *f.*
normal ['noːməl] *adj* normal. *n* normale *f.*
north [noːθ] *n* nord *m. adj also* **northerly, northern** nord *invar*; au *or* du nord. *adv* au nord. **northbound** *adj* nord *invar.* **north-east** *nm, adj* nord-est. **north-west** *nm, adj* nord-ouest.
Norway ['noːwei] *n* Norvège *f.* **Norwegian** *nm, adj* norvégien; *n* (*people*) Norvégien, -enne *m, f.*
nose [nouz] *n* nez *m.* **blow one's nose** se moucher. **have a nosebleed** saigner du nez. **nosebag** *n* musette mangeoire *f.* **nose-dive** *n* piqué *m.* **nose to tail** (*cars*) pare-choc contre pare-choc. *v* **nose out** flairer. **nosy** *adj* (*coll*) fouinard.
nostalgia [no'staldʒə] *n* nostalgie *f.* **nostalgic** *adj* nostalgique.
nostril ['nostrəl] *n* narine *f*; (*horse, etc.*) naseau *m.*
not [not] *adv* (ne...) pas; non. **I hope not** j'espère que non. **not at all** pas du tout; (*acknowledging thanks*) de rien.
notable ['noutəbl] *adj* notable. **notably** *adv* notamment.
notary ['noutəri] *n* notaire *m.*
notch [notʃ] *n* entaille *f*; (*belt*) cran *m*; (*wheel, saw*) dent *f. v* encocher; cranter; denteler.
note [nout] *n* note *f*; (*short letter*) mot *m*; (*money*) billet *m.* **notebook** *n* carnet *m.* **notepaper** *n* papier à lettres *m.* **noteworthy** *adj* notable. *v* noter; (*notice*) remarquer. **noted** *adj* célèbre.
nothing ['nʌθiŋ] *pron* (ne...) rien; (*with adjective*) rien de. *n* zéro *m*; (*void*) néant *m.* **nothing but** rien que.
notice ['noutis] *n* (*poster*) affiche *f*; (*in newspaper*) annonce *f*; (*warning*) préavis *m,* délai *m*; (*dismissal*) congé *m*; (*resignation*) démission *f.* **notice-board** *n* panneau d'affichage *m.* **take no notice of** ne tenir aucun compte de. *v* s'apercevoir de, remarquer. **noticeable** *adj* perceptible; évident.
notify ['noutifai] *v* (*make known*) notifier, signaler; (*inform*) aviser. **notification** *n* avis *m,* annonce *f.*
notion ['nouʃən] *n* idée *f.*
notorious [nou'toːriəs] *adj* notoire. **notoriety** *n* notoriété *f.*
notwithstanding [notwið'standiŋ] *prep* malgré. *adv* néanmoins.
nougat ['nuːgaː] *n* nougat *m.*
nought [noːt] *n* zéro *m.*
noun [naun] *n* nom *m.*
nourish ['nʌriʃ] *v* nourrir. **nourishment** *n* nourriture *f.*
novel[1] ['novəl] *n* roman *m.* **novelist** *n* romancier, -ère *m, f.*
novel[2] ['novəl] *adj* nouveau, -elle; original. **novelty** *n* nouveauté *f*; innovation *f.*
November [nə'vembə] *n* novembre *m.*
novice ['novis] *n* novice *m, f.*
now [nau] *adv* maintenant; (*immediately*) tout de suite. **from now on** à partir de maintenant. **nowadays** *adv* de nos jours. **now and then** de temps en temps. **up to now** jusqu'ici.
nowhere ['nouweə] *adv* nulle part.
noxious ['nokʃəs] *adj* nocif.
nozzle ['nozl] *n* ajutage *m.*
nuance ['njuːãs] *n* nuance *f.*
nuclear ['njuːkliə] *adj* nucléaire.
nucleus ['njuːkliəs] *n* noyau *m*; (*of cell*) nucléus *m.*
nude ['njuːd] *n, adj* nu, -e. **in the nude** nu. **nudist** *n* nudiste *m, f.* **nudity** *n* nudité *f.*
nudge [nʌdʒ] *v* pousser du coude. *n* coup de coude *m.*
nugget ['nʌgit] *n* pépite *f.*
nuisance ['njuːsns] *n* (*thing*) ennui *m*; (*person*) peste *f.* **be a nuisance** embêter. **what a nuisance!** (*coll*) quelle barbe!
null [nʌl] *adj* nul, nulle. **null and void** nul et non avenu.
numb [nʌm] *adj* engourdi; (*with fear*) transi. *v* engourdir; transir. **numbness** *n* engourdissement *m.*
number ['nʌmbə] *n* nombre *m*; (*of house, page, etc.*) numéro *m.* **number plate** plaque de police *f. v* compter; (*house, etc.*) numéroter.
numeral ['njuːmərəl] *n* chiffre *m.*
numerate ['njuːmərət] *adj* **be numerate** savoir compter. **numeracy** *n* notions de calcul *f pl.* **numerator** *n* numérateur *m.*
numerical [njuː'merikl] *adj* numérique. **in numerical order** dans l'ordre numérique.
numerous ['njuːmərəs] *adj* nombreux.
nun [nʌn] *n* religieuse *f.*
nurse [nəːs] *n* infirmier, -ère *m, f. v* (*med*) soigner; (*cradle*) bercer; (*hope*) nourrir. **nursing home** clinique *f.*

nursery ['nəːsəri] *n* (*room*) nursery *f*; crèche *f*; (*trees, etc.*) pépinière *f*. **nursery rhyme** comptine *f*. **nursery school** école maternelle *f*. **nursery slopes** (*skiing*) pentes pour débutants *f pl*.
nurture ['nəːtʃə] *v* (*rear*) élever; (*feed*) nourrir.
nut [nʌt] *n* (*bot*) noix *f*; (*tech*) écrou *m*. **in a nutshell** en un mot. **nutcase** *n* (*slang*) dingue *m, f*. **nutcracker** *n* casse-noix *m invar*. **nutmeg** *n* muscade *f*.
nutrient ['njuːtriənt] *n* substance nutritive *f*.
nutrition [nju'triʃən] *n* nutrition *f*. **nutritional** *adj* alimentaire. **nutritious** *adj* nutritif.
nuzzle ['nʌzl] *v* (*dog*) renifler; (*pig*) fouiner.
nylon ['nailon] *n* nylon *m*.
nymph [nimf] *n* nymphe *f*.

O

oak [ouk] *n* chêne *m*.
oar [oː] *n* rame *f*. **oarsman** *n* rameur *m*.
oasis [ou'eisis] *n* oasis *f*.
oath [ouθ] *n* (*law*) sermon *m*; (*expletive*) juron *m*. **take the oath** prêter serment.
oats [outs] *pl n* avoine *f sing*. **oatmeal** *n* flocons d'avoine *m pl*.
obedient [ə'biːdiənt] *adj* obéissant. **obedience** *n* obéissance *f*.
obelisk ['obəlisk] *n* obélisque *m*.
obese [ə'biːs] *adj* obèse. **obesity** *n* obésité *f*.
obey [ə'bei] *v* obéir (à).
obituary [ə'bitjuəri] *n* nécrologie *f*.
object ['obʒikt; *v* əb'ʒekt] *n* objet *m*; (*gramm*) complément *m*; (*aim*) but *m*. *v* élever une objection (contre); protester. **objection** *n* objection *f*. **objectionable** *adj* insupportable. **objective** *nm, adj* objectif.
oblige [ə'blaidʒ] *v* obliger. **be obliged to** (*have to*) être obligé de; (*be grateful*) être reconnaissant à. **obligation** *n* obligation *f*, devoir *m*. **obligatory** *adj* obligatoire.
oblique [ə'bliːk] *adj* oblique; indirect.
obliterate [ə'blitəreit] *v* effacer. **obliteration** *n* effacement *m*.
oblivion [ə'bliviən] *n* oubli *m*. **oblivious** *adj* inconscient.
oblong ['obloŋ] *adj* oblong, -ongue. *n* rectangle *m*.
obnoxious [əb'nokʃəs] *adj* odieux, détestable.
oboe ['oubou] *n* hautbois *m*. **oboist** *n* hautboïste *m, f*.
obscene [əb'siːn] *adj* obscène. **obscenity** *n* obscénité *f*.
obscure [əb'skjuə] *adj* obscur. *v* obscurcir; (*hide*) cacher. **obscurity** *n* obscurité *f*.
observe [əb'zəːv] *v* observer; remarquer. **observant** *adj* observateur, -trice. **observation** *n* observation *f*. **observatory** *n* observatoire *m*. **observer** *n* observateur, -trice *m, f*.
obsess [əb'ses] *v* obséder. **obsession** *n* obsession *f*.
obsolescent [obsə'lesnt] *adj* obsolescent. **obsolescence** *n* obsolescence *f*. **built-in obsolescence** désuétude calculée *f*.
obsolete ['obsəliːt] *adj* dépassé, désuet, -ète.
obstacle ['obstəkl] *n* obstacle *m*.
obstetrics [ob'stetriks] *n* obstétrique *f*. **obstetrician** *n* obstétricien, -enne *m, f*.
obstinate ['obstinət] *adj* obstiné, têtu. **obstinacy** *n* obstination *f*.
obstruct [əb'strʌkt] *v* obstruer; (*hinder*) entraver. **obstruction** *n* obstruction *f*; obstacle *m*.
obtain [əb'tein] *v* obtenir, procurer.
obtrusive [əb'truːsiv] *adj* importun. **obtrusion** *n* intrusion *f*.
obtuse [əb'tjuːs] *adj* obtus.
obverse ['obvəːs] *n* (*coin*) face *f*; (*statement, etc.*) contrepartie *f*. *adj* de face; correspondant.
obvious ['obviəs] *adj* évident.
occasion [ə'keiʒən] *n* occasion *f*; (*event*) événement *m*. *v* occasionner. **occasional** *adj* intermittent. **occasionally** *adv* de temps en temps.
occult ['okʌlt] *adj* occulte. *n* **the occult** le surnaturel.
occupy ['okjupai] *v* occuper. **occupant** *or* **occupier** *n* occupant, -e *m, f*. **occupation** *n* occupation *f*; profession *f*; (*trade*) métier *m*. **occupational hazard** risque du métier *m*. **occupational therapy** ergothérapie *f*.
occur [ə'kəː] *v* (*happen*) se produire, avoir lieu; (*be found*) se trouver; (*come to mind*) venir à l'esprit (de). **occurrence** *n* événement *m*.

ocean ['ouʃən] *n* océan *m*. **oceanic** *adj* océanique.
ochre ['oukə] *n* (*colour*) ocre *m*; (*substance*) ocre *f*.
o'clock [ə'klok] *adv* **one o'clock** une heure. **two/three/etc. o'clock** deux/trois/etc. heures.
octagon ['oktəgən] *n* octogone *m*. **octagonal** *adj* octogonal.
octane ['oktein] *n* octane *m*. **octane number** indice d'octane *m*.
octave ['oktiv] *n* octave *f*.
October [ok'toubə] *n* octobre *m*.
octopus ['oktəpəs] *n* pieuvre *f*.
oculist ['okjulist] *n* oculiste *m, f*.
odd [od] *adj* bizarre, étrange; (*number*) impair; (*from pair*) déparié. **odd jobs** menus travaux *m pl*. **odd man out** exception *f*. **oddity** *n* (*person*) excentrique *m, f*; (*thing*) curiosité *f*; (*oddness*) singularité *f*. **oddment** *n* fin de série *f*.
odds [odz] *pl n* (*betting*) cote *f sing*; chances *f pl*. **be at odds with** ne pas être d'accord avec. **it makes no odds** ça ne fait rien. **odds and ends** bouts *m pl*, restes *m pl*.
ode [oud] *n* ode *f*.
odious ['oudiəs] *adj* odieux.
odour ['oudə] *n* odeur *f*. **odourless** *adj* inodore.
oesophagus [iː'sofəgəs] *n* œsophage *m*.
of [ov] *prep* de. **of it** *or* **them** en: *j'en ai deux*.
off [of] *adj* absent; (*light*) éteint; (*gas, water, etc.*) coupé; (*cancelled*) annulé; (*food*) mauvais. **a day off** un jour de congé. *prep* de, sur; (*distant*) éloigné de.
offal ['ofəl] *n* abats *m pl*.
off chance ['oftʃaːns] *n* **on the off chance (that)** (*coll*) au cas où.
off-colour [of'kʌlə] *adj* **be off-colour** ne pas être dans son assiette.
offend [ə'fend] *v* offenser, offusquer. **offence** *n* (*law*) délit *m*. **take offence** se froisser. **offender** *n* délinquant, -e *m, f*; contrevenant, -e *m, f*. **offensive** *adj* offensant; déplaisant.
offer ['ofə] *n* offre *f*. *v* offrir, proposer. **offering** *n* offre *f*.
offhand [of'hand] *adj* (*casual*) désinvolte; brusque. *adv* à l'improviste.
office ['ofis] *n* (*place*) bureau *m*; (*post*) fonction *f*. **take office** entrer en fonctions. **officer** *n* officier *m*; (*police*) agent *m*.
official [ə'fiʃəl] *adj* officiel. *n* officiel *m*, fonctionnaire *m, f*; employé, -e *m, f*.
officious [ə'fiʃəs] *adj* empressé.
offing ['ofiŋ] *n* **in the offing** en vue; (*naut*) au large.
off-licence ['oflaisns] *n* magasin de vins et spiritueux *m*.
off-peak [of'piːk] *adj, adv* aux heures creuses.
off-putting ['of,putiŋ] *adj* (*coll*) peu engageant.
off-season [of'siːzn] *n* morte-saison *f*. *adv, adj* hors-saison.
offset [of'set; *n* 'ofset] *v* contrebalancer. *n* (*printing*) offset *m*.
offshore ['offoː] *adj* (*breeze*) de terre; (*waters*) côtier.
offside [of'said] *n* (*mot: right*) côté droit *m*; (*mot: left*) côté gauche *m*; (*sport*) hors-jeu *m invar*.
offspring ['ofspriŋ] *n* progeniture *f*; résultat *m*.
offstage ['ofsteidʒ] *adv, adj* dans les coulisses.
off-the-cuff [ofðə'kʌf] *adv, adj* au pied levé.
off-white [of'wait] *nm, adj* blanc cassé *invar*.
often ['ofn] *adv* souvent. **as often as not** le plus souvent. **every so often** de temps en temps.
ogre ['ougə] *n* ogre *m*. **ogress** *n* ogresse *f*.
oil [oil] *n* huile *f*; pétrole *m*. *v* graisser. **oily** *adj* huileux; (*hands, clothes*) graisseux; (*food*) gras, grasse; (*manners*) onctueux.
oilcan ['oilkan] *n* burette à huile *f*; (*storage*) bidon à huile *m*.
oilfield ['oilfiːld] *n* gisement pétrolifère *m*.
oil-fired [oil'faiəd] *adj* à mazout.
oil-painting ['oil,peintiŋ] *n* peinture à l'huile *f*.
oil pump *n* pompe à huile *f*.
oil refinery *n* raffinerie *f*.
oil rig *n* (*at sea*) plate-forme pétrolière *f*; (*on land*) derrick *m*.
oilskin ['oil,skin] *n* toile cirée *f*. **oilskins** *pl n* ciré *m sing*. *adj* en toile cirée.
oil-slick ['oilslik] *n* nappe de pétrole *f*.
oil-tanker ['oi,taŋkə] *n* (*ship*) pétrolier *m*; (*lorry*) camion-citerne *m*.
oil-well ['oilwel] puits de pétrole *m*.
ointment ['ointmənt] *n* onguent *m*, pommade *f*.

O.K. [ou'kei] *interj* d'accord!

old [ould] *adj* vieux, vieille; âgé; (*former*) ancien. **he is nine years old** il a neuf ans. **how old is he?** quel âge a-t-il? **old age** vieillesse *f*. **old-age pensioner** retraité, -e *m*, *f*. **old-fashioned** *adj* démodé, vieux jeu *invar*. **old maid** vieille fille *f*. **old master** (*painting*) tableau de maître *m*. **Old Testament** Ancien Testament *m*. **old wives' tale** conte de bonne femme *m*.

olive ['oliv] *n* (*fruit*) olive *f*; (*tree*) olivier *m*. **olive green** *nm*, *adj* vert olive. **olive oil** huile d'olive *f*.

Olympic [ə'limpik] *adj* olympique. **Olympic Games** Jeux olympiques *m pl*.

omelette ['omlit] *n* omelette *f*.

omen ['oumən] *n* présage *m*, augure *m*.

ominous ['ominəs] *adj* menaçant, sinistre.

omit [ou'mit] *v* omettre. **omission** *n* omission *f*.

omnipotent [om'nipətənt] *adj* omnipotent.

on [on] *prep* sur, à. *adj* (*elec*) allumé; (*tap*) ouvert. **oncoming** *adj* (*traffic*) qui approche. **onlooker** *n* spectateur, -trice *m*, *f*. **onset** *n* début *m*; attaque *f*. **onshore** *adj* du large. **onslaught** *n* attaque *f*. **onward(s)** *adj*, *adv* en avant. **from now onwards** désormais.

once [wʌns] *adv* une fois; (*formerly*) jadis. *conj* une fois que. **at once** tout de suite. **once again** encore une fois. **once and for all** une fois pour toutes.

one [wʌn] *n*, *adj* un, -e. *pron* un; (*impersonal*) on. **be one up on** avoir l'avantage sur. **one-armed bandit** machine à sous *f*. **one by one** un à un. **one-man band** homme-orchestre *m*. **one-sided** *adj* inégal, partial. **one-way** *adj* à sens unique. **that one** celui-là, celle-là *m*, *f*. **this one** celui-ci, celle-ci *m*, *f*. **which one** lequel, laquelle *m*, *f*.

oneself [wʌn'self] *pron* se; (*emphatic*) soi-même. **by oneself** tout seul.

onion ['ʌnjən] *n* oignon *m*.

only ['ounli] *adj* seul, unique. **only child** enfant unique *m*. *adv* seulement; (ne...) que. *conj* mais.

onus ['ounəs] *n* responsabilité *f*.

onyx ['oniks] *n* onyx *m*.

ooze [uːz] *v* suinter, exsuder.

opal ['oupəl] *n* opale *f*.

opaque [ə'paik] *adj* opaque; obscur. **opacity** *n* opacité *f*; obscurité *f*.

open ['oupən] *v* (s')ouvrir. *adj* ouvert; (*meeting*) public, -ique; (*question*) non résolu. **open-air** *adj* de *or* en plein air. **open-minded** *adj* sans parti pris. **open-mouthed** *adj*, *adv* bouche bée. **open-plan** *adj* sans cloisons.

opening ['oupəniŋ] *n* ouverture *f*; (*door, window*) embrasure *f*; (*ceremony*) inauguration *f*; (*opportunity*) occasion *f*. *adj* inaugural; préliminaire. **opening time** l'heure d'ouverture *f*.

opera ['opərə] *n* opéra *m*. **opera glasses** jumelles de théâtre *f pl*. **opera house** opéra *m*. **opera singer** chanteur, -euse d'opéra *m*, *f*. **operatic** *adj* d'opéra. **operetta** *n* opérette *f*.

operate ['opəreit] *v* opérer; (*machine*) (faire) marcher. **operable** *adj* opérable. **operating theatre** salle d'opération *f*. **operation** *n* opération *f*; marche *f*, fonctionnement *m*. **in operation** en service; en application. **operational** *adj* opérationnel. **operative** *adj* en vigueur; (*med*) opératoire. **the operative word** le mot clef. **operator** *n* opérateur, -trice *m*, *f*; (*phone*) standardiste *m*, *f*.

ophthalmic [of'θalmik] *adj* (*nerve*) ophtalmique; (*surgeon*) ophtalmologique.

opinion [ə'pinjən] *n* opinion *f*. **in my opinion** à mon avis. **opinion poll** sondage d'opinion *m*.

opium ['oupiəm] *n* opium *m*.

opponent [ə'pounənt] *n* adversaire *m*, *f*.

opportune [opə'tjuːn] *adj* opportun.

opportunity [opə'tjuːnəti] *n* occasion *f*, chance *f*.

oppose [ə'pouz] *v* s'opposer à. **opposed** *adj* opposé. **as opposed to** par opposition à. **opposition** *n* opposition *f*.

opposite ['opəzit] *adj* opposé; d'en face. **the opposite sex** l'autre sexe *m*. *prep* en face de. *n* opposé *m*, contraire *m*.

oppress [ə'pres] *v* opprimer; (*heat, etc.*) oppresser. **oppression** *n* oppression *f*. **oppressive** *adj* tyrannique; (*tax, etc.*) oppressif; (*heat*) accablant. **oppressor** *n* oppresseur *m*.

opt [opt] *v* opter. **opt out** se retirer; choisir de ne pas participer.

optical ['optikl] *adj* optique. **optical illusion** illusion d'optique *f*. **optician** *n* opticien, -enne *m*, *f*.

optimism ['optimizəm] *n* optimisme *m*. **optimist** *n* optimiste *m*, *f*. **optimistic** *adj* optimiste.

optimum ['optiməm] *nm, adj* optimum.
option ['opʃən] *n* option *f*, choix *m*. **optional** *adj* facultatif.
opulent ['opjulənt] *adj* opulent; abondant. **opulence** *n* opulence *f*; abondance *f*.
or [oː] *conj* ou; (*negative*) ni. **or else** ou bien; (*threat*) sinon.
oracle ['orəkl] *n* oracle *m*.
oral ['oːrəl] *nm, adj* oral.
orange ['orindʒ] *n* (*fruit*) orange *f*; (*tree*) oranger *m*. (*colour*) orange *m*. *adj* (*colour*) orange; (*flavour*) d'orange. **orangeade** *n* orangeade *f*.
orator ['orətə] *n* orateur, -trice *m, f*. **orate** *v* discourir. **oration** *or* **oratory** *n* discours *m*.
orbit ['oːbit] *n* orbite *f*. *v* orbiter.
orchard ['oːtʃəd] *n* verger *m*.
orchestra ['oːkəstrə] *n* orchestre *m*. **orchestral** *adj* orchestral. **orchestrate** *v* orchestrer. **orchestration** *n* orchestration *f*.
orchid ['oːkid] *n* orchidée *f*.
ordain [oː'dein] *v* (*rel*) ordonner; (*fate*) décréter. **ordination** *n* ordination *f*.
ordeal [oː'diːl] *n* supplice *m*.
order ['oːdə] *n* ordre *m*; (*comm*) commande *f*. **in order to** pour. **out of order** en panne. *v* ordonner; commander.
orderly ['oːdəli] *adj* rangé; méthodique; en ordre. *n* (*mil*) planton *m*; (*med*) garçon de salle *m*.
ordinal ['oːdinl] *adj* ordinal.
ordinary ['oːdənəri] *adj* ordinaire, normal; (*average*) moyen. *n* ordinaire *m*. **out of the ordinary** hors du commun, insolite.
ore [oː] *n* minerai *m*.
oregano [ori'gaːnou] *n* origan *m*.
organ ['oːgən] *n* organe *m*; (*music*) orgue *m*. **organist** *n* organiste *m, f*.
organic [oː'ganik] *adj* organique; fondamental.
organism ['oːgənizəm] *n* organisme *m*.
organize ['oːgənaiz] *v* organiser. **organization** *n* organisation *f*. **organizer** *n* organisateur, -trice *m, f*.
orgasm ['oːgazəm] *n* orgasme *m*.
orgy ['oːdʒi] *n* orgie *f*.
oriental [oːri'entl] *adj* oriental, d'Orient.
orientate ['oːriənteit] *v* orienter. **orientation** *n* orientation *f*.
orifice ['orifis] *n* orifice *m*.
origin ['oridʒin] *n* origine *f*. **originate** *v* être l'auteur de. **originate from** (*person*) être originaire de; (*thing*) provenir de; (*idea*) émaner de. **originator** *n* auteur *m*.
original [ə'ridʒinl] *adj* (*first*) originel; (*idea, play, etc.*) original. *n* original *m*. **originally** *adv* originairement, à l'origine.
ornament ['oːnəmənt] *n* (*decoration*) ornement *m*; (*vase, etc.*) bibelot *m*. *v* orner, décorer. **ornamental** *adj* ornemental, décoratif.
ornate [oː'neit] *adj* très orné.
ornithology [oːni'θolədʒi] *n* ornithologie *f*. **ornithological** *adj* ornithologique. **ornithologist** *n* ornithologiste *m, f*.
orphan ['oːfən] *n, adj* orphelin, -e. *v* rendre orphelin. **be orphaned** devenir orphelin. **orphanage** *n* orphelinat *m*.
orthodox ['oːθədoks] *adj* orthodoxe.
orthopaedic [oːθə'piːdik] *adj* orthopédique.
oscillate ['osileit] *v* osciller; fluctuer. **oscillation** *n* oscillation *f*.
Oslo ['ozlou] *n* Oslo.
ostensible [o'stensəbl] *adj* prétendu. **ostensibly** *adv* en apparence.
ostentatious [osten'teiʃəs] *adj* prétentieux; exagéré. **ostentation** *n* ostentation *f*.
osteopath ['ostiəpaθ] *n* ostéopathe *m, f*.
ostracize ['ostrəsaiz] *n* frapper d'ostracisme.
ostrich ['ostritʃ] *n* autruche *f*.
other ['ʌðə] *pron, adj* autre. *adv* autrement.
otherwise ['ʌðəwaiz] *adv, conj* autrement.
Ottawa ['otəwə] *n* Ottawa.
otter ['otə] *n* loutre *f*.
***ought** [oːt] *v* devoir.
our [auə] *pron* nous. *adj* notre; (*pl*) nos.
ours [auəz] *pron* le nôtre, la nôtre.
ourselves [auə'selvz] *pron* nous; (*emphatic*) nous-mêmes. **by ourselves** tout seuls.
oust [aust] *v* évincer.
out [aut] *adj* (*flower*) en fleur; (*light, etc.*) éteint. *adv* dehors. **out loud** tout haut. **out of** en dehors de, hors de; (*through*) par; (*from*) de, sur; (*without*) sans.
outboard [autboːd] *n* hors-bord *m*.
outbreak ['autbreik] *n* début *m*, déclenchement *m*.
outbuilding ['autbildiŋ] *n* appentis *m*, dépendance *f*.
outburst [autbəːst] *n* explosion *f*, accès *m*.

outcast ['autkaːst] *n* exilé, -e *m, f*; proscrit, -e *m, f.*
outcome ['autkʌm] *n* issue *f*; conséquence *f.*
outcry ['autkrai] *n* tollé *m.*
***outdo** [aut'duː] *v* surpasser.
outdoor ['autdoː] *adj* de *or* en plein air. **outdoors** *adv* dehors.
outer ['autə] *adj* extérieur, -e. **outer space** espace cosmique *m.*
outfit ['autfit] *n* (*clothes*) tenue *f*; équipement *m*; (*coll*) équipe *f.*
outgoing ['autgouiŋ] *adj* (*person*) ouvert; (*tide*) descendant; (*train, mail, etc.*) en partance. **outgoings** *pl n* dépenses *f pl.*
***outgrow** [aut'grou] *v* devenir trop grand pour; perdre *or* abandonner en grandissant.
outhouse ['authaus] *n* appentis *m.*
outing ['autiŋ] *n* sortie *f*, excursion *f.*
outlandish [aut'landiʃ] *adj* exotique; bizarre.
outlaw ['autloː] *n* hors-la-loi *m invar. v* proscrire.
outlay ['autlei] *n* frais *m pl*, dépenses *f pl.*
outlet ['autlit] *n* sortie *f*; (*comm*) débouché *m*; (*for emotions, etc.*) exutoire *m.*
outline ['autlain] *n* contour *m*; (*summary*) esquisse *f. v* délinéer; esquisser *or* exposer à grands traits.
outlive [aut'liv] *v* survivre à.
outlook ['autluk] *n* perspective *f*; attitude *f.*
outlying ['autlaiiŋ] *adj* périphérique; (*distant*) écarté.
outnumber [aut'nʌmbə] *v* surpasser en nombre.
out-of-date [autəv'deit] *adj* (*ticket, etc.*) périmé; (*clothes*) démodé.
outpatient ['autpeiʃənt] *n* malade en consultation externe *m, f.*
outpost ['autpoust] *n* avant-poste *m.*
output ['autput] *n* production *f*, rendement *m*; (*elec*) puissance fournie *f.*
outrage ['autreidʒ] *n* scandale *m. v* outrager.
outrageous [aut'reidʒəs] *adj* scandaleux, outrageant.
outright [aut'rait; *adj* 'autrait] *adv* complètement; catégoriquement; franchement. *adj* complet, -ète; franc, franche; (*winner*) incontesté; (*sale*) au comptant.
outset ['autset] *n* début *m.*
outside [aut'said; *adj* 'autsaid] *adv* dehors, à l'extérieur. *prep* à l'extérieur de, hors de; (*beyond*) en dehors de. *n* extérieur *m*, dehors *m. adj* extérieur, -e. **outsider** *n* étranger, -ère *m, f*; (*horse*) outsider *m.*
outsize ['autsaiz] *adj* (*clothes*) grande taille *invar*; énorme.
outskirts ['autskəːtz] *pl n* (*town*) faubourgs *m pl*; (*forest*) lisière *f sing.*
outspoken [aut'spoukən] *adj* carré. **be outspoken** avoir son franc-parler. **outspokenness** *n* franc-parler *m.*
outstanding [aut'standiŋ] *adj* exceptionnel; mémorable; (*debt*) impayé.
outstrip [aut'strip] *v* devancer.
outward ['autwəd] *adj* vers l'extérieur; (*appearance*) extérieur, -e. **outward bound** en partance. **outwardly** *adv* en apparence. **outwards** *adv* vers l'extérieur.
outweigh [aut'wei] *v* l'emporter sur.
outwit [aut'wit] *v* se montrer plus malin que; (*dodge*) dépister.
oval ['ouvəl] *nm, adj* ovale.
ovary ['ouvəri] *n* ovaire *m.*
ovation [ou'veiʃən] *n* ovation *f.*
oven ['ʌvn] *n* four *m.* **oven glove** gant isolant *m.* **ovenproof** *adj* allant au four. **oven-ready** *adj* prêt à cuire.
over ['ouvə] *adv* (par-)dessus; (*remaining*) en plus. *adj* fini. *prep* sur, par-dessus; (*above*) au-dessus de; (*during*) au cours de; (*more than*) plus de. **over and over again** à maintes reprises. **over here** ici. **over there** là-bas.
overall ['ouvəroːl] *adj* global; total. *n* blouse *f.* **overalls** *pl n* salopette *f sing.*
overbalance [ouvə'baləns] *v* basculer; perdre l'équilibre.
overbearing [ouvə'beəriŋ] *adj* autoritaire.
overboard ['ouvəboːd] *adv* (*fall*) à la mer; (*throw*) par-dessus bord. **go overboard** (*coll*) s'emballer.
overcast [ouvə'kaːst] *adj* couvert.
overcharge [ouvə'tʃaːdʒ] *v* faire payer un prix excessif; (*elec*) surcharger.
overcoat ['ouvəkout] *n* pardessus *m.*
***overcome** [ouvə'kʌm] *v* surmonter, triompher de. **be overcome by** succomber à.
overcrowded [ouvə'kraudid] *adj* surpeuplé, surchargé. **overcrowding** *n* surpeuplement *m.*
***overdo** [ouvə'duː] *v* exagérer; (*overcook*) trop cuire.
overdose ['ouvədous] *n* surdose *f.*

overdraft ['ouvədra:ft] *n* découvert *m*.
***overdraw** [ouvə'dro:] *v* dépasser son crédit. **overdrawn** *adj* à découvert.
overdue [ouvə'dju:] *adj* (*payment*) arriéré; (*train, bus*) en retard.
overestimate [ouvə'estimeit] *v* surestimer; exagérer.
overexpose [ouvəik'spouz] *v* surexposer. **overexposure** *n* surexposition *f*.
overflow [ouvə'flou; *n* 'ouvəflou] *v* déborder. *n* débordement *m*; (*of sink*) trop-plein *m*; (*excess*) excédent *m*.
overgrown [ouvə'groun] *adj* envahi, recouvert.
***overhang** [ouvə'haŋ; *n* 'ouvəhaŋ] *v* surplomber; faire saillie. *n* surplomb *m*. **overhanging** *adj* en saillie, en surplomb.
overhaul [ouvə'ho:l] *v* réviser. *n* révision *f*.
overhead [ouvə'hed] *adv* au-dessus; dans le ciel. *adj* aérien. **overheads** *pl n* frais généraux *m pl*.
***overhear** [ouvə'hiə] *v* surprendre, entendre par hasard.
overheat [ouvə'hi:t] *v* surchauffer; (*mot*) chauffer.
overjoyed [ouvə'dʒoid] *adj* ravi.
overland [ouvə'land] *adj, adv* par voie de terre.
overlap ['ouvəlap; *v* ouvə'lap] *n* chevauchement *m*. *v* se chevaucher.
***overlay** [ouvə'lei; *n* 'ouvəlei] *v* recouvrir. *n* revêtement *m*.
overleaf [ouvə'li:f] *adv* au verso.
overload [ouvə'loud; *n* 'ouvəloud] *v* surcharger. *n* surcharge *f*.
overlook [ouvə'luk] *v* (*miss*) oublier; (*house, etc.*) donner sur; (*ignore*) laisser passer.
overnight [ouvə'nait] *adv* jusqu'au lendemain, pendant la nuit; (*suddenly*) du jour au lendemain. *adj* (*journey*) de nuit; (*stay*) d'une nuit; (*sudden*) soudain.
overpower [ouvə'pauə] *v* subjuguer; dominer. **overpowering** *adj* irrésistible; suffocant.
overrated [ouvə'reitid] *adj* surfait.
***override** [ouvə'raid] *v* passer outre à, outrepasser; annuler. **overriding** *adj* prépondérant.
overrule [ouvə'ru:l] *v* annuler; rejeter.
***overrun** [ouvə'rʌn] *v* envahir; (*go beyond*) dépasser.
overseas [ouvə'si:z] *adv* outre-mer. *adj* d'outre-mer; (*trade*) extérieur, -e.
overseer [ouvə'siə] *n* contremaître *m*.
overshadow [ouvə'ʃadou] *v* ombrager; (*render insignificant*) éclipser.
***overshoot** [ouvə'ʃu:t] *v* dépasser.
oversight ['ouvəsait] *n* omission *f*. **through an oversight** par négligence.
***oversleep** [ouvə'sli:p] *v* dormir trop longtemps, se réveiller tard.
overspill ['ouvəspil] *n* excédent de population *m*.
overt [ou'və:t] *adj* déclaré. **overtly** *adv* ouvertement.
***overtake** [ouvə'teik] *v* (*pass*) doubler, dépasser; (*catch up*) rattraper.
***overthrow** [ouvə'θrou; *n* 'ouvəθrou] *v* renverser, vaincre. *n* chute *f*.
overtime ['ouvətaim] *n* heures supplémentaires *f pl*.
overtone ['ouvətoun] *n* note *f*, sous-entendu *m*.
overture ['ouvətjuə] *n* ouverture *f*.
overturn [ouvə'tə:n] *v* (se) renverser; (*car*) capoter.
overweight [ouvə'weit] *adj* trop lourd. **be overweight** peser trop.
overwhelm [ouvə'welm] *v* accabler; (*flood*) submerger; (*conquer*) écraser. **overwhelmed** *adj* bouleversé, confus, accablé. **overwhelming** *adj* accablant; irrésistible; dominant.
overwork [ouvə'wə:k] *n* surmenage *m*. *v* (se) surmener.
overwrought [ouvə'ro:t] *adj* excédé.
ovulation [ovju'leiʃn] *n* ovulation *f*.
owe [ou] *v* devoir. **owing** *adj* dû, due. **owing to** à cause de.
owl [aul] *n* hibou *m*.
own [oun] *adj* propre. **get one's own back** prendre sa revanche. **on one's own** tout seul. *v* posséder. **own up** avouer. **owner** *n* propriétaire *m, f*. **ownership** *n* possession *f*.
ox [oks] *n, pl* **oxen** bœuf *m*. **oxtail** *n* queue de bœuf *f*.
oxygen ['oksidʒən] *n* oxygène *m*.
oyster ['oistə] *n* huître *f*.

P

pace [peis] *n* pas *m*. **keep pace with** marcher de pair avec. *v* arpenter. **pace up and down** faire les cent pas.
Pacific [pə'sifik] *nm, adj* Pacifique.
pacify ['pasifai] *v* calmer, pacifier. **pacific** *adj* pacifique. **pacifism** *n* pacifisme *m*. **pacifist** *n*(*m*+*f*), *adj* pacifiste.
pack [pak] *n* (*group*) bande *f*; (*hounds*) meute *f*; (*cards*) jeu *m*; (*packet*) paquet *m*. **packhorse** *n* cheval de charge *m*. *v* emballer; (*cram*) tasser, bourrer; (*suitcase*) faire; (*for holiday*) faire ses bagages. **packed lunch** panier-repas *m*. **packing** *n* emballage *m*.
package ['pakidʒ] *n* paquet *m*. *adj* (*deal, contract*) global; (*holiday, tour*) organisé. *v* emballer.
packet ['pakit] *n* paquet *m*; (*sweets*) sachet *m*.
pact [pakt] *n* pacte *m*.
pad[1] [pad] *n* bourrelet *m*; (*writing*) bloc *m*; (*ink*) tampon encreur *m*. *v* rembourrer, capitonner. **pad out** (*speech, essay*) délayer. **padding** *n* bourre *f*; délayage *m*.
pad[2] [pad] *v* aller à pas feutrés.
paddle[1] ['padl] *n* (*canoe*) pagaie *f*; (*of waterwheel*) aube *f*. **paddle boat** *or* **steamer** bateau à aubes *m*. *v* pagayer.
paddle[2] ['padl] *v* barboter. **paddling pool** petite piscine *f*.
paddock ['padək] *n* enclos *m*; (*racing*) paddock *m*.
paddy-field ['padifiːld] *n* rizière *f*.
padlock ['padlok] *n* cadenas *m*. *v* cadenasser.
paediatric [piːdi'atrik] *adj* de pédiatrie; infantile. **paediatrician** *n* pédiatre *m, f*. **paediatrics** *n* pédiatrie *f*.
pagan ['peigən] *n, adj* païen, -enne.
page[1] [peidʒ] *n* (*book*) page *f*.
page[2] [peidʒ] *n also* **page-boy** (*hotel*) groom *m*; (*court*) page *m*. *v* (*person*) faire appeler.
pageant ['padʒənt] *n* spectacle historique *m*. **pageantry** *n* apparat *m*.
paid [peid] *V* **pay**.
pail [peil] *n* seau *m*.
pain [pein] *n* douleur *f*. **pain-killer** *n* calmant *m*. **pains** *pl n* (*trouble*) peine *f sing*. **painstaking** *adj* assidu, soigné. *v* peiner. **painful** *adj* douloureux; (*distressing*) pénible. **painless** *adj* sans douleur; (*easy*) inoffensif.
paint [peint] *n* peinture *f*. **paintbox** *n* boîte de couleurs *f*. **paintbrush** *n* pinceau *m*. **paints** *pl n* couleurs *f pl*. **paint-stripper** *n* décapant *m*. **paintwork** *n* peintures *f pl*. *v* peindre; (*describe*) dépeindre. **painter** *n* peintre *m*. **painting** *n* peinture *f*; (*picture*) tableau *m*.
pair [peə] *n* paire *f*; couple *m*. *v* (*socks, etc.*) appareiller; (*mate*) (s')accoupler. **pair off** (*people*) s'arranger deux par deux.
pal [pal] *n* (*coll*) copain, copine *m, f*.
palace ['paləs] *n* palais *m*. **palatial** *adj* grandiose.
palate ['palit] *n* palais *m*. **palatable** *adj* acceptable.
pale [peil] *adj* pâle; (*unnaturally*) blême. *v* pâlir; devenir blême. **paleness** *n* pâleur *f*.
palette ['palit] *n* palette *f*.
pall[1] [poːl] *v* perdre son charme (pour).
pall[2] [poːl] *n* drap mortuaire *m*; (*smoke*) voile *m*; (*snow*) manteau *m*.
pallid ['palid] *adj* blafard.
palm[1] [paːm] *n* (*of hand*) paume *f*. *v* **palm off** (*coll*) refiler (à). **palmist** *n* chiromancien, -enne *m, f*. **palmistry** *n* chiromancie *f*.
palm[2] [paːm] *n* (*tree*) palmier *m*. **Palm Sunday** dimanche des Rameaux *m*.
palpitate ['palpiteit] *v* palpiter. **palpitation** *n* palpitation *f*.
paltry ['poːltri] *adj* misérable.
pamper ['pampə] *v* dorloter, choyer.
pamphlet ['pamflit] *n* brochure *f*.
pan [pan] *n* casserole *f*.
pancake ['pankeik] *n* crêpe *f*. **Pancake Tuesday** mardi gras *m*.
pancreas ['paŋkriəs] *n* pancréas *m*. **pancreatic** *adj* pancréatique.
panda ['pandə] *n* panda *m*.
pandemonium [pandi'mouniəm] *n* tohu-bohu *m*.
pander ['pandə] *v* **pander to** se plier à.
pane [pein] *n* vitre *f*, carreau *m*.
panel ['panl] *n* panneau *m*; (*dress*) pan *m*; jury *m*; (*radio, TV*) invités *m pl*. *v* lambrisser. **panellist** *n* invité, -e *m, f*; membre d'un jury *m*. **panelling** *n* panneaux *m pl*.
pang [paŋ] *n* serrement de cœur *m*; (*conscience*) remords *m pl*; (*hunger*) tiraillement d'estomac *m*.
panic ['panik] *n* panique *f*. **panic-stricken** *adj* affolé. *v* (s')affoler.
panorama [ˌpanə'raːmə] *n* panorama *m*. **panoramic** *adj* panoramique.

pansy ['panzi] *n* pensée *f*.
pant [pant] *v* haleter. *n* halètement *m*.
panther ['panθə] *n* panthère *f*.
pantomime ['pantəmaim] *n* spectacle de Noël *m*; (*mime*) pantomime *f*.
pantry ['pantri] *n* garde-manger *m invar*.
pants [pants] *pl n* slip *m sing*; (*coll*: *trousers*) pantalon *m sing*.
papal ['peipl] *adj* papal, du Pape.
paper ['peipə] *n* papier *m*; (*news*) journal *m*; (*exam*) épreuve *f*; article *m*. **paperback** *n* livre de poche *m*. **paper bag** pochette *f*. **paper-boy** *n* livreur de journaux *m*. **paper-clip** *n* trombone *m*. **paper-knife** *n* coupe-papier *m invar*. **paper-mill** *n* papeterie *f*. **paper shop** (*coll*) marchand de journaux *m*. **paperweight** *n* presse-papiers *m invar*. **paperwork** *n* écritures *f pl*; (*derog*) paperasserie *f*. *v* (*room*) tapisser.
paprika ['paprikə] *n* paprika *m*.
par [paː] *n* pair *m*. **be on a par with** aller de pair avec. **feel under par** ne pas se sentir en forme.
parable ['parəbl] *n* parabole *f*.
parachute ['parəʃuːt] *n* parachute *m*. *v* descendre en parachute; parachuter. **parachutist** *n* parachutiste *m*, *f*.
parade [pə'reid] *n* défilé *m*; (*ceremony*) parade *f*. *v* défiler; (*display*) faire étalage de.
paradise ['parədais] *n* paradis *m*.
paradox ['parədoks] *n* paradoxe *m*. **paradoxical** *adj* paradoxal.
paraffin ['parəfin] *n* paraffine *f*; (*fuel*) pétrole *m*.
paragraph ['parəgraːf] *n* paragraphe *m*. **start a new paragraph** aller à la ligne.
parallel ['parəlel] *nm*, *adj* parallèle. **parallelogram** *n* parallélogramme *m*.
paralyse ['parəlaiz] *v* paralyser. **paralysis** *n* paralysie *f*; immobilisation *f*. **paralytic** *adj* paralytique; (*slang*: *drunk*) ivre mort.
paramilitary [ˌparə'militəri] *adj* paramilitaire.
paramount ['parəmaunt] *adj* souverain, suprême.
paranoia [ˌparə'noiə] *n* paranoïa *f*. **paranoid** *adj* paranoïde.
parapet ['parəpit] *n* parapet *m*.
paraphernalia [ˌparəfə'neiliə] *n* attirail *m*.
paraphrase ['parəfreiz] *n* paraphrase *f*. *v* paraphraser.
paraplegic [ˌparə'pliːdʒik] *n*(*m*+*f*), *adj* paraplégique.
parasite ['parəsait] *n* parasite *m*. **parasitic** *adj* parasite.
parasol ['parəsol] *n* ombrelle *f*.
paratrooper ['parəˌtruːpə] *n* parachutiste *m*.
parcel ['paːsəl] *n* colis *m*; (*portion*) parcelle *f*. **parcel office** bureau de messageries *m*. **parcel post** service de colis postaux *m*. *v also* **parcel up** emballer.
parch [paːtʃ] *v* (*land*) dessécher (*person*) altérer. **be parched** (*coll*) mourir de soif.
parchment ['paːtʃmənt] *n* parchemin *m*.
pardon ['paːdn] *n* pardon *m*; (*law*) grâce *f*. *v* pardonner; gracier. *interj* pardon?
pare [peə] *v* réduire; (*fruit*) peler.
parent ['peərənt] *n* père, mère *m*, *f*. **parents** parents *m pl*. **parental** *adj* des parents. **parenthood** *n* paternité *f*, maternité *f*.
parenthesis [pərenθəsis] *n* parenthèse *f*. **in parenthesis** entre parenthèses.
Paris ['paris] *n* Paris.
parish ['pariʃ] *n* paroisse *f*; (*civil*) commune *f*. **parish church** église paroissiale *f*.
parishioner *n* paroissien, -enne *m*, *f*.
parity ['pariti] *n* parité *f*.
park [paːk] *n* jardin public *m*; (*of mansion*) parc *m*. *v* (se) garer. **parking** *n* stationnement *m*. **parking lot** (*US*) parking *m*. **parking meter** parcomètre *m*. **parking ticket** procès-verbal *m*.
parliament ['paːləmənt] *n* parlement *m*. **parliamentary** *adj* parlementaire.
parlour ['paːlə] *n* petit salon *m*.
parochial [pə'roukiəl] *adj* paroissial; (*derog*) de clocher.
parody ['parədi] *n* parodie *f*. *v* parodier.
parole [pə'roul] *n* (*law*) liberté conditionnelle *f*.
paroxysm ['parəksizəm] *n* paroxysme *m*; (*anger*) accès *m*; (*joy*) transport *m*.
parrot ['parət] *n* perroquet *m*. **parrot fashion** comme un perroquet.
parsley ['paːsli] *n* persil *m*.
parsnip ['paːsnip] *n* panais *m*.
parson ['paːsn] *n* pasteur *m*. **parson's nose** croupion *m*. **parsonage** *n* presbytère *m*.
part [paːt] *n* partie *f*; (*behalf*) part *f*, parti *m*; rôle *m*; episode *m*. **part exchange** reprise en compte *f*. **part-time** *adj*, *adv* à mi-temps, à temps partiel. *v* (se) séparer; se quitter. **part one's hair** se faire une raie. **part with** se défaire de. **parting** *n*

séparation *f*; (*hair*) raie *f*. **partly** *adv* partiellement.
***partake** [paːteik] *v* **partake of** prendre.
partial ['paːʃəl] *adj* partiel; (*biased*) partial. **be partial to** avoir un faible pour. **partiality** *n* partialité *f*; (*liking*) prédilection *f*.
participate [paːtisipeit] *v* participer. **participant** *n* participant, -e *m, f*. **participation** *n* participation *f*.
participle ['paːtisipl] *n* participe *m*.
particle ['paːtikl] *n* particule *f*; (*dust, etc.*) grain *m*.
particular [pə'tikjulə] *adj* particulier; méticuleux; (*choosy*) pointilleux. *n* détail *m*. **in particular** en particulier. **particularity** *n* particularité *f*.
partisan [paːti'zan] *n* partisan *m*.
partition [paːtiʃən] *n* (*in room*) cloison *f*; division *f*, partage *m*. *v* cloisonner; diviser, partager.
partner ['paːtnə] *n* (*comm*) associé, -e *m, f*; (*sport*) partenaire *m, f*; (*dancing*) cavalier, -ère *m, f*; (*marriage*) époux, -ouse *m, f*. *v* être l'associé de; être le partenaire de; danser avec. **partnership** *n* association *f*. **go into partnership** s'associer.
partridge ['paːtridʒ] *n* perdrix *f*; (*cookery*) perdreau *m*.
party ['paːti] *n* (*pol*) parti *m*; (*law*) partie *f*; groupe *m*; (*celebration*) réunion *f*, fête *f*, soirée *f*. **party line** (*phone*) ligne commune à deux abonnés *f*; (*pol*) ligne du parti *f*.
pass [paːs] *v* passer; (*go beyond*) dépasser; (*exam*) être reçu à. **pass away** *or* **on** (*die*) s'éteindre. **pass out** s'évanouir. **pass round** faire passer; distribuer. *n* (*permit*) laissez-passer *m invar*; (*exam*) moyenne *f*; (*mountain*) col *m*; (*sport*) passe *f*.
passage ['pasidʒ] *n* passage *m*; voyage *m*; (*corridor*) couloir *m*.
passenger ['pasindʒə] *n* passager, -ère *m, f*; (*train*) voyageur, -euse *m, f*.
passer-by [ˌpaːsə'bai] *n* passant, -e *m, f*.
passion ['paʃən] *n* passion *f*. **passionate** *adj* passionné.
passive ['pasiv] *nm, adj* passif. **passiveness** *n* passivité *f*.
Passover ['paːsouvə] *n* Pâque des Juifs *f*.
passport ['paːspoːt] *n* passeport *m*.
password ['paːswəːd] *n* mot de passe *m*.
past [paːst] *nm, adj* passé. *prep* (*time*) plus de; (*beyond*) au delà de; (*in front of*) devant. **ten past four** quatre heures dix. *adv* devant. **go past** passer.
pasta ['pastə] *n* pâtes *f pl*.
paste [peist] *n* pâte *f*; (*meat*) pâté *m*; (*glue*) colle *f*; (*jewellery*) strass *m*. *v* coller.
pastel ['pastəl] *n* pastel *m*.
pasteurize ['pastʃəraiz] *v* pasteuriser. **pasteurization** *n* pasteurisation *f*.
pastime ['paːstaim] *n* passe-temps *m invar*.
pastoral ['paːstərəl] *adj* pastoral.
pastry ['peistri] *n* pâte *f*; (*cake*) pâtisserie *f*. **puff pastry** pâte feuilletée *f*. **shortcrust pastry** pâte brisée *f*.
pasture ['paːstʃə] *n* pâture *f*, pâturage *m*. *v* paître.
pasty[1] ['peisti] *adj* pâteux; (*face*) terreux.
pasty[2] ['pasti] *n* petit pâté *m*.
pat [pat] *v* tapoter; caresser. *n* petite tape *f*; caresse *f*; (*of butter*) noix *f*.
patch [patʃ] *n* morceau *m*; (*of colour*) tache *f*; (*on clothes*) pièce *f*; (*of land*) parcelle *f*. **patchwork** *n* patchwork *m*. *v* rapiécer. **patchy** *adj* inégal.
patent ['peitənt] *adj* patent. **patent leather** cuir verni *m*. *n* brevet *m*. *v* faire breveter. **patently** *adv* manifestement.
paternal [pə'təːnl] *adj* paternel. **paternity** *n* paternité *f*.
path [paːθ] *n* sentier *m*; (*garden*) allée *f*; (*of river*) cours *m*; (*of missile, etc.*) trajectoire *f*.
pathetic [pə'θetik] *adj* pitoyable.
pathology [pə'θolədʒi] *n* pathologie *f*. **pathological** *adj* pathologique. **pathologist** *n* pathologiste *m, f*.
patient ['peiʃənt] *adj* patient. *n* malade *m, f*; client, -e *m, f*. **patience** *n* patience *f*; (*game*) réussite *f*.
patio ['patiou] *n* patio *m*.
patriarchal ['peitriaːkəl] *adj* patriarcal.
patriot ['patriət] *n* patriote *m, f*. **patriotic** *adj* (*deed*) patriotique; (*person*) patriote. **patriotism** *n* patriotisme *m*.
patrol [pə'troul] *n* patrouille *f*. **patrol car** voiture de police *f*. *v* patrouiller (dans).
patron ['peitrən] *n* (*arts*) protecteur, -trice *m, f*; (*charity*) patron, -onne *m, f*; (*shop*) client, -e *m, f*. **patron saint** saint patron, sainte patronne *m, f*. **patronage** *n* patronage *m*. **patronize** *v* (*comm*) se fournir chez. **patronizing** *adj* condescendant.

patter[1] ['patə] *v* (*footsteps*) trottiner; (*rain*) crépiter. *n* petit bruit *m*; crépitement *m*.
patter[2] ['patə] *n* (*comedian*, *etc*.) bavardage *m*; (*salesman*) boniment *m*.
pattern ['patən] *n* dessin *m*, motif *m*; (*sewing*) patron *m*; modèle *f*. *v* modeler. **patterned** *adj* à motifs.
paunch [poːntʃ] *n* panse *f*.
pauper ['poːpə] *n* indigent, -e *m*, *f*.
pause [poːz] *n* pause *f*; silence *m*. *v* faire une pause, s'arrêter un instant; hésiter.
pave [peiv] *v* paver. **pave the way** préparer le chemin. **pavement** *n* trottoir *m*; (*US*) chaussée *f*. **paving** *n* pavage *m*, dallage *m*. **paving stone** pavé *m*.
pavilion [pə'viljən] *n* pavillon *m*.
paw [poː] *n* patte *f*. *v* donner un coup de patte à; (*coll*: *person*) tripoter.
pawn[1] [poːn] *v* mettre en gage. *n* gage *m*. **pawnbroker** *n* prêteur, -euse sur gages *m*, *f*. **pawnshop** *n* mont-de-piété *m*.
pawn[2] [poːn] *n* pion *m*.
***pay** [pei] *v* payer; (*attention*, *compliment*) faire. **pay back** rembourser. **pay in** verser. **pay off** (*debt*) régler; (*be worthwhile*) rapporter. *n* paie *f*. **pay-day** *n* jour de paie *m*. **pay rise** augmentation de salaire *f*. **pay-roll** *n* registre du personnel *m*. **pay-slip** *n* feuille de paie *f*. **payable** *adj* payable. **payee** *n* bénéficiaire *m*, *f*. **payment** *n* paiement *m*; récompense *f*.
pea [piː] *n* petit pois *m*.
peace [piːs] *n* paix *f*. **peacemaker** *n* pacificateur, -trice *m*, *f*. **peace offering** cadeau de réconciliation *m*. **peaceful** *adj* paisible.
peach [piːtʃ] *n* (*fruit*) pêche *f*; (*tree*) pêcher *m*.
peacock ['piːkok] *n* paon *m*.
peak [piːk] *n* pic *m*; sommet *m*; (*on cap*) visière *f*. **peak hours** heures d'affluence *f pl*, heures de pointe *f pl*.
peal [piːl] *n* (*bells*) carillon *m*; (*thunder*) coup *m*; (*laughter*) éclat *m*. *v* carillonner; (*thunder*) gronder; éclater.
peanut ['piːnʌt] *n* cacahouète *f*.
pear [peə] *n* (*fruit*) poire *f*; (*tree*) poirier *m*.
pearl [pəːl] *n* perle *f*; nacre *f*. *v* perler. **pearly** *adj* nacré.
peasant ['peznt] *n* paysan, -anne *m*, *f*.
peat [piːt] *n* tourbe *f*.
pebble ['pebl] *n* caillou *m*; (*on beach*) galet *m*. **pebbledash** *n* crépi moucheté *m*. **pebbly** *adj* caillouteux.
peck [pek] *v* becqueter, picorer; donner un coup de bec à. *n* coup de bec *m*; (*coll*: *kiss*) bise *f*.
peckish ['pekiʃ] *adj* **feel peckish** (*coll*) avoir la dent.
peculiar [pi'kjuːljə] *adj* bizarre; particulier. **peculiarity** *n* bizarrerie *f*; particularité *f*.
pedal ['pedl] *n* pédale *f*. *v* pédaler.
pedantic [pi'dantik] *adj* pédant.
peddle ['pedl] *v* colporter; (*drugs*) faire le trafic de.
pedestal ['pedistl] *n* piédestal *m*.
pedestrian [pi'destriən] *n* piéton *m*. **pedestrian crossing** passage clouté *m*. **pedestrian precinct** zone piétonnière *f*. *adj* (*style*) prosaïque.
pedigree ['pedigriː] *n* pedigree *m*; (*of person*) ascendance *f*. *adj* de pure race.
pedlar ['pedlə] *n* colporteur *m*.
peel [piːl] *v* (*se*) peler, éplucher. **peel off** (*covering*, *etc*.) décoller. *n* pelure *f*, épluchure *f*; (*orange*) écorce *f*; (*candied*) écorce confite *f*. **peeler** *n* éplucheur *m*. **peelings** *pl n* pelures *f pl*, épluchures *f pl*.
peep [piːp] *n* coup d'œil *m*. *v* jeter un coup d'œil, regarder furtivement. **peeping Tom** voyeur *m*. **peep out** se montrer.
peer[1] [piə] *v* regarder d'un air interrogateur. **peer at** scruter du regard.
peer[2] [piə] *n* pair *m*. **peerage** *n* pairie *f*. **peerless** *adj* sans pareil.
peevish ['piːviʃ] *adj* grincheux, maussade.
peg [peg] *n* cheville *f*; (*washing*) pince *f*; (*coat*, *hat*) patère *f*; (*tent*) piquet *m*. **off the peg** *adj* prêt-à-porter. *v* cheviller; (*prices*) stabiliser.
pejorative [pə'dʒorətiv] *adj* péjoratif.
Peking [piː'kiŋ] *n* Pékin.
pelican ['pelikən] *n* pélican *m*.
pellet ['pelit] *n* boulette *f*; (*for gun*) plomb *m*.
pelmet ['pelmit] *n* (*wood*) lambrequin *m*; (*fabric*) cantonnière *f*.
pelt[1] [pelt] *v* bombarder; (*coll*: *rain*) tomber des cordes; (*coll*: *run*) galoper. *n* **at full pelt** à toute vitesse.
pelt[2] [pelt] *n* peau *f*; fourrure *f*.
pelvis ['pelvis] *n* bassin *m*. **pelvic** *adj* pelvien.
pen[1] [pen] *n* plume *f*, stylo *m*. **penfriend** *n* correspondant, -e *m*, *f*. **penknife** *n* canif *m*. **pen-name** *n* pseudonyme *m*.

pen² [pen] *n* (*enclosure*) parc *m*. *v* parquer.
penal ['piːnl] *adj* pénal. **penal colony** colonie pénitentiaire *f*. **penalize** *v* pénaliser. **penalty** *n* pénalité *f*. peine *f*; (*sport*) pénalisation *f*.
penance ['penəns] *n* pénitence *f*.
pencil ['pensl] *n* crayon *m*. **pencil-case** *n* trousse *f*. **pencil-sharpener** *n* taille-crayon *m*. *v* crayonner.
pendant ['pendənt] *n* pendentif *m*.
pending ['pendiŋ] *adj* pendant, en suspens. *prep* en attendant; durant.
pendulum ['pendjuləm] *n* pendule *m*.
penetrate ['penitreit] *v* pénétrer. **penetrable** *adj* pénétrable. **penetration** *n* pénétration *f*.
penguin ['peŋgwin] *n* pingouin *m*.
penicillin [peni'silin] *n* pénicilline *f*.
peninsula [pə'ninsjulə] *n* péninsule *f*. **peninsular** *adj* péninsulaire.
penis ['piːnis] *n* pénis *m*.
penitent ['penitənt] *n*, *adj* pénitent, -e. **penitence** *n* pénitence *f*.
pennant ['penənt] *n* banderole *f*.
penniless ['peniləs] *adj* sans le sou.
pension ['penʃən] *n* pension *f*; (*from company*) retraite *f*. **pension book** livret de retraite *m*. **pension scheme** caisse de retraite *f*. *v* pensionner. **pension off** mettre à la retraite. **pensioner** *n* retraité, -e *m*, *f*.
pensive ['pensiv] *adj* pensif.
pentagon ['pentəgən] *n* pentagone *m*. **pentagonal** *adj* pentagonal.
penthouse ['penthaus] *n* appentis *m*. **penthouse flat** appartement de grand standing *m*.
pent-up [ˌpent'ʌp] *adj* refoulé.
penultimate [pi'nʌltimit] *adj* avant-dernier.
people ['piːpl] *n* peuple *m*. *pl n* gens *m pl*, *f pl*; personnes *f pl*; (*inhabitants*) peuple *m sing*; (*coll*) famille *f sing*. *v* peupler.
pepper ['pepə] *n* (*spice*) poivre *m*; (*vegetable*) poivron *m*. **peppercorn** *n* grain de poivre *m*. **peppermint** *n* (*flavour*) menthe *f*; (*sweet*) pastille de menthe *f*. **pepper-pot** *n* poivrier *m*. *v* poivrer. **peppery** *adj* poivré.
per [pəː] *prep* par. **per cent** pour cent. **percentage** *n* pourcentage *m*.
perceive [pə'siːv] *v* percevoir; (*notice*) remarquer.
perceptible [pə'septibl] *adj* perceptible. **perceptibly** *adv* sensiblement.
perception [pə'sepʃən] *n* perception *f*; sensibilité *f*; perspicacité *f*. **perceptive** *adj* percepteur, -trice; perspicace.
perch [pəːtʃ] *n* perchoir *m*. *v* (se) percher.
percolate ['pəːkəleit] *v* passer. **percolator** *n* cafetière à pression *f*.
percussion [pə'kʌʃən] *n* percussion *f*.
perennial [pə'reniəl] *adj* perpétuel; (*plant*) vivace. *n* plante vivace *f*.
perfect ['pəːfikt; *v* pə'fekt] *nm*, *adj* parfait. *v* achever, mettre au point. **perfection** *n* perfection *f*; (*perfecting*) perfectionnement *m*. **perfectionist** *n* perfectionniste *m*, *f*.
perforate ['pəːfəreit] *v* perforer. **perforation** *n* perforation *f*.
perform [pə'foːm] *v* accomplir, exécuter; (*theatre*) jouer, donner; (*machine*) marcher. **performance** *n* (*theatre*) représentation *f*, séance *f*; (*of individual*) interprétation *f*; (*sport*) performance *f*; (*of car*) fonctionnement *m*; exécution *f*; (*coll*: *fuss*) histoire *f*. **performer** *n* artiste *m*, *f*.
perfume ['pəːfjuːm] *n* parfum *m*. *v* parfumer.
perhaps [pə'haps] *adv* peut-être.
peril ['peril] *n* péril *m*. **perilous** *adj* périlleux.
perimeter [pə'rimitə] *n* périmètre *m*.
period ['piəriəd] *n* période *f*, époque *f*; (*school*) cours *m*; (*menstrual*) règles *f pl*. **periodic** *adj* périodique. **periodical** *nm*, *adj* périodique.
peripheral [pə'rifərəl] *adj* périphérique. **periphery** *n* périphérie *f*.
periscope ['periskoup] *n* périscope *m*.
perish ['periʃ] *v* périr; (*rubber*, *food*) se détériorer. **be perished** (*coll*) crever de froid. **perishable** *adj* périssable.
perjure ['pəːdʒə] *v* **perjure oneself** se parjurer; (*law*) faire un faux serment. **perjurer** *n* parjure *m*, *f*. **perjury** *n* parjure *m*, faux serment *m*.
perk [pəːk] *v* **perk up** (se) ragaillardir. **perky** *adj* vif, éveillé.
perm [pəːm] *n* permanente *f*. **have a perm** se faire faire une permanente.
permanent ['pəːmənənt] *adj* permanent. **permanence** *n* permanence *f*. **permanently** *adv* en permanence, à titre définitif.
permeate ['pəːmieit] *v* pénétrer; (*spread*)

se répandre (dans). **permeable** *adj* perméable.

permit [pə'mit; *n* 'pəːmit] *v* permettre. *n* permis *m*; autorisation écrite *f*. **permissible** *adj* permis; acceptable. **permission** *n* permission *f*; autorisation *f*. **permissive** *adj* tolérant; laxiste.

permutation [pəːmju'teiʃən] *n* permutation *f*.

pernicious [pə'niʃəs] *adj* (*med*) pernicieux; nuisible.

perpendicular [ˌpəːpen'dikjulə] *nf*, *adj* perpendiculaire.

perpetrate ['pəːpitreit] *v* perpétrer. **perpetration** *n* perpétration *f*. **perpetrator** *n* auteur *m*, coupable *m*, *f*.

perpetual [pə'petʃuəl] *adj* perpétual.

perpetuate [pə'petʃueit] *v* perpétuer. **perpetuation** *n* perpétuation *f*.

perplex [pə'pleks] *v* rendre perplexe; compliquer. **perplexed** *adj* perplexe. **perplexing** *adj* embarrassant. **perplexity** *n* perplexité *f*; complexité *f*.

persecute ['pəːsikjuːt] *v* persécuter; tourmenter. **persecution** *n* persécution *f*.

persevere [ˌpəːsi'viə] *v* persévérer. **perseverance** *n* persévérance *f*. **persevering** *adj* persévérant.

persist [pə'sist] *v* persister. **persistence** *n* persistance *f*. **persistent** *adj* continuel; (*person*) persévérant, obstiné.

person ['pəːsn] *n* personne *f*. **personal** *adj* personnel. **personality** *n* personnalité *f*. **personally** *adv* personnellement; en personne.

personify [pə'sonifai] *v* personnifier. **personification** *n* personnification *f*.

personnel [pəːsə'nel] *n* personnel *m*.

perspective [pə'spektiv] *n* perspective *f*.

perspire [pə'spaiə] *v* transpirer. **perspiration** *n* transpiration *f*, sueur *f*.

persuade [pə'sweid] *v* persuader. **persuasion** *n* persuasion *f*. **persuasive** *adj* persuasif; convaincant.

pert [pəːt] *adj* impertinent; (*hat*) coquin.

pertain [pə'tein] *v* se rapporter. **pertinent** *adj* pertinent, approprié.

perturb [pə'təːb] *v* perturber.

peruse [pə'ruːz] *v* lire attentivement. **perusal** *n* lecture attentive *f*.

pervade [pə'veid] *v* pénétrer dans, s'étendre dans.

perverse [pə'vəːs] *adj* pervers; obstiné; contrariant. **perversity** *n* perversité *f*; obstination *f*.

pervert [pə'vəːt; *n* 'pəːvəːt] *v* pervertir, dénaturer. *n* perverti sexuel, pervertie sexuelle *m*, *f*. **perversion** *n* perversion *f*.

pessimism ['pesimizəm] *n* pessimisme *m*. **pessimist** *n* pessimiste *m*, *f*. **pessimistic** *adj* pessimiste.

pest [pest] *n* animal *or* insecte nuisible *m*; (*coll*: *person*) casse-pieds *m*. **pesticide** *n* pesticide *m*.

pester ['pestə] *v* harceler.

pet [pet] *n* animal familier *m*; (*coll*: *favourite*) chouchou, -oute *m*, *f*; (*as endearment*) chou *m*. *adj* favori, -ite. *v* (*coll*) chouchouter; (*slang*: *sexually*) (se) peloter.

petal ['petl] *n* pétale *m*.

petition [pə'tiʃən] *n* pétition *f*. *v* pétitionner, adresser une pétition à.

petrify ['petrifai] *v* pétrifier de peur.

petrol ['petrəl] *n* essence *f*. **petrol pump** pompe d'essence *f*. **petrol station** station-service *f*. **petrol tank** réservoir d'essence *m*.

petroleum [pə'trouliəm] *n* pétrole *m*.

petticoat ['petikout] *n* jupon *m*; (*slip*) combinaison *f*.

petty ['peti] *adj* mesquin, petit; insignifiant. **petty cash** petite monnaie *f*. **petty officer** second maître *m*. **pettiness** *n* mesquinerie *f*; insignifiance *f*.

petulant ['petjulənt] *adj* irritable. **petulance** *n* irritabilité *f*.

pew [pjuː] *n* banc d'église *m*.

pewter ['pjuːtə] *n* étain *m*.

phantom ['fantəm] *n* fantôme *m*.

pharmacy ['faːməsi] *n* pharmacie *f*. **pharmaceutical** *adj* pharmaceutique. **pharmacist** *n* pharmacien, -enne *m*, *f*.

pharynx ['fariŋks] *n* pharynx *m*. **pharyngitis** *n* pharyngite *f*.

phase [feiz] *n* phase *f*. *v* **phase in** introduire progressivement. **phase out** retirer progressivement.

pheasant ['feznt] *n* faisan *m*.

phenomenon [fə'nomənən] *n*, *pl* **-ena** phénomène *m*. **phenomenal** *adj* phénoménal.

phial ['faiəl] *n* fiole *f*.

philanthropy [fi'lanθrəpi] *n* philanthropie *f*. **philanthropic** *adj* philanthropique. **philanthropist** *n* philanthrope *m*, *f*.

philately [fi'latəli] *n* philatélie *f*. **philatelist** *n* philatéliste *m*, *f*.

philosophy [fi'losəfi] *n* philosophie *f*. **philosopher** *n* philosophe *m, f*. **philosophical** *adj* philosophique; (*resigned*) philosophe. **philosophize** *v* philosopher.
phlegm [flem] *n* flegme *m*.
phlegmatic [fleg'matik] *adj* flegmatique.
phobia ['foubiə] *n* phobie *f*.
phone [foun] (*coll*) *n* téléphone *m*. *v* téléphoner (à).
phonetic [fə'netik] *adj* phonétique. **phonetics** *n* phonétique *f*.
phoney ['founi] *adj* (*coll*) faux, fausse.
phosphate ['fosfeit] *n* phosphate *m*.
phosphorescence [fosfə'resəns] *n* phosphorescence *f*. **phosphorescent** *adj* phosphorescent.
phosphorus ['fosfərəs] *n* phosphore *m*. **phosphorous** *adj* phosphoreux.
photo ['foutou] *n* (*coll*) photo *f*.
photocopy ['foutou,kopi] *n* photocopie *f*. *v* photocopier. **photocopier** *n* photocopieur *m*. **photocopying** *n* reprographie *f*.
photogenic [,foutou'dʒenik] *adj* photogénique.
photograph ['foutəgraːf] *n* photographie *f*. **photograph album** album de photos *m*. *v* photographier. **photographer** *n* photographe *m, f*. **photographic** *adj* photographique. **photography** *n* photographie *f*.
phrase [freiz] *n* expression *f*; (*gramm*) locution *f*; (*music*) phrase *f*. **phrase-book** *n* recueil d'expressions *m*. *v* exprimer.
physical ['fizikəl] *adj* physique. *n* (*coll*) examen médical *m*.
physician [fi'ziʃən] *n* médecin *m*.
physics ['fiziks] *n* physique *f*. **physicist** *n* physicien, -enne *m, f*.
physiology [,fizi'olədʒi] *n* physiologie *f*. **physiological** *adj* physiologique. **physiologist** *n* physiologiste *m, f*.
physiotherapy [,fiziou'θerəpi] *n* kinésithérapie *f*. **physiotherapist** *n* kinésithérapeute *m, f*.
physique [fi'ziːk] *n* constitution *f*; (*appearance*) physique *m*.
piano [pi'anou] *n* piano *m*. **pianist** *n* pianiste *m, f*.
piccolo ['pikəlou] *n* piccolo *m*.
pick[1] [pik] *n* choix *m*; (*best*) meilleur, -e *m, f*. **take one's pick** faire son choix. *v* choisir; (*fruit, flowers*) cueillir; (*lock*) crocheter. **pick at** (*food*) chipoter. **pick-me-up** *n* (*coll*) remontant *m*. **pick out** choisir; distinguer; (*highlight*) rehausser. **pickpocket** *n* pick-pocket *m*. **pick up** ramasser; (*collect*) passer prendre; s'améliorer; (*learn*) apprendre; (*coll: arrest*) cueillir.
pick[2] [pik] *n* (*tool*) pioche *f*.
picket ['pikit] *n* piquet *m*. **picket line** cordon de piquet de grève *m*. *v* organiser un piquet de grève; mettre un piquet de grève.
pickle ['pikl] *v* conserver dans du vinaigre. **pickles** *pl n* pickles *m pl*.
picnic ['piknik] *n* pique-nique *m*. *v* pique-niquer. **picnicker** *n* pique-niqueur, -euse *m, f*.
pictorial [pik'toːriəl] *adj* en images; illustré.
picture ['piktʃə] *n* image *f*; (*painting*) tableau *m*. **picture frame** cadre *m*. **picture rail** cimaise *f*. **pictures** *n* (*coll*) cinéma *m*. **picture window** fenêtre panoramique *f*. *v* (s')imaginer; décrire.
picturesque [piktʃə'resk] *adj* pittoresque.
pidgin ['pidʒən] *n* pidgin *m*. **pidgin French** petit-nègre *m*.
pie [pai] *n* tourte *f*, pâté en croûte *m*.
piece [piːs] *n* morceau *m*; (*item*) pièce *f*. **piecemeal** *adv* par bribes, petit à petit. **piecework** *n* travail à la pièce *m*. *v* **piece together** rassembler.
pier [piə] *n* jetée *f*; (*landing-stage*) appontement *m*.
pierce [piəs] *v* percer, transpercer. **piercing** *adj* perçant; glacial.
piety ['paiəti] *n* piété *f*.
pig [pig] *n* cochon *m*. **pigheaded** *adj* entêté. **pig-iron** *n* saumon de fonte *m*. **pigskin** *n* peau de porc *f*. **pigsty** *n* porcherie *f*. **pigtail** *n* natte *f*.
pigeon ['pidʒən] *n* pigeon *m*. **pigeon-hole** *n* casier *m*.
pigment ['pigmənt] *n* pigment *m*. **pigmentation** *n* pigmentation *f*. **pigmented** *adj* pigmenté.
pike [paik] *n* (*fish*) brochet *m*.
pilchard ['piltʃəd] *n* pilchard *m*.
pile[1] [pail] *n* (*heap*) pile *f*, tas *m*. **piles of** (*coll*) des masses de. *v* empiler, entasser. **pile up** (s')amonceler. **pile-up** *n* carambolage *m*.
pile[2] [pail] *n* (*post*) pieu *m*.
pile[3] [pail] *n* (*of carpet, etc.*) poils *m pl*.
piles [pailz] *pl n* (*med*) hémorroïdes *f pl*.

pilfer ['pilfə] (*coll*) *v* chaparder. **pilfering** *n* chapardage *m.*
pilgrim ['pilgrim] *n* pèlerin *m.* **pilgrimage** *n* pèlerinage *m.*
pill [pil] *n* pilule *f.*
pillage ['pilidʒ] *n* pillage *m.* *v* piller.
pillar ['pilə] *n* pilier *m*, colonne *f.* **pillar-box** *n* boîte aux lettres *f.*
pillion ['piljən] *n* siège arrière *m.*
pillow ['pilou] *n* oreiller *m.* **pillowcase** *n* taie d'oreiller *f.*
pilot ['pailət] *n* pilote *m.* **pilot-light** *n* veilleuse *f.* **pilot scheme** projet-pilote *m.* *v* piloter.
pimento [pi'mentou] *n* piment *m.*
pimp [pimp] *n* souteneur *m.*
pimple ['pimpl] *n* bouton *m.* **pimply** *adj* boutonneux.
pin [pin] *n* épingle *f*; (*tech*) goupille *f*; (*elec*: *in plug*) fiche *f.* **have pins and needles** avoir des fourmis. **pin-ball** *n* flipper *m.* **pincushion** *n* pelote à épingles *f.* **pin money** argent de poche *m.* **pinpoint** *v* mettre le doigt sur. **pin-stripe** *n* rayure très fine *f.* *v* épingler. **pin down** coincer. **pin up** (*notice*) afficher. **pin-up** *n* pin-up *f invar.*
pinafore ['pinəfoː] *n* (*apron*) tablier *m.* **pinafore dress** robe-chasuble *f.*
pincers ['pinsəz] *pl n* (*tool*) tenailles *f pl*; (*of crab*) pinces *f pl.*
pinch [pintʃ] *n* pincement *m*; (*of salt*) pincée *f.* **at a pinch** au besoin. *v* pincer; (*shoes, etc.*) serrer; (*coll*: *steal*) chiper.
pine[1] [pain] *n* pin *m.* **pine-cone** *n* pomme de pin *f.*
pine[2] [pain] *v* languir. **pine for** désirer ardemment.
pineapple ['painapl] *n* ananas *m.*
ping-pong ['piŋpoŋ] *n* ping-pong *m.* **ping-pong ball** balle de ping-pong *f.*
pinion[1] ['pinjən] *n* aileron *m.* *v* lier.
pinion[2] ['pinjən] *n* (*tech*) pignon *m.*
pink [piŋk] *n* (*colour*) rose *m*; (*flower*) œillet *m.* *adj* rose.
pinnacle ['pinəkl] *n* pinacle *m.*
pioneer [ˌpaiə'niə] *n* pionnier *m*; explorateur, -trice *m, f.*
pious ['paiəs] *adj* pieux.
pip[1] [pip] *n* (*seed*) pépin *m.*
pip[2] [pip] *n* (*phone, etc.*) top *m.* **the pips** le bip-bip *m sing.*
pipe [paip] *n* (*water, etc.*) tuyau *m*; tube *m*; (*for smoking*) pipe *f*; (*music*) pipeau *m.* **pipe-cleaner** *n* cure-pipe *m.* **pipeline** *n* pipeline *m.* **in the pipeline** en route. *v* transporter par tuyau. **pipe down** (*coll*) mettre la sourdine. **piping** *n* tuyauterie *f*; (*sewing*) passepoil *m.*
piquant ['piːkənt] *adj* piquant. **piquancy** *n* (*taste*) goût piquant *m*; (*of story*) piquant *m.*
pique [piːk] *n* dépit *m.* *v* dépiter.
pirate ['paiərət] *n* pirate *m*; (*comm*) contrefacteur *m.* *v* contrefaire, piller. **piracy** *n* piraterie *f*; contrefaçon *f*; pillage *m.*
pirouette [piru'et] *n* pirouette *f.* *v* pirouetter.
Pisces ['paisiːz] *n* Poissons *m pl.*
piss [pis] (*impol*) *v* pisser. *n* pisse *f.* **piss off!** fous-moi le camp! **pissed** *adj* (*drunk*) bituré. **be pissed off** en avoir marre.
pistachio [pi'staːʃiou] *n* pistache *f.*
pistol ['pistl] *n* pistolet *m.*
piston ['pistən] *n* piston *m.*
pit [pit] *n* fosse *f*; mine *f*; (*hole*) trou *m*; (*theatre*) orchestre *m.* *v* trouer, grêler. **pit one's wits against** se mesurer avec.
pitch[1] [pitʃ] *n* (*throw*) lancement *m*; degré *m*; (*music*) ton *m*; (*sport*) terrain *m.* *v* lancer; (*music*) donner le ton de; (*tent*) dresser; (*fall*) tomber. **pitchfork** *n* fourche à foin *f.*
pitch[2] [pitʃ] *n* poix *f.* **pitch-black** *adj* noir ébène *invar.*
pitfall ['pitfoːl] *n* piège *m.*
pith [piθ] *n* (*of orange*) peau blanche *f*; (*of plant*) moelle *f*; essence *f.* **pithy** *adj* concis, piquant.
pittance ['pitəns] *n* maigre revenu *m.*
pituitary [pi'tjuːitəri] *adj* pituitaire.
pity ['piti] *n* pitié *f*; (*shame*) dommage *m.* **take pity on** avoir pitié de. **what a pity!** quel dommage! *v* plaindre. **piteous** *adj* pitoyable. **pitiful** *adj* pitoyable; (*bad*) lamentable. **pitiless** *adj* sans pitié. **pitying** *adj* compatissant.
pivot ['pivət] *n* pivot *m.* *v* (faire) pivoter.
placard ['plakaːd] *n* affiche *f.* *v* placarder.
placate [plə'keit] *v* calmer.
place [pleis] *n* endroit *m*, lieu *m*; (*seat, position*) place *f.* **all over the place** partout. **out of place** déplacé; (*remark*) hors de propos. **take place** avoir lieu. *v* placer, mettre; situer; (*order*) passer.
placenta [plə'sentə] *n* placenta *m.*
placid ['plasid] *adj* placide. **placidity** *n* placidité *f.*

plagiarize ['pleidʒəraiz] *v* plagier. **plagiarism** *n* plagiat *m*. **plagiarist** *n* plagiaire *m, f*.
plague [pleig] *n* peste *f*; (*nuisance*) fléau *m*. *v* harceler, tourmenter.
plaice [pleis] *n* carrelet *m*.
plaid [plad] *n* tissu écossais *m*. *adj* écossais.
plain [plein] *adj* clair; simple; (*not patterned*) uni; sans beauté; (*utter*) pur. **plain-clothes** *adj* en civil. *n* plaine *f*.
plaintiff ['pleintif] *n* demandeur, -eresse *m, f*.
plaintive ['pleintiv] *adj* plaintif.
plait [plat] *n* natte *f*, tresse *f*. *v* natter, tresser.
plan [plan] *n* plan *m*, projet *m*. *v* projeter; organiser; préparer à l'avance. **planning** *n* planification *f*; (*comm*) planning *m*. **planning permission** permis de construire *m*.
plane[1] [plein] *n* (*level*) plan *m*; (*coll*: *aeroplane*) avion *m*. *adj* plan.
plane[2] [plein] *n* (*tool*) rabot. *v* raboter.
planet ['planit] *n* planète *f*. **planetarium** *n* planétarium *m*. **planetary** *adj* planétaire.
plank [plaŋk] *n* planche *f*.
plankton ['plaŋktən] *n* plancton *m*.
plant [plaːnt] *n* (*bot*) plante *f*; (*tech*) matériel *m*, installation *f*; (*factory*) usine *f*. *v* planter; (*hide*) cacher. **plantation** *n* plantation *f*.
plaque [plaːk] *n* plaque *f*.
plasma ['plazmə] *n* plasma *m*.
plaster ['plaːstə] *n* plâtre *m*; (*for wound*) sparadrap *m*. **plaster of Paris** plâtre de moulage *m*. *v* plâtrer; couvrir. **plasterer** *n* plâtrier *m*.
plastic ['plastik] *nm, adj* plastique. **plastic surgery** chirurgie esthétique *f*.
plate [pleit] *n* (*dish*) assiette *f*; (*of metal*) plaque *f*; (*in book*) gravure *f*. *v* plaquer; (*silver*) argenter; (*gold*) dorer. **plateful** *n* assiettée *f*.
plateau ['platou] *n* plateau *m*.
platform ['platfoːm] *n* plate-forme *f*; (*in hall*) estrade *f*, tribune *f*; (*rail*) quai *m*. **platform-soled** *adj* (*shoes*) à semelles compensées. **platform ticket** billet de quai *m*.
platinum ['platinəm] *n* platine *m*.
platonic [plə'tonik] *adj* platonique.
platoon [plə'tuːn] *n* (*mil*) section *f*.
plausible ['ploːzəbl] *adj* plausible; (*person*) convaincant. **plausibility** *n* plausibilité *f*.
play [plei] *n* jeu *m*; (*theatre*) pièce *f*. *v* jouer. **player** *n* joueur, -euse *m, f*. **playful** *adj* enjoué. **playfulness** *n* enjouement *m*, badinage *m*.
play-back ['pleibak] *n* réécoute *f*. **play back** *v* réécouter.
playboy ['pleiboi] *n* playboy *m*.
playground ['pleigraund] *n* cour de récréation *f*.
play-group ['pleigruːp] *n* garderie *f*.
playing card *n* carte à jouer *f*.
playing field *n* terrain de sport *m*.
playmate ['pleimeit] *n* camarade *m, f*.
play-pen ['pleipen] *n* parc *m*.
plaything ['plei,θiŋ] *n* jouet *m*.
playtime ['pleitaim] *n* récréation *f*.
playwright ['pleirait] *n* dramaturge *m*.
plea [pliː] *n* appel *m*; (*law*) argument *m*; excuse *f*.
plead [pliːd] *v* supplier, implorer; (*law*) plaider; (*as excuse*) alléguer.
pleasant ['pleznt] *adj* agréable.
please [pliːz] *v* plaire (à). **please oneself** faire comme on veut. *adv* s'il vous plaît. **pleased** *adj* content. **pleasing** *adj* plaisant.
pleasure ['pleʒə] *n* plaisir *m*. **pleasure boat** bateau de plaisance *m*. **pleasurable** *adj* agréable.
pleat [pliːt] *n* pli *m*. *v* plisser.
plectrum ['plektrəm] *n* plectre *m*.
pledge [pledʒ] *n* gage *m*; promesse *f*. *v* engager; promettre.
plenty ['plenti] *n* abondance *f*. **plenty of** bien assez de. **plentiful** *adj* abondant, copieux.
pleurisy ['pluərisi] *n* pleurésie *f*.
pliable ['plaiəbl] *adj* flexible; (*person*) souple. **pliability** *n* flexibilité *f*; souplesse *f*.
pliers ['plaiəz] *pl n* pinces *f pl*, tenailles *f pl*.
plight [plait] *n* état critique *m*, crise *f*.
plimsoll ['plimsəl] *n* tennis *m*.
plod [plod] *v* marcher d'un pas lourd; (*coll*: *work*) bûcher. **plod on** persévérer. **plodder** *n* (*coll*) bûcheur *m*.
plonk [ploŋk] *n* (*coll*) vin ordinaire *m*.
plop [plop] *n* ploc *m*. *v* faire ploc.
plot[1] [plot] *n* (*story, etc*) intrigue *f*; (*conspiracy*) complot *m*. *v* comploter; (*route*) déterminer.
plot[2] [plot] *n* (*land*) terrain *m*, lotissement *m*.

plough [plau] *n* charrue *f*. *v* labourer; (*furrow*) creuser. **ploughing** *n* labour *m*.
pluck [plʌk] *n* courage *m*. *v* (*music*) pincer; (*fruit*) cueillir; (*fowl*) plumer; (*eyebrows*) épiler. **pluck out** arracher. **pluck up courage** prendre son courage à deux mains. **plucky** *adj* courageux.
plug [plʌg] *n* (*stopper*) bouchon *m*, tampon *m*; (*sink, bath*) bonde *f*; (*elec*) fiche *f*; (*mot*) bougie *f*. *v* boucher. **plug in** (se) brancher.
plum [plʌm] *n* (*fruit*) prune *f*; (*tree*) prunier *m*. *adj* (*colour*) lie de vin *invar*. **plum pudding** pudding *m*.
plumage ['plu:midʒ] *n* plumage *m*.
plumb [plʌm] *n* plomb *m*. **plumbline** *n* fil à plomb *m*. *adj* vertical. *adv* en plein. *v* sonder. **plumb in** faire le raccordement de. **plumber** *n* plombier *m*. **plumbing** *n* plomberie *f*.
plume [plu:m] *n* plume *f*; (*smoke*) panache *m*. *v* lisser.
plummet ['plʌmit] *n* plomb *m*. *v* plonger; (*price, etc.*) dégringoler.
plump[1] [plʌmp] *adj* grassouillet, -ette, potelé. **plumpness** *n* rondeur *f*.
plump[2] [plʌmp] *v* tomber lourdement. **plump for** se décider pour.
plunder ['plʌndə] *v* piller. *n* (*loot*) butin *m*. **plunderer** *n* pillard *m*. **plundering** *n* pillage *m*.
plunge [plʌndʒ] *n* plongeon *m*; (*fall*) chute *f*. **take the plunge** se jeter à l'eau. *v* plonger; (*rush*) se jeter; (*fall*) tomber.
pluperfect [plu:'pəfikt] *n* plus-que-parfait *m*.
plural ['pluərəl] *nm, adj* pluriel.
plus [plʌs] *nm, prep* plus. *adj* positif.
plush [plʌʃ] *n* peluche *f*. *adj* pelucheux; (*coll*) rupin.
ply[1] [plai] *v* (*tool*) manier; (*trade*) exercer; (*with questions, etc.*) presser; (*ship, etc.*) faire la navette.
ply[2] [plai] *n* (*wood*) feuille *f*; (*wool*) fil *m*; (*rope*) brin *m*. **plywood** *n* contre-plaqué *m*.
pneumatic [nju'matik] *adj* pneumatique. **pneumatic drill** marteau-piqueur *m*.
pneumonia [nju'mouniə] *n* pneumonie *f*.
poach[1] [poutʃ] *v* braconner. **poacher** *n* braconnier *m*. **poaching** *n* braconnage *m*.
poach[2] [poutʃ] *v* (*egg*) pocher.
pocket ['pokit] *n* poche *f*. **pocket-money** *n* argent de poche *m*. *v* empocher.
pod [pod] *n* cosse *f*.
podgy ['podʒi] *adj* (*coll*) rondelet.
poem ['pouim] *n* poème *m*.
poet ['pouit] *n* poète *m*. **poetess** *n* poétesse *f*. **poetic** *adj* poétique. **poetry** *n* poésie *f*.
poignant ['poinjənt] *adj* poignant.
point [point] *n* point *m*; (*sharp end*) pointe *f*; (*decimal*) virgule *f*; (*elec: socket*) prise *f*; (*meaning*) sens *m*. **beside the point** hors de propos. **come to the point** en venir au fait. **make a point of** ne pas manquer de. **point-blank** *adv* (*shoot*) à bout portant; (*refuse*) tout net; (*demand*) de but en blanc. **what's the point?** à quoi bon? *v* indiquer; (*aim*) pointer, braquer. **point out** (*show*) montrer; (*say*) signaler. **pointed** *adj* pointu; (*remark*) lourd de sens. **pointless** *adj* inutile.
poise [poiz] *n* équilibre *m*; (*of body*) port *m*; calme *m*, assurance *f*. *v* tenir en équilibre. **be poised** être en équilibre; être suspendu.
poison ['poizən] *n* poison *m*. *v* empoisonner. **poisoning** *n* empoisonnement *m*. **poisonous** *adj* toxique; (*animal*) venimeux; (*plant*) vénéneux.
poke [pouk] *n* poussée *f*, coup *m*. *v* pousser, enfoncer; (*fire*) tisonner. **poker** *n* tisonnier *m*.
poker ['poukə] *n* (*cards*) poker *m*. **poker-faced** *adj* au visage impassible.
Poland ['pouland] *n* Pologne *f*. **Pole** *n* Polonais, -e *m, f*. **Polish** *nm, adj* polonais.
polar ['poulə] *adj* polaire. **polar bear** ours blanc *m*. **polarize** *v* polariser.
pole[1] [poul] *n* perche *f*; (*fixed*) poteau *m*, mât *m*. **pole-vault** *n* saut à la perche *m*.
pole[2] [poul] *n* (*geog, elec*) pôle *m*. **pole star** étoile polaire *f*.
police [pə'li:s] *n* police *f*, gendarmerie *f*. **the police force** la police *f*, les gendarmes *m pl*. **policeman** *n* agent de police *m*, gendarme *m*. **police station** poste de police *m*, gendarmerie *f*. **policewoman** *n* femme-agent *f*.
policy[1] ['poləsi] *n* politique *f*; ligne *f*, règle *f*.
policy[2] ['poləsi] *n* (*insurance*) police *f*.
polio ['pouliou] *n* polio *f*.
polish ['poliʃ] *n* (*shoes*) cirage *m*; (*floor, etc.*) cire *f*; (*shine*) poli *m*. *v* polir; cirer, faire briller. **polish off** finir. **polish up** perfectionner.

polite [pə'lait] *adj* poli. **politeness** *n* politesse *f*.
politics ['politiks] *n* politique *f*. **political** *adj* politique. **politician** *n* homme politique, femme politique *m, f*.
polka ['polkə] *n* polka *f*.
poll [poul] *n* vote *m*; élection *f*; (*survey*) sondage *m*. *v* voter. **polling booth** isoloir *m*. **polling day** jour des élections *m*. **polling station** bureau de vote *m*.
pollen ['polən] *n* pollen *m*. **pollinate** *v* féconder. **pollination** *n* pollinisation *f*.
pollute [pə'luːt] *v* polluer. **pollution** *n* pollution *f*.
polo ['poulou] *n* polo *m*. **polo-neck** *n* col roulé *m*.
polyester [ˌpoli'estə] *n* polyester *m*.
polygamy [pə'ligəmi] *n* polygamie *f*. **polygamous** *adj* polygame.
polygon ['poligən] *n* polygone *m*.
polystyrene [ˌpoli'staiəriːn] *n* polystyrène *m*.
polytechnic [ˌpoli'teknik] *n* Institut Universitaire de Technologie *m*.
polythene ['poliθiːn] *n* polyéthylène *m*. **polythene bag** sac en plastique *m*.
pomegranate ['pomigranit] *n* (*fruit*) grenade *f*; (*tree*) grenadier *m*.
pomp [pomp] *n* pompe *f*. **pompous** *adj* pompeux.
pond [pond] *n* étang *m*; (*artificial*) bassin *m*.
ponder ['pondə] *v* réfléchir (à), méditer.
pony ['pouni] *n* poney *m*. **pony-tail** *n* queue de cheval *f*. **pony-trekking** *n* randonnée équestre *f*.
poodle ['puːdl] *n* caniche *m*.
poof [puːf] *n* (*derog*) tante *f*, tapette *f*.
pool[1] [puːl] *n* (*liquid*) flaque *f*; (*swimming*) piscine *f*.
pool[2] [puːl] *n* (*money*) cagnotte *f*; (*things*) fonds commun *m*; (*ideas*) réservoir *m*; (*comm*) pool *m*. *v* mettre en commun; unir.
poor [puə] *adj* pauvre; médiocre; faible.
poorly ['puəli] *adj* malade. *adv* pauvrement; (*badly*) mal.
pop[1] [pop] *n* pan *m*, bruit sec *m*; (*drink*) boisson gazeuse *f*. **popcorn** *n* pop-corn *m*. *v* (*balloon*) crever; (*cork*) (faire) sauter. **pop in** entrer en passant.
pop[2] [pop] *nm, adj* (*music, etc.*) pop *invar*.
pope [poup] *n* pape *m*.
poplar ['poplə] *n* peuplier *m*.
poplin ['poplin] *n* popeline *f*.
poppy ['popi] *n* pavot *m*, coquelicot *m*.
popular ['popjulə] *adj* populaire. **popularity** *n* popularité *f*. **popularize** *v* populariser.
population [ˌpopju'leiʃən] *n* population *f*. **populate** *v* peupler.
porcelain ['poːslin] *n* porcelaine *f*.
porch [poːtʃ] *n* porche *m*.
porcupine ['poːkjupain] *n* porc-épic *m*.
pore[1] [poː] *n* (*anat*) pore *m*.
pore[2] [poː] *v* **pore over** s'absorber dans.
pork [poːk] *n* porc *m*.
pornography [poː'nogrəfi] *n* pornographie *f*. **pornographic** *adj* pornographique.
porous ['poːrəs] *adj* poreux.
porpoise ['poːpəs] *n* marsouin *m*.
porridge ['poridʒ] *n* porridge *m*.
port[1] [poːt] *n* (*harbour*) port *m*.
port[2] [poːt] *n* (*naut*: *left*) bâbord *m*.
port[3] [poːt] *n* (*wine*) porto *m*.
portable ['poːtəbl] *adj* portatif.
portent ['poːtent] *n* présage *m*.
porter ['poːtə] *n* (*rail, etc.*) porteur *m*; (*in flats, etc.*) concierge *m, f*, portier *m*.
portfolio [poːt'fouliou] *n* serviette *f*; (*pol*) portefeuille *f*.
porthole ['poːthoul] *n* hublot *m*.
portion ['poːʃən] *n* portion *f*; partie *f*.
portrait ['poːtrət] *n* portrait *m*.
portray [poː'trei] *v* peindre; représenter. **portrayal** *n* peinture *f*; représentation *f*.
Portugal ['poːtjugl] *n* Portugal *m*. **Portuguese** *nm, adj* portugais. **the Portuguese** les Portugais.
pose [pouz] *n* pose *f*. *v* poser. **pose as** se faire passer pour.
posh [poʃ] *adj* chic *invar*.
position [pə'ziʃən] *n* position *f*, place *f*; situation *f*. *v* placer, mettre en place.
positive ['pozətiv] *adj* positif; catégorique, réel; sûr, certain.
possess [pə'zes] *v* posséder. **possession** *n* possession *f*. **possessive** *nm, adj* possessif.
possible ['posəbl] *adj* possible. **possibility** *n* possibilité *f*. **possibly** *adv* (*perhaps*) peut-être.
post[1] [poust] *n* (*pole*) poteau *m*. *v* afficher.
post[2] [poust] *n* (*sentry, job*) poste *m*. *v* poster; (*send*) affecter. **posting** *n* affectation *f*.
post[3] [poust] *n* (*mail*) poste *f*; (*letters*) courrier *m*. **post-box** *n* boîte aux lettres *f*. **postcard** *n* carte postale *f*. **post-code** *n* code postal *m*. **postman** *n* facteur *m*.

postmark *n* cachet de la poste *m*. **postmarked** *adj* timbré. **post office** poste *f*. *v* envoyer par la poste, poster. **postage** *n* tarifs postaux *m pl*. **postage stamp** timbre-poste *m*. **postal** *adj* postal, par la poste. **postal order** mandat *m*.
poster ['poustə] *n* affiche *f*; (*as decoration*) poster *m*. **poster paint** gouache *f*.
posterior [po'stiəriə] *adj* postérieur, -e. *n* (*coll*) derrière *m*.
posterity [po'sterəti] *n* postérité *f*.
postgraduate [poust'gradjuit] *adj* de troisième cycle. *n* étudiant, -e de troisième cycle *m, f*.
posthumous ['postjuməs] *adj* posthume.
post-mortem [poust'moːtəm] *n* autopsie *f*.
postpone [pous'poun] *v* remettre, ajourner. **postponement** *n* ajournement *m*.
postscript ['pousskript] *n* post-scriptum *m*.
postulate ['postjuleit; *n* 'postjulət] *v* postuler, poser comme principe. *n* postulat *m*.
posture ['postʃə] *n* posture *f*; attitude *f*.
pot [pot] *n* pot *m*; (*for cooking*) marmite *f*. **pot-roast** *n* rôti braisé *m*. **pots and pans** batterie de cuisine *f sing*. **take pot luck** manger à la fortune du pot. *v* mettre en pot.
potassium [pə'tasjəm] *n* potassium *m*.
potato [pə'teitou] *n* pomme de terre *f*.
potent ['poutənt] *adj* puissant; (*drink*) fort.
potential [pə'tenʃəl] *adj* potentiel; possible. *n* (*phys, elec, etc.*) potentiel *m*; (*promise*) potentialités *f pl*.
pot-hole ['pothoul] *n* (*in road*) fondrière *f*; (*underground*) caverne *f*, grotte *f*. **potholer** *n* spéléologue *m, f*. **pot-holing** *n* spéléologie *f*.
potion ['pouʃən] *n* potion *f*.
potter[1] ['potə] *v* (*coll*) bricoler.
potter[2] ['potə] *n* potier *m*. **potter's wheel** tour de potier *m*.
pottery ['potəri] *n* (*place, craft*) poterie *f*; (*things made*) poteries *f pl*.
potty ['poti] *n* (*coll*) pot de bébé *m*.
pouch [pautʃ] *n* petit sac *m*; (*kangaroo*) poche *f*; (*tobacco*) blague *f*.
poultice ['poultis] *n* cataplasme *m*.
poultry ['poultri] *n* volaille *f*.
pounce [pauns] *v* bondir, sauter. *n* bond *m*.
pound[1] [paund] *v* battre, piler, pilonner, marteler.
pound[2] [paund] *n* livre *f*.
pour [poː] *v* verser; (*flow copiously*) couler à flots, ruisseler; (*rain*) tomber à verse; (*people, etc.*) affluer.
pout [paut] *n* moue *f*. *v* faire la moue.
poverty ['povəti] *n* pauvreté *f*.
powder ['paudə] *n* poudre *f*. **powder puff** houppette *f*. **powder room** toilettes pour dames *f pl*. *v* poudrer; pulvériser. **powdery** *adj* poudreux.
power ['pauə] *n* (*authority, capacity*) pouvoir *m*; (*energy, force*) puissance *f*; faculté *f*. **power cut** coupure de courant *f*. **power station** centrale électrique *f*. *v* faire marcher. **powerful** *adj* puissant. **powerless** *adj* impuissant.
practicable ['praktikəbl] *adj* praticable.
practical ['praktikəl] *adj* pratique. **practical joke** farce *f*.
practice ['praktis] *n* pratique *f*; (*training*) entraînement *m*; (*medicine, etc.*) exercice *m*; clientèle *f*.
practise ['praktis] *v* pratiquer; s'entraîner (à); (*music*) travailler, s'exercer (à); (*doctor, lawyer*) exercer.
practitioner [prak'tiʃənə] *n* praticien, -enne *m, f*.
pragmatic [prag'matik] *adj* pragmatique; dogmatique.
Prague [praːg] *n* Prague.
prairie ['preəri] *n* plaine *f*, prairie *f*.
praise [preiz] *n* éloge *m*. *v* louer. **praiseworthy** *adj* louable.
pram [pram] *n* voiture d'enfant *f*.
prance [praːns] *v* caracoler.
prank [praŋk] *n* frasque *f*; (*joke*) farce *f*.
prattle ['pratl] *v* jaser, babiller; (*chat*) jacasser. *n* babil *m*; jacasserie *f*.
prawn [proːn] *n* crevette rose *f*. **prawn cocktail** salade de crevettes *f*.
pray [prei] *v* prier. **prayer** *n* prière *f*. **prayer-book** *n* livre de messe *m*.
preach [priːtʃ] *v* prêcher. **preacher** *n* prédicateur *m*. **preaching** *n* predication *f*.
precarious [pri'keəriəs] *adj* precaire.
precaution [pri'koːʃən] *n* precaution *f*. **take precautions** prendre ses précautions.
precede [pri'siːd] *v* précéder. **precedence** *n* préséance *f*, priorité *f*. **precedent** *n* précédent *m*.
precinct ['priːsiŋkt] *n* enceinte *f*; limite *f*; (*shopping*) zone commerciale *f*.

precious ['preʃəs] *adj* précieux.
precipice ['presipis] *n* précipice *m*.
precipitate [pri'sipiteit; *adj* pri'sipitət] *v* (*hasten*) hâter; (*throw*) précipiter. *adj* irréfléchi. **precipitation** *n* précipitation *f*.
précis ['preisi] *n* précis *m*, résumé *m*.
precise [pri'sais] *adj* précis; méticuleux. **precision** *n* précision *f*.
preclude [pri'kluːd] *v* écarter; prévenir; exclure.
precocious [pri'kouʃəs] *adj* précoce. **precocity** *n* précocité *f*.
preconceive [ˌpriːkən'siːv] *v* préconcevoir. **preconception** *n* idée préconçue *f*.
precursor [ˌpriː'kəːsə] *n* (*person*) précurseur *m*; (*thing*) annonce *f*.
predator ['predətə] *n* prédateur *m*. **predatory** *adj* rapace, de prédateur.
predecessor ['priːdisesə] *n* prédécesseur *m*.
predestine [pri'destin] *v* prédestiner. **predestination** *n* prédestination *f*.
predicament [pri'dikəmənt] *n* situation difficile *f*.
predicate ['predikət] *n* prédicat *m*. *v* affirmer.
predict [pri'dikt] *v* prédire. **predictable** *adj* prévisible. **prediction** *n* prédiction *f*.
predominate [pri'domineit] *v* prédominer. **predominance** *n* prédominance *f*. **predominant** *adj* prédominant.
pre-eminent [priː'eminənt] *adj* prééminent. **pre-eminence** *n* prééminence *f*.
preen [priːn] *v* lisser. **preen oneself** se pomponner.
prefabricate [priː'fabrikeit] *v* préfabriquer. **prefab** *n* (*coll*) maison préfabriquée *f*.
preface ['prefis] *n* (*book*) préface *f*; (*speech*) introduction *f*. *v* faire précéder.
prefect ['priːfekt] *n* (*school*) élève chargé de la discipline *m*.
prefer [pri'fəː] *v* préférer, aimer mieux. **preferable** *adj* préférable. **preference** *n* préférence *f*. **preferential** *adj* préférentiel.
prefix ['priːfiks] *n* préfixe *m*. *v* préfixer.
pregnant ['pregnənt] *adj* (*woman*) enceinte; (*animal*) pleine. **pregnancy** *n* (*woman*) grossesse *f*; (*animal*) gestation *f*.
prehistoric [ˌpriːhi'storik] *adj* préhistorique.
prejudice ['predʒədis] *n* préjugé *m*. *v* prévenir; (*damage*) nuire à. **prejudiced** *adj* de parti pris.
preliminary [pri'liminəri] *adj* préliminaire; premier. **preliminaries** *pl n* préliminaires *m pl*.
prelude ['preljuːd] *n* prélude *m*.
premarital [priː'maritl] *adj* avant le mariage.
premature [premə'tʃuə] *adj* prématuré.
premeditate [priː'mediteit] *v* préméditer. **premeditation** *n* préméditation *f*.
premier ['premiə] *adj* premier. *n* premier ministre *m*.
première ['premieə] *n* première *f*.
premise ['premis] *n* prémisse *f*. **premises** *pl n* lieux *m pl*, locaux *m pl*.
premium ['priːmiəm] *n* prime *f*. **premium bond** bon à lots *m*.
premonition [ˌpremə'niʃən] *n* prémonition *f*.
preoccupied [priː'okjupaid] *adj* préoccupé. **preoccupation** *n* préoccupation *f*.
prepare [pri'peə] *v* (se) préparer. **preparation** *n* préparation. **preparations** *pl n* préparatifs *m pl*. **preparatory** *adj* préparatoire; préliminaire. **preparatory school** école primaire privée *f*.
preposition [ˌprepə'ziʃən] *n* préposition *f*.
preposterous [pri'postərəs] *adj* absurde, ridicule.
prerogative [pri'rogətiv] *n* prérogative *f*.
prescribe [pri'skraib] *v* prescrire. **prescription** *n* (*med*) ordonnance *f*; prescription *f*.
presence ['prezns] *n* présence *f*.
present[1] ['preznt] *adj* présent; actuel. *n* présent *m*. **at present** actuellement. **presently** *adv* tout à l'heure.
present[2] [pri'zent] *v* présenter; (*film, play*) donner; (*gift*) offrir; (*medal*) remettre. *n* cadeau *m*. **presentable** *adj* présentable. **presentation** *n* présentation *f*; (*of gift, medal*) remise *f*. **presenter** *n* présentateur, -trice *m, f*.
preserve [pri'zəːv] *v* conserver; (*from harm*) préserver. **preserved** *adj* en conserve. **preserves** *pl n* conserves *f pl*; (*jam*) confiture *f sing*. **preservation** *n* conservation *f*; préservation *f*. **preservative** *n* agent de conservation *m*.
preside [pri'zaid] *v* présider.
president ['prezidənt] *n* président *m*. **presidency** *n* présidence *f*. **presidential** *adj* présidentiel.
press [pres] *n* presse *f*; (*wine, cider*) pressoir *m*. **press conference** conférence de presse *f*. **press release** communiqué de presse *m*. *v* appuyer (sur), presser; (*iron*)

repasser; insister. **press for** faire pression pour. **press-gang** *v* faire pression sur. **press on** continuer. **press-stud** *n* bouton-pression *m*. **press-up** *n* traction *f*. **pressing** *adj* urgent.
pressure ['preʃə] *n* pression *f*. **pressure-cooker** *n* autocuiseur *m*. **pressure gauge** manomètre *m*. **pressurize** *v* (*cabin, etc.*) pressuriser; (*force*) contraindre.
prestige [pre'stiːʒ] *n* prestige *m*. **prestigious** *adj* prestigieux.
presume [pri'zjuːm] *v* présumer. **presumption** *n* présomption *f*. **presumptuous** *adj* présomptueux.
pretend [pri'tend] *v* faire semblant; (*claim*) prétendre. **pretence** *n* feinte *f*, prétexte *m*; (*claim*) prétention *f*. **pretension** *n* prétention *f*. **pretentious** *adj* prétentieux.
pretext ['priːtekst] *n* prétexte *m*.
pretty ['priti] *adj* joli. *adv* assez.
prevail [pri'veil] *v* prévaloir, prédominer. **prevail upon** persuader. **prevailing** *adj* (*wind*) dominant; courant, actuel. **prevalent** *adj* répandu.
prevent [pri'vent] *v* empêcher. **prevention** *n* prévention *f*. **preventive** *adj* préventif.
preview ['priːvjuː] *n* avant-première *f*.
previous ['priːviəs] *adj* précédent. **previously** *adv* auparavant.
prey [prei] *n* proie *f*. **be a prey to** être en proie à. *v* **prey on** (*animal*) faire sa proie de; (*fear*) ronger.
price [prais] *n* prix *m*. **price-list** *n* tarif *m*. *v* fixer le prix de; marquer le prix de. **priceless** *adj* inestimable.
prick [prik] *n* piqûre *f*. *v* piquer. **prick up one's ears** dresser l'oreille.
prickle ['prikl] *n* piquant *m*. *v* piquer; (*sensation*) picoter. **prickly** *adj* hérissé.
pride [praid] *n* orgueil *m*; (*satisfaction*) fierté *f*. *v* **pride oneself on** être fier de.
priest [priːst] *n* prêtre *m*. **priesthood** *n* prêtrise *f*.
prim [prim] *adj* guindé.
primary ['praiməri] *adj* (*first*) primaire, premier; principal. **primary school** école primaire *f*.
primate ['praimət] *n* (*zool*) primate *m*; (*rel*) primat *m*.
prime [praim] *adj* principal; excellent, de premier choix; (*math*) premier. **prime minister** premier ministre *m*. *v* préparer; (*for painting*) apprêter. **primer** *n* apprêt *m*; (*book*) premier livre *m*.
primitive ['primitiv] *adj* primitif.
primrose ['primrouz] *n* primevère *f*.
prince [prins] *n* prince *m*. **princely** *adj* princier. **princess** *n* princesse *f*.
principal ['prinsəpəl] *adj* principal. *n* (*school*) directeur, -trice *m, f*.
principle ['prinsəpəl] *n* principe *m*. **on principle** par principe.
print [print] *n* (*mark*) empreinte *f*; (*type*) caractères *m pl*; (*art*) gravure *f*; (*phot*) épreuve *f*. **out of print** épuisé. *v* imprimer; (*phot*) tirer. **print-out** *n* listage *m*. **printed matter** imprimés *m pl*. **printer** *n* imprimeur *m*. **printing** *n* impression *f*; (*phot*) tirage *m*. **printing press** presse typographique *f*.
prior ['praiə] *adj* antérieur, -e **prior to** antérieurement à. **priority** *n* priorité *f*.
prise [praiz] *v* **prise off/open** enlever/ouvrir en faisant levier; forcer.
prism ['prizm] *n* prisme *m*.
prison ['prizn] *n* prison *f*. **prisoner** *n* prisonnier, -ère *m, f*.
private ['praivət] *adj* privé; confidentiel; (*lesson, car, etc.*) particulier; personnel. *n* simple soldat *m*. **privacy** *n* intimité *f*, solitude *f*. **privately** *adv* en privé; à titre personnel.
privet ['privət] *n* troène *m*.
privilege ['privəlidʒ] *n* privilège *m*. **privileged** *adj* privilégié.
prize [praiz] *n* prix *m*. **prizewinner** *n* lauréat, -e *m, f*. *adj* primé. *v* priser.
probable ['probəbl] *adj* probable; (*believable*) vraisemblable. **probability** *n* probabilité *f*. **probably** *adv* probablement.
probation [prə'beiʃən] *n* (*law*) mise à l'épreuve *f*, liberté surveillée *f*. **on probation** (*job*) engagé à l'essai. **probationary** *adj* d'essai.
probe [proub] *n* sonde *f*; enquête *f*. *v* sonder, explorer.
problem ['probləm] *n* problème *m*. **problem child** enfant difficile *m, f*. **problem page** courrier du cœur *m*. **problematic** *adj* problématique.
proceed [prə'siːd] *v* aller, continuer, avancer. **proceed to** se mettre à. **proceeds** *pl n* produit *m sing*. **procedure** *n* procédure *f*. **proceedings** *pl n* cérémonie *f sing*; (*law*) mesures *f pl*.
process ['prouses] *n* processus *m*; (*method*) procédé *m*. **in the process of** en

train de, au cours de. *v* traiter; (*phot*) développer; (*admin*) s'occuper de.
procession [prə'seʃən] *n* cortège *m*, défilé *m*.
proclaim [prə'kleim] *v* proclamer; démontrer. **proclamation** *n* proclamation *f*.
procreate ['proukrieit] *v* procréer. **procreation** *n* procréation *f*.
procure [prə'kjuə] *v* obtenir; (*prostitute*) procurer.
prod [prod] *n* petit coup *m*. *v* pousser doucement; (*rouse*) aiguillonner.
prodigal ['prodigəl] *adj* prodigue.
prodigy ['prodidʒi] *n* prodige *m*. **prodigious** *adj* prodigieux.
produce [prə'djuːs; *n* 'prodjuːs] *v* produire; (*theatre*) mettre en scène. *n* produits *m pl*. **producer** *n* producteur, -trice *m, f*; metteur en scène *m*. **product** *n* produit *m*. **production** *n* production *f*; mise en scène *f*. **productive** *adj* productif; fécond. **productivity** *n* productivité *f*.
profane [prə'fein] *adj* profane. *v* profaner. **profanity** *n* (*oath*) juron *m*.
profess [prə'fes] *v* professer, affirmer, déclarer.
profession [prə'feʃən] *n* profession *f*. **professional** *n, adj* professionnel, -elle.
professor [prə'fesə] *n* professeur *m*. **professorship** *n* chaire *f*.
proficient [prə'fiʃənt] *adj* compétent. **proficiency** *n* compétence *f*.
profile ['proufail] *n* profil *m*; (*biographical sketch*) portrait *m*.
profit ['profit] *n* profit *m*, bénéfice *m*. **profit-making** *adj* à but lucratif. *v* **profit by** *or* **from** tirer profit de. **profitable** *adj* rentable; (*useful*) fructueux.
profound [prə'faund] *adj* profond. **profoundly** *adv* profondément.
profuse [prə'fjuːs] *adj* abondant, profus. **profusely** *adv* abondamment, à profusion. **profusion** *n* abondance *f*, profusion *f*.
programme ['prougram] *n* programme *m*; (*broadcast*) émission *f*. *v* programmer. **programmer** *n* programmeur, -euse *m, f*. **programming** *n* programmation *f*.
progress ['prougres] *n* progrès *m*. **in progress** en cours. **make progress** faire des progrès. *v* progresser, avancer. **progression** *n* progression *f*. **progressive** *adj* progressif; (*outlook, etc.*) progressiste.
prohibit [prə'hibit] *v* interdire, défendre; (*prevent*) empêcher. **prohibition** *n* prohibition *f*.
project ['prodʒekt; *v* prə'dʒekt] *n* projet *m*; opération *f*; (*school*) dossier *m*. *v* projeter; (*protrude*) faire saillie. **projectile** *n* projectile *m*. **projecting** *adj* saillant. **projection** *n* projection *f*; saillie *f*. **projector** *n* projecteur *m*.
proletarian [proulə'teəriən] *n* prolétaire *m*. *adj* prolétarien. **proletariat** *n* prolétariat *m*.
proliferate [prə'lifəreit] *v* proliférer. **proliferation** *n* prolifération *f*.
prolific [prə'lifik] *adj* prolifique.
prologue ['proulog] *n* prologue *m*.
prolong [prə'loŋ] *v* prolonger. **prolongation** *n* (*time*) prolongation *f*; (*space*) prolongement *m*.
promenade [promə'naːd] *n* promenade *f*.
prominent ['prominənt] *adj* proéminent; important; (*striking*) frappant. **prominence** *n* proéminence *f*; importance *f*.
promiscuous [prə'miskjuəs] *adj* léger, immoral; (*person*) de mœurs faciles. **promiscuity** *n* promiscuité *f*.
promise ['promis] *n* promesse *f*. *v* promettre. **promising** *adj* prometteur, -euse.
promontory ['proməntəri] *n* promontoire *m*.
promote [prə'mout] *v* promouvoir; (*comm*) lancer. **promotion** *n* promotion *f*; lancement *m*.
prompt [prompt] *adj* rapide, prompt; ponctuel. *v* pousser, inciter; (*theatre*) souffler. **prompter** *n* souffleur, -euse *m, f*.
prone [proun] *adj* enclin; (*lying*) prostré.
prong [proŋ] *n* dent *f*.
pronoun ['prounaun] *n* pronom *m*.
pronounce [prə'nauns] *v* prononcer. **pronouncement** *n* déclaration *f*. **pronunciation** *n* prononciation *f*.
proof [pruːf] *n* preuve *f*; (*of book, photo, etc.*) épreuve *f*. **proof-read** *v* corriger les épreuves de. **proof-reading** *n* correction des épreuves *f*. *adj* (*resistant*) à l'épreuve de.
prop[1] [prop] *n* support *m*. *v* (*lean*) appuyer; (*support*) étayer; (*financially*) soutenir.
prop[2] [prop] *n* (*coll: theatre*) accessoire *m*.
propaganda [propə'gandə] *n* propagande *f*.
propagate ['propəgeit] *v* (se) propager. **propagation** *n* propagation *f*.

propel [prə'pel] *v* propulser; (*push*) pousser. **propeller** *n* hélice *f*. **propelling pencil** porte-mine *m invar*.
proper ['propə] *adj* convenable, correct; (*real*) véritable. **proper noun** nom propre *m*. **properly** *adv* comme il faut.
property ['propəti] *n* propriété *f*; (*possessions*) biens *m pl*.
prophecy ['profəsi] *n* prophétie *f*. **prophesy** *v* prédire, prophétiser.
prophet ['profit] *n* prophète *m*. **prophetic** *adj* prophétique.
proportion [prə'poːʃən] *n* proportion *f*; part *f*. **out of proportion** mal proportionné; hors de proportion. *v* proportionner. **proportional** *adj* proportionnel.
propose [prə'pouz] *v* proposer; (*marriage*) faire sa demande; (*intend*) se proposer (de). **proposal** *n* proposition *f*; demande en mariage *f*; projet *m*. **proposition** *n* proposition *f*; affaire *f*.
proprietor [prə'praiətə] *n* propriétaire *m*, *f*.
propriety [prə'praiəti] *n* bienséance *f*; (*correctness*) justesse *f*.
propulsion [prə'pʌlʃən] *n* propulsion *f*.
prose [prouz] *n* prose *f*; (*translation*) thème *m*.
prosecute ['prosikjuːt] *v* poursuivre. **prosecution** *n* poursuites judiciaires *f pl*; (*side*) partie plaignante *f*.
prospect ['prospekt; *v* prə'spekt] *n* perspective *f*. **prospects** *pl n* (*of job, etc.*) avenir *m sing*. *v* prospecter. **prospective** *adj* futur; possible.
prospectus [prə'spektəs] *n* prospectus *m*.
prosper ['prospə] *v* prospérer. **prosperity** *n* prospérité *f*. **prosperous** *adj* prospère.
prostitute ['prostitjuːt] *n* prostituée *f*. *v* prostituer. **prostitution** *n* prostitution *f*.
prostrate ['prostreit; *v* pro'streit] *adj* prosterné, prostré; (*lying*) à plat ventre. *v* (*overcome*) accabler. **prostrate oneself** se prosterner. **prostration** *n* prosternation *f*; (*exhaustion*) prostration *f*.
protagonist [prou'tagənist] *n* protagoniste *m*.
protect [prə'tekt] *v* protéger. **protection** *n* protection *f*. **protective** *adj* protecteur, -trice; de protection.
protein ['proutiːn] *n* protéine *f*.
protest ['proutest; *v* prə'test] *n* protestation *f*. *v* protester. **protester** *n* (*on march*) manifestant, -e *m*, *f*.
Protestant ['protistənt] *n*, *adj* protestant, -e *m*, *f*.
protocol ['proutəkol] *n* protocole *m*.
prototype ['proutətaip] *n* prototype *m*.
protractor [prə'traktə] *n* rapporteur *m*.
protrude [prə'truːd] *v* dépasser, avancer. **protruding** *adj* saillant, en saillie.
proud [praud] *adj* fier; orgueilleux.
prove [pruːv] *v* prouver; se révéler.
proverb ['provəːb] *n* proverbe *m*. **proverbial** *adj* proverbial.
provide [prə'vaid] *v* fournir, pourvoir. **provided that** pourvu que.
provident ['providənt] *adj* prévoyant. **providence** *n* providence *f*.
province ['provins] *n* province *f*; domaine *m*. **the provinces** la province *f sing*. **provincial** *adj* provincial.
provision [prə'viʒən] *n* (*supply*) provision *f*; (*providing*) fourniture *f*; (*of contract, law, etc.*) disposition *f*. **make provision for** pourvoir aux besoins de. **provisions** *pl n* provisions *f pl*. **provisional** *adj* provisoire.
proviso [prə'vaizou] *n* stipulation *f*, condition *f*.
provoke [prə'vouk] *v* provoquer. **provocation** *n* provocation *f*. **provocative** *adj* provocant.
prow [prau] *n* proue *f*.
prowess ['prauis] *n* prouesse *f*.
prowl [praul] *v* rôder. **prowler** *n* rôdeur, -euse *m*, *f*.
proximity [prok'siməti] *n* proximité *f*.
proxy ['proksi] *n* procuration *f*. **by proxy** par procuration.
prude [pruːd] *n* prude *f*. **prudish** *adj* prude.
prudent ['pruːdənt] *adj* prudent. **prudence** *n* prudence *f*.
prune[1] [pruːn] *n* (*fruit*) pruneau *m*.
prune[2] [pruːn] *v* tailler, élaguer.
pry [prai] *v* être indiscret. **pry into** fourrer son nez dans. **prying** *adj* fureteur, -euse.
psalm [saːm] *n* psaume *m*.
pseudonym ['sjuːdənim] *n* pseudonyme *m*.
psychedelic [ˌsaikə'delik] *adj* psychédélique.
psychiatry [sai'kaiətri] *n* psychiatrie *f*. **psychiatric** *adj* psychiatrique. **psychiatrist** *n* psychiatre *m*, *f*.
psychic ['saikik] *adj* métapsychique; (*psych*) psychique.

psychoanalysis [ˌsaikouə'naləsis] *n* psychanalyse *f*. **psychoanalyse** *v* psychanalyser. **psychoanalyst** *n* psychanalyste *m, f*.
psychology [sai'kolədʒi] *n* psychologie *f*. **psychological** *adj* psychologique. **psychologist** *n* psychologue *m, f*.
psychopath ['saikəpaθ] *n* psychopathe *m, f*. **psychopathic** *adj* psychopathe.
psychosis [sai'kousis] *n* psychose *f*. **psychotic** *n*(*m*+*f*), *adj* psychotique.
psychosomatic [ˌsaikəsə'matik] *adj* psychosomatique.
psychotherapy [ˌsaikə'θerəpi] *n* psychothérapie *f*.
pub [pʌb] *n* pub *m*. **pub-crawl** *n* tournée des bistrots *f*.
puberty ['pjuːbəti] *n* puberté *f*.
pubic ['pjuːbik] *adj* pubien.
public ['pʌblik] *adj* public, -ique. *n* public *m*.
publican ['pʌblikən] *n* patron de bistrot *m*.
publication [ˌpʌbli'keiʃən] *n* publication *f*.
public bar *n* bar *m*.
public conveniences *pl n* toilettes *f pl*.
public footpath *n* sentier public *m*.
public holiday *n* jour férié *m*.
publicity [pʌb'lisəti] *n* publicité *f*.
publicize ['pʌblisaiz] *v* rendre public; (*advertise*) faire de la publicité pour.
public library *n* bibliothèque municipale *f*.
public relations *pl n* relations publiques *f pl*. **public relations officer** *n* public-relations *m*.
public school *n* collège secondaire privé *m*.
public speaking *n* art oratoire *m*.
public-spirited *adj* **be public-spirited** faire preuve de civisme.
public transport *n* transport en commun *m*.
publish ['pʌbliʃ] *v* publier. **publisher** *n* éditeur, -trice *m, f*. **publishing** *n* édition *f*; publication *f*. **publishing house** maison d'édition *f*.
pucker ['pʌkə] *v* (se) plisser; (*sewing*) (faire) goder. *n* (*sewing*) faux pli *m*.
pudding ['pudiŋ] *n* dessert *m*.
puddle ['pʌdl] *n* flaque d'eau *f*.
puerile ['pjuərail] *adj* puéril.
puff [pʌf] *n* bouffée *f*, souffle *m*; (*cake*) feuilleté *m*; (*for powder*) houppe *f*. **puff sleeves** manches bouffantes *f pl*. *v* souffler. **puff out** *or* **up** (se) gonfler. **puffy** *adj* gonflé.
pull [pul] *n* traction *f*; attraction *f*; (*action*) coup *m*. *v* tirer; (*trigger*) presser; (*muscle*) se déchirer. **pull away** démarrer, s'éloigner. **pull down** baisser, descendre; démolir. **pull off** enlever; (*deal*) conclure; (*trick*) réussir. **pull oneself together** se reprendre. **pull out** (*car, etc.*) déboîter; (*extract*) arracher; (*mil*) retirer. **pull to pieces** démolir. **pull up** (*car, etc.*) s'arrêter; (*socks, etc.*) remonter.
pulley ['puli] *n* poulie *f*.
pullover ['pulˌouvə] *n* pull *m*.
pulp [pʌlp] *n* pulpe *f*. *v* réduire en pulpe. **pulpy** *adj* pulpeux.
pulpit ['pulpit] *n* chaire *f*.
pulsate [pʌl'seit] *v* battre, palpiter; (*music*) vibrer. **pulsation** *n* pulsation *f*, battement *m*.
pulse [pʌls] *n* (*med*) pouls *m*; (*phys, elec*) vibration. *v* battre, palpiter.
pulverize ['pʌlvəraiz] *v* pulvériser. **pulverization** *n* pulvérisation *f*.
pump [pʌmp] *n* pompe *f*. *v* pomper. **pump up** gonfler.
pumpkin ['pʌmpkin] *n* citrouille *f*.
pun [pʌn] *n* calembour *m*.
punch[1] [pʌntʃ] *n* coup de poing *m*. **punch line** astuce *f*. *v* donner un coup de poing à.
punch[2] [pʌntʃ] *n* (*drink*) punch *m*.
punch[3] [pʌntʃ] *n* (*tool*) poinçonneuse *f*; perforateur *m*. *v* poinçonner; perforer.
punctual ['pʌŋktʃuəl] *adj* ponctuel, à l'heure. **punctuality** *n* ponctualité *f*, exactitude *f*.
punctuate ['pʌŋktʃueit] *v* ponctuer. **punctuation** *n* ponctuation *f*.
puncture ['pʌŋktʃə] *n* (*tyre*) crevaison *f*; (*leather, skin*) piqûre *f*. **have a puncture** crever. *v* crever; piquer.
pungent ['pʌndʒənt] *adj* âcre, piquant; (*remark*) mordant. **pungency** *n* âcreté *f*; mordant *m*.
punish ['pʌniʃ] *v* punir. **punishment** *n* punition *f*.
punt[1] [pʌnt] *n* (*boat*) bachot *m*.
punt[2] [pʌnt] *v* (*bet*) parier; (*cards*) ponter. **punter** *n* parieur, -euse *m, f*; ponte *m*.
puny ['pjuːni] *adj* chétif.
pupil[1] ['pjuːpl] *n* élève *m, f*.
pupil[2] ['pjuːpl] *n* (*eye*) pupille *f*.

puppet ['pʌpit] *n* marionnette *f.*
puppy ['pʌpi] *n* chiot *m.*
purchase ['pəːtʃəs] *n* achat *m.* *v* acheter.
pure ['pjuə] *adj* pur. **purify** *v* épurer, purifier. **purity** *n* pureté *f.*
purée ['pjuərei] *n* purée *f.*
purgatory ['pəːgətəri] *n* purgatoire *m.*
purge [pəːdʒ] *n* purge *f.* *v* purger. **purgative** *nm, adj* purgatif.
puritan ['pjuəritən] *n, adj* puritain, -e. **puritanical** *adj* puritain.
purl [pəːl] *n* maille à l'envers *f.* *v* tricoter à l'envers.
purple ['pəːpl] *nm, adj* pourpre, violet.
purpose ['pəːpəs] *n* (*aim*) but *m*; (*use*) usage *m.* **on purpose** exprès. **purposeful** *adj* résolu. **purposely** *adv* exprès.
purr [pəː] *v* ronronner. *n* ronronnement *m.*
purse [pəːs] *n* porte-monnaie *m invar*, bourse *f.* *v* **purse one's lips** se pincer les lèvres.
purser ['pəːsə] *n* commissaire du bord *m.*
pursue [pə'sjuː] *v* poursuivre; (*seek*) rechercher. **pursuer** *n* poursuivant, -e *m, f.* **pursuit** *n* poursuite *f*; recherche *f*; occupation *f.*
pus [pʌs] *n* pus *m.*
push [puʃ] *n* poussée *f.* **push-chair** *n* poussette *f.* *v* pousser; (*press*) appuyer (sur). **be pushed for** être à court de.
***put** [put] *v* mettre, poser; (*say*) dire, exprimer; (*case, etc.*) présenter. **put across** faire comprendre, communiquer. **put away** ranger. **put back** remettre. **put down** déposer; noter; attribuer; (*kill*) faire piquer. **put off** retarder, renvoyer à plus tard; (*distract*) dérouter. **put on** mettre. **put out** (*fire*) éteindre; (*bother*) déranger; (*annoy*) contrarier. **put up** (*tent*) dresser; construire; augmenter; loger; (*picture*) mettre. **put-up job** (*coll*) coup monté *m.* **put up with** supporter.
putrid ['pjuːtrid] *adj* putride.
putt [pʌt] *n* putt *m.* *v* putter. **putting** *n* putting *m.*
putty ['pʌti] *n* mastic *m.*
puzzle ['pʌzl] *n* énigme *f*; (*game*) casse-tête *m invar.* *v* rendre perplexe. **puzzle out** comprendre; éclaircir. **puzzled** *adj* perplexe. **puzzling** *adj* curieux.
pyjamas [pə'dʒaːməz] *pl n* pyjama *m sing.*
pylon ['pailən] *n* pylône *m.*
pyramid ['pirəmid] *n* pyramide *f.*
python ['paiθən] *n* python *m.*

Q

quack[1] [kwak] *n* (*duck*) coin-coin *m.* *v* faire coin-coin.
quack[2] [kwak] *n* charlatan *m.*
quadrangle ['kwodraŋgl] *n* cour *f*; (*math*) quadrilatère *m.*
quadrant ['kwodrənt] *n* quadrant *m.*
quadrilateral [kwodrə'latərəl] *nm, adj* quadrilatère.
quadruped ['kwodruped] *nm, adj* quadrupède.
quadruple [kwod'ruːpl] *nm, adj* quadruple. *v* quadrupler.
quadruplet ['kwodruːplit] *n* quadruplé, -e *m, f.*
quagmire ['kwagmaiə] *n* bourbier *m.*
quail[1] [kweil] *n* (*bird*) caille *f.*
quail[2] [kweil] *v* perdre courage.
quaint [kweint] *adj* au charme vieillot; bizarre; pittoresque.
quake [kweik] *v* trembler.
qualify ['kwolifai] *v* qualifier; obtenir son diplôme; (*modify*) mitiger. **qualification** *n* capacité *f*; réserve *f.* **qualifications** *pl n* titres *m pl*, diplômes *m pl.* **qualified** *adj* qualifié, diplômé; mitigé.
quality ['kwoləti] *n* qualité *f.*
qualm [kwaːm] *n* scrupule *m*; appréhension *f*; nausée *f.*
quandary ['kwondəri] *n* embarras *m*, dilemme *m.*
quantify ['kwontifai] *v* déterminer la quantité de.
quantity ['kwontəti] *n* quantité *f.*
quarantine ['kworəntiːn] *n* quarantaine *f.* *v* mettre en quarantaine.
quarrel ['kworəl] *n* querelle *f.* *v* se disputer. **quarrelsome** *adj* querelleur, -euse.
quarry[1] ['kwori] *n* (*stone*) carrière *f.* *v* extraire; exploiter (une carrière).
quarry[2] ['kwori] *n* proie *f*; (*game*) gibier *m.*
quarter ['kwoːtə] *n* quart *m*; (*of year*) trimestre *m*; (*of town*) quartier *m.* **quarter-final** *n* quart de finale *m.* **quartermaster** *n* (*naut*) maître de manœuvre *m.* **quarter past two** deux heures et quart. **quarters** *pl n* (*mil*) quartiers *m pl.* **quarter to two** deux heures moins le quart. *v* diviser en quatre; (*mil*) caserner. **quarterly** *adj* trimestriel.

quartet [kwoɪ'tet] *n* quatuor *m*.
quartz [kwoɪts] *n* quartz *m*.
quash [kwoʃ] *v* annuler; rejeter; (*riot*) étouffer.
quaver ['kweivə] *n* (*music*) croche *f*; tremblement *m*. *v* chevroter.
quay [kiɪ] *n* quai *m*.
queasy ['kwiɪzi] *adj* (*stomach*) délicat. **feel queasy** avoir mal au cœur. **queasiness** *n* mal au cœur *m*.
queen [kwiɪn] *n* reine *f*; (*cards*) dame *f*. **Queen Mother** reine mère *f*.
queer [kwiə] *adj* étrange; suspect; (*slang*) homosexuel. *n* (*slang*) pédé *m*.
quell [kwel] *v* réprimer.
quench [kwentʃ] *v* (*fire*) éteindre; (*hope*) réprimer. **quench one's thirst** se désaltérer.
query ['kwiəri] *n* question *f*. *n* mettre en doute.
quest [kwest] *n* quête *f*.
question ['kwestʃən] *n* question *f*; doute *m*. **it's out of the question** il n'en est pas question. **question mark** point d'interrogation *m*. *v* interroger; mettre en doute. **questionable** *adj* douteux. **questioning** *n* interrogation *f*. **questionnaire** *n* questionnaire *m*.
queue [kjuɪ] *n* queue *f*, file *f*. **queue-jumper** *n* resquilleur, -euse *m*, *f*. *v* faire la queue.
quibble ['kwibl] *n* chicane *f*. *v* chicaner.
quick [kwik] *adj* rapide, prompt. **quicksand** *n* sable mouvant *m*. **quickstep** *n* fox *m*. **quick-tempered** *adj* prompt à s'emporter. **quick-witted** *adj* à l'esprit vif. *n* vif *m*. **quicken** *v* (s')accélérer; stimuler. **quickly** *adv* vite, sans tarder.
quid [kwid] *n* (*coll*) livre *f*.
quiet ['kwaiət] *adj* tranquille; (*subdued*) doux, douce; (*voice*) bas, basse. *n also* **quietness** silence *m*; tranquillité *f*. **quieten** *v* calmer. **quietly** *adv* silencieusement, doucement.
quill [kwil] *n* penne *f*; (*pen*) plume d'oie *f*; (*of porcupine*) piquant *m*.
quilt [kwilt] *n* édredon piqué *m*. *v* ouater, ouatiner.
quince [kwins] *n* (*fruit*) coing *m*; (*tree*) cognassier *m*.
quinine [kwi'niɪn] *n* quinine *f*.
quinsy ['kwinzi] *n* amygdalite purulente *f*.
quintet [kwin'tet] *n* quintette *m*.
quintuplet [kwin'tuɪplit] *n* quintuplé, -e *m*, *f*.
quirk [kwəɪk] *n* bizarrerie *f*.
***quit** [kwit] *v* (*leave*) quitter; (*give up*) se rendre, renoncer. **quits** *adj* quitte.
quite [kwait] *adv* complètement, tout; (*fairly*) plutôt, assez.
quiver[1] ['kwivə] *v* trembler, frémir. *n* frémissement *m*, tremblement *m*.
quiver[2] ['kwivə] *n* (*for arrows*) carquois *m*.
quiz [kwiz] *n* quiz *m*, jeu-concours *m*. *v* interroger.
quizzical ['kwizikl] *adj* moqueur, -euse; amusant; bizarre.
quorum ['kwoɪrəm] *n* quorum *m*.
quota ['kwoutə] *n* quota *m*; (*share*) quote-part *f*.
quote [kwout] *v* citer; (*reference number*) rappeler; (*comm*) indiquer. **quotation** *n* citation *f*; (*comm*) devis *m*. **quotation marks** guillemets *m pl*.

R

rabbi ['rabai] *n* rabbin *m*.
rabbit ['rabit] *n* lapin *m*.
rabble ['rabl] *n* cohue *f*; (*derog*) populace *f*.
rabies ['reibiɪz] *n* rage *f*. **rabid** *adj* enragé.
race[1] [reis] *n* (*sport*) course *f*. **racecourse** *n* champ de courses *m*. **racehorse** *n* cheval de course *m*. *v* (*person*) faire une course avec; (*horse*) faire courir; (*rush*) courir; (*pulse*) être très rapide. **racing car** voiture de course *f*. **racing driver** coureur automobile *m*.
race[2] [reis] *n* race *f*. **racial** *adj* racial. **racialism** *or* **racism** *n* racisme *m*. **racialist** *or* **racist** *n*(*m*+*f*), *adj* raciste.
rack [rak] *n* (*bottles*) casier *m*; (*food*) râtelier *m*; (*shelves*) étagère *f*; (*torture*) chevalet *m*. *v* torturer. **rack one's brains** se creuser la tête.
racket[1] ['rakit] *n* (*sport*) raquette *f*.
racket[2] ['rakit] *n* (*noise*) tapage *m*, vacarme *m*; (*scheme*) combine *f*, escroquerie *f*.
radar ['reidaɪ] *n* radar *m*. **radar trap** piège radar *m*.
radial ['reidiəl] *adj* radial. **radial tyre** pneu à carcasse radiale *m*.

radiant ['reidiənt] *adj* radieux, rayonnant. **radiance** *n* éclat *m*, rayonnement *m*.
radiate ['reidieit] *v* irradier, rayonner; (*heat*) émettre. **radiation** *n* (*heat*) rayonnement *m*; (*light*) irradiation *f*; (*radioactive*) radiation *f*. **radiator** *n* radiateur *m*.
radical ['radikəl] *nm*, *adj* radical.
radio ['reidiou] *n* radio *f*, poste *m*. **radio contact** contact radio *m*. **radio station** poste émetteur *m*. **radio wave** onde hertzienne *f*. *v* appeler par radio; signaler par radio.
radioactive [reidiou'aktiv] *adj* radioactif. **radioactivity** *n* radioactivité *f*.
radiography [reidi'ogrəfi] *n* radiographie *f*. **radiographer** *n* radiologue *m*, *f*.
radiology [reidi'olədʒi] *n* radiologie *f*. **radiologist** *n* radiologue *m*, *f*.
radiotherapy [reidiou'θerəpi] *n* radiothérapie *f*.
radish ['radiʃ] *n* radis *m*.
radium ['reidiəm] *n* radium *m*.
radius ['reidiəs] *n* rayon *m*.
raffia ['rafiə] *n* raphia *m*.
raffle ['rafl] *n* loterie *f*. *v* mettre en loterie.
raft [raːft] *n* radeau *m*.
rafter ['raːftə] *n* chevron *m*.
rag[1] [rag] *n* (*piece*) loque *f*; (*for cleaning*) chiffon *m*; (*derog*: *newspaper*) torchon *m*. **rag doll** poupée de chiffon *f*. **rag-and-bone man** chiffonnier *m*. **rags** *pl n* haillons *m pl*. **ragged** *adj* (*clothes*) en loques; (*edge*) déchiqueté.
rag[2] [rag] (*coll*) *v* taquiner. *n* blague *f*.
rage [reidʒ] *n* rage *f*. **be all the rage** faire fureur. *v* (*person*) être furieux; (*storm*) faire rage. **raging** *adj* (*person*) furieux; (*pain*) atroce; (*storm*) déchaîné.
raid [reid] *n* raid *m*; (*police*) descente *f*; (*bandits*) razzia *f*. *v* faire un raid dans; faire une descente dans; razzier; (*orchard*) marauder dans; (*larder*) dévaliser. **raider** *n* pillard *m*.
rail [reil] *n* (*bar*) garde-fou *m*, balustrade *f*; (*for curtains*) tringle *m*; (*for train*) rail *m*. **by rail** par train. **railway** *or US* **railroad** chemin de fer *m*; (*track*) voie ferrée *f*.
railings ['reiliŋz] *pl n* grille *f sing*.
rain [rein] *n* pluie *f*. **rainbow** *n* arc-en-ciel *m*. **raincoat** *n* imperméable *m*. **raindrop** *n* goutte de pluie *f*. **rainfall** *n* hauteur des précipitations *f*. *v* pleuvoir. **rainy** *adj* pluvieux.
raise [reiz] *v* lever; augmenter; (*build*, *rear*) élever; (*question*) soulever; (*money*) se procurer.
raisin ['reizən] *n* raisin sec *m*.
rake [reik] *n* râteau *m*. *v* (*ground*) ratisser; (*leaves*) râteler. **rake in** (*coll*) amasser.
rally ['rali] *n* rassemblement *m*; (*mot*) rallye *m*; (*tennis*) échange *m*. *v* (se) rallier; (*get better*) aller mieux. **rally round** venir en aide.
ram [ram] *n* bélier *m*. *v* enfoncer; (*pack in*) tasser; (*car*) emboutir.
ramble ['rambl] *n* randonnée *f*. *v* faire une randonnée. **ramble on** discourir.
ramp [ramp] *n* rampe *f*.
rampage [ram'peidʒ] *n* **be on the rampage** se déchaîner.
rampant ['rampənt] *adj* (*plant*) exubérant; (*heraldry*) rampant. **be rampant** sévir.
rampart ['rampaːt] *n* rempart *m*.
ramshackle ['ramʃakl] *adj* délabré.
ran [ran] *V* **run**.
ranch [raːntʃ] *n* ranch *m*.
rancid ['ransid] *adj* rance. **go rancid** rancir.
rancour ['raŋkə] *n* rancœur *f*.
random ['randəm] *n* **at random** au hasard. *adj* fait au hasard. **random sample** échantillon prélevé au hasard *m*.
rang [raŋ] *V* **ring**[2].
range [reindʒ] *n* (*scope*) portée *f*; (*mountains*) chaîne *f*; (*extent*) étendue *f*; gamme *f*; choix *m*; (*stove*) fourneau *m*; (*mil*) champ de tir *m*. *v* ranger; (*extend*) s'étendre; (*roam*) parcourir.
rank[1] [raŋk] *n* rang *m*. **the rank and file** la masse *f*; (*mil*) les hommes de troupe *m pl*. *v* compter, (se) classer.
rank[2] [raŋk] *adj* (*smell*) fétide; (*plants*) exubérant; flagrant.
rankle ['raŋkl] *v* rester sur le cœur.
ransack ['ransak] *v* saccager; (*search*) fouiller.
ransom ['ransəm] *n* rançon *f*. **hold to ransom** rançonner. *v* racheter.
rap [rap] *v* frapper. *n* petit coup sec *m*.
rape [reip] *n* viol *m*. *v* violer. **rapist** *n* violeur *m*.
rapid ['rapid] *adj* rapide. **rapids** *pl n* rapides *m pl*. **rapidity** *n* rapidité *f*.
rapier ['reipiə] *n* rapière *f*.
rapport [ra'poː] *n* rapport *m*.
rapture ['raptʃə] *n* ravissement *m*, extase *f*. **go into raptures over** s'extasier sur.

rare[1] ['reə] *adj* rare. **rarity** *n* rareté *f.*
rare[2] ['reə] *adj* (*meat*) saignant.
rascal ['raːskəl] *n* polisson, -onne *m, f*; (*rogue*) coquin *m.*
rash[1] [raʃ] *adj* imprudent. **rashness** *n* imprudence *f.*
rash[2] [raʃ] *n* (*med*) éruption *f.*
rasher ['raʃə] *n* mince tranche *f.*
raspberry ['raːzbəri] *n* (*fruit*) framboise *f*; (*bush*) framboisier *m.*
rat [rat] *n* rat *m.* **rat poison** mort-aux-rats *m.* **rat race** foire d'empoigne *f.*
rate [reit] *n* taux *m*; (*speed*) train *m.* **at any rate** en tout cas. **ratepayer** *n* contribuable *m, f.* **rates** *pl n* impôts locaux *m pl.* *v* évaluer; considérer; se classer.
rather ['raːðə] *adv* plutôt; (*fairly*) assez, un peu. **I would rather . . .** j'aimerais mieux . . . .
ratify ['ratifai] *v* ratifier. **ratification** *n* ratification *f.*
ratio ['reiʃiou] *n* proportion *f*, raison *f.*
ration ['raʃən] *n* ration *f.* *v* rationner. **rationing** *n* rationnement *m.*
rational ['raʃənl] *adj* raisonnable, rationnel, logique. **rationale** *n* raisonnement *m.* **rationalize** *v* justifier après coup; (*organize*) rationaliser.
rattle ['ratl] *n* bruit *m*, fracas *m*; (*chains, etc.*) cliquetis *m*; (*toy*) hochet *m.* *v* faire du bruit; (*objects*) (faire) s'entrechoquer; (faire) cliqueter; (*coll*) déconcerter.
raucous ['roːkəs] *adj* rauque.
ravage ['ravidʒ] *n* ravage *m.* *v* ravager.
rave [reiv] *v* délirer, divaguer; s'extasier (sur). **raving** *adj* délirant; furieux.
raven ['reivən] *n* corbeau *m.*
ravenous ['ravənəs] *adj* vorace. **be ravenous** avoir un faim de loup.
ravine [rə'viːn] *n* ravin *m.*
ravish ['raviʃ] *v* ravir.
raw [roː] *adj* cru; (*unprocessed*) brut; novice; (*sore*) à vif. **raw deal** (*coll*) sale coup *m.* **raw edge** bord coupé *m.* **raw materials** matières premières *f pl.*
ray [rei] *n* rayon *m.*
rayon ['reion] *n* rayonne *f.*
razor ['reizə] *n* rasoir *m.* **razor blade** lame de rasoir *f.*
reach [riːtʃ] *v* atteindre, arriver à; (*extend*) s'étendre. **reach out** étendre le bras. *n* portée *f.* **out of reach** hors de portée. **within reach** à portée.
react [ri'akt] *v* réagir. **reaction** *n* réaction *f.* **reactionary** *n*(*m*+*f*), *adj* réactionnaire.
reactor *n* réacteur *m.*
***read** [riːd] *v* lire; étudier. **reader** *n* lecteur, -trice *m, f*; (*anthology*) recueil de textes *m.* **reading** *n* lecture *f.*
readjust [riːə'dʒʌst] *v* rajuster, (se) réadapter. **readjustment** *n* réadaptation *f*, rajustement *m.*
ready ['redi] *adj* prêt; prompt. **get ready** (se) préparer. **ready cash** argent liquide *m.* **ready-made** *adj* tout fait, tout prêt. **readily** *adv* volontiers. **readiness** *n* empressement *m.*
real [riəl] *adj* réel, vrai. **realism** *n* réalisme *m.* **realist** *n* réaliste *m, f.* **realistic** *adj* réaliste. **reality** *n* réalité *f.* **really** *adv* vraiment.
realize ['riəlaiz] *v* se rendre compte de; (*make real*) réaliser. **realization** *n* prise de conscience *f*; réalisation *f.*
realm [relm] *n* domaine *m*; (*kingdom*) royaume *m.*
reap [riːp] *v* moissonner; (*profit*) récolter. **reaping** *n* moisson *f.* **reaping machine** moissonneuse *f.*
reappear [riːə'piə] *v* réapparaître. **reappearance** *n* réapparition *f.*
rear[1] [riə] *nm, adj* arrière. **bring up the rear** fermer la marche. **rear-admiral** *n* contre-amiral *m.* **rearguard** *n* arrière-garde *f.* **rear-view mirror** rétroviseur *m.*
rear[2] [riə] *n* (*family*) élever; (*lift up*) dresser; (*horse, etc.*) se cabrer.
rearrange [riːə'reindʒ] *v* réarranger. **rearrangement** *n* réarrangement *m.*
reason ['riːzn] *n* raison *f.* *v* raisonner. **reasonable** *adj* raisonnable. **reasoning** *n* raisonnement *m.*
reassure [riə'ʃuə] *v* rassurer. **reassurance** *n* réconfort *m.* **reassuring** *adj* rassurant.
rebate ['riːbeit] *n* (*discount*) rabais *m*; remboursement *m.*
rebel ['rebl] *n*(*m*+*f*), *adj* rebelle. *v* se rebeller. **rebellion** *n* rébellion *f.* **rebellious** *adj* rebelle; désobéissant.
rebound [ri'baund; *n* 'riːbaund] *v* rebondir. *n* rebond *m*; ricochet *m.*
rebuff [ri'bʌf] *n* rebuffade *f.* *v* repousser.
***rebuild** [riː'bild] *v* rebâtir.
rebuke [ri'bjuːk] *n* reproche *m.* *v* réprimander.
recall [ri'koːl] *v* (se) rappeler. *n* rappel *m.*
recant [ri'kant] *v* (se) rétracter; (*rel*) abjurer.

recap ['riːkap] (*coll*) *v* faire un résumé (de). *n* récapitulation *f*.
recapture [ri'kaptʃə] *v* reprendre; (*atmosphere*) recréer. *n* arrestation *f*.
recede [ri'siːd] *v* s'éloigner; (*tide*) descendre.
receipt [rə'siːt] *n* (*receiving*) réception *f*; (*slip of paper*) reçu *m*, accusé de réception *m*.
receive [rə'siːv] *v* recevoir. **receiver** *n* (*phone*) récepteur *m*; (*law*) administrateur judiciaire *m*.
recent ['riːsnt] *adj* récent. **recently** *adv* récemment.
receptacle [rə'septəkl] *n* récipient *m*.
reception [rə'sepʃən] *n* réception *f*. **receptionist** *n* réceptionniste *m, f*.
recess [ri'ses] *n* renfoncement *m*, alcôve *f*; (*pol, law*) vacances *f pl*; (*of mind*) recoin *m*.
recession [rə'seʃən] *n* (*econ*) récession *f*; recul *m*.
recharge [riː'tʃaːdʒ] *v* recharger.
recipe ['resəpi] *n* recette *f*.
recipient [rə'sipiənt] *n* (*letter*) destinataire *m, f*; (*cheque*) bénéficiaire *m, f*.
reciprocate [rə'siprəkeit] *v* retourner; offrir en retour. **reciprocating engine** moteur alternatif *m*. **reciprocal** *nf, adj* réciproque.
recite [rə'sait] *v* réciter. **recital** *n* (*music*) récital *m*. **recitation** *n* récitation *f*.
reckless ['rekləs] *adj* insouciant; imprudent. **recklessness** *n* insouciance *f*; imprudence *f*.
reckon ['rekən] *v* compter, calculer; considérer, estimer; (*coll*) penser. **reckoning** *n* compte *m*, calcul *m*; estimation *f*.
reclaim [ri'kleim] *v* réclamer; (*land*) assécher, défricher; (*by-product*) récupérer. **reclamation** *n* réclamation *f*; assèchement *m*, défrichement *m*; récupération *f*.
recline [rə'klain] *v* reposer; être allongé.
recluse [rə'kluːs] *n* reclus, -e *m, f*.
recognize ['rekəgnaiz] *v* reconnaître. **recognition** *n* reconnaissance *f*. **recognizable** *adj* reconnaissable.
recoil [rə'koil; *n* 'riːkoil] *v* reculer; (*spring*) se détendre. *n* recul *m*; détente *f*; dégoût *m*.
recollect [rekə'lekt] *v* se souvenir (de). **recollection** *n* souvenir *m*.
recommence [riːkə'mens] *v* recommencer.
recommend [rekə'mend] *v* recommander, conseiller. **recommendation** *n* recommandation *f*.
recompense ['rekəmpens] *n* récompense *f*; (*law*) dédommagement *m*. *v* récompenser; dédommager.
reconcile ['rekənsail] *v* réconcilier; (*ideas*) concilier; (*argument*) arranger **reconcile oneself to** se résigner à. **reconciliation** *n* réconciliation *f*; conciliation *f*.
reconstruct [riːkən'strʌkt] *v* reconstruire; (*crime*) reconstituer. **reconstruction** *n* reconstruction *f*; reconstitution *f*.
record [rə'koːd; *n* 'rekoːd] *v* enregistrer. *n* disque *m*; (*sport, etc.*) record *m*; registre *m*, rapport *m*; dossier *m*. **record-player** *n* électrophone *m*. **record token** chèque-disque *m*. **recorded** *adj* enregistré. **by recorded delivery** avec avis de réception. **recorder** *n* (*music*) flûte à bec *f*. **recording** *n* enregistrement *m*.
recount [ri'kaunt] *v* raconter.
recoup [ri'kuːp] *v* récupérer.
recover [rə'kʌvə] *v* (*get back*) retrouver, récupérer; (*get well*) se remettre, se rétablir. **recovery** *n* récupération *f*; (*from illness*) guérison *f*.
recreation [rekri'eiʃən] *n* récréation *f*.
recruit [rə'kruːt] *n* recrue *f*. *v* recruter. **recruitment** *n* recrutement *m*
rectangle ['rektaŋgl] *n* rectangle *m*. **rectangular** *adj* rectangulaire.
rectify ['rektifai] *v* rectifier.
rectum ['rektəm] *n* rectum *m*.
recuperate [rə'kjuːpəreit] *v* (*person*) se rétablir; (*get back*) récupérer. **recuperation** *n* rétablissement *m*; récupération *f*.
recur [ri'kəː] *v* se reproduire, se retrouver; (*illness*) réapparaître. **recurrence** *n* répétition *f*. **recurrent** *or* **recurring** *adj* périodique.
red [red] *n* rouge *m*. **in the red** à découvert. *adj* rouge; (*hair*) roux, rousse. **go red** rougir. **redcurrant** *n* groseille rouge *f*. **red-handed** *adv* en flagrant délit. **redhead** *n* roux, rousse *m, f*. **red-hot** *adj* chauffé au rouge. **Red Indian** *n* peau-rouge *m, f*. **red tape** paperasserie *f*.
redeem [rə'diːm] *v* racheter; (*from pawn*) dégager. **redemption** *n* rachat *m*; dégagement *m*; (*rel*) rédemption *f*. **beyond redemption** irréparable; irrémédiable.
redirect [riːdai'rekt] *v* (*letter, etc.*) faire suivre.
redress [rə'dres] *v* redresser. *n* redressement *m*, réparation *f*.

reduce [rə'djuːs] *v* réduire; diminuer; (*lower*) abaisser. **reduction** *n* réduction *f*; (*comm*) remise *f*, rabais *m*.
redundant [rə'dʌndənt] *adj* superflu, redondant, en surnombre. **be made redundant** être licencié. **redundancy** *n* superfluité *f*; licenciement *m*.
reed [riːd] *n* (*bot*) roseau *m*; (*of wind instrument*) anche *f*.
reef [riːf] *n* récif *m*.
reek [riːk] *v* puer. *n* puanteur *f*.
reel[1] [riːl] *n* (*thread*) bobine *f*; (*film*) bande *f*. *v* **reel off** débiter.
reel[2] [riːl] *v* chanceler, tituber.
refectory [rə'fektəri] *n* réfectoire *m*.
refer [rə'fəː] *v* parler; faire allusion; s'appliquer; (*consult*) se reporter; (*pass*) soumettre. **reference** *n* référence *f*; allusion *f*; (*in book*) renvoi *m*. **reference book** ouvrage de référence *m*. **reference number** numéro de référence *m*.
referee [refə'riː] *n* arbitre *m*; (*job application*) répondant, -e *m, f*. *v* arbitrer.
referendum [refə'rendəm] *n* référendum *m*.
refill [riː'fil; *n* 'riːfil] *v* recharger. *n* recharge *f*, cartouche *f*.
refine [rə'fain] *v* affiner, raffiner. **refinement** *n* (*person*) raffinement *m*; (*refining*) raffinage *m*, affinage *m*; perfectionnement *m*. **refinery** *n* raffinerie *f*, affinerie *f*.
reflation [rə'fleiʃn] *n* (*econ*) relance *f*.
reflect [rə'flekt] *v* (*light*) refléter; (*mirror*) réfléchir; (*think*) penser; méditer. **reflection** *n* réflexion *f*; image *f*, reflet *m*. **reflector** *n* réflecteur *m*.
reflex ['riːfleks] *nm, adj* réflexe. **reflexive** *adj* réfléchi.
reform [rə'foːm] *n* réforme *f*. *v* (se) réformer. **reformation** *n* réforme *f*. **reformed** *adj* réformé; (*person*) amendé.
refract [rə'frakt] *v* réfracter. **refraction** *n* réfraction *f*.
refrain[1] [rə'frein] *v* s'abstenir.
refrain[2] [rə'frein] *n* refrain *m*.
refresh [rə'freʃ] *v* rafraîchir; (*rest*) reposer. **refresher course** cours de recyclage *m*. **refreshments** *pl n* rafraîchissements *m pl*.
refrigerator [rə'fridʒəreitə] *n* réfrigérateur *m*. **refrigerate** *v* réfrigérer. **refrigeration** *n* réfrigération *f*.
refuel [riː'fjuːəl] *v* (se) ravitailler.
refuge ['refjuːdʒ] *n* refuge *m*. **take refuge** se refugier. **refugee** *n* réfugié, -e *m, f*.
refund [ri'fʌnd; *n* 'riːfʌnd] *v* rembourser. *n* remboursement *m*.
refuse[1] [rə'fjuːz] *v* refuser. **refusal** *n* refus *m*.
refuse[2] ['refjuːs] *n* détritus *m pl*, déchets *m pl*, ordures *f pl*.
refute [ri'fjuːt] *v* réfuter.
regain [ri'gein] *v* regagner; (*health*) recouvrer; (*consciousness*) reprendre.
regal ['riːgəl] *adj* royal.
regard [rə'gaːd] *v* regarder; considérer. **as regards** en ce qui concerne. *n* égard *m*, attention *f*; respect *m*, estime *f*. **regards** *pl n* (*in letter*) amitiés *f pl*. **regarding** *prep* quant à. **regardless** *adv* quand même. **regardless of** sans regarder à.
regatta [rə'gatə] *n* régate *f*.
regent ['riːdʒənt] *n* régent, -e *m, f*. **regency** *n* régence *f*.
regime [rei'ʒiːm] *n* régime *m*.
regiment ['redʒimənt] *n* régiment *m*. **regimental** *adj* régimentaire.
region ['riːdʒən] *n* région *f*. **regional** *adj* régional.
register ['redʒistə] *n* registre *m*. *v* (*record*) enregistrer; (*as member, etc.*) s'inscrire; (*birth, death*) déclarer; (*meter*) indiquer; (*letter*) recommander. **registrar** *n* officier de l'état civil *m*; (*med*) interne *m, f*. **registration** *n* enregistrement *m*, inscription *f*. **registration number** numéro d'immatriculation *m*. **registry office** bureau de l'état civil *m*.
regress [ri'gres] *v* régresser; reculer. **regression** *n* recul *m*; régression *f*.
regret [rə'gret] *v* regretter. *n* regret *m*. **regrettable** *adj* regrettable.
regular ['regjulə] *adj* régulier; habituel, normal. *n* habitué, -e *m, f*. **regularity** *n* régularité *f*.
regulate ['regjuleit] *v* régler.
regulation [regju'leiʃən] *n* réglement *m*. *adj* réglementaire.
rehabilitate [riːhə'biliteit] *v* réhabiliter; (*for work*) réadapter. **rehabilitation** *n* réhabilitation *f*; réadaptation *f*.
rehearse [rə'həːs] *v* répéter. **rehearsal** *n* répétition *f*.
rehouse [riː'hauz] *v* reloger.
reign [rein] *n* règne *m*. *v* régner.
reimburse [riːim'bəːs] *v* rembourser.
rein [rein] *n* rêne *f*; (*control*) bride *f*.
reincarnation [riːinkaː'neiʃən] *n* réincarnation *f*.

reindeer ['reindiə] *n* renne *m*.
reinforce [riːin'fɔːs] *v* renforcer. **reinforcement** *n* renforcement *m*. **reinforcements** *pl n* renforts *m pl*.
reinstate [riːin'steit] *v* réintégrer. **reinstatement** *n* réintégration *f*.
reinvest [riːin'vest] *v* réinvestir.
reissue [riː'iʃuː] *v* (*book*) rééditer; (*film*) ressortir. *n* réédition *f*.
reject [rə'dʒekt; *n* 'riːdʒekt] *v* refuser, rejeter. *n* pièce de rebut *f*. *adj* de rebut. **rejection** *n* refus *m*, rejet *m*.
rejoice [rə'dʒois] *v* (se) réjouir. **rejoicing** *n* réjouissance *f*.
rejoin [rə'dʃoin] *v* rejoindre.
rejuvenate [rə'dʒuːvəneit] *v* rajeunir.
relapse [rə'laps] *n* rechute *f*. *v* rechuter.
relate [rə'leit] *v* raconter; (*be connected*) se rapporter; (*associate*) établir un rapport entre. **related** *adj* apparenté. **relating to** concernant.
relation [rə'leiʃn] *n* (*family*) parent, -e *m*, *f*; (*connection*) rapport *m*; (*business, etc.*) relation *f*. **relationship** *n* liens de parenté *m pl*; (*personal*) rapports *m pl*, relations *f pl*.
relative ['relətiv] *adj* relatif; respectif. *n* parent, -e *m*, *f*. **relatively** *adv* relativement; (*rather*) assez. **relativity** *n* relativité *f*.
relax [rə'laks] *v* (se) relâcher; (*person*) (se) détendre; (*rules*) modérer. **relaxation** *n* relâchement *m*; détente *f*, relaxation *f*. **relaxing** *adj* délassant, relaxant.
relay ['riːlei; *v* ri'lei] *n* relais *m*. **relay race** course de relais *f*. *v* relayer.
release [rə'liːs] *v* libérer; (*let go*) lâcher; (*record, film*) sortir. *n* libération *f*; sortie *f*.
relegate ['religeit] *v* reléguer. **relegation** *n* relégation *f*.
relent [rə'lent] *v* s'adoucir; revenir sur sa décision. **relentless** *adj* implacable.
relevant ['reləvənt] *adj* pertinent; approprié; significatif. **relevance** *n* rapport *m*; pertinence *f*.
reliable [ri'laiəbl] *adj* sérieux; (*machine*) solide. **reliability** *n* sérieux *m*; sûreté *f*; solidité *f*.
relic ['relik] *n* relique *f*.
relief [rə'liːf] *n* soulagement *m*; (*help*) secours *m*; (*geog, art*) relief *m*. *adj* supplémentaire.
relieve [rə'liːv] *v* soulager; (*help*) secourir; (*take over*) relayer; (*take away*) débarrasser, décharger.
religion [rə'lidʒən] *n* religion *f*. **religious** *adj* religieux; scrupuleux.
relinquish [rə'liŋkwiʃ] *v* (*give up*) renoncer à, abandonner; (*let go*) lâcher.
relish ['reliʃ] *n* goût *m*, attrait *m*. *v* (*food, drink*) savourer; (*enjoy*) se délecter à.
relive [riː'liv] *v* revivre.
reluctant [rə'lʌktənt] *adj* peu disposé. **reluctance** *n* répugnance *f*. **reluctantly** *adv* à contrecœur.
rely [rə'lai] *v* **rely on** compter sur.
remain [rə'mein] *v* rester. **remainder** *n* reste *m*. **remains** *pl n* restes *m pl*.
remand [rə'maːnd] *v* renvoyer. *n* renvoi *m*. **on remand** en prévention.
remark [rə'maːk] *n* remarque *f*; observation *f*. *v* remarquer; faire une remarque. **remarkable** *adj* remarquable.
remarry [riː'mari] *v* se remarier. **remarriage** *n* remariage *m*.
remedial [rə'miːdiəl] *adj* réparateur, -trice; (*teaching, class*) de rattrapage.
remedy ['remədi] *n* remède *m*. *v* remédier à.
remember [ri'membə] *v* se souvenir (de), se rappeler. **remembrance** *n* souvenir *m*.
remind [rə'maind] *v* rappeler. **reminder** *n* mémento *m*; (*comm*) lettre de rappel *f*.
reminiscence [remə'nisəns] *n* réminiscence *f*. **reminiscent of** qui rappelle.
remiss [rə'mis] *adj* négligent.
remission [rə'miʃn] *n* rémission *f*; (*law*) remise *f*.
remit [rə'mit] *v* (*law, rel*) remettre; (*money*) envoyer; (*lessen*) (se) relâcher. **remittance** *n* versement *m*, paiement *m*.
remnant ['remnənt] *n* reste *m*; (*fabric*) coupon *m*.
remorse [rə'mɔːs] *n* remords *m*. **remorseless** *adj* sans remords; implacable.
remote [rə'mout] *adj* lointain; isolé; vague. **remote control** télécommande *f*.
remould ['riːmould; *v* riː'mould] *n* pneu rechapé *m*. *v* remouler; rechaper.
remove [rə'muːv] *v* enlever; (*move house*) déménager. **removal** *n* enlèvement *m*; déménagement *m*.
remunerate [rə'mjuːnəreit] *v* rémunérer. **remuneration** *n* rémunération *f*. **remunerative** *adj* rémunérateur, -trice.
renaissance [rə'neisəns] *n* renaissance *f*.
rename [riː'neim] *v* rebaptiser.

render ['rendə] *v* rendre; remettre; (*fat*) faire fondre. **rendering** *or* **rendition** *n* interprétation *f*.
rendezvous ['rondivuː] *n* rendez-vous *m*. *v* se retrouver.
renegade ['renigeid] *n* renégat, -e *m*, *f*.
renew [rə'njuː] *v* renouveler; remplacer. **renewal** renouvellement *m*; remplacement *m*; (*of subscription*) réabonnement *m*.
renounce [ri'nauns] *v* renoncer à, renier. **renunciation** *n* renonciation *f*, reniement *m*.
renovate ['renəveit] *v* rénover, remettre à neuf. **renovation** *n* rénovation *f*; remise à neuf *f*.
renown [rə'naun] *n* renommée *f*; renom *m*. **renowned** *adj* renommé.
rent [rent] *n* loyer *m*. *v* louer. **rental** *n* prix de location *m*.
reopen [riː'oupən] *v* rouvrir; (*recommence*) reprendre. **reopening** *n* réouverture *f*.
reorganize [riː'oːgənaiz] *v* (se) réorganiser. **reorganization** *n* réorganisation *f*.
rep [rep] *n* (*coll*) représentant, -e *m*, *f*.
repair [ri'peə] *v* réparer. *n* réparation *f*. **beyond repair** irréparable. **in good/bad repair** en bon/mauvais état. **repairer** *n* réparateur, -trice *m*, *f*.
repartee [repaː'tiː] *n* repartie *f*.
repatriate [riː'patrieit; *n* riː'patriət] *v* rapatrier. *n* rapatrié, -e *m*, *f*. **repatriation** *n* rapatriement *m*.
***repay** [ri'pei] *v* rembourser; récompenser; (*debt*) s'acquitter de. **repayment** *n* remboursement *m*; récompense *f*.
repeal [rə'piːl] *v* abroger, annuler. *n* abrogation *f*, annulation *f*.
repeat [rə'piːt] *v* répéter; réciter; (*music*) reprendre. *n* répétition *f*; (*broadcast, music*) reprise *f*.
repel [rə'pel] *v* repousser. **repellent** *adj* repoussant.
repent [rə'pent] *v* se repentir (de). **repentance** *n* repentir *m*. **repentant** *adj* repentant.
repercussion [riːpə'kʌʃən] *n* répercussion *f*.
repertoire ['repətwaː] *n* répertoire *m*.
repertory ['repətəri] *n* théâtre de répertoire *m*. **repertory company** compagnie de répertoire *f*.
repetition [repə'tiʃn] *n* répétition *f*. **repetitive** *adj* (*person*) rabâcheur, -euse; (*work*) monotone.
replace [rə'pleis] *v* (*substitute*) remplacer; (*put back*) replacer. **replacement** *n* remplacement *m*; (*person*) remplaçant, -e *m*, *f*; replacement *m*.
replay [riː'plei; *n* 'riːplei] *v* rejouer. *n* match rejoué *m*.
replenish [rə'pleniʃ] *v* remplir. **replenishment** *n* remplissage *m*.
replica ['replikə] *n* (*picture*) réplique *f*; (*document*) fac-similé *m*.
reply [rə'plai] *n* réponse *f*. *v* répondre.
report [rə'poːt] *n* rapport *m*, compte rendu *m*; (*press*) reportage *m*; bulletin scolaire *m*; détonation *f*. *v* rapporter; faire un reportage; (*notify*) signaler; se présenter. **reporter** *n* reporter *m*; journaliste *m*, *f*.
repose [rə'pouz] *n* repos *m*. *v* (se) reposer.
represent [reprə'zent] *v* représenter. **representation** *n* représentation *f*.
representative [reprə'zentətiv] *adj* représentatif. *n* représentant, -e *m*, *f*.
repress [rə'pres] *v* réprimer. **repression** *n* répression *f*. **repressive** *adj* répressif.
reprieve [rə'priːv] *n* sursis *m*; (*law*) grâce *f*. *v* accorder du répit à.
reprimand ['reprimaːnd] *n* réprimande *f*. *v* réprimander.
reprint [riː'print; *n* 'riːprint] *v* réimprimer. *n* réimpression *f*.
reprisal [rə'praizəl] *n* représailles *f pl*.
reproach [rə'proutʃ] *n* reproche *m*. *v* réprocher à. **reproachful** *adj* réprobateur, -trice.
reproduce [riːprə'djuːs] *v* (se) reproduire. **reproduction** *n* reproduction *f*. **reproductive** *adj* reproducteur, -trice.
reprove [rə'pruːv] *v* (*person*) blâmer; (*action*) reprouver. **reproof** *n* réprimande *m*.
reptile ['reptail] *n* reptile *m*.
republic [rə'pʌblik] *n* république *f*. **republican** *n*, *adj* républicain, -e.
repudiate [rə'pjuːdieit] *v* répudier; (*person*) renier. **repudiation** *n* répudiation *f*; reniement *m*.
repugnant [rə'pʌgnənt] *adj* répugnant. **repugnance** *n* répugnance *f*.
repulsion [rə'pʌlʃn] *n* répulsion *f*. **repulsive** *adj* répulsif, répoussant.
repute [rə'pjuːt] *n* réputation *f*. **reputable** *adj* honorable, de bonne réputation. **rep-**

utation *n* réputation *f*. **reputed** *adj* réputé, censé.
request [ri'kwest] *n* demande *f*. *v* demander. **request stop** arrêt facultatif *m*.
requiem ['rekwiəm] *n* requiem *m*.
require [rə'kwaiə] *v* (*need*) demander, avoir besoin de; (*order*) exiger. **requirement** *n* (*need*) exigence *f*; condition *f*.
requisition [ˌrekwi'ziʃən] *n* demande *f*; réquisition *f*. *v* réquisitionner.
***reread** [riː'riːd] *v* relire.
re-route [riː'ruːt] *v* dérouter.
***rerun** [riː'rʌn; *n* 'riːrʌn] *v* (*film*) passer de nouveau; (*race*) courir de nouveau. *n* reprise *f*.
resale [riː'seil] *n* revente *f*.
rescue ['reskjuː] *n* sauvetage *m*; (*help*) secours *m*; (*freeing*) délivrance *f*. *v* sauver; secourir; délivrer. **rescuer** *n* sauveteur *m*.
research [ri'səːtʃ] *n* recherche *f*. *v* faire des recherches. **researcher** *n* chercheur, -euse *m, f*.
***resell** [riː'sel] *v* revendre.
resemble [rə'zembl] *v* ressembler à. **resemblance** *n* ressemblance *f*.
resent [ri'zent] *v* s'offusquer de. **resentful** *adj* rancunier. **resentment** *n* ressentiment *m*.
reserve [rə'zəːv] *v* réserver. *n* réserve *f*; (*sport*) remplaçant, -e *m, f*. **reservation** *n* réserve *f*; (*booking*) réservation *f*. **reserved** *adj* réservé; (*person*) renfermé.
reservoir ['rezəvwaː] *n* réservoir *m*.
reside [rə'zaid] *v* résider. **residence** *n* résidence *f*; (*hostel*) foyer *m*; (*stay*) séjour *m*. **resident** *n* habitant, -e *m, f*; (*in hotel*) pensionnaire *m, f*. **residential** *adj* résidentiel.
residue ['rezidjuː] *n* reste *m*; (*chem*) résidu *m*. **residual** *adj* restant; résiduaire.
resign [rə'zain] *v* (*from job*) donner sa démission (de), démissionner. **resign oneself to** se résigner à. **resignation** *n* démission *f*; résignation *f*. **resigned** *adj* résigné.
resilient [rə'ziliənt] *adj* (*rubber, etc.*) élastique. **be resilient** (*person*) avoir du ressort. **resilience** *n* elasticité *f*; ressort *m*.
resin ['rezin] *n* résine *f*.
resist [rə'zist] *v* résister (à). **resistance** *n* résistance *f*. **resistant** *adj* résistant.
***resit** [riː'sit; *n* 'riːsit] *v* (*exam*) repasser. *n* deuxième session *f*.
resolute ['rezəluːt] *adj* résolu.
resolution [rezə'luːʃən] *n* résolution *f*.
resolve [rə'zolv] *v* (se) résoudre. *n* résolution *f*.
resonant ['rezənənt] *adj* sonore; (*phys*) résonant. **resonance** *n* résonance *f*. **resonate** *v* résonner.
resort [rə'zoːt] *n* recours *m*, ressource *f*; (*place*) station *f*, lieu de vacances *m*. **as a last resort** en dernier ressort. *v* **resort to** avoir recours à.
resound [rə'zaund] *v* retentir, résonner. **resounding** *adj* sonore; (*victory, etc.*) retentissant
resource [rə'zoːs] *n* ressource *f*. **resourceful** *adj* ingénieux.
respect [rə'spekt] *n* respect *m*; (*aspect*) égard *m*, rapport *m*. **pay one's respects** présenter ses respects. **with respect to** en ce qui concerne. *v* respecter. **respectable** *adj* respectable; (*dress, behaviour*) convenable. **respectful** *adj* respectueux. **respective** *adj* respectif.
respiration [respə'reiʃn] *n* respiration *f*.
respite ['respait] *n* répit *m*.
respond [rə'spond] *v* répondre. **response** *n* réponse *f*. **be responsive** réagir bien.
responsible [rə'sponsəbl] *adj* responsable; digne de confiance. **responsibility** *n* responsabilité *f*.
rest[1] [rest] *n* repos *m*; (*music*) silence *m*; support *m*. *v* (se) reposer; (*lean*) (s')appuyer; (*land, put*) (se) poser. **restful** *adj* reposant. **restive** *adj* agité; impatient. **restless** *adj* agité.
rest[2] [rest] *n* **the rest** (*remaining part*) le reste *m*; (*remaining ones*) les autres *m pl*. *v* rester.
restaurant ['restront] *n* restaurant *m*. **restaurant car** (*on train*) wagon-restaurant *m*.
restore [rə'stoː] *v* rendre; (*order, rights, etc.*) rétablir; (*building, etc.*) restaurer. **restoration** *n* rétablissement *m*; restauration *f*.
restrain [rə'strein] *v* retenir; (*temper, etc.*) contenir. **restraint** *n* contrainte *f*; (*moderation*) retenue *f*.
restrict [rə'strikt] *v* restreindre. **restricted** *adj* restreint; confidentiel; (*narrow*) étroit. **restriction** *n* restriction *f*; limitation *f*. **restrictive** *adj* restrictif.
result [rə'zʌlt] *n* résultat *m*; conséquence *f*. *v* résulter. **result in** aboutir à. **resultant** *adj* résultant.

resume [rə'zjuːm] *v* reprendre. **resumption** *n* reprise *f*.
résumé ['reizumei] *n* résumé *m*.
resurgence [ri'səːdʒəns] *n* réapparition *f*.
resurrect [rezə'rekt] *v* ressusciter; (*coll*) remettre en service. **resurrection** *n* résurrection *f*.
resuscitate [rə'sʌsəteit] *v* ranimer.
retail ['riːteil] *n* détail *m*. *v* (se) vendre au détail. **retailer** *n* détaillant, -e *m, f*.
retain [rə'tein] *v* (*keep*) garder; (*hold*) retenir.
retaliate [rə'talieit] *v* se venger. **retaliation** *n* revanche *f*. **in retaliation** par représailles.
retard [rə'taːd] *v* retarder. **retarded** *adj* retardé; (*mentally*) arriéré.
reticent ['retisənt] *adj* réticent. **reticence** *n* réticence *f*.
retina ['retinə] *n* rétine *f*.
retinue ['retinjuː] *n* suite *f*.
retire [rə'taiə] *v* se retirer; (*from work*) prendre sa retraite; (*go to bed*) se coucher. **retired** *adj* retraité. **retirement** *n* retraite *f*.
retort[1] [rə'toːt] *v* rétorquer. *n* réplique *f*.
retort[2] [rə'toːt] *n* (*chem*) cornue *f*.
retrace [ri'treis] *v* reconstituer, retracer. **retrace one's steps** rebrousser chemin.
retract [rə'trakt] *v* (se) rétracter.
retreat [rə'triːt] *n* retraite *f*; (*place*) asile *m*. *v* se retirer; (*mil*) battre en retraite.
retrial [riː'traiəl] *n* nouveau procès *m*.
retrieve [rə'triːv] *v* récupérer; sauver. **retrieval** *n* récupération *f*. **retriever** *n* (*dog*) retriever *m*.
retrograde ['retrəgreid] *adj* rétrograde.
retrospect ['retrəspekt] *n* **in retrospect** rétrospectivement. **retrospective** *adj* rétrospectif.
return [rə'təːn] *v* retourner; (*come back*) revenir; (*give back*) rendre; (*pol*) élire. *n* retour *m*; (*ticket*) aller et retour *m*; (*from investments, etc.*) rapport *m*; (*tax*) déclaration *f*. **in return** en revanche. **in return for** en récompense de.
reunite [riːju'nait] *v* (se) réunir. **reunion** *n* réunion *f*.
rev [rev] (*mot*) *n* tour *m*. *v* **rev up** emballer.
reveal [rə'viːl] *v* révéler; laisser voir. **revealing** *adj* révélateur, -trice. **revelation** *n* révélation *f*.
revel ['revl] *v* se délecter (à). **revelry** *n* festivités *f pl*.
revenge [rə'vendʒ] *n* vengeance *f*. *v* venger.
revenue ['revinjuː] *n* revenu *m*.
reverberate [rə'vəːbəreit] *v* (*sound*) retentir, (se) répercuter; (*heat, light*) (se) réverbérer. **reverberation** *n* répercussion *f*; réverbération *f*.
reverence ['revərəns] *n* vénération *f*.
revere *v* révérer. **reverent** *adj* respectueux.
reverse [rə'vəːs] *adj* contraire, opposé. *n* contraire *m*, opposé *m*; (*coin*) revers *m*; (*page*) verso *m*; (*mot*) marche arrière *f*. *v* renverser, retourner; (*order*) inverser; (*mot*) faire marche arrière. **reverse the charges** (*phone*) téléphoner en P.C.V. **reversal** *n* renversement *m*. **reversible** *adj* réversible.
revert [rə'vəːt] *v* revenir, retourner.
review [rə'vjuː] *n* revue *f*; révision *f*; critique *f*. *v* passer en revue; réconsidérer; faire la critique de. **reviewer** *n* critique *m*.
revise [rə'vaiz] *v* réviser; corriger. **revision** *n* révision *f*.
revive [rə'vaiv] *v* ranimer; reprendre connaissance; (*custom*) rétablir; (*trade*) reprendre. **revival** *n* reprise *f*.
revoke [rə'vouk] *v* révoquer, revenir sur; (*withdraw*) retirer.
revolt [rə'voult] *n* révolte *f*. *v* (se) révolter. **revolting** *adj* dégoûtant.
revolution [revə'luːʃən] *n* révolution *f*. **revolutionary** *n*(*m*+*f*), *adj* révolutionnaire. **revolutionize** *v* révolutionner.
revolve [rə'volv] *v* (faire) tourner. **revolver** *n* revolver *m*. **revolving door** tambour *m*.
revue [rə'vjuː] *n* revue *f*.
revulsion [rə'vʌlʃən] *n* dégoût *m*.
reward [rə'woːd] *n* récompense *f*. *v* récompenser.
***rewind** [riː'waind] *v* (*film, tape*) réembobiner. **rewinding** *n* réembobinage *m*.
***rewrite** [riː'rait] *v* récrire; recopier.
Reykjavik ['reikjəˌviːk] *n* Reykjavik.
rhesus ['riːsəs] *n* rhésus *m*. **rhesus negative/positive** rhésus négatif/positif.
rhetoric ['retərik] *n* rhétorique *f*. **rhetorical** *adj* rhétorique. **rhetorical question** question pour la forme *f*.
rheumatism ['ruːmətizəm] *n* rhumatisme *m*. **rheumatic** *adj* rhumatismal.
rhinoceros [rai'nosərəs] *n* rhinocéros *m*.

rhododendron [roudə'dendrən] *n* rhododendron *m*.
rhubarb ['ru:ba:b] *n* rhubarbe *f*.
rhyme [raim] *n* rime *f*; (*poetry*) vers *m pl*. *v* (faire) rimer.
rhythm ['riðəm] *n* rythme *m*. **rhythmic** *adj* rythmique; (*music*) rythmé.
rib [rib] *n* côte *f*.
ribbon ['ribən] *n* ruban *m*. **in ribbons** en lambeaux.
rice [rais] *n* riz *m*. **rice paper** papier de riz *m*. **rice pudding** riz au lait *m*.
rich [ritʃ] *adj* riche. **riches** *pl n* richesses *f pl*. **richness** *n* richesse *f*.
rickety ['rikəti] *adj* branlant.
***rid** [rid] *v* débarrasser. **get rid of** se débarrasser de. **riddance** *n* débarras *m*.
ridden ['ridn] *V* **ride**.
riddle[1] ['ridl] *n* énigme *f*.
riddle[2] ['ridl] *v* cribler.
***ride** [raid] *v* monter; (*horse*) monter à cheval. *n* promenade *f*, tour *m*; (*journey*) trajet *m*. **rider** *n* (*horse*) cavalier, -ère *m*, *f*; (*addition*) annexe *f*. **riding** *n* équitation *f*. **riding school** manège *m*.
ridge [ridʒ] *n* (*hills*) faîte *m*; (*roof*) arête *f*; (*on surface*) strie *f*.
ridicule ['ridikju:l] *n* ridicule *m*. *v* ridiculiser. **ridiculous** *adj* ridicule.
rife [raif] *adj* répandu.
rifle[1] ['raifl] *n* fusil *m*. **rifle range** champ de tir *m*.
rifle[2] ['raifl] *v* piller; (*house, drawer*) dévaliser.
rift [rift] *n* fissure *f*; division *f*.
rig [rig] *n* (*naut*) gréement *m*. **rig-out** *n* (*coll*) tenue *f*. *v* gréer; (*falsify*) truquer. **rigging** *n* gréement *m*; truquage *m*.
right [rait] *adj* (*not left*) droit; juste; approprié; (*correct*) bon, bonne. **be right** avoir raison. *adv* à droite; (*straight*) droit; (*completely*) tout à fait; (*well*) bien. *n* droite *f*; (*entitlement*) droit *m*; (*good*) bien *m*. *v* redresser. **right angle** angle droit *m*. **right-handed** *adj* droitier *m*. **right-of-way** *n* (*public*) droit de passage *m*; (*mot*) priorité *f*. **right-wing** *adj* (*pol*) de droite.
righteous ['raitʃəs] *adj* vertueux; juste.
rightful [raitfəl] *adj* légitime.
rigid ['ridʒid] *adj* rigide; strict. **rigidity** *n* rigidité *f*.
rigmarole ['rigməroul] *n* (*coll*) comédie *f*; (*speech*) galimatias *m*.
rigour ['rigə] *n* rigueur *f*. **rigorous** *adj* rigoureux.
rim [rim] *n* bord *m*; (*wheel*) jante *f*.
rind [raind] *n* (*fruit*) peau *f*; (*cheese*) croûte *f*; (*bacon*) couenne *f*.
ring[1] [riŋ] *n* anneau *m*; (*with gem*) bague *f*; cercle *m*, rond *m*; (*circus*) piste *f*; (*boxing*) ring *m*. *v* entourer d'un cercle. **ringleader** *n* meneur *m*. **ring road** route de ceinture *f*.
***ring**[2] [riŋ] *v* (*bell*) sonner; téléphoner (à); résonner. **ring off** (*phone*) raccrocher. **ring up** (*coll*: *phone*) donner un coup de fil à. *n* sonnerie *f*; (*coll*: *phone*) coup de fil *m*.
rink [riŋk] *n* patinoire *f*.
rinse [rins] *v* rincer. *n* rinçage *m*.
riot ['raiət] *n* émeute *f*. *v* faire une émeute.
rip [rip] *v* (se) déchirer. **rip off** *or* **out** arracher. *n* déchirure *f*.
ripe [raip] *adj* mûr. **ripen** *v* mûrir. **ripeness** *n* maturité *f*.
ripple ['ripl] *n* ondulation *f*, ride *f*; (*laughter*) cascade *f*. *v* (se) rider, (faire) onduler.
***rise** [raiz] *n* (*sun, etc.*) lever *m*; (*increase*) hausse *f*; (*in salary*) augmentation *f*; (*in importance*) essor *m*. **give rise to** engendrer. *v* se lever, s'élever; augmenter, être en hausse; (*rebel*) se soulever. **rising** *adj* levant; en hausse; (*anger*) croissant.
risen ['rizn] *V* **rise**.
risk [risk] *n* risque *m*. **at risk** en danger. *v* risquer. **risky** *adj* risqué.
rissole ['risoul] *n* croquette *f*.
rite [rait] *n* rite *m*.
ritual ['ritʃuəl] *nm*, *adj* rituel.
rival ['raivəl] *n*, *adj* rival, -e. *v* rivaliser avec. **rivalry** *n* rivalité *f*.
river ['rivə] *n* rivière *f*; (*larger*) fleuve *m*. **riverside** *n* bord de l'eau *m*.
rivet ['rivit] *n* rivet *m*. *v* (*tech*) riveter; fixer, clouer. **riveting** *adj* fascinant.
Riviera [rivi'eərə] *n* **the Riviera** (*French*) la Côte d'Azur *f*; (*Italian*) a Riviera *f*.
road [roud] *n* route *f*; (*to success, etc.*) voie *f*, chemin *m*. **road-block** *n* barrage routier *m*. **road safety** sécurité routière *f*. **roadside** *n* bord de la route *m*. **road sign** panneau de signalisation *m*. **road-works** *pl n* travaux *m pl*.
roam [roum] *v* parcourir, errer.
roar [ro:] *v* (*lion*) rugir; (*crowd*) hurler; (*bull, wind*) mugir; (*engine*) vrombir;

(*thunder*) gronder. **roar with laughter** éclater de rire. *n* rugissement *m*; hurlement *m*; mugissement *m*; vrombissement *m*; grondement *m*.
roast [roust] *v* (*meat*) rôtir; (*coffee, chestnuts*) griller. *nm, adj* rôti.
rob [rob] *v* voler, dévaliser. **robber** *n* voleur *m*. **robbery** *n* vol *m*.
robe [roub] *n* robe *f*. *v* revêtir.
robin ['robin] *n* rouge-gorge *m*.
robot ['roubot] *n* robot *m*.
robust [rə'bʌst] *adj* robuste, vigoureux, solide.
rock[1] [rok] *n* (*stone*) roche *f*; (*hard*) roc *m*; (*boulder*) rocher *m*. **rock bun** *or* **cake** rocher *m*. **rock-climbing** *n* varappe *f*. **rock-plant** *n* plante alpestre *f*. **rockery** *n* rocaille *f*. **rocky** *adj* rocheux, rocailleux.
rock[2] [rok] *v* (*sway*) bercer, (se) balancer; (*shake*) ébranler. *n* (*music*) rock *m*. **rocking-chair** *n* fauteuil à bascule *m*. **rocking-horse** *n* cheval à bascule *m*.
rocket ['rokit] *n* fusée *f*. *v* (*prices*) monter en flèche.
rod [rod] *n* (*wood*) baguette *f*; (*metal*) tringle *f*; (*fishing*) canne *f*.
rode [roud] *V* **ride**.
rodent ['roudənt] *n* rongeur *m*.
roe [rou] n (*hard*) œufs de poisson *m pl*; (*soft*) laitance *f*.
rogue [roug] *n* coquin, -e *m*, *f*. **roguish** *adj* espiègle.
role [roul] *n* rôle *m*.
roll [roul] *n* rouleau *m*; (*bread*) petit pain *m*; (*drums*) roulement *m*; (*register*) liste *f*. **roll-call** *n* appel *m*. *v* rouler. **roll in** (*coll*) affluer; (*coll*: *person*) s'amener. **roll over** (se) retourner. **roll up** rouler; (*sleeves*) retrousser. **roller** *n* rouleau *m*. **roller-coaster** *n* montagnes russes *f pl*. **roller-skate** *n* patin à roulettes *m*. **rolling-pin** *n* rouleau *m*.
romance [rou'mans] *n* (*love*) idylle f, amour *m*; (*story*) roman à l'eau de rose *m*. **Romance** *adj* (*language*) roman. **romantic** *n*(*m*+*f*), *adj* romantique.
Romania [ruː'meinjə] *n* Roumanie *f*. **Romanian** *nm*, *adj* roumain; *n* (*people*) Roumain, -e *m*, *f*.
Rome [roum] *n* Rome. **Roman** *n* Romain, -e *m*, *f*; *adj* romain. **Roman Catholic** *n*(*m*+*f*), *adj* catholique. **Roman numeral** chiffre romain *m*.
romp [romp] *n* ébats *m pl*. *v* s'ébattre. **rompers** *pl n* barboteuse *f sing*.
roof [ruːf] *n*, *pl* **roofs** toit *m*. **roof of the mouth** voûte du palais *f*. **roof-rack** *n* galerie *f*.
rook [ruk] *n* (*bird*) corneille *f*. *v* (*slang*) rouler.
room [ruːm] *n* pièce *f*; (*larger*) salle *f*; (*hotel*) chambre *f*; (*space*) place *f*. **at room temperature** (*wine*) chambré. **room-mate** *n* camarade de chambre *m*, *f*. **room service** service des chambres *m*. **roomy** *adj* spacieux.
roost [ruːst] *n* perchoir *m*. *v* (se) jucher. **rooster** *n* coq *m*.
root[1] [ruːt] *n* racine *f*; origine *f*. *v* (s')enraciner.
root[2] [ruːt] *v* fouiller. **root for** (*slang*) encourager. **root out** (*find*) dénicher.
rope [roup] *n* corde *f*. **know the ropes** être au courant. **rope-ladder** *n* échelle de corde *f*. *v* corder, lier. **rope in** (*coll*) embringuer. **ropy** *adj* (*coll*) pas fameux.
rosary ['rouzəri] *n* chapelet *m*.
rose[1] [rouz] *V* **rise**.
rose[2] [rouz] *n* rose *f*. **rose-bush** *n* rosier *m*. **rose garden** roseraie *f*. **rosewood** *n* bois de rose *m*. **rosy** *adj* rose.
rosemary ['rouzməri] *n* romarin *m*.
rosette [rou'zet] *n* rosette *f*; (*prize*) cocarde *f*.
rot [rot] *n* pourriture *f*, carie *f*; (*coll*: *rubbish*) bêtises *f pl*. *v* pourrir. **rotten** *adj* pourri; (*coll*: *bad*) moche, sale; (*coll*: *ill*) mal fichu.
rota ['routə] *n* liste *f*.
rotate [rou'teit] *v* (faire) tourner, (faire) pivoter; (*crops*) alterner. **rotary** *adj* rotatif. **rotation** *n* rotation *f*.
rotor ['routə] *n* rotor *m*.
rouge [ruːʒ] *n* rouge *m*.
rough [rʌf] *adj* (*surface*) rugueux; (*coarse*) rude; brutal, dur; (*draft*) ébauché; approximatif. **rough-and-ready** *adj* rudimentaire. **rough copy** *or* **draft** brouillon *m*. *v* **rough it** (*coll*) vivre à la dure. **roughly** *adv* à peu près. **roughness** *n* rugosité *f*; rudesse *f*; brutalité *f*.
roulette [ruː'let] *n* roulette *f*.
round [raund] *adj* rond. *prep* autour de. *n* rond *m*; (*of bread*) tranche *f*; (*drinks, postman, etc.*) tournée *f*; (*game, competition*) partie *f*. **round-necked** *adj* (*pullover*) ras du cou. **round-shouldered** *adj* voûté. *v* arrondir. **round off** terminer. **round up** rassembler; (*figure*) arrondir.

roundabout ['raundəbaut] *n* (*mot*) rond-point *m*; (*fair*) manège *m*. *adj* détourné, indirect.
rouse [rauz] *v* éveiller; stimuler.
route [ruːt] *n* itinéraire *m*.
routine [ruː'tiːn] *n* routine *f*; (*theatre*) numéro *m*. *adj* d'usage; ordinaire.
rove [rouv] *v* errer (dans), vagabonder.
row[1] [rou] *n* (*side by side*) rang *m*; (*queue*) file *f*; (*trees, figures*) rangée *f*.
row[2] [rou] *v* (*boat*) ramer. *n* promenade en canot *f*. **rowing** *n* (*sport*) aviron *m*; (*for fun*) canotage *m*. **rowing boat** canot *m*.
row[3] [rau] *n* querelle *f*; (*noise*) tapage *m*. *v* se quereller.
rowdy ['raudi] *adj* chahuteur, -euse. **rowdiness** *n* tapage *m*.
royal ['roiəl] *adj* royal. **royal blue** bleu roi *invar*. **royalist** *n*(*m*+*f*), *adj* royaliste. **royalties** *pl n* droits d'auteur *m pl*. **royalty** *n* royauté *f*.
rub [rʌb] *n* frottement *m*; (*with duster*) coup de chiffon *m*. *v* frotter. **rub in** faire pénétrer; insister sur. **rub out** (s')effacer. **rub up the wrong way** prendre à rebrousse-poil. **rubbing** *n* (*brass, etc.*) frottis *m*.
rubber ['rʌbə] *n* caoutchouc *m*; (*eraser*) gomme *f*. **rubber band** élastique *m*. **rubber stamp** tampon *m*. **rubber tree** arbre à gomme *m*. **rubbery** *adj* caoutchouteux.
rubbish ['rʌbiʃ] *n* détritus *m pl*, ordures *f pl*; (*derog*) camelote *f*; (*nonsense*) bêtises *f pl*.
rubble ['rʌbl] *n* décombres *m pl*.
ruby ['ruːbi] *n* rubis *m*.
rucksack ['rʌksak] *n* sac à dos *m*.
rudder ['rʌdə] *n* gouvernail *m*.
rude [ruːd] *adj* impoli, grossier; (*sudden*) brusque; primitif. **rudeness** *n* impolitesse *f*, grossièreté *f*.
rudiment ['ruːdimənt] *n* rudiment *m*. **rudimentary** *adj* rudimentaire.
rueful ['ruːfəl] *adj* triste. **ruefully** *adv* avec regret.
ruff [rʌf] *n* (*dress*) fraise *f*; (*bird*) collier *m*.
ruffian ['rʌfiən] *n* voyou *m*.
ruffle ['rʌfl] *v* (*hair*) ébouriffer; (*surface*) agiter; (*clothes*) froisser; (*worry*) troubler.
rug [rʌg] *n* carpette *f*, petit tapis *m*; (*blanket*) couverture *f*.
rugby ['rʌgbi] *n* rugby *m*.
rugged ['rʌgid] *adj* (*cliff*) déchiqueté; (*landscape*) accidenté; (*person*) rude; (*determination*) acharné.
ruin ['ruːin] *n* ruine *f*. *v* ruiner.
rule [ruːl] *n* règle *f*; autorité *f*. **as a rule** normalement. *v* gouverner; régner; dominer; (*lines*) régler. **rule out** exclure. **ruler** *n* souverain, -e *m, f*; (*measuring*) règle *f*. **ruling** *n* décision *f*.
rum [rʌm] *n* rhum *m*.
rumble ['rʌmbl] *n* grondement *m*; (*stomach*) gargouillement *m*. *v* gronder; gargouiller.
rummage ['rʌmidʒ] *n* fouiller. *n* **rummage sale** vente de charité *f*.
rumour ['ruːmə] *n* rumeur *f*, bruit *m*.
rump [rʌmp] *n* (*animal*) croupe *f*; (*beef*) culotte *f*. **rump steak** romsteck *m*.
***run** [rʌn] *n* course *f*; (*outing*) tour *m*; (*track*) piste *f*; séquence *f*, série *f*; (*demand*) ruée *f*. **in the long run** à la longue. *v* courir; (*flow*) couler; (*colour*) s'étaler; (*function*) marcher; (*organize*) diriger; passer. **run away** *v* se sauver. **runaway** *n, adj* fugitif, -ive. **run down** *v* (*car, etc.*) renverser; (*coll*) dénigrer. **run-down** *adj* (*coll*) à plat, surmené. **run in** (*mot*) roder. **run out** expirer, s'épuiser. **run over** (*car, etc.*) écraser. **runway** *n* piste *f*. **runner** *n* coureur *m*. **runner bean** haricot à rames *m*. **runner-up** *n* second, -e *m, f*. **running** *adj* (*water, etc.*) courant; (*in succession*) de suite. **running commentary** commentaire suivi *m*. **running costs** frais d'exploitation *m pl*.
rung[1] [rʌŋ] *V* **ring**[2].
rung[2] [rʌŋ] *n* barreau *m*.
rupture ['rʌptʃə] *n* rupture *f*. *v* (se) rompre.
rural ['ruərəl] *adj* rural; de la campagne.
ruse [ruːz] *n* ruse *f*.
rush[1] [rʌʃ] *n* ruée *f*; hâte *f*. *v* se précipiter; (*do quickly*) dépêcher. **rush hour** heure de pointe *f*.
rush[2] [rʌʃ] *n* (*bot*) jonc *m*.
rusk [rʌsk] *n* biscotte *f*.
Russia ['rʌʃə] *n* Russie *f*. **Russian** *nm, adj* russe; *n* (*people*) Russe *m, f*.
rust [rʌst] *n* rouille *f*. *v* (se) rouiller. **rusty** *adj* rouillé.
rustic ['rʌstik] *adj* rustique.
rustle ['rʌsl] *v* (*leaves*) (faire) bruire; (*paper*) froisser. *n* bruissement *m*; froissement *m*.

rut [rʌt] *n* ornière *f*. **be in a rut** suivre l'ornière.
ruthless ['ruːθlis] *adj* impitoyable, sans pitié.
rye [rai] *n* seigle *m*.

S

sabbath ['sabəθ] *n* sabbat *m*.
sabbatical [sə'batikəl] *adj* sabbatique. *n* année sabbatique *f*.
sable ['seibl] *n* zibeline *f*.
sabotage ['sabətaːʒ] *n* sabotage *m*. *v* saboter. **saboteur** *n* saboteur, -euse *m, f*.
sabre ['seibə] *n* sabre *m*.
saccharin ['sakərin] *n* saccharine *f*.
sachet ['saʃei] *n* sachet *m*.
sack [sak] *n* sac *m*. **get the sack** (*coll*) être sacqué. *v* (*coll*) sacquer.
sacrament ['sakrəmənt] *n* sacrement *m*.
sacred ['seikrid] *adj* sacré.
sacrifice ['sakrifais] *n* sacrifice *m*. *v* sacrifier.
sacrilege ['sakrəlidʒ] *n* sacrilège *m*. **sacrilegious** *adj* sacrilège.
sad [sad] *adj* triste. **sadden** *v* attrister. **sadly** *adv* tristement; (*very*) bien, fort; (*unfortunately*) fâcheusement. **sadness** *n* tristesse *f*.
saddle ['sadl] *n* selle *f*. **saddle-bag** *n* (*horse*) sacoche de selle *f*; (*bicycle*) sacoche de bicyclette *f*. *v* seller. **saddle with** (*coll*) coller à. **saddler** *n* sellier *m*. **saddlery** *n* sellerie *f*.
sadism ['seidizəm] *n* sadisme *m*. **sadist** *n* sadique *m, f*. **sadistic** *adj* sadique.
safari [sə'faːri] *n* safari *m*. **safari park** réserve *f*.
safe [seif] *adj* (*person*) en sécurité; (*toy, etc.*) sans danger; sûr; solide. **safe and sound** sain et sauf. **safe keeping** bonne garde *f*. **to be on the safe side** par précaution. *n* coffre-fort *m*. **safely** *adv* sans danger; en sûreté. **safety** *n* sécurité *f*; solidité *f*. **safety-belt** *n* ceinture de sécurité *f*. **safety first** la sécurité d'abord. **safety-pin** *n* épingle de sûreté *f*.
safeguard ['seifgaːd] *n* sauvegarde *f*. *v* sauvegarder.
saffron ['safrən] *n* safran *m*.
sag [sag] *v* s'affaisser, fléchir. *n* affaissement *m*, fléchissement *m*.
saga ['saːgə] *n* saga *f*.
sage[1] [seidʒ] *nm, adj* (*wise*) sage.
sage[2] [seidʒ] *n* (*herb*) sauge *f*.
Sagittarius [sadʒi'teəriəs] *n* Sagittaire *m*.
sago ['seigou] *n* sagou *m*; (*pudding*) sagou au lait *m*.
said [sed] *V* **say**.
sail [seil] *n* voile *f*; (*trip*) tour en bateau *m*; (*windmill*) aile *f*. **sailcloth** *n* toile à voile *f*. **set sail** partir. *v* (*leave*) partir; (*cross*) traverser; (*boat*) piloter. **sail through** (*coll*) réussir haut la main. **sailing** *n* navigation *f*; (*sport, hobby*) voile *f*. **sailing boat** bateau à voiles *m*. **sailor** *n* marin *m*.
saint [seint] *n* saint, -e *m, f*.
sake [seik] *n* **for the sake of** pour l'amour de, par égard pour; pour le plaisir de.
salad ['saləd] *n* salade *f*. **salad cream** mayonnaise *f*. **salad dressing** vinaigrette *f*.
salami [sə'laːmi] *n* salami *m*.
salary ['saləri] *n* traitement *m*, salaire *m*. **salary scale** échelle des traitements *f*.
sale [seil] *n* vente *f*; (*reductions*) soldes *m pl*. **for sale** à vendre. **on sale** en vente. **sale-room** *n* salle des ventes *f*. **sales department** service des ventes *m*. **salesman** *n* (*shop*) vendeur *m*; représentant *m*. **salesmanship** *n* art de la vente *m*.
saline ['seilain] *adj* salin. **salinity** *n* salinité *f*.
saliva [sə'laivə] *n* salive *f*. **salivary** *adj* salivaire. **salivate** *v* saliver.
sallow ['salou] *adj* jaunâtre.
salmon ['samən] *n* saumon *m*.
salon ['salon] *n* salon *m*.
saloon [sə'luːn] *n* salle *f*, salon *m*. **saloon bar** bar *m*. **saloon car** conduite intérieure *f*.
salt [soːlt] *n* sel *m*. **salt-cellar** *n* salière *f*. *v* saler. **salty** *adj* salé.
salute [sə'luːt] *n* salut *m*; (*guns*) salve *f*. *v* saluer.
salvage ['salvidʒ] *n* sauvetage *m*; récupération *f*. *v* sauver; récupérer.
salvation [sal'veiʃən] *n* salut *m*. **Salvation Army** Armée du Salut *f*.
same [seim] *adj, pron* même. **all the same** quand même. **at the same time** en même temps.
sample ['saːmpl] *n* échantillon *m*; (*blood*) prélèvement *m*. *v* goûter.

sanatorium [sanə'tɔːriəm] *n* sanatorium *m*.
sanctify ['saŋktifai] *v* sanctifier. **sanctification** *n* sanctification *f*.
sanctimonious [saŋkti'mouniəs] *adj* moralisateur, -trice.
sanction ['saŋkʃən] *n* sanction *f*. *v* sanctionner.
sanctity ['saŋktəti] *n* sainteté *f*; inviolabilité *f*.
sanctuary ['saŋktʃuəri] *n* sanctuaire *m*; (*refuge*) asile *m*; (*birds, etc.*) réserve *f*.
sand [sand] *n* sable *m*. **sandbank** *n* banc de sable *m*. **sand-castle** *n* château de sable *m*. **sandpaper** *n* papier de verre *m*. **sandstone** *n* grès *m*. *v* sabler; (*with sandpaper*) frotter au papier de verre. **sandy** *adj* sablonneux; (*beach*) de sable; (*hair*) couleur sable.
sandal ['sandl] *n* sandale *f*.
sandwich ['sanwidʒ] *n* sandwich *m*. **sandwich board** panneau publicitaire *m*. **sandwich course** cours de formation professionnelle *m*.
sane [sein] *adj* sain d'esprit; raisonnable. **sanity** *n* santé mentale *f*.
sang [saŋ] *V* **sing**.
sanitary ['sanitəri] *adj* sanitaire; hygiénique. **sanitary towel** serviette hygiénique *f*.
sank [saŋk] *V* **sink**.
sap [sap] *n* sève *f*.
sapphire ['safaiə] *n* saphir *m*.
sarcasm ['saːkazəm] *n* sarcasme *m*. **sarcastic** *adj* sarcastique.
sardine [saː'diːn] *n* sardine *f*.
Sardinia [saː'dinjə] *n* Sardaigne *f*. **Sardinian** *nm, adj* sarde; *n* (*people*) Sarde *m, f*.
sardonic [saː'donik] *adj* sardonique.
sash[1] [saʃ] *n* (*uniform*) écharpe *f*; (*dress*) large ceinture *f*.
sash[2] [saʃ] *n* (*frame*) chassis à guillotine *m*. **sash-window** *n* fenêtre à guillotine *f*.
sat [sat] *V* **sit**.
Satan ['seitən] *n* Satan *m*. **satanic** *adj* satanique.
satchel ['satʃəl] *n* cartable *m*.
satellite ['satəlait] *n* satellite *m*.
satin ['satin] *n* satin *m*.
satire ['sataiə] *n* satire *f*. **satirical** *adj* satirique. **satirize** *v* faire la satire de.
satisfy ['satisfai] *v* satisfaire; convaincre. **satisfaction** *n* satisfaction *f*. **satisfactory** *adj* satisfaisant.
saturate ['satʃəreit] *v* saturer; (*soak*) tremper. **saturation** *n* saturation *f*. **reach saturation point** arriver à saturation.
Saturday ['satədi] *n* samedi *m*.
sauce [soːs] *n* sauce *f*; (*slang*) toupet *m*. **saucy** *adj* impertinent; coquin.
saucepan ['soːspən] *n* casserole *f*.
saucer ['soːsə] *n* soucoupe *f*.
sauerkraut ['sauəkraut] *n* choucroute *f*.
sauna [soːnə] *n* sauna *m*.
saunter [soːntə] *v* flâner, se balader. *n* flânerie *f*, balade *f*.
sausage ['sosidʒ] *n* saucisse *f*. **sausagemeat** *n* chair à saucisse *f*. **sausage roll** friand *m*.
savage ['savidʒ] *adj* féroce, brutal; primitif, sauvage. *n* sauvage *m, f*. *v* attaquer férocement. **savagery** *n* sauvagerie *f*.
save[1] [seiv] *v* sauver; (*put aside*) mettre de côté, garder; économiser, épargner. **savings** *pl n* économies *f pl*. **savings bank** caisse d'épargne *f*.
save[2] [seiv] *prep* sauf.
saviour ['seivjə] *n* sauveur *m*.
savour ['seivə] *v* savourer. *n* saveur *f*. **savoury** *adj* savoureux, appétissant; (*not sweet*) salé.
saw[1] [soː] *V* **see**[1].
***saw**[2] [soː] *n* scie *f*. **sawdust** *n* sciure *f*. **sawmill** *n* scierie *f*. *v* scier.
sawn [soːn] *V* **saw**[2].
saxophone ['saksəfoun] *n* saxophone *m*.
***say** [sei] *v* dire. **saying** *n* dicton *m*, proverbe *m*.
scab [skab] *n* croûte *f*; (*derog: non-striker*) jaune *m*. *v* se cicatriser; (*derog*) faire le jaune.
scaffold ['skafəld] *n* échafaud *m*. **scaffolding** *n* échafaudage *m*.
scald [skoːld] *v* échauder, ébouillanter. *n* brûlure *f*. **scalding** *adj* brûlant.
scale[1] [skeil] *n* (*fish, etc.*) écaille *f*; (*deposit*) tartre *m*. **scaly** *adj* écailleux; entartré.
scale[2] [skeil] *n* échelle *f*; (*music*) gamme *f*. **scale drawing** dessin à l'échelle *m*. *v* escalader. **scale down** réduire (proportionnellement).
scales [skeilz] *pl n* balance *f sing*.
scallop ['skaləp] *n* coquille Saint-Jacques *f*; (*sewing*) feston *m*. **scallop shell** coquille *f*. *v* festonner.
scalp [skalp] *n* cuir chevelu *m*. *v* scalper.
scalpel ['skalpəl] *n* bistouri *m*.
scamper ['skampə] *v* (*child*) galoper; (*mouse*) trottiner.

scampi ['skampi] *n* langoustines *f pl.*
scan [skan] *v* scruter; (*glance over*) parcourir des yeux; (*poetry*) (se) scander.
scandal ['skandl] *n* scandale *m*; (*gossip*) cancans *m pl.* **scandalize** *v* scandaliser. **scandalous** *adj* scandaleux.
Scandinavia [ˌskandi'neivjə] *n* Scandinavie *f.* **Scandinavian** *n* Scandinave *m, f*; *adj* scandinave.
scant [skant] *or* **scanty** *adj* insuffisant.
scapegoat ['skeipgout] *n* bouc émissaire *m.*
scar [skaː] *n* cicatrice *f*; (*from knife*) balafre *f.* *v* marquer d'une cicatrice; balafrer.
scarce [skeəs] *adj* peu abondant; rare. **scarcely** *adv* à peine. **scarcity** *n* manque *m*; rareté *f.*
scare [skeə] *n* peur *f*; alarme *f.* *v* effrayer. **be scared** avoir peur. **scarecrow** *n* épouvantail *m.*
scarf [skaːf] *n* écharpe *f*; (*square*) foulard *m.*
scarlet ['skaːlit] *nf, adj* écarlate. **scarlet fever** scarlatine *f.*
scathing ['skeiðiŋ] *adj* acerbe, cinglant.
scatter ['skatə] *v* éparpiller, répandre; (se) disperser. **scatterbrained** *adj* écervelé.
scavenge ['skavindʒ] *v* fouiller. **scavenger** *n* éboueur *m*; insecte *or* animal nécrophage *m.*
scene [siːn] *n* scène *f*; (*place*) lieu *m*; spectacle *m*, vue *f.*
scenery ['siːnəri] *n* paysage *m*; (*theatre*) décor *m.*
scent [sent] *n* parfum *m*; (*track*) piste *f.* *v* parfumer; (*smell*) flairer.
sceptic ['skeptik] *n* sceptique *m, f.* **sceptical** *adj* sceptique. **scepticism** *n* scepticisme *m.*
sceptre ['septə] *n* sceptre *m.*
schedule ['ʃedjuːl] *n* programme *m*; (*timetable*) horaire *m.* *v* prévoir.
scheme [skiːm] *n* plan *m*, projet *m*; (*plot*) complot *m*; arrangement *m.* *v* combiner, comploter.
schizophrenia [ˌskitsə'friːniə] *n* schizophrénie *f.* **schizophrenic** *n*(*m*+*f*), *adj* schizophrène.
scholar ['skolə] *n* érudit, -e *m, f*; (*pupil*) écolier, -ère *m, f.* **scholarly** *adj* érudit. **scholarship** *n* (*award*) bourse *f*; érudition *f.*
scholastic [skə'lastik] *adj* scolaire; scolastique.
school[1] [skuːl] *n* école *f*; (*secondary*) collège *m*, lycée *m.* **schoolboy** *n* élève *m*, écolier *m.* **school-days** *pl n* années d'école *f pl.* **schoolgirl** *n* élève *f*, écolière *f.* **school-leaving age** âge de fin de scolarité *m.* **school year** année scolaire *f.* *v* dresser. **schooling** *n* scolarité *f*; instruction *f*; dressage *m.*
school[2] [skuːl] *n* (*of fish*) banc *m.*
schooner ['skuːnə] *n* schooner *m.*
sciatica [sai'atikə] *n* sciatique *f.* **sciatic** *adj* sciatique.
science ['saiəns] *n* science *f.* **science fiction** *n* science-fiction *f.* **scientific** *adj* scientifique. **scientist** *n* scientifique *m, f.*
scintillating ['sintileitiŋ] *adj* scintillant; (*remark, etc.*) brillant.
scissors ['sizəz] *pl n* ciseaux *m pl.*
scoff[1] [skof] *v* se moquer.
scoff[2] [skof] *v* (*coll*) bouffer.
scold [skould] *v* attraper, gronder. **scolding** *n* gronderie *f.*
scone [skon] *n* petit pain au lait *m.*
scoop [skuːp] *n* pelle *f*, cuiller *f*; (*press*) scoop *m.* *v* (*pick up*) ramasser; (*water*) écoper; (*hole*) creuser.
scooter ['skuːtə] *n* scooter *m*; (*child's*) trottinette *f.*
scope [skoup] *n* (*range*) étendue *f*; (*opportunity*) possibilité *f.*
scorch [skoːtʃ] *n* brûlure légère *f.* *v* roussir, brûler.
score [skoː] *n* (*sport*) score *m*; (*game*) marque *f*; (*subject*) titre *m*; (*music*) partition *f*; (*twenty*) vingtaine *f*; (*cut*) rayure *f.* **scoreboard** *n* tableau *m.* *v* marquer; rayer, strier. **scorer** *n* marqueur *m.*
scorn [skoːn] *n* mépris *m*, dédain *m.* *v* mépriser, dédaigner. **scornful** *adj* méprisant, dédaigneux.
Scorpio ['skoːpiou] *n* Scorpion *m.*
scorpion ['skoːpiən] *n* scorpion *m.*
Scotland ['skotlənd] *n* Ecosse *f.* **Scot** *n* Ecossais, -e *m, f.* **Scotch** *n* whisky *m*, scotch *m.* **Scottish** *or* **Scots** *adj* écossais.
scoundrel ['skaundrəl] *n* vaurien *m.*
scour[1] [skauə] *v* (*clean*) récurer. **scourer** *n* (*powder*) poudre à récurer *f*; (*pad*) tampon abrasif *m.*
scour[2] [skauə] *v* (*search*) parcourir.
scourge [skəːdʒ] *n* fléau *m.*
scout [skaut] *n* scout *m*, éclaireur *m.* **scoutmaster** *n* chef scout *m.* **scouting** *n* scoutisme *m.*

scowl [skaul] *v* se renfrogner. *n* mine renfrognée *f*.
scramble ['skrambl] *v* avancer avec difficulté; (*rush*) se bousculer; (*eggs, phone*) brouiller. *n* bousculade *f*.
scrap [skrap] *n* bout *m*, fragment *m*; (*metal*) ferraille *f*. **scrap-book** *n* album *m*. **scrap-merchant** *n* ferrailleur *m*. **scrap paper** brouillon *m*. **scraps** *pl n* restes *m pl*. *v* mettre au rebut; abandonner.
scrape [skreip] *n* (*noise*) grattement *m*; (*graze*) éraflure *f*. *v* gratter, racler; érafler. **scrape through** (*exam*) réussir de justesse.
scratch [skratʃ] *v* (*for itch*) (se) gratter; (*with claw*) griffer; (*graze*) érafler; (*glass, record, etc.*) rayer. *n* grattement *m*; éraflure *f*; rayure *f*; zéro *m*.
scrawl [skroːl] *v* gribouiller. *n* gribouillage *m*.
scream [skriːm] *n* cri aigu *m*, hurlement *m*. *v* crier, hurler.
screech [skriːtʃ] *n* cri strident *m*, hurlement *m*; (*brakes*) grincement *m*. *v* crier, hurler; grincer.
screen [skriːn] *n* (*TV, film*) écran *m*; (*hospital, room*) paravent *m*; masque *m*. **screen-play** *n* scénario *m*. **screen test** essai filmé *m*. *v* masquer, cacher; (*film*) projeter; protéger.
screw [skruː] *n* vis *m*. **screwdriver** *n* tournevis *m*. *v* visser. **screw up** (*paper*) chiffonner.
scribble ['skribl] *v* gribouiller, griffonner. **scribble out** raturer. *n* gribouillage *m*, griffonage *m*.
script [skript] *n* (*play*) texte *m*; (*film*) scénario *m*; (*writing*) script *m*.
scripture ['skriptʃə] *n* (*school*) instruction religieuse *f*; (*holy*) écriture sainte *f*.
scroll [skroul] *n* rouleau *m*; manuscrit *m*; (*arch*) volute *f*.
scrounge [skraundʒ] (*coll*) *v* chiper, taper. **scrounger** *n* parasite *m*.
scrub[1] [skrʌb] *n* nettoyage *m*. *v* nettoyer à la brosse, frotter; (*coll: cancel*) annuler. **scrubbing brush** brosse dure *f*.
scrub[2] [skrʌb] *n* broussailles *f pl*.
scruff [skrʌf] *n* **by the scruff of the neck** par la peau du cou.
scruffy ['skrʌfi] *adj* négligé, débraillé. **scruffiness** *n* débraillé *m*.
scrum [skrʌm] *n* mêlée *f*.
scruple ['skruːpl] *n* scrupule *m*. **scrupulous** *adj* scrupuleux.
scrutiny ['skruːtəni] *n* examen minutieux *m*. **scrutinize** *v* scruter.
scuffle ['skʌfl] *n* bagarre *f*. *v* se bagarrer.
scull [skʌl] *n* aviron *m*, godille *f*. *v* ramer, godiller.
scullery ['skʌləri] *n* arrière-cuisine *f*.
sculpt [skʌlpt] *v* sculpter. **sculptor** *n* sculpteur *m*. **sculpture** *n* sculpture *f*.
scum [skʌm] *n* écume *f*; (*derog*) rebut *m*.
scurf [skəːf] *n* pellicules *f pl*.
scurvy ['skəːvi] *n* scorbut *m*.
scuttle[1] ['skʌtl] *n* (*coal*) seau à charbon *m*.
scuttle[2] ['skʌtl] *v* (*naut*) saborder.
scuttle[3] ['skʌtl] *v* courir précipitamment.
scythe [saið] *n* faux *f*. *v* faucher.
sea [siː] *n* mer *f*.
sea bed *n* fond de la mer *m*.
seafaring ['siːˌfeəriŋ] *adj* marin.
seafood ['siːfuːd] *n* fruits de mer *m pl*.
sea front *n* bord de mer *m*.
seagull ['siːgʌl] *n* mouette *f*.
seahorse ['siːhoːs] *n* hippocampe *m*.
seal[1] [siːl] *n* sceau *m*, cachet *m*. *v* sceller; (*stick down*) coller; (*fate*) décider. **sealing wax** cire à cacheter *f*.
seal[2] [siːl] *n* (*zool*) phoque *m*. **sealskin** *n* peau de phoque *f*.
sea-level *n* niveau de la mer *m*.
sea-lion *n* otarie *f*.
seam [siːm] *n* couture *f*; joint *m*; (*coal*) veine *f*.
seaman ['siːmən] *n* marin *m*.
séance ['seiɑ̃s] *n* séance de spiritisme *f*.
sear [siə] *v* flétrir; (*burn*) brûler. **searing** *adj* (*pain*) aigu, -guë.
search [səːtʃ] *n* recherche *f*; (*of house, etc.*) fouille *f*. **searchlight** *n* projecteur *m*. **search-party** *n* équipe de secours *f*. **search-warrant** *n* mandat de perquisition *m*. *v* fouiller, chercher. **searching** *adj* (*look*) pénétrant; (*examination*) rigoureux.
sea shell *n* coquillage *m*.
seashore ['siːʃoː] *n* rivage *m*, plage *f*.
seasick ['siːsik] *adj* **be seasick** avoir le mal de mer. **seasickness** *n* mal de mer *m*.
seaside ['siːsaid] *n* bord de la mer *m*. **seaside resort** station balnéaire *f*.
season ['siːzn] *n* saison *f*. **season ticket** carte d'abonnement *f*. *v* (*food*) assaisonner; (*wood*) faire sécher. **seasonal** *adj* saisonnier. **seasoning** *n* assaisonnement *m*.

seat [siːt] *n* siège *m*; place *f*. **seat-belt** *n* ceinture de sécurité *f*. *v* (faire) asseoir; placer.
seaweed ['siːwiːd] *n* algue *f*.
seaworthy ['siːwəːði] *adj* en état de naviguer.
secluded [si'kluːdid] *adj* à l'écart, retiré. **seclusion** *n* solitude *f*.
second[1] ['sekənd] *n* (*time*) seconde *f*. **second hand** trotteuse *f*.
second[2] ['sekənd] *n* deuxième *m*, *f*, second, -e *m*, *f*; (*comm*) article de second choix *m*. *adj*, *adv* deuxième, second. **on second thoughts** réflexion faite. **second-class** *adj* de deuxième classe; (*mail*) tarif réduit. **second-hand** *adj*, *adv* d'occasion. **second-rate** *adj* médiocre. **second to none** sans pareil. *v* appuyer (la motion de). **secondly** *adv* deuxièment, en second lieu.
secondary ['sekəndəri] *adj* secondaire.
secret ['siːkrit] *n* secret *m*. *adj* secret, -ète. **secrecy** *n* secret *m*. **secretive** *adj* réservé, dissimulé. **secretly** *adv* en secret.
secretary ['sekrətəri] *n* secrétaire *m*, *f*. **secretarial** *adj* de secrétariat, de secrétaire.
secrete [si'kriːt] *v* sécréter; (*hide*) çacher. **secretion** *n* sécrétion *f*.
sect [sekt] *n* secte *f*. **sectarian** *adj* sectaire.
section ['sekʃən] *n* section *f*, partie *f*.
sector ['sektə] *n* secteur *m*.
secular ['sekjulə] *adj* séculier, laïque.
secure [si'kjuə] *adj* solide; sûr, assuré; tranquille. *v* fixer; se procurer; garantir; assurer. **security** sécurité *f*; (*for loan*) caution *f*.
sedate [si'deit] *adj* posé, calme. **sedation** *n* sédation *f*. **sedative** *nm*, *adj* calmant.
sediment ['sedimənt] *n* (*geol*) sédiment *m*; (*wine, etc.*) dépôt *m*.
seduce [si'djuːs] *v* séduire. **seduction** *n* séduction *f*. **seductive** *adj* séduisant.
***see**[1] [siː] *v* voir. **see to** s'occuper de. **see you later!** à tout à l'heure!
see[2] [siː] *n* évêché *m*.
seed [siːd] *n* graine *f*; (*source*) germe *m*. **seedless** *adj* sans pépins. **seedling** *n* semis *m*. **seedy** *adj* miteux; (*coll: ill*) mal fichu.
***seek** [siːk] *v* chercher, rechercher; demander.
seem [siːm] *v* sembler, paraître. **seeming** *adj* apparent. **seemingly** *adv* apparemment; à ce qu'il paraît.
seen [siːn] *V* **see**[1].
seep [siːp] *v* suinter, filtrer. **seepage** *n* suintement *m*; (*leak*) fuite *f*.
seesaw ['siːsoː] *n* bascule *f*. *v* osciller.
seethe [siːð] *v* bouillir, bouillonner. **seething** *adj* (*coll*) furibond.
segment ['segmənt] *n* segment *m*; (*orange, etc.*) quartier *m*.
segregate ['segrigeit] *v* séparer, isoler. **segregation** *n* ségrégation *f*.
seize [siːz] *v* saisir; (*with force*) s'emparer de. **seize up** (*tech*) se gripper; (*med*) s'ankyloser. **seizure** *n* saisie *f*; capture *f*; (*med*) crise *f*.
seldom ['seldəm] *adv* rarement.
select [sə'lekt] *v* selectionner, choisir. *adj* choisi; (*club, etc.*) fermé. **selection** *n* sélection *f*. **selective** *adj* sélectif.
self [self] *n* moi *m*.
self-adhesive *adj* auto-adhésif.
self-assured *adj* plein d'assurance. **self-assurance** *n* assurance *f*.
self-centred *adj* égocentrique.
self-coloured *adj* uni.
self-confident *adj* sûr de soi. **self-confidence** *n* confiance en soi *f*.
self-conscious *adj* gêné. **self-consciousness** *n* gêne *f*.
self-contained *adj* indépendant.
self-control *n* maîtrise de soi *f*. **self-controlled** *adj* maître de soi, maîtresse de soi.
self-defence *n* légitime défense *f*.
self-discipline *n* discipline personelle *f*.
self-employed *adj* **be self-employed** travailler à son compte.
self-evident *adj* qui va de soi.
self-explanatory *adj* évident en soi.
self-expression *n* expression libre *f*.
self-important *adj* suffisant. **self-importance** *n* suffisance *f*.
self-interest *n* intérêt personnel *m*.
selfish ['selfiʃ] *adj* égoïste. **selfishness** *n* égoïsme *m*.
selfless ['selflis] *adj* désintéressé.
self-opinionated *adj* opiniâtre.
self-pity *n* apitoiement sur soi-même *m*.
self-portrait *n* autoportrait *m*.
self-possessed *adj* assuré. **self-possession** *n* sang-froid *m*.
self-raising flour *n* farine à levure *f*.
self-respect *n* respect de soi *m*.
self-righteous *adj* pharisaïque. **self-righteousness** *n* pharisaïsme *m*.
self-sacrifice *n* abnégation *f*.

selfsame ['selfseim] *adj* même.
self-satisfied *adj* content de soi.
self-service *n* libre-service *m*.
self-sufficient *adj* indépendant. **self-sufficiency** *n* indépendance *f*.
self-taught *adj* autodidacte.
self-willed *adj* entêté.
***sell** [sel] *v* (se) vendre; (*coll*) faire accepter. **sell off** solder, liquider. **seller** *n* vendeur, -euse *m, f*; marchand, -e *m, f*.
sellotape ® ['selәteip] *n* scotch ® *m*. *v* scotcher.
semantic [sә'mantik] *adj* sémantique. **semantics** *n* sémantique *f*.
semaphore ['semәfoː] *n* signaux à bras *m pl*; (*rail*) semaphore *m*.
semblance ['semblәns] *n* semblant *m*.
semen ['siːmәn] *n* sperme *m*, semence *f*.
semibreve ['semibriːv] *n* ronde *f*.
semicircle ['semisәːkl] *n* demi-cercle *m*. **semicircular** *adj* demi-circulaire.
semicolon [ˌsemi'koulәn] *n* point-virgule *m*.
semi-conscious *adj* à demi conscient.
semi-detached house *n* maison jumelée *f*.
semifinal [semi'fainl] *n* demi-finale *f*.
seminar ['seminaː] *n* séminaire *m*.
semi-precious *adj* semi-précieux.
semiquaver ['semikweivә] *n* double croche *f*.
semitone ['semitoun] *n* demi-ton *m*.
semolina [ˌsemә'liːnә] *n* semoule *f*; (*pudding*) semoule au lait *f*.
senate ['senit] *n* sénat *m*. **senator** *n* sénateur *m*.
***send** [send] *v* envoyer; rendre. **send back** renvoyer. **send for** faire venir; (*mail-order*) se faire envoyer.
senile ['siːnail] *adj* sénile. **senility** *n* sénilité *f*.
senior ['siːnjә] *adj* (*age*) aîné; (*rank*) supérieur, -e. *n* aîné, -e *m, f*; (*school*) grand, -e *m, f*. **seniority** *n* (*rank*) supériorité *f*; (*service*) ancienneté *f*; priorité d'âge *f*.
sensation [sen'seiʃәn] *n* sensation *f*. **sensational** *adj* sensationnel; (*newspaper*) à sensation.
sense [sens] *n* sens *m*; sensation *f*; (*feeling*) sentiment *m*; (*wisdom*) bon sens *m*. **senses** *pl n* raison *f sing*. *v* sentir. **senseless** *adj* insensé; (*unconscious*) sans connaissance.
sensible ['sensәbl] *adj* sensé, raisonnable; (*clothes*) pratique.
sensitive ['sensitiv] *adj* sensible; susceptible; délicat. **sensitivity** *n* sensibilité *f*; susceptibilité *f*, délicatesse *f*.
sensual ['sensjuәl] *adj* sensuel. **sensuality** *n* sensualité *f*.
sensuous ['sensjuәs] *adj* sensuel.
sent [sent] *V* **send**.
sentence ['sentәns] *n* (*gramm*) phrase *f*; (*law*) condamnation *f*. *v* condamner.
sentiment ['sentimәnt] *n* sentiment *m*; opinion *f*; sentimentalité *f*. **sentimental** *adj* sentimental.
sentry ['sentri] *n* sentinelle *f*.
separate ['sepәrәt; *v* 'sepәreit] *adj* séparé; indépendant; différent. *v* (se) séparer; diviser. **separation** *n* séparation *f*.
September [sep'tembә] *n* septembre *m*.
septic ['septik] *adj* septique (*wound*) infecté. **go septic** s'infecter.
sequel ['siːkwәl] *n* suite *f*, conséquence *f*.
sequence ['siːkwәns] ordre *m*; (*cards, music*) séquence *f*; (*series*) suite *f*.
sequin ['siːkwin] *n* paillette *f*.
serenade [serә'neid] *n* sérénade *f*.
serene [sә'riːn] *adj* serein. **serenity** *n* sérénité *f*.
serf [sәːf] *n* serf, serve *m, f*.
sergeant ['saːdʒәnt] *n* (*mil*) sergent *m*; (*police*) brigadier *m*. **sergeant-major** *n* sergent-major *m*.
serial ['siәriәl] *n* feuilleton *m*. *adj* de série. **serialize** *v* adapter en feuilleton; publier en feuilleton.
series ['siәriːz] *n* série *f*.
serious ['siәriәs] *adj* sérieux, grave. **seriousness** *n* sérieux *m*, gravité *f*.
sermon ['sәːmәn] *n* sermon *m*.
serpent ['sәːpәnt] *n* serpent *m*
serrated [sә'reitid] *adj* dentelé.
servant ['sәːvәnt] *n* domestique *m, f*.
serve [sәːv] *v* servir. **it serves you right** c'est bien fait pour toi.
service ['sәːvis] *n* service *m*; (*mot*) révision *f*. **service area** (*mot*) aire de services *f*. **service charge** service *m*. **serviceman** *n* militaire *m*. **service station** (*mot*) station-service *f*. *v* réviser. **serviceable** *adj* pratique, commode.
serviette [ˌsәːvi'et] *n* serviette *f*. **serviette ring** rond de serviette *m*.
servile ['sәːvail] *adj* servile. **servility** *n* servilité *f*.

session ['seʃən] *n* séance *f*, session *f*.
***set** [set] *n* jeu *m*, série *f*; collection *f*; (*people*) groupe *m*; (*TV*) poste *m*; (*cinema*) plateau *m*; (*hair*) mise en plis *f*; (*tennis*) set *m*. *adj* fixe. *v* (*put*) mettre; (*clock*) régler; fixer; (*mount*) monter; (*jelly*, *etc.*) prendre; (*sun*) se coucher; (*type*) composer. **set about** se mettre à. **setback** *n* contretemps *m*, revers *m*. **set off** (*leave*) partir; faire exploser; (*enhance*) mettre en valeur. **set out** partir; exposer. **set up** dresser; établir; s'installer. **setting** *n* cadre *m*; (*gem*) monture *f*; (*sun*) coucher *m*.
settee [se'tiː] *n* canapé *m*.
settle ['setl] *v* (*problem*, *account*, *etc.*) régler; calmer; (*bird*) se poser; (*person*) s'installer. **settle down** se calmer; s'installer. **settle up** (*bill*) régler. **settlement** *n* règlement *m*; accord *m*; colonie *f*.
seven ['sevn] *nm*, *adj* sept. **seventh** *n*(*m*+*f*), *adj* septième.
seventeen [sevn'tiːn] *nm*, *adj* dix-sept. **seventeenth** *n*(*m*+*f*), *adj* dix-septième.
seventy ['sevnti] *nm*, *adj* soixante-dix. **seventieth** *n*(*m*+*f*), *adj* soixante-dixième.
sever ['sevə] *v* (*cease*) rompre, cesser; (*cut*) couper.
several ['sevrəl] *adj*, *pron* plusieurs.
severe [sə'viə] *adj* sévère; (*hard*) dur; (*illness*) grave. **severity** *n* sévérité *f*; intensité *f*.
***sew** [sou] *v* coudre. **sewing** *n* couture *f*. **sewing machine** machine à coudre *f*.
sewage ['sjuidʒ] *n* vidanges *f pl*. **sewage farm** champ d'épandage *m*.
sewer ['sjuə] *n* égout *m*.
sewn [soun] *V* **sew**.
sex [seks] *n* sexe *m*. **sexual** *adj* sexuel. **sexual intercourse** rapports sexuels *m pl*. **sexuality** *n* sexualité *f*.
sextet [seks'tet] *n* sextuor *m*.
shabby ['ʃabi] *adj* râpé, minable; (*behaviour*) mesquin.
shack [ʃak] *n* cabane *f*.
shade [ʃeid] *n* ombre *f*; nuance *f*; (*lamp*) abat-jour *m invar*. *v* ombrager; (*painting*) ombrer; (*drawing*) hachurer. **shady** *adj* ombragé; (*dishonest*) louche.
shadow ['ʃadou] *n* ombre *f*. **shadow cabinet** cabinet fantôme *m*. *v* (*follow*) filer. **shadowy** *adj* ombragé; indistinct.
shaft [ʃaːft] *n* (*tool*) manche *m*; (*light*) trait *m*; (*lift*) cage *f*; (*mine*, *ventilation*) puits *m*; (*spear*) hampe *f*.
shaggy ['ʃagi] *adj* hirsute.
***shake** [ʃeik] *n* secousse *f*; tremblement *m*. *v* secouer; (*bottle*) agiter; trembler; (*weaken*) ébranler. **shake hands** serrer la main. **shake off** se débarrasser de. **shaky** *adj* tremblant; (*weak*, *unsure*) chancelant.
shaken ['ʃeikn] *V* **shake**.
shall [ʃal] *aux translated by future tense.*
shallot [ʃə'lot] *n* échalote *f*.
shallow ['ʃalou] *adj* peu profond; superficiel.
sham [ʃam] *n* imitation *f*; comédie *f*. *adj* faux, fausse; feint, simulé. *v* feindre, simuler; jouer la comédie.
shame [ʃeim] *n* honte *f*; (*pity*) dommage *m*. *v* faire honte à. **shamefaced** *adj* honteux; timide. **shameful** *adj* honteux. **shameless** *adj* éhonté; impudique.
shampoo [ʃam'puː] *n* shampooing *m*. *v* faire un shampooing à.
shamrock ['ʃamrok] *n* trèfle *m*.
shandy ['ʃandi] *n* panaché *m*.
shanty[1] ['ʃanti] *n* (*hut*) baraque *f*. **shanty town** bidonville *m*.
shanty[2] ['ʃanti] *n* chanson de marins *f*.
shape [ʃeip] *n* forme *f*. *v* façonner; prendre forme. **shapeless** *adj* informe. **shapely** *adj* bien fait, bien proportionné.
share [ʃeə] *n* part *f*; (*comm*) action *f*. **shareholder** *n* actionnaire *m*, *f*. *v* partager.
shark [ʃaːk] *n* requin *m*.
sharp [ʃaːp] *adj* aigu, -guë; (*point*) pointu; (*edge*) tranchant; (*sudden*) brusque; (*outline*) net, nette; (*pain*, *wind*) vif. *n* (*music*) dièse *m*. **sharpen** *v* aiguiser; (*pencil*) tailler; (*outline*) rendre plus net. **sharpness** *n* tranchant *m*; netteté *f*.
shatter ['ʃatə] *v* (se) fracasser; briser, ruiner. **shattered** *adj* bouleversé; (*tired*) éreinté. **shattering** *adj* bouleversant.
shave [ʃeiv] *v* (se) raser. **shaving** *n* (*of wood*, *metal*) copeau *m*. **shaving brush** blaireau *m*. **shaving cream** crème à raser *f*.
shawl [ʃoːl] *n* châle *m*.
she [ʃiː] *pron* elle. **she who** celle qui. *n* (*coll*) femelle *f*.
sheaf [ʃiːf] *n* (*corn*) gerbe *f*; (*papers*) liasse *f*; (*arrows*) faisceau *m*.
***shear** [ʃiə] *v* tondre. **shears** *pl n* cisailles *f pl*.

sheath [ʃiːθ] *n* gaine *f*; (*sword*) fourreau *m*; (*scissors*) étui *m*. **sheathe** *v* rengainer; recouvrir.

***shed**[1] [ʃed] *v* (*drop*) perdre; (*radiate*) répandre.

shed[2] [ʃed] *n* remise *f*, hutte *f*.

sheen [ʃiːn] *n* lustre *m*, éclat *m*.

sheep [ʃiːp] *n* mouton *m*. **sheep-dog** *n* chien de berger *m*. **sheepskin** *n* peau de mouton *f*. **sheepish** *adj* penaud.

sheer[1] [ʃiə] *adj* pur, absolu; (*cliff*) à pic; (*stockings*) extrêmement fin.

sheer[2] [ʃiə] *v* (*naut*) faire une embardée.

sheet [ʃiːt] *n* (*bed*) drap *m*; (*paper*) feuille *f*; (*ice*, *metal*) plaque *f*. **sheet lightning** éclair en nappe *m*. **sheet music** partitions *f pl*.

sheikh [ʃeik] *n* cheik *m*.

shelf [ʃelf] *n* rayon *m*, étagère *f*.

shell [ʃel] *n* coquille *f*; (*tortoise*, *crab*) carapace *f*; (*from beach*) coquillage *m*; (*mil*) obus *m*. **shellfish** *n* coquillage *m*; (*pl*: *as food*) fruits de mer *m pl*. *v* (*nut*, *shrimp*) décortiquer; (*peas*) écosser; (*mil*) bombarder.

shelter [ˈʃeltə] *n* abri *m*. *v* (s')abriter; protéger; (*lodge*) recueillir.

shelve [ʃelv] *v* (*project*) mettre en sommeil. **shelving** *n* rayonnage *m*.

shepherd [ˈʃepəd] *n* berger *m*. **shepherd's pie** hachis Parmentier *m*.

sheriff [ˈʃerif] *n* shérif *m*.

sherry [ˈʃeri] *n* xérès *m*.

shield [ʃiːld] *n* bouclier; (*screen*) écran *m*. *v* protéger.

shift [ʃift] *n* changement *m*; (*work*) poste *m*. **shift key** touche de majuscule *f*. **shift work** travail en équipe *m*. *v* déplacer, bouger; changer (de place). **shifty** *adj* louche.

shimmer [ˈʃimə] *v* miroiter, chatoyer. *n* miroitement *m*, chatoiement *m*.

shin [ʃin] *n* tibia *m*.

***shine** [ʃain] *n* éclat *m*, brillant *m*. *v* briller. **shiny** *adj* brillant, reluisant.

shingle [ˈʃiŋgl] *n* galets *m pl*.

ship [ʃip] *n* bateau *m*; (*larger*) navire *m*. **shipbuilding** *n* construction navale *f*. **shipshape** *adj* bien rangé. **shipwreck** *n* naufrage *m*. **be shipwrecked** faire naufrage. **shipyard** *n* chantier naval *m*. *v* transporter; (*send*) expédier; (*take on*) embarquer. **shipment** *n* cargaison *m*. **shipping** *n* navigation *f*.

shirk [ʃəːk] *v* esquiver. **shirker** *n* (*coll*) tire-au-flanc *m invar*.

shirt [ʃəːt] *n* chemise *f*. **in one's shirt sleeves** en bras de chemise. **shirtwaister** *n* robe chemisier *f*.

shit [ʃit] *nf*, *interj* (*vulgar*) merde.

shiver [ˈʃivə] *v* frissonner. *n* frisson *m*. **shivery** *adj* frissonnant; fiévreux.

shoal [ʃoul] *n* (*fish*) banc *m*.

shock [ʃok] *n* choc *m*; (*elec*) décharge *f*. **shock absorber** amortisseur *m*. **shock-proof** *adj* anti-choc *invar*. **shock treatment** électrochoc *m*. *v* secouer, bouleverser; dégoûter; (*scandalize*) choquer. **shocking** *adj* affreux, atroce; scandaleux.

shod [ʃod] *V* **shoe**.

shoddy [ˈʃodi] *adj* de mauvaise qualité. **shoddiness** *n* mauvaise qualité *f*.

***shoe** [ʃuː] *n* chaussure *f*, soulier *m*. **shoe-horn** *n* chausse-pied *m*. **shoe-lace** *n* lacet de soulier *m*. **shoemaker** *n* cordonnier *m*. **shoe repairer's** cordonnerie *f*. *v* (*horse*) ferrer.

shone [ʃon] *V* **shine**.

shook [ʃuk] *V* **shake**.

***shoot** [ʃuːt] *v* (*fire*) tirer, lancer; (*kill*) abattre; (*hit*) atteindre d'un coup de fusil; (*goal*) shooter; (*film*) tourner; (*go quickly*) aller en flèche. *n* (*bot*) pousse *f*. **shooting** *n* fusillade *f*; (*hunting*) chasse *f*.

shop [ʃop] *n* magasin *m*; (*smaller*) boutique *f*; (*in factory*) atelier *m*. **shop assistant** vendeur, -euse *m*, *f*. **shop-floor** *n* ouvriers *m pl*. **shopkeeper** *n* marchand, -e. **shoplifting** *n* vol à l'étalage *m*. **shop-soiled** *adj* défraîchi. **shop-steward** *n* délégué syndical *m*. **shop-window** *n* vitrine *f*. *v* faire ses courses. **shopping** *n* achats *m pl*. **go shopping** faire des courses. **shopping bag** sac à provisions *m*. **shopping centre** centre commercial *m*.

shore [ʃoː] *n* (*beach*) plage *f*; (*of sea*) rivage *m*; (*coast*) littoral *m*.

shorn [ʃoːn] *V* **shear**.

short [ʃoːt] *adj* court; bref, brève; insuffisant; brusque. **in short** en bref. **shortage** *n* manque *m*, pénurie *f*. **shorten** *v* raccourcir. **shortly** *adv* bientôt.

shortbread [ˈʃoːtbred] *n* sable *m*.

short-circuit *n* court-circuit *m*. *v* court-circuiter.

shortcoming [ˈʃoːtkʌmiŋ] *n* défaut *m*.

short cut *n* raccourci *m*.

shorthand ['ʃoːthand] *n* sténographie *f.* **shorthand typist** sténodactylo *m, f.*
short list *n* liste de candidats sélectionnés *f.*
short-lived [ʃoːt'livd] *adj* de courte durée.
shorts [ʃoːts] *pl n* short *m sing.*
short-sighted *adj* myope.
short story *n* nouvelle *f.*
short-tempered *adj* coléreux.
short-term *adj* à court terme.
short wave *n* ondes courtes *f pl. adj* à *or* sur ondes courtes.
shot[1] [ʃot] *V* **shoot.**
shot[2] [ʃot] *n* coup *m*; (*lead*) plomb *m*; (*try*) essai *m*; photo *f.* **shotgun** *n* fusil de chasse *m.*
should[1] [ʃud] *aux translated by conditional tense.*
should[2] [ʃud] *aux translated by conditional tense of* devoir.
shoulder ['ʃouldə] *n* épaule *f*; (*road*) accotement *m.* **shoulder-bag** *n* sac à bandoulière *m.* **shoulder-blade** *n* omoplate *f. v* endosser.
shout [ʃaut] *n* cri *m. v* crier.
shove [ʃʌv] *n* poussée *f. v* pousser.
shovel ['ʃʌvl] *n* pelle *f. v* pelleter.
***show** [ʃou] *n* démonstration *f*; (*flowers, etc.*) exposition *f*; (*theatre*) spectacle *m*; apparence *f*; (*ostentation*) parade *f.* **show business** le monde du spectacle *m.* **showcase** *n* vitrine *f.* **show-down** *n* épreuve de force *f.* **show-jumping** *n* concours hippique *m.* **show-room** *n* salle d'exposition *f. v* montrer; (*be visible*) se voir. **show in** faire entrer. **show off** (*coll*) crâner. **show up** être visible; (*coll: arrive*) se pointer; (*embarrass*) faire honte à.
shower ['ʃauə] *n* (*rain*) averse *f*; (*bath*) douche *f.* **shower-proof** *adj* imperméable. *v* combler, accabler. **showery** *adj* pluvieux.
shown [ʃoun] *V* **show.**
shrank [ʃraŋk] *V* **shrink.**
shred [ʃred] *n* lambeau *m*; (*small amount*) grain *m. v* déchiqueter.
shrew [ʃruː] *n* (*zool*) musaraigne *f*; (*woman*) mégère *f.*
shrewd [ʃruːd] *adj* perspicace, astucieux.
shriek [ʃriːk] *n* hurlement *m*, cri perçant *m. v* hurler, crier.
shrill [ʃril] *adj* perçant; (*whistle*) strident.
shrimp [ʃrimp] *n* crevette *f.*
shrine [ʃrain] *n* châsse *f*; lieu saint *m.*
***shrink** [ʃriŋk] *v* rétrécir; reculer. **shrinkage** *n* rétrécissement *m.*
shrivel ['ʃrivl] *v* se ratatiner, se flétrir.
shroud [ʃraud] *n* linceul *m*; (*mist*) voile *m. v* ensevelir.
Shrove Tuesday [ʃrouv] *n* mardi gras *m.*
shrub [ʃrʌb] *n* arbrisseau *m*, arbuste *m.* **shrubbery** *n* massif d'arbustes *m.*
shrug [ʃrʌg] *v* hausser (les épaules). *n* haussement d'épaules *m.*
shrunk [ʃrʌŋk] *V* **shrink.**
shudder ['ʃʌdə] *n* frisson *m*; (*engine*) vibration *f. v* frissonner, frémir; vibrer.
shuffle ['ʃʌfl] *v* traîner les pieds; (*cards*) battre. *n* battage *m*; réorganisation *f.*
shun [ʃʌn] *v* fuir, éviter.
shunt [ʃʌnt] *v* (*rail*) aiguiller, manœuvrer.
***shut** [ʃʌt] *v* fermer. **shut in** enfermer, entourer. **shut up** (*coll*) se taire, faire taire.
shutter ['ʃʌtə] *n* (*window*) volet *m*; (*phot*) obturateur *m.*
shuttle ['ʃʌtl] *n* navette *f.* **shuttlecock** *n* volant *m.* **shuttle service** service de navette *m.*
shy [ʃai] *adj* timide. *v* (*horse*) se cabrer. **shyness** *n* timidité *f.*
Siamese [ˌsaiə'miːz] *adj* (*cat, twin*) siamois.
sick [sik] *adj* malade; (*mind, humour*) malsain. **be sick** vomir. **be sick of** (*coll*) avoir marre de. **feel sick** avoir mal au cœur. **sick bay** infirmerie *f.* **sicken** *v* écœurer. **sicken for** couver. **sickening** *adj* écœurant; (*coll*) agaçant. **sickly** *adj* (*person*) maladif; pâle; (*cake*) écœurant. **sickness** *n* maladie *f*; vomissements *m pl.*
sickle ['sikl] *n* faucille *f.*
side [said] *n* côté *m*; (*hill, animal*) flanc *m*; (*edge*) bord *m*; (*team*) équipe *f*; (*in argument, etc.*) camp *m. v* **side with** prendre parti pour.
sideboard ['saidboːd] *n* buffet *m.*
side-effect *n* effet secondaire *m.*
sidelight ['saidlait] *n* (*mot*) lanterne *f.*
sideline ['saidlain] *n* activité secondaire *f*; (*sport*) touche *f.*
sidelong ['saidloŋ] *adj, adv* de côté.
side-show *n* attraction *f.*
side-step *v* éviter.
side-street *n* petite rue *f.*
side-track *v* faire dévier.
sidewalk ['saidwoːk] *n* (*US*) trottoir *m.*
sideways ['saidweiz] *adj* oblique. *adv* de côté; (*walk*) en crabe.

siding ['saidiŋ] *n* (*rail*) voie de garage *f*.
sidle ['saidl] *v* marcher de côté; avancer furtivement. **sidle up to** se glisser vers.
siege [siːdʒ] *n* siège *m*.
sieve [siv] *n* tamis *m*; (*coal*) crible *m*. *v* tamiser; cribler.
sift [sift] *v* (*food*) tamiser; (*coal*) cribler; (*evidence*) passer au crible. **sift out** dégager. **sifter** *n* (*flour*) saupoudreuse *f*.
sigh [sai] *n* soupir *m*. *v* soupirer.
sight [sait] *n* vue *f*; spectacle *m*; (*on gun*) mire *f*. **sight-read** *v* déchiffrer. **sightseeing** *n* tourisme *m*. *v* apercevoir.
sign [sain] *n* signe *m*; (*notice*) panneau *m*. **signpost** *n* poteau indicateur *m*. *v* signer.
signal ['signəl] *n* signal *m*. *v* faire signe (à); faire des signaux.
signature ['signətʃə] *n* signature *f*. **signature tune** indicatif musical *m*.
signify ['signifai] *v* signifier. **significance** *n* signification *f*. **significant** *adj* significatif; considérable.
silence ['sailəns] *n* silence *m*. *v* réduire au silence, faire taire. **silencer** *n* silencieux *m*. **silent** *adj* silencieux.
silhouette [silu'et] *n* silhouette *f*. *v* **be silhouetted against** se découper contre.
silk [silk] *n* soie *f*. **silkworm** *n* ver à soie *m*. **silky** *adj* soyeux.
sill [sil] *n* rebord *m*; (*mot*) bas de marche *m*.
silly ['sili] *adj* bête, idiot. **silliness** *n* sottise *f*.
silt [silt] *n* vase *f*. *v* **silt up** envaser.
silver ['silvə] *n* argent *m*; (*cutlery, etc.*) argenterie *f*; (*change*) monnaie *f*. *adj* d'argent; en argent. **silver birch** bouleau argenté *m*. **silver paper** papier d'argent *m*. **silversmith** *n* orfèvre *m*, *f*. *v* argenter. **silvery** *adj* argenté.
similar ['similə] *adj* semblable. **similarity** *n* ressemblance *f*.
simile ['siməli] *n* comparaison *f*.
simmer ['simə] *v* (faire) cuire à feu doux, mijoter; (*anger*) couver. **simmer down** (*coll*) se calmer.
simple ['simpl] *adj* simple. **simpleton** *n* nigaud, -e *m*, *f*. **simplicity** *n* simplicité *f*. **simplify** *v* simplifier. **simply** *adv* simplement; absolument.
simulate ['simjuleit] *v* simuler. **simulation** *n* simulation *f*.
simultaneous [ˌsiməl'teinjəs] *adj* simultané.
sin [sin] *n* péché *m*. *v* pécher. **sinful** *adj* coupable; scandaleux. **sinner** *n* pécheur, -eresse *m*, *f*.
since [sins] *prep*, *adv* depuis. *conj* depuis que; (*because*) puisque.
sincere [sin'siə] *adj* sincère. **sincerity** *n* sincérité *f*.
sinew ['sinjuː] *n* tendon *m*.
***sing** [siŋ] *v* chanter. **singer** *n* chanteur, -euse *m*, *f*. **singing** *n* chant *m*.
singe [sindʒ] *v* brûler légèrement, roussir. *n* légère brûlure *f*.
single ['siŋgl] *adj* seul; (*not double*) simple; célibataire. **single bed** lit d'une personne *m*. **single file** file indienne *f*. **single-handed** *adv* tout seul; (*sail*) en solitaire. **single-minded** *adj* résolu. **single ticket** aller simple *m*. **single room** chambre à un lit *f*. *n* (*ticket*) aller simple *m*; (*record*) 45 tours *m*. **singles** *n* (*sport*) simple *m*. *v* **single out** distinguer; choisir.
singular ['siŋgjulə] *nm*, *adj* singulier.
sinister ['sinistə] *adj* sinistre.
***sink** [siŋk] *v* (*go under*) couler; (*collapse*) s'affaisser; (*go down*) baisser; (*mine*) creuser. **sink in** (*idea, etc.*) rentrer, pénétrer. *n* évier *m*. **sink unit** bloc-évier *m*.
sinuous ['sinjuəs] *adj* sinueux.
sinus ['sainəs] *n* sinus *m invar*. **sinusitis** *n* sinusite *f*.
sip [sip] *n* petite gorgée *f*. *v* boire à petites gorgées.
siphon ['saifən] *n* siphon *m*. *v* siphonner.
sir [səː] *n* monsieur *m*; (*knight*) sir *m*.
siren ['saiərən] *n* sirène *f*.
sirloin ['səːloin] *n* aloyau *m*.
sister ['sistə] *n* sœur *f*; religieuse *f*; (*hospital*) infirmière en chef *f*. **sister-in-law** *n* belle-sœur *f*.
***sit** [sit] *n* (s')asseoir; (*clothes*) tomber; (*committee*) être en séance; (*exam*) passer. **sit down** s'asseoir. **sit-in** *n* sit-in *m invar*. **sit up** se redresser; (*stay up*) ne pas se coucher. **sitting** *n* séance *f*; (*meal*) service *m*. **sitting room** salon *m*. **sitting tenant** locataire en place *m*, *f*.
site [sait] *n* emplacement *m*; (*building*) chantier *m*; camping *m*. *v* placer.
situation [sitju'eiʃən] *n* situation *f*; emploi *m*. **situate** *v* placer, situer.
six [siks] *nm*, *adj* six. **sixth** *n*(*m*+*f*), *adj* sixième. **sixth form** classes de première et terminale *f pl*.
sixteen [siks'tiːn] *nm*, *adj* seize. **sixteenth** *n*(*m*+*f*), *adj* seizième.

sixty ['siksti] *nm, adj* soixante. **sixtieth** *n(m+f), adj* soixantième.
size [saiz] *n* taille *f*; grandeur *f*, dimensions *f pl*; (*shoes*) pointure *f*. *v* **size up** mesurer, juger. **sizeable** *adj* assez grand.
sizzle ['sizl] *v* grésiller. *n* grésillement *m*.
skate[1] [skeit] *n* patin *m*. **skateboard** *n* planche à roulettes *f*. *v* patiner. **skater** *n* patineur, -euse *m, f*. **skating** *n* patinage *m*.
skate[2] [skeit] *n* (*fish*) raie *f*.
skeleton ['skelitn] *n* squelette *m*. *adj* (*staff, etc.*) squelettique. **skeleton key** passe-partout *m invar*.
sketch [sketʃ] *n* croquis *m*; (*rough*) ébauche *f*; (*theatre*) sketch *m*. *v* esquisser. **sketchy** *adj* incomplet, -ète.
skewer ['skjuə] *n* brochette *f*. *v* embrocher.
ski [skiː] *n* ski *m*. **ski-lift** *n* remonte-pente *m*, remontée mécanique *f*. *v* faire du ski. **skier** *n* skieur, -euse *m, f*. **skiing** *n* ski *m*.
skid [skid] *n* dérapage *m*. *v* déraper.
skill [skil] *n* habileté *f*; technique *f*. **skilful** *adj* habile. **skilled** *adj* habile, adroit; (*worker*) qualifié.
skim [skim] *v* (*milk*) écrémer; (*surface*) raser; (*reading*) parcourir.
skimp [skimp] *v* lésiner (sur), économiser. **skimpy** *adj* insuffisant, maigre.
skin [skin] *n* peau *f*. **skin-diving** *n* plongée sous-marine *f*. **skin-tight** *adj* collant. *v* (*animal*) dépouiller; (*fruit, vegetable*) éplucher. **skinny** *adj* maigrelet.
skip [skip] *n* petit saut *m*. *v* gambader; sauter à la corde; (*miss*) sauter. **skipping** *n* saut à la corde *m*. **skipping rope** corde à sauter *f*.
skipper ['skipə] *n* capitaine *m*.
skirmish ['skəːmiʃ] *n* escarmouche *f*.
skirt [skəːt] *n* jupe *f*. *v* contourner. **skirting board** plinthe *f*.
skittle ['skitl] *n* quille *f*. **skittles** *n* jeu de quilles *m*.
skull [skʌl] *n* crâne *m*. **skull and crossbones** tête de mort *f*.
skunk [skʌŋk] *n* mouffette *f*.
sky [skai] *n* ciel *m*. **sky-blue** *nm, adj* bleu ciel. **skylark** *n* alouette *f*. **skylight** *n* lucarne *f*. **skyline** *n* ligne d'horizon *f*. **skyscraper** *n* gratte-ciel *m invar*.
slab [slab] *m* bloc *m*, plaque *f*; (*paving*) dalle *f*; (*butcher's*) étal *m*.
slack [slak] *adj* (*loose*) lâche; (*trade*) faible; (*person*) négligent, peu sérieux. *n* mou *m*. **slacken** *v* (se) relâcher; diminuer. **slacker** *n* (*coll*) flemmard, -e *m, f*.
slacks [slaks] *pl n* pantalon *m sing*.
slag [slag] *n* scories *f pl*. **slag heap** (*mining*) terril *m*.
slalom ['slaːləm] *n* slalom *m*.
slam [slam] *n* claquement *m*. *v* claquer. **slam on the brakes** freiner à mort.
slander ['slaːndə] *n* calomnie *f*; (*law*) diffamation *f*. *v* calomnier; diffamer. **slanderous** *adj* calomnieux; diffamatoire.
slang [slaŋ] *n* argot *m*.
slant [slaːnt] *n* inclinaison *f*; angle *m*. *v* (faire) pencher. **slanting** *adj* incliné, penché.
slap [slap] *n* claque *f*; (*on face*) gifle *f*. *v* donner une claque à; gifler; (*coll: put*) flanquer. **slapdash** *adj* (*person*) négligent; (*work*) bâclé. **slapstick** *n* grosse farce *f*. **slap-up meal** (*coll*) repas fameux *m*.
slash [slaʃ] *n* entaille *f*. *v* entailler, taillader; (*coll: prices*) casser.
slat [slat] *n* lame *f*; (*of blind*) lamelle *f*.
slate [sleit] *n* ardoise *f*. *v* ardoiser; (*coll: criticize*) éreinter.
slaughter [sloːtə] *n* abattage *m*; (*people*) carnage *m*. **slaughterhouse** *n* abattoir *m*. *v* abattre; massacrer.
slave [sleiv] *n* esclave *m, f*. **slave-driver** *n* négrier, -ère *m, f*. *v* trimer. **slavery** *n* esclavage *m*.
sledge [sledʒ] *n* luge *f*; (*drawn by animal*) traîneau *m*.
sledgehammer ['sledʒˌhamə] *n* marteau de forgeron *m*.
sleek [sliːk] *adj* lisse, brillant.
***sleep** [sliːp] *n* sommeil *m*. **go to sleep** s'endormir. **sleepwalker** *n* somnambule *m, f*. *v* dormir; (*spend the night*) coucher. **sleep in** faire la grasse matinée. **sleeper** *n* train-couchettes *m*; (*wooden beam*) traverse *f*. **sleeping-bag** *n* sac de couchage *m*. **sleeping-pill** *n* somnifère *m*. **sleepless night** nuit blanche *f*. **sleepy** *adj* endormi, somnolent.
sleet [sliːt] *n* neige fondue *f*.
sleeve [sliːv] *n* manche *f*; (*record*) pochette *f*. **sleeveless** *adj* sans manches.
sleigh [slei] *n* traîneau *m*.
slender ['slendə] *adj* svelte; fin; faible; maigre.
slept [slept] *V* **sleep**.
slice [slais] *n* tranche *f*; partie *f*. *v* couper en tranches.

slick [slik] *adj* (*derog*) facile, superficiel.
slid [slid] *V* **slide.**
***slide** [slaid] *n* glissade *f*; (*chute*) toboggan *m*; (*microscope*) porte-objet *m*; (*phot*) diapositive *f*; (*hair*) barrette *f*. **slide-rule** *n* règle à calcul *f*. *v* (se) glisser. **sliding** *adj* glissant; (*door, etc.*) coulissant.
slight [slait] *adj* petit, faible; (*person*) mince. *v* offenser. *n* offense *f*. **slightest** *adj* moindre. **slightly** *adv* un peu.
slim [slim] *adj* mince; faible. *v* (faire) maigrir. **slimming** *adj* (*diet, etc.*) amaigrissant.
slime [slaim] *n* vase *f*, limon *m*. **slimy** *adj* visqueux.
***sling** [sliŋ] *n* (*med*) écharpe *f*; (*weapon*) fronde *f*. *v* lancer; suspendre.
***slink** [sliŋk] *v* **slink away** s'en aller furtivement.
slip [slip] *n* erreur *f*; (*of paper*) bout *m*, fiche *f*; (*underskirt*) combinaison *f*. **slip of the tongue** *or* **pen** lapsus *m*. *v* (se) glisser. **slip-knot** *n* nœud coulant *m*. **slip-road** *n* bretelle d'accès *f*. **slipshod** *adj* négligé, négligent. **slipway** *n* cale *f*.
slipper ['slipə] *n* pantoufle *f*.
slippery ['slipəri] *adj* glissant.
***slit** [slit] *n* fente *f*, incision *f*. *v* fendre, inciser.
slither ['sliðə] *v* glisser, déraper.
slobber ['slobə] *v* baver. *n* bave *f*.
sloe [slou] *n* prunelle *f*.
slog [slog] *n* gros effort *m*. *v* travailler très dur; (*ball*) donner un grand coup à.
slogan ['slougən] *n* slogan *m*.
slop [slop] *v* (*spill*) répandre; (*overflow*) déborder.
slope [sloup] *n* inclinaison *f*; (*hill*) côte *f*. *v* être incliné. **sloping** *adj* en pente, incliné.
sloppy ['slopi] *adj* (*food*) liquide; (*dress*) négligé; (*garment*) mal ajusté; (*coll: work*) bâclé.
slot [slot] *n* fente *f*. **slot-machine** *n* (*vending*) distributeur automatique *m*; (*gambling*) machine à sous *f*. *v* (s')emboîter; (s')insérer.
slouch [slautʃ] *v* se tenir mal.
slovenly ['slʌvnli] *adj* négligé.
slow [slou] *adj* lent. *adv* lentement. **in slow motion** au ralenti. **slowcoach** *n* (*coll*) lambin, -e *m, f*. *v* **slow down** ralentir.
slug [slʌg] *n* (zool) limace *f*; (*bullet*) balle *f*.
sluggish ['slʌgiʃ] *adj* lent, paresseux.
sluice [sluːs] *n* écluse *f*. *v* laver à grande eau.
slum [slʌm] *n* taudis *m*. **slums** *pl n* quartiers pauvres *m pl*.
slumber ['slʌmbə] *n* sommeil paisible *m*. *v* dormir paisiblement.
slump [slʌmp] *n* baisse soudaine *f*; récession *f*, crise *f*. *v* s'effondrer.
slung [slʌŋ] *V* **sling.**
slunk [slʌŋk] *V* **slink.**
slur [sləː] *n* tache *f*; insulte *f*; (*music*) liaison *f*. *v* mal articuler; (*music*) lier.
slush [slʌʃ] *n* neige fondante *f*.
slut [slʌt] *n* souillon *f*.
sly [slai] *adj* rusé, sournois.
smack[1] [smak] *n* tape *f*, claque *f*; (*sound*) claquement *m*. *v* donner une tape *or* claque à.
smack[2] [smak] *v* **smack of** sentir. *n* léger goût *m*.
small [smoːl] *adj* petit; peu nombreux. **feel small** se sentir honteux. **small change** petite monnaie *f*. **smallholding** *n* petite ferme *f*. **smallpox** *n* variole *f*. **small talk** papotage *m*. *n* **small of the back** creux des reins *m*.
smart [smaːt] *adj* chic *invar*, élégant; intelligent, astucieux; rapide, vif. *v* brûler, piquer. **smarten up** devenir plus élégant; rendre plus élégant. **smartness** *n* élégance *f*; intelligence *f*.
smash [smaʃ] *n* (*sound*) fracas *m*; accident *m*, collision *f*; (*blow*) coup violent *m*. *v* (se) briser (en mille morceaux), (se) fracasser. **smashing** *adj* (*slang*) formidable.
smear [smiə] *n* tache *f*. *v* (se) salir, barbouiller.
***smell** [smel] *n* odeur *f*; (*sense*) odorat *m*. *v* sentir; (*sniff*) flairer. **smelly** *adj* malodorant.
smelt [smelt] *V* **smell.**
smile [smail] *n* sourire *m*. *v* sourire.
smirk [smaːk] *n* petit sourire satisfait *m*. *v* sourire d'un air satisfait.
smock [smok] *n* blouse *f*. **smocking** *n* smocks *m pl*.
smog [smog] *n* brouillard enfumé *m*.
smoke [smouk] *n* fumée *f*. **smoke-screen** *n* paravent *m*. *v* fumer. **smoker** *n* fumeur, -euse *m, f*. **no smoking** défense de fumer. **smoky** *adj* enfumé.

smooth [smuːð] *adj* lisse; régulier; (*person*) doucereux. *v* lisser. **smooth out** faire disparaître. **smoothly** *adv* facilement, doucement; (*move*) sans secousses; sans incident.
smother ['smʌðə] *v* étouffer.
smoulder ['smouldə] *v* couver.
smudge [smʌdʒ] *n* tache *f. v* (s')étaler, (se) maculer.
smug [smʌg] *adj* suffisant.
smuggle ['smʌgl] *v* passer en contrebande; passer clandestinement. **smuggler** *n* contrebandier, -ère *m, f.* **smuggling** *n* contrebande *f.*
snack [snak] *n* casse-croûte *m invar.* **snack-bar** *n* snack-bar *m.*
snag [snag] *n* inconvénient *m,* obstacle caché *m*; (*in cloth*) accroc *m. v* accrocher.
snail [sneil] *n* escargot *m.*
snake [sneik] *n* serpent *m. v* serpenter.
snap [snap] *n* bruit sec *m,* claquement *m,* craquement *m*; photo *f. adj* subit, irréfléchi. **snapdragon** *n* gueule-de-loup *f.* **snapshot** *n* photo *f. v* (se) casser net; (faire) claquer; (*dog*) essayer de mordre; (*person*) parler d'un ton brusque.
snare [sneə] *n* piège *m. v* attraper.
snarl [snaːl] *n* grondement *m. v* gronder.
snatch [snatʃ] *n* fragment *m*; (*theft*) vol *m. v* saisir, arracher (à).
sneak [sniːk] *v* se faufiler; (*slang: school*) moucharder. **sneak in/out** entrer/sortir furtivement. *n* (*coll*) mouchard, -e *m, f.*
sneer [sniə] *v* ricaner. *n* ricanement *m.* **sneering** *adj* ricaneur, -euse.
sneeze [sniːz] *n* éternuement *m. v* éternuer.
sniff [snif] *n* reniflement *m. v* renifler; (*air, aroma*) humer.
snigger ['snigə] *n* petit rire moqueur *m. v* pouffer de rire.
snip [snip] *v* couper à petits coups.
snipe [snaip] *n* bécassine *f. v* canarder. **sniper** *n* canardeur *m.*
snivel ['snivl] *v* pleurnicher. **snivelling** *adj* pleurnicheur, -euse.
snob [snob] *n* snob *m, f.* **snobbish** *adj* snob *invar.*
snooker ['snuːkə] *n* jeu de billard *m.*
snoop [snuːp] *v* (*coll*) fureter, fourrer son nez.
snooty ['snuːti] *adj* (*coll*) hautain.
snooze [snuːz] *n* roupillon *m. v* piquer un roupillon.
snore [snoː] *n* ronflement *m. v* ronfler. **snoring** *n* ronflements *m pl.*
snorkel ['snoːkəl] *n* (*swimmer*) tuba *m*; (*submarine*) schnorchel *m.*
snort [snoːt] *n* (*person*) grognement *m*; (*animal*) ébrouement *m. v* grogner; s'ébrouer.
snout [snaut] *n* museau *m.*
snow [snou] *n* neige *f.* **snow-drift** *n* congère *f.* **snowdrop** *n* perce-neige *m.* **snowflake** *n* flocon de neige *m.* **snowman** *n* bonhomme de neige *m.* **snow-plough** *n* chasse-neige *m invar.* **snow-shoe** *n* raquette *f.* **snowstorm** *n* tempête de neige *f. v* neiger. **be snowed under with** être submergé de. **snowy** *adj* neigeux; de neige.
snowball ['snouboːl] *n* boule de neige *f. v* (*increase*) faire boule de neige.
snub [snʌb] *n* rebuffade *f. v* (*person*) snober; repousser.
snuff [snʌf] *n* tabac à priser. **snuffbox** *n* tabatière *f.* **take snuff** priser.
snug [snʌg] *adj* douillet, -ette, confortable.
snuggle ['snʌgl] *v* se blottir, se pelotonner.
so [sou] *adv* si, tellement, aussi; (*thus*) ainsi. *conj* donc. **and so on** et ainsi de suite. **if so** si oui. **is that so?** vraiment? **... or so** à peu près .... **so as to** afin de. **so-called** *adj* soi-disant *invar.* **so much** *or* **many** tant (de). **so-so** *adj* (*coll*) comme ci comme ça. **so that** pour (que). **so what?** et alors?
soak [souk] *v* (faire) tremper. **soak in** pénétrer. **soak up** absorber. **soaking** *n* trempage *m.* **soaking wet** trempé.
soap [soup] *n* savon *m.* **soap-box** *n* tribune improvisée *f.* **soap-dish** *n* porte-savon *m.* **soap opera** (*coll*) mélo à épisodes *m.* **soap powder** lessive *f. v* savonner. **soapy** *adj* savonneux.
soar [soː] *v* monter en flèche; (*hope*) grandir.
sob [sob] *n* sanglot *m. v* sangloter.
sober ['soubə] *n* sérieux; modéré; (*not drunk*) pas ivre. *v* **sober up** désenivrer.
soccer ['sokə] *n* football *m.*
sociable ['souʃəbl] *adj* sociable.
social ['souʃəl] *adj* social; (*life, etc.*) mondain. **social club** association amicale *f.* **social science** sciences humaines *f pl.* **social security** aide sociale *f.* **social work** assistance sociale *f.* **socialism** *n* social-

isme *m.* **socialist** *n(m+f). adj* socialiste. **socialize** *v* fréquenter des gens.
society [sə'saiəti] *n* société *f.*
sociology [sousi'olədʒi] *n* sociologie *f.* **sociological** *adj* sociologique. **sociologist** *n* sociologue *m, f.*
sock [sok] *n* chaussette *f.*
socket ['sokit] *n* cavité *f*; (*elec*) prise de courant *f.*
soda ['soudə] *n* (*chem*) soude *f*; (*water*) eau de Seltz *f.*
sodden ['sodn] *adj* détrempé.
sofa ['soufə] *n* sofa *m.*
Sofia ['soufjə] *n* Sofia.
soft [soft] *adj* doux, douce; (*butter, clay, etc.*) mou, molle; (*coll*) stupide. **soft-boiled** *adj* (*egg*) à la coque. **soft drink** boisson non alcoolisée *f.* **soft toy** jouet de peluche *m.* **soften** *v* (s')adoucir; (se) ramollir. **softness** *n* douceur *f*; mollesse *f.*
soggy ['sogi] *adj* détrempé.
soil[1] [soil] *n* sol *m,* terre *f.*
soil[2] [soil] *v* salir.
solar ['soulə] *adj* solaire, du soleil.
sold [sould] *V* **sell.**
solder ['soldə] *n* soudure *f. v* souder. **soldering iron** fer à souder *m.*
soldier ['souldʒə] *n* soldat *m. v* **soldier on** persévérer.
sole[1] [soul] *adj* seul, unique; exclusif.
sole[2] [soul] *n* (*of shoe*) semelle *f*; (*of foot*) plante *f. v* ressemeler.
sole[3] [soul] *n* (*fish*) sole *f.*
solemn ['soləm] *adj* solennel. **solemnity** *n* solennité *f.*
solicitor [sə'lisitə] *n* avocat *m.*
solicitude [sə'lisitjuːd] *n* sollicitude *f.*
solid ['solid] *adj* solide; (*not hollow*) plein; (*line*) continu. *n* solide *m.* **solids** *pl n* (*food*) aliments solides *m pl.* **solidarity** *n* solidarité *f.* **solidify** *v* (se) solidifier; (se) congeler.
solitary ['solitəri] *adj* solitaire; seul, unique.
solitude ['solitjuːd] *n* solitude *f.*
solo ['soulou] *n* solo *m. adj* solo *invar*; (*flight*) en solitaire. **soloist** *n* soliste *m, f.*
solstice ['solstis] *n* solstice *m.*
soluble ['soljubl] *adj* soluble.
solution [sə'luːʃən] *n* solution *f.*
solve [solv] *v* résoudre, trouver la solution de.
solvent ['solvənt] *adj* (*finance*) solvable. *n* (*chem*) solvant *m.* **solvency** *n* solvabilité *f.*
sombre ['sombə] *adj* sombre, morne.
some [sʌm] *adj* du, de la; (*pl*) des; certains; (*unspecified*) quelque. *pron* quelques-uns; (*before verb*) en. *adv* environ. **somebody** *or* **someone** *pron* quelqu'un. **somehow** *adv* d'une façon ou d'une autre. **something** *pron* quelque chose. **sometime** *adv* un de ces jours. **sometimes** *adv* quelquefois. **somewhat** *adv* quelque peu. **somewhere** *adv* quelque part. **somewhere else** ailleurs.
somersault ['sʌməsoːlt] *n* culbute *f. v* faire la culbute.
son [sʌn] *n* fils *m.* **son-in-law** *n* gendre *m.*
sonata [sə'naːtə] *n* sonate *f.*
song [soŋ] *n* chanson *f*; (*birds*) chant *m.*
sonic ['sonik] *adj* sonique. **sonic boom** détonation supersonique *f.*
sonnet ['sonit] *n* sonnet *m.*
soon [suːn] *adv* bientôt; (*early*) tôt. **as soon as** dès que. **sooner or later** tôt ou tard.
soot [sut] *n* suie *f.*
soothe [suːð] *v* calmer, apaiser. **soothing** *adj* apaisant; (*ointment*) lénitif.
sophisticated [sə'fistikeitid] *adj* raffiné; élégant; (*machinery*) sophistiqué.
sopping ['sopiŋ] *adj* trempé.
soprano [sə'praːnou] *n* soprano *m, f.*
sordid ['soːdid] *adj* sordide.
sore [soː] *adj* douloureux. **sore point** point délicat *m. n* plaie *f.* **sorely** *adv* (*bitterly*) amèrement; (*greatly*) fortement. **soreness** *n* endolorissement *m.*
sorrow ['sorou] *n* peine *f,* chagrin *m. v* se lamenter. **sorrowful** *adj* triste, affligé.
sorry ['sori] *adj* désolé; (*plight*) triste. **feel sorry for** plaindre. *interj* pardon!
sort [soːt] *n* sorte *f,* genre *m*; (*brand*) marque *f. v* trier, classer. **sort out** ranger; (*problem*) régler; arranger. **sorting office** bureau de tri *m.*
soufflé ['suːflei] *n* soufflé *m.*
sought [soːt] *V* **seek.**
soul [soul] *n* âme *f.* **soul-destroying** *adj* démoralisant. **soulful** *adj* expressif.
sound[1] [saund] *n* (*noise*) son *m,* bruit *m.* **sound barrier** mur du son *m.* **sound effects** bruitage *m sing.* **soundproof** *adj* insonorisé. **sound-track** *n* piste sonore *f. v* sonner, retentir; (*seem*) sembler.
sound[2] [saund] *adj* sain, solide; (*advice,*

etc.) sensé; (*sleep*) profond. **be sound asleep** être profondément endormi.
sound³ [saund] *v* (*depth*) sonder.
soup [suːp] *n* soupe *f*, potage *m*. **soup-plate** *n* assiette creuse *f*.
sour [sauə] *adj* aigre, acide; (*person*) acerbe, revêche. *v* (s')aigrir.
source [soːs] *n* source *f*.
south [sauθ] *n* sud *m*. *adj also* **southerly, southern** sud *invar*; au *or* du sud. *adv* au sud; vers le sud. **southbound** *adj* sud *invar*. **south-east** *nm*, *adj* sud-est. **south-west** *nm*, *adj* sud-ouest.
souvenir [suːvəˈniə] *n* souvenir *m*.
sovereign [ˈsovrin] *n*, *adj* souverain, -e.
***sow¹** [sou] *v* semer, ensemencer.
sow² [sau] *n* truie *f*.
sown [soun] *V* **sow¹**.
soya [ˈsoiə] *n* soja *m*. **soya bean** graine de soja *f*. **soy sauce** sauce au soja *f*.
spa [spaː] *n* station thermale *f*.
space [speis] *n* espace *m*, place *f*. **spaceman** *n* astronaute *m*. **spaceship** *n* engin spatial *m*. *v* espacer. **spacious** *adj* spacieux.
spade¹ [speid] *n* bêche *f*, pelle *f*.
spade² [speid] *n* (*cards*) pique *m*.
spaghetti [spəˈgeti] *n* spaghetti *m pl*.
Spain [spein] *n* Espagne *f*. **Spaniard** *n* Espagnol, -e *m*, *f*. **Spanish** *nm*, *adj* espagnol.
span [span] *n* envergure *f*, portée *f*; (*bridge*) travée *f*; (*time*) espace *m*, durée *f*. *v* enjamber.
spaniel [ˈspanjəl] *n* épagneul *m*.
spank [spaŋk] *v* donner une fessée à. **spanking** *n* fessée *f*.
spanner [ˈspanə] *n* clef (à écrous) *f*.
spare [speə] *adj* de réserve, de trop. **spare part** (*mot*) pièce détachée *f*. **spare-rib** *n* (*cookery*) côtelette dans l'échine *f*. **spare room** chambre d'ami *f*. **spare time** temps libre *m*. **spare tyre** pneu de réchange *m*; (*coll*) bourrelet *m*. **spare wheel** roue de secours *f*. *v* se passer de; (*save*) épargner. **sparing** *adj* limité, modéré.
spark [spaːk] *n* étincelle *f*. **spark-plug** *n* bougie *f*. *v* jeter des étincelles. **spark off** provoquer.
sparkle [ˈspaːkl] *n* scintillement *m*; (*in eye*) étincelle *f*. *v* étinceler, scintiller. **sparkling** *adj* (*drink*) pétillant.
sparrow [ˈsparou] *n* moineau *m*.
sparse [spaːs] *adj* clairsemé. **sparsely** *adv* peu.
spasm [ˈspazəm] *n* spasme *m*; (*fit*) accès *m*. **spasmodic** *adj* (*med*) spasmodique; irrégulier.
spastic [ˈspastik] *n*, *adj* handicapé, -e moteur.
spat [spat] *V* **spit¹**.
spatial [ˈspeiʃl] *adj* spatial.
spatula [ˈspatjulə] *n* spatule *f*.
spawn [spoːn] *n* frai *m*. *v* frayer.
***speak** [spiːk] *v* parler. **speak up** parler fort. **speaker** *n* orateur *m*; (*loudspeaker*) haut-parleur *m*.
spear [spiə] *n* lance *f*; (*asparagus*) pointe *f*.
special [ˈspeʃəl] *adj* spécial, particulier; extraordinaire. **specialist** *n* spécialiste *m*, *f*. **speciality** *n* spécialité *f*. **specialize** *v* se spécialiser.
species [ˈspiːʃiːz] *n* espèce *f*.
specify [ˈspesifai] *v* spécifier. **specific** *adj* précis; (*science*) spécifique. **specification** *n* spécification *f*; stipulation *f*.
specimen [ˈspesimin] *n* spécimen *m*; (*urine*) échantillon *m*; (*blood*) prélèvement *m*.
speck [spek] *n* grain *m*; petite tache *f*. **speckle** *v* tacheter.
spectacle [ˈspektəkl] *n* spectacle *m*. **spectacles** *pl n* lunettes *f pl*. **spectacular** *adj* spectaculaire.
spectator [spekˈteitə] *n* spectateur, -trice *m*, *f*.
spectrum [ˈspektrəm] *n* spectre *m*; (*range*) gamme *f*.
speculate [ˈspekjuleit] *v* spéculer; s'interroger. **speculation** *n* spéculation *f*; conjecture *f*. **speculative** *adj* spéculatif.
sped [sped] *V* **speed**.
speech [spiːtʃ] *n* (*faculty*) parole *f*; articulation *f*; (*address*) discours *m*. **speech day** distribution des prix *f*. **speech impediment** défaut d'élocution *m*. **speech therapy** orthophonie *f*. **speechless** *adj* muet.
***speed** [spiːd] *n* vitesse *f*; rapidité *f*. **speedboat** *n* vedette *f*. **speed limit** limitation de vitesse *f*. **speedometer** *n* compteur de vitesse *m*. *v* (*mot*) conduire trop vite. **speed along** aller à toute vitesse. **speed up** aller plus vite; accélérer. **speeding** *n* excès de vitesse *m*. **speedy** *adj* rapide.
***spell¹** [spel] *v* épeler; (*write*) écrire; signifier. **spelling** *n* orthographe *f*.

spell[2] [spel] *n* (*magic*) charme *m*, formule magique *f*. **spellbound** *adj* subjugué, envoûté.
spell[3] [spel] *n* période *f*; (*turn*) tour *m*.
spelt [spelt] *V* **spell**[1].
***spend** [spend] *v* (*money*) dépenser; (*time*) passer. **spendthrift** *n* dépensier, -ère *m*, *f*. **spending** *n* dépenses *f pl*. **spending money** argent de poche *m*.
spent [spent] *V* **spend**.
sperm [spəːm] *n* sperme *m*.
spew [spjuː] *v* vomir.
sphere [sfiə] *n* sphère *f*; domaine *m*. **spherical** *adj* sphérique.
spice [spais] *n* épice *f*. *v* épicer. **spicy** *adj* épicé.
spider ['spaidə] *n* araignée *f*.
spike [spaik] *n* pointe *f*.
***spill** [spil] *v* renverser, (se) répandre.
spilt [spilt] *V* **spill**.
***spin** [spin] *n* tournoiement *m*; (*drying*) essorage *m*; (*coll: ride*) balade *f*. *v* (*wool, etc.*) filer; (*turn*) (faire) tourner, tournoyer. **spin-dry** *v* essorer. **spin-dryer** *n* essoreuse *f*. **spin out** faire durer. **spinning** *n* filage *m*. **spinning top** toupie *f*. **spinning wheel** rouet *m*.
spinach ['spinidʒ] *n* (*bot*) épinard *m*; (*cookery*) épinards *m pl*.
spindle ['spindl] *n* (*spinning*) fuseau *m*, broche *f*; (*tech*) axe *m*, tige *f*. **spindly** *adj* grêle.
spine [spain] *n* (*anat*) colonne vertébrale; épine *f*; (*book*) dos *m*. **spinal** *adj* spinal, vertébral. **spiny** *adj* épineux.
spinster ['spinstə] *n* célibataire *f*.
spiral ['spaiərəl] *adj* en spirale. **spiral staircase** escalier tournant *m*. *n* spirale *f*.
spire ['spaiə] *n* flèche *f*.
spirit ['spirit] *n* esprit *m*; courage *m*; alcool *m*. **spirit-level** *n* niveau à bulle *m*. **spirited** *adj* fougueux. **spiritual** *adj* spirituel. **spiritualism** *n* spiritisme *m*. **spiritualist** *n* spirite *m*, *f*.
***spit**[1] [spit] *n* crachat *m*; salive *f*. *v* cracher.
spit[2] [spit] *n* (*cookery*) broche *f*; (*geog*) pointe *f*.
spite [spait] *n* rancune *f*. **in spite of** malgré. *v* vexer. **spiteful** *adj* malveillant.
splash [splaʃ] *n* éclaboussement *m*; (*sound*) plouf *m*; (*mark*) éclaboussure *f*, tache *f*. *v* éclabousser.
spleen [spliːn] *n* (*anat*) rate *f*; mauvaise humeur *f*.
splendid ['splendid] *adj* splendide; excellent. **splendour** *n* splendeur *f*.
splice [splais] *v* épisser.
splint [splint] *n* éclisse *f*.
splinter ['splintə] *n* éclat *m*; (*in finger*) écharde *f*. *v* (se) fendre en éclats, (se) briser en éclats.
***split** [split] *n* fente *f*, fissure *f*. *v* (se) fendre; (se) diviser; (*share*) (se) partager. **split second** fraction de seconde *f*.
splutter ['splʌtə] *v* (*person*) bredouiller; (*engine*) bafouiller; (*fire, fat, etc.*) crépiter. *n* bredouillement *m*; bafouillage *m*; crépitement *m*.
***spoil** [spoil] *v* gâter; (*damage*) (s')abîmer. **spoil-sport** *n* trouble-fête *m*, *f*. **spoils** *pl n* butin *m sing*.
spoke[1] [spouk] *V* **speak**.
spoke[2] [spouk] *n* rayon *m*.
spoken ['spoukn] *V* **speak**.
spokesman ['spouksmən] *n* porte-parole *m invar*.
sponge [spʌndʒ] *n* éponge *f*; (*cake*) gâteau de Savoie *m*. **sponge bag** sac de toilette *m*. *v* éponger. **sponge on** vivre aux crochets de. **spongy** *adj* spongieux.
sponsor ['sponsə] *n* personne (*f*) *or* organisme (*m*) qui assure le patronage; (*for loan*) répondant, -e *m*, *f*; (*fund-raising*) donateur, -trice *m*, *f*. *v* patronner. **sponsorship** *n* patronage *m*.
spontaneous [spon'teinjəs] *adj* spontané. **spontaneity** *n* spontanéité *f*.
spool [spuːl] *n* bobine *f*.
spoon [spuːn] *n* cuiller *f*. **spoonful** *n* cuillerée *f*.
sporadic [spə'radik] *adj* sporadique.
sport [spoːt] *n* sport *m*. **sports car** voiture de sport *f*. **sports jacket** veste sport *f*. **sportsman** *n* sportif *m*. **sportswoman** *n* sportive *f*. *v* exhiber. **sporting** *adj* sportif. **sportive** *adj* folâtre.
spot [spot] *n* (*mark*) tache *f*; (*pimple*) bouton *m*; (*polka dot*) pois *m*; (*place*) endroit *m*; (*small amount*) goutte *f*, grain *m*. **on the spot** sur le champ. **spot check** *n* contrôle intermittent *m*. **spotlight** *n* (rayon de) projecteur *m*. *v* tacher; (*see*) apercevoir. **spotless** *adj* immaculé. **spotted** *adj* tacheté; à pois. **spotty** *adj* boutonneux.
spouse [spaus] *n* (*law*) conjoint, -e *m*, *f*.
spout [spaut] *n* bec *m*; jet *m*. *v* (faire) jaillir; (*coll: recite*) débiter.

sprain [sprein] *n* entorse *f*. *v* fouler.
sprang [spraŋ] *V* **spring**.
sprawl [sproːl] *v* s'étaler, être affalé.
spray[1] [sprei] *n* gouttelettes *f pl*; (*from aerosol*) pulvérisation *f*; bombe *f*, aérosol *m*. *v* (*water*) asperger; vaporiser, pulvériser.
spray[2] [sprei] *n* (*flowers*) gerbe *f*; branche *f*.
***spread** [spred] *n* propagation *f*, diffusion *f*; (*span*) envergure *f*; (*paste*) pâte *f*; (*coll: meal*) festin *m*. *v* (s')étaler, (s')étendre; (se) propager, (se) communiquer. **spread-eagled** *adj* vautré. **spread out** (s')étaler; se disperser.
spree [spriː] *n* fête *f*.
sprig [sprig] *n* brin *m*.
sprightly ['spraitli] *adj* alerte.
***spring** [spriŋ] *n* (*leap*) bond *m*; (*coil*) ressort *m*; (*water*) source *f*; (*season*) printemps *m*. **spring-board** *n* tremplin *m*. **spring-cleaning** *n* grand nettoyage *m*. **spring onion** ciboule *f*. *v* bondir. **spring up** surgir, jaillir. **springy** *adj* souple.
sprinkle ['spriŋkl] *v* asperger; (*sugar, etc.*) saupoudrer. **sprinkler** *n* (*garden*) arroseur *m*; (*fire*) diffuseur *m*. **sprinkling** *n* aspersion *f*; légère couche *f*.
sprint [sprint] *n* sprint *m*. *v* (*sport*) sprinter; foncer un sprint.
sprout [spraut] *n* pousse *f*, germe *m*. **Brussels sprouts** choux de Bruxelles *m pl*. *v* pousser, germer.
spruce [spruːs] *v* **spruce up** faire beau *or* belle.
sprung [sprʌŋ] *V* **spring**.
spun [spʌn] *V* **spin**.
spur [spəː] *n* éperon *m*. **on the spur of the moment** sous l'impulsion du moment. *v* éperonner.
spurious ['spjuəriəs] *adj* faux, fausse.
spurn [spəːn] *v* repousser.
spurt [spəːt] *n* (*water*) jet *m*; (*energy*) sursaut *m*; effort soudain *m*. *v* jaillir.
spy [spai] *n* espion, -onne *m, f*. *v* espionner; (*see*) apercevoir. **spying** *n* espionnage *m*.
squabble ['skwobl] *n* chamaillerie *f*. *v* se chamailler.
squad [skwod] *n* escouade *f*, groupe *m*.
squadron ['skwodrən] *n* (*mil*) escadron *m*; (*naut*) escadrille *f*.
squalid ['skwolid] *adj* misérable, sordide; (*dirty*) sale.
squall [skwoːl] *n* rafale *f*.
squander ['skwondə] *v* gaspiller.
square [skweə] *n* carré *m*; (*on chessboard, grid*) case *f*; (*in town*) place *f*. *adj* carré; en ordre. *v* carrer; (*settle*) régler.
squash [skwoʃ] *n* (*sport*) squash *m*; (*drink*) sirop *m*; (*crush*) cohue *f*. *v* (s')écraser; (*together*) (se) serrer.
squat [skwot] *adj* ramassé, courtaud. *v* s'accroupir; (*in house*) faire du squattage. **squatter** *n* squatter *m*.
squawk [skwoːk] *v* pousser des gloussements. *n* gloussement *m*, cri rauque *m*.
squeak [skwiːk] *n* grincement *m*; (*mouse, etc.*) petit cri aigu *m*. *v* grincer; (*mouse*) vagir.
squeal [skwiːl] *n* cri aigu *m*; (*brakes*) grincement *m*. *v* pousser un cri aigu; grincer.
squeamish ['skwiːmiʃ] *adj* délicat, facilement dégoûté.
squeeze [skwiːz] *n* pression *f*. *v* presser, serrer; (*extract*) exprimer.
squid [skwid] *n* calmar *m*.
squiggle ['skwigl] *n* gribouillis *m*. *v* gribouiller.
squint [skwint] *n* (*med*) strabisme *m*; (*glance*) coup d'œil *m*. *v* loucher.
squirm [skwəːm] *v* se tortiller; (*person*) avoir un haut-le-corps.
squirrel ['skwirəl] *n* écureuil *m*.
squirt [skwəːt] *n* jet *m*. *v* (faire) jaillir; asperger.
stab [stab] *n* coup de couteau *m*. *v* poignarder; donner un coup de couteau à.
stabilize ['steibilaiz] *v* stabiliser. **stabilizer** *n* stabilisateur *m*.
stable[1] ['steibl] *n* écurie *f*.
stable[2] ['steibl] *adj* stable; solide; constant. **stability** *n* stabilité *f*; solidité *f*.
staccato [stə'kaːtou] *adv* staccato. *adj* (*voice, sounds, etc.*) saccadé.
stack [stak] *n* (*pile*) tas *m*; (*hay, etc.*) meule *f*; (*chimneys*) souche de cheminée *f*. **stacks of** (*coll*) un tas de. *v* empiler, entasser.
stadium ['steidiəm] *n* stade *m*.
staff [staːf] *n* personnel *m*; bâton *m*. **staff-room** *n* (*school*) salle des professeurs *f*.
stag [stag] *n* cerf *m*. **stag party** (*coll*) réunion entre hommes *f*.
stage [steidʒ] *n* (*theatre*) scène *f*; (*platform*) estrade *f*; (*point*) étape *f*. **stage fright** trac *m*. **stage-manager** *n* régisseur

m. **stage name** nom de théâtre *m.* **stage whisper** aparté *m.* *v* monter; organiser.
stagger ['stagə] *v* chanceler; (*amaze*) stupéfier; (*payments, etc.*) échelonner. **staggering** *adj* renversant.
stagnant ['stagnənt] *adj* stagnant. **stagnate** *v* croupir, stagner. **stagnation** *n* stagnation *f.*
staid [steid] *adj* (*person*) posé; (*opinion*) pondéré.
stain [stein] *n* tache *f*; colorant *m.* **stain remover** détachant *m.* *v* tacher; (*wood*) teinter. **stained glass** verre coloré *m*; (*windows*) vitraux *m pl.* **stainless steel** acier inoxydable *m.*
stair [steə] *n* marche *f.* **staircase** *n* escalier *m.* **stairs** *pl n* escalier *m sing.*
stake[1] [steik] *n* (*post*) pieu *m*; (*for execution*) bûcher *m.* *v* jalonner.
stake[2] [steik] *n* (*betting*) enjeu *m*; intérêt *m.* **at stake** en jeu. *v* jouer.
stale [steil] *adj* (*bread*) rassis; (*air*) confiné; (*joke*) rebattu. **staleness** *n* manque de fraîcheur *m.*
stalemate ['steilmeit] *n* (*chess*) pat *m*; impasse *f.*
stalk[1] [stoːk] *n* (*plant*) tige *f*; (*fruit*) queue *f.*
stalk[2] [stoːk] *v* traquer. **stalk in/out** entrer/sortir avec raideur.
stall[1] [stoːl] *n* (*market*) éventaire *m*; kiosque *m*; (*theatre*) fauteuil d'orchestre *m*; (*cowshed*) stalle *f.* **stalls** *pl n* orchestre *m sing.* *v* (*car, etc.*) caler.
stall[2] [stoːl] *v* (*delay*) atermoyer. **stall off** tenir à distance.
stallion ['staljən] *n* étalon *m.*
stamina ['staminə] *n* vigueur *f*, résistance *f.*
stammer ['stamə] *n* bégaiement *m.* *v* bégayer.
stamp [stamp] *n* timbre *m*; (*mark*) cachet *m*; (*with foot*) trépignement *m.* **stamp-collecting** *n* philatélie *f.* *v* timbrer, tamponner; (*with foot*) taper du pied, trépigner.
stampede [stam'piːd] *n* débandade *f*; (*rush*) ruée *f.* *v* fuir à la débandade; se ruer.
***stand** [stand] *n* position *f*; support *m*; (*comm*) étalage *m*; (*at exhibition*) stand *m.* *v* être debout; (*get up*) se lever; (*put*) mettre; (*tolerate*) supporter; (*be based*) reposer. **stand for** représenter; tolérer. **stand out** ressortir. **standstill** *n* arrêt *m.* **come to a standstill** s'immobiliser, s'arrêter. **stand up for** défendre.
standard ['standəd] *n* norme *f*, critère *m*, niveau (voulu) *m*; (*flag*) étendard *m.* *adj* normal, ordinaire; (*comm*) standard *invar*; (*measure*) étalon *invar*; correct. **standard lamp** lampadaire *m.* **standardize** *v* standardiser.
standing ['standiŋ] *adj* debout; fixe; permanent. **standing order** (*bank*) virement automatique *m.* *n* importance *f*, standing *m*; durée *f.*
stank [staŋk] *V* **stink**.
stanza ['stanzə] *n* strophe *f.*
staple[1] [steipl] *n* (*papers*) agrafe *f*; (*tech*) crampon *m.* *v* agrafer; cramponner.
staple[2] [steipl] *adj* principal; de base.
star [staː] *n* étoile *f*; astérisque *m*; (*cinema, etc.*) vedette *f.* **starfish** *n* étoile de mer *f.* *v* étoiler; (*film*) avoir pour vedette; (*person*) être la vedette. **stardom** *n* célébrité *f.* **starry** *adj* étoilé.
starboard ['staːbəd] *n* tribord *m.*
starch [staːtʃ] *n* amidon *m.* *v* amidonner. **starchy** *adj* (*food*) féculent; (*person*) guindé.
stare [steə] *n* regard fixe *m.* *v* dévisager, regarder fixement.
stark [staːk] *adj* désolé, austère; (*stiff*) raide; (*utter*) pur. **stark naked** complètement nu.
starling ['staːliŋ] *n* étourneau *m.*
start [staːt] *n* commencement *m*, départ *m*; (*jump*) sursaut *m.* *v* commencer; (*clock, etc.*) mettre en marche; (*leave*) partir; (*car*) démarrer; sursauter. **starter** *n* (*sport*) starter *m*; (*mot*) démarreur *m*; (*meal*) hors-d'œuvre *m.*
startle ['staːtl] *v* faire sursauter. **startling** *adj* surprenant.
starve [staːv] *v* manquer de nourriture; (*to death*) (faire) mourir de faim; (*deliberately*) affamer; (*deprive*) priver. **starvation** *n* inanition *f*, famine *f.* **starving** *adj* affamé. **be starving** (*coll*) avoir une faim de loup.
state [steit] *n* état *m*; pompe *f.* **statesman** *n* homme d'État *m.* *v* déclarer; formuler; fixer. **stately** *adj* majestueux. **statement** *n* déclaration; (*law*) déposition *f*; (*bank*) relevé *m.*
static ['statik] *adj* statique. *n* (*elec, radio, etc.*) parasites *m pl.*

station ['steiʃən] *n* (*rail*) gare *f*; (*radio, underground*) station *f*; (*position*) poste *m*; (*in life*) rang *m*. *v* poster, placer.
stationary ['steiʃənəri] *adj* stationnaire.
stationer ['steiʃənə] *n* papetier, -ère *m, f*. **stationer's** *n* papeterie *f*. **stationery** *n* articles de bureau *m pl*; papier à lettres *m*.
statistics [stə'tistiks] *n* (*science*) statistique *f*. *pl n* statistiques *f pl*. **statistical** *adj* statistique.
statue ['statjuː] *n* statue *f*.
stature ['statʃə] *n* stature *f*; importance *f*, envergure *f*.
status ['steitəs] *n* situation *f*; prestige *m*.
statute ['statjuːt] *n* loi *f*. **statutory** *adj* statutaire; légal.
staunch [stoːntʃ] *adj* loyal, dévoué.
stay [stei] *n* séjour *m*. *v* rester; loger.
steadfast ['stedfaːst] *adj* ferme; constant.
steady ['stedi] *adj* stable, solide; constant, régulier. *v* maintenir; (*person*) reprendre son aplomb; (se) calmer. **steadily** *adv* fermement; progressivement; sans arrêt. **steadiness** *n* stabilité *f*; constance *f*.
steak [steik] *n* bifteck *m*; (*of pork, fish*) tranche *f*.
***steal** [stiːl] *v* voler. **stealing** *n* vol *m*.
stealthy ['stelθi] *adj* furtif.
steam [stiːm] *n* vapeur *f*. **steam-roller** *n* rouleau compresseur *m*. *v* fumer; (*cookery*) cuire à la vapeur. **steam up** se couvrir de buée.
steel [stiːl] *n* acier *m*. **steel wool** paille de fer *f*. **steelworks** *n* aciérie *f*. **steely** *adj* dur, d'acier.
steep[1] [stiːp] *adj* raide.
steep[2] [stiːp] *v* tremper.
steeple ['stiːpl] *n* clocher *m*. **steeplechase** *n* steeple *m*.
steer [stiə] *v* (*ship*) gouverner; (*car*) conduire; (*person*) guider. **steering** *n* conduite *f*. **steering-wheel** *n* volant *m*.
stem[1] [stem] *n* tige *f*; (*glass*) pied *m*. *v* **stem from** provenir de.
stem[2] [stem] *v* (*stop*) contenir, endiguer.
stench [stentʃ] *n* puanteur *f*.
stencil ['stensl] *n* pochoir *m*; (*typing*) stencil *m*.
step [step] *n* pas *m*; mesure *f*; (*stair*) marche *f*. **step-ladder** *n* escabeau *m*. *v* faire un pas; marcher. **step up** augmenter, intensifier.
stepbrother ['stepbrʌðə] *n* demi-frère *m*.
stepdaughter ['stepdoːtə] *n* belle-fille *f*.
stepfather ['stepfaːðə] *n* beau-père *m*.
stepmother ['stepmʌðə] *n* belle-mère *f*.
stepsister ['stepsistə] *n* demi-sœur *f*.
stepson ['stepsʌn] *n* beau-fils *m*.
stereo ['steriou] *nf, adj* stéréo. **stereophonic** *adj* stéréophonique.
stereotype ['steriətaip] *n* stéréotype *m*; (*printing*) cliché *m*. *v* stéréotyper; clicher.
sterile ['sterail] *adj* stérile. **sterility** *n* stérilité *f*. **sterilization** *n* stérilisation *f*. **sterilize** *v* stériliser.
sterling ['stəːliŋ] *n* livres sterling *f pl*. *adj* (*silver*) fin; (*character*) solide.
stern[1] [stəːn] *adj* sévère.
stern[2] [stəːn] *n* arrière *m*.
stethoscope ['steθəskoup] *n* stéthoscope *m*.
stew [stjuː] *n* ragoût *m*. *v* (*meat*) cuire en ragoût; (*fruit*) faire cuire.
steward ['stjuəd] *n* intendant *m*; (*plane, ship*) steward *m*. **stewardess** *n* hôtesse *f*.
stick[1] [stik] *n* bâton *m*; petite branche *f*; (*walking*) canne *f*.
***stick**[2] [stik] *v* (*stab*) planter, enfoncer; (*glue*) coller (*put*) mettre; (*get jammed*) être bloqué; (*slang*: *put up with*) supporter; (*stay*) rester. **stick out** sortir, (faire) dépasser. **stick up for** défendre. **sticky** *adj* poisseux, gluant.
stickler ['stiklə] *n* **be a stickler for** insister sur; être pointilleux sur.
stiff [stif] *adj* raide, rigide; (*hard to move*) dur; (*exam*) difficile; (*cool*) froid. **stiff neck** torticolis *m*. **stiffen** *v* (se) raidir; renforcer. **stiffness** *n* raideur *f*.
stifle ['staifl] *v* étouffer; (*smile, etc.*) réprimer. **stifling** *adj* suffocant.
stigma ['stigmə] *n* stigmate *m*.
stile [stail] *n* échalier *m*.
still[1] [stil] *adv* encore; (*anyway*) quand même; (*sit, stand*) sans bouger. *adj* calme, tranquille. **stillborn** *adj* mort-né. **still life** nature morte. *n* (*cinema*) photo *f*.
still[2] [stil] *n* alambic *m*; distillerie *f*.
stilt [stilt] *n* échasse *f*. **stilted** *adj* guindé.
stimulus ['stimjuləs] *n, pl* **-li** stimulus (*pl* -li) *m*; impulsion *f*, stimulant *m*. **stimulant** *nm, adj* stimulant. **stimulate** *v* stimuler. **stimulation** *n* stimulation *f*.
***sting** [stiŋ] *n* (*insect*) dard *m*; (*wound*) piqûre *f*; (*iodine*) brûlure. *v* piquer; brûler; (*whip*) cingler.

***stink** [stiŋk] *n* puanteur *f*. *v* puer, empester.
stint [stint] *n* ration de travail *f*. *v* lésiner sur.
stipulate ['stipjuleit] *v* stipuler. **stipulation** *n* stipulation *f*.
stir [stəː] *n* agitation *f*, sensation *f*. *v* (*tea, etc.*) tourner; (*move*) agiter, remuer; exciter.
stirrup ['stirəp] *n* étrier *m*.
stitch [stitʃ] *n* (*sewing*) point *m*; (*knitting*) maille *f*; (*med*) point de suture *m*; (*pain*) point de côté *m*. *v* coudre; (*med*) suturer.
stoat [stout] *n* hermine *f*.
stock [stok] *n* réserve *f*; (*farm*) cheptel *m*; (*cookery*) bouillon *m*; (*lineage*) souche *f*. **stockbroker** *n* agent de change *m*. **Stock Exchange** Bourse *f*. **stockpile** *v* stocker. **stocks and shares** valeurs *f pl*. **stocktaking** *n* inventaire *m*. *v* approvisionner.
Stockholm ['stokhoum] *n* Stockholm.
stocking ['stokiŋ] *n* bas *m*. **in one's stocking feet** sans chaussures.
stocky ['stoki] *adj* trapu.
stodge [stodʒ] (*coll*) *n* aliment bourratif *m*. **stodgy** *adj* bourratif.
stoical ['stouikl] *adj* stoïque.
stoke [stouk] *v* (*fire*) garnir; (*furnace*) alimenter; (*boiler*) chauffer.
stole[1] [stoul] *V* **steal**.
stole[2] [stoul] *n* étole *f*.
stolen ['stoulən] *V* **steal**.
stomach ['stʌmək] *n* estomac *m*; (*abdomen*) ventre *m*. **stomach-ache** *n* mal à l'estomac *m*. *v* supporter.
stone [stoun] *n* pierre *f*; (*of fruit*) noyau *m*; (*med*) calcul *m*. **stone-cold** *adj* complètement froid. *v* lapider; dénoyauter. **stony** *adj* pierreux; dur.
stood [stud] *V* **stand**.
stool [stuːl] *n* tabouret *m*.
stoop [stuːp] *v* se pencher, se courber; avoir le dos voûté; (*descend*) s'abaisser (jusqu'à).
stop [stop] *n* arrêt *m*. *v* (s')arrêter; cesser; (*block*) boucher; (*prevent*) empêcher. **stop-press** *n* dernière heure *f*. **stop thief!** au voleur! **stop-watch** *n* chronomètre *m*. **stoppage** *n* arrêt *m*; obstruction *f*; (*strike*) grève *f*. **stopper** *n* bouchon *m*.
store [stoː] *n* provision *f*; (*depot*) entrepôt *m*; (*shop*) magasin *m*. *v* mettre en réserve; emmagasiner. **storage** *n* entreposage *m*. **storage space** espace de rangement *m*.
storey ['stoːri] *n* étage *m*.
stork [stoːk] *n* cicogne *f*.
storm [stoːm] *n* tempête *f*; (*thunder*) orage *m*. *v* (*mil*) prendre d'assaut; (*wind, rain*) faire rage; (*person*) fulminer. **stormy** *adj* orageux.
story ['stoːri] *n* histoire *f*.
stout [staut] *adj* gros, grosse; solide; intrépide. *n* stout *m*.
stove [stouv] *n* (*cooker*) fourneau *m*; (*heater*) poêle *m*.
stow [stou] *v* ranger. **stow away** voyager clandestinement. **stowaway** *n* passager clandestin, passagère clandestine *m, f*.
straddle ['stradl] *v* enfourcher, enjamber, être à califourchon (sur).
straggle ['stragl] *v* (*plant*) pousser au hasard; (*hair*) être en désordre; (*village*) s'étendre en longueur. **straggler** *n* traînard, -e *m, f*.
straight [streit] *adj* droit; en ordre; franc, franche. *adv* droit; (*directly*) tout droit. **straight ahead** tout droit. **straight away** tout de suite. **straightforward** *adj* simple; honnête. **straighten** *v* redresser; mettre en ordre.
strain[1] [strein] *n* tension *f*, effort *m*; (*med*) entorse *f*. *v* forcer, tendre fortement; (*med*) froisser, filtrer; s'efforcer, peiner. **strainer** *n* passoire *f*.
strain[2] [strein] *n* race *f*; tendance *f*.
strait [streit] *n* détroit *m*.
strand[1] [strand] *n* brin *m*, fibre *f*, fil *m*.
strand[2] [strand] *v* laisser en rade; (*ship*) échouer.
strange [streindʒ] *adj* étrange; (*unfamiliar*) inconnu. **stranger** *n* inconnu, -e *m, f*.
strangle ['strangl] *v* étrangler.
strap [strap] *n* lanière *f*, sangle *f*; (*on garment*) bretelle *f*. *v* attacher avec une sangle. **strapping** *adj* costaud.
strategy ['stratədʒi] *n* stratégie *f*. **strategic** *adj* stratégique.
stratum ['straːtəm] *n*, *pl* **-ta** strate *f*, couche *f*.
straw [stroː] *n* paille *f*. **it's the last straw!** c'est le comble!
strawberry ['stroːbəri] *n* (*fruit*) fraise *f*; (*plant*) fraisier *m*.
stray [strei] *n* animal errant *m*. *adj* errant, perdu; isolé. *v* s'égarer, errer.
streak [striːk] *n* raie *f*; tendance *f*. *v* zébrer, strier.

stream [striːm] *n* ruisseau *m*; courant *m*; flot *m*, torrent *m*. **streamlined** *adj* (*aero*) fuselé; (*mot*) aérodynamique; (*efficient*) rationalisé. *v* ruisseler; (*school*) répartir par niveau. **streamer** *n* serpentin *m*.

street [striːt] *n* rue *f*.

strength [streŋθ] *n* force *f*. **strengthen** *v* fortifier; consolider; augmenter.

strenuous ['strenjuəs] *adj* ardu; vigoureux, acharné.

stress [stres] *n* pression *f*; accent *m*; tension *f*; insistance *f*; (*tech*) travail *m*. *v* insister sur; accentuer.

stretch [stretʃ] *n* (*action*) étirement *m*; (*distance*) étendue *f*; période *f*. *v* (s')étirer, (se) tendre; (*reach*) s'étendre. **stretcher** *n* brancard *m*.

stricken ['strikən] *adj* affligé.

strict [strikt] *adj* strict; exact. **strictly** *adv* strictement. **strictly speaking** à proprement parler. **strictness** *n* sévérité *f*; exactitude *f*.

***stride** [straid] *n* grand pas *m*, enjambée *f*. *v* marcher à grands pas.

strident ['straidənt] *adj* strident.

strife [straif] *n* conflit *m*; querelles *f pl*.

***strike** [straik] *n* (*industry*) grève *f*; (*hit*) coup *m*; (*oil, etc.*) découverte *f*. *v* (*hit*) frapper, heurter; faire grève; (*clock*) sonner; découvrir; (*match*) allumer, frotter. **striker** *n* grèviste *m, f*. **striking** *adj* frappant; en grève.

***string** [striŋ] *n* ficelle *f*; (*violin, racket, etc.*) corde *f*. **string bag** filet à provisions *m*. **string quartet** quatuor à cordes *m*. **string vest** gilet de coton à grosses mailles *m*. *v* (*beads*) enfiler; (*hang*) suspendre. **stringy** *adj* filandreux.

stringent ['strindʒənt] *adj* rigoureux.

strip[1] [strip] *v* dépouiller; (*undress*) (se) déshabiller; (*bed*) défaire. **strip off** enlever. **strip-tease** *n* strip-tease *m*. **stripper** *n* strip-teaseuse *f*; (*paint*) décapant *m*.

strip[2] [strip] *n* bande *f*. **strip cartoon** bande dessinée *f*.

stripe [straip] *n* raie *f*, rayure *f*. **striped** *adj* rayé.

***strive** [straiv] *v* s'efforcer (de).

strode [stroud] *V* **stride**.

stroke[1] [strouk] *n* coup *m*; (*swimming*) nage *f*; (*mark*) trait *m*; (*med*) attaque d'apoplexie *f*.

stroke[2] [strouk] *v* caresser. *n* caresse *f*.

stroll [stroul] *n* petite promenade *f*, tour *m*. *v* se promener nonchalamment, flâner.

strong [stroŋ] *adj*, *adv* fort; solide. **stronghold** *n* bastion *m*; (*mil*) forteresse *f*. **strong-minded** *adj* résolu. **strong-room** *n* chambre forte.

strove [strouv] *V* **strive**.

struck [strʌk] *V* **strike**.

structure ['strʌktʃə] *n* structure *f*; construction *f*. **structural** *adj* structural; de construction.

struggle ['strʌgl] *n* lutte *f*. *v* lutter; (*to escape*) se débattre. **struggle in/out** entrer/sortir avec peine.

strum [strʌm] *v* (*guitar*) racler; (*piano*) tapoter (de).

strung [strʌŋ] *V* **string**.

strut[1] [strʌt] *v* se pavaner.

strut[2] [strʌt] *n* étai *m*, support *m*.

stub [stʌb] *n* bout *m*; (*tree*) souche *f*; (*cheque*) talon *m*. *v* (*toe, etc.*) cogner. **stub out** écraser.

stubble ['stʌbl] *n* chaume *m*.

stubborn ['stʌbən] *adj* obstiné, opiniâtre. **stubbornness** *n* obstination *f*, opiniâtreté *f*.

stuck [stʌk] *V* **stick**[2].

stud[1] [stʌd] *n* clou (à grosse tête) *m*. *v* clouter. **studded with** parsemé de.

stud[2] [stʌd] *n* écurie *f*; (*farm*) haras *m*. **be at stud** étalonner.

student ['stjuːdənt] *n* étudiant, -e *m, f*; (*trainee*) stagiaire *m, f*.

studio ['stjuːdiou] *n* studio *m*.

study ['stʌdi] *n* étude *f*; (*room*) bureau *m*. *v* étudier, faire des études. **studious** *adj* studieux.

stuff [stʌf] *n* choses *f pl*; substance *f*; (*fabric*) étoffe *f*. *v* rembourrer; (*cram*) bourrer; (*thrust*) fourrer; (*cookery*) farcir; (*animal*) empailler. **stuffing** *n* bourre *f*, farce *f*; paille *f*. **stuffy** *adj* mal ventilé; (*person*) collet monté *invar*.

stumble [stʌmbl] *v* trébucher.

stump [stʌmp] *n* (*tree*) souche *f*; (*limb*) moignon *m*; (*pencil, etc.*) bout *m*; (*cricket*) piquet *m*. *v* (*sport*) mettre hors jeu; (*coll*) coller, faire sécher.

stun [stʌn] *v* étourdir; (*amaze*) abasourdir. **stunning** *adj* stupéfiant; (*coll*) sensationnel.

stung [stʌŋ] *V* **sting**.

stunk [stʌŋk] *V* **stink**.

stunt[1] [stʌnt] *v* retarder (la croissance de). **stunted** *adj* rabougri.

stunt[2] [stʌnt] *n* tour de force *m*; (*aero*) acrobatie *f*; (*trick, publicity*) truc *m*. **stunt man** cascadeur *m*.

stupid ['stjuːpid] *adj* stupide. **stupidity** *n* stupidité *f*.

stupor ['stjuːpə] *n* stupeur *f*.

sturdy ['stəːdi] *adj* robuste, vigoureux. **sturdiness** *n* robustesse *f*, vigueur *f*.

sturgeon ['stəːdʒən] *n* esturgeon *m*.

stutter ['stʌtə] *n* bégaiement *m*. *v* bégayer.

sty [stai] *n* porcherie *f*.

style [stail] *n* style *m*; (*dress*) mode *f*; (*hair*) coiffure *f*; (*type*) genre *m*. *v* créer; (*call*) appeler. **stylish** *adj* élégant, chic *invar*.

stylus ['stailəs] *n* (*tool*) style *m*; (*record player*) pointe de lecture *f*.

suave [swaːv] *adj* doucereux.

subconscious [sʌb'konʃəs] *nm, adj* subconscient.

subcontract [sʌbkən'trakt] *v* sous-traiter. **subcontractor** *n* sous-traitant *m*.

subdivide [sʌbdi'vaid] *v* (se) subdiviser. **subdivision** *n* subdivision *f*.

subdue [səb'djuː] *v* (*riot*) subjuguer; (*feelings*) contenir; (*light*) adoucir. **subdued** *adj* contenu; faible; (*voice*) bas, basse; (*lighting*) tamisé.

subject ['sʌbdʒikt; *v* səb'dʒekt] *n* sujet *m*; (*school*) matière *f*; (*people*) sujet, -ette *m, f*. *adj, adv* **subject to** sujet à; à condition de; exposé à. *v* soumettre; exposer. **subjection** *n* sujétion *f*. **subjective** *adj* subjectif.

subjunctive [səb'dʒʌŋktiv] *nm, adj* subjonctif.

sublet [sʌb'let] *v* sous-louer.

sublime [sə'blaim] *nm, adj* sublime.

submarine ['sʌbməriːn] *n* sous-marin *m*.

submerge [səb'məːdʒ] *v* submerger. **submersion** *n* submersion *f*.

submit [səb'mit] *v* (se) soumettre. **submission** *n* soumission *f*. **submissive** *adj* soumis.

subnormal [sʌb'noːməl] *adj* au-dessous de la normale; (*person*) arriéré.

subordinate [sə'boːdinət] *adj* subalterne; (*gramm*) subordonné. *n* subalterne *m, f*; subordonné, -e *m, f*. *v* subordonner. **subordination** *n* subordination *f*.

subscribe [səb'skraib] *v* **subscribe to** souscrire à; (*newspaper*) s'abonner à. **subscriber** *n* souscripteur, -trice *m, f*; abonné, -e *m, f*. **subscription** *n* souscription *f*; (*club*) cotisation *f*; abonnement *m*.

subsequent ['sʌbsikwənt] *adj* ultérieur, -e, suivant; résultant.

subservient [səb'səːviənt] *adj* subalterne; (*derog*) obséquieux.

subside [səb'said] *v* (*land*) s'affaisser; (*flood*) baisser; (*wind*) se calmer. **subsidence** *n* affaissement *m*.

subsidiary [səb'sidiəri] *adj* subsidiaire, accessoire. *n* (*comm*) filiale *f*.

subsidize ['sʌbsidaiz] *v* subventionner. **subsidy** *n* subvention *f*.

subsist [səb'sist] *v* subsister. **subsistence** *n* subsistance *f*.

substance ['sʌbstəns] *n* substance *f*. **substantial** *adj* important, substantiel.

substandard [sʌb'standəd] *adj* de qualité inférieure.

substitute ['sʌbstitjuːt] *n* (*person*) remplaçant, -e *m, f*; (*thing*) succédané *m*. *v* substituer, remplacer. **substitution** *n* substitution *f*.

subtitle ['sʌbtaitl] *n* sous-titre *m*. *v* sous-titrer.

subtle ['sʌtl] *adj* subtil. **subtlety** *n* subtilité *f*.

subtract [səb'trakt] *v* soustraire. **subtraction** *n* soustraction *f*.

suburb ['sʌbəːb] *n* faubourg *m*. **suburbs** *pl n* banlieue *f sing*. **suburban** *adj* suburbain.

subvert [səb'vəːt] *v* bouleverser; corrompre. **subversion** *n* subversion *f*. **subversive** *adj* subversif.

subway ['sʌbwei] *n* passage souterrain *m*; (*US*) métro *m*.

succeed [sək'siːd] *v* réussir; (*follow*) succéder à. **succeeding** *adj* suivant; à venir. **success** *n* succès *m*, réussite *f*. **successful** *adj* couronné de succès, qui a réussi. **successfully** *adv* avec succès. **succession** *n* succession *f*. **successive** *adj* successif, consécutif. **successor** *n* successeur *m*.

succinct [sək'siŋkt] *adj* succinct.

succulent ['sʌkjulənt] *adj* succulent.

succumb [sə'kʌm] *v* succomber.

such [sʌtʃ] *adj* tel, pareil; (*so much*) tant (de). **such as** tel que. *adv* si, tellement; (*as*) aussi. *pron* (*those*) ceux, celles; tel, telle.

suck [sʌk] *v* sucer; (*baby*) téter. **suck up to** (*slang*) faire de la lèche à

swagger ['swagə] *n* air important *m*. *v* plastronner; (*boast*) se vanter.
swallow[1] ['swolou] *v* avaler. **swallow up** engloutir. *n* avalement *m*; (*amount*) gorgée *f*.
swallow[2] ['swolou] *n* (*bird*) hirondelle *f*.
swam [swam] *V* **swim**.
swamp [swomp] *n* marais *m*. *v* inonder, submerger. **swampy** *adj* marécageux.
swan [swon] *n* cygne *m*.
swank [swaŋk] (*coll*) *n* esbroufe *f*. *v* faire de l'esbroufe. **swank about** se vanter de.
swap *or* **swop** [swop] *n* troc *m*; double *m*. *v* échanger.
swarm [swoːm] *n* essaim *m*; (*ants*) fourmillement *m*. *v* essaimer; fourmiller. **swarm in/out** entrer/sortir en masse.
swarthy ['swoːði] *adj* basané.
swat [swot] *v* écraser.
sway [swei] *n* balancement *m*, oscillation *f*. *v* (se) balancer, osciller; influencer.
***swear** [sweə] *v* jurer. **swear in** assermenter. **swear-word** *n* juron *m*.
sweat [swet] *n* sueur *f*. *v* suer. **sweater** *n* tricot *m*.
swede [swiːd] *n* rutabaga *m*.
Sweden ['swiːdn] *n* Suède *f*. **Swede** *n* Suédois, -e *m*, *f*. **Swedish** *nm*, *adj* suédois.
***sweep** [swiːp] *n* (*chimney*) ramoneur *m*; coup de balai *m*; grand geste *m*; (*curve*) grande courbe *f*. *v* balayer; ramoner. **sweep in/out** entrer/sortir rapidement *or* majestueusement. **sweeping** *adj* large; radical. **sweeping statement** généralisation hâtive *f*.
sweet [swiːt] *adj* doux, douce; (*taste*) sucré; (*kind*) gentil, -ille; (*attractive*) mignon, -onne. *n* bonbon *m*; dessert *m*. **sweetbread** *n* ris de veau *m*. **sweet corn** maïs sucré *m*. **sweetheart** *n* bien-aimé, -e *m*, *f*. **sweet pea** pois de senteur *m*. **sweet-shop** *n* confiserie *f*. **sweeten** *v* sucrer. **sweetly** *adj* (*sing*) mélodieusement; (*smile*) gentiment. **sweetness** *n* goût sucré *m*; douceur *f*.
***swell** [swel] *n* (*sea*) houle *f*. *v* (se) gonfler, (s')enfler, grossir. **swelling** *n* enflure *f*.
swelter ['sweltə] *v* étouffer de chaleur. **sweltering** *adj* étouffant.
swept [swept] *V* **sweep**.
swerve [swəːv] *v* dévier; (*car*, *ship*) faire une embardée. *n* embardée *f*.
swift [swift] *adj* prompt, rapide. *n* (*bird*) martinet *m*. **swiftness** *n* rapidité *f*.
swill [swil] *v* laver à grande eau, rincer. *n* (*for pigs*) pâtée *f*.
***swim** [swim] *v* nager; (*cross*) traverser à la nage. *n* baignade *f*. **swimmer** *n* nageur, -euse *m*, *f*. **swimming** *n* nage *f*, natation *f*. **swimming baths** *or* **pool** piscine *f*. **swimming costume** maillot de bain *m*.
swindle ['swindl] *n* escroquerie *f*. *v* escroquer. **swindler** *n* escroc *m*.
swine [swain] *n* pourceau; (*impol*) salaud *m*.
***swing** [swiŋ] *n* balancement *m*; (*pol*) revirement *m*; rythme *m*; (*in playground*) balançoire *f*. **be in full swing** battre son plein. **swing-door** *n* porte battante *f*. *v* (se) balancer, (faire) osciller; (*turn*) virer; influencer.
swipe [swaip] (*coll*) *n* grand coup *m*. *v* (*hit*) frapper à toute volée; (*take*) calotter.
swirl [swəːl] *n* tourbillon *m*, volute *f*. *v* tourbillonner.
swish [swiʃ] *n* bruissement *m*, sifflement *m*. *v* bruire, siffler.
Swiss [swis] *adj* suisse. **Swiss roll** gâteau roulé *m*. **the Swiss** les Suisses.
switch [switʃ] *n* bouton électrique *m*, interrupteur *m*; changement *m*; (*stick*) baguette *f*. **switchboard** *n* standard *m*. *v* changer, échanger; (*rail*) aiguiller. **switch off** éteindre. **switch on** allumer.
Switzerland ['switsələnd] *n* Suisse *f*.
swivel ['swivl] *v* (faire) pivoter. *n* pivot *m*.
swollen ['swoulən] *V* **swell**.
swoop [swuːp] *n* descente (en piqué) *f*. **at one fell swoop** d'un seul coup. *v* fondre, piquer.
swop *V* **swap**.
sword [soːd] *n* épée *f*. **swordfish** *n* espadon *m*.
swore [swoː] *V* **swear**.
sworn [swoːn] *V* **swear**.
swot [swot] (*coll*) *n* bûcheur, -euse *m*, *f*. *v* bûcher, potasser. **swotting** *n* bachotage *m*.
swum [swʌm] *V* **swim**.
swung [swʌŋ] *V* **swing**.
sycamore ['sikəmoː] *n* sycomore *m*.
syllable ['siləbl] *n* syllabe *f*. **syllabic** *adj* syllabique.
syllabus ['siləbəs] *n* programme *m*.
symbol ['simbl] *n* symbole *m*. **symbolic**

adj symbolique. **symbolism** *n* symbolisme *m*. **symbolize** *v* symboliser.
symmetry ['simitri] *n* symétrie *f*. **symmetrical** *adj* symétrique.
sympathy ['simpəθi] *n* compassion *f*; solidarité *f*. **sympathetic** *adj* compatissant, bien disposé. **sympathize with** *v* compatir à, plaindre.
symphony ['simfəni] *n* symphonie *f*. **symphonic** *adj* symphonique.
symposium [sim'pouziəm] *n* symposium *m*.
symptom ['simptəm] *n* symptôme *m*. **symptomatic** *adj* symptomatique.
synagogue ['sinəgog] *n* synagogue *f*.
synchromesh ['siŋkroumeʃ] *n* synchronisation *f*.
synchronize ['siŋkrənaiz] *v* synchroniser. **synchronization** *n* synchronisation *f*.
syncopate ['siŋkəpeit] *v* syncoper. **syncopation** *n* syncope *f*.
syndicate ['sindikit] *n* syndicat *m*.
syndrome ['sindroum] *n* syndrome *m*.
synonym ['sinənim] *n* synonyme *m*. **synonymous** *adj* synonyme.
synopsis [si'nopsis] *n, pl* **-ses** résumé *m*.
syntax ['sintaks] *n* syntaxe *f*.
synthesis ['sinθisis] *n, pl* **-ses** synthèse *f*. **synthesize** *v* synthétiser. **synthetic** *adj* synthétique.
syphilis ['sifilis] *n* syphilis *f*.
syringe [si'rindʒ] *n* seringue *f*. *v* seringuer.
syrup ['sirəp] *n* sirop *m*; (*golden*) mélasse raffinée *f*. **syrupy** *adj* sirupeux.
system ['sistəm] *n* système *m*; méthode *f*. **systematic** *adj* systématique.

T

tab [tab] *n* étiquette *f*, patte *f*. **keep tabs on** (*coll*) avoir à l'œil.
tabby ['tabi] *n* chat tigré *m*.
table ['teibl] *n* table *f*. **table-cloth** *n* nappe *f*. **table-mat** *n* dessous-de-plat *m invar*. **table salt** sel fin *m*. **tablespoon** *n* cuiller de service *f*. **tablespoonful** *n* cuillerée à soupe *f*. **table tennis** ping-pong *m*.
table d'hôte [taːblə'dout] *adj* à prix fixe.
tablet ['tablit] *n* (*pill*) comprimé *m*; (*stone*) plaque *f*; (*soap*) pain *m*.
taboo [ta'buː] *nm, adj* tabou. *v* proscrire.
tabulate ['tabjuleit] *v* mettre sous forme de table, classifier.
tacit ['tasit] *adj* tacite.
taciturn ['tasitəːn] *adj* taciturne.
tack [tak] *n* (*nail*) broquette *f*; (*sewing*) point de bâti *m*; (*naut*) bord *m*. *v* clouer; bâtir; faire un bord. **tacking** *n* bâtissage *m*.
tackle ['takl] *n* (*lifting*) appareil de levage *m*; équipement *m*; (*sport*) plaquage *m*. *v* s'attaquer à; plaquer.
tact [takt] *n* tact *m*. **tactful** *adj* plein de tact, discret, -ète. **tactless** *adj* peu délicat, indiscret, -ète.
tactics ['taktiks] *pl n* tactique *f sing*. **tactical** *adj* tactique.
tadpole ['tadpoul] *n* têtard *m*.
taffeta ['tafitə] *n* taffetas *m*.
tag [tag] *n* étiquette *f*, patte *f*; (*shoelace*) ferret *m*. *v* **tag along** (*coll*) suivre; traîner derrière.
tail [teil] *n* queue *f*; (*shirt*) pan *m*. **tail-end** *n* bout *m*, fin *f*. **tails** *pl n* (*coin*) pile *f sing*. *v* (*coll*) suivre.
tailor ['teilə] *n* tailleur *m*. *v* façonner; adapter.
taint [teint] *v* infecter, polluer *n* infection *f*; corruption *f*; (*moral*) tache *f*.
***take** [teik] *v* prendre; (*exam*) passer; accepter; contenir; (*accompany*) emmener. **take after** ressembler à. **take away** emporter; soustraire. **take-away** *adj* (*food*) à emporter. **take in** prendre; (*dress*) reprendre; (*understand*) saisir; inclure, couvrir; (*coll: deceive*) rouler. **take off** (*aero*) décoller; (*clothes, etc.*) enlever. **take-off** *n* décollage *m*; pastiche *m*. **take out** sortir; (*insurance*) prendre. **take-over** *n* rachat *m*.
taken ['teikn] *V* **take**.
talcum powder ['talkəm] *n* talc *m*.
tale [teil] *n* conte *m*, histoire *f*. **tell tales** (*coll*) cafarder.
talent ['talənt] *n* talent *m*. **talented** *adj* talentueux, doué.
talk [toːk] *n* propos *m pl*; conversation *f*; (*lecture*) exposé *m*. *v* parler; (*chat*) causer. **talk about** parler de. **talk into** persuader de. **talk over** discuter. **talkative** *adj* bavard.
tall [toːl] *adj* grand; (*high*) haut. **tallboy** *n* commode *f*. **tallness** *n* grande taille *f*; hauteur *f*.

tally ['tali] *n* compte *m*. *v* s'accorder.
talon ['talən] *n* serre *f*.
tambourine [tambə'riːn] *n* tambourin *m*.
tame [teim] *adj* apprivoisé; (*not exciting*) insipide. *v* apprivoiser; (*lion*) dompter.
tamper ['tampə] *v* **tamper with** toucher à; falsifier.
tampon ['tampon] *n* tampon *m*.
tan [tan] *n* bronzage *m*. *adj* ocre. *v* (*hide*) tanner; (*sun*) bronzer, hâler.
tandem ['tandəm] *n* tandem *m*.
tangent ['tandʒənt] *n* tangente *f*. **go off at a tangent** partir dans une digression.
tangerine [tandʒə'riːn] *nf*, *adj* mandarine.
tangible ['tandʒəbl] *adj* tangible.
tangle ['taŋgl] *n* enchevêtrement *m*, confusion *f*. *v* (s')enchevêtrer, (s')embrouiller.
tank [taŋk] *n* réservoir *m*; (*mil*) char *m*. **tanker** *n* (*lorry*) camion-citerne *m*; (*ship*) pétrolier *m*.
tankard ['taŋkəd] *n* chope *f*.
tantalize ['tantəlaiz] *v* tourmenter. **tantalizing** *adj* terriblement tentant.
tantamount ['tantəmaunt] *adj* **tantamount to** équivalent à.
tantrum ['tantrəm] *n* crise de colère *f*. **throw a tantrum** piquer une colère.
tap[1] [tap] *n* petit coup *m*. **tap-dance** *n* claquettes *f pl*. **tap-dancer** *n* danseur, -euse de claquettes *m*, *f*. *v* frapper légèrement, tapoter.
tap[2] [tap] *n* robinet *m*. *v* (*barrel*) percer; (*tree*) inciser; (*phone*) mettre sur écoute; exploiter.
tape [teip] *n* ruban *m*, bande *f*; (*recording*) bande magnétique *f*. **tape-measure** *n* mètre à ruban *m*. **tape-recorder** *n* magnétophone *m*. **tapeworm** *n* ténia *m*. *v* (*record*) enregistrer; attacher.
taper ['teipə] *n* bougie fine *f*. *v* (s')effiler. **tapered** *adj* fuselé.
tapestry ['tapəstri] *n* tapisserie *f*.
tapioca [tapi'oukə] *n* tapioca *m*.
tar [taː] *n* goudron *m*. *v* goudronner.
tarantula [tə'rantjulə] *n* tarentule *f*.
target ['taːgit] *n* cible *f*; objectif *m*.
tariff ['tarif] *n* tarif *m*.
tarmac ® ['taːmak] *n* macadam goudronné *m*.
tarnish ['taːniʃ] *v* (se) ternir. *n* ternissure *f*.
tarpaulin [taː'poːlin] *n* bâche *f*, prélart *m*.
tarragon ['tarəgən] *n* estragon *m*.
tart[1] [taːt] *adj* aigrelet, acerbe.
tart[2] [taːt] *n* tarte *f*; (*small*) tartelette *f*; (*slang*) poule *f*.
tartan ['taːtən] *n* tartan *m*. *adj* écossais.
tartar ['taːtə] *n* tartre *m*.
task [taːsk] *n* tâche *f*.
tassel ['tasəl] *n* gland *m*.
taste [teist] *n* goût *m*. *v* goûter; (*wine*) déguster. **taste of** avoir un goût de. **tasteful** *adj* de bon goût. **tasteless** *adj* (*flavourless*) sans saveur; insipide; (*in bad taste*) de mauvais goût. **tasty** *adj* savoureux.
tattered ['tatəd] *adj* en lambeaux.
tattoo[1] [tə'tuː] *v* tatouer. *n* tatouage *m*.
tattoo[2] [tə'tuː] *n* parade militaire *f*; (*drumming*) battements *m pl*.
tatty ['tati] *adj* (*coll*) fatigué, défraîchi.
taught [toːt] *V* **teach**.
taunt [toːnt] *n* raillerie *f*. *v* railler. **taunting** *adj* railleur, -euse.
Taurus ['toːrəs] *n* Taureau *m*.
taut [toːt] *adj* tendu. **tautness** *n* tension *f*.
tawny ['toːni] *adj* fauve.
tax [taks] *n* impôt *m*, taxe *f*. **tax-free** *adj* exempt d'impôts. **tax haven** refuge fiscal *m*. **taxpayer** *n* contribuable *m*, *f*. **tax return** déclaration de revenus *f*. *v* imposer, taxer; (*patience*) mettre à l'épreuve. **taxable** *adj* imposable. **taxation** *n* taxation *f*; (*taxes*) impôts *m pl*.
taxi ['taksi] *n* taxi *m*. **taxi-driver** *n* chauffeur de taxi *m*. **taxi rank** station de taxis *f*. *v* (*aero*) rouler lentement.
tea [tiː] *n* thé *m*; (*snack*) goûter *m*.
tea-bag ['tiːbag] *n* sachet de thé *m*.
teacake ['tiːkeik] *n* petit pain brioché *m*.
tea-cosy ['tiːkouzi] *n* couvre-théière *m*.
tea-leaf ['tiːliːf] *n* feuille de thé *f*.
teapot ['tiːpot] *n* théière *f*.
tea-room ['tiːruːm] *n* salon de thé *m*.
tea-set ['tiːset] *n* service à thé *m*.
teaspoon ['tiːspuːn] *n* petite cuiller *f*. **teaspoonful** *n* cuillerée à café *f*.
tea-towel ['tiːtauəl] *n* torchon *m*.
tea-urn ['tiːəːn] *n* fontaine à thé *f*.
***teach** [tiːtʃ] *v* apprendre, enseigner. **teacher** professeur *m*; (*primary school*) instituteur, -trice *m*, *f*. **teaching** *n* enseignement *m*.
teak [tiːk] *n* teck *m*.
team [tiːm] *n* équipe *f*; (*horses*) attelage *m*. **team-member** *n* équipier, -ère *m*, *f*. **team spirit** esprit d'équipe *m*. **team-work** *n* collaboration *f*.

***tear**[1] [teə] *n* déchirure *f*. *v* (se) déchirer; (*snatch*) arracher. **tear along/out** filer/sortir à toute allure.
tear[2] [tiə] *n* larme *f*. **burst into tears** fondre en larmes. **tear-gas** *n* gaz lacrymogène *m*. **tearful** *adj* larmoyant.
tease [tiːz] *v* taquiner. **teasing** *n* taquineries *f pl*.
teat [tiːt] *n* tétine *f*.
technique [tek'niːk] *n* technique *f*. **technical** *adj* technique. **technicality** *n* détail technique *m*. **technician** *n* technicien, -enne *m, f*. **technological** *adj* technologique. **technology** *n* technologie *f*.
teddy bear ['tedi,beə] *n* nounours *m*.
tedious ['tiːdiəs] *adj* ennuyeux.
tee [tiː] *n* tee *m*. *v* **tee off** partir du tee.
teem [tiːm] *v* (*swarm*) grouiller; (*rain*) pleuvoir à verse.
teenage ['tiːneidʒ] *adj* adolescent. **teenager** *n* adolescent, -e *m, f*. **teens** *pl n* adolescence *f sing*.
teeth [tiːθ] *V* **tooth**.
teethe [tiːð] *v* faire ses dents. **teething** *n* dentition *f*. **teething troubles** difficultés de croissance *f pl*.
teetotaller [tiː'toutələ] *n* personne qui ne boit jamais d'alcool *f*.
telecommunications [,telikəmjuːni'keiʃənz] *pl n* télécommunications *f pl*.
telegram ['teligram] *n* télégramme *m*.
telegraph ['teligraːf] *n* télégraphe *m*. **telegraph pole** poteau télégraphique *m*. *v* télégraphier. **telegraphic** *adj* télégraphique.
telepathy [tə'lepəθi] *n* télépathie *f*. **telepathic** *adj* télépathique.
telephone ['telifoun] *n* téléphone *m*. **telephone box** cabine téléphonique *f*. **telephone call** coup de téléphone *m*. **telephone directory** annuaire *m*. **telephone number** numéro de téléphone *m*. *v* téléphoner. **telephonist** *n* téléphoniste *m, f*.
telescope ['teliskoup] *n* télescope *m*. **telescopic** *adj* télescopique.
television ['teliviʒən] *n* télévision *f*. **televise** *v* téléviser.
telex ['teleks] *n* télex *m*.
***tell** [tel] *v* dire; (*story*) raconter; (*know*) savoir. **tell off** (*coll*) gronder.
temper ['tempə] *n* tempérament *m*, humeur *f*; (*anger*) colère *f*. **lose one's temper** se mettre en colère. *v* tempérer.
temperament ['tempərəmənt] *n* tempérament *m*. **temperamental** *adj* capricieux.
temperate ['temperət] *adj* tempéré.
temperature ['temprətʃə] *n* température *f*.
tempestuous [tem'pestjuəs] *adj* orageux.
template ['templət] *n* patron *m*.
temple[1] ['templ] *n* (*rel*) temple *m*.
temple[2] ['templ] *n* (*anat*) tempe *f*.
tempo ['tempou] *n* tempo *m*.
temporary ['tempərəri] *adj* temporaire; provisoire; (*secretary*) intérimaire.
tempt [tempt] *v* tenter. **temptation** *n* tentation *f*.
ten [ten] *nm, adj* dix. **tenth** *n(m+f), adj* dixième.
tenacious [tə'neiʃəs] *adj* tenace. **tenacity** *n* ténacité *f*.
tenant ['tenənt] *n* locataire *m f*. **tenancy** *n* location *f*.
tend[1] [tend] *v* avoir tendance, incliner. **tendency** *n* tendance *f*.
tend[2] [tend] *v* (*look after*) garder, soigner.
tender[1] ['tendə] *adj* tendre; délicat; (*heart, bruise*) sensible. **tenderize** *v* attendrir. **tenderness** *n* tendresse *f*; (*meat*) tendreté *f*.
tender[2] ['tendə] *v* offrir; (*comm*) faire une soumission. *n* soumission *f*. **legal tender** cours légal *m*.
tendon ['tendən] *n* tendon *m*.
tendril ['tendril] *n* vrille *f*.
tenement ['tenəmənt] *n* logement *m*. **tenement block** bâtiment *m*.
tennis ['tenis] *n* tennis *m*. **tennis-court** *n* court de tennis *m*.
tenor ['tenə] *n* (*music*) ténor *m*; sens *m*; (*wording*) teneur *f*.
tense[1] [tens] *adj* tendu, crispé. *v* tendre. **tension** *n* tension *f*.
tense[2] [tens] *n* temps *m*.
tent [tent] *n* tente *f*.
tentacle ['tentəkl] *n* tentacule *m*.
tentative ['tentətiv] *adj* hésitant; expérimental; provisoire.
tenterhooks ['tentəhuks] *pl n* **be on tenterhooks** être sur des charbons ardents.
tenuous ['tenjuəs] *adj* ténu.
tepid ['tepid] *adj* tiède. **tepidness** *n* tiédeur *f*.
term [təːm] *n* terme *m*; (*school*) trimestre *m*. **terms** *pl n* (*comm*) conditions *f pl*. **come to terms with** faire face à. **on good/bad terms** en bons/mauvais termes. *v* appeler.

terminal ['təːminəl] *adj* terminal. *n* terminus *m invar*; (*elec*) borne *f*.
terminate ['təːmineit] *v* (se) terminer. **termination** *n* fin *f*.
terminology [təːmi'nolədʒi] *n* terminologie *f*.
terminus ['təːminəs] *n* terminus *m invar*.
terrace ['terəs] *n* terrasse *f*; (*houses*) rangée de maisons *f*.
terrain [tə'rein] *n* terrain *m*.
terrestrial [tə'restriəl] *adj* terrestre.
terrible ['terəbl] *adj* terrible; atroce; abominable. **terribly** *adv* (*coll*: *very*) drôlement.
terrier ['teriə] *n* terrier *m*.
terrify ['terifai] *v* terrifier. **terrific** *adj* (*coll*: *excellent*) formidable; (*coll*: *extreme*) énorme, terrible.
territory ['teritəri] *n* territoire *m*. **territorial** *adj* territorial.
terror ['terə] *n* terreur *f*. **terrorism** *n* terrorisme *m*. **terrorist** *n*(*m*+*f*), *adj* terroriste. **terrorize** *v* terroriser.
terse [təːs] *adj* laconique.
test [test] *n* essai *m*; (*physical, mental*) épreuve *f*; analyse *f*; (*school*) interrogation *f*. **test card** (*TV*) mire *f*. **test case** (*law*) conflit-test *m*. **test drive** *n* essai de route *m*. **test flight** vol d'essai *m*. **test-tube** *n* éprouvette *f*. *v* essayer, mettre à l'essai; mettre à l'épreuve; analyser; mesurer.
testament ['testəmənt] *n* testament *m*.
testicle ['testikl] *n* testicule *m*.
testify ['testifai] *v* témoigner, porter témoignage.
testimony ['testiməni] *n* témoignage *m*; déclaration *f*. **testimonial** *n* recommandation *f*.
tetanus ['tetənəs] *n* tétanos *m*.
tether ['teðə] *n* longe *f*. *v* attacher.
text [tekst] *n* texte *m*. **textbook** *n* manuel *m*. **textual** *adj* textuel.
textile ['tekstail] *nm*, *adj* textile.
texture ['tekstjuə] *n* contexture *f*; (*wood, paper, etc.*) grain *m*.
Thames [temz] *n* **the Thames** la Tamise *f*.
than [ðən] *conj* que, de.
thank [θaŋk] *v* remercier. **thank you** merci. **thanks** *pl n* remerciements *m pl*. **thanksgiving** *n* action de grâce *f*. **thanks to** grâce à. **thankful** *adj* reconnaissant. **thankless** *adj* ingrat.
that [ðat] *adj* ce, cette; (*emphatic*) ce ... -là, cette ... -là: *ce livre-là*. *pron* cela, ça; ce; (*that one*) celui-là, celle-là; (*who, which*) qui, que, lequel, laquelle; (*when*) où. **that is** c'est-à-dire. *conj* que.
thatch [θatʃ] *n* chaume *m*. **thatched cottage** chaumière *f*.
thaw [θoː] *v* (faire) dégeler, (faire) fondre. *n* dégel *m*.
the [ðə] *art* le, la; (*pl*) les.
theatre ['θiətə] *n* théâtre *m*. **theatrical** *adj* théâtral.
theft [θeft] *n* vol *m*.
their [ðeə] *adj* leur.
theirs [ðeəz] *pron* le leur, la leur.
them [ðem] *pron* eux, elles; (*direct object*) les; (*indirect object*) leur.
theme [θiːm] *n* thème *m*. **thematic** *adj* thématique.
themselves [ðəm'selvz] *pron* se; (*emphatic*) eux-mêmes, elles-mêmes. **by themselves** tout seuls.
then [ðen] *adv* alors; (*next*) ensuite, puis; (*in that case*) en ce cas. *n* (*that time*) ce moment-là, cette époque-là.
theology [θi'olədʒi] *n* théologie *f*. **theologian** *n* théologien, -enne *m, f*. **theological** *adj* théologique.
theorem ['θiərəm] *n* théorème *m*.
theory ['θiəri] *n* théorie *f*. **theoretical** *adj* théorique.
therapy ['θerəpi] *n* thérapie *f*, thérapeutique *f*. **therapeutic** *adj* thérapeutique. **therapist** *n* thérapeute *m, f*.
there [ðeə] *adv* y, là. **thereabouts** *adv* environ; (*place*) par là. **thereby** *adv* de cette façon. **there is** *or* **are** il y a; (*showing*) voilà. **thereupon** *adv* sur ce.
therefore ['ðeəfoː] *adv* donc.
thermal ['θəːməl] *adj* thermal; (*phys*) thermique. *n* courant ascendant *m*.
thermodynamics [θəːmoudai'namiks] *n* thermodynamique *f*.
thermometer [θə'momitə] *n* thermomètre *m*.
thermonuclear [θəːmou'njukliə] *adj* thermonucléaire.
thermos ® ['θəːməs] *n* thermos ® *m*.
thermostat ['θəːməstat] *n* thermostat *m*. **thermostatic** *adj* thermostatique.
these [ðiːz] *adj* ces; (*emphatic*) ces ... -ci: *ces robes-ci*. *pron* ce; ceux-ci, celles-ci.
thesis ['θiːsis] *n*, *pl* **-ses** thèse *f*.
they [ðei] *pron* ils, elles; (*emphatic*) eux, elles; (*impersonal*) on.

thick [θik] *adj* épais, -aisse; (*stupid*) bête. **thick-skinned** *adj* peu sensible. **thicken** *v* (s')épaissir. **thickness** *n* épaisseur *f*.
thief [θiːf] *n* voleur, -euse *m, f*.
thigh [θai] *n* cuisse *f*.
thimble ['θimbl] *n* dé à coudre *m*.
thin [θin] *adj* mince, fin; (*person*) maigre; (*liquid*) peu épais, -aisse; (*hair*) clairsemé. *v* (s')éclaircir; (*dilute*) délayer. **thinness** *n* minceur *f*; maigreur *f*.
thing [θiŋ] *n* chose *f*. **things** *pl n* affaires *f pl*. **thingumajig** *n* (*coll*) machin *m*.
***think** [θiŋk] *v* penser; imaginer. **I think so** je pense que oui. **think about** penser à. **think over** réfléchir à.
third [θəːd] *adj* troisième. *n* troisième *m, f*; (*fraction*) tiers *m*; (*musique*) tierce *f*. **third party** (*law*) tiers *m*. **third-party insurance** assurance au tiers *f*. **third-rate** *adj* de qualité très inférieure. **Third World** Tiers-Monde *m*.
thirst [θəːst] *n* soif. *v* avoir soif. **be thirsty** avoir soif.
thirteen [θəː'tiːn] *nm, adj* treize. **thirteenth** *n*(*m*+*f*), *adj* treizième.
thirty ['θəːti] *nm, adj* trente. **thirtieth** *n*(*m*+*f*), *adj* trentième.
this [ðis] *adj* ce, cette; (*emphatic*) ce ... -ci, cette ... -ci: *cette maison-ci*. *pron* ceci, ce; (*this one*) celui-ci, celle-ci.
thistle ['θisl] *n* chardon *m*.
thong [θoŋ] *n* lanière *f*.
thorn [θoːn] *n* épine *f*.
thorough ['θʌrə] *adj* profond; minutieux. **thoroughbred** *n* (*horse*) pur-sang *m invar*; bête de race *f*. **thoroughfare** *n* voie publique *f*. **thoroughly** *adv* à fond; (*completely*) tout à fait. **thoroughness** *n* minutie *f*.
those [ðouz] *adj* ces; (*emphatic*) ces ... -là: *ces chaises-là*. *pron* ce; ceux-là, celles-là.
though [ðou] *conj* bien que. *adv* pourtant. **as though** comme si.
thought [θoːt] *V* **think**. *n* pensée *f*; idée *f*; opinion *f*; considération *f*. **thoughtful** *adj* pensif; sérieux; (*considerate*) prévenant, gentil, -ille. **thoughtless** *adj* étourdi; irréfléchi.
thousand ['θauzənd] *nm, adj* mille. **thousandth** *n*(*m*+*f*), *adj* millième.
thrash [θraʃ] *v* rosser, battre violemment; (*sport, etc.*) battre à plates coutures. **thrash about** se débattre. **thrash out** (*problem, etc.*) débattre de. **thrashing** *n* correction *f*.
thread [θred] *n* fil *m*; (*screw*) pas *m*. *v* enfiler; faire passer. **threadbare** *adj* usé, râpé.
threat [θret] *n* menace *f*. **threaten** *v* menacer.
three [θriː] *nm, adj* trois. **three-dimensional** *adj* à trois dimensions. **three-point turn** demi-tour en trois manœuvres *m*.
thresh [θreʃ] *v* battre. **threshing machine** batteuse *f*.
threshold ['θreʃould] *n* seuil *m*.
threw [θruː] *V* **throw**.
thrift [θrift] *n* économie *f*. **thrifty** *adj* économe.
thrill [θril] *n* frisson *m*. *v* transporter. **thriller** *n* roman *or* film à suspense *m*. **thrilling** *adj* palpitant.
thrive [θraiv] *v* se développer bien, pousser bien; prospérer. **thriving** *adj* robuste; prospère.
throat [θrout] *n* gorge *f*. **clear one's throat** s'éclaircir la voix. **throaty** *adj* guttural.
throb [θrob] *n* (*heart*) pulsation *f*; (*engine*) vibration *f*. *v* palpiter; vibrer; (*pain*) lanciner.
thrombosis [θrom'bousis] *n* thrombose *f*.
throne [θroun] *n* trône *m*.
throng [θroŋ] *n* foule *f*, multitude *f*. *v* affluer, se presser.
throttle ['θrotl] *v* étrangler. *n* (*tech*) papillon des gaz *m*; (*mot*) accélérateur *m*.
through [θruː] *prep* par; (*place*) à travers; (*time*) pendant. *adv* à travers. *adj* direct. **no through road** impasse *f*. **throughout** *prep* (*place*) partout dans; (*time*) pendant.
***throw** [θrou] *n* jet *m*. *v* jeter, lancer; (*hurl*) projeter. **throw away** jeter; (*waste*) gâcher, gaspiller. **throw out** rejeter; expulser. **throw up** vomir.
thrown [θroun] *V* **throw**.
thrush [θrʌʃ] *n* grive *f*.
***thrust** [θrʌst] *n* poussée *f*; coup *m*. *v* pousser brusquement, enfoncer; imposer.
thud [θʌd] *n* bruit sourd *m*. *v* faire un bruit sourd.
thumb [θʌm] *n* pouce *m*. *v* also **thumb through** feuilleter. **thumb a lift** (*coll*) faire du stop.
thump [θʌmp] *n* bruit lourd *m*; (*blow*) grand coup *m*. *v* cogner (à *or* sur); (*heart*) battre fort; (*person*) assener un coup à.

thunder ['θʌndə] *n* tonnerre *m*; (*noise*) fracas *m*. **thunderstorm** *n* orage *m*. **thunderstruck** *adj* abasourdi. *v* tonner. **thundery** *adj* orageux.
Thursday ['θəːzdi] *n* jeudi *m*.
thus [ðʌs] *adv* ainsi.
thwart [θwoːt] *v* contrecarrer, contrarier.
thyme [taim] *n* thym *m*.
thyroid ['θairoid] *nf*, *adj* thyroïde.
tiara [ti'aːrə] *n* diadème *m*.
tick[1] [tik] *n* (*mark*) coche *f*; (*sound*) tic-tac *m*; (*coll*) instant *m*. *v* cocher; faire tic-tac. **tick off** (*coll*: *scold*) attraper. **tick over** (*mot*) tourner au ralenti.
tick[2] [tik] *n* (*insect*) tique *f*.
ticket ['tikit] *n* billet *m*; (*bus*) ticket *m*; (*library*) carte *f*; (*label*) étiquette *f*. **ticket collector** contrôleur *m*. **ticket office** guichet *m*.
tickle ['tikl] *v* chatouiller. *n* chatouillement *m*. **ticklish** *adj* chatouilleux.
tide [taid] *n* marée *f*. **tide-mark** *n* ligne de marée haute *f*; (*of dirt*) ligne de crasse *f*. *v* **tide over** dépanner.
tidy ['taidi] *adj* en ordre, bien rangé; (*writing, appearance*) net, nette. *v* ranger. **tidily** *adv* soigneusement. **tidiness** *n* propreté *f*.
tie [tai] *n* attache *f*; (*neck*) cravate *f*; (*link*) lien *m*; (*draw*) égalité *f*, match nul *m*. *v* attacher; lier; (*ribbon, etc.*) nouer; faire match nul.
tier [tiə] *n* étage *m*; (*seating*) gradin *m*.
tiger ['taigə] *n* tigre *m*.
tight [tait] *adj* raide, serré, étroit; (*seal*) étanche; (*coll*: *drunk*) soûl; (*coll*: *mean*) radin. **tight-fisted** *adj* avare. **tightrope** *n* corde raide *f*. **tightrope walker** funambule *m, f*. *adv also* **tightly** bien; hermétiquement. **tighten** *v* (se) resserrer; (*rope*) (se) tendre; (*control*) renforcer. **tights** *pl n* collant *m sing*.
tile [tail] *n* (*roof*) tuile *f*; (*wall, floor*) carreau *m*. *v* couvrir de tuiles; carreler.
till[1] [til] *V* **until**.
till[2] [til] *n* caisse *f*.
till[3] [til] *v* labourer.
tiller ['tilə] *n* (*naut*) barre du gouvernail *f*.
tilt [tilt] *n* inclinaison *f*. *v* pencher, incliner.
timber ['timbə] *n* bois d'œuvre *m*. **timbered** *adj* (*house*) en bois.
time [taim] *n* temps *m*; (*clock*) heure *f*; (*occasion*) fois *f*; époque *f*; moment *m*; (*music*) mesure *f*. **a long time** longtemps. **a short time** peu de temps. **at the same time** à la fois. **from time to time** de temps en temps. **in time** à temps; (*music*) en mesure. **on time** à l'heure. **time bomb** bombe à retardement *f*. **time-sheet** *n* feuille de présence *f*. **time-switch** *n* minuteur *m*. **timetable** *n* (*rail*) horaire *m*; (*school*) emploi du temps *m*. **time zone** fuseau horaire *m*. *v* fixer; (*runner, etc.*) chronométrer; (*programme, etc.*) minuter. **timeless** *adj* éternel. **timely** *adj* à propos. **timer** *n* (*cooking*) compte-minutes *m invar*.
timid ['timid] *adj* timide, craintif. **timidity** *n* timidité *f*.
timpani ['timpəni] *pl n* timbales *f pl*.
tin [tin] *n* étain *m*; (*can*) boîte *f*; (*baking*) moule *m*; (*roasting*) plat *m*. **tin foil** papier d'étain *m*. **tin-opener** *n* ouvre-boîtes *m*. **tin soldier** soldat de plomb *m*. *v* mettre en boîte. **tinny** *adj* métallique.
tinge [tindʒ] *n* teinte *f*. *v* teinter.
tingle ['tiŋgl] *v* picoter. *n* picotement *m*.
tinker ['tiŋkə] *n* romanichel, -elle *m, f*. *v* bricoler.
tinkle ['tiŋkl] *v* (faire) tinter. *n* tintement *m*.
tinsel ['tinsəl] *n* clinquant *m*.
tint [tint] *n* teinte *f*; (*hair*) shampooing colorant *m*. *v* teinter.
tiny ['taini] *adj* tout petit, minuscule.
tip[1] [tip] *n* (*end*) bout *m*, pointe *f*. **on tiptoe** sur la pointe des pieds. *v* mettre un embout à.
tip[2] [tip] *v* (se) pencher, incliner; (*overturn*) (se) renverser; (*pour*) verser, déverser. *n* (*rubbish*) dépotoir *m*.
tip[3] [tip] *n* (*hint*) suggestion *f*, conseil *m*; (*money*) pourboire *m*. *v* donner un pourboire (à). **tip off** (*warn*) prévenir. **tip-off** *n* (*coll*) tuyau *m*.
tipsy ['tipsi] *adj* (*coll*) éméché.
Tirana [ti'raːnə] *n* Tirana.
tire[1] ['taiə] *v* (se) fatiguer. **tire out** épuiser. **tired** *adj* fatigué; las, lasse. **be tired of** en avoir assez de. **tiredness** *n* fatigue *f*. **tiresome** *adj* ennuyeux.
tire[2] (*US*) *V* **tyre**.
tissue ['tiʃuː] *n* tissu *m*; (*handkerchief*) mouchoir en papier *m*. **tissue paper** papier de soie *m*.
title ['taitl] *n* titre *m*; (*law*) droit *m*. **title-deed** *n* titre de propriété *m*. **title-page** *n* page de titre *f*. *v* intituler. **titled** *adj* titré.

titter ['titə] *n* gloussement *m*. *v* glousser.
to [tu] *prep* à; (*home, shop*) chez; (*in order to*) pour. **ten to four** quatre heures moins dix. **to-do** *n* (*coll*) histoire *f*.
toad [toud] *n* crapaud *m*. **toadstool** *n* champignon vénéneux *m*.
toast [toust] *n* pain grillé *m*; (*speech*) toast *m*. **toast-rack** *n* porte-toast *m*. *v* griller; porter un toast à. **toaster** *n* grille-pain *m invar*.
tobacco [tə'bakou] *n* tabac *m*. **tobacconist's** *n* tabac *m*.
toboggan [tə'bogən] *n* toboggan *m*.
today [tə'dei] *nm, adv* aujourd'hui.
toddler ['todlə] *n* petit, -e qui commence à marcher *m, f*.
toe [tou] *n* orteil *m*. **toe-nail** *n* ongle du pied *m*. *v* **toe the line** obéir, se plier.
toffee ['tofi] *n* caramel *m*. **toffee-apple** *n* pomme caramélisée *f*.
together [tə'geðə] *adv* ensemble; (*simultaneously*) à la fois.
toil [toil] *n* dur travail *m*. *v* travailler dur.
toilet ['toilit] *n* toilettes *f pl*, cabinets *m pl*. **toilet-paper** *n* papier hygiénique *m*. **toilet water** eau de toilette *f*.
token ['toukən] *n* marque *f*; (*disc*) jeton *m*; (*voucher*) bon *m*. **as a token of** en gage de. *adj* symbolique.
Tokyo ['toukiou] *n* Tokio.
told [tould] *V* **tell**.
tolerate ['toləreit] *v* tolérer, supporter. **tolerable** *adj* tolérable; passable. **tolerance** *or* **toleration** *n* tolérance *f*. **tolerant** *adj* tolérant.
toll[1] [toul] *n* péage *m*. **toll-gate** *n* barrière de péage *f*.
toll[2] [toul] *v* sonner.
tomato [tə'maːtou] *n* tomate *f*.
tomb [tuːm] *n* tombeau *m*. **tombstone** *n* pierre tombale *f*.
tomorrow [tə'morou] *nm, adv* demain. **the day after tomorrow** après-demain.
ton [tʌn] *n* tonne *f*.
tone [toun] *n* ton *m*; (*phone*) tonalité *f*; classe *f*; sonorité *f*. *v* (*colour*) s'harmoniser. **tone down** baisser, adoucir.
tongs [toŋz] *pl n* pinces *f pl*, pincettes *f pl*.
tongue [tʌŋ] *n* langue *f*. **tongue-tied** *adj* muet, -ette.
tonic ['tonik] *adj* tonique. *n* (*med*) tonique *m*; (*music*) tonique *f*.
tonight [tə'nait] *n, adv* cette nuit; (*evening*) ce soir.
tonsil ['tonsil] *n* amygdale *f*. **tonsillitis** *n* amygdalite *f*.
too [tuː] *adv* trop; (*also*) aussi; (*moreover*) en plus.
took [tuk] *V* **take**.
tool [tuːl] *n* outil *m*. **tool-shed** *n* cabane à outils *f*.
tooth [tuːθ] *n, pl* **teeth** dent *f*. **toothache** *n* mal de dents *m*. **have toothache** avoir mal aux dents. **tooth-brush** *n* brosse à dents *f*. **toothpaste** *n* dentifrice *m*. **toothpick** *n* cure-dent *m*. **toothless** *adj* édenté.
top[1] [top] *n* haut *m*; sommet *m*; (*lid*) couvercle *m*; surface *f*, dessus *m*; (*list*) tête *f*. **at the top of one's voice** à tue-tête. *adj* du haut; (*first*) premier; (*last*) dernier. **top hat** haut-de-forme *m*. **top-heavy** *adj* trop lourd du haut. **top secret** ultra-secret, -ète. **topside** *n* (*meat*) gîte *m*. **topsoil** *n* couche arable *f*. *v* surmonter; (*exceed*) dépasser. **top up** remplir, rajouter.
top[2] [top] *n* (*toy*) toupie *f*.
topaz ['toupaz] *n* topaze *f*.
topic ['topik] *n* sujet *m*. **topical** *adj* d'actualité.
topography [tə'pogrəfi] *n* topographie *f*. **topographical** *adj* topographique.
topple ['topl] *v* (faire) basculer, (faire) tomber.
topsy-turvy [topsi'təːvi] *adj, adv* sens dessus dessous.
torch [toːtʃ] *n* (*electric*) lampe de poche *f*; (*burning*) torche *f*.
tore [toː] *V* **tear**[1].
torment ['toːment; *v* toː'ment] *n* supplice *m*. *v* tourmenter.
torn [toːn] *V* **tear**[1].
tornado [toː'neidou] *n* tornade *f*.
torpedo [toː'piːdou] *n* torpille *f*. *v* torpiller.
torrent ['torənt] *n* torrent *m*. **torrential** *adj* torrentiel.
torso ['toːsou] *n* torse *m*; (*sculpture*) buste *m*.
tortoise ['toːtəs] *n* tortue *f*. **tortoise-shell** *n* écaille *f*.
tortuous ['toːtʃuəs] *adj* tortueux.
torture ['toːtʃə] *n* torture *f*. *v* torturer. **torturer** *n* tortionnaire *m*.
toss [tos] *n* lancement *m*; (*coin*) coup de pile ou face *m*. *v* lancer; (*pancake*) faire sauter; (s')agiter; (*coin*) jouer à pile ou face.

tot[1] [tot] *n* (*child*) petit enfant *m*; (*drink*) goutte *f*.
tot[2] [tot] *v* **tot up** additionner.
total ['toutəl] *nm*, *adj* total. *v* (*add up*) totaliser; (*add up to*) s'élever à. **totalitarian** *n*(*m*+*f*), *adj* totalitaire.
totter ['totə] *v* chanceler.
touch [tʌtʃ] *n* toucher *m*; contact *m*; (*artist's*) touche *f*. *v* toucher (à), se toucher. **touchy** *adj* susceptible; délicat.
tough [tʌf] *adj* dur; (*strong*) résistant; (*struggle*) acharné. **toughen** *v* rendre plus solide; (*person*) (s')endurcir. **toughness** *n* dureté *f*; résistance *f*.
toupee ['tuːpei] *n* postiche *m*.
tour [tuə] *n* voyage *m*; (*of town, museum, etc.*) visite *f*; (*by musicians, etc.*) tournée *f*. *v* visiter. **touring** *or* **tourism** *n* tourisme *m*. **tourist** *n* touriste *m*, *f*. **tourist's guide** guide touristique *f*.
tournament ['tuənəmənt] *n* tournoi *m*.
tousled ['tauzld] *adj* échevelé.
tow [tou] *n* remorque *f*. *v* remorquer; (*trailer*) tirer. **tow-path** *n* chemin de halage *m*. **tow-rope** *n* remorque *f*.
towards [tə'woːdz] *prep* vers; (*attitude*) envers.
towel ['tauəl] *n* serviette *f*; (*for hands*) essuie-mains *m*. **towel-rail** *n* porte-serviettes *m invar*. **towelling** *n* tissu éponge *m*.
tower ['tauə] *n* tour *f*. **tower block** immeuble-tour *m*. *v* **tower over** dominer. **towering** *adj* imposant.
town [taun] *n* ville *f*. **town centre** centre de la ville *m*. **town hall** hôtel de ville *m*. **town planning** urbanisme *m*.
toxic ['toksik] *adj* toxique.
toy [toi] *n* jouet *m*. *adj* petit, miniature; d'enfant. *v* **toy with** jouer avec; (*idea*) caresser.
trace [treis] *n* trace *f*. *v* tracer; (*find*) retrouver; (*through paper*) décalquer. **tracing** *n* calque *m*. **tracing paper** papier-calque *m invar*.
track [trak] *n* (*marks*) trace *f*; (*path*) chemin *m*; (*sport*) piste *f*; (*rail*) voie *f*. **track suit** survêtement *m*. *v* suivre la trace de. **track down** traquer. **tracker** *n* traqueur *m*.
tract[1] [trakt] *n* (*region*) étendue *f*; (*anat*) système *m*.
tract[2] [trakt] *n* (*treatise*) tract *m*.
tractor ['traktə] *n* tracteur *m*.
trade [treid] *n* commerce *m*; (*job*) métier *m*. **trademark** *n* marque *f*. **tradesman** *n* commerçant *m*. **trade union** syndicat *m*. **trade-unionist** *n* syndicaliste *m*, *f*. *v* faire le commerce (de); commercer (avec); échanger. **trade in** faire reprendre. **trader** *n* commerçant, -e *m*, *f*; négociant, -e *m*, *f*.
tradition [trə'diʃən] *n* tradition *f*. **traditional** *adj* traditionnel.
traffic ['trafik] *n* (*mot*) circulation *f*; (*aero, naut, etc.*) trafic *m*; commerce *m*. **traffic jam** embouteillage *m*. **traffic-light** *n* feu *m*. **traffic warden** contractuel, -elle *m*, *f*.
tragedy ['tradʒədi] *n* tragédie *f*. **tragic** *adj* tragique.
trail [treil] *n* traînée *f*; (*tracks*) trace *f*; (*path*) sentier *m*. *v* (*drag*) traîner; (*follow*) suivre la piste de. **trailer** *n* (*mot*) remorque *f*; film publicitaire *m*.
train [trein] *n* train *m*; (*series*) suite *f*; (*of dress*) traîne *f*. *v* (*teach*) former; (*learn*) recevoir sa formation; (*sport*) (s')entraîner; (*animal*) dresser. **trainee** *n* stagiaire *m*, *f*. **trainer** *n* (*sport*) entraîneur, -euse *m*, *f*; (*animal*) dresseur, -euse *m*, *f*; (*shoe*) chaussure de sport *f*. **training** *n* formation *f*; entraînement *m*; dressage *m*.
trait [treit] *n* trait *m*.
traitor ['treitə] *n* traître, -esse *m*, *f*.
tram [tram] *n* tram *m*.
tramp [tramp] *n* (*person*) clochard, -e *m*, *f*; (*hike*) randonnée *f*; (*sound*) martèlement des pas *m*. *v* marcher d'un pas lourd.
trample ['trampl] *v* piétiner, fouler aux pieds.
trampoline ['trampəliːn] *n* tremplin *m*.
trance [traːns] *n* transe *f*.
tranquil ['traŋkwil] *adj* tranquille. **tranquillity** *n* tranquillité *f*. **tranquillize** *v* tranquilliser. **tranquillizer** *n* tranquillisant *m*.
transact [tran'zakt] *v* traiter, régler. **transaction** *n* (*econ*) transaction *f*; (*comm*) opération *f*.
transcend [tran'send] *v* transcender; surpasser. **transcendental** *adj* transcendantal.
transcribe [tran'skraib] *v* transcrire. **transcription** *n* transcription *f*.
transept ['transept] *n* transept *m*.
transfer [trans'fəː; *n* 'transfəː] *v* transférer, être transféré. *n* transfert *m*; (*picture*) décalcomanie *f*. **not transferable** personnel.

transfixed [trans'fikst] *adj* cloué sur place.
transform [trans'fo:m] *v* transformer. **transformation** *n* transformation *f*. **transformer** *n* (*elec*) transformateur *m*.
transfuse [trans'fju:z] *v* transfuser. **transfusion** *n* transfusion *f*.
transient ['tranziənt] *adj* transitoire.
transistor [tran'zistə] *n* transistor *m*. **transistorize** *v* transistoriser.
transit ['transit] *n* transit *m*. **in transit** en transit.
transition [tran'ziʃən] *n* transition *f*. **transitional** *adj* de transition.
transitive ['transitiv] *adj* transitif.
transitory ['transitəri] *adj* transitoire.
translate [trans'leit] *v* traduire. **translation** *n* traduction *f*; (*school*) version *f*. **translator** *n* traducteur, -trice *m*, *f*.
translucent [trans'lu:snt] *adj* translucide. **translucence** *n* translucidité *f*.
transmit [tranz'mit] *v* transmettre; (*broadcast*) émettre. **transmission** *n* transmission *f*. **transmitter** *n* transmetteur *m*; émetteur *m*.
transparent [trans'peərənt] *adj* transparent. **transparency** (*phot*) diapositive *f*; transparence *f*.
transplant [trans'pla:nt; *n* 'transpla:nt] *v* transplanter. *n* transplantation *f*.
transport ['transpo:t; *v* trans'po:t] *n* transport *m*. *v* transporter. **transportation** *n* transport *m*.
transpose [trans'pouz] *v* transposer. **transposition** *n* transposition *f*.
transverse ['tranzvə:s] *adj* transversal.
transvestite [tranz'vestait] *n* travesti, -e *m*, *f*.
trap [trap] *n* piège *m*. **trapdoor** *n* trappe *f*. *v* prendre au piège; bloquer.
trapeze [trə'pi:z] *n* trapèze *m*. **trapeze artist** trapéziste *m*, *f*.
trash [traʃ] *n* (*worthless*) camelote *f*; (*waste*) ordures *f pl*. **trash can** (*US*) poubelle *f*.
trauma ['tro:mə] *n* traumatisme *m*; (*med*) trauma *m*. **traumatic** *adj* traumatisant; (*med*) traumatique.
travel ['travl] *v* voyager; (*go*) aller; (*cover*) parcourir. *n* voyage *m*. **travel agency** agence de voyages *f*. **travel brochure** dépliant touristique *m*. **travel-sickness** *n* mal de la route. **traveller** *n* voyageur, -euse *m*, *f*; (*comm*) représentant *m*. **traveller's cheque** chèque de voyage *m*.
travesty ['travəsti] *n* simulacre *m*, parodie *f*.
trawler ['tro:lə] *n* chalutier *m*. **trawling** *n* chalutage *m*.
tray [trei] *n* plateau *m*. **tray-cloth** *n* napperon *m*.
treachery ['tretʃəri] *n* traîtrise *f*. **treacherous** *adj* traître, -esse.
treacle ['tri:kl] *n* mélasse *f*.
***tread** [tred] *n* (bruit de) pas *m*; (*tyre*) chape *f*. *v* marcher. **tread on** mettre le pied sur; (*crush*) écraser du pied.
treason ['tri:zn] *n* trahison *f*.
treasure ['treʒə] *n* trésor *m*. *v* tenir beaucoup à; garder précieusement. **treasurer** *n* trésorier, -ère *m*, *f*. **treasury** *n* trésorerie *f*.
treat [tri:t] *v* traiter; (*med*) soigner. *n* plaisir *m*. **treatment** *n* traitement *m*.
treatise ['tri:tiz] *n* traité *m*.
treaty ['tri:ti] *n* traité *m*.
treble ['trebl] *adj* triple; de soprano. *n* soprano *m*. *v* tripler. *adv* trois fois plus.
tree [tri:] *n* arbre *m*.
trek [trek] *v* cheminer. *n* randonnée *f*.
trellis ['trelis] *n* treillis *m*, treillage *m*. *v* treillisser.
tremble ['trembl] *v* trembler, frémir. *n* tremblement *m*, frémissement *m*.
tremendous [trə'mendəs] *adj* énorme; (*terrible*) épouvantable; (*coll*: *excellent*) formidable.
tremor ['tremə] *n* tremblement *m*.
trench [trentʃ] *n* tranchée *f*.
trend [trend] *n* tendance *f*; mode *f*; direction *f*. **trendy** *adj* (*coll*) à la mode, dans le vent.
trespass ['trespəs] *v* s'introduire sans permission. *n* entrée non autorisée *f*. **trespasser** *n* intrus, -e *m*, *f*. **trespassers will be prosecuted** défense d'entrer sous peine de poursuites.
trestle ['tresl] *n* tréteau *m*. **trestle table** table à tréteaux *f*.
trial ['traiəl] *n* (*law*) procès *m*; (*test*) essai *m*; (*trouble*) épreuve *f*. **by trial and error** par tâtonnements. *adj* d'essai.
triangle ['traiaŋgl] *n* triangle *m*. **triangular** *adj* triangulaire.
tribe [traib] *n* tribu *f*. **tribal** *adj* tribal. **tribesman** *n* membre d'une tribu *m*.
tribunal [trai'bju:nl] *n* tribunal *m*.
tributary ['tribjutəri] *n* affluent *m*. *adj* tributaire.

tribute ['tribjuːt] *n* tribut *m*.
trick [trik] *n* tour *m*; ruse *f*; (*cards*) levée *f*. **do the trick** (*coll*) faire l'affaire. **trick photograph** photographie truquée *f*. **trick question** question-piège *f*. *v* attraper. **trickery** *n* ruse *f*. **tricky** *adj* délicat, difficile.
trickle ['trikl] *n* filet *m*. *v* couler, dégouliner.
tricycle ['traisikl] *n* tricycle *m*.
trifle ['traifl] *n* bagatelle *f*; (*sweet*) diplomate *m*. *v* **trifle with** traiter à la légère. **trifling** *adj* insignifiant.
trigger ['trigə] *n* détente *f*, gâchette *f*. *v* déclencher, provoquer.
trigonometry [trigə'nomətri] *n* trigonométrie *f*.
trill [tril] *n* trille *m*. *v* triller.
trim [trim] *adj* net, nette; (*tidy*) bien tenu. **in trim** en forme. *v* tailler légèrement; (*hair*) rafraîchir; (*decorate*) garnir. **trimmings** *pl n* garnitures *f pl*; accessoires *m pl*.
trinket ['triŋkit] *n* bibelot *m*.
trio ['triːou] *n* trio *m*.
trip [trip] *n* voyage *m*; (*stumble*) faux pas *m*; (*slang*: *drugs*) trip *m*. *v* trébucher. **trip up** (faire) trébucher; (*on purpose*) faire un croche-pied à.
tripe [traip] *n* tripes *f pl*; (*coll*) bêtises *f pl*.
triple ['tripl] *nm*, *adj* triple. *v* tripler. *adv* trois fois plus.
triplet ['triplit] *n* (*music*) triolet *m*; (*poetry*) tercet *m*; (*person*) triplé, -e *m*, *f*.
tripod ['traipod] *n* trépied *m*.
trite [trait] *adj* banal. **triteness** *n* banalité *f*.
triumph ['traiʌmf] *n* triomphe *m*. *v* triompher. **triumphant** *adj* triomphant. **triumphantly** *adv* triomphalement.
trivial ['triviəl] *adj* insignifiant; banal. **trivia** *or* **trivialities** *pl n* bagatelles *f pl*.
trod [trod] *V* **tread**.
trodden ['trodn] *V* **tread**.
trolley ['troli] *n* chariot *m*; (*shopping*) poussette *f*; (*tea*) table roulante *f*.
trombone [trom'boun] *n* trombone *m*.
troop [truːp] *n* bande *f*, troupe *f*. **troops** *pl n* (*mil*) troupes *f pl*. *v* **troop in/out** entrer/sortir en bande. **trooping the colour** le salut au drapeau.
trophy ['troufi] *n* trophée *m*.
tropic ['tropik] *n* tropique *m*. **tropical** *adj* tropical.
trot [trot] *n* trot *m*. **on the trot** (*coll*) de suite. *v* trotter. **trotter** *n* pied de porc *m*.
trouble ['trʌbl] *n* ennui *m*; (*bother*) peine *f*; difficulté *f*. **be in trouble** avoir des ennuis. **that's the trouble!** c'est ça l'ennui! **troublemaker** *n* fauteur, -trice de troubles *m*, *f*. **troublesome** *adj* fatigant, gênant. *v* (*bother*) (se) déranger; (*upset*) affliger, gêner; (*worry*) inquiéter.
trough [trof] *n* (*drinking*) abreuvoir *m*; (*food*) auge *f*; dépression *f*, creux *m*.
trousers ['trauzəz] *pl n* pantalon *m sing*; (*short*) culottes *f pl*. **trouser-suit** *n* tailleur-pantalon *m*.
trout [traut] *n* truite *f*.
trowel ['trauəl] *n* truelle *f*; (*gardening*) déplantoir *m*.
truant ['truːənt] *n* **play truant** faire l'école buissonnière. **truancy** *n* absence non autorisée *f*.
truce [truːs] *n* trêve *f*. **call a truce** faire trêve.
truck [trʌk] *n* camion *m*; (*rail*) wagon *m*. **truck-driver** *n* camionneur *m*.
trudge [trʌdʒ] *v* se traîner, marcher péniblement.
true [truː] *adj* vrai; exact; (*accurate*) fidèle; réel; (*straight*) droit; (*note*) juste. **truly** *adv* vraiment. **well and truly** bel et bien.
truffle ['trʌfl] *n* truffe *f*.
trump [trʌmp] *n* atout *m*. **turn up trumps** (*coll*) faire des merveilles. *v* couper.
trumpet ['trʌmpit] *n* trompette *f*. *v* (*elephant*) barrir. **trumpeter** *n* trompettiste *m*, *f*.
truncate [trʌŋ'keit] *v* tronquer.
truncheon ['trʌntʃən] *n* matraque *f*; (*police*) bâton *m*.
trunk [trʌŋk] *n* tronc *m*; (*elephant*) trompe *f*; (*case*) malle *f*. **trunk call** communication interurbaine *f*. **trunk road** route nationale *f*. **trunks** *pl n* slip de bain *m sing*.
truss [trʌs] *n* (*hay*) botte *f*; (*fruit*) grappe *f*; (*med*) bandage herniaire *m*. *v* trousser.
trust [trʌst] *n* confiance *f*; charge *f*; (*comm*) trust *m*; (*law*) fidéicommis *m*. **trustworthy** *adj* digne de confiance. *v* avoir confiance en, se fier à; (*hope*) espérer. **trustee** *n* (*law*) fidéicommissaire *m*; (*of school*) administrateur, -trice *m*, *f*. **trusting** *adj* confiant. **trusty** *adj* fidèle.

truth [truːθ] *n* verité *f*. **truthful** *adj* véridique. **truthfulness** *n* véracité *f*.
try [trai] *n* essai *m*. *v* essayer; juger; (*strain*) mettre à l'épreuve; tester. **try on** essayer. **trying** *adj* pénible.
tsar [zaː] *n* tsar *m*.
T-shirt ['tiːʃəːt] *n* T-shirt *m*.
tub [tʌb] *n* cuve *f*, baquet *m*; (*bath*) tub *m*.
tuba ['tjuːbə] *n* tuba *m*.
tube [tjuːb] *n* tube *m*; (*rail*) métro *m*. **tubeless** *adj* (*tyre*) sans chambre à air.
tuber ['tjuːbə] *n* tubercule *m*.
tuberculosis [tjubəːkju'lousis] *n* tuberculose *f*.
tuck [tʌk] *n* (*sewing*) rempli *m*. **tuck-shop** *n* (*school*) boutique à provisions *f*. *v* mettre. **tuck in** (*flap*) rentrer; (*bedclothes*) border; (*coll*: *eat*) boulotter. **tuck up** (*in bed*) border; (*skirt*) remonter.
Tuesday ['tjuːzdi] *n* mardi *m*.
tuft [tʌft] *n* touffe *f*; (*feathers*) huppe *f*.
tug [tʌg] *n* saccade *f*; (*boat*) remorqueur *m*. **tug-of-war** *n* lutte à la corde *f*. *v* tirer; remorquer.
tuition [tju'iʃən] *n* cours *m pl*.
tulip ['tjuːlip] *n* tulipe *f*.
tumble ['tʌmbl] *n* chute *f*, culbute *f*. *v* culbuter, dégringoler; (*knock over*) faire tomber, renverser. **tumbledown** *adj* en ruines. **tumble-dryer** *n* séchoir à air chaud *m*. **tumble out** tomber en vrac. **tumbler** *n* verre droit *m*.
tummy ['tʌmi] *n* (*coll*) ventre *m*.
tumour ['tjuːmə] *n* tumeur *f*.
tumult ['tjuːmʌlt] *n* tumulte *m*. **tumultuous** *adj* tumultueux.
tuna ['tjuːnə] *n also* **tunny** thon *m*.
tune [tjuːn] *n* air *m*. **in tune** accordé; (*sing*) juste. **out of tune** désaccordé; (*sing*) faux. *v* régler; (*music*) accorder. **tuneful** *adj* mélodieux. **tuner** *n* (*person*) accordeur *m*; (*radio*) radio-préamplificateur *m*. **tuning** *n* réglage *m*; accord *m*. **tuning fork** diapason *m*.
tunic ['tjuːnik] *n* tunique *f*.
tunnel ['tʌnl] *n* tunnel *m*. *v* percer un tunnel.
turban ['təːbən] *n* turban *m*.
turbine ['təːbain] *n* turbine *f*.
turbot ['təːbət] *n* turbot *m*.
turbulent ['təːbjulənt] *adj* turbulent. **turbulence** *n* turbulence *f*.
tureen [tə'riːn] *n* soupière *f*.
turf [təːf] *n* gazon *m*; (*sport*) turf *m*. **turf accountant** bookmaker *m*. *v* gazonner. **turf out** (*coll*: *thing*) bazarder; (*coll*: *person*) flanquer à la porte.
turkey ['təːki] *n* dindon *m*; (*cookery*) dinde *f*.
Turkey ['təːki] *n* Turquie *f*. **Turk** *n* Turc, Turque *m*, *f*. **Turkish** *nm*, *adj* turc, turque. **Turkish bath** bain turc *m*. **Turkish delight** loukoum *m*.
turmeric ['təːmərik] *n* curcuma *m*.
turmoil ['təːmoil] *n* agitation *f*, trouble *m*.
turn [təːn] *n* tour *m*; (*in road*) tournant *m*, virage *m*; (*med*) crise *f*; (*theatre*) numéro *m*. **do a good turn** rendre un service (à). *v* (faire) tourner; (se) retourner; changer. **turn away** (se) détourner; refuser, rejeter. **turn down** rejeter; (*lower*) baisser. **turn off** fermer, éteindre. **turn on** allumer, brancher; attaquer. **turn out** (*end up*) s'averer; (*light*) éteindre; (*empty*) vider; (*expel*) mettre à la porte. **turnover** *n* (*comm*) roulement *m*; (*cookery*) chausson *m*. **turnstile** *n* tourniquet *m*. **turntable** *n* (*record-player*) platine *f*; (*trains, etc.*) plaque tournante *f*. **turn up** arriver; (*be found*) être trouvé; (*raise*) mettre plus fort, monter. **turning** *n* (*side road*) route latérale *f*; (*bend*) coude *m*. **turning point** tournant *m*, moment décisif *m*.
turnip ['təːnip] *n* navet *m*.
turpentine ['təːpəntain] *n* térébenthine *f*.
turquoise ['təːkwoiz] *n* (*stone*) turquoise *f*; (*colour*) turquoise *m*. *adj* (*colour*) turquoise *invar*.
turret ['tʌrit] *n* tourelle *f*.
turtle ['təːtl] *n* tortue marine *f*. **turn turtle** chavirer. **turtle-neck** *n* (*jumper*) col montant *m*.
tusk [tʌsk] *n* défense *f*.
tussle ['tʌsl] *n* lutte *f*. *v* se battre.
tutor ['tjuːtə] *n* (*private*) précepteur, -trice *m*, *f*; (*university*) directeur, -trice d'études *m*, *f*. *v* donner des cours particuliers (à).
tuxedo [tʌk'siːdou] *n* smoking *m*.
tweed [twiːd] *n* tweed *m*.
tweezers ['twiːzəz] *pl n* pinces fines *f pl*.
twelve [twelv] *nm*, *adj* douze. **twelfth** *n*(*m*+*f*), *adj* douzième. **Twelfth Night** la fête des Rois *f*.
twenty ['twenti] *nm*, *adj* vingt. **twentieth** *n*(*m*+*f*), *adj* vingtième.

twice [twais] *adv* deux fois.
twiddle ['twidl] *v* tripoter. **twiddle one's thumbs** se tourner les pouces.
twig [twig] *n* brindille *f*.
twilight ['twailait] *n* crépuscule *m*.
twin [twin] *n*, *adj* jumeau, -elle. **twin beds** lits jumeaux *m pl*. **twin town** ville jumelée *f*. *v* jumeler.
twine [twain] *n* ficelle *f*. *v* (*weave*) tresser; (s')enrouler; serpenter.
twinge [twindʒ] *n* (*pain*) élancement *m*; (*sadness*) pincement *m*; remords *m*.
twinkle ['twiŋkl] *v* scintiller, briller. *n* scintillement *m*; (*eyes*) pétillement *m*.
twirl [twəːl] *v* (faire) tournoyer. *n* tournoiement *m*.
twist [twist] *n* torsion *f*; (*med*) entorse *f*; (*in wire, etc.*) tortillon *m*; (*in road*) tournant *m*; (*story*) coup de théâtre *m*. *v* (s')entortiller, tordre; (*turn*) tourner; (*road*) serpenter.
twit [twit] *n* (*slang*) idiot, -e *m*, *f*.
twitch [twitʃ] *n* tic *m*; (*pull*) coup sec *m*. *v* se convulser; avoir un tic; tirer d'un coup sec.
twitter ['twitə] *v* gazouiller. *n* gazouillement *m*.
two [tuː] *nm*, *adj* deux. **two-faced** *adj* hypocrite. **two-legged** *adj* bipède. **two-time** *v* (*coll*) doubler.
tycoon [tai'kuːn] *n* magnat *m*.
type [taip] *n* type *m*; (*sort*) genre *m*. **typesetting** *n* composition *f*. **typewriter** *n* machine à écrire *f*. *v* taper (à la machine). **typical** *adj* typique. **typing** *n* dactylo *f*. **typist** *n* dactylo *m*, *f*.
typhoid ['taifoid] *n* typhoïde *f*.
typhoon [tai'fuːn] *n* typhon *m*.
tyrant ['tairənt] *n* tyran *m*. **tyrannical** *adj* tyrannique. **tyranny** *n* tyrannie *f*.
tyre *or US* **tire** ['taiə] *n* pneu *m*.

U

ubiquitous [ju'bikwitəs] *adj* omniprésent.
udder ['ʌdə] *n* pis *m*, mamelle *f*.
ugly ['ʌgli] *adj* laid, vilain; répugnant. **ugliness** *n* laideur *f*.
ulcer ['ʌlsə] *n* ulcère *m*.
ulterior [ʌl'tiəriə] *adj* ultérieur, -e. **ulterior motive** arrière-pensée *f*.
ultimate ['ʌltimət] *adj* ultime; final; suprême. **ultimately** *adv* à la fin; (*basically*) en fin de compte. **ultimatum** *n* ultimatum *m*.
ultraviolet [ʌltrə'vaiələt] *adj* ultra-violet.
umbilical [ʌm'bilikəl] *adj* ombilical.
umbrage ['ʌmbridʒ] *n* ombrage *m*. **take umbrage** prendre ombrage.
umbrella [ʌm'brelə] *n* parapluie *m*.
umpire ['ʌmpaiə] *n* arbitre *m*. *v* arbitrer.
umpteen [ʌmp'tiːn] (*coll*) *adj* je ne sais combien (de). **umpteenth** *adj* énième.
unable [ʌn'eibl] *adj* incapable. **be unable to** (*lack means*) ne pas pouvoir; (*lack knowledge*) ne pas savoir.
unabridged [ʌnə'bridʒd] *adj* intégral.
unacceptable [ʌnək'septəbl] *adj* inacceptable; inadmissible.
unaccompanied [ʌnə'kumpənid] *adj* non accompagné; (*music*) sans accompagnement, seul.
unadulterated [ʌnə'dʌltəreitid) *adj* pur.
unaided [ʌn'eidid] *adj* sans aide.
unanimous [ju'naniməs] *adj* unanime. **unanimity** *n* unanimité *f*.
unarmed [ʌn'aːmd] *adj* (*combat*) sans armes; (*person*) non armé.
unattached [ʌnə'tatʃt] *adj* libre; indépendant.
unattractive [ʌnə'traktiv] *adj* peu attrayant, déplaisant.
unauthorized [ʌn'oːθəraizd] *adj* non autorisé.
unavoidable [ʌnə'voidəbl] *adj* inévitable.
unaware [ʌnə'weə] *adj* inconscient. **be unaware of** ignorer. **unawares** *adv* à l'improviste.
unbalanced [ʌn'balənst] *adj* mal équilibré; (*mentally*) déséquilibré.
unbearable [ʌn'beərəbl] *adj* insupportable.
unbelievable [ʌnbi'liːvəbl] *adj* incroyable.
***unbend** [ʌn'bend] *v* redresser; (*person*) se détendre. **unbending** *adj* inflexible.
unbiased [ʌn'baiəst] *adj* impartiel.
unbreakable [ʌn'breikəbl] *adj* incassable.
unbridled [ʌn'braidld] *adj* débridé.
unbutton [ʌn'butn] *v* déboutonner.
uncalled-for [ʌn'koːldfoː] *adj* injustifié, déplacé.
uncanny [ʌn'kani] *adj* étrange, troublant.
uncertain [ʌn'səːtn] *adj* incertain. **uncertainty** *n* incertitude *f*.

uncle ['ʌŋkl] *n* oncle *m*.
uncomfortable [ʌn'kʌmfətəbl] *adj* inconfortable; mal à l'aise.
uncommon [ʌn'komən] *adj* rare.
uncompromising [ʌn'komprəmaiziŋ] *adj* intransigeant.
unconditional [ʌnkən'diʃənl] *adj* inconditionnel.
unconscious [ʌn'konʃəs] *adj* (*med*) sans connaissance; (*unaware*) inconscient.
unconventional [ʌnkən'venʃənl] *adj* peu conventionnel.
uncooked [ʌn'kukt] *adj* non cuit.
uncouth [ʌn'kuːθ] *adj* grossier.
uncover [ʌn'kʌvə] *v* découvrir.
uncut [ʌn'kʌt] *adj* non coupé, non taillé.
undecided [ʌndi'saidid] *adj* indécis.
undeniable [ʌndi'naiəbl] *adj* indéniable, incontestable.
under ['ʌndə] *adv* au-dessous. *prep* sous; au dessous de; (*less*) moins de; (*according to*) selon.
underarm ['ʌndəraːm] *adj, adv* par en-dessous.
undercharge [ʌndə'tʃaːdʒ] *v* ne pas faire payer assez à.
underclothes ['ʌndəklouðz] *pl n* sous-vêtements *m pl*.
undercoat ['ʌndəkout] *n* couche de fond *f*.
undercover [ʌndə'kʌvə] *adj* secret, -ète.
undercut [ʌndə'kʌt] *v* vendre moins cher que.
underdeveloped [ʌndədi'veləpt] *adj* sous-développé.
underdog ['ʌndədog] *n* (*loser*) perdant *m*; (*oppressed*) opprimé *m*.
underdone [ʌndə'dʌn] *adj* (*meat*) saignant; pas assez cuit.
underestimate [ʌndə'estimeit] *v* sous-estimer. **underestimation** *n* sous-estimation *f*.
underfoot [ʌndə'fut] *adv* sous les pieds.
***undergo** [ʌndə'gou] *v* subir, éprouver.
undergraduate [ʌndə'gradjuət] *n* étudiant, -e *m, f*.
underground [ʌndə'graund; *adj, n* 'ʌndəgraund] *adv* sous terre; clandestinement. *adj* sous terre, souterrain; clandestin. *n* (*rail*) métro *m*.
undergrowth ['ʌndəgrouθ] *n* broussailles *f pl*.
underhand [ʌndə'hand] *adj* en sous-main, sournois.
***underlie** [ʌndə'lai] *v* être à la base de. **underlying** *adj* sous-jacent.
underline [ʌndə'lain] *v* souligner. **underlining** *n* soulignage *m*.
undermine [ʌndə'main] *v* saper, miner.
underneath [ʌndə'niːθ] *prep* sous, au-dessous de. *nm, adv* dessous. *adj* d'en dessous.
underpaid [ʌndə'peid] *adj* sous-payé.
underpants ['ʌndəpants] *pl n* caleçon *m sing*.
underpass ['ʌndəpaːs] *n* (*cars*) passage inférieur *m*; (*people*) passage souterrain *m*.
underprivileged [ʌndə'privilidʒd] *adj* défavorisé.
underrate [ʌndə'reit] *v* sous-estimer.
underskirt ['ʌndəskəːt] *n* jupon *m*.
understaffed [ʌndə'staːft] *adj* à court de personnel.
***understand** [ʌndə'stand] *v* comprendre; (*imply*) sous-entendre. **understandable** *adj* compréhensible. **understanding** *n* compréhension *f*; (*agreement*) accord *m*.
understate [ʌndə'steit] *n* minimiser. **make an understatement** ne pas assez dire. **that's an understatement!** c'est peu dire!
understudy ['ʌndəstʌdi] *n* doublure *f*. *v* doubler.
***undertake** [ʌndə'teik] *v* entreprendre, se charger de. **undertaker** *n* ordonnateur des pompes funèbres *m*. **undertaking** *n* entreprise *f*; promesse *f*.
undertone ['ʌndətoun] *n* **in an undertone** à demi-voix.
underwater [ʌndə'woːtə] *adj* sous-marin. *adv* sous l'eau.
underwear ['ʌndəweə] *n* sous-vêtements *m pl*.
underweight [ʌndə'weit] *adj* (*goods*) d'un poids insuffisant; (*person*) trop maigre.
underworld ['ʌndəwəːld] *n* (*criminal*) milieu *m*; (*hell*) enfers *m pl*.
***underwrite** [ʌndə'rait] *v* garantir; (*insurance*) souscrire.
undesirable [ʌndi'zaiərəbl] *adj* peu souhaitable. *n* indésirable *m, f*.
***undo** [ʌn'duː] *v* défaire; (*destroy*) détruire. **come undone** se défaire. **undoing** *n* ruine *f*.
undoubted [ʌn'dautid] *adj* indubitable.
undress [ʌn'dres] *v* (se) déshabiller.
undue [ʌn'djuː] *adj* indu. **unduly** *adv* trop.
undulate ['ʌndjuleit] *v* onduler. **undulating** *adj* onduleux. **undulation** *n* ondulation *f*.

unearth [ʌn'əːθ] *v* déterrer. **unearthly** *adj* surnaturel; (*coll*: *hour*) impossible, indu.
uneasy [ʌn'iːzi] *adj* mal à l'aise; troublé; anxieux.
uneducated [ʌn'edjukeitid] *adj* sans éducation.
unemployed [ʌnem'ploid] *adj* en chômage. **the unemployed** les chômeurs *m pl*. **unemployment** *n* chômage *m*.
unenthusiastic [ʌnenθjuːzi'astik] *adj* peu enthusiaste.
unequal [ʌn'iːkwəl] *adj* inégal.
uneven [ʌn'iːvn] *adj* inégal; (*number*) impair.
uneventful [ʌni'ventfəl] *adj* peu mouvementé.
unexpected [ʌneks'pektid] *adj* inattendu.
unfailing [ʌn'feiliŋ] *adj* inépuisable; infaillible.
unfair [ʌn'feə] *adj* injuste. **unfairness** *n* injustice *f*.
unfaithful [ʌn'feiθfəl] *adj* infidèle. **unfaithfulness** *n* infidélité *f*.
unfamiliar [ʌnfə'miljə] *adj* peu familier, inconnu.
unfasten [ʌn'faːsn] *v* défaire, ouvrir.
unfavourable [ʌn'feivərəbl] *adj* défavorable.
unfinished [ʌn'finiʃt] *adj* inachevé; à finir.
unfit [ʌn'fit] *adj* inapte, impropre; (*ill*) souffrant.
unfold [ʌn'fould] *v* déplier; exposer; (*story, countryside*) se dérouler.
unforeseen [ʌnfoː'siːn] *adj* imprévu.
unforgivable [ʌnfə'givəbl] *adj* impardonnable.
unfortunate [ʌn'foːtʃənət] *adj* malheureux, fâcheux.
unfounded [ʌn'faundid] *adj* sans fondement; injustifié.
unfriendly [ʌn'frendli] *adj* froid; hostile.
unfurnished [ʌn'fəːniʃd] *adj* non meublé.
ungainly [ʌn'geinli] *adj* gauche.
ungrateful [ʌn'greitfəl] *adj* ingrat.
unhappy [ʌn'hapi] *adj* triste, malheureux. **unhappiness** *n* tristesse *f*.
unhealthy [ʌn'helθi] *adj* malsain; (*person*) maladif.
unheard-of [ʌn'həːdov] *adj* inouï, sans précédent.
unhurt [ʌn'həːt] *adj* indemne, sain et sauf.
unhygienic [ʌnhai'dʒiːnik] *adj* non hygiénique.
unicorn ['juːnikoːn] *n* licorne *f*.
unidentified [ʌnai'dentifaid] *adj* non identifié. **unidentified flying object (UFO)** objet volant non identifié (OVNI) *m*.
uniform ['juːnifoːm] *nm, adj* uniforme. **uniformity** *n* uniformité *f*.
unify ['juːnifai] *v* unifier. **unification** *n* unification *f*.
unilateral [juːni'latərəl] *adj* unilatéral.
unimaginative [ʌni'madʒinətiv] *adj* peu imaginatif.
unimportant [ʌnim'poːtnt] *adj* peu important.
uninhabited [ʌnin'habitid] *adj* inhabité.
uninhibited [ʌnin'hibitid] *adj* sans inhibitions.
unintentional [ʌnin'tenʃənl] *adj* involontaire.
uninterested [ʌn'intristid] *adj* indifférent.
uninteresting *adj* inintéressant.
union ['juːnjən] *n* union *f*; (*trade*) syndicat *m*.
unique [juː'niːk] *adj* unique.
unisex ['juːniˌseks] *adj* (*coll*) unisexe.
unison ['juːnisn] *n* unisson *m*. **in unison** en chœur.
unit ['juːnit] *n* unité *f*; bloc *m*, groupe *m*.
unite [juː'nait] *v* (s')unir, unifier. **united** *adj* uni. **United Kingdom** Royaume-Uni *m*. **United Nations** Nations Unies *f pl*. **United States of America** Etats-Unis *m pl*.
unity ['juːniti] *n* unité *f*.
universe ['juːnivəːs] *n* univers *m*. **universal** *adj* universel.
university [juːni'vəːsəti] *n* université *f*. *adj* universitaire.
unjust [ʌn'dʒʌst] *adj* injuste.
unkempt [ʌn'kempt] *adj* débraillé; (*hair*) mal peigné.
unkind [ʌn'kaind] *adj* peu aimable, méchant, cruel. **unkindness** *n* méchanceté *f*.
unknown [ʌn'noun] *nm, adj* inconnu.
unlawful [ʌn'loːfəl] *adj* illégal, illégitime.
unless [ʌn'les] *conj* à moins que.
unlike [ʌn'laik] *adj* dissemblable, différent. *prep* à la différence de.
unlikely [ʌn'laikli] *adj* peu probable; (*story*) invraisemblable.
unlimited [ʌn'limitid] *adj* illimité.
unload [ʌn'loud] *v* décharger; (*get rid of*) se défaire de.
unlock [ʌn'lok] *v* ouvrir.

unlucky [ʌn'lʌki] *adj* malchanceux, malheureux; (*number, etc.*) qui porte malheur.
unmarried [ʌn'marid] *adj* célibataire.
unnatural [ʌn'natʃərəl] *adj* anormal; contre nature.
unnecessary [ʌn'nesəsəri] *adj* inutile; superflu.
unnerving [ʌn'nəːviŋ] *adj* déconcertant.
unnoticed [ʌn'noutist] *adj* inaperçu. **go unnoticed** passer inaperçu.
unobtainable [ʌnəb'teinəbl] *adj* impossible à obtenir.
unobtrusive [ʌnəb'truːsiv] *adj* discret, -ète.
unoccupied [ʌn'okjupaid] *adj* inoccupé, (*seat*) libre.
unofficial [ʌnə'fiʃəl] *adj* officieux, non officiel.
unorthodox [ʌn'oːθədoks] *adj* peu orthodoxe.
unpack [ʌn'pak] *v* (*case*) défaire (sa valise); (*contents*) déballer (ses affaires).
unpaid [ʌn'peid] *adj* impayé, non acquitté; (*worker*) non retribué.
unpleasant (ʌn'pleznt] *adj* désagréable, déplaisant.
unpopular [ʌn'popjulə] *adj* impopulaire.
unprecedented [ʌn'presidentid] *adj* sans précédent.
unpredictable [ʌnprə'diktəbl] *adj* imprévisible; incertain.
unqualified [ʌn'kwolifaid] *adj* non qualifié, non diplômé; (*absolute*) sans réserve.
unravel [ʌn'ravəl] *v* (s')effiler; (*mystery*) débrouiller.
unreal [ʌn'riəl] *adj* irréel.
unreasonable [ʌn'riːzənəbl] *adj* déraisonnable; excessif.
unrelenting [ʌnri'lentiŋ] *adj* implacable.
unreliable [ʌnri'laiəbl] *adj* sur qui on ne peut compter; (*machine*) peu fiable; (*source*) douteux.
unrest [ʌn'rest] *n* agitation *f*.
unruly [ʌn'ruːli] *adj* indiscipliné.
unsafe [ʌn'seif] *adj* dangereux.
unsatisfactory [ʌnsatis'faktəri] *adj* peu satisfaisant.
unscrew [ʌn'skruː] *v* (se) dévisser.
unscrupulous [ʌn'skruːpjuləs] *adj* sans scrupules, malhonnête.
unselfish [ʌn'selfiʃ] *adj* non égoïste, désintéressé.
unsettle [ʌn'setl] *v* perturber. **unsettled** *adj* perturbé; incertain; instable.
unsightly [ʌn'saitli] *adj* disgrâcieux.
unskilled [ʌn'skild] *adj* inexpérimenté. **unskilled worker** manœuvre *m*.
unsound [ʌn'saund] *adj* peu solide; (*health*) précaire; (*reasoning*) mal fondé.
unspeakable [ʌn'spiːkəbl] *adj* indescriptible.
unspecified [ʌn'spesifaid] *adj* non spécifié.
unstable [ʌn'steibl] *adj* instable.
unsteady [ʌn'stedi] *adj* instable, mal assuré.
unstuck [ʌn'stʌk] *adj* **come unstuck** se décoller.
unsuccessful [ʌnsək'sesfəl] *adj* infructueux; (*candidate*) refusé; (*marriage*) malheureux. **unsuccessfully** *adv* sans succès.
unsuitable [ʌn'suːtəbl] *adj* qui ne convient pas; inopportun; peu appropié.
unsure [ʌn'ʃuə] *adj* incertain.
untangle [ʌn'taŋgl] *v* démêler.
untidy [ʌn'taidi] *adj* négligé, débraillé; (*writing*) brouillon; (*room*) en désordre. **untidiness** *n* débraillé *m*; désordre *m*.
untie [ʌn'tai] *v* défaire.
until [ən'til] *prep* jusqu'à; (*before*) avant. *conj* jusqu'à ce que.
untoward [ʌntə'woːd] *adj* fâcheux.
untrue [ʌn'truː] *adj* faux, fausse; inexact.
unusual [ʌn'juːʒuəl] *adj* insolite; bizarre; exceptionnel.
unwanted [ʌn'wontid] *adj* superflu; non désiré.
unwell [ʌn'wel] *adj* indisposé, souffrant.
unwilling [ʌn'wiliŋ] *adj* peu disposé. **unwillingly** *adv* à contrecœur.
***unwind** [ʌn'waind] *v* (se) dérouler; (*relax*) se détendre.
unwise [ʌn'waiz] *adj* imprudent.
unworthy [ʌn'wəːði] *adj* indigne.
unwrap [ʌn'rap] *v* défaire.
up [ʌp] *adv* en haut, en l'air; (*standing*) debout; (*out of bed*) levé; terminé. **up there** là-haut. **up to** jusqu'à. *prep* dans, sur. **go up** monter. *n* **ups and downs** hauts et bas *m pl*.
upbringing ['ʌpbriŋiŋ] *n* éducation *f*.
update [ʌp'deit] *v* mettre à jour.
upheaval [ʌp'hiːvl] *n* bouleversement *m*; (*domestic*) branle-bas *m*; (*pol*) perturbation *f*.

uphill [ʌp'hil] *adj* qui monte; (*struggle*) pénible. *adv* **go uphill** monter.
***uphold** [ʌp'hould] *v* soutenir, maintenir.
upholster [ʌp'houlstə] *v* rembourrer. **upholstery** *n* tapisserie *f*; (*material*) rembourrage *m*; (*in car*) garniture *f*.
upkeep ['ʌpkiːp] *n* entretien *m*.
uplift [ʌp'lift] *v* élever.
upon [ə'pon] *prep* sur.
upper ['ʌpə] *adj* supérieur, -e, du dessus. **upper-class** *adj* aristocratique. **uppermost** *adj* le plus haut; en dessus.
upright ['ʌprait] *adj*, *adv* droit. *n* montant *m*.
uprising ['ʌpraiziŋ] *n* soulèvement *m*.
uproar ['ʌproː] *n* tumulte *m*, vacarme *m*. **uproarious** *adj* tumultueux; hilarant.
uproot [ʌp'ruːt] *v* déraciner.
***upset** [ʌp'set; *n* 'ʌpset] *v* (*knock over*) renverser; (*plans, etc.*) déranger; (*person*) faire de la peine à, contrarier. *adj* (*angry*) fâché; (*sad*) peiné; (*stomach*) dérangé. *n* désordre *m*; dérangement *m*; chagrin *m*.
upshot ['ʌpʃot] *n* résultat *m*.
upside down [ʌpsai'daun] *adv*, *adj* sens dessus dessous, à l'envers.
upstairs [ʌp'steəz] *adv* en haut. **go upstairs** monter (l'escalier). *adj* du dessus, d'en haut.
upstream [ʌp'striːm; *adj* 'ʌpstriːm] *adv* vers l'amont, en amont; (*swim*) contre le courant. *adj* d'amont.
uptight ['ʌptait] *adj* (*coll*) crispé.
up-to-date [ʌptə'deit] *adj* moderne.
upward ['ʌpwəd] *adj* ascendant. **upwards** *adv* vers le haut, en montant.
uranium [ju'reiniəm] *n* uranium *m*.
urban ['əːbən] *adj* urbain.
urchin ['əːtʃin] *n* polisson, -onne *m*, *f*.
urge [əːdʒ] *n* désir ardent *m*, forte envie *f*. *v* pousser, conseiller vivement.
urgent ['əːdʒənt] *adj* urgent; insistant. **urgency** *n* urgence *f*; insistance *f*. **urgently** *adv* d'urgence.
urine ['juːrin] *n* urine *f*. **urinate** *v* uriner.
urn [əːn] *n* urne *f*.
us [ʌs] *pron* nous.
usage ['juːzidʒ] *n* usage *m*.
use [juːs; *v* juːz] *n* usage *m*, emploi *m*. **it's no use** ça ne sert à rien. *v* se servir de, employer. **use up** user, consommer, épuiser. **used** *adj* (*car*) d'occasion. **be used to** être habitué à. **get used to** s'habituer à. **useful** *adj* utile. **useless** *adj* inutile. **user** *n* usager *m*.
usher ['ʌʃə] *n* (*law*) huissier *m*; (*church*) placeur *m*. *v* **usher in** introduire; inaugurer. **usherette** *n* ouvreuse *f*.
usual ['juːzuəl] *adj* habituel. **as usual** comme d'habitude. **usually** *adv* d'habitude, généralement.
usurp [ju'zəːp] *v* usurper.
utensil [ju'tensl] *n* ustensile *m*.
uterus ['juːtərəs] *n* utérus *m*.
utility [ju'tiləti] *n* utilité *f*. *adj* utilitaire.
utilize ['juːtilaiz] *v* utiliser.
utmost ['ʌtmoust] *adj* le plus grand; suprême; extrême. *n* plus haut point. **do one's utmost** faire tout son possible.
utter[1] ['ʌtə] *v* proférer; (*cry*) pousser.
utter[2] ['ʌtə] *adj* complet, -ète; pur; (*fool*) fini.
U-turn ['juːtəːn] *n* demi-tour *m*.

V

vacant ['veikənt] *adj* vacant, libre; (*stare*) vague. **vacancy** *n* (*room*) chambre à louer *f*; (*job*) vacance *f*. **no vacancies** complet.
vacate [vei'keit] *v* quitter.
vacation [vei'keiʃn] *n* vacances *f pl*.
vaccine ['vaksiːn] *n* vaccin *m*. **vaccinate** *v* vacciner. **vaccination** *n* vaccination *f*.
vacillate ['vasileit] *v* vaciller. **vacillation** *n* indécision *f*, vacillation *f*.
vacuum ['vakjum] *n* vide *m*; (*phys*) vacuum *m*. **vacuum cleaner** aspirateur *m*. **vacuum flask** bouteille thermos ® *f*. **vacuum-packed** *adj* emballé sous vide. *v* passer à l'aspirateur.
vagina [və'dʒainə] *n* vagin *m*. **vaginal** *adj* vaginal.
vagrant ['veigrənt] *n*, *adj* vagabond, -e. **vagrancy** *n* vagabondage *m*.
vague [veig] *adj* vague, flou, imprécis.
vain [vein] *adj* vain, inutile, futile; (*conceited*) vaniteux. **in vain** en vain.
valiant ['valiənt] *adj* courageux.
valid ['valid] *adj* valide, valable. **validity** *n* validité *f*; force *f*.
Valletta [və'letə] *n* La Valette.
valley ['vali] *n* vallée *f*; (*smaller*) vallon *m*.
value ['valjuː] *n* valeur *f*. *v* évaluer; apprécier, tenir à. **valuable** *adj* de valeur, précieux. **valuables** *pl n* objets de valeur *m pl*. **valuation** *n* évaluation *f*, expertise *f*.

valve [valv] *n* soupape *f*, valve *f*.
vampire ['vampaiə] *n* vampire *m*.
van [van] *n* camionnette *f*; (*rail*) fourgon *m*.
vandal ['vandl] *n* vandale *m*, *f*. **vandalism** *n* vandalisme *m*. **vandalize** *v* saccager.
vanilla [və'nilə] *n* vanille *f*.
vanish ['vaniʃ] *v* disparaître.
vanity ['vanəti] *n* vanité *f*. **vanity case** sac de toilette *m*.
vapour ['veipə] *n* vapeur *f*. **vaporize** *v* vaporiser.
varicose veins ['varikous] *pl n* varices *f pl*.
variety [və'raiəti] *n* variété *f*; quantité *f*. **variety show** spectacle de variétés *m*.
various ['veəriəs] *adj* divers.
varnish ['vaːniʃ] *n* vernis *m*. *v* vernir.
vary ['veəri] *v* varier, changer. **vary from** différer de. **variable** *nf*, *adj* variable. **variant** *n* variante *f*. **variation** *n* variation *f*.
vase [vaːz] *n* vase *m*.
vasectomy [və'sektəmi] *n* vasectomie *f*.
vast [vaːst] *adj* vaste. **vastness** *n* immensité *f*.
vat [vat] *n* cuve *f*.
Vatican ['vatikən] *n* Vatican *m*. **Vatican City** la Cité du Vatican *f*.
vault[1] [voːlt] *n* (*cellar*) cave *f*; (*tomb*) caveau *m*; (*bank*) coffre-fort *m*; (*arch*) voûte *f*.
vault[2] [voːlt] *v* sauter. *n* saut *m*. **vaulting horse** cheval d'arçons *m*.
veal [viːl] *n* veau *m*.
veer [viə] *v* tourner, virer.
vegetable ['vedʒtəbl] *n* légume *m*. *adj* végétal. **vegetable garden** potager *m*. **vegetarian** *n*, *adj* végétarien, -enne. **vegetation** *n* végétation *f*.
vehement ['viːəmənt] *adj* ardent; violent. **vehemence** *n* ardeur *f*; violence *f*. **vehemently** *adv* avec passion; avec violence.
vehicle ['viəkl] *n* véhicule *m*.
veil [veil] *n* voile *m*. *v* voiler.
vein [vein] *n* veine *f*.
velocity [və'losəti] *n* vélocité *f*.
velvet ['velvit] *n* velours *m*. **velvety** *adj* velouteux, velouté.
vending machine ['vendiŋ] *n* distributeur automatique *m*.
veneer [və'niə] *n* placage *m*; (*superficiality*) vernis *m*. *v* plaquer.
venerate ['venəreit] *v* vénérer. **venerable** *adj* vénérable. **veneration** *n* vénération *f*.
venereal disease [və'niəriəl] *n* maladie vénérienne *f*.
Venetian blind [və'niːʃən] *n* store vénitien *m*.
vengeance ['vendʒəns] *n* vengeance *f*. **with a vengeance** (*coll*) pour de bon.
venison ['venisn] *n* venaison *f*.
venom ['venəm] *n* venin *m*. **venomous** *adj* venimeux.
vent [vent] *n* orifice *m*, trou *m*. **give vent to** donner libre cours à. *v* décharger.
ventilate ['ventileit] *v* ventiler, aérer. **ventilation** *n* aération *f*, ventilation *f*.
ventriloquist [ven'triləkwist] *n* ventriloque *m*, *f*.
venture ['ventʃə] *n* aventure *f*; entreprise (risquée) *f*. *v* (se) risquer, (se) hasarder.
venue ['venjuː] *n* lieu de rendez-vous *m*.
veranda [və'randə] *n* véranda *f*.
verb [vəːb] *n* verbe *m*. **verbal** *adj* verbal.
verdict ['vəːdikt] *n* verdict *m*.
verge [vəːdʒ] *n* bord *m*. **on the verge of** sur le point de; à deux doigts de. *v* **verge on** approcher de, frôler.
verify ['verifai] *v* vérifier. **verification** *n* vérification *f*.
vermin ['vəːmin] *n* animaux nuisibles *m pl*; (*insects*, *people*) vermine *f*.
vermouth ['vəːməθ] *n* vermouth *m*.
vernacular [və'nakjulə] *adj* vernaculaire. *n* langue vernaculaire *f*.
versatile ['vəːsətail] *adj* aux talents variés; (*mind*) souple. **versatility** *n* variété de talents *f*; souplesse *f*.
verse [vəːs] *n* (*stanza*) strophe *f*; (*poetry*) vers *m pl*; (*bible*) verset *m*.
version ['vəːʃən] *n* version *f*.
versus ['vəːsəs] *prep* contre.
vertebra ['vəːtibrə] *n*, *pl* **-brae** vertèbre *f*. **vertebral** *adj* vertébral. **vertebrate** *nm*, *adj* vertébré.
vertical ['vəːtikl] *adj* vertical. *n* verticale *f*.
vertigo ['vəːtigou] *n* vertige *m*.
very ['veri] *adv* très, fort, bien; (*absolutely*) tout. **very much** beaucoup. *adj* (*exact*) même; (*extreme*) tout; (*mere*) seul.
vessel ['vesl] *n* vaisseau *m*.
vest [vest] *n* tricot de corps *m*; (*US*) gilet *m*.
vestibule ['vestibjuːl] *n* vestibule *m*.
vestige ['vestidʒ] *n* vestige *m*; grain *m*.
vestry ['vestri] *n* sacristie *f*.
vet [vet] (*coll*) *n* vétérinaire *m*, *f*. *v* examiner de près.
veteran ['vetərən] *n* vétéran *m*. **veteran car** voiture d'époque *f*. **war veteran** ancien combattant *m*.

veterinary ['vetərinəri] *adj* vétérinaire. **veterinary surgeon** vétérinaire *m, f.*
veto ['viːtou] *n* veto *m.* *v* mettre son veto à.
vex [veks] *v* contrarier, fâcher. **vexation** *n* ennui *m.*
via [vaiə] *prep* par, via.
viable ['vaiəbl] *adj* viable. **viability** *n* viabilité *f.*
viaduct ['vaiədʌkt] *n* viaduc *m.*
vibrate [vai'breit] *v* vibrer. **vibration** *n* vibration *f.*
vicar ['vikə] *n* pasteur *m.* **vicarage** *n* presbytère *m.*
vicarious [vi'keəriəs] *adj* délégué; indirect.
vice[1] [vais] *n* (*evil*) vice *m*; (*fault*) défaut *m.*
vice[2] [vais] *n* (*tool*) étau *m.*
vice-chancellor [vais'tʃaːnsələ] *n* vice-chancelier *m*; (*university*) recteur *m.*
vice-consul [vais'konsl] *n* vice-consul *m.*
vice-president [vais'prezidənt] *n* vice-president, -e *m, f.*
vice versa [vaisi'vəːsə] *adv* vice versa.
vicinity [vi'sinəti] *n* environs *m pl,* alentours *m pl.*
vicious ['viʃəs] *adj* (*remark*) méchant; (*attack*) brutal; (*animal*) vicieux. **vicious circle** cercle vicieux *m.* **viciousness** *n* méchanceté *f*; brutalité *f.*
victim ['viktim] *n* victime *f.* **victimize** *v* prendre pour victime.
victory ['viktəri] *n* victoire *f.* **victorious** *adj* victorieux.
video-tape ['vidiouteip] *n* bande de magnétoscope *f.* *v* enregistrer sur magnétoscope.
vie [vai] *v* lutter, rivaliser.
Vienna [vi'enə] *n* Vienne.
view [vjuː] *n* vue *f.* **in view of** étant donné, vu. **viewfinder** *n* viseur *m.* **viewpoint** *n* point de vue *m.* **with a view to** dans l'intention de, afin de. *v* visiter; considérer; regarder. **viewer** *n* (*TV*) téléspectateur, -trice *m, f*; (*slides*) visionneuse *f.*
vigil ['vidʒil] *n* veille *f.* **vigilance** *n* vigilance *f.* **vigilant** *adj* vigilant.
vigour ['vigə] *n* vigueur *f.* **vigorous** *adj* vigoureux.
vile [vail] *adj* vil; abominable.
villa ['vilə] *n* villa *f*; (*country*) maison de campagne *f.*
village ['vilidʒ] *n* village *m.* **villager** *n* villageois, -e *m, f.*
villain ['vilən] *n* scélérat *m.* **villainy** *n* infamie *f.*
vindictive [vin'diktiv] *adj* vindicatif.
vine [vain] *n* vigne *f.* **vineyard** *n* vignoble *m.*
vinegar ['vinigə] *n* vinaigre *m.*
vintage ['vintidʒ] *n* (*year*) année *f*; (*harvest*) vendange *f.* **vintage car** voiture d'époque *f.* **vintage wine** grand vin *m.*
vinyl ['vainil] *n* vinyle *m.*
viola [vi'oulə] *n* alto *m.*
violate ['vaiəleit] *v* violer. **violation** *n* violation *f.*
violence ['vaiələns] *n* violence *f.* **violent** *adj* violent.
violet ['vaiəlit] *n* (*flower*) violette *f*; (*colour*) violet *m.* *adj* violet, -ette.
violin [vaiə'lin] *n* violon *m.* **violinist** *n* violoniste *m, f.*
viper ['vaipə] *n* vipère *f.*
virgin ['vəːdʒin] *nf, adj* vierge. **virginity** *n* virginité *f.*
Virgo ['vəːgou] *n* Vierge *f.*
virile ['virail] *adj* viril. **virility** *n* virilité *f.*
virtually ['vəːtʃuəli] *adv* en fait, pratiquement.
virtue ['vəːtʃuː] *n* vertu *f*; mérite *m.* **by virtue of** en vertu de. **virtuous** *adj* vertueux.
virus ['vaiərəs] *n* virus *m.*
visa ['viːzə] *n* visa *m.*
viscount ['vaikaunt] *n* vicomte *m.* **viscountess** *n* vicomtesse *f.*
visible ['vizəbl] *adj* visible. **visibility** *n* visibilité *f.*
vision ['viʒən] *n* vision *f.* **visionary** *n*(*m*+*f*), *adj* visionnaire.
visit ['vizit] *n* visite *f*; (*stay*) séjour *m.* *v* (*call on*) aller voir, rendre visite à; (*stay with*) faire un séjour chez; (*place*) aller à; (*go round*) visiter. **visitor** *n* visiteur, -euse *m, f.*
visor ['vaizə] *n* visière *f.*
visual ['viʒuəl] *adj* visuel. **visualize** *v* se représenter.
vital ['vaitl] *adj* vital. **vitality** *n* vitalité *f.* **vitally** *adv* absolument.
vitamin ['vitəmin] *n* vitamine *f.*
vivacious [vi'veiʃəs] *adj* vif, enjoué. **vivacity** *n* vivacité *f.*
vivid ['vivid] *adj* vif, éclatant; (*description*) vivant. **vividness** *n* vivacité *f,* éclat *m,* clarté *f.*

vivisection [vivi'sekʃən] *n* vivisection *f.*
vixen ['viksn] *n* renarde *f.*
vocabulary [və'kabjuləri] *n* vocabulaire *m*; glossaire *m.*
vocal ['voukəl] *adj* vocal. **vocalist** *n* chanteur, -euse *m, f.*
vocation [vou'keiʃən] *n* vocation *f.* **vocational** *adj* professionnel.
vociferous [və'sifərəs] *adj* bruyant.
vodka ['vodkə] *n* vodka *f.*
voice [vois] *n* voix *f.* *v* exprimer.
void [void] *n* vide *m.* *adj* vide; (*law*) nul, nulle. *v* évacuer.
volatile ['volətail] *adj* (*chem*) volatil; (*person*) versatile; (*situation*) explosif.
volcano [vol'keinou] *n* volcan *m.* **volcanic** *adj* volcanique.
volley ['voli] *n* volée *f*; torrent *m.* **volley-ball** *n* volley *m.* *v* (*sport*) renvoyer une volée.
volt [voult] *n* volt *m.* **voltage** *n* voltage *m,* tension *f.*
volume ['voljum] *n* volume *m.*
volunteer [volən'tiə] *n* volontaire *m, f.* *v* s'offrir; offrir *or* fournir spontanément. **voluntary** *adj* volontaire; (*unpaid*) bénévole.
voluptuous [və'lʌptʃuəs] *adj* voluptueux. **voluptuousness** *n* volupté *f.*
vomit ['vomit] *n* vomissement *m.* *v* vomir.
voodoo ['vuːduː] *nm, adj* vaudou.
voracious [və'reiʃəs] *adj* vorace; avide. **voracity** *n* voracité *f.*
vote [vout] *n* vote *m,* voix *f.* **vote of thanks** discours de remerciement *m.* *v* voter; élire. **voter** *n* électeur, -trice *m, f.*
vouch [vautʃ] *v* **vouch for** se porter garant de, garantir.
voucher ['vautʃə] *n* bon *m*; (*receipt*) reçu *m.*
vow [vau] *n* vœu *m.* *v* jurer, vouer.
vowel ['vauəl] *n* voyelle *f.*
voyage ['voiidʒ] *n* voyage (par mer) *m.* *v* traverser, voyager (par mer).
vulgar ['vʌlgə] *adj* vulgaire, grossier. **vulgarity** *n* vulgarité *f,* grossièreté *f.*
vulnerable ['vʌlnərəbl] *adj* vulnérable.
vulture ['vʌltʃə] *n* vautour *m.*

W

wad [wod] *n* tampon *m*; (*papers*) liasse *f.* **wadding** *n* bourre *f,* rembourrage *m,* ouate *f.*
waddle ['wodl] *v* se dandiner. *n* dandinement *m.*
wade [weid] *v* avancer dans l'eau.
wafer ['weifə] *n* gaufrette *f.* **wafer-thin** *adj* mince comme du papier à cigarette.
waft [woft] *n* (*carry*) porter; (*float*) flotter. *n* bouffée *f.*
wag [wag] *v* agiter, remuer. *n* remuement *m.*
wage [weidʒ] *n* salaire *m.* *v* **wage war** faire la guerre.
wager ['weidʒə] *n* pari *m.* *v* parier.
waggle ['wagl] *v* agiter, frétiller.
wagon ['wagən] *n* chariot *m*; (*rail*) wagon *m.*
waif [weif] *n* enfant abandonné *m.*
wail [weil] *n* gémissement *m,* vagissement *m.* *v* gémir, vagir.
waist [weist] *n* taille *f,* ceinture *f.* **waistband** *n* ceinture *f.* **waistcoat** *n* gilet *m.* **waistline** *n* taille *f.*
wait [weit] *n* attente *f.* **lie in wait for** guetter. *v* attendre; servir. **waiter** *n* garçon *m.* **waiting** *n* attente *f.* **waiting-list** *n* liste d'attente *f.* **waiting-room** *n* salle d'attente *f.* **waitress** *n* serveuse *f.*
waive [weiv] *v* renoncer à, abandonner.
wake[1] [weik] *n* sillage *m.*
***wake**[2] [weik] *v* *also* **wake up** (se) réveiller.
Wales [weilz] *n* pays de Galles *m.*
walk [woːk] *n* promenade *f*; (*gait*) démarche *f.* *v* (faire) marcher; (*go on foot*) aller à pied; (*for pleasure*) se promener; (*distance*) faire à pied. **walk-out** *n* grève surprise *f.* **walkover** *n* walk-over *m,* victoire facile *f.* **walker** *n* promeneur, -euse *m, f.* **walking** *n* marche à pied *f.* **walking-stick** *n* canne *f.*
wall [woːl] *n* mur *m,* muraille *f.* *v* entourer d'un mur.
wallet ['wolit] *n* portefeuille *m.*
wallflower ['woːlflauə] *n* giroflée *f.* **be a wallflower** faire tapisserie.
wallop ['woləp] (*coll*) *n* coup *m,* beigne *f.* *v* cogner, rosser. **walloping** *adj* sacré.
wallow ['wolou] *v* se vautrer.
wallpaper ['woːlpeipə] *n* papier peint *m.* *v* tapisser.
walnut ['woːlnʌt] *n* (*nut*) noix *f*; (*tree, wood*) noyer *m.*

walrus ['wɔːlrəs] *n* morse *m*.
waltz [wɔːlts] *n* valse *f*. *v* valser.
wan [wɔn] *adj* pâle.
wand [wɔnd] *n* baguette *f*.
wander ['wɔndə] *v* errer; (*stray*) s'égarer. *n* tour *m*.
wane [wein] *v* décroître; diminuer.
wangle ['waŋgl] (*coll*) *n* combine *f*. *v* resquiller, se débrouiller pour avoir.
want [wɔnt] *n* (*lack*) manque *m*; (*need*) besoin *m*. **for want of** faute de. *v* vouloir, désirer; (*ask for*) demander; (*need*) avoir besoin de. **wanted** *adj* (*police*) recherché.
wanton ['wɔntən] *adj* (*woman*) dévergondé; (*cruelty, etc.*) gratuit. **wantonness** *n* dévergondage *m*; gratuité *f*.
war [wɔː] *n* guerre *f*. **be on the war-path** chercher la bagarre. **war-dance** *n* danse guerrière *f*. **warfare** *n* guerre *f*. **war memorial** monument aux morts *m*. **warship** *n* navire de guerre *m*. **wartime** *n* temps de guerre *m*.
warble ['wɔːbl] *n* gazouillis *m*. *v* gazouiller. **warbler** *n* oiseau chanteur *m*.
ward [wɔːd] *n* (*hospital*) salle *f*; section électorale *f*; (*law*) pupille *m, f*. *v* **ward off** parer.
warden ['wɔːdn] *n* directeur, -trice *m, f*; gardien, -enne *m, f*.
warder ['wɔːdə] *n* gardien de prison *m*. **wardress** *n* gardienne de prison *f*.
wardrobe ['wɔːdroub] *n* garde-robe *f*; (*theatre*) costumes *m pl*.
warehouse ['weəhaus] *n* entrepôt *m*. *v* entreposer.
warm [wɔːm] *adj* chaud; (*welcome, etc.*) chaleureux. *v* (se) chauffer. **warm up** s'échauffer. **warming-pan** *n* bassinoire *f*. **warmth** *n* chaleur *f*; cordialité *f*.
warn [wɔːn] *v* prévenir, avertir. **warning** *n* avertissement *m*; (*written*) avis *m*. **warning light** voyant avertisseur *m*.
warp [wɔːp] *v* (se) voiler, gauchir; pervertir; débaucher. *n* voilure *f*; (*cloth*) chaîne *f*.
warrant ['worənt] *n* (*police*) mandat *m*; justification *f*; (*voucher*) bon *m*. *v* justifier; garantir. **warranty** *n* garantie *f*.
warren ['worən] *n* garenne *f*.
warrior ['woriə] *n* guerrier, -ère *m, f*.
Warsaw ['wɔːsɔː] *n* Varsovie.
wart [wɔːt] *n* verrue *f*.
wary ['weəri] *adj* prudent, précautionneux.
was [woz] *V* **be**.
wash [woʃ] *n* (*clothes*) lavage *m*; (*face, etc.*) toilette *f*; (*paint*) badigeon *m*, lavis *m*. *v* (se) laver. **wash-basin** *n* lavabo *m*. **wash off** *or* **out** (faire) partir au lavage. **wash-out** *n* (*slang*) fiasco *m*. **wash-room** *n* toilettes *f pl*. **wash up** faire la vaisselle. **washable** *adj* lavable. **washing** *n* lessive *f*. **washing-machine** *n* machine à laver *f*. **washing-powder** *n* lessive *f*. **washing-up** *n* vaisselle *f*.
washer ['woʃə] *n* rondelle *f*.
Washington ['woʃiŋtən] *n* Washington.
wasp [wosp] *n* guêpe *f*.
waste [weist] *n* gaspillage *m*; (*time*) perte *f*; (*scrap*) déchets *m pl*; désert *m*. *adj* de rebut; (*lost*) perdu; (*extra*) superflu. **waste disposal unit** broyeur d'ordures *m*. **waste land** terrain vague *m*. **waste paper** vieux papiers *m pl*. **waste-paper basket** corbeille *f*. *v* gaspiller; perdre. **waste away** dépérir. **wasteful** *adj* gaspilleur, -euse; peu économique.
watch [wotʃ] *n* (*time*) montre *f*; garde *f*; surveillance *f*; (*naut*) quart *m*. **keep watch** faire le guet. **watch-dog** *n* chien de garde *m*. **watch-strap** *n* bracelet de montre *m*. *v* regarder; surveiller; faire attention (à); guetter. **watchful** *adj* vigilant.
water ['wɔːtə] *n* eau *f*. *v* (*plant, etc.*) arroser; (*eyes*) larmoyer. **water down** couper d'eau. **watery** *adj* aqueux; (*tea, etc.*) trop faible; pâle; insipide.
water-biscuit *n* craquelin *m*.
water-closet *n* cabinets *m pl*.
water-colour *n* aquarelle *f*.
watercress ['wɔːtəkres] *n* cresson *m*.
waterfall ['wɔːtəfɔːl] *n* chute d'eau *f*.
water-ice *n* sorbet *m*.
watering-can *n* arrosoir *m*.
water-lily *n* nénuphar *m*.
waterlogged ['wɔːtəlogd] *adj* (*land*) détrempé; (*wood*) imprégné d'eau.
water-main *n* conduite principale d'eau *f*.
watermark ['wɔːtəmaːk] *n* (*paper*) filigrane *m*; (*tide*) laisse de haute mer *f*.
water-melon *n* melon d'eau *m*.
water-pistol *n* pistolet à eau *m*.
waterproof ['wɔːtəpruːf] *nm, adj* imperméable. *v* imperméabiliser.
water-rate *n* taxe sur l'eau *f*.
watershed ['wɔːtəʃed] *n* moment critique *m*; (*geog*) ligne de partage des eaux *f*.
water-ski *v* faire du ski nautique. *n* ski nautique *m*. **water-skiing** *n* ski nautique *m*.

watertight ['wɔːtətait] *adj* étanche; (*excuse, etc.*) inattaquable.
water-way *n* voie navigable *f.*
waterworks ['wɔːtəwəːks] *n* système hydraulique *m.*
watt [wɒt] *n* watt *m.*
wave [weiv] *n* (*sea*) vague *f*; (*hair*) ondulation *f*; (*phys, radio, etc.*) onde *f*; geste de la main *m.* **waveband** *n* bande de fréquences *f.* **wavelength** *n* longueur d'ondes *f* *v* agiter, brandir; faire signe de la main; onduler. **wavy** *adj* (*hair*) ondulé; (*line*) onduleux.
waver ['weivə] *v* vaciller; trembler; (*weaken*) lâcher pied.
wax[1] [waks] *n* cire *f.* **waxwork** *n* personnage en cire *m.* **waxworks** *n* musée de cire *m.* *v* cirer. **waxy** *adj* cireux.
wax[2] [waks] *v* croître.
way [wei] *n* (*path*) chemin *m*, voie *f*; (*manner*) façon *f*, manière *f*; passage *m*; distance *f*; direction *f*, sens *m*. **be in the way** gêner. **by the way** à propos. **give way** céder; laisser la priorité. **on the way** en route. **this way** par ici. **under way** en cours, en marche. **way in** entrée *f.* **way out** sortie *f.*
***waylay** [wei'lei] *v* arrêter au passage.
wayside ['weisaid] *n* bord de la route. *adj* au bord de la route.
wayward ['weiwəd] *adj* capricieux, rebelle.
we [wiː] *pron* nous.
weak [wiːk] *adj* faible. **weaken** *v* faiblir, (s')affaiblir. **weakling** *n* gringalet *m.* **weakness** *n* faiblesse *f*; point faible *m*; (*liking*) faible *m.*
wealth [welθ] *n* richesse *f*; abondance *f.* **wealthy** *adj* riche.
wean [wiːn] *v* (*baby*) sevrer. **wean off** détourner de.
weapon ['wepən] *n* arme *f.*
***wear** [weə] *n* usage *m*; (*deterioration*) usure *f*; (*clothes*) vêtements *m pl.* **wear and tear** usure *f.* *v* porter; (s')user. **wear off** passer, se dissiper. **wear out** épuiser.
weary ['wiəri] *adj* las, lasse. *v* (se) lasser. **wearily** *adv* avec lassitude. **weariness** *n* lassitude *f.*
weasel ['wiːzl] *n* belette *f.*
weather ['weðə] *n* temps *m.* **weather-beaten** *adj* hâlé. **weathercock** *n* girouette *f.* **weather forecast** prévisions météorologiques *f pl.* *v* (*survive*) réchapper à.
***weave** [wiːv] *v* tisser; entrelacer; (*through traffic, etc.*) se faufiler. *n also* **weaving** tissage *m.*
web [web] *n* (*spider*) toile *f*; (*on feet*) palmure *f*; (*cloth*) tissu *m.* **web-footed** *adj* palmipède.
wedding ['wediŋ] *n* mariage *m*; noces *f pl.* **wedding-dress** *n* robe de mariée *f.* **wedding-ring** *n* alliance *f.*
wedge [wedʒ] *n* cale *f*, coin *m.* *v* caler; (*push in*) enfoncer; (*jam*) coincer.
Wednesday ['wenzdi] *n* mercredi *m.*
weed [wiːd] *n* mauvaise herbe *f.* **weedkiller** *n* désherbant *m.* *v* désherber. **weeding** *n* désherbage *m.*
week [wiːk] *n* semaine *f.* **a week today/tomorrow** aujourd'hui/demain en huit. **weekday** *n* jour de semaine *m.* **weekend** *n* week-end *m.*
weekly ['wiːkli] *adv* chaque semaine, tous les huit jours. *nm, adj* hebdomadaire.
***weep** [wiːp] *v* pleurer. **weeping willow** saule pleureur *m.*
weigh [wei] *v* peser. **weighbridge** *n* pont-bascule *m.* **weight** *n* poids *m.* **lose weight** maigrir. **put on weight** grossir. **weight-lifting** *n* haltérophilie *f.* **weighting** *n* indemnité *f.* **weightlessness** *n* apesanteur *f.*
weir [wiə] *n* barrage *m.*
weird [wiəd] *adj* surnaturel; bizarre. **weirdness** *n* étrangeté *f.*
welcome ['welkəm] *adj* opportun. **be welcome** être le bienvenu. **you're welcome!** (*acknowledging thanks*) il n'y a pas de quoi! *n* accueil *m.* *v* accueillir; souhaiter la bienvenue à; (*news, etc.*) se réjouir de.
weld [weld] *v* souder. *n* soudure *f.* **welder** *n* soudeur *m.* **welding** *n* soudage *m.*
welfare ['welfeə] *n* bien *m.* **Welfare State** Etat-providence *m.* **welfare work** travail social *m.*
well[1] [wel] *n* puits *m.* *v* **well up** monter.
well[2] [wel] *adj, adv* bien. **as well** aussi.
well-behaved *adj* sage, obéissant.
well-being *n* bien-être *m.*
well-bred *adj* bien élevé.
well-built *adj* solide.
well-informed *adj* bien informé; instruit.
wellington ['weliŋtən] *n* botte de caoutchouc *f.*
well-known *adj* célèbre.
well-meaning *adj* bien intentionné.
well-nigh *adv* presque.
well-off *adj* riche, aisé.

well-paid *adj* bien payé.
well-spent *adj* (*time*) bien employé.
well-spoken *adj* poli. **be well-spoken** avoir une élocution soignée.
well-timed *adj* opportun.
well-to-do *adj* aisé, riche.
well-trodden *adj* battu.
well-worn *adj* usagé.
Welsh [welʃ] *nm, adj* gallois. **the Welsh** les Gallois *m pl.*
went [went] *V* **go.**
wept [wept] *V* **weep.**
were [wəː] *V* **be.**
west [west] *n* ouest *m.* **the West** l'Occident *m. adj also* **westerly** occidental; ouest *invar*; à *or* de l'ouest. *adv* à l'ouest, vers l'ouest. **westbound** *adj* ouest *invar.*
western ['westən] *adj* ouest *invar*; de l'ouest; occidental. *n* (*film*) western *m.*
wet [wet] *adj* mouillé; (*damp*) humide; (*soaked*) trempé; (*weather*) pluvieux. **wet blanket** rabat-joie *m invar.* **wet suit** combinaison de plongée *f. n* pluie *f. v* mouiller.
whack [wak] (*coll*) *n* grand coup *m. v* donner un grand coup à.
whale [weil] *n* baleine *f.*
wharf [woːf] *n* quai *m.*
what [wot] *pron* (*subject*) (qu'est-ce) qui; (*object*) (qu'est-ce) que; (*after prep*) quoi; (*relative*) ce qui, ce que. *adj* quel, quelle. *interj* quoi!
whatever [wot'evə] *pron* tout ce que, quoi que. *adj, adv* quel que soit. **none whatever** pas le moindre.
wheat [wiːt] *n* blé *m,* froment *m.*
wheel [wiːl] *n* roue *f.* **wheelbarrow** *n* brouette *f.* **wheelchair** *n* fauteuil roulant *m. v* pousser, rouler; (*turn*) tournoyer.
wheeze [wiːz] *n* respiration bruyante *f. v* respirer bruyamment. **wheezy** *adj* poussif, asthmatique.
whelk [welk] *n* buccin *m.*
when [wen] *adv* quand. *conj* quand, lorsque; (*relative*) où, que. **whenever** *conj* chaque fois que.
where [weə] *adv* où. *conj* (là) où. **whereabouts** *adv* où. **whereas** *conj* alors que. **whereupon** *adv* sur quoi. **wherever** *conj* où que; (*anywhere*) là où; (*everywhere*) partout où.
whether ['weðə] *conj* si.
which [witʃ] *pron* lequel, laquelle; (*the one that*) celui qui *or* que, celle qui *or* que; (*relative*) (ce) qui, (ce) que. *adj* quel, quelle.
whichever [witʃ'evə] *pron* (quel que soit) celui qui *or* que, (quelle que soit) celle qui *or* que. *adj* n'importe quel; quel que soit . . . que.
whiff [wif] *n* bouffée *f,* odeur *f.*
while [wail] *conj* pendant que; (*as long as*) tant que. *n* quelque temps. *v* **while away** passer.
whim [wim] *n* caprice *m.*
whimper ['wimpə] *n* faible geignement *m. v* pleurnicher, geindre faiblement.
whimsical ['wimzikl] *adj* capricieux; étrange.
whine [wain] *n* gémissement *m*; (*siren, etc.*) plainte *f. v* gémir; (*complain*) se lamenter.
whip [wip] *n* fouet *m.* **whip-round** *n* (*coll*) collecte *f. v* fouetter. **whip away/out** enlever/sortir brusquement. **whipping** *n* correction *f.*
whippet ['wipit] *n* whippet *m.*
whirl [wəːl] *n* tourbillon *m. v* (faire) tourbillonner. **whirlpool** *n* tourbillon *m.* **whirlwind** *n* tornade *f,* trombe *f.*
whirr [wəː] *n* (*wings*) bruissement *m*; (*machinery*) vrombissement *m. v* bruire; vrombir.
whisk [wisk] *n* (*cookery*) fouet *m. v* fouetter; (*snatch*) enlever brusquement.
whisker ['wiskə] *n* poil *m.* **whiskers** *pl n* moustaches *f pl.*
whisky ['wiski] *n* whisky *m.*
whisper ['wispə] *v* chuchoter. *n* chuchotement *m.*
whist [wist] *n* whist *m.* **whist drive** tournoi de whist *m.*
whistle ['wisl] *n* sifflet *m*; (*sound*) sifflement *m. v* siffler.
Whit [wit] *n also* **Whitsun** la Pentecôte *f. adj* de Pentecôte.
white [wait] *adj* blanc, blanche. **white elephant** objet superflu *m. n* blanc *m*; (*person*) Blanc, Blanche *m, f.* **whiten** *v* blanchir. **whiteness** *n* blancheur *f.*
whitewash ['waitwoʃ] *n* blanc de chaux *m. v* blanchir à la chaux; (*cover up*) justifier, blanchir.
whiting ['waitiŋ] *n* merlan *m.*
whittle ['witl] *v* tailler au couteau. **whittle down** (*expenses, etc.*) rogner.
whizz [wiz] *n* sifflement *m.* **whizz-kid** (*coll*) petit prodige *m. v* aller comme une flèche.

who [huː] *pron* (qui est-ce) qui. **whoever** *pron* quiconque; qui que ce soit qui *or* que.
whole [houl] *n* totalité *f*; tout *m*. **on the whole** dans l'ensemble. *adj* entier; intact. **wholehearted** *adj* sans réserve. **wholeheartedly** *adv* de tout cœur. **wholemeal** *adj* (*flour*) brut; (*bread*) complet, -ète. **wholesome** *adj* sain.
wholesale ['houlseil] *n* vente en gros *f*. *adj* de gros; en masse, en bloc. *adv* en gros; en masse.
whom [huːm] *pron* qui; (*relative*) que, lequel, laquelle. **of whom** dont.
whooping cough ['huːpiŋ] *n* coqueluche *f*.
whore [hoː] *n* (*derog*) putain *f*.
whose [huːz] *pron* à qui. *adj* à qui, de qui; (*relative*) dont.
why [wai] *adv*, *conj* pourquoi. *interj* tiens!
wick [wik] *n* mèche *f*.
wicked ['wikid] *adj* mauvais, méchant, vilain. **wickedness** *n* méchanceté *f*.
wicker ['wikə] *n* osier *m*.
wicket ['wikit] *n* (*cricket*) guichet *m*.
wide [waid] *adj* large; grand; vaste. *adv* loin du but. **wide awake** bien éveillé. **widespread** *adj* répandu. **widely** *adv* largement; (*much*) beaucoup; généralement; radicalement. **widen** *v* (s')élargir.
widow ['widou] *n* veuve *f*. **be widowed** devenir veuf *or* veuve. **widower** *n* veuf *m*.
width [widθ] *n* largeur *f*.
wield [wiːld] *v* manier; brandir; exercer.
wife [waif] *n* femme *f*, épouse *f*.
wig [wig] *n* perruque *f*.
wiggle ['wigl] *v* tortiller; agiter, remuer. **wiggly** *adj* (*line*) ondulé.
wild [waild] *adj* sauvage; violent; (*unrestrained*) fou, folle. **like wildfire** comme une traînée de poudre. **wildlife** *n* faune *f*. **wildly** *adv* violemment; fiévreusement; follement.
wilderness ['wildənəs] *n* désert *m*; région sauvage *f*.
wilful ['wilfəl] *adj* (*stubborn*) entêté; volontaire; prémédité.
will[1] [wil] *aux translated by future tense*.
will[2] [wil] *v* vouloir; léguer. *n* volonté *f*; testament *m*. **against one's will** à contrecœur. **willpower** *n* volonté *f*.
willing ['wiliŋ] *adj* de bonne volonté. **be willing to** être disposé à, vouloir bien. **willingly** *adv* volontiers. **willingness** *n* bonne volonté *f*, empressement *m*.
willow ['wilou] *n* saule *m*. **willow-pattern** *n* motif chinois *m*. **willowy** *adj* svelte.
wilt [wilt] *v* (se) faner, (se) dessécher; (*person*) s'affaiblir.
wily ['waili] *adj* rusé, malin, -igne.
***win** [win] *n* victoire *f*. *v* gagner. **winner** *n* gagnant, -e *m*, *f*. **winning** *adj* gagnant; (*smile, etc.*) charmeur, -euse. **winnings** *pl n* gains *m pl*.
wince [wins] *v* tressaillir; grimacer. *n* tressaillement *m*; grimace *f*.
winch [wintʃ] *n* treuil *m*. *v* **winch up/down** monter/descendre au treuil.
wind[1] [wind] *n* vent *m*; (*breath*) souffle *m*; (*med*) vents *m pl*. *v* couper le souffle à. **windy** *adj* (*place*) battu par les vents; (*day*) de vent.
***wind**[2] [waind] *v* enrouler; (*clock, etc.*) remonter; serpenter. **wind up** (se) terminer; (*comm*) liquider; (*clock, etc.*) remonter. **winder** *n* remontoir *m*. **winding** *adj* sinueux.
wind-break *n* pare-vent *m invar*.
windfall ['windfoːl] *n* fruit abattu par le vent *m*; (*surprise*) aubaine *f*.
wind instrument *n* instrument à vent *m*.
windlass ['windləs] *n* guindeau *m*.
windmill ['wind,mil] *n* moulin à vent *m*.
window ['windou] *n* fenêtre *f*; (*car*) vitre *f*; (*shop*) vitrine *f*; (*cashier's*) guichet *m*. **window-box** *n* jardinière *f*. **window-cleaner** *n* laveur, -euse de vitres *m*, *f*. **window-dresser** *n* étalagiste *m*, *f*. **window-shopping** *n* lèche-vitrine *m*. **window-sill** *n* (*inside*) appui de fenêtre *m*; (*outside*) rebord de fenêtre *m*.
windpipe ['windpaip] *n* (*anat*) trachée *f*.
windscreen ['windskriːn] *n* pare-brise *m invar*. **windscreen wiper** essuie-glace *m invar*.
wind-sock *n* manche à air *f*.
windswept ['windswept] *adj* venteux, balayé par le vent.
wind tunnel *n* tunnel aérodynamique *m*.
wine [wain] *n* vin *m*. **wineglass** *n* verre à vin *m*. **wine list** carte des vins *f*. **wine-tasting** *n* dégustation *f*. **wine waiter** sommelier *m*.
wing [wiŋ] *n* aile *f*. **wing commander** lieutenant-colonel *m*. **wing-mirror** *n* rétroviseur de côté *m*. **wings** *pl n* (*theatre*) coulisses *f pl*. **wingspan** *n* envergure *f*.
wink [wiŋk] *n* clin d'œil. *v* faire un clin d'œil; (*light*) clignoter.

winkle ['wiŋkl] *n* bigorneau *m*. *v* **winkle out** extirper.
winter ['wintə] *n* hiver *m*. *v* hiverner. **wintry** *adj* d'hiver.
wipe [waip] *n* coup de torchon *m*. *v* essuyer. **wipe out** effacer; anéantir.
wire [waiə] *n* fil *m*; télégramme *m*. **wire-brush** *n* brosse métallique *f*. **wire-cutters** *pl n* cisaille *f sing*. **wireless** *n* T.S.F. *f*. **wire netting** treillis métallique *m*. *v* télégraphier. **wiring** *n* installation électrique *f*. **wiry** *adj* (*hair*) dru; (*person*) noueux.
wisdom ['wizdəm] *n* sagesse *f*; prudence *f*. **wisdom tooth** dent de sagesse *f*.
wise [waiz] *adj* sage; prudent; (*learned*) savant.
wish [wiʃ] *v* souhaiter, désirer. *n* souhait *m*, vœu *m*; désir *m*. **wishbone** *n* bréchet *m*.
wisp [wisp] *n* brin *m*; (*hair*) fine mèche *f*; (*smoke*) mince volute *f*. **wispy** *adj* fin.
wistful ['wistfəl] *adj* nostalgique, mélancolique. **wistfully** *adv* avec nostalgie *or* mélancolie.
wit [wit] *n* esprit *m*, intelligence *f*; (*person*) homme d'esprit, femme d'esprit *m*, *f*. **be at one's wits' end** ne plus savoir que faire.
witch [witʃ] *n* sorcière *f*. **witchcraft** *n* sorcellerie *f*. **witch-doctor** *n* sorcier *m*. **witch-hunt** *n* chasse aux sorcières *f*.
with [wið] *prep* avec; (*having*) à; (*because of*) de; (*despite*) malgré.
***withdraw** [wið'droː] *v* (se) retirer. **withdrawal** *n* retrait *m*, retraction *f*; (*med*) manque *m*. **withdrawn** *adj* renfermé.
wither ['wiðə] *v* (se) flétrir, (se) faner. **withered** *adj* flétri; desséché; (*limb*) atrophié. **withering** *adj* (*look*) méprisant; (*remark*) cinglant.
***withhold** [wið'hould] *v* (*keep back*) retenir; (*put off*) remettre; refuser; (*hide*) cacher.
within [wi'ðin] *adv* dedans, à l'intérieur. *prep* à l'intérieur de; dans; (*less than*) (à) moins de.
without [wi'ðaut] *prep* sans. *adv* à l'extérieur.
***withstand** [wið'stand] *v* résister à.
witness ['witnis] *n* (*person*) témoin *m*; (*evidence*) témoignage *m*. *v* (*accident, etc.*) être le témoin de; (*document*) attester l'authenticité de. **witness to** témoigner de.
witty ['witi] *adj* spirituel. **witticism** *n* mot d'esprit *m*.
wizard ['wizəd] *n* magicien *m*.
wobble ['wobl] *v* (faire) trembler, (faire) osciller, (faire) branler. **wobbly** *adj* bancal.
woke [wouk] *V* **wake**².
woken ['woukn] *V* **wake**².
wolf [wulf] *n* loup *m*. **wolfhound** *n* chien-loup *m*. **wolf-whistle** sifflement admiratif *m*. *v* **wolf down** engloutir.
woman ['wumən] *n*, *pl* **women** femme *f*. **Women's Lib** (*coll*) M.L.F. *m*. **womanhood** *n* féminité *f*. **womanly** *adj* féminin.
womb [wuːm] *n* utérus *m*.
won [wʌn] *V* **win**.
wonder ['wʌndə] *n* émerveillement *m*; miracle *m*, merveille *f*. **no wonder** (ce n'est) pas étonnant. *v* se demander; (*muse*) songer; (*marvel*) s'émerveiller. **wonderful** *adj* merveilleux.
wood [wud] *n* bois *m*. **wooden** *adj* de *or* en bois; (*stiff*) raide. **woody** *adj* boisé; (*stem*) ligneux.
woodcock ['wudkok] *n* bécasse *f*.
woodcut ['wudkʌt] *n* gravure sur bois *f*.
woodland ['wudlənd] *n* région boisée *f*.
wood-louse *n*, *pl* **-lice** cloporte *m*.
woodpecker ['wudpekə] *n* pic *m*.
wood-pigeon *n* ramier *m*.
wood-shed *n* bûcher *m*.
wood-wind *n* (*music*) bois *m pl*.
woodwork ['wudwəːk] *n* menuiserie *f*.
woodworm ['wudwəːm] *n* vers du bois *m*.
wool [wul] *n* laine *f*. **woollen** *adj* de *or* en laine. **woolly** *adj* laineux; (*ideas*) confus.
word [wəːd] *n* mot *m*, parole *f*. **be word-perfect in** savoir sur le bout des doigts. **in other words** autrement dit. *v* formuler, rédiger. **wording** *n* termes *m pl*. **wordy** *adj* verbeux.
wore [woː] *V* **wear**.
work [wəːk] *n* travail *m*, œuvre *f*, ouvrage *m*. **out of work** en chômage. **work-force** *n* main d'œuvre *f*. **workman** *n* ouvrier *m*. **workmanship** *n* maîtrise *f*. **work permit** permis de travail *m*. **works** *n* usine *f*. **workshop** *n* atelier *m*. **work-to-rule** *n* grève du zèle *f*. *v* travailler; (*machine, etc.*) (faire) marcher; exploiter. **work out** résoudre; (*plan*) élaborer; calculer. **worker** *n* travailleur, -euse *m*, *f*. **working-class** *adj* ouvrier. **workings** *pl n* mécanisme *m*.

world [wəːld] *n* monde *m*. **First/Second World War** Première/Deuxième guerre mondiale *f*. **world-wide** *adj* mondial. **worldly** *adj* terrestre; matérialiste.

worm [wəːm] *n* ver *m*.

worn [woːn] *V* **wear**.

worry ['wʌri] *n* souci *m*. *v* (s')inquiéter; (*sheep*) harceler. **don't worry!** ne vous en faites pas! **worried** *adj* inquiet, -ète.

worse [wəːs] *adj* pire, plus mauvais. *adv* plus mal. **get worse** empirer, se détériorer. **to make matters worse** pour comble de malheur. *n* pire *m*. **worsen** *v* empirer, se détériorer.

worship ['wəːʃip] *n* adoration *f*; culte *m*. *v* adorer, vénérer; faire ses dévotions.

worst [wəːst] *adj* le pire, la pire, le plus mauvais, la plus mauvaise. *adv* le plus mal. *n* pire *m*. **at worst** au pis aller.

worsted ['wustid] *n* worsted *m*.

worth [wəːθ] *n* valeur *f*. *adj* **be worth** valoir. **be worth it** valoir la peine. **worthwhile** *adj* qui en vaut la peine; utile; notable. **worthless** *adj* qui ne vaut rien. **worthy** *adj* digne; (*effort, cause*) louable.

would [wud] *aux translated by conditional or imperfect tense.*

wound[1] [waund] *V* **wind**[2].

wound[2] [wuːnd] *n* blessure *f*. *v* blesser.

wove [wouv] *V* **weave**.

woven ['wouvn] *V* **weave**.

wrangle ['raŋgl] *n* dispute *f*. *v* se disputer.

wrap [rap] *v* envelopper; (*parcel*) emballer. **wrapper** *n* papier *m*. **wrapping** *n* emballage *m*. **wrapping paper** papier d'emballage *m*; (*fancy*) papier cadeau *m*.

wreath [riːθ] *n* guirlande *f*, couronne *f*.

wreck [rek] *n* (*ship*) naufrage *m*; (*car*) voiture accidenté *f*; (*person*) épave *f*. *v* démolir, détruire; (*hopes, etc.*) ruiner, briser. **wreckage** *n* débris *m pl*.

wren [ren] *n* roitelet *m*.

wrench [rentʃ] *n* (*tool*) clef à écrous *f*; mouvement de torsion *m*; (*emotional*) déchirement *m*. *v* tirer violemment, arracher; (*med*) tordre.

wrestle ['resl] *v* lutter. **wrestle with** (*problem*) se débattre avec. **wrestler** *n* lutteur, -euse *m, f*; catcheur, -euse *m, f*. **wrestling** *n* lutte *f*, catch *m*.

wretch [retʃ] *n* malheureux, -euse *m, f*; misérable *m, f*. **wretched** *adj* misérable; (*coll: annoying*) maudit.

wriggle ['rigl] *v* (se) tortiller, remuer; (*fish*) frétiller.

***wring** [riŋ] *v* tordre; (*wet clothes*) essorer. **wringer** *n* essoreuse *f*. **wringing wet** trempé.

wrinkle ['riŋkl] *n* ride *f*; (*in cloth*) pli *m*. *v* rider; (se) plisser.

wrist [rist] *n* poignet *m*. **wrist-watch** *n* montre-bracelet *f*.

writ [rit] *n* acte judiciaire *m*. **issue a writ against** assigner.

***write** [rait] *v* écrire. **writer** *n* auteur *m*, écrivain *m*. **writing** *n* écriture *f*. **in writing** par écrit. **writing-case** *n* correspondancier *m*. **writing-pad** *n* bloc-notes *m*. **writing-paper** *n* papier à lettres *m*.

writhe [raið] *v* se tordre, frémir.

written ['ritn] *V* **write**.

wrong [roŋ] *adj* (*bad*) mal; erroné; incorrect, faux, fausse; (*end, side, etc.*) mauvais. **be wrong** avoir tort, se tromper; (*amiss*) ne pas aller. *adv* mal *n* mal *m*, tort *m*; injustice *f*. **wrongful** *adj* injustifié.

wrought iron [ˌroːt'aiən] *n* fer forgé *m*.

wrote [rout] *V* **write**.

wrung [rʌŋ] *V* **wring**.

wry [rai] *adj* désabusé.

X

xenophobia [ˌzenə'foubiə] *n* xénophobie *f*. **xenophobic** *adj* xénophobe.

Xerox ® ['ziəroks] *n* (*machine*) photocopieuse *f*; (*copy*) photocopie *f*. *v* photocopier.

Xmas ['krisməs] *V* **Christmas**.

X-ray ['eksrei] *n* (*photo*) radio *f*; (*ray*) rayon X *m*. **have an X-ray** se faire radiographier. *v* radiographier.

xylophone ['zailəfoun] *n* xylophone *m*.

Y

yacht [jot] *n* yacht *m*. **yachting** *n* yachting *m*.

yank [jaŋk] *n* coup sec *m.* *v* tirer d'un coup sec.
yap [jap] *v* japper. *n* jappement *m.*
yard [jaːd] *n* cour *f*; (*site*) chantier *m.*
yarn [jaːn] *n* fil *m*; (*tale*) histoire *f.*
yawn [joːn] *v* bâiller; (*hole*) s'ouvrir. *n* bâillement *m.*
year [jiə] *n* an *m*, année *f.* **yearly** *adj* annuel.
yearn [jəːn] *v* languir (après), aspirer (à). **yearning** *n* désir ardent *m*, envie *f.*
yeast [jiːst] *n* levure *f.*
yell [jel] *n* hurlement *m.* *v* hurler.
yellow ['jelou] *nm, adj* jaune. *v* jaunir.
yelp [jelp] *v* glapir, japper. *n* glapissement *m*, jappement *m.*
yes [jes] *adv* oui; (*after negative*) si. *n* oui *m invar.*
yesterday ['jestədi] *nm, adv* hier. **the day before yesterday** avant-hier *m.*
yet [jət] *adv* encore; (*already*) déjà. *conj* cependant, toutefois.
yew [juː] *n* if *m.*
yield [jiːld] *v* produire, rapporter; céder. *n* production *f*, rapport *m.*
yodel ['joudl] *v* jodler. *n* tyrolienne *f.*
yoga ['jougə] *n* yoga *m.*
yoghurt ['yogət] *n* yaourt *m.*
yoke [jouk] *n* joug *m*; (*dress*) empiècement *m.* *v* accoupler.
yolk [jouk] *n* jaune *m.*
yonder ['jondə] *adv* là-bas.
you [juː] *pron* (*subject*: *fam*) tu; (*subject*: *pl or fml*) vous; (*after prep*) toi, vous; (*before verb*) te, vous; (*impersonal*) on.
young [jʌŋ] *adj* jeune. *pl n* (*people*) jeunes *m pl*; (*animals*) petits *m pl.* **youngster** *n* jeune *m.*
your [joː] *adj* (*fam*) ton, ta, (*pl*) tes; (*pl or fml*) votre, (*pl*) vos; (*impersonal*) son, sa, (*pl*) ses. **yours** *pron* (*fam*) le tien, la tienne; (*pl or fml*) le vôtre, la vôtre.
yourself [jə'self] *pron* (*fam*) te; (*pl or fml*) vous; (*impersonal*) se; (*emphatic*) toi-même, vous-même, soi-même. **by yourself** tout seul.
youth [juːθ] *n* jeunesse *f*; (*boy*) jeune homme *m.* **youth hostel** auberge de la jeunesse *f.*
yo-yo ['joujou] *n* yo-yo *m.*
Yugoslavia [juːgou'slaːviə] *n* Yougoslavie *f.* **Yugoslav** *adj* yougoslave; *n* Yougoslave *m, f.* **Yugoslavian** *adj* yougoslave.

Z

Zaire [zaɪ'iːə] *n* Zaïre *m.*
zany ['zeini] *adj* (*coll*) toqué.
zeal [ziːl] *n* zèle *m.* **zealous** *adj* zélé; dévoué.
zebra ['zebrə] *n* zèbre *m.* **zebra crossing** passage pour piétons *m.*
zero ['ziərou] *n* zéro *m.*
zest [zest] *n* entrain *m*; saveur *f.*
zigzag ['zigzag] *n* zigzag *m.* *v* zigzaguer.
zinc [ziŋk] *n* zinc *m.*
zip [zip] *n* fermeture éclair *f.* **zip code** (*US*) code postal *m.* *v* **zip up** (se) fermer avec une fermeture éclair.
zodiac ['zoudiak] *n* zodiaque *m.*
zone [zoun] *n* zone *f.* *v* diviser en zones.
zoo [zuː] *n* zoo *m.*
zoology [zou'olədʒi] *n* zoologie *f.* **zoological** *adj* zoologique. **zoologist** *n* zoologiste *m, f.*
zoom [zuːm] *n* vrombissement *m.* **zoom lens** zoom *m.* *v* vrombir. **zoom past/through** (*coll*) passer/traverser en trombe.

French–Anglais

A

à [a] *prep* (*vers*) to; (*position*) at; (*ville*) in; (*d'après*) according to; (*transport*) by; (*pour*) for.
abaisser [abese] *v* lower. **s'abaisser** *v* fall; (*personne*) humble oneself. **abaissement** *nm* fall; (*personne*) subservience; degradation.
abandon [abɑ̃dɔ̃] *nm* desertion; renunciation, giving up; neglect. **à l'abandon** in a state of neglect. **avec abandon** without constraint.
abandonner [abɑ̃dɔne] *v* abandon, give up. **s'abandonner à** give way to, indulge in.
abasourdir [abazurdir] *v* stun. **abasourdissement** *nm* stupefaction.
abat-jour *nm invar* lampshade.
abats [aba] *nm pl* offal *sing*; (*volaille*) giblets *pl*.
abattoir [abatwar] *nm* abattoir.
***abattre** [abatrə] *v* pull *or* knock down; (*arbre*) fell; (*tuer*) kill; (*affaiblir*) weaken. **s'abattre** fall, collapse. **abattement** *nm* depression, low spirits *pl*; (*fatigue*) exhaustion; (*rabais*) reduction. **abattu** *adj* exhausted; feeble; depressed.
abbaye [abei] *nf* abbey.
abbé [abe] *nm* abbot. **abbesse** *nf* abbess.
abcès [apsɛ] *nm* abscess.
abdiquer [abdike] *v* abdicate. **abdication** *nf* abdication.
abdomen [abdɔmɛn] *nm* abdomen. **abdominal** *adj* abdominal.
abeille [abɛj] *nf* bee.
abhorrer [abɔre] *v* abhor.
abîme [abim] *nm* abyss, gulf.
abîmer [abime] *v* spoil, damage.
abject [abʒɛkt] *adj* despicable, abject.
abnégation [abnegɑsjɔ̃] *nf* self-denial.
aboiement [abwamɑ̃] *nm* bark.
abois [abwa] *nm pl* **aux abois** at bay.
abolir [abɔlir] *v* abolish. **abolition** *nf* abolition.
abominable [abɔminablə] *adj* abominable. **abomination** *nf* abomination. **avoir en abomination** loathe.
abonder [abɔ̃de] *v* abound, be plentiful. **abondance** *nf* abundance; (*richesse*) wealth. **abondant** *adj* plentiful, profuse; (*cheveux*) thick; (*repas*) copious.
s'abonner [abɔne] *v* subscribe. **abonné, -e** *nm, nf* subscriber; (*gaz, etc.*) consumer. **abonnement** *nm* subscription; (*rail, sport, etc.*) season ticket.
abord [abɔr] *nm* manner; access. **abords** *nm pl* surroundings *pl*. **au premier abord** at first sight. **d'abord** *adv* (at) first.
aborder [abɔrde] *v* approach; (*arriver à*) reach; (*problème, etc.*) tackle. **abordable** *adj* reasonable; approachable; accessible.
aborigène [abɔriʒɛn] *n*(*m*+*f*) aborigine. *adj* aboriginal.
aboutir [abutir] *v* succeed. **aboutir à** end up in *or* at, come to. **aboutissement** *nm* result; success.
aboyer [abwaje] *v* bark.
abrasif [abrazif] *nm, adj* abrasive. **abrasion** *nf* abrasion.
abréger [abreʒe] *v* shorten; (*texte*) abridge. **abrégé** *nm* summary.
abreuver [abrœve] *v* (*animal*) water; (*tremper*) soak; (*inonder*) shower, swamp. **s'abreuver** *v* quench one's thirst.
abréviation [abrevjɑsjɔ̃] *nf* abbreviation.
abri [abri] *nm* shelter; protection. **à l'abri** sheltered, safe.
abricot [abriko] *nm* apricot. **abricotier** *nm* apricot (tree).
abriter [abrite] *v* shelter; (*du soleil*) shade. **s'abriter** *v* take cover.

... v repeal. **abrogation** *nf*

...] *v* exhaust, daze, stupefy.

..., **-e** *nm, nf* absentee. *adj*
... *manque*) missing. **absence** *nf*

...psid] *nf* apse.

... [apsɛ̃t] *nf* absinthe.

... [apsɔly] *nm, adj* absolute.

...**ber** [apsɔrbe] *v* absorb; (*temps, etc.*) ...upy, take up. **absorbant** *adj* absorb...g; (*matière*) absorbent. **absorption** *nf* ...bsorption.

absoudre [apsudrə] *v* absolve. **absolution** *nf* absolution.

***s'abstenir** [apstənir] *v* abstain, refrain. **abstention** *nf* abstention. **abstinence** *nf* abstinence.

abstrait [apstrɛ] *adj* abstract. *nm* abstract; abstract art; abstract artist. **abstraction** *nf* abstraction; abstract idea. **faire abstraction de** disregard.

absurde [apsyrd] *nm, adj* absurd. **absurdité** *nf* absurdity.

abus [aby] *nm* abuse; over-use, over-indulgence. **abuser de** *v* abuse, misuse; exploit; over-use, over-indulge. **abusif** *adj* excessive; improper.

académie [akademi] *nf* academy; school. **académique** *adj* academic.

acajou [akaʒu] *nm* mahogany.

acariâtre [akarjɑtrə] *adj* sour-tempered.

accabler [akɑble] *v* overwhelm, overcome; (*questions, injures*) shower. **accablant** *adj* overwhelming; (*chaleur, travail*) exhausting. **accablement** *nm* exhaustion; depression.

accaparer [akapare] *v* monopolize; (*absorber*) take up completely.

accéder [aksede] *v* **accéder à** (*lieu*) reach, get to; attain; (*désirs*) comply with.

accélérer [akselere] *v* accelerate, speed up. **accélérateur** *nm* accelerator. **accélération** *nf* acceleration.

accent [aksɑ̃] *nm* accent; emphasis, stress; tone.

accentuer [aksɑ̃tɥe] *v* accent; emphasize, accentuate; intensify.

accepter [aksɛpte] *v* accept; (*être d'accord*) agree. **acceptable** *adj* acceptable; satisfactory. **acceptation** *nf* acceptance.

accès [aksɛ] *nm* access, approach; (*crise*) fit, bout. **accessible** *adj* accessible; (*personne*) approachable.

accessoire [akseswar] *adj* secondary; additional. *nm* accessory.

accident [aksidɑ̃] *nm* accident, mishap. **accidenté** *adj* (*terrain*) uneven. **accidentel** *adj* accidental.

acclamer [aklame] *v* acclaim, cheer. **acclamations** *nf pl* cheers *pl*.

acclimater [aklimate] *v* acclimatize. **s'acclimater** *v* adapt (oneself), become acclimatized.

accommoder [akɔmɔde] *v* adapt; (*cuisine*) prepare. **s'accommoder de** put up with.

accompagner [akɔ̃paɲe] *v* accompany. **accompagnement** *nm* accompaniment.

accomplir [akɔ̃plir] *v* accomplish, carry out, achieve; complete. **accomplissement** *nm* accomplishment, fulfilment; completion.

accord [akɔr] *nm* agreement; harmony; (*musique*) chord. **d'accord** (*fam*) O.K. **être d'accord** agree.

accordéon [akɔrdeɔ̃] *nm* accordion.

accorder [akɔrde] *v* grant, give; (*musique*) tune. **s'accorder** *v* agree; match, be in harmony.

accotement [akɔtmɑ̃] *nm* (*auto*) shoulder, verge. **accotement stabilisé** hard shoulder.

accoucher [akuʃe] *v* give birth. **accouchement** *nm* childbirth, delivery. **accoucheuse** *nf* midwife.

accouder [akude] *v* **s'accouder à** *or* **sur** lean one's elbows on.

***accourir** [akurir] *v* rush up, hurry.

accoutumer [akutyme] *v* accustom. **s'accoutumer à** get used to.

accroc [akro] *nm* tear; (*tache*) blot; (*anicroche*) hitch.

accrocher [akrɔʃe] *v* catch; (*tableau, etc.*) hang; (*voiture*) bump into. **s'accrocher à** cling to. **accrocheur, -euse** *adj* persistent; (*affiche, etc.*) eye-catching, catchy.

***accroître** [akrwatrə] *v* increase. **accroissement** *nm* increase.

s'accroupir [akrupir] *v* squat, crouch.

***accueillir** [akœjir] *v* (*aller chercher*) welcome; receive; meet; (*loger*) accommodate. **accueil** *nm* reception, welcome.

accumuler [akymyle] *v* accumulate. **accumulateur** *nm* accumulator. **accumulation** *nf* accumulation.

accuser [akyze] *v* accuse, blame; accentuate; (*montrer*) show. **accuser réception de** acknowledge receipt of. **accusation** *nf*

accusation. **accusé, -e** *nm, nf* accused, defendant.
acerbe [asɛrb] *adj* caustic.
acharner [aʃarne] *v* **s'acharner à** *or* **sur** try desperately to, work furiously at. **s'acharner contre** hound, set oneself against. **acharné** *adj* relentless; determined, set; (*combat*) fierce. **acharnement** *nm* relentlessness; determination; fierceness.
achat [aʃa] *nm* purchase. **faire des achats** go shopping.
acheminer [aʃmine] *v* forward, dispatch; transport. **s'acheminer vers** head for.
acheter [aʃte] *v* buy. **acheteur, -euse** *nm, nf* buyer.
achever [aʃve] *v* finish. **s'achever** end. **achevé** *adj* downright; accomplished. **achèvement** *nm* completion.
acide [asid] *nm, adj* acid. **acidité** *nf* acidity.
acier [asje] *nm* steel. **acier inoxydable** stainless steel. **aciérie** *nf* steelworks.
acné [akne] *nf* acne.
acompte [akɔ̃t] *nm* (*arrhes*) deposit, down payment; (*versement partiel*) instalment.
acoustique [akustik] *adj* acoustic. *nf* acoustics *pl.*
***acquérir** [akerir] *v* acquire; (*gagner*) win, gain. **acquéreur** *nm* purchaser.
acquiescer [akjese] *v* acquiesce, assent; approve. **acquiescement** *nm* acquiescence; approval.
acquis [aki] *adj* acquired; established. *nm* experience.
acquisition [akizisjɔ̃] *nf* acquisition.
acquit [aki] *nm* receipt.
acquitter [akite] *v* acquit; pay. **s'acquitter de** (*dette*) discharge. (*promesse, tâche*) fulfil. **acquittement** *nm* acquittal; payment; discharge; fulfilment.
âcre [akrə] *adj* acrid. **âcreté** *nf* acridity.
acrimonie [akrimɔni] *nf* acrimonie. **acrimonieux** *adj* acrimonious.
acrobate [akrɔbat] *n(m+f)* acrobat. **acrobatie** *nf* acrobatics. **acrobatique** *adj* acrobatic.
acrylique [akrilik] *adj* acrylic.
acte[1] [akt] *nm* action, act; (*jur*) deed, certificate. **acte de décès/mariage/naissance** death/marriage/birth certificate.
acte[2] [akt] *nm* (*théâtre*) act.
acteur [aktœr] *nm* actor. **actrice** *nf* actress.
actif [aktif] *adj* active. *nm* credit.
action [aksjɔ̃] *nf* action, act, deed; (*comm*) share. **actionnaire** *n(m+f)* shareholder.
activer [aktive] *v* speed up; (*chim*) activate. **activiste** *n(m+f)* activist. **activité** *nf* activity. **être en activité** function, be in operation.
actuaire [aktɥɛr] *n(m+f)* actuary.
actualité [aktɥalite] *nf* topicality; current events *pl.* **les actualités** the news *sing.*
actuel [aktɥɛl] *adj* current, present; (*livre, etc.*) topical. **actuellement** *adv* at the moment.
acupuncture [akypɔ̃ktyr] *nf* acupuncture.
adapter [adapte] *v* adapt, fit. **adaptable** *adj* adaptable. **adaptateur** *nm* adapter. **adaptation** *nf* adaptation.
addenda [adɛ̃da] *nm* addenda.
additif [aditif] *nm* additive; (*clause*) rider.
additionner [adisjɔne] *v* add (up). **addition** *nf* addition; (*facture*) bill. **additionnel** *adj* additional.
adénoïde [adenɔid] *adj* adenoidal. **végétations adénoïdes** *nf pl* adenoids *pl.*
adhérer [adere] *v* adhere, stick. **adhérer à** (*pneu, etc.*) grip; support; (*parti*) join, be a member of. **adhérence** *nf* adhesion; grip. **adhérent, -e** *nm, nf* adherent, member. **adhésif** *nm, adj* adhesive. **adhésion** *nf* support; membership.
adieu [adjø] *nm* farewell. *interj* goodbye! **faire ses adieux** say goodbye.
adjacent [adʒasɑ̃] *adj* adjacent.
adjectif [adʒɛktif] *nm* adjective. *adj* adjectival.
adjoint [adʒwɛ̃], **-e** *nm, nf* assistant.
adjudication [adʒydikasjɔ̃] *nf* sale by auction. **offrir par adjudication** put up for tender.
adjuger [adʒyʒe] *v* auction; (*contrat, etc.*) award. **une fois, deux fois, trois fois, adjugé!** going, going, gone!
***admettre** [admɛtrə] *v* admit; receive; (*candidat*) pass; accept; suppose.
administrer [administre] *v* administer; (*gérer*) manage, run. **administrateur, -trice** *nm, nf* administrator; director. **administratif** *adj* administrative. **administration** *nf* administration; management, government.
admirer [admire] *v* admire. **admirable** *adj* admirable. **admirateur, -trice** *nm, nf* admirer. **admiration** *nf* admiration.

admission [admisjɔ̃] *nf* admission, admittance; entry; acceptance. **admissible** *adj* admissible; acceptable; (*candidat*) eligible.
adolescence [adɔlesɑ̃s] *nf* adolescence. **adolescent, -e** *n, adj* adolescent.
adonner [adɔne] *v* **s'adonner à** devote oneself to; (*boisson, etc.*) take to.
adopter [adɔpte] *v* adopt. **adoptif** *adj* (*enfant*) adopted; (*parent*) adoptive. **adoption** *nf* adoption.
adorer [adɔre] *v* adore; (*rel*) worship. **adorable** *adj* adorable; delightful. **adorateur, -trice** *nm, nf* worshipper. **adoration** *nf* adoration; worship.
adosser [adose] *v* **adosser à** *or* **contre** lean *or* stand against.
adoucir [adusir] *v* soften; sweeten; ease, soothe.
adrénaline [adrenalin] *nf* adrenalin.
adresse[1] [adrɛs] *nf* skill, dexterity.
adresse[2] [adrɛs] *nf* address. **adresser** *v* address, direct. **s'adresser à** apply to; (*parler*) speak to.
adroit [adrwa] *adj* skilful, deft, clever.
adulation [adylɑsjɔ̃] *nf* adulation.
adulte [adylt] *n*(*m*+*f*), *adj* adult.
adultère [adyltɛr] *adj* adulterous. *nm* adultery.
***advenir** [advənir] *v* happen. **advenir de** become of.
adverbe [advɛrb] *nm* adverb. **adverbial** *adj* adverbial.
adverse [advɛrs] *adj* opposing, adverse. **adversité** *nf* adversity.
aérer [aere] *v* air; (*terre*) aerate. **aérateur** *nm* ventilator. **aération** *nf* airing; ventilation; aeration.
aérien [aerjɛ̃] *adj* aerial, air. *nm* aerial.
aérodynamique [aerɔdinamik] *adj* aerodynamic, streamlined. *nf* aerodynamics.
aéroglisseur [aerɔglisør] *nm* hovercraft.
aéronautique [aerɔnotik] *adj* aeronautical. *nf* aeronautics.
aéroport [aerɔpɔr] *nm* airport.
aéroporté [aerɔpɔrte] *adj* airborne.
aérosol [aerɔsɔl] *nm* aerosol.
affable [afablə] *adj* affable. **affabilité** *nf* affability.
affaiblir [afeblir] *v* weaken. **s'affaiblir** grow weaker; (*son*) fade; (*tempête*) die down. **affaiblissement** *nm* weakening.
affaire [afɛr] *nf* affair, matter, business; transaction, deal. **affaires** *nf pl* (*commerce*) business *sing*; (*effets personnels*) things *pl*, belongings *pl*. **avoir affaire à** have to deal with. **faire l'affaire** do nicely, come in handy. **occupe-toi de tes affaires!** mind your own business! **affairé** *adj* busy.
s'affaisser [afese] *v* sink, subside; (*personne*) collapse. **affaissement** *nm* subsidence.
affamer [afame] *v* starve. **affamé** *adj* starving, ravenous.
affecter[1] [afɛkte] *v* feign; (*adopter*) take on, assume. **affectation** *nf* affectation.
affecter[2] [afɛkte] *v* allocate, assign; (*nommer*) appoint. **affectation** *nf* allocation; appointment.
affecter[3] [afɛkte] *v* affect, touch, move.
affection [afɛksjɔ̃] *nf* affection; (*méd*) ailment. **affectionner** *v* be fond of. **affectueux** *adj* affectionate.
affiche [afiʃ] *nf* poster, bill. **afficher** *v* stick up; (*péj*) flaunt, display.
affilier [afilje] *v* affiliate. **affiliation** *nf* affiliation.
affiner [afine] *v* refine.
affinité [afinite] *nf* affinity.
affirmer [afirme] *v* assert, affirm. **affirmatif** *adj* affirmative; positive. **affirmation** *nf* assertion. **affirmative** *nf* affirmative.
affliction [afliksjɔ̃] *nf* affliction.
affliger [afliʒe] *v* distress. **être affligé de** be afflicted with.
affluence [aflyɑ̃s] *nf* crowd.
affoler [afɔle] *v* throw into a panic, terrify. **s'affoler** panic. **affolant** *adj* alarming. **affolé** *adj* panic-stricken. **affolement** *nm* panic.
affranchir [afrɑ̃ʃir] *v* (*lettre*) stamp; (*timbre*) frank; (*libérer*) free, emancipate.
affréter [afrete] *v* charter, hire.
affreux [afrø] *adj* dreadful, horrible, ghastly.
affronter [afrɔ̃te] *v* confront, face, brave.
afin [afɛ̃] *prep* **afin de** so as to, in order to. **afin que** so that, in order that.
Afrique [afrik] *nf* Africa. **africain** *adj* African. **Africain, -e** *nm, nf* African.
agacer [agase] *v* irritate, annoy. **agacement** *nm* irritation, annoyance.
âge [ɑʒ] *nm* age. **quel âge avez-vous?** how old are you? **âgé** *adj* old, elderly. **âgé de quatre ans** four years old.
agence [aʒɑ̃s] *nf* agency, office, bureau.
agenda [aʒɛ̃da] *nm* diary.

s'agenouiller [aʒnuje] *v* kneel (down).
agent [aʒɑ̃] *nm* agent; policeman; officer. **agent de change** stockbroker. **agent immobilier** estate agent.
agglomération [aglɔmerɑsjɔ̃] *nf* built-up area, town; conglomeration.
aggraver [agrave] *v* aggravate, worsen; (*redoubler*) increase. **aggravation** *nf* aggravation, worsening; increase.
agile [aʒil] *adj* agile, nimble. **agilité** *nf* agility.
agir [aʒir] *v* act. **s'agir de** be a matter *or* question of, be about.
agiter [aʒite] *v* shake, wave, flap; trouble; debate, discuss. **s'agiter** fidget, get restless. **agitation** *nf* agitation; restlessness. **agité** *adj* troubled; restless; (*mer*) rough.
agneau [aɲo] *nm* lamb.
agnostique [agnɔstik] *n(m+f)*, *adj* agnostic.
agoniser [agɔnize] *v* be dying. **agonie** *nf* mortal agony; (*déclin*) death throes *pl*. **à l'agonie** at death's door.
agrafe [agraf] *nf* hook; (*papiers*) staple. **agrafer** *v* hook, fasten; staple. **agrafeuse** *nf* stapler.
agrandir [agrɑ̃dir] *v* enlarge; (*développer*) expand, extend. **agrandissement** *nm* (*phot*) enlargement; expansion, extension.
agréable [agreablə] *adj* pleasant.
agréer [agree] *v* accept. **agréer à** please. **agrément** *nm* charm, pleasantness.
agression [agrɛsjɔ̃] *nf* aggression; attack. **agressif** *adj* aggressive.
agricole [agrikɔl] *adj* agricultural.
agriculture [agrikyltyr] *nf* agriculture.
agrumes [agrym] *nm pl* citrus fruits *pl*.
aguets [agɛ] *nm pl* **aux aguets** on the look-out.
ahurir [ayrir] *v* astound. **ahurissement** *nm* stupefaction.
aide [ɛd] *nf* help, aid, assistance. *n(m+f)* assistant. **à l'aide!** help! **à l'aide de** with the help of. **venir en aide à** come to the assistance of.
aider [ede] *v* help, aid, assist.
aïeux [ajø] *nm pl* forefathers *pl*.
aigle [ɛglə] *nm* eagle.
aiglefin [egləfɛ̃] *nm* haddock.
aigre [ɛgrə] *adj* sour; (*son*) shrill; (*froid*) bitter. **aigre-doux, -douce** *adj* bittersweet; (*cuisine*) sweet and sour. **aigreur** *nf* sourness.
aigrir [egrir] *v* embitter, sour.
aigu, -uë [egy] *adj* acute, sharp; (*son*) high-pitched.
aiguille [egɥij] *nf* needle; (*horloge*) hand. **travail à l'aiguille** *nm* needlework.
aiguillon [egɥijɔ̃] *nm* (*insecte*) sting; (*plante*) thorn; stimulus. **aiguillonner** *v* spur on.
aiguiser [egize] *v* sharpen; stimulate.
ail [aj] *nm*, *pl* **aulx** garlic.
aile [ɛl] *nf* wing; (*moulin*) sail. **ailé** *adj* winged.
ailleurs [ajœr] *adv* elsewhere. **d'ailleurs** *adv* besides. **par ailleurs** otherwise.
aimable [ɛmablə] *adj* kind, nice.
aimant [ɛmɑ̃] *nm* magnet. **aimanter** *v* magnetize.
aimer [eme] *v* like; (*d'amour*) love. **aimer mieux** prefer.
aine [ɛn] *nf* groin.
aîné [ene], **-e** *adj* elder, eldest. *nm*, *nf* eldest child; senior.
ainsi [ɛ̃si] *adv* in this way, thus, so. **ainsi que** just as, as well as. **et ainsi de suite** and so on. **pour ainsi dire** as it were.
air[1] [ɛr] *nm* air; atmosphere.
air[2] [ɛr] *nm* (*apparence*) air, look. **avoir l'air de** look *or* seem like.
air[3] [ɛr] *nm* (*musique*) tune, air; (*opéra*) aria.
aire [ɛr] *nf* area.
aise [ɛz] *nf* pleasure, joy. **à l'aise** at ease, comfortable. **mal à l'aise** ill at ease, uncomfortable. *adj* glad. **aisance** *nf* ease; (*richesse*) affluence. **aisé** *adj* easy.
aisselle [ɛsɛl] *nf* armpit.
ajonc [aʒɔ̃] *nm* gorse.
ajourner [aʒurne] *v* adjourn, postpone. **ajournement** *nm* adjournment, postponement.
ajouter [aʒute] *v* add. **s'ajouter à** add to.
ajuster [aʒyste] *v* adjust, fit; adapt.
alarme [alarm] *nf* alarm. **alarmer** *v* alarm. **alarmiste** *n(m+f)*, *adj* alarmist.
Albanie [albani] *nf* Albania. **albanais** *nm*, *adj* Albanian. **Albanais, -e** *nm*, *nf* Albanian.
albatros [albatros] *nm* albatross.
album [albɔm] *nm* album. **album à colorier** colouring book.
alcali [alkali] *nm* alkali. **alcalin** *adj* alkaline.
alchimie [alʃimi] *nf* alchemy. **alchimiste** *nm* alchemist.

alcool [alkɔl] *nm* alcohol. **alcool à brûler** methylated spirits. **alcoolique** *n(m+f)*, *adj* alcoholic. **alcoolisme** *nm* alcoholism.
alcôve [alkov] *nf* alcove.
aléatoire [aleatwar] *adj* uncertain, chancy.
alentour [alɑ̃tur] *adv* around. **alentours** *nm pl* surroundings *pl*, neighbourhood *sing*.
alerte [alɛrt] *adj* agile, alert, brisk. *nf* alert, alarm, warning. **alerter** *v* alert, notify, warn.
algèbre [alʒɛbrə] *nf* algebra. **algèbrique** *adj* algebraic.
Alger [alʒe] *n* Algiers.
Algérie [alʒeri] *nf* Algeria. **algérien** *adj* Algerian. **Algérien, -enne** *nm, nf* Algerian.
algue [alg] *nf* seaweed.
alias [aljɑs] *adv* alias.
alibi [alibi] *nm* alibi.
aliéner [aljene] *v* alienate; (*droits, etc.*) give up. **aliénation** *nf* alienation; (*méd*) derangement. **alienė, -e** *nm, nf* insane person.
aligner [aliɲe] *v* align, line up. **alignement** *nm* alignment.
aliment [alimɑ̃] *nm* food. **alimentation** *nf* feeding; (*comm*) foodstuffs *pl*. **alimenter** *v* feed, supply.
alinéa [alinea] *nm* paragraph.
aliter [alite] *v* confine to bed. **alité** *adj* bedridden.
allaiter [alete] *v* (*femme*) (breast-)feed; (*animal*) suckle. **allaitement** *nm* (breast-) feeding; suckling.
allée [ale] *nf* path.
alléger [aleʒe] *v* alleviate; (*poids*) lighten, make lighter. **allégement** *nm* alleviation.
allégorie [alegɔri] *nf* allegory. **allégorique** *adj* allegorical.
allègre [alɛgrə] *adj* cheerful, lively. **allégresse** *nf* elation.
alléguer [alege] *v* allege; (*excuse*) put forward. **allégation** *nf* allegation.
alléluia [aleluja] *nm, interj* hallelujah.
Allemagne [almaɲ] *nf* Germany. **allemand** *nm, adj* German. **Allemand, -e** *nm, nf* German.
***aller** [ale] *v* go; (*futur*) be going to. **aller à** (*style*) suit; (*mesure*) fit. **aller chercher** fetch. **aller de soi** be obvious. **allez-y!** go on! **allons!** come on! **allons-y!** let's go! **ça va** all right. **comment allez-vous?** how are you? **s'en aller** go away. *nm* (*trajet*) outward journey; (*billet*) single. **aller-retour** *nm* return.
allergie [alɛrʒi] *nf* allergy. **allergique** *adj* allergic.
allier [alje] *v* ally; unite, combine. **alliage** *nm* alloy. **alliance** *nf* alliance; union; (*bague*) wedding ring; combination. **allié, -e** *nm, nf* ally.
alligator [aligatɔr] *nm* alligator.
allitération [aliterɑsjɔ̃] *nf* alliteration.
allô [alo] *interj* hello!
allocation [alɔkɑsjɔ̃] *nf* allocation; (*somme*) allowance. **allocation de chômage** unemployment benefit. **allocations familiales** family allowance *sing*.
allocution [alɔkysjɔ̃] *nf* short speech.
allonger [alɔ̃ʒe] *v* lengthen; (*étendre*) stretch out; (*cuisine*) thin. **allonger le cou** crane one's neck.
allouer [alwe] *v* allocate, allot.
allumer [alyme] *v* light; (*lampe, etc.*) turn on. **allumage** *nm* lighting; (*auto*) ignition. **allumette** *nf* match.
allure [alyr] *nf* (*vitesse*) speed, pace; (*démarche*) walk, bearing; air, appearance. **à toute allure** at full speed.
allusion [alyzjɔ̃] *nf* allusion. **faire allusion à** allude to.
almanach [almana] *nm* almanac.
aloi [alwa] *nm* **de bon aloi** respectable, worthy. **de mauvais aloi** of doubtful reputation *or* quality.
alors [alɔr] *adv* then; so; in that case. **alors même que** even if *or* though. **alors que** while.
alouette [alwɛt] *nf* lark.
alourdir [alurdir] *v* make heavy, weigh down.
aloyau [alwajo] *nm* sirloin.
alphabet [alfabɛ] *nm* alphabet. **alphabétique** *adj* alphabetical.
alpinisme [alpinismə] *nm* mountaineering. **alpiniste** *n(m+f)* mountaineer.
altercation [altɛrkɑsjɔ̃] *nf* altercation.
altérer [altere] *v* (*donner soif*) make thirsty; falsify; (*abîmer*) spoil, debase. **altération** *nf* deterioration; falsification.
alterner [altɛrne] *v* alternate. **alternance** *nf* alternation. **alternatif** *adj* alternate; (*élec*) alternating. **alternative** *nf* alternative.
Altesse [altɛs] *nf* Highness.
altier [altje] *adj* haughty.

altitude [altityd] *nf* altitude, height.
alto [alto] *nm* viola.
aluminium [alyminjɔm] *nm* aluminium.
amabilité [amabilite] *nf* kindness.
amadouer [amadwe] *v* coax, cajole.
amaigrir [amegrir] *v* make thin *or* thinner. **amaigrissant** *adj* (*régime*) slimming. **amaigrissement** *nm* thinness; slimming.
amalgamer [amalgame] *v* combine; (*métal*) amalgamate.
amande [amɑ̃d] *nf* almond. **amandier** *nm* almond (tree).
amant [amɑ̃] *nm* lover.
amarrer [amare] *v* (*naut*) moor; (*fixer*) make fast. **amarrage** *nm* mooring.
amas [amɑ] *nm* heap, mass. **amasser** *v* amass, accumulate.
amateur [amatœr] *nm* (*non-professionnel*) amateur; enthusiast. **d'amateur** *adj* amateurish.
ambassade [ɑ̃basad] *nf* embassy; mission. **ambassadeur, -drice** *nm, nf* ambassador.
ambiance [ɑ̃bjɑ̃s] *nf* atmosphere.
ambidextre [ɑ̃bidekstrə] *adj* ambidextrous.
ambigu, -uë [ɑ̃bigy] *adj* ambiguous. **ambiguïté** *nf* ambiguity.
ambition [ɑ̃bisjɔ̃] *nf* ambition. **ambitieux** *adj* ambitious.
ambivalent [ɑ̃bivalɑ̃] *adj* ambivalent. **ambivalence** *nf* ambivalence.
ambre [ɑ̃brə] *nm* amber.
ambulance [ɑ̃bylɑ̃s] *nf* ambulance. **ambulancier** *nm* ambulance man.
ambulant [ɑ̃bylɑ̃] *adj* itinerant, travelling.
âme [ɑm] *nf* soul.
améliorer [ameljɔre] *v* improve. **amélioration** *nf* improvement.
aménager [amenaʒe] *v* fit out *or* up; (*parc*) lay out; develop. **aménagement** *nm* fitting-out; development.
amender [amɑ̃de] *v* amend. **amende** *nf* fine.
amener [amne] *v* bring; cause.
amer [amer] *adj* bitter. **amertume** *nf* bitterness.
Amérique [amerik] *nf* America. **américain** *adj* American. **Américain, -e** *nm, nf* American.
améthyste [ametist] *nf, adj* amethyst.
ameublement [amœbləmɑ̃] *nm* furnishing; (*meubles*) furniture.
ami [ami], **-e** *nm, nf* friend. *adj* friendly.
amiable [amjablə] *adj* amicable.
amiante [amjɑ̃t] *nm* asbestos.
amibe [amib] *nf* amoeba.
amical [amikal] *adj* friendly. **amicale** *nf* association.
amidon [amidɔ̃] *nm* starch. **amidonner** *v* starch.
amiral [amiral] *nm* admiral.
amitié [amitje] *nf* friendship. **amitiés** *nf pl* best wishes *pl*. **prendre en amitié** befriend.
ammoniaque [amɔnjak] *nf* ammonia.
amnésie [amnezi] *nf* amnesia.
amnistie [amnisti] *nf* amnesty.
amoindrir [amwɛ̃drir] *v* reduce, weaken, diminish.
amollir [amɔlir] *v* soften, weaken.
amonceler [amɔ̃sle] *v* pile up, accumulate. **amoncellement** *nm* heap; accumulation.
amont [amɔ̃] *nm* **d'amont** *adj* (*eau*) upstream; (*pente*) uphill. **en amont** *adv* upstream; uphill.
amoral [amɔral] *adj* amoral.
amorcer [amɔrse] *v* bait; (*commencer*) begin. **amorce** *nf* bait; beginning.
amorphe [amɔrf] *adj* (*roche*) amorphous; (*personne*) passive, lifeless.
amortir [amɔrtir] *v* absorb, cushion, deaden; (*dette*) pay off. **amortisseur** *nm* shock absorber.
amour [amur] *nm* love. **amour-propre** *nm* pride, self-esteem. **amoureux** *adj* (*personne*) in love; (*tendre*) loving.
ampère [ɑ̃per] *nm* amp.
amphétamine [ɑ̃fetamin] *nf* amphetamine.
amphibie [ɑ̃fibi] *adj* amphibious. *nm* amphibian.
amphithéâtre [ɑ̃fiteɑtrə] *nm* amphitheatre; (*université*) lecture theatre.
ample [ɑ̃plə] *adj* ample, full. **ampleur** *nf* (*importance*) scale, extent; fullness.
amplifier [ɑ̃plifje] *v* develop, expand; (*son*) amplify. **amplificateur** *nm* amplifier.
ampoule [ɑ̃pul] *nf* (*élec*) bulb; (*méd*) blister.
amputer [ɑ̃pyte] *v* amputate; (*texte, etc.*) reduce drastically.
Amsterdam [amsterdam] *n* Amsterdam.
amuser [amyze] *v* amuse. **s'amuser** enjoy oneself, have fun. **amusement** *nm* entertainment, amusement; pastime.
amygdale [amidal] *nf* tonsil. **amygdalite** *nf* tonsillitis.

an [ɑ̃] *nm* year. **avoir 15 ans** be 15 years old.
anachronisme [anakrɔnisme] *nm* anachronism.
anagramme [anagram] *nf* anagram.
anal [anal] *adj* anal.
analogie [analɔʒi] *nf* analogy.
analphabète [analfabɛt] *adj* illiterate. **analphabétisme** *nm* illiteracy.
analyser [analize] *v* analyse; (*méd*) test. **analyse** *nf* analysis; test. **analytique** *adj* analytical.
ananas [anana] *nm* pineapple.
anarchie [anarʃi] *nf* anarchy. **anarchiste** *n*(*m*+*f*) anarchist.
anatomie [anatɔmi] *nf* anatomy.
ancêtre [ɑ̃sɛtrə] *n*(*m*+*f*) ancestor.
anchois [ɑ̃ʃwa] *nm* anchovy.
ancien [ɑ̃sjɛ̃], **-enne** *adj* (*vieux*) ancient; (*d'autrefois*) former. *nm*, *nf* elder; (*élève*) old boy, old girl. **ancienneté** *nf* seniority; great age.
ancre [ɑ̃krə] *nf* anchor. **ancrer** *v* anchor.
Andorre [ɑ̃dɔr] *nm* Andorra.
âne [ɑn] *nm* donkey, ass.
anéantir [aneɑ̃tir] *v* annihilate; destroy; (*accabler*) overwhelm. **anéanti** *adj* (*fatigué*) exhausted; overwhelmed. **anéantissement** *nm* annihilation; destruction; exhaustion.
anecdote [anɛkdɔt] *nf* anecdote.
anémie [anemi] *nf* anaemia. **anémique** *adj* anaemic.
anémone [anemɔn] *nf* anemone.
anesthésier [anɛstezje] *v* anaesthetize. **anesthésique** *nm*, *adj* anaesthetic. **anesthésiste** *n*(*m*+*f*) anaesthetist.
ange [ɑ̃ʒ] *nm* angel.
angélique[1] [ɑ̃ʒelik] *adj* angelic.
angélique[2] [ɑ̃ʒelik] *nf* angelica.
angine [ɑ̃ʒin] *nf* sore throat. **angine de poitrine** angina.
angle [ɑ̃glə] *nm* angle; (*coin*) corner. **angle droit** right angle.
Angleterre [ɑ̃glətɛr] *nf* England. **anglais** *nm*, *adj* English. **les Anglais** the English.
anglican [ɑ̃glikɑ̃], **-e** *n*, *adj* Anglican.
angoisse [ɑ̃gwas] *nf* anguish, distress; (*peur*) dread. **angoissant** *adj* harrowing. **angoissé** *adj* anguished, distressed.
anguille [ɑ̃gij] *nf* eel.
anguleux [ɑ̃gylø] *adj* angular, bony.
anicroche [anikrɔʃ] *nf* (*fam*) hitch, snag.
animal[1] [animal] *nm* animal.
animal[2] [animal] *adj* animal.
animer [anime] *v* animate; (*discussion, etc.*) lead; (*pousser*) drive, impel; (*soirée, etc.*) liven up. **s'animer** come to life, liven up. **animateur**, **-trice** *nm*, *nf* compère; (*cinéma*) animator. **animation** *nf* animation; liveliness. **animé** *adj* busy, lively.
animosité [animozite] *nf* animosity.
anis [ani] *nm* aniseed.
annales [anal] *nf pl* annals *pl*.
anneau [ano] *nm* ring; (*chaîne*) link.
année [ane] *nf* year. **année bissextile** leap year. **année-lumière** *nf* light year.
annexer [anɛkse] *v* annex. **annexe** *nf* annexe.
annihiler [aniile] *v* destroy, ruin, annihilate. **annihilation** *nf* annihilation, destruction, ruin.
anniversaire [anivɛrsɛr] *nm* (*naissance*) birthday; (*événement*) anniversary. **anniversaire de mariage** (wedding) anniversary.
annoncer [anɔ̃se] *v* announce; (*prédire*) forecast, foreshadow; indicate. **s'annoncer** approach. **s'annoncer bien** look promising. **annonce** *nf* announcement; sign, indication; (*publicité*) advertisement.
annoter [anɔte] *v* annotate. **annotation** *nf* annotation.
annuaire [anɥɛr] *nm* annual, yearbook; telephone directory.
annuel [anɥɛl] *adj* annual.
annuler [anyle] *v* (*rendre nul*) nullify; (*mariage*) annul; (*commande, etc.*) cancel. **annulation** *nf* nullification; annulment; cancellation.
anode [anɔd] *nf* anode.
anodin [anɔdɛ̃] *adj* insignificant, trivial; (*sans danger*) harmless.
anomalie [anɔmali] *nf* anomaly.
anonyme [anɔnim] *adj* anonymous; impersonal. **anonymat** *nm* anonymity.
anormal [anɔrmal] *adj* abnormal.
anse [ɑ̃s] *nf* handle; (*géog*) cove.
antagonist [ɑ̃tagɔnist] *n*(*m*+*f*) antagonist. *adj* antagonistic. **antagonisme** *nm* antagonism.
antarctique [ɑ̃tarktik] *adj* antarctic. **l'Antarctique** *nm* the Antarctic.
antenne [ɑ̃tɛn] *nf* antenna; (*TV*, *radio*) aerial. **sur** *or* **à l'antenne** on the air.
antérieur, -e [ɑ̃terjœr] *adj* previous; (*patte*, *membre*) front, fore. **antérieur à** prior to.

anthologie [ɑ̃tɔlɔʒi] *nf* anthology.
anthropologie [ɑ̃trɔpɔlɔʒi] *nf* anthropology. **anthropologique** *adj* anthropological. **anthropologiste** *n(m+f)* anthropologist.
antiaérien [ɑ̃tiaerjɛ̃] *adj* anti-aircraft; (*abri*) air-raid.
antialcoolique [ɑ̃tialkɔlik] *adj* against alcohol *or* alcoholism. **ligue antialcoolique** *nf* temperance league.
antibiotique [ɑ̃tibjɔtik] *nm, adj* antibiotic.
antichoc [ɑ̃tiʃɔk] *adj* shockproof.
anticiper [ɑ̃tisipe] *v* anticipate. **anticipation** *nf* anticipation. **par anticipation** in advance.
anticonceptionnel [ɑ̃tikɔ̃sɛpsjɔnɛl] *adj* contraceptive.
anticorps [ɑ̃tikɔr] *nm* antibody.
anticyclone [ɑ̃tisiklon] *nm* anticyclone.
antidater [ɑ̃tidate] *v* backdate.
antidote [ɑ̃tidɔt] *nm* antidote.
antigel [ɑ̃tiʒɛl] *nm* antifreeze.
antihistaminique [ɑ̃tiistaminik] *nm, adj* antihistamine.
antilope [ɑ̃tilɔp] *nf* antelope.
antipathique [ɑ̃tipatik] *adj* unpleasant.
antique [ɑ̃tik] *adj* antique, ancient. **antiquaire** *n(m+f)* antique dealer. **antiquité** *nf* antiquity. **antiquités** *nf pl* (*meubles, etc.*) antiques *pl.*
antisémite [ɑ̃tisemit] *adj* anti-Semitic. *n(m+f)* anti-Semite. **antisémitisme** *nm* anti-Semitism.
antiseptique [ɑ̃tisɛptik] *nm, adj* antiseptic.
antisocial [ɑ̃tisɔsjal] *adj* antisocial.
antithèse [ɑ̃titɛz] *nf* antithesis. **antithétique** *adj* antithetical.
antonyme [ɑ̃tɔnim] *nm* antonym.
antre [ɑ̃trə] *nm* den.
anus [anys] *nm* anus.
anxiété [ɑ̃ksjete] *nf* anxiety. **anxieux** *adj* anxious.
août [u] *nm* August.
apaiser [apeze] *v* calm, soothe; (*soif*) quench. **s'apaiser** die down; calm down; be satisfied.
aparté [aparte] *nm* aside.
apathie [apati] *nf* apathy. **apathique** *adj* apathetic.
***apercevoir** [apɛrsəvwar] *v* see; (*brièvement*) catch sight of. **s'apercevoir de** notice. **aperçu** *nm* outline; (*coup d'œil*) glimpse.
apéritif [aperitif] *nm* aperitif.
aphrodisiaque [afrɔdizjak] *nm, adj* aphrodisiac.
aplanir [aplanir] *v* level; (*problèmes*) smooth away, iron out.
aplatir [aplatir] *v* flatten. **s'aplatir devant** grovel to. **aplati** *adj* flat.
aplomb [aplɔ̃] *nm* self-assurance; balance, equilibrium. **d'aplomb** *adv* (*stable*) steady; (*vertical*) straight down.
apogée [apɔʒe] *nm* peak, apogee.
apologie [apɔlɔʒi] *nf* apologia, defence.
apostrophe [apɔstrɔf] *nf* apostrophe; (*interpellation*) rude remark.
apôtre [apotrə] *nm* apostle.
***apparaître** [aparɛtrə] *v* appear; seem.
apparat [apara] *nm* pomp. **d'apparat** *adj* ceremonial.
appareil [aparɛj] *nm* device, apparatus, appliance; (*TV, radio*) set; (*fam*) phone; (*dents*) brace; (*fracture*) splint; (*anat*) system. **à l'appareil** (*téléphone*) speaking. **appareil-photo** *nm* camera. **appareil à sous** slot machine.
apparence [aparɑ̃s] *nf* appearance; semblance. **en apparence** apparently. **apparent** *adj* obvious; visible.
apparenter [aparɑ̃te] *v* **s'apparenter à** ally oneself with; marry into; (*ressembler*) be similar to.
apparition [aparisjɔ̃] *nf* appearance; vision, apparition.
appartement [apartəmɑ̃] *nm* flat; (*hôtel*) suite.
***appartenir** [apartənir] *v* **appartenir à** belong to; (*impersonnel*) be up to.
appât [apɑ] *nm* (*pêche*) bait; lure. **appâter** *v* lure; (*piège*) bait.
appeler [aple] *v* call; summon, send for; telephone. **en appeler à/de** appeal to/against. **s'appeler** be called. **comment vous appelez-vous?** what is your name? **appel** *nm* appeal; (*cri*) call; (*école*) register. **faire appel** appeal.
appendice [apɛ̃dis] *nm* appendix. **appendicite** *nf* appendicitis.
appentis [apɑ̃ti] *nm* lean-to; (*toit*) sloping roof.
appétit [apeti] *nm* appetite. **appétissant** *adj* appetizing.
applaudir [aplodir] *v* applaud. **s'applaudir** congratulate oneself. **applaudissements** *nm pl* applause *sing.*
appliquer [aplike] *v* apply. **applicable** *adj* applicable. **application** *nf* application. **appliqué** *adj* industrious.

appointements [apwɛ̃tmɑ̃] *nm pl* salary *sing*.
apporter [apɔrte] *v* bring.
apposer [apoze] *v* affix.
apprécier [apresje] *v* appreciate; value, assess. **appréciable** *adj* appreciable. **appréciation** *nf* assessment.
appréhender [apreɑ̃de] *v* apprehend; (*craindre*) dread. **appréhensif** *adj* apprehensive. **appréhension** *nf* apprehension.
***apprendre** [aprɑ̃drə] *v* learn; (*enseigner*) teach; (*aviser*) inform (of).
apprenti [aprɑ̃ti], **-e** *nm*, *nf* apprentice; (*débutant*) beginner. **apprentissage** *nm* apprenticeship.
apprivoiser [aprivwaze] *v* tame. **apprivoisé** *adj* tame.
approbation [aprɔbɑsjɔ̃] *nf* approval. **approbateur, -trice** *adj* approving.
approcher [aprɔʃe] *v* approach, draw *or* go near; (*objet*) move near. **s'approcher de** come *or* go near to, approach. **approche** *nf* approach.
approfondir [aprɔfɔ̃dir] *v* deepen; (*étudier*) go into. **approfondi** *adj* thorough.
approprier [aprɔprije] *v* suit, adapt. **s'approprier** appropriate. **s'approprier à** be appropriate to, suit. **approprié** *adj* appropriate.
approuver [apruve] *v* approve (of).
approvisionner [aprɔvizjɔne] *v* supply.
approximatif [aprɔksimatif] *adj* approximate. **approximation** *nf* approximation.
appui [apɥi] *nm* support. **appui-bras** *nm* armrest.
appuyer [apɥije] *v* press; support; (*poser*) lean, rest. **appuyer sur** press; rest on; stress, accentuate. **s'appuyer sur** rely on.
âpre [ɑprə] *adj* pungent, acrid; (*cruel*) bitter; (*dur*) grim; (*rude*) harsh.
après [aprɛ] *prep* after. *adv* afterwards. **après-demain** *adv* the day after tomorrow. **après-midi** *nm* afternoon. **après-rasage** *nm* after-shave. **d'après** (*selon*) according to; (*suivant*) next, following.
à-propos [aprɔpo] *nm* aptness.
apte [aptə] *adj* **apte à** capable of, fit for. **aptitude** *nf* aptitude, ability.
aquarelle [akwarɛl] *nf* watercolour.
aquarium [akwarjɔm] *nm* aquarium.
aquatique [akwatik] *adj* aquatic.
aqueduc [akdyk] *nm* aqueduct.
aqueux [akø] *adj* aqueous.
arable [arablə] *adj* arable.
arachide [araʃid] *nf* peanut.
araignée [areɲe] *nf* spider.
arbitrer [arbitre] *v* arbitrate; (*sport*) referee, umpire. **arbitrage** *nm* arbitration. **arbitraire** *adj* arbitrary. **arbitre** *nm* judge; (*sport*) referee, umpire.
arbre [arbrə] *nm* tree; (*tech*) shaft. **arbre à cames** camshaft. **arbre de Noël** Christmas tree. **arbre généalogique** family tree.
arbrisseau [arbriso] *nm* shrub.
arbuste [arbyst] *nm* bush.
arc [ark] *nm* arc; (*arme*) bow; arch. **arc-en-ciel** *nm* rainbow.
arcade [arkad] *nf* archway. **arcades** *nf pl* arcade *sing*, arches *pl*.
archaïque [arkaik] *adj* archaic.
arche[1] [arʃ] *nf* arch.
arche[2] [arʃ] *nf* (*rel*) ark.
archéologie [arkeɔlɔʒi] *nf* archaeology. **archéologique** *adj* archaeological. **archéologue** *n*(*m*+*f*) archaeologist.
archet [arʃɛ] *nm* bow.
archevêque [arʃəvɛk] *nm* archbishop.
archi- [arʃi] *prefix* tremendously, utterly. **archiplein** *adj* (*fam*) chock-a-block.
archiduc [arʃidyk] *nm* archduke.
archipel [arʃipɛl] *nm* archipelago.
architecte [arʃitɛkt] *nm* architect. **architectural** *adj* architectural. **architecture** *nf* architecture.
archives [arʃiv] *nf pl* archives *pl*.
arctique [arktik] *adj* arctic. **l'arctique** *nm* the Arctic.
ardent [ardɑ̃] *adj* burning; passionate; ardent.
ardeur [ardœr] *nf* ardour; passion.
ardoise [ardwaz] *nf* slate.
ardu [ardy] *adj* arduous.
arène [arɛn] *nf* arena.
arête [arɛt] *nf* fishbone; (*bord*) ridge; (*cube*) edge.
argent [arʒɑ̃] *nm* money; (*métal*) silver. **argent comptant** cash. **argent de poche** pocket money. **argent liquide** ready money. **argenté** *adj* silvery, silvered. **argenterie** *nf* silverware.
argile [arʒil] *nf* clay.
argot [argo] *nm* slang. **argotique** *adj* slang.
argument [argymɑ̃] *nm* argument. **argumenter** *v* argue, reason.
aride [arid] *adj* arid, dry. **aridité** *nf* aridity.

aristocratie [aristɔkrasi] *nf* aristocracy. **aristocrate** *n(m+f)* aristocrat. **aristocratique** *adj* aristocratic.
arithmétique [aritmetik] *nf* arithmetic. *adj* arithmetical.
arme [arm] *nf* weapon, arm. **armes** *nf pl* coat of arms *sing.*
armée [arme] *nf* army. **armée de l'air** air force. **Armée du Salut** Salvation Army.
armer [arme] *v* arm; equip; reinforce; (*fusil*) cock.
armoire [armwar] *nf* cupboard.
armure [armyr] *nf* armour.
arôme [arom] *nm* aroma; fragrance.
arpenter [arpɑ̃te] *v* (*terrain*) measure; pace up and down. **arpentage** *nm* surveying.
arquer [arke] *v* curve; arch. **arqué** *adj* curved; arched. **avoir les jambes arquées** be bow-legged.
arracher [araʃe] *v* snatch; (*extraire*) pull up *or* out; (*déchirer*) tear off *or* out. **d'arrache-pied** *adv* relentlessly.
arranger [arɑ̃ʒe] *v* arrange; (*régler*) settle; be convenient; (*réparer*) fix. **s'arranger** manage; (*se mettre d'accord*) come to an agreement; (*situation*) work out. **arrangement** *nm* arrangement; agreement.
arrérages [areraʒ] *nm pl* arrears *pl.*
arrestation [arɛstɑsjɔ̃] *nf* arrest.
arrêt [arɛ] *nm* stop; stopping; judgment. **arrêt d'autobus** bus stop. **arrêt du cœur** cardiac arrest. **arrêt de mort** death sentence.
arrêté [arete] *adj* firm, fixed. *nm* order, decree.
arrêter [arete] *v* stop; (*abandonner*) give up; (*police*) arrest; fix, decide on. **s'arrêter (de)** stop.
arrhes [ar] *nf pl* deposit *sing.*
arrière [arjɛr] *nm* rear, back; (*naut*) stern. **en arrière** backwards; (*derrière*) behind. *adj* rear, back. **arrière-goût** *nm* aftertaste. **arrière-pensée** *nf* ulterior motive. **arrière-plan** *nm* background. **arriéré** *adj* (*comm*) overdue, in arrears; (*personne, pays*) backward.
arriver [arive] *v* arrive; (*se passer*) happen. **arriver à** reach; (*réussir à*) manage. **j'arrive!** I'm coming! **arrivée** *nf* arrival.
arrogance [arɔgɑ̃s] *nf* arrogance. **arrogant** *adj* arrogant.
arrondir [arɔ̃dir] *v* round (off), make rounded. **arrondi** *adj* round.
arrondissement [arɔ̃dismɑ̃] *nm* district.
arroser [aroze] *v* water, spray; (*fam: repas*) wash down. **arrosoir** *nm* watering-can.
arsenal [arsənal] *nm* arsenal.
arsenic [arsənik] *nm* arsenic.
art [ar] *nm* art; (*adresse*) skill. **arts ménagers** domestic science *sing.*
artère [artɛr] *nf* artery. **artériel** *adj* arterial.
arthrite [artrit] *nf* arthritis. **arthritique** *adj* arthritic.
artichaut [artiʃo] *nm* globe artichoke.
article [artiklə] *nm* article, item. **article réclame** special offer. **articles de Paris** fancy goods *pl.* **articles de toilette** toiletries *pl.*
articuler [artikyle] *v* articulate. **articulation** *nf* (*anat*) joint; articulation. **articulation du doigt** knuckle. **articulé** *adj* articulate; jointed.
artifice [artifis] *nm* device, trick, artifice.
artificiel [artifisjɛl] *adj* artificial.
artillerie [artijri] *nf* artillery.
artisan [artizɑ̃] *nm* craftsman, artisan.
artiste [artist] *n(m+f)* artist; (*théâtre*) performer. **artistique** *adj* artistic.
as [ɑs] *nm* ace.
asbeste [asbɛst] *nm* asbestos
ascendant [asɑ̃dɑ̃] *adj* upward, rising. *nm* influence, ascendancy. **ascendance** *nf* ancestry.
ascenseur [asɑ̃sœr] *nm* lift.
ascension [asɑ̃sjɔ̃] *nf* ascent.
Asie [azi] *nf* Asia. **asiatique** *adj* Asian. **Asiatique** *n(m+f)* Asian.
asile [azil] *nm* refuge, asylum, sanctuary; (*vieillards*) home.
aspect [aspɛ] *nm* aspect; appearance, look.
asperge [aspɛrʒ] *nf* asparagus.
asperger [aspɛrʒe] *v* spray, sprinkle.
asphalte [asfalt] *nm* asphalt.
asphyxie [asfiksi] *nf* suffocation, asphyxia.
aspirer [aspire] *v* inhale; (*liquide*) suck up. **aspirer à** aspire to, long for. **aspirant, -e** *nm, nf* candidate. **aspirateur** *nm* vacuum cleaner. **aspiration** *nf* aspiration.
aspirine [aspirin] *nf* aspirin.
***assaillir** [asajir] *v* assail, attack.
assainir [asenir] *v* clean up; purify.
assaisonner [asɛzɔne] *v* season. **assaisonnement** *nm* seasoning.

assassiner [asasine] *v* murder; (*pol*) assassinate. **assassin, -e** *nm, nf* murderer; assassin. **assassinat** *nm* murder; assassination.
assaut [aso] *nm* assault, attack. **prendre d'assaut** take by storm.
assembler [asɑ̃ble] *v* assemble. **assemblage** *nm* assembling, assembly. **assemblée** *nf* assembly, meeting.
assentiment [asɑ̃timɑ̃] *nm* assent.
***asseoir** [aswar] *v* sit; establish. **s'asseoir** (*chaise, etc.*) sit down; (*lit*) sit up.
assez [ase] *adv* enough; (*plutôt*) rather, fairly. **en avoir assez de** be fed up with.
assidu [asidy] *adj* assiduous; regular.
assiéger [asjeʒe] *v* besiege, beset.
assiette [asjɛt] *nf* plate; (*cavalier*) seat. **assiette creuse** soup dish. **assiette plate** dinner plate. **ne pas être dans son assiette** be off-colour.
assigner [asiɲe] *v* assign, allot, allocate; (*jur*) summons. **assignation** *nf* assignation; summons.
assimiler [asimile] *v* assimilate, absorb. **assimiler à** liken to. **assimilation** *nf* assimilation.
assis [asi] *adj* sitting, seated.
assises [asiz] *nf pl* assizes *pl.*
assister [asiste] *v* assist. **assister à** attend, witness. **assistance** *nf* (*aide*) assistance; (*assemblée*) audience, attendance. **assistant, -e** *nm, nf* assistant.
associer [asɔsje] *v* associate, combine. **s'associer** join together; (*comm*) form a partnership. **association** *nf* association; partnership. **associé, -e** *nm, nf* associate; partner.
assombrir [asɔ̃brir] *v* darken; (*personne*) make gloomy. **assombri** *adj* gloomy, sombre.
assommer [asɔme] *v* knock out; (*fam*) bore stiff.
assortir [asɔrtir] *v* (*couleurs, etc.*) match; accompany; (*comm*) supply. **assorti** *adj* assorted; matched. **assortiment** *nm* assortment; arrangement; (*vaisselle, etc.*) set.
assoupir [asupir] *v* numb, dull, deaden. **s'assoupir** (*s'endormir*) doze off. **assoupissement** *nm* drowsiness.
assourdir [asurdir] *v* deafen; (*amortir*) muffle.
assujettir [asyʒetir] *v* subject, subjugate; (*fixer*) secure.
assumer [asyme] *v* assume, take on.
assuré [asyre], **-e** *adj* assured; certain, sure. *nm, nf* insured person, policyholder.
assurer [asyre] *v* assure; (*maison, etc.*) insure; maintain, provide; (*rendre sûr*) secure, ensure. **s'assurer** make sure, check; insure oneself. **assurance** *nf* assurance; self-confidence; (*contrat*) insurance.
astérisque [asterisk] *nm* asterisk.
asthme [asmə] *nm* asthma. **asthmatique** *adj* asthmatic.
astre [astrə] *nm* star.
***astreindre** [astrɛ̃drə] *v* force, compel.
astringent [astrɛ̃ʒɑ̃] *nm, adj* astringent.
astrologie [astrɔlɔʒi] *nf* astrology. **astrologique** *adj* astrological. **astrologue** *nm* astrologer.
astronaute [astrɔnot] *n(m+f)* astronaut.
astronomie [astrɔnɔmi] *nf* astronomy. **astronome** *nm* astronomer. **astronomique** *adj* astronomical.
astucieux [astysjø] *adj* shrewd. **astuce** *nf* shrewdness; (*truc*) trick.
asymétrique [asimetrik] *adj* asymmetric.
atelier [atəlje] *nm* workshop; (*art*) studio.
athée [ate] *adj* atheistic. *n(m+f)* atheist. **athéisme** *nm* atheism.
Athènes [atɛn] *n* Athens. **athénien** *adj* Athenian. **Athénien, -enne** *nm, nf* Athenian.
athlète [atlɛt] *n(m+f)* athlete. **athlétique** *adj* athletic. **athlétisme** *nm* athletics.
atlantique [atlɑ̃tik] *adj* Atlantic. **l'Atlantique** *nm* the Atlantic (Ocean).
atlas [atlɑs] *nm* atlas.
atmosphère [atmɔsfɛr] *nf* atmosphere. **atmosphérique** *adj* atmospheric.
atome [atom] *nm* atom. **atomique** *adj* atomic.
atout [atu] *nm* trump; (*avantage*) asset, trump card.
âtre [ɑtrə] *nm* hearth.
atroce [atrɔs] *adj* atrocious, dreadful. **atrocité** *nf* atrocity.
s'attabler [atable] *v* sit (down) at table.
attacher [ataʃe] *v* attach; (*lier*) tie up, fasten. **s'attacher** (*fermeture*) fasten, do up. **attachant** *adj* engaging. **attache** *nf* fastener, string; (*lien*) tie. **à l'attache** tied up. **attaché** *nm* attached.
attaquer [atake] *v* attack; (*problème*) tackle; (*travail*) set about. **s'attaquer à** attack. **attaque** *nf* attack.

attarder [atarde] *v* make late. **s'attarder** *v* linger.
***atteindre** [atɛ̃drə] *v* reach; (*balle, etc.*) hit; (*maladie*) affect. **être atteint de** be suffering from. **atteinte** *nf* attack.
atteler [atle] *v* harness. **s'atteler à** get down to.
attenant [atnɑ̃] *adj* adjoining.
attendre [atɑ̃drə] *v* wait (for); (*compter sur*) expect. **faire attendre** keep waiting. **s'attendre à** expect. **en attendant** meanwhile.
attendrir [atɑ̃drir] *v* (*personne*) move; (*viande*) tenderize. **s'attendrir sur** feel sorry for. **attendrissant** *adj* touching, moving. **attendrissement** *nm* emotion; pity. **attendrisseur** *nm* tenderizer.
attendu [atɑ̃dy] *adj* long-awaited; expected. *prep* considering. **attendu que** seeing that.
attentat [atɑ̃ta] *nm* murder attempt; attack; (*jur*) violation; offence.
attente [atɑ̃t] *nf* wait, waiting; expectation.
attention [atɑ̃sjɔ̃] *nf* attention, care. **avec attention** carefully. **faire attention** take care. **faire attention à** pay attention to. *interj* watch out! careful! **attentif** *adj* attentive; (*scrupuleux*) careful; (*prévenant*) thoughtful.
atténuer [atenɥe] *v* tone down, lighten; (*douleur*) alleviate; (*faute*) mitigate. **s'atténuer** die down, subside.
atterrer [atere] *v* appal.
atterrir [aterir] *v* land. **atterrissage** *nm* landing.
attester [ateste] *v* testify to, attest.
attirail [atiraj] *nm* (*fam*) gear.
attirer [atire] *v* attract; (*appâter*) lure, entice; cause. **attirance** *nf* attraction; lure. **attirant** *adj* attractive.
attiser [atize] *v* poke, stir up.
attitré [atitre] *adj* accredited; regular.
attitude [atityd] *nf* attitude.
attraction [atraksjɔ̃] *nf* attraction.
attrait [atrɛ] *nm* appeal, attraction.
attraper [atrape] *v* catch, get; (*tromper*) take in; (*gronder*) tell off. **attrape** *nf* trick.
attrayant [atrɛjɑ̃] *adj* appealing, attractive.
attribuer [atribɥe] *v* attribute; allocate, accord, award. **s'attribuer** claim. **attribut** *nm* attribute.
attrister [atriste] *v* sadden.
s'attrouper [atrupe] *v* flock together.
au [o] *contraction of* **à le**.
aubaine [obɛn] *nf* godsend, windfall.
aube[1] [ob] *nf* (*du jour*) dawn.
aube[2] [ob] *nf* (*bateau*) paddle; (*moulin*) vane.
aubépine [obepin] *nf* hawthorn.
auberge [obɛrʒ] *nf* inn. **auberge de la jeunesse** youth hostel. **aubergiste** *nm* innkeeper, landlord.
aubergine [ɔbɛrʒin] *nf* aubergine.
aucun [okœ̃] *adj, pron* any. **ne . . . aucun** not any, no, none. **aucunement** *adv* in no way, not in the least.
audace [odas] *nf* audacity, daring. **audacieux** *adj* daring, bold, audacious.
au-delà [odla] *nm, adv* beyond.
au-dessous [odəsu] *adv* below, underneath.
au-dessus [odəsy] *adv* above, over.
au-devant [odəvɑ̃] *adv* ahead. **aller au-devant de** anticipate; (*personne*) go and meet.
audible [odiblə] *adj* audible.
audience [odjɑ̃s] *nf* audience, hearing.
auditeur [oditœr], **-trice** *nm, nf* listener.
audition [odisjɔ̃] *nf* (*essai*) audition; recital; (*ouïe*) hearing.
auditoire [oditwar] *nm* audience.
auge [oʒ] *nf* trough.
augmenter [ɔgmɑ̃te] *v* increase. **augmentation** *nf* increase, rise.
aujourd'hui [oʒurdɥi] *adv* today. **aujourd'hui en huit** a week today.
aulx [o] *V* **ail**.
aumône [ɔmon] *nf* alms; charity. **aumônier** *nm* chaplain.
auparavant [oparavɑ̃] *adv* before, previously.
auprès [oprɛ] *prep* **auprès de** next to, close to; compared with; in the opinion of.
auquel [okɛl] *contraction of* **à lequel**.
aura [ɔra] *nf* aura.
auréole [ɔreɔl] *nf* halo.
Aurigny [ɔriɲi] *nf* Alderney.
aurore [ɔrɔr] *nf* dawn, daybreak.
aussi [osi] *adv* too, also; (*comparaison*) as; (*si*) so. **aussi bien** just as well. *conj* therefore.
aussitôt [osito] *adv* straight away. **aussitôt que** as soon as.
austère [ɔstɛr] *adj* austere. **austérité** *nf* austerity.

Australie [ɔstrali] *nf* Australia. **australien** *adj* Australian. **Australien, -enne** *nm, nf* Australian.
autant [otɑ̃] *adv* as much, so much. **autant de** as much, as many; (*tant*) so much, so many. **autant que** as much as. **autant que possible** as far as possible. **d'autant plus** all the more.
autel [ɔtɛl] *nm* altar.
auteur [otœr] *nm* author, writer; (*musique*) composer.
authentique [ɔtɑ̃tik] *adj* authentic, genuine. **authenticité** *nf* authenticity.
autistique [ɔtistik] *adj* autistic.
auto [ɔto] *nf* car. **auto-école** *nf* driving school. **auto-stop** *nm* hitch-hiking. **faire de l'auto-stop** hitch-hike. **auto-stoppeur, -euse** *nm, nf* hitch-hiker.
autobiographie [ɔtɔbjɔgrafi] *nf* autobiography. **autobiographique** *adj* autobiographical.
autobus [ɔtɔbys] *nm* bus.
autocar [ɔtɔkar] *nm* coach.
autodidacte [ɔtɔdidakt] *adj* self-taught.
autographe [ɔtɔgraf] *nm* autograph.
automatique [ɔtɔmatik] *adj* automatic. **automation** *or* **automatisation** *nf* automation. **automatiser** *v* automate.
automne [ɔtɔn] *nm* autumn. **automnal** *adj* autumnal.
automobile [ɔtɔmɔbil] *nf* motor car. **l'automobile** *nf* the motor industry; (*sport*) motoring. **automobiliste** *n(m+f)* motorist.
autonome [ɔtɔnɔm] *adj* autonomous. **autonomie** *nf* autonomy.
autopont [ɔtɔpɔ̃] *nm* flyover.
autopsie [ɔtɔpsi] *nf* post-mortem.
autoriser [ɔtɔrize] *v* authorize, give permission. **autorisation** *nf* authorization, permission. **autorisé** *adj* authorized; official.
autorité [ɔtɔrite] *nf* authority. **autoritaire** *n(m+f)*, *adj* authoritarian.
autoroute [ɔtɔrut] *nf* motorway.
autour [otur] *adv* around. *prep* **autour de** around.
autre [otrə] *adj* other; different. **autre chose** something else. **autre part** somewhere else. **d'autre part** on the other hand. *pron* another. **d'autres** others. **rien/personne d'autre** nothing/nobody else.
autrefois [otrəfwa] *adv* in the past. **d'autrefois** of the past.
autrement [otrəmɑ̃] *adv* differently, in another way; (*sinon*) otherwise. **autrement dit** in other words, that is.
Autriche [otriʃ] *nf* Austria. **autrichien** *adj* Austrian. **Autrichien, -enne** *nm, nf* Austrian.
autruche [otryʃ] *nf* ostrich.
autrui [otrɥi] *pron* others.
auvent [ovɑ̃] *nm* awning, canopy.
aux [o] *contraction of* **à les.**
auxiliaire [ɔksiljɛr] *adj* auxiliary, secondary. *n(m+f)* assistant, auxiliary.
auxquels, auxquelles [okɛl] *contractions of* **à lesquels, à lesquelles.**
aval [aval] *nm* **d'aval** *adj* (*eau*) downstream; (*pente*) downhill. **en aval** *adv* downstream; downhill.
avalanche [avalɑ̃ʃ] *nf* avalanche; torrent, flood.
avaler [avale] *v* swallow.
avancer [avɑ̃se] *v* advance; move *or* bring forward; (*accélérer*) speed up; make progress; (*montre*) gain. **avance** *nf* advance; lead. **à l'avance** in advance, beforehand. **d'avance** in advance. **en avance** (*heure*) early; ahead. **avancement** *nm* promotion; progress.
avant [avɑ̃] *prep* before. *adv* before; (*mouvement*) forward. *nm* front; (*naut*) bow. **avant tout** above all. **d'avant** *adj* previous. **en avant** (*mouvement*) forward; (*position*) ahead.
avantage [avɑ̃taʒ] *nm* advantage. **avantageux** *adj* worthwhile.
avant-bras *nm invar* forearm.
avant-coureur *nm* forerunner.
avant-dernier, -ère *n, adj* last but one.
avant-garde *nf* avant-garde. **d'avant-garde** *adj* avant-garde.
avant-goût *nm* foretaste.
avant-hier *adv* the day before yesterday.
avant-poste *nm* outpost.
avant-première *nf* preview.
avant-propos *nm invar* foreword.
avant-veille *nf* two days before.
avare [avar] *adj* miserly. *n(m+f)* miser. **avarice** *nf* avarice.
avarie [avari] *nf* damage. **avarié** *adj* rotting, damaged.
avec [avɛk] *prep* with.
avènement [avɛnmɑ̃] *nm* advent; (*roi*) accession.
avenir [avnir] *nm* future. **à l'avenir** from now on.

Avent [avɑ̃] *nm* Advent.
aventure [avɑ̃tyr] *nf* adventure; (*entreprise*) venture. **à l'aventure** at random, aimlessly. **s'aventurer** *v* venture. **aventureux** *adj* adventurous; risky. **aventurier** *nm* adventurer.
avenue [avny] *nf* avenue.
s'avérer [avere] *v* prove to be, turn out to be.
averse [avɛrs] *nf* shower.
aversion [avɛrsjɔ̃] *nf* aversion, loathing. **avoir en aversion** loathe.
avertir [avɛrtir] *v* warn; (*renseigner*) inform. **avertissement** *nm* warning; notice.
aveu [avø] *nm* confession, admission.
aveugle [avœglə] *adj* blind. *n*(*m+f*) blind person. **aveugler** *v* blind; (*éblouir*) dazzle. **s'aveugler sur** shut one's eyes to. **à l'aveuglette** blindly.
aviateur [avjatœr] *nm* airman. **aviation** *nf* aviation, flying; (*mil*) air force.
avide [avid] *adj* eager, avid; (*cupide*) greedy. **avidité** *nf* eagerness; greed.
avilir [avilir] *v* degrade, debase.
avion [avjɔ̃] *nm* aeroplane. **par avion** by airmail.
aviron [avirɔ̃] *nm* oar; (*sport*) rowing. **faire de l'aviron** row.
avis [avi] *nm* opinion; (*conseil*) advice; notice. **à mon avis** in my opinion. **avis au lecteur** foreword.
aviser [avize] *v* inform, notify; (*apercevoir*) notice. **aviser à** see to. **s'aviser de** realize suddenly; (*oser*) dare to. **avisé** *adj* sensible.
avocat[1] [avɔka], **-e** *nm, nf* (*jur*) barrister; advocate.
avocat[2] [avɔka] *nm* avocado (pear). **avocatier** *nm* avocado (tree).
avoine [avwan] *nf* oats *pl*.
***avoir**[1] [avwar] *v* have; (*obtenir*) get; (*être*) be. **il y a** there is *or* are; (*temps écoulé*) ago. **il n'y a pas de quoi** don't mention it. **qu'est-ce qu'il y a?** what's the matter?
avoir[2] [avwar] *nm* assets *pl*; (*comm*) credit.
avoisiner [avwazine] *v* border on, be close to. **avoisinant** *adj* neighbouring, nearby.
avorter [avɔrte] *v* abort; (*projet*) fail. **se faire avorter** have an abortion. **avortement** *nm* abortion. **avorteur, -euse** *nm, nf* abortionist.
avouer [avwe] *v* confess, admit. **avoué** *nm* solicitor.
avril [avril] *nm* April.
axe [aks] *nm* axis; (*tech*) axle.
azalée [azale] *nf* azalea.
azote [azɔt] *nf* nitrogen.

B

babiller [babije] *v* (*personne*) chatter; (*ruisseau*) babble; (*oiseau*) twitter. **babillage** *nm* chatter; babble; twitter. **babillard, -e** *nm, nf* chatterbox.
babines [babin] *nf pl* lips *pl*, chops *pl*.
bâbord [babɔr] *nm* (*naut*) port (side).
babouin [babwɛ̃] *nm* baboon.
bac [bak] *nm* ferry-boat; (*récipient*) tub, tray, sink.
baccalauréat [bakalɔrea] *nm* examination equivalent to A-levels.
bâche [bɑʃ] *nf* canvas cover. **bâche goudronnée** tarpaulin.
bâcler [bɑkle] *v* hurry through; (*travail*) botch. **bâclé** *adj* slapdash.
bactérie [bakteri] *nf* bacterium (*pl* -ria).
badigeonner [badiʒɔne] *v* (*mur*) distemper, whitewash; (*méd*) paint. **badigeon** *nm* distemper, whitewash.
badiner [badine] *v* banter; (*avec négatif*) treat lightly, trifle with. **badinage** *nm* banter.
bafouiller [bafuje] *v* splutter; (*bredouiller*) stammer.
bagage [bagaʒ] *nm* bag, piece of luggage. **bagages** *nm pl* luggage *sing*. **bagages à main** hand baggage *sing*.
bagarre [bagar] *nf* fight. **(se) bagarrer** *v* (*fam*) fight, scrap.
bagatelle [bagatɛl] *nf* trifle; (*objet*) trinket.
bagne [baɲ] *nm* hard labour.
bagnole [baɲɔl] *nf* (*fam*) old banger.
bague [bag] *nf* ring.
baguette [bagɛt] *nf* stick (*musique*) baton; (*pour manger*) chopstick; (*pain*) thin French loaf; (*magique*) wand.
bahut [bay] *nm* chest; (*argot*) school.
bai [bɛ] *adj* bay.
baie[1] [bɛ] *nf* (*géog*) bay.

baie[2] [bɛ] *nf* (*bot*) berry.
baigner [beɲe] *v* bathe; (*bébé*) bath; (*tremper*) soak. **se baigner** (*mer, piscine*) go swimming; (*se laver*) have a bath. **baignade** *nf* bathe, bathing. **baigneur, -euse** *nm, nf* bather. **baignoire** *nf* bath.
bail [baj] *nm, pl* **baux** lease.
bâiller [bɑje] *v* yawn; (*couture, col, etc.*) gape; (*porte*) be ajar. **bâillement** *nm* yawn.
bâillonner [bɑjɔne] *v* gag. **bâillon** *nm* gag.
bain [bɛ̃] *nm* (*baignoire*) bath; (*piscine, mer*) swim, bathe. **bain de foule** walkabout. **bain de mousse** bubble bath. **prendre un bain de soleil** sunbathe.
baïonnette [bajɔnɛt] *nf* bayonet.
baiser [beze] *nm* kiss. *v* (*embrasser*) kiss; (*vulgaire*) screw.
baisser [bese] *v* (*mettre plus bas*) lower; (*décliner*) fall, drop. **se baisser** bend down. **baisse** *nf* fall, drop.
bal [bal] *nm, pl* **bals** dance, ball; (*lieu*) dance hall. **bal costumé** fancy-dress ball.
balader [balade] (*fam*) *v* trail round. **se balader** go for a walk; (*en voiture*) go for a drive. **balade** *nf* walk; drive.
balafrer [balafre] *v* gash. **balafre** *nf* gash; (*cicatrice*) scar. **balafré** *adj* scarred.
balai [balɛ] *nm* broom, brush. **balai mécanique** carpet sweeper.
balance [balɑ̃s] *nf* scales *pl*; (*comm*) balance. **Balance** *nf* Libra.
balancer [balɑ̃se] *v* swing, rock; (*compte*) balance; (*argot*) chuck (out). **se balancer** sway, swing. **balancier** *nm* pendulum. **balançoire** *nf* swing; (*bascule*) seesaw.
balayer [baleje] *v* sweep.
balbutier [balbysje] *v* stammer, mumble.
balcon [balkɔ̃] *nm* balcony; (*théâtre*) dress circle.
baldaquin [baldakɛ̃] *nm* canopy.
baleine [balɛn] *nf* whale.
balise [baliz] *nf* beacon; (*flottante*) buoy.
balistique [balistik] *adj* ballistic. *nf* ballistics.
balivernes [balivɛrn] *nf pl* nonsense *sing*.
ballade [balad] *nf* ballad.
ballant [balɑ̃] *adj* dangling.
balle [bal] *nf* (*projectile*) bullet; (*sport*) ball.
ballet [balɛ] *nm* ballet. **ballerine** *nf* ballerina.
ballon [balɔ̃] *nm* balloon; (*sport*) ball.
ballotter [balɔte] *v* jolt, toss *or* shake about.
balnéaire [balneɛr] *adj* bathing. **station balnéaire** *nf* seaside resort.
balustrade [balystrad] *nf* handrail.
bambou [bɑ̃bu] *nm* bamboo.
banal [banal] *adj* banal, commonplace. **banalité** *nf* banality; (*propos*) platitude.
banane [banan] *nf* banana. **bananier** *nm* banana (tree).
banc [bɑ̃] *nm* bench, seat; (*géol*) layer, bed. **banc d'église** pew. **banc de sable** sandbank. **banc des accusés** dock.
bancal [bɑ̃kal] *adj* wobbly, shaky; (*personne*) bandy-legged.
bandage [bɑ̃daʒ] *nm* bandage.
bande[1] [bɑ̃d] *nf* strip, band; (*magnétophone*) tape; (*méd*) bandage. **bande dessinée** comic strip. **bande sonore** sound-track.
bande[2] [bɑ̃d] *nf* band, group, gang.
bandeau [bɑ̃do] *nm* (*ruban*) headband; (*yeux*) blindfold.
bander [bɑ̃de] *v* bandage; (*tendre*) stretch. **bander les yeux à** blindfold.
bandit [bɑ̃di] *nm* bandit, thief; (*escroc*) crook.
banlieue [bɑ̃ljø] *nf* suburbs *pl*.
banne [ban] *nf* (*magasin*) awning; (*manne*) hamper.
bannière [banjɛr] *nf* banner.
bannir [banir] *v* banish. **banni, -e** *nm, nf* exile. **bannissement** *nm* banishment.
banque [bɑ̃k] *nf* bank; (*métier*) banking. **banquier** *nm* banker.
banqueroute [bɑ̃krut] *nf* bankruptcy. **faire banqueroute** go bankrupt. **banqueroutier, -ère** *nm, nf* bankrupt.
banquet [bɑ̃kɛ] *nm* banquet.
banquette [bɑ̃kɛt] *nf* seat.
baptême [batɛm] *nm* baptism, christening.
baptiser [batize] *v* baptize, christen.
bar [bar] *nm* bar.
baragouiner [baragwine] *v* (*fam*) gabble; talk gibberish. **baragouin** *nm* gibberish.
baraque [barak] *nf* stand, stall; (*abri*) shed; (*fam*: *maison*) place.
baratte [barat] *nf* churn. **baratter** *v* churn.
barbare [barbar] *adj* barbarous, barbaric. *nm* barbarian. **barbarie** *nf* barbarity.
barbe [barb] *nf* beard. **barbe à papa** candy floss. **quelle barbe!** (*fam*) what a drag!
barbecue [barbəkju] *nm* barbecue.

barbelé [barbəle] *adj* **fil de fer barbelé** barbed wire.
barbier [barbje] *nm* barber.
barbiturique [barbityrik] *nm* barbiturate.
barboter [barbɔte] *v* paddle, splash about; (*fam*) pinch. **barboteuse** *nf* rompers *pl*.
barbouiller [barbuje] *v* smear, daub; (*écrire*) scribble. **barbouillis** *nm* daub; scribble.
barbu [barby] *adj* bearded. *nm* bearded man.
barème [barɛm] *nm* list, scale, table.
bariolé [barjɔle] *adj* gaudy, multicoloured.
baromètre [barɔmɛtrə] *nm* barometer.
baron [barɔ̃] *nm* baron. **baronne** *nf* baroness. **baronnet** *nm* baronet.
baroque [barɔk] *adj* weird, strange; (*arch*) baroque. *nm* baroque.
barque [bark] *nf* small boat.
barrage [baraʒ] *nm* (*rivière*) dam; barrier; barricade.
barre [bar] *nf* bar, rod; (*trait*) stroke; (*naut*) helm, tiller.
barreau [baro] *nm* (*échelle*) rung; (*cage, jur*) bar.
barrer [bare] *v* bar, obstruct; (*rayer*) cross (out); (*naut*) steer.
barrette [barɛt] *nf* hair-slide.
barricade [barikad] *nf* barricade. **barricader** *v* barricade.
barrière [barjɛr] *nf* (*porte*) gate; (*clôture*) fence; (*obstacle*) barrier.
baryton [baritɔ̃] *nm, adj* baritone.
bas[1], **basse** [bɑ, bɑs] *adj* low. *adv* low; (*parler*) in a low voice. *nm* bottom. **en bas** down, below; (*maison*) downstairs. **basse** *nf* bass.
bas[2] [bɑ] *nm* stocking.
basculer [baskyle] *v* fall over, topple; (*renverser*) tip up *or* out. **bascule** *nf* (*jeu*) see-saw. **cheval/fauteuil à bascule** *nm* rocking-horse/chair.
base [bɑz] *nf* base; (*fondement*) basis. **de base** basic.
base-ball [bɛzbol] *nm* baseball.
baser [bɑze] *v* base.
basilic [bazilik] *nm* basil.
basket-ball [baskɛtbol] *nm* basketball.
bassin [basɛ̃] *nm* pond, pool; (*géog*) basin; (*anat*) pelvis; (*naut*) dock.
basson [bɑsɔ̃] *nm* bassoon.
bastille [bastij] *nf* fortress.
bataclan [bataklɑ̃] *nm* (*fam*) junk.
bataille [bataj] *nf* battle, fight. **bataillon** *nm* battalion.
bâtard [bɑtar], **-e** *n, adj* bastard.
bateau [bato] *nm* boat. **bateau à voiles** sailing boat. **bateau de sauvetage** lifeboat.
bâtiment [bɑtimɑ̃] *nm* building; (*naut*) ship.
bâtir [bɑtir] *v* build; (*couture*) tack. **bâti** *nm* frame; tacking.
bâton [bɑtɔ̃] *nm* stick.
battant [batɑ̃] *nm* flap; (*porte*) door; (*cloche*) clapper.
batte [bat] *nf* (*sport*) bat.
battement [batmɑ̃] *nm* beat, beating; interval, pause. **battement de paupières** blink.
batterie [batri] *nf* battery; (*musique*) percussion, drums.
***battre** [batrə] *v* beat; (*parcourir*) scour; (*cartes*) shuffle. **battre des mains** clap. **battre son plein** be at its height. **se battre** fight.
baux [bo] *V* **bail**.
bavard [bavar], **-e** *adj* talkative. *nm, nf* (*fam*) chatterbox.
bavarder [bavarde] *v* chatter; (*papoter*) gossip. **bavardage** *nm* chatter, gossip.
baver [bave] *v* dribble, slobber. **bave** *nf* dribble, slobber. **bavette** *nf* bib.
béant [beɑ̃] *adj* gaping, wide open.
béat [bea] *adj* smug; (*sourire*) blissful.
beau [bo], **belle** *adj* beautiful, fine, lovely. **bel et bien** well and truly. **de plus belle** all the more. **beauté** *nf* beauty.
beaucoup [boku] *adv* (very) much, a great deal, a lot; (*personnes*) many. **de beaucoup** by far.
beau-fils *nm* son-in-law; (*remariage*) stepson.
beau-frère *nm* brother-in-law.
beau-père *nm* father-in-law; (*remariage*) stepfather.
beaux-arts [bozar] *nm pl* fine arts *pl*.
bébé [bebe] *nm* baby.
bec [bɛk] *nm* beak; (*plume*) nib; (*carafe*) lip; (*théière*) spout.
bécane [bekan] *nf* (*fam*) bike
bécasse [bekas] *nf* woodcock. **bécassine** *nf* snipe.
bêcher [beʃe] *v* dig. **bêche** *nf* spade.
becqueter [bɛkte] *v* peck.
bedaine [bədɛn] *nf* (*fam*) paunch.

bée [be] *adj* **bouche bée** open-mouthed.
beffroi [befrwa] *nm* belfry.
bégayer [begeje] *v* stammer, stutter.
bégueule [begœl] *nf* prude. *adj* prudish.
béguin [begɛ̃] *nm* bonnet. **avoir le béguin pour** (*fam*) have a crush on, take a fancy to.
beige [bɛʒ] *nm, adj* beige.
beignet [bɛɲɛ] *nm* fritter; (*soufflé*) doughnut.
bel [bɛl] *form of* **beau** *used before vowel or mute h.*
bêler [bele] *v* bleat.
belette [bəlɛt] *nf* weasel.
Belgique [bɛlʒik] *nf* Belgium. **belge** *adj* Belgian. **belge** *n(m+f)* Belgian.
Belgrade [bɛlgrad] *n* Belgrade.
bélier [belje] *nm* ram. **Bélier** *nm* Aries.
belle [bɛl] *V* **beau.**
belle-fille *nf* daughter-in-law; (*remariage*) stepdaughter.
belle-mère *nf* mother-in-law; (*remariage*) stepmother.
belle-sœur *nf* sister-in-law.
bémol [bemɔl] *nm* flat.
bénédicité [benedisite] *nm* grace.
bénédiction [benediksjɔ̃] *nf* blessing.
bénéfice [benefis] *nm* (*comm*) profit; advantage, benefit. **bénéficiaire** *n(m+f)* beneficiary; (*chèque*) payee. **bénéficier de** *v* benefit from; (*jouir de*) enjoy; (*obtenir*) get.
bénévole [benevɔl] *adj* voluntary, unpaid.
benin, -igne [benɛ̃, -iɲ] *adj* mild, slight; (*tumeur*) benign.
bénir [benir] *v* bless. **bénit** *adj* consecrated, holy.
béquille [bekij] *nf* crutch.
bercer [bɛrse] *v* rock; (*apaiser*) lull. **se bercer** delude oneself. **berceau** *nm* cradle. **berceuse** *nf* lullaby.
berger [bɛrʒe] *nm* shepherd; (*chien*) sheepdog. **berger allemand** alsatian. **bergère** *nf* shepherdess.
Berlin [bɛrlɛ̃] *n* Berlin.
Berne [bɛrn] *n* Bern.
besogne [bəzɔɲ] *nf* work.
besoin [bəzwɛ̃] *nm* need. **au besoin** if necessary. **avoir besoin de** need.
bétail [betaj] *nm* livestock; (*bovins*) cattle.
bête [bɛt] *nf* animal, creature, beast. **bête à bon dieu** ladybird. **bête noire** pet hate. **faire la bête** act stupid. *adj* stupid. **bêtise** *nf* stupidity; (*erreur*) blunder; (*action*) silly thing. **dire des bêtises** talk nonsense.
béton [betɔ̃] *nm* concrete. **bétonner** *v* concrete.
betterave [bɛtrav] *nf* beet. **betterave rouge** beetroot. **betterave sucrière** sugar beet.
beugler [bøgle] *v* bellow; (*radio*) blare; (*vache*) low.
beurre [bœr] *nm* butter. **beurrer** *v* butter.
bévue [bevy] *nf* blunder.
biais [bjɛ] *nm* (*détour*) expedient, device; (*aspect*) angle; (*couture*) bias; (*oblique*) slant. **de biais** at an angle; indirectly. **en biais** diagonally, at an angle.
bibelot [biblo] *nm* trinket, knick-knack.
biberon [bibrɔ̃] *nm* feeding bottle. **élevé au biberon** bottle-fed.
Bible [biblə] *nf* Bible. **biblique** *adj* biblical.
bibliographie [biblijɔgrafi] *nf* bibliography.
bibliothécaire [biblijɔtekɛr] *n(m+f)* librarian.
bibliothèque [biblijɔtɛk] *nf* library; (*meuble*) bookcase.
biceps [bisɛps] *nm* biceps.
biche [biʃ] *nf* doe.
bicyclette [bisiklɛt] *nf* bicycle; (*sport*) cycling. **aller à bicyclette** cycle.
bidon [bidɔ̃] *nm* can, tin.
bien [bjɛ̃] *adv* well; (*très*) very; (*beaucoup*) very much; (*plutôt*) rather; certainly, indeed; (*tout à fait*) properly, carefully. *adj* good; (*beau*) nice. *nm* good; possession. **bien de** much. **bien que** although. **biens** *nm pl* goods *pl*; property *sing*.
bien-aimé [bjɛ̃neme], **-e** *n, adj* beloved.
bien-être [bjɛ̃nɛtrə] *nm* well-being.
bienfaisant [bjɛ̃fəzɑ̃] *adj* beneficial; (*personne*) kind. **bienfaisance** *nf* charity.
bienfaiteur [bjɛ̃fɛtœr] *nm* benefactor. **bienfaitrice** *nf* benefactress.
bienheureux [bjɛ̃nœrø] *adj* (*rel*) blessed; happy.
biennal [bjenal] *adj* biennial.
bienséance [bjɛ̃seɑ̃s] *nf* propriety. **bienséant** *adj* proper, seemly.
bientôt [bjɛ̃to] *adv* soon. **à bientôt!** see you!
bienveillance [bjɛ̃vɛjɑ̃s] *nf* kindness, benevolence. **bienveillant** *adj* benevolent, kindly.
bienvenu [bjɛ̃vny], **-e** *adj* well-chosen. *nm, nf* welcome person *or* thing. **être le bienvenu** be welcome. **bienvenue** *nf* welcome.

bière[1] [bjɛr] *nf* (*boisson*) beer. **bière (à la) pression** draught beer. **bière blonde** lager.
bière[2] [bjɛr] *nf* coffin.
biffer [bife] *v* cross out.
bifocal [bifɔkal] *adj* bifocal. **lunettes bifocales** *nf pl* bifocals *pl*.
bifteck [biftɛk] *nm* steak.
bifurcation [bifyrkɑsjɔ̃] *nf* fork, branching off. **bifurquer** *v* fork, branch off.
bigame [bigam] *adj* bigamous. *n(m+f)* bigamist. **bigamie** *nf* bigamy.
bigorneau [bigɔrno] *nm* winkle.
bigot [bigo], **-e** *adj* bigoted. *nm, nf* bigot.
bigoudi [bigudi] *nm* curler, roller.
bijou [biʒu] *nm, pl* **-oux** jewel. **bijouterie** *nf* jewellery; (*boutique*) jeweller's. **bijoutier, -ère** *nm, nf* jeweller.
bikini [bikini] *nm* bikini.
bilan [bilɑ̃] *nm* assessment; consequence; (*comm*) balance sheet. **bilan de santé** check-up.
bile [bil] *nf* bile. **se faire de la bile** get worried.
bilingue [bilɛ̃g] *adj* bilingual.
billard [bijar] *nm* billiards; billiard table.
bille [bij] *nf* marble; billiard ball.
billet [bijɛ] *nm* ticket; note. **billet de banque** banknote.
billot [bijo] *nm* block.
binaire [binɛr] *adj* binary.
biner [bine] *v* hoe. **binette** *nf* hoe.
biographie [bjɔgrafi] *nf* biography. **biographe** *n(m+f)* biographer. **biographique** *adj* biographical.
biologie [bjɔlɔʒi] *nf* biology. **biologique** *adj* biological. **biologiste** *n(m+f)* biologist.
bis [bis] *nm, interj* encore. *adv* (*musique*) repeat.
bisannuel [bizanɥɛl] *adj* biennial.
biscornu [biskɔrny] *adj* irregular; (*bizarre*) peculiar.
biscotte [biskɔt] *nf* rusk.
biscuit [biskɥi] *nm* biscuit; (*gâteau*) sponge cake.
bise[1] [biz] *nf* (*vent*) north wind.
bise[2] [biz] *nf* kiss.
bistouri [bisturi] *nm* scalpel.
bistro [bistro] *nm* pub, café.
bizarre [bizar] *adj* strange, odd. **bizarrerie** *nf* strangeness, oddness.
blafard [blafar] *adj* pale, wan.
blague [blag] *nf* joke; (*farce*) trick. **sans blague?** really? **blaguer** (*fam*) *v* (*taquiner*) tease; (*plaisanter*) be joking.
blaireau [blɛro] *nm* badger; (*brosse*) shaving brush.
blâmer [blɑme] *v* blame; reprimand. **blâme** *nm* blame, reprimand.
blanc, blanche [blɑ̃, blɑ̃ʃ] *nm, adj* (*couleur*) white; (*page, etc.*) blank. **blanc cassé** off-white. **blancheur** *nf* whiteness.
blanchir [blɑ̃ʃir] *v* whiten; (*mur*) whitewash; (*toile*) bleach; (*linge*) launder; (*devenir blanc*) go *or* turn white. **blanchisserie** *nf* laundry.
blasé [blɑze] *adj* blasé. **être blasé de** be bored with.
blason [blazɔ̃] *nm* coat of arms; heraldry.
blasphémer [blasfeme] *v* blaspheme. **blasphématoire** *adj* blasphemous. **blasphème** *nm* blasphemy.
blatte [blat] *nf* cockroach.
blé [ble] *nm* wheat, corn.
blêmir [blemir] *v* turn *or* go pale. **blême** *adj* pallid, wan.
blessé [blese], **-e** *adj* wounded. *nm, nf* casualty.
blesser [blese] *v* hurt, injure, wound. **blessure** *nf* wound.
blet, blette [blɛ, blɛt] *adj* overripe.
bleu [blø] *adj* blue. *nm* blue; (*meurtrissure*) bruise; (*vêtement*) overalls *pl*; (*débutant*) beginner. **bleu marine** navy blue. **bleu roi** royal blue.
bleuet [bløɛ] *nm* cornflower.
blindé [blɛ̃de] *adj* armoured, reinforced.
bloc [blɔk] *nm* (*pierre, bois*) block; (*papier*) pad; group; (*d'éléments*) unit. **à bloc** fully, properly. **en bloc** outright.
blocage [blɔkaʒ] *nm* (*prix, etc.*) freeze; (*blocaille*) rubble.
blocus [blɔkys] *nm* blockade. **faire le blocus de** blockade.
blond [blɔ̃] *adj* fair, blond; (*sable*) golden. **blonde** *nf* blonde.
bloquer [blɔke] *v* block, jam, wedge; group together; (*salaires, etc.*) freeze.
se blottir [blɔtir] *v* snuggle up.
blouse [bluz] *nf* overall; (*chemisier*) blouse.
blue-jean [bludʒin] *nm* jeans *pl*.
bluff [blœf] *nm* (*fam*) bluff. **bluffer** *v* bluff.
bobine [bɔbin] *nf* spool, reel, bobbin; (*élec*) coil. **bobiner** *v* wind.
bocage [bɔkaʒ] *nm* grove; (*geog*) bocage.
bocal [bɔkal] *nm* jar; (*poissons*) bowl.

bock [bɔk] *nm* glass of beer.
bœuf [bœf] *nm* (*animal*) bullock, ox; (*viande*) beef.
bohème [bɔɛm] *n*(*m+f*), *adj* bohemian.
***boire** [bwar] *v* drink; absorb.
bois [bwa] *nm* wood; (*cerf*) antler; (*musique*) wood-wind instrument. **bois de chauffage** firewood. **de** *or* **en bois** wooden. **boisé** *adj* wooded, woody. **boiserie** *nf* panelling.
boisson [bwasɔ̃] *nf* drink. **boisson alcoolisée** alcoholic drink.
boîte [bwat] *nf* box; (*métal*) tin, can. **boîte à lettres** pillar-box. **boîte à ordures** dustbin. **boîte de nuit** night-club. **boîte de vitesses** gearbox.
boiter [bwate] *v* limp. **boiteux** *adj* lame; (*meuble*) wobbly; (*projet*) shaky.
bol [bɔl] *nm* bowl.
bombarder [bɔ̃barde] *v* bombard; bomb. **bombardier** *nm* (*avion*) bomber.
bombe [bɔ̃b] *nf* bomb; aerosol, spray. **bombe atomique** atom bomb.
bomber [bɔ̃be] *v* bulge, stick out; (*route*) camber. **bombé** *adj* rounded, bulging. **bombement** *nm* bulge; camber.
bon [bɔ̃], **bonne** *adj* good; (*agréable*) nice; (*gentil*) kind; (*valable*) valid; (*correct*) right. **à quoi bon?** what's the use? **bon à** *or* **pour** fit for. **de bonne heure** early. **pour de bon** for good. *nm* good person; good part. *interj* right!
bon² [bɔ̃] *nm* form; coupon, voucher; (*titre*) bond.
bon anniversaire *interj* happy birthday!
bonasse [bɔnas] *adj* meek.
bonbon [bɔ̃bɔ̃] *nm* sweet. **bonbon à la menthe** mint.
bond [bɔ̃] *nm* leap, bound; (*balle*) bounce.
bonde [bɔ̃d] *nf* plug, stopper.
bondé [bɔ̃de] *adj* packed, crammed.
bondir [bɔ̃dir] *v* leap (up), jump (up); (*balle*) bounce; (*sursauter*) start.
bon enfant *adj invar* good-natured.
bonheur [bɔnœr] *nm* happiness; joy; (*chance*) luck. **au petit bonheur** haphazardly. **par bonheur** fortunately.
bonhomie [bɔnɔmi] *nf* good nature.
bonhomme [bɔnɔm] *nm* (*fam*) chap, bloke. **bonhomme de neige** (*fam*) snowman. *adj invar* good-natured.
boni [bɔni] *nm* profit.
bonjour [bɔ̃ʒur] *nm*, *interj* hello; (*matin*) good morning; (*après-midi*) good afternoon.
bon marché *adj invar* cheap.
Bonn [bɔn] *n* Bonn.
bonne [bɔn] *V* **bon¹**. *nf* maid.
bonne année *interj* happy New Year!
bonne-maman *nf* (*fam*) granny, grandma.
bonnet [bɔnɛ] *nm* hat, bonnet; (*soutien-gorge*) cup. **bonnet d'âne** dunce's cap. **bonnet de bain** bathing cap. **bonneterie** *nf* hosiery.
bon-papa *nm* (*fam*) grand-dad, grandpa.
bon sens *nm* common sense.
bonsoir [bɔ̃swar] *nm*, *interj* good evening; (*en se couchant*) goodnight.
bonté [bɔ̃te] *nf* kindness, goodness.
bord [bɔr] *nm* edge, side; (*verre*) rim. **à bord** on board, aboard. **à ras bord** to the brim. **au bord de** (*lac, etc.*) by, alongside; (*larmes, ruine*) on the verge *or* brink of. **au bord de la mer** at the seaside. **bord du trottoir** kerb. **bordure** *nf* edge, border.
bordeaux [bɔrdo] *nm* Bordeaux. **bordeaux rouge** claret. *adj invar* maroon.
bordel [bɔrdɛl] *nm* brothel.
border [bɔrde] *v* edge; (*rue*) line; (*lit*) tuck in.
bordereau [bɔrdəro] *nm* note, slip; (*relevé*) statement.
borgne [bɔrɲə] *adj* one-eyed; (*louche*) shady.
borner [bɔrne] *v* limit; (*terrain*) mark out. **se borner à** content oneself with, confine oneself to. **borne** *nf* limit; (*kilométrique*) milestone. **sans bornes** limitless. **borné** *adj* narrow-minded; limited.
bosquet [bɔskɛ] *nm* copse.
bosse [bɔs] *nf* bump, lump; (*bossu*) hump. **avoir la bosse de** (*fam*) be good at, have a flair for.
bosseler [bɔsle] *v* emboss; (*déformer*) dent. **bosselé** *adj* dented, battered; (*sol*) bumpy. **bosselure** *nf* dent.
bossu [bɔsy], **-e** *adj* hunchbacked. *nm, nf* hunchback.
bot [bo] *adj* **pied bot** club foot.
botanique [bɔtanik] *adj* botanical. *nf* botany. **botaniste** *n*(*m+f*) botanist.
botte¹ [bɔt] *nf* boot. **botte de caoutchouc** wellington, gumboot. **bottillon** *nm* bootee.
botte² [bɔt] *nf* bunch, bundle.
botte³ [bɔt] *nf* (*escrime*) thrust.
botter [bɔte] *v* put boots on; (*fam, sport*) kick.

Bottin ® [bɔtɛ̃] *nm* directory.
bouc [buk] *nm* goat. **bouc émissaire** scapegoat.
boucaner [bukane] *v* (*viande*) cure; (*peau*) tan.
bouche [buʃ] *nf* mouth. **bouche à bouche** *nm invar* kiss of life. **bouchée** *nf* mouthful.
boucher[1] [buʃe] *v* block; (*bouteille*) cork; (*trou*) plug, fill up. **boucher le passage** be in the way. **bouché** *adj* (*temps*) cloudy; (*argot*) stupid, thick.
boucher[2] [buʃe] *nm* butcher. **boucherie** *nf* butcher's.
bouchon [buʃɔ̃] *nm* stopper, top; (*liège*) cork; (*évier*) plug; (*auto*) traffic jam.
boucler [bukle] *v* (*fermer*) buckle, fasten up; complete; (*cheveux*) curl. **boucler la boucle** (*aéro*) loop the loop; come full circle; complete. **boucle** *nf* buckle; curl; (*ruban, etc.*) loop. **boucle d'oreille** earring. **bouclé** *adj* curly.
bouclier [buklije] *nm* shield.
bouddhisme [budismə] *nm* Buddhism. **bouddhiste** *n*(*m*+*f*), *adj* Buddhist.
bouder [bude] *v* sulk. **boudeur, -euse** *adj* sulky.
boudin [budɛ̃] *nm* black pudding.
boue [bu] *nf* mud.
bouée [bwe] *nf* buoy. **bouée de sauvetage** lifebuoy.
boueux [bwø] *adj* muddy. *nm* dustman.
bouffer [bufe] *v* puff out; (*fam*) eat. **bouffant** *adj* (*manche*) full; (*pantalon, etc.*) baggy. **bouffe** *nf* (*argot*) grub. **bouffée** *nf* puff; (*vent*) gust; (*parfum*) whiff.
bouffir [bufir] *v* puff up. **bouffi** *adj* bloated, swollen; (*yeux*) puffy. **bouffissure** *nf* puffiness.
bouffon, -onne [bufɔ̃, -ɔn] *adj* comical. *nm* buffoon, clown. **bouffonnerie** *nf* clowning.
bouger [buʒe] *v* move, stir.
bougie [buʒi] *nf* candle; (*auto*) spark plug. **bougeoir** *nm* candlestick.
***bouillir** [bujir] *v* boil. **bouilloire** *nf* kettle.
bouillon [bujɔ̃] *nm* broth, stock; (*bulle*) bubble. **bouillon cube** stock cube.
bouillonner [bujɔne] *v* bubble, foam, seethe.
bouillotte [bujɔt] *nf* hot-water bottle.
boulanger [bulɑ̃ʒe] *nm* baker. **boulangerie** *nf* baker's, bakery.
boule [bul] *nf* ball. **boule de neige** snowball. **boules** *nf pl* (*jeu*) bowls *sing*.
bouleau [bulo] *nm* birch.
bouledogue [buldɔg] *nm* bulldog.
boulet [bulɛ] *nm* cannon-ball.
boulette [bulɛt] *nf* pellet.
boulevard [bulvar] *nm* boulevard.
bouleverser [bulvɛrse] *v* (*renverser*) turn upside down; disrupt, change completely; (*personne*) overwhelm, distress deeply. **bouleversement** *nm* upheaval.
boulon [bulɔ̃] *nm* bolt. **boulonner** *v* bolt.
boulot[1], **-otte** [bulo, -ɔt] *adj* plump.
boulot[2] [bulo] *nm* (*fam*) work.
boulotter [bulɔte] *v* (*fam*) eat.
bouquet[1] [bukɛ] *nm* bouquet, bunch; (*arbres*) clump. **c'est le bouquet!** that's the last straw!
bouquet[2] [bukɛ] *nm* (*crevette*) prawn.
bouquin [bukɛ̃] *nm* (*fam*) book. **bouquiniste** *nm* second-hand bookseller.
bourbe [burb] *nf* mire, mud. **bourbeux** *adj* miry, muddy.
bourdon [burdɔ̃] *nm* bumble-bee; (*musique*) drone.
bourdonner [burdɔne] *v* hum, buzz. **bourdonnement** *nm* buzz, hum.
bourg [bur] *nm* market town.
bourgeois [burʒwa], **-e** *adj* middle-class; (*péj*) bourgeois, conventional. *nm, nf* middle-class person. **bourgeoisie** *nf* middle class.
bourgeon [burʒɔ̃] *nm* bud. **bourgeonner** *v* bud.
bourgogne [burgɔɲ] *nm* burgundy.
bourrade [burad] *nf* thump, prod.
bourrage [buraʒ] *nm* stuffing, filling.
bourrasque [burask] *nf* gust of wind.
bourre [bur] *nf* stuffing, wadding.
bourreau [buro] *nm* torturer; executioner.
bourrelet [burlɛ] *nm* (*porte, etc.*) draught excluder; (*chair*) roll.
bourrer [bure] *v* stuff, cram.
bourriche [buriʃ] *nf* hamper.
bourru [bury] *adj* surly, gruff.
bourse [burs] *nf* purse; (*d'étudiant*) grant. **la Bourse** the Stock Exchange.
boursoufler [bursufle] *v* puff up. **se boursoufler** (*peinture*) blister. **boursouflé** *adj* puffy, swollen; blistered; (*style*) turgid. **boursouflure** *nf* puffiness; blister; turgidity.
bousculer [buskyle] *v* jostle; (*heurter*) bump into; (*renverser*) knock over. **bousculade** *nf* hustle, crush; (*hâte*) rush.

bousiller [buzije] (*fam*) *v* (*travail*) botch; (*abîmer*) wreck.
boussole [busɔl] *nf* compass.
bout [bu] *nm* end, tip; (*morceau*) piece, bit. **à bout** at the end of one's tether. **à bout de souffle** out of breath. **à bout portant** point-blank. **au bout de** at the end of; (*après*) after. **au bout du compte** all things considered. **de bout en bout** from start to finish. **jusqu'au bout** to the (bitter) end.
bouteille [butɛj] *nf* bottle. **en bouteille** bottled.
boutique [butik] *nf* shop. **boutiquier, -ère** *nm, nf* shopkeeper.
bouton [butɔ̃] *nm* button; (*élec*) switch; (*porte*) handle; (*fleur*) bud; (*méd*) pimple. **bouton de col** collar stud. **bouton de manchette** cuff-link. **bouton d'or** buttercup. **bouton-pression** *nm* press stud. **boutonner** *v* button. **boutonneux** *adj* pimply. **boutonnière** *nf* buttonhole.
bouture [butyr] *nf* cutting. **faire des boutures** take cuttings.
bouvier [buvje] *nm* herdsman.
bovin [bɔvɛ̃] *adj* bovine. **bovins** *nm pl* cattle *pl*.
boxer [bɔkse] *v* box. **boxe** *nf* boxing. **boxeur** *nm* boxer.
boyau [bwajo] *nm* gut; passageway. **boyaux** *nm pl* entrails *pl*.
boycotter [bɔjkɔte] *v* boycott. **boycottage** *nm* boycott.
bracelet [braslɛ] *nm* bracelet; (*montre*) strap. **bracelet-montre** *nm* wristwatch.
braconner [brakɔne] *v* poach. **braconnage** *nm* poaching. **braconnier** *nm* poacher.
braguette [bragɛt] *nf* (*pantalon*) fly.
braille [brɑj] *nm* braille.
brailler [brɑje] *v* bawl, yell.
***braire** [brɛr] *v* bray.
braise [brɛz] *nf* embers *pl*.
braiser [breze] *v* braise.
brancard [brɑ̃kar] *nm* stretcher; (*bras*) shaft.
branche [brɑ̃ʃ] *nf* branch.
brancher [brɑ̃ʃe] *v* plug in, connect up.
brandir [brɑ̃dir] *v* brandish.
branle-bas [brɑ̃lbɑ] *nm invar* bustle, commotion.
branler [brɑ̃le] *v* be shaky *or* unsteady; (*dent*) be loose. **branle** *nm* swing. **mettre en branle** set in motion, get moving.
braquer [brake] *v* aim, point; (*auto*) turn (the wheel).
bras [bra] *nm* arm; (*tech*) handle; (*travailleur*) worker. **bras dessus, bras dessous** arm in arm. **en bras de chemise** in shirt sleeves.
brasero [brɑzero] *nm* brazier.
brasier [brɑzje] *nm* inferno.
brasse [bras] *nf* breast-stroke. **brasse papillon** butterfly.
brassée [brase] *nf* armful.
brasser [brase] *v* stir, mix; (*bière*) brew. **brasserie** *nf* brewery; (*café*) brasserie.
brave [brav] *adj* good, nice; brave, courageous.
braver [brave] *v* brave, defy, stand up to.
bravoure [bravur] *nf* bravery.
break [brɛk] *nm* estate car.
brebis [brəbi] *nf* ewe, sheep. **brebis galeuse** black sheep.
brèche [brɛʃ] *nf* breach, gap.
bredouiller [brəduje] *v* stammer, mumble. **bredouille** *adj* empty-handed.
bref, brève [brɛf, brɛv] *adj* brief, short. **(en) bref** in short.
breloque [brəlɔk] *nf* charm.
Bretagne [brətaɲ] *nf* Brittany.
bretelle [brətɛl] *nf* strap. **bretelles** *nf pl* braces *pl*.
breuvage [brœvaʒ] *nm* drink, beverage.
brevet [brəvɛ] *nm* certificate, diploma; (*d'invention*) patent. **breveter** *v* patent.
bribe [brib] *nf* scrap, snatch, bit.
bricoler [brikɔle] *v* potter about, do odd jobs; (*réparer*) mend. **bricolage** *nm* do-it-yourself; makeshift repair. **bricoleur** *nm* handyman.
brider [bride] *v* bridle, restrain. **bride** *nf* bridle, rein; (*bonnet*) string, strap. **à bride abattue** (*fam*) flat out. **tenir en bride** keep a tight rein on.
bridge [bridʒ] *nm* bridge.
brièvement [brijɛvmɑ̃] *adv* briefly. **brièveté** *nf* brevity.
brigade [brigad] *nf* brigade; (*police*) squad; (*équipe*) team.
brigand [brigɑ̃] *nm* (*péj*) crook; (*enfant*) rascal. **brigandage** *nm* (armed) robbery.
brigue [brig] *nf* intrigue. **briguer** *v* covet, crave; solicit.
brillant [brijɑ̃] *adj* brilliant; (*luisant*) shiny, bright; outstanding, excellent. *nm* brilliance; shine, brightness.
briller [brije] *v* shine, sparkle.
brin [brɛ̃] *nm* sprig; (*herbe*) blade; (*fil*) strand. **un brin de** a bit of.

brindille [brɛ̃dij] *nf* twig.
brioche [brijɔʃ] *nf* bun.
brique [brik] *nf* brick.
briquet [brikɛ] *nm* cigarette lighter.
brise [briz] *nf* breeze.
briser [brize] *v* break, smash; (*espérance, rebelle*) crush. **brise-lames** *nm invar* breakwater.
britannique [britanik] *adj* British. **les Britanniques** the British.
broc [bro] *nm* pitcher.
brocanter [brɔkɑ̃te] *v* deal in second-hand goods. **brocante** *nf* second-hand goods *pl*; (*commerce*) second-hand trade. **brocanteur, -euse** *nm, nf* second-hand dealer.
broche [brɔʃ] *nf* (*bijou*) brooch; (*cuisine*) spit; (*tech*) pin.
broché [brɔʃe] *adj* **livre broché** paperback book.
brochet [brɔʃɛ] *nm* pike.
brochette [brɔʃɛt] *nf* (*broche*) skewer; (*plat*) kebab.
brochure [brɔʃyr] *nf* brochure, booklet.
brocoli [brɔkɔli] *nm* broccoli.
broder [brɔde] *v* embroider. **broder sur** elaborate on. **broderie** *nf* embroidery.
broncher [brɔ̃ʃe] *v* (*cheval*) stumble. **sans broncher** (*sans peur*) without flinching; (*sans faute*) without faltering.
bronchite [brɔ̃ʃit] *nf* bronchitis.
bronzer [brɔ̃ze] *v* tan; (*métal*) bronze. **bronzage** *nm* suntan. **bronze** *nm* bronze.
brosser [brɔse] *v* brush. **brosse** *nf* brush; (*cheveux*) crew-cut. **brosse à cheveux/dents/ongles** hair/tooth/nailbrush.
brouette [bruɛt] *nf* wheelbarrow.
brouhaha [bruaa] *nm* hubbub.
brouillard [brujar] *nm* fog. **il fait du brouillard** it's foggy.
brouiller [bruje] *v* (*troubler*) blur; (*mêler*) mix *or* muddle up. **se brouiller** become confused; (*se fâcher*) fall out. **brouille** *nf* quarrel.
brouillon, -onne [brujɔ̃, -ɔn] *adj* untidy; unsystematic. *nm* rough copy.
broussailles [brusɑj] *nf pl* undergrowth *sing*, scrub *sing*. **broussailleux** *adj* bushy.
brouter [brute] *v* graze.
broyer [brwaje] *v* grind, crush.
bru [bry] *nf* daughter-in-law.
bruiner [brɥine] *v* drizzle. **bruine** *nf* drizzle.
bruire [brɥir] *v* rustle; (*eau*) murmur. **bruissement** *nm* rustle; murmur.
bruit [brɥi] *nm* noise; rumour; (*histoires*) fuss. **bruitage** *nm* sound effects *pl*.
brûler [bryle] *v* burn. **brûlant** *adj* burning, scorching; (*objet*) red hot; (*liquid*) boiling hot. **brûlure** *nf* burn.
brume [brym] *nf* mist. **brumeux** *adj* misty.
brun [brœ̃] *adj* brown, dark. *nm* brown. **brune** *nf* brown ale; (*femme*) brunette.
brunir [brynir] *v* darken; (*peau*) tan, get sunburnt.
brusque [brysk] *adj* brusque, abrupt. **brusquerie** *nf* brusqueness, abruptness.
brut [bryt] *adj* crude, raw, rough; (*comm*) gross. **brute** *nf* brute.
brutal [brytal] *adj* rough, brutal; (*franc*) blunt, plain. **brutalité** *nf* brutality.
brutaliser [brytalize] *v* bully, ill-treat.
Bruxelles [brysɛl] *n* Brussels.
bruyant [brɥijɑ̃] *adj* noisy.
bruyère [bryjɛr] *nf* heather.
Bucarest [bykarɛst] *n* Bucharest.
buccin [byksɛ̃] *nm* whelk.
bûche [byʃ] *nf* log; (*fam*) blockhead.
bûcher[1] [byʃe] *nm* (*remise*) woodshed; (*supplice*) stake.
bûcher[2] [byʃe] *v* (*fam*) swot.
bucheron [byʃrɔ̃] *nm* woodcutter, lumberjack.
Budapest [bydapɛst] *n* Budapest.
budget [bydʒɛ] *nm* budget.
buée [bɥe] *nf* steam, condensation. **couvert de buée** misted up.
buffet [byfɛ] *nm* buffet; (*meuble*) sideboard. **buffet de cuisine** dresser.
buffle [byflə] *nm* buffalo.
buisson [bɥisɔ̃] *nm* bush.
bulbe [bylbə] *nm* bulb. **bulbeux** *adj* bulbous.
Bulgarie [bylgari] *nf* Bulgaria. **bulgare** *nm, adj* Bulgarian. **Bulgare** *nm, nf* Bulgarian.
bulle [byl] *nf* bubble; (*méd*) blister.
bulletin [byltɛ̃] *nm* bulletin; ticket; certificate; (*école*) report. **bulletin de vote** ballot paper. **bulletin météorologique** weather report.
bungalow [bœ̃galo] *nm* bungalow; (*motel*) chalet.
bureau [byro] *nm* (*meuble*) desk; (*cabinet*) study; (*lieu*) office; (*section*) department. **bureau de location** booking office. **bureau**

de poste post office. **bureau de vote** polling station.
bureaucratie [byrokrasi] *nf* bureaucracy. **bureaucrate** *n(m+f)* bureaucrat. **bureaucratique** *adj* bureaucratic.
buriner [byrine] *v* engrave.
burlesque [byrlɛsk] *adj* comical, ludicrous.
buste [byst] *nm* bust, chest.
but [by] *nm* goal, aim. **de but en blanc** point-blank, suddenly.
buter [byte] *v* stumble; (*sport*) score a goal; (*mur*) prop up. **se buter à** bump into. **buté** *adj* stubborn.
butin [bytɛ̃] *nm* booty, spoils.
butoir [bytwar] *nm* buffer.
butte [byt] *nf* mound. **être en butte à** be exposed to.
buvard [byvar] *nm* blotting paper.
buvette [byvɛt] *nf* refreshment bar.
buveur [byvœr], **-euse** *nm, nf* drinker.
byzantin [bizɑ̃tɛ̃] *adj* Byzantine.

C

c' [s] *V* **ce**[2].
ça [sa] *informal contraction of* **cela**.
çà [sa] *adv* **çà et là** here and there.
cabale [kabal] *nf* cabal.
cabane [kaban] *nf* hut, shed, cabin. **cabane à outils** toolshed. **cabane en rondins** log cabin.
cabaret [kabarɛ] *nm* night-club, cabaret.
cabillaud [kabijo] *nm* fresh cod.
cabine [kabin] *nf* cabin; (*réduit*) cubicle, booth. **cabine de bain** beach hut. **cabine téléphonique** telephone box.
cabinet [kabinɛ] *nm* (*bureau*) office; (*médecin, dentiste*) surgery; (*meuble, pol*) cabinet. **cabinet de débarras** box-room. **cabinet de toilette** toilet. **cabinet de travail** study.
câble [kɑblə] *nm* cable. **câbler** *v* cable.
cabosser [kabɔse] *v* dent.
se cabrer [kɑbre] *v* rear up; rebel.
cabriole [kabrijɔl] *nf* caper; (*danse*) cabriole; (*culbute*) somersault. **cabrioler** *v* caper about.
cacahouette [kakawɛt] *nf* peanut.
cacao [kakao] *nm* cocoa.
cachemire [kaʃmir] *nm* cashmere.
cacher [kaʃe] *v* hide, conceal. **cache-cache** *nm invar* hide-and-seek. **cache-col** *or* **cache-nez** *nm invar* scarf. **se cacher de** hide from.
cachet [kaʃɛ] *nm* seal, stamp; (*comprimé*) tablet; style. **cachet de la poste** postmark. **cacheter** *v* seal.
cachette [kaʃɛt] *nf* hiding-place. **en cachette** on the quiet, secretly.
cachot [kaʃo] *nm* dungeon.
cactus [kaktys] *nm invar* cactus (*pl* -ti).
cadavre [kadɑvrə] *nm* corpse; (*animal*) carcass. **cadavéreux** *or* **cadavérique** *adj* deathly.
cadeau [kado] *nm* present, gift.
cadenas [kadnɑ] *nm* padlock. **cadenasser** *v* padlock.
cadence [kadɑ̃s] *nf* rhythm; (*musique*) cadence; (*vitesse*) rate. **cadencé** *adj* rhythmic.
cadet, -ette [kadɛ, -ɛt] *adj* younger, youngest. *nm, nf* (*famille*) youngest child; junior.
cadran [kadrɑ̃] *nm* dial, face. **cadran solaire** sundial.
cadre [kɑdrə] *nm* frame; (*milieu*) setting; (*formulaire*) space; scope, limits *pl*; context; (*responsable*) executive. **les cadres** management *sing*.
cadrer [kɑdre] *v* tally, conform; (*phot*) centre.
caduc, -uque [kadyk] *adj* (*feuilles*) deciduous; (*jur*) null and void; (*périmé*) outmoded.
cafard [kafar] *nm* (*insecte*) cockroach; (*tristesse*) depression; (*mouchard*) sneak. **avoir le cafard** be down in the dumps. **cafarder** *v* sneak, tell tales.
café [kafe] *nm* coffee; (*lieu*) café. **café au lait** white coffee. **café noir** *or* **nature** black coffee. **café soluble** instant coffee.
caféine [kafein] *nf* caffeine.
cafetière [kaftjɛr] *nf* coffee-pot.
cage [kaʒ] *nf* cage; (*tech*) casing. **cage à poules** hen-coop.
cagneux [kaɲø] *adj* knock-kneed.
cagnotte [kaɲɔt] *nf* kitty.
cagoule [kagul] *nf* hood.
cahier [kaje] *nm* notebook, exercise book.
cahin-caha [kaɛ̃kaa] *adv* (*fam*) so-so.
cahot [kao] *nm* jolt, bump. **cahotant** *or* **cahoteux** *adj* bumpy. **cahoter** *v* jolt.
caille [kɑj] *nf* quail.

cailler [kɑje] *v* (*lait*) curdle; (*sang*) clot. **caillé** *nm* curds *pl*. **caillot** *nm* clot.
caillou [kaju] *nm*, *pl* **-oux** stone, pebble. **caillouteux** *adj* stony, pebbly.
caisse [kɛs] *nf* box, case; (*argent*) cash-box, till; (*guichet*) cash-desk; (*tambour*) drum. **caisse d'épargne** savings bank. **caissier, -ère** *nm, nf* cashier.
cajoler [kaʒɔle] *v* coax, cajole; (*câliner*) make a fuss of.
cake [kɛk] *nm* fruit cake.
calamité [kalamite] *nf* calamity, disaster.
calcaire [kalkɛr] *adj* chalky; (*eau*) hard. *nm* limestone.
calcium [kalsjɔm] *nm* calcium.
calculer [kalkyle] *v* calculate, work out. **calcul** *nm* calculation, sum; arithmetic.
cale[1] [kal] *nf* (*naut*) hold; (*plan incliné*) slipway. **cale sèche** dry dock.
cale[2] [kal] *nf* wedge.
caleçon [kalsɔ̃] *nm* underpants *pl*. **caleçon de bain** bathing trunks *pl*.
calembour [kalɑ̃bur] *nm* pun.
calendrier [kalɑ̃drije] *nm* calendar; (*programme*) timetable, schedule.
calepin [kalpɛ̃] *nm* notebook.
caler [kale] *v* wedge; prop up, support; (*moteur*) stall; (*fam*) give up.
calfeutrer [kalfɶtre] *v* stop up; (*pièce*) draughtproof.
calibre [kalibrə] *nm* calibre; (*qualité*) grade; (*grosseur*) size; (*instrument*) gauge. **calibrer** *v* gauge; grade.
califourchon [kalifurʃɔ̃] *nm* **à califourchon** astride.
câlin [kɑlɛ̃] *adj* cuddly; tender. *nm* cuddle. **câliner** *v* fondle, cuddle. **câlinerie** *nf* tenderness; caress.
calleux [kalø] *adj* callous.
calmant [kalmɑ̃] *adj* soothing. *nm* tranquillizer; (*analgésique*) pain-killer.
calmar [kalmar] *nm* squid.
calme [kalmə] *adj* quiet, calm, peaceful. *nm* stillness, peace, calmness.
calmer [kalme] *v* calm, soothe. **se calmer** calm down; (*diminuer*) ease, subside.
calomnier [kalɔmnje] *v* slander; (*par écrit*) libel. **calomnie** *nf* slander; libel. **calomnieux** *adj* slanderous; libellous.
calorie [kalɔri] *nf* calorie.
calorifuger [kalɔrifyʒe] *v* lag, insulate. **calorifugeage** *nm* lagging, insulation.
calquer [kalke] *v* trace; copy exactly. **calque** *nm* tracing; exact copy. **papier-calque** *nm* tracing paper.
calvitie [kalvisi] *nf* baldness.
camarade [kamarad] *n(m+f)* companion, friend. **camarade de jeu** playmate.
cambrer [kɑ̃bre] *v* arch, bend. **se cambrer** arch one's back. **cambrure** *nf* curve, arch.
cambrioler [kɑ̃brijɔle] *v* break into, burgle. **cambriolage** *nm* burglary. **cambrioleur** *nm* burglar.
camée [kame] *nm* cameo.
caméléon [kameleɔ̃] *nm* chameleon.
camelote [kamlɔt] *nf* (*fam*) junk.
caméra [kamera] *nf* cine-camera.
Cameroun [kamrun] *nm* Cameroon.
camion [kamjɔ̃] *nm* lorry. **camion-citerne** *nm* tanker. **camionnette** *nf* van. **camionneur** *nm* lorry driver.
camoufler [kamufle] *v* camouflage; (*cacher*) conceal; disguise. **camouflage** *nm* camouflage.
camp [kɑ̃] *nm* camp; (*parti*) side. **camp de concentration** concentration camp.
campagne [kɑ̃paɲ] *nf* country, countryside; (*pol, mil, etc.*) campaign. **campagnard, -e** *n, adj* rustic.
camper [kɑ̃pe] *v* camp. **se camper** plant oneself. **campeur, -euse** *nm, nf* camper. **camping** *nm* camping; (*lieu*) campsite.
campus [kɑ̃pys] *nm* campus.
Canada [kanada] *nm* Canada. **canadien** *adj* Canadian. **Canadien, -enne** *nm, nf* Canadian.
canaille [kanɑj] *adj* coarse. *nf* scoundrel, rogue.
canal [kanal] *nm* channel; (*artificiel, anat*) canal. **canaliser** *v* channel.
canapé [kanape] *nm* sofa, settee; (*cuisine*) canapé.
canard [kanar] *nm* duck; false report; (*musique*) false note. **canardeau** *nm* duckling. **canardière** *nf* duck-pond.
canari [kanari] *nm* canary.
cancan [kɑ̃kɑ̃] *nm* gossip. **cancaner** *v* gossip. **cancanier, -ère** *nm, nf* gossip, scandalmonger.
cancer [kɑ̃sɛr] *nm* cancer. **Cancer** *nm* Cancer. **cancérigène** *adj* carcinogenic.
cancre [kɑ̃krə] *nm* (*fam*) dunce.
candeur [kɑ̃dœr] *nf* naivety.
candidat [kɑ̃dida], **-e** *nm, nf* candidate, applicant.
candide [kɑ̃did] *adj* naive, ingenuous.
cane [kan] *nf* (female) duck. **caneton** *nm* duckling.

canevas [kanva] *nm* (*toile*) canvas; (*ébauche*) framework.
caniche [kaniʃ] *nm* poodle.
canif [kanif] *nm* penknife.
canin [kanɛ̃] *adj* canine.
caniveau [kanivo] *nm* gutter.
canne [kan] *nf* cane; walking stick. **canne à pêche** fishing rod. **canne à sucre** sugar cane.
canneler [kanle] *v* flute. **cannelure** *nf* groove.
cannelle [kanɛl] *nf* cinnamon.
canoë [kanɔe] *nm* canoe. **faire du canoë** go canoeing.
canon[1] [kanɔ̃] *nm* gun, cannon; (*tube*) barrel.
canon[2] [kanɔ̃] *nm* canon; model.
cañon [kaɲɔ̃] *nm* canyon.
canoniser [kanɔnize] *v* canonize.
canot [kano] *nm* boat, dinghy. **canot automobile** motor boat. **canot de sauvetage** lifeboat. **canot pneumatique** rubber dinghy. **canotage** *nm* boating, rowing. **faire du canotage** go boating *or* rowing. **canotier** *nm* boater.
cantatrice [kɑ̃tatris] *nf* singer.
cantine [kɑ̃tin] *nf* canteen.
canton [kɑ̃tɔ̃] *nm* canton, district; section.
cantonnier [kɑ̃tɔnje] *nm* road-mender.
canular [kanylar] *nm* hoax. **faire un canular à** hoax, play a hoax on.
caoutchouc [kautʃu] *nm* rubber. **caoutchouc mousse** foam rubber. **caoutchouteux** *adj* rubbery.
cap [kap] *nm* cape; headland.
capable [kapablə] *adj* capable, able.
capacité [kapasite] *nf* capacity; ability.
cape [kap] *nf* cape, cloak.
capitaine [kapitɛn] *nm* captain.
capital [kapital] *adj* major, chief; fundamental. *nm* capital; fund. **capitale** *nf* capital (letter); capital (city). **capitaliser** *v* amass, accumulate. **capitalisme** *nm* capitalism. **capitaliste** *n(m+f)*, *adj* capitalist.
capiteux [kapitø] *adj* heady; (*femme*) alluring.
capitonner [kapitɔne] *v* pad. **capitonnage** *nm* padding. **capitonné de** lined with.
caporal [kapɔral] *nm* corporal.
capot [kapo] *nm* (*auto*) bonnet *or US* hood.
capote [kapɔt] *nf* (*auto*) hood; (*manteau*) greatcoat.
câpre [kɑprə] *nf* caper.
caprice [kapris] *nm* whim, caprice. **capricieux** *adj* capricious, temperamental.
Capricorne [kaprikɔrn] *nm* Capricorn.
capsule [kapsyl] *nf* capsule; (*pistolet*) cap.
capter [kapte] *v* win, gain; (*émission*) pick up.
captieux [kapsjø] *adj* specious.
captif [kaptif], **-ive** *n*, *adj* captive. **captivité** *nf* captivity.
captiver [kaptive] *v* captivate, fascinate.
capuchon [kapyʃɔ̃] *nm* hood; (*stylo*) cap.
capucine [kapysin] *nf* nasturtium.
caquet [kakɛ] *nm* cackle. **caqueter** *v* cackle.
car[1] [kar] *nm* coach.
car[2] [kar] *conj* because, for.
carabine [karabin] *nf* rifle.
caractère [karaktɛr] *nm* character, nature. **caractériser** *v* characterize. **caractéristique** *nf*, *adj* characteristic.
carafe [karaf] *nf* carafe, decanter.
caramboler [karɑ̃bɔle] *v* collide with. **carambolage** *nm* pile-up.
caramel [karamɛl] *nm* caramel; (*dur*) toffee.
carapace [karapas] *nf* shell.
carat [kara] *nm* carat.
caravane [karavan] *nf* caravan.
carbone [karbɔn] *nm* carbon.
carboniser [karbɔnize] *v* (*forêt*) burn to the ground; (*cuisine*) burn to a cinder. **carbonisé** *adj* charred.
carburant [karbyrɑ̃] *nm* fuel.
carburateur [karbyratœr] *nm* carburettor.
carcasse [karkas] *nf* carcass; (*charpente*) frame.
cardiaque [kardjak] *adj* cardiac. **être cardiaque** have heart trouble, suffer from heart disease.
cardinal [kardinal] *nm*, *adj* cardinal.
carême [karɛm] *nm* fast. **Carême** *nm* Lent.
carence [karɑ̃s] *nf* deficiency.
carène [karɛn] *nf* hull.
caresser [karese] *v* caress, stroke; (*projet*) toy with. **caresse** *nf* caress.
cargaison [kargɛzɔ̃] *nf* cargo.
caricaturer [karikatyre] *v* caricature. **caricature** *nf* caricature.
carier [karje] *v* decay. **carie** *nf* tooth decay.

carillon [karijɔ̃] *nm* chime. **carillonner** *v* chime, ring. **carillonneur** *nm* bell-ringer.
carnage [karnaʒ] *nm* carnage.
carnassier [karnasje] *adj* carnivorous. *nm* carnivore.
carnaval [karnaval] *nm* carnival.
carnet [karnɛ] *nm* notebook. **carnet de chèques** chequebook. **carnet de billets/timbres** book of tickets/stamps.
carnivore [karnivɔr] *adj* carnivorous. *nm* carnivore.
carotte [karɔt] *nf* carrot.
carpette [karpɛt] *nf* rug.
carquois [karkwa] *nm* quiver.
carré [kare] *adj* square; (*franc*) straight, forthright. *nm* square. **carrément** *adv* bluntly, straight.
carreau [karo] *nm* (*mur, sol*) tile; (*vitre*) pane; (*tissu*) check; (*papier*) square; (*cartes*) diamond.
carrefour [karfur] *nm* crossroads.
carreler [karle] *v* tile; (*papier*) square. **carrelage** *nm* tiling.
carrelet [karlɛ] *nm* plaice.
carrer [kare] *v* square. **se carrer** ensconce oneself.
carrière[1] [karjɛr] *nf* (*pierre*) quarry.
carrière[2] [karjɛr] *nf* (*profession*) career.
carrosse [karɔs] *nm* coach. **carrosserie** *nf* (*auto*) body, bodywork.
carrure [karyr] *nf* build; stature.
cartable [kartablə] *nm* schoolbag, satchel.
carte [kart] *nf* card; (*géog*) map; menu. **carte à jouer** playing card. **carte de crédit** credit card. **carte des vins** wine list. **carte d'identité** identity card. **carte postale** postcard.
cartilage [kartilaʒ] *nm* cartilage; (*viande*) gristle. **cartilagineux** *adj* cartilaginous; gristly.
carton [kartɔ̃] *nm* cardboard; (*boîte*) box.
cartouche [kartuʃ] *nf* cartridge; (*cigarettes*) carton.
carvi [karvi] *nm* caraway.
cas [kɑ] *nm* case; situation. **au cas où** in case. **cas limite** borderline case. **cas urgent** emergency. **en aucun cas** under no circumstances. **en tout cas** in any case. **faire cas de** attach importance to.
cascade [kaskad] *nf* waterfall; torrent. **cascadeur** *nm* stuntman.
case [kɑz] *nf* (*papier, échiquier*) square; compartment; hut.
caser [kɑze] *v* find a place for; fix up; (*fam*) put. **se caser** settle down; find a job.
caserne [kazɛrn] *nf* barracks. **caserne de pompiers** fire station.
casier [kɑzje] *nm* compartment; (*courrier*) pigeon-hole; (*fermant à clef*) locker; (*bouteilles*) rack. **casier judiciaire** police record.
casino [kazino] *nm* casino.
casque [kask] *nm* helmet; (*à écouteurs*) headphones *pl*.
casquette [kaskɛt] *nf* cap.
casse [kɑs] *nf* breakage, damage. **mettre à la casse** scrap.
casser [kɑse] *v* break; (*jur*) annul, quash. **casse-cou** *nm invar* (*fam*) reckless person. **casse-croûte** *nm invar* snack. **casse-noisettes** *nm invar* nutcracker. **casse-pieds** *n(m+f) invar* (*fam*) nuisance. **cassable** *adj* breakable. **cassant** *adj* brittle; brusque, abrupt. **cassure** *nf* break.
casserole [kasrɔl] *nf* saucepan.
cassette [kasɛt] *nf* casket; (*magnétophone*) cassette.
cassis [kasis] *nm* blackcurrant.
cassonade [kasɔnad] *nf* brown sugar.
caste [kast] *nf* caste.
castor [kastɔr] *nm* beaver.
cataloguer [katalɔge] *v* catalogue, list. **catalogue** *nm* catalogue, list.
catalyseur [katalizœr] *nm* catalyst.
catamaran [katamarɑ̃] *nm* catamaran.
cataphote [katafɔt] *nm* reflector; (*route*) cat's-eye.
cataplasme [kataplasmə] *nm* poultice.
cataracte [katarakt] *nf* cataract.
catarrhe [katar] *nm* catarrh.
catastrophe [katastrɔf] *nf* disaster, catastrophe.
catch [katʃ] *nm* wrestling. **catcheur, -euse** *nm, nf* wrestler.
catéchisme [kateʃismə] *nm* catechism. **aller au catéchisme** go to Sunday school.
catégoriser [kategɔrize] *v* categorize. **catégorie** *nf* category. **catégorique** *adj* categorical.
cathédrale [katedral] *nf* cathedral.
cathode [katɔd] *nf* cathode.
catholique [katɔlik] *n(m+f), adj* Catholic. **catholicism** *nm* Catholicism.
cauchemar [koʃmar] *nm* nightmare. **cauchemardesque** *adj* nightmarish.
cause [koz] *nf* cause; (*jur*) case, brief. **à cause de** because of. **en cause** in question. **pour cause de** on account of.

causer[1] [koze] *v* (*occasionner*) cause.
causer[2] [koze] *v* (*bavarder*) chat, talk. **causant** *adj* (*fam*) talkative. **causerie** *nf* chat, talk.
caustique [kostik] *adj* caustic.
cauteleux [kotlø] *adj* wily.
caution [kosjɔ̃] *nf* guarantee; (*jur*) bail; support. **sous caution** on bail.
cautionnement [kosjɔnmɑ̃] *nm* guarantee.
cavalerie [kavalri] *nf* cavalry.
cavalier [kavalje], **-ère** *adj* offhand. *nm, nf* (*cheval*) rider; (*bal*) partner. *nm* escort; (*échecs*) knight.
cave[1] [kav] *nf* cellar.
cave[2] [kav] *adj* hollow, sunken.
caveau [kavo] *nm* vault.
caverne [kavɛrn] *nf* cave. **caverneux** *adj* cavernous.
caviar [kavjar] *nm* caviar.
cavité [kavite] *nf* cavity.
ce[1] [sə], **cette** *adj* (*ci*) this; (*là*) that.
ce[2] [sə], **c'** *pron* it; (*homme*) he; (*femme*) she. **ce que** *or* **qui** what, which.
ceci [səsi] *pron* this.
cécité [sesite] *nf* blindness.
céder [sede] *v* give up *or* in; (*fléchir, succomber*) give way.
cédille [sedij] *nf* cedilla.
cèdre [sɛdrə] *nm* cedar.
***ceindre** [sɛ̃drə] *v* encircle; (*mettre*) put on.
ceinture [sɛ̃tyr] *nf* belt; (*gaine*) girdle; (*écharpe*) sash; (*anat*) waist. **ceinture de securité** seat *or* safety belt.
cela [səla] *pron* that; it. **cela** *or* **ça ne fait rien** it doesn't matter.
célèbre [selɛbrə] *adj* famous. **célébrité** *nf* celebrity.
célébrer [selebre] *v* celebrate. **célébration** *nf* celebration.
celer [sle] *v* conceal.
céleri [sɛlri] *nm* celery.
céleste [selɛst] *adj* celestial, heavenly.
célibataire [selibatɛr] *adj* single. *nm* bachelor, single man. *nf* single girl *or* woman. **celibat** *nm* celibacy.
cellule [selyl] *nf* cell.
celte [sɛlt] *adj also* **celtique** Celtic. **Celte** *n*(*m*+*f*) Celt.
celui, celle [səlɥi, sɛl] *pron* the one. **celui-ci, celle-ci** this one; (*dernier*) the latter. **celui-là, celle-là** that one; (*premier*) the former.
cendre [sɑ̃drə] *nf* ash. **cendrier** *nm* ashtray.
cène [sɛn] *nf* (*rel*) Communion. **la Cène** the Last Supper.
censé [sɑ̃se] *adj* supposed.
censeur [sɑ̃sœr] *nm* censor; critic; (*lycée*) deputy head.
censurer [sɑ̃syre] *v* (*film, etc.*) censor; (*critiquer*) censure. **censure** *nf* censorship; censure.
cent [sɑ̃] *nm, adj* a hundred. **faire les cent pas** pace up and down. **pour cent** per cent. **une centaine (de)** about a hundred. **centième** *n*(*m*+*f*), *adj* hundredth.
centenaire [sɑ̃tnɛr] *adj* hundred-year-old. *n*(*m*+*f*) centenarian. *nm* centenary.
centigrade [sɑ̃tigrad] *adj* centigrade.
centime [sɑ̃tim] *nm* centime.
centimètre [sɑ̃timɛtrə] *nm* centimetre; (*ruban*) tape measure.
central [sɑ̃tral] *adj* central. *nm* telephone exchange. **centrale** *nf* power station.
centraliser [sɑ̃tralize] *v* centralize. **centralisation** *nf* centralization.
centre [sɑ̃trə] *nm* centre. **centre commercial** shopping centre. **centre-ville** *nm* town centre.
cep [sɛp] *nm* stock.
cependant [səpɑ̃dɑ̃] *conj* however, nevertheless.
céramique [seramik] *nf, adj* ceramic. **la céramique** ceramics.
cerceau [sɛrso] *nm* hoop.
cercle [sɛrklə] *nm* circle; club; (*étendue*) range. **cercle vicieux** vicious circle.
cercueil [sɛrkœj] *nm* coffin.
céréale [sereal] *nf* cereal.
cérébral [serebral] *adj* cerebral; mental.
cérémonie [seremɔni] *nf* ceremony. **faire des cérémonies** stand on ceremony; (*fam*) make a fuss. **sans cérémonie** informal, informally. **cérémonieux** *adj* ceremonious, formal.
cerf [sɛr] *nm* stag. **cerf-volant** *nm* kite.
cerise [səriz] *nf* cherry. **cerisier** *nm* cherry (tree).
cerner [sɛrne] *v* encircle, surround. **avoir les yeux cernés** have rings under one's eyes.
certain [sɛrtɛ̃] *adj* certain; definite. **certains** *pron, adj* some, certain. **certainement** *adv* certainly; most probably.
certes [sɛrt] *adv* indeed, most certainly; admittedly.
certifier [sɛrtifje] *v* certify; (*signature*) witness; assure. **certificat** *nm* certificate.

certitude [sɛrtityd] *nf* certainty.
cerveau [sɛrvo] *nm* brain; (*intelligence*) mind; (*personne*) mastermind.
cervelle [sɛrvɛl] *nf* brains *pl*.
Cervin [sɛrvɛ̃] *nm* Matterhorn.
ces [se] *adj* (*ci*) these; (*là*) those.
cesse [sɛs] *nf* **sans cesse** continually; incessantly.
cesser [sese] *v* stop, cease. **faire cesser** put a stop to.
cet [sɛt] *form of* **ce**[1] *used before vowel or mute h.*
cette [sɛt] *V* **ce**[1].
ceux, celles [sø, sɛl] *pron* the ones, those. **ceux-ci, celles-ci** these; (*derniers*) the latter. **ceux-là, celles-là** those; (*premiers*) the former.
chacal [ʃakal] *nm, pl* **-als** jackal.
chacun [ʃakœ̃] *pron* each; (*tout le monde*) everyone.
chagrin [ʃagrɛ̃] *adj* despondent; morose. *nm* sorrow, grief.
chagriner [ʃagrine] *v* distress, worry.
chahut [ʃay] *nm* rumpus. **chahuteur, -euse** *n, adj* rowdy.
chaîne [ʃɛn] *nf* chain; (*montagnes*) range; (*usine*) production line (*TV*) channel.
chair [ʃɛr] *nf* flesh. **chair à saucisse** sausage-meat. **chair de poule** goose-flesh.
chaire [ʃɛr] *nf* (*rel*) pulpit; (*université*) chair.
chaise [ʃɛz] *nf* chair.
chaland [ʃalɑ̃] *nm* barge.
châle [ʃal] *nm* shawl.
chalet [ʃalɛ] *nm* chalet.
chaleur [ʃalœr] *nf* heat, warmth; fervour. **chaleureux** *adj* warm.
chaloupe [ʃalup] *nf* launch. **chaloupe de sauvetage** lifeboat.
chalumeau [ʃalymo] *nm* (*tech*) blowlamp; (*musique*) pipe.
chalut [ʃaly] *nm* trawl. **pêcher au chalut** trawl. **chalutier** *nm* trawler.
se chamailler [ʃamɑje] *v* (*fam*) squabble. **chamailleur, -euse** *adj* quarrelsome.
chambellan [ʃɑ̃belɑ̃] *nm* chamberlain.
chambranle [ʃɑ̃brɑ̃l] *nm* frame; (*cheminée*) mantelpiece.
chambre [ʃɑ̃brə] *nf* room; (*à coucher*) bedroom; (*tech, admin*) chamber; (*pol*) house. **chambre d'ami** spare room. **chambre d'enfants** nursery. **chambre noire** dark-room. **chambrer** *v* (*vin*) bring to room temperature; (*personne*) corner.
chameau [ʃamo] *nm* camel.
chamois [ʃamwa] *nm* chamois. *adj invar* buff.
champ [ʃɑ̃] *nm* field. **champ d'aviation** airfield. **champ de courses** racecourse. **champ de foire** fairground.
champagne [ʃɑ̃paɲ] *nm* champagne.
champêtre [ʃɑ̃pɛtrə] *adj* rural.
champignon [ʃɑ̃piɲɔ̃] *nm* mushroom; (*vénéneux*) toadstool; (*terme générique*) fungus; (*fam*) accelerator.
champion, -onne [ʃɑ̃pjɔ̃, -ɔn] *nm, nf* champion. *adj* (*fam*) first-rate. **championnat** *nm* championship.
chance [ʃɑ̃s] *nf* luck; (*possibilité*) chance. **avoir de la chance** be lucky. **pas de chance!** hard luck! **chanceux** *adj* lucky.
chanceler [ʃɑ̃sle] *v* totter, falter. **chancelant** *adj* unsteady, shaky.
chancelier [ʃɑ̃səlje] *nm* chancellor.
chandail [ʃɑ̃daj] *nm* sweater.
chandelle [ʃɑ̃dɛl] *nf* candle. **chandelier** *nm* candlestick.
changer [ʃɑ̃ʒe] *v* change; exchange; (*modifier*) alter. **change** *nm* exchange; (*taux*) exchange rate. **changeant** *adj* changeable. **changement** *nm* change; alteration.
chanoine [ʃanwan] *nm* canon.
chanson [ʃɑ̃sɔ̃] *nf* song.
chant [ʃɑ̃] *nm* singing; (*chanson*) song. **chant de Noël** Christmas carol.
chanter [ʃɑ̃te] *v* sing. **faire chanter** blackmail. **chantage** *nm* blackmail. **chanteur, -euse** *nm, nf* singer.
chantier [ʃɑ̃tje] *nm* yard, site; (*route*) roadworks *pl*. **chantier naval** shipyard.
chantonner [ʃɑ̃tɔne] *v* hum, croon.
chanvre [ʃɑ̃vrə] *nm* hemp.
chaos [kao] *nm* chaos.
chape [ʃap] *nf* (*pneu*) tread; (*rel*) cope.
chapeau [ʃapo] *nm* hat. **chapeau melon** bowler hat.
chapelain [ʃaplɛ̃] *nm* chaplain.
chapelet [ʃaplɛ] *nm* rosary.
chapelle [ʃapɛl] *nf* chapel.
chapelure [ʃaplyr] *nf* breadcrumbs *pl*.
chaperon [ʃaprɔ̃] *nm* chaperon. **chaperonner** *v* chaperon.
chapitre [ʃapitrə] *nm* chapter; subject.
chaque [ʃak] *adj* every, each.
char [ʃar] *nm* (*mil*) tank; (*carnaval*) float.
charabia [ʃarabja] *nm* (*fam*) gibberish.
charbon [ʃarbɔ̃] *nm* coal. **charbon de bois** charcoal. **charbonnage** *nm* coal-mining. **charbonnier** *nm* coalman.

charcuterie [ʃarkytri] *nf* (*magasin*) pork butcher's, delicatessen; (*viande*) cooked pork meats. **charcutier, -ère** *nm, nf* pork butcher.
chardon [ʃardɔ̃] *nm* thistle.
chardonneret [ʃardɔnrɛ] *nm* goldfinch.
charger [ʃarʒe] *v* load; (*mil, élec*) charge. **charger de** ask to, put in charge of. **se charger de** see to, take care of. **charge** *nf* load; charge; responsibility; (*frais*) expense. **à charge de** on condition that. **chargé** *adj* loaded, laden; (*rempli, occupé*) full, heavy. **chargement** *nm* loading.
chariot [ʃarjo] *nm* trolley; (*charrette*) wagon; (*tech*) carriage.
charité [ʃarite] *nf* charity; (*gentillesse*) kindness.
charivari [ʃarivari] *nm* hullabaloo.
charlatan [ʃarlatɑ̃] *nm* charlatan; (*médecin*) quack.
charmer [ʃarme] *v* charm, enchant. **charmant** *adj* charming, delightful. **charme** *nm* charm; (*magique*) spell.
charnel [ʃarnɛl] *adj* carnal.
charnière [ʃarnjɛr] *nf* hinge.
charnu [ʃarny] *adj* fleshy.
charpente [ʃarpɑ̃t] *nf* framework, structure; (*carrure*) build. **charpenté** *adj* built.
charrette [ʃarɛt] *nf* cart.
charrue [ʃary] *nf* plough.
charte [ʃart] *nf* charter.
chasse [ʃas] *nf* hunting, hunt; (*au fusil*) shooting; (*poursuite*) chase; (*d'eau*) flush. **tirer la chasse** pull the chain.
châsse [ʃɑs] *nf* shrine.
chasser [ʃase] *v* hunt; (*au fusil*) shoot; (*faire partir*) drive out, chase away; (*dissiper*) dispel. **chasse-neige** *nm invar* snowplough. **chasseur** *nm* hunter; (*hôtel*) page.
châssis [ʃɑsi] *nm* frame; (*auto*) chassis.
chaste [ʃast] *adj* chaste. **chasteté** *nf* chastity.
chat, chatte [ʃa, ʃat] *nm, nf* cat. **chaton** *nm* (*zool*) kitten; (*bot*) catkin.
châtaigne [ʃɑtɛɲ] *nf* chestnut. **châtaignier** *nm* chestnut (tree).
châtain [ʃɑtɛ̃] *adj* chestnut, auburn.
château [ʃɑto] *nm* castle; (*manoir*) mansion.
châtier [ʃɑtje] *v* punish; refine. **châtiment** *nm* punishment.
chatouiller [ʃatuje] *v* tickle. **chatouillement** *nm* tickle. **chatouilleux** *adj* ticklish; (*irritable*) touchy, sensitive.
chatoyer [ʃatwaje] *v* glisten, shimmer, sparkle. **chatoiement** *nm* glistening, shimmer, sparkle.
châtrer [ʃɑtre] *v* castrate.
chaud [ʃo] *adj* warm, hot. *nm* heat, warmth. **avoir chaud** be warm *or* hot.
chaudière *nf* boiler.
chauffer [ʃofe] *v* warm (up), heat (up); (*moteur*) overheat. **chauffe-eau** *nm invar* water-heater. **chauffe-plats** *nm invar* hotplate. **chauffage** *nm* heating. **chauffage central** central heating.
chauffeur [ʃofœr] *nm* driver; (*privé*) chauffeur.
chaume [ʃom] *nm* stubble; (*toit*) thatch. **chaumière** *nf* thatched cottage.
chaussée [ʃose] *nf* road; causeway.
chausser [ʃose] *v* (*mettre*) put (shoes) on; (*marchand*) supply with shoes; (*chaussure*) fit. **chausse-pied** *nm* shoehorn. **chaussette** *nf* sock. **chausson** *nm* slipper. **chaussure** *nf* shoe, boot; footwear.
chauve [ʃov] *adj* bald. **chauve-souris** *nf* bat.
chauvin [ʃovɛ̃], **-e** *nm, nf* chauvinist. *adj* chauvinistic. **chauvinisme** *nm* chauvinism.
chaux [ʃo] *nf* lime. **blanchir à la chaux** whitewash.
chavirer [ʃavire] *v* capsize, overturn.
chef [ʃɛf] *nm* head; (*patron*) boss; (*tribu*) chief; (*révolte, etc.*) leader; (*cuisine*) chef. **chef d'équipe** foreman; (*sport*) captain. **chef de gare** station-master. **chef de train** guard. **chef-d'œuvre** *nm* masterpiece. **chef d'orchestre** conductor. **chef-lieu** *nm* county town.
cheik [ʃɛk] *nm* sheik.
chelem [ʃlɛm] *nm* (*cartes*) slam.
chemin [ʃəmɛ̃] *nm* way, path; (*campagne*) lane. **chemin de fer** railway. **chemin faisant** on the way. **se mettre en chemin** set off.
chemineau [ʃəmino] *nm* tramp.
cheminée [ʃəmine] *nf* chimney; (*foyer*) fireplace; (*encadrement*) mantelpiece; (*paquebot*) funnel.
cheminer [ʃəmine] *v* walk; (*péniblement*) trudge along; (*eau, sentier*) make its way.
chemise [ʃəmiz] *nf* shirt; (*dossier*) folder; (*tech*) lining, jacket. **chemise de nuit** nightdress. **chemisier** *nm* blouse.

chenal [ʃənal] *nm* channel; canal.
chêne [ʃɛn] *nm* oak.
chenille [ʃənij] *nf* caterpillar.
chèque [ʃɛk] *nm* cheque. **chèque-cadeau** *nm* gift token. **chèque de voyage** traveller's cheque. **chèque en blanc** blank cheque. **chéquier** *nm* cheque book.
cher [ʃɛr] *adj* dear; (*coûteux*) expensive. *adv* dearly. **coûter/payer cher** cost/pay a lot. **cherté** *nf* high price *or* cost.
chercher [ʃɛrʃe] *v* look for, seek. **chercher à** try to. **chercheur, -euse** *nm, nf* researcher.
chéri [ʃeri] **-e** *adj* beloved. *nm, nf* darling.
chérir [ʃerir] *v* cherish.
chérubin [ʃerybɛ̃] *nm* cherub.
chétif [ʃetif] *adj* (*enfant, etc.*) puny; (*repas, etc.*) meagre.
cheval [ʃəval] *nm* horse; (*auto*) horsepower. **à cheval** on horseback; (*chaise, etc.*) astride, straddling. **cheval à bascule** rocking horse. **cheval de course** racehorse.
chevalerie [ʃəvalri] *nf* chivalry. **chevaleresque** *adj* chivalrous.
chevalet [ʃəvalɛ] *nm* (*peinture*) easel; (*menuiserie*) trestle; (*violon*) bridge.
chevalier [ʃəvalje] *nm* knight. **chevalière** *nf* signet ring.
chevaucher [ʃəvoʃə] *v* be astride, straddle; (*tuile, pan*) overlap.
chevelu [ʃəvly] *adj* long-haired, hairy. **chevelure** *nf* (head of) hair.
chevet [ʃəvɛ] *nm* bedside.
cheveu [ʃəvø] *nm* hair. **cheveux** *nm pl* hair *sing.* **tiré par les cheveux** far-fetched.
cheville [ʃəvij] *nf* ankle; (*fiche*) peg, pin.
chèvre [ʃɛvrə] *nf* goat. **chevreau** *nm* kid.
chèvrefeuille [ʃɛvrəfœj] *nm* honeysuckle.
chevron [ʃəvrɔ̃] *nm* rafter; (*motif*) chevron.
chevroter [ʃəvrɔte] *v* quaver.
chez [ʃe] *prep* at *or* to the house of; (*avec*) with, in, among; (*docteur, etc.*) at, to; (*adresse*) care of, c/o. **chez soi** at home. **faites comme chez vous!** make yourself at home!
chic [ʃik] *nm* style. **avoir le chic pour** have the knack of. *adj invar* smart; (*fam*) nice, decent. *interj* great! terrific!
chicaner [ʃikane] *v* quibble. **chicanerie** *nf* quibbling.
chiche [ʃiʃ] *adj* niggardly, paltry, mean.
chicorée [ʃikɔre] *nf* (*salade*) endive; (*café*) chicory.
chien [ʃjɛ̃] *nm* dog. **chien d'aveugle** guide dog. **chien de berger** sheepdog. **chien de garde** guard dog. **entre chien et loup** in the twilight. **temps de chien** *nm* filthy weather. **chienne** *nf* bitch.
chiffon [ʃifɔ̃] *nm* rag; (*de papier*) scrap; (*à poussière*) duster.
chiffonner [ʃifɔne] *v* crumple, crease; (*fam*) bother, worry.
chiffre [ʃifrə] *nm* figure; total; code. **chiffre d'affaires** turnover.
chiffrer [ʃifre] *v* code; (*évaluer*) assess; (*pages*) number. **se chiffrer à** add up to.
chignon [ʃiɲɔ̃] *nm* bun.
chimère [ʃimɛr] *nf* dream, fancy. **chimérique** *adj* fanciful; imaginary.
chimie [ʃimi] *nf* chemistry. **chimique** *adj* chemical. **chimiste** *n(m+f)* chemist.
chimpanzé [ʃɛ̃pɑ̃ze] *nm* chimpanzee.
Chine [ʃin] *nf* China. **chinois** *nm, adj* Chinese. **les Chinois** the Chinese.
chiot [ʃjo] *nm* puppy.
chiper [ʃipe] *v* (*fam*) pinch.
chipoter [ʃipɔte] (*fam*) *v* haggle, quibble; (*manger*) pick at.
chips [ʃip] *nm pl* crisps *pl.*
chiquenaude [ʃiknod] *nf* flick, flip.
chiromancie [kirɔmɑ̃si] *nf* palmistry. **chiromancien, -enne** *nm, nf* palmist.
chirurgie [ʃiryrʒi] *nf* surgery. **chirurgical** *adj* surgical. **chirurgien** *nm* surgeon.
chlore [klɔr] *nm* chlorine. **chlorer** *v* chlorinate.
chloroforme [klɔrɔfɔrm] *nm* chloroform. **chloroformer** *v* chloroform.
chlorophylle [klɔrɔfil] *nf* chlorophyll.
choc [ʃɔk] *nm* shock; impact, crash; (*conflit*) clash.
chocolat [ʃɔkɔla] *nm* chocolate. **chocolat à croquer** plain chocolate. **chocolat au lait** milk chocolate. **chocolat en poudre** drinking chocolate. *adj invar* chocolate-coloured.
chœur [kœr] *nm* chorus; (*chanteurs*) choir. **en chœur** in chorus.
***choir** [ʃwar] *v* fall.
choisir [ʃwazir] *v* choose, select. **choisi** *adj* chosen; (*raffiné*) select.
choix [ʃwa] *nm* choice, selection. **de choix** choice.
choléra [kɔlera] *nm* cholera.
cholestérol [kɔlɛsterɔl] *nm* cholesterol.
chômer [ʃome] *v* be idle; (*travailleur*) be unemployed; (*usine, etc.*) be at a standstill. **chômage** *nm* unemployment. **au**

chômage unemployed. **mettre au chômage** make redundant. **chômeur, -euse** *nm, nf* unemployed person.
chope [ʃɔp] *nf* tankard.
choquer [ʃɔke] *v* shock, appal; (*offusquer*) offend; (*commotionner*) shake up; (*heurter*) knock, clink. **se choquer** be shocked.
choral [kɔral] *adj* choral. *nm* chorale. **chorale** *nf* choral society, choir.
chorégraphie [kɔregrafi] *nf* choreography. **chorégraphe** *n(m+f)* choreographer.
chose [ʃoz] *nf* thing. *nm* (*fam*) thingumajig. **être tout chose** (*fam*) feel peculiar.
chou [ʃu] *nm, pl* **choux** cabbage; (*ruban*) rosette; (*cuisine*) puff. **chou de Bruxelles** Brussels sprout. **chou-fleur** *nm* cauliflower.
choucas [ʃukɑ] *nm* jackdaw.
chouchou, -oute [ʃuʃu, -ut] *nm, nf* (*fam*) pet.
choucroute [ʃukrut] *nf* sauerkraut.
chouette[1] [ʃwɛt] *adj, interj* (*fam*) smashing, great.
chouette[2] [ʃwɛt] *nf* owl.
choyer [ʃwaje] *v* pamper; cherish.
chrétien [kretjɛ̃] *adj* Christian. **Chrétien, -enne** *nm, nf* Christian.
christianisme [kristjanismə] *nm* Christianity.
chromatique [krɔmatik] *adj* chromatic.
chrome [krom] *nm* chromium, chrome. **chromé** *adj* chromium-plated.
chromosome [krɔmozom] *nm* chromosome.
chronique[1] [krɔnik] *adj* chronic.
chronique[2] [krɔnik] *nf* chronicle; (*journal*) column.
chronologique [krɔnɔlɔʒik] *adj* chronological.
chronométrer [krɔnɔmetre] *v* time. **chronomètre** *nm* stopwatch.
chrysalide [krizalid] *nf* chrysalis.
chrysanthème [krizɑ̃tɛm] *nm* chrysanthemum.
chuchoter [ʃyʃɔte] *v* whisper. **chuchotement** *nm* whisper.
chuinter [ʃɥɛ̃te] *v* hiss softly; (*chouette*) hoot.
chut [ʃyt] *interj* hush!
chute [ʃyt] *nf* fall; (*ruine*) collapse, downfall. **chute d'eau** waterfall.
Chypre [ʃiprə] *n* Cyprus.
ci [si] *adv* this; here. **ci-après** *adv* below. **ci-contre** *adv* opposite. **ci-dessous** below. **ci-dessus** *adv* above. **ci-devant** *adv* formerly. **ci-inclus** *adj* enclosed. **ci-joint** *adj* enclosed, attached.
cible [siblə] *nf* target.
ciboule [sibul] *nf* spring onion. **ciboulette** *nf* chive.
cicatrice [sikatris] *nf* scar.
cidre [sidrə] *nm* cider.
ciel [sjɛl] *nm, pl* **ciels** *or* **cieux** sky; (*rel*) heaven.
cierge [sjɛrʒ] *nm* candle.
cigale [sigal] *nf* cicada.
cigare [sigar] *nm* cigar. **cigarette** *nf* cigarette.
cigogne [sigɔɲ] *nf* stork.
cil [sil] *nm* eyelash.
cime [sim] *nf* peak; (*montagne*) summit; (*arbre*) top.
ciment [simɑ̃] *nm* cement. **cimenter** *v* cement.
cimetière [simtjɛr] *nm* cemetery, graveyard.
cinéaste [sineast] *n(m+f)* film-maker.
cinéma [sinema] *nm* cinema.
cinétique [sinetik] *adj* kinetic. *nf* kinetics.
cingler [sɛ̃gle] *v* lash, whip. **cinglant** *adj* biting; (*pluie*) driving. **cinglé** *adj* (*fam*) mad, crazy.
cinq [sɛ̃k] *nm, adj* five. **cinquième** *n(m+f), adj* fifth.
cinquante [sɛ̃kɑ̃t] *nm, adj* fifty. **cinquantième** *n(m+f), adj* fiftieth.
cintrer [sɛ̃tre] *v* arch; bend. **cintre** *nm* arch; (*vêtements*) coat-hanger.
cirage [siraʒ] *nm* shoe polish.
***circoncire** [sirkɔ̃sir] *v* circumcize. **circoncision** *nf* circumcision.
circonférence [sirkɔ̃ferɑ̃s] *nf* circumference.
circonflexe [sirkɔ̃flɛks] *adj* circumflex.
circonscription [sirkɔ̃skripsjɔ̃] *nf* district; (*électorale*) constituency.
***circonscrire** [sirkɔ̃skrir] *v* confine; (*math*) circumscribe.
circonspect [sirkɔ̃spɛkt] *adj* circumspect, cautious.
circonstance [sirkɔ̃stɑ̃s] *nf* circumstance; occasion. **de circonstance** appropriate.
circuit [sirkɥi] *nm* circuit; (*excursion*) tour.
circuler [sirkyle] *v* circulate; (*voiture, piéton*) go, move along. **circulaire** *nf, adj* circular. **circulation** *nf* circulation; (*auto*) traffic.

cirer [sire] *v* polish. **cire** *nf* wax; (*meubles*) polish. **ciré** *nm* oilskin. **cireux** *adj* waxy.
cirque [sirk] *nm* circus.
cisaille [sizaj] *nf* shears *pl*.
ciseau [sizo] *nm* chisel. **ciseaux** *nm pl* scissors *pl*.
ciseler [sizle] *v* chisel, carve.
cité [site] *nf* city, town. **cité universitaire** halls of residence *pl*.
citer [site] *v* quote, cite; (*jur*) summon. **citation** *nf* quotation; summons.
citerne [sitern] *nf* tank.
cithare [sitar] *nf* zither.
citoyen [sitwajɛ̃] **-enne** *nm*, *nf* citizen.
citron [sitrɔ̃] *nm*, *adj* lemon. **citron pressé** lemon juice. **citronnade** *nf* lemon squash. **citronnier** *nm* lemon tree.
citrouille [sitruj] *nf* pumpkin.
civette [sivet] *nf* chive.
civière [sivjer] *nf* stretcher.
civil [sivil] *adj* civil; civilian. *nm* civilian. **en civil** in plain clothes.
civiliser [sivilize] *v* civilize. **civilisation** *nf* civilization.
civique [sivik] *adj* civic.
clair [kler] *adj* clear; (*lumineux*) light, bright; (*sauce*, *tissu*) thin; (*couleur*) pale; (*evident*) plain. *adv* clearly. *nm* light. **clair de lune** moonlight.
clairière [klerjer] *nf* clearing.
clairon [klerɔ̃] *nm* bugle.
clairsemé [klersəme] *adj* scattered, sparse.
clairvoyant [klervwajɑ̃] *adj* perceptive, clear-sighted.
clameur [klamœr] *nf* clamour.
clan [klɑ̃] *nm* clan.
clandestin [klɑ̃destɛ̃] *adj* secret, clandestine, underground.
clapier [klapje] *nm* hutch.
clapoter [klapɔte] *v* lap. **clapotement** *or* **clapotis** *nm* lapping.
claquemurer [klakmyre] *v* coop up, shut away.
claquer [klake] *v* (*son*) bang, snap, crack; (*gifler*) slap; (*fam*: *fatiguer*) tire out; (*fam*: *mourir*) die. **claque** *nf* slap. **claquement** *nm* bang, snap, crack.
clarifier [klarifje] *v* clarify. **clarification** *nf* clarification.
clarinette [klarinet] *nf* clarinet.
clarté [klarte] *nf* brightness, clearness; (*lumière*) light; (*netteté*) clarity.
classe [klɑs] *nf* class; (*salle*) classroom; (*école*) school. **aller en classe** go to school. **faire la classe** teach. **sans classe** classless.
classer [klɑse] *v* class, classify; (*ranger*) file; (*élève*, *fruits*) grade. **classement** *nm* classification; filing; grading. **classeur** *nm* file; (*meuble*) filing cabinet.
classifier [klasifje] *v* classify. **classification** *nf* classification.
classique [klasik] *adj* classic; (*art*, *musique*, *etc*.) classical; (*habituel*) usual. *nm* (*ouvrage*) classic; (*auteur*) classicist.
claustrophobie [klostrɔfɔbi] *nf* claustrophobia.
clavecin [klavsɛ̃] *nm* harpsichord.
clavicule [klavikyl] *nf* collarbone.
clavier [klavje] *nm* keyboard.
clef *or* **clé** [kle] *nf* key; (*tech*) spanner; (*musique*) clef. **clef de contact** ignition key. **sous clef** under lock and key.
clémence [klemɑ̃s] *nf* clemency; (*temps*) mildness. **clément** *adj* lenient; mild.
clerc [kler] *nm* clerk.
clergé [klerʒe] *nm* clergy.
clérical [klerikal] *adj* clerical.
cliché [kliʃe] *nm* cliché; (*phot*) negative.
client [klijɑ̃], **-e** *nm*, *nf* customer, client; (*hôtel*) guest; (*médecin*) patient. **clientèle** *nf* clientèle; (*magasin*) customers *pl*; (*médecin*) practice; (*comm*) custom.
cligner [kliɲe] *v* **cligner les yeux** blink; (*fermer à demi*) screw up one's eyes. **clignement** *nm* blink.
clignoter [kliɲɔte] *v* (*yeux*) blink; (*étoile*) twinkle; (*vaciller*) flicker; (*signal*) flash. **clignotant** *nm* (*auto*) indicator.
climat [klima] *nm* climate. **climatique** *adj* climatic.
climatiser [klimatize] *v* air-condition. **climatisation** *nf* air-conditioning. **climatiseur** *nm* air-conditioner.
clin [klɛ̃] *nm* **clin d'œil** wink.
clinique [klinik] *adj* clinical. *nf* nursing home.
clinquant [klɛ̃kɑ̃] *adj* flashy. *nm* tinsel.
cliqueter [klikte] *v* rattle, clatter; (*métal*) clink, jingle. **cliquetis** *nm* clatter; clink, jingle.
clitoris [klitɔris] *nm* clitoris.
clochard [klɔʃar], **-e** *nm*, *nf* (*fam*) tramp.
cloche [klɔʃ] *nf* bell; cover.
clocher[1] [klɔʃe] *nm* church tower, steeple.
clocher[2] [klɔʃe] *v* (*fam*) be wrong.
cloison [klwazɔ̃] *nf* partition; barrier.

cloître [klwatrə] *nm* cloister.
clopiner [klɔpine] *v* hobble along. **clopin-clopant** *adv* hobbling. **entrer/sortir clopin-clopant** hobble in/out.
cloporte [klɔpɔrt] *nm* wood-louse (*pl* -lice).
***clore** [klɔr] *v* close, end, conclude.
clos [klo] *adj* closed, enclosed. *nm* enclosed field; vineyard.
clôture [klotyr] *nf* (*fermeture*) closure, closing; (*enceinte*) fence.
clou [klu] *nm* nail; (*chaussée*) stud; (*méd*) boil; (*théâtre*) star turn. **clou de girofle** clove.
clouer [klue] *v* nail down, pin down. **cloué au lit** confined to bed. **cloué sur place** rooted to the spot.
clouter [klute] *v* stud.
clovisse [klɔvis] *nf* clam.
clown [klun] *nm* clown.
club [klœb] *nm* club.
coaguler [kɔagyle] *v* congeal; (*sang*) coagulate; (*lait*) curdle.
coalition [kɔalisjɔ̃] *nf* coalition.
coasser [kɔase] *v* croak. **coassement** *nm* croak.
cobaye [kɔbaj] *nm* guinea-pig.
cobra [kɔbra] *nm* cobra.
cocarde [kɔkard] *nf* rosette.
cocasse [kɔkas] *adj* comical.
coccinelle [kɔksinɛl] *nf* ladybird.
cocher[1] [kɔʃe] *v* (*crayon*) tick; (*entaille*) notch.
cocher[2] [kɔʃe] *nm* coachman.
cochon, -onne [kɔʃɔ̃, -ɔn] *nm* pig. **cochon d'Inde** guinea-pig. *adj* (*argot*) dirty. **cochonnerie** (*fam*) *nf* rubbish; (*saleté*) filth; (*tour*) dirty trick.
cocktail [kɔktɛl] *nm* cocktail; cocktail party.
cocon [kɔkɔ̃] *nm* cocoon.
cocotier [kɔkɔtje] *nm* coconut palm.
cocotte[1] [kɔkɔt] *nf* (*poule*) hen; (*péj: femme*) tart.
cocotte[2] [kɔkɔt] *nf* casserole.
code [kɔd] *nm* code. **code de la route** highway code. **se mettre en code** (*auto*) dip one's headlights.
cœur [kœr] *nm* heart; courage; (*fruit*) core. **avoir mal au cœur** feel sick. **de bon cœur** willingly. **parler à cœur ouvert** have a heart-to-heart.
coexister [kɔɛgziste] *v* coexist. **coexistence** *nf* coexistence.
coffre [kɔfrə] *nm* chest; (*auto*) boot. **coffre-fort** *nm* safe.
cognac [kɔɲak] *nm* cognac.
cogner [kɔɲe] *v* hit, knock; (*plus fort*) hammer, bang.
cohabiter [kɔabite] *v* live together.
cohérent [kɔerɑ̃] *adj* coherent, consistent. **cohérence** *nf* coherence, consistency.
cohue [kɔy] *nf* crowd.
coiffer [kwafe] *v* (*mettre*) put (a hat) on; cover. **coiffer quelqu'un** do someone's hair. **se coiffer** do one's hair. **se coiffer de** put on; (*péj*) become infatuated with. **coiffeur** *nm* hairdresser; (*hommes*) barber. **coiffeuse** *nf* hairdresser; (*meuble*) dressing table. **coiffure** *nf* hair-style; (*métier*) hairdressing.
coin [kwɛ̃] *nm* corner; (*lieu*) spot, area. **au coin du feu** by the fireside. **du coin** local.
coincer [kwɛ̃se] *v* wedge, jam.
coïncider [kɔɛ̃side] *v* coincide. **coïncidence** *nf* coincidence.
coin-coin [kwɛ̃kwɛ̃] *nm, interj* quack.
coing [kwɛ̃] *nm* quince.
col [kɔl] *nm* (*vêtement*) collar; (*géog*) pass; (*vase*) neck. **col roulé** polo-neck.
coléoptère [kɔleɔptɛr] *nm* beetle.
colère [kɔlɛr] *nf* anger, rage. **en colère** angry. **coléreux** *adj* quick-tempered.
colimaçon [kɔlimasɔ̃] *nm* snail. **en colimaçon** spiral.
colin [kɔlɛ̃] *nm* hake.
colique [kɔlik] *nf* stomach-ache; colic; diarrhoea.
colis [kɔli] *nm* parcel. **par colis postal** by parcel post.
collaborer [kɔlabɔre] *v* collaborate. **collaborateur, -trice** *nm, nf* collaborator; (*journal*) contributor. **collaboration** *nf* collaboration; contribution.
collant [kɔlɑ̃] *nm* (*bas*) tights *pl*; (*acrobate*) leotard. *adj* sticky; (*vêtement*) close-fitting, clinging.
colle [kɔl] *nf* glue, paste; (*fam: question*) poser.
collectif [kɔlɛktif] *adj* collective; (*hystérie*) mass; (*billet*) group. **collectivité** *nf* group; community.
collection [kɔlɛksjɔ̃] *nf* collection.
collectionner [kɔlɛksjɔne] *v* collect. **collectionneur, -euse** *nm, nf* collector.
collège [kɔlɛʒ] *nm* secondary school; college. **collégien** *nm* schoolboy. **collégienne** *nf* schoolgirl.

collègue [kɔlɛg] *n(m+f)* colleague.
coller [kɔle] *v* stick, cling.
collet [kɔlɛ] *nm* (*piège*) snare; (*tech*) collar, neck. **collet monté** prim, strait-laced.
collier [kɔlje] *nm* (*femme*) necklace; (*animal*) collar.
colline [kɔlin] *nf* hill.
collision [kɔlizjɔ̃] *nf* collision; (*conflit*) clash.
colombe [kɔlɔ̃b] *nf* dove. **colombier** *nm* dovecote.
colonel [kɔlɔnɛl] *nm* colonel.
colonie [kɔlɔni] *nf* colony. **colonie de vacances** holiday camp for children. **colonial** *nm, adj* colonial. **coloniser** *v* colonize.
colonne [kɔlɔn] *nf* column; (*arch*) pillar. **colonne vertébrale** spine.
colorer [kɔlɔre] *v* colour; (*tissu*) dye; (*bois*) stain. **coloration** *nf* colouring. **coloré** *adj* colourful; (*teint*) ruddy. **colorier** *v* colour in.
coloris [kɔlɔri] *nm* colour, colouring.
colosse [kɔlɔs] *nm* giant, colossus. **colossal** *adj* colossal.
colporter [kɔlpɔrte] *v* peddle. **colporteur, -euse** *nm, nf* pedlar.
coma [kɔma] *nm* coma.
combat [kɔ̃ba] *nm* fight, combat; (*sport*) match.
***combattre** [kɔ̃batrə] *v* fight, combat.
combien [kɔ̃bjɛ̃] *adv* (*quantité*) how much; (*nombre*) how many. **combien de temps** how long. **le combien sommes-nous?** what date is it?
combinaison [kɔ̃binɛzɔ̃] *nf* combination; (*sous-vêtement*) slip; (*astuce*) device, scheme.
combiner [kɔ̃bine] *v* combine; (*élaborer*) devise, plan. **combine** *nf* (*truc*) trick; (*péj*) scheme. **combiné** *nm* (*chim*) compound; (*téléphone*) receiver.
comble[1] [kɔ̃blə] *nm* height, climax, peak; (*toit*) roof timbers *pl*. **c'est le comble!** that's the last straw! **pour comble** to cap it all.
comble[2] [kɔ̃blə] *adj* packed.
combler [kɔ̃ble] *v* fill; (*déficit*) make good; (*désir*) fulfil.
combustible [kɔ̃bystiblə] *adj* combustible. *nm* fuel. **combustion** *nf* combustion.
comédie [kɔmedi] *nf* comedy, play; (*fam*) fuss. **comédie musicale** musical. **jouer la comédie** put on an act. **comédien** *nm* comedian; actor; comedy actor. **comédienne** *nf* comedienne; actress; comedy actress.
comestible [kɔmɛstiblə] *adj* edible. **comestibles** *nm pl* food *sing*.
comète [kɔmɛt] *nf* comet.
comique [kɔmik] *adj* comic; (*drôle*) comical. *nm* comedy; (*artiste*) comic.
comité [kɔmite] *nm* committee, board.
commander [kɔmɑ̃de] *v* order; command; control. **commandant** *nm* commander; (*mil*) major; (*naut*) captain. **commande** *nf* order; control. **de commande** affected, forced. **fait sur commande** made to order. **commandement** *nm* command; (*rel*) commandment.
commanditer [kɔmɑ̃dite] *v* finance.
comme [kɔm] *conj* as; (*tel que*) like, such as. *adv* how. **comme ça** like that. **comme ci comme ça** so-so. **comme si** as if, as though. **comme il faut** properly. **... comme tout** as ... as can be.
commémorer [kɔmemɔre] *v* commemorate. **commémoratif** *adj* commemorative, memorial. **commémoration** *nf* commemoration.
commencer [kɔmɑ̃se] *v* begin, start. **commencement** *nm* beginning, start.
comment [kɔmɑ̃] *adv* how. **comment allez-vous?** how are you? **comment s'appelle-t-il?** what's his name? *interj* what.
commenter [kɔmɑ̃te] *v* comment on; (*sport*) give a commentary on. **commentaire** *nm* comment; (*exposé*) commentary. **commentateur, -trice** *nm, nf* (*sport*) commentator; (*journal*) correspondent.
commérage [kɔmeraʒ] *nm* gossip.
commerçant [kɔmɛrsɑ̃], **-e** *adj* commercial; (*rue*) shopping. *nm, nf* shopkeeper, tradesman.
commerce [kɔmɛrs] *nm* trade, commerce, business. **commercial** *adj* commercial. **commerciale** *nf* van.
***commettre** [kɔmɛtrə] *v* commit.
commis [kɔmi] *nm* assistant; (*bureau*) clerk.
commissaire [kɔmisɛr] *nm* commissioner; (*surveillant*) steward. **commissaire de police** police superintendant. **commissaire-priseur** *nm* auctioneer.
commissariat [kɔmisarja] *nm* police station.

commission [kɔmisjɔ̃] *nf* commission; message; (*course*) errand; committee. **commissions** *nf pl* shopping.
commissionnaire [kɔmisjɔnɛr] *nm* messenger; (*livreur*) delivery man; (*hôtel*) commissionnaire; (*comm*) agent.
commode [kɔmɔd] *adj* handy, convenient; (*facile*) easy; (*personne*) easy-going. *nf* chest of drawers. **commodité** *nf* convenience.
commotion [kɔmosjɔ̃] *nf* shock. **commotion cérébrale** concussion. **commotionner** *v* shock, shake.
commun [kɔmœ̃] *adj* common; (*partagé*) shared, communal. **hors du commun** out of the ordinary. **peu commun** uncommon.
communauté [kɔmynote] *nf* community; (*cohabitation*) commune.
commune [kɔmyn] *nf* district, borough; parish. **communal** *adj* local; council.
communiant [kɔmynjɑ̃], **-e** *nm, nf* communicant.
communication [kɔmynikɑsjɔ̃] *nf* communication; message; telephone call. **communication interurbaine/en PCV/avec préavis** trunk/reverse-charge/personal call.
communion [kɔmynjɔ̃] *nf* communion.
communiquer [kɔmynike] *v* communicate; pass on; transmit. **se communiquer** spread; (*personne*) be communicative.
communisme [kɔmynismə] *nm* communism. **communiste** *n(m+f)*, *adj* communist.
compact [kɔ̃pakt] *adj* compact; dense.
compagnie [kɔ̃paɲi] *nf* company. **compagnon, compagne** *nm, nf* companion.
comparer [kɔ̃pare] *v* compare. **comparable** *adj* comparable. **comparaison** *nf* comparison. **comparatif** *nm, adj* comparative.
compartiment [kɔ̃partimɑ̃] *nm* compartment.
compas [kɔ̃pa] *nm* compass; (*math*) pair of compasses.
compassion [kɔ̃pɑsjɔ̃] *nf* compassion, sympathy.
compatible [kɔ̃patiblə] *adj* compatible. **compatibilité** *nf* compatibility.
compatir [kɔ̃patir] *v* sympathize. **compatissant** *adj* compassionate, sympathetic.
compenser [kɔ̃pɑ̃se] *v* compensate (for). **compensation** *nf* compensation.
compère [kɔ̃pɛr] *nm* accomplice.
compétent [kɔ̃petɑ̃] *adj* competent. **compétence** *nf* competence.
compétition [kɔ̃petisjɔ̃] *nf* competition; event, race. **compétiteur, -trice** *nm, nf* competitor. **compétitif** *adj* competitive.
compiler [kɔ̃pile] *v* compile. **compilation** *nf* compilation.
complaisance [kɔ̃plɛzɑ̃s] *nf* kindness; servility; indulgence; self-satisfaction. **complaisant** *adj* kind; servile; indulgent; self-satisfied.
complément [kɔ̃plemɑ̃] *nm* complement. **complémentaire** *adj* complementary; additional.
complet, -ète [kɔ̃plɛ, -ɛt] *adj* complete; (*plein*) full. *nm* suit.
compléter [kɔ̃plete] *v* complete; (*augmenter*) supplement, add to.
complexe [kɔ̃plɛks] *nm, adj* complex. **complexité** *nf* complexity.
complication [kɔ̃plikɑsjɔ̃] *nf* complication.
complice [kɔ̃plis] *n(m+f)* accomplice. *adj* knowing. **être complice de** be a party to. **complicité** *nf* complicity.
compliment [kɔ̃plimɑ̃] *nm* compliment. **compliments** *nm pl* congratulations *pl.* **complimenter** *v* compliment; congratulate.
compliquer [kɔ̃plike] *v* complicate. **se compliquer** get complicated.
complot [kɔ̃plo] *nm* plot. **comploter** *v* plot.
comporter [kɔ̃pɔrte] *v* consist of; (*impliquer*) entail; include. **se comporter** behave, perform. **comportement** *nm* behaviour, performance.
composer [kɔ̃poze] *v* compose, make up; (*numéro*) dial. **composer avec** come to terms with. **se composer de** consist of. **composé** *nm, adj* compound. **compositeur, -trice** *nm, nf* composer. **composition** *nf* composition.
compote [kɔ̃pɔt] *nf* stewed fruit.
compréhensif [kɔ̃preɑ̃sif] *adj* understanding. **comprehension** *nf* understanding, comprehension.
***comprendre** [kɔ̃prɑ̃drə] *v* understand; consist of, comprise; include. **se faire comprendre** make oneself understood. **compris** *adj* included. **tout compris** all inclusive. **y compris** including.

compresse [kɔ̃prɛs] *nf* compress. **compression** [kɔ̃prɛsjɔ̃] *nf* compression; (*réduction*) cut-back.
comprimer [kɔ̃prime] *v* compress; (*réduire*) cut back; (*contenir*) hold back.
***compromettre** [kɔ̃prɔmɛtrə] *v* compromise; (*santé, etc.*) jeopardize. **compromis** *nm* compromise.
comptable [kɔ̃tablə] *adj* accounts; (*responsable*) accountable.
compte [kɔ̃t] *nm* account; number; (*calcul*) count. **compte à rebours** countdown. **compte rendu** report, review. **tenir compte de** take into account.
compter [kɔ̃te] *v* count; (*escompter*) reckon; pay; (*facturer*) charge for. **comptant** *nm, adv* cash.
compteur [kɔ̃tœr] *nm* meter. **compteur de vitesse** speedometer. **compteur kilométrique** milometer.
comptine [kɔ̃tin] *nf* nursery rhyme.
comptoir [kɔ̃twar] *nm* counter; bar.
comte [kɔ̃t] *nm* count. **comtesse** *nf* countess.
comté [kɔ̃te] *nm* county.
concave [kɔ̃kav] *adj* concave.
concéder [kɔ̃sede] *v* concede, grant.
concentrer [kɔ̃sɑ̃tre] *v* concentrate. **concentration** *nf* concentration. **concentré** *nm* concentrate, extract.
concentrique [kɔ̃sɑ̃trik] *adj* concentric.
concept [kɔ̃sɛpt] *nm* concept.
conception [kɔ̃sɛpsjɔ̃] *nf* conception; idea.
concerner [kɔ̃sɛrne] *v* concern.
concert [kɔ̃sɛr] *nm* concert. **de concert** together, in unison.
concerté [kɔ̃sɛrte] *adj* concerted.
concertina [kɔ̃sɛrtina] *nm* concertina.
concerto [kɔ̃sɛrto] *nm* concerto.
concession [kɔ̃sesjɔ̃] *nf* concession.
***concevoir** [kɔ̃səvwar] *v* conceive; (*comprendre*) understand; (*rédiger*) express.
concierge [kɔ̃sjɛrʒ] *n*(*m*+*f*) caretaker. **conciergerie** *nf* caretaker's lodge.
concilier [kɔ̃silje] *v* reconcile; (*attirer*) win, gain.
concis [kɔ̃si] *adj* concise.
***conclure** [kɔ̃klyr] *v* conclude. **concluant** *adj* conclusive. **conclusion** *nf* conclusion.
concombre [kɔ̃kɔ̃brə] *nm* cucumber.
concorder [kɔ̃kɔrde] *v* agree, tally. **concordance** *nf* agreement. **concorde** *nf* concord.
***concourir** [kɔ̃kurir] *v* compete; converge.
concours [kɔ̃kur] *nm* competition; (*examen*) competitive examination; aid.
concret, -ète [kɔ̃krɛ, -ɛt] *adj* concrete.
concurrence [kɔ̃kyrɑ̃s] *nf* competition. **faire concurrence à** compete with. **concurrent, -e** *nm, nf* competitor; (*examen*) candidate. **concurrentiel** *adj* competitive.
condamner [kɔ̃dɑne] *v* condemn; (*jur*) sentence; (*porte, etc.*) block up. **condamnation** *nf* condemnation; sentence.
condenser [kɔ̃dɑ̃se] *v* condense. **condensation** *nf* condensation.
condescendre [kɔ̃desɑ̃drə] *v* condescend. **condescendance** *nf* condescension.
condition [kɔ̃disjɔ̃] *nf* condition; (*comm*) term; (*rang*) station. **à condition** on approval. **à condition de** provided that. **conditionnel** *nm, adj* conditional.
conditionner [kɔ̃disjɔne] *v* condition; (*emballer*) package. **conditionnement** *nm* conditioning; packaging.
condoléances [kɔ̃dɔleɑ̃s] *nf pl* condolences *pl*.
conducteur [kɔ̃dyktœr], **-trice** *nm, nf* driver; (*chef*) leader. *nm* (*élec*) conductor. **conduction** *nf* conduction.
***conduire** [kɔ̃dɥir] *v* (*véhicule*) drive; (*emmener*) take; (*guider*) lead; (*élec*) conduct; (*diriger*) run. **se conduire** behave. **conduit** *nm* duct, pipe. **conduite** *nf* driving; running; behaviour, conduct; pipe. **conduite d'eau/de gaz** water/gas main. **conduite intérieure** saloon car.
cône [kon] *nm* cone.
confectionner [kɔ̃fɛksjɔne] *v* make. **confection** *nf* making; clothing industry. **de confection** ready-made, off-the-peg.
confédéré [kɔ̃federe] *adj* confederate. **confédération** *nf* confederation.
conférer [kɔ̃fere] *v* confer; compare. **conférence** *nf* conference; (*exposé*) lecture. **conférencier, -ère** *nm, nf* lecturer.
confesser [kɔ̃fese] *v* confess. **confession** *nf* confession.
confetti [kɔ̃feti] *nm* confetti.
confiance [kɔ̃fjɑ̃s] *nf* confidence, trust. **avec confiance** confidently. **avoir confiance en** trust. **confiance en soi** self-confidence. **de confiance** trustworthy. **confiant** *adj* confident
confidence [kɔ̃fidɑ̃s] *nf* confidence, personal secret. **confidentiel** *adj* confidential.

confier [kɔ̃fje] *v* confide. **se confier à** (*se livrer*) confide in; (*se fier*) put one's trust in.
confiner [kɔ̃fine] *v* confine. **confiner à** border on. **confins** *nm pl* borders *pl*.
***confire** [kɔ̃fir] *v* preserve.
confirmer [kɔ̃firme] *v* confirm. **confirmation** *nf* confirmation.
confiserie [kɔ̃fizri] *nf* confectionery; (*magasin*) confectioner's, sweet-shop. **confiseur, -euse** *nm, nf* confectioner.
confisquer [kɔ̃fiske] *v* confiscate. **confiscation** *nf* confiscation.
confit [kɔ̃fi] *adj* candied.
confiture [kɔ̃fityr] *nf* jam. **confiture d'oranges** marmalade.
conflit [kɔ̃fli] *nm* conflict, clash.
confluer [kɔ̃flye] *v* join, converge. **confluence** *nf* mingling. **confluent** *nm* confluence.
confondre [kɔ̃fɔ̃drə] *v* mix up, confuse; (*ennemi*) confound; (*étonner*) astound; join, meet. **se confondre** merge. **se confondre en excuses/remerciements** apologize/thank profusely. **confondu** *adj* overwhelmed.
conforme [kɔ̃fɔrm] *adj* **conforme à** true to; in accordance with; in keeping with. **conformément à** in accordance with.
conformer [kɔ̃fɔrme] *v* model. **se conformer à** conform to. **conformité** *nf* conformity; similarity.
confort [kɔ̃fɔr] *nm* comfort. **confortable** *adj* comfortable.
confrère [kɔ̃frɛr] *nm* colleague.
confronter [kɔ̃frɔ̃te] *v* confront; compare. **confrontation** *nf* confrontation; comparison.
confus [kɔ̃fy] *adj* confused; (*honteux*) ashamed. **confusion** *nf* confusion; (*honte*) embarrassment.
congé [kɔ̃ʒe] *nm* holiday, leave; (*renvoi*) notice. **prendre congé** take one's leave.
congédier [kɔ̃ʒedje] *v* dismiss.
congeler [kɔ̃ʒle] *v* freeze. **congélateur** *nm* freezer.
congestion [kɔ̃ʒɛstjɔ̃] *nf* congestion. **congestionné** *adj* congested; (*visage*) flushed.
congrès [kɔ̃grɛ] *nm* congress.
conifère [kɔ̃nifɛr] *nm* conifer.
conique [kɔnik] *adj* conical.
conjoint [kɔ̃ʒwɛ̃], **-e** *nm, nf* spouse. *adj* joint.
conjonction [kɔ̃ʒɔ̃ksjɔ̃] *nf* conjunction.
conjugal [kɔ̃ʒygal] *adj* conjugal.
conjuguer [kɔ̃ʒyge] *v* conjugate; combine. **conjugaison** *nf* conjugation.
connaissance [kɔnɛsɑ̃s] *nf* knowledge; (*personne*) acquaintance; (*conscience*) consciousness. **sans connaissance** unconscious.
connaisseur [kɔnɛsœr], **-euse** *adj* expert. *nm, nf* connoisseur.
***connaître** [kɔnɛtrə] *v* know; be acquainted *or* familiar with; (*éprouver*) experience. **faire connaître** make known.
connu [kɔny] *adj* known; (*répandu, fameux*) well-known.
***conquérir** [kɔ̃kerir] *v* conquer.
conquête [kɔ̃kɛt] *nf* conquest.
consacrer [kɔ̃sakre] *v* consecrate; (*dédier*) devote, dedicate. **consacré** *adj* consecrated, hallowed; accepted, established. **consécration** *nf* consecration.
conscience [kɔ̃sjɑ̃s] *nf* consciousness; (*morale*) conscience. **avoir conscience de** be aware of. **consciencieux** *adj* conscientious. **conscient** *adj* conscious.
conscription [kɔ̃skripsjɔ̃] *nf* conscription.
conscrit [kɔ̃skri] *nm* conscript.
consécutif [kɔ̃sekytif] *adj* consecutive.
conseil [kɔ̃sɛj] *nm* advice; (*organisme*) board, council. **conseil d'administration** board of directors. **conseil de guerre** court-martial. **conseiller, -ère** *nm, nf* adviser; councillor.
conseiller [kɔ̃seje] *v* recommend; advise.
***consentir** [kɔ̃sɑ̃tir] *v* consent, agree. **consentement** *nm* consent.
conséquence [kɔ̃sekɑ̃s] *nf* consequence, result. **conséquent** *adj* logical; consistent. **par conséquent** consequently.
conservateur [kɔ̃sɛrvatœr], **-trice** *adj* conservative. *nm, nf* (*musée*) curator; (*pol*) Conservative.
conservatoire [kɔ̃sɛrvatwar] *nm* academy, school.
conserve [kɔ̃sɛrv] *nf* **en conserve** tinned, canned. **mettre en conserve** can.
conserver [kɔ̃sɛrve] *v* keep, retain, conserve; (*aliments, etc.*) preserve. **conservation** *nf* preservation.
considérer [kɔ̃sidere] *v* consider; regard; respect. **considérable** *adj* considerable. **considération** *nf* consideration; reflection; respect.
consigner [kɔ̃siɲe] *v* (*par écrit*) record; (*en dépôt*) deposit; (*soldat*) confine to barracks. **consignation** *nf* deposit; (*comm*) consignment. **consigne** *nf* orders

pl; (*bagages*) left-luggage office; (*comm*) deposit. **consigné** *adj* (*bouteille, etc.*) returnable.
consister [kɔ̃siste] *v* consist. **consister en** consist of. **consistance** *nf* consistency. **consistant** *adj* solid.
consoler [kɔ̃sɔle] *v* console. **consolation** *nf* consolation.
consolider [kɔ̃sɔlide] *v* strengthen, consolidate. **consolidation** *nf* strengthening, consolidation.
consommer [kɔ̃sɔme] *v* consume; use; (*manger*) eat; (*mariage*) consummate. **consommateur, -trice** *nm, nf* consumer; (*café*) customer. **consommation** *nf* consumption; (*café*) drink; consummation. **consommé** *nm* consommé.
consonne [kɔ̃sɔn] *nf* consonant.
conspirer [kɔ̃spire] *v* conspire. **conspirateur, -trice** *nm, nf* conspirator. **conspiration** *nf* conspiracy.
conspuer [kɔ̃spɥe] *v* shout down.
constant [kɔ̃stɑ̃] *adj* constant. **constamment** *adv* constantly. **constance** *nf* constancy.
constater [kɔ̃state] *v* note, notice; (*consigner*) record, certify. **constatation** *nf* observation.
constellation [kɔ̃stelɑsjɔ̃] *nf* constellation.
consterner [kɔ̃sterne] *v* dismay. **consternation** *nf* consternation, dismay.
constipation [kɔ̃stipɑsjɔ̃] *nf* constipation. **constipé** *adj* constipated.
constituer [kɔ̃stitɥe] *v* constitute; (*fonder*) put together, set up; (*jur*) appoint. **constituent** *adj* constituent. **constitution** *nf* constitution; composition.
construction [kɔ̃stryksjɔ̃] *nf* construction; (*bâtiment*) building. **constructif** *adj* constructive.
***construire** [kɔ̃strɥir] *v* construct; build.
consul [kɔ̃syl] *nm* consul. **consulat** *nm* consulate.
consulter [kɔ̃sylte] *v* consult. **consultation** *nf* consultation.
consumer [kɔ̃syme] *v* consume; destroy.
contact [kɔ̃takt] *nm* contact; (*auto*) ignition.
contagieux [kɔ̃taʒjø] *adj* contagious, infectious. **contagion** *nf* contagion.
contaminer [kɔ̃tamine] *v* contaminate. **contamination** *nf* contamination.
conte [kɔ̃t] *nm* tale, story. **conte de fée** fairy tale.
contempler [kɔ̃tɑ̃ple] *v* contemplate. **contemplatif** *adj* contemplative. **contemplation** *nf* contemplation.
contemporain [kɔ̃tɑ̃pɔrɛ̃], **-e** *n, adj* contemporary.
contenance [kɔ̃tnɑ̃s] *nf* capacity; attitude. **faire bonne contenance** put on a brave face.
***contenir** [kɔ̃tnir] *v* contain; (*récipient*) hold.
content [kɔ̃tɑ̃] *adj* pleased, happy; satisfied, content.
contenter [kɔ̃tɑ̃te] *v* satisfy. **se contenter de** content oneself with. **contentement** *nm* contentment, satisfaction.
contenu [kɔ̃tny] *adj* restrained *nm* content; (*récipient*) contents *pl*.
conter [kɔ̃te] *v* recount, relate. **conteur, -euse** *nm, nf* storyteller.
contester [kɔ̃teste] *v* contest, dispute; protest. **contestable** *adj* questionable. **contestation** *nf* dispute.
contexte [kɔ̃tekst] *nm* context.
contigu, -uë [kɔ̃tigy] *adj* adjacent, adjoining.
continent [kɔ̃tinɑ̃] *nm* continent. **continental** *adj* continental.
contingent [kɔ̃tɛ̃ʒɑ̃] *nm* contingent; quota; (*part*) share.
continuer [kɔ̃tinɥe] *v* continue. **continu** *adj* continuous. **continuel** *adj* continual; continuous. **continuité** *nf* continuity; continuation.
contourner [kɔ̃turne] *v* skirt round, bypass; (*façonner*) shape; (*déformer*) twist.
contraception [kɔ̃trasɛpsjɔ̃] *nf* contraception. **contraceptif** *nm, adj* contraceptive.
contracter[1] [kɔ̃trakte] *v* (*raidir*) tense, contract. **contraction** *nf* contraction.
contracter[2] [kɔ̃trakte] *v* contract; (*dette*) incur; (*alliance*) enter into.
contractuel [kɔ̃traktɥɛl], **-elle** *adj* contractual. *nm, nf* traffic warden.
contradiction [kɔ̃tradiksjɔ̃] *nf* contradiction; debate, argument. **contradictoire** *adj* contradictory.
***contraindre** [kɔ̃trɛ̃drə] *v* force, compel. **contrainte** *nf* constraint.
contraire [kɔ̃trɛr] *adj* contrary; opposite; conflicting. *nm* opposite. **au contraire** on the contrary.
contrarier [kɔ̃trarje] *v* (*irriter*) annoy; (*gêner*) thwart. **contrariant** *adj* tiresome; (*personne*) contrary.

contraster [kɔ̃traste] *v* contrast. **contraste** *nm* contrast.
contrat [kɔ̃tra] *nm* contract, agreement.
contravention [kɔ̃travɑ̃sjɔ̃] *nf* (*amende*) fine; (*procès-verbal*) parking ticket; (*jur*) contravention.
contre [kɔ̃trə] *prep* against; (*protection*) from; (*échange*) for; (*rapport*) to. **par contre** on the other hand.
contre-amiral *nm* rear admiral.
contre-attaque *nf* counter-attack. **contre-attaquer** *v* counter-attack.
contre-avion *adj* anti-aircraft.
contrebande [kɔ̃trəbɑ̃d] *nf* contraband; (*activité*) smuggling. **faire la contrebande de** smuggle. **contrebandier, -ère** *nm, nf* smuggler.
contrebasse [kɔ̃trəbɑs] *nf* double bass.
contre-boutant *nm* buttress.
contrecarrer [kɔ̃trəkare] *v* thwart.
contrecœur [kɔ̃trəkœr] *adv* **à contrecœur** grudgingly.
contrecoup [kɔ̃trəku] *nm* repercussions *pl*.
***contredire** [kɔ̃trədir] *v* contradict.
contrée [kɔ̃tre] *nf* region.
contrefaçon [kɔ̃trəfasɔ̃] *nf* forgery, counterfeit, imitation.
***contrefaire** [kɔ̃trəfɛr] *v* counterfeit, forge; disguise; imitate. **contrefait** *adj* deformed.
contre-interrogatoire *nm* cross-examination.
contremaître [kɔ̃trəmɛtrə] *nm* foreman.
contremander [kɔ̃trəmɑ̃de] *v* cancel.
contre-manifestation *nf* counter-demonstration.
contre-pied *nm* opposite.
contre-plaqué *nm* plywood.
contrepoids [kɔ̃trəpwa] *nm* counterbalance.
contre-poil *adv* **à contre-poil** the wrong way.
contrepoison [kɔ̃trəpwazɔ̃] *nm* antidote.
contresens [kɔ̃trəsɑ̃s] *nm* misinterpretation. **à contresens** the wrong way. **à contresens de** against.
contretemps [kɔ̃trətɑ̃] *nm* hitch. **à contretemps** at an inconvenient time.
contre-torpilleur *nm* destroyer.
***contrevenir** [kɔ̃trəvnir] *v* contravene.
contrevent [kɔ̃trəvɑ̃] *nm* shutter.
contre-voie *adv* **à contre-voie** (*rail*) on the wrong side.
contribuer [kɔ̃tribɥe] *v* contribute. **contribuable** *n(m+f)* taxpayer. **contribution** *nf* contribution. **contributions** *nf pl* (*à l'état*) taxes *pl*; (*à la commune*) rates *pl*; (*bureau*) tax office *sing*.
contrôler [kɔ̃trole] *v* control; (*vérifier*) check; (*argent, or*) hallmark. **contrôle** *nm* control; check, inspection; list; hallmark. **contrôleur** *nm* inspector; bus conductor; ticket collector.
controverse [kɔ̃trɔvɛrs] *nf* controversy.
contusion [kɔ̃tyzjɔ̃] *nf* bruise. **contusionner** *v* bruise.
***convaincre** [kɔ̃vɛ̃krə] *v* convince, persuade; (*jur*) convict.
convalescence [kɔ̃valesɑ̃s] *nf* convalescence. **convalescent, -e** *nm, nf* convalescent.
***convenir** [kɔ̃vnir] *v* suit; (*être utile*) be convenient; (*être approprié*) be suitable; (*avouer*) acknowledge; admit; (*s'accorder*) agree on. **convenable** *adj* fitting, suitable, appropriate; decent, acceptable, proper. **convenance** *nf* convenience; preference. **les convenances** propriety *sing*. **convenu** *adj* agreed.
convention [kɔ̃vɑ̃sjɔ̃] *nf* convention; (*accord*) understanding; (*pacte*) agreement. **conventionnel** *adj* conventional.
converger [kɔ̃vɛrʒe] *v* converge.
convers [kɔ̃vɛr] *adj* lay.
conversation [kɔ̃vɛrsɑsjɔ̃] *nf* conversation.
conversion [kɔ̃vɛrsjɔ̃] *nf* conversion.
convertir [kɔ̃vɛrtir] *v* convert. **converti, -e** *nm, nf* convert. **convertible** *adj* convertible.
convexe [kɔ̃vɛks] *adj* convex.
conviction [kɔ̃viksjɔ̃] *nf* conviction.
convier [kɔ̃vje] *v* invite, urge.
convive [kɔ̃viv] *n(m+f)* guest.
convocation [kɔ̃vɔkasjɔ̃] *nf* summons.
convoi [kɔ̃vwa] *nm* convoy.
convoiter [kɔ̃vwate] *v* covet. **convoitise** *nf* lust.
convoquer [kɔ̃vɔke] *v* (*assemblée*) convene; (*personne*) summon.
convulsion [kɔ̃vylsjɔ̃] *nf* convulsion. **convulsif** *adj* convulsive.
coopérer [kɔɔpere] *v* cooperate. **coopératif** *adj* cooperative. **coopération** *nf* cooperation. **coopérative** *nf* cooperative.
coordination [kɔɔrdinɑsjɔ̃] *nf* coordination.
coordonner [kɔɔrdɔne] *v* coordinate.

copain, copine [kɔpɛ̃, kɔ̃pin] *nm, nf* (*fam*) pal, mate.
Copenhague [kɔpənag] *n* Copenhagen.
copier [kɔpje] *v* copy. **copie** *nf* copy; (*examen*) paper.
copieux [kɔpjø] *adj* copious.
copuler [kɔpyle] *v* copulate. **copulation** *nf* copulation.
coq [kɔk] *nm* cock.
coque [kɔk] *nf* shell; (*mollusque*) cockle; (*bateau*) hull.
coquelicot [kɔkliko] *nm* poppy.
coqueluche [kɔklyʃ] *nf* whooping cough.
coquet, -ette [kɔke, -ɛt] *adj* flirtatious; clothes-conscious; charming; (*fam: somme*) tidy.
coquetier [kɔktje] *nm* egg-cup.
coquille [kɔkij] *nf* shell; (*récipient*) scallop; (*erreur*) misprint. **coquille Saint-Jacques** scallop. **coquillage** *nm* shellfish.
coquin [kɔkɛ̃], **-e** *adj* mischievous, naughty. *nm, nf* rascal.
cor [kɔr] *nm* (*musique*) horn; (*méd*) corn. **cor anglais** cor anglais. **cor d'harmonie** French horn.
corail [kɔraj] *nm, pl* **-aux** coral.
corbeau [kɔrbo] *nm* crow.
corbeille [kɔrbɛj] *nf* basket. **corbeille à papier** wastepaper basket.
corbillard [kɔrbijar] *nm* hearse.
cordages [kɔrdaʒ] *nm pl* ropes *pl*, rigging *sing*.
corde [kɔrd] *nf* rope; (*musique, raquette*) string; (*tissu*) thread. **corde à linge** clothes-line. **corde à sauter** skipping-rope. **corde raide** tightrope. **cordes vocales** vocal cords *pl*.
corder [kɔrde] *v* twist; (*raquette*) string.
cordon [kɔrdɔ̃] *nm* cord, string; (*soldats, police*) cordon. **cordonnier** *nm* cobbler.
coriace [kɔrjas] *adj* tough.
corne [kɔrn] *nf* horn. **corne de brume** foghorn.
corneille [kɔrnɛj] *nf* crow.
cornemuse [kɔrnəmyz] *nf* bagpipes *pl*.
cornet [kɔrnɛ] *nm* (*papier, glace*) cone, cornet. **cornet à pistons** cornet.
cornichon [kɔrniʃɔ̃] *nm* gherkin.
Cornouailles [kɔrnwaj] *nf* Cornwall.
cornu [kɔrny] *adj* horned.
corporation [kɔrpɔrasjɔ̃] *nf* guild, corporate body.
corporel [kɔrpɔrɛl] *adj* corporal.
corps [kɔr] *nm* body; (*mil*) corps; (*cadavre*) corpse. **corps à corps** *adv* hand-to-hand. **le corps enseignant/médical** the teaching/medical profession.
corpulent [kɔrpylɑ̃] *adj* stout, corpulent.
corpuscule [kɔrpyskyl] *nm* corpuscle.
correct [kɔrɛkt] *adj* correct, accurate, right. **correction** *nf* correction; (*châtiment*) thrashing; accuracy.
correspondant [kɔrɛspɔ̃dɑ̃], **-e** *adj* corresponding. *nm, nf* correspondent. **correspondance** *nf* correspondence; (*transport*) connection.
correspondre [kɔrɛspɔ̃drə] *v* correspond; connect. **correspondre à** fit, agree with, suit.
corrida [kɔrida] *nf* bullfight.
corridor [kɔridɔr] *nm* corridor.
corriger [kɔriʒe] *v* correct; (*punir*) thrash.
corroborer [kɔrɔbɔre] *v* corroborate. **corroboration** *nf* corroboration.
corroder [kɔrɔde] *v* corrode. **corrodant** *adj* corrosive.
corrompre [kɔrɔ̃prə] *v* corrupt; (*eau, aliments*) taint; (*soudoyer*) bribe. **corrompu** *adj* corrupt.
corruption [kɔrypsjɔ̃] *nf* corruption; bribery; decomposition.
corsage [kɔrsaʒ] *nm* bodice.
corrosion [kɔrozjɔ̃] *nf* corrosion. **corrosif** *adj* corrosive; (*ironie, etc.*) scathing.
Corse [kɔrs] *nf* Corsica. *n(m+f)* Corsican. **corse** *nm, adj* Corsican.
corset [kɔrsɛ] *nm* corset.
cortège [kɔrtɛʒ] *nm* procession.
corvée [kɔrve] *nf* chore; (*mil*) fatigue.
cosmétique [kɔsmetik] *adj* cosmetic.
cosmique [kɔsmik] *adj* cosmic.
cosmopolite [kɔsmɔpɔlit] *adj* cosmopolitan.
cosmos [kɔsmɔs] *nm* cosmos.
cosse [kɔs] *nf* pod, hull.
cossu [kɔsy] *adj* well-off, opulent.
costaud [kɔsto] *adj* strong, sturdy.
costume [kɔstym] *nm* costume, dress; (*complet*) suit.
cote [kɔt] *nf* rating, popularity; (*comm*) quotation; (*courses*) odds *pl*; mark.
côte [kot] *nf* (*anat, tricot*) rib; (*pente*) slope, hill; (*littoral*) coast, coastline.
côté [kote] *nm* side; way, direction. **à côté** (*maison, pièce*) next door; (*près*) nearby. **à côté de** beside; compared to. **de côté** sideways; aside.
coteau [kɔto] *nm* hill, slope.

côtelette [kotlɛt] *nf* chop, cutlet.
coter [kɔte] *v* rate, mark; (*comm*) quote.
côtier [kotje] *adj* coastal, inshore.
se cotiser [kɔtize] *v* subscribe; (*groupe*) club together. **cotisant, -e** *nm, nf* (*club*) subscriber; (*pension*) contributor. **cotisation** *nf* subscription; contribution; collection.
coton [kɔtɔ̃] *nm* cotton. **coton à broder/repriser** embroidery/darning thread.
côtoyer [kotwaje] *v* skirt, run alongside; (*frôler*) be close to, be verging on.
cou [ku] *nm* neck. **cou-de-pied** *nm* instep.
couchant [kuʃɑ̃] *adj* setting. *nm* west; sunset.
couche [kuʃ] *nf* layer; (*peinture*) coat; (*bébé*) nappy. **couches** *nf pl* (*méd*) confinement *sing*.
coucher [kuʃe] *v* lay down; (*loger*) put up; (*séjourner*) sleep; (*mettre au lit*) put to bed. **se coucher** go to bed; (*s'étendre*) lie down; (*soleil*) set. *nm* **coucher du soleil** sunset. **couché** *adj* lying down; in bed; (*penché*) sloping. **couchette** *nf* couchette, berth.
coucou [kuku] *nm* cuckoo.
coude [kud] *nm* elbow; (*rivière, tuyau*) bend.
***coudre** [kudr] *v* sew, stitch.
coudrier [kudrije] *nm* hazel tree.
couenne [kwan] *nf* rind.
couic [kwik] *interj* squeak!
couler [kule] *v* run, flow; (*fuir*) leak; (*bateau*) sink; (*verser*) pour. **se couler** slip. **coulant** *adj* smooth, flowing. **coulé** *nm* (*musique*) slur. **coulée** *nf* casting.
couleur [kulœr] *nf* colour; (*cartes*) suit; (*peinture*) paint.
couleuvre [kulœvrə] *nf* grass snake.
coulisse [kulis] *nf* runner, slide. **coulisses** *nf pl* wings *pl*. **dans les coulisses** behind the scenes. **porte à coulisse** *nf* sliding door.
couloir [kulwar] *nm* corridor; (*voie*) lane; (*pol*) lobby.
coup [ku] *nm* blow, knock; (*pinceau, plume*) stroke; (*bruit*) sound; (*essai*) try; (*tour*) trick. **à coup sûr** definitely. **après coup** afterwards. **du coup** suddenly. **du premier coup** first time. **tout à coup** suddenly.
coupable [kupablə] *adj* guilty. *n(m+f)* culprit.
coup de bec *nm* peck.
coup de coude *nm* nudge.
coup de feu *nm* shot.
coup de fil *nm* (*fam*) phone call.
coup de froid *nm* chill.
coup de main *nm* (helping) hand.
coup d'envoi *nm* kick-off.
coup de pied *nm* kick.
coup de poing *nm* punch.
coup de soleil *nm* sunburn.
coup de sonnette *nm* ring.
coup de téléphone *nm* telephone call.
coup de vent *nm* gust.
coup d'œil *nm* glance.
coupe[1] [kup] *nf* (*dessert*) dish; (*boire*) goblet; (*sport*) cup.
coupe[2] [kup] *nf* cut, cutting. **coupe transversale** cross section.
couper [kupe] *v* cut; (*eau, élec, etc.*) cut off; (*traverser*) cross; (*voyage*) break; (*vin*) dilute, blend. **coupe-papier** *nm* paper knife. **coupant** *adj* sharp. **coupure** *nf* cut; (*journal*) cutting; (*courant*) power cut.
couple [kuplə] *nm* couple, pair. **coupler** *v* couple.
couplet [kuplɛ] *nm* verse.
coupon [kupɔ̃] *nm* coupon; (*reste*) remnant.
cour [kur] *nf* court; (*bâtiment*) yard, courtyard; (*école*) playground; (*gare*) forecourt; (*femme*) courtship. **cour de ferme** farmyard. **faire la cour** (**à**) court.
courage [kuraʒ] *nm* courage; spirit, will. **perdre courage** lose heart. **courageux** *adj* brave, courageous.
couramment [kuramɑ̃] *adv* fluently; commonly.
courant [kurɑ̃] *adj* (*normal*) ordinary, standard; (*fréquent*) common; (*actuel*) current. *nm* current; movement; course. **au courant** well-informed, up to date. **courant d'air** draught.
courbature [kurbatyr] *nf* ache. **courbaturé** *adj* aching, stiff.
courbe [kurb] *adj* curved. *nf* curve.
courber [kurbe] *v* bend, curve. **se courber** bend down; (*saluer*) bow.
courge [kurʒ] *nf* marrow. **courgette** *nf* courgette.
***courir** [kurir] *v* run; (*sport*) race; (*aller vite*) rush, speed; (*chasser*) hunt; (*parcourir*) roam. **coureur, -euse** *nm, nf* runner; (*sport*) competitor. **coureur automobile** racing driver.

couronner [kurɔne] *v* crown; (*ceindre*) encircle; award a prize to. **couronne** *nf* crown; (*fleurs*) wreath. **couronnement** *nm* coronation.
courrier [kurje] *nm* mail, letters *pl*; (*journal*) column, page.
courroie [kurwa] *nf* belt, strap. **courroie de ventilateur** fan belt.
courroux [kuru] *nm* wrath.
cours [kur] *nm* course; (*monnaie*) currency; (*leçon*) class. **au cours de** during. **avoir cours** be current. **cours du change** exchange rate. **en cours** in progress.
course [kurs] *nf* run, running; (*épreuve*) race; (*achat*) shopping, errand; (*voyage*) journey. **faire des courses** go shopping.
court[1] [kur] *adj, adv* short. **à court de** short of. **court-circuit** *nm* short-circuit.
court[2] [kur] *nm* tennis court.
courtier [kurtje], **-ère** *nm, nf* broker.
courtisan [kurtizɑ̃] *nm* courtier; (*flatteur*) sycophant.
courtois [kurtwa] *adj* courteous.
cousin[1] [kuzɛ̃], **-e** *nm, nf* cousin. **cousin germain** first cousin.
cousin[2] [kuzɛ̃] *nm* gnat.
coussin [kusɛ̃] *nm* cushion. **coussinet** *nm* pad; (*tech*) bearing.
cousu [kuzy] *adj* sewn, stitched.
coût [ku] *nm* cost.
couteau [kuto] *nm* knife. **couteau à découper** carving knife. **couteau de poche** pocket knife. **couteau-éplucheur** *nm* peeler.
coutellerie [kutɛlri] *nf* cutlery.
coûter [kute] *v* cost. **coûte que coûte** at all costs. **coûter cher** be expensive. **coûteux** *adj* expensive.
coutume [kutym] *nf* custom. **coutumier** *adj* customary.
couture [kutyr] *nf* sewing; (*confection*) dressmaking; (*suite de points*) seam. **couturier** *nm* fashion designer. **couturière** *nf* dressmaker.
couvent [kuvɑ̃] *nm* convent.
couver [kuve] *v* (*feu, haine*) smoulder; (*émeute*) brew; (*poule*) brood, sit on; (*œufs*) hatch. **couvée** *nf* brood, clutch. **couveuse** *nf* incubator.
couvercle [kuvɛrklə] *nm* lid, cover, top.
couvert [kuvɛr] *adj* covered; (*ciel*) overcast. *nm* place setting; (*restaurant*) cover charge; (*abri*) cover, shelter. **mettre le couvert** lay the table.
couverture [kuvɛrtyr] *nf* cover; (*lit*) blanket. **couverture chauffante** electric blanket.
***couvrir** [kuvrir] *v* cover; (*cacher*) conceal. **se couvrir** (*vêtements*) wrap up; (*chapeau*) put on one's hat; (*ciel*) cloud over. **couvre-feu** *nm* curfew. **couvre-lit** *nm* bedspread.
crabe [krɑb] *nm* crab.
crac [krak] *interj* crack!
cracher [kraʃe] *v* spit (out). **crachat** *nm* spit, spittle. **crachement** *nm* spitting.
crachiner [kraʃine] *v* drizzle. **crachin** *nm* drizzle.
craie [krɛ] *nf* chalk.
***craindre** [krɛ̃drə] *v* fear, be afraid (of).
crainte [krɛ̃t] *nf* fear. **craintif** *adj* timid.
cramoisi [kramwazi] *adj* crimson.
crampe [krɑ̃p] *nf* cramp.
cramponner [krɑ̃pɔne] *v* clamp; (*fam*) cling to. **se cramponner à** clutch, cling to. **crampon** *nm* clamp; (*chaussure*) stud.
cran [krɑ̃] *nm* notch; (*fusil*) catch; (*cheveux*) wave; (*fam*) guts *pl*.
crâne [krɑn] *nm* skull, head.
crâner [krɑne] (*fam*) *v* show off. **craneur, -euse** *nm, nf* show-off.
crapaud [krapo] *nm* toad.
crapuleux [krapylø] *adj* (*vie*) dissolute; (*action*) villainous.
craquer [krake] *v* crack; (*neige*) crunch; (*parquet*) creak; (*bas, pantalon*) rip. **craquement** *nm* crack, creak.
crasse [kras] *nf* grime, filth. **crasseux** *adj* grimy, filthy.
cratère [kratɛr] *nm* crater.
cravate [kravat] *nf* tie.
crawl [krol] *nm* crawl. **dos crawlé** *nm* backstroke.
crayon [krɛjɔ̃] *nm* pencil; (*dessin*) pencil sketch. **crayon de couleur** crayon.
crayonner [krɛjɔne] *v* jot down, scribble; (*dessin*) sketch.
créance [kreɑ̃s] *nf* debt, claim. **créancier, -ère** *nm, nf* creditor.
créateur [kreatœr] **-trice** *adj* creative. *nm, nf* creator.
création [kreɑsjɔ̃] *nf* creation.
créature [kreatyr] *nf* creature.
crèche [krɛʃ] *nf* crèche; (*rel*) crib.
crédit [kredi] *nm* credit; bank; trust. **créditer** *v* credit. **créditeur, -trice** *adj* credit.
crédule [kredyl] *adj* gullible. **crédulité** *nf* gullibility.

créer [kree] *v* create.
crémaillère [kremajɛr] *nf* (*tech*) rack. **pendre la crémaillère** have a house-warming party.
crématoire [krematwar] *nm* crematorium. **crémation** *nf* cremation.
crème [krɛm] *nf, adj* cream. **crème anglaise** custard. **crème à raser** shaving cream. **crème patissière** confectioner's custard. **crémerie** *nf* dairy. **crémeux** *adj* creamy.
crénelé [krɛnle] *adj* notched; (*bordure*) scalloped; (*mur*) crenellated.
crêpe[1] [krɛp] *nf* (*cuisine*) pancake. **crêperie** *nf* pancake shop *or* café.
crêpe[2] [krɛp] *nm* (*tissu*) crepe.
crépiter [krepite] *v* crackle.
crépuscule [krepyskyl] *nm* twilight.
cresson [kresɔ̃] *nm* cress.
crête [krɛt] *nf* ridge, crest; (*coq*) comb; (*mur*) top.
creuser [krøze] *v* dig (out), hollow (out); (*problème*) go into thoroughly.
creux [krø] *adj* hollow; (*vide*) empty; (*visage*) gaunt; (*jours*) slack. **heures creuses** off-peak periods *pl. nm* hollow; slack period. **creux des reins** small of the back.
crevaison [krəvɛzɔ̃] *nf* puncture.
crevasser [krəvase] *v* crack; (*mains*) chap. **crevasse** *nf* crack, crevice.
crever [krəve] *v* burst; (*pneu*) puncture; (*fam: fatiguer*) wear out; (*fam: mourir*) die.
crevette [krəvɛt] *nf* shrimp; (*rose*) prawn.
cri [kri] *nm* cry, shout.
criailler [kriɑje] *v* squawk, screech; (*bébé*) bawl; (*rouspéter*) grumble.
criard [krijar] *adj* yelling, squawking; (*couleur*) garish; (*son*) piercing.
cribler [krible] *v* sift; (*percer*) riddle. **crible** *nm* sieve, riddle. **passer au crible** examine closely. **criblé de** riddled with; covered with; (*dettes*) crippled with.
cric [krik] *nm* jack. **soulever au cric** jack up.
cricket [krikɛt] *nm* cricket.
cri-cri [krikri] *nm* (*grillon*) cricket.
criée [krije] *nf* auction.
crier [krije] *v* shout, cry, scream; (*oiseau*) call; (*grincer*) squeak, squeal.
crime [krim] *nm* crime. **criminel, -elle** *n, adj* criminal.
crin [krɛ̃] *nm* hair, horsehair. **crinière** *nf* mane; (*personne*) mop of hair.
crique [krik] *nf* creek.
criquet [krikɛ] *nm* locust.
crise [kriz] *nf* crisis; (*accès*) attack, fit; (*pénurie*) shortage. **crise cardiaque** heart attack. **crise de foie** bilious attack. **piquer une crise** (*fam*) fly off the handle.
crisper [krispe] *v* tense, clench; (*plisser*) shrivel up. **se crisper** become tense, clench. **crispation** *nf* contraction; (*nervosité*) tension; (*spasme*) twitch. **crispé** *adj* nervous, tense, on edge.
crisser [krise] *v* (*gravier*) crunch; (*freins*) screech; (*soie*) rustle. **crisser des dents** grind one's teeth.
cristal [kristal] *nm* crystal. **cristal taillé** cut glass. **cristallin** *adj* crystalline; (*son*) crystal-clear.
cristalliser [kristalize] *v* crystallize. **cristallisation** *nf* crystallization.
critère [kritɛr] *nm* criterion.
critique [kritik] *adj* critical; crucial. *nf* criticism; (*analyse*) critique, review. *n(m+f)* critic. **critiquer** *v* criticize.
croasser [krɔase] *v* caw. **croassement** *nm* caw.
croc [kro] *nm* fang, tooth; (*grappin*) hook. **faire un croc-en-jambe à** trip up.
croche [krɔʃ] *nf* quaver.
crochet [krɔʃɛ] *nm* hook; (*technique*) crochet; detour; (*véhicule*) swerve. **crochets** *nm pl* square brackets *pl.* **faire du crochet** crochet. **vivre aux crochets de** sponge on, live off.
crochu [krɔʃy] *adj* hooked.
crocodile [krɔkɔdil] *nm* crocodile.
crocus [krɔkys] *nm* crocus.
***croire** [krwar] *v* believe, think. **croire à** *or* **en** believe in.
croisade [krwazad] *nf* crusade.
croiser [krwaze] *v* cross; pass; (*naut*) cruise. **croisé** *adj* double-breasted. **croisement** *nm* crossing; (*carrefour*) crossroads. **croisière** *nf* cruise.
croissance [krwasɑ̃s] *nf* growth, development.
croissant [krwasɑ̃] *nm* crescent; (*pain*) croissant. *adj* growing, increasing, rising.
***croître** [krwatrə] *v* grow, increase; (*rivière, vent*) rise.
croix [krwa] *nf* cross. **croix gammée** swastika.
croquer [krɔke] *v* crunch, munch; (*salade, fruit*) be crisp; (*dessiner*) sketch. **croquant** *adj* crisp, crunchy. **croque-monsieur** *nm invar* toasted cheese and ham sandwich.

croquet [krɔkɛ] *nm* croquet.
croquis [krɔki] *nm* sketch.
crosse [krɔs] *nf* (*sport*) club, stick; (*fusil*) butt; (*rel*) crook.
crotter [krɔte] *v* dirty, make muddy, soil. **crotte** *nf* droppings *pl*, dung.
crouler [krule] *v* collapse; (*délabré*) be tumbledown; (*empire, etc.*) totter. **croulant** *adj* crumbling, tumbledown.
croupe [krup] *nf* rump, hindquarters *pl*; (*colline*) hilltop. **monter en croupe** ride pillion.
croupir [krupir] *v* stagnate; (*personne*) wallow. **croupi** *adj* stagnant.
croustiller [krustije] *v* be crisp *or* crunchy; (*pain*) be crusty. **croustillant** *adj* crisp, crunchy; crusty; (*grivois*) spicy.
croûte [krut] *nf* (*pain*) crust; (*fromage*) rind; (*plaie*) scab. **croûton** *nm* crust; (*cuisine*) crouton.
croyable [krwajablə] *adj* credible.
croyance [krwajɑ̃s] *nf* belief. **croyant, -e** *nm, nf* believer.
cru[1] [kry] *adj* raw, crude; (*lumière*) harsh; (*franc*) blunt.
cru[2] [kry] *nm* (*vignoble*) vineyard; (*vin*) vintage, wine.
cruauté [kryote] *nf* cruelty.
cruche [kryʃ] *nf* jug, pitcher.
crucifier [krysifje] *v* crucify. **crucifixion** *nf* crucifixion.
crucifix [krysifi] *nm* crucifix.
crudité [krydite] *nf* crudeness; harshness. **crudités** *nf pl* coarse remarks *pl*; (*cuisine*) salads *pl*.
crue [kry] *nf* swelling, rising.
cruel [kryɛl] *adj* cruel.
crûment [krymɑ̃] *adv* bluntly.
crustacé [krystase] *nm* shellfish. **crustacés** *nm pl* (*cuisine*) seafood *sing*.
crypte [kript] *nf* crypt.
cube [kyb] *nm* cube; (*d'enfant*) block, brick. *adj* cubic. **cubique** *adj* cubic.
***cueillir** [kœjir] *v* pick, gather; (*attraper*) catch.
cuiller [kɥijɛr] *nf* spoon. **cuiller à café** teaspoon. **cuiller de service** tablespoon. **cuillerée** *nf* spoonful. **cuillerée à soupe** tablespoonful.
cuir [kɥir] *nm* leather; (*avant tannage*) hide. **cuir chevelu** scalp. **cuir suédé** suede. **cuir verni** patent leather.
cuirasse [kɥiras] *nf* armour; (*chevalier*) breastplate.
cuirassé [kɥirase] *adj* armoured. *nm* battleship.
***cuire** [kɥir] *v* cook; (*pain*) bake; (*porcelaine*) fire; (*brûler*) smart. **à cuire** *adj* cooking. **cuire à feu doux** simmer. **cuire à l'eau** boil. **cuire au four** (*viande*) roast; (*pain*) bake.
cuisant [kɥizɑ̃] *adj* burning, stinging; (*regret*) bitter.
cuisine [kɥizin] *nf* (*pièce*) kitchen; (*art*) cookery, cooking. **faire la cuisine** cook. **cuisinier** *nm* cook. **cuisinière** *nf* (*personne*) cook; (*fourneau*) cooker.
cuisse [kɥis] *nf* thigh; (*cuisine*) leg.
cuit [kɥi] *adj* cooked, ready. **cuit à point** done to a turn.
cuivre [kɥivrə] *nm* copper. **cuivre jaune** brass.
cul [ky] *nm* bottom; (*vulgaire*) arse.
culasse [kylas] *nf* cylinder head.
culbuter [kylbyte] *v* somersault; (*tomber*) tumble, topple; (*renverser*) knock over. **culbute** *nf* somersault; tumble, fall; (*fam: banque, etc.*) collapse.
culinaire [kylinɛr] *adj* culinary.
culminer [kylmine] *v* culminate, reach its highest point.
culot [kylo] *nm* cap, base; (*fam*) cheek.
culotte [kylɔt] *nf* short trousers *pl*; (*slip*) pants *pl*.
culpabilité [kylpabilite] *nf* guilt.
culte [kylt] *nm* cult, worship.
cultiver [kyltive] *v* cultivate. **cultivateur, -trice** *nm, nf* farmer. **cultivé** *adj* cultured.
culture [kyltyr] *nf* (*champ, etc.*) cultivation; (*esprit*) culture. **culturel** *adj* cultural.
cupide [kypid] *adj* greedy. **cupidité** *nf* greed.
cure [kyr] *nf* cure; course of treatment.
curé [kyre] *nm* parish priest.
curer [kyre] *v* clean out; (*nez*) pick. **cure-dent** *nm* toothpick. **cure-pipe** *nm* pipe cleaner.
curieux [kyrjø], **-euse** *adj* curious; interested, keen; (*indiscret*) inquisitive. *nm* strange thing. *nm, nf* inquisitive person.
curiosité [kyrjozite] *nf* curiosity; inquisitiveness; (*d'une ville, etc.*) strange sight *or* feature; (*bibelot*) curio.
curry [kyri] *nm* curry. **au curry** curried.
cuver [kyve] *v* ferment. **cuve** *nf* vat, tank. **cuvée** *nf* vintage. **cuvette** *nf* basin.
cycle[1] [siklə] *nm* (*révolution*) cycle.

cycle[2] [siklə] *nm* (*bicyclette*) cycle. **cyclisme** *nm* cycling. **cycliste** *n*(*m+f*) cyclist.
cyclomoteur [siklɔmɔtœr] *nm* moped.
cyclone [siklon] *nm* cyclone.
cygne [siɲ] *nm* swan.
cylindre [silɛ̃drə] *nm* cylinder; roller. **cylindrique** *adj* cylindrical.
cymbale [sɛ̃bal] *nf* cymbal.
cynique [sinik] *adj* cynical. *nm* cynic.
cyprès [siprɛ] *nm* cypress.
cypriote [siprijɔt] *adj* Cypriot. **Cypriote** *n*(*m+f*) Cypriot.

D

d' [d] *V* de.
dactylographier [daktilɔgrafje] *v* type. **dactylo** *nf* typist. **dactylographie** *nf* typing.
dague [dag] *nm* dagger.
daigner [deɲe] *v* condescend, deign.
daim [dɛ̃] *nm* (*animal*) deer; (*cuir*) suede.
dais [dɛ] *nm* canopy.
daller [dale] *v* pave. **dallage** *nm* paving. **dalle** *nf* (*pierre*) slab; (*trottoir*) paving stone.
daltonien [daltɔnjɛ̃] *adj* colour-blind. **daltonisme** *nm* colour-blindness.
damas [dama] *nm* damask. **prune de Damas** *nf* damson.
dame [dam] *nf* lady; (*cartes*) queen. **dames** *nf pl* (*jeu*) draughts *sing*.
damier [damje] *nm* draughtboard.
damner [dɑne] *v* damn. **damnation** *nf* damnation. **damné** *adj* (*fam*) confounded.
se dandiner [dɑ̃dine] *v* waddle. **dandinement** *nm* waddle.
Danemark [danmark] *nm* Denmark.
danger [dɑ̃ʒe] *nm* danger. **mettre en danger** endanger. **sans danger** *adv* safely. **dangereux** *adj* dangerous.
danois [danwa] *nm*, *adj* Danish. **Danois, -e** *nm*, *nf* Dane.
dans [dɑ̃] *prep* in; into.
danser [dɑ̃se] *v* dance. **danse** *nf* dance; (*art*) dancing. **danseur, -euse** *nm*, *nf* dancer.
dard [dar] *nm* sting.
darder [darde] *v* (*lancer*) shoot; (*dresser*) point.
dater [date] *v* date. **date** *nf* date. **date limite** deadline.
datte [dat] *nf* date. **dattier** *nm* date palm.
daube [dob] *nf* stew, casserole.
dauphin [dofɛ̃] *nm* dolphin.
davantage [davɑ̃taʒ] *adv* (*plus*) more, any more; (*plus longtemps*) longer, any longer.
de [də], **d'** *prep* of; from. **de/du/de la/des** some, any.
dé [de] *nm* dice. **couper en dés** dice. **dé à coudre** thimble.
débâcle [debɑklə] *nf* collapse; (*mil*) rout; (*glace*) breaking up.
déballer [debale] *v* unpack. **déballage** *nm* unpacking.
se débander [debɑ̃de] *v* disperse, scatter. **débandade** *nf* scattering. **à la débandade** in disorder.
débarbouiller [debarbuje] *v* wash. **se débarbouiller** wash one's face.
débarcadère [debarkadɛr] *nm* landing stage.
débardeur [debardœr] *nm* docker.
débarquer [debarke] *v* land; (*navire*) disembark; (*décharger*) unload. **débarquement** *nm* landing; unloading.
débarras [debara] *nm* lumber room. **bon débarras!** good riddance!
débarrasser [debarase] *v* rid; (*table*) clear. **se débarrasser de** get rid of.
débat [deba] *nm* debate; discussion.
***débattre** [debatrə] *v* debate; discuss. **se débattre** struggle.
débaucher [deboʃe] *v* lead astray; (*ouvriers*) lay off, make redundant. **débauche** *nf* debauchery. **debauché** *adj* debauched.
débile [debil] *adj* weak, feeble.
débit[1] [debi] *nm* (*comm*) turnover; (*fluide*) flow, output; (*élocution*) delivery. **débit de boissons** bar. **débit de tabac** tobacconist's.
débit[2] [debi] *nm* debit.
débiter[1] [debite] *v* (*comm*) retail; (*fluide*) produce; recite; (*couper*) cut up.
débiter[2] [debite] *v* debit.
déblai [deblɛ] *nm* clearing. **déblais** *nm pl* rubble *sing*, debris *sing*.
déblayer [debleje] *v* clear.
déboîter [debwate] *v* (*méd*) dislocate; (*séparer*) disconnect; (*auto*) pull out. **déboîtement** *nm* dislocation.

débonnaire [debɔnɛr] *adj* easy-going.
déborder [debɔrde] *v* (*liquide*) overflow; (*dépasser*) go beyond, jut out; (*drap*) untuck. **débordant** *adj* exuberant, unbounded. **débordé de** (*fam*) snowed under with. **débordement** *nm* overflowing; outburst.
déboucher[1] [debuʃe] *v* (*tuyau*) unblock; (*bouteille*) uncork.
déboucher[2] [debuʃe] *v* emerge. **débouché** *nm* opening; (*comm*) outlet.
débourser [deburse] *v* pay out. **débours** *nm* outlay.
debout [dəbu] *adv, adj* standing. **être debout** stand. **se mettre debout** stand up.
déboutonner [debutɔne] *v* unbutton.
débraillé [debrɑje] *adj* slovenly, untidy. *nm* slovenliness.
débrancher [debrɑ̃ʃe] *v* disconnect; (*appareil électrique*) unplug.
débrayer [debreje] *v* (*auto*) let out the clutch; (*fam*) knock off work.
débris [debri] *nm pl* fragments *pl*; (*restes*) remains *pl*; debris *sing*.
débrouiller [debruje] *v* sort out; (*fils*) disentangle. **se débrouiller** manage, cope.
début [deby] *nm* beginning. **au début** at first. **débuts** *nm pl* début *sing*. **débutant, -e** *nm, nf* beginner. **débuter** *v* start.
deçà [dəsa] *adv* **en deçà de** on this side of.
décade [dekad] *nf* decade.
décadent [dekadɑ̃] *adj* decadent. **décadence** *nf* decadence.
décaler [dekale] *v* shift; (*avancer*) bring forward; (*reculer*) put back. **décalage** *nm* gap; (*temps*) interval; (*concepts*) discrepancy; (*horaire, etc.*) change.
décamper [dekɑ̃pe] *v* (*fam*) clear off.
décanter [dekɑ̃te] *v* (*liquide*) allow to settle; (*verser*) decant. **se décanter** settle; (*idées*) become clear. **décanteur** *nm* decanter.
décapotable [dekapɔtablə] *adj* (*voiture*) convertible.
décéder [desede] *v* die. **décédé, -e** *n, adj* deceased.
déceler [desle] *v* detect; reveal.
décembre [desɑ̃brə] *nm* December.
décent [desɑ̃] *adj* decent; (*acceptable*) proper. **décence** *nf* decency.
déception [desɛpsjɔ̃] *nf* disappointment.
décerner [desɛrne] *v* award.
décès [desɛ] *nm* decease.
***décevoir** [desvwar] *v* disappoint.
déchaîner [deʃene] *v* (*colère, etc.*) unleash; (*enthousiasme*) rouse. **se déchaîner** (*personne*) rage; (*tempête*) break out. **déchaînement** *nm* fury.
décharger [deʃarʒe] *v* discharge; (*bagages*) unload; (*tirer*) fire. **décharger de** relieve of, release from. **décharge** *nf* discharge; (*arme*) volley of shots; (*ordures*) rubbish tip.
décharné [deʃarne] *adj* bony, emaciated.
se déchausser [deʃose] *v* take one's shoes off. **déchaussé** *adj* barefooted.
déchéance [deʃeɑ̃s] *nf* decline; degeneration; (*pol*) deposition.
déchet [deʃɛ] *nm* (*reste*) scrap; (*comm*) waste. **déchets** *nm pl* rubbish, waste.
déchiffrer [deʃifre] *v* decipher, decode; (*musique*) sight-read.
déchiqueter [deʃikte] *v* tear to pieces, shred. **déchiqueté** *adj* jagged.
déchirer [deʃire] *v* tear. **déchirant** *adj* heartrending. **déchirure** *nf* tear.
***déchoir** [deʃwar] *v* (*se dégrader*) demean oneself; decline.
décibel [desibɛl] *nm* decibel.
décider [deside] *v* decide; persuade; determine. **se décider** (*personne*) make up one's mind; (*question*) be settled. **décidé** *adj* determined; settled. **décidément** *adv* undoubtedly.
décimal [desimal] *adj* decimal. **décimale** *nf* decimal.
décisif [desizif] *adj* decisive.
décision [desizjɔ̃] *nf* decision.
déclarer [deklare] *v* declare, announce; (*naissance*) register. **déclaration** *nf* declaration; (*discours*) statement; (*aveu*) admission; registration.
déclencher [deklɑ̃ʃe] *v* (*mécanisme*) release, activate; (*attaque*) launch; (*entraîner*) trigger off.
déclin [deklɛ̃] *nm* decline; (*jour*) close; (*lune*) wane.
décliner [dekline] *v* decline. **déclinaison** *nf* declension.
décoiffé [dekwafe] *adj* dishevelled.
décoller [dekɔle] *v* unstick; (*avion*) take off. **se décoller** come unstuck. **décollage** *nm* take-off.
décolorer [dekɔlɔre] *v* fade; (*cheveux*) bleach.
décombres [dekɔ̃brə] *nm pl* rubble *sing*.
décommander [dekɔmɑ̃de] *v* cancel.

décomposer [dekɔ̃poze] *v* split up; (*visage*) distort. **se décomposer** decompose. **décomposition** *nf* decomposition.
décompte [dekɔ̃t] *nf* deduction; (*compte*) breakdown. **décompter** *v* deduct.
déconcerter [dekɔ̃sɛrte] *v* disconcert.
décongeler [dekɔ̃ʒle] *v* thaw out.
déconseiller [dekɔ̃seje] *v* advise against. **déconseillé** *adj* inadvisable.
décontracter [dekɔ̃trakte] *v* relax. **décontraction** *nf* relaxation.
déconvenue [dekɔ̃vny] *nf* disappointment.
décor [dekɔr] *nm* scenery; (*maison*) décor; (*cadre*) setting.
décorer [dekɔre] *v* decorate. **décorateur, -trice** *nm, nf* decorator. **décoratif** *adj* decorative. **décoration** *nf* decoration.
découper [dekupe] *v* cut out *or* up. **se découper** stand out.
décourager [dekuraʒe] *v* discourage. **découragement** *nm* discouragement.
décousu [dekuzy] *adj* disjointed; (*couture*) undone.
découvert [dekuvɛr] *adj* uncovered; (*terrain*) exposed, open. *nm* overdraft, deficit. **découverte** *nf* discovery.
***découvrir** [dekuvrir] *v* (*trouver*) discover, find out; (*exposer*) uncover.
décrasser [dekrase] *v* clean.
décret [dekrɛ] *nm* decree. **décréter** *v* decree, order.
***décrire** [dekrir] *v* describe.
décrocher [dekrɔʃe] *v* take down; (*téléphone*) pick up (the receiver).
***décroître** [dekrwatrə] *v* decrease, decline, (*lune*) wane. **décroissance** *nf* decrease, decline.
dédaigner [dedeɲe] *v* despise, scorn. **dédaigneux** *adj* scornful, contemptuous.
dédain [dedɛ̃] *nm* contempt, scorn.
dédale [dedal] *nm* maze.
dedans [dədɑ̃] *adv* inside, indoors. *nm* inside.
dédicace [dedikas] *nf* dedication. **dédicacer** *v* sign, autograph.
dédier [dedje] *v* dedicate.
se *dédire [dedir] *v* go back on (one's word); retract.
dédit [dedi] *nm* forfeit; retraction.
dédommager [dedɔmaʒe] *v* compensate. **dédommagement** *nm* compensation.
déduction [dedyksjɔ̃] *nf* deduction; conclusion.
***déduire** [dedɥir] *v* (*comm*) deduct; (*conclure*) deduce.
déesse [deɛs] *nf* goddess.
***défaillir** [defajir] *v* weaken, fail; (*s'évanouir*) faint. **défaillance** *nf* (*faiblesse*) weakness; (*incapacité*) failure; faint.
***défaire** [defɛr] *v* (*couture, nœud*) undo; (*valise*) unpack; (*construction*) dismantle. **se défaire** come undone *or* apart. **se défaire de** get rid of.
défaite [defɛt] *nf* defeat.
défalquer [defalke] *v* deduct.
défaut [defo] *nm* fault, flaw, defect; (*manque*) lack. **faire défaut** be lacking; (*jur*) default.
défection [defɛksjɔ̃] *nf* desertion, defection.
défectueux [defɛktɥø] *adj* defective, faulty.
défendre [defɑ̃drə] *v* (*protéger*) defend; (*interdire*) forbid.
défense [defɑ̃s] *nf* defence. **défense de fumer/stationner** no smoking/parking. **défense d'entrer** keep out.
déférer [defere] *v* defer; (*jur*) hand over. **déférence** *nf* deference. **déférent** *adj* deferential.
défi [defi] *nm* challenge; (*bravade*) defiance.
déficeler [defisle] *v* untie.
déficit [defisit] *nm* deficit.
défier [defje] *v* defy, challenge. **se défier de** distrust. **défiance** *nf* distrust. **défiant** *adj* distrustful.
défigurer [defigyre] *v* disfigure, spoil; (*verité*) distort; (*monument*) deface. **défiguration** *nf* distortion; disfigurement.
défilé [defile] *nm* procession; (*géog*) gorge, pass.
définir [definir] *v* define. **défini** *adj* definite. **définitif** *adj* final, definitive. **définition** *nf* definition; (*mots croisés*) clue.
défoncer [defɔ̃se] *v* smash in, break up.
déformer [defɔrme] *v* deform, distort; (*métal, etc.*) bend *or* put out of shape. **déformation** *nf* deformation, distortion.
défraîchi [defreʃi] *adj* faded.
défricher [defriʃe] *v* clear. **défricher le terrain** prepare the ground.
défunt [defœ̃], **-e** *n, adj* deceased.
dégager [degaʒe] *v* clear; (*libérer*) free; (*exhaler*) give off. **dégagé** *adj* clear; (*allure*) casual.

dégarnir [degarnir] *v* strip, clear, empty. **dégarni** *adj* bare.
dégât [degɑ] *nm* damage.
dégel [deʒɛl] *nm* thaw. **dégeler** *v* thaw (out).
dégénérer [deʒenere] *v* degenerate. **dégénéré** *adj* degenerate. **dégénérescence** *nf* degeneration, degeneracy.
dégivrer [deʒivre] *v* defrost, de-ice. **dégivreur** *nm* defroster, de-icer.
dégonfler [degɔ̃fle] *v* deflate. **se dégonfler** go down; (*fam*) back out. **dégonflé** *adj* (*pneu*) flat; (*fam*) chicken.
dégorger [degɔrʒe] *v* discharge, pour out; (*déboucher*) clear out.
dégouliner [deguline] *v* trickle, drip. **dégoulinade** *nf* trickle.
dégourdir [degurdir] *v* warm up. **se dégourdir** stretch one's legs. **dégourdi** *adj* (*fam*) smart, bright.
dégoûter [degute] *v* disgust. **dégoût** *nm* disgust.
dégoutter [degute] *v* drip.
dégrader [degrade] *v* degrade, debase; (*mur, monument*) deface, damage. **se degrader** debase oneself; deteriorate. **dégradation** *nf* degradation.
dégrafer [degrafe] *v* unfasten.
dégraisser [degrese] *v* remove the fat *or* grease from. **dégraissage** *nm* cleaning.
degré [dəgre] *nm* degree; stage.
dégringoler [degrɛ̃gɔle] *v* tumble (down). **dégringolade** *nf* tumble.
dégriser [degrize] *v* sober up.
déguenillé [degnije] *adj* ragged.
déguerpir [degerpir] *v* (*fam*) clear off.
dégueulasse [degœlas] *adj* (*argot*) lousy, rotten, revolting.
déguiser [degize] *v* disguise. **se déguiser** (en) dress up (as). **déguisé** *adj* in disguise; (*travesti*) in fancy dress. **déguisement** *nm* disguise; fancy dress.
déguster [degyste] *v* taste, sample; savour, enjoy. **dégustation** *nf* wine-tasting.
dehors [dəɔr] *adv* outside, outdoors. **en dehors de** outside; (*sauf*) apart from. *nm* outside; appearance.
déjà [deʒa] *adv* already; (*encore*) yet.
déjeuner [deʒœne] *v* have lunch. *nm* lunch.
delà [dəla] *adv* **au delà** beyond. **en delà** beyond, outside. **par delà** beyond. *prep* **au delà de** beyond, over.
délabré [delɑbre] *adj* dilapidated, falling down; (*vêtements*) ragged.
délai [delɛ] *nm* delay; time limit, deadline. **à bref délai** at short notice; (*bientôt*) very soon.
délaisser [delese] *v* abandon; neglect; (*jur*) relinquish. **délaissement** *nm* desertion; neglect.
délasser [delɑse] *v* refresh, relax. **délassement** *nm* relaxation.
délavé [delave] *adj* faded, washed-out.
délayer [deleje] *v* mix; dilute, thin down; (*péj*) spin out.
déléguer [delege] *v* delegate. **delégation** *nf* delegation. **délégué, -e** *nm, nf* delegate.
délibérer [delibere] *v* deliberate, confer, consider. **délibération** *nf* deliberation; resolution. **délibéré** *adj* deliberate; resolute.
délicat [delika] *adj* delicate; refined; scrupulous; sensitive; (*difficile*) fussy. **délicatesse** *nf* delicacy; tact; refinement.
délice [delis] *nm* delight. **délicieux** *adj* delightful; (*goût*) delicious.
délier [delje] *v* untie, loosen. **délié** *adj* agile; fine, slender.
délinquant [delɛ̃kɑ̃], **-e** *n, adj* delinquent. **délinquance** *nf* delinquency.
délire [delir] *nm* delirium; frenzy. **avoir le délire** be delirious. **délirer** *v* be delirious.
délit [deli] *nm* offence.
délivrer [delivre] *v* (*libérer*) free; (*débarrasser*) relieve; (*livrer*) issue. **délivrance** *nf* release; relief; issue.
déloyal [delwajal] *adj* disloyal; (*procédé*) unfair. **déloyauté** *nf* disloyalty; unfairness.
delta [dɛlta] *nm* delta.
déluge [delyʒ] *nm* deluge, flood; (*pluie*) downpour.
déluré [delyre] *adj* smart, resourceful.
se démailler [demɑje] *v* (*bas*) ladder; (*tricot*) unravel.
demain [dəmɛ̃] *adv* tomorrow. **à demain!** see you tomorrow! **demain en huit** a week tomorrow.
demander [dəmɑ̃de] *v* ask for; enquire, ask; (*médecin, etc.*) send for; (*avoir besoin de*) require, need. **se demander** wonder. **demande** *nf* request; (*emploi*) application; (*remboursement*) claim; (*comm*) demand. **demande** *adj* in demand.
démanger [demɑ̃ʒe] *v* itch. **démangeaison** *nf* itch.

démaquiller [demakije] *v* remove make-up from. **démaquillant** *nm* make-up remover.
démarche [demarʃ] *nf* gait; procedure, step; approach.
démarrer [demare] *v* (*auto*) start; (*partir*) move off. **bien démarrer** get off to a good start. **démarreur** *nm* (*auto*) starter.
démêler [demele] *v* untangle. **démêlé** *nm* dispute.
démembrer [demɑ̃bre] *v* dismember, carve up.
déménager [demenaʒe] *v* move (house). **déménagement** *nm* removal, move. **déménageur** *nm* removal man.
démence [demɑ̃s] *nf* madness.
se démener [dɛmne] *v* struggle; make an effort.
***démentir** [demɑ̃tir] *v* refute, deny, contradict. **démenti** *nm* denial.
démesuré [deməzyre] *adj* immoderate; enormous.
***démettre** [demɛtrə] *v* dislocate; (*renvoyer*) dismiss. **se démettre** resign.
demeurer [dəmœre] *v* (*rester*) remain; (*habiter*) live. **au demeurant** for all that. **demeure** *nf* residence. **à demeure** permanent.
demi [dəmi], **-e** *n*, *adj* half. **à demi** *adv* half.
demi-bouteille *nf* half-bottle.
demi-cercle *nm* semicircle. **en demi-cercle** semicircular.
demi-douzaine *nf* half-dozen. **une demi-douzaine** half-a-dozen.
demi-finale *nf* semifinal. **demi-finaliste** *n(m+f)* semifinalist.
demi-frère *nm* half-brother.
demi-heure *nf* half-hour. **une demi-heure** half an hour.
demi-pension *nf* half-board.
demi-sœur *nf* half-sister.
démission [demisjɔ̃] *nf* resignation; abdication. **donner sa démission** hand in one's notice. **démissionner** *v* resign.
demi-tarif *nm* half-price; (*transport*) half-fare.
demi-teinte *nf* half-tone.
demi-tour *nm* about-turn; (*auto*) U-turn.
démocratie [demɔkrasi] *nf* democracy. **démocrate** *n(m+f)* democrat. **démocratique** *adj* democratic.
démodé [demɔde] *adj* old-fashioned.
demoiselle [dəmwazɛl] *nf* young lady. **demoiselle d'honneur** bridesmaid.
démolir [demɔlir] *v* demolish; destroy. **démolition** *nf* demolition.
démon [demɔ̃] *nm* demon.
démonter [demɔ̃te] *v* dismantle, take apart; disconcert.
démontrer [demɔ̃tre] *v* demonstrate. **démonstratif** *adj* demonstrative. **démonstration** *nf* demonstration.
démoraliser [demɔralize] *v* demoralize. **se démoraliser** lose heart. **démoralisation** *nf* demoralization.
démordre [demɔrdrə] *v* give up. **ne pas démordre de** stick to.
démunir [demynir] *v* deprive, divest. **démuni de** without.
dénaturer [denatyre] *v* distort. **dénaturé** *adj* unnatural.
dénégation [denegɑsjɔ̃] *nf* denial.
dénicher [deniʃe] (*fam*) *v* discover; (*personne*) track down; (*objet*) unearth.
dénigrer [denigre] *v* denigrate, run down.
dénivellation [denivɛlɑsjɔ̃] *nf* unevenness; (*pente*) slope; (*auto*) ramp.
dénombrer [denɔ̃bre] *v* count; enumerate.
dénominateur [denɔminatœr] *nm* denominator.
dénommer [denɔme] *v* name.
dénoncer [denɔ̃se] *v* denounce; (*coupable*) give away; (*révéler*) expose.
dénoter [denɔte] *v* denote, indicate.
dénouer [denwe] *v* (*nœud*) undo; (*intrigue*) untangle, resolve. **se dénouer** come undone; be resolved. **dénouement** *nm* outcome; (*théâtre*) dénouement.
denrée [dɑ̃re] *nf* foodstuff.
dense [dɑ̃s] *adj* dense; compact.
densité [dɑ̃site] *nf* density.
dent [dɑ̃] *nf* tooth (*pl* teeth); (*fourche*) prong; (*roue*) cog. **avoir la dent** (*fam*) be peckish. **avoir une dent contre** have a grudge against. **du bout des dents** half-heartedly. **en dents de scie** serrated. **faire ses dents** teethe. **dentaire** *adj* dental.
denteler [dɑ̃tle] *v* indent. **dentelé** *adj* jagged.
dentelle [dɑ̃tɛl] *nf* lace.
dentier [dɑ̃tje] *nm* denture.
dentifrice [dɑ̃tifris] *nm* toothpaste.
dentiste [dɑ̃tist] *n(m+f)* dentist.
dénuder [denyde] *v* strip, bare. **dénudé** *adj* bare; (*crâne*) bald.
dénué [denɥe] *adj* **dénué de** devoid of, lacking in.

déodorant [deɔdɔrɑ̃] *nm, adj* deodorant.
dépanner [depane] *v* fix, repair. **dépannage** *nm* repairing. **service de dépannage** *nm* breakdown service. **dépanneuse** *nf* breakdown lorry.
dépaqueter [depakte] *v* unpack.
dépareillé [depareje] *adj* (*objet*) odd; (*collection*) incomplete.
départ [depar] *nm* departure; (*début*) start.
département [departəmɑ̃] *nm* department.
départir [departir] *v* assign. **se départir de** abandon, depart from.
dépasser [depɑse] *v* pass; (*auto*) overtake; exceed, go beyond; (*clou, rocher, etc.*) stick out. **dépassé** *adj* outmoded; (*fam*) out of one's depth. **dépassement** *nm* overtaking.
dépaysé [depeize] *adj* disorientated. **sentir dépaysé** not feel at home.
dépêcher [depeʃe] *v* dispatch. **se dépêcher** hurry. **dépêche** *nf* dispatch; telegram.
***dépeindre** [depɛ̃drə] *v* depict.
dépendance [depɑ̃dɑ̃s] *nf* dependence, dependency; subordination; (*bâtiment*) outbuilding. **dépendant de** (*employé*) answerable to; dependent on.
dépendre[1] [depɑ̃drə] *v* **dépendre de** depend on, be dependent on; (*employé*) be answerable to; (*appartenir*) belong to.
dépendre[2] [depɑ̃drə] *v* take down.
dépens [depɑ̃] *nm pl* costs *pl*. **aux dépens de** at the expense of.
dépenser [depɑ̃se] *v* (*argent*) spend; (*consumer*) use (up). **se dépenser** exert oneself. **dépense** *nf* expenditure, expense; consumption. **dépensier** *adj* extravagant. **être dépensier** be a spendthrift.
dépérir [deperir] *v* decline; (*personne*) waste away; (*plante*) wither.
dépêtrer [depetre] *v* extricate, free.
dépister [depiste] *v* (*découvrir*) detect, track down; (*détourner*) throw off the scent.
dépit [depi] *nm* vexation, resentment. **en dépit de** in spite of.
déplacer [deplase] *v* move, shift; (*air, eau, etc.*) displace. **se déplacer** move (around); (*voyager*) travel. **déplacé** *adj* uncalled-for; out of place. **déplacement** *nm* displacement; moving, movement; travel.
***déplaire** [deplɛr] *v* **déplaire à** be disliked by, displease. **se déplaire** be unhappy, dislike it. **déplaisant** *adj* unpleasant. **déplaisir** *nm* displeasure.
déplantoir [deplɑ̃twar] *nm* trowel.
déplier [deplije] *v* unfold, open out. **dépliant** *nm* leaflet, folder.
déplorer [deplɔre] *v* regret, deplore. **déplorable** *adj* deplorable.
déployer [deplwaje] *v* spread out; (*troupes*) deploy; (*étaler*) display.
se déplumer [deplyme] *v* moult.
déporter [depɔrte] *v* deport. **déportation** *nf* deportation.
déposer[1] [depoze] *v* set *or* put down; (*argent, sédiment*) deposit; (*admin*) file, register; (*roi*) depose. **déposant, -e** *nm, nf* depositor. **déposition** *nf* deposition.
dépositaire [depozitɛr] *n*(*m*+*f*) guardian; agent.
dépôt [depo] *nm* deposit; (*train, autobus*) depot; (*entrepôt*) warehouse; (*garde*) trust.
dépouiller [depuje] *v* strip; (*examiner*) peruse, study. **se dépouiller de** shed. **dépouille** *nf* skin, hide. **dépouillé** *adj* bare.
dépourvu [depurvy] *adj* **dépourvu de** devoid of, lacking in, without. *nm* **au dépourvu** unprepared.
dépraver [deprave] *v* deprave. **dépravation** *nf* depravity.
déprécier [depresje] *v* depreciate; (*dénigrer*) belittle. **dépréciation** *nf* depreciation.
dépression [depresjɔ̃] *nf* depression.
déprimer [deprime] *v* depress.
depuis [dəpɥi] *prep* since, from. *adv* ever since.
députation [depytɑsjɔ̃] *nf* deputation.
député [depyte] *nm* member of parliament; (*envoyé*) delegate.
déraciner [derasine] *v* (*détruire*) eradicate; (*arbre*) uproot. **déracinement** *nm* eradication.
dérailler [deraje] *v* be derailed. **déraillement** *nm* derailment.
déraisonnable [derezɔnablə] *adj* unreasonable.
déranger [derɑ̃ʒe] *v* disturb; (*coiffure*) ruffle; (*gêner*) trouble; (*routine*) upset. **se déranger** put oneself out; move aside. **dérangement** *nm* trouble; disorder.
déraper [derape] *v* skid. **dérapage** *nm* skid.

derechef [dərəʃɛf] *adv* once more.
dérégler [deregle] *v* disturb, unsettle, upset. **se dérégler** go wrong. **déréglé** *adj* out of order; (*mœurs*) dissolute; upset. **dérèglement** *nm* disturbance; dissoluteness.
dérision [derizjɔ̃] *nf* derision, mockery. **dérisoire** *adj* derisory.
dériver[1] [derive] *v* derive; (*rivière*) divert. **dérivation** *nf* derivation; diversion. **dérivé** *nm* derivative, by-product.
dériver[2] [derive] *v* drift. **dérive** *nf* drift. **à la dérive** adrift.
dernier [dɛrnje], **-ère** *adj* last; (*plus récent*) latest; (*extrême*) utmost; (*pire*) bottom; (*ultime*) top. *nm, nf* last. **ce dernier, cette dernière** the latter. **dernièrement** *adv* recently.
dérober [derɔbe] *v* (*cacher*) hide; (*voler*) steal. **se dérober** shy away; (*échapper*) slip away; (*s'effondrer*) give way. **dérobé** *adj* secret. **à la dérobée** secretly.
déroger [derɔʒe] *v* **déroger à** (*jur*) go against; (*s'abaisser*) lower oneself.
dérouler [derule] *v* unroll, unwind. **se dérouler** (*fil*) unwind, unroll; develop, progress; (*se passer*) take place.
dérouter [derute] *v* (*avion*) divert; disconcert. **déroute** *nf* rout. **déroutement** *nm* diversion.
derrière [dɛrjɛr] *prep* behind. *adv* behind, at the back. *nm* back, rear; (*fam*) behind.
des [de] *contraction of* **de les.**
dès [dɛ] *prep* from, since. **dès lors** from then on, from that moment. **dès que** as soon as.
désabuser [dezabyze] *v* disillusion. **désabusé** *adj* disenchanted. **désabusement** *nm* disillusionment.
désaccord [dezakɔr] *nm* discord; conflict, disagreement; (*contradiction*) discrepancy.
désaffecter [dezafɛkte] *v* close down. **désaffecté** *adj* disused.
désagréable [dezagreablə] *adj* unpleasant.
désagréger [dezagreʒe] *v* disintegrate, break up. **désagrégation** *nf* disintegration.
désagrément [dezagremɑ̃] *nm* annoyance, trouble.
se désaltérer [dezaltere] *v* quench one's thirst. **désaltérant** *adj* thirst-quenching.
désappointer [dezapwɛ̃te] *v* disappoint.
désapprobation [dezaprɔbasjɔ̃] *nf* disapproval. **désapprobateur, -trice** *adj* disapproving.
désapprouver [dezapruve] *v* disapprove of.
désarmer [dezarme] *v* disarm.
désarroi [dezarwa] *nm* confusion.
désassorti [dezasɔrti] *adj* unmatching.
désastre [dezastrə] *nm* disaster. **désastreux** *adj* disastrous.
désavantage [dezavɑ̃taʒ] *nm* disadvantage, handicap.
désaveu [dezavø] *nm* disavowal, repudiation; retraction.
désavouer [dezavwe] *v* disown, repudiate. **se désavouer** retract.
désaxé [dezakse] *adj* unbalanced.
descendant [desɑ̃dɑ̃], **-e** *adj* downward, descending. *nm, nf* descendant.
descendre [desɑ̃drə] *v* go down, come down; (*transport*) get out *or* off; (*tomber*) fall; (*baisser*) lower; (*porter*) take down. **descendre de** be descended from.
descente [desɑ̃t] *nf* descent; raid; (*pente*) downward slope. **descente de lit** bedside rug.
description [dɛskripsjɔ̃] *nf* description. **descriptif** *adj* descriptive.
désemparer [dezɑ̃pare] *v* (*naut*) disable. **sans désemparer** without stopping. **désemparé** *adj* bewildered; (*navire, avion*) crippled.
désencombrer [dezɑ̃kɔ̃bre] *v* clear.
désenfler [dezɑ̃fle] *v* go down, become less swollen.
désengager [dezɑ̃gaʒe] *v* free, release; (*mil*) disengage.
désenivrer [dezɑ̃nivre] *v* sober up.
déséquilibré [dezekilibre] *adj* unbalanced.
désert [dezɛr] *adj* deserted. *nm* desert.
déserter [dezɛrte] *v* desert. **déserteur** *nm* deserter. **désertion** *nf* desertion.
désespérer [dezɛspere] *v* despair, lose hope; (*désoler*) drive to despair. **désespérant** *adj* maddening. **désespéré** *adj* desperate.
désespoir [dezɛspwar] *nm* despair.
déshabiller [dezabije] *v* undress. **déshabillé** *nm* negligee.
désherber [dezɛrbe] *v* weed. **désherbage** *nm* weeding. **désherbant** *nm* weed-killer.
déshériter [dezerite] *v* disinherit; (*désavantager*) deprive.
déshonneur [dezɔnœr] *nm* disgrace, dishonour.

déshonorer [dezɔnɔre] *v* disgrace, dishonour.
déshydrater [dezidrate] *v* dehydrate. **déshydratation** *nf* dehydration.
désigner [dezipe] *v* designate; (*montrer*) point out; (*nommer*) name, appoint. **désignation** *nf* designation; appointment.
désillusionner [dezilyzjɔne] *v* disillusion. **désillusion** *nf* disillusionment.
désinfecter [dezɛ̃fɛkte] *v* disinfect. **désinfectant** *nm*, *adj* disinfectant. **désinfection** *nf* disinfection.
désintégrer [dezɛ̃tegre] *v* split *or* break up. **se désintégrer** disintegrate. **désintégration** *nf* disintegration.
désintéressé [dezɛ̃terese] *adj* disinterested, unselfish. **désintéressement** *nm* unselfishness.
désinvolte [dezɛ̃vɔlt] *adj* casual. **avec désinvolture** casually.
désirer [dezire] *v* desire, want. **désir** *nm* desire, wish. **désirable** *adj* desirable. **désireux de** anxious to.
désobéir [dezɔbeir] *v* disobey. **désobéissance** *nf* disobedience. **désobéissant** *adj* disobedient.
désodorisant [dezɔdɔrizɑ̃] *nm*, *adj* deodorant.
désœuvré [dezœvre] *adj* idle. **désœuvrement** *nm* idleness.
désoler [dezɔle] *v* distress, upset; devastate. **désolation** *nf* distress, grief; devastation. **désolé** sorry, distressed; (*endroit*) desolate.
désopilant [dezɔpilɑ̃] *adj* hilarious.
désordonné [dezɔrdɔne] *adj* disorderly, untidy, muddled.
désordre [dezɔrdrə] *nm* disorder, untidiness; confusion. **désordres** *nm pl* disturbances *pl*.
désorganiser [dezɔrganize] *v* disorganize, disrupt. **désorganisation** *nf* disorganization.
désorienter [dezɔrjɑ̃te] *v* disorientate, bewilder.
désormais [dezɔrmɛ] *adv* in future, from now on.
désosser [dezɔse] *v* bone.
desquels, desquelles [dekɛl] *contractions of* **de lesquels, de lesquelles.**
dessécher [deseʃe] *v* dry out, parch; (*feuille*) wither; (*aliments*) dehydrate; (*amaigrir*) emaciate.
dessein [desɛ̃] *nm* intention, plan. **à dessein** intentionally. **avoir des desseins sur** have designs on.
desserrer [desere] *v* loosen, release. **desserrer les dents** open one's mouth, speak. **desserré** *adj* loose.
dessert [desɛr] *nm* dessert, sweet.
***desservir**[1] [desɛrvir] *v* clear the table; (*nuire*) harm, do a disservice to.
***desservir**[2] [desɛrvir] *v* (*transport*) serve; (*porte*) lead into.
dessin [desɛ̃] *nm* drawing; (*motif*) pattern; (*contour*) outline. **dessin animé** cartoon (film). **dessin humoristique** cartoon. **dessinateur, -trice** *nm*, *nf* draughtsman; designer; cartoonist.
dessiner [desine] *v* draw; design. **se dessiner** stand out; become apparent.
dessous [dəsu] *adv* under, below. *nm* bottom, underside. **avoir le dessous** get the worst of it. **dessous de plat** table mat. **dessous de verre** coaster.
dessus [dəsy] *adv* above, over, on top. *nm* top. **avoir le dessus** have the upper hand. **dessus de lit** bedspread.
destin [dɛstɛ̃] *nm* fate, destiny.
destination [dɛstinɑsjɔ̃] *nf* destination. **à destination de** bound for.
destiner [dɛstine] *v* destine; intend. **destinée** *nf* fate, destiny.
destituer [dɛstitɥe] *v* dismiss. **destitution** *nf* dismissal, discharge.
destruction [dɛstryksjɔ̃] *nf* destruction. **destructif** *adj* destructive.
désuet, -ète [desɥɛ, -ɛt] *adj* outdated. **désuétude** *nf* disuse. **tomber en désuétude** become obsolete.
désunir [dezynir] *v* divide, disunite.
détacher[1] [detaʃe] *v* (*dénouer*) untie, undo; (*ôter*) remove; separate. **se détacher** come undone; come off *or* away; (*ressortir*) stand out. **se détacher de** renounce. **détachable** *adj* detachable. **détachement** *nm* detachment.
détacher[2] [detaʃe] *v* clean, remove stains from. **détachant** *nm* stain remover.
détail [detaj] *nm* detail; (*facture*) breakdown; (*comm*) retail.
détailler [detaje] *v* explain in detail; (*articles*) sell separately; (*comm*) retail. **détaillant, -e** *nm*, *nf* retailer. **détaillé** *adj* detailed.
détective [detɛktiv] *nm* **détective privé** private detective.
***déteindre** [detɛ̃drə] *v* (*au soleil*) fade; (*au lavage*) run.

détendre [detɑ̃drə] *v* release, loosen. **se détendre** relax.
***détenir** [detnir] *v* have, hold; (*prisonnier*) detain. **détenteur, -trice** *nm, nf* holder. **détenu, -e** *nm, nf* prisoner.
détente [detɑ̃t] *nf* relaxation; (*élan*) spring; (*gâchette*) trigger.
détergent [detɛrʒɑ̃] *nm, adj* detergent.
détériorer [deterjɔre] *v* damage. **se détériorer** deteriorate. **détérioration** *nf* damage; deterioration.
déterminer [detɛrmine] *v* determine; fix; decide. **se déterminer** make up one's mind. **détermination** *nf* determination; resolution. **déterminé** *adj* determined; specific.
déterrer [detere] *v* dig up, unearth.
détester [deteste] *v* hate, detest. **détestable** *adj* loathsome.
détoner [detɔne] *v* detonate. **détonant** *nm, adj* explosive. **détonateur** *nm* detonator.
détonner [detɔne] *v* clash, be out of place; (*musique*) go out of tune.
détour [detur] *nm* detour; (*courbe*) bend. **sans détours** straight out.
détourner [deturne] *v* divert; (*regard*) turn away; (*avion*) hijack; (*argent*) embezzle. **détourné** *adj* indirect, roundabout. **détournement** *nm* diversion; hijacking; embezzlement.
détraqué [detrake] *adj* broken down, out of order; (*temps*) unsettled; (*fam: personne*) crazy.
détremper [detrɑ̃pe] *v* soak; dilute, mix with water.
détresse [detrɛs] *nf* distress.
détritus [detritys] *nm pl* rubbish *sing*, refuse *sing*.
***détruire** [detrɥir] *v* destroy; ruin.
dette [dɛt] *nf* debt.
deuil [dœj] *nm* mourning; (*perte*) bereavement.
deux [dø] *adj* two; (*quelques*) a couple of; (*épelant*) double. *nm* two. **deux-points** *nm invar* colon. **(tous) les deux** both. **tous les deux jours** every other day. **deuxième** *n(m+f), adj* second.
dévaler [devale] *v* rush *or* hurtle down.
dévaliser [devalize] *v* burgle, rob.
dévaluer [devalɥe] *v* devalue. **dévaluation** *nf* devaluation.
devancer [dəvɑ̃se] *v* forestall; (*question, etc.*) anticipate; (*coureur*) get ahead of, leave behind. **devancier, -ère** *nm, nf* precursor.
devant [dəvɑ̃] *prep* in front of, before. *adv* in front, ahead. *nm* front. **aller au-devant de** anticipate.
devanture [dəvɑ̃tyr] *nf* (*étalage*) window, display; (*façade*) shop front. **à la devanture** in the window.
dévaster [devaste] *v* devastate. **dévastation** *nf* devastation.
développer [devlɔpe] *v* develop; (*industrie, etc.*) expand. **se développer** develop, spread. **développement** *nm* development; expansion.
***devenir** [dəvnir] *v* become.
dévergondé [devɛrgɔ̃de] *adj* shameless; licentious.
déverser [devɛrse] *v* pour out. **déversoir** *nm* overflow.
dévêtir [devetir] *v* undress.
dévier [devje] *v* deviate, veer off course; divert. **déviation** *nf* deviation; diversion.
deviner [dəvine] *v* guess; (*énigme*) solve. **devinette** *nf* riddle.
devis [dəvi] *nm* estimate.
dévisager [devizaʒe] *v* stare at.
devise [dəviz] *nf* motto; (*comm*) slogan. **devises** *nf pl* currency *sing*.
dévisser [devise] *v* unscrew.
dévoiler [devwale] *v* unveil; reveal, disclose.
***devoir** [dəvwar] *v* have to, must; (*argent, etc.*) owe. *nm* duty; (*école*) homework.
dévorer [devɔre] *v* devour; consume.
dévot [devo], **-e** *adj* devout, pious. *nm, nf* pious person. **dévotion** *nf* devoutness.
se dévouer [devwe] *v* devote oneself; sacrifice oneself. **dévouement** *nm* devotion.
dextérité [dɛksterite] *nf* skill, dexterity.
diabète [djabɛt] *nm* diabetes. **diabétique** *n(m+f), adj* diabetic.
diable [djɑblə] *nm* devil. **diablerie** *nf* mischief. **diabolique** *adj* diabolical.
diablotin [djɑblɔtɛ̃] *nm* (*enfant*) imp; (*pétard*) cracker.
diadème [djadɛm] *nm* diadem; (*bijou*) tiara.
diagnostiquer [djagnɔstike] *v* diagnose. **diagnostic** *nm* diagnosis.
diagonal [djagɔnal] *adj* diagonal. **diagonale** *nf* diagonal.
dialecte [djalɛkt] *nm* dialect.
dialogue [djalɔg] *nm* dialogue, conversation.
diamant [djamɑ̃] *nm* diamond.

diamètre [djamɛtrə] *nm* diameter. **diamétralement opposé** diametrically opposed.
diaphragme [djafragmə] *nm* diaphragm.
diapositive [djapozitiv] *nf* slide, transparency.
diapré [djapre] *adj* mottled.
diarrhée [djare] *nf* diarrhoea.
dictateur [diktatœr] *nm* dictator. **dictature** *nf* dictatorship.
dicter [dikte] *v* dictate. **dictée** *nf* dictation.
dictionnaire [diksjɔnɛr] *nm* dictionary.
dicton [diktɔ̃] *nm* saying.
dièse [djɛz] *nm, adj* sharp.
diesel [djezɛl] *nm* diesel.
diète [djɛt] *nf* diet.
dieu [djø] *nm* god.
diffamer [difame] *v* slander; (*par écrit*) libel. **diffamation** *nf* slander; libel. **diffamatoire** *adj* slanderous; libellous.
différence [diferɑ̃s] *nf* difference. **à la différence de** unlike. **différent** *adj* different.
différencier [diferɑ̃sje] *v* differentiate. **différenciation** *nf* differentiation.
différend [diferɑ̃] *nm* disagreement, difference of opinion.
différentiel [diferɑ̃sjɛl], **-elle** *n, adj* differential.
différer [difere] *v* differ; (*renvoyer*) defer, postpone.
difficile [difisil] *adj* difficult. **difficulté** *nf* difficulty.
difforme [difɔrm] *adj* deformed. **difformité** *nf* deformity.
diffuser [difyze] *v* diffuse, spread; (*émission*) broadcast.
digérer [diʒere] *v* digest.
digestion [diʒɛstjɔ̃] *nf* digestion.
digitale [diʒital] *nf* **digitale pourprée** foxglove.
digne [diɲ] *adj* worthy; (*grave*) dignified.
dignité [diɲite] *nf* dignity.
dique [dig] *nf* dyke.
dilapider [dilapide] *v* squander; (*détourner*) embezzle.
dilater [dilate] *v* dilate, distend. **se dilater** swell, expand. **dilatation** *nf* dilation.
dilemme [dilɛm] *nm* dilemma.
diluer [dilɥe] *v* dilute. **dilution** *nf* dilution.
dimanche [dimɑ̃ʃ] *nm* Sunday. **dimanche des Rameaux** Palm Sunday.
dimension [dimɑ̃sjɔ̃] *nf* dimension, size, measurement.
diminuer [diminɥe] *v* diminish, reduce, decrease. **diminutif** *nm, adj* diminutive. **diminution** *nf* reduction, decrease.
dinde [dɛ̃d] *nf* turkey. **dindon** *nm* turkey.
dîner [dine] *v* have dinner, dine. *nm* dinner. **dineur, -euse** *nm, nf* diner.
dingue [dɛ̃g] (*fam*) *adj* barmy, crazy. *n(m+f)* nutcase.
dinosaure [dinozɔr] *nm* dinosaur.
diocèse [djɔsɛz] *nm* diocese.
diphtongue [diftɔ̃g] *nf* diphthong.
diplomate [diplɔmat] *adj* diplomatic. *n(m+f)* diplomat. *nm* (*cuisine*) trifle. **diplomatie** *nf* diplomacy. **diplomatique** *adj* diplomatic.
diplôme [diplom] *nm* diploma; examination.
diplômé [diplome], **-e** *adj* qualified. *nm, nf* holder of a diploma.
***dire** [dir] *v* say, tell. **c'est-à-dire** that is. **vouloir dire** mean.
direct [dirɛkt] *adj* direct, straight, immediate. *nm* fast train, express. **directement** *adv* directly, straight, immediately.
directeur [dirɛktœr] *nm* director; (*responsable*) manager; (*école*) headmaster. **directeur général** managing director. **directrice** *nf* director; manageress; headmistress.
direction [dirɛksjɔ̃] *nf* direction; (*gestion*) management; (*auto*) steering.
diriger [diriʒe] *v* direct; (*gérer*) run, manage; (*arme*) point, aim; steer. **se diriger** find one's way. **se diriger vers** head for.
discerner [disɛrne] *v* discern; distinguish.
disciple [disiplə] *nm* disciple.
discipline [disiplin] *nf* discipline. **disciplinaire** *adj* disciplinary. **discipliner** *v* discipline, control.
discontinu [diskɔ̃tiny] *adj* discontinuous; intermittent.
discorde [diskɔrd] *nf* discord, dissension. **discordant** *adj* discordant.
discothèque [diskɔtɛk] *nf* record collection; (*club*) discotheque.
discours [diskur] *nm* speech.
discréditer [diskredite] *v* discredit. **discrédit** *nm* discredit.
discret, -ète [diskrɛ, -ɛt] *adj* discreet; quiet, sober; (*quantité*) discrete. **discrétion** *nf* discretion. **avec discrétion** discreetly. **discrétionnaire** *adj* discretionary.
discrimination [diskriminasjɔ̃] *nf* discrimination.
discussion [diskysjɔ̃] *nf* discussion; (*querelle*) argument.

discuter [diskyte] *v* discuss; question, dispute; (*protester*) argue. **discutable** *adj* debatable; questionable.
disette [dizɛt] *nf* scarcity, shortage.
disgrâce [disgrɑs] *nf* disgrace. **disgracié** *adj* in disgrace.
disgracieux [disgrasjø] *adj* inelegant; (*laid*) unsightly.
disloquer [dislɔke] *v* (*méd*) dislocate; (*désunir*) dismantle; (*briser*) break up; (*dissoudre*) disperse. **dislocation** *nf* dislocation.
***disparaître** [disparɛtrə] *v* disappear, vanish. **faire disparaître** get rid of, remove. **disparition** *nf* disappearance.
disparate [disparat] *adj* disparate, ill-assorted. **disparité** *nf* disparity.
disparu [dispary], **-e** *adj* vanished; (*époque*) bygone; (*mort*) dead; (*mil, etc.*) missing. *nm, nf* dead person; missing person.
dispendieux [dispɑ̃djø] *adj* extravagant, expensive.
dispenser [dispɑ̃se] *v* dispense; exempt. **se dispenser de** avoid, get out of. **dispense** *nf* exemption.
disperser [disperse] *v* disperse, scatter.
disponible [dispɔniblə] *adj* available, free. **disponibilité** *nf* availability.
dispos [dispo] *adj* alert, in good form.
disposer [dispoze] *v* arrange, lay out; (*engager*) dispose, incline. **disposer de** have at one's disposal. **se disposer à** be about to, prepare to. **disposition** *nf* arrangement; disposal; (*humeur*) mood; tendancy; aptitude; (*jur*) clause.
dispositif [dispozitif] *nm* device; plan of action.
disputer [dispyte] *v* fight, contest; (*fam*) tell off. **se disputer** quarrel; fight over. **dispute** *nf* quarrel.
disqualifier [diskalifje] *v* disqualify; (*discréditer*) dishonour. **disqualification** *nf* disqualification.
disque [disk] *nm* disc; (*musique*) record.
dissemblable [disɑ̃blablə] *adj* dissimilar, different. **dissemblance** *nf* dissimilarity.
disséminer [disemine] *v* scatter.
dissentiment [disɑ̃timɑ̃] *nm* disagreement.
disséquer [diseke] *v* dissect.
dissident [disidɑ̃], **-e** *n, adj* dissident. **dissidence** *nf* dissidence, rebellion.
dissimuler [disimyle] *v* conceal; disguise. **dissimulation** *nf* dissimulation.
dissiper [disipe] *v* dispel, disperse; (*gaspiller*) waste, squander. **dissipation** *nf* dissipation; dispersal.
dissocier [disɔsje] *v* dissociate. **dissociation** *nf* dissociation.
***dissoudre** [disudrə] *v* dissolve.
dissuader [disɥade] *v* dissuade. **dissuasion** *nf* dissuasion.
distance [distɑ̃s] *nf* distance. **distant** *adj* distant.
distiller [distile] *v* distil. **distillerie** *nf* distillery.
distinct [distɛ̃] *adj* distinct. **distinctif** *adj* distinctive. **distinction** *nf* distinction.
distinguer [distɛ̃ge] *v* distinguish; honour. **distingué** *adj* distinguished; eminent.
distraction [distraksjɔ̃] *nf* absent-mindedness, lack of attention; (*détente*) recreation, entertainment.
***distraire** [distrɛr] *v* distract; (*divertir*) entertain. **se distraire** amuse oneself. **distrait** *adj* absent-minded.
distribuer [distribɥe] *v* distribute; arrange; (*cartes*) deal; (*courrier*) deliver. **distributeur** *nm* distributor. **distributeur automatique** slot machine. **distribution** *nf* distribution; arrangement; delivery; (*acteurs*) cast.
divaguer [divage] *v* ramble.
divan [divɑ̃] *nm* divan.
diverger [divɛrʒe] *v* diverge. **divergence** *nf* divergence.
divers [divɛr] *adj* diverse; different; (*plusieurs*) various, several. **diversité** *nf* diversity, variety.
divertir [divɛrtir] *v* amuse, entertain. **divertissement** *nm* amusement, entertainment.
dividende [dividɑ̃d] *nm* dividend.
divin [divɛ̃] *adj* divine. **divinité** *nf* divinity.
diviser [divize] *v* divide. **divisible** *adj* divisible. **division** *nf* division; discord.
divorcer [divɔrse] *v* get divorced. **divorce** *nm* divorce. **divorcé, -e** *nm, nf* divorcee.
divulguer [divylge] *v* divulge, disclose.
dix [dis] *nm, adj* ten. **dixième** *n(m+f), adj* tenth.
dix-huit [dizɥit] *nm, adj* eighteen. **dix-huitième** *n(m+f), adj* eighteenth.
dix-neuf [diznœf] *nm, adj* nineteen. **dix-neuvième** *n(m+f), adj* nineteenth.
dix-sept [disɛt] *nm, adj* seventeen. **dix-septième** *n(m+f), adj* seventeenth.

dizaine [dizɛn] *nf* **une dizaine (de)** about ten.
docile [dɔsil] *adj* docile.
docte [dɔktə] *adj* learned.
docteur [dɔktœr] *nm* doctor.
doctrine [dɔktrin] *nf* doctrine.
document [dɔkymɑ̃] *nm* document. **documentaire** *nm, adj* documentary. **documentation** *nf* documentation, information, research. **documenter** *v* document, research.
dodu [dɔdy] *adj* (*fam*) plump, chubby.
dogmatique [dɔgmatik] *adj* dogmatic.
dogme [dɔgmə] *nm* dogma.
doigt [dwa] *nm* finger. **doigt de pied** toe. **doigté** *nm* (*musique*) fingering; tact.
doit [dwa] *nm* debit.
doléances [dɔleɑ̃s] *nf pl* complaints *pl*.
dollar [dɔlar] *nm* dollar.
domaine [dɔmɛn] *nm* domain; property, estate; sphere, field.
dôme [dom] *nm* dome.
domestique [dɔmɛstik] *n*(*m*+*f*) servant. *adj* domestic.
domestiquer [dɔmɛstike] *v* domesticate. **domestication** *nf* domestication.
domicile [dɔmisil] *nm* home, place of residence; address.
dominer [dɔmine] *v* dominate; surpass; (*contrôler*) master; prevail; (*donner sur*) overlook. **dominant** *adj* dominant, main. **dominateur, -trice** *adj* domineering. **domination** *nf* domination.
dominion [dɔminjɔn] *nm* dominion.
domino [dɔmino] *nm* domino.
dommage [dɔmaʒ] *nm* harm, damage. **dommages-intérêts** *nm pl* damages *pl*. **quel dommage!** what a pity!
dompter [dɔ̃te] *v* tame; subdue; master. **dompteur, -euse** *nm, nf* tamer.
don [dɔ̃] *nm* gift; talent; (*argent*) donation. **faire don de** donate. **donateur, -trice** *nm, nf* donor.
donc [dɔk] *conj* so, then, thus. **dis donc** I say; tell me. **tais-toi donc!** do be quiet!
donner [dɔne] *v* give; (*cartes*) deal; produce. **donner dans** fall into. **donner pour** present as, make out to be. **donner sur** overlook, open onto. **se donner à** devote oneself to. **donne** *nf* (*cartes*) deal. **donné** *adj* given. **étant donné que** seeing that. **données** *nf pl* data *pl*, facts *pl*. **donneur, -euse** *nm, nf* dealer; (*méd*) donor.
dont [dɔ̃] *pron* whose; (*objet*) of which; (*personne*) of whom.
dorénavant [dɔrenavɑ̃] *adv* from now on.
dorer [dɔre] *v* gild; (*cuisine*) brown; (*peau*) tan. **doré** *adj* gilt; (*blé, etc.*) golden.
dorloter [dɔrlɔte] *v* pamper, cosset.
***dormir** [dɔrmir] *v* sleep, be asleep. **dormir à poings fermés** sleep soundly.
dortoir [dɔrtwar] *nm* dormitory.
dorure [dɔryr] *nf* gilt, gilding.
dos [do] *nm* back; (*livre*) spine.
dose [doz] *nf* dose, dosage.
dossier [dosje] *nm* file; (*siège*) back.
dot [dɔt] *nf* dowry.
doter [dɔte] *v* endow; equip.
douane [dwan] *nf* customs *pl*. **exempté de douane** duty-free. **douanier, -ère** *nm, nf* customs officer.
double [dublə] *adj, adv* double. *nm* double; copy; duplicate.
doubler [duble] *v* double; (*école*) repeat; (*film*) dub; (*acteur*) stand in for; (*revêtir*) line; (*auto*) overtake. **doubler le pas** speed up. **doublage** *nm* dubbing; lining. **doublure** *nf* lining; (*acteur*) stand-in, understudy.
douceur [dusœr] *nf* softness; (*clémence*) mildness; (*goût, son, etc.*) sweetness; (*personne*) gentleness.
douche [duʃ] *nf* shower.
douer [dwe] *v* endow. **doué** *adj* gifted, talented.
douille [duj] *v* socket; cartridge case.
douillet, -ette [dujɛ, -ɛt] *adj* cosy, soft.
douleur [dulœr] *nf* pain; (*chagrin*) sorrow, distress. **douloureux** *adj* painful; distressing.
douter [dute] *v* **douter de** doubt. **se douter de** suspect. **doute** *nm* doubt. **mettre en doute** question. **sans doute** doubtless. **douteux** *adj* doubtful; uncertain; (*péj*) dubious.
douve [duv] *nf* moat, ditch.
Douvres [duvrə] *n* Dover.
doux, douce [du, dus] *adj* soft; (*clément, pas fort*) mild; (*agréable, sucré*) sweet; (*personne, pente*) gentle.
douze [duz] *nm, adj* twelve. **douzaine** *nf* dozen. **douzième** *n*(*m*+*f*), *adj* twelfth.
doyen [dwajɛ̃], **-enne** *nm, nf* dean; senior member.
drachme [drakmə] *nf* drachma.
dragée [draʒe] *nf* sugared almond.
dragon [dragɔ̃] *nm* dragon.

draguer [drage] *v* dredge, drag.
dramatiser [dramatize] *v* dramatize. **dramatique** *adj* dramatic.
dramaturge [dramatyrʒ] *nm, nf* dramatist, playwright.
drame [dram] *nm* drama.
drap [dra] *nm* sheet.
drapeau [drapo] *nm* flag.
draper [drape] *v* drape. **draperie** *nf* drapery. **drapier** *nm* draper.
dresser [drese] *v* put up, erect; (*liste, plan*) draw up; (*lever*) raise; (*animal*) train. **dresser l'oreille** prick up one's ears. **se dresser** stand (up); rise (up). **dressage** *nm* training. **dressoir** *nm* dresser.
drogue [drɔg] *nf* drug. **drogué, -e** *nm, nf* drug addict. **se droguer** take drugs.
droit[1] [drwa] *adj* (*côté*) right; (*ligne*) straight; (*vertical*) upright; honest. *adv* straight. **droitier** *adj* right-handed.
droit[2] [drwa] *nm* right; (*taxe*) duty; (*d'entrée, etc.*) fee, charge; (*jur*) law. **droits d'auteur** royalties *pl*. **droit de passage** right of way.
droite [drwat] *nf* right, right-hand side.
drôle [drol] *adj* funny. **drôlement** *adv* (*fam*) terribly, awfully.
dromadaire [drɔmadɛr] *nm* dromedary.
dru [dry] *adj* thick, dense. *adv* thick and fast; (*pluie*) heavily.
du [dy] *contraction of* **de le**.
dû, due [dy] *adj* owing, due. *nm* due.
duc [dyk] *nm* duke. **duchesse** *nf* duchess.
duel [dɥɛl] *nm* duel.
dûment [dymɑ̃] *adv* duly.
dune [dyn] *nf* dune.
Dunkerque [dœ̃kɛrk] *n* Dunkirk.
duo [dɥo] *nm* duet.
duper [dype] *v* dupe, deceive.
duquel [dykɛl] *contraction of* **de lequel**.
dur [dyr] *adj* hard, stiff, tough; (*pénible*) harsh. *adv* (*fam*) hard. **à la dure** rough. **durcir** *v* harden. **dureté** *nf* hardness.
durer [dyre] *v* last. **durable** *adj* lasting. **durant** *prep* during, for. **durée** *nf* duration, length; (*ampoule, pile, etc.*) life.
duvet [dyvɛ] *nm* down; sleeping-bag.
dynamique [dinamik] *adj* dynamic. *nf* dynamics. **dynamisme** *nm* dynamism.
dynamite [dinamit] *nf* dynamite.
dynamo [dinamo] *nf* dynamo.
dynastie [dinasti] *nf* dynasty.
dysenterie [disɑ̃tri] *nf* dysentery.
dyslexie [dislɛksi] *nf* dyslexia. **dyslexique** *n*(*m*+*f*), *adj* dyslexic.
dyspepsie [dispɛpsi] *nf* dyspepsia.

E

eau [o] *nf* water. **eau de Javel** bleach. **eau de vie** brandy. **eau douce** fresh water. **eau gazeuse** soda water. **eau minérale** mineral water. **eau potable** drinking water. **eau salée** salt water. **faire eau** leak. **prendre l'eau** leak.
ébahir [ebair] *v* astound. **ébahi** *adj* flabbergasted, dumbfounded. **ébahissement** *nm* astonishment.
ébats [eba] *nm pl* frolics *pl*.
ébaucher [eboʃe] *v* sketch out, outline. **s'ébaucher** take shape. **ébauche** *nf* outline, rough draft.
ébène [ebɛn] *nf* ebony.
éberlué [ebɛrlɥe] *adj* astounded, flabbergasted.
éblouir [ebluir] *v* dazzle. **éblouissement** *nm* dazzle; (*méd*) dizzy turn.
éboulement [ebulmɑ̃] *nm* landslide.
ébouriffer [eburife] *v* tousle, ruffle; (*fam*) amaze.
ébranler [ebrɑ̃le] *v* shake; (*affaiblir*) weaken. **s'ébranler** move off. **ébranlement** *nm* (*choc*) shock; weakening.
ébrécher [ebreʃe] *v* chip, nick; (*fortune*) break into. **ébréchure** *nf* chip, nick.
ébrouer [ebrue] *v* snort; (*s'agiter*) shake oneself. **ébrouement** *nm* snort.
ébullition [ebylisjɔ̃] *nf* boiling point; (*agitation*) turmoil. **en ébullition** boiling; (*ville, personne*) seething.
écailler [ekaje] *v* scale. **s'écailler** flake, peel. **écaille** *nf* scale; (*peinture*) flake; (*de tortue*) tortoise-shell. **écailleux** *adj* scaly; flaky.
écaler [ekale] *v* shell. **écale** *nf* shell.
écarlate [ekarlat] *nf, adj* scarlet.
écarquiller [ekarkije] *v* open wide.
écart [ekar] *nm* gap; difference; (*contradiction*) discrepancy; (*faute*) lapse. **à l'écart** on one side; (*isolé*) out of the way; (*distant*) aloof. **à l'écart de** well away from. **faire le grand écart** do the splits. **faire un écart** (*cheval*) shy; (*auto*) swerve.

écarter [ekarte] *v* separate, open; (*exclure*) dismiss; (*éloigner*) push aside, lead away from. **s'écarter** (*séparer*) part; (*s'éloigner*) move away; deviate, wander. **écarté** *adj* remote.
ecclésiastique [eklezjastik] *adj* ecclesiastical. *nm* ecclesiastic.
écervelé [esɛrvəle], **-e** *adj* scatterbrained. *nm*, *nf* scatterbrain.
échafaud [eʃafo] *nm* scaffold. **échafaudage** *nm* scaffolding.
échalier [eʃalje] *nm* stile.
échalote [eʃalɔt] *nf* shallot.
échancré [eʃɑ̃kre] *adj* (*robe*) V-necked, with a scooped neckline; (*côte*) indented; (*feuille*) serrated.
échanger [eʃɑ̃ʒe] *v* exchange. **échange** *nm* exchange. **échangeable** *adj* exchangeable.
échantillon [eʃɑ̃tijɔ̃] *nm* sample.
échapper [eʃape] *v* escape. **échapper à** escape (from). **laisser échapper** let out, let slip. **échappatoire** *nf* loophole, way out. **échappement** *nm* (*auto*) exhaust.
écharde [eʃard] *nf* splinter.
écharpe [eʃarp] *nf* scarf; (*méd*) sling; (*maire*) sash.
échasse [eʃɑs] *nf* stilt.
échauder [eʃode] *v* scald; (*laver*) wash in hot water; (*théière*) warm.
échauffer [eʃofe] *v* make hot; (*moteur*) overheat; excite. **s'échauffer** (*sport*) warm up; (*s'animer*) become heated. **échauffement** *nm* overheating; warm-up.
échéance [eʃeɑ̃s] *nf* expiry date; date of payment; term. **échéant** *adj* due, payable. **le cas échéant** if the case arises.
échec [eʃɛk] *nm* failure; (*revers*) setback; (*jeu*) check. **échec et mat** checkmate. **échecs** *nm pl* (*jeu*) chess *sing*.
échelle [eʃɛl]*nf* ladder; (*carte, etc.*) scale.
échelon [eʃlɔ̃] *nm* rung; step, grade; (*niveau*) level.
échelonner [eʃlɔne] *v* space *or* spread out; (*vacances, etc.*) stagger.
échevelé [eʃəvle] *adj* dishevelled; (*effréné*) wild.
échine [eʃin] *nf* spine.
échiquier [eʃikje] *nm* chessboard.
écho [eko] *nm* echo.
***échoir** [eʃwar] *v* fall due; expire.
échouer [eʃwe] *v* fail; (*naut*) run aground; (*aboutir*) end up. **faire échouer** foil, thwart.
éclabousser [eklabuse] *v* splash. **éclaboussure** *nf* splash; (*tache*) stain, smear.
éclair [eklɛr] *nm* flash; (*temps*) lightning; (*cuisine*) eclair.
éclaircir [eklɛrsir] *v* lighten; (*soupe, plantes*) thin; (*question, mystère*) explain, clarify. **s'éclaircir** (*temps*) clear up; thin out, become thin. **éclaircie** *nf* bright interval, break. **éclaircissement** *nm* clarification.
éclairer [eklere] *v* light up; (*problème, texte*) throw light on; (*personne*) enlighten. **s'éclairer** light up; (*rue, maison, etc.*) be lit. **éclairage** *nm* lighting. **éclaireur** *nm* scout. **éclaireuse** *nf* guide.
éclat [ekla] *nm* brightness; splendour, glamour; fragment, splinter; (*rire, colère*) burst; (*scandale*) fuss.
éclater [eklate] *v* (*pneu*) burst; (*bombe*) explode; (*briser*) break up, shatter; (*guerre*) break out. **éclater de rire** burst out laughing. **faire éclater** blow up. **éclatant** *adj* bright; (*fort*) loud; (*victoire*) resounding.
éclipse [eklips] *nf* eclipse. **éclipser** *v* eclipse.
éclisse [eklis] *nf* splint.
éclopé [eklɔpe] *adj* lame.
***éclore** [eklɔr] *v* hatch; (*fleur*) open out. **éclosion** *nf* hatching; (*apparition*) birth, dawn.
écluse [eklyz] *nf* lock.
écœurer [ekœre] *v* nauseate, sicken; disgust. **écœurant** *adj* disgusting; (*gâteau*) sickly. **écœurement** *nm* nausea; disgust; discouragement.
école [ekɔl] *nf* school. **école de secrétariat** secretarial college. **école maternelle** nursery school. **école normale** college of education. **faire l'école buissonnière** play truant. **écolier** *nm* schoolboy. **écolière** *nf* schoolgirl.
écologie [ekɔlɔʒi] *nf* ecology. **écologique** *adj* ecological.
***éconduire** [ekɔ̃dɥir] *v* dismiss; reject.
économe [ekɔnɔm] *adj* thrifty. **économie** *nf* economy; (*science*) economics; (*épargne*) saving. **faire des économies** save. **économique** *adj* economic.
économiser [ekɔnɔmize] *v* economize, save. **économiste** *n*(*m*+*f*) economist.
écoper [ekɔpe] *v* bale out.
écorcer [ekɔrse] *v* peel; (*arbre*) bark. **écorce** *nf* peel; bark.
écorcher [ekɔrʃe] *v* (*animal*) skin; (*égratigner*) graze, scratch; (*frotter*) chafe;

(*fam*: *estamper*) fleece. **écorchure** *nf* graze, scratch.
écorné [ekɔrne] *adj* (*livre*) dog-eared.
Écosse [ekɔs] *nf* Scotland. **écossais** *adj* Scottish, Scots; (*whisky*) Scotch; (*tissu*) tartan. **Écossais, -e** *nm, nf* Scot.
écot [eko] *nm* share.
écouler [ekule] *v* get rid of; (*comm*) move, sell. **s'écouler** (*liquide*) flow, ooze; pass; sell. **écoulement** *nm* flow; (*méd*) discharge; passing.
écourter [ekurte] *v* shorten.
écouter [ekute] *v* listen (to). **écouter aux portes** eavesdrop.
écouteur, -euse [ekutœr, -øz] *nm, nf* listener; eavesdropper. *nm* (*telephone*) receiver. **écouteurs** *nm pl* headphones *pl*.
écran [ekrɑ̃] *nm* screen.
écraser [ekrɑze] *v* crush; (*voiture*) run over; (*accabler*) overcome. **s'écraser** (*voiture, avion*) crash. **se faire écraser** get run over. **écrasant** *adj* overwhelming; (*poids*) crushing; (*travail*) gruelling.
écrémer [ekreme] *v* cream, skim.
écrevisse [ekrəvis] *nf* crayfish.
s'écrier [ekrije] *v* exclaim.
écrin [ekrɛ̃] *nm* jewel case.
***écrire** [ekrir] *v* write. **écrit** *nm* writing; (*examen*) written paper. **par écrit** in writing. **écriteau** *nm* notice. **écritoire** *nf* writing case. **écriture** *nf* writing; (*comm*) entry.
écrivain [ekrivɛ̃] *nm* writer.
écrou [ekru] *nm* nut.
s'écrouler [ekrule] *v* collapse, crumble, fall (down). **écroulement** *nm* collapse, fall.
écru [ekry] *adj* raw; (*toile*) unbleached.
écu [eky] *nm* shield.
écueil [ekœj] *nm* reef; (*piège*) pitfall.
écuelle [ekɥɛl] *nf* bowl.
écumer [ekyme] *v* skim; (*mousser*) foam, froth; pillage, scour. **écume** *nf* foam, froth; (*crasse*) scum. **écumeux** *adj* frothy.
écureuil [ekyrœj] *nm* squirrel.
écurie [ekyri] *nf* stable.
écuyer [ekɥije], **-ère** *nm* rider.
eczéma [ɛgzema] *nm* eczema.
édenté [edɑ̃te] *adj* toothless.
édifice [edifis] *nm* building; structure.
édifier [edifje] *v* edify; construct, build.
Edimbourg [edɛ̃bur] *n* Edinburgh.
édit [edi] *nm* edict.
éditer [edite] *v* publish; (*annoter*) edit. **éditeur, -trice** *nm, nf* publisher; editor.
édition *nf* publishing; edition. **éditorial** *nm* leading article.
édredon [edrədɔ̃] *nm* eiderdown.
éducation [edykɑsjɔ̃] *nf* education; (*familiale*) upbringing. **éducatif** *adj* educational.
éduquer [edyke] *v* educate; (*élever*) bring up.
effacer [efase] *v* erase, obliterate. **s'effacer** fade, wear away; (*s'écarter*) step aside. **effacé** *adj* faded; (*personne*) retiring.
effarer [efare] *v* alarm. **effarement** *nm* alarm.
effaroucher [efaruʃe] *v* scare; shock. **s'effaroucher** take fright; be shocked.
effectif [efɛktif] *adj* effective, actual, real. *nm* size, strength.
effectuer [efɛktɥe] *v* carry out, make, execute.
efféminé [efemine] *adj* effeminate.
effervescence [efɛrvesɑ̃s] *nf* effervescence; agitation, turmoil.
effet [efɛ] *nm* effect; impression; (*comm*) bill. **effets** *nm pl* things *pl*, clothes *pl*. **en effet** indeed.
s'effeuiller [efœje] *v* shed its leaves.
efficace [efikas] *adj* effective; (*personne*) efficient. **efficacité** *nf* effectiveness; efficiency.
effigie [efiʒi] *nf* effigy.
effiler [efile] *v* (*amincir*) taper; (*forme*) streamline; (*étoffe*) fray.
effleurer [eflœre] *v* touch lightly.
s'effondrer [efɔ̃dre] *v* collapse, cave in. **effondrement** *nm* collapse.
s'efforcer [efɔrse] *v* try hard, do one's best.
effort [efɔr] *nm* effort; (*tech*) stress.
effrayer [efreje] *v* frighten.
effréné [efrene] *adj* wild, frantic.
effriter [efrite] *v* crumble.
effroi [efrwɑ] *nm* terror. **effroyable** *adj* appalling.
effronté [efrɔ̃te] *adj* insolent, cheeky; (*ehonté*) brazen. **effronterie** *nf* insolence.
égal [egal], **-e** *adj* equal; (*constant*) even. **ça m'est égal** I don't mind. *nm, nf* equal. **également** *adv* equally; (*aussi*) also. **égaler** *v* equal, match. **égalité** *nf* equality; evenness.
égaliser [egalize] *v* equalize; (*sol*) level out.
égard [egar] *nm* respect, consideration. **à l'égard de** (*envers*) towards; concerning. **avoir égard à** take into account.

égarer [egare] *v* lead astray; (*perdre*) mislay. **s'égarer** get lost. **égaré** *adj* lost; (*animal*) stray; (*isolé*) remote; (*éperdu*) distraught.
égayer [egeje] *v* brighten up; (*divertir*) amuse.
église [egliz] *nf* church.
égocentrique [egɔsɑ̃trik] *adj* self-centred.
égoïste [egɔist] *adj* selfish. **égoïsme** *nm* selfishness.
égorger [egɔrʒe] *v* cut the throat of.
égout [egu] *nm* sewer, drain.
égoutter [egute] *v* drain; (*linge*) drip. **égouttoir** *nm* draining board.
égratigner [egratiɲe] *v* scratch, scrape. **égratignure** *nf* scratch.
égrener [egrəne] *v* (*écosser*) shell; (*raisins*) pick off; (*chapelet*) say.
éhonté [eɔ̃te] *adj* shameless, brazen.
éjaculer [eʒakyle] *v* ejaculate. **éjaculation** *nf* ejaculation.
éjecter [eʒɛkte] *v* eject.
élaborer [elabɔre] *v* work out, elaborate.
élaguer [elage] *v* prune. **élagage** *nm* pruning.
élan [elɑ̃] *nm* rush, surge; (*vitesse*) momentum; vigour, spirit.
s'élancer [elɑ̃se] *v* rush, dash. **élancé** *adj* slender. **élancement** *nm* sharp pain.
élargir [elarʒir] *v* widen, stretch; (*jur*) release.
élastique [elastik] *adj* elastic; flexible. *nm* elastic; rubber band.
élection [elɛksjɔ̃] *nf* election; choice. **élection partielle** by-election.
électoral [elɛktɔral] *adj* electoral. **électorat** *nm* electorate.
électricité [elɛktrisite] *nf* electricity. **électricien** *nm* electrician.
électrique [elɛktrik] *adj* electric.
électriser [elɛktrize] *v* electrify.
électrocuter [elɛktrɔkyte] *v* electrocute. **électrocution** *nf* electrocution.
électrode [elɛktrɔd] *nf* electrode.
électronique [elɛktrɔnik] *adj* electronic. *nf* electronics.
électrophone [elɛktrɔfɔn] *nm* record player.
élégant [elegɑ̃] *adj* elegant. **élégance** *nf* elegance.
élégie [eleʒi] *nf* elegy.
élément [elemɑ̃] *nm* element; fact; (*préfabriqué*) unit. **éléments** *nm pl* rudiments *pl*. **élémentaire** *adj* elementary, basic.
éléphant [elefɑ̃] *nm* elephant.
élevage [ɛlvaʒ] *nm* breeding, rearing; farm. **faire l'élevage de** breed, rear.
élévation [elevɑsjɔ̃] *nf* elevation; (*action*) raising; erection.
élève [elɛv] *n(m+f)* pupil, student.
élever [ɛlve] *v* raise; (*enfant*) bring up; (*animal*) rear, breed; erect. **s'élever** rise, go up. **s'élever à** add up to. **élevé** *adj* high, lofty. **bien/mal élevé** well-/ill-mannered.
elfe [ɛlf] *nm* elf.
éligible [eliʒiblə] *adj* eligible.
éliminer [elimine] *v* eliminate. **élimination** *nf* elimination.
***élire** [elir] *v* elect.
élite [elit] *nf* elite.
elle [ɛl] *pron* (*sujet*: *personne*) she; (*objet*: *personne*) her; (*chose*, *animal*) it. **elle-même** *pron* herself; itself. **elles** *pron* (*sujet*) they; (*objet*) them. **elles-mêmes** *pron* themselves.
ellipse [elips] *nf* ellipse. **elliptique** *adj* elliptical.
élocution [elɔkysjɔ̃] *nf* elocution, diction. **défaut d'élocution** *nm* speech impediment.
éloge [elɔʒ] *nm* praise. **faire l'éloge de** praise.
éloigner [elwaɲe] *v* remove; move *or* take away; (*ajourner*) postpone. **s'éloigner** go away. **éloigné** *adj* distant, far. **éloignement** *nm* distance; removal; absence; postponement.
éloquent [elɔkɑ̃] *adj* eloquent. **éloquence** *nf* eloquence.
élu [ely], **-e** *adj* elected, chosen. *nm*, *nf* elected member *or* representative.
éluder [elyde] *v* evade, elude.
émaciation [emasjɑsjɔ̃] *nf* emaciation. **émacié** *adj* emaciated.
émail [emaj] *nm*, *pl* **-aux** enamel. **émailler** *v* enamel; (*parsemer*) dot.
émanciper [emɑ̃sipe] *v* emancipate, liberate. **émancipation** *nf* emancipation, liberation.
emballer [ɑ̃bale] *v* pack, wrap; (*fam*) thrill. **s'emballer** (*moteur*) race; (*cheval*) bolt; (*fam*) get worked up. **emballage** *nm* packing, wrapping; (*comm*) package.
embarcadère [ɑ̃barkadɛr] *nm* landing stage, pier.
embardée [ɑ̃barde] *nf* swerve. **faire une embardée** swerve.

embargo [ɑ̃bargo] *nm* embargo.
embarquer [ɑ̃barke] *v* embark, board; (*cargaison*) load. **s'embarquer dans** (*fam*) get involved in. **embarquement** *nm* boarding; loading.
embarras [ɑ̃bara] *nm* obstacle; (*gêne*) embarrassment; (*situation difficile*) predicament; dilemma. **faire des embarras** make a fuss.
embarrasser [ɑ̃barase] *v* hinder, hamper; put in a predicament. **s'embarrasser** be troubled; (*s'emmêler*) get tangled up. **embarrassant** *adj* awkward. **embarrassé** *adj* embarrassed, ill-at-ease; confused.
embaucher [ɑ̃boʃe] *v* take on, hire.
embaumer [ɑ̃bome] *v* embalm; perfume; (*sentir bon*) be fragrant.
embellir [ɑ̃belir] *v* make attractive; embellish. **embellissement** *nm* embellishment.
embêter [ɑ̃bete] (*fam*) *v* bother, annoy. **s'embêter** be fed up. **embêtement** *nm* nuisance, annoyance.
emblée [ɑ̃ble] *adv* **d'emblée** straight away.
emblème [ɑ̃blɛm] *nm* emblem.
emboîter [ɑ̃bwate] *v* fit together.
embouchure [ɑ̃buʃyr] *nf* (*fleuve*) mouth; (*musique*) mouthpiece.
embouteiller [ɑ̃buteje] *v* block. **embouteillage** *nm* traffic jam.
emboutir [ɑ̃butir] *v* crash into.
embrancher [ɑ̃brɑ̃ʃe] *v* join up. **embranchement** *nm* branch; junction.
embraser [ɑ̃brɑze] *v* set ablaze. **s'embraser** blaze up, flare up. **embrasement** *nm* blaze.
embrasser [ɑ̃brase] *v* embrace; (*donner un baiser*) kiss.
embrayer [ɑ̃breje] *v* (*auto*) let in the clutch. **embrayage** *nm* clutch.
embrouiller [ɑ̃bruje] *v* muddle (up); (*ficelle*) tangle (up).
embryon [ɑ̃brijɔ̃] *nm* embryo.
embuscade [ɑ̃byskad] *nf* ambush.
éméché [emeʃe] *adj* tipsy.
émeraude [ɛmrod] *nf*, *adj* emerald.
émerger [emɛrʒe] *v* emerge.
émerveiller [emɛrveje] *v* fill with wonder. **s'émerveiller de** marvel at. **émerveillement** *nm* wonder.
***émettre** [emɛtrə] *v* give out, emit; (*TV, radio*) transmit, broadcast; (*monnaie, etc.*) issue. **émetteur** *nm* transmitter.
émeu [emø] *nm* emu.
émeute [emøt] *nf* riot.
émietter [emjete] *v* crumble; split up, disperse.
émigrer [emigre] *v* emigrate; (*oiseau*) migrate. **émigrant, -e** *nm, nf* emigrant. **émigration** *nf* emigration.
éminent [eminɑ̃] *adj* eminent.
émission [emisjɔ̃] *nf* (*radio, TV*) programme, broadcast; emission; issue.
emmagasiner [ɑ̃magazine] *v* store (up). **emmagasinage** *nm* storage.
emmancher [ɑ̃mɑ̃ʃe] *v* put a handle on; (*fam*) make a start (on).
emmanchure [ɑ̃mɑ̃ʃyr] *nf* armhole.
emmêler [ɑ̃mele] *v* tangle; confuse, muddle.
emménager [ɑ̃menaʒe] *v* move in.
emmener [ɑ̃mne] *v* take (away), (*équipe*) lead.
emmitoufler [ɑ̃mitufle] *v* muffle up.
émoi [emwa] *nm* agitation, commotion.
émonder [emɔ̃de] *v* prune.
émotion [emosjɔ̃] *nf* emotion; (*peur*) fright. **émotif** *or* **émotionnel** *adj* emotional.
émousser [emuse] *v* blunt, dull. **émoussé** *adj* blunt.
***émouvoir** [emuvwar] *v* move, affect; (*indigner*) rouse; (*troubler*) upset. **émouvant** *adj* (*compassion*) moving, touching; (*admiration*) stirring.
empailler [ɑ̃pɑje] *v* stuff.
empaqueter [ɑ̃pakte] *v* pack, wrap up. **empaquetage** *nm* packing.
emparer [ɑ̃pare] *v* **s'emparer de** seize, take possession of.
empâter [ɑ̃pɑte] *v* thicken, fatten.
empêcher [ɑ̃peʃe] *v* prevent, stop. **n'empêche (que)** all the same.
empereur [ɑ̃prœr] *nm* emperor.
empeser [ɑ̃pəze] *v* starch.
empester [ɑ̃pɛste] *v* stink.
s'empêtrer [ɑ̃petre] *v* get entangled *or* involved.
empiéter [ɑ̃pjete] *v* encroach.
s'empiffrer [ɑ̃pifre] *v* (*fam*) stuff oneself.
empiler [ɑ̃pile] *v* pile, stack.
empire [ɑ̃pir] *nm* empire; influence.
empirer [ɑ̃pire] *v* worsen.
empirique [ɑ̃pirik] *adj* empirical.
emplacement [ɑ̃plasmɑ̃] *nm* site.
emplâtre [ɑ̃plɑtrə] *nm* plaster.
emplette [ɑ̃plɛt] *nf* purchase. **faire des emplettes** do some shopping.

emplir [ɑ̃plir] *v* fill.
emploi [ɑ̃plwa] *nm* use; (*poste*) job, employment. **emploi du temps** timetable, schedule.
employer [ɑ̃plwaje] *v* use; (*ouvrier*) employ. **s'employer à** apply oneself to. **employé, -e** *nm, nf* employee; (*bureau*) clerk. **employeur, -euse** *nm, nf* employer.
empoigner [ɑ̃pwaɲe] *v* grasp, grab; (*lecture, etc.*) grip.
empoisonner [ɑ̃pwazɔne] *v* poison; (*empester*) stink; (*fam*) annoy, aggravate. **empoisonnement** *nm* poisoning; (*fam*) bother.
emporter [ɑ̃pɔrte] *v* take (away); (*entraîner*) carry away *or* along; (*gagner*) win. **l'emporter sur** get the better of. **s'emporter** lose one's temper. **emporté** *adj* angry; (*personne*) quick-tempered. **emportement** *nm* anger.
s'empourprer [ɑ̃purpre] *v* flush, turn crimson.
***empreindre** [ɑ̃prɛ̃drə] *v* imprint; (*marquer*) stamp, tinge.
empreinte [ɑ̃prɛ̃t] *nf* impression; mark, stamp; (*animal*) track. **empreinte de pas** footprint. **empreinte digitale** fingerprint.
s'empresser [ɑ̃prese] *v* (*se hâter*) hurry; (*s'affairer*) bustle around. **empressé** *adj* attentive; (*péj*) over-zealous. **empressement** *nm* attentiveness; (*hâte*) eagerness.
emprisonner [ɑ̃prizɔne] *v* imprison. **emprisonnement** *nm* imprisonment.
emprunter [ɑ̃prœ̃te] *v* borrow; derive. **emprunt** *nm* loan. **d'emprunt** (*nom*) assumed. **emprunté** *adj* ill-at-ease, awkward.
ému [emy] *adj* moved, touched; excited; emotional.
emulsion [emylsjɔ̃] *nf* emulsion.
en[1] [ɑ̃] *prep* in; (*à*) to; (*transport*) by; (*comme*) as; (*composition*) made of; (*durée*) while, when.
en[2] [ɑ̃] *pron* of it *or* them; (*lieu*) from there; (*cause*) about it; (*des*) some, any.
encadrer [ɑ̃kadre] *v* frame; (*entourer*) surround; (*instruire*) train. **encadrement** *nm* frame; training.
encaisser [ɑ̃kese] *v* collect; (*chèque*) cash. **encaisse** *nf* cash in hand.
enceinte[1] [ɑ̃sɛ̃t] *adj* pregnant.
enceinte[2] [ɑ̃sɛ̃t] *nf* enclosure; (*mur*) surrounding wall; (*palissade*) fence.
encens [ɑ̃sɑ̃] *nm* incense.
encercler [ɑ̃sɛrkle] *v* surround, encircle.
enchaîner [ɑ̃ʃene] *v* chain up; (*lier*) link together; continue, carry on. **enchaînement** *nm* series, chain.
enchanter [ɑ̃ʃɑ̃te] *v* enchant; (*ravir*) delight. **enchanté** *adj* delighted; (*salutation*) pleased to meet you. **enchantement** *nm* enchantment; magic; delight.
enchère [ɑ̃ʃɛr] *nf* bid. **enchères** *nf pl* auction *sing*.
enchérir [ɑ̃ʃerir] *v* **enchérir sur** (*comm*) bid higher than; (*dépasser*) go further than. **enchérisseur, -euse** *nm, nf* bidder.
enchevêtrer [ɑ̃ʃəvetre] *v* entangle; confuse, muddle.
enclin [ɑ̃klɛ̃] *adj* inclined, prone.
***enclore** [ɑ̃klɔr] *v* enclose, shut in.
enclos [ɑ̃klo] *nm* enclosure; (*chevaux*) paddock.
enclume [ɑ̃klym] *nf* anvil.
encoche [ɑ̃kɔʃ] *nf* notch.
encoignure [ɑ̃kɔɲyr] *nf* corner.
encolure [ɑ̃kɔlyr] *nf* neck; (*comm*) collar size.
encombrer [ɑ̃kɔ̃bre] *v* clutter, obstruct; (*ligne téléphonique*) block. **s'encombrer de** load oneself with. **encombrant** *adj* cumbersome. **sans encombre** without mishap. **encombrement** *nm* congestion; clutter.
encontre [ɑ̃kɔ̃trə] *prep* **à l'encontre de** against, counter to; contrary to.
encore [ɑ̃kɔr] *adv* (*toujours*) still; (*de nouveau*) again; (*en plus*) more; (*aussi*) also; (*même*) even. **pas encore** not yet.
encorner [ɑ̃kɔrne] *v* gore.
encourager [ɑ̃kuraʒe] *v* encourage. **encouragement** *nm* encouragement.
***encourir** [ɑ̃kurir] *v* incur.
encrasser [ɑ̃krase] *v* clog (up); (*salir*) dirty.
encre [ɑ̃krə] *nf* ink.
encroûter [ɑ̃krute] *v* encrust. **s'encroûter** (*fam*) get into a rut.
encyclopédie [ɑ̃siklɔpedi] *nf* encyclopedia.
endémique [ɑ̃demik] *adj* endemic.
s'endetter [ɑ̃dete] *v* get into debt. **endetté** *adj* in debt.
endiablé [ɑ̃djable] *adj* boisterous, wild.
s'endimancher [ɑ̃dimɑ̃ʃe] *v* put on one's Sunday best.
endive [ɑ̃div] *nf* endive; chicory.
endoctriner [ɑ̃dɔktrine] *v* indoctrinate. **endoctrination** *nf* indoctrination.

endolori [ɑ̃dɔlɔri] *adj* painful.
endommager [ɑ̃dɔmaʒe] *v* damage. **endommagement** *nm* damage.
***endormir** [ɑ̃dɔrmir] *v* send to sleep; (*douleur*) deaden. **s'endormir** *v* fall asleep. **endormi** *adj* asleep.
endosser [ɑ̃dose] *v* (*vêtement*) put on; (*chèque, etc.*) endorse. **endossement** *nm* endorsement.
endroit [ɑ̃drwa] *nm* place; (*roman, film, etc.*) point, part. **à l'endroit** (*vêtement*) the right side out; (*objet*) the right way round.
***enduire** [ɑ̃dɥir] *v* coat. **enduit** *nm* coating.
endurcir [ɑ̃dyrsir] *v* harden.
endurer [ɑ̃dyre] *v* endure. **endurance** *nf* endurance.
énergie [enɛrʒi] *nf* energy; (*fermeté*) spirit, force. **énergique** *adj* energetic; forceful.
énerver [enɛrve] *v* irritate. **s'énerver** get excited.
enfant [ɑ̃fɑ̃] *n(m+f)* child (*pl* children). **enfant unique** only child. **enfance** *nf* childhood; (*bébé*) infancy. **enfantin** *adj* childlike; (*puéril*) childish.
enfanter [ɑ̃fɑ̃te] *v* give birth (to).
enfer [ɑ̃fɛr] *nm* hell.
enfermer [ɑ̃fɛrme] *v* shut up *or* in; (*sous clef*) lock up.
enfiler [ɑ̃file] *v* thread; (*fam*: *vêtement*) slip on; (*rue, etc.*) take.
enfin [ɑ̃fɛ̃] *adv* at last, finally; (*bref*) in short; (*après tout*) after all.
enflammer [ɑ̃flame] *v* (*allumer*) set fire to; (*irriter*) inflame. **s'enflammer** catch fire; (*colère, désir*) flare up. **enflammé** *adj* blazing; inflamed.
enfler [ɑ̃fle] *v* swell. **enflé** *adj* swollen. **enflure** *nf* swelling.
enfoncer [ɑ̃fɔ̃se] *v* (*clou, etc.*) drive in; (*porte*) break down. **s'enfoncer** sink, plunge.
enfouir [ɑ̃fwir] *v* bury.
***enfreindre** [ɑ̃frɛ̃drə] *v* infringe.
***s'enfuir** [ɑ̃fɥir] *v* run away.
engager [ɑ̃gaʒe] *v* engage; (*lier*) bind; (*entraîner*) involve; (*clef, etc.*) insert. **s'engager** (*promettre*) commit oneself, undertake; (*mil*) enlist. **engagement** *nm* (*promesse*) agreement; enlistment; (*acteur*) engagement.
engelure [ɑ̃ʒlyr] *nf* chilblain.
engendrer [ɑ̃ʒɑ̃dre] *v* generate, create.
engin [ɑ̃ʒɛ̃] *nm* machine; (*outil*) tool.
englober [ɑ̃glɔbe] *v* include.
engloutir [ɑ̃glutir] *v* (*navire*) swallow up; (*manger*) gulp down.
engorger [ɑ̃gɔrʒe] *v* block.
engouffrer [ɑ̃gufre] *v* engulf; (*fam*: *manger*) wolf down. **s'engouffrer** rush.
engourdir [ɑ̃gurdir] *v* numb; (*esprit*) dull. **engourdi** *adj* numb. **engourdissement** *nm* numbness.
engrais [ɑ̃grɛ] *nm* fertilizer; (*organique*) manure.
engraisser [ɑ̃grese] *v* (*animal*) fatten up; (*terre*) fertilize.
engrenage [ɑ̃grənaʒ] *nm* (*tech*) gearing; (*enchaînement*) chain.
engueuler [ɑ̃gœle] (*fam*) *v* shout at. **s'engueuler** have a row. **engueulade** *nf* shouting at; (*dispute*) row.
enhardir [ɑ̃ardir] *v* embolden. **s'enhardir** become bolder.
énigme [enigmə] *nf* (*mystère*) enigma; (*devinette*) riddle, puzzle. **énigmatique** *adj* enigmatic.
enivrer [ɑ̃nivre] *v* intoxicate. **s'enivrer** get drunk. **enivrement** *nm* intoxication.
enjamber [ɑ̃ʒɑ̃be] *v* step over; (*pont*) straddle. **enjambée** *nf* stride.
enjeu [ɑ̃ʒø] *nm* stake.
enjôler [ɑ̃ʒole] *v* coax.
enjoliveur [ɑ̃ʒɔlivœr] *nm* (*auto*) hub cap.
enjoué [ɑ̃ʒwe] *adj* jolly, playful. **enjouement** *nm* jollity, playfulness.
enlacer [ɑ̃lase] *v* entwine. **s'enlacer** (*fils*) intertwine; (*amants*) embrace.
enlaidir [ɑ̃ledir] *v* (*déparer*) make ugly; (*personne*) become ugly.
enlever [ɑ̃lve] *v* remove, take off *or* away; kidnap. **s'enlever** come off. **enlèvement** *nm* kidnapping; removal.
enliser [ɑ̃lize] *v* get stuck. **s'enliser** sink.
ennemi [ɛnmi], **-e** *nm, nf* enemy. *adj* hostile. **être ennemi de** be opposed to.
ennui [ɑ̃nɥi] *nm* boredom; (*difficulté*) trouble.
ennuyer [ɑ̃nɥije] *v* (*lasser*) bore; (*inquiéter*) worry; (*importuner*) bother; (*agacer*) annoy. **s'ennuyer** be bored. **ennuyeux** *adj* boring, annoying.
énoncer [enɔ̃se] *v* state.
enorgueillir [ɑ̃nɔrgœjir] *v* make proud. **s'enorgueillir de** boast about.
énorme [enɔrm] *adj* enormous. **énormément** *adv* tremendously. **énormément de** a tremendous amount of.

s'enquérir [ɑ̃kerir] *v* inquire. **s'enquérir de** ask after.
enquête [ɑ̃kɛt] *nf* inquiry; (*police*) investigation; (*sondage*) survey; (*mort*) inquest. **enquêter** *v* investigate.
enraciné [ɑ̃rasine] *adj* deep-rooted, entrenched.
enragé [ɑ̃raʒe], **-e** *nm, nf* (*fam*) fanatic. *adj* furious; (*fam*) mad keen. **enrager** *v* be furious.
enrayer [ɑ̃reje] *v* (*maladie*) check; (*machine*) jam. **s'enrayer** jam.
enregistrer [ɑ̃rʒistre] *v* register; (*son*) record. **enregistrement** *nm* registration; recording.
s'enrhumer [ɑ̃ryme] *v* catch a cold. **être enrhumé** have a cold.
enrichir [ɑ̃riʃir] *v* enrich. **enrichissement** *nm* enrichment.
enrôler [ɑ̃role] *v* enrol; (*mil*) enlist. **enrôlé** *nm* recruit. **enrôlement** *nm* enrolment; enlistment.
enroué [ɑ̃rwe] *v* hoarse.
enseigne [ɑ̃sɛɲ] *nf* sign; (*mil, naut*) ensign.
enseigner [ɑ̃seɲe] *v* teach. **enseignant, -e** *nm, nf* teacher. **enseignement** *nm* education; teaching.
ensemble [ɑ̃sɑ̃blə] *adv* together. *nm* whole; unity; (*groupe*) set; (*vêtements*) outfit. **dans l'ensemble** on the whole. **d'ensemble** overall.
ensemencer [ɑ̃smɑ̃se] *v* sow.
ensevelir [ɑ̃səvlir] *v* bury; (*cacher*) shroud, hide.
ensoleillé [ɑ̃sɔleje] *adj* sunny.
ensorceler [ɑ̃sɔrsəle] *v* bewitch, cast a spell on.
ensuite [ɑ̃sɥit] *adv* then, next; afterwards.
***s'ensuivre** [ɑ̃sɥivrə] *v* follow.
entaille [ɑ̃taj] *nf* cut, gash, notch. **entailler** *v* cut, gash, notch.
entamer [ɑ̃tame] *v* start (on), open; (*couper*) cut into.
entasser [ɑ̃tase] *v* pile up; amass; (*serrer*) cram.
entendre [ɑ̃tɑ̃drə] *v* hear; (*écouter*) listen to; (*comprendre*) understand; intend, mean. **entendre parler de** hear of. **s'entendre** agree; (*s'accorder*) get on. **entendu** *adj* agreed; understood. **bien entendu** of course.
entente [ɑ̃tɑ̃t] *nf* understanding; (*accord*) agreement; harmony.
enterrer [ɑ̃tere] *v* bury. **enterrement** *nm* burial; (*cérémonie*) funeral.
en-tête *nm* heading. **papier à lettres à en-tête** *nm* headed notepaper.
entêté [ɑ̃tete] *adj* stubborn. **entêtement** *nm* stubbornness.
enthousiaste [ɑ̃tuzjast] *n*(*m*+*f*) enthusiast. *adj* enthusiastic. **enthousiasme** *nm* enthusiasm. **s'enthousiasmer** *v* be enthusiastic.
enticher [ɑ̃tiʃe] *v* **s'enticher de** become infatuated with.
entier [ɑ̃tje] *adj* entire, whole; intact; absolute. **en entier** totally. **tout entier** entirely, completely.
entité [ɑ̃tite] *nf* entity.
entonnoir [ɑ̃tɔnwar] *nm* funnel.
entorse [ɑ̃tɔrs] *nf* sprain, twist.
entortiller [ɑ̃tɔrtije] *v* twist, wind; (*fam*: *enjôler*) get round. **s'entortiller** twist; get entangled.
entourer [ɑ̃ture] *v* surround. **entourage** *nm* circle, entourage; (*bordure*) surround.
entracte [ɑ̃trakt] *nm* interval, interlude.
entrailles [ɑ̃traj] *nf pl* entrails *pl*.
entrain [ɑ̃trɛ̃] *nm* spirit, gusto.
entraîner [ɑ̃trene] *v* carry along; (*causer*) bring about; (*athlète*) train; (*influencer*) lead. **entraînement** *nm* training; force, impetus. **entraîneur, -euse** *nm, nf* trainer, coach.
entraver [ɑ̃trave] *v* hinder; (*animal*) shackle. **entrave** *nf* hindrance; shackle.
entre [ɑ̃trə] *prep* between; (*parmi*) among; (*dans*) in.
entrebâillé [ɑ̃trəbɑje] *adj* ajar.
s'entrechoquer [ɑ̃trəʃɔke] *v* knock together; (*verres*) clink.
entrecouper [ɑ̃trəkupe] *v* interrupt, intersperse. **s'entrecouper** intersect.
s'entrecroiser [ɑ̃trəkrwaze] *v* (*fils*) intertwine; (*lignes*) intersect.
entrée [ɑ̃tre] *nf* entry, entrance; (*accès*) admission; (*début*) outset; (*cuisine*) first course, entrée.
entrefaites [ɑ̃trəfɛt] *nf pl* **sur ces entrefaites** at that moment.
entrefilet [ɑ̃trəfilɛ] *nm* paragraph; (*journal*) item.
entremets [ɑ̃trəmɛ] *nm* dessert.
***s'entremettre** [ɑ̃trəmɛtrə] *v* intervene. **entremise** *nf* intervention.
entrepôt [ɑ̃trəpo] *nm* warehouse.
***entreprendre** [ɑ̃trəprɑ̃drə] *v* undertake;

(*commencer*) begin, embark upon. **entreprenant** *adj* enterprising.
entrepreneur, -euse [ɑ̃trəprənœr, -øz] *nm, nf* contractor. **entrepreneur de pompes funèbres** undertaker.
entreprise [ɑ̃trəpriz] *nf* firm; enterprise, venture.
entrer [ɑ̃tre] *v* enter, go *or* come in. **faire entrer** (*personne*) show in; (*objet*) put in. **laisser entrer** let in.
entre-temps *adv* meanwhile.
***entretenir** [ɑ̃trətnir] *v* maintain; (*famille*) support; (*sentiment*) keep alive. **s'entretenir** converse; support oneself. **entretien** *nm* maintenance, upkeep; (*subsistance*) keep; discussion, conversation; interview.
***entrevoir** [ɑ̃trəvwar] *v* make out, glimpse.
entrevue [ɑ̃trəvy] *nf* meeting; interview.
entrouvert [ɑ̃truvɛr] *adj* half-open.
envahir [ɑ̃vair] *v* invade; (*occuper*) overrun. **envahissement** *nm* invasion. **envahisseur, -euse** *nm, nf* invader.
envelopper [ɑ̃vlɔpe] *v* wrap; (*entourer*) envelop, shroud. **enveloppe** *nf* envelope; (*emballage*) wrapping, covering.
envenimer [ɑ̃vnime] *v* poison; aggravate. **s'envenimer** fester.
envergure [ɑ̃vɛrgyr] *nf* scope, range; (*ailes*) wingspan; calibre.
envers[1] [ɑ̃vɛr] *prep* towards, to.
envers[2] [ɑ̃vɛr] *nm* wrong side; (*médaille*) reverse. **à l'envers** (*vêtement*) inside out; (*dessus dessous*) upside down; (*devant derrière*) back to front.
envier [ɑ̃vje] *v* envy. **enviable** *adj* enviable. **envie** *nf* desire; envy; (*anat*) birthmark. **avoir envie de** want, fancy. **envieux** *adj* envious.
environ [ɑ̃virɔ̃] *adv* about. **environs** *nm pl* surroundings *pl*, vicinity *sing*.
environnement [ɑ̃virɔnmɑ̃] *nm* environment.
envisager [ɑ̃vizaʒe] *v* envisage; consider.
envoi [ɑ̃vwa] *nm* sending; (*colis*) parcel, consignment.
s'envoler [ɑ̃vɔle] *v* fly away; (*avion*) take off; disappear, vanish.
***envoyer** [ɑ̃vwaje] *v* send. **envoyer chercher** send for. **envoyé, -e** *nm, nf* messenger; (*pol*) envoy; (*journal*) correspondent.
enzyme [ɑ̃zim] *nm* enzyme.
épagneul [epaɲœl] *nm* spaniel.
épais, -aisse [epɛ, -ɛs] *adj* thick. **épaisseur** *nf* thickness; (*neige, nuit*) depth. **épaissir** *v* thicken.
épancher [epɑ̃ʃe] *v* (*sentiments*) pour out; (*colère*) vent.
épandre [epɑ̃drə] *v* spread.
s'épanouir [epanwir] *v* blossom, open out; (*visage*) light up. **épanoui** *adj* (*fleur*) in full bloom; (*sourire*) radiant.
épargner [eparɲe] *v* save, spare. **épargne** *nf* saving.
éparpiller [eparpije] *v* scatter, disperse.
épars [epar] *adj* scattered.
épater [epate] (*fam*) *v* amaze, stagger. **épatement** *nm* amazement.
épaule [epol] *nf* shoulder.
épave [epav] *nf* wreck, ruin; (*débris*) wreckage.
épée [epe] *nf* sword.
épeler [ɛple] *v* spell.
éperdu [epɛrdy] *adj* distraught, frantic; passionate.
éperon [eprɔ̃] *nm* spur. **éperonner** *v* spur on.
éphémère [efemɛr] *adj* ephemeral, short-lived.
épi [epi] *nm* (*blé*) ear; (*cheveux*) tuft.
épice [epis] *nf* spice.
épicier [episje], **-ère** *nm, nf* grocer. **épicerie** *nf* grocer's; (*aliments*) groceries *pl*.
épidémie [epidemi] *nf* epidemic. **épidémique** *adj* epidemic; contagious.
épier [epje] *v* spy on; (*guetter*) watch for.
épilepsie [epilɛpsi] *nf* epilepsy. **épileptique** *n(m+f)*, *adj* epileptic.
épiler [epile] *v* remove hair from; (*sourcils*) pluck.
épilogue [epilɔg] *nm* epilogue; conclusion.
épinards [epinar] *nm pl* spinach *sing*.
épine [epin] *nf* (*plante*) thorn; (*animal*) spine, quill. **épine dorsale** backbone. **épineux** *adj* thorny; (*situation*) tricky.
épingle [epɛ̃glə] *nf* pin. **épingle à cheveux** hairpin. **épingle de nourrice** *or* **sûreté** safety-pin. **épingler** *v* pin.
Épiphanie [epifani] *nf* Twelfth Night, Epiphany.
épique [epik] *adj* epic.
épiscopal [episkɔpal] *adj* episcopal.
épisode [epizɔd] *nm* episode. **épisodique** *adj* episodic, occasional; secondary, minor.

épitaphe [epitaf] *nf* epitaph.
éploré [eplɔre] *adj* tearful, in tears.
éplucher [eplyʃe] *v* (*légumes*) peel; (*salade*) clean; (*texte*) examine closely. **éplucheur** *nm* peeler. **épluchures** *nf pl* peelings *pl*.
épointé [epwɛ̃te] *adj* blunt.
éponger [epɔ̃ʒe] *v* mop (up). **éponge** *nf* sponge.
épopée [epɔpe] *nf* epic.
époque [epɔk] *nf* time; (*passé*) age, era; (*géol*) period.
épouser [epuze] *v* marry. **épouse** *nf* wife.
épousseter [epuste] *v* dust. **époussetage** *nm* dusting.
épouvanter [epuvɑ̃te] *v* terrify, appal. **épouvantable** *adj* dreadful, terrible. **épouvantail** *nm* scarecrow. **épouvante** *nf* terror, dread. **film d'épouvante** *nm* horror film.
époux [epu] *nm* husband.
***éprendre** [eprɑ̃drə] *v* **s'éprendre de** fall in love with.
épreuve [eprœv] *nf* test; (*peine*) ordeal; (*sport*) event; (*texte*) proof; (*phot*) print.
éprouver [epruve] *v* feel, experience; (*subir*) suffer; test. **éprouvette** *nf* test tube.
épuiser [epɥize] *v* exhaust; use up. **épuisé** *adj* worn out; (*comm*) sold out. **épuisement** *nm* exhaustion.
épurer [epyre] *v* purify, refine. **épuration** *nf* purification, refinement.
équateur [ekwatœr] *nm* equator. **équatorial** *adj* equatorial.
équation [ekwasjɔ̃] *nf* equation.
équerre [ekɛr] *nf* set square. **en équerre** at right angles.
équestre [ekɛstrə] *adj* equestrian.
équilatéral [ekɥilateral] *adj* equilateral.
équilibre [ekilibrə] *nm* balance; (*mental, tech*) equilibrium; harmony. **en équilibre** balanced. **équilibré** *adj* well-balanced. **équilibrer** *v* balance; counterbalance.
équinoxe [ekinɔks] *nm* equinox.
équiper [ekipe] *v* equip, fit out. **équipage** *nm* crew; equipment. **équipe** *nf* team; (*usine*) shift. **équipement** *nm* equipment.
équitable [ekitablə] *adj* fair.
équitation [ekitasjɔ̃] *nf* riding.
équité [ekite] *nf* equity.
équivalent [ekivalɑ̃] *nm, adj* equivalent.
***équivaloir** [ekivalwar] *v* be equivalent.
équivoque [ekivɔk] *adj* ambiguous; (*louche*) dubious. *nf* ambiguity; doubt.
érable [erablə] *nm* maple.
érafler [erɑfle] *v* scratch, graze. **éraflure** *nf* scratch, graze.
éraillé [erɑje] *adj* scratched; (*voix*) hoarse, rasping.
ère [ɛr] *nf* era.
érection [erɛksjɔ̃] *nf* erection.
éreinter [erɛ̃te] *v* exhaust; (*fam critiquer*) slate.
ergoter [ɛrgɔte] *v* quibble.
ériger [eriʒe] *v* establish, set up; (*monument*) erect.
ermite [ɛrmit] *nm* hermit.
éroder [erɔde] *v* erode. **érosif** *adj* erosive. **érosion** *nf* erosion.
érotique [erɔtik] *adj* erotic.
errer [ɛre] *v* wander, stray.
erreur [ɛrœr] *nf* mistake, error.
éruption [erypsjɔ̃] *nf* eruption. **entrer en éruption** erupt.
ès [ɛs] *prep* in the. **licencié ès lettres/sciences** *nm* Bachelor of Arts/Science.
escabeau [ɛskabo] *nm* stool; (*échelle*) step-ladder.
escadron [ɛskadrɔ̃] *nm* squadron.
escalader [ɛskalade] *v* climb, scale. **escalade** *nf* climbing.
escale [ɛskal] *nf* stop; (*naut*) port of call.
escalier [ɛskalje] *nm* staircase, stairs. **escalier de secours** fire escape. **escalier roulant** escalator. **escalier tournant** spiral staircase.
escalope [ɛskalɔp] *nf* escalope.
escamoter [ɛskamɔte] *v* (*esquiver*) dodge, evade; (*carte, etc.*) make disappear; (*fam*) pinch. **escamoteur, -euse** *nm, nf* conjuror.
escarbille [ɛskarbij] *nf* smut.
escargot [ɛskargo] *nm* snail.
escarmouche [ɛskarmuʃ] *nf* skirmish.
escarpé [ɛskarpe] *adj* steep.
escient [esjɑ̃] *nm* **à bon escient** advisedly. **à mauvais escient** ill-advisedly.
esclandre [ɛsklɑ̃drə] *nm* scene.
esclave [ɛsklav] *nm* slave. **esclavage** *nm* slavery.
escompter [ɛskɔ̃te] *v* discount; (*attendre*) expect, count on. **escompte** *nm* discount.
escorte [ɛskɔrt] *nf* escort. **escorter** *v* escort.
escrime [ɛskrim] *nf* fencing. **faire de l'escrime** fence.

escroc [ɛskro] *nm* swindler.
escroquer [ɛskrɔke] *v* swindle. **escroquerie** *nf* swindle, fraud.
espace [ɛspas] *nm* space. **espacer** *v* space out.
espadon [ɛspadɔ̃] *nm* swordfish.
Espagne [ɛspaɲ] *nf* Spain. **espagnol** *nm, adj* Spanish. **Espagnol, -e** *nm, nf* Spaniard.
espèce [ɛspɛs] *nf* sort, kind; (*bot, zool*) species. **espèces** *nf pl* cash *sing*.
espérer [ɛspere] *v* hope (for). **espérer en** trust in. **espérance** *nf* hope, expectation.
espiègle [ɛspjɛglə] *adj* mischievous. **espièglerie** *nf* mischief.
espion, -onne [ɛspjɔ̃, -ɔn] *nm, nf* spy. **espionnage** *nm* espionage. **espionner** *v* spy on.
esplanade [ɛsplanad] *nf* esplanade.
espoir [ɛspwar] *nm* hope.
esprit [ɛspri] *nm* spirit; (*pensée*) mind; (*humour*) wit. **avoir l'esprit large/étroit** be broad-/narrow-minded.
esquimau, -aude [ɛskimo, -od] *nm, adj* Eskimo. **Esquimau, -aude** *nm, nf* Eskimo.
esquisser [ɛskise] *v* sketch, outline. **esquisse** *nf* sketch, outline.
esquiver [ɛskive] *v* dodge, evade. **s'esquiver** slip away.
essai [esɛ] *nm* try, attempt; (*produit, voiture*) trial, test; (*littéraire*) essay. **à l'essai** on trial.
essaim [esɛ̃] *nm* swarm. **essaimer** *v* swarm; (*se disperser*) scatter, spread.
essayer [eseje] *v* try; test; (*vêtement*) try on.
essence [esɑ̃s] *nf* (*carburant*) petrol; (*extrait*) oil, essence.
essentiel [esɑ̃sjɛl] *adj* essential. *nm* main thing, essentials *pl*. **l'essentiel de** the best part of.
essieu [esjø] *nm* axle.
essor [esɔr] *nm* development, expansion; (*oiseau*) flight.
essorer [esɔre] *v* wring (out); (*machine*) spin-dry. **essoreuse** *nf* spin-dryer; (*à rouleaux*) mangle.
essoufflé [esufle] *adj* breathless, out of breath.
essuyer [esɥije] *v* wipe; (*sécher*) dry; (*subir*) suffer. **essuie-glace** *nm* windscreen wiper. **essuie-mains** *nm* hand towel. **essuie-pieds** doormat.
est [ɛst] *nm* east. *adj invar* east; (*région*) eastern; (*direction*) eastward.
estaminet [ɛstaminɛ] *nm* tavern.
estamper [ɛstɑ̃pe] *v* stamp; (*fam*) diddle. **estampe** *nf* engraving, print.
estampille [ɛstɑ̃pij] *nf* stamp.
esthétique [ɛstetik] *adj* aesthetic. **esthéticien, -enne** *nm, nf* beautician.
estimer [ɛstime] *v* estimate; value; respect, esteem; consider. **estime** *nf* esteem, respect.
estivant [ɛstivɑ̃], **-e** *nm, nf* holiday-maker.
estomac [ɛstɔma] *nm* stomach.
estomper [ɛstɔ̃pe] *v* blur.
estrade [ɛstrad] *nf* platform.
estragon [ɛstragɔ̃] *nm* tarragon.
estropier [ɛstrɔpje] *v* cripple. **estropié, -e** *nm, nf* cripple.
estuaire [ɛstɥɛr] *nm* estuary.
esturgeon [ɛstyrʒɔ̃] *nm* sturgeon.
et [e] *conj* and.
étable [etablə] *nf* cowshed.
établir [etablir] *v* establish, set up; (*liste, plan*) draw up. **s'établir** become established; (*s'installer*) settle. **établissement** *nm* establishment.
étage [etaʒ] *nm* floor, storey; (*gâteau*) tier. **étagère** *nf* shelf; (*meuble*) set of shelves.
étai [etɛ] *nm* stay, prop.
étain [etɛ̃] *nm* tin; (*alliage*) pewter.
étaler [etale] *v* spread (out); (*comm*) display; parade, flaunt. **s'étaler** stretch out. **étalage** *nm* display; (*vitrine*) shop window. **étalagiste** *n*(*m*+*f*) window-dresser.
étalon[1] [etalɔ̃] *nm* (*cheval*) stallion.
étalon[2] [etalɔ̃] *nm* standard.
étancher [etɑ̃ʃe] *v* stem, staunch; make watertight. **étanche** *adj* watertight. **étanche à l'air** airtight.
étang [etɑ̃] *nm* pond.
étape [etap] *nf* stage; (*arrêt*) stop.
état [eta] *nm* state; condition; (*comm*) statement. **état-major** *nm* (*mil*) staff; (*comm*) senior management.
États-Unis [etazyni] *nm pl* United States *sing*.
étau [eto] *nm* (*tech*) vice.
étayer [eteje] *v* support, prop up.
été [ete] *nm* summer.
***éteindre** [etɛ̃drə] *v* extinguish; (*lampe, radio, etc.*) switch *or* turn off; (*calmer*) quench. **s'éteindre** (*feu, etc.*) go out; (*mourir*) die out. **éteint** *adj* dull, faded; feeble; (*disparu*) extinct.

étendard [etɑ̃dar] *nm* standard.
étendre [etɑ̃drə] *v* extend, expand; (*étaler*) spread (out), stretch out; dilute. **étendu** *adj* vast, extensive. **étendue** *nf* (*terre*) expanse, area; (*pouvoir*) scope, extent.
éternel [etɛrnɛl] *adj* eternal; perpetual.
éternité [etɛrnite] *nf* eternity.
éternuer [etɛrnɥe] *v* sneeze. **éternuement** *nm* sneeze.
éther [etɛr] *nm* ether.
éthique [etik] *adj* ethical. *nf* ethics *pl.*
ethnique [ɛtnik] *adj* ethnic.
étinceler [etɛ̃sle] *v* sparkle, glitter. **étincelle** *nf* spark. **étincellement** *nm* sparkle, gleam.
étiquette [etikɛt] *nf* label; (*protocole*) etiquette. **etiqueter** *v* label.
étirer [etire] *v* stretch.
étoffe [etɔf] *nf* material. **avoir l'étoffe de** have the makings of.
étoile [etwal] *nf* star. **étoile de mer** starfish.
étole [etɔl] *nf* stole.
étonner [etɔne] *v* surprise, amaze. **étonnement** *nm* surprise, amazement.
étouffer [etufe] *v* stifle, suffocate; (*bruit*) muffle; (*sentiments, révolte*) suppress. **étouffement** *nm* suffocation; suppression.
étourdir [eturdir] *v* stun, daze; (*altitude, etc.*) make dizzy; (*douleur*) deaden; (*bruit*) deafen. **étourderie** *nf* thoughtlessness. **étourdi** *adj* scatterbrained, thoughtless. **étourdissement** *nm* dizzy spell.
étourneau [eturno] *nm* starling.
étrange [etrɑ̃ʒ] *adj* strange.
étranger [etrɑ̃ʒe], **-ère** *adj* foreign; (*inconnu*) strange, unfamiliar. *nm* foreign country. **à l'étranger** abroad. *nm, nf* foreigner; stranger.
étrangler [etrɑ̃gle] *v* strangle, choke. **étranglement** *nm* strangulation.
étrave [etrav] *nf* stem.
***être** [ɛtrə] *v* be. **être à** belong to. *nm* being; (*âme*) soul. **être humain** *nm* human being.
***étreindre** [etrɛ̃drə] *v* embrace; (*serrer*) grasp, grip. **étreinte** *nf* embrace; grasp, grip.
étrenne [etrɛn] *nf* New Year's gift.
étrier [etrije] *nm* stirrup.
étriqué [etrike] *adj* narrow, cramped, tight.
étroit [etrwa] *adj* narrow; (*vêtement*) tight; (*intime*) close; strict. **étroitesse** *nf* narrowness; tightness.
étude [etyd] *nf* study.
étudier [etydje] *v* study; examine. **étudiant, -e** *nm, nf* student.
étui [etɥi] *nm* case.
étymologie [etimɔlɔʒi] *nf* etymology. **étymologique** *adj* etymological.
eucalyptus [økaliptys] *nm* eucalyptus.
Eucharistie [økaristi] *nf* Eucharist.
eunuque [ønyk] *nm* eunuch.
euphémisme [øfemismə] *nm* euphemism. **euphémique** *adj* euphemistic.
euphorie [øfɔri] *nf* euphoria. **euphorique** *adj* euphoric.
Europe [ørɔp] *nf* Europe. **européen** *adj* European. **Européen, -enne** *nm, nf* European.
euthanasie [øtanazi] *nf* euthanasia.
eux [ø] *pron* (*sujet*) they; (*objet*) them. **eux-mêmes** *pron* themselves.
évacuer [evakɥe] *v* evacuate. **évacuation** *nf* evacuation. **evacué -e** *nm, nf* evacuee.
s'évader [evade] *v* escape.
évaluer [evalɥe] *v* (*bijou*) value; (*dégâts*) assess; estimate.
évangélique [evɑ̃ʒelik] *adj* evangelical. **évangéliste** *nm* evangelist.
évangile [evɑ̃ʒil] *nm* gospel.
s'évanouir [evanwir] *v* (*personne*) faint; (*disparaître*) vanish. **évanouissement** *nm* loss of consciousness; disappearance.
évaporer [evapɔre] *v* evaporate. **évaporation** *nf* evaporation.
évasé [evɑze] *adj* flared.
évasion [evazjɔ̃] *nf* escape. **évasif** *adj* evasive.
éveiller [eveje] *v* arouse, awaken. **éveil** *nm* alert, alarm. **en éveil** on the alert. **éveillé** *adj* alert; awake.
événement [evɛnmɑ̃] *nm* event.
éventail [evɑ̃taj] *nm* fan.
éventer [evɑ̃te] *v* fan, air; discover. **s'éventer** go flat *or* stale. **éventé** *adj* stale, flat.
éventrer [evɑ̃tre] *v* tear open; (*taureau*) gore.
éventuel [evɑ̃tɥɛl] *adj* possible. **éventualité** *nf* possibility, eventuality
évêque [evɛk] *nm* bishop.
s'évertuer [evɛrtɥe] *v* strive, do one's utmost.
évidence [evidɑ̃s] *nf* evidence; (*fait*) obvious fact. **en evidence** conspicuous.

évidemment *adv* obviously, of course. **évident** *adj* obvious, evident.
évider [evide] *v* hollow out.
évier [evje] *nm* sink.
évincer [evɛ̃se] *v* oust.
éviter [evite] *v* avoid. **évitable** *adj* avoidable.
évocateur, -trice [evɔkatœr, -tris] *adj* evocative.
évoluer [evɔlɥe] *v* evolve, develop; move about, manoeuvre. **évolution** *nf* evolution, development; movement, manoeuvre.
évoquer [evɔke] *v* evoke, recall.
exacerber [ɛgzasɛrbe] *v* exacerbate.
exact [ɛgzakt] *adj* exact; correct; (*vrai*) true; precise, accurate; punctual. **exactitude** *nf* exactness; precision; accuracy; punctuality.
exagérer [ɛgzaʒere] *v* exaggerate; (*abuser*) go too far. **exagération** *nf* exaggeration.
exalter [ɛgzalte] *v* excite; (*glorifier*) exalt. **exaltation** *nf* great excitement. **exalté** *adj* excited, elated; (*imagination*) vivid; fanatical.
examen [ɛgzamɛ̃] *nm* examination; test.
examiner [ɛgzamine] *v* examine.
exaspérer [ɛgzaspere] *v* exasperate, aggravate. **exaspération** *nf* exasperation.
exaucer [ɛgzose] *v* grant.
excaver [ɛkskave] *v* excavate. **excavation** *nf* excavation.
excéder [ɛksede] *v* exceed; exasperate. **excédent** *nm* surplus, excess.
excellent [ɛksɛlɑ̃] *adj* excellent. **excellence** *nf* excellence. **Excellence** *nf* Excellency.
exceller [ɛksele] *v* excel.
excentrique [ɛksɑ̃trik] *n(m+f)*, *adj* eccentric. **excentricité** *nf* eccentricity.
excepter [ɛksɛpte] *v* exclude. **excepté** *prep* except. **exception** *nf* exception. **exceptionnel** *adj* exceptional.
excès [ɛksɛ] *nm* excess; surplus. **excès de vitesse** (*auto*) speeding. **excessif** *adj* excessive.
exciter [ɛksite] *v* excite; (*provoquer*) arouse; stimulate; (*encourager*) urge. **s'exciter** (*fam*) get worked up. **excitation** *nf* excitement; stimulation.
s'exclamer [ɛksklame] *v* exclaim. **exclamation** *nf* exclamation.
***exclure** [ɛksklyr] *v* exclude; (*chasser*) expel. **exclusif** *adj* exclusive; sole. **exclusion** *nf* exclusion; expulsion.
excommunier [ɛkskɔmynje] *v* excommunicate. **excommunication** *nf* excommunication.
excréter [ɛkskrete] *v* excrete. **excrément** *nm* excrement. **excrétion** *nf* excretion.
excursion [ɛkskyrsjɔ̃] *nf* excursion, trip.
excuser [ɛkskyze] *v* excuse; pardon, forgive. **excusez-moi** I'm sorry. **s'excuser** apologize. **excuse** *nf* excuse. **excuses** *nf pl* apology *sing*.
exécrer [ɛgzekre] *v* loathe. **exécrable** *adj* atrocious.
exécuter [ɛgzekyte] *v* execute, perform, carry out. **exécutif** *adj* executive. **exécution** *nf* execution.
exemplaire [ɛgzɑ̃plɛr] *adj* exemplary. *nm* copy; specimen.
exemple [ɛgzɑ̃plə] *nm* example. **par exemple** for example; (*surprise*) indeed, really.
exempt [ɛgzɑ̃] *adj* exempt, free. **exempter** *v* exempt. **exemption** *nf* exemption.
exercer [ɛgzɛrse] *v* exercise; practise; (*force*) exert; (*entraîner*) train. **s'exercer** practise.
exercice [ɛgzɛrsis] *nm* exercise; practice; (*mil*) drill.
exhaler [ɛgzale] *v* exhale; (*odeur*) give off; (*soupir*) utter.
exhiber [ɛgzibe] *v* exhibit, show, display. **exhibition** *nf* exhibition; show. **exhibitionniste** *n(m+f)*, *adj* exhibitionist.
exiger [ɛgziʒe] *v* demand, insist; (*nécessiter*) need, require. **exigences** *nf pl* demands *pl*, requirements *pl*.
exigu, -uë [ɛgzigy] *adj* cramped.
exiler [ɛgzile] *v* exile, banish. **exil** *nm* exile.
exister [ɛgziste] *v* exist; (*être*) be. **existence** *nf* existence. **existentialisme** *nm* existentialism.
exorbitant [ɛgzɔrbitɑ̃] *adj* exorbitant.
exorciser [ɛgzɔrsize] *v* exorcize. **exorcisme** *nm* exorcism. **exorciste** *nm* exorcist.
exotique [ɛgzɔtik] *adj* exotic.
expansion [ɛkspɑ̃sjɔ̃] *nf* expansion. **expansif** *adj* expansive.
expatrier [ɛkspatrije] *v* expatriate. **expatrié, -e** *n*, *adj* expatriate.
expédier [ɛkspedje] *v* send, dispatch; (*fam*) dispose of. **expédient** *nm*, *adj* expedient. **expéditeur, -trice** *nm*, *nf* sender. **expédition** *nf* dispatch; (*paquet*) consignment; (*voyage*) expedition.

expérience [ɛksperjɑ̃s] *nf* experience; (*scientifique*) experiment.
expérimenter [ɛksperimɑ̃te] *v* experiment; test, try out. **expérimental** *adj* experimental. **expérimenté** *adj* experienced.
expert [ɛkspɛr] *nm, adj* expert. **expert-comptable** *nm* chartered accountant.
expier [ɛkspje] *v* atone for. **expiation** *nf* atonement.
expirer [ɛkspire] *v* expire; (*air*) breathe out. **expiration** *nf* expiry.
explication [ɛksplikɑsjɔ̃] *nf* explanation; (*texte*) analysis, commentary. **explicatif** *adj* explanatory.
explicite [ɛksplisit] *adj* explicit.
expliquer [ɛksplike] *v* explain; (*texte*) analyse.
exploit [ɛksplwa] *nm* exploit.
exploiter [ɛksplwate] *v* exploit; operate, run.
explorer [ɛksplɔre] *v* explore; examine. **explorateur, -trice** *nm, nf* explorer. **exploration** *nf* exploration.
exploser [ɛksploze] *v* explode. **explosif** *nm, adj* explosive. **explosion** *nf* explosion.
exporter [ɛkspɔrte] *v* export. **exportation** *nf* export.
exposer [ɛkspoze] *v* expose; exhibit, display; (*expliquer*) explain. **exposant, -e** *nm, nf* exhibitor. **exposé** *nm* talk, account. **exposition** *nf* exhibition; (*à l'air, etc.*) exposure; (*maison*) aspect.
exprès [ɛksprɛ] *adj invar* express. *adv* on purpose; specially.
express [ɛksprɛs] *nm* fast train.
expression [ɛksprɛsjɔ̃] *nf* expression. **expressif** *adj* expressive.
exprimer [ɛksprime] *v* express.
expulser [ɛkspylse] *v* expel; (*locataire*) evict. **expulsion** *nf* expulsion; eviction.
exquis [ɛkski] *adj* exquisite, delightful.
extase [ɛkstɑz] *nf* ecstasy. **extasié** *adj* ecstatic.
extension [ɛkstɑ̃sjɔ̃] *nf* extension, expansion.
exténuer [ɛkstenɥe] *v* exhaust.
extérieur, -e [ɛksterjœr] *adj* outer, external, outside; (*étranger*) foreign. *nm* exterior, outside. **à l'extérieur** outside. **en extérieur** on location.
exterminer [ɛkstɛrmine] *v* exterminate. **extermination** *nf* extermination.
externe [ɛkstɛrn] *adj* external. **pour l'usage externe** for external use only. *n(m+f)* day pupil. **externat** *nm* day school.
extinction [ɛkstɛ̃ksjɔ̃] *nf* extinction. **extincteur** *nm* extinguisher.
extirper [ɛkstirpe] *v* eradicate; (*arracher*) pull out.
extorquer [ɛkstɔrke] *v* extort. **extorsion** *nf* extortion.
extra [ɛkstra] *adj invar* first-rate, top-quality; (*fam*) fantastic. *adv* extra.
extraction [ɛkstraksjɔ̃] *nf* extraction.
extrader [ɛkstrade] *v* extradite. **extradition** *nf* extradition.
***extraire** [ɛkstrɛr] *v* extract; (*charbon*) mine; (*pierre*) quarry. **extrait** *nm* extract.
extraordinaire [ɛkstraɔrdinɛr] *adj* extraordinary; exceptional.
extravagant [ɛkstravagɑ̃] *adj* extravagant; (*prix*) excessive; (*idée*) crazy. **extravagance** *nf* extravagance.
extraverti [ɛkstraverti], **-e** *n, adj* extrovert.
extrême [ɛkstrɛm] *nm* extreme. *adj* extreme; (*loin*) far; intense; (*suprême*) utmost. **Extrême-Orient** *nm* Far East. **extrémiste** *n(m+f), adj* extremist. **extremité** *nf* end, tip; limit. **extremités** *nf pl* (*anat*) extremities *pl*.
exubérant [ɛgzyberɑ̃] *adj* exuberant. **exubérance** *nf* exuberance.

F

fable [fɑblə] *nf* fable.
fabricant [fabrikɑ̃] *nm* manufacturer. **fabrication** *nf* manufacture.
fabriquer [fabrike] *v* manufacture, make; (*mensonge*) fabricate. **fabrique** *nf* factory.
fabuleux [fabylø] *adj* fabulous.
fac [fak] *nf* (*argot*) university, college.
façade [fasad] *nf* façade, front.
face [fas] *nf* face; (*côté*) side. **de face** frontal. **en face (de)** opposite. **face à** facing. **faire face à** face.
facétie [fasesi] *nf* joke, trick. **facétieux** *adj* mischievous; humorous.
facette [fasɛt] *nf* facet.
fâcher [fɑʃe] *v* make angry. **se fâcher** get angry; (*se brouiller*) fall out. **fâché** *adj*

angry; (*désolé*) sorry. **fâcheux** *adj* unfortunate; (*ennuyeux*) annoying.
facile [fasil] *adj* easy; (*spontané*) ready.
faciliter [fasilite] *v* facilitate, make easier. **facilité** *nf* ease, easiness; aptitude; tendency. **facilités** *nf pl* facilities *pl*.
façon [fasɔ̃] *nf* way, manner; (*robe*) cut. **de façon à** so as to. **de toute façon** anyway. **façons** *nf pl* (*conduite*) behaviour *sing*; (*chichis*) fuss *sing*.
façonner [fasɔne] *v* shape, form; (*fabriquer*) manufacture, make.
fac-similé [faksimile] *nm* facsimile.
facteur [faktœr] *nm* factor; postman.
factice [faktis] *adj* artificial, false.
faction [faksjɔ̃] *nf* faction; guard, sentry.
facture [faktyr] *nf* bill; (*comm*) invoice. **facturer** *v* invoice; (*compter*) charge for.
facultatif [fakyltatif] *adj* optional; (*arrêt*) request.
faculté [fakylte] *nf* faculty; (*pouvoir*) power; (*droit*) right; (*argot*) university, college.
fadaises [fadɛz] *nf pl* nonsense *sing*.
fade [fad] *adj* insipid, dull.
fagot [fago] *nm* bundle of sticks.
fagoter [fagɔte] *v* (*péj*) rig out.
faible [fɛblə] *adj* weak, feeble; (*petit*) low, small, slight. *nm* (*personne*) weakling; (*penchant*) weakness. **faiblesse** *nf* weakness.
faiblir [feblir] *v* weaken, fail.
faïence [fajɑ̃s] *nf* earthenware.
faillible [fajiblə] *adj* fallible. **faillibilité** *nf* fallibility.
***faillir** [fajir] *v* fail. **faillir faire** almost do, narrowly miss doing. **failli, -e** *n, adj* bankrupt. **faillite** *nf* bankruptcy; (*chute*) collapse. **faire faillite** go bankrupt.
faim [fɛ̃] *nf* hunger. **avoir faim** be hungry.
fainéant [fɛneɑ̃], **-e** *adj* lazy, idle. *nm, nf* idler. **fainéantise** *nf* idleness.
***faire** [fɛr] *v* make; do; (*mesurer, temps*) be; (*sport, théâtre*) play; (*paraître*) look; (*dire*) say. **ça ne fait rien** it doesn't matter. **faire faire** have done. **faire-part** *nm invar* announcement. **faire voir** show. **se faire à** get used to.
faisable [fəzablə] *adj* feasible.
faisan [fəzɑ̃] *nm* pheasant.
faisceau [fɛso] *nm* bundle; (*rayon*) beam.
fait[1] [fɛ] *nm* fact; event; act. **au fait** (*à propos*) by the way; (*au courant*) informed. **en fait** in fact. **fait divers** news item.
fait[2] [fɛ] *adj* made; done; (*mûr*) ripe. **c'est bien fait pour toi!** it serves you right!
faîte [fɛt] *nm* summit, top.
faix [fɛ] *nm* burden.
falaise [falɛz] *nf* cliff.
***falloir** [falwar] *v* be necessary. **il faut le faire** it must be done. **s'en falloir (de)** be lacking.
falsifier [falsifje] *v* falsify, alter. **falsification** *nf* falsification.
famé [fame] *adj* **mal famé** disreputable.
fameux [famø] *adj* famous; first-rate, excellent; (*rude*) real. **pas fameux** not so good.
familial [familjal] *adj* family, domestic.
familiariser [familjarize] *v* familiarize. **familiarité** *nf* familiarity.
familier [familje] *adj* familiar; (*amical*) informal; (*mot*) colloquial. *nm* regular visitor.
famille [famij] *nf* family.
famine [famin] *nf* famine.
fanal [fanal] *nm* lantern.
fanatique [fanatik] *adj* fanatical. *n(m+f)* fanatic.
faner [fane] *v* make hay. **se faner** fade, wither.
fanfare [fɑ̃far] *nf* fanfare, flourish; (*orchestre*) brass band.
fanfaron, -onne [fɑ̃farɔ̃, -ɔn] *adj* boastful.
fange [fɑ̃ʒ] *nf* mire.
fantaisie [fɑ̃tezi] *nf* fantasy, fancy; (*caprice*) whim; extravagance; imagination.
fantastique [fɑ̃tastik] *adj* fantastic; (*bizarre*) weird, uncanny.
fantoche [fɑ̃tɔʃ] *nm* puppet.
fantôme [fɑ̃tom] *nm* ghost, phantom. **cabinet fantôme** *nm* shadow cabinet.
faon [fɑ̃] *nm* fawn.
farce[1] [fars] *nf* joke, prank; (*théâtre*) farce. **farceur, -euse** *nm, nf* practical joker.
farce[2] [fars] *nf* stuffing.
farcir [farsir] *v* stuff.
fard [far] *nm* make-up.
fardeau [fardo] *nm* burden.
farder [farde] *v* make up; disguise.
farfouiller [farfuje] *v* (*fam*) rummage about.
farine [farin] *nf* flour. **farine d'avoine** oatmeal. **farine de maïs** cornflour. **farineux** *adj* floury.

farouche [faruʃ] *adj* fierce; timid; savage, wild; unsociable.
fart [far] *nm* wax. **farter** *v* wax.
fascicule [fasikyl] *nm* volume; part, instalment.
fasciner [fasine] *v* fascinate. **fascination** *nf* fascination.
fascisme [fasismə] *nm* fascism. **fasciste** *n(m+f)*, *adj* fascist.
faste [fast] *nm* splendour.
fastidieux [fastidjø] *adj* tedious.
fastueux [fastɥø] *adj* sumptuous, luxurious.
fatal [fatal] *adj* fatal; inevitable. **fatalité** *nf* fate.
fatiguer [fatige] *v* tire, strain; (*agacer*) annoy. **se fatiguer** get tired. **fatigant** *adj* tiring; (*agaçant*) tiresome. **fatigue** *nf* fatigue, tiredness.
fatras [fatra] *nm* jumble.
faubourg [fobur] *nm* suburb.
faucher [foʃe] *v* mow, cut; (*fam*) pinch, nick. **fauché** *adj* (*fam*) broke, hard up.
faucon [fokɔ̃] *nm* falcon; hawk.
faufiler [fofile] *v* tack. **se faufiler** thread *or* edge one's way.
faune [fon] *nm* fauna.
fausser [fose] *v* distort, alter; (*courber*) bend, buckle. **fausser compagnie à** slip away from.
fausset [fose] *nm* falsetto.
faute [fot] *nf* fault; mistake, error; (*jur*) offence. **faute de** for lack of. **fautif** *adj* at fault, guilty; incorrect.
fauteuil [fotœj] *nm* armchair; (*théâtre*) seat. **fauteuil à bascule** rocking chair. **fauteuil roulant** wheelchair.
fauve [fov] *adj* tawny, fawn. *nm* wild animal; (*couleur*) fawn.
faux[1], **fausse** [fo, fos] *adj* false; (*incorrect*) wrong; (*argent, etc.*) fake, forged. **fausse alerte** false alarm. **fausse couche** miscarriage. **faux-filet** *nm* sirloin. **faux pli** crease. *adv* out of tune. *nm* falsehood; forgery. **à faux** wrongly. **fausseté** *nf* falseness, falsity.
faux[2] [fo] *nf* scythe.
faveur [favœr] *nf* favour. **billet de faveur** *nm* complimentary ticket. **en faveur de** on behalf of. **favorable** *adj* favourable.
favori, -ite [favɔri, -it] *n*, *adj* favourite. **favoriser** *v* favour.
fébrile [febril] *adj* feverish. **fébrilité** *nf* feverishness.
fécond [fekɔ̃] *adj* fertile; prolific. **fécondité** *nf* fertility.
fécule [fekyl] *nf* starch. **féculent** *adj* starchy.
fédérer [federe] *v* federate. **fédéral** *adj* federal. **fédération** *nf* federation.
fée [fe] *nf* fairy. **féerique** *adj* magical.
***feindre** [fɛ̃drə] *v* feign. **feindre de** pretend.
fêler [fele] *v* crack. **fêlure** *nf* crack.
féliciter [felisite] *v* congratulate. **félicitations** *nf pl* congratulations *pl*.
félin [felɛ̃] *adj* feline.
femelle [fəmɛl] *nf*, *adj* female.
féminin [feminɛ̃] *adj* feminine, female. *nm* feminine. **féminisme** *nm* feminism. **féministe** *n(m+f)*, *adj* feminist. **féminité** *nf* femininity.
femme [fam] *nf* woman; (*épouse*) wife. **femme de chambre** chambermaid. **femme de ménage** cleaner.
fémur [femyr] *nm* femur.
fendre [fɑ̃drə] *v* split, crack.
fenêtre [fənɛtrə] *nf* window. **fenêtre à guillotine** sash window. **fenêtre en saillie** bay window.
fenouil [fənuj] *nm* fennel.
fente [fɑ̃t] *nf* crack, fissure; (*interstice*) slit; slot.
féodal [feɔdal] *adj* feudal.
fer [fɛr] *nm* iron. **fer à cheval** horseshoe. **fer à repasser** iron. **fer-blanc** *nm* tin. **fer forgé** wrought iron.
férié [ferje] *adj* **jour férié** *nm* public holiday.
ferme[1] [fɛrm] *adj* firm; (*solide*) steady. *adv* hard. **fermeté** *nf* firmness, steadiness.
ferme[2] [fɛrm] *nf* farm; (*maison*) farmhouse. **fermier** *nm* farmer. **fermière** *nf* farmer's wife.
fermenter [fɛrmɑ̃te] *v* ferment. **ferment** *nm* ferment. **fermentation** *nf* fermentation.
fermer [fɛrme] *v* close, shut; (*boucher*) block; (*gaz, eau, etc.*) turn off. **fermer à clef** lock. **fermeture** *nf* (*vêtement, sac, etc.*) fastener, catch; (*action*) closing. **fermeture à glissière** zip.
féroce [ferɔs] *adj* ferocious, fierce. **férocité** *nf* ferocity.
ferraille [fɛraj] *nf* scrap iron.
ferré [fere] *adj* (*canne*) steel-tipped; (*soulier*) hobnailed. **voie ferrée** *nf* railway track *or* line.

ferroviaire [fɛrɔvjɛr] *adj* railway.
fertile [fɛrtil] *adj* fertile. **fertilisation** *nf* fertilization. **fertiliser** *v* fertilize. **fertilité** *nf* fertility.
fervent [fɛrvɑ̃] *adj* fervent. **ferveur** *nm* fervour.
fesser [fese] *v* spank. **fesse** *nf* buttock. **fesses** *nf pl* bottom *sing*. **fessée** *nf* spanking.
festin [fɛstɛ̃] *nm* feast.
festival [fɛstival] *nm* festival.
feston [fɛstɔ̃] *nm* festoon; (*couture*) scallop. **festonner** *v* festoon; scallop.
fête [fɛt] *nf* festival; (*congé*) holiday; (*rel*) feast day; (*foire*) fair; celebration. **fête des Mères** Mothers' Day. **fête foraine** funfair.
fêter [fete] *v* celebrate.
fétiche [fetiʃ] *nm* fetish; mascot.
fétide [fetid] *adj* fetid.
feu[1] [fø] *nm* fire; (*lumière, lampe*) light; (*cuisine*) ring, burner; (*chaleur*) heat. **feu d'artifice** firework. **feu de joie** bonfire. **feu de position** sidelight. **feux** *nm pl* (*auto*) traffic lights *pl*.
feu[2] [fø] *adj* late, deceased.
feuille [fœj] *nf* leaf; (*papier, etc.*) sheet; form; (*bulletin*) slip. **feuillage** *nm* foliage. **feuillet** *nm* (*livre*) leaf, page.
feuilleter [fœjte] *v* leaf *or* skim through. **pâte feuilletée** *nf* puff pastry.
feuilleton [fœjtɔ̃] *nm* serial.
feutre [føtrə] *nm* felt; (*stylo*) felt-tip pen. **feutré** *adj* muffled.
fève [fɛv] *nf* broad bean.
février [fevrije] *nm* February.
fiacre [fjakrə] *nm* cab.
fiancé [fjɑ̃se] *adj* engaged. *nm* fiancé. **fiancée** *nf* fiancée.
se fiancer [fjɑ̃se] *v* get engaged. **fiançailles** *nf pl* engagement *sing*.
fiasco [fjasko] *nm* fiasco.
fibre [fibrə] *nf* fibre.
ficeler [fisle] *v* tie up. **ficelle** *nf* string.
ficher[1] [fiʃe] *v* (*enfoncer*) stick, drive in; (*mettre en fiche*) file. **fiche** *nf* (*cheville*) peg; (*élec*) pin; index card; form, slip. **fichier** *nm* file.
ficher[2] [fiʃe] (*fam*) *v* do, be up to; (*donner*) give; (*mettre*) put. **ficher le camp** clear off. **se ficher de** (*se moquer*) make fun of; (*être indifférent*) not care about. **fichu** *adj* (*mauvais*) rotten; (*perdu*) done for; capable, likely.
fiction [fiksjɔ̃] *nf* fiction. **fictif** *adj* fictitious; false; imaginary.
fidèle [fidɛl] *adj* faithful; loyal; (*habituel*) regular. *n*(*m*+*f*) (*rel*) believer; regular. **fidélité** *nf* faithfulness; loyalty; (*conjugale*) fidelity.
fiel [fjɛl] *nm* gall.
fiente [fjɑ̃t] *nm* droppings *pl*.
fier[1] [fjɛr] *adj* proud. **fierté** *nf* pride.
fier[2] [fje] *v* **se fier à** trust.
fièvre [fjɛvrə] *nf* fever. **fievreux** *adj* feverish.
figer [fiʒe] *v* congeal, clot, coagulate; (*paralyser*) freeze, stiffen.
figue [fig] *nf* fig. **figuier** *nm* fig tree.
figure [figyr] *nf* figure; (*visage*) face; (*image*) picture.
figurer [figyre] *v* represent; appear. **se figurer** imagine. **figurant, -e** *nm, nf* (*cinéma*) extra; (*théâtre*) walk-on; (*pantin*) puppet. **figuré** *adj* figurative.
fil [fil] *nm* thread; (*élec*) wire; (*linge, pêche*) line; (*bois*) grain; (*tranchant*) edge; current. **fil à plomb** plumbline. **fil de fer** wire.
filament [filamɑ̃] *nm* filament; (*fil*) thread.
file [fil] *nf* line; (*auto*) lane; (*d'attente*) queue. **à la file** in single file; one after the other.
filer [file] *v* spin; prolong, draw out; (*liquide, sable*) flow, run; (*bas*) ladder; (*fam: courir*) fly, dash; (*fam: s'en aller*) slip away.
filet[1] [filɛ] *nm* streak; (*eau*) trickle; (*fumée*) wisp.
filet[2] [filɛ] *nm* (*viande, etc.*) fillet.
filet[3] [filɛ] *nm* (*sport, pêche*) net; (*bagages*) rack. **filet à provisions** string bag.
filial [filjal] *adj* filial. **filiale** *nf* subsidiary company.
filigrane [filigran] *nm* (*papier*) watermark; (*argent, verre, etc.*) filigree.
fille [fij] *nf* girl; (*opposé à fils*) daughter. **fillette** *nf* little girl.
filleul [fijœl] *nm* (*garçon*) godson; (*enfant*) godchild. **filleule** *nf* goddaughter.
film [film] *nm* film. **film fixe** filmstrip. **filmer** *v* film.
filou [filu] *nm* rogue.
filouter [filute] (*fam*) *v* diddle; (*tricher*) cheat; (*voler*) filch.
fils [fis] *nm* son; (*après nom*) junior.

filtrer [filtre] *v* filter. **filtre** *nm* filter; (*cigarette*) filter-tip.
fin[1] [fɛ̃] *adj* fine; (*mince*) thin; (*vue*) sharp; (*personne*) shrewd, astute; (*aliments*) choice; (*habile*) expert. **fines herbes** *nf pl* mixed herbs *pl*.
fin[2] [fɛ̃] *nf* end; (*but*) purpose. **en fin de compte** in the end. **fin de série** oddment.
final [final] *adj* final. **finale** *nf* (*sport*) final. **finalement** *adv* in the end, finally. **finaliste** *n(m+f)* finalist.
finance [finɑ̃s] *nf* finance. **financer** *v* finance.
financier [finɑ̃sje] *adj* financial. *nm* financier.
finaud [fino] *adj* wily.
finesse [finɛs] *nf* fineness; (*vue*) sharpness; (*broderie*) delicacy; subtlety.
finir [finir] *v* finish, end; (*arrêter*) stop. **fini** *adj* finished; (*terminé*) over; (*complet*) utter.
Finlande [fɛ̃lɑ̃d] *nf* Finland. **finlandais** *adj* Finnish. **Finlandais, -e** *nm, nf* Finn. **finnois** *nm, adj* Finnish. **Finnois, -e** *nm, nf* Finn, Finnish speaker.
fioriture [fjɔrityr] *nf* flourish.
firme [firm] *nf* firm.
fisc [fisk] *nm* Inland Revenue. **fiscal** *adj* tax, fiscal.
fission [fisjɔ̃] *nf* fission.
fissure [fisyr] *nf* crack, fissure.
fixer [fikse] *v* fix; decide, settle; arrange, set. **fixation** *nf* fixation; (*attache*) fastening; (*ski*) binding. **fixe** *adj* fixed, set.
flacon [flakɔ̃] *nm* bottle.
flageller [flaʒele] *v* flog. **flagellation** *nf* flogging.
flagrant [flagrɑ̃] *adj* blatant, glaring. **prendre en flagrant délit** catch red-handed.
flairer [flere] *v* smell, sniff (at); (*discerner*) sense, scent. **flair** *nm* sense of smell; intuition.
flamand [flamɑ̃] *nm, adj* Flemish. **les Flamands** the Flemish.
flamant [flamɑ̃] *nm* flamingo.
flambeau [flɑ̃bo] *nm* torch; candlestick.
flamber [flɑ̃be] *v* blaze; (*cheveux*) singe. **flambée** *nf* blaze; (*colère, etc.*) outburst.
flamboyant [flɑ̃bwajɑ̃] *adj* blazing, fiery.
flamme [flam] *nf* flame; (*ardeur, éclat*) fire. **flammèche** *nf* spark.
flan [flɑ̃] *nm* (*cuisine*) egg custard; (*tech*) mould.
flanc [flɑ̃] *nm* side, flank.
flanelle [flanɛl] *nf* flannel.
flâner [flɑne] *v* stroll; (*péj*) dawdle.
flanquer [flɑ̃ke] *v* flank; (*fam*) fling, chuck.
flaque [flak] *nf* pool. **flaque d'eau** puddle.
flasque [flask] *adj* flaccid, flabby, limp; (*personne*) spineless.
flatter [flate] *v* flatter; encourage; (*caresser*) stroke. **se flatter** delude oneself. **se flatter de** pride oneself on. **flatterie** *nf* flattery. **flatteur, -euse** *adj* flattering.
flatulence [flatylɑ̃s] *nf* flatulence.
fléau [fleo] *nm* scourge; (*fam*) plague.
flèche [flɛʃ] *nf* arrow; (*église*) spire. **monter en flèche** soar, rocket. **fléchette** *nf* dart.
fléchir [fleʃir] *v* bend, sag; (*personne*) yield.
flegme [flɛgmə] *nm* composure. **flegmatique** *adj* phlegmatic.
flet [flɛ] *nm* flounder.
flétan [fletɑ̃] *nm* halibut.
flétrir[1] [fletrir] *v* (*faner*) wither, fade.
flétrir[2] [fletrir] *v* condemn; (*marquer*) brand. **flétrissure** *nf* (*tache*) stain, blemish; brand.
fleur [flœr] *nf* flower; (*arbre*) blossom; (*meilleur*) prime. **à fleur de** just above, on the surface of. **fleurist** *n(m+f)* florist.
fleurir [flœrir] *v* flower, bloom; blossom; flourish, prosper; decorate with flowers. **fleuri** *adj* flowery; (*plante*) in flower; (*teint*) florid.
fleuve [flœv] *nm* river.
flexible [flɛksiblə] *adj* flexible.
flibustier [flibystje] *nm* buccaneer, pirate.
flic [flik] *nm* (*fam*) copper, policeman.
flirter [flœrte] *v* flirt. **flirteur, -euse** *nm, nf* flirt.
flocon [flɔkɔ̃] *nm* flake.
floral [flɔral] *adj* floral.
flore [flɔr] *nf* flora.
florissant [flɔrisɑ̃] *adj* flourishing; (*santé*) blooming.
flot [flo] *nm* flood, stream. **à flot** afloat. **à flots** in torrents.
flotter [flɔte] *v* float; (*brume*) drift; (*parfum*) waft; (*drapeau*) flutter, fly; hesitate. **flottabilité** *nf* buoyancy **flottable** *adj* buoyant. **flottant** *adj* floating; (*vêtement*) loose; irresolute. **flotte** *nf* fleet. **flotteur** *nm* float.
flou [flu] *adj* blurred; vague.

fluctuer [flyktɥe] *v* fluctuate. **fluctuation** *nf* fluctuation.
fluet, -ette [flyɛ, -ɛt] *adj* slender.
fluide [flɥid] *nm, adj* fluid. **fluidité** *nf* fluidity, flow.
fluorescent [flyɔresɑ̃] *adj* fluorescent. **fluorescence** *nf* fluorescence.
flûte [flyt] *nf* flute; (*pain*) long thin loaf. **flûte à bec** recorder. **flûtiste** *n(m+f)* flautist.
flux [fly] *nm* flood; (*méd*) flow; (*phys*) flux.
fluxion [flyksjɔ̃] *nf* inflammation, swelling. **fluxion dentaire** gumboil. **fluxion de poitrine** pneumonia.
focal [fɔkal] *adj* focal.
fœtus [fetys] *nm* foetus. **fœtal** *adj* foetal.
foi [fwa] *nf* faith; (*parole*) word.
foie [fwa] *nm* liver.
foin [fwɛ̃] *nm* hay.
foire [fwar] *nf* fair.
fois [fwa] *nf* time. **à la fois** at once. **des fois** (*fam*) sometimes. **deux fois** twice. **une fois** once.
foisonner [fwazɔne] *v* abound. **à foison** in abundance.
fol [fɔl] *form of* **fou** *used before vowel or mute h.*
folâtre [fɔlɑtrə] *adj* playful, lively.
folie [fɔli] *nf* (*méd*) madness; (*bêtise*) folly; (*dépense*) extravagance.
folklore [fɔlklɔr] *nm* folklore. **folklorique** *adj* folk; (*fam*) weird, outlandish.
folle [fɔl] *V* **fou**.
follet, -ette [fɔlɛ, -ɛt] *adj* scatter-brained.
follicule [fɔlikyl] *nm* follicle.
foncer [fɔ̃se] *v* charge, rush; (*fam*) tear along; (*puits*) sink; (*couleur*) go darker. **foncé** *adj* dark.
foncier [fɔ̃sje] *adj* land; fundamental.
fonction [fɔ̃ksjɔ̃] *nf* function; post, office. **faire fonction de** act as. **fonctionnaire** *n(m+f)* civil servant. **fonctionnel** *adj* functional.
fonctionner [fɔ̃ksjɔne] *v* function, work, operate.
fond [fɔ̃] *nm* bottom; (*pièce*) back; (*tableau*) background; (*essentiel*) heart, core; (*profondeur*) depth; (*lie*) sediment. **à fond** thoroughly. **au fond** deep down, basically. **de fond** basic.
fondamental [fɔ̃damɑ̃tal] *adj* fundamental, basic.
fondant [fɔ̃dɑ̃] *adj* melting. *nm* fondant.
fonder [fɔ̃de] *v* found; base; (*foyer*) start, set up; justify. **se fonder sur** (*idée*) be based on; (*personne*) go on. **fondateur, -trice** *nm, nf* founder. **fondation** *nf* foundation. **fondement** *nm* foundation, base, grounds *pl.*
fonderie [fɔ̃dri] *nf* foundry.
fondre [fɔ̃drə] *v* melt; (*dans l'eau*) dissolve; (*statue, etc.*) cast; (*couleur*) merge. **fondre sur** swoop down on.
fondrière [fɔ̃drijɛr] *nf* pothole, rut.
fonds [fɔ̃] *nm* fund, collection; (*comm*) business. *nm pl* funds *pl.*
fontaine [fɔ̃tɛn] *nf* fountain.
fonts [fɔ̃] *nm pl* **fonts baptismaux** font *sing.*
football [futbol] *nm* football. **footballeur** *nm* footballer.
footing [futiŋ] *nm* jogging. **faire du footing** go jogging.
for [fɔr] *nm* **dans son for intérieur** in one's heart of hearts.
forain [fɔrɛ̃] *nm* (*marchand*) stallholder; fairground entertainer.
forçat [fɔrsa] *nm* convict.
force [fɔrs] *nf* force, strength. **à force de** by dint of.
forcené [fɔrsəne], **-e** *adj* (*fou*) deranged; (*acharné*) frenzied. *nm, nf* fanatic, maniac.
forceps [fɔrsɛps] *nm* forceps *pl.*
forcer [fɔrse] *v* force; (*claquer*) strain, overdo. **forcé** *adj* forced; inevitable. **forcément** *adv* inevitably, of course. **pas forcément** not necessarily.
forer [fɔre] *v* drill, bore. **foreuse** *nf* drill.
forêt [fɔre] *nf* forest. **forestier** *nm* forester.
forfait[1] [fɔrfɛ] *nm* (*sport*) withdrawal; serious crime. **déclarer forfait** withdraw.
forfait[2] [fɔrfɛ] *nm* fixed price; contract. **forfaitaire** *adj* inclusive.
forger [fɔrʒe] *v* forge; create, form; (*mot*) coin; (*inventer*) contrive, concoct. **forge** *nf* forge. **forgeron** *nm* blacksmith.
se formaliser [fɔrmalize] *v* take offence.
format [fɔrma] *nm* format, size.
former [fɔrme] *v* form; make up; (*éduquer*) train; develop. **formalité** *nf* formality. **formation** *nf* formation; training. **forme** *nf* form; (*contour*) shape. **être en forme** be fit. **formel** *adj* formal; definite.
formidable [fɔrmidablə] *adj* tremendous; (*fam*) incredible, fantastic.
formuler [fɔrmyle] *v* formulate; (*sentiment*) express; (*ordonnance*) draw up.

formulaire *nm* form. **formule** *nf* formula; expression; system, method; form.
fort [fɔr] *adj* strong; (*gros*) large; (*bruit*) loud; (*grand*) great; (*violent*) hard; (*doué*) good, able. *adv* loudly; hard; (*très*) very, most; (*beaucoup*) greatly, very much. *nm* strong point, forte; (*forteresse*) fort; (*milieu*) height, depths *pl*.
forteresse [fɔrtərɛs] *nf* fortress, stronghold.
fortifier [fɔrtifje] *v* fortify, strengthen. **fortification** *nf* fortification.
fortuit [fɔrtɥi] *adj* fortuitous, chance.
fortune [fɔrtyn] *nf* fortune; (*chance*) luck. **de fortune** makeshift. **fortuné** *adj* (*riche*) wealthy; (*heureux*) fortunate.
fosse [fos] *nf* pit; (*tombe*) grave. **fossé** *nm* ditch; (*écart*) gulf. **fossette** *nf* dimple. **fossoyeur** *nm* gravedigger.
fossile [fosil] *nm* fossil. *adj* fossilized.
fou [fu], **folle** *adj* mad; (*fam*) terrific, tremendous. **avoir le fou rire** have the giggles. *nm, nf* lunatic.
foudre [fudrə] *nf* lightning. **coup de foudre** love at first sight.
foudroyer [fudrwaje] *v* strike (down). **foudroyant** *adj* (*vitesse, attaque*) lightning; violent; (*succès*) thundering.
fouet [fwɛ] *nm* whip; (*cuisine*) whisk. **fouetter** *v* whip.
fougère [fuʒɛr] *nf* fern.
fougue [fug] *nf* ardour, spirit. **fougueux** *adj* fiery, spirited.
fouiller [fuje] *v* search; (*creuser*) dig, excavate. **fouiller dans** rummage in, go through. **fouille** *nf* excavation; search.
fouillis [fuji] *nm* jumble, muddle.
fouir [fwir] *v* dig, burrow.
foulard [fular] *nm* scarf.
foule [ful] *nf* crowd, mob.
fouler [fule] *v* trample, tread; (*méd*) sprain. **foulure** *nf* sprain.
four [fur] *nm* oven; (*usine*) furnace; (*poterie*) kiln.
fourbe [furb] *adj* deceitful, treacherous. **fourberie** *nf* deceit, treachery.
fourche [furʃ] *nf* fork; (*foin*) pitchfork; (*anat*) crotch. **fourcher** *v* split. **fourchette** *nf* fork. **fourchu** *adj* forked; (*pied*) cloven.
fourgon [furgɔ̃] *nm* coach, wagon, van.
fourmi [furmi] *nf* ant. **avoir des fourmis** have pins and needles. **fourmilier** *nm* anteater. **fourmilière** *nf* ant-hill.
fourmiller [furmije] *v* swarm.
fourneau [furno] *nm* furnace; (*cuisine*) stove.
fournir [furnir] *v* supply, provide. **fourni** *adj* bushy, thick. **fournisseur** *nm* tradesman, stockist; (*comm*) supplier. **fournitures** *nf pl* supplies *pl*.
fourrer [fure] *v* (*cuisine*) stuff, fill; (*vêtement*) line with fur; (*fam*) shove, stick. **fourreau** *nm* sheath. **fourre-tout** *nm invar* (*pièce*) lumber room; (*sac*) holdall. **fourreur** *nm* furrier. **fourrure** *nf* fur.
***foutre** [futrə] (*impol*) *v* do. **fous-moi le camp!** bugger off! **se foutre de** not give a damn about. **va te faire foutre!** fuck off! **foutaise** *nf* rubbish.
foyer [fwaje] *nm* home; (*âtre*) hearth; (*jeunes*) hostel; (*théâtre*) foyer; (*phys*) focus; (*infection, etc.*) seat, centre.
fracas [fraka] *nm* crash, din.
fracasser [frakase] *v* smash, shatter.
fraction [fraksjɔ̃] *nf* fraction.
fracturer [fraktyre] *v* fracture, break. **fracture** *nf* fracture.
fragile [fraʒil] *adj* fragile, delicate, frail. **fragilité** *nf* fragility, frailty.
fragment [fragmɑ̃] *nm* fragment, bit.
frai [frɛ] *nm* spawn.
frais[1], **fraîche** [frɛ, frɛʃ] *adj* fresh; (*froid*) cool; (*nouveau*) new. **fraîcheur** *nf* freshness; coolness.
frais[2] [frɛ] *nm pl* costs *pl*, expenses *pl*.
fraise[1] [frɛz] *nf* (*fruit*) strawberry. **fraisier** *nm* strawberry plant.
fraise[2] [frɛz] *nf* (*col*) ruff; (*dentiste*) drill.
framboise [frɑ̃bwaz] *nf* raspberry. **framboisier** *nm* raspberry bush.
franc[1] [frɑ̃] *nm* franc.
franc[2], **franche** [frɑ̃, frɑ̃ʃ] *adj* frank, candid; (*libre*) free; (*péj*) utter, downright; (*net*) clear. **franc-parler** *nm invar* outspokenness.
France [frɑ̃s] *nf* France. **français** *nm, adj* French. **les Français** the French.
franchir [frɑ̃ʃir] *v* (*obstacle*) clear, get over; (*traverser*) cross; pass.
franchise [frɑ̃ʃiz] *nf* frankness; exemption; (*bagages*) allowance.
franco [frɑ̃ko] *adv* post-free, carriage-paid.
frange [frɑ̃ʒ] *nf* fringe.
frapper [frape] *v* hit, strike; (*glacer*) chill, ice; (*porte*) knock.
fraternel [fratɛrnɛl] *adj* brotherly, fraternal. **fraternité** *nf* brotherhood, fraternity.

fraterniser [fraternize] *v* fraternize.
fraude [frod] *nf* fraud, cheating. **passer en fraude** smuggle in. **frauder** *v* defraud, cheat. **frauduleux** *adj* fraudulent.
frayer [freje] *v* clear, open up; (*poisson*) spawn. **frayer avec** mix *or* associate with.
fredaine [frədɛn] *nf* mischief.
fredonner [frədɔne] *v* hum.
frein [frɛ̃] *nm* brake; (*cheval*) bit. **frein à main** handbrake. **mettre le frein à** curb, check. **freiner** *v* slow down; (*auto*) brake; (*contrarier*) check.
frêle [frɛl] *adj* frail, flimsy.
frelon [frəlɔ̃] *nm* hornet.
frémir [fremir] *v* shudder, tremble; (*de froid*) shiver. **frémissement** *nm* shudder, shiver.
frêne [frɛn] *nm* ash.
frénésie [frenezi] *nf* frenzy. **frénétique** *adj* frenzied, frenetic.
fréquence [frekɑ̃s] *nf* frequency. **fréquent** *adj* frequent.
fréquenter [frekɑ̃te] *v* frequent; (*amis, etc.*) go around with, see often.
frère [frɛr] *nm* brother; (*moine*) friar.
fresque [frɛsk] *nf* fresco.
fret [frɛ] *nm* freight.
fréter [frete] *v* charter.
frétiller [fretije] *v* wriggle; (*queue*) wag.
friable [frijablə] *adj* crumbly.
friand [frijɑ̃] *adj* **friand de** fond of, partial to. **friandise** *nf* sweet, delicacy.
fricoter [frikɔte] *v* (*fam*) cook up.
friction [friksjɔ̃] *nf* friction. **frictionner** *v* rub.
frigide [friʒid] *adj* frigid. **frigidité** *nf* frigidity.
frigo [frigo] *nm* (*fam*) fridge.
frileux [frilø] *adj* sensitive to cold, chilly.
friper [fripe] *v* crumple.
fripon, -onne [fripɔ̃, -ɔn] *adj* cheeky, mischievous. *nm, nf* (*fam*) rascal.
***frire** [frir] *v* fry.
frise [friz] *nf* frieze.
friser [frize] *v* curl; (*frôler*) skim; (*approcher*) verge on. **frisé** *adj* curly.
frisquet, -ette, [friskɛ, -ɛt] *adj* chilly.
frissonner [frisɔne] *v* tremble, shudder; (*de froid*) shiver; (*feuillage*) rustle. **frisson** *nm* shiver.
frit [fri] *adj* fried. **frites** *nf pl* chips *pl*. **friteuse** *nf* chip pan, deep-fryer. **friture** *nf* frying; fried food.
frivole [frivɔl] *adj* frivolous. **frivolité** *nf* frivolity.
froid [frwa] *adj* cold. *nm* cold. **avoid froid** be cold. **froideur** *nf* coldness.
froisser [frwase] *v* crumple, crease; (*personne*) offend. **se froisser** take offence.
frôler [frole] *v* brush against, skim.
fromage [frɔmaʒ] *nm* cheese. **fromage blanc** cream cheese. **fromage maigre** cottage cheese.
froment [frɔmɑ̃] *nm* wheat.
froncer [frɔ̃se] *v* gather. **froncer les sourcils** frown. **fronce** *nm* gather. **froncement de sourcils** *nm* frown.
fronde [frɔ̃d] *nf* sling.
front [frɔ̃] *nm* front; (*anat*) forehead. **de front** head-on; (*côte à côte*) abreast. **faire front à** face up to. **frontal** *adj* frontal.
frontière [frɔ̃tjɛr] *nf* frontier, border.
frotter [frɔte] *v* rub; (*nettoyer*) scrub; (*allumette*) strike.
fructueux [fryktɥø] *adj* fruitful, profitable.
frugal [frygal] *adj* frugal. **frugalité** *nf* frugality.
fruit [frɥi] *nm* fruit. **fruits de mer** seafood *sing*. **fruits secs** dried fruit *sing*.
fruste [fryst] *adj* unpolished, crude.
frustrer [frystre] *v* frustrate. **frustration** *nf* frustration.
fugace [fygas] *adj* fleeting.
fugitif [fyʒitif], **-ive** *nm, nf* fugitive. *adj* runaway; (*fugace*) fleeting.
***fuir** [fɥir] *v* run away, escape; (*éviter*) shun, avoid; (*gaz, liquide*) leak. **fuite** *nf* escape, flight; leak.
fumer [fyme] *v* smoke; (*vapeur*) steam. **fumée** *nf* smoke; steam. **fumeur, -euse** *nm, nf* smoker.
fumier [fymje] *nf* dung, manure.
funambule [fynɑ̃byl] *n*(*m*+*f*) tightrope walker.
funèbre [fynɛbrə] *adj* funeral; (*lugubre*) mournful, gloomy.
funérailles [fynerɑj] *nf pl* funeral *sing*.
funeste [fynɛst] *adj* disastrous; fatal, deadly.
fur [fyr] *nm* **au fur et à mesure** as, as soon as, as fast as.
furet [fyrɛ] *nm* ferret.
fureter [fyrte] *v* ferret about; (*fouiller*) rummage.
fureur [fyrœr] *nf* fury, rage; passion, mania. **furibond** *adj* furious, mad. **furie** *nf* fury; mania. **furieux** *adj* furious.

furoncle [fyrɔ̃klə] *nm* boil.
furtif [fyrtif] *adj* furtive.
fusée [fyze] *nf* rocket; (*mine*) fuse; (*tech*) spindle.
fusil [fyzi] *nm* gun, rifle. **fusil de chasse** shotgun. **fusiller** *v* shoot.
fusion [fyzjɔ̃] *nf* fusion; (*métal, glace*) melting.
fusionner [fyzjɔne] *v* merge, amalgamate.
fustiger [fystiʒe] *v* censure.
fût [fy] *nm* (*arbre*) bole; (*tonneau*) barrel; (*colonne*) shaft.
futaie [fytɛ] *nf* forest, plantation of timber trees.
futaille [fytɑj] *nf* barrel.
futile [fytil] *adj* futile; (*frivole*) trivial. **futilité** *nf* futility; triviality.
futur [fytyr] *adj* future, prospective. **future maman** *nf* mother-to-be. **futur mari** *nm* husband-to-be. *nm* future.
fuyant [fɥijɑ̃] *adj* elusive; (*menton, etc.*) receding.

G

gâcher [gɑʃe] *v* (*gaspiller*) waste; (*gâter*) spoil; (*travail*) botch. **gâchis** *nm* mess; waste.
gâchette [gɑʃɛt] *nf* trigger.
gaffe [gaf] *nf* (*impair*) blunder; (*naut*) boat-hook.
gage [gaʒ] *nm* guarantee, security; (*preuve*) proof, evidence; (*jeu*) forfeit. **gages** *nm pl* wages *pl*. **gager** *v* wager; guarantee.
gagner [gaɲe] *v* (*toucher, mériter*) earn; (*être vainqueur*) win; (*obtenir*) gain; (*arriver à*) reach. **gagnant, -e** *nm, nf* winner.
gai [ge] *adj* cheerful, gay, merry. **gaieté** *nf* gaiety, cheerfulness.
gaillard [gajar] *adj* strong; (*alerte*) lively, sprightly; (*grivois*) ribald. *nm* strapping fellow. **gaillardise** *nf* ribald remark.
gain [gɛ̃] *nm* gain; (*salaire*) earnings *pl*. **gains** *nm pl* profits *pl*; (*jeu*) winnings *pl*.
gaine [gɛn] *nf* sheath; (*vêtement*) girdle. **gainer** *v* sheathe, cover.
galant [galɑ̃] *adj* gallant; courteous; romantic. **galanterie** *nf* gallantry.
galaxie [galaksi] *nf* galaxy.
galbe [galbə] *nm* curve.
gale [gal] *nf* mange, scabies. **galeux** *adj* mangy; (*sordide*) squalid, seedy.
galère [galɛr] *nf* galley.
galerie [galri] *nf* gallery; (*auto*) roof rack.
galet [galɛ] *nm* pebble. **galets** *nm pl* shingle *sing*.
galette [galɛt] *nf* (*crêpe*) pancake; biscuit; (*gâteau*) cake.
galion [galjɔ̃] *nm* galleon.
Galles [gal] *nf pl* **pays de Galles** *nm* Wales. **gallois** *nm, adj* Welsh. **les Gallois** the Welsh.
gallon [galɔ̃] *nm* gallon.
galon [galɔ̃] *nm* braid; (*mil*) stripe.
galop [galo] *nm* gallop. **petit galop** canter. **galoper** *v* gallop.
galvaniser [galvanize] *v* galvanize.
gambader [gɑ̃bade] *v* gambol, leap about. **gambade** *nf* leap, caper.
gamin [gamɛ̃], **-e** *adj* playful; (*puéril*) childish. *nm, nf* (*fam*) kid.
gamme [gam] *nf* scale; (*série*) range.
gangrène [gɑ̃grɛn] *nf* gangrene.
gangster [gɑ̃gstɛr] *nm* gangster.
gant [gɑ̃] *nm* glove. **gant de toilette** facecloth, flannel.
garage [garaʒ] *nm* garage. **garagiste** *nm* garage owner; garage mechanic.
garant [garɑ̃], **-e** *nm, nf* (*personne*) guarantor; (*chose*) guarantee. **se porter garant de** stand bail for.
garantir [garɑ̃tir] *v* guarantee; assure; protect. **garantie** *nf* guarantee.
garce [gars] *nf* (*impol*) bitch.
garçon [garsɔ̃] *nm* boy; (*magasin*) assistant; (*restaurant*) waiter; (*célibataire*) bachelor. **garçon d'honneur** best man.
garde [gard] *nf* guard; (*jur*) custody; (*surveillance*) care. **garde-à-vous!** (*mil*) attention! **prendre garde** be careful, take care. *nm* guard; (*château*) warden. **garde du corps** bodyguard.
garder [garde] *v* (*surveiller*) look after, guard; (*conserver, retenir*) keep. **garde-boue** *nm invar* mudguard. **garde-chasse** *nm* gamekeeper. **garde-feu** *nm invar* fireguard. **garde-fou** *nm* railing, parapet. **garde-manger** *nm invar* pantry, larder. **garde-nappe** *nm* tablemat. **garde-robe** *nf* wardrobe. **se garder de** beware of, be careful not to. **garderie** *nf* crèche, day nursery.

gardien [gardjɛ̃], **-enne** *nm, nf* guard; (*prison*) warder; (*château*) warden; (*zoo*) keeper; (*musée*) attendant; (*défenseur*) guardian. **gardien de but** goalkeeper. **gardien de nuit** night watchman.
gare[1] [gar] *nf* station. **gare routière** bus station.
gare[2] [gar] *interj* look out! beware!
garenne [garɛn] *nf* rabbit warren.
garer [gare] *v* (*voiture*) park: (*bateau*) dock. **se garer** park; (*piéton*) move aside. **se garer de** avoid.
se gargariser [gargarize] *v* gargle. **gargarisme** *nm* gargle.
gargouiller [garguje] *v* gurgle; (*intestin*) rumble. **gargouille** *nf* gargoyle.
garnir [garnir] *v* (*remplir*) fill, stock; (*équiper*) fit; (*doubler*) line; cover; decorate; (*cuisine*) garnish. **garnison** *nm* garrison. **garniture** *nf* fittings *pl*; (*cuisine*) garnish, trimmings *pl*; (*légumes*) vegetables *pl*; lining.
gars [gɑ] *nm* (*fam*) lad.
gaspiller [gaspije] *v* waste. **gaspillage** *nm* waste. **gaspilleur, -euse** *adj* wasteful.
gastrique [gastrik] *adj* gastric.
gastronomie [gastrɔnɔmi] *nf* gastronomy. **gastronomique** *adj* gastronomic.
gâteau [gɑto] *nm* cake; (*dessert*) gâteau. **petit gâteau (sec)** biscuit.
gâter [gɑte] *v* spoil, ruin. **se gâter** go bad *or* off; take a turn for the worse.
gauche [goʃ] *adj* left; (*maladroit*) awkward, clumsy. *nf* left, left-hand side. **gaucher** *adj* left-handed. **gaucherie** *nf* awkwardness, clumsiness.
gauchir [goʃir] *v* warp; (*fausser*) distort.
gaz [gɑz] *nm invar* gas. **gazeux** *adj* gaseous; (*boisson*) fizzy.
gaze [gɑz] *nf* gauze.
gazéifier [gazeifje] *v* aerate.
gazelle [gazɛl] *nf* gazelle.
gazon [gɑzɔ̃] *nm* lawn; (*motte*) turf.
gazouiller [gazuje] *v* (*oiseau*) chirp; (*bébé*) gurgle; (*ruisseau*) babble.
géant [ʒeɑ̃] *adj* gigantic, giant. *nm* giant.
***geindre** [ʒɛ̃drə] *v* groan, moan, whine.
gel [ʒɛl] *nm* frost.
gélatine [ʒelatin] *nf* gelatine.
geler [ʒəle] *v* freeze, be frozen. **gelé** *adj* frozen; (*membre*) frostbitten. **gelée** *nf* frost; (*cuisine*) jelly. **gelure** *nf* frostbite.
gélignite [ʒelignit] *nf* gelignite.
Gémeaux [ʒemo] *nm pl* Gemini *sing*.
gémir [ʒemir] *v* groan, moan, whine; (*grincer*) creak. **gémissement** *nm* groan, moan.
gemme [ʒɛm] *nf* gem.
gencive [ʒɑ̃siv] *nf* gum.
gendarme [ʒɑ̃darm] *nm* policeman.
gendre [ʒɑ̃drə] *nm* son-in-law.
gène [ʒɛn] *nm* gene.
gêne [ʒɛn] *nf* trouble, bother; embarrassment; (*physique*) discomfort; financial difficulties *pl*.
généalogie [ʒenealɔʒi] *nf* genealogy. **généalogique** *adj* genealogical.
gêner [ʒene] *v* bother, embarrass; (*obstacle*) hamper; inconvenience. **se gêner** put oneself out. **gênant** *adj* embarrassing, awkward. **gêné** *adj* embarrassed, uncomfortable; short of money.
général [ʒeneral] *nm, adj* general. **en général** in general, usually. **général de brigade** brigadier. **généralisation** *nf* generalization. **généraliser** *v* generalize. **généraliste** *nm* general practitioner.
génération [ʒenerɑsjɔ̃] *nf* generation.
génératrice [ʒeneratris] *nf* generator.
généreux [ʒenerø] *adj* generous. **générosité** *nf* generosity.
générique [ʒenerik] *adj* generic. *nm* (*cinéma*) credits *pl*.
génétique [ʒenetik] *adj* genetic. *nf* genetics.
génie [ʒeni] *nm* genius; spirit. **le génie** (*mil*) the Engineers. **génial** *adj* brilliant, inspired.
genièvre [ʒənjɛvrə] *nm* (*arbre*) juniper; (*fruit*) juniper berry; (*boisson*) gin.
génital [ʒenital] *adj* genital. **organes génitaux** *nm pl* genitals *pl*.
genou [ʒənu] *nm, pl* **-oux** knee. **à genoux** kneeling.
genre [ʒɑ̃r] *nm* kind, sort; (*gramm*) gender; (*art, etc.*) genre; family, genus. **le genre humain** mankind.
gens [ʒɑ̃] *nm pl* people *pl*.
gentiane [ʒɑ̃sjan] *nf* gentian.
gentil, -ille [ʒɑ̃ti, -ij] *adj* nice; (*personne*) kind; (*sage*) good. **gentillesse** *nf* kindness; favour. **gentiment** *adv* nicely; kindly.
génuflexion [ʒenyflɛksjɔ̃] *nf* genuflexion.
géographie [ʒeɔgrafi] *nf* geography. **géographe** *n(m+f)* geographer. **géographique** *adj* geographical.
geôle [ʒol] *nf* jail. **geôlier, -ère** *nm, nf* jailer.

géologie [ʒeɔlɔʒi] *nf* geology. **géologique** *adj* geological. **géologue** *n(m+f)* geologist.
géométrie [ʒeɔmetri] *nf* geometry. **géomètre** *nm* surveyor. **géométrique** *adj* geometrical.
géranium [ʒeranjɔm] *nm* geranium.
gerbe [ʒɛrb] *nf* sheaf, bundle; (*fleurs*) spray; (*eau, étincelles*) shower.
gercer [ʒɛrse] *v* chap, crack. **gerçure** *nf* crack.
gérer [ʒere] *v* manage. **gérance** *nf* management. **gérant** *nm* manager. **gérante** *nf* manageress.
gériatrie [ʒerjatri] *nf* geriatrics. **gériatrique** *adj* geriatric.
germanique [ʒɛrmanik] *adj* Germanic.
germer [ʒɛrme] *v* germinate; (*plante*) sprout, shoot. **germe** *nm* germ; (*source*) seed. **germination** *nf* germination.
gérondif [ʒerɔ̃dif] *nm* gerund, gerundive.
***gésir** [ʒezir] *v* lie, be lying.
geste [ʒɛst] *nm* gesture; act, deed.
gesticuler [ʒɛstikyle] *v* gesticulate. **gesticulation** *nf* gesticulation.
gestion [ʒɛstjɔ̃] *nf* management, administration.
geyser [ʒɛzɛr] *nm* geyser.
ghetto [gɛto] *nm* ghetto.
gibet [ʒibɛ] *nm* gallows.
gibier [ʒibje] *nm* game.
giboulée [ʒibule] *nf* shower.
gicler [ʒikle] *v* spurt, squirt. **giclée** *nf* spurt, squirt.
gifler [ʒifle] *v* slap in the face. **gifle** *nf* slap in the face.
gigantesque [ʒigɑ̃tɛsk] *adj* gigantic, immense.
gigot [ʒigo] *nm* leg of lamb.
gigue [ʒig] *nf* jig.
gilet [ʒilɛ] *nm* waistcoat; cardigan. **gilet de sauvetage** life-jacket.
gin [dʒin] *nm* gin.
gingembre [ʒɛ̃ʒɑ̃brə] *nm* ginger.
girafe [ʒiraf] *nf* giraffe.
girofle [ʒirɔflə] *nm* clove.
giron [ʒirɔ̃] *nm* lap.
girouette [ʒirwɛt] *nf* weathercock.
gisement [ʒizmɑ̃] *nm* deposit.
gitan [ʒitɑ̃] *adj* gipsy. **Gitan, -e** *nm, nf* gipsy.
gîte [ʒit] *nm* shelter.
givre [ʒivrə] *nm* hoar-frost. **givrer** *v* ice up.

glabre [glɑbrə] *adj* hairless; (*rasé*) clean-shaven.
glacer [glase] *v* freeze; (*boissons, etc.*) chill; (*cuisine*) glaze; (*gâteau*) ice. **glaçage** *nm* icing. **glace** *nf* ice; (*crème*) ice cream; mirror; (*vitre*) window; (*verre*) glass. **glacé** *adj* frozen, icy; (*boisson*) iced. **glacial** *adj* icy, frosty. **glacière** *nf* icebox. **glaçon** *nm* icicle; (*boisson*) ice cube.
glacier [glasje] *nm* glacier. **glaciation** *nf* glaciation.
glaise [glɛz] *nf* clay.
gland [glɑ̃] *nm* acorn; (*ornement*) tassel.
glande [glɑ̃d] *nf* gland. **glandulaire** *adj* glandular.
glaner [glane] *v* glean.
glapir [glapir] *v* yelp, squeal.
glisser [glise] *v* slide, slip; (*voilier, patineur*) glide; (*véhicule*) skid. **se glisser** slip, creep. **glissade** *nf* slide, slip; skid. **glissant** *adj* slippery. **glissière** *nf* groove, channel. **à glissière** sliding. **glissoire** *nf* slide.
globe [glɔb] *nm* globe. **globe oculaire** eyeball. **global** *adj* global, overall, total.
gloire [glwar] *nf* glory; (*renommée*) fame; distinction, credit. **glorieux** *adj* glorious.
glorifier [glɔrifje] *v* glorify. **se glorifier de** glory in. **glorification** *nf* glorification.
glossaire [glɔsɛr] *nm* glossary.
glouglouter [gluglute] *v* (*eau*) gurgle; (*dindon*) gobble. **glouglou** *nm* gurgling; gobbling.
glousser [gluse] *v* (*poule*) cluck; (*personne*) chuckle. **gloussement** *nm* cluck; chuckle.
glouton, -onne [glutɔ̃, -ɔn] *adj* greedy. *nm, nf* glutton. **gloutonnerie** *nf* gluttony, greed.
gluant [glyɑ̃] *adj* sticky.
glucose [glykoz] *nm* glucose.
glycine [glisin] *nf* wisteria.
gnome [gnom] *nm* gnome.
go [go] *adv* (*fam*) **tout de go** straight; (*dire*) straight out.
gobelet [gɔblɛ] *nm* beaker; (*verre*) tumbler; (*papier*) cup.
gober [gɔbe] *v* swallow whole; (*mensonge*) swallow, believe. **se gober** fancy oneself.
godasse [gɔdas] *nf* (*fam*) shoe.
godet [gɔdɛ] *nm* pot, jar.
godiche [gɔdiʃ] *adj* awkward, oafish.
goéland [gɔelɑ̃] *nm* seagull.
goélette [gɔelɛt] *nf* schooner.

gogo [gɔgo] *adv* **à gogo** (*fam*) galore.
golf [gɔlf] *nm* golf; (*terrain*) golf course. **golfeur, -euse** *nm, nf* golfer.
golfe [gɔlf] *nm* gulf, bay.
gommer [gɔme] *v* (*effacer*) erase, rub out; (*coller*) gum. **gomme** *nf* eraser, rubber; gum. **gommeux** *adj* sticky.
gond [gɔ̃] *nm* hinge.
gondole [gɔ̃dɔl] *nf* gondola. **gondolier, -ère** *nm, nf* gondolier.
gonfler [gɔ̃fle] *v* swell; (*d'air*) inflate. **gonflé** *adj* swollen; (*yeux*) puffy; (*ventre*) bloated. **gonflement** *nm* swelling; inflation.
gong [gɔ̃] *nm* gong.
gorge [gɔrʒ] *nf* (*gosier*) throat; (*poitrine*) breast; (*défilé*) gorge; (*rainure*) groove. **gorgée** *nf* mouthful. **petite gorgée** sip. **se gorger** *v* gorge.
gorille [gɔrij] *nm* gorilla.
gosier [gozje] *nm* throat.
gosse [gɔs] *n(m+f)* (*fam*) kid.
gothique [gɔtik] *nm* Gothic.
goudron [gudrɔ̃] *nm* tar. **goudronner** *v* tar.
gouffre [gufrə] *nm* abyss.
goulot [gulo] *nm* neck.
goulu [guly] *adj* greedy.
gourde [gurd] *nf* gourd; (*bidon*) flask; (*fam*) clot.
gourmand [gurmɑ̃] *adj* greedy. **gourmandise** *nf* greed.
gourmet [gurmɛ] *nm* gourmet.
gousse [gus] *nf* pod. **gousse d'ail** clove of garlic.
goût [gu] *nm* taste; (*penchant*) liking; style. **de bon/mauvais goût** in good/bad taste.
goûter [gute] *v* taste; savour, enjoy. **goûter à** taste, sample. *nm* afternoon tea.
goutte [gut] *nf* drop; (*méd*) gout. **goutte-à-goutte** *nm invar* (*méd*) drip. **tomber goutte à goutte** drip. **gouttière** *nf* gutter.
gouvernail [guvɛrnaj] *nm* rudder; (*barre*) helm.
gouverner [guvɛrne] *v* govern, rule; control; (*naut*) steer. **gouvernante** *nf* housekeeper; (*des enfants*) governess. **gouvernement** *nm* government. **gouverneur** *nm* governor.
grâce [grɑs] *nf* grace; favour; charm; pardon, mercy. **de bonne grâce** willingly. **grâce à** thanks to. **gracieux** *adj* graceful; amiable, kindly.
gracile [grasil] *adj* slender.
grade [grad] *nm* grade; (*échelon*) rank; (*titre*) degree.
gradin [gradɛ̃] *nm* terrace, step; (*théâtre*) tier.
graduer [gradɥe] *v* increase gradually; (*exercices*) grade; (*règle, etc.*) graduate. **graduel** *adj* gradual; progressive.
graffiti [grafiti] *nm pl* graffiti *pl.*
grain [grɛ̃] *nm* grain; (*café*) bean; (*collier*) bead. **grain de beauté** mole. **grain de poivre** peppercorn. **grain de raisin** grape.
graine [grɛn] *nf* seed.
graisser [grese] *v* grease. **graisse** *nf* fat, grease. **graisse de rognon** suet. **graisse de viande** dripping. **graisseux** *adj* greasy, fatty.
grammaire [gramɛr] *nf* grammar. **grammatical** *adj* grammatical.
gramme [gram] *nm* gram.
grand [grɑ̃], **-e** *adj* large, big; (*personne*) tall; (*intense, important*) great; (*principal*) main; (*réception, etc.*) grand. *nm, nf* senior *or* older pupil. **grandeur** *nf* greatness; (*dimension*) size.
grand-chose *n(m+f) invar* much.
Grande-Bretagne *nf* Great Britain.
grande ligne *nf* (*rail*) main line.
grandes vacances *nf pl* summer holidays *pl.*
grandiose [grɑ̃djoz] *adj* grand, imposing.
grandir [grɑ̃dir] *v* grow; (*augmenter*) increase; exaggerate; (*grossir*) magnify; (*hausser*) make taller.
grand magasin *nm* department store.
grand-mère *nf* grandmother.
grand ouvert *adj* wide open.
grand-parent *nm* grandparent.
grand-père *nm* grandfather.
grand-route *nf* main road.
grand-voile *nf* mainsail.
grange [grɑ̃ʒ] *nf* barn.
granit [granit] *nm* granite.
graphique [grafik] *adj* graphic. *nm* graph.
grappe [grap] *nf* cluster. **grappe de raisin** bunch of grapes.
gras, grasse [grɑ, grɑs] *adj* fat; (*graisseux*) greasy; (*épais*) thick; rich. **faire la grasse matinée** have a lie-in. *nm* fat. **grassouillet, -ette** *adj* (*fam*) plump, podgy.
gratifier [gratifje] *v* present, give, favour. **gratification** *nf* bonus.
gratin [gratɛ̃] *nm* **au gratin** topped with breadcrumbs or grated cheese.

gratitude [gratityd] *nf* gratitude.
gratter [grate] *v* scratch, scrape. **gratte-ciel** *nm invar* skyscraper.
gratuit [gratɥi] *adj* free; (*injustifié*) gratuitous.
grave [grav] *adj* serious, grave; (*digne*) solemn; (*son*) deep, low. **gravité** *nf* gravity, seriousness.
graver [grave] *v* engrave; (*disque*) cut. **graver à l'eau-forte** etch. **graveur** *nm* engraver. **gravure** *nf* engraving; (*illustration*) plate; (*réproduction*) print.
gravier [gravje] *nm* gravel.
gravir [gravir] *v* climb.
gré [gre] *nm* (*volonté*) will; (*goût*) taste, liking.
Grèce [grɛs] *nf* Greece. **grec, grecque** *nm, adj* Greek. **Grec, Grecque** *nm, nf* Greek.
gréer [gree] *v* rig. **gréement** *nm* rigging.
greffer [grefe] *v* graft; (*organe*) transplant. **greffe** *nf* graft; transplant.
greffier [grefje] *nm* clerk of the court.
grégaire [gregɛr] *adj* gregarious.
grêle[1] [grɛl] *adj* spindly, lanky; (*son*) shrill.
grêle[2] [grɛl] *nf* hail. **grêler** *v* hail. **grêlon** *nm* hailstone.
grelotter [grələte] *v* shiver; (*tinter*) jingle.
grenade[1] [grənad] *nf* (*fruit*) pomegranate. **grenadier** *nm* pomegranate tree.
grenade[2] [grənad] *nf* grenade. **grenade à main** hand grenade. **grenadier** *nm* grenadier.
grenier [grənje] *nm* attic, loft.
grenouille [grənuj] *nf* frog.
grès [grɛ] *nm* sandstone.
grésiller [grezije] *v* sizzle; (*phone, radio*) crackle.
grève[1] [grɛv] *nf* (*rivière*) bank; (*mer*) shore.
grève[2] [grɛv] *nf* strike. **faire grève** be on strike. **grève de la faim** hunger strike. **grève du zèle** work-to-rule. **grève perlée** go-slow. **se mettre en grève** strike, go on strike. **gréviste** *n(m+f)* striker.
grever [grəve] *v* burden, put a strain on.
gribouiller [gribuje] *v* scribble; (*dessiner*) doodle. **gribouillage** *nm* scribble; doodle.
grief [grijɛf] *nm* grievance. **grièvement blessé** seriously injured.
griffer [grife] *v* scratch. **griffe** *nf* claw; signature.
griffonner [grifɔne] *v* scribble. **griffonnage** *nm* scribble.
grignoter [griɲɔte] *v* nibble (at).
gril [gril] *nm* grill pan.
grille [grij] *nf* grid; (*claire-voie*) grille; (*prison*) bars *pl*; (*clôture*) gate; (*égout*) grating.
griller [grije] *v* grill; (*pain*) toast; (*brûler*) burn, scorch. **grille-pain** *nm invar* toaster. **grillade** *nm* grill.
grillon [grijɔ̃] *nm* cricket.
grimacer [grimase] *v* grimace, pull a face; (*sourire*) grin. **grimace** *nf* grimace.
grimer [grime] *v* (*théâtre*) make up. **grimage** *nm* make-up.
grimper [grɛ̃pe] *v* climb (up).
grincer [grɛ̃se] *v* (*métal*) grate; (*bois*) creak. **grincer des dents** gnash one's teeth.
grincheux [grɛ̃ʃø] *adj* grumpy.
grippe [grip] *nf* flu, influenza. **prendre en grippe** take a sudden dislike to.
gris [gri] *adj* grey; (*morne*) dull; (*ivre*) drunk. *nm* grey. **griser** *v* intoxicate. **se griser** get drunk. **grisonner** *v* go grey.
grive [griv] *nf* thrush.
grivois [grivwa] *adj* saucy.
Groënland [groɛnlɑ̃d] *nm* Greenland. **Groënlandais, -e** *nm, nf* Greenlander.
grogner [grɔɲe] *v* (*chien*) growl; (*cochon*) grunt; (*grommeler*) grumble. **grognement** *nm* growl, grunt.
groin [grwɛ̃] *nm* snout.
grommeler [grɔmle] *v* mutter, grumble.
gronder [grɔ̃de] *v* (*enfant*) scold; (*train, orage*) rumble; (*chien*) growl.
gros, grosse [gro, gros] *adj* big, large; (personne) fat; (*épais*) thick, heavy; (*important*) great; (*rude*) coarse. **gros lot** *nm* jackpot. **gros plan** *nm* close-up. **gros titre** *nm* headline. *nm* fat man; (*principal*) main part, bulk; (*comm*) wholesale. **en gros** wholesale; broadly, roughly. **grosse** *nf* fat woman; (*comm*) gross.
groseille [grozɛj] *nf* (*rouge*) red currant; (*blanche*) white currant. **groseille à maquereau** gooseberry. **groseillier** *nm* currant bush.
grossier [grosje] *adj* coarse, rough, crude. **grossièreté** *nf* coarseness, crudeness.
grossir [grosir] *v* swell, grow; (*personne*) put on weight; (*augmenter*) increase; exaggerate; (*agrandir*) enlarge, magnify.
grotesque [grɔtɛsk] *adj* grotesque; (*risible*) ludicrous. *nm* grotesque
grotte [grɔt] *nf* cave; (*artificielle*) grotto.

grouiller [gruje] *v* mill about. **grouiller de** be swarming *or* crawling with.
grouper [grupe] *v* group, put together. **groupe** *nm* group.
grue [gry] *nf* crane.
grumeau [grymo] *nm* lump.
se grumeler [grymle] *v* go lumpy; (*lait*) curdle. **grumeleux** *adj* lumpy.
gué [ge] *nm* ford. **passer à gué** ford.
guenille [gənij] *nf* rag.
guépard [gepar] *nm* cheetah.
guêpe [gɛp] *nf* wasp. **guêpier** *nm* wasp's nest; (*piège*) trap.
guère [gɛr] *adv* hardly, scarcely; not much.
guérilla [gerija] *nf* guerrilla warfare. **guérillero** *nm* guerilla.
guérir [gerir] *v* (*maladie*) cure; (*blessure*) heal; (*malade*) get better. **guérison** *nf* recovery.
Guernesey [gɛrnəzɛ] *nf* Guernsey.
guerre [gɛr] *nf* war; (*stratégie*) warfare. **en guerre** at war. **guerre mondiale** world war. **guerrier, -ère** *nm, nf* warrior.
guerroyer [gɛrwaje] *v* wage war.
guet [gɛ] *nm* watch. **faire le guet** be on the look-out. **guet-apens** *nm* ambush, trap.
guetter [gete] *v* watch (for); (*menace*) lie in wait for.
gueuler [gœle] *v* (*argot*) bawl, yell. **gueule** *nf* mouth; (*fam*: *figure*) face. **gueule de bois** (*fam*) hangover. **gueule-de-loup** *nf* snapdragon.
gueux [gø], **gueuse** *nm, nf* beggar.
gui [gi] *nm* mistletoe.
guichet [giʃɛ] *nm* window, counter; (*théâtre*) box office; (*gare*) ticket office; (*porte*) hatch, grille.
guide [gid] *nm* guide; (*livre*) guidebook. *nf* rein; (*jeune fille*) girl guide. **guider** *v* guide.
guidon [gidɔ̃] *nm* handlebars *pl*.
guigne [giɲ] *nf* (*fam*) bad luck.
guillemets [gijmɛ] *nm pl* inverted commas *pl*, quotation marks *pl*. **entre guillemets** in inverted commas.
guilleret, -ette [gijrɛ, -ɛt] *adj* perky, lively; (*propos*) saucy.
guillotine [gijɔtin] *nf* guillotine. **guillotiner** *v* guillotine.
guimauve [gimov] *nf* marshmallow.
guindé [gɛ̃de] *v* (*air*) stiff; (*style*) stilted.
Guinée [gine] *nf* Guinea.
guingois [gɛ̃gwa] *adv* **de guingois** (*fam*) askew, lop-sided.
guirlande [girlɑ̃d] *nf* garland. **guirlande de Noël** tinsel. **guirlande électrique** *or* **lumineuse** fairy lights *pl*.
guise [giz] *nf* **à sa guise** as one pleases. **en guise de** by way of.
guitare [gitar] *nf* guitar. **guitariste** *n(m+f)* guitarist.
gymnase [ʒimnɑz] *nm* gymnasium. **gymnaste** *n(m+f)* gymnast. **gymnastique** *nf* (*sport*) gymnastics; exercises *pl*.
gynécologie [ʒinekɔlɔʒi] *nf* gynaecology. **gynécologique** *adj* gynaecological. **gynécologue** *n(m+f)* gynaecologist.
gypse [ʒips] *nm* gypsum.
gyroscope [ʒirɔskɔp] *nm* gyroscope.

H

habile [abil] *adj* skilful, clever; (*malin*) cunning. **habileté** *nf* skill, cleverness.
habiller [abije] *v* dress, clothe; cover. **s'habiller** get dressed. **s'habiller en** dress up as. **habillement** *nm* clothing; outfit.
habit [abi] *nm* (*costume*) dress, outfit; (*soirée*) formal dress; (*rel*) habit. **habits** *nm pl* clothes *pl*.
habiter [abite] *v* live (in). **habitable** *adj* habitable. **habitant, -e** *nm, nf* inhabitant; (*maison*) occupant. **habitat** *nm* habitat. **habitation** *nf* residence, home; (*logement*) housing.
habitude [abityd] *nf* habit; custom. **avoir l'habitude de** be used to. **comme d'habitude** as usual. **d'habitude** usually.
habituer [abitɥe] *v* accustom. **s'habituer à** get used to. **habitué** *nm* regular. **habituel** *adj* usual, habitual.
hâbleur, -euse ['ɑblœr, -øz] *adj* boastful. *nm, nf* braggart. **hablerie** *nf* bragging, boasting.
hacher ['aʃe] *v* chop; (*menu*) mince. **hache** *nf* axe. **haché** *adj* minced; (*phrases*) jerky. **hachette** *nf* hatchet. **hachis** *nm* mince. **hachis Parmentier** cottage pie. **hachoir** *nm* chopper; mincer.
hagard ['agar] *adj* wild, distraught.
haie ['ɛ] *nf* hedge; (*sport*) hurdle, fence; (*rangée*) line.

haillon ['ɑjɔ̃] *nm* rag.
haine ['ɛn] *nf* hatred.
***haïr** ['air] *v* detest, hate.
Haïti [aiti] *nf* Haiti.
halage ['alaʒ] *nm* towing. **chemin de halage** *nm* towpath.
hâle ['ɑl] *nm* sunburn, tan. **hâlé** *adj* sunburnt, tanned.
haleine [alɛn] *nf* breath. **hors d'haleine** out of breath. **reprendre haleine** get one's breath back.
haler ['ale] *v* tow; (*ancre*) haul in.
haleter ['alte] *v* pant, gasp for breath. **haletant** *adj* panting, breathless.
hall ['ol] *nm* hall.
halle ['al] *nf* covered market.
hallucination [alysinɑsjɔ̃] *nf* hallucination.
halte ['alt] *nf* stop, pause; (*rail*) halt. **faire halte** stop, halt. *interj* stop! halt!
haltérophilie [alterɔfili] *nf* weight-lifting.
hamac ['amak] *nm* hammock.
hameau ['amo] *nm* hamlet.
hameçon [amsɔ̃] *nm* hook.
hampe ['ɑ̃p] *nf* pole, shaft.
hamster ['amstɛr] *nm* hamster.
hanche ['ɑ̃ʃ] *nf* hip; (*cheval*) haunch.
handicaper ['ɑ̃dikape] *v* handicap. **handicap** *nm* handicap. **handicapé, -e** *nm, nf* handicapped person. **handicapé moteur** spastic.
hangar ['ɑ̃gar] *nm* shed; (*aéro*) hangar.
hanter ['ɑ̃te] *v* haunt. **hantise** *nf* obsession.
happer ['ape] *v* snatch, grab.
haras ['arɑ] *nm* stud farm.
harassé ['arase] *adj* exhausted.
harceler ['arsəle] *v* harass, pester.
harde ['ard] *nf* herd.
hardes ['ard] *nf pl* old clothes *pl.*
hardi ['ardi] *adj* bold, daring. **hardiesse** *nf* boldness; effrontery, audacity.
hareng ['arɑ̃] *nm* herring. **hareng fumé** kipper.
hargneux ['arɲø] *adj* aggressive.
haricot ['ariko] *nm* bean. **haricot à rames** runner bean. **haricot beurre/blanc/rouge/vert** butter/haricot/kidney/French bean.
harmonica [armɔnika] *nm* harmonica.
harmonie [armɔni] *nf* harmony. **harmonieux** *adj* harmonious. **harmonique** *nm, adj* harmonic. **harmoniser** *v* harmonize.
harnacher ['arnaʃe] *v* harness.
harnais ['arnɛ] *nm* harness.
harpe ['arp] *nf* harp. **harpiste** *n(m+f)* harpist.
harpon ['arpɔ̃] *nm* harpoon.
hasard ['azar] *nm* chance, luck; risk, hazard; coincidence. **au hasard** at random. **par hasard** by accident. **hasarder** *v* risk. **hasardeux** *adj* risky, dangerous.
haschich ['aʃiʃ] *nm* hashish.
hâter ['ɑte] *v* hasten, hurry. **hâte** *nf* haste, hurry; impatience. **à la hâte** hurriedly. **hâtif** *adj* hasty, hurried; precocious, early.
hausser ['ose] *v* raise. **hausser les épaules** shrug one's shoulders. **hausse** *nf* rise, increase.
haut ['o] *adj* high; (*arbre, édifice*) tall; noble. *adv* high; (*fort*) loudly. *nm* top. **à haute voix** aloud. **de haut en bas** downwards; (*regarder*) up and down. **en haut** at the top; (*dessus*) above; (*maison*) upstairs. **haut-de-forme** *nm* top hat. **haut fourneau** blast furnace. **haut-parleur** *nm* loudspeaker.
hautain ['otɛ̃] *adj* haughty.
hautbois ['obwɑ] *nm* oboe. **hauboïste** *n(m+f)* oboist.
hauteur ['otœr] *nf* height; (*son*) pitch; nobility; (*arrogance*) haughtiness. **à la hauteur de** level with; equal to.
hâve ['ɑv] *adj* haggard, gaunt.
havre ['ɑvrə] *nm* haven.
havresac ['ɑvrəsak] *nm* haversack.
Haye ['ɛ] *nf* **La Haye** the Hague.
hebdomadaire [ɛbdɔmadɛr] *nm, adj* weekly.
héberger [ebɛrʒe] *v* lodge, take in.
hébéter [ebete] *v* daze, numb. **hébétement** *nm* stupor.
hébraïque [ebraik] *adj* Hebrew.
hébreu [ebrø] *nm, adj* Hebrew. **Hebreu** *nm* Hebrew.
hectare [ɛktar] *nm* hectare.
hein ['ɛ̃] *interj* (*fam*) eh?
hélas ['elɑs] *interj* alas!
héler ['ele] *v* hail.
hélice [elis] *nf* propeller.
hélicoptère [elikɔptɛr] *nm* helicopter.
hémisphère [emisfɛr] *nm* hemisphere.
hémorragie [emɔraʒi] *nf* haemorrhage.
hémorroïdes [emɔrɔid] *nf pl* haemorrhoids *pl.*
henné ['ene] *nm* henna.

hennir ['enir] *v* neigh. **hennissement** *nm* neigh.
héraldique [eraldik] *adj* heraldic. *nf* heraldry.
héraut ['ero] *nm* herald.
herbe [ɛrb] *nf* grass; (*cuisine*) herb. **en herbe** (*plante*) unripe; (*personne*) budding. **herbeux** *or* **herbu** *adj* grassy. **herbicide** *nm* weed-killer.
hérédité [eredite] *nf* heredity. **héréditaire** *adj* hereditary.
hérésie [erezi] *nf* heresy.
hérétique [eretik] *adj* heretical. *n(m+f)* heretic.
hérisser ['erise] *v* bristle, spike; (*personne*) ruffle. **se hérisser** stand on end, bristle up. **hérissé** *adj* bristly, prickly.
hérisson ['erisɔ̃] *nm* hedgehog.
hériter [erite] *v* inherit. **héritage** *nm* inheritance; (*civilisation*) heritage. **héritier** *nm* heir. **héritière** *nf* heiress.
hermétique [ɛrmetik] *adj* sealed; (*étanche*) watertight; (*à l'air*) airtight; impenetrable.
hermine [ɛrmin] *nf* ermine; (*animal*) stoat.
hernie ['ɛrni] *nf* hernia. **hernie discale** slipped disc.
héroïne[1] [erɔin] *nf* (*femme*) heroine.
héroïne[2] [erɔin] *nf* (*drogue*) heroin.
héroïsme [erɔismə] *nm* heroism. **héroïque** *adj* heroic.
héron ['erɔ̃] *nm* heron.
héros ['ero] *nm* hero.
hésiter [ezite] *v* hesitate. **hésitant** *adj* hesitant. **hésitation** *nf* hesitation.
hétéroclite [eterɔklit] *adj* sundry, assorted; (*personne*) eccentric.
hétérosexual [eterɔsɛksɥɛl] *adj* heterosexual.
hêtre ['ɛtrə] *nm* beech.
heure [œr] *nf* time; (*mesure*) hour. **à l'heure** on time. **deux/trois etc. heures** two/three etc. o'clock. **heure d'affluence** rush hour. **heures creuses** off-peak periods *pl*. **heures supplémentaires** overtime *sing*. **tout à l'heure** (*passé*) just now; (*futur*) shortly.
heureux [œrø] *adj* happy; fortunate, lucky.
heurter ['œrte] *v* strike, hit; (*sentiments, idées*) conflict with, go against. **se heurter** collide; (*s'opposer*) clash. **heurt** *nm* collision; clash. **sans heurts** smoothly. **heurtoir** *nm* door-knocker.
hexagone [ɛgzagɔn] *nm* hexagon. **hexagonal** *adj* hexagonal.
hiberner [ibɛrne] *v* hibernate. **hibernation** *nf* hibernation.
hibou ['ibu] *nm*, *pl* **-oux** *nm* owl.
hideux ['idø] *adj* hideous.
hier [jɛr] *adv* yesterday. **hier soir** yesterday evening, last night.
hiérarchie ['jerarʃi] *nf* hierarchy. **hiérarchique** *adj* hierarchical.
hilare [ilar] *adj* merry, mirthful. **hilarité** *nf* hilarity.
hindou [ɛ̃du] *adj* Hindu. **Hindou, -e** *nm, nf* Hindu. **hindouisme** *nm* Hinduism.
hippique [ipik] *adj* horse, equestrian. **concours hippique** *nm* show-jumping. **hippisme** *nm* (*courses*) horse-racing; (*équitation*) horse-riding.
hippocampe [ipɔkɑ̃p] *nm* sea-horse.
hippodrome [ipɔdrom] *nm* racecourse.
hippopotame [ipɔpɔtam] *nm* hippopotamus.
hirondelle [irɔ̃dɛl] *nf* swallow.
hisser ['ise] *v* hoist. **se hisser** heave *or* haul oneself up.
histoire [istwar] *nf* history; (*conte*) story; (*fam: affaire*) business. **histoires** *nf pl* (*fam*) fuss *sing*, trouble *sing*. **historien, -enne** *nm, nf* historian. **historique** *adj* historical; (*événement*) historic.
hiver [ivɛr] *nm* winter. **hivernal** *adj* winter; (*temps*) wintry.
hocher ['ɔʃe] *v* **hocher la tête** (*oui*) nod; (*non*) shake one's head. **hochement de tête** *nm* nod; shake of the head.
hochet ['ɔʃɛ] *nm* rattle.
hockey ['ɔkɛ] *nm* hockey.
Hollande ['ɔlɑ̃d] *nf* Holland. **hollandais** *nm, adj* Dutch. **les Hollandais** the Dutch.
homard ['ɔmar] *nm* lobster.
homicide [ɔmisid] *nm* murder. **homicide involontaire** manslaughter.
hommage [ɔmaʒ] *nm* homage, tribute; (*témoignage*) token. **hommages** *nm pl* respects *pl*.
homme [ɔm] *nm* man (*pl* men); (*espèce*) mankind. **homme à tout faire** odd-job man. **homme d'affaires** businessman. **homme de loi** lawyer. **homme d'État** statesman. **homme-grenouille** *nm* frogman. **homme politique** politician.
homogène [ɔmɔʒɛn] *adj* homogeneous.
homonyme [ɔmɔnim] *nm* homonym; (*personne*) namesake.

homosexuel [ɔmɔsɛksɥɛl], **-elle** *n, adj* homosexual. **homosexualité** *nf* homosexuality.
Hongrie ['ɔ̃gri] *nf* Hungary. **hongrois** *nm, adj* Hungarian. **Hongrois, -e** *nm, nf* Hungarian.
honnête [ɔnɛt] *adj* honest; decent; (*juste*) fair, reasonable. **honnêteté** *nf* honesty; decency; fairness.
honneur [ɔnœr] *nm* honour; (*mérite*) credit.
honorer [ɔnɔre] *v* honour; do credit to; respect. **honorable** *adj* honourable, worthy. **honoraire** *adj* honorary.
honte ['ɔ̃t] *nf* shame; (*déshonneur*) disgrace. **avoir honte** be ashamed. **faire honte à** put to shame. **honteux** *adj* (*penaud*) ashamed; (*scandaleux*) shameful, disgraceful.
hôpital [ɔpital] *nm* hospital.
hoquet ['ɔkɛ] *nm* hiccup. **avoir le hoquet** have hiccups. **hoqueter** *v* hiccup.
horaire [ɔrɛr] *adj* hourly. *nm* timetable.
horde ['ɔrd] *nf* horde.
horizon [ɔrizɔ̃] *nm* horizon; (*paysage*) landscape, view.
horizontal [ɔrizɔ̃tal] *adj* horizontal. **horizontale** *nf* horizontal.
horloge [ɔrlɔʒ] *nf* clock.
hormis ['ɔrmi] *prep* but, save.
hormone [ɔrmɔn] *nf* hormone.
horoscope [ɔrɔskɔp] *nm* horoscope.
horreur [ɔrœr] *nf* horror. **avoir horreur de** loathe, detest. **faire horreur à** disgust.
horrible [ɔriblə] *adj* horrible, dreadful.
horrifier [ɔrifje] *v* horrify.
hors ['ɔr] *prep* except, apart from. **hors-bord** *nm invar* speedboat. **hors de** out of; (*dehors*) outside; (*loin de*) away from. **être hors de soi** be beside oneself. **hors d'œuvre** *nm invar* hors d'oeuvre, starter. **hors-jeu** *nm, adj invar* offside. **hors-la-loi** *nm invar* outlaw. **hors-taxe** *adv, adj invar* duty-free.
horticulture [ɔrtikyltyr] *nf* horticulture. **horticole** *adj* horticultural.
hospice [ɔspis] *nm* home.
hospitalier [ɔspitalje] *adj* (*service*) hospital; (*accueillant*) hospitable. **hospitalité** *nf* hospitality.
hostile [ɔstil] *adj* hostile.
hôte [ot] *nm* host. *n(m+f)* (*invité*) guest. **hôtesse** *nf* hostess. **hôtesse de l'air** air hostess.
hôtel [otɛl] *nm* hotel; (*particulier*) mansion. **hôtel de ville** town hall. **hôtel-Dieu** *nm* general hospital. **hôtelier, -ère** *nm, nf* hotelier.
houblon ['ublɔ̃] *nm* hop.
houe ['u] *nf* hoe.
houille ['uj] *nf* coal. **houille blanche** hydro-electric power. **houillère** *nf* coalmine.
houle ['ul] *nf* swell. **houleux** *adj* turbulent, stormy.
houppe ['up] *nf* tuft, tassel. **houppette** *nf* powder puff.
houspiller ['uspije] *v* scold, tell off.
housse ['us] *nf* cover.
houx ['u] *nm* holly.
hublot ['yblo] *nm* porthole.
huer ['ɥe] *v* boo; (*chouette*) hoot. **huées** *nf pl* boos *pl*.
huile [ɥil] *nf* oil. **huile de coude** (*fam*) elbow grease. **huile de ricin** castor oil. **huile solaire** suntan oil. **huiler** *v* oil. **huileux** *adj* oily.
huis [ɥi] *nm* **à huis clos** in camera.
huissier [ɥisje] *nm* usher; (*jur*) bailiff.
huit ['ɥit] *nm, adj* eight. **huit jours** a week. **... en huit** a week on ... . **huitaine** *nf* about eight; about a week. **huitième** *n(m+f), adj* eighth.
huître [ɥitrə] *nf* oyster.
humain [ymɛ̃] *adj* human; (*compatissant*) humane. *nm* human. **humanitaire** *adj* humanitarian. **humanité** *nf* humanity.
humble [œblə] *adj* humble.
humecter [ymɛkte] *v* dampen, moisten.
humer ['yme] *v* smell; (*air*) inhale.
humeur [ymœr] *nf* mood, humour; temperament, temper; (*colère*) bad temper. **d'humeur égale** even-tempered
humide [ymid] *adj* damp, moist; (*climat*) humid. **humidité** *nf* humidity; dampness, damp.
humilier [ymilje] *v* humiliate. **humiliation** *nf* humiliation. **humilité** *nf* humility, humbleness.
humour [ymur] *nm* humour; sense of humour. **humoriste** *n(m+f)* humorist. **humoristique** *adj* humorous.
huppe ['yp] *nf* crest.
hurler ['yrle] *v* yell, roar; (*chien*) howl. **hurlement** *nm* yell, roar; howl.
hussard ['ysar] *nm* hussar.
hutte ['yt] *nf* hut.
hybride [ibrid] *nm, adj* hybrid.

hydrate [idrat] *nm* **hydrate de carbone** carbohydrate.
hydraulique [idrolik] *adj* hydraulic.
hydro-électrique [idrɔelɛktrik] *adj* hydroelectric.
hydrofoil [idrɔfɔjl] *nm* hydrofoil.
hydrogène [idrɔʒɛn] *nm* hydrogen.
hydromel [idrɔmɛl] *nm* mead.
hydrophile [idrɔfil] *adj* absorbent.
hyène [jɛn] *nf* hyena.
hygiène [iʒjɛn] *nf* hygiene. **hygiénique** *adj* hygienic.
hymne [imnə] *nm* hymn. **hymne national** national anthem.
hypermétropie [ipɛrmetrɔpi] *nf* longsightedness. **hypermétrope** *adj* longsighted.
hypertension [ipɛrtɑ̃sjɔ̃] *nf* high blood pressure.
hypnose [ipnoz] *nf* hypnosis. **hypnotique** *adj* hypnotic. **hypnotiser** *v* hypnotize. **hypnotiseur** *nm* hypnotist. **hypnotisme** *nm* hypnotism.
hypocondrie [ipɔkɔ̃dri] *nf* hypochondria. **hypocondriaque** *n(m+f)*, *adj* hypochondriac.
hypocrite [ipɔkrit] *adj* hypocritical. *n(m+f)* hypocrite. **hypocrisie** *nf* hypocrisy.
hypodermique [ipɔdɛrmik] *adj* hypodermic.
hypotension [ipɔtɑ̃sjɔ̃] *nf* low blood pressure.
hypothéquer [ipɔteke] *v* mortgage. **hypothèque** *nf* mortgage.
hypothèse [ipɔtɛz] *nf* hypothesis. **hypothétique** *adj* hypothetical.
hystérectomie [iskerɛktɔmi] *nf* hysterectomy.
hystérie [isteri] *nf* hysteria. **hystérique** *adj* hysterical.

I

iceberg [ajsbɛrg] *nm* iceberg.
ici [isi] *adv* (*lieu*) here; (*temps*) now. **d'ici là** before then. **d'ici peu** before long. **par ici** this way.
icône [ikon] *nf* icon.
idéal [ideal] *nm*, *adj* ideal.
idéaliste [idealist] *adj* idealistic. *n(m+f)* idealist.
idée [ide] *nf* idea; (*esprit*) mind. **idée fixe** obsession. **idée lumineuse** brainwave.
identifier [idɑ̃tifje] *v* identify. **identification** *nf* identification.
identique [idɑ̃tik] *adj* identical. **identité** *nf* identity.
idéologie [ideɔlɔʒi] *nf* ideology.
idiome [idjom] *nm* idiom. **idiomatique** *adj* idiomatic.
idiosyncrasie [idjɔsɛ̃krazi] *nf* idiosyncrasy.
idiot [idjo], **-e** *adj* idiotic. *nm*, *nf* idiot. **idiotie** *nf* idiocy, stupidity; (*action, propos*) idiotic *or* stupid thing.
idiotisme [idjɔtismə] *nm* idiom.
idolâtrer [idɔlɑtre] *v* idolize. **idolâtrie** *nf* idolatry.
idole [idɔl] *nf* idol.
idyllique [idilik] *adj* idyllic.
if [if] *nm* yew.
igloo [iglu] *nm* igloo.
ignifuger [ignifyʒe] *v* fireproof. **ignifuge** *adj* fireproof.
ignorer [iɲɔre] *v* not know, be unaware of. **ignorance** *nf* ignorance. **ignorant** *adj* ignorant. **ignorant de** unaware of. **ignoré** *adj* unknown.
il [il] *pron* it; (*personne*) he. **il y a** (*sing*) there is; (*pl*) there are.
île [il] *nf* island. **les îles anglo-normandes** the Channel Islands.
illégal [ilegal] *adj* illegal. **illégalité** *nf* illegality.
illégitime [ileʒitim] *adj* illegitimate. **illégitimité** *nf* illegitimacy.
illettré [iletre], **-e** *n*, *adj* illiterate.
illicite [ilisit] *adj* illicit.
illimité [ilimite] *adj* unlimited, boundless.
illisible [iliziblə] *adj* (*écriture*) illegible; (*livre*) unreadable.
illogique [ilɔʒik] *adj* illogical.
illuminer [ilymine] *v* light up, illuminate. **illumination** *nf* illumination, lighting.
illusion [ilyzjɔ̃] *nf* illusion. **illusion d'optique** optical illusion.
illustre [ilystrə] *adj* illustrious.
illustrer [ilystre] *v* illustrate. **illustrateur, -trice** *nm*, *nf* illustrator. **illustration** *nf* illustration.
ils [il] *pron* they.
image [imaʒ] *nf* image; (*dessin*) picture; reflection.

imaginer [imaʒine] *v* imagine; (*inventer*) think up. **s'imaginer** imagine; (*croire*) think. **imaginaire** *adj* imaginary. **imaginatif** *adj* imaginative. **imagination** *nf* imagination.
imbécile [ɛ̃besil] *adj* stupid. *n(m+f)* imbecile.
imbiber [ɛ̃bibe] *v* saturate, impregnate, soak. **s'imbiber** absorb.
imbu [ɛ̃by] *adj* **imbu de** full of, steeped in.
imiter [imite] *v* imitate; copy; (*signature*) forge; (*ressembler*) look like; (*célébrité*) impersonate. **imitation** *nf* imitation; forgery; impersonation.
immaculé [imakyle] *adj* immaculate, spotless.
immanquable [ɛ̃mɑ̃kablə] *adj* inevitable; infallible.
immatriculer [imatrikyle] *v* register. **immatriculation** *nf* registration.
immédiat [imedja] *adj* immediate.
immense [imɑ̃s] *adj* vast, immense; (*espace*) boundless.
immerger [imɛrʒe] *v* immerse, submerge. **immersion** *nf* immersion, submersion.
immeuble [imœblə] *nm* building; (*appartements*) block of flats; (*bureaux*) office block.
immigrer [imigre] *v* immigrate. **immigrant, -e** *nm, nf* immigrant. **immigration** *nf* immigration.
imminent [iminɑ̃] *adj* imminent, impending.
immiscer [imise] *v* **s'immiscer dans** interfere with.
immobile [imɔbil] *adj* immobile, motionless, still. **immobilier** *adj* property. **immobiliser** *v* immobilize. **s'immobiliser** come to a standstill.
immonde [imɔ̃d] *adj* vile, foul; (*rel*) unclean. **immondices** *nf pl* refuse *sing*.
immoral [imɔral] *adj* immoral. **immoralité** *nf* immorality.
immortel [imɔrtɛl] *adj* immortal. **immortaliser** *v* immortalize. **immortalité** *nf* immortality.
immuniser [imynize] *v* immunize. **immunisation** *nf* immunization. **immunisé** *adj* immune. **immunité** *nf* immunity.
impact [ɛ̃pakt] *nm* impact.
impair [ɛ̃pɛr] *adj* odd, uneven. *nm* blunder.
imparfait [ɛ̃parfɛ] *nm, adj* imperfect.
impartial [ɛ̃parsjal] *adj* impartial, unbiased. **impartialité** *nf* impartiality.
impasse [ɛ̃pɑs] *nf* dead end, no through road; (*situation*) impasse, deadlock.
impassible [ɛ̃pasiblə] *adj* impassive.
impatience [ɛ̃pasjɑ̃s] *nf* impatience. **impatient** *adj* impatient; (*avide*) eager.
impatienter [ɛ̃pasjɑ̃te] *v* irritate. **s'impatienter** lose one's patience.
impeccable [ɛ̃pekablə] *adj* perfect, impeccable.
imper [ɛ̃pɛr] *nm* (*fam*) mac.
impératif [ɛ̃peratif] *nm, adj* imperative.
impératrice [ɛ̃peratris] *nf* empress.
impérial [ɛ̃perjal] *adj* imperial. **impériale** *nf* (*autobus*) top deck. **autobus à impériale** double-decker.
imperméable [ɛ̃pɛrmeablə] *adj* waterproof; (*roches*) impervious. *nm* raincoat. **imperméabiliser** *v* waterproof.
impersonnel [ɛ̃pɛrsɔnɛl] *adj* impersonal.
impertinent [ɛ̃pɛrtinɑ̃] *adj* impertinent. **impertinence** *nf* impertinence.
impétueux [ɛ̃petɥø] *adj* impetuous.
impitoyable [ɛ̃pitwajablə] *adj* merciless, ruthless.
implicite [ɛ̃plisit] *adj* implicit.
impliquer [ɛ̃plike] *v* imply; (*mêler*) involve.
implorer [ɛ̃plɔre] *v* implore.
impoli [ɛ̃pɔli] *adj* impolite.
impopulaire [ɛ̃pɔpylɛr] *adj* unpopular. **impopularité** *nf* unpopularity.
importer[1] [ɛ̃pɔrte] *v* (*comm*) import. **importation** *nf* import.
***importer**[2] [ɛ̃pɔrte] *v* matter. **n'importe** never mind, it doesn't matter. **n'importe comment/où/quand/quel/qui/quoi** anyhow/anywhere/anytime/any/anybody/anything. **importance** *nf* importance; (*grandeur*) size, extent. **important** *adj* important; considerable.
importuner [ɛ̃pɔrtyne] *v* bother, trouble.
imposer [ɛ̃poze] *v* impose; (*prescrire*) set; tax. **imposable** *adj* taxable. **imposant** *adj* imposing, impressive.
impossible [ɛ̃pɔsiblə] *adj* impossible.
imposteur [ɛ̃pɔstœr] *nm* impostor.
impôt [ɛ̃po] *nm* tax; taxation.
impotent [ɛ̃pɔtɑ̃], **-e** *adj* disabled, crippled. *nm, nf* disabled person. **impotence** *nf* disability.
imprécis [ɛ̃presi] *adj* imprecise.
imprégner [ɛ̃preɲe] *v* impregnate; (*air*) pervade. **s'imprégner de** absorb, soak up.

impression [ɛ̃presjɔ̃] *nf* impression; (*imprimerie*) printing. **impressionable** *adj* impressionable. **impressionnant** *adj* impressive. **impressionner** *v* impress; (*bouleverser*) upset.
imprévu [ɛ̃prevy] *adj* unexpected, unforeseen.
imprimer [ɛ̃prime] *v* print; (*cachet*) stamp; (*marquer*) imprint; publish. **imprimé** *nm* (*poste*) printed matter; (*tissu*) print. **imprimerie** *nf* printing; printing house *or* works. **imprimeur** *nm* printer.
improbable [ɛ̃prɔbablə] *adj* improbable, unlikely.
impromptu [ɛ̃prɔ̃pty] *adj*, *adv* impromptu.
improviser [ɛ̃prɔvize] *v* improvise. **improvisation** *nf* improvisation.
improviste [ɛ̃prɔvist] *nm* **à l'improviste** without warning, unexpectedly.
imprudent [ɛ̃prydɑ̃] *adj* unwise, foolish, careless. **imprudence** *nf* foolishness, carelessness.
impudent [ɛ̃pydɑ̃] *adj* impudent. **impudence** *nf* impudence.
impuissant [ɛ̃pɥisɑ̃] *adj* powerless; (*effort*) ineffectual; (*sexuellement*) impotent. **impuissance** *nf* impotence.
impulsion [ɛ̃pylsjɔ̃] *nf* impulse; impetus. **impulsif** *adj* impulsive.
impur [ɛ̃pyr] *adj* impure. **impureté** *nf* impurity.
imputer [ɛ̃pyte] *v* impute, attribute; (*frais*) charge.
inaccessible [inaksesiblə] *adj* inaccessible.
inactif [inaktif] *adj* inactive, idle.
inadapté [inadapte], **-e** *nm*, *nf* misfit. *adj* (*psychol*) maladjusted.
inadvertance [inadvɛrtɑ̃s] *nf* oversight. **par inadvertance** inadvertently.
inanimé [inanime] *adj* inanimate; (*personne*) unconscious.
inaperçu [inapɛrsy] *adj* unnoticed. **passer inaperçu** go unnoticed.
inappréciable [inapresjablə] *adj* invaluable; imperceptible.
inapte [inapt] *adj* incapable, unfit.
inarticulé [inartikyle] *adj* inarticulate.
inattendu [inatɑ̃dy] *adj* unexpected.
inaudible [inodiblə] *adj* inaudible.
inaugurer [inɔgyre] *v* inaugurate; (*plaque*) unveil; (*exposition*) open. **inaugural** *adj* inaugural; (*voyage*) maiden. **inauguration** *nf* inauguration; unveiling; opening.
incapable [ɛ̃kapablə] *adj* incapable, unable.
incapacité [ɛ̃kapasite] *nf* incapacity; incompetence; inability; (*invalidité*) disability.
incendier [ɛ̃sɑ̃dje] *v* set fire to, burn. **incendiaire** *adj* incendiary. **incendie** *nm* fire. **incendie volontaire** arson.
incertain [ɛ̃sɛrtɛ̃] *adj* uncertain. **incertitude** *nf* uncertainty.
incessant [ɛ̃sɛsɑ̃] *adj* incessant. **incessamment** *adv* very soon.
inceste [ɛ̃sɛst] *nm* incest. **incestueux** *adj* incestuous.
incident [ɛ̃sidɑ̃] *adj* incidental. *nm* incident; (*anicroche*) setback, hitch. **incidemment** *adv* incidentally.
incinérer [ɛ̃sinere] *v* (*ordures*) incinerate; (*cadavre*) cremate. **incinérateur** *nm* incinerator. **incinération** *nf* incineration; cremation.
inciter [ɛ̃site] *v* incite, encourage.
incliner [ɛ̃kline] *v* slope, tilt; tend, be inclined. **s'incliner** bow. **inclinaison** *nm* slope, incline. **inclination** *nf* inclination.
***inclure** [ɛ̃klyr] *v* include; (*joindre*) enclose; insert. **inclus** *adj* enclosed; included, inclusive. **inclusion** *nf* inclusion; insertion. **inclusivement** *adv* inclusively.
incognito [ɛ̃kɔɲito] *adv* incognito.
incohérent [ɛ̃kɔerɑ̃] *adj* incoherent.
incolore [ɛ̃kɔlɔr] *adj* colourless.
incommoder [ɛ̃kɔmɔde] *v* disturb, bother. **incommode** *adj* inconvenient, awkward; (*siège*) uncomfortable. **incommodité** *nf* inconvenience.
incompatible [ɛ̃kɔ̃patiblə] *adj* incompatible. **incompatibilité** *nf* incompatibility.
incompétent [ɛ̃kɔ̃petɑ̃] *adj* incompetent. **incompétence** *nf* incompetence; (*ignorance*) lack of knowledge.
incomplet, -ète [ɛ̃kɔ̃plɛ, -ɛt] *adj* incomplete.
inconcevable [ɛ̃kɔ̃svablə] *adj* inconceivable.
inconfort [ɛ̃kɔ̃fɔr] *nm* discomfort. **inconfortable** *adj* uncomfortable.
inconnu [ɛ̃kɔny], **-e** *adj* unknown; strange. *nm*, *nf* stranger. **l'inconnu** the unknown.
inconscience [ɛ̃kɔ̃sjɑ̃s] *nf* unconsciousness; (*folie*) thoughtlessness, rashness. **inconscient** *adj* unconscious; thoughtless, rash.

inconséquent [ɛ̃kɔ̃sekɑ̃] *adj* inconsistent; (*irréfléchi*) thoughtless
inconstant [ɛ̃kɔ̃stɑ̃] *adj* fickle.
incontestable [ɛ̃kɔ̃tɛstablə] *adj* unquestionable, undeniable.
inconvenant [ɛ̃kɔ̃vnɑ̃] *adj* improper, unseemly.
inconvénient [ɛ̃kɔ̃venjɑ̃] *nm* disadvantage, drawback; risk.
incorporer [ɛ̃kɔrpɔre] *v* incorporate; mix.
incorrect [ɛ̃kɔrɛkt] *adj* incorrect; impolite.
incrédule [ɛ̃kredyl] *adj* incredulous. *n(m+f)* (*rel*) unbeliever. **incrédulité** *nf* incredulity.
incriminer [ɛ̃krimine] *v* incriminate.
incroyable [ɛ̃krwajablə] *adj* incredible.
incuber [ɛ̃kybe] *v* incubate, hatch. **incubation** *nf* incubation.
inculper [ɛ̃kylpe] *v* charge. **inculpation** *nf* charge.
inculte [ɛ̃kylt] *adj* uncultivated; (*négligé*) unkempt.
incurable [ɛ̃kyrablə] *adj* incurable.
Inde [ɛ̃d] *nf* India.
indécent [ɛ̃desɑ̃] *adj* indecent. **indécence** *nf* indecency.
indécis [ɛ̃desi] *adj* (*irrésolu*) indecisive; (*hésitant*) undecided; (*douteux*) unsettled; vague.
indéfini [ɛ̃defini] *adj* indefinite.
indemne [ɛ̃dɛmnə] *adj* unharmed, unhurt.
indemniser [ɛ̃dɛmnize] *v* compensate, reimburse. **indemnité** *nf* compensation, indemnity; (*frais*) allowance.
indépendant [ɛ̃depɑ̃dɑ̃] *adj* independent; (*appartement*) self-contained; (*journaliste, etc.*) freelance. **indépendance** *nf* independence.
index [ɛ̃dɛks] *nm* index; (*aiguille*) needle, pointer; (*doigt*) index finger.
indicatif [ɛ̃dikatif] *adj* indicative. *nm* (*musical*) signature tune; (*téléphonique*) dialling code; (*gramm*) indicative.
indication [ɛ̃dikɑsjɔ̃] *nf* indication; (*renseignement*) information; instruction, direction. **indicateur** *nm* indicator; (*horaire*) timetable; guide; gauge.
indice [ɛ̃dis] *nm* indication, sign; (*clef*) clue; index, rating.
indien [ɛ̃djɛ̃] *adj* Indian. **Indien, -enne** *nm, nf* Indian.
indifférent [ɛ̃diferɑ̃] *adj* indifferent; (*sans importance*) immaterial. **indifférence** *nf* indifference.
indigence [ɛ̃diʒɑ̃s] *nf* poverty. **indigent** *adj* poor, destitute.
indigène [ɛ̃diʒɛn] *n(m+f)*, *adj* native.
indigestion [ɛ̃diʒɛstjɔ̃] *nf* indigestion.
indigne [ɛ̃diɲ] *adj* unworthy.
indigner [ɛ̃diɲe] *v* make indignant. **s'indigner** be indignant. **indignation** *nf* indignation. **indigné** *adj* indignant.
indiquer [ɛ̃dike] *v* indicate, show, point out.
indirect [ɛ̃dirɛkt] *adj* indirect.
indiscipliné [ɛ̃disipline] *adj* unruly.
indiscret, -ète [ɛ̃diskrɛ, -ɛt] *adj* indiscreet. **indiscrétion** *nf* indiscretion.
indispensable [ɛ̃dispɑ̃sablə] *adj* essential.
indisposé [ɛ̃dispoze] *adj* unwell.
individu [ɛ̃dividy] *nm* individual. **individualité** *nf* individuality. **individuel** *adj* individual; personal, private.
indolent [ɛ̃dɔlɑ̃] *adj* idle, indolent. **indolence** *nf* idleness, indolence.
indolore [ɛ̃dɔlɔr] *adj* painless.
***induire** [ɛ̃dɥir] *v* infer. **induire en erreur** mislead.
indulgence [ɛ̃dylʒɑ̃s] *nf* indulgence, leniency. **indulgent** *adj* indulgent, lenient.
industrie [ɛ̃dystri] *nf* industry. **industrialiser** *v* industrialize. **industriel** *adj* industrial.
inébranlable [inebrɑ̃lablə] *adj* steadfast; solid.
inefficace [inefikas] *adj* (*mesure*) ineffective; (*employé*) inefficient.
inégal [inegal] *adj* (*irrégulier*) uneven; (*différent*) unequal. **inégalité** *nf* inequality; unevenness; difference.
inepte [inɛpt] *adj* inept.
inerte [inɛrt] *adj* inert, lifeless; passive, apathetic. **inertie** *nf* inertia; apathy.
inestimable [inɛstimablə] *adj* invaluable.
inévitable [inevitablə] *adj* inevitable; (*accident*) unavoidable.
inexact [inɛgzakt] *adj* inaccurate; unpunctual. **inexactitude** *nf* inaccuracy; unpunctuality.
inexpérimenté [inɛksperimɑ̃te] *adj* (*personne*) inexperienced; (*produit*) untested.
infaillible [ɛ̃fajiblə] *adj* infallible.
infâme [ɛ̃fɑm] *adj* infamous; (*odieux*) vile, despicable. **infamie** *nf* infamy.
infanterie [ɛ̃fɑ̃tri] *nf* infantry.
infarctus [ɛ̃farktys] *nm* **infarctus du myocarde** coronary thrombosis.

infatué [ɛ̃fatɥe] *adj* conceited, vain.
inféond [ɛ̃fekɔ̃] *adj* sterile, infertile. **infécondité** *nf* sterility, infertility.
infect [ɛ̃fɛkt] *adj* vile, revolting.
infecter [ɛ̃fɛkte] *v* infect, contaminate. **s'infecter** turn septic. **infectieux** *adj* infectious. **infection** *nf* infection; (*puanteur*) stench.
inférieur, -e [ɛ̃ferjœr] *adj* (*plus bas*) lower; (*qualité*) inferior; (*quantité*) smaller. *nm, nf* inferior. **infériorité** *nf* inferiority.
infester [ɛ̃fɛste] *v* infest. **infestation** *nf* infestation.
infidèle [ɛ̃fidɛl] *adj* unfaithful; (*inexact*) inaccurate. **infidélité** *nf* unfaithfulness; (*mari, femme*) infidelity; inaccuracy.
s'infiltrer [ɛ̃filtre] *v* infiltrate; (*liquide*) percolate; (*lumière*) filter through. **infiltration** *nf* infiltration.
infime [ɛ̃fim] *adj* tiny, minute.
infini [ɛ̃fini] *adj* infinite; interminable. *nm* infinity. **infinité** *nf* infinity; infinite number. **infinitif** *nm, adj* infinitive.
infirme [ɛ̃firm] *adj* crippled, disabled; (*vieillards*) infirm. *nm, nf* cripple, disabled person. **infirmerie** *nf* (*école*) sick bay. **infirmier, -ère** *nm, nf* nurse. **infirmité** *nf* disability; infirmity.
inflammable [ɛ̃flamablə] *adj* inflammable. **inflammation** *nf* inflammation.
inflation [ɛ̃flɑsjɔ̃] *nf* inflation.
inflexion [ɛ̃flɛksjɔ̃] *nf* inflection; (*courbe*) bend.
infliger [ɛ̃fliʒe] *v* inflict; impose.
influencer [ɛ̃flyɑ̃se] *v* influence. **influence** *nf* influence. **influent** *adj* influential.
influer [ɛ̃flye] *v* **influer sur** have an influence on.
informe [ɛ̃fɔrm] *adj* shapeless.
informer [ɛ̃fɔrme] *v* inform. **s'informer** inquire, find out. **information** *nf* information; (*jur*) inquiry. **informations** *nf pl* news *sing*.
infortune [ɛ̃fɔrtyn] *nf* misfortune. **infortuné** *adj* ill-fated, wretched.
infraction [ɛ̃fraksjɔ̃] *nf* offence; (*loi*) infringement, breach.
infroissable [ɛ̃frwasablə] *adj* crease-resistant.
infuser [ɛ̃fyze] *v* (*thé*) brew, infuse.
ingénieur [ɛ̃ʒenjœr] *nm* engineer.
ingénieux [ɛ̃ʒenjø] *adj* ingenious. **ingéniosité** *nf* ingenuity.
ingénu [ɛ̃ʒeny] *adj* naïve, ingenuous.
s'ingérer [ɛ̃ʒere] *v* interfere, meddle. **ingérence** *nf* interference.
ingrat [ɛ̃gra] *adj* ungrateful; (*tâche*) thankless; (*déplaisant*) unattractive. **ingratitude** *nf* ingratitude.
ingrédient [ɛ̃gredjɑ̃] *nm* ingredient.
inhabile [inabil] *adj* clumsy, inept.
inhabité [inabite] *adj* uninhabited, unoccupied.
inhaler [inale] *v* inhale.
inhérent [inerɑ̃] *adj* inherent.
inhiber [inibe] *v* inhibit. **inhibition** *nf* inhibition.
inhumain [inymɛ̃] *adj* inhuman.
inimitié [inimitje] *nf* enmity.
initial [inisjal] *adj* initial. **initiale** *nf* initial.
initiative [inisjativ] *nf* initiative.
initier [inisje] *v* initiate. **initiation** *nf* initiation.
injecter [ɛ̃ʒɛkte] *v* inject. **injection** *nf* injection.
injurier [ɛ̃ʒyrje] *v* abuse, insult. **injure** *nf* abuse, insult. **injurieux** *adj* abusive, insulting.
injuste [ɛ̃ʒyst] *adj* unjust, unfair. **injustice** *nf* injustice, unfairness.
inné [ine] *adj* innate.
innocent [inɔsɑ̃], **-e** *adj* innocent. *nm, nf* innocent (person); idiot, simpleton. **innocence** *nf* innocence.
innovation [inɔvɑsjɔ̃] *nf* innovation.
inoccupé [inɔkype] *adj* unoccupied.
inoculer [inɔkyle] *v* inoculate. **inoculation** *nf* inoculation.
inonder [inɔ̃de] *v* flood; (*tremper*) soak. **inondation** *nf* flood.
inopiné [inɔpine] *adj* unexpected.
inouï [inwi] *adj* incredible, unheard-of.
inoxydable [inɔksidablə] *adj* stainless; (*couteau, etc.*) stainless steel.
inquiéter [ɛ̃kjete] *v* worry, bother. **inquiet, -ète** *adj* worried, anxious. **inquiétude** *nf* worry, anxiety.
inquisition [ɛ̃kizisjɔ̃] *nf* inquisition.
inscription [ɛ̃skripsjɔ̃] *nf* inscription; (*club, cours, etc.*) enrolment, registration.
***inscrire** [ɛ̃skrir] *v* write down, enrol, register; (*graver*) inscribe.
insecte [ɛ̃sɛkt] *nm* insect. **insecticide** *nm* insecticide.
insécurité [ɛ̃sekyrite] *nf* insecurity.
inséminer [ɛ̃semine] *v* inseminate. **insémination** *nf* insemination.

insensé [ɛ̃sɑ̃se] *adj* insane, crazy.
insensible [ɛ̃sɑ̃siblə] *adj* insensitive; imperceptible. **insensibilité** *nf* insensitivity.
insérer [ɛ̃sere] *v* insert. **s'insérer dans** fit into. **insertion** *nf* insertion.
insidieux [ɛ̃sidjø] *adj* insidious.
insigne [ɛ̃siɲ] *adj* distinguished, notable. *nm* badge, insignia.
insignifiant [ɛ̃siɲifjɑ̃] *adj* insignificant. **insignifiance** *nf* insignificance.
insinuer [ɛ̃sinɥe] *v* insinuate, imply. **s'insinuer dans** worm one's way into. **insinuation** *nf* insinuation.
insipide [ɛ̃sipid] *adj* insipid.
insister [ɛ̃siste] *v* insist. **insister sur** stress. **insistance** *nf* insistence. **insistant** *adj* insistent.
insolation [ɛ̃sɔlɑsjɔ̃] *nf* (*méd*) sunstroke; (*temps*) sunshine.
insolent [ɛ̃sɔlɑ̃] *adj* insolent. **insolence** *nf* insolence.
insolite [ɛ̃sɔlit] *adj* strange, unusual.
insomnie [ɛ̃sɔmni] *nf* insomnia. **insomniaque** *n(m+f)*, *adj* insomniac.
insonore [ɛ̃sɔnɔr] *adj* soundproof. **insonoriser** *v* soundproof.
insouciant [ɛ̃susjɑ̃] *adj* carefree, happy-go-lucky.
inspecter [ɛ̃spɛkte] *v* inspect. **inspecteur, -trice** *nm, nf* inspector. **inspection** *nf* inspection.
inspirer [ɛ̃spire] *v* inspire; (*respirer*) breathe in. **inspiration** *nf* inspiration.
instable [ɛ̃stablə] *adj* unstable. **instabilité** *nf* instability.
installer [ɛ̃stale] *v* install; (*pièce*) fit out. **s'installer** settle in (*or* down); (*emménager*) move in, set up home. **installation** *nf* installation. **installations** *nf pl* fittings *pl*, facilities *pl*; (*usine*) plant *sing*.
instant [ɛ̃stɑ̃] *nm* moment, instant. **à l'instant** at this moment; (*passé*) a moment ago. **par instants** at times. **pour l'instant** for the time being. **instantané** *adj* instantaneous; (*café*) instant.
instar [ɛ̃star] *nm* **à l'instar de** after the fashion of.
instigation [ɛ̃stigɑsjɔ̃] *nf* instigation. **instigateur, -trice** *nm, nf* instigator.
instinct [ɛ̃stɛ̃] *nm* instinct. **instinctif** *adj* instinctive.
instituer [ɛ̃stitɥe] *v* institute. **institut** *nm* institute. **instituteur, -trice** *nm, nf* primary school teacher. **institution** *nf* institution; (*école*) private school.
instruction [ɛ̃stryksjɔ̃] *nf* education. **instructions** *nf pl* instructions *pl*. **instructif** *adj* instructive.
***instruire** [ɛ̃strɥir] *v* teach, instruct; educate; inform.
instrument [ɛ̃strymɑ̃] *nm* instrument; (*outil*) tool. **instrumental** *adj* instrumental.
insu [ɛ̃sy] *nm* **à l'insu de** unknown to. **à mon insu** without my knowing it.
insubordonné [ɛ̃sybɔrdɔne] *adj* insubordinate. **insubordination** *nf* insubordination.
insuccès [ɛ̃syksɛ] *nm* failure.
insuffisant [ɛ̃syfizɑ̃] *adj* inadequate; (*quantité*) insufficient. **insuffisance** *nf* inadequacy; insufficiency.
insulaire [ɛ̃sylɛr] *adj* insular. *n(m+f)* islander.
insuline [ɛ̃sylin] *nf* insulin.
insulter [ɛ̃sylte] *v* insult. **insulte** *nf* insult.
insupportable [ɛ̃sypɔrtablə] *adj* unbearable, intolerable.
s'insurger [ɛ̃syrʒe] *v* rebel. **insurgé, -e** *nm, nf* rebel. **insurrection** *nf* revolt.
intact [ɛ̃takt] *adj* intact.
intègre [ɛ̃tɛgrə] *adj* honest. **intégrité** *nf* integrity.
intégrer [ɛ̃tegre] *v* integrate. **intégral** *adj* complete, full; (*texte*) unabridged. **intégration** *nf* integration.
intellect [ɛ̃telɛkt] *nm* intellect. **intellectuel, -elle** *n, adj* intellectual.
intelligence [ɛ̃teliʒɑ̃s] *nf* intelligence; (*compréhension*) understanding. **intelligent** *adj* intelligent, clever.
intelligible [ɛ̃teliʒiblə] *adj* intelligible.
intendant [ɛ̃tɑ̃dɑ̃] *nm* (*école*) bursar; (*maison*) steward; (*mil*) quartermaster.
intense [ɛ̃tɑ̃s] *adj* intense. **intensif** *adj* intensive. **intensifier** *v* intensify. **intensité** *nf* intensity.
intention [ɛ̃tɑ̃sjɔ̃] *nf* intention. **à l'intention de** for the benefit of, for. **avoir l'intention de** intend to. **intentionnel** *adj* intentional.
intercéder [ɛ̃tɛrsede] *v* intercede.
intercepter [ɛ̃tɛrsɛpte] *v* intercept; (*boucher*) block, cut off. **interception** *nf* interception.
***interdire** [ɛ̃tɛrdir] *v* forbid, ban. **interdiction** *nf* ban. **interdit** *adj* prohibited.

intéresser [ɛ̃terese] *v* interest; concern. **s'intéresser à** be interested in. **intéressant** *adj* interesting; (*offre, prix*) attractive.
intérêt [ɛ̃terɛ] *nm* interest; importance.
intérieur, -e [ɛ̃terjœr] *adj* inner, internal, inside; (*pol*) domestic, home. *nm* interior, inside. **à l'intérieur** inside.
intérim [ɛ̃terim] *nm* interim. **intérimaire** *adj* temporary.
interjection [ɛ̃tɛrʒɛksjɔ̃] *nf* interjection.
interloquer [ɛ̃tɛrlɔke] *v* dumbfound, take aback.
intermède [ɛ̃tɛrmɛd] *nm* interlude.
intermédiaire [ɛ̃tɛrmedjɛr] *adj* intermediate. *n*(*m*+*f*) go-between; (*comm*) middleman. **sans intermédiaire** directly.
interminable [ɛ̃tɛrminablə] *adj* endless, interminable.
intermittent [ɛ̃tɛrmitɑ̃] *adj* intermittent.
internat [ɛ̃tɛrna] *nm* boarding school.
international [ɛ̃tɛrnasjɔnal] *adj* international.
interne [ɛ̃tɛrn] *adj* internal. *n*(*m*+*f*) boarder; (*méd*) houseman, intern. **internement** *nm* internment. **interner** *v* intern.
interpeller [ɛ̃tɛrpele] *v* (*appeler*) call out to; (*apostropher*) shout at; question.
interphone [ɛ̃tɛrfɔn] *nm* intercom.
interposer [ɛ̃tɛrpoze] *v* interpose. **s'interposer** intervene.
interpréter [ɛ̃tɛrprete] *v* interpret; (*théâtre, musique*) perform. **interprétation** *nf* interpretation. **interprète** *n*(*m*+*f*) interpreter; performer.
interroger [ɛ̃terɔʒe] *v* question; examine; (*police, etc.*) interrogate. **interrogatif** *nm, adj* interrogative. **interrogation** *nf* questioning, interrogation; question; (*école*) test. **interrogatoire** *nm* questioning; (*jur*) cross-examination.
***interrompre** [ɛ̃terɔ̃prə] *v* interrupt; (*arrêter*) break off.
interruption [ɛ̃terypsjɔ̃] *nf* interruption. **interrupteur** *nm* switch.
interurbain [ɛ̃tɛryrbɛ̃] *adj* (*téléphone*) long-distance.
intervalle [ɛ̃tɛrval] *nm* interval; space. **dans l'intervalle** in the meantime.
***intervenir** [ɛ̃tɛrvənir] *v* intervene; (*survenir*) take place, occur. **intervention** *nf* intervention.
intervertir [ɛ̃tɛrvɛrtir] *v* invert, reverse.
interview [ɛ̃tɛrvju] *nf* interview.
intestin [ɛ̃tɛstɛ̃] *nm* intestine. **intestins** *nm pl* bowels *pl*. *adj* internal. **intestinal** *adj* intestinal.
intime [ɛ̃tim] *adj* intimate; private, personal; (*ami*) close. *n*(*m*+*f*) close friend. **intimité** *nf* intimacy; privacy.
intimider [ɛ̃timide] *v* intimidate. **intimidation** *nf* intimidation.
intituler [ɛ̃tityle] *v* entitle, call. **intitulé** *nm* title.
intolérable [ɛ̃tɔlerablə] *adj* intolerable. **intolérance** *nf* intolerance. **intolérant** *adj* intolerant.
intonation [ɛ̃tɔnɑsjɔ̃] *nf* intonation.
intoxiquer [ɛ̃tɔksike] *v* poison. **intoxication** *nf* poisoning. **intoxiqué, -e** *nm, nf* addict.
intransitif [ɛ̃trɑ̃zitif] *nm, adj* intransitive.
intraveineux [ɛ̃travɛnø] *adj* intravenous.
intrépide [ɛ̃trepid] *adj* intrepid, bold.
intriguer [ɛ̃trige] *v* intrigue; (*comploter*) scheme. **intrigue** *nf* scheme; (*film, livre, etc.*) plot.
intrinsèque [ɛ̃trɛ̃sɛk] *adj* intrinsic.
***introduire** [ɛ̃trɔdɥir] *v* introduce; insert; (*faire entrer*) show in. **s'introduire** get in. **introduction** *nf* introduction; insertion; admission.
introverti [ɛ̃trɔvɛrti], **-e** *adj* introverted. *nm, nf* introvert.
intrus [ɛ̃try], **-e** *nm, nf* intruder. *adj* intrusive. **intrusion** *nf* intrusion.
intuition [ɛ̃tɥisjɔ̃] *nf* intuition. **intuitif** *adj* intuitive.
inutile [inytil] *adj* useless; (*effort*) pointless; (*superflu*) needless.
invaincu [ɛ̃vɛ̃ky] *adj* unbeaten.
invalide [ɛ̃valid] *n*(*m*+*f*) disabled person. *adj* disabled. **invalidité** *nf* disability.
invariable [ɛ̃varjablə] *adj* invariable.
invasion [ɛ̃vɑzjɔ̃] *nf* invasion.
inventaire [ɛ̃vɑ̃tɛr] *nm* inventory; (*comm*) stocktaking.
inventer [ɛ̃vɑ̃te] *v* invent; (*forger*) make up; (*imaginer*) think up. **inventeur, -trice** *nm, nf* inventor. **invention** *nf* invention.
inverse [ɛ̃vɛrs] *nm, adj* opposite, reverse. **inversement** *adv* conversely. **inverser** *v* reverse, invert. **inversion** *nf* inversion.
invertébré [ɛ̃vɛrtebre] *nm, adj* invertebrate.
investigation [ɛ̃vɛstigɑsjɔ̃] *nf* investigation.
investir [ɛ̃vɛstir] *v* invest. **investissement** *nm* investment.

invisible [ɛ̃viziblə] *adj* invisible.
inviter [ɛ̃vite] *v* invite, ask. **invitation** *nf* invitation. **invité, -e** *nm, nf* guest.
involontaire [ɛ̃vɔlɔ̃tɛr] *adj* involuntary; unintentional.
invoquer [ɛ̃vɔke] *v* call upon; (*excuse*) put forward.
invraisemblable [ɛ̃vrɛsɑ̃blablə] *adj* unlikely, improbable; incredible.
iode [jɔd] *nm* iodine.
ion [jɔ̃] *nm* ion.
iris [iris] *nm* iris.
Irlande [irlɑ̃d] *nf* Ireland. **irlandais** *nm, adj* Irish. **les Irlandais** the Irish.
ironie [irɔni] *nf* irony. **ironique** *adj* ironic.
irrationnel [irasjɔnɛl] *adj* irrational.
irréel [ireɛl] *adj* unreal.
irréfléchi [irefleʃi] *adj* thoughtless, hasty.
irrégulier [iregylje] *adj* irregular. **irrégularité** *nf* irregularity.
irrésistible [irezistiblə] *adj* irresistible.
irrespect [irɛspɛ] *nm* disrespect. **irrespectueux** *adj* disrespectful.
irrévocable [irevɔkablə] *adj* irrevocable.
irriguer [irige] *v* irrigate. **irrigation** *nf* irrigation.
irriter [irite] *v* irritate; annoy. **irritable** *adj* irritable. **irritation** *nf* irritation.
irruption [irypsjɔ̃] *nf* **faire irruption** burst in.
Islam [islam] *nm* Islam. **islamique** *adj* Islamic.
Islande [islɑ̃d] *nf* Iceland. **islandais** *nm, adj* Icelandic. **Islandais, -e** *nm, nf* Icelander.
isoler [izɔle] *v* isolate; (*élec*) insulate. **isolation** *nf* insulation. **isolé** *adj* isolated, lonely, remote. **isolement** *nm* isolation. **isoloir** *nm* polling booth.
issu [isy] *adj* **issu de** descended from.
issue [isy] *nf* (*sortie*) exit; solution; (*fin*) outcome; (*eau*) outlet.
isthme [ismə] *nm* isthmus.
Italie [itali] *nf* Italy. **italien** *nm, adj* Italian. **Italien, -enne** *nm, nf* Italian.
italique [italik] *nm* italics *pl. adj* italic.
itinéraire [itinerɛr] *nm* itinerary, route.
ivoire [ivwar] *nm* ivory. **Côte d'Ivoire** *nf* Ivory Coast.
ivre [ivrə] *adj* drunk. **ivresse** *nf* drunkenness; ecstasy, exhilaration. **ivrogne** *n*(*m+f*) drunkard.

J

j' [ʒ] *V* **je.**
jabot [ʒabo] *nm* (*chemise*) jabot; (*zool*) crop.
jacasser [ʒakase] *v* chatter. **jacasse** *nf* magpie. **jacassement** *nm* chatter.
jachère [ʒaʃɛr] *nf* fallow.
jacinthe [ʒasɛ̃t] *nf* hyacinth. **jacinthe des bois** bluebell.
jade [ʒad] *nm* jade.
jadis [ʒadis] *adv* formerly, long ago.
jaguar [ʒagwar] *nm* jaguar.
jaillir [ʒajir] *v* gush forth, spurt out; (*rires, etc.*) burst out; (*surgir*) spring up. **jaillissement** *nm* spurt, gush.
jais [ʒɛ] *nm* jet.
jalonner [ʒalɔne] *v* mark out; (*border*) line.
jaloux, -ouse [ʒalu, -uz] *adj* jealous. **jalousie** *nf* jealousy; (*store*) blind.
jamais [ʒamɛ] *adv* ever; (*négatif*) never. **à tout jamais** for ever and ever. **ne ... jamais** never.
jambe [ʒɑ̃b] *nf* leg.
jambon [ʒɑ̃bɔ̃] *nm* ham.
jante [ʒɑ̃t] *nf* rim.
janvier [ʒɑ̃vje] *nm* January.
Japon [ʒapɔ̃] *nm* Japan. **japonais** *nm, adj* Japanese. **les Japonais** the Japanese.
japper [ʒape] *v* yap. **jappement** *nm* yap.
jaquette [ʒakɛt] *nf* jacket; (*homme*) morning coat.
jardin [ʒardɛ̃] *nm* garden. **jardin d'enfants** nursery school. **jardin maraîcher** market garden. **jardin public** park.
jardiner [ʒardine] *v* garden. **jardinage** *nm* gardening. **jardinier** *nm* gardener. **jardinière** *nf* gardener; (*caisse*) window box.
jargon [ʒargɔ̃] *nm* jargon.
jarret [ʒarɛ] *nm* (*anat*) back of the knee; (*zool*) hock; (*cuisine*) knuckle.
jarretelle [ʒartɛl] *nf* suspender *or US* garter.
jarretière [ʒartjɛr] *nf* garter.
jars [ʒar] *nm* gander.
jaser [ʒɑze] *v* chatter; (*médire*) gossip; (*ruisseau*) babble.
jasmin [ʒasmɛ̃] *nm* jasmine.
jatte [ʒat] *nf* bowl.
jauger [ʒoʒe] *v* measure, gauge; (*personne*) size up. **jauge** *nf* gauge; capacity.

jauge d'essence petrol gauge. **jauge d'huile** dipstick.
jaune [ʒon] *adj* yellow. *nm* yellow; (*œuf*) yolk; (*péj*) blackleg. **jaunir** *v* turn yellow. **jaunisse** *nf* jaundice.
javelot [ʒavlo] *nm* javelin.
jazz [dʒɑz] *nm* jazz.
je [ʒə], **j'** *pron* I.
jean [dʒin] *nm* jeans *pl*.
jeep [ʒip] *nf* jeep.
jersey [ʒɛrzɛ] *nm* jersey, jumper.
Jersey [ʒɛrzɛ] *nf* Jersey.
jet[1] [ʒɛ] *nm* (*liquide*) jet, spurt, stream; (*lumière*) beam; (*pierre*) throw; (*fam: coup*) go.
jet[2] [dʒɛt] *nm* (*aéro*) jet.
jetée [ʒəte] *nf* jetty; pier.
jeter [ʒəte] *v* throw.
jeton [ʒətɔ̃] *nm* token; (*jeu*) counter.
jeu [ʒø] *nm* play; game; (*série*) set; (*casino*) gambling. **jeu de cartes** (*ensemble*) pack of cards; (*partie*) card game. **jeu de mots** pun.
jeudi [ʒødi] *nm* Thursday. **jeudi saint** Maundy Thursday.
jeun [ʒœ̃] *adv* **à jeun** on an empty stomach.
jeune [ʒœn] *adj* young; (*cadet*) junior, younger. *n*(*m*+*f*) young person. **jeunesse** *nf* youth; (*personnes*) young people *pl*.
jeûner [ʒøne] *v* go without food; (*rel*) fast. **jeûne** *nm* fast.
joaillier [ʒɔɑje], **-ère** *nm, nf* jeweller. **joaillerie** *nf* jewellery; (*magasin*) jeweller's.
jockey [ʒɔkɛ] *nm* jockey.
jodler [ʒɔdle] *v* yodel.
joie [ʒwa] *nf* joy, delight.
***joindre** [ʒwɛ̃drə] *v* join; (*unir*) combine; (*inclure*) attach, enclose; (*personne*) contact.
joint [ʒwɛ̃] *nm* joint; (*auto*) gasket; (*robinet*) washer. *adj* joint. **jointure** *nf* joint.
joli [ʒɔli] *adj* pretty, nice. **joliment** *adv* nicely; (*fam*) pretty, jolly.
jonc [ʒɔ̃] *nm* (*plante*) rush; cane; (*bracelet*) bangle; (*baque*) ring.
joncher [ʒɔ̃ʃe] *v* strew, litter.
jonction [ʒɔ̃ksjɔ̃] *nf* junction.
jongler [ʒɔ̃gle] *v* juggle. **jonglerie** *nf* juggling, jugglery. **jongleur, -euse** *nm, nf* juggler.
jonquille [ʒɔ̃kij] *nf* daffodil.
joue [ʒu] *nf* cheek.
jouer [ʒwe] *v* play; (*théâtre*) act; (*clef, etc.*) be loose; (*casino*) gamble; (*argent*) stake. **jouer de** use, make use of. **se jouer de** (*tromper*) deceive; (*moquer*) scoff at. **jouet** *nm* toy. **joueur, -euse** *nm, nf* player; gambler.
joufflu [ʒufly] *adj* chubby-cheeked.
joug [ʒu] *nm* yoke.
jouir [ʒwir] *v* **jouir de** enjoy. **jouissance** *nf* pleasure, delight; (*jur*) use.
jour [ʒur] *nm* day; (*lumière*) light; (*ouverture*) gap. **de nos jours** nowadays. **jour de congé** day off. **jour ferié** bank holiday. **jour ouvrable** weekday. **le jour de l'An** New Year's day. **quinze jours** a fortnight. **vivre au jour le jour** live from hand to mouth. **journée** *nf* day.
journal [ʒurnal] *nm* newspaper; magazine, journal; (*intime*) diary. **journalier** *adj* daily; (*banal*) everyday. **journalisme** *nm* journalism. **journaliste** *n*(*m*+*f*) journalist.
jovial [ʒɔvjal] *adj* jovial, jolly. **jovialité** *nf* joviality, jollity.
joyau [ʒwajo] *nm* jewel, gem.
joyeux [ʒwajø] *adj* joyful, merry.
jubilé [ʒybile] *nm* jubilee.
jubiler [ʒybile] *v* (*fam*) be jubilant. **jubilation** *nf* jubilation.
jucher [ʒyʃe] *v* perch.
judaïsme [ʒydaismə] *nm* Judaism.
judiciaire [ʒydisjɛr] *adj* judicial.
judicieux [ʒydisjø] *adj* judicious.
judo [ʒydo] *nm* judo.
juger [ʒyʒe] *v* judge; (*jur*) try; consider; decide. **au jugé** by guesswork. **juge** *nm* judge. **juge de paix** Justice of the Peace. **jugement** *nm* judgment; (*jur*) sentence.
juif [ʒɥif] *adj* Jewish. **Juif, Juive** *nm, nf* Jew.
juillet [ʒɥijɛ] *nm* July.
juin [ʒɥɛ̃] *nm* June.
jumeau, -elle [ʒymo, -ɛl] *adj* twin; (*maisons*) semi-detached. *nm, nf* twin. **vrais jumeaux, vraies jumelles** identical twins. **jumelles** *nf pl* binoculars *pl*.
jumeler [ʒymle] *v* twin; join. **jumelé** *adj* double; twin.
jument [ʒymɑ̃] *nf* mare.
jungle [ʒɔ̃glə] *nf* jungle.
junte [ʒœ̃t] *nf* junta.
jupe [ʒyp] *nf* skirt. **jupon** *nm* waist slip.
jurer [ʒyre] *v* swear, vow; (couleurs) clash. **juré, -e** *nm, nf* juror.

juridique [ʒyridik] *adj* legal. **juridiction** *nf* jurisdiction.
juron [ʒyrɔ̃] *nm* oath, curse.
jury [ʒyri] *nm* jury.
jus [ʒy] *nm* juice. **jus de viande** gravy.
jusant [ʒyzɑ̃] *nm* ebb.
jusque [ʒyskə] *prep* up to. **jusqu'à** up to; (*lieu*) as far as; (*temps*) until; (*même*) even. **jusqu'à ce que** until. **jusqu'au bout** to the bitter end. **jusqu'ici** so far; (*lieu*) up to here; (*temps*) until now. **jusqu'où?** how far?
juste [ʒyst] *adj* just, fair; exact, accurate, right; (*pertinent*) sound; (*musique*) in tune; (*trop petit*) tight, barely enough. *adv* just; exactly; accurately; in tune. **au juste** exactly. **tout juste** only just, barely; exactly. **justesse** *nf* accuracy; soundness.
justice [ʒystis] *nf* justice, fairness; (*pol*) law.
justifier [ʒystifje] *v* justify; prove. **justifiable** *adj* justifiable. **justification** *nf* justification; proof.
jute [ʒyt] *nm* jute.
juteux [ʒytø] *adj* juicy.
juvénile [ʒyvenil] *adj* young, youthful.
juxtaposer [ʒykstapoze] *v* juxtapose. **juxtaposition** *nf* juxtaposition.

K

kaki [kaki] *nm, adj* khaki.
kaléidoscope [kaleidɔskɔp] *nm* kaleidoscope.
kangourou [kɑ̃guru] *nm* kangaroo.
karaté [karate] *nm* karate.
kayak [kajak] *nm* kayak.
kermesse [kɛrmɛs] *nf* fair, bazaar.
kidnapper [kidnape] *v* kidnap. **kidnappeur, -euse** *nm, nf* kidnapper.
kilo [kilo] *nm* kilo.
kilogramme [kilɔgram] *nm* kilogram.
kilomètre [kilɔmɛtrə] *nm* kilometre. **kilométrage** *nm* mileage.
kilowatt [kilɔwat] *nm* kilowatt.
kimono [kimɔno] *nm* kimono.
kinésithérapie [kineziterapi] *nf* physiotherapy. **kinésithérapeute** *n(m+f)* physiotherapist.
kiosque [kjɔsk] *nm* kiosk; (*jardin*) summer-house.
kiwi [kiwi] *nm* kiwi.
klaxon ® [klaksɔn] *nm* horn. **klaxonner** *v* sound one's horn, hoot.
kleptomanie [klɛptɔmani] *nf* kleptomania. **kleptomane** *n(m+f), adj* kleptomaniac.
kyste [kist] *nm* cyst.

L

l' [l] *V* **la, le.**
la [la], **l'** *art* the. *pron* (*personne*) her; (*animal, chose*) it.
là [la] *adv* there; (*ici*) here; (*temps*) then; (*cela*) that. **là-bas** *adv* over there. **là-dedans** *adv* inside, in it. **là-dessous** *adv* underneath. **là-dessus** *adv* on that; (*à ce sujet*) about that; (*alors*) at that point. **là-haut** up there.
laboratoire [labɔratwar] *nm* laboratory.
laborieux [labɔrjø] *adj* (*pénible*) laborious; (*diligent*) hard-working.
labourer [labure] *v* plough. **laboureur** *nm* ploughman.
labyrinthe [labirɛ̃t] *nm* labyrinth, maze.
lac [lak] *nm* lake.
lacer [lɑse] *v* lace (up). **lacet** *nm* lace; (*route*) sharp bend; (*piège*) snare. **en lacet** winding.
lacérer [lasere] *v* tear up; (*corps*) lacerate. **lacération** *nf* laceration.
lâche [lɑʃ] *adj* loose; (*personne*) cowardly. *n(m+f)* coward. **lâcheté** *nf* cowardice.
lâcher [lɑʃe] *v* release, let go (of); (*ceinture*) loosen; (*fam: abandonner*) give up, drop. **lâcher pied** give way. **lâcher prise** let go.
lacrymogène [lakrimɔʒɛn] *adj* **gaz lacrymogène** *nm* tear-gas.
lacté [lakte] *adj* milky.
lacune [lakyn] *nf* gap.
ladre [lɑdrə] *adj* mean. *n(m+f)* miser.
lagune [lagyn] *nf* lagoon.
laid [lɛ] *adj* ugly. **laideur** *nf* ugliness.
laine [lɛn] *nf* wool. **de laine** woollen. **laineux** *adj* woolly.
laïque [laik] *adj* lay, secular. *nm* layman. **laïques** *nm pl* laity *sing*.
laisse [lɛs] *nf* lead, leash.

laisser [lese] *v* leave; let. **laisser-aller** *nm invar* carelessness. **laissez-passer** *nm invar* pass.
lait [lɛ] *nm* milk. **lait caillé** curds *pl.* **lait concentré** evaporated milk. **laiterie** *nf* dairy. **laiteux** *adj* milky. **laitier** *nm* milkman.
laiton [lɛtɔ̃] *nm* brass.
laitue [lety] *nf* lettuce.
lama [lama] *nm* llama.
lambeau [lɑ̃bo] *nm* scrap, shred.
lambrequin [lɑ̃brəkɛ̃] *nm* pelmet.
lame [lam] *nf* (*bande*) strip; (*tranchant*) blade; (*vague*) wave.
se lamenter [lamɑ̃te] *v* lament, moan. **lamentable** *adj* lamentable, awful; (*cri*) pitiful. **lamentation** *nf* lament.
lampadaire [lɑ̃padɛr] *nm* standard lamp.
lampe [lɑ̃p] *nf* lamp, light. **lampe de poche** torch.
lamper [lɑ̃pe] (*fam*) *v* swig. **lampée** *nf* swig.
lance [lɑ̃s] *nf* spear.
lancer [lɑ̃se] *v* throw, hurl; (*émettre*) send out; (*mettre en mouvement*) launch. **lance-pierres** *nm invar* catapult. **se lancer** (*sauter*) leap; (*se précipiter*) dash. **se lancer dans** embark on.
lanciner [lɑ̃sine] *v* throb; obsess, torment.
landau [lɑ̃do] *nm* pram.
lande [lɑ̃d] *nf* moor.
langage [lɑ̃gaʒ] *nm* language.
langouste [lɑ̃gust] *nf* crayfish. **langoustines** *nf pl* scampi *pl.*
langue [lɑ̃g] *nf* (*anat*) tongue; language.
languir [lɑ̃gir] *v* languish; (*conversation*) flag; (*désirer*) pine, long. **languissant** *adj* (*personne*) listless; (*récit*) dull.
lanière [lanjɛr] *nf* strap, thong.
lanterne [lɑ̃tɛrn] *nf* lantern; lamp, light; (*auto*) sidelight.
Laos [laɔs] *nm* Laos.
laper [lape] *v* lap (up).
lapin [lapɛ̃] *nm* rabbit.
Laponie [lapɔni] *nf* Lapland. **lapon** *nm, adj* Lapp. **Lapon, -e** *nm, nf* Lapp.
lapsus [lapsys] *nm* (*parlé*) slip of the tongue; (*écrit*) slip of the pen.
laque [lak] *nf* lacquer. **laquer** *v* lacquer.
laquelle [lakɛl] *V* **lequel**.
larcin [larsɛ̃] *nm* (*vol*) theft.
lard [lar] *nm* bacon; (*gras*) fat.
large [larʒ] *adj* wide, broad; generous. *nm* width; (*place*) space, room; (*naut*) open sea. **largement** *adv* widely; generously; (*de loin*) greatly; (*au moins*) at least, easily. **largesse** *nf* generosity. **largeur** *nf* width, breadth.
larme [larm] *nf* tear.
larmoyer [larmwaje] *v* whimper; (*yeux*) water. **larmoyant** *adj* tearful.
larve [larv] *nf* larva, grub.
larynx [larɛ̃ks] *nm* larynx. **laryngite** *nf* laryngitis.
las, lasse [lɑ, lɑs] *adj* weary.
lascif [lasif] *adj* lascivious.
laser [lazɛr] *nm* laser.
lasser [lɑse] *v* weary. **se lasser de** grow tired of.
lasso [laso] *nm* lasso. **prendre au lasso** lasso.
latent [latɑ̃] *adj* latent.
latéral [lateral] *adj* lateral.
latin [latɛ̃] *nm, adj* Latin.
latitude [latityd] *nf* latitude.
laurier [lɔrje] *nm* laurel; (*cuisine*) bay leaves *pl.*
lavable [lavablə] *adj* washable.
lavabo [lavabo] *nm* washbasin. **lavabos** *nm pl* toilets *pl.*
lavage [lavaʒ] *nm* wash, washing. **lavage de cerveau** brainwashing.
lavande [lavɑ̃d] *nf* lavender.
lave [lav] *nf* lava.
laver [lave] *v* wash; (*plaie*) bathe. **lave-vaisselle** *nm invar* dishwasher. **se laver** have a wash. **laverie automatique** *nf* launderette. **lavette** *nf* dishcloth. **laveur de vitres** *nm* window-cleaner.
laxatif [laksatif] *nm, adj* laxative.
le [lə], **l'** *art* the. *pron* (*personne*) him; (*animal, chose*) it.
lécher [leʃe] *v* lick. **faire du lèche-vitrines** go window-shopping.
leçon [ləsɔ̃] *nf* lesson.
lecteur, -trice [lɛktœr, -tris] *nm, nf* reader. **lecture** *nf* reading.
ledit, ladite [lədi, ladit] *adj, pl* **lesdits, lesdites** the aforementioned *or* aforesaid.
légal [legal] *adj* legal; official. **légaliser** *v* legalize. **légalité** *nf* legality.
légende [leʒɑ̃d] *nf* legend; (*illustration*) caption. **légendaire** *adj* legendary.
léger [leʒe] *adj* light; (*petit*) slight; agile; (*licencieux*) ribald. **à la légère** thoughtlessly; not seriously. **légèreté** *nf* lightness.
légiférer [leʒifere] *v* legislate.

légion [leʒjɔ̃] *nf* legion; vast number. **être légion** be numberless.
législation [leʒislɑsjɔ̃] *nf* legislation.
légitime [leʒitim] *adj* legitimate, lawful.
legs [lɛg] *nm* legacy.
léguer [lege] *v* bequeath.
légume [legym] *nm* vegetable.
Léman [lemɑ̃] *nm* **lac Léman** *nm* Lake Geneva.
lendemain [lɑ̃dmɛ̃] *nm* day after, next day; future. **le lendemain matin/soir** the next morning/evening.
lent [lɑ̃] *adj* slow. **lenteur** *nf* slowness.
lentille [lɑ̃tij] *nf* lentil; (*optique*) lens.
léopard [leɔpar] *nm* leopard.
lépreux [leprø], **-euse** *adj* leprous. *nm, nf* leper. **lèpre** *nf* leprosy.
lequel [ləkɛl], **laquelle** *pron, pl* **lesquels, lesquelles** which; (*personne*) who, whom.
les [le] *art* the. *pron* them.
lesbienne [lɛsbjɛn] *nf* lesbian.
léser [leze] *v* wrong; injure.
lésiner [lezine] *v* skimp.
lessive [lesiv] *nf* washing; (*substance*) washing powder.
lest [lɛst] *nm* ballast.
leste [lɛst] *adj* nimble, sprightly; risqué; (*cavalier*) offhand.
léthargie [letarʒi] *nf* lethargy. **léthargique** *adj* lethargic.
lettre [lɛtrə] *nf* letter. **au pied de la lettre** literally. **lettres** *nf pl* (*université*) arts *pl*; literature *sing*. **lettres de créance** credentials *pl*.
leu [lø] *nm* **à la queue leu leu** in single file.
leucémie [løsemi] *nf* leukaemia.
leur [lœr] *pron* them, to them. *adj* their. **le** *or* **la leur** theirs.
leurrer [lœre] *v* deceive, delude. **leurre** *nm* delusion; (*appât*) lure; (*piège*) trap.
levé [ləve] *nm* survey. *adj* raised.
lever [ləve] *v* raise, lift; (*impôts*) levy; (*séance*) close; (*cuisine*) rise. **se lever** rise, get up. *nm* rising. **lever du soleil** sunrise. **levée** *nf* raising; closing; (*poste*) collection; (*cartes*) trick.
levier [ləvje] *nm* lever. **levier de vitesse** gear lever.
lèvre [lɛvrə] *nf* lip.
lévrier [levrije] *nm* greyhound.
levure [ləvyr] *nf* yeast.
lézard [lezar] *nm* lizard. **lézarde** *nf* crack. **lézarder** *v* crack; (*au soleil*) bask in the sun.
liaison [ljɛzɔ̃] *nf* (*d'affaires*) relationship; contact; (*rapport*) connection, link; (*amoureuse*) affair.
liasse [ljas] *nf* bundle, wad.
libelle [libɛl] *nm* libel; (*satire*) lampoon.
libellule [libelyl] *nf* dragonfly.
libéral [liberal], **-e** *adj* liberal; (*pol*) Liberal. *nm, nf* Liberal.
libérer [libere] *v* release, free, liberate. **libération** *nf* release, liberation.
liberté [liberte] *nf* freedom, liberty. **liberté conditionnelle** parole. **liberté sous caution** bail. **liberté surveillée** probation.
librairie [libreri] *nf* bookshop. **libraire** *n(m+f)* bookseller.
libre [librə] *adj* free. **libre-service** *nm* self-service shop or restaurant.
licence [lisɑ̃s] *nf* (*université*) degree; (*comm*) licence; permit. **licencié, -e** *nm, nf* graduate. **licencié ès lettres/sciences** Bachelor of Arts/Science.
licorne [likɔrn] *nf* unicorn.
licou [liku] *nm* halter.
lie [li] *nf* dregs *pl*.
Liechtenstein [liʃtɛnʃtajn] *nm* Liechtenstein.
liège [ljɛʒ] *nm* cork.
lien [ljɛ̃] *nm* (*attache*) bond; (*liaison*) link; (*de famille, etc.*) tie.
lier [lje] *v* tie up, bind; (*relier*) link up; unite; (*cuisine*) thicken.
lierre [ljɛr] *nm* ivy.
lieu [ljø] *nm* place. **au lieu de** instead of. **avoir lieu** take place. **avoir lieu de** have good reason to. **donner lieu à** give rise to. **sur les lieux** at the scene, on the spot. **tenir lieu de** take the place of.
lieutenant [ljøtnɑ̃] *nm* lieutenant. **lieutenant-colonel** *nm* wing commander.
lièvre [ljɛvrə] *nm* hare.
ligament [ligamɑ̃] *nm* ligament.
ligne [liɲ] *nf* line; (*rangée*) row; (*silhouette*) figure. **à la ligne** new paragraph. **hors ligne** outstanding. **ligne d'horizon** skyline.
ligoter [ligɔte] *v* tie, bind.
ligue [lig] *nf* league.
lilas [lilɑ] *nm, adj invar* lilac.
limace [limas] *nf* slug. **limaçon** *nm* snail.
limaille [limɑj] *nf* filings *pl*.
limbe [lɛ̃b] *nm* **les limbes** limbo *sing*. **dans les limbes** (*rel*) in limbo; (*projet*) in the air.

limer [lime] *v* file. **lime** *nf* file. **lime à ongles** nail-file.
limier [limje] *nm* bloodhound; (*policier*) sleuth.
limite [limit] *nf* limit; (*pays*) boundary. *adj* maximum. **cas limite** *nm* borderline case. **date limite** *nf* deadline.
limiter [limite] *v* limit, restrict; (*frontière*) border. **limitation** *nf* limitation, restriction.
limon [limɔ̃] *nm* silt.
limonade [limɔnad] *nf* lemonade.
lin [lɛ̃] *nm* flax.
linceul [lɛ̃sœl] *nm* shroud.
linéaire [lineɛr] *adj* linear.
linge [lɛ̃ʒ] *nm* linen; (*lessive*) washing; (*sous-vêtements*) underwear; (*torchon*) cloth. **lingerie** *nf* lingerie.
lingot [lɛ̃go] *nm* ingot.
linguistique [lɛ̃gɥistik] *nf* linguistics. *adj* linguistic. **linguiste** *n*(*m*+*f*) linguist.
linoléum [linɔleɔm] *nm* linoleum. **lino** *nm* (*fam*) lino.
lion [ljɔ̃] *nm* lion. **Lion** *nm* Leo. **lionceau** *nm* lion cub. **lionne** nf lioness.
liqueur [likœr] *nf* liqueur.
liquide [likid] *nm*, *adj* liquid. **liquidation** *nf* liquidation; (*règlement*) settlement. **liquider** *v* liquidate; settle.
***lire**[1] [lir] *v* read.
lire[2] [lir] *nf* lira.
lis [lis] *nm* lily.
Lisbonne [lisbɔn] *n* Lisbon.
lisible [liziblə] *adj* (*écriture*) legible; (*livre*) readable. **lisibilité** *nf* legibility.
lisière [lizjɛr] *nf* edge; (*tissu*) selvage.
lisse [lis] *adj* smooth. **lisser** *v* smooth.
liste [list] *nf* list.
lit [li] *nm* bed; (*couche*) layer. **lit de camp** camp-bed. **lit d'enfant** cot. **lit d'une personne** single bed. **literie** *nf* bedding.
litanie [litani] *nf* litany.
litée [lite] *nf* litter.
litre [litrə] *nm* litre.
littéraire [literɛr] *adj* literary.
littéral [literal] *adj* literal.
littérature [literatyr] *nf* literature.
littoral [litɔral] *adj* coastal. *nm* coast.
livide [livid] *adj* pallid, livid.
livraison [livrɛzɔ̃] *nm* delivery; (*revue*) part, issue.
livre[1] [livrə] *nm* book. **livre à succès** best-seller. **livre de bord** logbook. **livre de poche** paperback. **livre d'images** picture book. **livre d'or** visitors' book.
livre[2] [livrə] *nf* pound.
livrer [livre] *v* deliver; (*abandonner*) hand over, give up. **se livrer** confide. **se livrer à** (*s'adonner*) indulge in; (*se consacrer*) devote oneself to.
livret [livrɛ] *nm* (*musique*) libretto; (*carnet*) booklet, record book.
lobe [lɔb] *nm* lobe.
local [lɔkal] *adj* local. *nm* premises *pl*. **localiser** *v* localize; (*déterminer*) locate; (*limiter*) confine. **localité** *nf* locality.
locataire [lɔkatɛr] *n*(*m*+*f*) tenant.
location [lɔkɑsjɔ̃] *nf* (*maison*) renting; (*voiture*, *bateau*) hiring. **bureau de location** *nm* booking office.
locomotive [lɔkɔmɔtiv] *nf* locomotive, engine.
locuste [lɔkyst] *nf* locust.
locution [lɔkysjɔ̃] *nf* phrase.
logarithme [lɔgaritmə] *nm* logarithm.
loger [lɔʒe] *v* lodge; accommodate, put up; (*habiter*) live. **se loger** find accommodation; (*se coincer*) get stuck. **loge** *nf* lodge; (*artiste*) dressing room; (*spectateur*) box. **logement** *nm* housing; accommodation, lodgings *pl*. **logeur** *nm* landlord. **logeuse** *nf* landlady.
logique [lɔʒik] *nf* logic. *adj* logical.
logis [lɔʒi] *nm* dwelling.
loi [lwa] *nf* law.
loin [lwɛ̃] *adv* far. **au loin** in the distance. **de loin** from a distance; (*de beaucoup*) by far. **plus loin** further.
lointain [lwɛ̃tɛ̃] *adj* distant, remote. *nm* (*tableau*) background. **au lointain** in the distance.
loir [lwar] *nm* dormouse.
loisir [lwazir] *nm* leisure, spare time.
lombric [lɔ̃brik] *nm* earthworm.
Londres [lɔ̃drə] *n* London.
long, longue [lɔ̃, lɔ̃g] *adj* long. **à long terme** long-term. **à longue portée** long-range. **de longue date** long-standing. **longue-vue** *nf* telescope. *adv* **en savoir/dire long** know/say a lot. *nm* length. **de long en large** back and forth. **le long de** along. *nf* **à la longue** at last, in the end. **longueur** *nf* length. **longueur d'onde** wavelength.
longer [lɔ̃ʒe] *v* border; (*sentier*, *etc.*) run alongside; (*personne*) walk along.
longévité [lɔ̃ʒevite] *nf* longevity.
longitude [lɔ̃ʒityd] *nf* longitude.

longtemps [lɔ̃tɑ̃] *adv* (for) a long time, (for) long.
loque [lɔk] *nf* rag.
loquet [lɔkɛ] *nm* latch.
lorgner [lɔrɲe] *v* (*fam*) peer at, eye up.
lors [lɔr] *adv* **dès lors** from then on. **lors de** at the time of. **lors même que** even if.
lorsque [lɔrskə] *conj* when.
losange [lɔzɑ̃ʒ] *nm* diamond.
lot [lo] *nm* (*assortiment*) set, batch; (*portion*) share; (*prix*) prize.
loterie [lɔtri] *nf* lottery, raffle.
lotion [losjɔ̃] *nf* lotion.
lotus [lɔtys] *nm* lotus.
louange [lwɑ̃ʒ] *nf* praise.
louche[1] [luʃ] *adj* dubious, shady. **loucher** *v* have a squint.
louche[2] [luʃ] *nf* ladle.
louer[1] [lwe] *v* (*exalter*) praise. **louable** *adj* praiseworthy.
louer[2] [lwe] *v* rent, hire.
loufoque [lufɔk] *adj* (*fam*) crazy.
loup [lu] *nm* wolf. **loup-cervier** *nm* lynx. **loup-garou** *nm* werewolf.
loupe [lup] *nf* magnifying glass.
louper [lupe] (*fam*) *v* bungle, make a mess of; (*occasion*) miss; (*examen*) fail.
lourd [lur] *adj* heavy; (*temps*) close; (*important*) serious; (*gauche*) clumsy. **lourdeur** *nf* heaviness.
loutre [lutrə] *nf* otter.
louveteau [luvto] *nm* wolf cub; cub scout.
loyal [lwajal] *adj* loyal; (*honnête*) fair. **loyauté** *nf* loyalty; fairness.
loyer [lwaje] *nm* rent.
lubie [lybi] *nf* whim, fad.
lubrifier [lybrifje] *v* lubricate. **lubrifiant** *nm* lubricant. **lubrification** *nf* lubrication.
lucarne [lykarn] *nf* skylight, dormer window.
lucide [lysid] *adj* lucid. **lucidité** *nf* lucidity.
lucratif [lykratif] *adj* lucrative, profitable.
lueur [lɥœr] *nf* glimmer, glow.
luge [lyʒ] *nf* sledge, toboggan.
lugubre [lygybrə] *adj* gloomy, dismal.
lui [lɥi] *pron* (*homme*) him, to him; (*femme*) her, to her; (*chose, animal*) it, to it; (*sujet*) he. **lui-même** *pron* himself; itself.
***luire** [lɥir] *v* gleam, shine. **luisant** *nm* sheen, gloss.
lumbago [lɔ̃bago] *nm* lumbago.
lumière [lymjɛr] *nf* light.
lumineux [lyminø] *adj* luminous.
lundi [lœ̃di] *nm* Monday.
lune [lyn] *nf* moon. **lune de miel** honeymoon. **lunaire** *adj* lunar.
lunette [lynɛt] *nf* telescope. **lunettes** *nf pl* glasses *pl*. **lunettes de soleil** sunglasses *pl*. **lunettes protectrices** goggles *pl*.
lurette [lyrɛt] *nf* **il y a belle lurette** ages ago.
lustrer [lystre] *v* polish; make shiny. **lustre** *nm* lustre; (*appareil d'éclairage*) chandelier. **lustré** *adj* shiny.
luth [lyt] *nm* lute.
lutin [lytɛ̃] *nm* imp. *adj* impish, mischievous.
lutrin [lytrɛ̃] *nm* lectern.
lutter [lyte] *v* struggle, fight. **lutte** *nf* struggle, fight. (*sport*) wrestling. **lutteur, -euse** *nm, nf* fighter; wrestler.
luxe [lyks] *nm* luxury. **luxueux** *adj* luxurious.
Luxembourg [lyksɑ̃bur] *nm* Luxembourg.
luxure [lyksyr] *nf* lust. **luxurieux** *adj* lascivious.
lycée [lise] *nm* secondary school. **lycéen, -enne** *nm, nf* secondary school pupil.
lyncher [lɛ̃ʃe] *v* lynch.
lynx [lɛ̃ks] *nm* lynx.
lyre [lir] *nf* lyre.
lyrique [lirik] *adj* lyrical.

M

m' [m] *V* **me**.
ma [ma] *V* **mon**.
macabre [makɑbrə] *adj* macabre.
macaroni [makarɔni] *nm* macaroni.
macédoine [masedwan] *nf* (*fam*) jumble. **macédoine de fruits** fruit salad. **macédoine de légumes** mixed vegetables *pl*.
mâcher [mɑʃe] *v* chew, munch. **mâchoire** *nf* jaw.
machin [maʃɛ̃] (*fam*) *nm* thing, contraption; whatsit. **Machin** *nm* what's-his-name.
machine [maʃin] *nf* machine (*rail, naut*) engine. **machine à coudre/laver** sewing/washing machine. **machine à écrire** typewriter. **machine à sous** slot machine. **machinal** *adj* mechanical, automatic. **machinerie** *nf* machinery.

macis [masi] *nm* mace.
maçon [masɔ̃] *nm* (*pierre*) mason; (*construction*) builder; (*briques*) bricklayer. **maçonner** *v* build. **maçonnerie** *nf* masonry; building.
maculer [makyle] *v* stain. **macule** *nf* smudge.
madame [madam] *nf, pl* **mesdames** madam. **Madame** *nf* (*suivi du nom de famille*) Mrs.
mademoiselle [madmwazɛl] *nf, pl* **mesdemoiselles** miss, young lady. **Mademoiselle** *nf* (*suivi du nom de famille*) Miss.
madère [madɛr] *nm* (*vin*) Madeira. **Madère** *nf* (*île*) Madeira.
Madrid [madrid] *n* Madrid.
madrier [madrije] *nm* beam.
magasin [magazɛ̃] *nm* shop; (*entrepôt*) warehouse; (*fusil*) magazine. **magasin à succursales multiples** chain store.
magazine [magazin] *nm* magazine.
magie [maʒi] *nf* magic. **magicien, -enne** *nm, nf* magician. **magique** *adj* magic, magical.
magistral [maʒistral] *adj* masterly, brilliant; authoritative.
magistrat [maʒistra] *nm* magistrate.
magnanime [maɲanim] *adj* magnanimous. **magnanimité** *nf* magnanimity.
magnat [magna] *nm* tycoon, magnate.
magnétiser [maɲetize] *v* magnetize. **magnétique** *adj* magnetic. **magnétisme** *nm* magnetism.
magnétophone [maɲetɔfɔn] *nm* tape-recorder.
magnifique [maɲifik] *adj* magnificent.
mai [mɛ] *nm* May.
maigre [mɛgrə] *adj* thin; (*viande*) lean; (*petit*) meagre, slight; (*médiocre*) poor. *nm* lean meat. **maigreur** *nf* thinness. **maigrir** *v* lose weight; (*exprès*) slim.
maille [mɑj] *nf* stitch; (*armure*) link; (*filet*) mesh. **maille filée** ladder.
maillet [majɛ] *nm* mallet.
maillot [majo] *nm* vest; (*sport*) jersey; (*danse*) leotard. **maillot de bain** (*homme*) swimming trunks *pl*; (*femme*) bathing costume.
main [mɛ̃] *nf* hand. **à la main** by hand. **en venir aux mains** come to blows. **fait main** handmade. **main-d'œuvre** *nf* labour, manpower. **sous la main** to *or* at hand.
maint [mɛ̃] *adj* many (a). **maintes fois** time and again.
maintenant [mɛ̃tnɑ̃] *adv* now.
***maintenir** [mɛ̃tnir] *v* maintain; support; (*garder*) keep. **se maintenir** hold one's own, keep up; continue, persist. **maintien** *nm* maintenance, upholding; (*posture*) deportment.
maire [mɛr] *nm* mayor. **mairie** *nf* town hall.
mais [mɛ] *conj* but. *nm* objection.
maïs [mais] *nm* maize *or US* corn.
maison [mɛzɔ̃] *nf* house; (*foyer*) home; firm, company; (*domestiques*) household. *adj invar* home-made. **maison de repos** convalescent home. **maison de retraite** old people's home. **maison de santé** nursing home.
maître, -esse [mɛtrə, -ɛs] *adj* main, major. *nm* master. **être maître de** be in control of. **maître chanteur** blackmailer. **maître de chapelle** choirmaster. **maître d'hôtel** (*maison*) butler; (*hôtel*) head waiter. *nf* mistress.
maîtriser [mɛtrize] *v* control, master, overcome. **maîtrise** *nf* mastery; control. **maîtrise de soi** self-control.
majesté [maʒɛste] *nf* majesty. **majestueux** *adj* majestic.
majeur, -e [maʒœr] *adj* major; (*principal*) main; (*jur*) of age.
majorité [maʒɔrite] *nf*, majority. **être majoritaire** be in the majority.
majuscule [maʒyskyl] *nf, adj* capital.
mal [mal] *adv* badly; ill; (*incorrectement*) wrongly; with difficulty. **mal acquis** ill-gotten. **mal à l'aise** ill-at-ease. **mal comprendre** misunderstand. **mal élevé** ill-mannered. **mal interpréter** misinterpret. **pas mal** rather well, not badly. **pas mal de** (*fam*) quite a lot of. *adj invar* bad, wrong; (*malade*) ill; (*mal à l'aise*) uncomfortable. *nm* evil; (*douleur*) pain; (*maladie*) sickness; (*tristesse*) sorrow; difficulty, trouble; (*dommage*) harm. **avoir mal** be in pain, ache. **avoir mal à** have a pain in. **avoir mal aux dents/oreilles** have toothache/earache. **faire du mal à** hurt, harm. **mal de l'air** airsickness. **mal de mer** seasickness. **mal de tête** headache. **mal du pays** homesickness. **se faire mal** hurt oneself.
malade [malad] *adj* ill, sick. *n*(*m*+*f*) invalid, sick person; (*d'un médecin*) patient. **maladie** *nf* illness, disease. **maladif** *adj* sickly.

maladresse [maladrɛs] *nf* clumsiness, awkwardness; (*gaffe*) blunder.
maladroit [maladrwa] *adj* clumsy; (*indélicat*) tactless.
malaise [malɛz] *nm* discomfort; (*trouble*) uneasiness.
malappris [malapri] *adj* ill-mannered.
malaria [malarja] *nf* malaria.
malavisé [malavize] *adj* unwise, ill-advised.
malchance [malʃɑ̃s] *nf* misfortune, bad luck. **malchanceux** *adj* unlucky.
malcommode [malkɔmɔd] *adj* inconvenient; (*peu pratique*) unsuitable.
mâle [mɑl] *adj* male; virile. *nm* male.
malédiction [malediksjɔ̃] *nf* curse.
malentendu [malɑ̃tɑ̃dy] *nm* misunderstanding.
malfaisant [malfəzɑ̃] *adj* evil, harmful.
malgré [malgre] *prep* despite, in spite of.
malheur [malœr] *nm* misfortune; (*épreuve*) hardship; (*accident*) mishap. **malheureux** *adj* unfortunate; miserable.
malhonnête [malɔnɛt] *adj* dishonest; (*impoli*) rude. **malhonnêteté** *nf* dishonesty; rudeness.
Mali [mali] *nm* Mali.
malice [malis] *nf* mischief; (*malignité*) malice. **malicieux** *adj* mischievous.
malin, -igne [malɛ̃, -iɲ] *adj* cunning, shrewd; (*fam*) difficult; (*mauvais*) malicious; (*méd*) malignant.
malingre [malɛ̃grə] *adj* sickly, puny.
malle [mal] *nf* trunk; (*auto*) boot.
malmener [malməne] *v* manhandle.
malotru [malɔtry], **-e** *nm, nf* uncouth person, lout.
malpropre [malprɔprə] *adj* dirty; (*travail*) slovenly; (*indélicat*) unsavoury. **malpropreté** *nf* dirtiness; (*propos*) unsavoury remark; (*acte*) low trick.
malsain [malsɛ̃] *adj* unhealthy.
malséant [malseɑ̃] *adj* unseemly.
malt [malt] *nm* malt.
Malte [malt] *nf* Malta. **maltais** *nm, adj* Maltese. **les Maltais** the Maltese.
maltraiter [maltrete] *v* ill-treat, manhandle; misuse.
malveillant [malvɛjɑ̃, -ɑ̃t] *adj* malevolent, malicious. **malveillance** *nf* malevolence.
maman [mamɑ̃] *nf* (*fam*) mummy, mum.
mamelle [mamɛl] *nf* (*femme*) breast; (*animal*) teat; (*pis*) udder. **mamelon** *nm* nipple.
mammifère [mamifɛr] *nm* mammal.
mammouth [mamut] *nm* mammoth.
manche[1] [mɑ̃ʃ] *nf* sleeve. **à manches courtes/longues** short-/long-sleeved. **la Manche** the English Channel. **manchette** *nf* cuff; (*journal*) headline. **manchon** *nm* muff.
manche[2] [mɑ̃ʃ] *nf* handle. **manche à balai** broomstick; (*aéro*) joystick.
manchot [mɑ̃ʃo] *adj* one-armed; (*sans bras*) armless. *nm* penguin.
mandarine [mɑ̃darin] *nf* mandarin, tangerine.
mandat [mɑ̃da] *nm* mandate; (*police*) warrant. **mandat-poste** *nm* postal order.
mandater *v* commission; elect.
mandoline [mɑ̃dɔlin] *nf* mandolin.
manège [manɛʒ] *nm* (*fête foraine*) roundabout; (*équitation*) riding school; (*jeu*) game.
manette [manɛt] *nf* lever.
manger [mɑ̃ʒe] *v* eat; (*fortune*) squander. *nm* food. **mangeable** *adj* edible.
mangue [mɑ̃g] *nf* mango. **manguier** *nm* mango tree.
maniaque [manjak] *adj* fussy, fanatical. *n*(*m*+*f*) fanatic.
manie [mani] *nf* odd habit; (*obsession*) mania.
manier [manje] *v* handle. **maniable** *adj* manageable; easily influenced; (*accommodant*) amenable. **maniement** *nm* handling.
manière [manjɛr] *nf* way, manner; style. **de manière à** so as to. **d'une manière ou d'une autre** somehow or other. **manières** *nf pl* manners *pl*, behaviour *sing*. **maniéré** *adj* affected.
manifeste [manifɛst] *adj* obvious, evident. *nm* manifesto.
manifester [manifɛste] *v* show, indicate; (*pol*) demonstrate. **manifestant, -e** *nm, nf* demonstrator. **manifestation** *nf* demonstration; expression; appearance.
manipuler [manipyle] *v* manipulate; (*objet*) handle. **manipulation** *nf* manipulation; handling.
manivelle [manivɛl] *nf* crank.
manne [man] *nf* hamper.
mannequin [mankɛ̃] *nm* (*personne*) model; (*objet*) dummy.
manœuvre [manœvrə] *nf* manoeuvre, operation; (*intrigue*) scheme. *nm* labourer. **manœuvrer** *v* manoeuvre; (*machine*) operate.

manoir [manwar] *nm* manor house.
manquer [mɑ̃ke] *v* miss; (*rater*) make a mess of, botch; (*faire défaut*) be lacking; be absent; (*échouer*) fail. **manquer à** be missed by. **manquer de** lack. **manquer de faire** almost do. **ne pas manquer de** be sure to. **manque** *nm* lack, shortage; (*lacune*) gap; (*méd*) withdrawal.
mansarde [mɑ̃sard] *nf* attic.
manteau [mɑ̃to] *nm* coat.
manuel [manɥɛl] *nm, adj* manual.
manuscrit [manyskri] *adj* handwritten. *nm* manuscript.
manutention [manytɑ̃sjɔ̃] *nf* handling.
maquereau[1] [makro] *nm* (*poisson*) mackerel.
maquereau[2] [makro] *nm* (*argot*) pimp.
maquette [makɛt] *nf* model.
maquiller [makije] *v* make up; (*document, etc.*) fake. **maquillage** *nm* make-up.
maquis [maki] *nm* scrub, bush.
maraîcher [mareʃe], **-ère** *nm, nf* market gardener.
marais [marɛ] *nm* marsh.
marathon [maratɔ̃] *nm* marathon.
marbre [marbrə] *nm* marble.
marchand [marʃɑ̃], **-e** *nm, nf* (*boutiquier*) shopkeeper, tradesman; dealer, merchant. **marchand de journaux** newsagent. **marchand de légumes** greengrocer. **marchand de poissons** fishmonger. *adj* (*valeur*) market; (*navire*) merchant.
marchander [marʃɑ̃de] *v* haggle (over), bargain.
marchandise [marʃɑ̃diz] *nf* merchandise, goods *pl.*
marche [marʃ] *nf* walk, walking; (*mil, etc.*) march; (*machine, véhicule*) running; progress; (*escalier*) step. **marche arrière** reverse. **mettre en marche** start, set going.
marché [marʃe] *nm* market; (*contrat*) bargain, deal. **Marché commun** Common Market. **marché noir** black market.
marcher [marʃe] *v* walk; (*mil*) march; (*mettre le pied*) step, tread; (*fonctionner*) work.
mardi [mardi] *nm* Tuesday. **Mardi gras** Shrove Tuesday.
mare [mar] *nf* (*étang*) pond; (*flaque*) pool.
marécage [marekaʒ] *nm* marsh, bog. **marécageux** *adj* marshy.
maréchal [mareʃal] *nm* marshal, field marshal. **maréchal-ferrant** *nm* blacksmith.
marée [mare] *nf* tide. **marée noire** oil slick.
margarine [margarin] *nf* margarine.
marge [marʒ] *nf* margin. **marginal** *adj* marginal.
marguerite [margərit] *nf* daisy.
mari [mari] *nm* husband.
mariage [marjaʒ] *nm* marriage; (*cérémonie*) wedding.
marié [marje], **-e** *adj* married. *nm* bridegroom. *nf* bride.
marier [marje] *v* marry; (*couleurs, etc.*) blend. **se marier** get married.
marihuana [mariɥana] *nf* marijuana.
marin [marɛ̃] *adj* sea, marine. *nm* sailor.
marina [marina] *nf* marina.
marine [marin] *nf, adj invar* navy. **marine marchande** merchant navy.
mariner [marine] *v* marinade. **marinade** *nf* marinade.
marionnette [marjɔnɛt] *nf* puppet.
marital [marital] *adj* marital.
maritime [maritim] *adj* maritime; (*ville*) coastal; (*commerce, etc.*) shipping.
marjolaine [marʒɔlɛn] *nf* marjoram.
mark [mark] *nm* mark.
marmite [marmit] *nf* pot.
marmonner [marmɔne] *v* mumble, mutter.
marmot [marmo] *nm* (*fam*) kid, brat.
marmotter [marmɔte] *v* mumble, mutter.
Maroc [marɔk] *nm* Morocco. **marocain** *adj* Moroccan. **Marocain, -e** *nm, nf* Moroccan.
marotte [marɔt] *nf* hobby, craze.
marquer [marke] *v* mark; indicate, show; (*écrire*) write *or* note down; (*événement*) stand out. **marque** *nf* mark; (*comm*) brand, make; (*sport*) score. **de marque** (*produit*) high-class; (*personne*) distinguished, important. **marque de fabrique** trademark.
marqueterie [markətri] *nf* marquetry.
marquis [marki] *nm* marquis *or* marquess. **marquise** *nf* marchioness.
marraine [marɛn] *nf* godmother.
marre [mar] (*fam*) *adv* **en avoir marre** be fed up. **marrant** *adj* funny. **se marrer** *v* laugh.
marron [marɔ̃] *nm* chestnut; (*couleur*) brown. **marron d'Inde** horse-chestnut. *adj invar* brown. **marronnier** *nm* chestnut tree.

mars [mars] *nm* March.
Mars [mars] *nm* Mars. **martien, -enne** *n, adj* Martian.
marsouin [marswɛ̃] *nm* porpoise.
marsupial [marsypjal] *nm, adj* marsupial.
marteau [marto] *nm* hammer; (*porte*) knocker. **marteau-piqueur** *nm* pneumatic drill.
marteler [martəle] *v* hammer, pound.
martial [marsjal] *adj* martial, warlike.
martinet [martinɛ] *nm* swift.
martin-pêcheur [martɛ̃pɛʃœr] *nm* kingfisher.
martre [martrə] *nf* marten. **martre zibeline** sable.
martyr [martir], **-e** *nm, nf* martyr. **martyre** *nm* martyrdom; (*souffrance*) agony. **martyriser** *v* (*rel*) martyr; torture; (*bébé*) batter.
mascara [maskara] *nm* mascara.
mascarade [maskarad] *nf* masquerade.
mascotte [maskɔt] *nf* mascot.
masculin [maskylɛ̃] *nm, adj* masculine. **masculinité** *nf* masculinity.
masochiste [mazɔʃist] *n*(*m*+*f*) masochist. *adj* masochistic. **masochisme** *nm* masochism.
masquer [maske] *v* hide, mask. **masque** *nm* mask; air, façade. **masque de beauté** face-pack.
massacrer [masakre] *v* massacre; (*animaux*) slaughter; (*fam*) make a mess of. **massacre** *nm* massacre; slaughter.
masse[1] [mas] *nf* mass; (*élec*) earth.
masse[2] [mas] *nf* (*maillet*) sledge-hammer; (*bâton*) mace.
massepain [maspɛ̃] *nm* marzipan.
masser[1] [mase] *v* assemble, gather together.
masser[2] [mase] *v* massage. **massage** *nm* massage. **masseur** *nm* masseur. **masseuse** *nf* masseuse.
massif [masif] *adj* massive; solid, heavy. *nm* clump; (*géog*) massif.
massue [masy] *nf* club.
mastic [mastik] *nm* putty.
mastiquer[1] [mastike] *v* (*mâcher*) chew.
mastiquer[2] [mastike] *v* apply putty to.
mastodonte [mastɔdɔ̃t] *nm* (*camion*) juggernaut; (*personne*) colossus.
se masturber [mastyrbe] *v* masturbate. **masturbation** *nf* masturbation.
mat[1] [mat] *nm* checkmate. *adj invar* checkmated. **faire mat** checkmate.
mat[2] [mat] *adj* matt, dull.
mât [mɑ] *nm* (*naut*) mast; (*poteau*) pole.
match [matʃ] *nm* match. **match nul** draw.
matelas [matla] *nm* mattress. **matelas pneumatique** air-bed. **matelasser** *v* pad.
matelot [matlo] *nm* sailor.
se matérialiser [materjalize] *v* materialize.
matérialiste [materjalist] *adj* materialistic. *n*(*m*+*f*) materialist.
matériaux [materjo] *nm pl* material(s).
matériel [materjɛl] *adj* material. *nm* equipment, materials *pl*; (*tech*) plant.
maternel [matɛrnɛl] *adj* maternal; (*soin, geste*) motherly. **école maternelle** *nf* nursery school. **maternité** *nf* maternity, motherhood; maternity hospital.
mathématique [matematik] *adj* mathematical. **mathématiques** *nf pl* mathematics *sing*. **mathématicien, -enne** *nm, nf* mathematician. **maths** *nf pl* (*fam*) maths *sing*.
matière [matjɛr] *nf* matter; subject; material. **matière grasse** fat. **matières premières** raw materials *pl*.
matin [matɛ̃] *nm* morning. **de bon matin** early in the morning. **matinal** *adj* morning, early. **matinée** *nf* morning; (*théâtre*) afternoon performance, matinée.
matois [matwa] *adj* wily, sly.
matraque [matrak] *nf* truncheon, cosh.
matriarcal [matrijarkal] *adj* matriarchal.
matrice [matris] *nf* matrix; (*utérus*) womb.
matrimonial [matrimɔnjal] *adj* matrimonial.
maturité [matyrite] *nf* maturity.
***maudire** [modir] *v* curse.
mausolée [mozɔle] *nm* mausoleum.
maussade [mosad] *adj* sullen, morose; (*triste*) gloomy.
mauvais [mɔvɛ] *adj* bad; (*erroné*) wrong; (*vilain*) wicked, evil; (*désagreable*) nasty, unpleasant. **mauvaise herbe** *nf* weed.
mauve [mov] *nm, adj* mauve.
maxime [maksim] *nf* maxim.
maximum [maksimɔm] *nm, adj* maximum.
mayonnaise [majɔnɛz] *nf* mayonnaise.
mazout [mazut] *nm* oil.
me [mə], **m'** *pron* me, to me; (*réfléchi*) myself.
méandre [meɑ̃drə] *nm* meander.
mec [mɛk] *nm* (*argot*) bloke.

mécanique [mekanik] *adj* mechanical. *nf* mechanics. **mécanicien, -enne** *nm, nf* mechanic; (*naut, aéro*) engineer. **mécaniser** *v* mechanize. **méchanisme** *nm* mechanism; mechanics *pl*.

méchant [meʃɑ̃] *adj* nasty; (*malveillant*) spiteful; (*enfant*) naughty; (*vilain*) wicked. **méchanceté** *nf* nastiness; (*propos*) spiteful remark.

mèche [mɛʃ] *nf* (*bougie*) wick; (*bombe*) fuse; (*cheveux*) lock; (*tech*) bit. **être de mèche avec** be in league with.

mécompte [mekɔ̃t] *nm* (*déception*) disappointment; (*erreur*) miscalculation.

mécontent [mekɔ̃tɑ̃] *adj* discontented, dissatisfied; (*contrarié*) annoyed. **mécontentement** *nm* dissatisfaction. **mécontenter** *v* displease, annoy.

médaille [medaj] *nf* medal.

médecin [medsɛ̃] *nm* doctor. **médecine** *nf* medicine.

media [medja] *nm pl* mass media *pl*.

médiation [medjɑsjɔ̃] *nf* mediation. **médiateur, -trice** *nm, nf* mediator.

médical [medikal] *adj* medical.

médicament [medikamɑ̃] *nm* medicine.

médication [medikɑsjɔ̃] *nf* treatment, medication.

médicinal [medisinal] *adj* medicinal.

médiéval [medjeval] *adj* medieval.

médiocre [medjɔkrə] *adj* mediocre, poor. **médiocrité** *nf* mediocrity.

***médire** [medir] *v* speak ill, malign. **médisance** *nf* scandal, gossip.

méditer [medite] *v* meditate, contemplate.

Méditerrané [mediterane] *nf* Mediterranean (Sea). **méditerranéen** *adj* Mediterranean.

méduse [medyz] *nf* jellyfish.

méfait [mefɛ] *nm* misdemeanour. **méfaits** *nm pl* ravages *pl*, damage *sing*.

se méfier [mefje] *v* be careful, look out. **se méfier de** mistrust, be suspicious of; beware of. **méfiance** *nf* distrust. **méfiant** *adj* suspicious.

mégarde [megard] *nf* **par mégarde** accidentally, inadvertently.

mégère [meʒɛr] *nf* shrew.

mégot [mego] *nm* (*fam*) fag end.

meilleur, -e [mɛjœr] *adj, adv* better. **le meilleur, la meilleure** (the) best.

mélancolie [melɑ̃kɔli] *nf* melancholy. **mélancolique** *adj* melancholy, melancholic.

mélanger [melɑ̃ʒe] *v* mix (up); (*couleurs, etc.*) blend. **mélange** *nm* mixture; blend.

mélasse [melas] *nf* treacle.

mêler [mele] *v* mix, mingle; (*cartes*) shuffle; (*impliquer*) involve. **se mêler à** join, mingle with; get involved in. **se mêler de** meddle with, interfere in. **mêle-toi de tes affaires!** mind your own business! **mêlée** *nf* fray, mêlée; (*rugby*) scrum. **mêlée générale** free-for-all.

mélèze [melɛz] *nm* larch.

mélodie [melɔdi] *nf* melody. **mélodieux** *adj* melodious. **mélodique** *adj* melodic.

mélodrame [melɔdram] *nm* melodrama. **mélodramatique** *adj* melodramatic.

melon [məlɔ̃] *nm* melon; (*chapeau*) bowler.

membrane [mɑ̃bran] *nf* membrane.

membre [mɑ̃brə] *nm* (*anat*) limb; (*société*) member.

même [mɛm] *adj* (*semblable*) same; very. *pron* same. *adv* even. **de même** likewise. **quand même** all the same.

mémé [meme] *nf* (*fam*) granny, grandma.

mémento [memɛ̃to] *nm* (*agenda*) engagement diary; note.

mémoire[1] [memwar] *nf* memory.

mémoire[2] [memwar] *nm* memorandum; report; (*comm*) bill; (*exposé*) paper. **mémoires** *nm pl* memoirs *pl*.

mémorable [memɔrablə] *adj* memorable.

mémorandum [memɔrɑ̃dɔm] *nm* memorandum.

menacer [mənase] *v* threaten. **menaçant** *adj* menacing, threatening. **menace** *nf* threat.

ménage [menaʒ] *nm* (*entretien*) housekeeping, housework; married couple; (*communauté*) household. **ménager** *adj* household, domestic. **ménagère** *nf* (*femme*) housewife; (*couverts*) canteen of cutlery.

ménager [menaʒe] *v* spare; (*personne*) show consideration for; (*argent, etc.*) use sparingly *or* carefully; (*amener*) bring about; arrange. **ménagement** *nm* care, consideration.

mendier [mɑ̃dje] *v* beg (for). **mendiant, -e** *nm, nf* beggar. **mendicité** *nf* begging.

mener [məne] *v* lead; (*emmener*) take; (*enquête, conversation*) conduct; (*affaires, entreprise*) manage, run. **menées** *nf pl* intrigues *pl*. **meneur, -euse** *nm, nf* leader.

ménestrel [menɛstrɛl] *nm* minstrel.

méningite [menɛ̃ʒit] *nf* meningitis.
ménopause [menɔpoz] *nf* menopause.
menottes [mənɔt] *nf pl* handcuffs *pl*.
mensonge [mɑ̃sɔ̃ʒ] *nm* lie. **mensonger** *adj* false.
menstruel [mɑ̃stryɛl] *adj* menstrual. **menstruation** *nf* menstruation.
mensuel [mɑ̃sɥɛl] *adj* monthly. **mensuellement** *adv* monthly.
mensuration [mɑ̃syrasjɔ̃] *nf* measurement.
mental [mɑ̃tal] *adj* mental. **mentalité** *nf* mentality.
menteur, -euse [mɑ̃tœr, -øz] *adj* false; illusory; (*personne*) untruthful. *nm, nf* liar.
menthe [mɑ̃t] *nf* mint.
menthol [mɛ̃tɔl] *nm* menthol.
mention [mɑ̃sjɔ̃] *nf* mention; note; (*examen*) grade, class. **avec mention très bien** with distinction. **mentionner** *v* mention.
***mentir** [mɑ̃tir] *v* lie.
menton [mɑ̃tɔ̃] *nm* chin.
menu [məny] *adj* (*fin*) small, slight; (*peu important*) petty, minor. *adv* finely, small. *nm* menu.
menuisier [mənɥizje] *nm* joiner, carpenter. **menuiserie** *nf* joinery, carpentry, woodwork.
se *méprendre [meprɑ̃drə] *v* make a mistake.
mépris [mepri] *nm* contempt, scorn.
méprise [mepriz] *nf* mistake.
mépriser [meprize] *v* scorn, despise. **méprisable** *adj* contemptible. **méprisant** *adj* contemptuous.
mer [mɛr] *nf* sea; (*marée*) tide. **en mer** at sea.
mercenaire [mɛrsənɛr] *nm, adj* mercenary.
mercerie [mɛrsəri] *nf* haberdashery.
merci [mɛrsi] *interj* thank you; (*refus*) no thank you. **merci beaucoup** *or* **bien** thank you very much. *nm* thank-you, thanks *pl*. *nf* mercy.
mercier [mɛrsje], **-ère** *nm, nf* haberdasher.
mercredi [mɛrkrədi] *nm* Wednesday. **mercredi des Cendres** Ash Wednesday.
mercure [mɛrkyr] *nm* mercury.
merde [mɛrd] (*vulgaire*) *nf* shit. *interj* hell! shit!
mère [mɛr] *nf* mother.
méridien [meridjɛ̃] *nm, adj* meridian.
méridional [meridjɔnal] *adj* southern; from the south of France. **Méridional, -e** *nm, nf* Southerner.
meringue [mərɛ̃g] *nf* meringue.
mériter [merite] *v* deserve, merit; (*exiger*) require; (*valoir*) be worth. **mérite** *nm* merit; (*respect*) credit; quality.
merlan [mɛrlɑ̃] *nm* whiting.
merle [mɛrl] *nm* blackbird.
merveille [mɛrvɛj] *nf* wonder marvel. **à merveille** perfectly, marvellously. **merveilleux** *adj* wonderful, marvellous.
mes [me] *V* **mon**.
mésaventure [mezavɑ̃tyr] *nf* misadventure, misfortune.
mesquin [mɛskɛ̃] *adj* mean, stingy; (*étroit*) petty. **mesquinerie** *nf* meanness; pettiness.
message [mesaʒ] *nm* message. **messager, -ère** *nm, nf* messenger. **messageries** *nf pl* parcels service *sing*. **bureau de messageries** *nm* parcel office.
messe [mɛs] *nf* mass.
mesurer [məzyre] *v* measure; (*évaluer*) assess; limit, ration. **mesure** *nf* measure; measurement; (*musique*) bar; (*cadence*) time; moderation. **à mesure que** as. **fait sur mesure** made-to-measure. **mesuré** *adj* measured; moderate; (*ton*) steady.
métabolisme [metabɔlismə] *nm* metabolism.
métal [metal] *nm* metal. **métallique** *adj* metallic. **métallurgie** *nf* metallurgy. **métallurgiste** *nm* metallurgist; (*ouvrier*) metal-worker.
métamorphose [metamɔrfoz] *nf* metamorphosis.
métaphore [metafɔr] *nf* metaphor. **métaphorique** *adj* metaphorical.
métaphysique [metafizik] *adj* metaphysical. *nf* metaphysics.
météore [meteɔr] *nm* meteor. **météorique** *adj* meteoric. **météorite** *nm* meteorite.
météorologie [meteɔrɔlɔʒi] *nf* meteorology. **météorologique** *adj* meteorological, weather. **météorologue** *n(m+f)* meteorologist.
méthane [metan] *nm* methane.
méthode [metɔd] *nf* method. **méthodique** *adj* methodical.
méthodiste [metɔdist] *n(m+f)*, *adj* Methodist. **méthodisme** *nm* Methodism.
méticuleux [metikylø] *adj* meticulous.
métier [metje] *nm* job, trade, profession; technique, experience; (*machine*) loom.

métis, -isse [metis] *n, adj* half-caste, half-breed. **métisser** *v* cross.
métrage [metraʒ] *nm* length; measurement.
mètre [mɛtrə] *nm* metre; (*règle*) rule. **mètre à ruban** tape measure. **métrique** *adj* metric.
métro [metro] *nm* underground, tube.
métronome [metrɔnɔm] *nm* metronome.
métropole [metrɔpɔl] *nf* metropolis. **métropolitain** *adj* metropolitan.
mets [mɛ] *nm* dish.
***mettre** [mɛtrə] *v* put; (*vêtements*) put on, wear; (*temps*) take, spend; suppose. **se mettre à** start. **metteur en scène** *nm* (*théâtre*) producer; (*cinéma*) director.
meubler [mœble] *v* furnish; (*remplir*) fill (out). **meuble** *nm* piece of furniture. **meubles** *nm pl* furniture *sing*.
meugler [møgle] *v* moo, low. **meuglement** *nm* lowing.
meule[1] [møl] *nf* (*moudre*) millstone; (*aiguiser*) grindstone.
meule[2] [møl] *nf* stack, rick. **meule de foin** haystack.
meunier [mønje] *nm* miller.
meurtre [mœtrə] *nm* murder.
meurtrier [mœrtrije], **-ère** *nm, nf* murderer. *adj* murderous, lethal.
meurtrir [mœrtrir] *v* bruise. **meurtrissure** *nf* bruise.
meute [møt] *nf* pack.
mi- [mi] *prefix* half-, mid-. **à mi-chemin** halfway. **à mi-corps** to the waist. **à mi-côte** halfway up *or* down. **à mi-temps** part-time. **à mi-voix** in an undertone. **mi-janvier, mi-février, etc.** mid-January, mid-February, etc.
miche [miʃ] *nf* round loaf.
micro [mikro] *nm* (*fam*) mike.
microbe [mikrɔb] *nm* germ, microbe.
microfilm [mikrɔfilm] *nm* microfilm.
microphone [mikrɔfɔn] *nm* microphone.
microscope [mikrɔskɔp] *nm* microscope. **microscopique** *adj* microscopic.
microsillon [mikrɔsijɔ̃] *nm* long-playing record.
midi [midi] *nm* midday, noon; lunchtime; (*géog*) south. **le Midi** the South of France.
mie [mi] *nf* soft part of bread.
miel [mjɛl] *nm* honey. **mielleux** *adj* (*péj*) sugary, smooth.
mien [mjɛ̃], **mienne** *pron* **le mien, la mienne** mine.
miette [mjɛt] *nf* crumb.
mieux [mjø] *adj, adv* better. **le** *or* **la mieux** (the) best.
mièvre [mjɛvrə] *adj* mawkish, affected.
mignon, -onne [miɲɔ̃, -ɔn] *adj* sweet, dainty. *nm, nf* darling.
migraine [migrɛn] *nf* headache; (*méd*) migraine.
migration [migrɑsjɔ̃] *nf* migration.
mijoter [miʒɔte] *v* simmer; (*fam*) plot, cook up.
mildiou [mildju] *nm* mildew.
milieu [miljø] *nm* middle; environment; (*social*) circle, background. **au milieu de** in the middle of. **juste milieu** happy medium.
militaire [militɛr] *adj* military. *nm* soldier.
militant [militɑ̃], **-e** *n, adj* militant.
mille[1] [mil] *nm, adj invar* (a) thousand. **mille-pattes** *nm invar* centipede. **milliard** *nm* thousand million. **millième** *n(m+f)*, *adj* thousandth. **millier** *nm* thousand or so. **des milliers de** thousands *or* millions of.
mille[2] [mil] *nm* mile.
millénaire [milenɛr] *nm* millennium, thousand years. *adj* thousand-year-old, ancient.
milligramme [miligram] *nm* milligram.
millilitre [mililitrə] *nm* millilitre.
millimètre [milimɛtrə] *nm* millimetre.
million [miljɔ̃] *nm* million. **millionnaire** *n(m+f)* millionnaire. **millionième** *n(m+f)*, *adj* millionth.
mimer [mime] *v* mime; (*imiter*) mimic. **mime** *nm* mime; mimic.
minable [minablə] *adj* (*lieu*) seedy, shabby; miserable, wretched; (*fam*: *piètre*) pathetic, hopeless.
minauder [minode] *v* mince, simper.
mince [mɛ̃s] *adj* thin; (*svelte*) slim, slender; (*insignifiant*) slight, small. *adv* thinly. *interj* blast! drat! **minceur** *nf* thinness.
mine[1] [min] *nf* expression; look, appearance. **avoir bonne/mauvaise mine** look well/unwell. **faire mine de** pretend to, make as if to.
mine[2] [min] *nf* mine; (*crayon*) lead. **miner** *v* (*mil*) mine; (*saper*) undermine. **mineur** *nm* miner. **minier** *adj* mining.
minerai [minrɛ] *nm* ore.
minéral [mineral] *nm, adj* mineral.
mineur, -e [minœr] *n, adj* minor.

miniature [minjatyr] *nf, adj* miniature.
minime [minim] *adj* minimal; (*insignifiant*) trivial; (*piètre*) paltry. **minimiser** *v* minimize. **minimum** *nm, adj* minimum.
ministère [minister] *nm* ministry; government. **ministériel** *adj* ministerial. **ministre** *nm* minister.
minorité [minorite] *nf* minority. **minoritaire** *adj* minority.
minuit [minɥi] *nm* midnight.
minuscule [minyskyl] *adj* minute, tiny; (*lettre*) small. *nf* small letter.
minute [minyt] *nf* minute; moment, instant.
minutieux [minysjø] *adj* meticulous, minute. **minutie** *nf* meticulousness; (*ouvrage*) minute detail.
mioche [mjɔʃ] *n*(*m+f*) (*fam*) kid, brat.
miracle [miraklə] *nm* miracle. **miraculeux** *adj* miraculous.
mirage [miraʒ] *nm* mirage.
mirer [mire] *v* mirror. **se mirer** be reflected.
miroir [mirwar] *nm* mirror.
miroiter [mirwate] *v* sparkle, gleam.
misanthrope [mizɑ̃trɔp] *n*(*m+f*) misanthropist. *adj* misanthropic. **misanthropie** *nf* misanthropy.
mise [miz] *nf* putting; (*enjeu*) stake; (*vêtements*) clothing. **être de mise** be acceptable. **mise en plis** set. **mise en scène** production. **miser** *v* stake, bet.
misérable [mizerablə] *adj* miserable; (*pitoyable*) wretched; (*pauvre*) destitute; (*minable*) paltry. *n*(*m+f*) wretch.
misère [mizɛr] *nf* (*malheur*) misery, misfortune; poverty. **faire des misères à** (*fam*) be nasty to.
miséricorde [mizerikɔrd] *nf* mercy. **miséricordieux** *adj* merciful.
misogyne [mizɔʒin] *n*(*m+f*) misogynist. **misogynie** *nf* misogyny.
missile [misil] *nm* missile.
mission [misjɔ̃] *nf* mission. **missionnaire** *n*(*m+f*) missionary.
mite [mit] *nf* clothes moth. **mité** *adj* moth-eaten. **miteux** *adj* seedy, shabby.
mitoyen [mitwajɛ̃] *adj* dividing, common. **mur mitoyen** *nm* party wall.
mitrailleuse [mitrɑjøz] *nf* machine gun.
mitre [mitrə] *nf* mitre.
mixte [mikst] *adj* mixed; (*école*) coeducational.
mobile [mɔbil] *adj* mobile, moving, movable. *nm* motive; (*art*) mobile. **mobiliser** *v* mobilize. **mobilité** *nf* mobility.
mobilier [mɔbilje] *adj* (*jur*) personal, movable. *nm* furniture.
mocassin [mɔkasɛ̃] *nm* moccasin.
moche [mɔʃ] (*fam*) *adj* (*mauvais*) rotten; (*laid*) ugly.
mode[1] [mɔd] *nf* fashion; style. **à la mode** fashionable.
mode[2] [mɔd] *nm* mode; method; (*gramm*) mood. **mode d'emploi** directions for use.
modeler [mɔdle] *v* model, shape, mould. **modèle** *nm, adj* model.
modérer [mɔdere] *v* moderate, restrain. **se modérer** control oneself. **modération** *nf* moderation; reduction. **modéré** *adj* moderate.
moderne [mɔdɛrn] *adj* modern. **modernisation** *nf* modernization. **moderniser** *v* modernize.
modeste [mɔdɛst] *adj* modest. **modestie** *nf* modesty.
modifier [mɔdifje] *v* modify. **modification** *nf* modification.
modique [mɔdik] *adj* modest, small.
module [mɔdyl] *nm* module.
moduler [mɔdyle] *v* modulate. **modulation** *nf* modulation.
moelle [mwal] *nf* (*anat*) marrow; pith. **moelle épinière** spinal cord. **moelleux** *adj* soft, smooth, mellow.
mœurs [mœr] *nf pl* morals *pl*; customs *pl*; habits *pl*; manners *pl*.
mohair [mɔɛr] *nm* mohair.
moi [mwa] *pron* me; (*sujet*) I. *nm* self, ego. **moi-même** *pron* myself.
moignon [mwaɲɔ̃] *nm* stump.
moindre [mwɛ̃drə] *adj* less; (*plus bas*) lower; (*inférieur*) poorer. **le** *or* **la moindre** the least, the slightest.
moine [mwan] *nm* monk.
moineau [mwano] *nm* sparrow.
moins [mwɛ̃] *nm, adv* less. **à moins de** barring, unless. **à moins que** unless. **au moins** at least. **du moins** at least. **le** *or* **la moins** (the) least. **moins de** less (than); (*heure*) before. *prep* minus. **six heures moins dix** ten to six.
mois [mwa] *nm* month. **au mois** by the month, monthly.
moisir [mwazir] *v* go mouldy. **moisi** *adj* mouldy. **sentir le moisi** smell musty. **moisissure** *nf* mould.
moisson [mwasɔ̃] *nf* harvest, crop. **mois-**

sonner *v* harvest, reap. **moissonneuse-batteuse** *nf* combine harvester.
moite [mwat] *adj* moist, clammy.
moitié [mwatje] *nf* half. **à moitié** half. **moitié moitié** half-and-half.
mol [mɔl] *form of* **mou** *used before a vowel or mute h.*
molécule [mɔlekyl] *nf* molecule. **moléculaire** *adj* molecular.
molester [mɔlɛste] *v* manhandle, maul.
mollasse [mɔlas] (*fam*) *adj* lethargic; (*flasque*) flabby.
molle [mɔl] *V* **mou.**
mollesse [mɔlɛs] *nf* softness; (*manque de fermeté*) limpness; lethargy, lifelessness.
mollet, -ette [mɔlɛ, -ɛt] *adj* soft; (*œuf*) soft-boiled. *nm* (*anat*) calf.
mollir [mɔlir] *v* soften; (*vent*) abate; (*fléchir*) yield; give way.
mollusque [mɔlysk] *nm* mollusc.
môme [mom] *n*(*m*+*f*) (*fam*) kid, brat.
moment [mɔmɑ̃] *nm* moment; time. **en ce moment** at the moment. **momentané** *adj* momentary, brief.
momie [mɔmi] *nf* mummy. **momification** *nf* mummification. **momifier** *v* mummify.
mon [mɔ̃], **ma** *adj*, *pl* **mes** my.
Monaco [mɔnako] *nm* Monaco.
monarque [mɔnark] *nm* monarch. **monarchie** *nf* monarchy. **monarchiste** *n*(*m*+*f*) monarchist.
monastère [mɔnastɛr] *nm* monastery. **monastique** *adj* monastic.
monceau [mɔ̃so] *nm* heap, pile.
monde [mɔ̃d] *nm* world; (*gens*) people; society, circle. **tout le monde** everybody. **mondain** *adj* fashionable; society; refined; (*rel*) worldly. **mondial** *adj* worldwide.
monétaire [mɔnetɛr] *adj* monetary.
mongolien [mɔ̃gɔljɛ̃], **-enne** *n*, *adj* mongol. **mongolisme** *nm* mongolism.
moniteur, -trice [mɔnitœr, -tris] *nm*, *nf* (*sport*) instructor; (*surveillant*) supervisor.
monnaie [mɔnɛ] *nf* (*devises*) currency; (*pièce*) coin; (*appoint*) change. **monnayer** *v* mint; (*tirer profit de*) capitalize on.
monogamie [mɔnɔgami] *nf* monogamy. **monogame** *adj* monogamous.
monogramme [mɔnɔgram] *nm* monogram.
monologue [mɔnɔlɔg] *nm* monologue.
monopole [mɔnɔpɔl] *nm* monopoly. **monopoliser** *v* monopolize.
monosyllabe [mɔnɔsilab] *nm* monosyllable. **monosyllabique** *adj* monosyllabic.
monotone [mɔnɔtɔn] *adj* monotonous. **monotonie** *nf* monotony.
monseigneur [mɔ̃sɛɲœr] *nm* Your *or* His Grace, Your *or* His Lordship.
monsieur [məsjø] *nm*, *pl* **messieurs** gentleman; (*titre*) sir. **Monsieur** *nm* (*suivi du nom de famille*) Mr.
monstre [mɔ̃strə] *nm* monster. *adj* (*fam*) colossal. **monstrueux** *adj* monstrous. **monstruosité** *nf* monstrosity.
mont [mɔ̃] *nm* mount. **mont-de-piété** *nm* pawnshop.
montagne [mɔ̃taɲ] *nf* mountain. **montagnes russes** big dipper *sing*. **montagneux** *adj* mountainous.
montant [mɔ̃tɑ̃] *adj* upward, rising; (*col*, *corsage*) high. *nm* (*portant*) upright; (*somme*) total.
monter [mɔ̃te] *v* mount; go up, rise; ascend, climb; (*porter*) take up; (*cheval*) ride; (*théâtre*) put on, produce; assemble; equip. **monter à cheval/bicyclette** ride a horse/bicycle. **monter dans** *or* **en** get on *or* into. **se monter à** amount to. **montage** *nm* assembly; (*cinéma*) editing. **montée** *nf* ascent, climb; rise; (*côte*) hill. **monture** *nf* frame, setting, mount.
montre [mɔ̃trə] *nf* watch. **faire montre de** show, display. **montre-bracelet** *nf* wristwatch.
montrer [mɔ̃tre] *v* show. **se montrer** appear; prove to be.
monument [mɔnymɑ̃] *nm* monument. **monumental** *adj* monumental.
moquer [mɔke] *v* **se moquer de** make fun of; (*mépriser*) not care about. **moquerie** *nf* mockery.
moral [mɔral] *adj* moral. *nm* morale. **morale** *or* **moralité** *nf* morality; (*mœurs*) morals *pl*; (*fable*) moral. **moraliser** *v* moralize. **moraliste** *n*(*m*+*f*) moralist.
morbide [mɔrbid] *adj* morbid.
morceau [mɔrso] *nm* piece; (*bout*) bit; extract, passage.
mordre [mɔrdrə] *v* bite. **mordant** *adj* biting; (*acerbe*) scathing, cutting. **mordu** *adj* (*fam*) mad keen.
se morfondre [mɔrfɔ̃drə] *v* mope.
morgue[1] [mɔrg] *nf* morgue, mortuary.
morgue[2] [mɔrg] *nf* (*arrogance*) pride, haughtiness.

moribond [mɔribɔ̃] *adj* dying.
mormon [mɔrmɔ̃], **-e** *n, adj* Mormon.
morne [mɔrn] *adj* gloomy, dismal.
morose [mɔroz] *adj* sullen, morose.
morphine [mɔrfin] *nf* morphine.
mors [mɔr] *nm* bit.
morse[1] [mɔrs] *nm* (*zool*) walrus.
morse[2] [mɔrs] *nm* Morse code.
morsure [mɔrsyr] *nf* bite.
mort[1] [mɔr], **-e** *adj* dead. *nm, nf* dead person. **morte-saison** *nf* off season. **mort-né** *adj* stillborn.
mort[2] [mɔr] *nf* death. **mort-aux-rats** *nf* rat poison.
mortalité [mɔrtalite] *nf* mortality; (*taux*) death rate.
mortel [mɔrtɛl] *adj* mortal; fatal; (*poison, etc.*) lethal, deadly.
mortier [mɔrtje] *nm* mortar.
mortifier [mɔrtifje] *v* mortify. **mortification** *nf* mortification.
mortuaire [mɔrtɥɛr] *adj* mortuary. **dépôt mortuaire** *nm* funeral parlour.
morue [mɔry] *nf* cod.
morveux [mɔrvø], **-euse** *nm, nf* (*argot*) kid, brat.
mosaïque [mɔzaik] *nf* mosaic.
Moscou [mɔsku] *n* Moscow.
mosquée [mɔske] *nf* mosque.
mot [mo] *nm* word; note; (*expression*) saying. **mot de passe** password. **mots croisés** crossword *sing.*
motel [mɔtɛl] *nm* motel.
moteur, -trice [mɔtœr, -tris] *nm* motor, engine. **moteur à explosion** internal combustion engine. **moteur à réaction** jet engine. *adj* (*anat*) motor; (*tech*) driving.
motif [mɔtif] *nm* motive, grounds *pl*; (*ornement, musique*) motif.
motion [mosjɔ̃] *nf* motion.
motiver [mɔtive] *v* motivate; justify; (*expliquer*) account for. **motivation** *nf* motivation.
moto [mɔto] *nf* (*fam*) motorbike. **motocycliste** *n*(*m+f*) motorcyclist.
motte [mɔt] *nf* lump; (*terre*) clod; (*gazon*) turf.
mou [mu], **molle** *adj* soft; (*sans fermeté*) limp; (*flasque*) flabby; feeble, weak; lethargic; (*temps*) muggy. *nm* softness. **avoir du mou** be slack.
mouche [muʃ] *nf* fly. **prendre la mouche** (*fam*) get in a huff. **moucheron** *nm* midge.
moucher [muʃe] *v* (*fam*) snub; (*chandelle*) snuff. **se moucher** blow one's nose.
moucheter [muʃte] *v* speckle. **moucheture** *nf* speck, spot.
mouchoir [muʃwar] *nm* handkerchief. **mouchoir en papier** tissue.
***moudre** [mudrə] *v* grind.
moue [mu] *nf* pout. **faire la moue** pout, pull a face.
mouette [mwɛt] *nf* sea-gull.
mouffette [mufɛt] *nf* skunk.
moufle [muflə] *nf* mitten.
mouiller [muje] *v* wet; (*naut*) moor, anchor. **mouillage** *nm* mooring, anchorage. **mouillé** *adj* wet.
moule[1] [mul] *nm* mould.
moule[2] [mul] *nf* (*zool, cuisine*) mussel.
mouler [mule] *v* mould, cast; (*vêtements*) hug, fit closely.
moulin [mulɛ̃] *nm* mill. **moulin à café** coffee-mill. **moulin à paroles** (*fam*) chatterbox. **moulin à vent** windmill. **moulinet** *nm* (*pêche*) reel.
moulu [muly] *adj* ground.
***mourir** [murir] *v* die.
mousquet [muskɛ] *nm* musket. **mousquetaire** *nm* musketeer.
mousse[1] [mus] *nf* (*bot*) moss; (*écume*) froth, foam; (*savon*) lather; (*cuisine*) mousse. **mousser** *v* froth, foam; lather; (*vin*) sparkle. **mousseux** *adj* frothy; sparkling. **moussu** *adj* mossy.
mousse[2] [mus] *nm* cabin boy.
mousseline [muslin] *nf* muslin.
mousson [musɔ̃] *nf* monsoon.
moustache [mustaʃ] *nf* moustache. **moustaches** *nf pl* (*animal*) whiskers *pl.*
moustique [mustik] *nm* mosquito.
moutarde [mutard] *nf* mustard.
mouton [mutɔ̃] *nm* sheep; (*cuisine*) mutton.
***mouvoir** [muvwar] *v* drive, move. **se mouvoir** move. **mouvant** *adj* changing, shifting. **mouvement** *nm* movement; activity; impulse. **mouvementé** *adj* lively, eventful.
moyen [mwajɛ̃], **-enne** *adj* medium, average; middle. **moyen âge** *nm* Middle Ages *pl.* **Moyen-Orient** *nm* Middle East. *nm* means, way. **au moyen de** by means of. **moyens** *nm pl* means *pl.* *nf* average.
moyennant [mwajɛnɑ̃] *prep* (in return) for.
moyeu [mwajø] *nm* hub.

muer [mɥe] *v* moult; (*voix*) break.
muet, -ette [mɥɛ, -ɛt] *adj* silent; (*infirme*) dumb. *nm, nf* mute, dumb person.
mufle [myflə] *nm* muzzle; (*argot*) lout.
mugir [myʒir] *v* bellow, roar; (*vache*) moo.
muguet [mygɛ] *nm* lily of the valley.
mule [myl] *nf* mule.
mulet [mylɛ] *nm* mule.
multicolore [myltikɔlɔr] *adj* multicoloured.
multiple [myltiplə] *adj* multiple, numerous, many. *nm* multiple.
multiplier [myltiplije] *v* multiply; (*augmenter*) increase. **multiplication** *nf* multiplication.
multitude [myltityd] *nf* multitude, vast number.
municipal [mynisipal] *adj* municipal; (*conseil*) local; (*piscine, etc.*) public. **municipalité** *nf* municipality; town council.
munir [mynir] *v* **munir de** provide with, equip with. **munitions** *nf pl* ammunition *sing.*
mur [myr] *nm* wall; barrier. **muraille** *nf* high wall.
mûr [myr] *adj* (*fruit*) ripe; (*personne*) mature.
mural [myral] *adj* mural. **peinture murale** *nf* mural.
mûre [myr] *nf* (*ronce*) blackberry; (*mûrier*) mulberry. **mûrier** *nm* mulberry bush; blackberry bush.
mûrir [myrir] *v* ripen; mature.
murmurer [myrmyre] *v* murmur. **murmure** *nm* murmur.
musc [mysk] *nm* musk.
muscade [myskad] *nf* nutmeg.
muscle [mysklə] *nm* muscle. **musclé** *adj* muscular.
museau [myzo] *nm* muzzle; (*porc*) snout.
musée [myze] *nm* museum; (*d'art*) art gallery.
museler [myzle] *v* muzzle. **muselière** *nf* muzzle.
muséum [myzeɔm] *nm* natural history museum.
musicien [myzisjɛ̃], **-enne** *nm, nf* musician. *adj* musical.
musique [myzik] *nf* music; (*mil*) band. **musical** *adj* musical.
musulman [myzylmɑ̃], **-e** *n, adj* Muslim.
mutiler [mytile] *v* mutilate; (*personne*) maim. **mutilation** *nf* mutilation. **mutilé, -e** *nm, nf* disabled person.
mutin [mytɛ̃] *adj* mischievous. *nm* rebel.
se mutiner [mytine] *v* mutiny; rebel. **mutiné** *adj* mutinous. **mutinerie** *nf* mutiny; rebellion.
mutisme [mytismə] *nm* silence; (*méd*) dumbness.
mutuel [mytɥɛl] *adj* mutual.
myope [mjɔp] *adj* short-sighted. **myopie** *nf* short-sightedness.
myrtille [mirtij] *nf* bilberry.
mystère [mistɛr] *nm* mystery. **mystérieux** *adj* mysterious.
mystifier [mistifje] *v* fool, take in.
mystique [mistik] *n(m+f)* mystic. *adj* mystical, mystic. **mysticisme** *nm* mysticism.
mythe [mit] *nm* myth. **mythique** adj mythical. **mythologie** *nf* mythology. **mythologique** *adj* mythological.

N

n' [n] *V* **ne.**
nabot [nabo], **-e** *adj* tiny. *nm, nf* dwarf.
nacre [nakrə] *nf* mother-of-pearl. **nacré** *adj* pearly.
nager [naʒe] *v* swim; float; (*naut*) row. **nage** *nf* (*action*) swimming; (*manière*) stroke. **nage libre** freestyle. **nageoire** *nf* (*poisson*) fin; (*phoque*) flipper. **nageur, -euse** *nm, nf* swimmer.
naguère [nagɛr] *adv* not long ago; (*autrefois*) formerly.
naïf [naif], **-ïve** *adj* naive. *nm, nf* gullible fool. **naïveté** *nf* naivety.
nain [nɛ̃], **-e** *n, adj* dwarf.
naissance [nɛsɑ̃s] *nf* birth; source.
***naître** [nɛtrə] *v* be born; (*surgir*) arise, spring up. **faire naître** arouse; create.
nappe [nap] *nf* tablecloth; (*eau*) sheet; (*brouillard*) blanket. **nappe de pétrole** oil slick. **napperon** *nm* mat.
narcotique [narkɔtik] *nm, adj* narcotic.
narine [narin] *nf* nostril.
narquois [narkwa] *adj* mocking, derisive.
narrer [nare] *v* narrate. **narrateur, -trice** *nm, nf* narrator. **narratif** *adj* narrative. **narration** *nf* narration; (*récit*) narrative.

nasal [nazal] *adj* nasal. **nasaliser** *v* nasalize. **naseau** *nm* nostril. **nasillard** *adj* nasal.
natal [natal] *adj* native. **natalité** *nf* birth rate.
natation [natasjɔ̃] *nf* swimming.
natif [natif] **-ive** *n, adj* native.
nation [nasjɔ̃] *nf* nation. **national, -e** *n, adj* national. **nationalisation** *nf* nationalization. **nationaliser** *v* nationalize. **nationalisme** *nm* nationalism. **nationaliste** *n(m+f)* nationalist. **nationalité** *nf* nationality.
nativité [nativite] *nf* nativity.
natter [nate] *v* plait. **natte** *nf* (*cheveux*) plait; (*paille, etc.*) mat.
naturalisme [natyralismə] *nm* naturalism. **naturaliste** *n(m+f)* naturalist.
nature [natyr] *nf* nature. **en nature** in kind. **nature morte** still life. *adj invar* plain, neat.
naturel [natyrɛl] *adj* natural. *nm* disposition.
naufrage [nofraʒ] *nm* shipwreck; ruin. **naufragé** *adj* shipwrecked.
nausée [noze] *nf* nausea. **avoir la nausée** feel sick. **nauséabond** *adj* nauseating.
nautique [notik] *adj* nautical.
naval [naval] *adj* naval.
navet [navɛ] *nm* turnip; (*fam*) rubbish.
navette [navɛt] *nf* shuttle (service). **faire la navette** commute; go backwards and forwards.
naviguer [navige] *v* (*bateau*) sail; (*avion*) fly; (*piloter*) navigate. **navigateur** *nm* navigator. **navigation** *nf* navigation; traffic.
navire [navir] *nm* ship.
navrer [navre] *v* distress; (*irriter*) annoy. **navré** *adj* sorry; distressed.
ne [nə], **n'** *adv* not. **ne ... guère** scarcely. **ne ... jamais** never. **ne ... pas** not. **ne ... personne** nobody. **ne ... plus** no longer. **ne ... que** only. **ne ... rien** nothing.
né [ne] *adj* born.
néanmoins [neɑ̃mwɛ̃] *adv* nevertheless, yet.
néant [neɑ̃] *nm* nothing, void.
nébuleux [nebylø] *adj* nebulous, vague; (*ciel*) cloudy.
nécessaire [nesesɛr] *adj* necessary; indispensable. *nm* essentials *pl*. **le nécessaire** what is needed. **nécessité** *nf* necessity. **nécessiter** *v* necessitate.
nécrologie [nekrɔlɔʒi] *nf* (*notice*) obituary; (*liste*) obituary column.
nectar [nɛktar] *nm* nectar.
néerlandais [neɛrlɑ̃dɛ] *nm, adj* Dutch. **les Néerlandais** the Dutch.
nef [nɛf] *nf* nave.
néfaste [nefast] *adj* (*nuisible*) harmful; (*funeste*) unlucky.
négatif [negatif] *nm, adj* negative.
négligé [negliʒe] *adj* neglected; (*tenue*) slovenly; (*travail*) careless. *nm* slovenliness; (*vêtement*) negligée.
négliger [negliʒe] *v* neglect; (*occasion*) miss. **négligeable** *adj* negligible. **négligence** *nf* negligence, carelessness. **négligent** *adj* negligent, careless.
négocier [negɔsje] *v* negotiate. **négoce** *nm* trade. **négociable** *adj* negotiable. **négociant, -e** *nm, nf* merchant. **négociation** *nf* negotiation.
nègre [nɛgrə] *nm, adj* Negro. **petit nègre** pidgin French. **négresse** *nf* Negress. **négrier** *nm* (*péj*) slave-driver.
neige [nɛʒ] *nf* snow. **neige fondue** sleet. **neiger** *v* snow. **neigeux** *adj* snowy.
nénuphar [nenyfar] *nm* water-lily.
néon [neɔ̃] *nm* neon.
néo-zélandais [neɔzelɑ̃dɛ] *adj* New Zealand. **Néo-Zélandais, -e** *nm, nf* New Zealander.
nerf [nɛr] *nm* nerve; spirit, energy. **nerveux** *adj* nervous; energetic, vigorous; (*musclé*) sinewy. **nervosité** *nf* nervousness; tension; irritability.
net, nette [nɛt] *adj* neat; (*propre*) clean; (*comm*) net; (*clair*) clear; distinct. *adv* net; frankly; (*sur le coup*) outright; (*s'arrêter*) dead. **netteté** *nf* neatness; clearness.
nettoyer [nɛtwaje] *v* clean. **nettoyer à sec** dry-clean. **nettoyage** *nm* cleaning.
neuf[1] [nœf] *nm, adj* nine. **neuvième** *n(m+f), adj* ninth.
neuf[2] [nœf] *adj* new. **à neuf** as good as new.
neutre [nøtrə] *nm, adj* neutral; (*genre*) neuter. **neutraliser** *v* neutralize. **neutralité** *nf* neutrality.
neveu [nəvø] *nm* nephew.
névralgie [nevralʒi] *nf* neuralgia.
névrose [nevroz] *nf* neurosis. **névrosé** *adj* neurotic.
nez [ne] *nm* nose; flair; (*figure*) face.
ni [ni] *conj* nor, or. **ni ... ni ...** neither ... nor ....

niais [njɛ], **-e** *adj* simple, silly. *nm*, *nf* simpleton. **niaiserie** *nf* silliness; (*propos*) foolish talk.
nicher [niʃe] *v* nest. **niche** *nf* niche; (*chien*) kennel. **nichée** *nf* brood.
nickel [nikɛl] *nm* nickel.
Nicosie [nikɔsi] *n* Nicosia.
nicotine [nikɔtin] *nf* nicotine.
nid [ni] *nm* nest. **nid de poule** pot-hole.
nièce [njɛs] *nf* niece.
nier [nje] *v* deny.
nigaud [nigo], **-e** *adj* silly, simple. *nm*, *nf* simpleton.
nimbe [nɛ̃b] *nm* halo.
nitouche [nituʃ] *nf* **sainte nitouche** hypocrite. **faire la sainte nitouche** look as if butter wouldn't melt in one's mouth.
niveau [nivo] *nm* level; (*degré*) standard. **niveau à bulle** spirit level. **niveau de vie** standard of living.
niveler [nivle] *v* level, even out.
noble [nɔblə] *nm*, *adj* noble. **noblesse** *nf* nobleness, nobility.
noce [nɔs] *nf* wedding. **faire la noce** (*fam*) live it up.
nocif [nɔsif] *adj* noxious, harmful.
nocturne [nɔktyrn] *adj* nocturnal.
Noël [nɔɛl] *nm* Christmas.
nœud [nø] *nm* knot; (*de ruban*) bow; (*lien*) bond; (*rail*, *route*) junction. **nœud coulant** slip-knot. **nœud papillon** bow tie.
noir [nwar] *adj* black; (*obscur*) dark; (*profond*) deep. *nm* black; darkness. **Noir** *nm* black man. **noire** *nf* crotchet. **Noire** *nf* black woman. **noircir** *v* blacken; darken.
noisette [nwazɛt] *nf* hazelnut. *adj invar* hazel. **noisetier** *nm* hazel tree.
noix [nwa] *nf* walnut. **noix de beurre** knob of butter. **noix de coco** coconut.
nom [nɔ̃] *nm* name; (*gramm*) noun. **nom de baptême** Christian name. **nom de famille** surname. **nom de jeune fille** maiden name. **nom d'emprunt** assumed name. **nom de théâtre** stage name. **nom propre** proper noun.
nomade [nɔmad] *adj* nomadic. *n*(*m*+*f*) nomad.
nombre [nɔ̃brə] *nm* number. **nombreux** *adj* numerous.
nombril [nɔ̃bri] *nm* navel.
nominal [nɔminal] *adj* nominal.
nomination [nɔminɑsjɔ̃] *nf* appointment, nomination.
nommer [nɔme] *v* name; (*désigner*) appoint.
non [nɔ̃] *adv* no; (*pas*) not. **non plus** neither. *nm invar* no.
nonchalant [nɔ̃ʃalɑ̃] *adj* nonchalant. **nonchalance** *nf* nonchalance.
non-conformiste [nɔ̃kɔ̃fɔrmist] *n*(*m*+*f*), *adj* nonconformist.
non-existant [nɔnɛgzistɑ̃] *adj* non-existent.
nonobstant [nɔnɔpstɑ̃] *prep*, *adv* notwithstanding.
nord [nɔr] *nm* north. *adj invar* north; (*région*) northern; (*direction*) northward. **nord-est** *nm*, *adj invar* north-east. **nord-ouest** *nm*, *adj invar* north-west.
normal [nɔrmal] *adj* normal. **normale** *nf* norm, normal.
norme [nɔrm] *nf* norm; standard.
Norvège [nɔrvɛʒ] *nf* Norway. **norvégien** *nm*, *adj* Norwegian. **Norvégien**, **-enne** *nm*, *nf* Norwegian.
nos [no] *V* **notre**.
nostalgie [nɔstalʒi] *nf* nostalgia. **nostalgique** *adj* nostalgic.
notable [nɔtablə] *adj* notable.
notaire [nɔtɛr] *nm* notary.
notamment [nɔtamɑ̃] *adv* notably, in particular.
notation [nɔtɑsjɔ̃] *nf* notation; (*devoir*) marking.
noter [nɔte] *v* (*écrire*) note down; (*remarquer*) notice, note; (*devoir*) mark. **note** *nf* note; mark; (*compte*) bill.
notice [nɔtis] *nf* note; instructions *pl*.
notifier [nɔtifje] *v* notify. **notification** *nf* notification.
notion [nosjɔ̃] *nf* notion.
notoire [nɔtwar] *adj* well-known; (*criminal*) notorious. **notoriété** *nf* fame; notoriety. **notoriété publique** common knowledge.
notre [nɔtrə] *adj*, *pl* **nos** our.
nôtre [notrə] *pron* **le** *or* **la nôtre** ours.
nouer [nwe] *v* tie, knot; (*amitié*, *etc.*) strike up; (*intrigue*) build up. **noueux** *adj* knotty, gnarled.
nouilles [nuj] *nf pl* noodles *pl*.
nounou [nunu] *nf* (*fam*) nanny.
nounours [nunurs] *nm* (*fam*) teddy.
nourrice [nuris] *nf* nurse. **nourricier** *adj* nutritive.
nourrir [nurir] *v* feed, nourish; (*espoir*, *etc.*) nurse, harbour. **nourrisson** *nm* infant. **nourriture** *nf* food, nourishment.

nous [nu] *pron* (*sujet*) we; (*objet*) us, to us; (*réfléchi*) ourselves, each other. **nous-mêmes** *pron* ourselves.

nouveau, -elle [nuvo, -ɛl] *adj* new; fresh. **à nouveau** afresh. **de nouveau** again. **nouveau-né** *adj* newborn. **Nouveau Testament** *nm* New Testament. **nouveau venu, nouvelle venue** *nm, nf* newcomer. **nouveaux-mariés** *nm pl* newly-weds *pl*. **nouvel an** *nm* New Year. **Nouvelle-Zélande** *nf* New Zealand. *nf* piece of news; (*récit*) short story. **nouvelles** *nf pl* news *sing*. **nouveauté** *nf* novelty; change; (*mode*) fashion.

nouvel [nuvɛl] *form of* **nouveau** *used before a vowel or mute h.*

novateur, -trice [nɔvatœr, -tris] *adj* innovative. *nm, nf* innovator.

novembre [nɔvɑ̃brə] *nm* November.

novice [nɔvis] *adj* inexperienced. *n(m+f)* novice.

noyau [nwajo] *nm* (*fruit*) stone; nucleus; (*tech*) core; small group.

noyer[1] [nwaje] *nm* (*arbre, bois*) walnut.

noyer[2] [nwaje] *v* drown; (*auto*) flood; (*submerger*) swamp. **noyade** *nf* drowning.

nu [ny] *adj* bare; (*sans vêtements*) naked; (*style*) plain. *nm* nude. **mettre à nu** expose, lay bare. **nu-pieds** *adv* barefoot.

nuage [nɥaʒ] *nm* cloud. **nuageux** *adj* cloudy.

nuance [nɥɑ̃s] *nf* nuance; (*couleur*) shade; slight difference. **nuancer** *v* shade.

nucléaire [nykleɛr] *adj* nuclear.

nudité [nydite] nudity; (*dénuement*) bareness. **nudiste** *n(m+f)* nudist.

nue [ny] *nf* **porter aux nues** praise to the skies. **tomber des nues** be flabbergasted.

nuée [nɥe] *nf* cloud; (*multitude*) horde.

***nuire** [nɥir] *v* **nuire à** harm. **nuisible** *adj* harmful. **animal** *or* **insecte nuisible** *nm* pest.

nuit [nɥi] *nf* night; (*obscurité*) darkness. **cette nuit** (*passé*) last night; (*futur*) tonight. **nuit blanche** sleepless night.

nul, nulle [nyl] *adj* (*aucun*) no; (*résultat*) nil; (*personne*) useless. **nul et non avenu** null and void. **nulle part** nowhere. *pron* no-one. **nullement** *adv* not at all.

numéral [nymeral] *nm* numeral.

numérique [nymerik] *adj* numerical.

numéro [nymero] *nm* number; (*journal*) issue. **numéro minéralogique** (*auto*) registration number.

numéroter [nymerɔte] *v* number.

nuptial [nypsjal] *adj* bridal, nuptial.

nuque [nyk] *nf* nape of the neck.

nutrition [nytrisjɔ̃] *nf* nutrition. **nutritif** *adj* nutritious, nourishing.

nylon [nilɔ̃] *nm* nylon.

nymphe [nɛ̃f] *nf* nymph.

O

oasis [ɔazis] *nf* oasis.

obéir [ɔbeir] *v* **obéir à** obey. **obéissance** *nf* obedience. **obéissant** *adj* obedient.

obélisque [ɔbelisk] *nm* obelisk.

obèse [ɔbɛz] *adj* obese. **obésité** *nf* obesity.

objecter [ɔbʒɛkte] *v* object; (*raison*) put forward; (*prétexter*) plead. **objection** *nf* objection.

objectif [ɔbʒɛktif] *adj* objective. *nm* objective; (*appareil-photo*) lens.

objet [ɔbʒɛ] *nm* object; (*but*) purpose; subject. **objets trouvés** lost property *sing*.

obliger [ɔbliʒe] *v* oblige; force, compel. **obligation** *nf* obligation; (*devoir*) duty. **obligatoire** *adj* compulsory; (*fam*) inevitable.

oblique [ɔblik] *adj* oblique. **regard oblique** *nm* sidelong glance.

oblitérer [ɔblitere] *v* cancel.

oblong, -ongue [ɔblɔ̃, -ɔ̃g] *adj* oblong.

obscène [ɔpsɛn] *adj* obscene. **obscénité** *nf* obscenity.

obscur [ɔpskyr] *adj* obscure; (*sombre*) dark; humble. **obscurité** *nf* obscurity; darkness.

obscurcir [ɔpskyrsir] *v* obscure; darken.

obséder [ɔpsede] *v* obsess, haunt. **obsédant** *adj* obsessive, haunting. **obsédé, -e** *nm, nf* (*fam*) fanatic.

obsèques [ɔpsɛk] *nf pl* funeral *sing*.

observateur, -trice [ɔpsɛrvatœr, -tris] *nm, nf* observer. *adj* observant.

observer [ɔpsɛrve] *v* observe; (*regarder*) watch; (*remarquer*) notice. **observation** *nf* observation; remark. **observatoire** *nm* observatory.

obsession [ɔpsesjɔ̃] *nf* obsession.

obstacle [ɔpstaklə] *nm* obstacle; (*hippisme*) fence

obstétrique [ɔpstetrik] *nf* obstetrics.

s'obstiner [ɔpstine] *v* insist. **s'obstiner à** persist obstinately in. **obstination** *nf* obstinacy. **obstiné** *adj* obstinate.

obstruer [ɔpstrye] *v* obstruct, block. **obstruction** *nf* obstruction.

***obtenir** [ɔptənir] *v* obtain, get; (*atteindre*) achieve.

obturateur [ɔptyratœr] *nm* (*phot*) shutter.

obtus [ɔbty] *adj* obtuse.

obus [ɔby] *nm* shell.

occasion [ɔkɑzjɔ̃] *nf* opportunity, chance; (*circonstance*) occasion; cause; (*comm*) bargain; (*marché*) second-hand market. **d'occasion** second-hand. **occasionnel** *adj* casual; (*fortuit*) chance. **occasionner** *v* cause.

occident [ɔksidɑ̃] *nm* west. **occidental** *adj* western.

occulte [ɔkylt] *adj* occult; secret, hidden.

occuper [ɔkype] *v* occupy. **s'occuper de** attend to, take care of. **occupant, -e** *nm, nf* occupant, occupier. **occupation** *nf* occupation. **occupé** *adj* busy; (*téléphone, toilettes*) engaged; (*mil*) occupied.

océan [ɔseɑ̃] *nm* ocean. **océanique** *adj* oceanic.

ocre [ɔkrə] *nf* ochre. *nm* (*couleur*) ochre.

octane [ɔktan] *nm* octane.

octave [ɔktav] *nf* octave.

octobre [ɔktɔbrə] *nm* October.

octogone [ɔktɔgɔn] *nm* octagon. **octogonal** *adj* octagonal.

octroyer [ɔktrwaje] *v* grant.

oculiste [ɔkylist] *n(m+f)* oculist.

ode [ɔd] *nf* ode.

odeur [ɔdœr] *nf* odour, smell; (*agréable*) fragrance, scent. **odorant** *adj* sweet-smelling. **odorat** *nm* sense of smell.

odieux [ɔdjø] *adj* obnoxious, odious.

œil [œj] *nm, pl* **yeux** eye; (*expression*) look. **œil poché** black eye. **œillade** *nf* wink. **œillères** *nf pl* blinkers *pl*. **œillet** *nm* carnation; (*trou*) eyelet.

œsophage [ezɔfaʒ] *nm* oesophagus.

œuf [œf] *nm* egg. **œuf à la coque** boiled egg. **œuf du jour** new-laid egg. **œuf dur** hard-boiled egg. **œuf mollet** soft-boiled egg. **œuf poché** poached egg. **œufs brouillés** scrambled eggs *pl*. **œuf sur le plat** fried egg.

œuvre [œvrə] *nf* work; (*tâche*) task; charity. **œuvre d'art** work of art.

offenser [ɔfɑ̃se] *v* offend. **s'offenser** take offence. **offensant** *adj* offensive. **offense** *nf* insult; (*rel*) trespass. **offensive** *nm* (*mil*) offensive.

office [ɔfis] *nm* office; bureau, agency; (*rel*) service. **faire office de** act as. **officiel, -elle** *n, adj* official. **officier** *nm* officer. **officieux** *adj* unofficial.

officine [ɔfisin] *nf* dispensary.

***offrir** [ɔfrir] *v* offer; present; (*cadeau*) give. **s'offrir** treat oneself to. **offrande** *nf* offering. **offre** *nf* offer; (*enchères*) bid; (*comm*) tender.

offusquer [ɔfyske] *v* offend.

ogre [ɔgrə] *nm* ogre. **ogresse** *nf* ogress.

oie [wa] *nf* goose.

oignon [ɔɲɔ̃] *nm* (*légume*) onion; (*bot*) bulb.

***oindre** [wɛ̃drə] *v* anoint.

oiseau [wazo] *nm* bird.

oisif [wazif] *adj* idle. **oisiveté** *nf* idleness.

oison [wazɔ̃] *nm* gosling.

olive [ɔliv] *nf* olive. **olivier** *nm* olive tree.

olympique [ɔlɛ̃pik] *adj* Olympic.

ombrage [ɔ̃braʒ] *nm* shade. **prendre ombrage** take umbrage. **ombrager** *v* shade. **ombrageux** *adj* touchy.

ombre [ɔ̃brə] *nf* shadow; (*ombrage*) shade; obscurity, dark. **ombrer** *v* shade.

omelette [ɔmlɛt] *nf* omelette.

***omettre** [ɔmɛtrə] *v* omit. **omission** *nf* omission.

omnibus [ɔmnibys] *nm* slow train.

omnipotent [ɔmnipɔtɑ̃] *adj* omnipotent.

omoplate [ɔmɔplat] *nf* shoulder blade.

on [ɔ̃] *pron* one, (*les gens*) they, people; (*tu, vous*) you; (*nous*) we; (*quelqu'un*) someone. **on demande . . .** . . . wanted. **on-dit** *nm invar* rumour, hearsay.

oncle [ɔ̃klə] *nm* uncle.

onde [ɔ̃d] *nf* wave. **grandes ondes** long wave(s). **ondes courtes/moyennes** short/medium wave(s). **sur les ondes** on the air.

ondoyer [ɔ̃dwaje] *v* ripple, wave. **ondoyant** *adj* undulating; (*flamme*) wavering; (*forme*) supple.

onduler [ɔ̃dyle] *v* undulate; (*cheveux*) be wavy. **ondulant** *adj* undulating; (*pouls*) uneven. **ondulation** *nf* undulation. **ondulé** *adj* (*cheveux*) wavy. **onduleux** *adj* wavy; (*movement*) sinuous.

ongle [ɔ̃glə] *nm* nail; (*animal*) claw.

onguent [ɔ̃gɑ̃] *nm* ointment.

onyx [ɔniks] *nm* onyx.

onze [ɔ̃z] *nm, adj* eleven. **onzième** *n(m+f), adj* eleventh.

opale [ɔpal] *nf* opal.
opaque [ɔpak] *adj* opaque. **opacité** *nf* opacity.
opéra [ɔpera] *nm* opera; (*édifice*) opera house. **opérette** *nf* operetta.
opérer [ɔpere] *v* operate; (*accomplir*) carry out; (*effectuer*) bring about; (*faire*) make; (*agir*) act, work. **se faire opérer** have an operation. **opérateur, -trice** *nm, nf* operator. **opération** *nf* operation; (*comm*) deal; (*tech*) process. **salle d'opération** *nf* operating theatre.
ophtalmique [ɔftalmik] *adj* ophthalmic.
s'opiniâtrer [ɔpinjɑtre] *v* persist stubbornly. **opiniâtre** *adj* stubborn, obstinate; persistent. **opiniâtreté** *nf* stubbornness, obstinacy.
opinion [ɔpinjɔ̃] *nf* opinion.
opium [ɔpjɔm] *nm* opium.
opportun [ɔpɔrtœ̃] *adj* opportune; appropriate. **opportunité** *nf* timeliness.
opposé [ɔpoze] *adj* opposite; conflicting, opposing; contrasting. **opposé à** opposed to. *nm* opposite.
opposer [ɔpoze] *v* place opposite; contrast. **s'opposer à** oppose. **opposition** *nf* opposition; conflict; contrast. **par opposition à** as opposed to.
opprimer [ɔprime] *v* oppress.
opprobre [ɔprɔbrə] *nm* disgrace.
opter [ɔpte] *v* opt, choose. **option** *nf* option.
opticien [ɔptisjɛ̃], **-enne** *nm, nf* optician.
optimiste [ɔptimist] *n(m+f)* optimist. *adj* optimistic. **optimisme** *nm* optimism.
optimum [ɔptimɔm] *nm, adj* optimum.
optique [ɔptik] *adj* optical, optic. *nf* optics.
opulent [ɔpylɑ̃] *adj* wealthy, rich, opulent. **opulence** *nf* richness, opulence.
or[1] [ɔr] *nm* gold. **d'or** golden.
or[2] [ɔr] *conj* now.
oracle [ɔrɑklə] *nm* oracle.
orage [ɔraʒ] *nm* storm. **orageux** *adj* stormy.
oraison [ɔrezɔ̃] *nf* prayer.
oral [ɔral] *nm, adj* oral.
orange [ɔrɑ̃ʒ] *nf* orange. *nm, adj invar* (*couleur*) orange. **oranger** *nm* orange tree.
orateur, -trice [ɔratœr, -tris] *nm, nf* orator, speaker.
orbite [ɔrbit] *nf* orbit. **orbiter** *v* orbit.
orchestre [ɔrkɛstrə] *nm* orchestra; (*danse, jazz*) band; (*théâtre*) stalls *pl*. **orchestral** *adj* orchestral. **orchestration** *nf* orchestration. **orchestrer** *v* orchestrate.
orchidée [ɔrkide] *nf* orchid.
ordinaire [ɔrdinɛr] *adj* ordinary; common; (*habituel*) usual. *nm* ordinary.
ordinal [ɔrdinal] *adj* ordinal.
ordinateur [ɔrdinatœr] *nm* computer.
ordonner [ɔrdɔne] *v* order; arrange, organize; (*méd*) prescribe; (*rel*) ordain. **ordonnance** *nf* order; prescription; organization. **ordonné** *adj* orderly, tidy.
ordre [ɔrdrə] *nm* order. **de premier/deuxième ordre** first-/second-rate. **en ordre** tidy. **ordre du jour** agenda.
ordure [ɔrdyr] *nf* dirt, filth. **ordures** *nf pl* rubbish *sing*, refuse *sing*; obscenities *pl*.
oreille [ɔrɛj] *nf* ear; (*ouïe*) hearing. **oreiller** *nm* pillow. **oreillons** *nm pl* mumps *sing*.
ores [ɔr] *adv* **d'ores et déjà** already, here and now.
orfèvre [ɔrfɛvrə] *nm* (*argent*) silversmith; (*or*) goldsmith.
organe [ɔrgan] *nm* organ; instrument; (*porte-parole*) spokesman, mouthpiece.
organique [ɔrganik] *adj* organic.
organiser [ɔrganize] *v* organize. **organisateur, -trice** *nm, nf* organizer. **organisation** *nf* organization. **organisme** *nm* organism; (*institution*) body.
organiste [ɔrganist] *n(m+f)* organist.
orgasme [ɔrgasmə] *nm* orgasm.
orge [ɔrʒ] *nf* barley.
orgie [ɔrʒi] *nf* orgy; (*excès*) profusion.
orgue [ɔrg] *nm* organ.
orgueil [ɔrgœj] *nm* pride, arrogance. **orgueilleux** *adj* proud, arrogant.
orient [ɔrjɑ̃] *nm* east. **oriental** *adj* eastern, oriental.
orienter [ɔrjɑ̃te] *v* orientate; direct; (*disposer*) position, adjust. **orienter vers** turn towards. **s'orienter** find one's bearings. **orientation** *nf* orientation; direction; positioning; (*maison, jardin*) aspect. **orientation professionnelle** careers guidance.
origan [ɔrigɑ̃] *nm* oregano.
origine [ɔriʒin] *nf* origin. **à l'origine** originally. **originaire** *adj* original; native. **original** *nm, adj* original; (*péj*) eccentric. **originalité** *nf* originality; eccentricity. **originel** *adj* original.
orme [ɔrm] *nm* elm.
ornement [ɔrnəmɑ̃] *nm* ornament. **orne-**

mental *adj* ornamental. **ornementation** *nf* ornamentation.
orner [ɔrne] *v* decorate; embellish. **orné** *adj* ornate.
ornière [ɔrnjɛr] *nf* rut.
ornithologie [ɔrnitɔlɔʒi] *nf* ornithology. **ornithologique** *adj* ornithological. **ornithologiste** *n(m+f)* ornithologist.
orphelin [ɔrfəlɛ̃], **-e** *n, adj* orphan. **orphelinat** *nm* orphanage.
orteil [ɔrtɛj] *nm* toe.
orthodoxe [ɔrtɔdɔks] *adj* orthodox.
orthographe [ɔrtɔgraf] *nf* spelling. **orthographier** *v* spell.
orthopédique [ɔrtɔpedik] *adj* orthopaedic.
orthophonie [ɔrtɔfɔni] *nf* (*méd*) speech therapy. **orthophoniste** *n(m+f)* speech therapist.
ortie [ɔrti] *nf* nettle.
os [ɔs] *nm* bone. **os à moelle** marrowbone. **trempé jusqu'aux os** soaked to the skin.
osciller [ɔsile] *v* oscillate; (*se balancer*) rock, swing; (*hésiter*) waver; (*prix, etc.*) fluctuate. **oscillation** *nf* oscillation; fluctuation.
oser [oze] *v* dare. **osé** *adj* bold, daring.
osier [ozje] *nm* wicker. **en osier** wickerwork.
ossature [ɔsatyr] *nf* (*corps*) frame; framework; (*visage*) bone structure.
osseux [ɔsø] *adj* bony.
ostentation [ɔstɑ̃tɑsjɔ̃] *nf* ostentation.
ostraciser [ɔstrasize] *v* ostracize. **ostracisme** *nm* ostracism.
otage [ɔtaʒ] *nm* hostage.
otarie [ɔtari] *nf* sea-lion.
ôter [ote] *v* take away *or* off, remove.
ou [u] *conj* or. **ou bien** or else. **ou ... ou ...** either ... or ... .
où [u] *adv* where; (*temps*) when.
ouate [wat] *nf* cotton wool; (*rembourrage*) wadding. **ouater** *v* quilt.
oublier [ublije] *v* forget. **oubli** *nm* oblivion; lapse of memory; omission, oversight.
ouest [wɛst] *nm* west. *adj invar* west; (*région*) western; (*direction*) westward.
oui [wi] *adv, nm invar* yes.
***ouïr** [wir] *v* hear. **ouï-dire** *nm invar* hearsay. **ouïe** *nf* hearing.
ouragan [uragɑ̃] *nm* hurricane.
ourdir [urdir] *v* (*complot*) hatch.
ourler [urle] *v* hem. **ourlet** *nm* hem.
ours [urs] *nm* bear. **ours blanc** polar bear.
outil [uti] *nm* tool, implement. **outillage** *nm* set of tools; equipment. **outiller** *v* provide with tools; equip.
outrager [utraʒe] *v* outrage; insult. **outrage** *nm* insult. **outrage à la pudeur** indecent behaviour. **outrage à magistrat** contempt of court.
outrance [utrɑ̃s] *nf* excess.
outre [utrə] *prep* as well as. **en outre** moreover, besides. **outre-mer** *adv* overseas.
outrer [utre] *v* outrage; exaggerate. **outré** *adj* excessive, overdone; outraged.
ouvert [uvɛr] *adj* open. **ouvertement** *adv* openly, overtly. **ouverture** *nf* opening; (*musique, avance*) overture.
ouvrable [uvrablə] *adj* **jour ouvrable** weekday.
ouvrage [uvraʒ] *nm* work, piece of work.
ouvreuse [uvrøz] *nf* usherette.
ouvrier [uvrije], **-ère** *adj* labour, industrial; working-class. *nm, nf* worker.
***ouvrir** [uvrir] *v* open; (*gaz, robinet, etc.*) turn on. **ouvre-boîte** *nm invar* tin-opener. **ouvre-bouteille** *nm invar* bottle-opener.
ovaire [ɔvɛr] *nm* ovary.
ovale [ɔval] *nm, adj* oval.
ovation [ɔvɑsjɔ̃] *nf* ovation.
ovulation [ɔvylɑsjɔ̃] *nf* ovulation.
oxygène [ɔksiʒɛn] *nm* oxygen.

P

pacage [pakaʒ] *nm* pasture.
pacifier [pasifje] *v* pacify. **pacifique** *adj* peaceful, peaceable. **pacifisme** *nm* pacifism. **pacifiste** *n(m+f), adj* pacifist.
Pacifique [pasifik] *nm, adj* Pacific.
pacte [paktə] *nm* pact, treaty.
pagaie [pagɛ] *nf* paddle. **pagayer** *v* paddle.
pagaïe [pagaj] *nf* mess; (*cohue*) chaos.
page[1] [paʒ] *nf* (*livre*) page. **à la page** up-to-date.
page[2] [paʒ] *nm* (*garçon*) page.
pagode [pagɔd] *nf* pagoda.
paie [pɛ] *nf* pay. **paiement** *nm* payment.
païen [pajɛ̃], **-enne** *n, adj* pagan, heathen.
paillasson [pɑjasɔ̃] *nm* doormat.

paille [paj] *nf* straw; (*défaut*) flaw. **paille de fer** steel wool. **paillette** *nf* speck; (*savon*) flake; (*ornement*) sequin; flaw.
pain [pɛ̃] *nm* bread; (*miche*) loaf; (*savon*) bar. **pain bis/complet** brown/wholemeal bread. **pain de mie** sandwich loaf. **pain d'épice** gingerbread. **pain grillé** toast. **petit pain** roll.
pair[1] [pɛr] *nm* peer. **au pair** *adj* au pair. **pairie** *nf* peerage.
pair[2] [pɛr] *adj* even.
paire [pɛr] *nf* pair.
paisible [pezibla] *adj* peaceful, quiet.
***paître** [pɛtrə] *v* graze.
paix [pɛ] *nf* peace.
palace [palas] *nm* luxury hotel.
palais[1] [palɛ] *nm* palace. **palais de justice** law courts *pl*.
palais[2] [palɛ] *nm* (*anat*) palate.
pâle [pal] *adj* pale; (*faible*) faint, weak. **paleur** *nf* paleness.
palefrenier [palfrənje] *nm* groom.
palette [palɛt] *nf* palette; (*aube*) paddle.
palier [palje] *nm* landing; (*étape*) stage.
pâlir [palir] *v* turn pale; (*couleur, etc.*) fade; (*lumière*) grow dim.
palissade [palisad] *nf* fence.
palmarès [palmarɛs] *nm* prize list.
palme [palmə] *nf* palm leaf; (*nageur*) flipper. **palmé** *adj* (*patte*) webbed. **palmier** *nm* palm tree. **palmipède** *adj* webfooted.
palombe [palɔ̃b] *nf* wood-pigeon.
palourde [palurd] *nf* clam.
palper [palpe] *v* feel, finger.
palpiter [palpite] *v* (*cœur*) beat; (*violemment*) pound, throb; (*frémir*) quiver. **palpitant** *adj* thrilling. **palpitation** *nf* palpitation.
paludisme [palydismə] *nm* malaria.
pâmer [pame] *v* **se pâmer de** be overcome with.
pamphlet [pɑ̃flɛ] *nm* lampoon.
pamplemousse [pɑ̃pləmus] *nm* grapefruit.
pan [pɑ̃] *nm* piece; (*côté*) side. **pan de chemise** shirt-tail.
panache [panaʃ] *nm* plume; gallantry.
panaché [panaʃe] *adj* multicoloured; mixed, motley. *nm* shandy. **panacher** *v* vary; (*mélanger*) blend.
panais [panɛ] *nm* parsnip.
pancarte [pɑ̃kart] *nf* sign; (*manifestation*) placard.
pancréas [pɑ̃kreas] *nm* pancreas. **pancréatique** *adj* pancreatic.
panda [pɑ̃da] *nm* panda.
paner [pane] *v* coat with breadcrumbs.
panier [panje] *nm* basket. **panier à salade** salad shaker; (*fam*) police van, Black Maria. **panier-repas** *nm* packed lunch.
panique [panik] *nf* panic.
panne [pan] *nf* breakdown, failure. **être en panne** break down. **être en panne de** run out of.
panneau [pano] *nm* panel; (*écriteau*) sign. **panneau d'affichage** notice-board. **panneau de signalisation** road sign. **panneau-réclame** *nm* hoarding.
panoplie [panɔpli] *nf* outfit.
panorama [panɔrama] *nm* panorama. **panoramique** *adj* panoramic.
panse [pɑ̃s] *nf* paunch.
panser [pɑ̃se] *v* (*plaie*) dress; bandage; (*cheval*) groom. **pansement** *nm* dressing; bandage; (*sparadrap*) plaster.
pantalon [pɑ̃talɔ̃] *nm* trousers *pl*; pair of trousers.
pantelant [pɑ̃tlɑ̃] *adj* panting; (*cœur*) throbbing.
panthère [pɑ̃tɛr] *nf* panther.
pantomime [pɑ̃tɔmim] *nf* mime.
pantoufle [pɑ̃tuflə] *nf* slipper.
paon [pɑ̃] *nm* peacock.
papa [papa] *nm* (*fam*) dad, daddy.
pape [pap] *nm* pope. **papal** *adj* papal. **papauté** *nf* papacy.
papeterie [papetri] *nf* stationery; (*magasin*) stationer's; (*fabrique*) paper mill. **papetier, -ère** *nm, nf* stationer.
papier [papje] *nm* paper.
papier à lettres *nm* notepaper.
papier à musique *nm* manuscript paper.
papier buvard *nm* blotting paper.
papier calque *nm* tracing paper.
papier d'aluminium *nm* kitchen foil.
papier de soie *nm* tissue paper.
papier de verre *nm* sandpaper.
papier hygiénique *nm* toilet paper.
papier millimétré *nm* graph paper.
papier peint *nm* wallpaper.
papillon [papijɔ̃] *nm* butterfly; (*police*) parking ticket. **papillon de nuit** moth.
paprika [paprika] *nm* paprika.
paquebot [pakbo] *nm* liner.
pâquerette [pakrɛt] *nf* daisy.
Pâques [pak] *nm* Easter.
paquet [pakɛ] *nm* packet, pack; (*colis*) parcel; (*tas*) pile, mass. **mettre en paquet** parcel up.

par [par] *prep* by; through; (*distribution*) per. **par-ci par-là** here and there; (*temps*) now and then. **par-dessous** *prep, adv* under. **par-dessus** *prep, adv* over. **par ici/là** this/that way.
parabole [parabɔl] *nf* (*rel*) parable; (*math*) parabola.
parachute [paraʃyt] *nm* parachute. **parachuter** *v* parachute. **parachutiste** *n(m+f)* parachutist; (*mil*) paratrooper.
parade [parad] *nf* parade; (*ostentation*) show. **faire parade de** show off, brag about.
paradis [paradi] *nm* paradise, heaven.
paradoxe [paradɔks] *nm* paradox. **paradoxal** *adj* paradoxical.
paraffine [parafin] *nf* paraffin (wax).
parages [paraʒ] *nm pl* vicinity *sing*. **dans les parages** round about, in the area.
paragraphe [paragraf] *nm* paragraph.
***paraître** [parɛtrə] *v* appear; (*sembler*) seem; be visible, show; be published.
parallèle [paralɛl] *nm, adj* parallel. *nf* parallel line. **parallélogramme** *nm* parallelogram.
paralyser [paralize] *v* paralyse. **paralysie** *nf* paralysis. **paralytique** *adj* paralytic.
paramilitaire [paramilitɛr] *adj* paramilitary.
paranoïa [paranɔja] *nf* paranoia. **paranoïde** *adj* paranoid.
parapet [parapɛ] *nm* parapet.
paraphraser [parafrɑze] *v* paraphrase. **paraphrase** *nf* paraphrase.
paraplégique [parapleʒik] *n(m+f), adj* paraplegic.
parapluie [paraplɥi] *nm* umbrella.
parasite [parazit] *nm* parasite. **parasites** *nm pl* (*radio*) interference *sing*. *adj* parasitic.
paratonnerre [paratɔnɛr] *nm* lightning conductor.
parc [park] *nm* park; (*château*) grounds *pl*; (*animal*) pen; (*bébé*) play-pen.
parcelle [parsɛl] *nf* fragment, bit. **parcelle de terre** plot of land.
parce que [parskə] *conj* because.
parchemin [parʃəmɛ̃] *nm* parchment. **parcheminé** *adj* wrinkled.
parcomètre [parkɔmɛtrə] *nm* parking meter.
***parcourir** [parkurir] *v* travel through, cover; (*livre*) glance through.
parcours [parkur] *nm* distance; (*trajet*) journey; course; (*itinéraire*) route.
pardessus [pardəsy] *nm* overcoat.
pardon [pardɔ̃] *nm* forgiveness, pardon. **demander pardon** apologize. *interj* (*comment*) pardon; (*désolé*) sorry, excuse me. **pardonner** *v* forgive, pardon; excuse.
pareil, -eille [parɛj] *adj* the same, alike; (*tel*) such. *nm, nf* equal, peer.
parement [parmɑ̃] *nm* facing.
parent [parɑ̃], **-e** *nm, nf* relation. **parents** *nm pl* (*père, mère*) parents *pl*. **parenté** *nf* relationship.
parenthèse [parɑ̃tɛz] *nf* parenthesis; digression; (*signe*) bracket. **entre parenthèses** in brackets; incidentally.
parer[1] [pare] *v* (*orner*) adorn; (*robe*) trim; (*préparer*) dress.
parer[2] [pare] *v* ward off. **pare-balles** *adj invar* bulletproof. **pare-brise** *nm invar* windscreen. **pare-chocs** *nm invar* bumper. **pare-étincelles** *nm invar* fireguard. **parer à** deal with; prepare for.
paresseux [parɛsø] *adj* lazy. **paresse** *nf* laziness.
parfait [parfɛ] *adj* perfect; complete; absolute.
parfois [parfwa] *adv* sometimes; occasionally.
parfum [parfœ̃] *nm* perfume, scent; (*glace*) flavour. **parfumer** *v* perfume; flavour.
pari [pari] *nm* bet. **parier** *v* bet.
Paris [pari] *n* Paris.
parité [parite] *nf* parity.
parjure [parʒyr] *adj* false. *nm* perjury, false witness. *n(m+f)* perjurer. **se parjurer** *v* perjure oneself, bear false witness.
parking [parkiŋ] *nm* car park.
parlement [parləmɑ̃] *nm* parliament. **parlementaire** *adj* parliamentary.
parler [parle] *v* talk, speak. **sans parler de** not to mention. **tu parles!** (*fam*) you're telling me! *nm* speech.
parmi [parmi] *prep* among.
parodie [parɔdi] *nf* parody. **parodier** *v* parodier.
paroi [parwa] *nf* wall; (*cloison*) partition; rock face; (*récipient*) inside surface.
paroisse [parwas] *nf* parish. **paroissial** *adj* parish. **salle paroissiale** *nf* church hall. **paroissien, -enne** *nm, nf* parishioner.
parole [parɔl] *nf* word; (*faculté*) speech; remark. **parolier, -ère** *nm, nf* lyricist.
paroxysme [parɔksismə] *nm* height, climax.

parquer [parke] *v* (*auto*) park; (*enfermer*) pen in; (*entasser*) pack in.
parquet [parkɛ] *nm* floor.
parrain [parɛ̃] *nm* godfather.
parsemer [parsəme] *v* scatter, sprinkle.
part [par] *nf* part; portion, share. **à part** (*de côté*) aside; separately; except for, apart from. **d'autre part** moreover. **de la part de** on behalf of. **faire part de** announce.
partager [partaʒe] *v* share; divide. **partage** *nm* share, portion; (*distribution*) sharing out; division.
partance [partɑ̃s] *nf* **en partance** outbound. **en partance pour** (bound) for.
partenaire [partənɛr] *n*(*m+f*) partner.
parterre [partɛr] *nm* border, flower-bed; (*théâtre*) stalls *pl*.
parti [parti] *nm* party, side; decision; (*mariage*) match. **parti pris** prejudice, bias. **prendre le parti de** stand up for. **prendre parti pour** side with. **tirer parti de** take advantage of, put to good use.
partial [parsjal] *adj* partial, biased. **partialité** *nf* partiality, bias.
participe [partisip] *nm* participle.
participer [partisipe] *v* **participer à** participate in, take part in; (*frais*) contribute to; (*profits, etc.*) share in. **participant, -e** *nm, nf* participant; (*concours*) entrant. **participation** *nf* participation; (*comm*) interest.
particularité [partikylarite] *nf* particularity, characteristic.
particule [partikyl] *nf* particle.
particulier [partikylje] *adj* particular; special, exceptional; (*étrange*) peculiar; private. *nm* person, individual.
partie [parti] *nf* part; (*sport, etc.*) game; (*droit, divertissement*) party. **faire partie de** belong to.
partiel [parsjɛl] *adj* partial.
***partir** [partir] *v* leave, go; (*fusil*) go off; (*commencer*) start. **à partir de** from.
partisan [partizɑ̃], **-e** *nm, nf* supporter, advocate. **être partisan de** be in favour of.
partition [partisjɔ̃] *nf* (*musique*) score.
partout [partu] *adv* everywhere. **partout où** wherever.
parure [paryr] *nf* finery; (*bijoux*) jewels *pl*; (*ensemble*) set; (*ornement*) trimming.
***parvenir** [parvənir] *v* **parvenir à** reach, get to; (*réussir*) manage to, succeed in. **parvenu, -e** *nm, nf* (*péj*) upstart.

pas[1] [pɑ] *nm* step; (*vitesse*) pace; (*trace*) footprint; (*géog*) pass. **à pas de loup** stealthily. **pas de la porte** doorstep.
pas[2] [pɑ] *adv* not. **ne . . . pas** not. **pas du tout** not at all. **pas mal de** (*fam*) quite a lot of.
passage [pɑsaʒ] *nm* passage; change, transition; (*traversée*) crossing. **passage à niveau** level crossing. **passage clouté** pedestrian crossing. **passage interdit** no thoroughfare. **passage souterrain** subway.
passager [pɑsaʒe], **-ère** *adj* passing, brief; (*oiseau*) migratory; (*rue*) busy. *nm, nf* passenger. **passager clandestin** stowaway.
passant [pɑsɑ̃], **-e** *nm, nf* passer-by.
passe [pɑs] *nf* pass. **en passe de** on the way to.
passé [pɑse] *adj* past; (*dernier*) last. *nm* past. *prep* after.
passe-partout *nm invar* skeleton key.
passeport [pɑspɔr] *nm* passport.
passer [pɑse] *v* pass; go past; (*aller*) go; (*franchir*) get through *or* over; (*examen*) sit, take; (*temps*) spend; (*film*) show; (*cuisine*) strain; (*traverser*) cross. **passer par** go through. **passer prendre** pick up, call for. **passer voir** call on. **se passer** happen, take place; (*finir*) be over. **se passer de** do without.
passerelle [pɑsrɛl] *nf* (*pont*) foot-bridge; (*naut*) gangway.
passe-temps *nm invar* pastime.
passif [pasif] *nm, adj* passive. **passivité** *nf* passiveness.
passion [pɑsjɔ̃] *nf* passion.
passionné [pɑsjɔne], **-e** *adj* passionate. *nm, nf* fanatic.
passionner [pɑsjɔne] *v* fascinate. **se passionner pour** be mad keen on.
passoire [pɑswar] *nf* sieve; (*plus grande*) colander.
pastel [pastɛl] *nm, adj invar* pastel.
pastèque [pastɛk] *nf* water-melon.
pasteuriser [pastœrize] *v* pasteurize. **pasteurisation** *nf* pasteurization.
pastille [pastij] *nf* pastille.
pastis [pastis] *nm* (*boisson*) pastis; (*argot*) jam, fix.
pastoral [pastɔral] *adj* pastoral.
pat [pat] *nm* stalemate.
pataud [pato] *adj* clumsy.
patauger [patoʒe] *v* wade, splash; (*se perdre*) flounder.

pâte [pɑt] *nf* paste; cream; (*tarte*) pastry; (*à frire*) batter; (*gâteau*) mixture; (*pain*) dough. **pâte à modeler** plasticine ®. **pâte brisée** shortcrust pastry. **pâte dentifrice** toothpaste. **pâte feuilletée** puff pastry. **pâtes** *nf pl* pasta *sing.*
pâté [pɑte] *nm* (*cuisine*) pâté; (*encre*) blot; (*maisons*) block; (*sable*) sand-castle. **pâté en croûte** pie.
patelin [patlɛ̃] *nm* (*fam*) village.
patelle [patɛl] *nf* limpet.
patent [patɑ̃] *adj* patent, obvious.
patenté [patɑ̃te] *adj* licensed.
patère [patɛr] *nf* peg.
paternel [patɛrnɛl] *adj* paternal; (*bienveillant*) fatherly. **paternité** *nf* paternity.
pâteux [pɑtø] *adj* pasty; (*langue*) furred; (*voix*) husky.
pathétique [patetik] *adj* pathetic. *nm* pathos.
pathologie [patɔlɔʒi] *nf* pathology. **pathologique** *adj* pathological. **pathologiste** *n*(*m*+*f*) pathologist.
patient [pasjɑ̃], **-e** *n, adj* patient. **patience** *nf* patience. **patienter** *v* wait.
patin [patɛ̃] *nm* skate; (*luge*) runner. **patin à glace** ice-skate. **patin à roulettes** roller-skate. **patinage** *nm* skating. **patiner** *v* skate; (*auto*) spin. **patineur, -euse** *nm, nf* skater. **patinoire** *nf* ice rink.
patio [patjo] *nm* patio.
pâtir [pɑtir] *v* suffer.
pâtisserie [pɑtisri] *nf* (*magasin*) cake shop; (*gâteau*) pastry, cake; (*métier*) confectionery. **pâtissier, -ère** *nm, nf* confectioner.
patois [patwa] *nm* patois, dialect.
patrie [patri] *nf* homeland.
patrimoine [patrimwan] *nm* inheritance, heritage.
patriote [patrijɔt] *n*(*m*+*f*) patriot. *adj* patriotic. **patriotique** *adj* patriotic. **patriotisme** *nm* patriotism.
patron, -onne [patrɔ̃, -ɔn] *nm, nf* proprietor; employer; (*fam*) boss; (*protecteur*) patron; (*naut*) skipper. *nm* pattern. **patronage** *nm* patronage. **patronat** *nm* management. **patronner** *v* support, sponsor.
patrouille [patruj] *nf* patrol. **patrouiller** *v* patrol.
patte [pat] *nf* (*jambe*) leg; (*pied*) paw, foot; (*languette*) flap, tongue. **patte de derrière** hind leg. **patte de devant** foreleg. **patte de mouche** scrawl.
pâture [pɑtyr] *nf* pasture; (*nourriture*) food. **pâturage** *nm* pasture.
paume [pom] *nf* palm.
paupière [popjɛr] *nf* eyelid.
pause [poz] *nf* break, pause. **pause-café** *nf* coffee break.
pauvre [povrə] *adj* poor; (*piètre*) weak. *n*(*m*+*f*) poor person. **pauvreté** *nf* poverty; poorness; weakness.
se pavaner [pavane] *v* strut about.
paver [pave] *v* pave; (*chaussée*) cobble. **pavé** *nm* paving stone; (*rond*) cobblestone.
pavillon [pavijɔ̃] *nm* pavilion; lodge; (*villa*) house; (*drapeau*) flag.
pavot [pavo] *nm* poppy.
payer [peje] *v* pay (for). **se payer** (*fam*) treat oneself to. **payable** *adj* payable.
pays [pei] *nm* country, land; region. **du pays** local. **les Pays-Bas** the Netherlands *pl.* **pays de Galles** Wales. **paysage** *nm* landscape; scenery. **paysan, -anne** *nm, nf* peasant.
péage [peaʒ] *nm* toll.
peau [po] *nf* skin; (*cuir*) hide; (*fruit*) peel. **peau de chamois** chamois leather. **peau de mouton** sheepskin. **Peau-Rouge** *n*(*m*+*f*) Red Indian.
pêche[1] [pɛʃ] *nf* (*fruit*) peach. **pêcher** *nm* peach tree.
pêche[2] [pɛʃ] *nf* fishing. **aller à la pêche** go fishing.
pécher [peʃe] *v* sin. **péché** *nm* sin. **pécheur, -eresse** *nm, nf* sinner.
pêcher [peʃe] *v* fish (for); (*attraper*) catch. **pêcheur** *nm* fisherman.
pédagogique [pedagɔʒik] *adj* educational.
pédaler [pedale] *v* pedal. **pédale** *nf* pedal.
pédant [pedɑ̃] *adj* pedantic.
pédéraste [pederast] *nm* homosexual. **pédé** *nm* (*argot*) queer. **pédérastie** *nf* homosexuality.
pédiatre [pedjatrə] *n*(*m*+*f*) paediatrician. **pédiatrie** *nf* paediatrics.
pédicure [pedikyr] *n*(*m*+*f*) chiropodist.
pedigree [pedigri] *nm* pedigree.
peigner [peɲe] *v* comb. **se peigner** comb one's hair. **mal peigné** dishevelled. **peigne** *nm* comb. **peignoir** *nm* dressing-gown.
***peindre** [pɛ̃drə] *v* paint; (*décrire*) depict, portray.
peine [pɛn] *nf* effort, trouble; (*tristesse*) sorrow; difficulty; punishment. **à peine** scarcely, hardly.

peiner [pene] *v* (*s'efforcer*) labour, struggle; (*affliger*) grieve, distress.
peintre [pɛ̃trə] *n(m+f)* painter. **peinture** *nf* painting; (*surface*) paintwork; (*matière*) paint.
péjoratif [peʒɔratif] *adj* derogatory.
Pékin [pekɛ̃] *n* Peking.
pelage [pəlaʒ] *nm* coat, fur.
pêle-mêle [pɛlmɛl] *adv* pell-mell, any old how. *nm invar* jumble.
peler [pəle] *v* peel.
pèlerin [pɛlrɛ̃] *nm* pilgrim. **pèlerinage** *nm* pilgrimage. **pèlerine** *nf* cape.
pélican [pelikɑ̃] *nm* pelican.
pelle [pɛl] *nf* shovel; (*d'enfant*) spade. **pelle à ordures** dustpan. **pelleter** *v* shovel (up).
pelletier [pɛltje], **-ère** *nm, nf* furrier.
pellicule [pelikyl] *nf* film. **pellicules** *nf pl* dandruff *sing*.
pelote [pəlɔt] *nf* ball; (*à épingles*) pincushion.
se peloter [pəlɔte] *v* (*fam*) pet, neck.
peloton [pəlɔtɔ̃] *nm* small ball; group, squad.
pelotonner [pəlɔtɔne] *v* (*laine*) wind into a ball. **se pelotonner** curl up, snuggle up.
pelouse [pəluz] *nf* lawn.
peluche [pəlyʃ] *nf* plush, fur fabric; (*poil, flocon*) bit of fluff. **en peluche** fluffy. **pelucheux** *adj* fluffy.
pelure [pəlyr] *nf* peel, peeling.
pénal [penal] *adj* penal. **pénaliser** *v* penalize. **pénalité** *nf* penalty.
penaud [pəno] *adj* sheepish, contrite.
pencher [pɑ̃ʃe] *v* tilt, lean (over), slant. **se pencher** lean (over); (*se baisser*) bend (down). **penchant** *nm* tendency; (*goût*) liking. **penché** *adj* sloping.
pendant[1] [pɑ̃dɑ̃] *adj* hanging, drooping; (*affaire*) pending. *nm* counterpart, match.
pendant[2] [pɑ̃dɑ̃] *prep* during, for. **pendant que** *conj* while.
pendentif [pɑ̃dɑ̃tif] *nm* pendant.
pendiller [pɑ̃dije] *v* flap about.
pendre [pɑ̃drə] *v* hang; (*s'affaisser*) sag; (*bras, jambes*) dangle. **pendaison** *nf* hanging.
pendule [pɑ̃dyl] *nf* clock. *nm* pendulum.
pêne [pɛn] *nm* bolt.
pénétrer [penetre] *v* penetrate. **pénétrer dans** enter. **pénétrable** *adj* penetrable. **pénétrant** *adj* piercing, penetrating; (*pluie*) drenching; (*esprit, personne*) shrewd. **pénétration** *nf* penetration.
pénible [penibl] *adj* hard, difficult; (*fatigant*) tiresome; (*douloureux*) painful.
péniche [peniʃ] *nf* barge.
pénicilline [penisilin] *nf* penicillin.
péninsule [penɛ̃syl] *nf* peninsula. **péninsulaire** *adj* peninsular.
pénis [penis] *nm* penis.
pénitent [penitɑ̃], **-e** *n, adj* penitent. **pénitence** *nf* penitence; (*peine*) penance; punishment.
penser [pɑ̃se] *v* think. **penser à** think of *or* about; (*réfléchir*) think over. **penser de** think of. **penser faire** be thinking of doing, expect to do. **pensée** *nf* thought; (*bot*) pansy. **pensif** *adj* pensive.
pension [pɑ̃sjɔ̃] *nf* (*allocation*) pension; (*hôtel*) guest house; (*école*) boarding school; (*hébergement*) board and lodging. **pension complète** full board. **pension de famille** boarding house. **pensionnaire** *n(m+f)* (*école*) boarder; (*maison*) lodger; (*hôtel*) resident. **pensionnat** *nm* boarding school.
pentagone [pɛ̃tagɔn] *nm* pentagon. **pentagonal** *adj* pentagonal.
pente [pɑ̃t] *nf* slope. **en pente** sloping, on a slope.
Pentecôte [pɑ̃tkot] *nf* Whitsun. **lundi de Pentecôte** *nm* Whit Monday.
pénurie [penyri] *nf* shortage.
pépé [pepe] *nm* (*fam*) grandad, grandpa.
pépier [pepje] *v* chirp, tweet. **pépiement** *nm* chirping.
pépin [pepɛ̃] *nm* pip; (*fam*) snag, hitch. **pépinière** *nf* nursery.
pépite [pepit] *nf* nugget.
percepteur, -trice [pɛrsɛptœr, -tris] *adj* perceptive. *nm* tax collector.
perception [pɛrsɛpsjɔ̃] *nf* perception; (*impôt, etc.*) collection; (*bureau*) tax office. **perceptible** *adj* perceptible; payable. **perceptif** *adj* perceptive.
percer [pɛrse] *v* pierce; (*avec perceuse*) drill, bore; penetrate; (*abcès*) burst; (*mil, soleil*) break through. **perce-neige** *nm invar* snowdrop. **perce-oreille** *nm* earwig. **percer des dents** cut one's teeth, be teething. **percée** *nf* opening, gap. **perceuse** *nf* drill.
***percevoir** [pɛrsəvwar] *v* perceive; (*impôt*) collect.
perche[1] [pɛrʃ] *nf* (*poisson*) perch.

perche[2] [pɛrʃ] *nf* pole.
percher [pɛrʃe] *v* perch. **perchoir** *nm* perch.
perclus [pɛrkly] *adj* paralysed.
percussion [pɛrkysjɔ̃] *nf* percussion.
perdre [pɛrdrə] *v* lose; (*gaspiller*) waste; (*manquer*) miss; (*réservoir, etc.*) leak; ruin. **se perdre** get lost; disappear; go to waste. **perdant, -e** *nm, nf* loser. **perdu** *adj* lost, wasted; missed; ruined; isolated.
perdrix [pɛrdri] *nf* partridge.
père [pɛr] *nm* father. **le père Noël** Father Christmas.
perfection [pɛrfɛksjɔ̃] *nf* perfection. **perfectionner** *v* improve, perfect. **perfectionniste** *n(m+f)* perfectionist.
perfide [pɛrfid] *adj* treacherous, false. **perfidie** *nf* perfidy.
perforer [pɛrfɔre] *v* perforate; (*poinçonner*) punch. **perforation** *nf* perforation.
péril [peril] *nm* peril. **périlleux** *adj* perilous.
périmé [perime] *adj* out-of-date.
périmètre [perimɛtrə] *nm* perimeter; (*zone*) area.
période [perjɔd] *nf* period.
périodique [perjɔdik] *adj* periodic, periodical; (*math, méd*) recurring. *nm* periodical.
péripétie [peripesi] *nf* event, episode.
périphérique [periferik] *adj* peripheral. *nm* ring road. **périphérie** *nf* periphery; (*ville*) outskirts *pl*.
périr [perir] *v* perish, die. **périssable** *adj* perishable.
périscope [periskɔp] *nm* periscope.
périssoire [periswar] *nf* canoe.
perle [pɛrl] *nf* pearl; (*grain*) bead; (*goutte*) drop; (*erreur*) howler.
permanence [pɛrmanɑ̃s] *nf* permanence; (*bureau*) office. **en permanence** permanently; continuously. **être de permanence** be on duty. **permanent** *adj* permanent; continuous. **permanente** *nf* perm.
perméable [pɛrmeablə] *adj* permeable, pervious.
***permettre** [pɛrmɛtrə] *v* allow, permit; (*rendre possible*) enable.
permis [pɛrmi] *adj* permitted. *nm* permit, licence. **permis de conduire** driving licence. **permis de construire** planning permission. **permis de séjour/travail** residence/work permit.
permission [pɛrmisjɔ̃] *nf* permission; (*mil*) leave.
permutation [pɛrmytɑsjɔ̃] *nf* permutation.
pernicieux [pɛrnisjø] *adj* pernicious; (*nuisible*) harmful.
pérorer [perɔre] *v* hold forth.
peroxyde [pɛrɔksid] *nm* peroxide.
perpendiculaire [pɛrpɑ̃dikylɛr] *nf, adj* perpendicular.
perpétrer [pɛrpetre] *v* perpetrate. **perpétration** *nf* perpetration.
perpétuer [pɛrpetɥe] *v* perpetuate, carry on. **se perpétuer** survive. **perpétuel** *adj* perpetual; constant; permanent. **perpétuité** *nf* perpetuity. **à perpétuité** for ever; (*jur*) for life.
perplexe [pɛrplɛks] *adj* perplexed, puzzled. **perplexité** *nf* perplexity, confusion.
perquisition [pɛrkizisjɔ̃] *nf* search. **perquisitionner** *v* search.
perron [pɛrɔ̃] *nm* steps *pl*.
perroquet [pɛrɔkɛ] *nm* parrot.
perruche [peryʃ] *nf* budgerigar.
perruque [peryk] *nf* wig.
persécuter [pɛrsekyte] *v* persecute; harass. **persécution** *nf* persecution.
persévérer [pɛrsevere] *v* persevere. **persévérance** *nf* perseverance. **persévérant** *adj* persevering.
persienne [pɛrsjɛn] *nf* shutter.
persifler [pɛrsifle] *v* mock. **persiflage** *nm* mockery.
persil [pɛrsi] *nm* parsley.
persister [pɛrsiste] *v* persist. **persister à** persist in. **persistance** *nf* persistence. **persistant** *adj* persistent. **à feuilles persistantes** (*arbre, plante*) evergreen.
personne [pɛrsɔn] *nf* person. *pron* anyone. **ne ... personne** nobody. **personnage** *nm* character; individual; celebrity, important person. **personnalité** *nf* personality.
personnel [pɛrsɔnɛl] *adj* personal. *nm* staff, personnel.
personnifier [pɛrsɔnifje] *v* personify. **personnification** *nf* personification, embodiment.
perspective [pɛrspɛktiv] *nf* perspective; view, angle; (*éventualité*) prospect.
perspicace [pɛrspikas] *adj* shrewd. **perspicacité** *nf* shrewdness, insight.
persuader [pɛrsɥade] *v* persuade; convince. **persuasif** *adj* persuasive. **persuasion** *nf* persuasion; (*croyance*) belief.

perte [pɛrt] *nf* loss; ruin; (*gaspillage*) waste. **à perte de vue** as far as the eye can see.
pertinent [pɛrtinɑ̃] *adj* pertinent, relevant; (*juste*) apt. **pertinence** *nf* pertinence, relevance; aptness.
perturbateur, -trice [pɛrtyrbatœr, -tris] *adj* disruptive. *nm, nf* troublemaker.
perturber [pɛrtyrbe] *v* disturb, disrupt; (*personne*) perturb. **perturbation** *nf* disturbance, disruption.
pervers [pɛrvɛr] *adj* perverse; depraved, perverted. **perversion** *nf* perversion. **perversité** *nf* perversity; depravity.
pervertir [pɛrvɛrtir] *v* pervert, corrupt. **perverti, -e** *nm, nf* pervert.
peser [pəze] *v* weigh; (*appuyer*) press. **pesant** *adj* heavy. **pesanteur** *nf* heaviness; (*phys*) gravity; (*poids*) weight.
pessimiste [pesimist] *adj* pessimistic. *n(m+f)* pessimist. **pessimisme** *nm* pessimism.
peste [pɛst] *nf* plague; (*personne*) nuisance, pest.
pet [pɛ] *nm* (*vulgaire*) fart.
pétale [petal] *nm* petal.
pétarader [petarade] *v* backfire.
pétard [petar] *nm* banger, firecracker; (*mil*) explosive charge; (*fam: tapage*) row, din.
péter [pete] *v* (*vulgaire*) fart; (*fam: casser*) bust; (*fam: exploser*) burst, go off.
pétiller [petije] *v* sparkle; (*champagne*) bubble; (*feu*) crackle. **pétillant** *adj* sparkling; bubbly.
petit [pəti], **-e** *adj* small, little; (*mince*) slim, thin; (*jeune*) young; (*court*) short; (*faible*) faint, slight; (*mesquin*) petty. **petit ami** *nm* boyfriend. **petit déjeuner** *nm* breakfast. **petite amie** *nf* girlfriend. **petite-fille** *nf* granddaughter. **petit-enfant** *nm* grandchild. **petit-fils** *nm* grandson. **petit gâteau** *nm* biscuit. **petit-pois** *nm* pea. *adv* **petit à petit** little by little. *nm, nf* young child; small person; (*animal*) young. **petitesse** *nf* smallness; pettiness.
pétrin [petrɛ̃] *nm* mess, fix.
pétrir [petrir] *v* knead; mould.
pétrole [petrɔl] *nm* oil, petroleum. **pétrole lampant** paraffin. **pétrolifère** *adj* oil-bearing. **gisement pétrolifère** *nm* oilfield.
pétrolier [petrɔlje] *adj* oil. *nm* tanker.
pétulant [petylɑ̃] *adj* vivacious. **pétulance** *nf* vivacity.
peu [pø] *nm* little. *adv* little; (*quantité*) not much; (*nombre*) few; (*pas très*) not very. **à peu près** about; (*presque*) almost. **peu à peu** little by little.
peupler [pœple] *v* populate, fill. **peuple** *nm* people; nation; (*foule*) crowd.
peuplier [pøplije] *nm* poplar.
peur [pœr] *nf* fear; fright. **avoir peur** be frightened *or* afraid. **faire peur à** frighten, scare. **peureux** *adj* fearful, timorous.
peut-être [pøtɛtrə] *adv* perhaps, maybe.
phallus [falys] *nm* phallus. **phallique** *adj* phallic. **phallocrate** *nm* (*fam*) male chauvinist pig.
phare [far] *nm* lighthouse; (*balise*) beacon; (*auto*) headlight. **phare antibrouillard** fog lamp.
pharmacie [farmasi] *nf* pharmacy; (*magasin*) chemist's; (*armoire*) medicine chest. **pharmaceutique** *adj* pharmaceutical. **pharmacien, -enne** *nm, nf* chemist, pharmacist.
pharynx [farɛ̃ks] *nm* pharynx. **pharyngite** *nf* pharyngitis.
phase [fɑz] *nf* phase; stage.
phénix [feniks] *nm* phoenix.
phénomène [fenɔmɛn] *nm* phenomenon (*pl* -ena); (*personne*) freak. **phénoménal** *adj* phenomenal.
philanthropie [filɑ̃trɔpi] *nf* philanthropy. **philanthrope** *n(m+f)* philanthropist. **philanthropique** *adj* philanthropic.
philatélie [filateli] *nf* philately. **philatéliste** *n(m+f)* philatelist.
philosophe [filɔzɔf] *adj* philosophical. *n(m+f)* philosopher. **philosophie** *nf* philosophy. **philosophique** *adj* philosophical.
phobie [fɔbi] *nf* phobia.
phonétique [fɔnetik] *adj* phonetic. *nf* phonetics.
phonographe [fɔnɔgraf] *nm* gramophone.
phoque [fɔk] *nm* seal.
phosphate [fɔsfat] *nm* phosphate.
phosphore [fɔsfɔr] *nm* phosphorus. **phosphoreux** *adj* phosphorous.
phosphorescence [fɔsfɔresɑ̃s] *nf* phosphorescence. **phosphorescent** *adj* phosphorescent, luminous.
photo [fɔto] *nf* photo.
photocopier [fɔtɔkɔpje] *v* photocopy. **photocopie** *nf* photocopy. **photocopieur** *nm* photocopier.
photogénique [fɔtɔʒenik] *adj* photogenic.
photographie [fɔtɔgrafi] *nf* (*image*) photograph; (*art*) photography. **photographe** *n(m+f)* photographer. **photographier** *v*

photograph, take a picture of. **photographique** *adj* photographic.
phrase [frɑz] *nf* phrase; (*gramm*) sentence.
physiologie [fizjɔlɔʒi] *nf* physiology. **physiologique** *adj* physiological. **physiologiste** *n*(*m*+*f*) physiologist.
physique[1] [fizik] *adj* physical. *nm* physique.
physique[2] [fizik] *nf* physics. **physicien, -enne** *nm, nf* physicist.
piaffer [pjafe] *v* stamp, paw the ground.
piailler [pjɑje] *v* (*fam*) squawk, screech.
piano [pjano] *nm* piano. **piano à queue** grand piano. **pianiste** *n*(*m*+*f*) pianist.
piauler [pjole] *v* whine; (*enfant*) whimper; (*oiseau*) cheep.
pic[1] [pik] *nm* (*oiseau*) woodpecker; (*instrument*) pick.
pic[2] [pik] *nm* (*cime*) peak. **à pic** sheer; (*arriver, tomber*) just at the right time.
piccolo [pikɔlo] *nm* piccolo.
picorer [pikɔre] *v* peck (at).
picoter [pikɔte] *v* (*yeux*) smart, sting; (*gorge*) tickle; (*peau*) prickle; (*picorer*) peck.
pie [pi] *nf* magpie.
pièce [pjɛs] *nf* piece; (*machine*) part; document; (*maison*) room; (*théâtre*) play; (*monnaie*) coin; (*couture*) patch. **à la pièce** separately. **pièce détachée** spare part.
pied [pje] foot; (*table*) leg; base; (*verre*) stem. **à pied** on foot. **au pied de la lettre** literally. **en pied** full-length. **être sur pied** be under way. **mettre les pieds dans le plat** put one's foot in it. **mettre sur pied** set up. **perdre pied** get out of one's depth. **pied bot** *adj* club-footed.
piédestal [pjedɛstal] *nm* pedestal.
piège [pjɛʒ] *nm* trap. **piéger** *v* trap; (*engin, etc.*) booby-trap. **lettre/voiture piégée** *nf* letter/car bomb.
pierre [pjɛr] *nf* stone. **pierre à briquet** flint. **pierre à chaux** limestone. **pierre d'achoppement** stumbling block. **pierre de gué** stepping stone. **pierre ponce** pumice stone. **pierre tombale** tombstone. **pierreux** *adj* stony.
piété [pjete] *nf* piety; devotion.
piétiner [pjetine] *v* (*fouler*) trample (on); (*trépigner*) stamp; make no progress.
piéton [pjetɔ̃] *nm* pedestrian.
piètre [pjɛtrə] *adj* paltry, very poor.
pieu [pjø] *nm* post; (*pointu*) stake.
pieuvre [pjœvrə] *nf* octopus.
pieux [pjø] *adj* pious, devout.
pigeon [piʒɔ̃] *nm* pigeon.
piger [piʒe] (*argot*) *v* cotton on, twig. **tu piges?** do you get it?
pigment [pigmɑ̃] *nm* pigment. **pigmentation** *nf* pigmentation.
pignon [piɲɔ̃] *nm* (*arch*) gable; (*tech*) pinion.
pile[1] [pil] *nf* (*tas*) pile; support; (*élec*) battery.
pile[2] [pil] *nf* (*pièce*) tails *pl*. **côté pile** *nm* reverse side. **pile ou face?** heads or tails? **tirer à pile ou face** toss up. *adv* (*fam*) dead, exactly.
piler [pile] *v* crush, pound.
pilier [pilje] *nm* pillar.
piller [pije] *v* pillage, plunder. **pillage** *nm* pillage, looting.
pilote [pilɔt] *nm* pilot; (*auto*) driver; guide. *adj* experimental. **piloter** *v* pilot; (*avion*) fly; drive; (*personne*) show round.
pilule [pilyl] *nf* pill.
piment [pimɑ̃] *nm* pimento; piquancy, spice. **piment doux** capsicum. **piment rouge** chilli. **pimenté** *adj* (*plat*) hot; (*récit*) spicy.
pimpant [pɛ̃pɑ̃] *adj* trim, smart.
pin [pɛ̃] *nm* pine.
pinacle [pinaklə] *nm* pinnacle.
pince [pɛ̃s] *nf* pliers *pl*; (*charbon, sucre*) tongs *pl*; (*levier*) crowbar; (*couture*) dart; (*crabe*) pincer, claw. **pince à épiler** eyebrow tweezers *pl*. **pince à linge** clothes peg. **pincé** *adj* stiff; (*sourire*) tight-lipped. **pincée** *nf* pinch. **pincer** *v* pinch, nip; (*serrer*) grip; (*musique*) pluck; (*fam*) catch.
pinceau [pɛ̃so] *nm* paintbrush.
pingouin [pɛ̃gwɛ̃] *nm* penguin.
ping-pong [piŋpɔ̃g] *nm* table tennis.
pinson [pɛ̃sɔ̃] *nm* chaffinch.
piocher [pjɔʃe] *v* dig with a pick; (*fam*) swot; (*cartes, etc.*) pick up. **pioche** *nf* pick, pickaxe.
pion [pjɔ̃] *nm* (*jeu*) piece; (*échecs*) pawn; student supervising schoolchildren.
pionnier [pjɔnje] *nm* pioneer.
pipe [pip] *nf* pipe.
piquant [pikɑ̃] *adj* (*tige*) prickly; (*goût*) hot, pungent; (*vin*) tart; (*mordant*) biting; (*sauce, détail*) piquant. *nm* prickle; (*hérisson*) spine; piquancy.
pique[1] [pik] *nf* (*arme*) pike. *nm* (*cartes*) spade.

pique[2] [pik] *nf* cutting remark.
pique-nique [piknik] *nm* picnic. **pique-niquer** *v* picnic. **pique-niqueur, -euse** *nm, nf* picnicker.
piquer [pike] *v* prick; sting; (*insecte, serpent*) bite; (*aiguille, etc.*) jab, stick; excite, arouse; (*fam: voler*) pinch; (*moutarde, etc.*) be hot *or* pungent; (*avion, oiseau*) swoop down. **piquer une colère** fly into a rage. **piquer une crise** throw a fit. **se faire piquer** have an injection. **se piquer** get stung; give oneself an injection; take offence. **piqué** *adj* (*couture*) quilted; (*marqué*) dotted, pitted; (*fam*) barmy. **piqûre** *nf* prick; sting; bite; injection; (*couture*) stitch; (*trou*) hole.
piquet [pikɛ] *nm* post, stake; (*tente*) peg; (*de grève*) picket.
pirate [pirat] *nm, adj* pirate. **pirate de l'air** hijacker. **piraterie** nf piracy.
pire [pir] *adj* worse. **le** *or* **la pire** (the) worst.
pirouette [pirwɛt] *nf* pirouette. **pirouetter** *v* pirouette.
pis[1] [pi] *nm* udder.
pis[2] [pi] *adj, adv* worse. **de pis en pis** worse and worse. *nm* worst. **au pis aller** if the worst comes to the worst. **pis-aller** *nm invar* makeshift.
piscine [pisin] *nf* swimming pool; (*publique*) baths *pl*.
pissenlit [pisɑ̃li] *nm* dandelion.
pisser [pise] (*vulgaire*) *v* piss. **pisse** *nf* piss.
pistache [pistaʃ] *nf* pistachio.
piste [pist] *nf* track; (*traces*) trail; (*aéro*) runway; (*ski*) run; (*police*) lead. **piste cavalière** bridle-path. **piste sonore** soundtrack.
pistolet [pistɔlɛ] *nm* pistol, gun.
piston [pistɔ̃] *nm* piston; (*musique*) valve. **avoir du piston** (*fam*) have friends in the right places.
pitié [pitje] *nf* pity. **avoir pitié de** take pity on; (*compâtir*) feel sorry for. **piteux** *adj* pitiful, sorry; (*honteux*) shamefaced. **pitoyable** *adj* pitiful.
pitre [pitrə] *nm* clown.
pittoresque [pitɔrɛsk] *adj* picturesque.
pivot [pivo] *nm* pivot. **pivoter** *v* pivot, revolve, swivel round.
placage [plakaʒ] *nm* (*bois*) veneer; (*pierre*) facing.
placard [plakar] *nm* (*armoire*) cupboard; (*affiche*) notice, placard. **placarder** *v* (*affiche*) stick up; (*mur*) placard.
place [plas] *nf* place; space; (*siège*) seat; (*prix*) fare; (*ville*) square; (*emploi*) job. **à la place de** instead of; (*personne*) on behalf of. **à ta** *or* **votre place** if I were you. **faire place à** give way to. **sur place** on the spot.
placenta [plasɛ̃ta] *nm* placenta.
placer [plase] *v* place, put; (*argent*) invest; (*vendre*) sell. **se placer** (*debout*) stand; (*assis*) sit; (*avoir lieu*) take place; find a job. **placement** *nm* investment. **placeur** *nm* usher.
placide [plasid] *adj* placid. **placidité** *nf* placidity.
plafond [plafɔ̃] *nm* ceiling.
plage [plaʒ] *nf* beach; (*ville*) seaside resort; (*disque*) track.
plagier [plaʒje] *v* plagiarize. **plagiaire** *n*(*m*+*f*) plagiarist. **plagiat** *nm* plagiarism.
plaider [plede] *v* plead.
plaie [plɛ] *nf* wound; (*fam*) nuisance.
***plaindre** [plɛ̃drə] *v* pity, feel sorry for. **se plaindre** moan, complain, grumble.
plaine [plɛn] *nf* plain.
plain-pied [plɛ̃pje] *adv* **de plain-pied avec** on the same level as.
plainte [plɛ̃t] *nf* complaint; (*gémissement*) moan. **plaintif** *adj* plaintive.
***plaire** [plɛr] *v* **plaire à** please; (*convenir à*) suit. **se plaire** be happy, enjoy oneself. **se plaire à** like, delight in. **s'il te** *or* **vous plaît** please.
plaisance [plɛzɑ̃s] *nf* **maison de plaisance** *nf* country house. **navigation de plaisance** *nf* boating; yachting.
plaisant [plɛzɑ̃] *adj* pleasant; amusing.
plaisanter [plɛzɑ̃te] *v* joke; (*taquiner*) tease. **plaisanterie** *nf* joke.
plaisir [plezir] *nm* pleasure. **faire plaisir à** please, make happy.
plan[1] [plɑ̃] *adj* flat, level, plane. *nm* plane, level; (*cinéma*) shot. **premier plan** foreground.
plan[2] [plɑ̃] *nm* plan; (*carte*) map.
planche [plɑ̃ʃ] *nf* board, plank; (*rayon*) shelf. **faire la planche** float on one's back. **planche à dessin/repasser** drawing/ironing board. **planche à pain** breadboard.
plancher [plɑ̃ʃe] *nm* floor.
plancton [plɑ̃ktɔ̃] *nm* plankton.
planer [plane] *v* glide, hover; (*monter*) soar. **planer sur** (*danger*) hang over;

(*regard*) look down over. **planeur** *nm* glider.
planète [planɛt] *nf* planet. **planétaire** *adj* planetary. **planétarium** *nm* planetarium.
plant [plɑ̃] *nm* seedling, young plant; (*arbres*) plantation; (*légumes, fleurs*) bed.
plantation [plɑ̃tɑsjɔ̃] *nf* plantation; (*action*) planting.
plante[1] [plɑ̃t] *nf* (*bot*) plant. **plante grimpante** creeper.
plante[2] [plɑ̃t] *nf* (*anat*) sole of the foot.
planter [plɑ̃te] *v* plant; (*enfoncer*) drive *or* stick in; (*mettre*) put, stick; (*installer*) put *or* set up. **planter là** (*fam*) dump, ditch.
planton [plɑ̃tɔ̃] *nm* orderly.
plantureux [plɑ̃tyrø] *adj* copious, lavish.
plaque [plak] *nf* plate, sheet; (*pierre, chocolat*) slab; (*tache*) patch, blotch; (*commémorative*) plaque; (*insigne*) badge. **plaque chauffante** hotplate. **plaque minéralogique** *or* **d'immatriculation** number plate.
plaquer [plake] *v* (*bois*) veneer; (*métal*) plate; (*fam*) ditch, chuck; (*aplatir*) plaster down, flatten; (*sport*) tackle.
plasma [plasma] *nm* plasma.
plastique [plastik] *nm, adj* plastic.
plat [pla] *adj* flat; (*fade*) dull; (*cheveux*) straight. **à plat** flat. **plate-bande** *nf* flowerbed. **plate-forme** *nf* platform. *nm* flat part; (*cuisine*) dish; (*partie d'un repas*) course.
plateau [plato] *nm* tray; (*géog*) plateau; (*théâtre*) stage. **plateau à** *or* **de fromages** cheeseboard.
platine [platin] *nm* platinum.
platonique [platɔnik] *adj* (*amour*) platonic; vain, futile.
plâtrer [plɑtre] *v* plaster; (*méd*) set in plaster. **plâtre** *nm* plaster; (*méd, art*) plaster cast. **plâtrier** *nm* plasterer.
plausible [plozibIə] *adj* plausible. **plausibilité** *nf* plausibility.
plectre [plɛktrə] *nm* plectrum.
plein [plɛ̃] *adj* full; complete; solid; (*animal*) pregnant. **en plein . . .** at the height of . . . , in the middle of . . . . **en plein jour** in broad daylight. **plein air** *nm* open air. **pleine mer** *nf* open sea; (*marée*) high tide. *adv* full. *nm* **faire le plein** fill up.
pleurer [plœre] *v* cry; (*yeux*) water; lament, bemoan; (*mort*) mourn. **pleureur, -euse** *adj* tearful; (*enfant*) whining.
pleurnicher [plœrniʃe] *v* snivel, whine.
***pleuvoir** [pløvwar] *v* rain.
pli [pli] *nm* fold; (*faux*) crease; (*couture*) pleat; (*genou*) bend; envelope; (*forme*) shape; habit.
plier [plije] *v* fold; (*courber*) bend; (*céder*) yield, give way. **se plier à** submit to. **pliant** *adj* collapsible, folding.
plinthe [plɛ̃t] *nf* skirting board.
plisser [plise] *v* (*jupe, etc.*) pleat; (*rider*) pucker, crease.
plomb [plɔ̃] *nm* lead; (*chasse*) shot; (*élec*) fuse. **à plomb** straight down. **de plomb** leaden; (*sommeil*) heavy. **plombage** *nm* filling. **plomber** *v* weight; (*dent*) fill. **plomberie** *nf* plumbing. **plombier** *nm* plumber.
plonger [plɔ̃ʒe] *v* plunge, dive. **plonge** *nf* washing-up. **plongé dans** *adj* immersed in, buried in. **plongée** *nf* diving. **plongée sous-marine** skin-diving. **plongeoir** *nm* diving board. **plongeon** *nm* dive. **plongeur, -euse** *nm, nf* diver; (*restaurant*) washer-up.
plouf [pluf] *nm, interj* splash.
ployer [plwaje] *v* bend; (*plancher*) sag; (*céder*) give way.
pluie [plɥi] *nf* rain; (*averse*) shower.
plume [plym] *nf* (*oiseau*) feather; (*écrire*) pen; (*bec*) nib. **plumage** *nm* plumage. **plumer** *v* pluck; (*argot*) fleece.
plupart [plypar] *nf* **la plupart** most, the majority. **pour la plupart** mostly.
pluriel [plyrjɛl] *nm, adj* plural.
plus [ply] *adv* more. **de** *or* **en plus** on top, extra, in addition, besides. **de plus en plus** more and more. **le** *or* **la plus** the most. **ne . . . plus** no more; (*temps*) no longer. **plus de** more than, over. **plus-que-parfait** *nm* pluperfect. *conj* plus.
plusieurs [plyzjœr] *adj* several.
plutôt [plyto] *adv* rather.
pluvieux [plyvjø] *adj* rainy, wet.
pneu [pnø] *nm* tyre. **pneu réchapé** remould.
pneumatique [pnømatik] *adj* pneumatic; (*canot, matelas*) inflatable.
pneumonie [pnømɔni] *nf* pneumonia.
pochard [pɔʃar], **-e** *nm, nf* (*argot*) drunk.
poche [pɔʃ] *nf* pocket; (*sac*) bag; (*zool*) pouch. **de poche** pocket; (*livre*) paperback. **pochette** *nf* pocket handkerchief; envelope, case.

pocher [pɔʃe] *v* poach. **pocher un œil à** give a black eye to. **pochade** *nf* quick sketch. **pochoir** *nm* stencil.
poêle[1] [pwɑl] *nf* frying pan.
poêle[2] [pwɑl] *nm* stove.
poème [pɔɛm] *nm* poem. **poésie** *nf* poetry. **poète** *nm* poet. **poétesse** *nf* poetess. **poétique** *adj* poetic.
poids [pwa] *nm* weight. **poids lourd** heavyweight; (*camion*) lorry. **prendre du poids** put on weight.
poignant [pwaɲɑ̃] *adj* poignant, harrowing.
poignard [pwaɲar] *nm* dagger. **poignarder** *v* stab, knife.
poigne [pwaɲ] *nf* grip; (*main*) hand. **poignée** *nf* (*valise, porte, etc.*) handle; (*quantité*) handful. **poignée de main** handshake. **poignet** *nm* wrist; (*vêtement*) cuff.
poil [pwal] *nm* hair; (*brosse*) bristle; (*tapis, tissu*) pile. **à poil** (*fam*) naked. **poilu** *adj* hairy.
poinçon [pwɛ̃sɔ̃] *nm* awl; (*or, etc.*) die, stamp; (*marque*) hallmark. **poinçonner** *v* stamp; hallmark; (*billet*) punch.
***poindre** [pwɛ̃drə] *v* (*jour*) dawn; (*aube*) break; (*plante*) come up.
poing [pwɛ̃] *nm* fist.
point[1] [pwɛ̃] *nm* point; (*marque*) dot; (*tache*) spot; (*ponctuation*) full stop; (*couture, tricot*) stitch. **à point** just right; (*bifteck*) medium. **au point** (*phot*) in focus; perfect. **être sur le point de** be just about to. **mettre au point** perfect; (*phot*) focus; finalize. **point de côté** stitch. **point de mire** focal point. **point de suture** (*méd*) stitch. **point d'exclamation** exclamation mark. **point d'interrogation** question mark. **point du jour** daybreak. **point mort** (*auto*) neutral. **point noir** (*visage*) blackhead; (*auto*) black spot. **point virgule** semicolon.
point[2] [pwɛ̃] *adv* not. **ne ... point** not at all.
pointe [pwɛ̃t] *nf* point; (*bout*) tip; (*maximum*) peak; (*soupçon*) touch, dash. **sur la pointe des pieds** on tiptoe.
pointer[1] [pwɛ̃te] *v* (*cocher*) tick off; (*braquer*) aim, point; (*employé*) clock in *or* out. **pointeur** *nm* timekeeper.
pointer[2] [pwɛ̃te] *v* (*piquer*) stick; appear; (*dresser*) soar up.
pointillé [pwɛ̃tije] *adj* dotted. *nm* dotted line. **pointiller** *v* (*art*) stipple.
pointilleux [pwɛ̃tijø] *adj* particular.
pointu [pwɛ̃ty] *adj* pointed; (*aigu*) sharp; (*péj*) touchy, peevish.
pointure [pwɛ̃tyr] *nf* size.
poire [pwar] *nf* pear; (*fam*) mug. **poirier** *nm* pear tree.
poireau [pwaro] *nm* leek.
pois [pwa] *nm* pea; (*point*) dot, spot. **pois cassés** split peas *pl*. **pois chiche** chickpea. **pois de senteur** sweet pea.
poison [pwazɔ̃] *nm* poison.
poisseux [pwasø] *adj* sticky.
poisson [pwasɔ̃] *nm* fish. **poisson d'avril** April fool. **poisson rouge** goldfish. **Poissons** *nm pl* Pisces *sing*. **poissonnerie** *nm* fish shop. **poissonnier, -ère** *nm, nf* fishmonger.
poitrine [pwatrin] *nf* chest; (*seins*) bust; (*cuisine*) breast.
poivre [pwavrə] *nm* pepper. **poivre de Cayenne** Cayenne pepper. **poivré** *adj* peppery; (*récit*) spicy. **poivrer** *v* pepper. **poivrier** *nm* pepper-pot. **poivron** *nm* pepper.
poix [pwa] *nf* pitch.
polaire [pɔlɛr] *adj* polar.
polariser [pɔlarize] *v* polarize; attract; (*concentrer*) focus. **se polariser sur** be centred on.
pôle [pol] *nm* pole.
polémique [pɔlemik] *adj* controversial. *nf* controversy, argument.
poli[1] [pɔli] *adj* polite.
poli[2] [pɔli] *adj* polished. *nm* shine.
police[1] [pɔlis] *nf* police. **faire la police** keep order.
police[2] [pɔlis] *nf* (*assurance*) policy.
policier [pɔlisje] *nm* policeman; (*roman*) detective novel. *adj* police; detective.
polio [pɔljo] *nf* polio.
polir [pɔlir] *v* polish.
polisson, -onne [pɔlisɔ̃, -ɔn] *nm, nf* rascal. *adj* (*enfant*) naughty; (*grivois*) saucy. **polissonnerie** *nf* naughty trick; saucy remark *or* action.
politesse [pɔlitɛs] *nf* politeness, courtesy; polite remark *or* gesture.
politique [pɔlitik] *adj* political. *nf* (*science*) politics; (*ligne de conduite*) policy. **politicien, -enne** *nm, nf* politician.
polka [pɔlka] *nf* polka.
pollen [pɔlɛn] *nm* pollen. **pollinisation** *nf* pollination.

polluer [pɔlɥe] *v* pollute. **pollution** *nf* pollution.
Pologne [pɔlɔɲ] *nf* Poland. **polonais** *nm, adj* Polish. **Polonais, -e** *nm, nf* Pole.
poltron, -onne [pɔltrɔ̃, -ɔn] *nm, nf* coward. *adj* cowardly. **poltronnerie** *nf* cowardice.
polycopier [pɔlikɔpje] *v* duplicate, stencil.
polyester [pɔliɛstɛr] *nm* polyester.
polyéthylène [pɔlietilɛn] *nm* polythene.
polygame [pɔligam] *adj* polygamous. *nm* polygamist. **polygamie** *nf* polygamy.
polyglotte [pɔliglɔt] *adj* multilingual. *n(m+f)* polyglot.
polygone [pɔligɔn] *nm* polygon.
pommade [pɔmad] *nf* ointment.
pomme [pɔm] *nf* apple; (*laitue, chou*) heart; (*arrosoir*) rose. **pomme à couteau/cuire** eating/cooking apple. **pomme d'Adam** Adam's apple. **pomme de pin** pine cone. **pomme de terre** potato. **pommes frites** chips *pl*. **pommier** *nm* apple tree.
pommelé [pɔmle] *adj* (*cheval*) dappled.
pommette [pɔmɛt] *nf* cheekbone.
pompe[1] [pɔ̃p] *nf* pump. **pompe à incendie** fire engine. **pomper** *v* pump. **pompier** *nm* fireman. **pompiste** *n(m+f)* petrol pump attendant.
pompe[2] [pɔ̃p] *nf* pomp. **pompeux** *adj* pompous.
poncer [pɔ̃se] *v* rub down, sandpaper.
ponctuel [pɔ̃ktɥɛl] *adj* punctual; (*assidu*) meticulous. **ponctualité** *nf* punctuality; meticulousness.
ponctuer [pɔ̃ktɥe] *v* punctuate. **ponctuation** *nf* punctuation.
pondérer [pɔ̃dere] *v* balance. **pondéré** *adj* level-headed.
pondre [pɔ̃drə] *v* lay; (*œuvre*) produce.
poney [pɔnɛ] *nm* pony.
pont [pɔ̃] *nm* bridge; (*naut*) deck. **pont aérien** airlift. **pont-levis** *nm* drawbridge. **pont suspendu** suspension bridge. **pont tournant** swing bridge.
popeline [pɔplin] *nf* poplin.
populace [pɔpylas] *nf* rabble.
populaire [pɔpylɛr] *adj* popular; (*république, etc.*) people's, of the people. **populariser** *v* popularize. **popularité** *nf* popularity.
population [pɔpylɑsjɔ̃] *nf* population.
porc [pɔr] *nm* pig; (*viande*) pork. **porc-épic** *nm* porcupine.
porcelaine [pɔrsəlɛn] *nf* porcelain, china.
porche [pɔrʃ] *nm* porch.
porcherie [pɔrʃəri] *nf* pigsty.
pore [pɔr] *nm* pore. **poreux** *adj* porous.
pornographie [pɔrnɔgrafi] *nf* pornography. **pornographique** *adj* pornographic.
port[1] [pɔr] *nm* port; (*bassin*) harbour.
port[2] [pɔr] *nm* carriage; postage; (*comportement*) bearing; (*casque, barbe, etc.*) wearing.
porte [pɔrt] *nf* door; (*aéro, jardin, écluse*) gate; (*embrasure*) doorway. **mettre à la porte** throw out; (*licencier*) sack.
porte-avions *nm invar* aircraft carrier.
porte-bagages *nm invar* luggage rack.
porte-bébé *nm* carrycot.
porte-bonheur *nm invar* lucky charm.
porte-clefs *nm invar* key ring.
porte d'entrée *nf* front door.
porte-fenêtre *nf* French window.
portefeuille [pɔrtəfœj] *nm* wallet; (*pol*) portfolio.
portemanteau [pɔrtmɑ̃to] *nm* coat rack.
porte-mine *nm* propelling pencil.
porte-monnaie *nm invar* purse.
porte-parole *nm invar* spokesman.
porter [pɔrte] *v* carry; bear; (*vêtement*) wear; (*amener*) take; direct, turn; (*comm*) put down, enter; (*ressentir*) feel; (*inciter*) prompt, induce; (*coup*) strike home. **se porter bien/mal** be well/ill. **portable** *adj* wearable. **portatif** *adj* portable. **porté** *adj* inclined, prone. **portée** *nf* range, reach; (*effet*) significance, consequences *pl*; (*animal*) litter; (*musique*) stave. **porteur, -euse** *nm, nf* bearer; (*valises*) porter; messenger.
porte-serviettes *nm invar* towel rail.
porte-voix *nm invar* megaphone.
portière [pɔrtjɛr] *nf* door.
portion [pɔrsjɔ̃] *nf* portion; part.
porto [pɔrto] *nm* port.
portrait [pɔrtrɛ] *nm* portrait.
Portugal [pɔrtygal] *nm* Portugal. **portugais** *nm, adj* Portuguese. **les Portugais** the Portuguese.
poser [poze] *v* put, lay; set down; (*question*) ask; (*tableau, étagères*) put up; (*art*) pose. **se poser** alight, come down; (*regard*) rest; (*question*) crop up, arise. **se poser en** pose as. **pose** *nf* pose; (*phot*) exposure; affectation; laying; (*chauffage, etc.*) installation. **posé** *adj* sedate, staid; (*allure*) steady.

positif [pozitif] *adj* positive; real; definite.
position [pɔzisjɔ̃] *nf* position.
posséder [pɔsede] *v* possess, have. **possessif** *nm, adj* possessive. **possession** *nf* possession.
possible [pɔsiblə] *adj* possible; feasible; potential. **possibilité** *nf* possibility.
poste[1] [pɔst] *nf* post; (*bureau*) post office. **mettre à la poste** post. **poste aérienne** air mail. **postal** *adj* postal.
poste[2] [pɔst] *nm* post; (*emploi*) job; (*TV, radio*) set; (*téléphone*) extension. **poste de police** police station. **poste d'essence** petrol station.
poster [pɔste] *v* post.
postérieur, -e [pɔsterjœr] *adj* (*temps*) later; (*espace*) back; (*pattes, etc.*) hind. *nm* (*fam*) behind.
postérité [pɔsterite] *nf* posterity.
posthume [pɔstym] *adj* posthumous.
postiche [pɔstiʃ] *adj* false. *nm* hairpiece.
postscolaire [pɔstskɔlɛr] *adj* **enseignement postscolaire** *nm* further education.
post-scriptum [pɔstskriptɔm] *nm invar* postscript.
postuler [pɔstyle] *v* (*emploi*) apply for; (*poser*) postulate. **postulant, -e** *nm, nf* applicant. **postulat** *nm* postulate.
posture [pɔstyr] *nf* posture, position.
pot [po] *nm* pot; (*verre*) jar; (*lait*) jug; carton; (*fam: chance*) luck. **pot à bière** tankard. **pot-au-feu** *nm invar* stew. **pot-de-vin** *nm* bribe.
potable [pɔtablə] *adj* drinkable; (*fam*) reasonable, decent.
potage [pɔtaʒ] *nm* soup.
potager [pɔtaʒe] *adj* vegetable; (*plante*) edible. *nm* vegetable garden.
potassium [pɔtasjɔm] *nm* potassium.
poteau [pɔto] *nm* post. **poteau indicateur** signpost. **poteau télégraphique** telegraph pole.
potelé [pɔtle] *adj* plump, chubby.
potence [pɔtɑ̃s] *nf* (*gibet*) gallows; (*support*) bracket.
potentiel [pɔtɑ̃sjɛl] *nm, adj* potential.
poterie [pɔtri] *nf* pottery. **potier** *nm* potter.
potin [pɔtɛ̃] *nm* din, racket. **potins** *nm pl* gossip *sing*. **potiner** *v* gossip.
potion [posjɔ̃] *nf* potion.
potiron [pɔtirɔ̃] *nm* pumpkin.
pou [pu] *nm, pl* **poux** louse (*pl* lice).
poubelle [pubɛl] *nf* bin.
pouce [pus] *nm* thumb; (*orteil*) big toe; (*mesure*) inch.
poudre [pudrə] *nf* powder. **poudre à canon** gunpowder. **poudre de riz** face powder. **poudrer** *v* powder. **poudreux** *adj* dusty. **poudrier** *nm* powder compact.
pouffer [pufe] *v* snigger.
poulain [pulɛ̃] *nm* foal.
poule [pul] *nf* hen; (*cuisine*) fowl. **poulailler** *nm* henhouse. **poulet** *nm* chicken.
pouliche [puliʃ] *nf* filly.
poulie [puli] *nf* pulley.
poulpe [pulp] *nm* octopus.
pouls [pu] *nm* pulse.
poumon [pumɔ̃] *nm* lung.
poupe [pup] *nf* stern.
poupée [pupe] *nf* doll.
pour [pur] *prep* for; (*comme*) as; (*but*) to. **pour cent** per cent. **pour que** so that.
pourboire [purbwar] *nm* tip.
pourceau [purso] *nm* (*péj*) swine.
pourcentage [pursɑ̃taʒ] *nm* percentage.
pourchasser [purʃase] *v* pursue.
pourpre [purprə] *nm, adj* crimson, purple.
pourquoi [purkwa] *conj, adv* why.
pourrir [purir] *v* rot, decay; (*fruit*) go rotten *or* bad; (*gâter*) spoil. **pourri** *adj* rotten, bad. **pourriture** *nf* rot.
***poursuivre** [pursɥivrə] *v* pursue; (*harceler*) hound; (*jur*) prosecute; continue, carry on. **poursuite** *nf* pursuit, chase. **poursuites** *nf pl* legal proceedings *pl*. **poursuivant, -e** *nm, nf* pursuer.
pourtant [purtɑ̃] *adv* yet, nevertheless.
pourtour [purtur] *nm* circumference; perimeter.
***pourvoir** [purvwar] *v* provide, equip, supply. **pourvoir à** provide for, cater for. **pourvoyeur, -euse** *nm, nf* supplier.
pourvu [purvy] *adj* **être pourvu de** (*personne*) be endowed with; (*chose*) be fitted *or* equipped with. **pourvu que** *conj* provided that, as long as.
pousser [puse] *v* push; (*stimuler, inciter*) drive, urge; continue, pursue; (*cri*) utter, let out; (*grandir*) grow. **pousser du coude** nudge. **pousse** *nf* growth; (*bot*) shoot. **poussé** *adj* advanced; elaborate; (*enquête*) exhaustive. **poussée** *nf* push, thrust; (*prix, pol*) upsurge. **poussette** *nf* push-chair.
poussière [pusjɛr] *nf* dust. **poussiéreux** *adj* dusty.

poussin [pusɛ̃] *nm* chick.
poutre [putrə] *nf* beam; (*métal*) girder.
***pouvoir** [puvwar] *v* can; (*permission*) may, be allowed to; (*capacité*) be able to; (*possibilité*) might, could. **n'en plus pouvoir** be tired out. **n'y rien pouvoir** be unable to do anything about it. **se pouvoir** be possible. *nm* power; (*capacité*) ability; influence.
pragmatique [pragmatik] *adj* pragmatic.
Prague [prag] *n* Prague.
prairie [preri] *nf* meadow, grassland; (*Amérique*) prairie.
praticable [pratikablə] *adj* practicable; feasible; (*chemin*) passable.
praticien [pratisjɛ̃], **-enne** *nm, nf* practitioner.
pratique[1] [pratik] *adj* practical; (*commode*) handy, convenient.
pratique[2] [pratik] *nf* practice.
pratiquer [pratike] *v* practise; (*faire*) make; (*employer*) use; (*rel*) go to church.
pré [pre] *nm* meadow.
préalable [prealablə] *adj* preliminary, prior. *nm* **au préalable** first.
préavis [preavi] *nm* (advance) notice.
précaire [prekɛr] *adj* precarious.
précaution [prekosjɔ̃] *nf* precaution; (*prudence*) care, caution.
précédent [presedɑ̃] *adj* previous. *nm* precedent.
précéder [presede] *v* precede.
précepteur [presɛptœr] *nm* tutor. **préceptrice** *nf* governess.
prêcher [preʃe] *v* preach. **prêche** *nm* sermon.
précieux [presjø] *adj* precious; affected.
précipice [presipis] *nm* precipice, chasm.
précipiter [presipite] *v* precipitate; (*lancer*) throw, hurl; (*hâter*) hasten, speed up. **se précipiter** rush. **précipitamment** *adv* hurriedly, hastily. **précipitation** *nf* precipitation; haste. **précipité** *adj* hurried, rapid; (*décision*) hasty; (*fuite*) headlong.
précis [presi] *adj* precise. *nm* précis, summary; (*manuel*) handbook. **précisément** *adv* precisely; exactly; just. **préciser** *v* specify, make clear; be more precise (about). **se préciser** become clear, take shape. **précision** *nf* precision; detail, point.
précoce [prekɔs] *adj* precocious; (*fruit, etc.*) early; (*sénilité*) premature. **précocité** *nf* precocity; earliness.
préconçu [prekɔ̃sy] *adj* preconceived.
préconiser [prekɔnize] *v* recommend; advocate.
précurseur [prekyrsœr] *nm* precursor.
prédateur, -trice [predatœr, -tris] *nm* predator. *adj* predatory.
prédécesseur [predesesœr] *nm* predecessor.
prédestiner [predestine] *v* predestine. **prédestination** *nf* predestination.
prédicat [predika] *nm* predicate.
prédicateur [predikatœr] *nm* preacher.
***prédire** [predir] *v* predict, foretell. **prédiction** *nf* prediction.
prédominer [predɔmine] *v* predominate, prevail. **prédominance** *nf* predominance. **prédominant** *adj* predominant, prevailing.
prééminent [preeminɑ̃] *adj* pre-eminent. **prééminence** *nf* pre-eminence.
préfabriqué [prefabrike] *adj* prefabricated.
préface [prefas] *nf* preface.
préfecture [prefɛktyr] *nf* prefecture. **préfecture de police** Paris police headquarters.
préférer [prefere] *v* prefer. **préférable** *adj* preferable. **préféré, -e** *n, adj* favourite. **préférence** *nf* preference. **préférentiel** *adj* preferential.
préfet [prefɛ] *nm* prefect, chief administrative officer of a French department. **préfet de police** chief of Paris police.
préfixe [prefiks] *nm* prefix. **préfixer** *v* prefix.
préhistorique [preistɔrik] *adj* prehistoric.
préjudice [preʒydis] *nm* harm, wrong; (*matériel*) loss. **au préjudice de** at the expense of. **préjudiciable** *adj* detrimental.
préjugé [preʒyʒe] *nm* prejudice.
prélever [prelve] *v* take; (*argent*) deduct. **prélèvement** *nm* taking; deduction. **faire un prélèvement de sang** take a blood sample.
préliminaire [preliminɛr] *adj* preliminary. **préliminaires** *nm pl* preliminaries *pl*.
prélude [prelyd] *nm* prelude.
prématuré [prematyre] *adj* premature.
préméditer [premedite] *v* premeditate. **préméditation** *nf* premeditation.
premier [prəmje], **-ère** *adj* first; (*le plus bas*) bottom; (*le plus haut*) top; (*le plus important*) greatest, foremost; (*fondamental*) basic; original. **premier ministre** *nm* prime minister. **premiers secours** *nm pl* first aid *sing*. *nm* first; (*étage*) first

floor. *nf* first; (*cinéma*) première; (*transport*) first class; (*lycée*) lower sixth form.
prémisse [premis] *nf* premise.
prémonition [premɔnisjɔ̃] *nf* premonition.
prenant [prənɑ̃] *adj* absorbing, fascinating.
***prendre** [prɑ̃drə] *v* take; (*aller chercher*) fetch, pick up; (*attraper*) catch; (*repas*) have; (*acheter*) buy; (*air*) assume, put on; (*manier*) handle; (*durcir*) set. **s'en prendre à** take it out on; blame; attack. **s'y prendre** set about it.
prénom [prenɔ̃] *nm* Christian name.
prénuptial [prenypsjal] *adj* premarital.
préoccuper [preɔkype] *v* (*absorber*) preoccupy; (*inquiéter*) worry. **se préoccuper de** be concerned with *or* about. **préoccupation** *nf* preoccupation; worry.
préparer [prepare] *v* prepare; (*faire*) make; (*apprêter*) get ready; (*réserver*) have in store. **préparatifs** *nm pl* preparations *pl*. **préparation** *nf* preparation. **préparatoire** *adj* preparatory.
préposé [prepoze], **-e** *nm*, *nf* employer, official; (*vestiaire*) attendant.
préposition [prepozisjɔ̃] *nf* preposition.
prérogative [prerɔgativ] *nf* prerogative.
près [prɛ] *adv* near, close. **à cela près** apart from that. **de près** closely. **près de** close to; (*presque*) almost.
présager [prezaʒe] *v* be an omen of; (*prédire*) predict. **présage** *nm* omen.
presbyte [prɛsbit] *adj* long-sighted. **presbytie** *nf* long-sightedness.
***prescrire** [prɛskrir] *v* prescribe; order; stipulate. **prescription** *nf* prescription; order.
préséance [preseɑ̃s] *nf* precedence.
présence [prezɑ̃s] *nf* presence; (*bureau, école*) attendance.
présent[1] [prezɑ̃] *nm*, *adj* present. **à présent** now. **d'à présent** of today, present-day.
présent[2] [prezɑ̃] *nm* present, gift.
présenter [prezɑ̃te] *v* present; introduce; (*exposer*) set out; turn. **se présenter** appear; (*occasion*) arise; (*élection*) stand; (*concours*) go in for; (*examen*) take. **présentable** *adj* presentable. **présentateur, -trice** *nm*, *nf* presenter. **présentation** *nf* presentation; introduction.
préserver [prezɛrve] *v* protect; save. **préservatif** *nm* condom. **préservation** *nf* preservation, protection.
président [prezidɑ̃] *nm* president; (*comité*) chairman. **présidence** *nf* presidency. **présidentiel** *adj* presidential.
présider [prezide] *v* preside (over); (*débat*) chair.
présomption [prezɔ̃psjɔ̃] *nf* presumption. **présomptueux** *adj* presumptuous.
presque [prɛskə] *adv* almost, nearly; (*guère*) scarcely, hardly.
presqu'île [prɛskil] *nf* peninsula.
presser [prese] *v* press; (*serrer*) squeeze; (*hâter*) speed up, hurry; be urgent. **presse-papiers** *nm invar* paperweight. **se presser** hurry; squeeze up, crowd together. **pressant** *adj* urgent. **presse** *nf* press. **pressé** *adj* hurried, in a hurry; urgent. **pression** *nf* pressure. **à la pression** on draught. **pressoir** *nm* press. **pressuriser** *v* pressurize.
preste [prɛst] *adj* nimble.
prestidigitateur, -trice [prɛstidiʒitatœr, -tris] *nm*, *nf* conjuror. **prestidigitation** *nf* conjuring.
prestige [prɛstiʒ] *nm* prestige. **prestigieux** *adj* prestigious.
présumer [prezyme] *v* presume.
prêt[1] [prɛ] *adj* ready. **prêt-à-porter** *nm* ready-to-wear clothes *pl*.
prêt[2] [prɛ] *nm* loan; advance; (*action*) lending.
prétendre [pretɑ̃drə] *v* claim; intend, mean. **prétendant, -e** *nm*, *nf* candidate. **prétendu** *adj* so-called, alleged. **prétention** *nf* claim, pretension; (*vanité*) pretentiousness. **prétentieux** *adj* pretentious.
prêter [prete] *v* lend; attribute; (*offrir*) give; (*tissu*) stretch. **prête-nom** *nm* figurehead. **prêter attention à** pay attention to. **prêter serment** take an oath. **prêteur, -euse** *nm*, *nf* lender. **prêteur sur gages** pawnbroker.
prétexte [pretɛkst] *nm* pretext, excuse.
prêtre [prɛtrə] *nm* priest. **prêtrise** *nf* priesthood.
preuve [prœv] *nf* proof, evidence.
***prévaloir** [prevalwar] *v* prevail. **se prévaloir de** (*profiter*) take advantage of; (*se flatter*) pride oneself on.
***prévenir** [prevnir] *v* (*avertir*) warn; inform; anticipate; (*éviter*) avert; (*influencer*) prejudice. **prévenance** *nf* kindness, consideration. **prévenant** *adj* kind, considerate. **prévenu, -e** *n*, *adj* accused.
préventif [prevɑ̃tif] *adj* preventive. **prévention** *nf* prevention; (*jur*) custody; (*préjugé*) prejudice.

prévision [previzjɔ̃] *nf* prediction, forecast. **prévisions météorologiques** weather forecast *sing*. **prévisible** *adj* foreseeable.
***prévoir** [prevwar] *v* anticipate; (*temps*) forecast; (*projeter*) plan; (*envisager*) allow; (*jur*) provide for. **prévoyance** *nf* foresight.
prier [prije] *v* pray; invite, ask; (*implorer*) beg. **je vous en prie** (*de rien*) don't mention it; (*faites donc*) please do. **prière** *nf* prayer; (*demande*) request, plea.
prieuré [prijœre] *nm* priory.
primaire [primɛr] *adj* primary.
prime[1] [prim] *nf* premium; bonus; (*cadeau*) free gift.
prime[2] [prim] *adj* first, earliest.
primer[1] [prime] *v* prevail over, outdo.
primer[2] [prime] *v* award a prize to.
primesautier [primsotje] *adj* impulsive.
primeurs [primœr] *nf pl* early fruit and vegetables *pl*.
primevère [primvɛr] *nf* primrose.
primitif [primitif] *adj* primitive; original.
primordial [primɔrdjal] *adj* primordial, essential.
prince [prɛ̃s] *nm* prince. **princesse** *nf* princess. **princier** *adj* princely.
principal [prɛ̃sipal] *adj* main, principal; (*employé*) chief, head. *nm* principal; main point.
principe [prɛ̃sip] *nm* principle. **par principe** on principle.
printanier [prɛ̃tanje] *adj* spring, springlike.
printemps [prɛ̃tɑ̃] *nm* spring, springtime.
priorité [prijɔrite] *nf* priority; (*auto*) right of way.
pris [pri] *adj* (*place*) taken, occupied; (*mains*) full; (*personne*) busy, engaged.
prise [priz] *nf* hold, grip; capture; (*élec*: *à fiches*) plug; (*élec*: *à douilles*) socket. **en prise** (*auto*) in gear. **prise multiple** adapter.
priser [prize] *v* prize.
prisme [prismə] *nm* prism.
prison [prizɔ̃] *nf* prison, jail; imprisonment. **prisonnier, -ère** *nm, nf* prisoner.
privé [prive] *adj* private.
priver [prive] *v* deprive. **se priver** deny oneself. **se priver de** do without. **privation** *nf* deprivation.
privilège [privilɛʒ] *nm* privilege. **privilégié** *adj* privileged.
prix [pri] *nm* price, cost; (*récompense*) prize. **à tout prix** at all costs. **prix fixe** set price.
probable [prɔbablə] *adj* probable, likely. **probabilité** *nf* probability, likelihood.
probe [prɔb] *adj* honest. **probité** *nf* integrity.
problème [prɔblɛm] *nm* problem. **problématique** *adj* problematic.
procéder [prɔsede] *v* proceed. **procédé** *nm* process; conduct, behaviour. **procédure** *nf* procedure.
procès [prɔsɛ] *nm* (*jur*) trial; (*poursuite*) proceedings *pl*, lawsuit; (*affaire*) case. **procès-verbal** *nm* minutes *pl*, report.
procession [prɔsesjɔ̃] *nf* procession.
processus [prɔsesys] *nm* process.
prochain [prɔʃɛ̃] *adj* next; (*départ, etc.*) imminent; (*proche*) near, nearby. **prochainement** *adv* soon.
proche [prɔʃ] *adj* near, close; (*village, rue, etc.*) nearby. **proches** *nm pl* close relations *pl*.
proclamer [prɔklame] *v* proclaim, declare; announce. **proclamation** *nf* proclamation.
procréer [prɔkree] *v* procreate. **procréation** *nf* procreation.
procurer [prɔkyre] *v* (*fournir*) provide; (*donner*) give; (*apporter*) bring. **se procurer** get, obtain. **procuration** *nf* proxy; power of attorney. **procureur** *nm* public prosecutor, attorney.
prodige [prɔdiʒ] *nm* wonder, marvel; (*personne*) prodigy. **prodigieux** *adj* fantastic, prodigious, phenomenal.
prodigue [prɔdig] *adj* prodigal, extravagant; generous, lavish. **prodigalité** *nf* extravagance.
***produire** [prɔdɥir] *v* produce. **se produire** happen. **producteur, -trice** *nm, nf* producer. **productif** *adj* productive. **production** *nf* production; (*produit*) product. **productivité** *nf* productivity. **produit** *nm* product. **produits** *nm pl* (*légumes, etc.*) produce *sing*; (*comm*) goods *pl*. **produits chimiques** chemicals *pl*. **produits de beauté** cosmetics *pl*.
proéminence [prɔeminɑ̃s] *nf* prominence. **proéminent** *adj* prominent.
profane [prɔfan] *adj* secular, profane. *n*(*m+f*) layman. **profaner** *v* desecrate, profane, debase.
professer [prɔfese] *v* profess, declare; (*enseigner*) teach.

professeur [prɔfɛsœr] *nm* teacher; (*université*) professor.
profession [prɔfɛsjɔ̃] *nf* profession; occupation.
professionnel [prɔfɛsjɔnɛl], **-elle** *adj* professional; (*formation*) vocational. *nm, nf* professional; (*ouvrier*) skilled worker.
profil [prɔfil] *nm* profile; contour, outline.
profit [prɔfi] *nm* profit; advantage, benefit. **tirer profit de** profit from. **profitable** *adj* beneficial.
profiter [prɔfite] *v* **profiter à** benefit, be beneficial to. **profiter de** take advantage of.
profond [prɔfɔ̃] *adj* deep; (*sentiment, remarque*) profound. **peu profond** shallow. **profondément** *adv* deeply; profoundly. **profondeur** *nf* depth.
profus [prɔfy] *adj* profuse. **profusion** *nf* profusion.
progéniture [prɔʒenityr] *nf* offspring.
programme [prɔgram] *nm* programme; (*scolaire*) curriculum, syllabus; (*ordinateur*) program. **programmation** *nf* programming. **programmer** *v* programme. **programmeur, -euse** *nm, nf* computer programmer.
progrès [prɔgrɛ] *nm* progress; advance, improvement.
progresser [prɔgrese] *v* progress; advance; make progress. **progressif** *adj* progressive. **progression** *nf* progression; progress. **progressiste** *n(m+f), adj* progressive.
prohiber [prɔibe] *v* prohibit. **prohibition** *nf* prohibition.
proie [prwa] *nf* prey. **être en proie à** be a prey to; be a victim of.
projecteur [prɔʒɛktœr] *nm* projector; (*théâtre*) spotlight; (*monument, sport*) floodlight; (*pour chercher*) searchlight.
projectile [prɔʒɛktil] *nm* missile, projectile.
projection [prɔʒɛksjɔ̃] *nf* projection.
projet [prɔʒɛ] *nm* plan; (*ébauche*) draft. **projeter** *v* project; plan.
prolétariat [prɔletarja] *nm* proletariat. **prolétaire** *nm* proletarian. **prolétarien** *adj* proletarian.
proliférer [prɔlifere] *v* proliferate. **prolifération** *nf* proliferation.
prolifique [prɔlifik] *adj* prolific.
prologue [prɔlɔg] *nm* prologue.
prolonger [prɔlɔ̃ʒe] *v* prolong, extend. **se prolonger** go on, persist. **prolongation** *nf* prolongation. **prolongement** *nm* extension.
promener [prɔmne] *v* take for a walk. **se promener** go for a walk; (*errer*) wander. **promenade** *nf* walk, stroll; (*en voiture*) drive; (*à cheval*) ride.
promesse [prɔmɛs] *nf* promise.
***promettre** [prɔmɛtrə] *v* promise. **prometteur, -euse** *adj* promising.
promotion [prɔmosjɔ̃] *nf* promotion.
***promouvoir** [prɔmuvwar] *v* promote.
prompt [prɔ̃] *adj* swift, prompt, quick. **promptitude** *nf* swiftness, promptness.
prône [pron] *nm* sermon.
pronom [prɔnɔ̃] *nm* pronoun.
prononcer [prɔnɔ̃se] *v* pronounce; (*dire*) utter; (*discours*) deliver. **se prononcer** come to a decision; give an opinion. **prononciation** *nf* pronunciation.
propagande [prɔpagɑ̃d] *nf* propaganda.
propager [prɔpaʒe] *v* propagate, spread. **propagation** *nf* propagation.
prophète [prɔfɛt] *nm* prophet. **prophétie** *nf* prophecy. **prophétique** *adj* prophetic. **prophétiser** *v* prophesy.
propice [prɔpis] *adj* favourable.
proportion [prɔpɔrsjɔ̃] *nf* proportion. **proportionnel** *adj* proportional. **proportionner** *v* proportion, make proportional.
propos [prɔpo] *nm* purpose, intention; subject. *nm pl* talk *sing*; remarks *pl*. **à propos** by the way; (*arriver*) at the right time; (*remarque*) apt. **à propos de** concerning, about.
proposer [prɔpoze] *v* propose; suggest; offer. **se proposer de** intend to. **proposition** *nf* proposal, proposition; suggestion; (*gramm*) clause.
propre [prɔprə] *adj* (*pas sale*) clean; (*net*) neat; (*chien, chat*) house-trained; honest; (*possessif*) own; appropriate, suitable. **propre à** suitable for; (*coutume, etc.*) peculiar to. **proprement** *adv* cleanly; neatly; (*comme il faut*) properly; strictly. **à proprement parler** strictly speaking. **propreté** *nf* cleanness; neatness.
propriétaire [prɔprijetɛr] *nm* owner; (*hôtel*) proprietor; (*location*) landlord. *nf* owner; proprietress; landlady. **propriété** *nf* property; (*droit*) ownership; correctness, suitability.
propulser [prɔpylse] *v* propel. **propulseur** *nm* propeller. **propulsion** *nf* propulsion.

***proscrire** [prɔskrir] *v* ban, prohibit; (*personne*) banish, exile. **proscrit, -e** *nm, nf* outlaw; exile.
prose [proz] *nf* prose.
prospectus [prɔspɛktys] *nm* leaflet, brochure.
prospérer [prɔspere] *v* thrive, flourish; (*personne*) prosper. **prospère** *adj* thriving, flourishing; prosperous. **prospérité** *nf* prosperity.
se prosterner [prɔstɛrne] *v* bow down, prostrate oneself; (*s'humilier*) grovel. **prosternation** *nf* prostration. **prosterné** *adj* prostrate.
prostituer [prɔstitɥe] *v* prostitute. **prostituée** *nf* prostitute. **prostitution** *nf* prostitution.
protagoniste [prɔtagɔnist] *nm* protagonist.
protecteur, -trice [prɔtɛktœr, -tris] *adj* protective. *nm, nf* protector; (*art*) patron. **protection** *nf* protection; patronage.
protéger [prɔteʒe] *v* protect; patronize, be a patron of.
protéine [prɔtein] *nf* protein.
protester [prɔtɛste] *v* protest; declare. **protestant, -e** *n, adj* Protestant. **protestation** *nf* protest.
protocole [prɔtɔkɔl] *nm* protocol; etiquette.
prototype [prɔtɔtip] *nm* prototype.
proue [pru] *nf* bow, prow.
prouesse [pruɛs] *nf* prowess; (*acte*) feat.
prouver [pruve] *v* prove.
***provenir** [prɔvnir] *v* **provenir de** come from; be the result of. **provenance** *nf* origin, source. **en provenance de** (coming) from.
proverbe [prɔvɛrb] *nm* proverb. **proverbial** *adj* proverbial.
providence [prɔvidɑ̃s] *nf* providence.
province [prɔvɛ̃s] *nf* province. **provincial** *adj* provincial.
proviseur [prɔvizœr] *nm* headmaster.
provision [prɔvizjɔ̃] *nf* stock, supply. **provisions** *nf pl* provisions *pl*, food *sing*.
provisoire [prɔvizwar] *adj* provisional, temporary.
provoquer [prɔvɔke] *v* provoke; cause; incite; (*duel*) challenge; (*colère, curiosité*) arouse. **provocant** *adj* provocative. **provocation** *nf* provocation.
proximité [prɔksimite] *nf* proximity.
prude [pryd] *nf* prude. *adj* prudish.
prudent [prydɑ̃] *adj* prudent; (*circonspect*) careful, cautious; (*sage*) sensible. **prudence** *nf* prudence; care, caution.
prune [pryn] *nf* plum. **pruneau** *nm* prune. **prunelle** *nf* (*bot*) sloe; (*anat*) pupil. **prunier** *nm* plum tree.
psaume [psom] *nm* psalm.
pseudonyme [psødɔnim] *nm* pseudonym.
psychanalyse [psikanaliz] *nf* psychoanalysis. **psychanalyser** *v* psychoanalyse. **psychanalyste** *n(m+f)* psychoanalyst.
psychédélique [psikedelik] *adj* psychedelic.
psychiatrie [psikjatri] *nf* psychiatry. **psychiatre** *n(m+f)* psychiatrist. **psychiatrique** *adj* psychiatric.
psychique [psiʃik] *adj* psychic.
psychologie [psikɔlɔʒi] *nf* psychology. **psychologique** *adj* psychological. **psychologue** *n(m+f)* psychologist.
psychopathe [psikɔpat] *n(m+f)* psychopath.
psychose [psikoz] *nf* psychosis. **psychotique** *n(m+f)*, *adj* psychotic.
psychosomatique [psikɔsɔmatik] *adj* psychosomatic.
psychothérapie [psikɔterapi] *nf* psychotherapy.
puanteur [pɥɑ̃tœr] *nf* stink.
puberté [pybɛrte] *nf* puberty.
pubien [pybjɛ̃] *nf* puberty.
public, -ique [pyblik] *adj* public. *nm* public; audience. **le grand public** the general public.
publicité [pyblisite] *nf* publicity; (*comm*) advertising; (*annonce*) advertisement. **publicitaire** *adj* advertising.
publier [pyblije] *v* publish. **publication** *nf* publication; publishing.
puce [pys] *nf* flea. **jeu de puce** *nm* tiddlywinks. **puceron** *nm* greenfly.
pucelle [pysɛl] *nf* virgin.
pudeur [pydœr] *nf* modesty, decency.
pudique [pydik] *adj* modest; discreet.
puer [pɥe] *v* stink.
puéril [pɥeril] *adj* childish.
puis [pɥi] *adv* then.
puiser [pɥize] *v* draw. **puiser dans** dip into.
puisque [pɥiskə] *conj* since, seeing that, as.
puissance [pɥisɑ̃s] *nf* power; (*jur*) authority. **en puissance** potentially. **puissant** *adj* powerful.

puits [pɥi] *nm* well; (*mine*) shaft.
pull [pyl] *nm* (*fam*) jumper.
pulluler [pylyle] *v* swarm, teem. **pullulation** *nf* swarm, multitude.
pulpe [pylp] *nf* pulp. **pulpeux** *adj* pulpy.
pulsation [pylsɑsjɔ̃] *nf* beat, pulsation. **pulsation du cœur** heartbeat.
pulvériser [pylverize] *v* pulverize; (*liquide*) spray; demolish. **pulvérisateur** *nm* spray. **pulvérisation** *nf* pulverization; spraying; demolition.
punaise [pynɛz] *nf* (*zool*) bug; (*clou*) drawing-pin.
punch [pɔ̃ʃ] *nm* punch.
punir [pynir] *v* punish. **punition** *nf* punishment.
pupille[1] [pypij] *nf* (*anat*) pupil.
pupille[2] [pypij] *n*(*m*+*f*) ward.
pupitre [pypitrə] *nm* desk; (*rel*) lectern; music stand.
pur [pyr] *adj* pure; (*boisson*) neat; honest; (*absolu*) sheer. **pur-sang** *nm* thoroughbred. **pureté** *nf* purity.
purée [pyre] *nf* (*tomates, etc.*) purée; (*pommes de terre*) mashed potato.
purgatoire [pyrgatwar] *nm* purgatory.
purger [pyrʒe] *v* purge; (*tech*) flush out, drain. **purgatif** *nm, adj* purgative. **purge** *nf* purge.
purifier [pyrifje] *v* purify, cleanse. **purification** *nf* purification.
puritain [pyritɛ̃], **-e** *adj* puritanical. *nm, nf* puritan.
pus [py] *nm* pus.
pusillanime [pyzilanim] *adj* faint-hearted.
putain [pytɛ̃] *nf* (*argot*) whore.
putride [pytrid] *adj* putrid.
puzzle [pœzlə] *nm* jigsaw.
pygmée [pigme] *nm* pygmy.
pyjama [piʒama] *nm* pyjamas *pl*.
pylône [pilon] *nm* pylon.
pyramide [piramid] *nf* pyramid.
python [pitɔ̃] *nm* python.

Q

qu' [k] *V* **que**.
quadrant [kadrɑ̃] *nm* quadrant.
quadrilatère [kadrilatɛr] *nm* quadrilateral.
quadrillé [kadrije] *adj* squared.
quadrupède [kadrypɛd] *nm, adj* quadruped.
quadrupler [kadryple] *v* quadruple. **quadruple** *nm, adj* quadruple. **quadruplé, -e** *nm, nf* quadruplet.
quai [ke] *nm* quay; (*gare*) platform; (*rivière*) embankment.
qualifier [kalifje] *v* qualify; describe, call. **qualification** *nf* qualification; description, label.
qualité [kalite] *nf* quality; (*don*) skill; (*fonction*) position, capacity.
quand [kɑ̃] *conj, adv* when. **quand même** all the same, nevertheless.
quant [kɑ̃] *adv* **quant à** as for; regarding.
quantité [kɑ̃tite] *nf* quantity, amount; great number, great deal.
quarantaine [karɑ̃tɛn] *nf* quarantine. **mettre en quarantaine** quarantine
quarante [karɑ̃t] *nm, adj* forty. **quarantième** *n*(*m*+*f*), *adj* fortieth.
quart [kar] *nm* quarter; (*naut*) watch. **... et quart** quarter past .... **... moins le quart** quarter to .... **quart de finale** quarter-final. **quart d'heure** quarter of an hour.
quartier [kartje] *nm* quarter; (*ville*) district, area; (*portion*) piece. **du quartier** local. **quartier général** headquarters.
quartz [kwarts] *nm* quartz.
quasi [kazi] *adv* almost.
quatorze [katɔrz] *nm, adj* fourteen. **quatorzième** *n*(*m*+*f*), *adj* fourteenth.
quatre [katrə] *nm, adj* four. **à quatre pattes** on all fours. **quatrième** *n*(*m*+*f*), *adj* fourth.
quatre-vingt-dix *nm, adj* ninety. **quatre-vingt-dixième** *n*(*m*+*f*), *adj* ninetieth.
quatre-vingts *nm, adj* eighty. **quatre-vingtième** *n*(*m*+*f*), *adj* eightieth.
quatuor [kwatɥɔr] *nm* quartet.
que[1] [kə] *conj* that; (*but*) so that; (*comparaison*) than; (*aussi*) as. **ne ... que** only. **que ... que ...** whether ... or ....
que[2] [kə] *adv* how.
que[3] [kə] *pron* that, which; (*temps*) when; (*personne*) that, whom; (*interrogatif*) what. **qu'est-ce que** *or* **qui** what.
quel [kɛl], **quelle** *pron, adj* what, which. **quel que** whatever; (*personne*) whoever.
quelconque [kɛlkɔ̃k] *adj* any, some; (*médiocre*) poor; ordinary.

quelque [kɛlkə] *adj, adv* some. **quelque chose** something. **quelquefois** *adv* sometimes. **quelque part** somewhere. **quelque peu** somewhat. **quelques** *adj* some, a few; (*peu de*) few. **quelques-uns, -unes** *pron* some, a few. **quelqu'un** *pron* somebody.
quémander [kemɑ̃de] *v* beg for.
querelle [kərɛl] *nf* quarrel. **se quereller** *v* quarrel. **querelleur, -euse** *adj* quarrelsome.
question [kɛstjɔ̃] *nf* question. **il n'en est pas question** it's out of the question. **questionnaire** *nm* questionnaire. **questionner** *v* question, interrogate.
quêter [kete] *v* collect money; (*chercher*) seek. **quête** *nf* collection; (*recherche*) quest, search. **en quête de** in search of. **faire la quête** collect for charity; (*rel*) take the collection.
queue [kø] *nf* tail; (*file*) queue; (*bout, fin*) end; (*liste*) bottom; (*fleur, fruit*) stalk; (*train*) rear; (*billard*) cue. **faire la queue** queue.
qui [ki] *pron* who; (*objet*) whom; (*chose*) which, that; (*quiconque*) whoever, anyone who. **à** *or* **de qui** (*possessif*) whose.
quiche [kiʃ] *nf* quiche.
quiconque [kikɔ̃k] *pron* whoever; (*personne*) anyone.
quignon [kiɲɔ̃] *nm* hunk of bread; (*croûton*) crust.
quille[1] [kij] *nf* (*jeu*) skittle; (*fam: jambe*) pin, leg. **jeu de quilles** skittles.
quille[2] [kij] *nf* (*naut*) keel.
quincaillerie [kɛ̃kɑjri] *nf* hardware; (*magasin*) hardware shop. **quincaillier, -ère** *nm, nf* ironmonger.
quinine [kinin] *nf* quinine.
quinte [kɛ̃t] *nf* coughing fit; (*musique*) fifth.
quintessence [kɛ̃tesɑ̃s] *nf* quintessence.
quintette [kɛ̃tɛt] *nm* quintet.
quintuplé [kɛ̃typle], **-e** *nm, nf* quintuplet.
quinze [kɛ̃z] *nm, adj* fifteen. **demain en quinze** a fortnight tomorrow. **quinze jours** a fortnight. **quinzaine** *nf* fortnight. **quinzième** *n(m+f), adj* fifteenth.
quiproquo [kiprɔko] *nm* mistake; (*malentendu*) misunderstanding.
quittance [kitɑ̃s] *nf* receipt.
quitter [kite] *v* leave; (*espoir*) give up. **ne quittez pas** (*téléphone*) hold the line. **se quitter** part. **quitte** *adj* quits, even; (*débarrassé*) clear, rid.
quoi [kwa] *pron* what. **à quoi bon?** what's the use? **avoir de quoi** have (the) means. **il n'y a pas de quoi** don't mention it. **quoi que** whatever.
quoique [kwakə] *conj* although.
quorum [kɔrɔm] *nm* quorum.
quote-part [kɔtpar] *nf* share, quota.
quotidien [kɔtidjɛ̃] *adj* daily; (*banal*) everyday. *nm* daily newspaper.

R

rabâcher [rabɑʃe] *v* harp on, keep repeating.
rabais [rabɛ] *nm* reduction, discount.
rabaisser [rabese] *v* belittle, disparage; reduce.
rabat [raba] *nm* flap.
***rabattre** [rabatrə] *v* (*fermer*) close; (*faire retomber*) pull *or* turn down; (*drap*) fold back; reduce; deduct. **rabat-joie** *nm invar* spoilsport. **se rabattre** close; (*voiture*) cut in.
rabbin [rabɛ̃] *nm* rabbi.
rabot [rabo] *nm* plane. **raboter** *v* plane; (*fam*) scrape. **raboteux** *adj* uneven, rough.
rabougri [rabugri] *adj* stunted; (*ratatiné*) shrivelled.
racaille [rakaj] *nf* rabble.
raccommoder [rakɔmɔde] *v* mend; (*fam*) reconcile. **se raccommoder** (*fam*) make it up. **raccommodage** *nm* (*action*) mending; (*endroit*) mend. **raccommodement** *nm* (*fam*) reconciliation.
raccorder [rakɔrde] *v* join, link up, connect. **raccord** *nm* join, link.
raccourcir [rakursir] *v* shorten; get shorter. **raccourci** *nm* (*résumé*) summary; (*chemin*) short cut. **en raccourci** in miniature.
raccrocher [rakrɔʃe] *v* (*téléphone*) hang up, ring off; (*attraper*) grab, get hold of; (*tableau, etc.*) hang up again. **se raccrocher à** cling to; (*relier*) link with.
race [ras] *nf* race; (*animal*) breed; (*famille*) stock, blood. **de race** pedigree, thoroughbred. **racial** *adj* racial. **racisme** *nm* racialism, racism. **raciste** *n(m+f), adj* racialist, racist.

racheter [raʃte] *v* buy back; (*dette*) redeem; (*otage*) ransom; (*péché*) atone for; (*faute*) make up for. **rachat** *nm* redemption; ransom; atonement.
racine [rasin] *nf* root.
racler [rɑkle] *v* scrape. **se racler la gorge** clear one's throat. **raclée** *nf* (*fam*) thrashing.
racoler [rakɔle] *v* (*prostituée*) solicit; (*vendeur*) tout for.
raconter [rakɔ̃te] *v* tell, relate. **racontar** *nm* story, piece of gossip. **raconteur, -euse** *nm, nf* story-teller, narrator.
se racornir [rakɔrniːr] *v* shrivel up; (*durcir*) become hard *or* tough.
radar [radar] *nm* radar.
rade [rad] *nf* harbour. **laisser en rade** leave stranded, abandon.
radeau [rado] *nm* raft.
radial [radjal] *adj* radial.
radiateur [radjatœr] *nm* radiator; (*à gaz*) heater. **radiateur électrique** electric fire. **radiateur soufflant** fan heater.
radiation [radjɑsjɔ̃] *nf* radiation.
radical [radikal] *nm, adj* radical.
radier [radje] *v* cross *or* strike off.
radieux [radjø] *adj* radiant.
radin [radɛ̃], **-e** (*fam*) *adj* stingy. *nm, nf* skinflint.
radio [radjo] *nf* radio; (*méd*) X-ray.
radioactif [radjɔaktif] *adj* radioactive. **radioactivité** *nf* radioactivity.
radiodiffuser [radjɔdifyze] *v* broadcast. **radiodiffusion** *nf* broadcasting.
radiographie [radjɔgrafi] *nf* radiography. **radiographier** *v* X-ray.
radiologie [radjɔlɔʒi] *nf* radiology.
radiothérapie [radjɔterapi] *nf* radiotherapy.
radis [radi] *nm* radish.
radium [radjɔm] *nm* radium.
radoter [radɔte] *v* (*péj*) ramble on. **radotage** *nm* drivel.
radoucir [radusir] *v* soften. **se radoucir** (*personne*) calm down; (*temps, voix*) become milder.
rafale [rafal] *nf* gust, blast.
raffermir [rafɛrmir] *v* strengthen; (*durcir*) harden; (*voix*) steady. **se raffermir** grow stronger; harden; become steady.
raffiner [rafine] *v* refine. **raffinage** *nm* refining. **raffinement** *nm* refinement. **raffinerie** *nf* refinery.
raffoler [rafɔle] *v* **raffoler de** be very fond of.
raffut [rafy] *nm* (*fam*) row, racket.
rafistoler [rafistɔle] *v* patch up.
rafle [rɑflə] *nf* police raid. **rafler** *v* (*fam*) swipe.
rafraîchir [rafreʃir] *v* refresh; (*visage*) freshen up; (*refroidir*) cool; (*vêtement, appartement, etc.*) brighten up; (*cheveux*) trim. **rafraîchissements** *nm pl* refreshments *pl*.
rage [raʒ] *nf* rage; mania; (*méd*) rabies. **rage de dents** raging toothache. **rager** *v* fume, be furious. **rageur, -euse** *adj* hot-tempered.
ragots [rago] *nm pl* (*fam*) gossip *sing*.
ragoût [ragu] *nm* stew.
raide [rɛd] *adj* stiff; (*cheveux*) straight; (*corde*) tight; (*pente*) steep; (*fam: histoire*) far-fetched; (*osé*) daring *adv* steeply. **raideur** *nf* stiffness; straightness; tightness; steepness. **raidir** *v* stiffen.
raie[1] [rɛ] *nf* line; (*bande*) stripe; (*cheveux*) parting; (*éraflure*) scratch.
raie[2] [rɛ] *nf* (*poisson*) skate, ray.
raifort [rɛfɔr] *nm* horse-radish.
rail [rɑj] *nm* rail.
railler [rɑje] *v* scoff at. **raillerie** *nf* mockery. **railleur, -euse** *adj* mocking.
rainure [renyr] *nf* groove; (*plus courte*) slot.
raisin [rɛzɛ̃] *nm* grape. **raisin de Corinthe** currant. **raisin de Smyrne** sultana. **raisin sec** raisin.
raison [rɛzɔ̃] *nf* reason; (*math*) ratio. **avoir raison** be right. **raisonnable** *adj* reasonable; (*sensé*) sensible. **raisonnement** *nm* reasoning; argument. **raisonner** *v* reason; (*convaincre*) reason with; argue.
rajeunir [raʒœnir] *v* rejuvenate; modernize; (*rafraîchir*) brighten up; (*personne*) look *or* feel younger.
rajuster [raʒyste] *v* readjust; rearrange, tidy.
ralenti [ralɑ̃ti] *adj* slow. *nm* (*cinéma*) slow motion; (*auto*) tick-over. **au ralenti** in slow motion. **tourner au ralenti** tick over, idle.
ralentir [ralɑ̃tir] *v* slow down.
rallier [ralje] *v* rally; unite; (*gagner*) win over. **se rallier à** join, side with.
rallonger [ralɔ̃ʒe] *v* lengthen, extend. **rallonge** *nf* extension; (*table*) leaf. **à rallonges** (*fam: nom*) double-barrelled.
ramasser [ramɑse] *v* pick up; collect; (*récolter*) gather. **ramassé** *adj* crouched, huddled up; (*trapu*) squat; compact.

rame[1] [ram] *nf* (*aviron*) oar. **ramer** *v* row. **rameur** *nm* oarsman.
rame[2] [ram] *nf* train; (*papier*) ream.
rame[3] [ram] *nf* (*branche*) stick, stake.
rameau [ramo] *nm* branch.
ramener [ramne] *v* bring back; (*tirer*) draw, pull.
ramier [ramje] *nm* wood-pigeon.
se ramifier [ramifje] *v* branch out.
ramollir [ramɔlir] *v* soften; (*courage, etc.*) weaken. **ramolli** *adj* soft.
ramoner [ramɔne] *v* sweep. **ramoneur** *nm* chimney-sweep.
ramper [rɑ̃pe] *v* crawl, creep. **rampe** *nf* ramp; (*côte*) slope; (*balustrade*) handrail; (*escalier*) banister; (*théâtre*) footlights *pl.*
rancart [rɑ̃kar] *nm* **mettre au rancart** (*argot*) scrap, chuck out.
rance [rɑ̃s] *adj* rancid.
rançon [rɑ̃sɔ̃] *nf* ransom. **rançonner** *v* hold to ransom.
rancune [rɑ̃kyn] *nf* spite; grudge.
randonnée [rɑ̃dɔne] *nf* (*voiture*) drive; (*bicyclette*) ride; (*pied*) walk, hike.
rang [rɑ̃] *nm* (*rangée*) row; (*place*) rank.
ranger [rɑ̃ʒe] *v* arrange; (*à sa place*) put away; (*en ordre*) tidy up; (*compter*) rank. **se ranger** (*s'écarter*) step aside; (*voiture*) pull over; (*soldats, etc.*) line up; (*fam*) settle down. **se ranger à** go along with, fall in with. **rangé** *adj* orderly; settled. **rangée** *nf* row.
ranimer [ranime] *v* revive; (*feu, amour*) rekindle.
rapace [rapas] *adj* (*avide*) rapacious; (*oiseau*) predatory.
rapatrier [rapatrije] *v* repatriate. **rapatrié, -e** *nm, nf* repatriate. **rapatriement** *nm* repatriation.
râper [rɑpe] *v* (*cuisine*) grate; (*bois*) rasp. **râpe** *nf* grater; rasp. **râpé** *adj* grated; (*usé*) threadbare. **râpeux** *adj* rough.
rapetisser [raptise] *v* shorten; (*vêtement*) take up *or* in; look smaller; (*vieillard*) shrink; (*dénigrer*) belittle.
raphia [rafja] *nm* raffia.
rapide [rapid] *adj* fast, rapid, quick. *nm* express train. **rapides** *nm pl* rapids *pl.* **rapidité** *nf* speed, rapidity.
rapiécer [rapjese] *v* patch, mend.
rappeler [raple] *v* call back; (*faire souvenir*) remind, recall. **se rappeler** remember. **rappel** *nm* recall; reminder.
rapport [rapɔr] *nm* connection; relationship; (*exposé*) report; revenue, yield; (*math*) ratio. **être en rapport avec** (*s'accorder*) be in keeping with; (*comm, etc.*) have dealings with. **par rapport à** in relation to; (*envers*) with regard to.
rapporter [rapɔrte] *v* bring back; (*revenu*) yield, bring in; report; (*argot*) tell tales, sneak. **se rapporter à** relate to, refer to. **s'en rapporter à** rely on. **rapporteur** *nm* (*fam*) sneak; (*géom*) protractor. **rapporteuse** *nf* (*fam*) sneak.
rapprocher [raprɔʃe] *v* bring together; (*approcher*) bring nearer; compare. **se rapprocher** come together; get closer, approach; be reconciled. **rapprochement** *nm* comparison, reconciliation; (*lien*) link, parallel.
raquette [rakɛt] *nf* racket.
rare [rar] *adj* rare; (*peu*) few; (*peu abondant*) scarce, sparse; exceptional. **rareté** *nf* rarity.
ras [rɑ] *adj* short; (*cheveux*) close-cropped. **à ras bords** to the brim. **au ras de** level with. **en avoir ras le bol** (*fam*) be fed up with.
raser [rɑze] *v* shave; (*effleurer*) skim, scrape; (*fam*) bore. **se raser** have a shave; (*fam*) be bored. **rasage** *nm* shaving. **raseur, -euse** *nm, nf* (*fam*) bore. **rasoir** *nm* razor; (*fam*) bore.
rassasier [rasazje] *v* satisfy. **se rassasier** eat one's fill. **se rassasier de** tire of.
rassembler [rasɑ̃ble] *v* collect, assemble, gather (together); (*remonter*) reassemble.
rassis [rasi] *adj* stale; (*personne*) composed, calm.
rassurer [rasyre] *v* reassure. **se rassurer** put one's mind at ease.
rat [ra] *nm* rat.
ratatiner [ratatine] *v* wrinkle, shrivel up.
râteau [rɑto] *nm* rake.
râtelier [rɑtəlje] *nm* rack; (*fam*) set of false teeth.
rater [rate] *v* (*fusil*) misfire; (*affaire*) go wrong; (*fam: manquer*) miss; (*fam: gâcher*) mess up; (*fam: échouer*) fail.
ratifier [ratifje] *v* ratify. **ratification** *nf* ratification.
ration [rɑsjɔ̃] *nf* ration.
rationaliser [rasjɔnalize] *v* rationalize. **rationnel** *adj* rational.
rationner [rasjɔne] *v* ration. **rationnement** *nm* rationing.
ratisser [ratise] *v* rake (up).

rattacher [rataʃe] *v* fasten again; join; (*relier*) link, relate.
rattraper [ratrape] *v* catch again; (*regagner, réparer*) make up for; (*rejoindre*) catch up with.
rature [ratyr] *nf* deletion, erasure.
rauque [rok] *adj* hoarse; (*cri*) raucous.
ravager [ravaʒe] *v* ravage, devastate. **ravages** *nm pl* ravages *pl*, devastation *sing*.
ravaler [ravale] *v* swallow; (*colère, larmes*) hold back; (*mur*) restore.
ravauder [ravode] *v* mend.
ravin [ravɛ̃] *nm* ravine, gully.
ravir [ravir] *v* delight; (*enlever*) carry off. **ravissant** *adj* delightful, beautiful. **ravissement** *nm* rapture.
se raviser [ravize] *v* change one's mind.
ravitailler [ravitɑje] *v* (*carburant*) refuel; (*vivres, etc.*) provide with fresh supplies.
rayer [reje] *v* (*marquer*) line; (*érafler*) scratch; (*biffer*) cross out. **rayé** *adj* (*papier*) ruled, lined; (*tissu*) striped; scratched.
rayon[1] [rɛjɔ̃] *nm* ray, beam; (*roue*) spoke; (*cercle*) radius. **rayon X** X-ray.
rayon[2] [rɛjɔ̃] *nm* (*planche*) shelf; (*comm*) department; (*comptoir*) counter; (*miel*) honeycomb.
rayon[3] [rɛjɔ̃] *nm* row, drill.
rayonne [rɛjɔn] *nf* rayon.
rayonner [rɛjɔne] *v* radiate; (*briller*) shine (forth), be radiant. **rayonnant** *adj* radiant. **rayonnement** *nm* radiance; radiation; influence.
rayure [rejyr] *nf* (*bande*) stripe; (*éraflure*) scratch.
razzia [razja] *nf* raid.
réaction [reaksjɔ̃] *nf* reaction. **moteur à réaction** jet engine. **réacteur** *nm* reactor. **réactionnaire** *n*(*m*+*f*), *adj* reactionary.
réadapter [readapte] *v* readjust; (*méd*) rehabilitate. **réadaptation** *nf* readjustment; rehabilitation.
réagir [reaʒir] *v* react.
réaliser [realize] *v* realize; (*ambition*) fulfil; (*projet*) carry out; (*cinéma*) produce. **réalisateur, -trice** *nm, nf* director. **réalisation** *nf* realization; fulfilment; production.
réaliste [realist] *adj* realistic. *n*(*m*+*f*) realist. **réalisme** *nm* realism.
réalité [realite] *nf* reality.
***réapparaître** [reaparɛtrə] *v* reappear. **réapparition** *nf* reappearance.
réarranger [rearɑ̃ʒe] *v* rearrange. **réarrangement** *nm* rearrangement
rébarbatif [rebarbatif] *adj* forbidding, daunting.
rebattu [rəbaty] *adj* hackneyed.
rebelle [rəbɛl] *adj* rebellious; (*cheveux*) unruly; (*virus*) resistant. *n*(*m*+*f*) rebel. **se rebeller** *v* rebel. **rébellion** *nf* rebellion.
rebondir [rəbɔ̃dir] *v* bounce, rebound. **rebond** *nm* bounce, rebound. **rebondi** *adj* (*personne*) plump, portly; (*forme*) rounded.
rebord [rəbɔr] *nm* edge; (*plat, assiette*) rim; (*vêtement*) hem. **rebord de fenêtre** window ledge *or* sill.
rebours [rəbur] *nm* **à rebours** the wrong way; (*compter*) backwards. **à rebours de** against.
rebrousser [rəbruse] *v* brush up *or* back. **à rebrousse-poil** the wrong way. **prendre à rebrousse-poil** rub up the wrong way. **rebrousser chemin** turn back, retrace one's steps.
rebuffade [rəbyfad] *nf* rebuff.
rebut [rəby] *nm* scrap. **mettre au rebut** throw out, discard.
rebuter [rəbyte] *v* discourage, put off; (*répugner*) repel.
receler [rəsəle] *v* (*secret*) conceal; (*malfaiteur*) harbour; (*objet volé*) receive.
recensement [rəsɑ̃smɑ̃] *nm* census.
récent [resɑ̃] *adj* recent; (*nouveau*) new. **récemment** *adv* recently.
récépissé [resepise] *nm* receipt.
récepteur, -trice [reseptœr, -tris] *adj* receiving. *nm* receiver.
réception [resɛpsjɔ̃] *nf* reception; (*d'une lettre, etc.*) receipt. **réceptionniste** *n*(*m*+*f*) receptionist.
récession [resesjɔ̃] *nf* recession.
recette [rəsɛt] *nf* (*cuisine*) recipe; (*comm*) takings *pl*. **recettes** *nf pl* receipts *pl*, revenue *sing*.
***recevoir** [rəsvwar] *v* receive; (*invité*) entertain; (*contenir*) take, hold. **être reçu (à)** (*examen*) pass. **receveur, -euse** *nm, nf* tax collector; bus conductor.
rechange [rəʃɑ̃ʒ] *nm* **de rechange** spare; alternative. **rechange de vêtements** change of clothes.
réchapper [reʃape] *v* **réchapper de** come through.
recharger [rəʃarʒe] *v* (*stylo, etc.*) refill; (*fusil, etc.*) reload; (*batterie*) recharge. **recharge** *nf* refill.

réchaud [reʃo] *nm* stove.
réchauffer [reʃofe] *v* warm up; (*cuisine*) reheat.
rêche [rɛʃ] *adj* rough, harsh.
rechercher [rəʃɛrʃe] *v* seek; (*chercher*) search for; (*viser*) strive for, pursue; (*s'informer*) inquire into. **recherche** *nf* search; pursuit; investigation; (*université*) research. **à la recherche de** in search of. **recherché** *adj* in demand; (*soigné*) meticulous; (*péj*) affected.
rechute [rəʃyt] *nf* relapse.
récif [resif] *nm* reef.
récipient [resipjɑ̃] *nm* container, receptacle.
réciproque [resiprɔk] *adj* reciprocal, mutual.
réciter [resite] *v* recite. **récit** *nm* story, account. **récital** *nm* recital. **récitation** *nf* recitation.
réclamer [reklame] *v* (*demander*) ask for, call for; (*protester*) complain; (*droit, etc.*) claim. **réclamation** *nf* complaint. **réclame** *nf* (*annonce*) advertisement; (*publicité*) advertising. **en réclame** on offer. **faire de la réclame** advertise.
reclus [rəkly], **-e** *nm, nf* recluse. *adj* cloistered.
recoin [rəkwɛ̃] *nm* nook, recess.
récolter [rekɔlte] *v* harvest; collect. **récolte** *nf* harvest, crop; collection.
recommander [rəkɔmɑ̃de] *v* recommend; (*conseiller*) advise; (*poste*) register. **recommandation** *nf* recommendation. **recommandé** *adj* recommended; advisable; registered. **en recommandé** by registered post; (*avec avis de réception*) recorded delivery.
recommencer [rəkɔmɑ̃se] *v* start again.
récompenser [rekɔ̃pɑ̃se] *v* reward. **récompense** *nf* reward.
réconcilier [rekɔ̃silje] *v* reconcile. **réconciliation** *nf* reconciliation.
***reconduire** [rəkɔ̃dɥir] *v* (*raccompagner*) take back; (*renouveler*) renew.
réconforter [rekɔ̃fɔrte] *v* comfort; (*remonter*) fortify. **réconfort** *nm* comfort.
***reconnaître** [rəkɔnɛtrə] *v* recognize; (*avouer*) admit, acknowledge; (*mil*) reconnoitre. **reconnaissable** *adj* recognizable. **reconnaissance** *nf* recognition; acknowledgement; (*mil*) reconnaissance; gratitude. **reconnaissant** *adj* grateful.
reconstituer [rəkɔ̃stitɥe] *v* (*crime*) reconstruct; (*édifice*) restore. **reconstitution** *nf* reconstruction; restoration.
***reconstruire** [rəkɔ̃strɥir] *v* rebuild, reconstruct. **reconstruction** *nf* reconstruction.
record [rəkɔr] *nm* record.
recours [rəkur] *nm* recourse, resort. **avoir recours à** resort to.
***recouvrir** [rəkuvrir] *v* cover.
récréation [rekreɑsjɔ̃] *nf* recreation; (*école*) break.
recrue [rəkry] *nf* recruit.
recruter [rəkryte] *v* recruit. **recrutement** *nm* recruitment.
rectangle [rɛktɑ̃glə] *nm* rectangle, oblong. *adj* right-angled. **rectangulaire** *adj* rectangular, oblong.
rectifier [rɛktifje] *v* rectify, correct; adjust; (*rendre droit*) straighten.
rectitude [rɛktityd] *nf* rectitude.
rectum [rɛktɔm] *nm* rectum.
reçu [rəsy] *adj* accepted; (*candidat*) successful. *nm* receipt.
recueil [rəkœj] *nm* collection; (*poèmes*) anthology. **recueil d'expressions** phrase-book.
***recueillir** [rəkœjir] *v* collect, gather; (*réfugié*) take in; (*enregistrer*) record, take down. **se recueillir** collect one's thoughts. **recueillement** *nm* meditation. **recueilli** *adj* meditative.
reculer [rəkyle] *v* move back; (*fusil*) recoil; (*mil*) retreat; (*diminuer*) decline, subside; (*date, décision*) postpone. **reculer devant** (*hésiter*) shrink from. **recul** *nm* retreat; recoil; decline; postponement; distance. **reculé** *adj* remote. **à reculons** backwards.
récupérer [rekypere] *v* recover; (*ferraille, etc.*) salvage, retrieve; (*heures*) make up. **récupération** *nf* recovery; salvage.
récurer [rekyre] *v* scour.
rédacteur, -trice [redaktœr, -tris] *nm, nf* editor; (*article*) writer. **rédaction** *nf* (*contrat*) drafting; writing; editing; (*personnel*) editorial staff; (*école*) essay.
rédiger [rediʒe] *v* write; (*contrat*) draft, draw up.
***redire** [rədir] *v* repeat. **trouver à redire à** find fault with.
redondant [rədɔ̃dɑ̃] *adj* redundant, superfluous.
redoubler [rəduble] *v* increase, intensify; (*école*) repeat a year.

redouter [rədute] *v* dread, fear. **redoutable** *adj* formidable.
redresser [rədrese] *v* straighten (up); (*relever*) right, set upright; rectify. **se redresser** stand up straight.
***réduire** [redɥir] *v* reduce. **se réduire à** amount to; limit oneself to. **se réduire en** be reduced to. **réduction** *nf* reduction.
réduit [redɥi] *adj* small-scale, miniature; (*prix*) reduced. *nm* tiny room; (*recoin*) recess.
réel [reɛl] *adj* real. *nm* reality.
***refaire** [rəfɛr] *v* do *or* make again; (*pièce, meuble*) do up, renovate. **se refaire** recover.
réfectoire [refɛktwar] *nm* canteen, refectory.
référence [referɑ̃s] *nf* reference. **faire référence à** refer to.
référendum [referɛ̃dɔm] *nm* referendum.
référer [refere] *v* **se référer à** refer to; consult.
réfléchir [refleʃir] *v* reflect; (*penser*) think. **réfléchir à** think over *or* about. **réfléchi** *adj* (*personne*) thoughtful; (*action*) well thought out; (*gramm*) reflexive.
réflecteur [reflɛktœr] *nm* reflector.
reflet [rəflɛ] *nm* reflection; (*lumière*) light, glint.
refléter [rəflete] *v* reflect, mirror.
réflexe [reflɛks] *nm, adj* reflex.
réflexion [reflɛksjɔ̃] *nf* reflection; (*pensée*) thought; remark. **réflexion faite** on second thoughts.
reflux [rəfly] *nm* ebb.
réformer [refɔrme] *v* reform; (*mil*) discharge. **réforme** *nf* reform; (*rel*) reformation; discharge.
refouler [rəfule] *v* force back, repress.
réfracter [refrakte] *v* refract. **réfraction** *nf* refraction.
refrain [rəfrɛ̃] *nm* refrain.
réfrigérer [refriʒere] *v* refrigerate. **réfrigérateur** *nm* refrigerator. **réfrigération** *nf* refrigeration.
refroidir [rəfrwadir] *v* cool (down). **refroidissement** *nm* cooling; (*méd*) chill.
refuge [rəfyʒ] *nm* refuge; (*pour piétons*) traffic island.
se réfugier [refyʒje] *v* take refuge. **réfugié, -e** *nm, nf* refugee.
refuser [rəfyze] *v* refuse; (*client*) turn away. **être refusé (à)** (*examen*) fail. **refus** *nm* refusal.
réfuter [refyte] *v* refute.
regagner [rəgaɲe] *v* regain; (*argent, etc.*) win back; (*temps*) make up; (*lieu*) get back to.
regain [rəgɛ̃] *nm* renewal, revival.
régal [regal] *nm, pl* **-als** delight, treat. **régaler** *v* treat.
regarder [rəgarde] *v* look at; (*action*) watch; concern, regard. **regarder fixement** stare at, gaze at. **regard** *nm* look, glance; expression; (*égout*) manhole. **regard fixe** gaze, stare. **regard furieux** glare.
régate [regat] *nf* regatta.
régent [reʒɑ̃], **-e** *nm, nf* regent. **régence** *nf* regency.
régie [reʒi] *nf* state control.
régime [reʒim] *nm* regime; system; government; (*méd*) diet.
régiment [reʒimɑ̃] *nm* regiment. **régimentaire** *adj* regimental.
région [reʒjɔ̃] *nf* region, area. **régional** *adj* regional.
régir [reʒir] *v* govern. **régisseur** *nm* (*théâtre*) stage manager; (*gérant*) steward.
registre [rəʒistrə] *nm* register.
régler [regle] *v* settle; adjust, regulate; (*papier*) rule. **réglage** *nm* adjustment; (*moteur, TV, etc.*) tuning. **règle** *nf* rule; (*instrument*) ruler. **en règle** (*papiers*) in order. **règle à calcul** slide rule. **règles** *nf pl* (*méd*) period *sing*. **réglé** *adj* regular; (*papier*) lined. **règlement** *nm* settlement; (*règle*) rule. **réglementaire** *adj* regulation; statutory.
réglisse [reglis] *nf* liquorice.
régner [reɲe] *v* reign. **règne** *nm* reign; (*bot, zool*) kingdom.
regret [rəgrɛ] *nm* regret. **regrettable** *adj* regrettable. **regretter** *v* regret; (*personne, pays, etc.*) miss; (*être désolé*) be sorry; deplore.
régulier [regylje] *adj* regular; (*constant*) steady; (*égal*) even. **régularité** *nf* regularity; steadiness; evenness.
réhabiliter [reabilite] *v* rehabilitate; restore to favour. **réhabilitation** *nf* rehabilitation.
rehausser [rəose] *v* (*relever*) raise, make higher; (*beauté, goût, etc.*) enhance, bring out.
rein [rɛ̃] *nm* kidney. **reins** *nm pl* back *sing*.
réincarnation [reɛ̃karnɑsjɔ̃] *nf* reincarnation.

reine [rɛn] *nf* queen. **reine-claude** *nf* greengage.
réintégrer [reɛ̃tegre] *v* reinstate; return to. **réintégration** *nf* reinstatement; return.
rejeter [rəʒte] *v* reject; (*relancer*) throw back; (*lave, déchets, etc.*) throw out; (*expulser*) cast out, expel. **se rejeter sur** fall back on. **rejet** *nm* rejection; expulsion; (*bot*) shoot.
***rejoindre** [rəʒwɛ̃drə] *v* rejoin; join; (*rattraper*) catch up with. **se rejoindre** meet.
réjouir [reʒwir] *v* delight, thrill. **se réjouir** be delighted; rejoice. **réjouissance** *nf* rejoicing. **réjouissant** *adj* amusing; (*nouvelle*) cheerful.
relâcher [rəlɑʃe] *v* relax; (*desserrer*) loosen; (libérer) release. **relâche** *nf* rest, respite; (*théâtre*) closure; (*naut*) port of call. **relâché** *adj* loose; (*discipline*) lax.
relais [rəlɛ] *nm* relay; (*usine*) shift.
relatif [rəlatif] *adj* relative. **relativité** *nf* relativity.
relation [rəlɑsjɔ̃] *nf* relationship; (*connaissance*) acquaintance, connection; (*récit*) account. **relations** *nf pl* relations *pl*.
relayer [rəleje] *v* (*remplacer*) relieve, take over from; (*TV, radio*) relay. **se relayer** take turns.
reléguer [rəlege] *v* relegate. **relégation** *nf* relegation.
relevé [rəlve] *adj* raised, elevated; (*manches*) rolled-up; (*col*) turned-up; (*cuisine*) highly-seasoned. *nm* summary, statement; list; (*facture*) bill. **relevé de compte** bank statement.
relever [rəlve] *v* (*redresser*) pick up, stand up; (*remonter*) raise; (*manche*) roll up; (*chaussette*) pull up; (*col*) turn up; (*cuisine*) season; (*relayer*) relieve; (*faute*) find; (*notes*) take down. **relever de** be a matter for, be the concern of. **relève** *nf* relief. **relève de la garde** changing of the guard.
relief [rəljɛf] *nm* relief. **en relief** in relief; (*en-tête*) embossed; (*phot*) three-dimensional. **mettre en relief** bring out, accentuate.
relier [rəlje] *v* link, connect, (*livre*) bind.
religieux [rəliʒjø] *adj* religious. *nm* monk. **religieuse** *nf* nun.
religion [rəliʒjɔ̃] *nf* religion; (*foi*) faith.
relique [rəlik] *nf* relic.
***relire** [rəlir] *v* re-read.
***reluire** [rəlɥir] *v* shine, gleam. **reluisant** *adj* shiny.
remanier [rəmanje] *v* revise, modify.
se remarier [rəmarje] *v* remarry. **remariage** *nm* remarriage.
remarquer [rəmarke] *v* notice; (*faire une remarque*) remark. **faire remarquer** point out. **remarquable** *adj* remarkable. **remarque** *nf* remark, comment.
remblai [rɑ̃blɛ] *nm* embankment.
rembourrer [rɑ̃bure] *v* stuff, pad. **rembourrage** *nm* stuffing, padding.
rembourser [rɑ̃burse] *v* repay; (*dépenses*) refund, reimburse. **remboursement** *nm* repayment; refund, reimbursement.
remède [rəmɛd] *nm* remedy, cure. **remédier à** *v* remedy.
remercier [rəmɛrsje] *v* thank. **remerciement** *nm* thanks *pl*.
***remettre** [rəmɛtrə] *v* put back; (*donner*) hand over; (*ajourner*) postpone; (*dette, péché*) remit. **se remettre** recover, get better.
réminiscence [reminisɑ̃s] *nf* reminiscence.
remise [rəmiz] *nf* (*rabais*) discount; (*livraison*) delivery; (*grâce*) remission; (*resserre*) shed; (*ajournement*) postponement.
rémission [remisjɔ̃] *nf* remission.
remonter [rəmɔ̃te] *v* go up (again); return, go back; (*cheval*) remount; (*relever*) raise; (*montre*) wind up; (*moral*) cheer up; (*machine, etc.*) reassemble. **remontant** *nm* tonic. **remontée** *nf* ascent, rise.
remords [rəmɔr] *nm* remorse.
remorquer [rəmɔrke] *v* tow. **remorque** *nf* towing; (*câble*) tow-rope; (*véhicule*) trailer. **en remorque** on tow. **remorqueur** *nm* tugboat.
remous [rəmu] *nm* (*eau*) wash, swirl; (*air*) eddy; (*foule*) bustle; (*agitation*) stir.
rempart [rɑ̃par] *nm* rampart.
remplacer [rɑ̃plase] *v* replace; (*acteur, etc.*) stand in for; be a substitute for. **remplaçant, -e** *nm, nf* replacement; substitute; (*sport*) reserve; (*théâtre*) understudy. **remplacement** *nm* replacement; substitution.
rempli [rɑ̃pli] *adj* full. *nm* (*vêtement*) tuck.
remplir [rɑ̃plir] *v* fill; (*à nouveau*) refill; (*devoir*) fulfil; (*travail*) carry out.

remporter [rɑ̃pɔrte] *v* take away; (*victoire*) win; (*prix*) carry off.

remuer [rəmɥe] *v* move; (*tourner*) stir. **remue-ménage** *nm invar* commotion.

rémunérer [remynere] *v* remunerate, pay. **rémunérateur, -trice** *adj* remunerative, lucrative. **rémunération** *nf* remuneration.

renâcler [rənɑkle] *v* (*animal*) snort; (*personne*) grumble.

renaissance [rənɛsɑ̃s] *nf* rebirth.

renard [rənar] *nm* fox.

renchérir [rɑ̃ʃerir] *v* (*prix*) get more expensive; (*ajouter*) add, go further; (*péj*) go one better.

rencontrer [rɑ̃kɔ̃tre] *v* meet; (*trouver*) come across; (*obstacle*) come up against, encounter. **rencontre** *nf* meeting, encounter.

rendez-vous [rɑ̃devu] *nm invar* appointment; (*lieu*) meeting place. **donner rendez-vous à** make an appointment with.

se *rendormir [rɑ̃dɔrmir] *v* go back to sleep.

rendre [rɑ̃drə] *v* return, give back; (*achat*) take *or* send back; render; (*faire*) make; (*mil*) surrender; (*terre*) yield. **se rendre** surrender. **se rendre à** go to. **se rendre compte de** realize. **rendement** *nm* yield, output.

rêne [rɛn] *nf* rein.

renégat [rənega], **-e** *nm, nf* renegade.

renfermer [rɑ̃fɛrme] *v* contain. **renfermé** *adj* withdrawn. **sentir le renfermé** smell stuffy.

renforcer [rɑ̃fɔrse] *v* reinforce, strengthen; intensify. **renforcement** *nm* reinforcement, strengthening; intensification.

renfort [rɑ̃fɔr] *nm* reinforcement. **de** *or* **en renfort** extra, additional. **renforts** *nm pl* supplies *pl*.

se renfrogner [rɑ̃frɔɲe] *v* scowl. **renfrogné** *adj* sullen, sulky.

rengaine [rɑ̃gɛn] *nf* hackneyed expression.

renier [rənje] *v* renounce, deny; repudiate, disown; (*promesse*) go back on. **reniement** *nm* renunciation, denial; repudiation.

renifler [rənifle] *v* sniff. **reniflement** *nm* sniff.

renne [rɛn] *nm* reindeer.

renom [rənɔ̃] *nm* renown, fame. **renommé** *adj* renowned, famous. **renommée** *nf* renown, fame.

renoncer [rənɔ̃se] *v* **renoncer à** give up, renounce, abandon. **renonciation** *nf* renunciation.

renoncule [rənɔ̃kyl] *nf* buttercup.

renouer [rənwe] *v* tie again; (*conversation, etc.*) renew, resume.

renouveler [rənuvle] *v* renew. **se renouveler** recur. **renouvellement** *nm* renewal; recurrence.

rénover [renɔve] *v* renovate; (*méthodes, etc.*) reform. **rénovation** *nf* renovation; restoration.

renseigner [rɑ̃seɲe] *v* inform, give information to. **se renseigner** find out, make inquiries. **renseignements** *nm pl* information *sing*; inquiries *pl*; (*mil*) intelligence *sing*.

rente [rɑ̃t] *nf* pension, allowance. **rentes** *nf pl* private income *sing*. **rentable** *adj* profitable.

rentrer [rɑ̃tre] *v* return, go *or* come back; (*chez soi*) go home; (*entrer*) go in; (*à nouveau*) go back in; (*amener*) bring *or* take in. **rentrer dans** go into; (*voiture*) crash into; be included in. **rentrée** *nf* return; reopening; beginning of school term; (*acteur*) comeback.

renverser [rɑ̃vɛrse] *v* (*faire tomber*) knock over; (*mettre à l'envers*) turn upside down; (*gouvernement*) overthrow; (*inverser*) invert, reverse; (*fam*) stagger, astound. **se renverser** overturn. **renversé** *adj* upside down; inverted. **renversement** *nm* inversion, reversal; overthrow.

***renvoyer** [rɑ̃vwaje] *v* send back; (*employé*) dismiss; (*élève*) expel; (*soldat*) discharge; refer; (*ajourner*) postpone; echo. **renvoi** *nm* dismissal; expulsion; discharge; cross-reference; postponement; (*rot*) belch.

réorganiser [reɔrganize] *v* reorganize. **réorganisation** *nf* reorganization.

repaire [rəpɛr] *nm* den.

répandre [repɑ̃drə] *v* (*renverser*) spill; (*disperser*) scatter; (*étendre*) spread; (*odeur, chaleur, etc.*) give off. **répandu** *adj* widespread.

***reparaître** [rəparɛtrə] *v* reappear.

réparer [repare] *v* mend, repair; correct; (*compenser*) make up for. **réparation** *nf* repair; correction; compensation.

repartie [rəparti] *nf* repartee; (*riposte*) retort.

répartir [repartir] *v* share out, divide up; distribute; (*étaler*) spread. **répartition** *nf* distribution; allocation.
repas [rəpa] *nm* meal. **repas léger** snack.
repasser [rəpase] *v* (*frontière*) go back across; (*souvenir, trait*) go (back) over; (*examen*) resit; (*film, émission*) show again; (*au fer*) iron; (*couteau*) sharpen. **repassage** *nm* ironing; sharpening.
se *repentir [rəpɑ̃tir] *v* repent. **se repentir de** regret, be sorry for. *nm* repentance. **repentant** *adj* repentant.
répercussion [repɛrkysjɔ̃] *nf* repercussion.
répercuter [repɛrkyte] *v* echo; reflect. **se répercuter** reverberate.
repérer [rəpere] *v* locate; (*fam*) spot, discover. **repère** *nm* mark, marker; (*monument, etc.*) landmark.
répertoire [repɛrtwar] *nm* index, list; (*carnet*) notebook; (*théâtre*) repertory; (*chanteur*) repertoire.
répéter [repete] *v* repeat; (*théâtre*) rehearse. **répétiteur, -trice** *nm, nf* tutor. **répétition** *nf* repetition; rehearsal. **répétition générale** dress rehearsal.
répit [repi] *nm* respite.
replacer [rəplase] *v* replace, put back; (*employé*) find a new job for.
replier [rəplije] *v* fold up; (*mil*) withdraw. **se replier** curl up; (*se renfermer*) withdraw. **repli** *nm* fold; withdrawal.
réplique [replik] *nf* reply, retort; counterattack; (*théâtre*) line, cue; (*art*) replica. **répliquer** *v* reply, retort; (*se venger*) retaliate.
répondre [repɔ̃drə] *v* answer, reply; (*réagir*) respond. **répondre de** answer for.
réponse [repɔ̃s] *nf* answer, reply; (*réaction*) response.
reporter[1] [rəpɔrte] *v* (*ramener*) take back; (*différer*) put off, postpone; transfer; copy out. **se reporter à** refer to; (*penser*) think back to.
reporter[2] [rəpɔrtɛr] *nm* reporter. **reportage** *nm* report; (*sport*) commentary.
repos [rəpo] *nm* rest; pause; (*tranquillité*) peace.
reposer[1] [rəpoze] *v* rest; (*être étendu*) lie. **se reposer** rest; (*compter*) rely. **reposant** *adj* restful.
reposer[2] [rəpoze] *v* put back; (*question*) repeat, raise again.
repousser [rəpuse] *v* repulse, repel; (*écarter*) push away; reject; (*différer*) put off, postpone; (*cheveux, etc.*) grow again. **repoussant** *adj* repulsive.
***reprendre** [rəprɑ̃drə] *v* take back; (*récupérer*) recover, get back; (*recommencer*) resume; (*attraper*) recapture; reprimand. **se reprendre** correct onself; (*se ressaisir*) pull oneself together.
représailles [rəprezaj] *nf pl* reprisals *pl*, retaliation *sing*.
représenter [rəprezɑ̃te] *v* represent; (*art*) depict, portray; (*théâtre*) perform. **se représenter** imagine; (*survenir*) occur *or* arise again; (*à un examen*) resit. **représentant, -e** *nm, nf* representative. **représentatif** *adj* representative. **représentation** *nf* representation; performance.
répressif [represif] *adj* repressive. **répression** *nf* repression.
réprimande [reprimɑ̃d] *nf* reprimand. **réprimander** *v* reprimand.
réprimer [reprime] *v* repress, suppress.
reprise [rəpriz] *nf* (*recommencement*) resumption, renewal; (*film, émission*) repeat; (*affaires, etc.*) recovery; (*chaussette*) darn; (*fois*) occasion, time. **à maintes reprises** many times. **repriser** *v* darn.
reprocher [rəprɔʃe] *v* reproach; criticize. **reproche** *nm* reproach.
reproduction [rəprɔdyksjɔ̃] *nf* reproduction.
***reproduire** [rəprɔdɥir] *v* reproduce. **se reproduire** recur.
réprouver [repruve] *v* reprove, condemn.
reptile [rɛptil] *nm* reptile.
républicain [repyblikɛ̃], **-e** *n, adj* republican.
république [repyblik] *nf* republic.
répudier [repydje] *v* repudiate, renounce. **répudiation** *nf* repudiation.
répugnant [repyɲɑ̃] *adj* repugnant, revolting. **répugnance** *nf* repugnance, loathing.
répulsif [repylsif] *adj* repulsive. **répulsion** *nf* repulsion.
réputation [repytasjɔ̃] *nf* reputation, repute. **réputé** *adj* reputable, renowned; (*prétendu*) reputed.
***requérir** [rəkerir] *v* require, call for; (*solliciter*) request.
requête [rəkɛt] *nf* request, petition.
requiem [rekɥijɛm] *nm invar* requiem.
requin [rəkɛ̃] *nm* shark.
requis [rəki] *adj* required, requisite.

réquisition [rekizisjɔ̃] *nf* requisition. **réquisitionner** *v* requisition.
rescapé [rɛskape], **-e** *nm, nf* survivor.
réseau [rezo] *nm* network.
réserver [rezɛrve] *v* reserve; (*mettre de côté*) keep, save; (*destiner*) have in store. **réservation** *nf* reservation. **réserve** *nf* reserve; (*restriction*) reservation; (*provision*) stock; (*entrepôt*) storeroom.
réservoir [rezɛrvwar] *nm* tank; (*étang*) reservoir; (*poissons*) fishpond.
résider [rezide] *v* reside. **résidence** *nf* residence. **résidentiel** *adj* residential.
résidu [rezidy] *nm* residue.
se résigner [reziɲe] *v* resign oneself. **résignation** *nf* resignation.
résilier [rezilje] *v* terminate, cancel.
résille [rezij] *nf* net; (*coiffure*) hairnet.
résine [rezin] *nf* resin.
résister [reziste] *v* **résister à** resist, withstand. **résistance** *nf* resistance. **résistant** *adj* strong, robust.
résolu [rezɔly] *adj* resolute, determined. **résolution** *nf* resolution; solution.
résonner [rezɔne] *v* resonate, resound. **resonance** *nf* resonance.
***résoudre** [rezudrə] *v* resolve; (*problème*) solve.
respect [rɛspɛ] *nm* respect. **respect de soi** self-respect. **respectable** *adj* respectable. **respecter** *v* respect. **respectif** *adj* respective. **respectueux** *adj* respectful.
respirer [rɛspire] *v* breathe. **respiration** *nf* breathing. **respiration artificielle** artificial respiration.
resplendir [rɛsplɑ̃dir] *v* beam, shine, gleam. **resplendissant** *adj* radiant.
responsable [rɛspɔ̃sablə] *adj* responsible. *n(m+f)* (*coupable*) culprit; (*dirigeant*) official. **responsabilité** *nf* responsibility.
resquiller [rɛskije] *v* get in without paying; jump the queue; (*carotter*) wangle.
se ressaisir [rəsezir] *v* pull oneself together.
ressembler [rəsɑ̃blə] *v* **ressembler à** resemble, be like. **se ressembler** be alike. **ressemblance** *nf* resemblance; similarity.
***ressentir** [rəsɑ̃tir] *v* feel. **se ressentir de** (*personne*) feel the effects of; (*travail*) show the effects of. **ressentiment** *nm* resentment.
resserrer [rəsere] *v* tighten.
ressort[1] [rəsɔr] *nm* spring.
ressort[2] [rəsɔr] *nm* scope, province.
***ressortir** [rəsɔrtir] *v* go *or* come out again; (*retirer*) bring *or* take out again; (*se détacher*) stand out. **ressortir de** be the result of.
ressource [rəsurs] *nf* resource; possibility; (*recours*) resort.
ressusciter [resysite] *v* revive; (*rel, péj*) resurrect.
restant [rɛstɑ̃] *adj* remaining. *nm* rest, remainder.
restaurant [rɛstɔrɑ̃] *nm* restaurant.
restaurer [rɛstɔre] *v* restore. **restauration** *nf* restoration.
rester [rɛste] *v* stay, remain; (*subsister*) be left; (*durer*) last. **en rester à** go no further than. **reste** *nm* rest, remainder; (*morceau*) piece left over. **du reste** moreover. **restes** *nm pl* remains *pl*; (*nourriture*) left-overs *pl*.
restituer [rɛstitɥe] *v* restore; (*rendre*) return.
***restreindre** [rɛstrɛ̃drə] *v* restrict, limit.
restriction [rɛstriksjɔ̃] *nf* restriction. **restrictif** *adj* restrictive.
résulter [rezylte] *v* result. **résultat** *nm* result.
résumer [rezyme] *v* summarize, sum up. **résumé** *nm* summary, résumé.
résurrection [rezyrɛksjɔ̃] *nf* resurrection.
rétablir [retablir] *v* restore; (*réintégrer*) reinstate. **se rétablir** (*malade*) recover. **rétablissement** *nm* recovery; restoration.
retard [rətar] *nm* delay; (*personne*) lateness; (*peuple, enfant*) backwardness. **en retard** late. **retardé** *adj* backward. **retarder** *v* delay; (*remettre*) put back; (*montre*) be slow.
***retenir** [rətnir] *v* hold back; (*garder*) keep, retain; (*retarder*) detain; (*réserver*) book; (*contenir*) restrain.
retentir [rətɑ̃tir] *v* ring, resound, echo. **retentissement** *nm* repercussion; effect.
retenue [rətny] *nf* restraint, reserve; (*prélèvement*) deduction; (*école*) detention.
réticent [retisɑ̃] *adj* reticent; hesitant. **réticence** *nf* reservation.
rétif [retif] *adj* restive.
rétine [retin] *nf* retina.
retirer [rətire] *v* remove, withdraw. **se retirer** retire, withdraw.
retomber [rətɔ̃be] *v* fall (again); (*fusée, etc.*) land, come down; (*pendre*) hang down.

rétorquer [retɔrke] *v* retort.
retors [rətɔr] *adj* sly, wily.
retoucher [rətuʃe] *v* touch up; (*vêtement*) alter. **retouche** *nf* alteration.
retour [rətur] *nm* return. **être de retour** be back.
retourner [rəturne] *v* return; (*renverser*) turn over; (*sens opposé*) turn round.
rétracter [retrakte] *v* retract.
retrait [rətrɛ] *nm* withdrawal. **en retrait** set back.
retraite [rətrɛt] *nf* retreat; (*vieux travailleur*) retirement; pension. **prendre sa retraite** retire.
retraité [rətrete], **-e** *adj* retired. *nm*, *nf* pensioner.
retrancher [rətrɑ̃ʃe] *v* deduct, take away; (*couper*) cut out *or* off. **se retrancher** (*mil*) entrench oneself; take refuge.
rétrécir [retresir] *v* (*tissu*) shrink; (*rue*) narrow; (*pupille*) contract. **rétrécissement** *nm* shrinkage; contraction.
rétribuer [retribɥe] *v* pay. **rétribution** *nf* payment.
rétrograder [retrɔgrade] *v* regress, go backward; (*officier*) demote. **rétrogradation** *nf* regression; demotion. **rétrograde** *adj* retrograde, backward.
rétrospectif [retrɔspɛktif] *adj* retrospective. **rétrospectivement** *adv* in retrospect.
retrousser [rətruse] *v* (*manche*) roll up; (*lèvre*) curl up; (*jupe, etc.*) hitch up; (*nez*) turn up.
retrouver [rətruve] *v* find (again); (*personne*) meet, join; (*santé*) regain. **se retrouver** meet up, get together.
rétroviseur [retrɔvizœr] *nm* driving mirror.
réunir [reynir] *v* collect, gather (together); join; (*ennemis, anciens amis*) reunite. **se réunir** unite; (*amis*) get together. **réunion** *nf* (*séance*) meeting; reunion; collection.
réussir [reysir] *v* succeed. **réussir à** succeed in; (*examen*) pass; (*air, nourriture*) agree with. **réussi** *adj* successful. **réussite** *nf* success; (*cartes*) patience.
revanche [rəvɑ̃ʃ] *nf* revenge. **en revanche** (*au contraire*) on the other hand; (*en retour*) in return.
rêvasser [rɛvase] *v* daydream.
rêve [rɛv] *nm* dream.
revêche [rəvɛʃ] *adj* surly.
réveiller [reveje] *v* wake (up); (*raviver*) rouse, reawaken, revive. **se réveiller** wake up, awake. **réveil** *nm* waking; (*à la réalité*) awakening; (*pendule*) alarm clock. **réveillé** *adj* awake.
révéler [revele] *v* reveal. **révélateur, -trice** *adj* revealing. **révélation** *nf* revelation.
revendiquer [rəvɑ̃dike] *v* claim, demand. **revendication** *nf* claim, demand.
***revenir** [rəvnir] *v* come back, return. **revenir à** come to, amount to. **revenir à soi** come round. **revenir de** get over. **revenir sur** (*promesse*) go back on; (*passé*) go back over. **revenant, -e** *nm*, *nf* ghost. **revenu** *nm* income, revenue.
rêver [reve] *v* dream. **rêverie** *nf* daydream. **rêveur, -euse** *adj* dreamy.
réverbérer [reverbere] *v* reverberate, reflect. **réverbération** *nf* reverberation. **réverbère** *nm* street lamp.
révérence [reverɑ̃s] *nf* (*homme*) bow; (*femme*) curtsy; (*respect*) reverence. **faire une révérence** bow; curtsy.
revers [rəvɛr] *nm* back; (*monnaie*) reverse; (*tissu*) wrong side; (*veste*) lapel; (*manche*) cuff. **réversible** *adj* reversible.
***revêtir** [rəvetir] *v* assume, take on; (*habiller*) clothe; cover, coat. **revêtement** *nm* covering, coating; surface.
revirement [rəvirmɑ̃] *nm* sudden change, reversal.
réviser [revize] *v* revise; (*examiner*) review; (*voiture, machine*) service, overhaul. **révision** *nf* revision; review; service.
***revivre** [rəvivrə] *v* relive. **faire revivre** revive.
***revoir** [rəvwar] *v* see again; revise. **au revoir!** goodbye!
révolter [revɔlte] *v* revolt, outrage. **se révolter** revolt, rebel. **révolte** *nf* revolt, rebellion.
révolution [revɔlysjɔ̃] *nf* revolution. **révolutionnaire** *n(m+f)*, *adj* revolutionary. **révolutionner** *v* revolutionize.
revolver [revɔlvɛr] *nm* gun, revolver.
révoquer [revɔke] *v* revoke; (*destituer*) dismiss.
revue [rəvy] *nf* review; (*spectacle*) revue; magazine; (*mil*) inspection.
rez-de-chaussée [redʃose] *nm invar* ground floor.
rhésus [rezys] *nm* rhesus. **rhésus négatif/positif** rhesus negative/positive.
rhétorique [retɔrik] *nf* rhetoric. *adj* rhetorical.

rhinocéros [rinɔserɔs] *nm* rhinoceros.
rhododendron [rɔdɔdɛ̃drɔ̃] *nm* rhododendron.
rhubarbe [rybarb] *nf* rhubarb.
rhum [rɔm] *nm* rum.
rhumatisme [rymatismə] *nm* rheumatism. **rhumatismal** *adj* rheumatic.
rhume [rym] *nm* cold. **rhume des foins** hay fever.
riant [rjɑ̃] *adj* cheerful, smiling.
ricaner [rikane] *v* snigger, sneer. **ricanement** *nm* snigger, sneer.
riche [riʃ] *adj* rich. *n(m+f)* rich person. **richesse** *nf* richness; (*argent*) wealth; abundance. **richesses** *nf pl* riches *pl*.
ride [rid] *nf* (*peau*) wrinkle; (*eau*) ripple. **rider** *v* wrinkle; ripple.
rideau [rido] *nm* curtain; (*écran*) screen. **rideau de fer** Iron Curtain.
ridicule [ridikyl] *adj* ridiculous. *nm* ridicule; absurdity. **ridiculiser** *v* ridicule.
rien [rjɛ̃] *pron* nothing; (*quelque chose*) anything. **ça ne fait rien** (*fam*) it doesn't matter. **de rien** (*fam*) not at all, you're welcome. **ne . . . rien** nothing. *nm* nothing; (*bagatelle*) trivial thing; (*goutte*) touch, hint.
rigide [riʒid] *adj* rigid, stiff; strict. **rigidité** *nf* rigidity, stiffness; strictness.
rigole [rigɔl] *nf* channel; (*d'écoulement*) drain; (*sillon*) furrow.
rigoler [rigɔle] (*fam*) *v* (*plaisanter*) joke; (*rire*) laugh; (*s'amuser*) have fun. **rigolo, -ote** *adj* funny, comical.
rigoureux [rigurø] *adj* rigorous, (*sévère*) harsh; strict.
rigueur [rigœr] *nf* rigour; (*sévérité*) harshness; strictness; precision. **à la rigueur** if need be; possibly. **de rigueur** compulsory; (*étiquette*) the done thing.
rime [rim] *nf* rhyme. **rimer** *v* rhyme.
rincer [rɛ̃se] *v* rinse. **rinçage** *nm* rinse.
riposter [ripɔste] *v* retort; (*contre-attaquer*) retaliate. **riposte** *nf* retort.
***rire** [rir] *v* laugh; (*plaisanter*) joke; (*s'amuser*) have fun. **se rire de** laugh at. *nm* laugh; (*éclat*) laughter. **petit rire** chuckle. **petit rire nerveux** giggle.
ris [ri] *nm* **ris de veau** sweetbread.
risée [rize] *nf* ridicule; (*personne*) laughing stock.
risquer [riske] *v* risk. **risquer de** may well. **risque-tout** *n(m+f) invar* daredevil. **se risquer** venture. **risque** *nm* risk. **risqué** *adj* risky; (*licencieux*) risqué.
ristourne [risturn] *nf* rebate, refund.
rite [rit] *nm* rite.
rituel [ritɥɛl] *nm, adj* ritual.
rival [rival], **-e** *n, adj* rival.
rivaliser [rivalize] *v* **rivaliser avec** rival, vie with. **rivalité** *nf* rivalry.
rive [riv] *nf* (*mer*) shore; (*rivière*) bank. **rivage** *nm* shore.
river [rive] *v* rivet; (*lier*) bind. **rivet** *nm* rivet.
rivière [rivjɛr] *nf* river.
rixe [riks] *nf* brawl.
riz [ri] *nm* rice. **riz au lait** rice pudding.
robe [rɔb] *nf* dress; (*magistrat*) robe; (*professeur*) gown; (*peau*) skin. **robe-chasuble** *nf* pinafore dress. **robe de chambre** dressing-gown. **robe de grossesse** maternity dress, smock. **robe de mariée** wedding dress. **robe du soir** evening dress.
robinet [rɔbinɛ] *nm* tap.
robot [rɔbo] *nm* robot.
robuste [rɔbyst] *adj* robust.
roc [rɔk] *nm* rock. **rocaille** *nf* (*jardin*) rockery.
roche [rɔʃ] *nf* rock. **rocher** *nm* rock; (*gros bloc*) boulder.
roder [rɔde] *v* (*auto*) run in. **en rodage** running in.
rôder [rode] *v* (*en maraude*) prowl; (*au hasard*) roam. **rôdeur, -euse** *nm, nf* prowler.
rogner [rɔɲe] *v* trim, clip; (*dépense*) whittle down.
rognon [rɔɲɔ̃] *nm* kidney.
rogue [rɔg] *adj* haughty, arrogant.
roi [rwa] *nm* king. **la fête des Rois** Twelfth Night.
roitelet [rwatlɛ] *nm* wren.
rôle [rol] *nm* role, part; (*liste*) roll.
romain [rɔmɛ̃] *adj* Roman. **Romain, -e** *nm, nf* Roman.
roman[1] [rɔmɑ̃] *nm* novel; (*récit*) story. **roman-feuilleton** *nm* serial. **roman policier** detective story. **romans** *nm pl* fiction *sing*. **romancier, -ère** *nm, nf* novelist.
roman[2] [rɔmɑ̃] *adj* (*langue*) Romance; (*arch*) Romanesque.
romanesque [rɔmanɛsk] *adj* (*personne*) romantic; (*récit*) fantastic; (*amour*) storybook.
romantique [rɔmɑ̃tik] *n(m+f)*, *adj* romantic.

romarin [rɔmarɛ̃] *nm* rosemary.
Rome [rɔm] *n* Rome.
rompre [rɔ̃prə] *v* break. **rompu** *adj* broken; (*fatigué*) exhausted. **rompu à** experienced in.
romsteck [rɔmstɛk] *nm* rump steak.
ronce [rɔs] *nf* bramble; (*mûrier*) blackberry bush.
rond [rɔ̃] *adj* round; (*gras*) chubby, plump; (*fam*) drunk. **rond-de-cuir** *nm* clerk. **rond-point** *nm* roundabout. *nm* ring; (*tranche*) slice. **en rond** in a circle. **ronde** *nf* patrol, rounds *pl*; (*musique*) semibreve. **rondelle** *nf* washer; disc. **rondement** *adv* (*promptement*) briskly; frankly. **rondeur** *nf* roundness; plumpness. **rondin** *nm* log.
ronfler [rɔ̃fle] *v* snore; (*rugir*) roar; (*vrombir*) hum. **ronflement** *nm* snore; roar; hum.
ronger [rɔ̃ʒe] *v* gnaw at, eat into; (*malade*) sap. **se ronger les ongles** bite one's nails. **rongeur** *nm* rodent.
ronronner [rɔ̃rɔne] *v* purr. **ronron** *or* **ronronnement** *nm* purr.
roquet [rɔkɛ] *nm* ill-tempered little dog.
roquette [rɔkɛt] *nf* rocket.
rosaire [rozɛr] *nm* rosary.
rosbif [rɔsbif] *nm* roast beef.
rose [roz] *nf* rose. *nm* pink. *adj* pink; (*joues*) rosy. **roseraie** *nf* rose garden. **rosier** *nm* rose-bush.
roseau [rozo] *nm* reed.
rosée [roze] *nf* dew.
rosette [rozɛt] *nf* rosette; (*nœud*) bow.
rosser [rɔse] *v* thrash. **rossée** *nf* (*fam*) thrashing, hiding.
rossignol [rɔsiɲɔl] *nm* nightingale; (*fam*) piece of junk.
rot [ro] (*fam*) *nm* burp. **roter** *v* burp.
rotatif [rɔtatif] *adj* rotary.
rôtir [rotir] *v* roast. **rôti** *nm* joint, roast. **rôtisserie** *nf* steak-house.
rotor [rɔtɔr] *nm* rotor.
rotule [rɔtyl] *nf* kneecap.
rouage [rwaʒ] *nm* cog; part. **rouages** *nm pl* works *pl*.
roublard [rublar] *adj* (*fam*) crafty, wily.
roucouler [rukule] *v* coo. **roucoulement** *nm* coo.
roue [ru] *nf* wheel. **faire la roue** (*se pavaner*) strut about; (*gymnaste*) do a cart-wheel. **roue de secours** spare wheel.
roué [rwe] *adj* cunning.
rouge [ruʒ] *adj* red. **rouge-gorge** *nm* robin. *nm* red; (*fard*) rouge. **rouge à lèvres** lipstick. **rougeur** *nf* redness; (*visage*) flush, flushing; (*de gêne, honte*) blush, blushing.
rougeole [ruʒɔl] *nf* measles.
rougir [ruʒir] *v* go *or* turn red, redden; (*visage*) flush; (*de gêne, honte*) blush.
rouiller [ruje] *v* rust, go rusty. **rouille** *nf* rust. **rouillé** *adj* rusty.
rouleau [rulo] *nm* roller; (*papier, pellicule, tabac, etc.*) roll; (*parchemin*) scroll. **rouleau à pâtisserie** rolling pin. **rouleau compresseur** steam-roller. **rouleau de papier hygiénique** toilet roll.
rouler [rule] *v* roll; (*enrouler*) roll up; (*pousser*) wheel; (*aller*) go, run; (*conduire*) drive; (*fam: duper*) con, diddle. **roulant** *adj* moving; (*meuble*) on wheels; (*argot*) hilarious. **roulement** *nm* roll; movement; (*bruit*) rumble. **roulement à billes** ball bearings *pl*. **roulette** *nf* castor; (*jeu*) roulette.
roulotte [rulɔt] *nf* caravan.
Roumanie [rumani] *nf* Romania. **roumain** *nm, adj* Romanian. **Roumain, -e** *nm, nf* Romanian.
roupiller [rupije] (*fam*) *v* snooze. **roupillon** *nm* snooze.
rouquin [rukɛ̃], **-e** (*fam*) *nm, nf* redhead. *adj* red-haired.
rouspéter [ruspete] *v* (*fam*) moan, grumble.
roussir [rusir] *v* (*brûler*) scorch, singe; (*feuilles*) go brown. **rousseur** *nf* redness.
route [rut] *nf* road; (*chemin*) way; (*ligne*) route. **en route** on the way. **en route pour** bound for. **se mettre en route** set off. **routier** *adj* road.
routine [rutin] *nf* routine. **routinier** *adj* humdrum, routine.
***rouvrir** [ruvrir] *v* reopen.
roux, rousse [ru, rus] *adj* reddish-brown; (*cheveux*) red, auburn, ginger. *nm, nf* redhead.
royal [rwajal] *adj* royal; majestic, regal. **royaliste** *n*(*m*+*f*), *adj* royalist. **royauté** *nf* royalty; monarchy.
royaume [rwajom] *nm* kingdom, realm. **Royaume-Uni** *nm* United Kingdom.
ruban [rybɑ̃] *nm* ribbon; band, tape.
rubéole [rybeɔl] *nf* German measles.
rubis [rybi] *nm* ruby.
rubrique [rybrik] *nf* (*article*) column; (*titre*) heading.

ruche [ryʃ] *nf* hive.
rude [ryd] *adj* (*pénible, dur*) hard, harsh; (*surface*) rough; (*grossier*) crude. **rudement** *adv* harshly; roughly; (*fam*) terribly, awfully. **rudesse** *nf* harshness; roughness; crudeness.
rudiment [rydimɑ̃] *nm* rudiment. **rudimentaire** *adj* rudimentary.
rudoyer [rydwaje] *v* treat roughly.
rue [ry] *nf* street. **rue à sens unique** one-way street. **ruelle** *nf* alley.
ruer [rɥe] *v* kick out. **se ruer** dash, rush, hurl oneself. **se ruer sur** pounce on. **ruée** *nf* rush, stampede.
rugby [rygbi] *nm* rugby.
rugir [ryʒir] *v* roar. **rugissement** *nm* roar.
rugueux [rygø] *adj* rough. **rugosité** *nf* roughness.
ruine [rɥin] *nf* ruin. **ruiner** *v* ruin.
ruisseau [rɥiso] *nm* stream; (*caniveau*) gutter.
ruisseler [rɥisle] *v* stream.
rumeur [rymœr] *nf* (*nouvelle*) rumour; (*son*) murmur, hum, hubbub.
rupture [ryptyr] *nf* rupture, break. **rupture de contrat** breach of contract.
rural [ryral] *adj* rural, country.
ruse [ryz] *nf* (*procédé*) trick, ruse; (*art*) cunning, guile. **ruses de guerre** tactics *pl*. **rusé** *adj* sly, cunning.
Russie [rysi] *nf* Russia. **russe** *nm, adj* Russian. **Russe** *n(m+f)* Russian.
rustique [rystik] *adj* rustic.
rustre [rystrə] *nm* lout.
rutabaga [rytabaga] *nm* swede.
rythme [ritmə] *nm* rhythm; (*vitesse*) rate. **rythmé** *or* **rythmique** *adj* rhythmic.

S

s' [s] *V* **se, si**[1].
sa [sa] *V* **son**[1].
sabbat [saba] *nm* sabbath.
sable[1] [sɑblə] *nm* sand. **sables mouvants** quicksands *pl*. **sabler** *v* sand. **sableux** *or* **sablonneux** *adj* sandy. **sablier** *nm* hourglass.
sable[2] [sɑblə] *nm* sable.
sablé [sɑble] *nm* shortbread.
saborder [sabɔrde] *v* scuttle.
sabot [sabo] *nm* (*chaussure*) clog; (*animal*) hoof.
saboter [sabɔte] *v* sabotage. **sabotage** *nm* sabotage. **saboteur, -euse** *nm, nf* saboteur.
sabre [sɑbrə] *nm* sabre.
sac [sak] *nm* bag; (*à charbon, etc.*) sack. **sac à dos** rucksack. **sac à main** handbag. **sac à provisions** shopping bag. **sac de couchage** sleeping bag.
saccade [sakad] *nf* jerk. **par saccades** jerkily, in fits and starts. **saccadé** *adj* jerky.
saccager [sakaʒe] *v* wreck, devastate; (*piller*) ransack. **saccage** *nm* havoc.
saccharine [sakarin] *nf* saccharin.
sacerdoce [sasɛrdɔs] *nm* priesthood.
sachet [saʃɛ] *nm* sachet; (*bonbons*) bag. **sachet de thé** tea-bag.
sacoche [sakɔʃ] *nf* bag; (*cycliste*) saddle-bag; (*écolier*) satchel.
sacquer [sake] (*fam*) *v* sack; (*recaler*) fail.
sacrement [sakrəmɑ̃] *nm* sacrament.
sacrer [sakre] *v* consecrate; (*roi*) crown; (*fam*) swear. **sacre** *nm* consecration; (*roi*) coronation. **sacré** *adj* sacred; (*fam*) blasted, damned.
sacrifier [sakrifje] *v* sacrifice. **sacrifice** *nm* sacrifice.
sacrilège [sakrilɛʒ] *nm* sacrilege *adj* sacrilegious.
sacristie [sakristi] *nf* vestry.
sadique [sadik] *adj* sadistic. *n(m+f)* sadist. **sadisme** *nm* sadism.
safari [safari] *nm* safari.
safran [safrɑ̃] *nm* saffron.
saga [saga] *nf* saga.
sagace [sagas] *adj* shrewd. **sagacité** *nf* shrewdness.
sage [saʒ] *adj* wise, sensible; (*enfant*) good; moderate. **sage-femme** *nf* midwife. **sois sage!** be good! behave yourself! *nm* wise man, sage. **sagesse** *nf* wisdom; good behaviour; moderation.
Sagittaire [saʒitɛr] *nm* Sagittarius.
sagou [sagu] *nm* sago.
saigner [seɲe] *v* bleed. **saignant** *adj* bleeding; (*viande*) rare, underdone.
saillir [sajir] *v* jut out, protrude. **saillant** *adj* prominent, protruding; (*frappant*) outstanding. **saillie** *nf* projection; (*boutade*) witticism. **en saillie** overhanging.
sain [sɛ̃] *adj* healthy; (*d'esprit*) sane;

(*robuste*) sound. **sain et sauf** safe and sound.
saindoux [sɛ̃du] *nm* lard.
saint [sɛ̃], **-e** *adj* holy; pious, saintly. *nm, nf* saint. **Saint-Esprit** *nm* Holy Spirit. **Saint-Jean** *nm* Midsummer Day. **saint patron** patron saint. **Saint-Sylvestre** *nf* New Year's Eve. **sainteté** *nf* holiness, sanctity; saintliness.
saisir [sezir] *v* seize, take hold of; (*comprendre*) grasp; (*serrer*) grip. **saisie** *nf* seizure; capture. **saisissant** *adj* (*spectacle*) gripping; (*frappant*) striking; (*froid*) biting. **saisissement** *nm* (*frisson*) shiver; rush of emotion.
saison [sɛzɔ̃] *nf* season. **hors de saison** out of season; (*prix*) low-season. **saisonnier** *adj* seasonal.
salade [salad] *nf* salad; (*laitue*) lettuce; (*fam*) muddle.
salaire [salɛr] *nm* pay; (*à la semaine*) wages *pl*; (*au mois*) salary; (*récompense*) reward.
salami [salami] *nm* salami.
salaud [salo] *nm* (*impol*) bastard, sod.
sale [sal] *adj* dirty; (*fam*) nasty, lousy. **saleté** *nf* dirt; obscenity; (*sale tour*) dirty trick; (*fam*: *camelote*) rubbish.
saler [sale] *v* salt; (*fam*) do, overcharge. **salé** *adj* salty; salted; (*fam*: *grivois*) spicy; (*fam*: *sévère*) stiff, steep. **salière** *nf* salt-cellar.
salin [salɛ̃] *adj* saline. **salinité** *nf* salinity.
salir [salir] *v* dirty, soil; corrupt, sully. **se salir** get dirty; tarnish one's reputation.
salive [saliv] *nf* saliva. **salivaire** *adj* salivary. **saliver** *v* salivate.
salle [sal] *nf* room; hall; auditorium; (*hôpital*) ward. **salle à manger** dining room. **salle d'attente** waiting room. **salle de bain** bathroom. **salle de bal** ballroom. **salle de classe** classroom. **salle de séjour** living room. **salle des professeurs** staffroom. **salle d'opération** operating theatre.
saloperie [salɔpri] (*argot*) *nf* (*camelote*) rubbish; (*ordure*) muck; (*sale tour*) dirty trick.
salopette [salɔpɛt] *nf* (*ouvrier*) overalls *pl*; (*enfant, femme*) dungarees *pl*; (*ski*) salopette.
saltimbanque [saltɛ̃bɑ̃k] *n*(*m*+*f*) acrobat, member of travelling circus.
salubre [salybrə] *adj* healthy.
saluer [salɥe] *v* greet; (*mil*) salute; (*acteur*) bow; (*acclamer*) hail.
salut [saly] *nm* (*mil*) salute; (*salutation*) greeting; (*révérence*) bow; (*sécurité*) safety; (*rel*) salvation. *interj* (*fam*: *bonjour*) hi! (*fam*: *au revoir*) bye! **salutation** *nf* greeting.
salutaire [salytɛr] *adj* salutary, beneficial; profitable; (*sain*) healthy.
samedi [samdi] *nm* Saturday.
sanatorium [sanatɔrjɔm] *nm* sanatorium.
sanctifier [sɑ̃ktifje] *v* hallow, sanctify. **sanctification** *nf* sanctification.
sanction [sɑ̃ksjɔ̃] *nf* sanction; (*peine*) punishment, penalty. **sanctionner** *v* sanction; punish.
sanctuaire [sɑ̃ktɥɛr] *nm* sanctuary.
sandale [sɑ̃dal] *nf* sandal.
sandwich [sɑ̃dwitʃ] *nm* sandwich.
sang [sɑ̃] *nm* blood. **à sang chaud/froid** warm-/cold-blooded. **sang-froid** *nm invar* calmness, coolness. **sang-mêlé** *n*(*m*+*f*) *invar* half-caste.
sanglant [sɑ̃glɑ̃] *adj* bloody; (*visage, habit, etc.*) covered in blood; cruel.
sangle [sɑ̃glə] *nf* strap; (*selle*) girth. **sangler** *v* strap up.
sanglier [sɑ̃glije] *nm* boar.
sanglot [sɑ̃glo] *nm* sob. **sangloter** *v* sob.
sangsue [sɑ̃sy] *nf* leech.
sanguin [sɑ̃gɛ̃] *adj* blood; (*visage*) ruddy; (*tempérament*) fiery. **sanguinaire** *adj* bloodthirsty.
sanitaire [sanitɛr] *adj* sanitary.
sans [sɑ̃] *prep* without; but for. **sans-abri** *n*(*m*+*f*) *invar* homeless person. **sans ça** or else. **sans faute** without fail. **sans-gêne** *adj invar* offhand. **sans quoi** otherwise. **sans-souci** *adj invar* carefree.
sansonnet [sɑ̃sɔnɛ] *nm* starling.
santé [sɑ̃te] *nf* health. **à votre santé!** cheers!
saper [sape] *v* undermine, sap.
sapeur [sapœr] *nm* (*mil*) sapper. **sapeur-pompier** *nm* fireman.
saphir [safir] *nm* sapphire.
sapin [sapɛ̃] *nm* fir.
sarcasme [sarkasmə] *nm* sarcasm. **sarcastique** *adj* sarcastic.
sarcler [sarkle] *v* weed. **sarclage** *nm* weeding.
Sardaigne [sardɛɲ] *nf* Sardinia. **sarde** *nm, adj* Sardinian. **Sarde** *n*(*m*+*f*) Sardinian.
sardine [sardin] *nf* sardine.
sardonique [sardɔnik] *adj* sardonic.

Satan [satɑ̃] *nm* Satan. **satanique** *adj* satanic.
satellite [satelit] *nm* satellite.
satin [satɛ̃] *nm* satin.
satire [satir] *nf* satire. **faire la satire de** satirize. **satirique** *adj* satirical.
satisfaction [satisfaksjɔ̃] *nf* satisfaction.
***satisfaire** [satisfɛr] *v* satisfy. **satisfaire à** satisfy; (*condition*) fulfil. **satisfaisant** *adj* satisfactory. **satisfait** *adj* satisfied.
saturer [satyre] *v* saturate. **saturation** *nf* saturation.
sauce [sos] *nf* sauce; (*jus de viande*) gravy.
saucée [sose] *nf* (*fam*) downpour.
saucisse [sosis] *nf* sausage. **saucisson** *nm* large sausage.
sauf [sof] *adj* unharmed; intact. *prep* except, but; (*à moins de*) unless.
sauge [soʒ] *nf* sage.
saugrenu [sogrəny] *adj* ludicrous.
saule [sol] *nm* willow.
saumon [somɔ̃] *nm* salmon.
saumure [somyr] *nf* brine.
sauna [sona] *nm* sauna.
saupoudrer [sopudre] *v* sprinkle. **saupoudreuse** *nf* dredger.
saut [so] *nm* jump, leap. **saut à la corde** skipping. **saut-de-lit** *nm invar* housecoat. **saut-de-mouton** *nm* flyover. **saut en hauteur/longueur** high/long jump. **saut périlleux** somersault.
sauter [sote] *v* jump, leap; explode; (*fusible*) blow; (*omettre*) skip. **faire sauter** (*mine, etc.*) blow up; (*crêpe*) toss. **saute-mouton** *nm* leapfrog. **saute** *nf* sudden change. **sauté** *adj* sauté. **sauterelle** *nf* grasshopper. **sauterie** *nf* party.
sautiller [sotije] *v* hop; (*enfant*) skip.
sauvage [sovaʒ] *adj* wild; (*brutal, primitif*) savage; unsociable. *n*(*m*+*f*) savage; recluse. **sauvagerie** *nf* savagery.
sauvegarder [sovgarde] *v* safeguard. **sauvegarde** *nf* safeguard.
sauver [sove] *v* save, rescue; (*récupérer*) salvage. **sauve-qui-peut** *nm invar* stampede. **se sauver** run away. **sauvetage** *nm* rescue; (*technique*) life-saving; salvage. **sauveur** *nm* saviour.
savant [savɑ̃] *adj* learned, scholarly; (*habile*) skilful; (*chien*) performing. *nm* scholar; scientist.
savate [savat] (*fam*) *nf* old shoe *or* slipper; (*maladroit*) clumsy oaf.
saveur [savœr] *nf* (*goût*) flavour; (*piment*) savour.
***savoir** [savwar] *v* know; (*être capable de*) know how to. **à savoir** namely, that is. **faire savoir à** inform. **sans le savoir** unknowingly. *nm* learning, knowledge.
savon [savɔ̃] *nm* soap. **savonner** *v* soap, lather. **savonneux** *adj* soapy.
savourer [savure] *v* savour. **savoureux** *adj* tasty; (*histoire*) spicy.
saxophone [saksɔfɔn] *nm* saxophone.
scabreux [skabrø] *adj* indecent, shocking; risky.
scandale [skɑ̃dal] *nm* scandal; scene, fuss. **scandaleux** *adj* scandalous. **scandaliser** *v* scandalize, shock.
Scandinavie [skɑ̃dinavi] *nf* Scandinavia. **scandinave** *adj* Scandinavian. **Scandinave** *n*(*m*+*f*) Scandinavian.
scaphandrier [skafɑ̃drije] *nm* diver.
scarlatine [skarlatin] *nf* scarlet fever.
sceau [so] *nm* seal; (*marque*) stamp.
scélérat [selera], **-e** *nm*, *nf* villain. *adj* wicked.
sceller [sele] *v* seal.
scénario [senarjo] *nm* scenario; (*dialogue, etc.*) screenplay.
scène [sɛn] *nf* scene; (*estrade, profession*) stage. **mettre en scène** present; (*pièce*) stage; (*film*) direct. **scénique** *adj* theatrical.
sceptique [sɛptik] *adj* sceptical. *n*(*m*+*f*) sceptic. **scepticisme** *nm* scepticism.
sceptre [sɛptrə] *nm* sceptre.
schéma [ʃema] *nm* diagram; (*résumé*) outline.
schizophrénie [skizɔfreni] *nf* schizophrenia. **schizophrène** *n*(*m*+*f*), *adj* schizophrenic.
sciatique [sjatik] *nf* sciatica. *adj* sciatic.
scie [si] *nf* saw; (*péj: personne*) bore. **scie à découper** fretsaw. **scie à métaux** hacksaw.
sciemment [sjamɑ̃] *adv* knowingly.
science [sjɑ̃s] *nf* science; (*savoir*) knowledge. **science-fiction** *nf* science fiction.
scientifique [sjɑ̃tifik] *adj* scientific. *n*(*m*+*f*) scientist.
scintiller [sɛ̃tije] *v* sparkle, glitter; (*esprit*) scintillate.
scolaire [skɔlɛr] *adj* school, scholastic. **scolarité** *nf* schooling.
scooter [skutœr] *nm* scooter.
scorpion [skɔrpjɔ̃] *nm* scorpion. **Scorpion** *nm* Scorpio.

scotch[1] [skɔtʃ] *nm* (*boisson*) Scotch.
scotch[2] ® [skɔtʃ] *nm* sellotape ®
scrupule [skrypyl] *nm* scruple. **sans scrupules** *adj* unscrupulous. **scrupuleux** *adj* scrupulous.
scruter [skryte] *v* scrutinize, examine.
scrutin [skrytɛ̃] *nm* (*vote*) ballot; (*élection*) poll.
sculpter [skylte] *v* sculpt. **sculpteur** *nm* sculptor. **sculpture** *nf* sculpture.
se [sə], **s'** *pron* (*réfléchi*) oneself; (*homme*) himself; (*femme*) herself; (*chose, animal*) itself; (*au pluriel*) themselves; (*réciproque*) each other.
séance [seɑ̃s] *nf* session; (*réunion*) meeting; (*théâtre*) performance.
séant [seɑ̃] *nm* (*fam*) behind, posterior. *adj* seemly.
seau [so] *nm* bucket.
sec, sèche [sɛk, sɛʃ] *adj* dry; (*raisin, etc.*) dried; (*maigre*) lean; (*dur*) hard, cold; (*bref*) curt; (*alcool*) neat. *nm* **à sec** dried-up; (*fam*) broke. **au sec** in a dry place. *nf* (*argot*) fag. *adv* hard. **sécheresse** *nf* dryness; hardness; coldness; curtness.
sécher [seʃe] *v* dry. **sèche-cheveux** *nm invar* hair-drier. **séchoir** *nm* drier. **séchoir à linge** clothes-horse.
second [səgɔ̃] *adj* second. *nm* second; (*étage*) second floor. **seconde** *nf* second; (*transport*) second class. **secondaire** *adj* secondary.
secouer [səkwe] *v* shake.
***secourir** [səkurir] *v* help.
secours [səkur] *nm* help, aid; (*mil*) relief. **au secours!** help! **de secours** (*de rechange*) spare; (*d'urgence*) emergency.
secousse [səkus] *nf* jolt, bump; shock; (*saccade*) jerk. **par secousses** jerkily.
secret, -ète [səkrɛ, -ɛt] *adj* secret; (*caché*) hidden. *nm* secret; (*silence, discrétion*) secrecy. **en secret** secretly, in secret.
secrétaire [səkretɛr] *n(m+f)* secretary. *nm* (*meuble*) writing desk.
sécréter [sekrete] *v* secrete. **sécrétion** *nf* secretion.
secte [sɛkt] *nf* sect. **sectaire** *adj* sectarian.
secteur [sɛktœr] *nm* sector; (*zone*) area; (*élec*) mains (supply).
section [sɛksjɔ̃] *nf* section; (*autobus*) fare stage.
séculaire [sekylɛr] *adj* a hundred years old; (*très vieux*) age-old; (*jeux, fête, etc.*) occurring once a century.
séculier [sekylje] *adj* secular.
sécurité [sekyrite] *nf* security; (*sûreté*) safety.
sédatif [sedatif] *nm, adj* sedative. **sédation** *nf* sedation.
sédiment [sedimɑ̃] *nm* sediment.
***séduire** [sedɥir] *v* seduce; (*attirer*) charm; (*plaire*) appeal to. **séduction** *nf* seduction; charm; appeal. **séduisant** *adj* seductive; appealing, attractive.
segment [sɛgmɑ̃] *nm* segment.
ségrégation [segregasjɔ̃] *nf* segregation.
seigle [sɛglə] *nm* rye.
seigneur [sɛɲœr] *nm* lord.
sein [sɛ̃] *nm* breast; (*milieu*) bosom.
séisme [seismə] *nm* earthquake; (*bouleversement*) upheaval.
seize [sɛz] *nm, adj* sixteen. **seizième** *n(m+f)*, *adj* sixteenth.
séjour [seʒur] *nm* stay; (*demeure*) abode. **séjourner** *v* stay.
sel [sɛl] *nm* salt; (*esprit*) wit; (*piquant*) spice. **sel de cuisine/table** cooking/table salt.
sélection [selɛksjɔ̃] *nf* selection. **sélectif** *adj* selective.
sélectionner [selɛksjɔne] *v* select.
selle [sɛl] *nf* saddle. **seller** *v* saddle. **sellerie** *nf* saddlery; (*lieu*) harness room. **sellier** *nm* saddler.
selon [səlɔ̃] *prep* according to.
Seltz [sɛls] *nf* **eau de Seltz** soda water.
semaine [səmɛn] *nf* week.
sémantique [semɑ̃tik] *adj* semantic. *nf* semantics.
sémaphore [semafɔr] *nm* semaphore.
sembler [sɑ̃ble] *v* seem. **semblable** *adj* similar; (*tel*) such. **semblable à** like. **semblant** *nm* semblance. **faire semblant de** pretend.
semelle [səmɛl] *nf* sole. **semelle intérieure** insole. **semelles compensées** platform soles *pl*.
semence [səmɑ̃s] *nf* seed.
semer [səme] *v* sow; (*en dispersant*) scatter; (*parsemer*) sprinkle, dot.
semestre [səmɛstrə] *nm* half-year. **semestriel** *adj* half-yearly.
séminaire [seminɛr] *nm* (*université*) seminar; (*rel*) seminary.
semi-précieux *adj* semi-precious.
semoule [səmul] *nf* semolina.
sempiternel [sɛ̃pitɛrnɛl] *adj* never-ending.
sénat [sena] *nm* senate. **sénateur** *nm* senator.

sénile [senil] *adj* senile. **sénilité** *nf* senility.

sens [sãs] *nm* sense; direction; (*signification*) meaning. **à sens unique** (*rue*) one-way. **bon sens** common sense. **dans le sens des aiguilles d'une montre** clockwise. **sens dessus dessous** upside down. **sens devant derrière** back to front. **sens interdit** no entry.

sensation [sãsasjɔ̃] *nf* sensation; (*impression*) feeling. **sensationnel** *adj* sensational; (*fam*) fantastic, terrific.

sensé [sãse] *adj* sensible.

sensible [sãsiblə] *adj* sensitive; perceptible, noticeable; (*cœur*) tender; (*impressionnable*) susceptible. **sensibilité** *nf* sensitivity.

sensuel [sãsɥɛl] *adj* (*charnel*) sensual; (*esthétique*) sensuous. **sensualité** *nf* sensuality; sensuousness.

sentence [sãtãs] *nf* (*jur*) sentence; maxim.

sentier [sãtje] *nm* path.

sentiment [sãtimã] *nm* feeling; (*péj*) sentiment. **sentimental** *adj* sentimental.

sentinelle [sãtinɛl] *nf* sentry.

***sentir** [sãtir] *v* feel; (*odeur*) smell; (*goût*) taste; (*pressentir*) sense; (*être conscient de*) be aware of.

***seoir** [swar] *v* be fitting. **seoir à** become.

séparer [separe] *v* separate; (*diviser*) part, split. **séparation** *nf* separation; parting; division. **séparé** *adj* separated; (*éloigné*) apart.

sept [sɛt] *nm*, *adj* seven. **septième** *n*(*m*+*f*), *adj* seventh.

septembre [sɛptãbrə] *nm* September.

septentrional [sɛptãtrijɔnal] *adj* northern.

septique [sɛptik] *adj* septic.

séquence [sekãs] *nf* sequence.

serein [sərɛ̃] *adj* serene, calm.

sérénade [serenad] *nf* serenade.

serf [sɛrf], **serve** *nm*, *nf* serf.

sergent [sɛrʒã] *nm* sergeant.

série [seri] *nf* series; (*ensemble*) set. **de série** standard. **fait en série** mass-produced. **hors série** (*machine*) custom-built; (*qualité*) outstanding.

sérieux [serjø] *adj* serious; (*sage*) responsible; (*sûr*) reliable; (*grand*) considerable. *nm* seriousness. **prendre au sérieux** take seriously.

serin [sərɛ̃] *nm* canary.

seringue [sərɛ̃g] *nf* syringe.

serment [sɛrmã] *nm* oath.

sermon [sɛrmɔ̃] *nm* sermon.

serpent [sɛrpã] *nm* snake, serpent. **serpent à sonnettes** rattlesnake.

serpenter [sɛrpãte] *v* snake, wind.

serre [sɛr] *nf* greenhouse; (*contiguë à une maison*) conservatory; (*griffe*) talon. **serre chaude** hothouse.

serrer [sere] *v* grip; (*dents, poings*) clench; (*vêtement*) be tight; (*nœud, écrou*) tighten; (*rester près de*) keep close to; (*rapprocher*) close up. **serrer la main à** shake hands with. **se serrer** squeeze up, crowd together. **serré** *adj* tight; (*personnes*) packed, crowded; dense.

serrure [seryr] *nf* lock. **serrurier** *nm* locksmith.

servante [sɛrvãt] *nf* servant, maid.

serveur [sɛrvœr] *nm* (*restaurant*) waiter; (*bar*) barman. **serveuse** *nf* waitress; barmaid.

service [sɛrvis] *nm* service; (*travail*) duty; department; (*ensemble*) set. **être de service** be on duty. **service à thé** tea-set.

serviette [sɛrvjɛt] *nf* (*de toilette*) towel; (*de table*) serviette; (*cartable*) briefcase. **serviette hygiénique** sanitary towel.

servile [sɛrvil] *adj* servile. **servilité** *nf* servility.

***servir** [sɛrvir] *v* serve; (*dîneur, patron*) wait on; (*client*) attend to; aid. **servir à** be used for; (*être utile*) be useful for. **servir de** act as. **se servir** help oneself. **se servir de** use.

serviteur [sɛrvitœr] *nm* servant.

ses [se] *V* **son**[1].

session [sesjɔ̃] *nf* session.

seuil [sœj] *nm* threshold; (*porte*) doorway; (*dalle*) doorstep.

seul [sœl] *adj* only; (*sans compagnie*) alone; (*isolé*) lonely; (*unique*) single, sole. *adv* by oneself. **seulement** *adv* only.

sève [sɛv] *nf* sap.

sévère [sevɛr] *adj* severe. **sévérité** *nf* severity.

sévir [sevir] *v* act ruthlessly; punish severely; (*régime, fléau*) rage.

sexe [sɛks] *nm* sex. **sexualité** *nf* sexuality. **sexuel** *adj* sexual, sex.

sextuor [sɛkstɥɔr] *nm* sextet.

shampooing [ʃãpwɛ̃] *nm* shampoo.

shérif [ʃerif] *nm* sheriff.

short [ʃɔrt] *nm* shorts *pl*.

si[1] [si], **s'** *conj* if.

si² [si] *adv* so; (*aussi*) as; (*oui*) yes. **si bien que** so that. **si . . . que** however.
siamois [sjamwa] *adj* Siamese.
sidérer [sidere] *v* (*fam*) stagger, shatter.
siècle [sjɛklə] *nm* century; (*époque*) age.
siège [sjɛʒ] *nm* seat; (*organisation*) headquarters; (*épiscopal*) see; (*mil*) siege. **siège éjectable** ejector seat.
siéger [sjeʒe] *v* be located; (*tenir séance*) sit.
sien [sjɛ̃], **sienne** *pron* **le sien, la sienne** (*homme*) his; (*femme*) hers; (*chose, animal*) its own; (*réfléchi*) one's own.
sieste [sjɛst] *nf* siesta; (*petit somme*) nap.
siffler [sifle] *v* whistle; (*serpent, gaz*) hiss. **sifflement** *nm* whistle, hiss. **sifflet** *nm* whistle.
signal [siɲal] *nm* signal.
signaler [siɲale] *v* indicate; (*faire un signe*) signal; (*faire un exposé*) report. **se signaler** stand out, distinguish oneself. **signalement** *nm* description.
signature [siɲatyr] *nf* signature; (*action*) signing.
signe [siɲ] *nm* sign; mark. **faire signe à** beckon. **signet** *nm* bookmark.
signer [siɲe] *v* sign.
signifier [siɲifje] *v* mean, signify. **significatif** *adj* significant. **signification** *nf* significance, meaning.
silence [silɑ̃s] *nm* silence; pause; (*musique*) rest.
silencieux [silɑ̃sjø] *adj* silent. *nm* silencer.
silex [silɛks] *nm* flint.
silhouette [silwɛt] *nf* silhouette, outline; figure.
sillage [sijaʒ] *nm* wake.
sillon [sijɔ̃] *nm* furrow; (*disque*) groove. **sillonner** *v* furrow; (*traverser*) cross.
simagrée [simagre] *nf* pretence. **simagrées** *nf pl* fuss *sing*, play-acting *sing*.
simple [sɛ̃plə] *adj* simple; (*billet*) single. **simplement** *adv* simply; (*seulement*) merely, just. **simplicité** *nf* simplicity. **simplifier** *v* simplify.
simulacre [simylakrə] *nm* pretence, show.
simuler [simyle] *v* simulate; feign. **simulation** *nf* simulation. **simulé** *adj* simulated; feigned, sham.
simultané [simyltane] *adj* simultaneous.
sincère [sɛ̃sɛr] *adj* sincere; (*authentique*) genuine, true. **sincérité** *nf* sincerity.
singe [sɛ̃ʒ] *nm* monkey, ape.
singer [sɛ̃ʒe] *v* mimic, ape. **singeries** *nf pl* antics *pl*, clowning *sing*.
singulier [sɛ̃gylje] *adj* (*gramm*) singular; remarkable; uncommon. *nm* singular. **singularité** *nf* peculiarity. **singulièrement** *adv* remarkably; strangely; particularly.
sinistre [sinistrə] *adj* sinister. *nm* disaster; (*assurances*) damage, loss.
sinon [sinɔ̃] *conj* if not; (*autrement*) otherwise; (*sauf*) except, other than.
sinueux [sinɥø] *adj* winding; (*ligne*) sinuous.
sinus [sinys] *nm invar* (*anat*) sinus. **sinusite** *nf* sinusitis.
siphon [sifɔ̃] *nm* siphon. **siphonner** *v* siphon.
sirène [sirɛn] *nf* siren; (*mythologie*) mermaid.
sirop [siro] *nm* syrup; (*boisson*) squash, cordial. **sirupeux** *adj* syrupy.
siroter [sirɔte] *v* sip.
site [sit] *nm* site; (*environnement*) setting; (*tourisme*) beauty spot, place of interest.
sitôt [sito] *adv* immediately, no sooner. **sitôt que** as soon as.
situer [sitɥe] *v* situate, locate; (*par la pensée*) place. **situation** *nf* situation; position; (*emploi*) job.
six [sis] *nm, adj* six. **sixième** *n(m+f), adj* sixth.
ski [ski] *nm* ski; (*sport*) skiing. **faire du ski** ski, go skiing. **ski nautique** water-skiing. **skieur, -euse** *nm, nf* skier.
slalom [slalɔm] *nm* slalom.
slip [slip] *nm* briefs *pl*, pants *pl*. **slip de bain** (*homme*) trunks *pl*.
slogan [slɔgɑ̃] *nm* slogan.
smoking [smɔkiŋ] *nm* dinner jacket.
snob [snɔb] *n(m+f)* snob. *adj* snobbish.
sobre [sɔbrə] *adj* temperate, abstemious; (*repas*) frugal; (*style*) sober. **sobriété** *nf* temperance; frugality; (*modération*) restraint; sobriety.
sobriquet [sɔbrikɛ] *nm* nickname.
sociable [sɔsjablə] *adj* sociable.
social [sɔsjal] *adj* social. **socialisme** *nm* socialism. **socialiste** *n(m+f), adj* socialist.
société [sɔsjete] *nf* society; club; company. **société anonyme** limited company. **sociétaire** *n(m+f)* member.
sociologie [sɔsjɔlɔʒi] *nf* sociology. **sociologique** *adj* sociological. **sociologue** *n(m+f)* sociologist.
socle [sɔklə] *nm* base; pedestal.

socquette [sɔkɛt] *nf* ankle sock.
sœur [sœr] *nf* sister; (*rel*) nun.
sofa [sɔfa] *nm* sofa.
soi [swa] *pron* one, oneself. **aller de soi** be obvious, stand to reason. **soi-même** *pron* oneself.
soi-disant *adj invar* so-called. *adv* supposedly.
soie [swa] *nf* silk; (*poil*) bristle.
soif [swaf] *nf* thirst. **avoir soif** be thirsty.
soigner [swaɲe] *v* look after, take care of; (*malade*) treat. **soigné** *adj* neat, tidy; (*consciencieux*) carefully done. **soigneux** *adj* careful; (*soigné*) neat, tidy.
soin [swɛ̃] *nm* care.
soir [swar] *nm* evening. **ce soir** this evening, tonight. **soirée** *nf* evening; party; (*théâtre*) evening performance.
soit [swa] *adv* very well, so be it. *conj* whether; (*à savoir*) that is to say. **soit que** whether. **soit . . . soit . . .** either . . . or . . . .
soixante [swasɑ̃t] *nm, adj* sixty. **soixantième** *n(m+f), adj* sixtieth.
soixante-dix *nm, adj* seventy. **soixante-dixième** *n(m+f), adj* seventieth.
soja [sɔʒa] *nm* soya.
sol [sɔl] *nm* ground; (*plancher*) floor; (*territoire*) soil.
solaire [sɔlɛr] *adj* solar; (*crème, etc.*) suntan.
soldat [sɔlda] *nm* soldier.
solde[1] [sɔld] *nf* pay.
solde[2] [sɔld] *nm* (*compte*) balance; (*vente*) sale; (*marchandises*) sale goods *pl*.
sole [sɔl] *nf* sole.
soleil [sɔlɛj] *nm* sun; (*lumière*) sunshine. **il fait du soleil** it's sunny.
solennel [sɔlanɛl] *adj* solemn; ceremonial. **solennité** *nf* solemnity; grand occasion.
solide [sɔlid] *adj* solid; (*sérieux, durable*) sound; robust, sturdy. *nm* solid. **solidarité** *nf* solidarity. **solidement** *adv* solidly; firmly. **solidifier** *v* solidify.
soliste [sɔlist] *n(m+f)* soloist.
solitaire [sɔlitɛr] *adj* solitary; deserted; (*seul, sans compagnie*) lonely. *n(m+f)* recluse. **solitairement** *adv* alone.
solitude [sɔlityd] *nf* solitude; loneliness.
solive [sɔliv] *nf* joist.
solliciter [sɔlisite] *v* appeal to; (*demander*) seek, request.
solo [sɔlo] *nm, adj invar* solo.
soluble [sɔlyblə] *adj* soluble.
solution [sɔlysjɔ̃] *nf* solution.
solvable [sɔlvablə] *adj* solvent. **solvabilité** *nf* solvency.
sombre [sɔ̃brə] *adj* dark; (*morne*) sombre, gloomy.
sombrer [sɔ̃bre] *v* sink, founder.
sommaire [sɔmɛr] *adj* brief, basic. *nm* summary.
sommation [sɔmɑsjɔ̃] *nf* (*jur*) summons; demand.
somme[1] [sɔm] *nf* **bête de somme** *nf* beast of burden.
somme[2] [sɔm] *nm* nap, snooze. **faire un petit somme** have a nap.
somme[3] [sɔm] *nf* sum, amount. **en somme** all in all; (*en résumé*) in short. **faire la somme de** add up. **somme toute** when all is said and done.
sommeil [sɔmɛj] *nm* sleep; (*envie de dormir*) sleepiness. **avoir sommeil** feel sleepy.
sommeiller [sɔmeje] *v* doze.
sommelier [sɔməlje] *nm* wine waiter.
sommer [sɔme] *v* (*jur*) summon.
sommet [sɔmɛ] *nm* summit, top.
somnambule [sɔmnɑ̃byl] *n(m+f)* sleepwalker. **somnambulisme** *nm* sleep-walking.
somnifère [sɔmnifɛr] *nm* sleeping-pill.
somnoler [sɔmnɔle] *v* doze. **somnolent** *adj* sleepy, drowsy.
son[1] [sɔ̃], **sa** *adj*, *pl* **ses** (*homme*) his, (*femme*) her; (*chose, animal*) its; (*indéfini*) one's.
son[2] [sɔ̃] *nm* (*bruit*) sound.
son[3] [sɔ̃] *nm* bran.
sonate [sɔnat] *nf* sonata.
sonder [sɔ̃de] *v* (*fouiller*) probe; (*naut*) sound; (*personne*) sound out; (*tech*) bore, drill. **sondage** *nm* probe; sounding; drilling; (*d'opinion*) poll. **sonde** *nf* probe; drill.
songer [sɔ̃ʒe] *v* (*rêver*) dream; reflect. **songer à** consider, think of. **songe** *nm* dream.
songeur, -euse [sɔ̃ʒœr, -øz] *adj* pensive. *nm, nf* dreamer.
sonique [sɔnik] *adj* sonic.
sonner [sɔne] *v* (*cloche, etc.*) ring; (*trompette, etc.*) sound; (*heure*) strike. **sonnerie** *nf* ringing; (*sonnette*) bell; (*pendule*) chimes *pl*. **sonnette** *nf* bell.
sonnet [sɔnɛ] *nm* sonnet.
sonore [sɔnɔr] *adj* resonant; (*rire, gifle, etc.*) resounding; (*film, onde, effet*) sound.

soprano [sɔprano] *n(m+f)* soprano.
sorcier [sɔrsje] *nm* sorcerer, wizard. **sorcière** *nf* witch. **sorcellerie** *nf* witchcraft, sorcery.
sordide [sɔrdid] *adj* sordid.
sort [sɔr] *nm* fate; (*condition*) lot; (*charme*) spell. **tirer au sort** draw lots.
sorte [sɔrt] *nf* sort, kind. **de la sorte** in that way. **de sorte que** so that. **en quelque sorte** in a way.
***sortir** [sɔrtir] *v* go out; come out; (*quitter, partir*) leave; (*retirer*) take *or* bring out; (*film, disque*) release. **sortie** *nf* (*endroit, porte*) way out, exit; (*promenade*) outing; (*emportement*) outburst; publication; release. **sortie de secours** emergency exit.
sot, sotte [so, sɔt] *adj* silly, foolish. *nm, nf* fool. **sottise** *nf* silliness; silly thing.
sou [su] *nm* penny. **sans le sou** penniless.
soubresaut [subrəso] *nm* jolt, start.
souche [suʃ] *nf* (*arbre*) stump; (*talon*) stub; (*famille*) founder.
souci[1] [susi] *nm* (*bot*) marigold.
souci[2] [susi] *nm* (*tracas*) worry; (*préoccupation*) concern.
se soucier [susje] *v* **se soucier de** care about. **soucieux** *adj* concerned.
soucoupe [sukup] *nf* saucer.
soudain [sudɛ̃] *adj* sudden. *adv* suddenly.
soude [sud] *nf* soda.
souder [sude] *v* (*autogène*) weld; (*avec fil à souder*) solder; unite. **se souder** (*os*) knit together. **soudeur** *nm* welder; solderer. **soudure** *nf* welding; soldering; (*substance*) solder; (*endroit*) weld.
soudoyer [sudwaje] *v* bribe.
souffler [sufle] *v* blow; (*bougie*) blow out; (*se reposer*) get one's breath back; (*haleter*) puff, pant; (*dire*) whisper; (*théâtre*) prompt; (*fam: voler*) pinch; (*fam: étonner*) stagger. **souffle** *nm* blow, puff; (*respiration*) breathing; (*haleine*) breath; inspiration. **être à bout de souffle** be out of breath.
soufflet[1] [suflɛ] *nm* bellows *pl*; (*couture*) gusset.
soufflet[2] [suflɛ] *nm* (*gifle*) slap (in the face). **souffleter** *v* slap (in the face).
***souffrir** [sufrir] *v* suffer; (*avoir mal*) be in pain; (*supporter*) endure, bear; (*permettre*) allow. **souffrance** *nf* suffering. **en souffrance** pending. **souffrant** *adj* suffering; (*malade*) unwell.
soufre [sufrə] *nm* sulphur.
souhait [swɛ] *nm* wish. **à souhait** to perfection, as well as one could wish. **souhaiter** *v* wish; (*espérer*) hope.
souiller [suje] *v* soil, dirty; (*réputation*) tarnish; (*profaner*) defile. **souillon** *nm* slut. **souillure** *nf* stain.
soûl [su] *adj* drunk. **tout son soûl** to one's heart's content. **soûlard, -e** *nm, nf* (*argot*) drunkard. **soûler** *v* intoxicate. **se soûler** get drunk.
soulager [sulaʒe] *v* relieve; (*conscience*) ease. **soulagement** *nm* relief.
soulever [sulve] *v* raise; (*lever*) lift; (*provoquer*) arouse, stir up. **soulèvement** *nm* uprising.
soulier [sulje] *nm* shoe.
souligner [suliɲe] *v* underline; accentuate, emphasize.
***soumettre** [sumɛtrə] *v* (*dompter*) subject; (*présenter*) submit. **se soumettre** submit. **soumis** *adj* submissive. **soumission** *nf* submission; (*comm*) tender.
soupape [supap] *nf* valve.
soupçon [supsɔ̃] *nm* suspicion; (*ombre*) touch, hint; (*goutte*) drop. **soupçonner** *v* suspect. **soupçonneux** *adj* suspicious.
soupe [sup] *nf* soup.
soupente [supɑ̃t] *nf* cupboard (under the stairs).
souper [supe] *nm* supper. *v* have supper.
soupir [supir] *nm* sigh. **soupirer** *v* sigh.
soupirail [supiraj] *nm, pl* **-aux** basement window.
souple [suplə] *adj* supple; flexible; (*gracieux*) lithe. **souplesse** *nf* suppleness; flexibility; litheness.
source [surs] *nf* source; (*point d'eau*) spring.
sourcil [sursi] *nm* eyebrow.
sourd [sur], **-e** *adj* deaf; (*son, couleur*) muted; (*douleur*) dull; (*caché*) hidden. *nm, nf* deaf person.
sourd-muet, sourde-muette *adj* deaf and dumb. *nm, nf* deaf mute.
sourdine [surdin] *nf* mute.
souricière [surisjɛr] *nf* mousetrap.
***sourire** [surir] *nm* smile. *v* smile.
souris [suri] *nf* mouse.
sournois [surnwa] *adj* underhand, deceitful; (*air*) shifty.
sous [su] *prep* under; (*temps*) within; (*pluie, soleil, etc.*) in.
sous-alimentation *nf* malnutrition.

***souscrire** [suskrir] *v* subscribe; sign. **souscripteur, -trice** *nm, nf* subscriber. **souscription** *nf* subscription.
sous-développé *adj* underdeveloped.
sous-entendre *v* imply, infer.
sous-entendu *adj* understood. *nm* innuendo.
sous-estimer *v* underestimate, underrate. **sous-estimation** *nf* underestimation.
sous-jacent *adj* underlying.
sous-louer *v* sublet.
sous-marin *adj* underwater. *nm* submarine.
sous-payé *adj* underpaid.
sous-sol *nm* (*maison*) basement; (*terre*) subsoil.
sous-titre *nm* subtitle. **sous-titrer** *v* subtitle.
***soustraire** [sustrεr] *v* take away; (*math*) subtract; (*cacher*) shield. **se soustraire à** shirk, escape. **soustraction** *nf* subtraction.
sous-traiter *v* subcontract. **sous-traitant** *nm* subcontractor.
sous-vêtements *nm pl* underwear *sing*.
soutane [sutan] *nf* cassock.
***soutenir** [sutnir] *v* support; (*faire durer*) sustain, keep up; (*résister à*) withstand; (*affirmer*) uphold. **soutenu** *adj* sustained; elevated.
souterrain [suterε̃] *adj* underground. *nm* underground passage.
soutien [sutjε̃] *nm* support. **soutien de famille** breadwinner. **soutien-gorge** *nm* bra.
***souvenir** [suvnir] *nm* memory; (*souvenance*) recollection; (*objet*) memento; (*pour touristes*) souvenir. *v* **se souvenir (de)** remember.
souvent [suvɑ̃] *adv* often. **peu souvent** seldom.
souverain [suvrε̃], **-e** *adj* supreme, sovereign. *nm, nf* sovereign.
soyeux [swajø] *adj* silky.
spacieux [spasjø] *adj* spacious.
spaghetti [spageti] *nm pl* spaghetti.
sparadrap [sparadra] *nm* sticking plaster.
spasme [spasmə] *nm* spasm. **spasmodique** *adj* spasmodic.
spatial [spasjal] *adj* spatial; (*voyage, engin, etc.*) space.
spatule [spatyl] *nf* spatula.
speaker, speakerine [spikœr, spikrin] *nm, nf* announcer.
spécial [spesjal] *adj* special; (*bizarre*) peculiar. **spécialement** *adv* particularly, especially; (*exprès*) specially. **se spécialiser** *v* specialize. **spécialiste** *n(m+f)* specialist. **spécialité** *nf* speciality.
spécieux [spesjø] *adj* specious.
spécifier [spesifje] *v* specify, state. **spécification** *nf* specification. **spécifique** *adj* specific.
spécimen [spesimεn] *nm* specimen; (*exemplaire*) sample copy.
spectacle [spεktaklə] *nm* sight, spectacle; (*représentation*) show. **spectaculaire** *adj* spectacular.
spectateur, -trice [spεktatœr, -tris] *nm, nf* onlooker; (*sport*) spectator. **spectateurs** *nm pl* (*théâtre*) audience *sing*.
spectre [spεktrə] *nm* (*fantôme*) spectre; (*phys*) spectrum.
spéculer [spekyle] *v* speculate. **spéculatif** *adj* speculative. **spéculation** *nf* speculation.
spéléologie [speleɔlɔʒi] *nf* pot-holing. **spéléologue** *n(m+f)* pot-holer.
sperme [spεrm] *nm* sperm.
sphère [sfεr] *nf* sphere. **sphérique** *adj* spherical.
spinal [spinal] *adj* spinal.
spiral [spiral] *adj* spiral. **spirale** *nf* spiral.
spirite [spirit] *n(m+f)* spiritualist. **spiritisme** *nm* spiritualism.
spirituel [spiritɥεl] *adj* spiritual; (*fin*) witty.
spiritueux [spiritɥø] *nm* (*liqueur*) spirit.
splendeur [splɑ̃dœr] *nf* splendour; glory. **splendide** *adj* splendid, magnificent.
spongieux [spɔ̃ʒjø] *adj* spongy.
spontané [spɔ̃tane] *adj* spontaneous. **spontanéité** *nf* spontaneity.
sporadique [spɔradik] *adj* sporadic.
sport [spɔr] *nm* sport. **de sport** sports.
sportif [spɔrtif] *adj* sports; competitive; (*personne*) athletic; (*attitude*) sporting. *nm* sportsman. **sportive** *nf* sportswoman.
square [skwar] *nm* square with public garden.
squelette [skəlεt] *nm* skeleton. **squelettique** *adj* skeletal; (*très maigre*) scrawny; (*exposé*) sketchy.
stabiliser [stabilize] *v* stabilize. **stabilisateur** *nm* stabilizer.
stable [stablə] *adj* stable. **stabilité** *nf* stability.
stade [stad] *nm* (*étape*) stage; (*sport*) stadium.

stage [staʒ] *nm* training period; training course. **stagiaire** *n(m+f)*, *adj* trainee, student.
stagnant [stagnɑ̃] *adj* stagnant. **stagnation** *nf* stagnation. **stagner** *v* stagnate.
stalle [stal] *nf* stall.
standard [stɑ̃dar] *nm* switchboard. *adj* standard. **standardiser** *v* standardize. **standardiste** *n(m+f)* switchboard operator.
starter [starter] *nm* (*auto*) choke; (*sport*) starter.
station [stɑsjɔ̃] *nf* station; (*halte*) stop; site; (*de vacances*) resort; posture. **station balnéaire** seaside resort. **station de taxis** taxi rank. **station-service** *nf* petrol station.
stationner [stasjɔne] *v* park. **stationnaire** *adj* stationary. **stationnement** *nm* parking.
statique [statik] *adj* static.
statistique [statistik] *nf* statistic; (*science*) statistics. *adj* statistical.
statue [staty] *nf* statue.
stature [statyr] *nf* stature.
statut [staty] *nm* status. **statuts** *nm pl* statutes *pl*, rules *pl*. **statutaire** *adj* statutory.
steeple [stiplə] *nm* steeplechase.
stencil [stɛnsil] *nm* stencil.
sténodactylo [stenɔdaktilo] *nf* (*personne*) shorthand typist; (*emploi*) shorthand typing.
sténographie [stenɔgrafi] *nf* shorthand.
stéréo [stereo] *nf*, *adj* stereo. **stéréophonique** *adj* stereophonic.
stéréotype [stereɔtip] *nm* stereotype.
stérile [steril] *adj* sterile; (*terre*) barren; (*effort*) fruitless. **stérilet** *nm* (*méd*) coil. **stérilisation** *nf* sterilization. **stériliser** *v* sterilize. **stérilité** *nf* sterility; barrenness; fruitlessness.
stéthoscope [stetɔskɔp] *nm* stethoscope.
stigmate [stigmat] *nm* stigma; mark.
stimulant [stimylɑ̃] *adj* stimulating. *nm* stimulant; stimulus (*pl* -li).
stimuler [stimyle] *v* stimulate. **stimulation** *nf* stimulation.
stimulus [stimylys] *nm*, *pl* **-li** stimulus (*pl* -li).
stipuler [stipyle] *v* stipulate, specify. **stipulation** *nf* stipulation.
stock [stɔk] *nm* stock. **stocker** *v* stock; (*amasser*) stockpile.
Stockholm [stɔkɔlm] *n* Stockholm.
stoïque [stɔik] *adj* stoical. **stoïcisme** *nm* stoicism.
stop [stɔp] *interj* stop! *nm* (*panneau*) stop sign; (*feu*) brake light; (*fam*) hitch-hiking. **faire du stop** hitch-hike.
store [stɔr] *nm* blind; (*magasin*) awning.
strabisme [strabismə] *nm* squint.
strapontin [strapɔ̃tɛ̃] *nm* folding seat.
strate [strat] *nf* stratum (*pl* -ta).
stratégie [strateʒi] *nf* strategy. **stratégique** *adj* strategic.
strict [strikt] *adj* strict; (*tenue*) plain.
strident [stridɑ̃] *adj* strident, shrill.
strié [strije] *adj* streaked; (*en relief*) ridged.
strophe [strɔf] *nf* verse, stanza.
structure [stryktyr] *nf* structure. **structural** *adj* structural.
studieux [stydjø] *adj* studious.
studio [stydjo] *nm* studio; (*logement*) flatlet.
stupéfiant [stypefjɑ̃] *adj* astounding. *nm* drug, narcotic.
stupéfier [stypefje] *v* stun, astound. **stupéfaction** *nf* amazement. **stupéfait** *adj* astounded, dumbfounded.
stupeur [stypœr] *nf* amazement; (*méd*) stupor.
stupide [stypid] *adj* stupid, silly. **stupidité** *nf* stupidity.
style [stil] *nm* style.
stylo [stilo] *nm* pen. **stylo à bille** ballpoint pen.
suaire [sɥɛr] *nm* shroud.
suant [sɥɑ̃] *adj* sweaty.
suave [sɥav] *adj* smooth; (*musique*, *etc.*) sweet. **suavité** *nf* smoothness; sweetness.
subalterne [sybaltɛrn] *n(m+f)*, *adj* subordinate.
subconscient [sypkɔ̃sjɑ̃] *nm*, *adj* subconscious.
subdiviser [sybdivize] *v* subdivide. **subdivision** *nf* subdivision.
subir [sybir] *v* undergo; endure; suffer.
subit [sybi] *adj* sudden. **subitement** *adv* suddenly. **subito** *adv* (*fam*) suddenly, at once.
subjectif [sybʒɛktif] *adj* subjective.
subjonctif [sybʒɔ̃ktif] *nm*, *adj* subjunctive.
subjuguer [sybʒyge] *v* captivate.
sublime [syblim] *nm*, *adj* sublime.
submerger [sybmɛrʒe] *v* submerge; (*ennemi*, *émotion*) overwhelm; (*travail*, *etc.*) swamp. **submersion** *nf* submersion.

subordonner [sybɔrdɔne] *v* subordinate. **subordination** *nf* subordination. **subordonné, -e** *n, adj* subordinate.
subreptice [sybrɛptis] *adj* surreptitious.
subsidiaire [sypsidjɛr] *adj* subsidiary.
subsister [sybziste] *v* survive, live; (*rester*) remain, subsist. **subsistance** *nf* subsistence, maintenance.
substance [sypstɑ̃s] *nf* substance. **substantiel** *adj* substantial
substituer [sypstitɥe] *v* substitute. **substitution** *nf* substitution.
subtil [syptil] *adj* subtle. **subtilité** *nf* subtlety.
suburbain [sybyrbɛ̃] *adj* suburban.
***subvenir** [sybvənir] *v* **subvenir à** meet, provide for.
subvention [sybvɑ̃sjɔ̃] *nf* grant, subsidy. **subventionner** *v* subsidize.
subversion [sybvɛrsjɔ̃] *nf* subversion. **subversif** *adj* subversive.
suc [syk] *nm* juice; essence, pith.
succédané [syksedane] *nm* substitute.
succéder [syksede] *v* **succéder à** succeed; (*suivre*) follow. **succès** *nm* success. **à succès** successful. **avec succès** successfully. **successeur** *nm* successor. **successif** *adj* successive. **succession** *nf* succession.
succinct [syksɛ̃] *adj* succinct.
succion [syksjɔ̃] *nf* suction.
succomber [sykɔ̃be] *v* succumb, yield; (*mourir*) die.
succulent [sykylɑ̃] *adj* succulent, delicious.
succursale [sykyrsal] *nf* branch.
sucer [syse] *v* suck. **sucette** *nf* lollipop; (*tétine*) dummy.
sucre [sykrə] *nm* sugar. **sucre d'orge** barley sugar. **sucre en poudre** caster sugar. **sucre glace** icing sugar. **sucre semoule** granulated sugar. **sucré** *adj* sweet. **sucrer** *v* sweeten; (*thé, café, etc.*) put sugar in. **sucrier** *nm* sugar-basin.
sud [syd] *nm* south. *adj invar* south; (*région*) southern; (*direction*) southward. **sud-est** *nm, adj invar* south-east. **sud-ouest** *nm, adj invar* south-west.
suède [sɥɛd] *nm* suede.
Suède [sɥɛd] *nf* Sweden. **suédois** *nm, adj* Swedish. **Suédois, -e** *nm, nf* Swede.
suer [sɥe] *v* sweat. **sueur** *nf* sweat.
***suffire** [syfir] *v* suffice, be enough *or* sufficient. **ça suffit** that will do, that's enough. **suffisant** *adj* sufficient; (*résultat*) satisfactory; (*personne*) self-important.
suffixe [syfiks] *nm* suffix.
suffoquer [syfɔke] *v* suffocate, choke. **suffocation** *nf* suffocation.
suffrage [syfraʒ] *nm* suffrage; (*voix*) vote; approbation, approval.
suggérer [sygʒere] *v* suggest. **suggestif** *adj* suggestive. **suggestion** *nf* suggestion.
se suicider [sɥiside] *v* commit suicide. **suicidaire** *adj* suicidal. **suicide** *nm* suicide. **suicidé, -e** *nm, nf* suicide.
suie [sɥi] *nf* soot.
suif [sɥif] *nm* tallow.
suinter [sɥɛ̃te] *v* ooze.
Suisse [sɥis] *nf* Switzerland. **les Suisses** the Swiss. **suisse** *adj* Swiss.
suite [sɥit] *nf* result, effect; succession, series; (*musique, appartement*) suite; (*feuilleton*) next episode, continuation; (*roman, film*) sequel; coherence, consistency. **de suite** in succession. **faire suite à** follow. **par la suite** afterwards, subsequently. **par suite** consequently. **suite à** (*comm*) further to. **tout de suite** at once, immediately.
suivant [sɥivɑ̃], **-e** *adj* next, following. *nm, nf* next (one). *prep* according to.
***suivre** [sɥivrə] *v* follow; (*cours*) attend; (*en classe*) keep up (with). **faire suivre** forward. **suivi** *adj* consistent; regular; coherent.
sujet, -ette [syʒɛ, -ɛt] *adj* subject, liable, prone. *nm* subject; (*d'examen*) question. **au sujet de** about, concerning. **sujet de** cause for. *nm, nf* (*personne*) subject. **sujétion** *nf* subjection.
sultan [syltɑ̃] *nm* sultan.
superbe [sypɛrb] *adj* superb, magnificent.
supercherie [sypɛrʃəri] *nf* trick.
superficie [sypɛrfisi] *nf* surface area.
superficiel [sypɛrfisjɛl] *adj* superficial.
superflu [sypɛrfly] *adj* superfluous.
supérieur, -e [syperjœr] *adj* upper; (*hautain, meilleur*) superior; (*plus grand*) greater; (*plus haut*) higher. *nm, nf* superior. **supériorité** *nf* superiority.
superlatif [sypɛrlatif] *nm, adj* superlative.
supermarché [sypɛrmarʃe] *nm* supermarket.
supersonique [sypɛrsɔnik] *adj* supersonic.
superstition [sypɛrstisjɔ̃] *nf* superstition. **superstitieux** *adj* superstitious.
suppléant [sypleɑ̃], **-e** *adj* temporary. *nm, nf* deputy; (*professeur*) supply teacher; (*médecin*) locum.

suppléer [syplee] *v* supply, provide; (*lacune*) fill in; (*manque*) make up (for); replace. **suppléer à** (*remédier*) make up for; (*remplacer*) substitute for.
supplément [syplemɑ̃] *nm* supplement; (*tarif*) extra charge; (*transport*) excess fare. **en supplément** extra. **supplémentaire** *adj* additional, extra, supplementary.
supplice [syplis] *nm* torture; torment. **dernier supplice** execution.
supplier [syplije] *v* implore, entreat.
support [sypɔr] *nm* support; (*moyen*) medium.
supporter [sypɔrte] *v* support; endure, bear; tolerate, put up with; (*résister à*) withstand. **supportable** *adj* bearable; tolerable.
supposer [sypoze] *v* suppose; imply. **supposition** *nf* supposition.
supprimer [syprime] *v* suppress; (*enlever*) remove; (*mot*) delete; abolish, do away with; (*train, etc.*) cancel. **suppression** *nf* suppression; removal; deletion; abolition; cancellation.
suprême [syprɛm] *adj* supreme. **suprématie** *nf* supremacy.
sur [syr] *prep* on; (*par-dessus*) over; (*au-dessus*) above; (*sujet*) about; (*proportion*) out of; (*mesure*) by; (*après*) after. **sur-le-champ** *adv* immediately.
sûr [syr] *adj* sure, certain; (*sans danger*) safe; (*sérieux*) reliable. **à coup sûr** definitely.
surabondance [syrabɔ̃dɑ̃s] *nf* overabundance. **surabondant** *adj* overabundant.
suranné [syrane] *adj* outdated, outmoded.
surcharger [syrʃarʒe] *v* overload. **surcharge** *nf* extra *or* excess load; (*surabondance*) surfeit; (*impôt*) surcharge.
surchauffer [syrʃofe] *v* overheat.
surcroît [syrkrwa] *nm* excess; (*augmentation*) increase. **par surcroît** in addition.
surdité [syrdite] *nf* deafness.
surdose [syrdoz] *nf* overdose.
sureau [syro] *nm* elder. **baie du sureau** elderberry.
surélever [syrɛlve] *v* raise, heighten.
surenchère [syrɑ̃ʃɛr] *nf* higher bid.
surestimer [syrɛstime] *v* overestimate.
sûreté [syrte] *nf* (*sécurité*) safety; (*précision*) reliability; guarantee.
surexposer [syrɛkspoze] *v* overexpose. **surexposition** *nf* overexposure.
surface [syrfas] *nf* surface; (*aire*) surface area. **faire surface** surface.
surfait [syrfɛ] *adj* overrated.
surgeler [syrʒəle] *v* deep-freeze.
surgir [syrʒir] *v* appear suddenly; (*jaillir*) spring up; (*problème, etc.*) arise.
surhumain [syrymɛ̃] *adj* superhuman.
surimpression [syrɛ̃presjɔ̃] *nf* superimposition. **en surimpression** superimposed.
surlendemain [syrlɑ̃dmɛ̃] *nm* next day but one. **le surlendemain** two days later.
surmener [syrməne] *v* overwork. **surmenage** *nm* overwork.
surmonter [syrmɔ̃te] *v* surmount; (*vaincre*) overcome; *dôme, etc.*) top.
surnaturel [syrnatyrɛl] *nm, adj* supernatural.
surnom [syrnɔ̃] *nm* nickname. **surnommer** *v* nickname.
surnombre [syrnɔ̃brə] *nm* **en surnombre** too many.
surpasser [syrpɑse] *v* surpass.
surpeuplé [syrpœple] *adj* overpopulated, overcrowded. **surpeuplement** *nm* overpopulation, overcrowding.
surplomb [syrplɔ̃] *nm* overhang. **surplomber** *v* overhang.
surplus [syrply] *nm* surplus. **au surplus** moreover.
***surprendre** [syrprɑ̃drə] *v* surprise; discover, detect; (*prendre*) catch (out). **surpris** *adj* surprised. **surprise** *nf* surprise.
surréaliste [syrrealist] *adj* surrealistic. *n*(*m*+*f*) surrealist. **surréalisme** *nm* surrealism.
sursaut [syrso] *nm* start, jump. **sursauter** *v* start, jump.
***surseoir** [syrswar] *v* **surseoir à** defer, postpone. **sursis** *nm* reprieve.
surtaxer [syrtakse] *v* surcharge. **surtaxe** *nf* surcharge.
surtout [syrtu] *adv* above all; especially, particularly.
surveiller [syrveje] *v* (*garder, épier*) watch; (*contrôler*) supervise. **surveillance** *nf* watch; supervision. **surveillant, -e** *nm, nf* supervisor; (*prison*) warder; (*école*) person in charge of discipline.
***survenir** [syrvənir] *v* occur, take place; (*problème*) arise; (*personne*) arrive unexpectedly.
survêtement [syrvɛtmɑ̃] *nm* tracksuit.
***survivre** [syrvivrə] *v* survive. **survivre à** outlive. **survivance** *nf* survival. **survivant, -e** *nm, nf* survivor.

sus [sy] *adv* **en sus** in addition.
susceptible [syseptiblə] *adj* sensitive, touchy. **susceptible à** (*possible*) likely to; capable of.
susciter [sysite] *v* arouse; (*obstacles, etc.*) create.
susdit [sysdi] *adj* aforesaid.
suspect [syspɛkt], **-e** *adj* suspicious; (*douteux*) suspect. **suspect de** suspected of. *nm, nf* suspect.
suspendre [syspɑ̃drə] *v* suspend; (*fixer, accrocher*) hang (up). **suspendu** *adj* suspended; hanging.
suspens [syspɑ̃] *nm* **en suspens** (*projet, etc.*) in abeyance; in suspense; in suspension. **suspense** *nm* suspense.
suspension [syspɑ̃sjɔ̃] *nf* suspension.
susurrer [sysyre] *v* murmur.
suture [sytyr] *nf* suture. **suturer** *v* (*méd*) stitch (up).
svelte [svɛlt] *adj* slender.
sycomore [sikɔmɔr] *nm* sycamore.
syllabe [silab] *nf* syllable **syllabique** *adj* syllabic.
sylvestre [silvɛstrə] *adj* forest, woodland.
sylviculture *nf* forestry.
symbole [sɛ̃bɔl] *nm* symbol. **symbolique** *adj* symbolic; (*donation contribution*) nominal. **symboliser** *v* symbolize. **symbolisme** *nm* symbolism.
symétrie [simetri] *nf* symmetry. **symétrique** *adj* symmetrical.
sympathie [sɛ̃pati] *nf* liking; affinity. **sympathique** *adj* nice, pleasant; (*personne*) likeable, friendly.
symphonie [sɛ̃fɔni] *nf* symphony. **symphonique** *adj* symphonic.
symposium [sɛ̃pozjɔm] *nm* symposium.
symptôme [sɛ̃ptɔm] *nm* symptom; sign. **symptomatique** *adj* symptomatic.
synagogue [sinagɔg] *nf* synagogue.
synchroniser [sɛ̃krɔnize] *v* synchronize. **synchronisation** *nf* synchronization.
syncoper [sɛ̃kɔpe] *v* (*musique*) syncopate. **syncope** *nf* syncopation; (*méd*) black-out, fainting fit.
syndicat [sɛ̃dika] *nm* syndicate; (*ouvrier*) union; association. **syndicat d'initiative** tourist information bureau. **syndical** *adj* union. **syndicaliste** *n(m+f)* trade unionist. **syndiqué, -e** *nm, nf* union member.
syndrome [sɛ̃drom] *nm* syndrome.
synonyme [sinɔnim] *nm* synonym. *adj* synonymous.
syntaxe [sɛ̃taks] *nf* syntax.
synthèse [sɛ̃tɛz] *nf* synthesis (*pl* -ses). **synthétique** *adj* synthetic. **synthétiser** *v* synthesize.
syphilis [sifilis] *nf* syphilis.
système [sistɛm] *nm* system. **systématique** *adj* systematic.

T

t' [t] *V* **te**.
ta [ta] *V* **ton'**.
tabac [taba] *nm* tobacco; (*magasin*) tobacconist's. **tabac à priser** snuff. **tabatière** *nf* snuffbox.
table [tablə] *nf* table; tablet. **faire table rase** make a clean sweep. **table basse** coffee table. **table des matières** table of contents. **table gigogne** nest of tables. **table roulante** trolley.
tableau [tablo] *nm* picture; (*peinture*) painting; scene; (*support, panneau*) board; list; (*graphique*) table, chart. **tableau de bord** dashboard. **tableau noir** blackboard.
tablette [tablɛt] *nf* tablet; (*rayon*) shelf; (*chocolat*) bar.
tablier [tablije] *nm* apron.
tabou [tabu] *nm, adj* taboo.
tabouret [taburɛ] *nm* stool.
tache [taʃ] *nf* mark, spot; (*sang, vin, etc.*) stain; (*pâté*) blot. **tache de rousseur** *or* **son** freckle. **tacher** *v* mark; stain.
tâche [tɑʃ] *nf* task, work. **tâcher** *v* try, endeavour.
tacheté [taʃte] *adj* speckled, spotted.
tacite [tasit] *adj* tacit.
taciturne [tasityrn] *adj* taciturn.
tact [takt] *nm* tact. **avoir du tact** be tactful.
tactique [taktik] *nf* tactics *pl*. *adj* tactical.
taffetas [tafta] *nm* taffeta.
taie [tɛ] *nf* **taie d'oreiller** pillowcase.
taillade [tɑjad] *nf* slash, gash. **taillader** *v* slash, gash.
taille [tɑj] *nf* size; (*hauteur*) height; (*corps, vêtement*) waist; (*coupe*) cutting, cut; (*tranchant*) edge. **à la taille de** in keeping with. **être de taille à** be up to.
tailler [tɑje] *v* cut; (*bois*) carve; (*barbe, haie, etc.*) trim; (*crayon*) sharpen. **taille-**

crayon *nm invar* pencil sharpener. **tailleur** *nm* (*personne*) tailor; (*costume*) suit.
taillis [taji] *nm* copse.
***taire** [tɛr] *v* conceal, hush up. **faire taire** silence. **se taire** be quiet.
talc [talk] *nm* talcum powder.
talent [talɑ̃] *nm* talent. **talentueux** *adj* talented.
talon [talɔ̃] *nm* heel; (*chèque*) stub; (*pain*) crust.
talonner [talɔne] *v* (*suivre*) follow closely; (*harceler*) hound; (*cheval*) spur on.
talus [taly] *nm* embankment.
tambour [tɑ̃bur] *nm* drum; (*joueur*) drummer. **tambourin** *nm* tambourine. **tambouriner** *v* drum.
tamis [tami] *nm* sieve. **tamiser** *v* sieve, sift; filter.
Tamise [tamiz] *nf* **la Tamise** the Thames.
tampon [tɑ̃pɔ̃] *nm* pad, wad; (*pour boucher*) plug; (*pour règles*) tampon; (*timbre*) stamp; (*rail*) buffer. **tamponner** *v* dab, mop; stamp; plug; (*heurter*) crash into.
tancer [tɑ̃se] *v* scold, reprimand.
tandem [tɑ̃dɛm] *nm* tandem; (*couple*) pair.
tandis [tɑ̃di] *conj* **tandis que** while; (*contraste*) whereas.
tangente [tɑ̃ʒɑ̃t] *nf* tangent.
tangible [tɑ̃ʒiblə] *adj* tangible.
tanguer [tɑ̃ge] *v* pitch, reel.
tanière [tanjɛr] *nf* den, lair.
tanner [tane] *v* tan; (*fam*) pester, annoy.
tan-sad [tɑ̃sad] *nm* pillion.
tant [tɑ̃] *adv* so much, so. **en tant que** as. **tant de** (*quantité*) so much; (*nombre*) so many; (*qualité*) such. **tant mieux** so much the better. **tant pis** too bad. **tant que** as long as, while. **tant s'en faut** far from it.
tante [tɑ̃t] *nf* aunt.
tantôt [tɑ̃to] *adv* this afternoon. **tantôt . . . tantôt . . .** sometimes . . . sometimes . . . .
taon [tɑ̃] *nm* horse-fly.
tapage [tapaʒ] *nm* (*vacarme*) uproar, din; (*scandale*) fuss. **tapageur, -euse** *adj* rowdy; (*criard*) showy, flashy.
taper [tape] *v* knock, hit; (*battre*) beat; (*à la machine*) type. **taper sur les nerfs de quelqu'un** get on someone's nerves. **tape** *nf* slap.
tapioca [tapjɔka] *nm* tapioca.
se tapir [tapir] *v* crouch; (*se cacher*) hide away.
tapis [tapi] *nm* carpet; (*carpette*) rug; (*natte*) mat; (*table*) cloth, covering. **tapis de sol** groundsheet. **tapis roulant** conveyor belt.
tapisser [tapise] *v* cover; (*sol*) carpet; (*mur*) paper. **tapisserie** *nf* tapestry; (*papier peint*) wallpaper. **tapissier** *nm* upholsterer; (*maison*) interior decorator.
tapoter [tapɔte] *v* pat, tap.
taquin [takɛ̃] *adj* teasing. **taquiner** *v* tease; (*inquiéter*) bother, worry. **taquinerie** *nf* teasing.
tard [tar] *adv* late.
tarder [tarde] *v* (*différer*) delay, put off; (*être lent*) take a long time, be long. **tardif** *adj* late; (*remords, etc.*) belated.
tarif [tarif] *nm* tariff, rate; (*tableau*) price list; (*transport*) fare.
tarir [tarir] *v* run dry, dry up.
tarte [tart] *nf* tart. **tartelette** *nf* tart. **tartine** *nf* slice of bread (and butter). **tartiner** *v* spread.
tartre [tartrə] *nm* tartar; (*bouilloire*) fur.
tas [tɑ] *nm* pile, heap; (*fam*: *foule*) crowd. **un tas de** (*fam*) loads of, lots of.
tasse [tɑs] *nf* cup. **tasse à thé/café** tea/coffee cup.
tasser [tɑse] *v* pack (down), cram. **se tasser** (*se serrer*) squeeze up; (*s'affaisser*) settle; (*corps*) shrink.
tâter [tɑte] *v* (*palper*) feel; (*opinion, etc.*) sound out; (*essayer*) try out.
tâtonner [tɑtɔne] *v* grop along *or* around, feel one's way. **par tâtonnements** by trial and error.
tâtons [tatɔ̃] *adv* **avancer à tâtons** feel one's way along. **chercher à tâtons** feel around for.
tatouer [tatwe] *v* tattoo. **tatouage** *nm* tattoo.
taudis [todi] *nm* slum.
taule [tol] *nf* (*argot*: *prison*) nick.
taupe [top] *nf* mole.
taureau [tɔro] *nm* bull. **Taureau** *nm* Taurus.
taux [to] *nm* rate; degree, level. **taux de change** exchange rate.
taxer [takse] *v* tax; (*comm*) fix the price of; accuse. **taxation** *nf* taxation. **taxe** *nf* tax; (*douane*) duty; fixed price.
taxi [taksi] *nm* taxi.
Tchécoslovaquie [tʃekɔslɔvaki] *nf* Czechoslovakia. **tchécoslovaque** *nm, adj* Czechoslovak. **Tchécoslovaque** *n(m+f)* Czech-

oslovak. **tchèque** *nm, adj* Czech. **Tchèque** *n(m+f)* Czech.
te [tə], **t'** *pron* you, to you; (*réfléchi*) yourself.
technique [teknik] *adj* technical. *nf* technique. **technicien, -enne** *nm, nf* technician. **technologie** *nf* technology. **technologique** *adj* technological.
teck [tek] *nm* teak.
***teindre** [tɛ̃drə] *v* dye; colour, tinge.
teint [tɛ̃] *adj* dyed. *nm* complexion, colouring. **teinte** *nf* shade, tint; colour; (*trace*) tinge, hint.
teinter [tɛ̃te] *v* (*verre*) tint; (*bois*) stain.
teinture [tɛ̃tyr] *nf* (*substance*) dye; (*action*) dyeing. **teinturerie** *nf* cleaner's.
tel [tel], **telle** *adj* such (a), like, as. **tel que** such as, like. **tel quel** as it stands, as it is. *pron* one, someone.
télécommande [telekɔmɑ̃d] *nf* remote control.
télécommunications [telekɔmynikɑsjɔ̃] *nf pl* telecommunications *pl.*
télégramme [telegram] *nm* telegram.
télégraphier [telegrafje] *v* telegraph, cable. **télégraphe** *nm* telegraph. **télégraphique** *adj* telegraphic; (*poteau*) telegraph.
télépathie [telepati] *nf* telepathy. **télépathique** *adj* telepathic.
téléphérique [teleferik] *nm* cable-car.
téléphone [telefɔn] *nm* telephone, phone. **téléphoner** *v* telephone, phone. **téléphonique** *adj* telephone. **téléphoniste** *n(m+f)* telephonist.
télescope [teleskɔp] *nm* telescope. **télescopique** *adj* telescopic.
télésiège [telesjɛʒ] *nm* chair-lift.
téléski [teleski] *nm* ski-lift.
téléviser [televize] *v* televise. **télévision** *nf* television. **téléviseur** *nm* television set.
télex [teleks] *nm* telex.
tellement [telmɑ̃] *adv* so (much). **pas tellement** not (very) much.
téméraire [temerer] *adj* rash, reckless. **témérité** *nf* rashness, recklessness.
témoigner [temwaɲe] *v* testify; (*montrer*) show; reveal. **témoigner de** bear witness to. **témoignage** *nm* evidence, testimony; (*récit*) account; expression; (*cadeau*) token. **témoin** *nm* witness; evidence, testimony; (*sport*) baton.
tempe [tɑ̃p] *nf* temple.
tempérament [tɑ̃peramɑ̃] *nm* temperament, disposition; constitution. **achat à tempérament** *nm* hire purchase.
température [tɑ̃peratyr] *nf* temperature.
tempérer [tɑ̃pere] *v* temper; (*douleur*) soothe. **tempéré** *adj* temperate.
tempête [tɑ̃pɛt] *nf* storm. **tempétueux** *adj* stormy, tempestuous.
temple [tɑ̃plə] *nm* temple; Protestant church.
tempo [tempo] *nm* tempo.
temporaire [tɑ̃pɔrer] *adj* temporary.
temporel [tɑ̃pɔrel] *adj* temporal, worldly.
temps [tɑ̃] *nm* time; (*météorologie*) weather; (*musique*) beat; (*gramm*) tense. **à temps** in time. **de temps en temps** now and again. **quel temps fait-il?** what's the weather like?
tenace [tənas] *adj* stubborn, persistent, tenacious. **ténacité** *nf* stubbornness, persistence, tenacity.
tenailles [tənɑj] *nf pl* pincers *pl.* **tenailler** *v* torture, torment.
tendance [tɑ̃dɑ̃s] *nf* tendency; (*évolution*) trend; (*opinions*) leanings *pl.* **avoir tendance à** tend to.
tendon [tɑ̃dɔ̃] *nm* tendon.
tendre[1] [tɑ̃drə] *v* (*raidir*) tighten; (*tirer sur*) stretch; (*muscle*) tense; (*poser*) set; (*tapisserie, etc.*) hang; (*présenter*) hold out. **tendre à** tend to; (*viser à*) aim at *or* to. **tendre le cou** crane one's neck. **tendre l'oreille** prick up one's ears. **tendu** *adj* taut, tight; tense; (*bras*) outstretched. **tendu de** hung with.
tendre[2] [tɑ̃drə] *adj* tender; soft, delicate. **tendresse** *nf* tenderness, affection. **tendreté** *nf* tenderness.
ténèbres [tenebrə] *nf pl* darkness *sing*, gloom *sing.* **ténébreux** *adj* dark, gloomy; obscure; mysterious.
***tenir** [tənir] *v* hold; (*garder*) keep; (*avoir*) have; (*magasin, etc.*) run; (*occuper*) take up; (*durer*) last. **se tenir** (*se conduire*) behave; (*debout*) stand. **se tenir à** hold on to. **tenir à** (*vouloir*) be anxious to, insist on; (*aimer*) be fond of; (*résulter*) stem from. **tenir compte de** take into account. **tenir de** take after. **tenir pour** regard as.
tennis [tenis] *nm* tennis; tennis court. *nf pl* plimsolls *pl.*
ténor [tenɔr] *nm* tenor.
tension [tɑ̃sjɔ̃] *nf* tension; (*méd*) blood pressure; (*élec*) voltage.

tentacule [tɑ̃takyl] *nm* tentacle.
tente [tɑ̃t] *nf* tent.
tenter [tɑ̃te] *v* (*tentation*) tempt; (*tentative*) attempt. **tentation** *nf* temptation. **tentative** *nf* attempt.
tenture [tɑ̃tyr] *nf* hanging; (*rideau*) curtain.
tenu [təny] *adj* **bien tenu** neat, well-kept. **être tenu de** be obliged to. **mal tenu** untidy, neglected. **tenue** *nf* (*habillement*) dress; (*maintien*) posture; (*conduite*) manners *pl*; (*magasin, etc.*) running; control.
ténu [teny] *adj* fine; (*subtil*) tenuous.
térébenthine [terebɑ̃tin] *nf* turpentine.
tergiverser [tɛrʒivɛrse] *v* prevaricate.
terme [tɛrm] *nm* term; (*date limite*) deadline; (*loyer*) rent. **avant terme** prematurely.
terminaison [tɛrminɛzɔ̃] *nf* ending.
terminal [tɛrminal] *adj* terminal. **terminale** *nf* (*classe*) upper sixth.
terminer [tɛrmine] *v* end, finish, terminate.
terminologie [tɛrminɔlɔʒi] *nf* terminology.
terminus [tɛrminys] *nm* terminus.
ternir [tɛrnir] *v* tarnish, dull. **terne** *adj* dull, drab.
terrain [tɛrɛ̃] *nm* ground, land; (*sport*) pitch, field; (*parcelle*) plot, site. **terrain de jeu** playing field. **terrain vague** wasteland.
terrasse [tɛras] *nf* terrace.
terrasser [tɛrase] *v* overcome, overwhelm.
terre [tɛr] *nf* earth; (*sol*) ground; (*étendue, pays*) land. **à terre** ashore. **par terre** on the ground. **terre-à-terre** *adj invar* down-to-earth.
terrestre [tɛrɛstrə] *adj* earthly, terrestrial.
terreur [tɛrœr] *nf* terror.
terrible [tɛriblə] *adj* terrible, dreadful; (*fam*) terrific.
terrier [tɛrje] *nm* hole; (*lapin*) burrow; (*renard*) earth; (*race de chien*) terrier.
terrifier [tɛrifje] *v* terrify.
terrine [tɛrin] *nf* earthenware dish; pâté.
territoire [tɛritwar] *nm* territory. **territorial** *adj* territorial.
terroir [tɛrwar] *nm* soil.
terroriser [tɛrɔrize] *v* terrorize. **terrorisme** *nm* terrorism. **terroriste** *n*(*m*+*f*), *adj* terrorist.
tes [te] *V* **ton**[1].
tesson [tesɔ̃] *nm* piece of broken glass.
testament [tɛstamɑ̃] *nm* testament; (*jur*) will.
testicule [tɛstikyl] *nm* testicle.
tétanos [tetanos] *nm* tetanus.
têtard [tɛtar] *nm* tadpole.
tête [tɛt] *nf* head; (*visage*) face; (*devant*) front; (*haut*) top; (*esprit*) mind. **en tête** in front; at the top. **tenir tête à** stand up to. **tête-à-tête** *nm invar* private conversation.
tétine [tetin] *nf* teat; (*vache*) udder; (*sucette*) dummy.
têtu [tety] *adj* stubborn.
texte [tɛkst] *nm* text; passage; subject. **textuel** *adj* textual.
textile [tɛkstil] *nm, adj* textile.
texture [tɛkstyr] *nf* texture.
thé [te] *nm* tea. **théière** *nf* teapot.
théâtre [teɑtrə] *nm* theatre; drama. **théâtral** *adj* theatrical; dramatic.
thème [tɛm] *nm* theme; (*traduction*) prose. **thématique** *adj* thematic.
théologie [teɔlɔʒi] *nf* theology. **théologien, -enne** *nm, nf* theologian. **théologique** *adj* theological.
théorème [teɔrɛm] *nm* theorem.
théorie [teɔri] *nf* theory. **théorique** *adj* theoretical.
thérapeutique [terapøtik] *adj* therapeutic. *nf also* **thérapie** therapy. **thérapeute** *n*(*m*+*f*) therapist.
thermal [tɛrmal] *adj* thermal. **station thermale** *nf* spa.
thermique [tɛrmik] *adj* thermal, heat.
thermodynamique [tɛrmɔdinamik] *nf* thermodynamics.
thermomètre [tɛrmɔmɛtrə] *nm* thermometer.
thermonucléaire [tɛrmɔnykleɛr] *adj* thermonuclear.
thermos ® [tɛrmos] *nm* thermos flask ®.
thermostat [tɛrmɔsta] *nm* thermostat.
thésauriser [tezɔrize] *v* hoard (money).
thèse [tɛz] *nf* thesis.
thon [tɔ̃] *nm* tuna.
thym [tɛ̃] *nm* thyme.
thyroïde [tirɔid] *nf, adj* thyroid.
tiare [tjar] *nf* tiara.
tic [tik] *nm* tic, twitch; (*manie*) mannerism.
ticket [tikɛ] *nm* ticket.
tic-tac [tiktak] *nm* tick, ticking. **faire tic-tac** tick.

tiède [tjɛd] *adj* lukewarm, tepid; (*doux*) mild.
tien [tjɛ̃], **tienne** *pron* **le tien, la tienne** yours.
tiens [tjɛ̃] *interj* well! (*en donnant*) here! (*en expliquant*) look!
tiers, tierce [tjɛr, tjɛrs] *adj* third. **Tiers-Monde** *nm* Third World. *nm* third; (*jur*) third party. *nf* (*musique*) third.
tige [tiʒ] *nf* stem, stalk; (*métal*) rod.
tigre [tigrə] *nm* tiger. **tigré** *adj* (*tacheté*) spotted; (*rayé*) striped. **chat tigré** *nm* tabby cat.
tilleul [tijœl] *nm* lime tree.
timbale [tɛ̃bal] *nf* kettledrum; (*gobelet*) metal tumbler. **timbales** *nf pl* timpani *pl*.
timbre [tɛ̃brə] *nm* stamp; (*son*) tone; (*sonnette*) bell. **timbrer** *v* stamp; (*d'un cachet*) postmark.
timide [timid] *adj* timid; (*mal à l'aise*) shy. **timidité** *nf* timidity; shyness.
tintamarre [tɛ̃tamar] *nm* din.
tinter [tɛ̃te] *v* ring; (*clochette*) tinkle; (*clefs, monnaie, etc.*) jingle; (*verres*) chink.
tir [tir] *nm* firing; (*feu*) fire; (*sport*) shooting. **tir à l'arc** archery.
tirailler [tirɑje] *v* tug *or* pull at; (*harceler*) plague; (*douleur*) gnaw *or* stab at. **tiraillement** *nm* pulling, tugging; conflict; stabbing *or* gnawing pain.
tirelire [tirlir] *nf* money-box.
tirer [tire] *v* pull, draw; extract, get out, take from; (*fusil*) fire, shoot; (*imprimer*) print. **se tirer de** (*s'échapper*) get out of; (*se débrouiller*) handle, cope with. **tire-bouchon** *nm* corkscrew. **tirage** *nm* printing; (*journal*) circulation; edition; (*loterie*) draw.
tiroir [tirwar] *nm* drawer. **tiroir-caisse** *nm* till.
tisane [tizan] *nf* herb tea.
tisonner [tizɔne] *v* poke. **tisonnier** *nm* poker.
tisser [tise] *v* weave. **tissage** *nm* weaving.
tissu [tisy] *nm* cloth, fabric, material; (*bot, anat*) tissue.
titre [titrə] *nm* title; (*diplôme*) qualification; (*bourse*) bond, security; (*droit*) right, claim. **à ce titre** as such. **à titre de** as, in the capacity of.
tituber [titybe] *v* stagger.
toast [tost] *nm* toast.
toboggan [tɔbɔgɑ̃] *nm* toboggan; (*glissière*) slide, chute.
toi [twa] *pron* you. **toi-même** *pron* yourself.
toile [twal] *nf* cloth; (*grosse*) canvas; linen; cotton; (*araignée*) web. **toile cirée** oilskin. **toile de fond** backcloth, backdrop.
toilette [twalɛt] *nf* (*soins de propreté*) wash; (*habillement*) outfit, clothes *pl*. **toilettes** *nf pl* toilet *sing*.
toison [twazɔ̃] *nf* fleece.
toit [twa] *nm* roof.
Tokio [tɔkjo] *n* Tokyo.
tôle [tol] *nf* metal sheet. **tôle onculée** corrugated iron.
tolérer [tɔlere] *v* tolerate; endure, stand. **tolérable** *adj* tolerable. **tolérance** *nf* tolerance, toleration. **tolérant** *adj* tolerant.
tomate [tɔmat] *nf* tomato.
tombe [tɔ̃b] *nf* grave, tomb. **tombeau** *nm* tomb.
tomber [tɔ̃be] *v* fall; (*baisser*) drop; (*pendre*) hang. **laisser tomber** drop. **tomber juste** be exactly right. **tomber sur** come across. **tombée** *nf* fall.
tome [tɔm] *nm* volume.
ton[1] [tɔ̃], **ta** *adj*, *pl* **tes** your.
ton[2] [tɔ̃] *nm* tone; (*hauteur*) pitch; (*échelle musicale*) key.
tondre [tɔ̃drə] *v* clip; (*mouton*) shear; (*pelouse*) mow. **tondeuse** *nf* shears *pl*; clippers *pl*; lawn-mower. **tondu** *adj* closely-cropped.
tonifier [tɔnifje] *v* tone up, invigorate. **tonifiant** *adj* invigorating, bracing.
tonique [tɔnik] *nm* tonic. *nf* (*musique*) tonic.
tonne [tɔn] *nf* ton.
tonneau [tɔno] *nm* barrel.
tonner [tɔne] *v* thunder. **tonnerre** *nm* thunder.
topaze [tɔpɑz] *nf* topaz.
toper [tɔpe] *v* agree. **tope-là!** (*fam*) it's a deal!
topographie [tɔpɔgrafi] *nf* topography. **topographique** *adj* topographical.
torche [tɔrʃ] *nf* torch.
torcher [tɔrʃe] *v* (*fam*) wipe.
torchon [tɔrʃɔ̃] *nm* cloth; (*à vaisselle*) tea towel; (*chiffon*) duster.
tordre [tɔrdrə] *v* twist; (*linge, cou*) wring; (*déformer*) distort. **se tordre de douleur/rire** be doubled up with pain/laughter. **tordu** *adj* twisted, crooked.

tornade [tɔrnad] *nf* tornado.

torpille [tɔrpij] *nf* torpedo. **torpiller** *v* torpedo.

torréfier [tɔrefje] *v* roast.

torrent [tɔrɑ̃] *nm* torrent. **torrentiel** *adj* torrential.

tors [tɔr] *adj* twisted, crooked.

torse [tɔrs] *nm* torso; (*poitrine*) chest.

tort [tɔr] *nm* wrong; fault; (*dommage*) harm. **à tort** wrongly. **avoir tort** be wrong.

torticolis [tɔrtikɔli] *nm* stiff neck.

tortiller [tɔrtije] *v* twist; (*cheveux, doigts*) twiddle; (*hanches*) wiggle. **se tortiller** wriggle; (*fumée*) curl.

tortue [tɔrty] *nf* tortoise. **tortue de mer** turtle.

tortueux [tɔrtɥø] *adj* (*chemin, etc.*) twisting, winding; (*oblique*) tortuous.

torturer [tɔrtyre] *v* torture. **torture** *nf* torture.

tôt [to] *adv* early, soon. **tôt ou tard** sooner or later.

total [tɔtal] *adj* total; complete, absolute. *nm* total. **totaliser** *v* total. **totalitaire** *adj* totalitarian. **totalité** *nf* whole. **la totalité de** all (of).

toucher [tuʃe] *v* touch; concern, affect; (*être contigu*) adjoin; (*frapper*) hit; contact, reach; (*pension, etc.*) draw; (*chèque*) cash; (*salaire*) get. **toucher à** touch; (*modifier*) meddle with; approach. *nm* touch. **touche** *nf* touch; (*piano*) key.

touffe [tuf] *nf* tuft; (*arbres, fleurs*) clump. **touffu** *adj* bushy, thick; (*roman*) complex.

toujours [tuʒur] *adv* always; (*encore*) still; (*en tout cas*) anyway.

toupet [tupɛ] *nm* (*cheveux*) quiff; (*fam*) nerve, cheek.

toupie [tupi] *nf* spinning-top.

tour[1] [tur] *nf* tower.

tour[2] [tur] *nm* turn; (*excursion*) trip; (*tourisme*) tour; (*poitrine, taille, etc.*) measurement; (*farce, ruse*) trick; (*tech*) lathe. **à tour de rôle** in turn. **faire le tour de** go round. **tour de main** knack. **tour de piste** lap.

tourbe [turb] *nf* peat.

tourbillon [turbijɔ̃] *nm* (*vent*) whirlwind; (*eau*) whirlpool; (*vie, plaisir, etc.*) whirl. **tourbillonner** *v* whirl, swirl.

tourelle [turɛl] *nf* turret.

tourisme [turismə] *nm* (*industrie*) tourism; (*activité*) sightseeing. **touriste** *n*(*m*+*f*) tourist. **touristique** *adj* tourist.

tourment [turmɑ̃] *nm* agony, torment. **tourmenter** *v* torment. **se tourmenter** fret, worry.

tourmente [turmɑ̃t] *nf* storm; (*pol*) upheaval.

tournant [turnɑ̃] *adj* (*pivotant*) revolving, swivel; (*escalier*) spiral; (*sinueux*) winding, twisting. *nm* bend; (*moment décisif*) turning point.

tourner [turne] *v* turn; (*film*) make, shoot; (*lait*) turn sour; (*disque, etc.*) revolve, go round; (*moteur*) run. **bien/mal tourner** turn out well/badly. **tourne-disque** *nm* record player. **tournevis** *nm* screwdriver. **tournée** *nf* round; tour.

tournesol [turnəsɔl] *nm* sunflower.

tourniquet [turnikɛ] *nm* (*barrière*) turnstile; (*méd*) tourniquet.

tournoi [turnwa] *nm* tournament.

tournoyer [turnwaje] *v* whirl, swirl.

tournure [turnyr] *nf* turn; turn of phrase; (*apparence*) shape, face.

tourte [turt] *nf* pie.

tourterelle [turtərɛl] *nf* turtle-dove.

Toussaint [tusɛ̃] *nf* All Saints' Day.

tousser [tuse] *v* cough.

tout [tu], **toute** *adj*, *pl* **tous, toutes** all; (*chaque*) every; (*n'importe quel*) any; (*total*) utmost, full. **de toute façon** in any case. **tous les deux** both. **tous risques** (*assurance*) fully comprehensive. *pron* everything, all. *nm* whole. **du tout** at all. **pas du tout** not at all. *adv* quite, completely; (*très*) very; (*quoique*) though, however. **tout à coup** suddenly. **tout à fait** quite, entirely. **tout à l'heure** (*futur*) presently; (*passé*) just now. **tout au plus/moins** at the very most/least. **tout de même** all the same. **tout de suite** at once. **tout en . . .** while . . . . **tout fait** ready-made. **tout neuf** brand new. **tout-puissant** *adj* omnipotent.

toutefois [tutfwa] *adv* however.

toux [tu] *nf* cough.

toxique [tɔksik] *adj* toxic.

trac [trak] *nm* fit of nerves; (*théâtre*) stage fright.

tracas [traka] *nm* worry, bother. **tracasser** *v* worry, bother.

trace [tras] *nf* trace; mark, sign; (*chemin*) track, path; (*empreinte*) tracks *pl*, trail. **suivre à la trace** track.

tracer [trase] *v* trace, draw; (*chemin*) mark out.
tract [trakt] *nm* pamphlet.
tracteur [traktœr] *nm* tractor.
tradition [tradisjɔ̃] *nf* tradition. **traditionnel** *adj* traditional.
***traduire** [tradɥir] *v* translate; express, convey. **traducteur, -trice** *nm, nf* translator. **traduction** *nf* translation.
trafic [trafik] *nm* traffic; (*péj*) dealings *pl*. **trafiquer** *v* traffic, trade illicitly.
tragédie [traʒedi] *nf* tragedy. **tragique** *adj* tragic.
trahir [trair] *v* betray; (*forces, etc.*) fail; (*mal exprimer*) misrepresent. **trahison** *nf* betrayal; (*crime*) treason.
train [trɛ̃] *nm* train; (*allure*) pace; (*file*) line. **en train** under way. **être en train de** be in the middle of.
train-train *nm* daily routine.
traîner [trene] *v* drag; (*mots*) drawl; (*s'attarder*) dawdle, lag behind; (*pendre*) trail; (*s'éterniser*) drag on; (*être éparpillé*) lie around. **se traîner** drag oneself, crawl. **traîneau** *nm* sledge, sleigh. **traînée** *nf* streak; (*trace*) trail.
***traire** [trɛr] *v* milk.
trait [trɛ] *nm* line; (*caractéristique*) trait; (*visage*) feature; (*de lumière, satire, etc.*) shaft; (*gorgée*) gulp. **d'un trait** at one go. **trait d'union** hyphen.
traiter [trete] *v* treat; (*qualifier*) call; (*s'occuper de*) deal with; (*négocier*) have dealings. **traité** *nm* (*convention*) treaty; (*livre*) treatise. **traitement** *nm* treatment; salary.
traître, -esse [trɛtrə, -ɛs] *adj* treacherous. *nm, nf* traitor. **traîtrise** *nf* treachery.
trajet [traʒɛ] *nm* (*voyage*) journey; distance.
trame [tram] *nf* (*tissu*) thread; (*vie*) texture, web. **tramer** *v* (*combiner*) plot; (*tisser*) weave.
tramway [tramwɛ] *nm* tram.
tranchant [trɑ̃ʃɑ̃] *adj* sharp; (*personne*) assertive. *nm* cutting edge.
trancher [trɑ̃ʃe] *v* cut, sever; resolve, settle; contrast sharply. **tranche** *nf* slice; section; (*bord*) edge. **tranché** *adj* clear-cut, distinct. **tranchée** *nf* trench.
tranquille [trɑ̃kil] *adj* quiet; calm, peaceful; (*esprit*) easy, at rest. **laisser tranquille** leave alone. **tranquillisant** *nm* tranquillizer. **tranquilliser** *v* reassure. **tranquillité** *nf* peace, tranquillity.
transaction [trɑ̃zaksjɔ̃] *nf* transaction; compromise.
transatlantique [trɑ̃zatlɑ̃tik] *adj* transatlantic. *nm* (*chaise*) deckchair.
transcender [trɑ̃sɑ̃de] *v* transcend. **transcendantal** *adj* transcendental.
***transcrire** [trɑ̃skrir] *v* transcribe; copy out. **transcription** *nf* transcription; copy.
transe [trɑ̃s] *nf* trance. **transes** *nf pl* agony *sing*.
transept [trɑ̃sɛpt] *nm* transept.
transférer [trɑ̃sfere] *v* transfer. **transfert** *nm* transfer.
transformer [trɑ̃sfɔrme] *v* change, alter; (*radicalement*) transform; convert. **transformateur** *nm* transformer. **transformation** *nf* change; transformation; conversion.
transfuge [trɑ̃sfyʒ] *n(m+f)* renegade.
transfuser [trɑ̃sfyze] *v* transfuse. **transfusion** *nf* transfusion.
transiger [trɑ̃ziʒe] *v* come to an agreement, compromise.
transir [trɑ̃zir] *v* numb; (*froid*) chill to the bone; (*peur*) transfix. **transi** *adj* numb with cold; transfixed with fear.
transistor [trɑ̃zistɔr] *nm* transistor. **transistoriser** *v* transistorize.
transit [trɑ̃zit] *nm* transit. **en transit** in transit.
transitif [trɑ̃zitif] *adj* transitive.
transition [trɑ̃zisjɔ̃] *nf* transition. **de transition** transitional.
transitoire [trɑ̃zitwar] *adj* transient, transitory; provisional.
translucide [trɑ̃slysid] *adj* translucent. **translucidité** *nf* translucence.
***transmettre** [trɑ̃smɛtrə] *v* pass on; (*tech*) transmit. **transmetteur** *nm* transmitter. **transmission** *nf* transmission.
transparent [trɑ̃sparɑ̃] *adj* transparent.
transpirer [trɑ̃spire] *v* sweat, perspire; (*secret*) come to light. **transpiration** *nf* perspiration.
transplanter [trɑ̃splɑ̃te] *v* transplant. **transplantation** *nf* transplant.
transport [trɑ̃spɔr] *nm* transport; (*marchandises*) carriage, transportation. **transporter** *v* carry, convey; (*avec un véhicule*) transport; (*exalter*) carry away.
transposer [trɑ̃spoze] *v* transpose. **transposition** *nf* transposition.
transvaser [trɑ̃svɑze] *v* decant.

transversal [trɑ̃svɛrsal] *adj* transverse.
trapèze [trapɛz] *nm* (*sport*) trapeze; (*géom*) trapezium. **trapéziste** *n(m+f)* trapeze artist.
trappe [trap] *nf* trapdoor.
trapu [trapy] *adj* squat, stocky.
traquer [trake] *v* track (down), hunt (out); (*harceler*) hound. **traquenard** *nm* trap; (*embûche*) pitfall.
trauma [troma] *nm* trauma. **traumatique** *adj* traumatic. **traumatisant** *adj* traumatic. **traumatisme** *nm* trauma.
travail [travaj] *nm, pl* **-aux** work; (*métier, tâche*) job; (*méd, ouvriers*) labour. **travaux d'aiguille** needlework *sing*.
travailler [travaje] *v* work; (*vin*) ferment; (*exercer*) practise, work at; (*agir sur*) work on; torment, distract. **travaillé** *adj* (*style*) polished; (*ornement*) intricate; (*façonné*) wrought.
travailleur, -euse [travajœr, -øz] *adj* hard-working. *nm, nf* worker.
travailliste [travajist] *adj* Labour. *n(m+f)* member of the Labour party. **les travaillistes** *nm pl* Labour *sing*.
travers [travɛr] *nm* failing, fault. **à travers** (*milieu*) through; (*surface*) across. **au travers** through. **de travers** (*pas droit*) crooked; (*mal*) wrong. **en travers** across.
traverser [travɛrse] *v* (*surface*) cross; (*milieu*) go through. **traverse** *nf* (*rail*) sleeper; (*tech*) strut, cross-piece. **traversée** *nf* crossing.
traversin [travɛrsɛ̃] *nm* bolster.
travestir [travɛstir] *v* dress up; (*vérité*) misrepresent. **se travestir** (*bal*) put on fancy dress; (*cabaret, psych*) dress up as a woman.
travesti [travɛsti], **-e** *adj* disguised; (*bal*) fancy-dress. *nm* fancy dress; (*cabaret*) drag artist. *nm, nf* (*psych*) transvestite.
trébucher [trebyʃe] *v* stumble. **faire trébucher** trip up. **trébuchant** *adj* staggering; (*voix*) halting.
trèfle [trɛflə] *nm* clover; (*cartes*) club.
treillis [trɛji] *nm* trellis, lattice. **treillis métallique** wire netting.
treize [trɛz] *nm, adj* thirteen. **treizième** *n(m+f), adj* thirteenth.
trembler [trɑ̃ble] *v* tremble, shake; (*de froid*) shiver; (*lumière*) flicker. **tremblement** *nm* tremble, tremor; shiver. **tremblement de terre** earthquake.
se trémousser [tremuse] *v* fidget, wriggle; (*se dandiner*) wiggle.
tremper [trɑ̃pe] *v* soak; (*plonger*) dip. **faire trempette** dunk one's bread *or* sugar.
tremplin [trɑ̃plɛ̃] *nm* spring-board; (*piscine*) diving-board.
trente [trɑ̃t] *nm, adj* thirty. **trentième** *n(m+f), adj* thirtieth.
trépas [trepɑ] *nm* death. **trépasser** *v* die, pass away.
trépider [trepide] *v* vibrate. **trépidation** *nf* vibration; (*agitation*) flurry.
trépied [trepje] *nm* tripod.
trépigner [trepiɲe] *v* stamp.
très [trɛ] *adv* very; (*devant un participe*) highly, very much.
trésor [trezɔr] *nm* treasure; (*source*) mine, wealth; (*endroit*) treasury; (*de l'état*) exchequer. **trésorerie** *nf* treasury; finances *pl*, funds *pl*. **trésorier, -ère** *nm, nf* treasurer.
***tressaillir** [tresajir] *v* quiver; (*de peur*) shudder; (*de douleur*) wince; (*sursauter*) start; vibrate, shake. **tressaillement** *nm* quiver; shudder; start; vibration.
tresser [trese] *v* (*cheveux*) plait; (*guirlande*) weave; (*corde*) twist. **tresse** *nf* plait; (*cordon*) braid.
tréteau [treto] *nm* trestle.
treuil [trœj] *nm* winch.
trêve [trɛv] *nf* (*mil, pol*) truce; respite. **sans trêve** unceasingly, relentlessly.
tri [tri] *nm* sorting; selection. **faire le tri de** sort; select. **triage** *nm* sorting, selection.
triangle [trijɑ̃glə] *nm* triangle. **triangulaire** *adj* triangular.
tribord [tribɔr] *nm* starboard.
tribu [triby] *nf* tribe.
tribunal [tribynal] *nm* court, tribunal. **tribune** *nf* (*église*) gallery; (*stade*) stand; platform; (*journal, radio, etc.*) forum.
tribut [triby] *nm* tribute.
tributaire [tribytɛr] *adj* tributary.
tricher [triʃe] *v* cheat. **tricherie** *nf* cheating. **tricheur, -euse** *nm, nf* cheat.
tricot [triko] *nm* (*technique*) knitting; (*vêtement*) jumper. **tricot de corps** vest. **tricoter** *v* knit.
trictrac [triktrak] *nm* backgammon.
tricycle [trisiklə] *nm* tricycle.
trier [trije] *v* sort (out); select. **trier sur le volet** hand-pick.
trille [trij] *nm* trill. **triller** *v* trill.

trimballer [trɛ̃bale] *v* (*fam*) cart around.
trimestre [trimɛstrə] *nm* quarter; (*école*) term. **trimestriel** *adj* quarterly; end-of-term.
tringle [trɛ̃glə] *nf* rod.
trinquer [trɛ̃ke] *v* clink glasses.
trio [trijo] *nm* trio.
triompher [trijɔ̃fe] *v* triumph, win. **triompher de** overcome, conquer. **triomphant** *adj* triumphant. **triomphe** *nm* triumph.
tripes [trip] *nf pl* (*cuisine*) tripe *sing*; (*fam*) guts *pl*.
triple [triplə] *adj* triple, treble. *nm* **le triple** three times as much. **triplé, -e** *nm, nf* triplet. **tripler** *v* triple, treble.
tripoter [tripɔte] *v* fiddle with; (*fouiller*) rummage about; (*affaire*) be involved in.
triste [trist] *adj* sad, miserable; (*sombre*) dreary, dismal. **tristesse** *nf* sadness, sorrow; dreariness.
triton [tritɔ̃] *nm* newt.
trivial [trivjal] *adj* (*grossier*) coarse; (*ordinaire*) mundane. **trivialité** *nf* coarseness; coarse remark *or* detail; mundane nature.
troc [trɔk] *nm* exchange; (*système économique*) barter.
trognon [trɔɲɔ̃] *nm* core.
trois [trwɑ] *nm, adj* three. **à trois dimensions** three-dimensional. **trois-quarts** *nm pl* three quarters. **troisième** *n*(*m*+*f*), *adj* third.
trombe [trɔ̃b] *nf* (*pluie*) downpour; (*tornade*) whirlwind.
trombone [trɔ̃bɔn] *nm* trombone; (*agrafe*) paper-clip.
trompe [trɔ̃p] *nf* (*éléphant*) trunk; (*musique*) horn.
tromper [trɔ̃pe] *v* deceive; (*par accident*) mislead; (*poursuivant*) elude; (*duper*) fool, trick. **se tromper** be wrong, make a mistake. **tromperie** *nf* deception, deceit. **trompeur, -euse** *adj* (*apparence*) deceptive, misleading; (*personne*) deceitful.
trompette [trɔ̃pɛt] *nf* trumpet. **trompettiste** *n*(*m*+*f*) trumpeter.
tronc [trɔ̃] *nm* trunk.
tronçon [trɔ̃sɔ̃] *nm* section.
trône [tron] *nm* throne.
tronquer [trɔ̃ke] *v* truncate; (*texte*) cut down; (*détails*) cut out.
trop [tro] *adv* too, too much. **de trop** (*quantité*) too much; (*nombre*) too many; (*importun*) in the way. **trop de** too much; too many. **trop-plein** *nm* overflow. *nm* excess.
trophée [trɔfe] *nm* trophy.
tropique [trɔpik] *nm* tropic. **tropical** *adj* tropical.
troquer [trɔke] *v* exchange, swap; (*transaction commerciale*) barter.
trot [tro] *nm* trot; (*souris*) scamper. **trotter** *v* trot. **trottinette** *nf* scooter.
trottoir [trɔtwar] *nm* pavement.
trou [tru] *nm* hole; (*vide*) gap. **trou de serrure** keyhole. **trou d'homme** manhole.
trouble[1] [trublə] *adj* (*eau*) cloudy; (*vue*) blurred, misty; (*affaire*) shady.
trouble[2] [trublə] *nm* (*agitation*) turmoil; discord; embarrassment; (*inquiétude*) distress; (*méd*) disorder.
troubler [truble] *v* disturb, trouble; (*eau*) make cloudy. **se troubler** (*personne*) get flustered; (*eau*) become cloudy. **trouble-fête** *n*(*m*+*f*) *invar* spoilsport.
trouer [true] *v* make a hole in; pierce; (*parsemer*) dot. **trouée** *nf* gap; (*mil*) breach.
troupe [trup] *nf* (*mil*) troop; (*chanteurs, etc.*) troupe; band, group. **troupeau** *nm* herd; (*moutons*) flock.
trousse [trus] *nf* case, kit; (*sac*) bag. **trousseau** *nm* (*clefs*) bunch; (*mariée*) trousseau. **trousser** *v* truss.
trouver [truve] *v* find. **se trouver** be; (*se sentir*) feel; (*arriver*) happen. **trouvaille** *nf* find.
truc [tryk] *nm* trick; (*fam*: *combine*) knack; (*fam*: *chose*) thing; (*fam*: *machin*) whatsit, thingummy.
truelle [tryɛl] *nf* trowel.
truffe [tryf] *nf* truffle.
truie [trɥi] *nf* sow.
truite [trɥit] *nf* trout.
truquer [tryke] *v* rig, fix. **truquage** *nm* rigging, fixing; (*cinéma*) trick photography, special effects *pl*.
tsar [dzar] *nm* tsar.
tu [ty] *pron* you.
tuba [tyba] *nm* tuba.
tube [tyb] *nm* tube; pipe; (*fam*: *chanson, disque*) hit.
tuberculose [tybɛrkyloz] *nf* tuberculosis.
tuer [tɥe] *v* kill. **à tue-tête** at the top of one's voice. **tuerie** *nf* slaughter. **tueur, -euse** *nm, nf* killer.
tuile [tɥil] *nf* tile; (*fam*) blow.

tulipe [tylip] *nf* tulip.
tumeur [tymœr] *nf* tumour.
tumulte [tymylt] *nm* tumult, commotion. **tumultueux** *adj* turbulent, stormy.
tunique [tynik] *nf* tunic.
tunnel [tynɛl] *nm* tunnel.
turban [tyrbɑ̃] *nm* turban.
turbine [tyrbin] *nf* turbine.
turbot [tyrbo] *nm* turbot.
turbulent [tyrbylɑ̃] *adj* turbulent; (*agité*) boisterous, unruly. **turbulence** *nf* turbulence.
turf [tyrf] *nm* (*hippisme*) racing; (*terrain*) racecourse.
turquoise [tyrkwaz] *nf*, *adj invar* turquoise.
tutelle [tytɛl] *nf* (*surveillance*) supervision; protection; (*jur*) guardianship.
tuteur, -trice [tytœr, -tris] *nm*, *nf* guardian. *nm* stake.
tutoyer [tytwaje] *v* address as 'tu'. **tutoiement** *nm* use of the 'tu' form.
tuyau [tɥijo] *nm* pipe; (*d'arrosage*) hose; (*fam*) tip. **tuyau d'échappement** exhaust pipe.
tympan [tɛ̃pɑ̃] *nm* eardrum.
type [tip] *nm* type; (*représentant*) classic example; (*fam*) bloke, chap.
typhoïde [tifɔid] *nf*, *adj* typhoid.
typhon [tifɔ̃] *nm* typhoon.
typique [tipik] *adj* typical.
tyran [tirɑ̃] *nm* tyrant. **tyrannie** *nf* tyranny. **tyrannique** *adj* tyrannical.

U

ulcérer [ylsere] *v* (*méd*) ulcerate; (*blesser*) wound, embitter. **ulcère** *nm* ulcer.
ultérieur, -e [ylterjœr] *adj* later, subsequent.
ultimatum [yltimatɔm] *nm* ultimatum.
ultime [yltim] *adj* ultimate, final.
ultrasonique [yltrasɔnik] *adj* ultrasonic.
ultraviolet, -ette [yltravjɔlɛ, -ɛt] *adj* ultraviolet.
un [œ̃], **une** *art* a, an. *n*, *adj*, *pron* one. **les uns** some. **l'un et l'autre** both. **l'un ou l'autre** either. **unième** *adj* first.
unanime [ynanim] *adj* unanimous. **unanimité** *nf* unanimity.
uni [yni] *adj* (*tissu*, *couleur*) plain; (*famille*) close; (*lisse*) smooth, even.
unifier [ynifje] *v* unify. **unification** *nf* unification.
uniforme [ynifɔrm] *adj* uniform; (*surface*) even. *nm* uniform. **uniformité** *nf* uniformity.
union [ynjɔ̃] *nf* union; association; combination.
unique [ynik] *adj* (*seul*) only; (*exceptionnel*) unique. **uniquement** *adv* only.
unir [ynir] *v* unite; combine; join. **unité** *nf* (*élément*) unit; (*cohésion*) unity.
unisexe [ynisɛks] *adj invar* unisex.
unisson [ynisɔ̃] *nm* unison. **à l'unisson** in unison.
univers [ynivɛr] *nm* universe. **universel** *adj* universal; (*outil*) all-purpose.
université [ynivɛrsite] *nf* university. **universitaire** *adj* university.
urbain [yrbɛ̃] *adj* urban, town. **urbanisme** *nm* town planning. **urbaniste** *n*(*m*+*f*) town planner.
urgent [yrʒɑ̃] *adj* urgent. **urgence** *nf* urgency; (*cas urgent*) emergency.
uriner [yrine] *v* urinate. **urine** *nf* urine. **urinoir** *nm* urinal.
urne [yrn] *nf* (*vase*) urn; (*pol*) ballot-box.
usage [yzaʒ] *nm* use; custom; (*gramm*) usage; (*politesse*) breeding. **usagé** *adj* (*usé*) worn, old; (*d'occasion*) second-hand, used.
user [yze] *v* wear out; (*consommer*) use. **user de** use, make use of. **usé** *adj* worn; (*banal*) hackneyed; (*râpé*) threadbare. **usure** *nf* wear.
usine [yzin] *nf* factory, works.
ustensile [ystɑ̃sil] *nm* implement; (*de cuisine*) utensil.
usuel [yzɥɛl] *adj* common, everyday; (*d'usage*) usual.
usurper [yzyrpe] *v* usurp. **usurpateur, -trice** *nm*, *nf* usurper. **usurpation** *nf* usurpation.
utérus [yterys] *nm* womb, uterus.
utile [ytil] *adj* useful. **utilité** *nf* use, usefulness.
utiliser [ytilize] *v* use, utilize. **utilisable** *adj* usable.

V

vacance [vakɑ̃s] *nf* vacancy. **vacances** *nf pl* holiday *sing*, vacation *sing*. **en vacances** on holiday. **vacant** *adj* vacant.
vacarme [vakarm] *nm* din, row.
vaccin [vaksɛ̃] *nm* vaccine. **vaccination** *nf* vaccination. **vacciner** *v* vaccinate.
vache [vaʃ] *nf* cow; (*argot*) bitch, swine. *adj* (*argot*) rotten. **vachement** *adv* (*argot*) bloody.
vaciller [vasije] *v* wobble, sway; (*flamme*) flicker; (*courage*) falter, fail. **vacillant** *adj* unsteady; flickering; (*santé*) shaky; indecisive.
va-et-vient [vaevjɛ̃] *nm invar* comings and goings *pl*; (*mécanisme*) movement to and fro.
vagabond [vagabɔ̃], **-e** *adj* (*errant*) roaming, restless; (*nomade*) wandering. *nm, nf* tramp, vagrant. **vagabondage** *nm* wandering; vagrancy. **vagabonder** *v* roam, wander.
vagin [vaʒɛ̃] *nm* vagina. **vaginal** *adj* vaginal.
vague[1] [vag] *adj* vague. *nm* vagueness. **regarder dans le vague** stare into space.
vague[2] [vag] *nf* wave; (*montée*) surge. **vague de chaleur** heat wave.
vaillant [vajɑ̃] *adj* brave, valiant; vigorous, robust.
vain [vɛ̃] *adj* vain; empty, futile. **en vain** in vain.
***vaincre** [vɛ̃krə] *v* conquer, defeat, overcome.
vainqueur [vɛ̃kœr] *nm* conqueror; (*sport*) winner. *adj* victorious.
vaisseau [vɛso] *nm* vessel; (*naut*) ship.
vaisselle [vɛsɛl] *nf* crockery, dishes *pl*; (*lavage*) washing-up. **faire la vaisselle** wash up.
val [val] *nm* valley.
valable [valablə] *adj* valid; (*notable*) worthwhile.
valet [valɛ] *nm* servant, valet; (*cartes*) jack. **valet d'écurie** groom. **valet de ferme** farm-hand.
valeur [valœr] *nf* value; (*qualité*) worth. **de valeur** valuable. **mettre en valeur** exploit; (*détail*) bring out, highlight. **objets de valeur** *nm pl* valuables *pl*. **valeurs** *nf pl* (*bourse*) securities *pl*.
valide [valid] *adj* (*billet*) valid; (*personne*) fit; able-bodied. **validité** *nf* validity.
valise [valiz] *nf* suitcase.
vallée [vale] *nf* valley.
***valoir** [valwar] *v* be worth; be valid, apply; (*équivaloir à*) be as good as; (*causer*) bring, earn. **faire valoir** exploit; (*caractéristique*) bring out, highlight. **il vaut mieux** it is better. **valoir la peine** be worth it.
valse [vals] *nf* waltz. **valser** *v* waltz.
valve [valv] *nf* valve.
vampire [vɑ̃pir] *nm* vampire.
vandale [vɑ̃dal] *n(m+f)* vandal. **vandalisme** *nm* vandalism.
vanille [vanij] *nf* vanilla.
vanité [vanite] *nf* vanity, conceit; futility. **vaniteux** *adj* vain, conceited.
vanter [vɑ̃te] *v* praise. **se vanter** boast. **se vanter de** pride oneself on. **vantard** *adj* boastful. **vantardise** *nf* boasting, boastfulness; (*propos*) boast.
vapeur [vapœr] *nf* vapour, steam. **bateau à vapeur** *nm* steamer. **cuire à la vapeur** steam. **vaporiser** *v* (*parfum*) spray; (*phys*) vaporize.
varice [varis] *nf* varicose vein.
varicelle [varisɛl] *nf* chicken-pox.
varier [varje] *v* vary. **variable** *nf, adj* variable. **variante** *nf* variant. **variation** *nf* variation. **variété** *nf* variety.
variole [varjɔl] *nf* smallpox.
Varsovie [varsɔvi] *n* Warsaw.
vase[1] [vɑz] *nm* vase.
vase[2] [vɑz] *nf* mud, sludge.
vaste [vast] *adj* vast, immense.
Vatican [vatikɑ̃] *nm* Vatican.
vau [vo] *nm* **à vau-l'eau** with the current; (*projets, etc.*) down the drain. **aller à vau-l'eau** be on the road to ruin.
vaudou [vodu] *nm, adj invar* voodoo.
vaurien [vorjɛ̃], **-enne** *nm, nf* good-for-nothing.
vautour [votur] *nm* vulture.
se vautrer [votrə] *v* sprawl. **se vautrer dans** wallow in.
veau [vo] *nm* calf; (*cuisine*) veal.
vedette [vədɛt] *nf* (*cinéma, etc.*) star; (*bateau*) launch.
végétal [veʒetal] *adj* plant, vegetable.
végétation [veʒetɑsjɔ̃] *nf* vegetation. **végétations adénoïdes** adenoids *pl*.
véhément [veemɑ̃] *adj* vehement. **véhémence** *nf* vehemence.

véhicule [veikyl] *nm* vehicle.
veille [vɛj] *nf* (*garde*) watch, vigil; (*jour précédent*) eve, day before; (*état*) wakefulness. **veillée** *nf* evening; (*mort*) watch. **veiller** *v* (*mort, malade*) sit up with, watch over; (*rester éveillé*) stay awake; be vigilant. **veiller à** attend to, see to. **veiller sur** watch over. **veilleuse** *nf* (*flamme*) pilot-light; (*lampe*) night-light.
veine [vɛn] *nf* vein; (*fam*) luck.
vélo [velo] *nm* (*fam*) bike.
vélocité [velɔsite] *nf* swiftness, nimbleness; (*vitesse*) velocity.
velours [vəlur] *nm* velvet. **velours côtelé** corduroy. **velouté** *adj* velvety, smooth.
velu [vəly] *adj* hairy.
venaison [vənɛzɔ̃] *nf* venison.
vendange [vɑ̃dɑ̃ʒ] *nf* grape harvest.
vendre [vɑ̃drə] *v* sell. **vendre la mèche** (*fam*) give the game away. **vendeur, -euse** *nm, nf* seller; (*magasin*) shop assistant.
vendredi [vɑ̃drədi] *nm* Friday. **vendredi saint** Good Friday.
vénéneux [venenø] *adj* poisonous.
vénérer [venere] *v* venerate, revere. **vénérable** *adj* venerable. **vénération** *nf* veneration.
vénérien [venerjɛ̃] *adj* venereal. **maladie vénérienne** venereal disease.
venger [vɑ̃ʒe] *v* avenge. **se venger** take one's revenge. **vengeance** *nf* vengeance, revenge.
venin [vənɛ̃] *nm* venom. **venimeux** *adj* venomous.
***venir** [vənir] *v* come. **en venir à** come to, resort to. **faire venir** send for. **venir de** come from; (*suivi d'un infinitif*) have just.
vent [vɑ̃] *nm* wind. **dans le vent** (*fam*) trendy, fashionable. **il fait du vent** it is windy. **venteux** *adj* windswept.
vente [vɑ̃t] *nf* sale. **vente aux enchères** auction. **vente de charité** bazaar, jumble sale.
ventiler [vɑ̃tile] *v* ventilate. **ventilateur** *nm* fan, ventilator. **ventilation** *nf* ventilation.
ventouse [vɑ̃tuz] *nf* sucker, suction pad.
ventre [vɑ̃trə] *nm* stomach, belly.
ventriloque [vɑ̃trilɔk] *n(m+f)* ventriloquist.
venue [vəny] *nf* coming.
ver [vɛr] *nm* worm; (*larve*) grub; (*asticot*) maggot. **ver à soie** silkworm. **ver du bois** woodworm.
véranda [verɑ̃da] *nf* veranda.
verbe [verb] *nm* verb. **verbal** *adj* verbal.
verdict [vɛrdikt] *nm* verdict.
verdir [vɛrdir] *v* turn green. **verdure** *nf* greenery.
verge [vɛrʒ] *nf* rod; penis.
verger [verʒe] *nm* orchard.
verglas [vɛrgla] *nm* black ice.
vergogne [vɛrgɔɲ] *nf* shame.
véridique [veridik] *adj* truthful.
vérifier [verifje] *v* check, verify; (*comptes*) audit; confirm, prove. **vérification** *nf* check, verification; auditing; confirmation.
vérité [verite] *nf* truth; (*sincérité*) truthfulness. **véritable** *adj* real, true, genuine.
vermeil, -eille [vɛrmɛj] *adj* bright red.
vermine [vɛrmin] *nf* vermin.
vermouth [vɛrmut] *nm* vermouth.
vernaculaire [vɛrnakylɛr] *adj* vernacular.
vernir [vɛrnir] *v* varnish. **verni** *adj* varnished; (*luisant*) glossy. **cuir verni** patent leather. **vernis** *nm* varnish; (*poterie*) glaze; (*éclat*) gloss; (*apparence*) veneer. **vernis à ongles** nail varnish *or* polish. **vernisser** *v* glaze.
vérole [verɔl] *nf* **petite vérole** smallpox.
verre [vɛr] *nm* glass; (*optique*) lens; (*boisson*) drink. **verres de contact** contact lenses *pl*.
verrou [vɛru] *nm* bolt.
verrouiller [vɛruje] *v* bolt.
verrue [vɛry] *nf* wart.
vers[1] [vɛr] *prep* towards, to; (*approximation*) about, around.
vers[2] [vɛr] *nm* line. *nm pl* verse *sing*.
versant [vɛrsɑ̃] *nm* side, slope.
verse [vɛrs] *nf* **à verse** in torrents. **il pleut à verse** it is pouring down.
Verseau [vɛrso] *nm* Aquarius.
verser [vɛrse] *v* pour; (*sang, larmes*) shed; pay; (*basculer*) overturn. **versement** *nm* payment; (*échelonné*) instalment.
version [vɛrsjɔ̃] *nf* version; (*traduction*) translation.
verso [vɛrso] *nm* back.
vert [vɛr] *adj* green; (*fruit*) unripe; (*propos*) spicy. *nm* green.
vertèbre [vɛrtɛbrə] *nf* vertebra (*pl* -brae). **vertébral** *adj* vertebral. **vertébré** *nm, adj* vertebrate.
vertical [vɛrtikal] *adj* vertical. **verticale** *nf* vertical.
vertige [vɛrtiʒ] *nm* vertigo, dizziness. **avoir le vertige** feel dizzy. **pris de vertige** dizzy, giddy. **vertigineux** *adj* breathtaking; (*hauteur*) giddy.

vertu [vɛrty] *nf* virtue. **vertueux** *adj* virtuous.
verve [vɛrv] *nf* vigour, zest; eloquence.
vessie [vesi] *nf* bladder.
veste [vɛst] *nf* jacket.
vestiaire [vɛstjɛr] *nm* cloakroom; (*piscine, etc.*) changing-room.
vestibule [vɛstibyl] *nm* hall, vestibule.
vestige [vɛstiʒ] *nm* vestige, remnant, trace.
veston [vɛstɔ̃] *nm* jacket.
vêtement [vɛtmɑ̃] *nm* garment. **vêtements** *nm pl* clothes *pl*, clothing *sing*.
vétéran [veterɑ̃] *nm* veteran.
vétérinaire [veterinɛr] *nm* vet. *adj* veterinary.
vétille [vetij] *nf* trifle.
***vêtir** [vetir] *v* clothe, dress. **vêtu de** wearing.
veto [veto] *nm* veto. **mettre son veto à** veto.
vétuste [vetyst] *adj* ancient, decrepit. **vétusté** *nf* age, decay.
veuf [vœf] *adj* widowed. *nm* widower. **veuve** *nf* widow. **veuvage** *nm* widowhood.
veule [vøl] *adj* spineless, weak.
vexer [vɛkse] *v* upset, hurt. **vexant** *adj* hurtful; (*contrariant*) annoying.
via [vja] *prep* via.
viable [vjablə] *adj* viable. **viabilité** *nf* viability; (*chemin*) practicability.
viaduc [vjadyk] *nm* viaduct.
viager [vjaʒe] *adj* for life.
viande [vjɑ̃d] *nf* meat.
vibrer [vibre] *v* vibrate; (*voix*) quiver. **vibration** *nf* vibration.
vicaire [vikɛr] *nm* curate.
vice [vis] *nm* vice; fault.
vice-chancelier *nm* vice-chancellor.
vice-consul *nm* vice-consul.
vice-président, -e *nm, nf* (*état*) vice-president; (*réunion*) vice-chairman.
vice versa [viseversa] *adv* vice versa.
vicier [visje] *v* pollute, taint; (*jur*) invalidate.
vicieux [visjø] *adj* licentious, depraved; (*animal*) unruly; (*fautif*) incorrect.
vicomte [vikɔ̃t] *nm* viscount. **vicomtesse** *nf* viscountess.
victime [viktim] *nf* victim.
victoire [viktwar] *nf* victory. **victorieux** *adj* victorious.
vidange [vidɑ̃ʒ] *nf* emptying; (*auto*) oil change. **vidanges** *nf pl* sewage *sing*. **vidanger** *v* empty, drain.
vide [vid] *adj* empty; (*disponible*) vacant. *nm* emptiness; (*espace*) void; (*sans air*) vacuum; (*creux*) gap. **vider** *v* empty; (*bassin, etc.*) drain; (*quitter*) vacate; (*cuisine*) gut; (*fam*: *épuiser*) wear out; (*fam*: *expulser*) throw out.
vie [vi] *nf* life; (*moyens*) living.
vieil [vjɛj] *form of* **vieux** *used before a vowel or mute h*.
vieillir [vjejir] *v* age, grow old. **vieillard** *nm* old man. **vieillesse** *nf* old age.
Vienne [vjɛn] *n* Vienna.
vierge [vjɛrʒ] *nf* virgin. **Vierge** *nf* Virgo. *adj* (*terre, etc.*) virgin; (*papier*) blank.
vieux, vieille [vjø, vjɛj] *adj* old. **vieille fille** spinster. **vieux jeu** *adj invar* old-fashioned. *nm* old man. *nf* old woman.
vif [vif] *adj* lively; brusque; (*aigu*) sharp, keen; intense, vivid; (*fort*) strong, great; (*froid*) biting; (*éclat*) bright; (*allure*) brisk. *nm* quick.
vigile [viʒil] *nf* vigil. **vigilance** *nf* vigilance. **vigilant** *adj* vigilant.
vigne [viɲ] *nf* vine. **vignoble** *nm* vineyard.
vignette [viɲɛt] *nf* label; (*auto*) tax disc.
vigoureux [vigurø] *adj* vigorous, robust, sturdy.
vigueur [vigœr] *nf* vigour; (*robustesse*) sturdiness; (*force*) strength. **entrer en vigueur** come into effect. **en vigueur** in force, current.
vil [vil] *adj* vile, base.
vilain [vilɛ̃] *adj* nasty; (*laid*) ugly; (*méchant*) mean, wicked.
vilebrequin [vilbrəkɛ̃] *nm* (*auto*) crankshaft; (*tech*) brace.
villa [villa] *nf* villa, detached house.
village [vilaʒ] *nm* village. **villageois, -e** *nm, nf* villager.
ville [vil] *nf* town; (*plus grande*) city. **ville d'eau** spa.
villégiature [vileʒatyr] *nf* holiday; (*lieu*) holiday resort.
vin [vɛ̃] *nm* wine. **grand vin** vintage wine.
vinaigre [vinɛgrə] *nm* vinegar. **vinaigrette** *nf* French dressing, vinaigrette.
vindicatif [vɛ̃dikatif] *adj* vindictive.
vingt [vɛ̃] *nm, adj* twenty. **vingtième** *n(m+f), adj* twentieth.
vinyle [vinil] *nm* vinyl.
viol [vjɔl] *nm* rape.
violent [vjɔlɑ̃] *adj* violent; (*effort*) strenuous; (*fort*) strong, intense. **violence** *nf* violence.

violer [vjɔle] *v* violate; (*femme*) rape; (*loi, promesse*) break. **violation** *nf* violation.
violet, -ette [vjɔlɛ, -ɛt] *adj* purple, violet. *nm* purple. *nf* violet.
violon [vjɔlɔ̃] *nm* violin. **violoncelle** *nm* cello. **violoniste** *n(m+f)* violinist.
vipère [vipɛr] *nf* adder, viper.
virage [viraʒ] *nm* bend, turn.
virer [vire] *v* turn; change; (*argent*) transfer. **virement** *nm* transfer.
virginité [virʒinite] *nf* virginity.
virgule [virgyl] *nf* comma; (*math*) decimal point.
viril [viril] *adj* virile, manly; masculine. **virilité** *nf* virility.
virtuel [virtɥɛl] *adj* potential. **virtuellement** *adv* potentially; (*pratiquement*) virtually.
virus [virys] *nm* virus.
vis [vis] *nf* screw.
visa [viza] *nm* (*passeport*) visa; (*timbre*) stamp; (*de censure*) certificate.
visage [vizaʒ] *nm* face.
vis-à-vis [vizavi] *adv* opposite, face to face. *nm* **en vis-à-vis** opposite each other. *prep* **vis-à-vis de** opposite; (*comparaison*) beside, next to; (*envers*) towards.
viser [vize] *v* aim (at); (*remarque*) be directed at. **visée** *nf* aim; design.
visible [viziblə] *adj* visible; (*évident*) obvious. **visibilité** *nf* visibility.
visière [vizjɛr] *nf* (*casquette*) peak; (*armure*) visor.
vision [vizjɔ̃] *nf* vision; (*faculté*) eyesight. **visionnaire** *n(m+f)*, *adj* visionary.
visiter [vizite] *v* visit; (*ville, château*) go round; examine; (*fouiller*) search. **visite** *nf* visit; tour; inspection, examination. **rendre visite à** visit, call on. **visiteur, -euse** *nm, nf* visitor.
vison [vizɔ̃] *nm* mink.
visser [vise] *v* screw down *or* on.
visuel [vizɥɛl] *adj* visual.
vital [vital] *adj* vital. **vitalité** *nf* vitality, energy.
vitamine [vitamin] *nf* vitamin.
vite [vit] *adv* fast, quickly; (*tôt*) soon. *interj* quick! **vitesse** *nf* speed; (*auto*) gear; velocity.
vitrer [vitre] *v* put glass in, glaze. **vitrail** *nm, pl* **-aux** stained-glass window. **vitre** *nf* pane of glass; (*fenêtre*) window. **vitrine** *nf* (*magasin*) shop-window; (*armoire*) display cabinet, glass case.
vivace [vivas] *adj* (*plante*) hardy; (*foi, haine*) undying. **vivacité** *nf* vivacity, liveliness; (*éclat*) brightness; (*mordant*) sharpness; intensity.
vivant [vivɑ̃] *adj* alive, living; (*vivace*) lively. *nm* living person; (*vie*) lifetime.
vivier [vivje] *nm* fish-pond.
vivifier [vivifje] *v* invigorate.
vivisection [vivisɛksjɔ̃] *nf* vivisection.
***vivre** [vivrə] *v* live, be alive. **vive . . . !** *interj* long live . . . ! three cheers for . . . ! **vivre de** live on. *nm* board. **vivres** *nm pl* provisions *pl*.
vocabulaire [vɔkabylɛr] *nm* vocabulary.
vocal [vɔkal] *adj* vocal.
vocation [vɔkɑsjɔ̃] *nf* vocation, calling.
vodka [vɔdka] *nf* vodka.
vœu [vø] *nm* (*souhait*) wish; (*promesse*) vow.
vogue [vɔg] *nf* fashion, vogue. **en vogue** fashionable.
voguer [vɔge] *v* sail; (*pensées, etc.*) drift.
voici [vwasi] *prep* (*sing*) here is, this is; (*pl*) here are, these are. **voici . . . que** it is . . . since. **voici une heure** an hour ago.
voie [vwa] *nf* way, road; (*rail*) track, line; (*autoroute, etc.*) lane. **voie d'eau** leak. **voie ferrée** railway line. **voie publique** public highway. **voie sans issue** no through road.
voilà [vwala] *prep* (*sing*) there is, that is; (*pl*) there are, those are. **voilà . . . que** it is . . . since. **voilà une heure** an hour ago.
voile[1] [vwal] *nf* sail; (*sport*) sailing. **voilier** *nm* sailing ship *or* boat.
voile[2] [vwal] *nm* veil; (*tissu*) net.
voiler [vwale] *v* veil, shroud. **se voiler** mist over, grow hazy.
***voir** [vwar] *v* see. **aller voir** call on, visit. **faire voir** show. **n'avoir rien à voir avec** have nothing to do with. **se voir** show, be obvious.
voire [vwar] *adv* indeed.
voirie [vwari] *nf* (*voies*) highways *pl*; (*entretien*) highway maintenance; (*enlèvement des ordures*) refuse collection; (*dépotoir*) refuse dump.
voisin [vwazɛ̃], **-e** *adj* neighbouring; (*adjacent*) adjoining; (*ressemblant*) akin. *nm, nf* neighbour. **voisinage** *nm* neighbourhood; proximity.
voiture [vwatyr] *nf* car; (*wagon*) coach, carriage. **voiture d'enfant** pram.
voix [vwa] *nf* voice; (*pol*) vote. **à voix basse/haute** in a low/loud voice. **être sans voix** be speechless.

vol[1] [vɔl] *nm* flight. **à vol d'oiseau** as the crow flies. **vol à voile** gliding. **vol libre** hang-gliding.
vol[2] [vɔl] *nm* theft. **vol à l'étalage** shoplifting. **vol à main armée** armed robbery.
volaille [vɔlɑj] *nf* poultry, fowl.
volant [vɔlɑ̃] *nm* (*auto*) steering wheel; (*tech*) flywheel; (*sport*) shuttlecock; (*robe*) flounce. *adj* flying.
volatil [vɔlatil] *adj* volatile.
volcan [vɔlkɑ̃] *nm* volcano. **volcanique** *adj* volcanic.
voler[1] [vɔle] *v* fly. **volée** *nf* flight; (*groupe*) flock, swarm; (*coups, sport*) volley.
voler[2] [vɔle] *v* (*chose*) steal; (*personne*) rob. **voleur, -euse** *nm, nf* thief. **au voleur!** stop thief!
volet [vɔlɛ] *nm* shutter; (*tech*) flap.
volière [vɔljɛr] *nf* aviary.
volontaire [vɔlɔ̃tɛr] *adj* voluntary; intentional; (*décidé*) headstrong, determined. *n*(*m*+*f*) volunteer.
volonté [vɔlɔ̃te] *nf* will; (*détermination*) willpower. **bonne volonté** goodwill, willingness. **volontiers** *adv* gladly, willingly.
volt [vɔlt] *nm* volt. **voltage** *nm* voltage.
volte-face [vɔltəfas] *nf invar* about-turn.
voltiger [vɔltiʒe] *v* flutter about.
volume [vɔlym] *nm* volume.
volupté [vɔlypte] *nf* sensual delight, voluptuousness. **voluptueux** *adj* voluptuous.
vomir [vɔmir] *v* vomit. **vomissement** *nm* vomiting; (*matière*) vomit.
vorace [vɔras] *adj* voracious. **voracité** *nf* voracity.
vos [vo] *V* **votre.**
voter [vɔte] *v* vote; (*loi*) pass. **vote** *nm* vote.
votre [vɔtrə] *adj, pl* **vos** your.
vôtre [votrə] *pron* **le** *or* **la vôtre** yours.
vouer [vwe] *v* (*promettre*) vow; (*consacrer*) devote; (*condamner*) doom.
***vouloir** [vulwar] *v* want; (*essayer*) try; require, need. **en vouloir à** have a grudge against. **vouloir bien** be willing. **vouloir dire** mean. *nm* will.
vous [vu] *pron* you, to you; (*réfléchi*) yourselves, each other. **vous-mêmes** *pron* yourselves.
voûter [vute] *v* arch. **voûte** *nf* vault, arch. **voûté** *adj* arched; (*personne*) stooped.
vouvoyer [vuvwaje] *v* address as 'vous'. **vouvoiement** *nm* use of the 'vous' form.
voyage [vwajaʒ] *nm* (*course*) journey, trip; (*action*) travel, travelling; (*par mer, d'exploration*) voyage. **voyage de noces** honeymoon. **voyage organisé** package tour. **voyager** *v* travel. **voyageur, -euse** *nm, nf* traveller; passenger.
voyant [vwajɑ̃] *adj* gaudy, garish.
voyelle [vwajɛl] *nf* vowel.
voyou [vwaju] *nm* hooligan, lout.
vrai [vrɛ] *adj* true; real. *nm* truth. **à vrai dire** to tell the truth, in actual fact. **pour de vrai** (*fam*) for real. **vraiment** *adv* really.
vraisemblable [vrɛsɑ̃blablə] *adj* likely, probable; (*histoire*) convincing, plausible. **vraisemblance** *nf* likelihood, probability; plausibility.
vrille [vrij] *nf* (*bot*) tendril; (*tech*) gimlet; spiral.
vrombir [vrɔ̃bir] *v* hum. **vrombissement** *nm* humming.
vu [vy] *adj* **bien vu** highly regarded. **mal vu** poorly thought of. *prep* in view of. *conj* **vu que** seeing that. **vue** *nf* view; (*sens, spectacle*) sight; (*projet*) plan, design.
vulgaire [vylgɛr] *adj* (*grossier*) vulgar; (*banal*) common. **vulgarité** *nf* vulgarity.
vulnérable [vylnerablə] *adj* vulnerable.

W

wagon [vagɔ̃] *nm* (*marchandises*) truck, wagon; (*voyageurs*) carriage. **wagon-lit** *nm* sleeping-car. **wagon-restaurant** *nm* restaurant-car.
watt [wat] *nm* watt.
week-end [wikɛnd] *nm* weekend.
western [wɛstɛrn] *nm* western.
whisky [wiski] *nm* whisky.
whist [wist] *nm* whist.

X

xénophobe [ksenɔfɔb] *adj* xenophobic. *n(m+f)* xenophobe. **xénophobie** *nf* xenophobia.
xérès [gzerɛs] *nm* sherry.
xylophone [ksilɔfɔn] *nm* xylophone.

Y

y [i] *adv* there. *pron* it, about it, to it, in it. **n'y être pour rien** have nothing to do with it.
yacht [jɔt] *nm* yacht.
yaourt [jaurt] *nm* yoghurt.
yeux [jø] *V* **œil**.
yoga [jɔga] *nm* yoga.
Yougoslavie [jugɔslavi] *nf* Yugoslavia. **yougoslave** *adj* Yugoslav, Yugoslavian. **Yougoslave** *n(m+f)* Yugoslav.
youyou [juju] *nm* dinghy.
yo-yo [jojo] *nm invar* yo-yo.

Z

zèbre [zɛbrə] *nm* zebra. **zébrer** *v* stripe. **zébrure** *nf* stripe; (*d'un coup*) weal.
zèle [zɛl] *nm* zeal. **zélé** *adj* zealous.
zéro [zero] *nm* zero, nought.
zeste [zɛst] *nm* peel, zest.
zézayer [zezeje] *v* lisp. **zézaiement** *nm* lisp.
zibeline [ziblin] *nf* sable.
zigzag [zigzag] *nm* zigzag. **zigzaguer** *v* zigzag.
zinc [zɛ̃g] *nm* zinc; (*fam*) bar, counter.
zodiaque [zɔdjak] *nm* zodiac.
zone [zɔn] *nf* zone, area.
zoo [zoo] *nm* zoo.
zoologie [zɔɔlɔʒi] *nf* zoology. **zoologique** *adj* zoological

Pan Languages

Travellers' **French**
Travellers' **German**
Travellers' **Italian**
Travellers' **Spanish**
Travellers' **Dutch**
Travellers' **Greek**
Travellers' **Portuguese**
Travellers' **Serbo-Croat** for Yugoslavia

A new series of *modern* phrase books developed from the results of a nationwide Gallup survey of the needs of modern travellers abroad. They will prove invaluable companions in any holiday or business situation.

Special features include:

- outstandingly clear and easy-to-use design
- specially prepared, simplified pronunciation
- helpful background information
- 'likely answers' sections
- unique section to help practise basic phrases

plus index, conversion tables, map, reference section.

Pan Study Aids

Published jointly by Heinemann Educational Books and Pan Books

Pan Study Aids is a major new series developed to help school and college students prepare for examinations. All of the authors are experienced teachers/examiners at O level, School Certificate and equivalent examinations and authors of textbooks used in schools and colleges worldwide.

Each volume in the series:

- explains its subject and covers clearly and concisely and with excellent illustrations the essential points of the syllabus, drawing attention to common areas of difficulty and to areas which carry most marks in the exam
- gives guidance on how to plan revision, and prepare for the exam, outlining what examiners are looking for
- provides practice by including typical exam questions and exercises

French
C. Beswick and P. J. Downes

German
D. Shotter

Spanish
D. Utley

Other titles available: Physics, Chemistry, Maths, Human Biology, English Language, Geography 1 & 2, Economics, Commerce, Accounts and Book-keeping, British Government and Politics, History 1 & 2, Effective Study Skills